The Penguin Guide to *the* European Treaties

Clive H. Church and David Phinnemore

PENGUIN BOOKS

PENGUIN BOOKS

Published by the Penguin Group
Penguin Books Ltd, 80 Strand, London WC2R 0RL, England
Penguin Putnam Inc., 375 Hudson Street, New York, New York 10014, USA
Penguin Books Australia Ltd, 250 Camberwell Road, Camberwell, Victoria 3124, Australia
Penguin Books Canada Ltd, 10 Alcorn Avenue, Toronto, Ontario, Canada M4V 3B2
Penguin Books India (P) Ltd, 11 Community Centre, Panchsheel Park, New Delhi – 110 017, India
Penguin Books (NZ) Ltd, Cnr Rosedale and Airborne Roads, Albany, Auckland, New Zealand
Penguin Books (South Africa) (Pty) Ltd, 24 Sturdee Avenue, Rosebank 2196, South Africa

Penguin Books Ltd, Registered Offices: 80 Strand, London WC2R 0RL, England

www.penguin.com

First published 2002
1

Set in Sabon and TheSans
Typeset by Rowland Phototypesetting Ltd, Bury St Edmunds, Suffolk
Printed in England by Clays Ltd, St Ives plc

For the Bennetts and the Southwells

For Antonia

Contents

IV The Treaty Establishing the European Community

V Other Treaties and Related Documents

VI Annexes

Preface

This *Guide* both is, and is not, a second edition. On the one hand, it draws generally and textually on a previous work, updated in the light of both new developments in the Union, up to and including Nice, and advances in information technology. It also remains essentially a commentary on the European Treaties. This reflects our continuing belief that the treaties and the changes which they undergo both matter and need to be publicized and explained. This is particularly so now that the Union is embarking on yet more debates about whether Nice is an acceptable legal foundation and what its future nature should be, beyond the next scheduled IGC in 2004. In other words, the general vision and approach which underlay the previous version are largely maintained. What we offer is not just lists of amendments, or even replacement articles as do the official versions, but the treaties as they will be if Nice comes into effect, with changes agreed in 2000 and 1997 highlighted.

On the other hand, the *Guide* appears with new publishers and under a new title. We are immensely grateful to Penguin Books for not merely rescuing our project but also giving it a new focus and outlook. Hence the *Guide* has a radically different structure, which derives solely from the treaties establishing the European Union and the European Community as they emerged from the Amsterdam and Nice negotiations. The first of the latter pioneered a new approach to treaty amendment and gave the two basic European Treaties a new appearance which deserves to be better known. The second has made limited but significant changes to the Union's decision-making arrangements ahead of enlargement and, assuming ratification, these will be added to the treaty base along with those of Amsterdam.

The Irish referendum of June 2001 came so late in the writing of the text that it posed a major problem. However, precedent suggests a way will be found to get Irish support both for enlargement and Nice. And since, as we argue later, the hard-fought compromises of Nice are bound to affect the Union one way or another, we have decided that there is no point in delaying further beyond the time of completion of the text, which was August 2001, given both that it may be quite late in 2002 before we actually know what will happen to Nice and that an official consolidated version may not be available until 2003. Hence we have proceeded on the basis that Nice will eventually be added to the European Treaties. Moreover, Nice has been so misinterpreted and traduced by opponents from very different points on the political compass, it deserves to be properly explained.

In any case, in order to make room for these two additions, the historical and contextual elements of the original book have been dropped. So we now think of this as very much a commentary on the European Treaties rather than a description of the Union as such. We are aware that this means we leave much unsaid about the actual working of the Union. But while this may be a loss here, it is made good by a host of excellent textbooks. And, in any case, the European Treaties deserve at least one attempt to explain them in full.

Overall, in its new form, the *Guide* starts by seeking to explain the nature of the treaties and the problems they pose, especially for the British. It then goes on to explore where the treaties have come from and how they have developed. The bulk of the *Guide* is then given over to printing the existing texts of the two key treaties, indicating what had been agreed at Maastricht and was then changed at Amsterdam and Nice. This reflects our belief that, even though the Treaty of Amsterdam has attracted much less attention than Maastricht, it was more significant than the muted response to it suggests. For us, it is significant not only because of the concrete amendments it made to the substance of the Union but also because it made significant changes both to the EU's treaty base and to the way the main treaties are presented. In turn, Nice made some interesting contributions of its own to the form and organization of the treaty base.

For the sake of simplicity, we avoid terms used to denote elements of the treaties themselves when describing our own text. We therefore treat our own elements as 'divisions' and 'subdivisions'. Treaty text is indented and printed in a smaller size than the commentary. Changes introduced by the Treaty of Amsterdam are, moreover, marked out in bold where they are wholly new and in italic where they represent essentially stylistic alterations to the text or alterations in the location of the text. A different typeface is used in much the same way to indicate changes resulting from Nice.

At the same time we try to explain the origins, meaning and significance of the present texts. This is done in a general and interpretative way rather than in a strictly legalistic manner. Whereas legal commentaries and texts seek to set out the current state of EC law, beginning with the treaties but going well beyond them, we have been more restrained. Hence the organization of the *Guide* reflects the sections of the treaties and does not necessarily proceed on a strict article-by-article basis as is common in legal commentaries. The aim is to make the treaties more comprehensible to ordinary readers, particularly in the United Kingdom and the English-speaking world. Had this book been available before the Gothenburg European Council in 2001 then Messrs Hague and Maude might not have made such a display of their ignorance of the process of treaty revision. Equally, Austin Mitchell's complaint during the second reading of the debate on Nice that there was no consolidated version available – although there was an unofficial one available at the Europa website – might also have been met. We hope that the inclusion of a synoptic table, which indicates where in our text articles and comments can be found, will also make them more accessible.

Obviously in drawing up the commentary we have our own views but we have sought to achieve a certain neutrality and hope that, as before, the commentary does not fall into the extremes of either Europhobia or over-enthusiastic support for further integration, come what may. This first attitude we would describe as 'sovereignist' since it rejects any, or all, decisions not made solely in national boundaries. Conversely we think of the second as a 'federationism', that is demanding that the Union be turned into one rather stereotyped state. We feel that it is wrong to call this 'federalism', because the Union's present 'in-between' network of ambiguous compromises is essentially federalist in political-science terms since it attempts to distribute power to various levels while trying to preserve the rights and identities of all those involved. Whether we are consistent in such an interpretation is for readers to judge, remembering that, as Louis observed in an earlier commentary, one can hardly demand total consistency when talking about a text which itself cannot make up its mind how to describe something as basic as the single market.

The final subdivisions of the *Guide* deal with both recent changes to other founding treaties and with certain other texts. These, though they are not formally part of the treaty base, are, in our view, necessary to explain the ultimate ground rules under which the Union operates, sometimes known as the 'meta' rules. The Annexes also contain a bibliography of further reading together with a set of tables to explain the changes made over the years to the original treaties of the 1950s. Special attention is also given to actual and projected processes of simplification, consolidation and codification of the treaties.

Clive Church is primarily responsible for divisions I, parts of II, III and IV, notably the final elements, and V ii and V vi, together with the first part of Annexe 3. David Phinnemore is responsible for parts of II and III, the policy elements of IV and V, the rest of the Annexes, the Synoptic Table and the Index. However, all of the text has been jointly read, added to, corrected and agreed by both of us.

C. H. C. *Thanington Without, Kent*
D. P. *Moira, Co. Down*

Acknowledgements

The *Guide* continues to owe a debt to the EU's Jean Monnet Action Programme, whose 1990 award to the University of Kent started the whole process off. Equally it continues to owe much to the University of Kent at Canterbury, to Liverpool Hope University College and, more recently, Queen's University Belfast, who have supported both versions, both as institutions and as gatherings of helpful colleagues. The process has also benefited from the activities of a study group on the EU's 2000 Inter-Governmental Conference, generously supported by the University Association for Contemporary European Studies (UACES). Help from Lisa Yates, Carmen Stoian, Frank Douglas and other postgraduate students must also be acknowledged, along with the advice of Therese Blanchet, Franklin Dehousse, Graham Horgan, Lee McGowan, Bill Nicoll, Handley Stevens and various UK officials. We hope that they, and the students with whom we have discussed it, will continue to find the finished product of use. Needless to say, as before, we shall be only too happy to receive suggestions about any future editions.

Our special thanks are due to Caroline Pretty, Martin Toseland, Emma Horton and others of Penguin who have helped bring the revised project to fruition.

Synoptic Table

IV The Treaty Establishing the European Community

Tables

Boxes

Abbreviations

ACP	African, Caribbean and Pacific countries
BBC	British Broadcasting Corporation
BEST	Business Environment Simplification Task Force
BSE	Bovine Spongiform Encephalopathy
CAP	Common Agricultural Policy
CCP	Common Commercial Policy
CCT	Common Customs Tariff
CDU/CSU	Christian Democratic Union/Christian Social Union (Germany)
CE	Compulsory Expenditure
CECAF	Committee for Eastern Central Atlantic Fisheries
CEDEFOP	European Centre for the Development of Vocational Training
CESDP	Common European Security and Defence Policy
CET	Common External Tariff
CFI	Court of First Instance
CFP	Common Fisheries Policy
CFSP	Common Foreign and Security Policy
CJD	Creutzfeldt–Jakob Disease
CMEA	Council for Mutual Economic Assistance (Comecon)
CoA	Court of Auditors
CoE	Council of Europe
COMETT	Programme of the Community in Education and Training for Technologies
CoR	Committee of the Regions
COREPER	Committee of Permanent Representatives
COSAC	Standing Conference of Parliamentary European Affairs Committees
CSCE	Conference on Security and Co-operation in Europe
CTP	Common Transport Policy
DB	Draft Budget

DG	Directorate General
EAEC	European Atomic Energy Community (Euratom)
EAGGF	European Agricultural Guidance and Guarantee Fund (often known by its French acronym, FEOGA)
EBRD	European Bank for Reconstruction and Development (often known by its French acronym, BERD)
EC	European Community
ECB	European Central Bank
ECHR	European Court (or Convention) on Human Rights
ECJ	European Court of Justice
ECOFIN	Economic and Finance Ministers
EcoSoc	Economic and Social Committee
ECSC	European Coal and Steel Community
ECU	European Currency Unit
EEA	European Economic Area/European Environment Agency
EEC	European Economic Community
EFC	Economic and Financial Committee
EFTA	European Free Trade Association
EIB	European Investment Bank
EMCF	European Monetary Co-operation Fund
EMI	European Monetary Institute
EMS	European Monetary System
EMU	Economic and Monetary Union
ENEL	Ente Nazionale dell'Electricita
EP	European Parliament
EPC (POCO)	European Political Co-operation
EPU	European Political Union
ERASMUS	European Action Scheme for the Mobility of University Students
ERDF	European Regional Development Fund
ERM	Exchange Rate Mechanism
ERRF	European Rapid Reaction Force
ERTA	European Road Transport Association
ESCB	European System of Central Banks
ESF	European Social Fund
ETA	Euskadi ta Azkatasuna [Basque Nation and Liberty]
ETUC	European Confederation of Trade Unions
EU	European Union
EUI	European University Institute, Florence
EUMC	European Union Military Committee
EUROSTAT	EC Statistical Office and its Publications
GATT	General Agreement on Tariffs and Trade

GDP	Gross Domestic Product
HMSO	Her Majesty's Stationery Office
ICJ	International Court of Justice
ICRI	International Commission for the Reform of the Institutions of the EU
IGC	Inter-Governmental Conference
ILO	International Labour Organization
IMP	Integrated Mediterranean Programme
JHA	Justice and Home Affairs
LFAs	Less-Favoured Areas
LINGUA	Action Programme to Promote Foreign Language Competence in the Community
MAG '92	Mutual Assistance Group '92 – customs
MCA	Monetary Compensation Amounts
MEP	Member of the European Parliament
MOT	Ministry of Transport (roadworthiness test)
MP	Member of Parliament
MT	Merger Treaty
NATO	North Atlantic Treaty Organization
NCE	Non-Compulsory Expenditure
NGO	Non-Governmental Organization
OCTs	Overseas Countries and Territories
OECD	Organization for Economic Co-operation and Development
OJ	*Official Journal*
OOPEC	Office for the Official Publications of the EC
OSCE	Organization for Security and Co-operation in Europe
PCB/PCT	polychlorinated biphenyls/polychlorinated triphenyls
PDB	Preliminary Draft Budget
PHARE	Assistance for the Economic Reconstruction of Central and Eastern Europe
PJCCM	Police and Judicial Co-operation in Criminal Matters
PMI	Philip Morris Institute, Brussels
PRINCE	Programme d'information des citoyens européens
PS	French Parti Socialiste
PSC	Political and Security Committee [COPS in French]
QMV	Qualified Majority Voting
QR	Quantitative Restrictions
RTD	Research and Technological Development
SDR	Special Drawing Rights
SEA	Single European Act
SEM	Single European Market
SIS	Schengen Information System

SLIM	Simpler Legislation for the Single Market Initiative
SME	Small and Medium-sized Enterprise
SoA	Statement of Assurance
SOS	Save Our Souls Democracy Movement
SPD	Social Democratic Party (Germany)
STABEX	Stabilisation of Exports Fund (Lomé and Cotonou)
STM	Supplementary Trade Mechanism
TA	Treaty of Amsterdam
TACs	Total Allowable Catches
TEAEC	Treaty establishing the European Atomic Energy Community
TEC	Treaty establishing the European Community
TECSC	Treaty establishing the European Coal and Steel Community
TENs	Trans-European Networks
TEU	Treaty on European Union
TN	Treaty of Nice
TREVI	Terrorisme, radicalisme, extremisme et violence internationale
UEF	European Union of Federalists
UK	United Kingdom of Great Britain and Northern Ireland
UN	United Nations Organization
UNCTAD	United Nations Conference on Trade and Development
UNESCO	United Nations Economic, Social and Cultural Organization
UNICE	Union of Industrial and Employers' Confederations of Europe
VAT	Value-Added Tax
WEU	Western European Union
WTO	World Trade Organization

1 Introduction

What are 'European Treaties' and why the need for a *Guide*? We understand them to be the international agreements which organize the European Union (EU) and its component bodies. This choice, clearly set out in our title, reflects the growing general tendency to restrict the term 'European' to things related to the EU. However, this is not a wholly healthy development and we are very aware that Europe is actually a larger and more diverse place than the Union, with many states and institutions, all of which have signed innumerable treaties. The Council of Europe alone is responsible for nearly 180 of its own. Yet, important though these latter are, and no matter how much they deserve the title 'European', they are not the subject of this *Guide*.

Overall importance, as well as usage, justifies our concentration on the Union's key treaties, notably the Treaty establishing the European Community (TEC) and the Treaty on European Union (TEU). For the EU is an unusual construction. It is not a single body but, as we shall see, one resting on several 'pillars', the most important of which is the European Community (EC). Hence, it is partly 'supra-national' in that its collective decisions have authority within the member states. At the same time it is 'inter-governmental' in that it is based on, and structured through, specific strategic agreements among the member states.

These agreements are enshrined in a growing series of rather special treaties. They are special because not merely are they different from the many other international agree-ments the Union has with outside bodies, but they are more constitutional in nature than most treaties, being designed to create or change the structures, processes and aims of the Union. In fact they provide the basis for Community and Union powers as well as providing a framework for economic – and to a lesser extent political – life in the member states of the Union. Taken together they 'constitute' the whole European enterprise, as Loveland says. And academic and political discourse, as well as everyday usage, reinforces the tendency of the EU's own website to talk of them as 'the European Treaties'.

These treaties can therefore be regarded as the basic blueprints for the European Union and the other supra-national organizations it comprises, notably the European Community. Because of the growing importance of the Union the treaties, which consti-tute and regulate it, are clearly significant. Yet they are often misunderstood. Thus in 1995 the European Court of Justice (ECJ) had to point out to a Spanish court that it was mixing up the treaties in its application for a preliminary ruling. In line with its general record of being probably the least well-informed country on matters European, the treaties are particularly poorly known in the United Kingdom (UK) and are rarely studied save during such moments of high passion as the Maastricht ratification crisis of 1992–3.

Nor are they generally well understood. Given that a quarter of the UK population cheerfully admit to knowing nothing of the Union this is hardly surprising. Indeed, even broadsheet newspapers can misconstrue their nature and relationships. So they need, and deserve, to be better publicized and explained. This is the major justification for having a guide to them. However, as the following pages show, we can find other reasons in the fact that their number, status and meaning are not self-evident and also because the texts themselves present us with a series of technical and cultural difficulties. Not everyone, in other words, can read a blueprint. And the 'European Treaties' are rarely self-explanatory. Neither, as we will see, do they tell us everything we need to know about the Union.

In many countries and in languages other than English, all this has usually led to the provision of detailed commentaries on the treaties. Indeed, Ludlow and Ersbøll have argued that treaty revisions really require a good commentary if they are to be successful. Our *Guide* seeks to provide this, even though we also recognize that, as Solana recently wrote, 'explaining EU treaties is a thankless task'. None the less, we hope that by making the treaties more easily available, they may become better known. And by adopting a straightforward approach, we hope that the *Guide* will also make the treaties more comprehensible and meaningful. However, whether as Peter Hain, the Minister for Europe, has suggested, this can be done in language so simple that it makes no use of acronyms is questionable. Things like the EU cannot survive without a minimum of formality. People may not find the treaties understandable but they could be even worse off with a document written by tabloid subeditors, demotic though this might be. Simplicity and precision do not always go together.

However, before plunging in to reproduce and comment on the treaties, there are three kinds of general considerations about the European Treaties as such which we need to take on board. The first set of questions begins with what are 'treaties' in the Union context and what are their characteristics? This raises the question of exactly which treaties we are talking about and why. But we also need to ask what precisely is the status of the two we focus on – the TEU, sometimes known, somewhat misleadingly, as the Maastricht Treaty, and the TEC, again slightly misleadingly known as the Rome Treaty. Are they, for example, truly constitutional documents?

Secondly, we need to face a number of problems about the European Treaties. As we have already suggested, there are very many of them. Also they do have some inherent difficulties, including the obscurity of the texts themselves. There is also the problem that they deal with a series of bodies whose relationships are not clear, drawing us to the question of what is the difference between the Union and the Community. At the same time the nature and existence of the treaties can go against the grain of English (and perhaps UK) political culture, based as this is on the lack of a codified constitution and a tendency to deride written constitutional documents.

Given all this there is a need, thirdly, to explain how we ourselves approach the treaties. For, no matter how much we try to be neutral, like everybody else we have our own assumptions and feelings about the treaties both technically and politically. This leads us to the questions of what the aims of the *Guide* are and how, and why, we go about achieving them. In other words, we also need to explain how the book is structured to bring this about.

Having done this we then go on, in the next division of the *Guide*, to explain exactly how the existing treaties actually came about. In fact they are the fruit of a continuous and ongoing evolution. The first treaty emerged in Paris in 1951. Further development at Rome in 1957 was followed by a period of limited change. However, a new phase of increasingly frequent amendments began in the 1980s and has continued right up to the changes introduced through the Treaty of Nice (TN), which are, at the time of writing, awaiting ratification. In other words, the treaties are very much in evolution and under-standing how the development of the Community and Union has shaped the treaties themselves is an important aid to explaining them. All of this completes the context for the more detailed study of the treaty texts themselves which make up the bulk of the *Guide*.

i Treaties: Their Characteristics and Status

When attention in the United Kingdom does focus on the European Treaties they are generally seen as historic events rather than documents. And often the practical impact they have is given more attention than the written acts themselves. We believe that this is a misguided approach. In fact, a first step towards understanding the European Treaties is to look more carefully at treaties *per se*. To begin with, what are treaties, especially in the Union context? And precisely which treaties do we have to deal with and what are they really like?

While this helps to explain the treaties, the more important question is that of their status. Are they, as many claim, the 'supra-national constitution' of the Union? Or are they simply international agreements, 'acts of the member states', as Hartley calls them? The answer, in fact, seems to lie somewhere between. As a result, the treaties do not play all the roles normally fulfilled by a national constitution. However, they are very influen-tial and can do much for the Union. In other words, questions about the treaties are more complicated than is often thought.

What are Treaties?

In diplomacy, treaties are normally understood as formally recorded, and binding, agreements between two or more states (or other international actors) defining their future relations. Treaties set out a series of propositions by which the actors agree to be bound in good faith: what is known as the *pacta sunt servanda* principle. Treaties therefore can only be concluded by those with the authority to do so, which means having what international law calls 'legal personality' or the recognized power to conclude and operate such contracts. Hence treaties must be authoritative written documents, officially negotiated, initialled and signed by all those involved, and then duly ratified by those to whom the negotiators are responsible. This explains the reference to full powers in most treaty preambles which indicates that those who sign them have the right to do so, something which is still important, as Aust says.

Whether described as agreements, charters, conventions, exchanges of notes, pacts or statutes, such treaties can cover a variety of subjects. They can be of a number of types such as contractual, which means that they create obligations only for their signatories, or law-making, which create rules for a wider international community. All of them are regulated, however, by international law, thanks to the Vienna Convention of 23 May 1969 on the law of treaties.

In the case of the EU its treaties are of at least two kinds. To begin with they can be agreements concluded between the Community and other international actors under its treaty-making powers. Article 281 TEC gives the Community (but not the Union as such) legal personality and Article 300 TEC specifies some of the procedures for concluding treaties with third parties. Some of these are negotiated simply by the Community while others, depending on their subject, are negotiated by the member states and the Community. The latter are known as mixed agreements. And this right to conclude agreements has been widely used, especially after the European Court of Justice's *AETR* ruling of 31 March 1971. Although the Union cannot sign binding treaties, because of its lack of formal legal personality, since the Treaty of Amsterdam (TA) the revised Article 24 TEU provides that the Presidency can be given authority to initiate negotiations for international agreements arising out of the Common Foreign and Security Policy (CFSP) and Police and Judicial Co-operation in Criminal Matters (PJCCM), albeit in ways somewhat altered by the TN.

However, the various association, co-operation and trade accords permitted by the EC's treaty-making power are rarely thought of as 'European' treaties in a formal sense. This term is usually reserved for treaties which deal with the Union and the various Communities as such, whether establishing, organizing or regulating their overall operations. Although these 'European Treaties' are legally multilateral international agreements between the member states, they also have a kind of foundational or constitutive nature. They first established, or constituted, the European Communities: the European Coal and Steel Community (ECSC), the European Economic Community (EEC) and the European Atomic Energy Community (EAEC or 'Euratom'), along with the European Union as such. They also decided what actions they should take and how, thereby, as suggested, giving life and shape to the whole enterprise. They are of a 'self-executing' nature, which means that they do not require national acts to make them operative. Conventional usage therefore talks of 'the treaties on which the Union is founded'. Indeed, were there no founding treaties, there could not really be a Union. The treaties are thus prescriptive contracts amongst the member states. They give the Union the three things it needs to operate successfully: statements on exactly what the states will do together; the institutions and decision-making procedures to implement these common enterprises; and means of enforcement of such commonly agreed aims and decisions. The Union, in other words, is what the Germans would call *zweckrational*, that is to say a body set up for particular reasons and hence to achieve specific purposes.

Treaties subsequent to the founding treaties have altered aims, processes and structures so as to bring the Communities and the Union into line with new aspirations and conditions. Because of this focus on ground rules and institutional powers, notably through the supra-national organizations set up inside the Union, these European Treaties have to be seen as 'constitutional' in the loose sense of the term used above. This point is reinforced by the fact that the treaties are the Union's primary law. Hence they are also the basis of the *acquis*, that is to say the overall corpus of Union legislation and objectives.

The Union is today based on a variety of treaties, signed at different times and for different reasons. Yet, as formally recorded agreements, they have a number of things in common. To begin with they all come into being in much the same way, being negotiated through one or more inter-governmental conferences (IGCs). This rather suggests a single self-contained assembly, but with the passing of time IGCs have become more a continuous series of special sessions of state representatives, of ministers meeting as part of the General Affairs Council, and increasingly of heads of government. Since Maastricht, the heads of government have served as a final, and crucial, level of the IGC adding an element of personality to the general domination of the process by national core executives. There can also be advisory, preparatory and technical groups.

So, although in theory the negotiations are supposed to be a unified process this is not always so. Moreover, the actual work is done mainly by special representatives, often officials meeting more regularly together, and not by the ministers themselves. Officials can also work bilaterally and in technical working groups. However, the pressures on them are such that their decisions are often somewhat contradictory. None the less, even though the Commission and European Parliament (EP) have a limited role, albeit a growing one in the case of the EP, the essential decisions are taken by government representatives. Hence the states are said to be 'the Masters of the Treaties'.

Second, most of the treaties have the same shape: a preamble, a main body (consisting of series of parts), a final act and additional materials such as annexes, declarations and protocols. Preambles encapsulate the strategic aims of the negotiators. They are considered essential to the drafting of treaties and not to have one has been described as the equivalent of a diplomat going out without wearing trousers. Individual aims or elements are usually known as 'recitals'. In some cases, like Amsterdam, the preamble may be a mere statement of fact but often it can give a very clear steer as to what the whole institutional or treaty enterprise is all about, and the Court of Justice has taken them very seriously as a means of interpreting the treaties. They clearly provide evidence of the intentions of the drafters of a treaty and this would be considered significant by the ECJ as it was in the *Van Gend en Loos* (1963) case. The Court then used the TEC's commitment to 'union' to show that a new legal order had been created. The official Community version of the collected treaties, moreover, includes the preambles as part of the 'text' of the various treaties. They are lofty statements of what the signatories wish to achieve by their agreement. They do not, in themselves, create rights but pave the way for them to appear in specific and binding treaty articles.

International law accepts that preambles can be used in the interpretation of a treaty if they are sufficiently precise, as are those of the TEU and the TEC. Hence they can, as Schepers notes, have legal force in themselves. Equally, preambles are a common element in legislative enactments in many countries, and are common in EC legislation. They can be used to justify or summarize the legislation. Continental practice often also involves specifying the various texts and decisions which have led the legislators to this new step. Hence the tendency of Westminster to disregard and denigrate them is doubly ill advised.

The main body of treaties can be long and so, for the sake of convenience and identification, are divided up in at least two ways. On the one hand, treaties can be split into manageable thematic chunks. The largest of these are usually known as Parts. In the case of the TEU there are no Parts but only Titles, a term generally used to describe major subsections of Parts. Titles in turn can be subdivided into Chapters and these into Sections. On the other hand, there is also usually a consecutive series of numbered articles within them. Where there are numbers within articles these are usually known as paragraphs and elements within them, or within articles which are not so subdivided, are often described as 'indents' or 'tirets' (and sometimes 'literas' in French) when they have a letter.

The last part of a treaty is conventionally described as the General and Final Provisions. These usually specify the validity of the text and the way it should come into force and for how long. The signatures of the negotiators, known as the testimonium, also appear here. A Final Act is slightly different. It is not actually part of the treaty as such but is the last operation of the negotiations which produced it, in the EU's case, of the IGC, summarizing the proceedings of the conference as Aust observes. It usually carries out three main functions: providing a record of when and why the IGC was convened; listing all documents adopted which give substance to its outcome, including the treaty and the protocols; and giving a home to declarations. Hence it too contains the signatures of the national representatives involved in approving the outcome of the IGC. All the European

Treaties, save that establishing the European Coal and Steel Community (TECSC), have such a final act.

Declarations which technically are statements made to or by the IGC about the treaties are left in the outhouse of the treaty because they have much less legal status than protocols and are not binding. They are not to be confused with the kind of 'declarations' made at Stuttgart and Copenhagen which lay down political goals for the Union. Indeed, in 1997 the House of Commons' Foreign Affairs Committee was told by its legal adviser that the declarations were not, in fact, part of the Treaty of Amsterdam. Declarations are simply adopted or noted by an IGC and then annexed to a final act. Hence, given that its jurisdiction does not extend to final acts, the European Court of Justice is not obliged to take any relevant declaration into consideration when interpreting the provisions of the European Treaties. Indeed, as Toth notes, it is debatable whether the ECJ should be permitted to consider the content of declarations at all. No provision equivalent to Article 311 TEC governing the legal standing of protocols (see below), for example, exists.

However, declarations can be politically significant since they can be formal indications by some, or all, of the 'High Contracting Parties', as the states agreeing to the treaty are called, as to how they will interpret the treaty. They can also be unilateral statements on things, such as animal welfare, which matter to a particular state. As such their inclusion can be instrumental in facilitating final agreement in an IGC, even though they can almost be a form of reservation to the treaty. Conversely, many of them read as if they were really interpretative glosses on the treaty text, almost taking the place of an official commentary. For Vibert they, along with protocols, are actually the key to interpreting the treaties. This is why, despite their lowly status, they have become increasingly popular, participants at Maastricht and Amsterdam noting the Christmas-tree effect member states created by freely adding declarations to the respective treaties. Nice, interestingly, made an innovative use of them to signal Union negotiating positions on the precise institutional changes to be brought in as enlargement takes place. And while these could be changed, they rather read as texts which the candidates will have to accept, like it or not.

The other main additional materials in a treaty are known as Protocols. These are documents which have the same legal authority as the main body of a treaty. And, in theory, they form an integral part of the treaty to which they are attached (as Article 311 TEC makes clear). However, Article 69 TEC suggests that there are still doubts in some quarters about how authoritative they actually are.

In any case, they are normally printed immediately after the treaty proper and not as part of it. This is done in order to avoid cluttering up the treaty text with too much detail, given that they usually deal with complex technical rules. As time has gone by negotiators have made increasing use of such documents. This protocolization of the treaties shows that governments are increasingly concerned to seek legally binding guarantees that they will get what they want out of a given treaty. Hence one negotiator has compared them to codicils to a will. But, while politically understandable, they do not make the treaties easier to follow.

A third common feature of all the European Treaties is that they are formally adopted through a specific procedure. Once agreed the treaties are initialled by the negotiators. Then, after any infelicities in the text have been eliminated and political agreements given legal form, they are formally signed by national representatives. The clean text is thereafter submitted to national parliaments and, sometimes, to national electorates for their approval, a process known as ratification. Having agreed the treaty, the EU's member states are bound to seek ratification whereas, in the case of many ordinary treaties, signatory states choose not to ratify them. The requirement for both unanimity in the IGC and ratification has been described as a 'double safety lock' for the member states.

Once approved, in the ways required by national constitutional provisions, the governments deposit formal documents of ratification with a specific government. This is normally that of Italy because the most important initial treaties were signed in Rome. There the originals stay in the Foreign Ministry archives, unless brought out for historical exhibitions. Once the last signatory state has deposited what are called its instruments of ratification, the treaties come into force normally at the beginning of the following month. In some states, like the United Kingdom, which are described as 'dualist' in legal terms, because it regards international and domestic law as entirely separate, there is a further step to be taken. Treaties can only come into effect once an Act of Parliament turns the ratified treaty into national law.

Fourth, most of the treaties are concluded for an unlimited duration. Only the TECSC – which is kept in Paris – has a finite life, of 50 years. It expired on 23 July 2002. So, contrary to many normal treaties, there is no real provision for the treaties to be denounced or even suspended. However, Greenland was relieved of its obligations under the Treaties in 1985. The territories to which treaties apply are specified in the texts. This is one of the elements which has to be changed after any accession to the Union. Versions in all official languages of the Community are equally valid. Amendment is almost invariably by procedures laid down in the constitutive treaties as with Article 48 TEU. This allows the Commission or the member states to propose changes. Should it be agreed to explore these, then a further IGC is convened. However, the TECSC did allow for some amendments without resort to such complicated procedures. Following Nice some *de facto* amendments to the TEC can also be made without an IGC.

Which are the European Treaties?

Even when we limit ourselves to looking at European Treaties only in the sense of those which deal with establishment and organization of the Union and the Communities, there are still a good many to choose from. The EP has talked of there being a 'multitude' of such treaties and certainly there are too many to be printed and analysed in a single-volume *Guide*. Moreover, others have pointed out that merely publishing one text, notably the Treaty on European Union, is unhelpful because it assumes knowledge of many other texts not normally printed alongside the TEU. Even though the Court of Justice has sought to construe what we take here to be the European Treaties as a single code, this has not prevented their variety causing much confusion. As Annex 3 shows, this has also led to a series of moves to clarify and, if possible, fuse the treaties into one, more comprehensible and authoritative document. This is why the *Guide* concentrates on the two key constitutive treaties, those which establish the EC and the EU and thus give shape to the Brussels-based enterprise: the TEU and the TEC. Other treaties are simply listed here and their evolution explained in the next division of the *Guide*.

However, because all these other 'European' agreements retain their validity even if they have been subsumed in later treaties we really have to think in terms of what can be called the 'treaty base', that is to say the collected body of agreements which have created or adapted the Communities and the Union. The exact dimensions of this are a trifle uncertain so that even the Union's own listings talk of 'Selected Instruments' so as to be on the safe side. Certainly the base includes many protocols as well as some constitutional acts which do not have formal treaty status. So it is not surprising that one journalist has talked of the Union 'collapsing under the weight of its own treaties'. What is more, over the last few years the treaties have been constantly growing in number and changing in nature. And all of them are, in fact, integral elements of EC primary law. Most authorities would include the following in their list:

Treaty Establishing the European Coal and Steel Community (TECSC) (18 April 1951), often referred to as the Treaty of Paris

Treaty Establishing the European Community (TEC) (25 March 1957), often referred to as the Treaty of Rome

Treaty Establishing the European Atomic Energy Community (TEAEC) (25 March 1957), also known as the second Treaty of Rome or the Euratom Treaty

Convention on Certain Institutions Common to the European Communities (25 March 1957)

Convention of 13 November 1962 Amending the Treaty Establishing the European Economic Community relating to elements of Part IV TEC applicable to the Netherlands Antilles

Treaty Establishing a Single Council and a Single Commission of the European Communities (8 April 1965), often referred to as the Merger Treaty

Treaty Amending Certain Budgetary Provisions (22 April 1970), also known as the Treaty of Luxembourg

Act Concerning the Conditions of Accession and the Adjustments to the Treaties – Accession to the Communities of the Kingdom of Denmark, Ireland and the United Kingdom of Great Britain and Northern Ireland (22 January 1972)

Treaty Amending Certain Financial Provisions (22 July 1975), also known as the Treaty of Brussels

Act Concerning the Election of Representatives of the Assembly by Direct Universal Suffrage (20 September 1976)

Act Concerning the Conditions of Accession and the Adjustments to the Treaties – Accession to the Communities of the Hellenic Republic (23 April 1979)

Treaty Amending, with Regard to Greenland, the Treaties Establishing the European Communities (13 March 1984), also known as the Greenland Treaty

Act Concerning the Conditions of Accession and the Adjustments to the Treaties – Accession to the Communities of the Kingdom of Spain and the Portuguese Republic (12 June 1985)

Single European Act (SEA) (17/28 February 1986)

Treaty on European Union (TEU) (7 February 1992), often referred to as the Maastricht Treaty

Agreement on the European Economic Area (EEA) (2 May 1992)

Act Concerning the Conditions of Accession and the Adjustments to the Treaties – Accession to the European Union of the Republic of Austria, the Republic of Finland and the Kingdom of Sweden (24 June 1994)

Council Decision on the System of the European Communities' Own Resources (31 October 1994)

Treaty of Amsterdam (TA) (2 October 1997)

Treaty of Nice (TN) (26 February 2001) – Not ratified at the time of writing

All of these came into operation subsequent to the dates given here, which are the dates when they were actually signed. Signature is usually some time after the treaty is actually negotiated. The Nice treaty was thus agreed on 11 December 2000. In fact the TEC came into force on 1 January 1958, the SEA on 1 July 1987, the TEU on 1 November 1993 and the TA on 1 May 1999. Thus in the latter two cases a long time elapsed between signature and implementation, as we explain below. It was hoped that the Treaty of Nice would come into effect in 2002.

Of the agreements listed the first three, along with the TEU, are normally regarded as the 'original or constitutive treaties'. With the SEA and the Amsterdam and Nice revisions, they are defined by the Europa website as the 'European Treaties' par excellence. Academics use much the same designation and selection. Most of their articles and protocols are still taken very seriously. Thus the 1965 Protocol on the Privileges and Immunities of the European Communities now appears, in an amended form, as Protocol 34 of the TEC (although it is designated as referring to the TECSC and the TEAEC as well). However, the 1957 Convention and the Merger Treaty, originally treated as supplementary agreements, were formally repealed by Article 9 TA. Amsterdam also introduced a new protocol on the location of the Union's institutions which had previously been regulated by a decision of representatives of the governments of the member states. At the same time it also brought into the treaty proper the amended 1976 Act on European Parliament Elections. Such acts had, in the past, been treated rather as footnotes to the key treaties, although they remained legally effective. Nice made further changes to the original protocols.

Partly because of the complexity of all this there has, as we have already suggested, been a tendency to concentrate on the TEU and the TEC. This reflects, to begin with, the facts that, of the other original treaties, the TEAEC is of diminishing importance and the TECSC expired in July 2002, something recognized by the TN. It also reflects the fact that the TEU and TEC are politically the most significant of all the European Treaties and are those to which people most often refer. Article 47 TEU underlines their significance. Equally, the concentration bears witness to the fact that the Accession Treaties basically involve only temporary arrangements together with minor amendments to the original treaties. However, some of the protocols and declarations do have continuing effect. The EEA Agreement is included because it applies EC law to other countries to whom the four freedoms are extended and ties in with the mention of Iceland and Norway in the TA. However, the trend to concentration was given a real impetus by the way the Amsterdam treaty, as we shall see, restructured the main treaties while encouraging thoughts of their fusion. None of this, of course, makes it clear what the European Treaties really are. Nor does it exhaust their difficulties.

What is their Nature?

The fact that there are so many treaties raises further questions about their characteristics. To start with, there are further technical questions, beginning with how much of the Union's operations the treaties cover. And are they all of the same kind? Finally, how integrated are the treaties? This leads us on to consider the actual status of the treaties and the roles they play. The question of why there are so many treaties in the first place will, as already noted, be dealt with later since it takes us into the past of the Community and the Union.

Here, to begin with, it is important to note that the European Treaties do not tell us everything about the Union and what it does. Like any other blueprint they are an outline and a starting point. They are not a self-sufficient explanation of what the Union is and does. All EU activities must have a justification in the treaties, since the Union ultimately depends on the transfer of specific authority by the member states and cannot act without this. The treaties thus create what is known as 'the doctrine of conferred powers'. None the less, the treaties do not spell out all the details of the way things actually work in the Union. Moreover, because of their origins, the treaties do not cover all the policy areas that we might expect to find in national constitutional documents. So they leave much to be decided in other, 'extra-treaty', ways. Hence other things also play a part in fine-tuning the Union and its operation: secondary legislation, the case law of the ECJ and precedent. In fact, Bulmer suggested in 1997 that nine-tenths of how the EU works lies outside the treaties.

But it is perhaps too easy to say that the European Treaties are simply framework accords, laying down general guidelines and allowing other actors a large autonomy. Certainly they set up institutions and processes and can often indicate general policy aims without specifying in minute detail how these should work or be achieved. And they have become increasingly declaratory, which means that implementing legislation is necessary to give them real impact. Yet, because they are contracts between states, the treaties can also be very detailed on some policy matters, notably Economic and Monetary Union (EMU). In this the treaties are rather like the old Swiss Constitution, which also cheerfully mixes the general and the specific. Both the TEU and the TA have added to the detailed policy coverage, reflecting the member states' suspicion of each other's goals, something which necessitates things being spelt out clearly. So, the European Treaties are absolutely essential in more than merely constitutional matters.

This leads us to a second observation: despite the family resemblances we have already seen, the treaties are not all of the same functional kind. They actually fall into at least three main types. The first of these are the original founding or constitutive treaties, using the latter term in a narrower sense. This is because these are the treaties which create, or constitute, a specific new body such as Euratom or the Union itself. Some authorities therefore accord them a higher status than other accords, in other words as constitutional treaties as Lasok and Bridge do. Certainly they tend to get more attention but legally their status is hardly different from that of other treaties. All of them are sovereign acts of will by the contracting states so they retain their validity until the states decide otherwise. So, to say, as Lord Pearson of Rannoch does, that they are 'collectively known as the Treaty of Rome' is to miss their essential individual nature and significance.

The second category comprises the amending treaties. These can be acts of accession annexed to accession treaties. These merely change a limited number of institutional details, so as to allow for new members, and specify how the latter will take the obligations laid down in the treaties. Amending treaties can also be acts which change specific powers and arrangements. Some of these, like the Budgetary Treaties and the 1976 Election Act, can be relatively minor as, in some ways, was the case with Nice.

In the case of three of the more recent European Treaties, that is to say the SEA, the TEU and the TA, large areas of the pre-existing treaties have been subject to alteration, often quite substantially. Nice, despite the importance of the changes in representation, seats and votes, only really rewrote the provisions on enhanced co-operation and judicial organization. And, in the case of the SEA and the TEU, new bodies have also been constituted: first European Political Co-operation (EPC) thanks to the former and then, by the latter, the Union itself with its pillars. They also brought about major changes in the policy spread and operation of the Communities. This gives these two European Treaties a mixed status both constitutive and amending.

Finally come Amsterdam and Nice. The former is at one and the same time a large-scale amending treaty and what we might call a rationalizing treaty, a new type of agreement. Its innovativeness lies in the fact that it treats the treaties as a single framework, partly by repealing existing acts and, more importantly, by becoming a kind of 'window treaty' which leaves virtually nothing behind itself. At the same time it simplifies and consolidates the treaties, producing new working versions shorn of some redundant elements and with new numbering. It also encourages ideas of fusing the original constitutive treaties into one document. Nice echoed some of these innovations although the nature of its amendments means that it left more behind it than Amsterdam.

Notwithstanding the work of the TA, the treaties remain individual acts, often very fragmentary ones since, like much EC legislation, they derive from what has been called the 'garbage-can' approach to policy-making in which, for political reasons, states throw all kinds of odd and often extraneous ideas into the negotiations. Hence the treaty base is fragmented and complex. Because they are all sovereign acts by the member states involved, the treaties all have equal and continuing legal status. Unless, as happened at Amsterdam, a new treaty formally repeals an earlier accord, treaties remain in being even if their contents are merely amendments to another act in which they are generally subsumed. One treaty cannot therefore be cited against another.

Each European Treaty is an autonomous element in the constitutional foundations of the Union, a fact which is not always understood. Moreover, each treaty has its own peculiarities. Thus, contrary to Cowgill, it is not really the case that, after Amsterdam, 'the complete Treaty on European Union is formed by the four treaties'. In fact the Union as such is a constituted body and not a set of treaties. Moreover, it was created by the TEU alone. However, the activities and institutions of its various components are regulated by the four treaties together. Equally, it is not true, as has been claimed, that the Union started as a treaty and became a Community.

Moreover, the way in which recent treaties have divided the Union up into pillars has increased the fragmentation. The proliferation of protocols does not help either. So it is not surprising that Allott talks about the Byzantine nature of the treaties. To some extent this reflects what many people see as the obscure way in which they are written. All this has implications for any assessment either of the actual status of the treaties or of the structures and policy strategies contained in them.

What is the Status of the Treaties?

If the European Treaties are special, even though they all count and usually have particular characteristics of their own, does this have implications for their standing? In fact their status has been much debated because this is a politically very sensitive matter. Even lawyers can be uncertain about this and about the difference between treaties and constitutions. For some the treaties remain just treaties, which means that the Union, whether rightly or wrongly, is essentially a body dominated by the member states. While some are happy with this, others are not and believe either that the treaties already are much more than this or should become so. In other words they see the treaties collectively as the constitution of an autonomous European polity.

Deciding which interpretation is right, of course, requires, firstly, being clear exactly what we mean by the term 'constitution'. Here, as may already have become evident, we find the word is often used loosely and uncertainly. People often fail to state clearly what they mean by the term and can conflate contradictory meanings in their usage. Although this makes any assessment rather difficult, what seems to emerge is that the treaties are only constitutional in certain senses and even then only to a limited extent. So the answer to the basic question about the status of the treaties is that they are only partial constitutions. Hence, as we shall see, they do not play all the political roles which national constitutions can do.

Although people often assume that 'everybody knows' what a constitution actually is, the fact remains, as Blondel, Snyder and others have pointed out, there are at least three uses of the term. Firstly, it can be used empirically to refer to the actual organization of the polity: its institutions, procedures and structures, something which is often referred to as the 'concrete' or 'material' constitution. In other words, a constitution can be the actual political system of a polity. Much British usage takes 'constitutional' to mean such strategic questions of substantive governance involving institutions, power and rights and the rules of the game by which the institutions have to play.

This points to a second, jurisprudential understanding of the term: of a set of prescriptive and overriding legal principles for political life. In the Western constitutionalist tradition these are seen as establishing the rule of law and limiting the power of the state, often through both the 'separation of powers' and the enshrining of civic rights. By not allowing one branch of the state to have authority in all dimensions of public life, but sharing this between several institutions, civil society can be protected from abuse. Equally, by detailing the legally enforceable rights of the citizen a further restraint on state power can be established. Rau talks of a constitution as a 'book of freedom' as a result. Hartley talks of this libertarian or instrumental meaning as constituting a constitution in the narrow sense of a self-validated legal system.

Yet, thirdly, the term constitution can be used in an instrumental way to describe an actual document, the single comprehensive document which is the ultimate founding act of a polity. This is what people mean by a compact, codified or written constitution. For Snyder this is part of a further, subjective, understanding of a constitution which brings all three definitions together when a people deliberate on their situation and future needs. This may be unduly complicated because, in political terms, the single document is usually seen as indissolubly linked to popular state-building. For many authorities such a document has to emerge from, or be duly approved by, the people of the polity. Hence it is the symbol of the creation of a state or new political order. In other words, the single document creates a polity by listing the various institutions and principles by which the citizens agree to be governed.

What this brings out is that arguments about whether the treaties are a constitution do not really turn on the question of whether or not there is either an actual structure of governance or legal rules on the exercise of power. As Harden shows, these clearly exist in the Union and this helps to distinguish the EU from other international bodies. The arguments essentially concern the linked questions of, partly, whether the treaties actually match up to the form, principles and scope of constitutional documents drawn up in nation-states. Secondly, the argument turns on the origin and status of the treaties. For some they remain treaties, rightly or wrongly, and not an emanation from a European people. Conversely others argue that the treaties either always did constitute a constitution in technical senses of the term or have become so with the passage of time.

The case for saying the treaties are not constitutions rests on three contentions. To begin with, many think that only states can have constitutions and that the Union is not a state founded by a European people. This assumes that in a treaty citizens have no place while, in a constitution, the citizenry is ultimately sovereign. In fact there is no real 'European people' as such and citizens of the various democracies which constitute the Union do not really recognize or legitimize the treaties as their ruling charter. The Union is, in other words, a limited association created not by popular will but by continual negotiation amongst pre-existing states which do have their own people or 'demoi'. Only the states can negotiate, sign and ratify changes to their collective contracts. And they do this largely outside the normal rules of the Union through a process, the IGC, which, many think incapable of producing a constitution in any meaningful sense.

Hence, secondly, ultimate authority over the Union still rests with the states. The former cannot decide its own rules and powers without reference to them. And the states, while accepting the rules they make in common, limit these to those areas in which they are prepared to pool sovereignty. Equally, only the states can implement the agreed rules. So their underlying constitutional principles and political independence are not affected by doing all this. In fact, in Hartley's view, the states could wind up the Union if they so chose.

Thirdly, the treaties are not just one visible, compact, holistic and codified document but a hotchpotch of agreements and other acts which merely bundle obligations together rather than create rights or impose proper restraints on the states. Moreover, they are incomprehensible, out of date and opaque documents very different, in the eyes of many, from the style of national constitutions. One description of them is as being confused, dense, unreadable and, as a result, invisible. For Olivier Duhamel – a member of the European Parliament (MEP) – although there are institutions, there is no constitution. Thus, even though treaties can provide constitutions, the European Treaties do not qualify as constitutions in terms of nature, origin or content.

Such views are put forward by some quite different groups. Thus some British Euro-sceptics can still cling to this position arguing, despite their growing fears of a 'federal superstate', that the Union remains essentially an economic contract. Many academics and practical statesmen more favourably disposed to the Union also reject the notion that there is already a constitution. And Jacques Delors argues that the very idea is inappropriate. More significantly, many disappointed supporters of deeper integration find themselves forced into accepting that the treaties are not a constitution because of the way the treaties are negotiated, the limited powers of the institutions they create and their failure to measure up to the ideals of European democracy.

Often such federationists can go beyond this and demand that the Union move from a treaty base to a true constitutional foundation. They feel that a 'real constitution' is now a necessity. By this they mean a single text with clearer statements of rights and powers and a different legitimacy from the treaties. Such a demand has been heard in the European Parliament since the early 1980s. More recently, at the beginning of the 1996 IGC process, some two hundred MEPs signed up to an Inter-Group calling for a constitution. Greens, non-governmental organizations (NGOs) and many pro-European academics go along with such calls as do some statesmen.

This pressure continued into 2000 with the EP twice calling for constitutionalization of the treaties, notably in a resolution of 25 October 2000. What they wanted was partly to slim the treaties down into one, two-part document, principles and practice, and partly to refine their contents in line with national constitutional models, notably by including the Charter of Fundamental Rights. This would provide a reference text for citizens and would simplify the EU's institutional procedures. In other words, a major motive is to ensure that there is a particular form of material constitution within the EU, one which both rewards the EP and shows that the Union now rests on popular legitimacy and not on national sovereignty. The belief is that the extension of EU activity means that it must be both democratized and controlled, in line with western constitutional traditions. Terminology and texts should reflect reality more closely than they do now. Such ideas also figure largely in thinking about the 2004 IGC as Division V and Annex 3 show.

However, it should not be assumed that all calls for endowing the Union with a constitution come from those who want to turn it into a federal state. In fact, conservatives like Chris Patten and Edmund Stoiber, the Bavarian premier, advocate a constitution in order to clarify transfers of sovereignty to Brussels and to make clear the limits to the Union's powers and desires. Hence Rau talks of a constitution as being 'a book of subsidiarity' because he believes that the Union needs a constitution in order to ensure that it does not become a single centralized state. This means a clear, and strictly policed, division of powers between states and Union. Similar views can also be found among those who, like the European Constitutional Group, endorse the libertarian 'constitutional economics' ideas of James Buchanan. They believe that state power must be restrained by popularly based constitutional rules. However, most British Eurosceptics dislike this approach since it suggests allowing the EU to determine national powers and not the national parliaments. And many also think, with Telo and Magnette, that the national analogy is neither appropriate nor wise, since constitutionalization could end the Union's creative, evolutionary ambiguity.

As well as this potentially divisive ambiguity, there is a further paradox about calls for a constitution or constitutionalization. For, at the same time that pro-integrationist voices are calling for a European constitution, others with similar sympathies are claiming this is not necessary because the treaties always were, or more often have now become, a 'true constitution'. The first assessment rests on assertions that the treaties are not 'ordinary' treaties, being self-executing and creating both unusually powerful institutions and a separate system of law. And neither are subject to international law as such. Similarly, they impose new and binding obligations on states. The latter thus cannot avoid having their acts reviewed, their law interpreted by the ECJ and their own internal operations restrained. Nor can they easily revise the treaties. The latter rest on traditional institutions and practices, often of a federal nature, not to mention on the constitutions of the member states themselves.

However, a more common view is that the treaties may not originally have been a constitution but that they have become one. They have cast off their initial diplomatic characteristics as a result of a purposive evolution over time. This partly reflects the fact that the treaties have a life of their own, partly in the way in which more and more people have become involved with the treaties and their ratification and, particularly, the activities of the Court of Justice. For Stone Sweet and others the ECJ has, through its jurisprudence (and notably its rights of preliminary judgments and review), transformed European law from something which affects states to 'a vertically integrated legal regime conferring judicially enforceable rights and obligations on all legal persons'. This process of legal 'constitutionalization' has created a new legal order which takes precedence over national law and is enforced by a quasi-constitutional ECJ. The latter has, of course, referred to the TEC as 'the constitutional charter' of the Community's legal order. Hence, for Gerkrath and Pernice, there is no need to draft a new constitutional document because one already exists, made up of a combination of the treaties, ECJ case law and national constitutional provisions.

Attitudes to this process diverge greatly. Many lawyers have welcomed it as a positive and remarkable achievement. So have constructivist academic supporters of integration such as Christiansen and Jørgensen. Conversely, many Eurosceptics denounce the process and the way the ECJ has abusively reinterpreted what the treaties were meant to be and achieve, deriving ideas of citizenship which ought to belong to member states and deciding the division of power between the states and the supra-national institutions. Their view is that this 'integration through interpretation', combined with the efforts of collaborationist and federalist politicians, has turned the Union from a simple free-trade area into a 'superstate', an all-powerful country called 'Europe'. Clearly, those who take this view, like those who believe that the treaties always were a constitution, assume that the Union is essentially a self-sufficient polity and not just the creation of the states. However, national courts do not always accept the outcome as a constitution while some authorities interpret constitutionalization itself in wider ways. In other words this is a very legalistic view and one which ignores several of the meanings of a constitution.

To sum up, there is precious little agreement about what a constitution actually is. Equally, there is no consensus as to whether the treaties actually form one, in whatever sense, and if so of what type, not to mention whether this is good or bad. Hence the status of the treaties remains uncertain. Because of this the debate is both confused and politically charged. And this is likely to become increasingly apparent in the context of the 2004 IGC.

The Treaties as Partial Constitutions in Form and Function

Despite the controversial nature of the subject we can perhaps clarify things by first asking in more detail whether the treaties measure up to the main understandings of the term 'constitution'. And, secondly, we can ask what roles the treaties actually play. On the first, the Union clearly does have a material constitution. We have only to go to Brussels and stand outside the gleaming Justus Lipsius Consilium Building or the recovering Berlaymont of the Commission, to see this. In other words, there is a frame of governance in the treaties. However, this is neither as extensive nor of the same type as most national constitutional structures. It centres on economic matters and applies more to the Communities than to the Union as such. The treaties tend to emphasize legal and policy commitments over institutions while the latter are endowed with specific duties and powers rather than with full autonomy of action, as the idea of conferred powers would suggest. In any case, the Union's concrete constitution is not really aligned on the conventional model of national political structures and the way they work whether these be rigid, pragmatic, unitary, bi-cameral or something else.

Equally, there is the rule of law and the treaties embrace some, although not all, the checks and balances normally written into the rules of the democratic game. Many, but again not all of these, are enforced by the ECJ. Given the strength of the member states, however, such enforcement can be no better than nominal. And states are only bound in those areas covered by the treaties and not generally. Also, the treaties proceed on a case-by-case basis rather than using the general principles favoured by national constitutions. So, even from these perspectives the treaties are only partly constitutional.

This is even more the case when we turn to the treaties as constitutions in Blondel's third sense. Clearly the treaties are not a single, codified constitutional document, despite recent proposals to condense them into one. There are a variety, not to say a labyrinth, of written treaties. Despite the way they have come together they are still far from providing a holistic view of the Union. Moreover, their institutional provisions are secondary to policy agreements and also lead to the creation of a variety of bodies and not a single polity. And, even if the treaties are the ultimate legal authority in the Union, they still have to be supplemented by a raft of other legislation and case judgments, enjoying varying statuses, what Schmid has called a 'maquis' of law. For Vibert, moreover, the treaties are actually silent on key constitutional norms whether because these have been established by the ECJ, because they are in annexes or because they rest on partly unspoken conventions

Nor, despite the use of parliamentary and popular ratification procedures, can they really be said to emerge from the people. Neither are they sufficiently well written to make them either accessible or, more important, subjectively popular. They can, in fact, be said to provide constitutionalism without a true constitution. Hence the demands for their constitutionalization.

In other words, even if the treaties are commonly accepted as a constitution because they look like one, it is even clearer here that they are at best partial, or pre-constitutions. One way of regarding the treaties is to take them collectively as forming, in Newman's words, a kind of social contract for the Union. Or, more persuasively, they can be regarded as something equivalent to the charters granted by medieval European monarchs to towns and corporations such as universities. These organized such bodies, gave them specific privileges and let them run their own affairs within the constraints laid down by the monarch. However, it left them and their freedoms ultimately dependent on the Crown's good will although, in theory, the ruler was obliged to respect the privileges which he had granted, since even the king was subject to 'the law'. So, while the treaties echo some of the functions of national constitutions they do so only partially, and have a lesser status. A House of Commons Select Committee thus argued in 2000 that there had to be a clear distinction between the recognition that the treaties to some extent function as the constitutional blueprint of the EU and their being treated as a written charter in the same way as one would do a member-state constitution.

Because of their partial nature the treaties do not, to take up the second point, perform all the roles that national constitutions usually do. They do, however, execute some of them. To begin with, they certainly reflect the balance of power within the IGCs and beyond at the time they were drafted. Indeed, their contents derive from the political map and balance at the time they were drafted. The treaties are thus very much a projection of state interests and power. And this fact has not declined with the passage of time.

Equally, the European Treaties set out the framework of governance of the Union and the basic institutions needed to run it. They provide the latter with their basic legitimacy. Like constitutions the treaties are also there to lay down the rules by which the political game should be played and to suggest what the political process should be. And, at the same time, they define a political code for the Union, specifying and circumscribing the powers and relations of the various components and institutions.

Finally, the European Treaties create a superior point for assessing ordinary decisions, together with the mechanisms of Community law and the ECJ for carrying out this assessment. So they do provide reference points for judging the acceptability of proposed political changes, both by laying down basic principles against which other legislation must be judged and also by preventing too easy change in essential values by giving a special status to constitutional and other basic laws. Equally, they open the way to the drafting of new laws. However, easy amendment of the treaties themselves is only partly excluded since, while the rules require a fairly strict process to be gone through before an IGC is called, there is nothing thereafter to stop states inserting whatever they like, irrespective of how relevant such things are, provided, that is, they gain the agreement of the other member states. So, with the partial exception of the more political codes needed for such an unusual body as the Union, the treaties do all these things, though not perfectly.

The situation is less clear-cut with another group of roles. Normally constitutions provide guarantees for the citizenry's political and other rights. In other words, they enshrine the compact between the people and the government. The European Treaties have only slowly moved towards doing this, first through court rulings and then with the introduction of citizenship in the TEU and the new emphases on rights introduced by the TA and the TN. But even then it is made clear that citizenship and rights are also the concern of other bodies such as the Council of Europe (CoE). In other words, there is a weak form of citizenship and rights. Equally, though the powers of the institutions are limited and rules of procedure are laid down, it is not clear on what basis this is done. Subsidiarity and flexibility are some way from the clear limitations on power typical of the Anglo-Saxon tradition.

When it comes to the last group of functions, the treaties fall a long way short. They are, as argued above, based on governmental decision and not on 'we the free peoples of Europe', as the Levellers would have put it. The treaties in other words create an agreement to act in common, they do not reflect the creation of a state by a self-conscious European people. They fail Snyder's subjectivity test in other words. This is Weiler's essential argument. He sees the treaties as not so much a constitution without a document but a constitution without a popular sanction. Nor, it might be added, do the treaties enshrine long-standing traditions which give the Union its identity in the way national charters do. Rather they point to the failure of national traditions and to changing needs in post-1945 Europe.

Despite the invocation of various values and aims in the preambles and elsewhere, the treaties do not really provide a moral and philosophical justification for the regime, often only setting out the aims which it is meant to achieve. Hence the treaties are not well known and, as just implied, they do not fulfil the affective and popular symbolic role that many national constitutions do. Equally, they lack the educational role of better drafted national documents which can be the basis for civic education. Hence it is hard to think of the treaties being called 'the first love of the European people', as the 1830 constitution of the Swiss canton of the Ticino is known. At best they are justified by the Commission and others as being a record of achievement to be defended against critics. So the treaties are only partial constitutions in a functional sense. They have many of the technical elements, albeit to a limited extent, but without the basic constitutive power, roots and status of popularly endorsed national constitutions.

ii Problems Presented by the Treaties

Even if we could agree on the status of the two key European Treaties, the TEC and the TEU, this would not end the difficulties they cause. In fact there are at least three obstacles to understanding them. The most obvious of these is the inherent difficulties presented by the texts themselves. But the fact that they cover two different structures, the Union and the Community, should not be overlooked either. Furthermore, there seem to be special problems for United Kingdom readers arising from the fact that there is no codified constitutional document in the country. And many of these problems have implications for the way this *Guide* is constructed.

The Inherent Difficulties of the Treaties

The treaties are difficult documents with which to come to terms. As we have already seen, there are many of them and their status and relationships are not always clear. Indeed, only slowly have they been brought to a coherent state. All too often the published versions of agreements such as the TA and the TN are actually lists of amendments to earlier texts. While these may be both available and familiar to specialists, most ordinary readers are often unaware of this history, and find comprehension difficult. Before the TA the treaties used to include both obsolete clauses and inserted elements of other constitutional-type acts, which caused further confusion. The fact that most recent treaties amend three or four existing treaties as well as protocols makes for even greater complexity. Hence understanding the actual effect of some of the treaties is not easy.

Even when consolidated texts have been published they can often fail to reproduce elements of the original treaties. Faced with the statements in the consolidated version of the TEU published in 1997 that the text, *inter alia*, of Article 8 (ex G) and various protocols are 'not reproduced', many readers might legitimately wonder why. (The answer is actually the reasonable one that these are either formal, or very detailed, elements which are not needed to make sense of the TEU because they are already incorporated in it and that to include them a second time, in their original form, would make the printed texts even more complicated and dense than they already are. But such reasoning is not always explained.)

If the proliferation of treaties, treaty changes and textual amendments, and the manifold protocols and declarations they generate, are the first difficulties, they are far from being the only ones. A related problem is that there are now three sets of numbers to the actual articles in the main treaties. Until the TA, articles in the TEU were given capital letters while those in the TEC had numbers and, where new elements had been added, lower-case letters. Thus in the provisions for Economic and Monetary Union, not only was there an Article 109 but there were also Articles 109a to 109m. This was complicated, but practitioners were used to it.

The Treaty of Amsterdam changed all this when it consolidated the constitutive treaties. Both the main constituent treaties were renumbered in a more rational way, eliminating both the TEC's lower-case letters and the TEU's capital letter based system. But both treaties were renumbered in separate single numerical sequences. So, whereas a reference to Article L automatically meant the Union treaty, today a reference to Article 7 could mean the provisions on suspending a state for infringing human rights under the Treaty on European Union or the listing of institutions in the Treaty establishing the European Community. As a result, references to articles now need to be followed by the acronym of the treaty being cited, for example Article 7 TEC. Again this is cumbersome, even if it makes for easier recognition and citation. A further problem is that the consolidated versions do not enjoy full legal status, being merely 'working versions'. Legal status remains with the original treaties as they were negotiated. Moreover, existing texts and commentaries using the older enumerations remain in circulation. And, as the Treaty of Nice has shown, changing the treaties can also mean interposing new articles with lower-case letters attached in order to avoid a further, and even more confusing, renumbering.

If we look at the contents there are a further set of difficulties. The first is the technical complexity of the structure of the European Treaties. Not merely are these divided into various parts and titles (and subordinate categories, often on an inconsistent basis), but not everything in them enjoys the same status. The treaties can be very detailed in some areas, as with EMU, but they can also be very sketchy in others, notably on the institutions. On top of this there are all the protocols and declarations, often attached to, or associated with, more than one final act. So the treaties can be uncomfortably long.

For many people an even greater problem is that, even though the treaties are available in all the legal languages of the Union, they are rarely an easy read. Even after the rationalizations brought about by the TA, they remain written in a style which does not lend itself to easy comprehension. Hence, as we might expect from documents which emerged from frantic late-night compromises among heads of government in assorted European cities, the texts are opaque and complicated. They are not written in plain terms but use the terminology and formulations of treaties and parliamentary bills with which most people are not familiar. In the case of the TEU some of the drafters were said to have admitted that if they had realized that it would be read by the public, they would have produced a different document altogether.

Given all this, the texts as such have been harshly criticized in the United Kingdom and beyond. One former Commission official said, 'Maastricht had all the readability of a railway timetable'; a French MEP that the Vatican would have drafted it better; and a member of the House of Lords castigated it as a 'shambles with which no lawyer or accountant would wish to be associated'. A former editor of *The Times* went so far as to call it the worst treaty since Versailles, presumably in form and in substance. And Commissioner Oreja was almost beside himself at the way that the 1996 IGC produced a text of extraordinary difficulty, which was almost impossible to understand, let alone explain. Similar criticisms were made by insiders and outsiders about Nice, even though this was a briefer document. The texts thus fail one of the main tasks of a constitutional document, which is to simplify rules so that people can understand and internalize them. There has been no equivalent of the UK's Plain Language Commission.

This has to be put down to the fact that the language used is not there by happenstance but as a result of hard political bargaining, and simpler language could easily change what is acceptable to the states. Words can matter a great deal even if they are hard to follow. As Commissioner Michel Barnier has said, the treaties are not made deliberately complicated so as to discourage the reader. They are the inevitable result of up to 15 states and to a lesser extent the institutions all seeking to have their say and to insert what matters to them in the texts. And they have to do this in conditions which are far from ideal. Many of the problems presented by the treaties reflect the way in which they are actually negotiated. Although much of the work is done by competent officials, the final decisions have, since the Maastricht summit, had to be taken by heads of government in a mad post-midnight rush to get finished. This is not the kind of careful consideration that constitutional conventions are supposed to provide, always assuming that the IGC is such a body. Indeed the IGC process has been attacked as bizarrely untransparent, ineffective and undemocratic, particularly because the negotiators are agents of the national governments and not free spirits. But whatever the justification, this simply compounds the inherent difficulties of the texts.

A final problem is that, as we have already seen, the treaties are not self-contained and self-explanatory. Although Margaret Thatcher once pledged herself to maintaining 'the treaties, the whole treaties and nothing but the treaties' this misses the point in three ways. First of all, while the treaties give guidance they cannot be a full explanation of how things work in practice. Understanding the treaties is not the same as knowing the day-to-day life of the Union. This has to be seen in terms of wider European realities. Secondly, the treaties have been extended by case law and other legislative enactments, so they do not provide a comprehensive guide to the basic law of the Union. Thirdly, the thinking of the treaties is often opaque. As a result, as Harden rightly says, the meaning of the treaties can only be looked at through interpretative argument. This is inherently controversial as well as difficult. It means that glosses are very necessary to help make sense of the treaties as they stand. This may be good for academics but not necessarily for the general public.

Union and/or Community?

Even if all this were not so, there is a further problem. This is that the concrete structures created by the various European Treaties are themselves inordinately complicated, as has probably already become clear. To begin with, the body which many people take to be a single entity known as 'Brussels', or even 'Europe', is not actually a unity. 'Brussels' can involve either, or both, the European Union and the European Community, not to mention the other two Communities. What makes things worse is that the term 'Union' has undergone a series of changes over time. At the outset, it was essentially an aspiration for those who wanted to see Europe unite after 1945. Then, once the TEC was agreed, 'ever closer union' became a process to which the Community was dedicated. Finally, with the TEU 'union' ceased to be merely a process and took on organizational form as the European Union.

However, the relationship between the new body and the existing Community is anything but simple. In fact it was only with the TEU that the singular term became official, replacing the previous references to the European Economic Community and to the Communities in the plural. The subsequent substantive and terminological mess has confused many sensible scholars, like those who claim that 'the EC has been officially renamed the "European Union"'. This is not, technically, true because what the TEU actually did was to create a new body, the European Union. The problem is that this was an odd kind of body, a loose tarpaulin over the three existing Communities and the new inter-governmental pillars, as Curtin has described it. Yet, though the Union is, as we suggested in the previous version of the *Guide*, superior to the other bodies so that new states can only apply to join the Union, it lacks real force. It possesses neither what is known as 'legal personality', that is to say the ability to take binding decisions in international law, nor the ability to implement its own desires. In fact, it is dependent on the European Community, not to mention on the other Communities and pillars, for getting things done. Hans Van den Broek was close to the truth when he told the Council of Europe that the EC 'is the legal personality of the EU', although the relationships between the two are actually more ambiguous and complex. Hence it is hardly surprising that many believe that the two should simply be merged.

A further complication is that the two terms can produce emotive responses. For some, the term 'Community' is the key to European integration and solidarity while 'Union' suggests inter-governmental control and national self-interest. Equally, the latter appeals to others for precisely this reason and they go to great lengths to distinguish between EC law and the EU which, to their minds, does not have any law, being an inter-governmental body. So when, after the TEU came into effect, the Council of Ministers seized on the term Union to describe itself since it is the only body which operates fully and freely across all three post-Maastricht pillars, Community fans were horrified. They would have preferred that the Council kept its old title, as most other Brussels institutions have done.

Despite such strong convictions, the desire for simplicity has largely overcome these reservations, initially among the general public and thereafter in elite circles. With the passage of time much general usage has ignored the difficulty and plumped for using the term Union as a portmanteau word in all situations relating to treaty-based integration, irrespective of technical niceties. Subsequently many lawyers have dropped their concentration on the EC so that textbooks now rarely use the term Community in their titles and even studies of European law are increasingly referring to this as Union law. And it is not uncommon to find people nowadays talking of the Union as though it existed in the 1950s or 1960s, rather than from November 1993. Furthermore, in some cases the Brussels institutions have themselves ignored the differences, for example attributing foreign-policy decisions to the Union as in the case of Mostar. Equally, the convention which drafted the Charter of Fundamental Rights assumed that its ideas applied across the whole Union. And Nice has encouraged this by changing the title of its main record to the *Official Journal of the European Union* and talking of Union institutions and values. More concretely it developed the status of the TEU by making it even more key to enhanced co-operation.

Some authorities like von Bogdandy would argue that there are sound reasons for going beyond this and regarding the Union and Community as one undifferentiated body, especially after the TA, which brought institutions closer together and transformed things into a real polity, albeit not a state. For example, it brought the European Council more into the Community mainstream while also shifting responsibilities from the third to the first pillar and changing the roles of the Community institutions in the inter-governmental pillars. This blurring of boundaries between the pillars has led de Witte to argue that the EU should be viewed not as a Greek temple with pillars but as a French-style Gothic cathedral with the EC as its central nave and the CFSP and PJCCM making up 'somewhat darker side aisles'. Legally though, the pillars remain intact. Some elements of inter-governmental activity have been transferred to the Community pillar, while the Community institutions have gained more say in the inter-governmental pillars. From this point of view there is neither fragmentation nor problem, but fusion, because, in practice, the Union does have legal personality, as Wessels argues, as well as a single institutional framework, a single means of treaty revision and a single legal code, as von Bogdandy and Nettesheim claim. This is very appealing, especially after Nice.

However, there are several reasons why we feel we cannot follow this line and treat the Union and the Community as identical. To begin with, von Bogdandy and Nettesheim themselves still call for further simplifications to make the unity clear, which suggests the identity is incomplete. Secondly, the negotiators at Amsterdam deliberately refused to give the Union legal personality, thus purposely maintaining the two bodies. Furthermore, to insist on the absolute identity of the two can give a false impression of the development of integration, playing down the earlier importance of the EC. Fourthly, it would make the overall treaty structure seem rather silly in providing for the two. The member states have clearly left us with both Union and Community as they are, locked into an extremely complex and obscure relationship deriving from the fact that the states cannot really decide what they want the European project to be. We have to assume a certain awareness, competence and rationality on the part of the drafters, which the fusion thesis does not do. Equally, it overlooks the strong political feelings the terms can evoke.

Lastly, there are a whole range of detailed questions which would present themselves when the treaties distinguish between Union and Community. In looking at the treaties the differences between the Union and the Community cannot be easily set aside. Treating the two as synonymous makes a nonsense of the texts, whose authors went to great pains to distinguish between the two, particularly, as noted, by refusing to give the Union legal personality. This would have more or less meant the Union absorbing the Community. This was unacceptable to many member governments and, though apparently remaining a possibility until late in the negotiations, was ultimately rejected. Those who opposed granting legal personality feared that to do so would have made the Union a more state-like body. In particular, it would have prevented the states from enjoying treaty-making powers under the second and third pillars, although they did partially finesse this by the provisions of the TEU's Article 24. Equally, full legal personality would have encouraged a switch of competences to the Union in a way which the TA went to some lengths to rule out. Pro-integrationists might also have feared that the Community *acquis* was being sacrificed to a Union which could be seen as too inter-governmental. Many, like Curtin and Dehousse, accuse those who negotiated the TEU and the TA of having dangerously fragmented the EC as it is.

So how should we proceed, given the confusion? The first thing is to accept that there will have to be some inconsistency, given what Curtin now rightly calls the multi-layered nature of the Union. In general discussion we will use the term Union even when this may not be wholly accurate. But where a treaty distinguishes between the two, so will we. Where it is necessary to discriminate, as in questions of the first pillar, the four freedoms and policies, along with specific institutions, we will talk of the Community even in today's context. Even if we keep to this, the confusion remains, but at least we are facing up to it.

The United Kingdom and the Treaties

As well as having such internal difficulties, the treaties also face further problems of understanding in the United Kingdom. This is not simply because Europhobia runs deep, although this does cause problems both in attitudes and in the availability of information. It is also a reflection of UK political culture which places little stress on formal documents and often has little time for written constitutions. This arises, finally, from the nature of the contemporary UK constitution itself and the strange ways that legislation can be handled.

One problem is that there is an underlying hostility to the Union. The April 2000 Eurobarometer showed the United Kingdom coming bottom in support for the Union, in trust in EU institutions and in the belief that their country had benefited from membership. This lack of public support, together with both the strength of movements which are viscerally opposed to all forms of European integration and the way the media portrays the Union, has three effects. Firstly, it discourages governments and others from putting over the opposing case. Any government- or Brussels-sourced provision of information is immediately denounced as 'propaganda'. This, secondly, results in a low level of information, with UK respondents seeing themselves as the least well informed of all where the Union is concerned. As a result very little attention is given to the treaties. Even at the time of the Maastricht and Amsterdam negotiations little was done to understand or explain the details of the finalized treaties and, in the latter case, the manifold versions generated. The Labour government thus did not think it worthwhile to produce any kind of guide either to the TA or to the TN. In fact things were even worse with Nice, when the opposition front bench clearly did not understand the difference between the treaty as such and the other decisions taken at the summit. All this means that understanding the treaties needs a good deal of effort, and this the British are generally unwilling to put in. And because they do not take the trouble to read the documents, ideas such as having been misled about the implications of integration in 1972 or 1987 can arise. The old English adage that 'ignorance of the law is no defence at law' is rarely applied to matters European.

Even when they do look at the treaties they have two problems to overcome. The first is that political culture in the UK seems to place little stress on formal documents. What seems to matter is personality, policy and struggles for power. The rules within which these take place, and the documents which enshrine them, are largely ignored when they are not actively misconstrued. Hence students of politics are somewhat unfamiliar with documents like the treaties, even though there are distinct similarities between the European Treaties and the ramshackle nature of the UK Constitution, as Nash points out. Indeed, most people in the United Kingdom have never even read an Act of Parliament. Hence, when John Major made two specific references to the TEU text in his speech during the November 1992 Paving Debate in the Commons, this was described by a radio commentator as 'virtually a line-by-line analysis'.

This is not just a matter of chance. It can often rest on a strongly held belief in the superiority of the UK Constitution and a corresponding assumption that written constitutions are, by definition, inefficient. Much British opinion, especially of a conservative bent, argues that the British system has worked very well, producing strong and successful government. As Lodge puts it, the British are inclined to ask: 'What is a constitution? Why do we need one? And what is its relevance to the citizen?'

Given this, many believe there is no need to change, especially since written constitutions are often perceived to be a reflection of national failure, whether in war or revolution, and hence needed only by lesser and more unstable breeds. Such crises have forced the French and others to decide what they want to do in a way which the British, who have avoided such crises since 1689, have no need of. And it has been said that calls for change come from those who have lost elections, so that constitutions are not democratic but represent the 'poetry of the impotent'. British linguistic insularity and incompetence plays a particular role here. Written constitutions are also seen as hard to reconcile with common law and also as likely to prove very rigid. They give power to the courts rather than to elected legislators. Hence they can prevent rapid and emphatic responses to changing circumstances, a charge often levelled against the United States, which can be seen as essentially old-fashioned. In any case, such constitutions do not last long and can conceal authoritarianism. In contrast the UK Constitution is 'nothing less than the way of life of a free people' according to Anderson and Kaltenthaler.

Such attitudes may now be changing. The UK Constitution was largely taken for granted until the 1970s. Since then it has been subject to a growing volume of criticism, partly from the modernizing left and partly from right-wing libertarians. There is growing unease at the way in which majorities have exploited the dominance of Parliament in a way probably not envisaged in 1688, as Loveland points out. Devolution, the incorporation of the European Convention on Human Rights into domestic law, electoral reform, freedom of information legislation and the fate of the House of Lords have all come on to the agenda. European integration and the need to co-ordinate these initiatives have also made constitutional questions more salient and bring nearer the day when a written constitution may have to be considered. There is evidence that the idea of a rights-based constitution has more appeal than used to be the case. This is in line with a general European trend to see rights rather than rules as the main characteristic of a constitution. All this may make it easier to come to terms with the European Treaties. However, there is a long history of ignorance and incomprehension to be overcome.

All this affects the assumptions the British bring to reading constitutional documents. The United Kingdom is clearly a constitutional country in the sense of one which has a series of rules to govern the exercise of power in the state and to ensure its democratic nature, rules which are largely written, whether in the form of statute or of legal precedent. However, the rules are not codified. There is no one single written constitutional document in the UK and never has been. Only England has ever had such a charter, and then a long time ago, with the Levellers' 'Agreement of the People' and the Cromwellian 'Instrument of Government' of the 1650s. Consequently, the UK Constitution is evolutionary and based on the sovereignty of the monarch in Parliament as interpreted by the courts and unwritten conventions. This is not a mere quirk of history, a piece of archaic colour, no more significant than the Beefeaters. It is a fact which shapes both the distribution of power in the United Kingdom and the way many people think about politics and the law.

The UK Constitution, according to both Finer and Bogdanor, is indeterminate, in the sense that there are no clear limits. Because of this, and the stress placed on parliamentary sovereignty (and the lack of stress on the separation of powers), virtually everything can be constitutional and what counts as constitutional is dictated by the party in power, and is not subject to the kind of arbitration provided by the US Supreme Court. The constitution is a pragmatic and changing matter. As Keating and Jones say, 'democracy and constitutionalism in Britain have become identified not with the limitation of govern-mental power but with the alternation of parties in power at the centre'. Thus the UK Constitution is an immensely party political matter in some senses. However, because there is no tradition of reverence for a single document, there is a tendency to play down concern for structures and rules of the game.

The UK Constitution is also indistinct in that there is no special category of consti-tutional laws. Because the constitution is uncodified, and rests on the supremacy of Parliament, all laws are of equal value. There is no difference in status between the European Communities Act of 1972, which gives EC law predominance in the UK, and acts regulating traffic in Thanington Without or Moira. Where there is a conflict the most recent law takes precedence. In other words, there is no sense of a hierarchy of norms, that is to say the acceptance that some laws are more important and binding than are others. People no longer think, as they did in Cromwell's day that 'In every government there must be Somewhat Fundamental. Somewhat like a Magna Carta. Which should be standing, be unalterable.' Therefore they do not see the need to think much about formal documents like the treaties as their importance is limited. This has the perverse effect that, contrary to most other member states, the United Kingdom has no clear and overriding rules on what powers can, or cannot, be transferred to the European Union. This makes the emergence of the European treaties as a parallel constitution, as Madgwick and Woodhouse term it, doubly difficult for some to accept.

A concomitant of this is that the constitution is un-entrenched, which means that basic rules can be easily changed. And, as Allott says, there is no tradition of fundamental rights. Hence UK governments have been able to undo basic constitutive institutions such as local government in ways which would be unthinkable in mainland Europe. This may be changing with the growing talk of requiring referenda for major changes. However, so far little of this encourages the British to pay special attention to a classic constitutional document.

A final reason why the British, and especially the English, are not very well versed in reading constitutional-type documents lies in the attitudes to legislation produced by the UK system. Politicians are used to the very precise and detailed legislative acts produced by UK parliamentary draftsmen which seek to cover all contingencies and leave little scope for interpretation. They assume therefore that the European Treaties are a totally rigid construction. In fact continental drafting is more a matter of principle and purpose. The treaties are, as we have seen, partly frameworks, indicating general objectives and ways of achieving them, but not laying down detailed provisions. They leave this to implementation and court rulings.

The way the treaties are applied is thus affected by circumstance and by judicial interpretation. This also makes British critics unhappy because this fluidity opens the way for the very different type of broad-brush interpretation of the spirit of the European Treaties practised by the ECJ. The tradition in the United Kingdom, for instance, until the case of *Pepper* v. *Hart* in late 1992, forbade judges even to consult reports of relevant parliamentary debates in Hansard when interpreting statutes. They were expected to work from the text alone, hence the slightly contradictory complaints about generalities, ambiguities and lack of precise definitions.

In any case, the UK system does not make it easy to get hold of basic legislation. While some free publication and photocopying of statutes has been allowed in the aftermath of privatization, this is still constrained. Legal texts are no longer provided free, as was traditional English practice. This is very different from other Commonwealth countries, where the principle that 'one of the cornerstones of democracy is that the people own the legislation' still applies so that there can be no copyright in laws. The underlying view in the UK has been one of the people as subjects and consumers, not as citizens. All this has deleterious effects on British democracy in general and, in particular, makes it difficult for the British to come to terms with the European Treaties. Nevertheless, the European Treaties are important and need to be understood, in their own terms and not just through the prism of British preconceptions. The question is, how can this be done?

iii The Nature of the *Guide*

Although the European Treaties are complex, enjoy an uncertain status and can be difficult to fit into the UK's ways of looking at things, this does not mean that they are not worth studying. As we have shown, they are important and indeed deserve to be better known. There are, though, limits to the problems to be faced in studying them. So we now set out our starting point in trying to do this, making clear both the presuppositions we have made and the aims we have set ourselves in reproducing and also commenting on the treaties. The structure that derives from these aims is then set out. We hope that this will make the *Guide* user-friendly and helpful.

Approaches and Presumptions

The fact that, as we have seen, there are such violently conflicting views of the Union makes it clear that no commentary can be neutral. All assessments, in other words, are marked by the authors' views. It is therefore important that we make clear the basis on which the *Guide* proceeds. Our view is that the treaties are important and should be seen as the fundamental blueprints of the Union but no more than a partial constitution. This is because we do not see the Union as a 'superstate' but as a much more complicated organization, a pluralist competitive network, both inter-governmental and supra-national aimed at specific functions. Consequently we believe it is necessary to go on distinguishing between Union and Community where this is relevant. The European Treaties, especially after Nice, reflect all this very clearly. And this is one of their weaknesses.

The European Treaties are important for a variety of reasons. They matter because they are constitutive and structure the Union and Community as a whole, in an institutional way. Moreover, they provide the basis for the whole range of policy-making since no legislation is possible without treaty authorization. The treaties are also the keys to the future of the Union, and indeed of the integration process, since changes in the nature of the Union must, ultimately at least, be formalized by treaty amendment. But, we cannot accept the argument that they are, or have become, actual constitutions in the sense of a single codified and self-confident national document. They are only partial constitutions and then mainly in functional senses. In terms of status we see them as, at heart, a grant from the member states, the modern-day equivalent of a medieval charter, in fact.

In other words, the Union remains a body which ultimately depends on the member states. Many of the Union's problems are, when examined closely, less the doings of an all-powerful socialist Brussels bureaucracy than of the divisions, hesitations and self-interest of member-state governments. While these may not play the simple dominating role spelt out by Moravscik, they are fundamental. But they are also much less uniform than is often assumed. Equally, they are caught up in both a whole series of decision-making networks, along with many other social forces, and a competitive political process in which governments, institutions and others engage to seek their own ends, as they do within states. The institutions, as well as involving a pooling of sovereignty, have a life and interests of their own. Hence the Union is a complex, in-between kind of institution, as Laffan says. And it is likely to remain so even after the Treaty of Nice.

The EU is, in fact, best seen as a body which is not easily classified, partly because it involves so many internal interactions and so many outputs, both internally regulatory and international. It is inherently messy, not to say post-modern in its nature, and differs from most other international (and national) organizations. Trying to appreciate its diversity and avoiding oversimplified and polemical approaches is the overriding aim here.

All this has its effects on the treaties. In our view they are very human documents, reflecting doubts and disagreements as much as shared aspirations. They are not all-powerful plans for a clear future. They represent the state of play at the time they were negotiated and the way in which this was done. They are far from perfect, like the Union itself. However, with the TA a much ignored attempt was made to tidy them up. So they are still there, and in our view their flaws are less significant than the fact that they structure a form of international co-operation in which the United Kingdom is rightly, if problematically, involved. And of course the meaning of the treaties has often to be teased out, whether by lawyers or others. Doing this often depends on circumstances and theoretical presuppositions.

Although the *Guide* does not seek to advance any particular theoretical approach to the Union, it does reflect our belief that many neat theories are limited and leave as much unexplained as they reveal. In particular too many ignore economics, public opinion and the wider patterns of social interaction which have distinguished post-1945 Europe. Equally, many of the decisions made are best explained as political compromises rather than rational preferences. A comprehensive approach, even if this means being eclectic, is advisable. Hence, while we need legal insights to help us to understand the European treaties, there are also clear political elements. The approach adopted here is a common-sense political one and not a technical legalistic one. It is hoped that this will continue to make the treaties more accessible and more comprehensible than has so far been the case.

Aims and Purposes

We see the *Guide*'s purpose as sevenfold. To begin with, we want to show that the treaties are evolving and historic documents, negotiated largely in a series of IGCs. In particular we want to update our original commentary on the treaties and explain what has happened since, and how and why the Treaties of Amsterdam and Nice came about. Secondly, we want to make it clear what was changed at each of these IGCs and what has been inherited from the past, particularly since our first commentary was published. In other words we want to make the Amsterdam and Nice changes clear.

Thirdly, by publishing the treaties in this very welcome format, we hope to make the texts more available than has often been the case. Few people use the Stationery Office (formerly known as HMSO) which publishes the UK versions and sells the Community editions. Because the treaties are parallel to, if different from, the British Constitution, they need to be known to UK and other citizens. In other words, we believe that people ought to know what 'Europe' is actually all about and not rely on the distorted views so often propagated by the media. We hope that this will allow people to go beyond the dangers of 'a little learning'.

However, because of their technical difficulties the treaties need explanation. So our fourth aim is to try to explain why the various articles are in the treaties, what they mean and what their consequences have been, or may be. This means we want to look at the whole of the treaties we are studying and not just the key institutional or policy elements. Equally, we want to make it possible to understand the meanings and inter-connections of the treaties, particularly by relating them to the policies pursued by the Union. And, as we have already said, we want to try and do all this simply and comprehensibly, and in as detached a way as possible, so that readers can make their own judgements on the texts. We hope to enable our readers, whether they are students or ordinary citizens, to cope with the problems of difficult texts, polemical interpretations and all too rapidly changing circumstances.

Because we are aware that the European Treaties are not the whole of the story and that the primary law of the Union goes wider, as does the Union itself, our fifth aim is to bring together a number of other fundamental documents in this one volume. Reproducing such texts as the new Charter of Fundamental Rights alongside the treaties makes possible a more convenient and fuller understanding of the rules governing the Union. By doing this and providing means to integrate both treaties and commentary we hope to make the primary law seem more of a unity than is sometimes the case, which is our sixth goal. However, we are very conscious that understanding the treaties does not give a complete and self-sufficient insight into the actual workaday Union.

Finally, we also want to provide a minimum of reference material which readers may need to set the treaties and their evolution in context. This obviously includes bibliographic listings to enable readers to follow up items of interest to them. On a technical level we feel we should provide details of the way that the basic treaties have changed over the years; an account of attempts to rationalize the treaty base; and a note on how recent changes have affected the two other constitutive treaties which are not printed in full here. We hope that all this will prove useful.

Structure

All this helps to explain the way the *Guide* is structured. It is divided into five main divisions along with some annexes. These are numbered but not called 'parts' or 'sections' because, as already noted, this could cause confusion with the use of terms such as part, title, chapter and section in the treaties themselves. Thus, having tried in this first division – the Introduction – to pick out the nature of the treaties, the problems they pose and the way we seek to overcome them, we move on to look at their evolution. The second division focuses on the genealogy of the treaties, beginning with the origins in the 1951 Treaty establishing the European Coal and Steel Community and going up to the TEU and beyond. It then goes into more detail on the Amsterdam and Nice treaties in themselves and not just as a series of amendments. In the case of Amsterdam, this is partly because not only did it make more significant changes to both the substance of the Union and the treaty base, but it also rationalized the treaties. As a result it is now hard to grasp what was actually in it and we try to assess this.

Nice also will tend to be lost against the background of the staged treaty revisions it brought about. So it too is assessed as a whole and characterized, after introducing the events of the 2000 IGC. And because it was so encouraging to enlargement its key provisions are presented here. Apart from this, because both treaties are essentially amending treaties, all that is reproduced in this division is the basic outline plus the final act of the relevant IGC.

This enables us to devote the next two divisions, which constitute the bulk of the *Guide*, to the two key European Treaties: the Treaty on European Union and the Treaty establishing the European Community in the form each will have if the Treaty of Nice is ratified. Owing to constraints of space not all the treaty base is included, but the TECSC and the TEAEC would, in any case, present an unnecessary complication. They duplicate material, complicate simplification and generally make texts such as the Treaty of Nice more difficult to follow, even though the changes are just the same as those made to the TEC. They are mentioned only where they differ substantially from the Treaty of Rome. Moreover, the TECSC will have expired before publication of the *Guide*.

Whereas in our earlier commentary we adopted a composite structure of our own in order to make the two treaties seem more integrated, here we have followed much more closely the arrangement of the two treaties themselves as consolidated by the Treaty of Amsterdam. The approach is to start with a brief overview and then to subdivide the division into elements largely paralleling the titles of the treaties. Thus on the TEU we look at the preamble and the common provisions. We then include a brief mention of Titles II, III and IV. These initially were lists of amendments to the other treaties. However, since their contents have now been subsumed in the consolidated versions, we have thought it an unnecessary complication and use of space to reproduce them.

We then go on to look at Titles V and VI, dealing with common foreign and security policy (V) and police and judicial co-operation in criminal matters (VI), in other words the two inter-governmental pillars of the Union. This is followed by the provisions of Title VII on enhanced co-operation or 'flexibility' and the final provisions of Title VIII on jurisdiction, enlargement and amendment, etc. Finally, we print the various binding protocols specifically attached to the treaty and the formal final act, a kind of appendix which provides a home to the various explanatory declarations. Relevant declarations adopted at the time of Amsterdam and Nice are also reproduced.

Within each of these elements our strategy has been, as with the TEC, to introduce the treaty text through a commentary which seeks to show how and why each part of the treaty is where it is, what we think it means and how policies flow legally and logically from it. Our focus is now on the treaties and not on what has been deduced from them. However, we do try to relate the text to key decisions of the ECJ. In doing all this we are drawing on the kind of documentary analysis now being brought into the national curriculum and with which lawyers, theologians and some political scientists will already be familiar.

The treaty text is indented and picked out in bold and italic where necessary. Bold type denotes wholly new material and italic material which, while present in the TEC and the TEU, has been subjected to some change as a result of the TA and TN. This can involve omissions, altered positions or other minor changes. The fact that all the articles (except numbers 1, 2, 3 and 105 of the TEC) were renumbered by the TA, as well as often being simplified, has not been signalled typographically since this would italicize the whole of the treaties and make it harder to see the impact of Amsterdam. A separate typeface has been used to pick out the relatively limited changes made at Nice but, as already noted, using bold and italic as appropriate to indicate new material and alterations respectively.

Throughout we use the new enumeration established at Amsterdam, although we print the old location in brackets. The old enumeration as such is repeated in an annex for comparison. For reasons of simplicity we have decided not to follow the ECJ in its May 2001 decision in using EU or EC after an article to denote post-Amsterdam numbers and 'of the EC treaty' to denote earlier numbers. To facilitate recognition of such changes and to provide both this and ease of access a Synoptic Table of treaty articles and commentary has been included above. This locates precisely elements of the *Guide* on a page-by-page basis.

When it comes to the TEC we again start with an overview and an examination of the Preamble. Thereafter the division is subdivided into elements covering either parts, where these are relatively brief as is the case of Principles, Citizenship and (later on) Association, or titles where this is not the case. Hence Part Three: Community Policies gives rise to 21 subdivisions covering the various policy areas where the Community has full competence, some of which, like EMU, are long and detailed. Part Five of the treaty occupies two subdivisions, the first dealing with the various institutions each analysed individually in the order given in the treaty. Similarly Part Six: General and Final Provisions is, like the treaty, split here, separating the external related policy questions from the more formal articles of legitimation in the final provisions proper. As with the TEU we then separately discuss the Protocols and Declarations, the latter being annexed to the Final Act.

The fifth division is given over firstly to a discussion of the ECSC and EAEC treaties and to the reproduction of other relevant documents. These include such items as the preamble to the SEA, the stability pacts linked to Economic and Monetary Union and the Charter of Fundamental Rights. Secondly, the division tries to pull the threads together by looking back at the treaties as a whole and then looking towards the future. For even before IGC 2000 entered the final straight, people were talking about another IGC in 2004. And this overlooks the need for further treaty adjustment to cope with the addition of new members. So the story of the European Treaties is clearly not yet complete.

Finally, a little like the TEC, the *Guide* also has a set of annexes. The first of these is a bibliography of works consulted and mentioned in the text. Then there are three technical annexes: showing how the TEC has changed over the years; discussing the various attempts to simplify, codify and redivide the treaties as a whole; and noting amendments to the TECSC and TEAEC. The *Guide* ends with an index, though readers will also find the Synoptic Table helpful when trying to track things down.

II The Evolution of the Treaties: From Paris to Nice

As well as being complex, the European Treaties are constantly changing. As the list in the previous division shows, the treaty base has rarely been static. To quote de Gaulle, 'treaties, like maidens and roses, each have their day'. In fact, the key European Treaties as we see them today owe some of their overall structure to the initial decisions of the 1950s; much of their detailed contents to an increasingly frequent series of recent treaty amendments, culminating with those agreed at Nice; and their numbering and repolishing to the simplification process undertaken in 1997 after the Amsterdam summit.

The reasons for this increasingly rapid evolution lie partly in internal dynamics, institutional constraints and unforeseen legacies from the past, as Christiansen and Jørgensen, along with Sverdrup, have argued. But the evolution also owes much to the way in which changing economic and political circumstances, domestic and external, have made new demands on the EU. Equally, national interests and strategies have played a major part in shaping the evolution of the European Treaties. National actors do matter, in other words, and IGCs are not simply the reflection of an underlying 'path dependent' logic of spillover or transnational exchange as Christiansen and Jørgensen and others including Stone Sweet and Sandholtz have claimed.

If the process is not as convoluted as that which produced the United Kingdom Constitution, it has been more erratic and conflictual than Lasok and Bridge's talk of each treaty revision being a self-conscious stage in integration would suggest. The European Treaties are the records of difficult political bargains. Indeed, at times, one treaty has to beget another because agreement cannot be reached in the time available, hence both the step-by-step development of the treaties and the ongoing pressures for further institutional changes. This has helped to institutionalize IGCs and to ensure that they are increasingly politicized. In other words, the way the treaties are negotiated does affect their contents. This helps to explain why they are often inconsistent, unclear and of varying types.

Coming to terms with the political history of the treaties establishing the European Community and creating the European Union is important for two other reasons. To begin with, it helps to place them more firmly within the wider treaty base. Secondly, and more significantly, unless we know something of what the treaties were like in the past, we cannot really assess the changes made at negotiations like those ending at Nice. We need to be aware that, because they are evolving, the treaties themselves have changed considerably over time. So appreciating the historical background contributes greatly to understanding not just the content of the treaties but their changing status and shape.

Tracing this evolution requires not merely looking at the various phases of treaty development which started with the original negotiations leading to the Treaty establishing the European Coal and Steel Community (TECSC) and which continued, at an increasing pace, up to the actual establishment of the Union after Maastricht, but also at what has happened since. Here, the Treaty of Amsterdam demands special attention, not only because it emerged after our previous commentary was published but because it is both undervalued and obscured by the success of the way it deliberately disappeared from view, leaving behind it two renumbered and repolished 'working versions' of the TEC and TEU. Hence as well as tracing how it came about (including the various stages through which the treaty documents went), we also offer first an initial overview of the treaty as such, leaving the examination of the detailed changes Amsterdam made to the major treaties to the divisions dealing with these later in the *Guide*. However, we do print below the details of those changes made in 1997 which need to be remembered separately from the TEU and the TEC. We apply the same approach to the Treaty of Nice, which followed some of the technical approach to the treaties introduced at Amsterdam as well as changing a surprising number of key facets of the Union as part of its contribution to preparation for eastwards enlargement.

i The Early Genealogy of the Treaties, to the Era of Maastricht

Nice can be regarded as simply the latest addition to the family of European Treaties. Indeed we can fairly view the treaty base not as static but as an evolving family tree with births, marriages and even some deaths across the generations. At the head of the genealogy of the present-day European Treaties stands the 1951 Treaty establishing the European Coal and Steel Community, the most successful of the original post-war experiments in integration. The next ancestral generation was formed by the two related treaties signed in Rome in 1957 establishing the European Economic Community and the European Atomic Energy Community.

An important generation of consolidation involving only minor treaty changes then followed, encompassing the 1965 Merger Treaty, three accession treaties and other, mainly budgetary, agreements. Thereafter there was an increasingly rapid period of gestation. This began with the Single European Act which made the first set of major changes to the treaty base and the Communities, including marrying various components together. It was rapidly followed by the Treaty on European Union agreed at Maastricht in 1991 which extended the scope of the treaty base. Maastricht also left a double legacy of political uncertainty and a commitment to further treaty negotiations. This not only brought about minor adaptations to accommodate the fourth enlargement but paved the way for Amsterdam and a new look at the form of the treaties.

Origins

Although there were practical and intellectual precedents for structured European co-operation beyond bilateral collaboration of states, it was only after 1945 that an intensive search for new structures which might help avoid a new world war breaking out in Europe began. Out of this came the Council of Europe, the North Atlantic Treaty

Organization (NATO) and the Organization for European Economic Co-operation, as it then was. Some would have preferred to see the first as an overarching supra-national body, to be known as the 'European Union'. This was not to be, however, and all three bodies remained largely inter-governmental and sectoral in nature. So our European Treaties did not emerge from these experiments, significant though they were.

The family history of the treaties constituting the Union really started in Paris with the signing in 1951 of the Treaty establishing the European Coal and Steel Community (TECSC). This grew out of Jean Monnet's realization that an oblique approach towards European unity through economic integration was more likely to succeed than a direct approach. It would also secure very real economic and political gains for France and other states. Enunciated in the Schuman Plan of May 1950, the TECSC was then negotiated by representatives from six states – Belgium, France, Germany, Italy, Luxembourg and the Netherlands – in Paris over several months in 1950–51. Monnet had thought of a quick outline treaty leaving details to be decided later, thus allowing a small technocratic team to push things forward, but the Six had ideas of their own and wanted something more formal. So what emerged after several months of negotiation was a much more detailed 100-article draft which provided both for the joint management of the coal and steel industries of the Six and for innovative but balanced institutional provisions. And, perhaps because it was the first treaty of its kind, it was concluded for a fixed period of 50 years, to end in 2002.

The completed treaty, operative from July 1952, consisted of a preamble, setting out the philosophy behind the ECSC, and four titles, which dealt with aims, institutions, economic and social policies and generalities (including finance), respectively. There were also a number of annexed conventions, letters and protocols (see V i). Subsequent changes are indicated in Annex 4.

The institutional arrangements centred on a High Authority of nine independent members, able to act directly on the participating industries, and with its own financial resources. To check that this supra-national body did not exceed its powers, the treaty also created a ministerial Council (assisted by a Liaison Committee of officials), a parliamentary assembly (drawn from delegates to the Council of Europe), a consultative committee representing the industries, and a court. This institutional pattern was to be repeated in the next two members of the family of European Treaties.

From Messina to Merger

Although it did not realize all Monnet's hopes, the ECSC generated experience of co-operation and a belief that it constituted a pointer for the future, and 1950–51 saw a crop of projects for other communities, most significantly in defence. Although the European Defence Community which emerged from this was rejected by the French, the Benelux leaders felt that there was still room for further progress along Monnet's lines by applying the ECSC method on a wider economic front. A resolution to this effect was passed by the foreign ministers of the Six at a meeting in Messina in June 1955. They set up a committee under the Belgian foreign minister, Paul-Henri Spaak, to examine the possibilities of further integration involving atomic energy and a common market. This met between July 1955 and March 1956 at Val Duchesse in Brussels.

In its report, published in 1956, the Spaak Committee argued that mere sectoral integration within the ECSC would not work. It therefore proposed the creation of a separate customs union cum common market among the Six plus an Atomic Energy

Community. Perhaps because of the way Jean Monnet's Action Committee lobbied political leaders, this met with approval from ECSC ministers and parliamentarians. Hence the report formed the basis for negotiations in an inter-governmental conference, again chaired by Spaak.

This met from June 1956 to February 1957 and, after some hard bargaining to protect national interests, produced treaties establishing the European Economic Community (TEC) and the European Atomic Energy Community (TEAEC). These were signed in Rome on 25 March 1957. They joined the ECSC as part of the early generations of constitutive treaties which form the basis of Community law. Despite some opposition, ratification proceeded relatively smoothly and the treaties came into operation on 1 January 1958. Economic means were again adopted in order to achieve essentially political ends while the institutional provisions were less supra-national than those in the TECSC. Thus, while the institutional structures of the new bodies mirrored those in the ECSC, the Commission was given less power than the High Authority and member states correspondingly more. Even so, the TEC was to eclipse the other two treaties because the EC itself was more wide ranging and dynamic than the other communities. So it has become very much the lead treaty of its generation, often dominating thinking about integration. However, the preliminary papers on which it was based have never been published and the Court of Justice has avoided asking what the states meant in agreeing what they did.

The TEC originally consisted of 248 articles in six parts, subdivided into titles, chapters and sometimes sections. The parts themselves dealt in turn with principles, foundations, policies, association, institutions and general matters. There were also 4 annexes, 13 protocols, 4 conventions and 9 declarations. The West German government also issued a unilateral, and rarely publicized, declaration stating its assumption that a re-evaluation of the two Rome treaties would be possible in the event of unification. Annex 2 in the *Guide* shows how these elements have changed with successive generational changes.

The TEAEC contained 225 articles divided into six titles and a section of final provisions. The titles covered tasks, encouragement to nuclear energy, institutions, finance and general and initial matters (see V ii and Annex 4). Other agreements were also produced at the time, notably the Convention on Certain Institutions of 25 March 1957, which ensured that, for reasons of efficiency, there would be only one court and one assembly between the various communities. The Convention also created one Economic and Social Committee for the two new communities, leaving the parallel ECSC Consultative Committee untouched. A few years later the treaties were extended to the Netherlands Antilles with the TEC gaining a new protocol too.

The three communities, and by implication the treaties, were brought closer together by the 1965 Merger Treaty (MT) which integrated the remaining institutions. Again, much hard bargaining was needed before this was agreed on 8 April 1965. The Merger Treaty laid down the principles of a single Commission and Council – which could be composed of a wide variety of ministers, depending on the matters in hand – while amending and repealing the relevant clauses of the three founding treaties accordingly. The Merger Treaty also took tentative decisions on relations between the Communities, the location of the various institutions, financing and, in a protocol, on the status of officials of the merged institutions. These new marriage contracts came into effect on 1 July 1967. However, although some thought was given to merging the three treaties themselves, this did not happen, because of the High Authority's unwillingness to see its supra-national status be reduced to that of the Commission as some governments would have liked. And merging the treaties was not a statutory requirement. In any case, from

1967 there was, in practice if not in law, only one Community with a single, shared, set of institutions.

This achievement was despite the crisis with de Gaulle over the growing ambitions of the EEC. The subsequent French withdrawal from the institutions led to an important informal addition to the way in which the Community worked: the 1965 Luxembourg Compromise. This was a recognition that there could be profound disagreement about the development and policies of the EC and that, when there was, a decision could not be thrust on a dissenting state. The matter at issue could only be left to lie on the table. Since in the first instance this blocked moves to build on the TEC by giving the EP budgetary powers, moving to majority voting and enhancing the role of the Commission, the Community took on a more inter-governmental tone. But the French were not able to force a formal revision of the treaties to enshrine this.

Consolidation in the 1970s and 1980s

The French failure did not, however, signal the end of the process of treaty development. Once de Gaulle had left office it became possible to consider moving things forward through major new initiatives such as foreign-policy development and monetary union. In the event the first was done outside the treaties under the title European Political Co-operation (EPC) and the second was not acted on because of an economic downturn, but there were to be further amendments to the treaties over the next few years through three types of changes.

To begin with, alterations were made by the accession treaties and related agreements allowing the next six states to join the Community. These were signed in January 1972, April 1979 and then June 1985. They adjusted the size of Community institutions in line with the number of new members. Accession treaties are always relatively short and formal, as Division Viv shows, and the details of actual changes are contained in an attached act of accession. Thus Article 1 of the 1972 Brussels Treaty on Accession recognized the new states as members consequent on their acceptance of the conditions laid down in the accompanying act. The other two articles provided for ratification procedures, allowing for the treaty to become operative even if not all applicants ratified, a wise decision given the outcome of the Norwegian referendum. The treaty was put into operation by a Council decision of 1 January 1973 supplemented by a second decision amending the act of accession in the light of the Norwegian 'no' vote. The act of accession specified the status of the new members and listed amendments to the treaties and other acts regulating the Community and finished by laying down measures for transition and implementation. This too was accompanied by a number of protocols and declarations. The Greek and Iberian accession treaties were to take much the same form, the latter introducing one innovative institutional reform: the alternating cycles which governed the rotation of the Council presidency until 1995.

Secondly, a number of small institutional changes were made to the budgetary provisions of the treaties, to the number of commissioners, and to miscellaneous matters including direct elections to the European Parliament in 1975. On two occasions, at Luxembourg in 1970 and at Brussels in 1975, changes in financing led to new treaties. Thirdly, minor changes were made following the signing of association agreements with former colonies and other states in the African–Caribbean–Pacific (ACP) group. It is also the case that the 1984 Greenland Treaty confirming Greenland's departure from the Community makes up part of the treaty base since it brought about amendments to the

TEC. Some authorities also believe, as already noted, that the European Economic Area (EEA) agreement of May 1992 extending the Single Market to most EFTA countries also makes up part of the treaty base, a view we largely accept.

In addition to these two sets of new amending treaties the period saw a growing number of key European Court of Justice rulings in the 1960s and 1970s which had to be considered when the treaty base was invoked, as did other informal precedents. As Golub and Ludlow argue, decision- and law-making was relatively effective while the Community also developed its operations and attitudes. As a result of all this the TEC continued to alter and, as it did so, the Economic Community came to eclipse its parallel communities. In other words, these changes were quite significant, even if they were not often enshrined in treaty changes. Certainly they argue against the period being one of 'sclerosis'.

The SEA and the First Major Changes to the Treaties

Even if the consolidation of the 1970s and early 1980s did not make a huge difference to the nature of the Communities as such, it did pave the way for wider and more rapid changes. Indeed, since the mid-1980s, the Community has been engaged in an almost unceasing attempt to reshape and revivify its institutional structures through treaty-based changes. These partly had their roots in outside developments which produced feelings that the Community was not moving fast enough to cope with a globalizing economy. The changes were to involve not merely substantive changes to the Community but the beginnings of what was to become the pillar system.

Following promptings, first from France and then from a joint German–Italian initiative, not to mention from the European Parliament's 1984 draft European Union Treaty, the member states moved towards new initiatives. Hence, building on the 1983 Stuttgart Solemn Declaration, two committees were set up at Fontainebleau in 1984 to look at a 'People's Europe' and institutional changes respectively. The latter, chaired by Senator James Dooge of Ireland, had a difficult life but reported largely in favour of strengthening the Commission, enhancing the role of the EP, limiting the use of unanimous voting in the Council and regularizing the role of the European Council. This reflected the way that, even without large-scale treaty revisions, things had moved on in the Community. While Britain and other states opposed making such changes through an IGC and formal treaty revision, Franco-German support led the 1985 Milan Council to take a majority vote to set up an inter-governmental conference (IGC) to look at foreign policy, decision-making and treaty amendments.

Despite reservations and divisions, reform was driven forward by the need to complete the Internal Market and prevent dissident states from vetoing necessary proposals. Concern for the uncertain status of foreign policy co-operation also encouraged them. Working from an early draft treaty ministers and, to a lesser extent, heads of government were able by December 1985 to reach acceptable compromises on many of the ideas circulating. The fact that these were brought together in one document rather than a series of separately documented amendments explains the undramatic title, the Single European Act (SEA). None the less, this bringing together of different strands of reform has been seen by some as marking a further move towards treaty unification.

In any case, in February 1986 the member states proceeded to sign the first major revision of the TEC. The SEA had a significant preamble (see V iii), 30 articles divided into four titles plus a final act. The titles covered general changes, amendments to the three treaties, arrangements for EPC, and general matters. Most of the articles amended clauses of the TEC and the other constitutive treaties. Included were 18 amendments to the TEC bringing about a co-operation procedure involving the EP, a new Court of First Instance, more use of qualified majority voting, a timetable for the Internal Market, and five other new policy areas: monetary co-operation, social policies, cohesion, research and development, and the environment.

Beyond this, of course, the SEA also consolidated and legitimized the EPC system, although it did not make this fully a part of the Community structures. It gave the system a treaty-based status, but only within the SEA as such. It did not incorporate EPC into the TEC proper. Hence it can be seen as the first experiment in pillar building although, because the SEA can be seen as a constitutive act, the status of EPC was a little ambiguous even if the SEA contained some provisions common to the treaties and EPC. Equally, a number of national declarations were also adopted or noted in the Final Act.

All this was significant both in its extension of the Community's scope and in the innovative ways it changed its *modus operandi*. Clearly the SEA went well beyond the changes made in the years of consolidation and encouraged an increased momentum in EC development. Hence many people, both Europhile and Europhobe, have seen it as the single most decisive constitutional change in the Community's history because of its resort to majority voting and the changes it made to the single common market. This belief may be related to the fact that this was one of the few occasions when treaty reform was really led by the Commission and drew on existing practices and economic ideas, rather than innovating. For this reason it has been called a 'driving mirror' treaty. It gave encouragement to the idea of 'mutual recognition' of national standards which had been circulating for some years but had never made much impact before then.

None the less, the SEA was a new treaty in its own right and one with specific characteristics and dynamics. It planted ideas of Economic and Monetary Union and increased social policy. So, even before the new treaty came into effect in the summer of 1987 after some Danish hiccups about ratification, thought was being given both to implementation and to further reform, reflecting not only the changes made to the TEC, TECSC and TEAEC but also the working of the provisions on EPC.

Maastricht and its Legacy

The SEA was not destined to have a long life as a freestanding treaty. In fact it was to prove merely a prelude to even more radical institutional and treaty change at Maastricht in the early 1990s. The treaty then signed has proved immensely significant and controversial. This is partly because of the substantive changes it made to the operations of the Community, changes which had more effect on ordinary people than had earlier accords. This was notably the case with the addition of EMU, which was to prove both more influential and more divisive than the Single Market especially as it was established in a period of economic recession and uncertainty. This added to the fact that the far-reaching changes the treaty made to the nature of the integration process, with the creation of the Union and its principles of citizenship and subsidiarity, awoke the public to the way the Community was developing. Hence, the post-Maastricht ratification crisis made the whole process of integration more politically salient and uncertain. Even though the TEU would not have been possible without the SEA, it was to have far more general impact than its predecessor, especially as it set up a further IGC.

The reasons why the SEA was soon left behind lie partly in the fact that, while the new treaty had more significant effects than Margaret Thatcher and others had expected, it did not satisfy all those who wanted to see more radical moves towards European unity. They were able to draw on the way that the move towards the Single Market encouraged the idea that this needed social and monetary underpinnings. Hence in 1988 Edouard Balladur, French Finance Minister, and Hans-Dietrich Genscher, Germany's Foreign Minister, suggested considering monetary unification, an initiative which was endorsed by the decision of the European Council at Hanover in June 1988 to create the Delors Committee of central bankers. In April 1989 this reported in favour of a three-stage move to Economic and Monetary Union. Eight months later at Strasbourg the twelve agreed to hold a new IGC on EMU, a decision which was upheld despite UK arguments in favour of a 'hard ECU' alternative. By then the Social Charter had also been signed committing eleven of the twelve member states to social measures felt necessary to offset the negative effects of the Single Market.

While all this was going on, the political context and balance changed dramatically with the breaching of the Berlin Wall, moves towards the unification of Germany and the Gulf War. In February 1990 the Belgian government came out in favour of institutional reform and this was then reinforced by Franco-German initiatives. Political reform was seen as a way both of winning support for EMU in Germany and of reassuring the other member states that a unified Germany would not abuse its new strength. The European Parliament also lobbied hard for change and a share in the reform process. With the Iraqi invasion of Kuwait adding a new concern for enhancing the Community's foreign policy potential, agreement was reached on holding what was effectively a second IGC, on European Political Union (EPU).

In the view of the Commission, set out in a memorandum of October 1990, this sought to aim primarily at providing the Community with a higher international profile through the establishment of a common foreign policy (including security and defence) in response to the events of 1989–90 in Eastern Europe and the Gulf. Article 30 (12) of the SEA had also pointed in this direction. There were also pressures, arising in part from concern about the effect of German unification, for extending the competences of the EC; increasing the democratic legitimacy of the Community's institutions and decision-making processes; and establishing closer links with the people of Europe through the concepts of European citizenship and subsidiarity. This was supported by the European and Italian Parliaments and by the Belgian, Greek and Spanish governments.

Whereas the IGC on EMU ran smoothly, drawing on a largely agreed draft, and encountering only technical differences, that on EPU was much more difficult. In fact it soon became clear that few, if any, member states accepted the Commission proposals in their entirety. Divisions existed over the extent to which a common foreign policy should be extended to security and defence matters; the extent to which the powers of the European Parliament should be increased; any increase in qualified majority voting within the Council of Ministers; and widening the policy competences of the EC. Many things they were willing to do but not through the traditional Community method, thus encouraging the development of a more formal pillar structure.

Despite the clear differences which existed, the Luxembourg presidency in April 1991 presented a 95-page draft treaty. Although this was sharply criticized by the Commission and the EP, it won the grudging assent of most member states. This was in part because it adopted the pillar approach suggested, apparently, by Pierre de Boissieu, the French permanent representative. Hence it opened the way for detailed bargaining and a formal draft Treaty on Political Union was tabled by the Luxembourg presidency on 20 June.

This established the structure found in the final version and contributed about 80% of the final package. It was based on the idea of a Union as a body embracing a series of 'pillars'. In sensitive areas of integration such as diplomacy and home affairs, Union action would be carried on outside the main Community framework using more inter-governmental methods and without the full participation of the EC institutions. These would, however, continue to operate in a reformed supra-national Community, which would be the main pillar of the Union.

Divisions between the member states meant that the Luxembourg presidency was unable to conclude the IGC before its term of office expired at the end of June 1991. However, the whole IGC process was almost put in jeopardy when, after a long silence over the summer, the Dutch government presented its own draft treaty on 24 September 1991. This played down the concept of a Union but insisted on it having a single-pillar structure. This annoyed both member states and the EP and the Dutch were forced to withdraw it, reverting to the Luxembourg draft. New versions were provided in late October and mid-November but these still gave rise to furious debate over federalism and other topics.

December had arrived and time was running out, the IGC being scheduled to end at the Maastricht European Council. Both the Commission and the EP were becoming increasingly unhappy about the process. Despite these hiccups, the tortuous IGC negoti-ations carried on although many questions were left unanswered until the summit itself. Arguments on cohesion funds, Commission powers, federalism, immigration, industrial policy, security and social action continued until the EC's leaders convened. Yet, despite fears that the British might not accept the emerging package, the European Council meeting at Maastricht on 9–10 December did reach agreement on a Treaty on European Union. However, 'its flustered improvisations', as Davidson called them on a radio programme, were only possible after long hours of negotiations and once significant opt-outs on EMU and the Social Chapter for the United Kingdom had been finalized. And, as Forster notes, it is not true that John Major himself hailed it 'as game, set and match to Britain'. The founding document of the Union was therefore very much a reflection of the balance of force among the governments involved at the end of 1991. For Moravscik, for instance, its external clauses reflected British positions while those on EMU were essentially German inspired.

It then remained to tidy up the agreements into a single agreed document compatible with the existing treaties. A preamble was thus added along with Article 138a (now Article 191) on the role of political parties in the Union and Declaration 33. Minor changes were also made to Article B (now 2 TEU), which had to be brought into line with J.4(1) (now 17(1) TEU), and 198a (now 263 TEC) which, at British behest, replaced the term 'authorities' with 'bodies'. This was done on 7 February 1992, again in Maastricht. Immediately prior to the new meeting there were also two further nominal conferences to amend the ECSC and Euratom treaties. A final addition was to be made in May 1992 when, to help the Irish government out of a problem with its abortion legislation, a final declaration was agreed.

The sprawling and often unrevealing Treaty on European Union, as finally agreed, involved seven titles and 19 articles, not to mention a host of protocols and declarations. As the next division shows, two titles referred directly to the Union, two dealt with the new pillars and the remaining three specified changes to be made to the existing European Treaties. So, even more than the SEA it was a constitutive treaty, as well as an amending one. Thus, firstly, it constituted a new body: the European Union, structured somewhat after the model introduced in the SEA with two semi-detached pillars for the common foreign and security policy (CFSP) on the one hand, and justice and home affairs (JHA) on the other, flanking the Community pillar. But, as we have already seen, this marriage between the Union and the Community is a curious affair. Thus the Union is partly superior to the revised EC because it has a legal existence and treaty of its own and because entry to the Community alone is no longer possible. Yet it is dependent on the latter for most of its actions and principles and the TEC enjoys equal status to the TEU. In other words, despite the way it has been demonized, the TEU cannot be seen as a simple exercise in strengthening the tendencies to federationism. It also started a trend to reinforce states' rights.

So, secondly, Maastricht had profound implications for the TEC which was amended by the incorporation of the long list of amendments in Title II, Article G (now 8 TEU). These changed the structure of the TEC somewhat, introduced new principles such as citizenship and subsidiarity, giving formal legal bases to some established policy areas and creating other new policy areas, notably EMU, all of which were now brought together in a new Part on policies, and provided new decision-making procedures notably co-decision. There were also some institutional adjustments. Where necessary these were written into the TECSC and the TEAEC. In other words, the TEU reconstituted the structures of EC integration. It also looked to yet more change through the commitment to call a further IGC in 1996.

All this was highly controversial. For some, though not all, it meant the end of national sovereignty and a dangerous turn in the process of integration. Hence the ratification process was thrown into confusion by the Danish rejection, by difficulties in France and the United Kingdom and by upheavals on the currency markets. All this caused considerable uncertainty within the Union. It also revealed both a groundswell of public disenchantment with integration and an increasingly vocal opposition.

The ratification process began with a brief honeymoon during which there seemed to be no problem in those countries where parliamentary processes got under way, and most of the criticisms came from frustrated supporters of more radical changes. Then the Danes very narrowly rejected the treaty at a referendum on 2 June 1992. This presented the other 11 with a real problem as there was no provision for anything other than unanimous ratification. The Danish result also encouraged opponents to come out of the woodwork, and they were encouraged in this by the way the 11 refused to abandon the project and the fact that President Mitterrand called a referendum in France to try to trump the one in Denmark. The treaty only narrowly scraped through in the autumn. By then opinion in Britain was turning against the TEU partly because of the way that currency speculation against the overvalued pound forced sterling out of the ERM. This, like German unease at the demise of the Deutschmark (DM), threatened the financial foundation of Maastricht.

As a result, while the Danes agreed on an informal revised understanding of Maastricht, there was mayhem in the UK Commons where a weak government was increasingly undermined by its Eurosceptic backbenchers. None the less, the Danes voted 'yes' at a second referendum in May 1993 and the Committee stage of the Bill was concluded in the UK. This opened the way for formal approval of the treaty, despite a rearguard Eurosceptic action in the Lords and a series of bizarre constitutional challenges. The fact that the French franc then came under attack and the ERM had effectively to be suspended added to the problems. Although the difficulties were eventually overcome, public suspicion and concern about integration became all too clear, despite the fact that 11 of the 12 states had by then ratified the treaty.

The impact of this alienation showed up in the autumn 1993 judgment by the German Constitutional Court, which had agreed to consider a handful of the many challenges brought before it. While rejecting challenges to ratification the Court both held that national democratic controls over EC decision-making should be increased and assumed for itself a role in monitoring the compatibility of EC/EU decisions with the guidelines laid down in the TEU. This allowed the Germans to ratify but reinforced an emerging tendency to seek to renew the Community's links with its citizens.

Moreover, almost as soon as the TEU came into effect on 1 November 1993 the treaties were subject to yet further, albeit generally minor, amendments. Thus some institutional elements were altered by the act of accession signed in 1994 by the four EFTA countries (including Norway) who looked set to join the Union. A new approach to the rotation of the Council presidency was also introduced. Difficulties with Britain and Spain meant that new understandings about qualified majority voting thresholds also had to be taken on board after Ioannina to satisfy them. This was done by a Council decision of 29 March 1994. And following the Norwegian 'no' to EU membership in November 1994, the envisaged changes had to be revised to account for only three EFTA states joining. So when all these came into effect in January 1995 there was also a Council decision of 1 January which, as before, formally established the redundancy of the clauses relating to Norway.

However, the continuing political and economic uncertainties were fuelled by the inherent importance and ambiguity of the Maastricht settlement. The TEU is more sweeping than most other treaties and has enjoyed a growing status both within the treaty base and beyond. At the same time, because it embraces inter-governmental, supra-national and freestanding institutional innovations, it is open to very different interpretations. Some thus still see it as restraining rather than encouraging integration. All this meant that the family-tree process was far from finished and it had become far more salient and open to question than ever before, even if the types of treaties and the way they were negotiated remained relatively unaffected.

ii The Amsterdam Remodelling of the Treaties

Compared to the SEA and TEU the next development in the family tree of the European Treaties, the deal agreed at Amsterdam in 1997, seems to be much less significant. For some it is a pathetic little squib compared to the 'big bang' of Maastricht and one which failed to ignite solutions to enlargement. So it is not unfair to call it, as we ourselves have done, a 'disappearing treaty'. This is partly because people have paid little attention to it, and so often denigrate, misunderstand or undervalue the settlement. They do this because they see the Treaty of Amsterdam (TA) as disappearing when it came to the key pre-enlargement institutional questions which the IGC had been called to resolve. Indeed, even during the final summit it allowed itself to be diverted into other issues such as employment and growth.

However, there is another, more technical, reason for the treaty being thus overlooked. This is because the TA seems to have little identity of its own: with no preamble and virtually no clauses which do not amend the existing constitutive European Treaties. This was no oversight. It was because Amsterdam, as well as making many substantive changes, deliberately adopted a new approach to the presentation of the treaties. These resulted in helpful new working versions of the TEC and the TEU, restructured and renumbered. Hence the actual TA itself disappears from view in another way since it leaves virtually nothing behind as a separate contribution to the family tree. One of its major achievements was significantly to rationalize, remodel and repolish the basic European Treaties. It is because it is a rationalizing treaty that we feel it necessary to outline both the changes it did make, whether technological or concrete, and the various protocols and declarations in its final act.

As well as pioneering this new approach to the treaties the TA was also a far from insignificant amending treaty. Although it does not contain any striking innovations like EMU, it does make over 100 changes which cumulatively are likely to prove quite influential. So, for all these reasons, the Amsterdam process, its evolution, the precise changes it made to the material constitution of the Union and its efforts at remodelling the treaties, deserves detailed attention. These did not, however, avoid adding yet more declarations and protocols. The questions also arise as to how all this was put into effect and how it should be assessed.

The '1996' Negotiations

Given the destabilizing furore generated by Maastricht it is surprising that the member states should have taken the risk of embarking on yet another IGC when they did. In fact it is probably the case that they would have preferred not to have done so, especially given the growing political difficulties with the UK Conservative government. However, they were forced to act by the TEU and by outside circumstances. In the relatively optimistic days of December 1991 the states had agreed to have a new IGC in 1996, a decision inescapably then enshrined in what was Article N TEU. Moreover, the latter talked elsewhere of giving further consideration to such subjects as the working of the JHA pillar, the hierarchy of norms, the extension of co-decision, enhancing civil rights and increasing the EC's policy responsibilities in the areas of civil protection, energy and tourism.

At the same time outside events encouraged the move to an IGC. Thus, once the Union accepted in the summer of 1993 that enlargement to the east was inevitable, the question arose of how the Union's institutions should be adjusted to make this possible. A related factor was the way continuing difficulties in former Yugoslavia showed up the Union's external weaknesses, especially in the defence field, despite the TEU's aspirations to strengthen Europe's place in the world. Many felt this weakness called for a reform of the CFSP provisions.

The fact that the TEU as a whole was also not working as well as it might be, notably where decision-making and subsidiarity were concerned, reinforced the need for treaty reform. Moreover, the reaction to Maastricht had convinced many that something ought to be done to revitalize the Union and undo the popular alienation visible in 1992–3. New policy initiatives relevant to ordinary people and a simplified and better-presented treaty package might be ways of doing this. Hence a further IGC could help develop Union identity. At the same time new institutional issues emerged, some of which were placed on the IGC agenda by various summit meetings. This was the case with the size of the Commission, the use of qualified majority voting and the idea of 'flexibility', that is of states integrating at different speeds and with different intensities. Its presence on the agenda was due to two opposing contributions in September 1994, the Schäuble–Lamers paper on a 'hard core' and John Major's Leiden 'variable geometry' speech.

Finally, there was also pressure from those who had been dissatisfied with the TEU and wanted to create a European federation, a desire echoed in the EP's unregarded draft constitution of 10 February 1994. This was, in fact, a prelude to an outpouring of proposals for reform from academics, federalist forces and special interest groups, not to mention those in the formal resolutions required of the Commission and the EP. Many of the states, who also published their own wish lists, called for radical changes. All this made the IGC more open but also denied it the few clear themes which had driven the SEA and the TEU.

So, while this meant that the member states could not escape a new IGC, their underlying reservations combined with the increasing range of the potential agenda and a difficult political climate seriously affected the Amsterdam process. It proved to be much longer, more politicized and more problematic than many of its predecessors. This was despite attempts to make the process more open and better prepared. Hence, as a first stage the European Council at Corfu asked the institutions to assess the working of the TEU. The aim was to help a projected Reflection Group to sift the agenda in the way Dooge had for the SEA but which had not been done for Maastricht. However, the institutions offered widely varying assessments and were often both critical of each other and more concerned with demanding further powers for themselves despite the need to put the citizen at the centre of their preoccupations.

The Reflection Group, chaired by Carlos Westendorp of Spain, consisted of a representative of each head of government and, unusually, two nominees of the EP. Unfortunately, as Dehousse says, the group, which started work in June 1995, did not really succeed in doing more than stating usually highly divergent national positions, notably where the United Kingdom was concerned. And the three suggested aims for the IGC which did emerge from its two reports in the second half of 1996 – bringing the Union closer to its citizens, making it work better in the run-up to enlargement and giving it greater external capacity – were truisms which did not engage with the detail. The group helped to float the idea of flexibility as a way of allowing at least some states to escape what threatened to be general stagnation, but even the conditions for embarking on closer co-operation proved to be a matter of dispute.

The IGC itself, which met from March 1996, was equally unable to produce real consensus or clarity, thanks in part to the shadow of domestic politics. Louis is critical of the lack of political guidance given by heads of government at the Turin launch of the IGC. Thus there was even less progress at the ministerial level than in the officials' working group, although McDonagh does credit it with giving some political direction at times. So, despite optimistic claims, the first few months of the IGC under the Italian presidency brought only a limited clarification of issues. Then, despite intensive efforts by the Irish to speed things up, a special summit had to be held in early October to give new impetus to the process by setting the Amsterdam European Council in June 1997 as the time by which a deal had to be struck. This helped the Irish to produce a user-friendly draft treaty for their main Dublin summit in December 1996.

Even so, many questions – some of them new – remained open for the Dutch presidency and neither public opinion nor the media were terribly interested in it all. Few noticed that a working party on simplification started work in January. Certainly the Dutch were much more cautious than in 1991, especially as the imminence of the general election made the UK government resistant to any real change. Many feared that there would be no agreement. However, the Dutch persevered with the negotiations. They saw the period up to April as one of hanging in and seeking a limited narrowing of gaps through a series of compromise papers, notably on flexibility. This included an addendum to the Irish draft treaty at the end of March. To an extent they were successful, though discussions of institutional change to facilitate enlargement showed continuing differences.

It seems that enough was done to allow a real breakthrough after Tony Blair's UK general election victory of 1 May 1997, the Dutch having already engaged in informal contacts with Labour. Things moved fast thereafter with a flurry of new treaty drafts being produced. Yet, even though the new UK government withdrew its opposition to the Social Chapter and other provisions, this merely brought into the open divisions amongst the other states. These showed in the growing numbers of protocols and declarations being tabled, it being easier to accept these than cause a rumpus. The Dutch have been criticized for seeking consensus at the expense of principle. None the less, although a good deal of progress was made, many issues were still left to the European Council at Amsterdam in mid-June. And this found it hard to concentrate on IGC questions thanks to the arrival of a new socialist-led government in France with its emphatic commitment to action on growth and employment.

Indeed, even though it overran by many hours, arguments on Schengen, flexibility and the CFSP meant that the summit neither addressed all the questions left over from Maastricht nor resolved the crucial institutional questions related to enlargement which were supposed to be the *raison d'être* of the IGC. This was despite convening a Friends of the Presidency Group and getting the Political Committee to work over the security texts. As a result some authorities, including Weiler, criticized the heads of government for not persevering irrespective of the Dutch insistence on finishing at the agreed time and place. And certainly the hasty end left a good deal of tidying up to be done, especially as new items were slipped in during the early hours, often without everybody being aware of them. Hence there was a certain amount of querying of what had actually been decided. The UK, French and Irish governments all felt that what was recorded by the Dutch was not accurate but the incoming Luxembourg presidency refused to accept any changes to the published text. Equally, as we will see below, there was insufficient will, or stamina, to make institutional changes felt necessary to facilitate enlargement.

The Substantive Changes

None the less, the IGC had met its timetable and the European Union had a deal. The Treaty of Amsterdam as then published was packaged, not as a traditional treaty, but in what it was hoped would be a more accessible way. The changes agreed were organized under six thematic headings, some deriving from initial suggestions by the Spanish and taken up by the Irish draft treaty. Changes to the objectives of the Union and Community were also updated. Each heading contained a list of treaty changes, not all of which were given numbers, and the protocols and declarations were printed together with the relevant treaty articles. The aim of all this was presumably to make the deal more comprehensible and attractive to the general public. This is certainly the impression given by the headings used.

The first of these was 'An Area of Freedom, Security and Justice'. This saw a shift in competences with the Union adopting a new commitment to the values and rights of democracy, a commitment with which new members would have to comply. This involved rights for individuals, including data protection within EC institutions, social protection and a new concern for the disadvantaged, whether women, the disabled or the ethnically excluded. The ECJ was given a new standing in these fields. Moreover, the commitment to democratic values was now reinforced by a new procedure for suspending member states which offend against them.

A related aim was to assure citizens that, while free movement was being enhanced and guaranteed, it would not be abused. To do this, elements of the third pillar were, after a five-year transition period, to be added to the TEC through a new title on asylum, immigration and visas. This led to the third pillar being radically altered and refocused on police and judicial co-operation in criminal matters, with member states being able to ask the ECJ to adjudicate on problems arising should they choose. At the same time the Schengen system was slated for incorporation into Union practice and legislation, with an undertaking that standards of protection would be no lower than in the past. However, the UK and Ireland, along with Denmark, insisted on various kinds of opt-out.

The second heading was 'The Union and the Citizen', another somewhat euphemistic description of a mass of not terribly closely related amendments. Great emphasis was given to what were actually limited commitments, in Title VIa (subsequently VIII) of Part Three TEC, to monitor employment. These seem mainly intended to show that the Union does care about its citizens' jobs. At the same time there were changes in social policy where many of the provisions of the Social Chapter were brought into the TEC in an altered but again limited and co-operative form. Thirdly, there were a whole gamut of provisions on things like animal welfare, anti-fraud activities, consumer protection, customs co-operation, environmental protection, island regions and public credit institutions. Some of these were written in by states and lobbies for their own reasons and thus ended up as protocols. The TA also reasserted the non-threatening nature of citizenship, redefined subsidiarity and made gestures towards transparency. Much of this was more a matter of tidying up Maastricht than of seriously addressing the relations between individual citizens and the Union.

The third heading covered 'An Effective and Coherent External Policy'. The changes made kept the existing structure and did not transfer new powers to the Union. However, they did involve a wholesale reorganization of the CFSP articles. The aim was to enhance consistency by involving the European Council more, encouraging member-state co-operation, seeking to develop long-term external strategies, clarifying the nature of the instruments used, and allowing for constructive abstention so that states which are unhappy might not block foreign policy initiatives. At the same time new structures, centring on the creation of a new high representative for external policy within the Council Secretariat, were introduced so as to make policy more effective. The presidency was also authorized to open diplomatic negotiations in specific circumstances. Equally, the Commission's profile was raised, even though it was not given responsibility for negotiations on services under the TEC.

On the military side there was a new commitment to the progressive evolution both of defence policy and even of a common defence, providing the European Council can agree on this. There was also to be closer co-operation with the Western European Union (WEU). At the same time the concept of security was widened to include the humanitarian missions, involving military personnel, known as the Petersberg tasks. The CFSP itself could now benefit from EC financing thanks to an associated inter-institutional agreement.

The fourth heading was 'The Union's Institutions'. While decisions on key questions such as the number of commissioners and the weightings used in majority voting were postponed, there were a number of far from insubstantial procedural and institutional changes. These focused on the EP which saw the assent and co-decision procedures extended to some new and to some old treaty provisions, including some where the Council decides by unanimity rather than by majority. This, although it was not said formally, reduced the co-operation process to a footnote role applicable only in certain areas of EMU. More significantly, the co-decision process was made the main form of decision-making, and the process itself was simplified. The Parliament was also given an enhanced voice in the appointment of the Commission, the right to set its own rules for MEPs and increased budgetary responsibilities. Its numbers were also to be limited to 700 while a new attempt was made to resolve the problem of divergent electoral procedures by allowing the EP to devise one which reflected the principles common to member states if it could not agree a single mode. All this was seen as enhancing democracy although it ducked the challenge of enlargement, simply postponing related changes to the Commission and to voting procedures until later dates.

At the same time there were changes to virtually all the other institutions. Thus where the Council was concerned, its use of qualified majority voting was extended again to new provisions, fourteen of them, and to five existing ones. The Council's own voting patterns and documentation were also partly opened to the public. At the same time the role of both the Committee of Permanent Representatives (COREPER) and the Secretariat General were changed. The former had a new quasi-legislative role while the latter acquired both another official and new staff. There was also a requirement for the Commission to submit plans for its own reorganization. This went along with giving the president, who had to be formally confirmed by the EP, formal political control of the College. Other elements of Amsterdam also widened the Commission's roles and responsibilities in ways which are apparent only on a very close reading of the text.

This is even more the case with the European Council and, to a lesser extent, the Council of Ministers and the ECJ. The latter gains some new oversight through the revised Final Provisions of the TEU and elsewhere. However, Amsterdam insisted both on the importance of Community law and on the role of national judiciaries. Finally the standing and powers of the Court of Auditors were both underlined by the treaty while the Committee of the Regions was freed from its administrative links with the Economic and Social Committee and was given a higher profile. Like the latter, it was to be consulted more. Conversely arrangements were made to bring national parliaments more into the integration process.

The fifth heading introduced what appeared to be a major substantive innovation: provisions on flexibility described as 'Closer Co-operation'. Because there was so much disagreement on developing integration, the resulting pressure finally resulted in three sets of criteria about how and when states might use the Community framework to seek enhanced co-operation. The first applied to the Union as a whole and required that such enhanced co-operation can only be a last resort, must involve a majority of member states and must be open to all states to join. Equally, such closer co-operation was to detract neither from the principles of the Union and the *acquis* nor from the rights of member states. These conditions are then subject to further limits where flexibility within the first and third pillars is concerned through new Articles 11 TEC and 40 TEU. The treaty also introduced a number of less-visible provisions for differential integration. All this worried many lawyers, who feared the proliferation of regimes within the allegedly uniform Union. In the event, the facility was not used, perhaps because of its complexity, along with the rights of the Commission to advise against it, not to mention the facility under Article 11 TEC for unhappy states to appeal to the European Council against the invocation of the new title.

Simplification, Consolidation and Codification

The final heading of the original treaty document did not relate to the Union's material constitution. Rather it simply noted that the second part of the final version of the treaty would contain simplifications of the treaties. The work of the IGC was not over. In fact the lawyers and linguists, meeting as the Friends of the Presidency Group, and working with COREPER, spent much of July and August 1997 turning June's institutional and policy changes into proper treaty form. This included changing the places in the treaties to which some of the amendments and protocols were attached. This unusual variant on the life and times of an IGC was possible partly because all the key political decisions had been taken at Amsterdam, leaving only technical questions to be resolved, and partly because those decisions themselves did not represent a grand new vision of Europe which might be challenged in the reworking. The limitations of the June deal thus facilitated both this new format and the simplification process.

The revised version of Amsterdam, as it emerged from the new work, was now after a list of plenipotentiaries serving and in the absence of a real preamble, a formal treaty of 15 articles divided into three parts, covering: substantive amendments (Articles 1–5); simplification (6–11); and general and final provisions (12–15). Then, after an annex and the protocols, there was a final act, a further annex and a crop of declarations. This structure was not substantially changed either in October when the treaty was signed or in November when the treaties were at last published in the *Official Journal* (OJ). However, small changes were made *en route* which went unnoticed by some of those most closely involved.

Article 1 within Part I covered the TEU, to which fifteen changes were each now listed in order as amendments. These included new Titles for the treaty. *Article 2* of Amsterdam then listed 59 changes to the Treaty Establishing the European Community. These included the insertion of new titles on 'Visa, Asylum, Immigration and Other Policies Related to Free Movement of Persons' and 'Employment'. A total of 26 further changes were made to the TECSC, the TEAEC and the 1976 Act on Elections to the EP through *Articles 2–6*.

Part II of the treaty took things into a new, and largely unexpected and unappreciated, dimension. It contained three articles amending the existing treaties establishing the European Communities in the light of 'simplification', leaving the TEU unchanged apart from what had already been agreed in Article 1. *Articles 6–8* are again simply lists, this time of small technical changes made to the treaties as a result of this process. 'Simplification' is a somewhat loose term and involves repealing redundant articles, deleting now otiose references and amending misleading wordings and headings. Two elements of the treaty base, the Convention on Certain Institutions Common to the European Communities (1957) and the Merger Treaty (1965), were also repealed by *Article 9* in the process of simplification, the first real deaths in the family tree of the European Treaties. However, the clause made it clear that the single institutions continued to form one administration, with the normal privileges of EU staff, even though they acted under different powers in different treaties, irrespective of the changes made to the latter.

Article 10 then emphasizes the point that repeal and deletions do not affect the legal status of the original treaties or of acts deriving from them. This is then underlined in Declaration 51 TA, which states that changes to the treaties do not affect the *acquis communautaire*. Questions arising from all this can be evoked before the ECJ thanks to *Article 11*, although some lawyers doubt whether this will be effective. Then *Article 12* further provides for the TEC and the TEU to be renumbered in the light of the changes made by simplification and the substantive changes made at Amsterdam. This means a certain amount of moving articles up to fill gaps, so the process is usually known as 'consolidation'. The clause also provides for mentions of old numbers to be understood as references to new ones.

The result of all this was consolidated versions of the TEC and TEU which are printed as an annex to the final act, along with an at times misleading table of equivalences (see Annex 3 below). Overall, therefore, the TEU turns into a treaty with eight consecutively numbered titles embracing 53 numbered articles. This makes it rather more of a treaty in its own right than it was before, when it was something of a set of book-ends to the TEC. The TEC itself was also slightly restructured because of the changes made and now runs from Article 1 to 314. The new treaty texts were described as 'illustrative' because, as

Article 10 TA makes clear, the changes do not affect the legal standing or effects of the existing treaties and thus of the *acquis*. However, the new 'working versions' can be used, as we do in the *Guide*, because they are reflections of the still-binding original treaty texts. Neither this nor the renumbering have caused the difficulties some initially anticipated since the cleaner, consolidated versions of the TEU and the TEC proved quite usable.

None the less, the changes are quite significant. They represent the first attempt to remodel the treaties and make them more accessible and usable. The TA does this, firstly, by rationalizing the existing documents and eschewing any claims to be a self-standing treaty. Hence its title is 'The Treaty of Amsterdam amending the Treaty on the European Union, the Treaties establishing the European Communities and certain related acts and signed on 2 October 1997'. Contrary to its predecessors it makes no claim to be making a specific thematic contribution to the treaty base. It was merely things which were done at a given time and in a given place. Hence it has no real preamble, merely a statement that the representatives meeting in Amsterdam agreed the following changes to the treaties.

Secondly, in line with recent Community thinking on legal consolidation, all that will survive are Articles 9–12 on the legal implications of simplification, which is much less than with the SEA. However, the treaty is, by *Article 13*, concluded for an unlimited period. It also had to be ratified in the normal way thanks to *Article 14*. All the various language versions are to be treated as equally valid under *Article 15*. In other words, it is very much a 'window' treaty, offering only a temporary view of changes made to the constitutive treaties.

Thirdly, the revisions treated the treaty base as much more of a unity than had previously been the case. They repealed some acts, rather than leaving references to them and earlier articles as had happened previously. Equally, the revisions implicitly brought some secondary decisions into the treaties, whether through the envisaged incorporation of the Schengen *acquis* into that of the Union, the adoption of much of the 'approach to subsidiarity' adopted at Edinburgh in 1992 as a protocol, or the indirect references to inter-institutional agreements such as that on the codification of legislation. This restyling suggests that the treaty base has become a little more 'constitutional' in form. Unfortunately the revisions did not do much to change the difficult language in which the treaties are written.

A further dimension was the note in a declaration to the June draft that technical work, started during the IGC, on 'codifying' the treaties should continue. As Annex 3 of the *Guide* explains in more detail, codifying involves going further than merely tidying up and reshaping existing treaties as such. It usually means melding the latter into a single document. Two variants of this were canvassed, one putting the TEC and the TEU together and the other marrying these with the TECSC and the TEAEC as well. The promised documents were eventually published in the spring of 2000.

Such consolidation and codification could be regarded as a complication. On the one hand it means that there are parallel versions of the treaties circulating, which could be confusing. On the other hand, the failure to codify left a major obstacle to comprehension in place. The complexity of the European Treaties therefore remained. Indeed, owing to the lack of political agreement at Amsterdam a plethora of protocols and declarations were added to the treaty base, adding to its complexity.

Protocols, Final Act and Declarations

These trends showed up not just in the protocols and declarations negotiated at Amsterdam itself but in the way that, after the summit, the draft treaty went on expanding. Thus, throughout the summer of 1997, new statements were tacked on to the treaties. For instance the Protocol on the Role of National Parliaments in the European Union was only a draft in July. Equally, in June there were 50 declarations, often of new types. By August the number had risen to 58 thanks to new declarations on credit institutions and subsidiarity while two further declarations were added at the time of signature. The first group of additions included a statement by the WEU on closer collaboration, a note on the need to extend transparency and the fight against fraud to the ECSC and Euratom, and, most importantly, a Belgian declaration insisting on institutional change before enlargement to which France and Italy subsequently signed up. Then, as the treaty was being signed, on 2 October in the Royal Palace in Amsterdam, six states declared that they would accept ECJ jurisdiction in criminal matters while the IGC also noted that, as with the 1994 Accession Treaty, the Belgian regions and language communities were themselves bound by the national signature. Here again the treaty process was elongated in a new way partly because the initial negotiations had failed to solve the basic problems of institutional reform.

When the process of tacking on new elements was complete, the resulting protocols were, as in most previous treaties, printed in sections related to the various treaties to which they are attached. This was done in a much more formal and clear way than at Maastricht. Thus the single protocol in Section A is limited in its application to the TEU, making it clear that any future common defence will not affect NATO. Section B, which is essentially the Schengen incorporation act and the British, Danish and Irish exceptions, is attached to both the TEC and the TEU.

Section C comprises protocols relating solely to the TEC. These include questions of asylum, borders, public welfare and subsidiarity. Most of these are due to the special interests of the member states. Thus the sixth protocol effectively says that the existence of both free movement and guarantees for democracy in the Union means that EU citizens cannot normally claim asylum in another member state. This was to satisfy Spain, which had objected to Belgium offering a haven to ETA militants. However, Belgium insisted in a declaration that it would still look at such cases on their merits. The protocols on public broadcasting and animal welfare seem slightly unusual. They are more declaratory than operational and probably reflect the fact that there was insufficient agreement to make these formal treaty-based policy responsibilities of the EC.

The last section covers protocols annexed to all four treaties. These include the key enlargement protocol, the protocol on seats, and the new arrangements for consulting national parliaments. The first of these can be seen as a kind of adaption of what was the old Article N(2) TEU. It actually proposed some institutional reforms and declared that a further IGC would be held at least one year before the EU admitted its twenty-first member. Belgium, France and Italy found it unsatisfactory, hence Declaration No. 6n TA. The second was one of the texts slipped through, almost unnoticed, at the very end of the Amsterdam summit whereas the third had been the subject of much discussion around the IGC. Given that all four constitutive treaties have institutional clauses, all need to take note of these changes.

All told, 13 protocols were listed in the final act, which compared with 17 for Maastricht. There are no protocols left with the TA itself, although this did repeal a number of earlier protocols. Yet the protocols, both new and old, seem to have escaped the simplification process since they still refer to the old numberings. In an attempt to alleviate the situation, the *Guide* inserts references to the new treaty numbers into the protocols it reproduces. Another unusual feature is that many of the protocols themselves have explanatory declarations associated with them. All this shows up the increasing sensitivity of IGC negotiations and the way that national uncertainties have led states to seek clarifications and guarantees about EU decisions. While this may provide reassurance to some, the resulting 'protocolarization', as Guggenbühl calls it, makes the treaties less transparent for ordinary readers.

Where declarations in general themselves are concerned, the TA at one stage also divided these up according to the treaties to which they were attached. However, the August version, as part of the final act, proffered an undifferentiated list of the 51 declarations 'adopted' by the Conference and the eight national declarations 'of which the Conference took note'. Despite the logic of the former approach, we have largely remained true to the structure of the final version of the TA. Hence, as well as listing them below, we print the texts in our discussion of the TEU and TEC. Further comment is provided under the various treaty articles to which they refer.

Of the conference-adopted declarations, which are those which normally carry most weight as a result, eleven relate to the TEU, mainly to Pillar III matters. There were a further 27, ranging from environmental impact assessments to helping people with disabilities, which go with the TEC. There is one declaration relating to the international negotiating role of the ECSC, one on the consolidation of the treaties and eight concerning protocols, mainly relating to the TEC.

Many of these are, again, statements of national concern, about the privileges of German savings banks, about Greek monasteries and about outlying regions. However, others are necessary codes for working the changes introduced at Amsterdam, whether these be the Planning and Early Warning Unit set up to support the CFSP, the extent of security to be provided after the incorporation of Schengen or the working of the co-decision procedures. They can be significant statements of intent or clarification. And without such declarations as those on the quality of legislative drafting (39), and on the consolidation of the treaties (42), the whole rationalization side of the TA would not have been possible. There is even Declaration 51, relating specifically to Article 10 TA. Because it is not concerned with any other treaty it needs to be printed here.

DECLARATION ON ARTICLE 10 OF THE TREATY OF AMSTERDAM

The Treaty of Amsterdam repeals and deletes lapsed provisions of the Treaty establishing the European Community, the Treaty establishing the European Coal and Steel Community and the Treaty establishing the European Atomic Energy Community as they were in force before the entry into force of the Treaty of Amsterdam and adapts certain of their provisions, including the insertion of certain provisions of the Treaty establishing a single Council and a single Commission of the European Communities and the Act concerning the election of the representatives of the European Parliament by direct universal suffrage. These operations do not affect the '*acquis communautaire*'.

In other words, it seeks to reassure people that the simplification process makes no substantive changes to the legal basis of the Union. Moreover, there is a note at the end of the final act agreeing to the consolidated treaty texts being attached, for illustrative purposes. This is something of a departure for a final act.

National statements on things like credit institutions, subsidiarity and overseas departments form a separate category of 'Declarations of which the Conference took note'. This type of declaration was only hinted at in the TEU and the SEA, where most declarations were acts of the Conference as a whole. Generally declarations of this new type are felt to be of a lesser status but in the case of the Belgian-sponsored warning on institutional reform this does not stop them being highly significant too. They are clear statements of intent, often betraying strong feelings in governments who felt they needed extra guarantees for their interests or that the overall agreement was incomplete and needed further action.

The fact that, in total, the treaty mustered almost 60 declarations shows, on the one hand, the extent of dissatisfaction and insecurity in many of the member states, notably Belgium. The way that other states latched on to resolutions from other countries, such as that on credit institutions, is also interesting. On the other, it shows the complexity of the IGC and treaty processes even after rationalization and remodelling. To some extent this is because states wish to appeal to their publics but whether these are aware of such declarations is doubtful.

Although so many of the key decisions were not in the treaty proper but in the attached materials, they deserve this attention. On the one hand, they reflect the political dynamics of the Amsterdam process and the way in which the treaties have become increasingly encumbered with what are often politically inspired protocols. On the other, they can easily be overlooked. Hence the *Guide* prints the protocols not with the TA but, in line with the new legislative style, with the existing treaties. The same is done for declarations agreed at both Amsterdam and Nice (see pp. 175–6 and 547–9). The final act, as printed below, helpfully lists both the protocols and declarations in their official orders.

FINAL ACT

THE CONFERENCE OF THE REPRESENTATIVES OF THE GOVERN-MENTS OF THE MEMBER STATES convened in Turin on the twenty-ninth day of March in the year nineteen hundred and ninety-six to adopt by common accord the amendments to be made to the Treaty on European Union, the Treaties establishing respectively the European Community, the European Coal and Steel Community and the European Atomic Energy Community and certain related Acts has adopted the following texts:

I.   The Treaty of Amsterdam amending the Treaty on European Union, the Treaties establishing the European Communities and certain related Acts

II.   Protocols

A.   Protocol annexed to the Treaty on European Union:

   1. Protocol on Article J.7 [now 21] of the Treaty on European Union

B.   Protocols annexed to the Treaty on European Union and to the Treaty establishing the European Community:

   2. Protocol integrating the Schengen *acquis* into the framework of the European Union

   3. Protocol on the application of certain aspects of Article 7a [now 14] of the Treaty establishing the European Community to the United Kingdom and to Ireland

   4. Protocol on the position of the United Kingdom and Ireland

   5. Protocol on the position of Denmark

C. <u>Protocols annexed to the Treaty establishing the European Community:</u>

    6. Protocol on asylum for nationals of Member States of the European Union
    7. Protocol on the application of the principles of subsidiarity and pro-
       portionality
    8. Protocol on external relations of the Member States with regard to the
       crossing of external borders
    9. Protocol on the system of public broadcasting in the Member States
   10. Protocol on protection and welfare of animals

D. <u>Protocols annexed to the Treaty on European Union and to the Treaties
establishing the European Community, the European Coal and Steel Community and the European Atomic Energy Community</u>

   11. Protocol on the institutions with the prospect of enlargement of the Euro-
      pean Union
   12. Protocol on the location of the seats of the institutions and of certain bodies
      and departments of the European Communities and of Europol
   13. Protocol on the role of national parliaments in the European Union

III.   Declarations

The Conference adopted the following declarations annexed to this Final Act:

    1. Declaration on the abolition of the death penalty
    2. Declaration on enhanced co-operation between the European Union and
       the Western European Union
    3. Declaration relating to the Western European Union
    4. Declaration on Articles J.14 [now 24] and K.10 [now 38] of the Treaty on
       European Union
    5. Declaration on Article J.15 [now 25] of the Treaty on European Union
    6. Declaration on the establishment of a policy planning and early warning
       unit
    7. Declaration on Article K.2 [now 30] of the Treaty on European Union
    8. Declaration on Article K.3(e) [now 31(e)] of the Treaty on European Union
    9. Declaration on Article K.6(2) [now 34(2)] of the Treaty on European Union
   10. Declaration on Article K.7 [now 35] of the Treaty on European Union
   11. Declaration on the status of churches and non-confessional organisations
   12. Declaration on environmental impact assessments
   13. Declaration on Article 7d [now 16] of the Treaty establishing the European
      Community
   14. Declaration on the repeal of Article [ex] 44 of the Treaty establishing the
      European Community
   15. Declaration on the preservation of the level of protection and security
      provided by the Schengen *acquis*
   16. Declaration on Article 73j(2)(b) [now 62(2)(b)] of the Treaty establishing
      the European Community
   17. Declaration on Article 73k [now 63] of the Treaty establishing the European
      Community
   18. Declaration on Article 73k(3)(a) [now 63(3)(a)] of the Treaty establishing
      the European Community
   19. Declaration on Article 73l(1) [now 64] of the Treaty establishing the
      European Community

20. Declaration on Article 73m [now 65] of the Treaty establishing the European Community
21. Declaration on Article 73o [now 67] of the Treaty establishing the European Community
22. Declaration regarding persons with a disability
23. Declaration on incentive measures referred to in Article 109r [now 129] of the Treaty establishing the European Community
24. Declaration on Article 109r [now 129] of the Treaty establishing the European Community
25. Declaration on Article 118 [now 137] of the Treaty establishing the European Community
26. Declaration on Article 118(2) [now 137(2)] of the Treaty establishing the European Community
27. Declaration on Article 118b(2) [now 139(2)] of the Treaty establishing the European Community
28. Declaration on Article 119(4) [now 141(4)] of the Treaty establishing the European Community
29. Declaration on sport
30. Declaration on island regions
31. Declaration relating to the Council Decision of 13 July 1987
32. Declaration on the organisation and functioning of the Commission
33. Declaration on Article 188c(3) [now 248(3)] of the Treaty establishing the European Community
34. Declaration on respect for time limits under the co-decision procedure
35. Declaration on Article 191a(1) [now 255(1)] of the Treaty establishing the European Community
36. Declaration on the Overseas Countries and Territories
37. Declaration on public credit institutions in Germany
38. Declaration on voluntary service activities
39. Declaration on the quality of the drafting of Community legislation
40. Declaration concerning the procedure for concluding international agreements by the European Coal and Steel Community
41. Declaration on the provisions relating to transparency, access to documents and the fight against fraud
42. Declaration on the consolidation of the Treaties
43. Declaration relating to the Protocol on the application of the principles of subsidiarity and proportionality
44. Declaration on Article 2 of the Protocol integrating the Schengen *acquis* into the framework of the European Union
45. Declaration on Article 4 of the Protocol integrating the Schengen *acquis* into the framework of the European Union
46. Declaration on Article 5 of the Protocol integrating the Schengen *acquis* into the framework of the European Union
47. Declaration on Article 6 of the Protocol integrating the Schengen *acquis* into the framework of the European Union
48. Declaration relating to the Protocol on asylum for nationals of Member States of the European Union
49. Declaration relating to subparagraph (d) of the Sole Article of the Protocol on asylum for nationals of Member States of the European Union

50. Declaration relating to the Protocol on the institutions with the prospect of enlargement of the European Union
51. Declaration on Article 10 of the Treaty of Amsterdam

The Conference also took note of the following declarations annexed to this Final Act:

1. Declaration by Austria and Luxembourg on credit institutions
2. Declaration by Denmark relating to Article K.14 [now 42] of the Treaty on European Union
3. Declaration by Germany, Austria and Belgium on subsidiarity
4. Declaration by Ireland on Article 3 of the Protocol on the position of the United Kingdom and Ireland
5. Declaration by Belgium on the Protocol on asylum for nationals of Member States of the European Union
6. Declaration by Belgium, France and Italy on the Protocol on the institutions with the prospect of enlargement of the European Union
7. Declaration by France concerning the situation of the overseas departments in the light of the Protocol integrating the Schengen *acquis* into the framework of the European Union
8. Declaration by Greece concerning the Declaration on the status of churches and non-confessional organisations

Finally, the Conference agreed to attach, for illustrative purposes, to this Final Act the texts of the Treaty on European Union and the Treaty establishing the European Community, as they result from the amendments made by the Conference.

Done at Amsterdam on the second day of October in the year one thousand nine hundred and ninety seven

Ratification, Implementation and Retrospect

Amsterdam was not followed by anything like the political crisis unleashed by Maastricht nor even the post-Nice difficulties. For although the treaty was subject to considerable criticism amongst the politically committed, it aroused little interest amongst the public and, indeed, many of the critics came round to accepting it at most as an interim measure. For, as we will see, they started to plan for a further and more radical IGC ahead of enlargement. As a result, the main problem about ratification was not the public concern it generated but the slowness of the process. Hence, the institutions began to work towards implementing it well before it came into effect. All this suggests that rather than meriting the more extreme judgements on it, Amsterdam needs to be seen as a fair reflection of the nature of the contemporary Union.

None the less, Amsterdam was clearly a great worry to supporters of further integration. For them it was a potentially catastrophic failure because it dodged the key question of providing for enlargement. At the same time it fragmented the Union and left its complexities untouched. Moreover, its policy and institutional changes were superficial and pointillist, not to mention bereft of any real vision for the Union. The European Social Observatory reckoned it was more a completion of the SEA's work on the internal market than a complement to the restructuring of Maastricht. Much of the trouble was blamed on the member states, notably on Chirac and Kohl, and their partial restoration of the national veto. Hence, there was much talk of replacing the IGC's 'garbage-can' method of treaty reform by something more considered and supra-national.

Conversely, critics of the Union saw the treaty as moving the EU too far towards a 'superstate', hence they sometimes called it 'Maastricht II'. Its many changes were seen as transferring yet more sovereignty to Brussels, and threatening the democratic rights of national parliaments. The British Conservatives were so incensed by its concessions on the ECJ, qualified majority voting (QMV), foreign relations, social policy and human rights that they demanded a referendum. Yet public opinion seems to have been much less worried. In fact, despite the Commission's campaigns such as PRINCE and Building Europe Together, very few people really knew about the treaty. EMU and the travail of the Commission proved much more interesting to both them and the media.

The passage of time also brought more nuanced opinions amongst the supporters of integration. The facts that the treaty did not alarm the masses while forces such as the Europe of the Nations Parliamentary Group called for it to be rejected no doubt encouraged them. The changes to the CFSP, the extension of rights of the EP and the improvements in decision-making were also seen as helpful. Equally, the treaty brought in policies attractive to ordinary people: on the environment, on jobs, in social matters and on controlling migration. Therefore it needed to be supported.

Ratification was never seriously in doubt. Notwithstanding many grumbles, the European Parliament gave its approval, fearing to lose real reforms in a search for more speculative gains. Similarly, despite the dozens of wrecking amendments tabled by the Conservative opposition, the Commons was the first chamber to approve the treaty, which it did on 19 January 1998 with a majority of 230. However, due to delays in the Lords the formal ratification was not until 15 June. By then both Germany and Sweden had ratified, the former on 7 May following a 561–34 vote in favour in the Bundestag, and the latter on 15 May, by 226 votes to 40.

All told, eight of the 15 member states ratified by the end of July, including Austria where a constitutional amendment was required. Even in Denmark and Ireland, both of which had held referenda, ratification was speedy and successful. The Danish referendum of 7 May resulted in a clear affirmative vote by 55.1% to 44.9%. A fortnight later the Irish also voted in favour by 61.7% to 38.3%. However, the size of the 'no' votes was a sign, not much noticed at the time, that public alienation from the Union was far from over. None the less, other states went on to ratify by the end of the year, leading to hopes that the treaty would become operative early in 1999.

The fact that it did not was due to difficulties in a number of countries. In Belgium it took the regional bodies until February to complete their consideration. In Portugal the process was delayed by thoughts, eventually set aside, that a referendum might be held. In the event the issue was shelved until January 1999 with ratification following on 19 March, four days ahead of that by Greece, which had had a stormy debate in January and February.

This left only France, where the problem was one of constitutional amendment. The authorities were slow first in submitting the text to the Constitutional Council and then in arranging to alter the constitution after the Council said the TA was incompatible with it, notably on questions of visas and border controls. This delay reflected the strength of opposition on the right, something which led Chirac to seek amendment through a parliamentary Congress rather than a referendum. The Congress agreed the requisite changes by 758–111 on 18 January, despite accusations of 'collaboration' from opponents.

Such caution may help to explain why there was so little opposition. By early 1999 the whole thing must have seemed very old hat. Mainstream parties were all in favour, and the opposition was divided between the far left and right-wing Eurosceptics. With the French presenting their instruments of ratification on 30 March, the treaty duly came into effect on 1 May 1999, nineteen months after it had been signed, and accompanied by rhetorical claims that it marked a victory for democracy and citizens' interests.

The delay caused problems. It forced the Union to start preparing for its implementation long before ratification was finished, notably where the restructuring of the third pillar was concerned. The Parliament for its part moved on those elements of the treaty which affected it. Even so, European Council meetings in 1998 urged more progress. However, although work was still going on when the treaty was finally implemented no major crises were reported, though not all the new provisions were actually used at first.

So what does all this tell us about the treaty? Clearly it was more than the minimalist deception some federationists claimed, let alone the death of supra-nationalism. The process of implementation makes it clear that, if viewed as a whole, it made many quite substantial and significant changes, and can be seen as tidying up and developing what was agreed at Maastricht. On the other hand, it was not revolutionary and has not deprived the member states of their last vestiges of sovereignty as Eurosceptics claimed. The states certainly got more drawn into the Brussels process as a result of parts of the treaty, but they also gained new powers and guarantees of their status within the Union.

So, if it is perhaps going a little far to talk of it as a creative inter-governmental bargain and a harbinger of a more constitutionally aware future, as Moravscik and Nicolaides do, it does seem to be the case that Amsterdam is an accurate and realistic reflection of the nature of the Union in the second half of the 1990s. It points in a number of directions even if it did not always follow them up consistently. Admittedly the treaty is messy and somewhat contradictory, but so is the Union. And, technically, Amsterdam did pioneer a way of managing the Union's garbage-can treaty-reform style. Indeed, one of its major – and undervalued – achievements was to change the form of the treaties for the better.

Unfortunately, the hopes that this new transparency and the treaty's 'relevant' policy changes would win over EU citizens and increase the EU's legitimacy soon proved false. This was in part because Amsterdam did not succeed in dealing with enlargement. It was also because the Union's constitutional agenda began to change well before the TA came into effect. So Amsterdam was hardly the 'stabilizing' treaty once claimed by a UK minister for Europe, any more than it was the socially balancing text claimed by others. In substantive terms it was another complex package deal while its technical innovations were not felt sufficient by many.

iii   IGC 2000 and the Treaty of Nice

Whatever its merits, the Treaty of Amsterdam neither resolved all the issues which had given rise to the IGC which preceded it nor stopped debate about the future institutional reforms needed by the Union. Indeed, almost before the ink was dry on it, pressure for further changes developed. This was one reason why there was a much more rapid calling of a further IGC than might have been expected from the enlargement protocol (see below and III ix). However, the agenda agreed was very narrow and the IGC was somewhat by-passed by a new debate on the future of the Union. None the less, the IGC persevered and ultimately delivered an agreement, despite an atmosphere of crisis and a near breakdown at the concluding Nice summit in December 2000. The agreement was by way of being an MOT certificate of roadworthiness for the Union which should remain valid until enlargement is well advanced. It had three main elements. The first, and most symbolic, was a further encouragement to relatively rapid enlargement. The second was a series of changes to decision-making weights and rules, described as completing what was begun at Amsterdam. These are supposed to ensure that the enlarged Union can function effectively. The third was a series of institutional improvements which responded not just to the potential needs of an enlarged EU but to perceived weaknesses in the way the Union of 15 was already working. However, like all MOT certificates, Nice will eventually expire and so a further process of institutional reflection was called for. This, like the treaty itself, may also have changed the political balance of the Union.

So we need to examine both the motives for the new IGC and the process of negotiation which actually led up to the Nice summit. And, because Nice built on the legacy of Amsterdam, not just by contributing the institutional decisions which could not be agreed in 1997, but in its self-effacing technical nature and the extent of the changes it made, it too deserves special attention. Hence, even if Nice is not quite so much of a window treaty as its predecessor, it is again necessary to outline its final act. Given what its protocols and declarations say about the future of enlargement and the Union this is doubly important. The final act not only points the way ahead but also helps us to a better understanding of the significance of the Nice settlement.

The Road to Nice

What started the new reform process was less the failure to address some of the more constitutional questions on the Amsterdam agenda, such as a hierarchy of norms or giving legal personality to the Union, than the heads of governments' inability to address the key institutional questions related to enlargement. All they could manage in 1997 was a protocol, jointly attached to all four constitutive treaties, which states that at the time of the next enlargement the Commission should be composed of one national from each member state provided compensation has been agreed in the form of increased voting weights in the Council of Ministers for those (larger) states which would lose their second Commissioner. Thereafter, at least one year before Union membership reached 20, there would be a comprehensive review of the institutional provisions of the treaties. And the Belgian-sponsored declaration (No. 6n TA) made it clear that some member states did not believe that Amsterdam had met the conditions laid down by the European Council at Madrid in 1995 for substantial institutional change. Hence they were determined to push for real change, notably in the extension of QMV, raising the possibility that enlargement might be blocked were there not to be changes.

At the same time there was a good deal of outside pressure for a more radical restructuring of the Union. This came from federationist think-tanks and movements. Thus the European Union of Federalists (UEF) talked in 1998 of collecting a million signatures calling for a European Constitution ahead of the 1999 EP elections. Like the Commission, the EP also produced reports on the kind of institutional changes it believed necessary while a number of study groups were set up to do similar things. Many of these believed that a group of 'Wise Men' was needed to produce proposals. Others talked about giving the Union a charter of rights.

All this encouraged the Luxembourg European Council of December 1997 to note that improving the operation of the institutions was a prerequisite for enlargement. The Cardiff European Council of June 1998 went on to agree that, once the Treaty of Amsterdam was ratified, there would need to be an early decision on how and when to tackle the institutional issues not resolved at Amsterdam. Then, after a preliminary discussion at Portschach, the Vienna European Council made institutional questions one of four primary issues for the Union. As a result the Cologne European Council of June 1999 was mandated to take the decisions identified at Cardiff.

To do so became increasingly urgent because of the way that the Union's policy on enlargement changed. At the end of 1997 it was agreed to start accession negotiations with a first wave of six applicant countries in March 1998. This implied that the Union could accept new members in the early years of the twenty-first century. But while talks began, the question of what to do about the other applicants, including Turkey, became ever more pressing particularly in the light of the Kosovo crisis in 1999 and the commitment made by Blair and others to open negotiations with more applicants. So, once a deal on financing the first wave within the Agenda 2000 framework was agreed at the spring 1999 Berlin European Council, more decisive steps on institutional change could be taken, going beyond the staged process outlined in the Amsterdam protocol. The tendency to leave this behind was reinforced by the decision taken at Helsinki in December 1999 to abandon the wave process and open negotiations with a further six countries. This required a single and prompt solution to the institutional questions.

Hence the Cologne European Council agreed that there should be an IGC in 2000, not to review the whole of the Union's structures but to address the key questions unresolved at Amsterdam: the size and composition of the Commission, the weighting of votes in the Council and the possible extension of qualified majority voting in the Council. This narrow focus, and the fact that the IGC would not, as some enthusiasts had wished, begin under the Finns, was bitterly attacked by non-governmental organizations (NGOs), federalist groups and MEPs even though the German presidency also took the initiative on discussing a charter of rights. Their disillusion was compounded by the fact that there was to be no group of Wise Men to prepare the way, reform being left very much to the member states. Indeed, at Helsinki, José Maria Aznar, the Spanish Prime Minister, is reputed to have said of himself and his fellow heads of government that 'we are the wise men'. The fact that the 1996 Reflection Group had not been very successful and had helped to delay the IGC process may also have been in their minds.

As a result the new president of the Commission, Romano Prodi, set up a group of his own under Jean-Luc Dehaene, to produce ideas, which it duly did in October 1999, its report ranging quite widely as did those of various think-tanks and the European Parliament. None the less, the Finnish presidency's report to the Helsinki European Council made it clear that the states preferred to focus on the three so-called Amsterdam 'leftovers'. The report explored technical solutions to them while making it clear that there was a fourth 'box' of issues which could be considered relating to the size of the EP, the speeding up of procedures within the ECJ and other matters including the Court of Auditors and, perhaps, defence co-operation. Moreover, the presidency saw all these things as a package which would have to be both balanced and agreed before the end of 2000. This would allow the Union to be ready to accept new members by the end of 2002. Hence the report recommended that a fifth box of issues including flexibility, splitting the treaties, and issues left over from earlier IGCs should not figure on the 2000 agenda. And the European Council so agreed, causing new criticism of a 'mini-IGC', so that widening the agenda became a major concern for federationists. They did not accept, as the governments did, that the proposed IGC was the wide-ranging one envisaged in the second clause of the Amsterdam protocol. This was understandable since the states clearly did not see the IGC as the prelude either to a great leap forward or to a long drawn-out process. They wanted it to keep to the late 2000 timetable.

Even this narrow agenda went too far for some. And no previous IGC had dared to tackle questions of voting weights and thresholds which, as Ioannina in 1994 had showed, were sensitive. A further concern came from the parallel debates on the Charter of Fundamental Rights which was being discussed as a possible (binding) addition to the treaties. Equally, some social interests wanted the Convention doing this to innovate by writing social and economic rights into the draft charter alongside existing political ones. All this was controversial because not merely are rights a very 'constitutional' question but the Convention was very different from an IGC. All this caused great difficulties for many nationalists, notably in Britain, who saw it all as a move to the much-heralded 'superstate'. Hence in April 2000 an 'SOS democracy group' was founded to try and block it all. This meant that the charter was a brooding presence in the background of the mainstream negotiations. A further complication arose from the way in which the entry of Jörg Haider's Freedom Party into the Austrian government caused a major stand-off among the states and raised questions about preserving both democratic values and the rights of states.

The IGC Process

In the end, the IGC started its stately progress in early 2000 on the Helsinki basis. Thus, in response to the invitation from the presidency, the Commission presented its opinion on 26 January and the Parliament on 3 February. This allowed the IGC meetings to start on 14 February. It met on two levels and, for the first time, the EP was allowed two representatives in the Preparatory Group of personal representatives. The president of the Parliament, Nicole Fontaine, was also allowed to address the ministerial meetings. The opinions of the candidate countries were sought but not really heeded. This was even more the case with the many pressures from outside.

There was no draft treaty before the IGC although the Commission's paper did propose a number of specimen articles which might be used to help resolve the 'leftovers'. In fact the IGC proceeded on the basis of presidency papers, working through the four 'boxes' in a reasonably systematic manner. Where necessary the presidency returned to the charge with revised and refocused opinions. The IGC also had the benefit of new submissions from the Commission, notably on the ECJ, and the Parliament. Similarly it resorted to using a Friends of the Presidency Group to work on possible reforms to the ECJ rather than going outside the member states.

The Portuguese presidency managed all this in a very open way. Thus all the candidate countries were invited to put in statements of their own opinion, as did most though not all of the member states. All these were published on a number of sites on the Europa web server, along with virtually all the conference working documents. Moreover, while from March the Commission started a 'dialogue' programme in an attempt to interest the general public, the EP representatives published their own account of the work of the IGC. There were also a large number of fringe meetings and reports.

Whether in spite or because of this, the IGC did not at first make great headway. So the Portuguese, who initially seemed to have hoped that the agenda could be widened, soon realized that there was no political will for radical change. Indeed, because nothing needed to be decided until December 2000 the states seemed unwilling to engage in meaningful negotiations. They were happy just to state their positions and to rule out solutions they were not willing to accept such as QMV on harmonizing tax rates, leaving the obvious differences between states – large and small, radical and moderate – unresolved. This led to the Portuguese calling for cards to be put on the table and for more momentum.

Some of the more radical states saw an opportunity for action. The Belgians sought to raise the question of changing Article 7 TEU to reflect the emerging difficulties with Austria after the Freedom Party joined the government while the Italians sounded a warning note about Commission reform, pointing out the need for a smaller and more effective body. The French and Germans also floated the idea of relaxing the Amsterdam conditions regarding flexibility clauses so as to make progress possible in the event of a post-Nice stalemate. This made both the Commission and other states very uneasy. At the same time those who did not like the idea of any further moves to supra-nationalism were calling for the new treaty to be equipped with a list of competences which would reinforce the existing prerogatives of regions and states. Such moves led to something of a speeding up as the Nice summit came nearer, but did not fully resolve matters.

Progress was slow because the states could not agree and were therefore reluctant to declare their hands too early. Even the Feira summit gave little attention to the IGC. The fact that talk of flexibility helped to stimulate a wider debate on the future of the Union, thanks mainly to speeches made in Germany by Joschka Fischer and Jacques Chirac, also distracted attention from the rather routine business before the IGC as did the emerging debate on the Charter of Fundamental Rights.

The Presidency's own view, set out in its report to the summit, was that it was at least now possible to analyse the main political questions on the agenda in depth. But it warned against getting sucked into the wider debate on the future of the Union. Hence the first part of its report was an analysis of the leftovers and the possible options which had emerged, stressing the differences of opinion and the unwillingness of the IGC to extend its agenda except on flexibility and one or two other things. The second part of the report provided a series of draft treaty articles and tables which could be used once the political disagreements had been sorted out. The European Council claimed, a little misleadingly, that this evidenced significant progress. It saw no problems in meeting the December deadline, even though the Conference was also now to take flexibility on board, and possibly defence collaboration as well.

It would be wrong to think that nothing had been achieved. The IGC clearly had eliminated some ideas, ensuring that fraud, legal personality and the composition of the Economic and Social Committee (EcoSoc), among other things, were not going to be discussed. It also struck out some possible solutions to the questions still on the agenda. Thus the idea of not having a representative of all member states on bodies such as the Commission and the Courts was effectively buried, as was the idea of having a double-majority voting system for the Council. At the same time the IGC did a good deal of technical preparatory work on some of the key issues. In the case of the ECJ real progress was made. And, the IGC seems to have become increasingly aware that Nice would have to be a real package deal, and one going well beyond the linked issues of Commission size and voting weights in the Council. The Portuguese view of their presidency as being a time for ground clearing was probably right.

Perhaps because of this the French set out in a forceful way, seeking more rapid and emphatic negotiations which would treat all the issues together. Their aim was a balanced agreement not just on the leftovers but on Article 7 TEU, the EP and the Court of Justice. Claiming that 'no treaty would be better than a bad treaty', notably where the size of the Commission was concerned, the French hoped to have an initial discussion of all the subjects before the Biarritz Council in October 2000 so that a further report could be made then. This was a risky strategy given that France was suspected of wishing to create a '*directoire*' and was faced with threats of vetoes from the German *Länder*, the Austrians and others if the treaty went too far. And the Poles were sufficiently concerned to put in a new paper stressing the need to ensure that all changes actually helped enlargement. Consequently Chirac had to backtrack on his Berlin speech so as to reassure the Commission and the small states even though those who, like the Belgian Senate, wanted more sweeping changes were also making threatening noises.

When the negotiations resumed after their August break they did not make much better progress. The Commission remained a secondary player while the states, particularly the smaller ones, camped on their positions (especially where the weighting of votes was concerned) and became increasingly critical of the French presidency. The fact that this was divided on party lines and between politicians in Paris and the professionals in Brussels encouraged it to be aggressive. Hence not only was there talk of possible walk-outs but the French found themselves accused of hypocrisy for on the one hand urging others to give ground and on the other refusing to yield either their veto or their absolute parity in the Council with Germany. French warnings that it would prefer no treaty to a bad treaty seem to have fallen on deaf ears.

All this also produced warnings against inter-governmentalism and calls for a better mode of treaty reform. This was the prelude to a bruising encounter at the informal Biarritz summit in mid-October. For Galloway this secured the acceptance from larger states that in a smaller Commission they could be absent and from small states that capping would have to come in at some stage. But this still left some states feeling aggrieved. So, despite some optimistic talk to the contrary, Biarritz did not greatly improve things. Hence there was great unease over the presidency's first progress report in early November. This managed to combine evasion on key issues like the Commission and weighting with obduracy on extending QMV. States therefore hardened their position, with talk of 'red lines in the sand' from the United Kingdom. Only on secondary issues such as judicial reform and flexibility was there progress. The latter gained considerable momentum because of the blockages.

At the end of the month a second progress report, which was closer to a set of treaty amendments than its predecessor, emerged. This moved things on a little in some areas but seemed regressive in others. Matters were then complicated by new German demands for an enhanced weighting which alarmed both Paris and the smaller states. As a result the run-up to Nice was increasingly difficult. Ministers failed to discuss the key issues at their early December meeting and Chirac's pre-summit tour of the capitals seems to have contributed little. Only about two-fifths of the issues had been resolved and key questions like voting thresholds were as bitterly contested as ever. This was despite 370 hours of negotiations in some thirty sessions. Not surprisingly, optimists like Prodi thought the outcome was very nicely balanced and pessimists talked of extending the summit or even of postponing decisions. The unexpected level of street protest, which included a Eurosceptic 'counter-summit', added to the general gloom even though Umberto Bossi's Northern League did not descend on Nice as had been threatened.

In fact the summit did succeed, even though it proved to be the longest ever. This was partly because it was successfully split into two, the first day and a half dealing mainly with normal European Council business and the IGC proper only formally starting on the Friday afternoon. It also clearly did go to the brink and was a real and not a manufactured crisis, as Jens-Peter Bonde has claimed. He subsequently attacked it as a sly plot by a well-organized presidency to use a withholding of the texts so as to push through things of which the other heads of government were not aware. More than most IGCs, Nice was about power, raw and relative, and this brought out divisions between large and small states in a way that policy questions are less likely to do, and some two-thirds of the time was spent on reweighting. Indeed, it seems that the bilateral discussions on the Friday evening made this all too clear to a somewhat surprised Chirac.

This was reinforced by the lukewarm response to the first version of the draft treaty circulated on the Saturday morning. Reservations were clearly expressed, especially by Spain, which led Blair to say that they had spent the best part of two days stating initial positions.

Some progress was made on the Saturday, notably where Commission organization, enlargement and flexibility were concerned. Concessions were granted to Spain and to Germany, which was rewarded by the promise of a new IGC focusing on the distribution of power in the Union in return for dropping its demand for an enhanced weighting. However, the smaller states rejected the mathematics behind the presidency's suggestions on weightings, with the Portuguese accusing the larger states of a coup at their expense. The refusal of the presidency to accept a double-majority voting system, because it would have informally recognized German pre-eminence, did not help things. And the concessions being offered destroyed the possibility of a principled solution to the institutional questions desired by some. A second draft treaty in the late afternoon annoyed others by its vagueness on weighting and its stance on QMV. So despite efforts by Schröder and Blair to help the presidency out, the acrimonious haggling continued into Sunday.

This was despite both more progress on side issues and the appearance of a third, and much less Francocentric, variant of the treaty in the morning. The smaller states still felt that they were being discriminated against when it came to voting weights. The presidency made further concessions but these were insufficient to avert talk of a break-down. Hence the presidency abandoned the question of weighting and went back to QMV, where a deal favourable to France and the UK was struck. This was badly received by the small states and Chirac nearly gave up the struggle. But he returned to the charge in the early hours of Monday morning with new proposals which helped the smaller states. Even then Guy Verhofstadt of Belgium refused the deal because it destroyed Belgian parity with the Netherlands and was unfair to the candidate countries. To avert a walk-out further concessions had to be made, which were then seized on by Greece and Portugal to extract further gains. Yet it was only with great difficulty that a final deal was accepted by the confused and exhausted negotiators at 4.30 a.m. on the Monday morning.

Despite Chirac's brave talk of a historic agreement the actual text, as posted on the Internet on 13 December, proved difficult to sell. This was because in the chaos of the summit's last hours its decisions on thresholds were inconsistent and had to be rectified by COREPER on 20–21 December. A second version was then posted. It too was difficult to sell because the overall package fell short of what some states and others had wanted, even if it scared Eurosceptics. Hence the EP condemned it by a three to one majority. However, some of the wilder threats soon faded and, contrary to Amsterdam, there were very few declarations added prior to the finalizing of the text by linguists and lawyers in mid-February.

This process of tidying-up changed what had been a relatively concise and concentrated document into a longer and less comprehensible standard treaty. The initial version set out the changes in a logical order, working through the TEU and TEC changes, grouping declarations with the articles to which they refer, usually under convenient headings. These were followed by annexes setting out the protocols and declarations. At the same time, as had been the case in the pre-summit versions, the new elements were picked out in bold and the instructions for change were printed in italics. All this made it relatively easy to assess the extent of change.

The treaty finally signed in a low-key ceremony on 26 February was less transparent. It contained a brief preamble, two Parts, a set of Protocols and a Final Act. The first part contained six articles, the first four of which listed 106 amendments to the TEU (*Article 1*), TEC (*Article 2*), TEAEC (*Article 3*) and TECSC (*Article 4*). This meant a good deal of repetition. The subtitles and highlighting of changes were also removed. Neither change was overhelpful. The next articles were also hard to follow. *Article 5* thus made a brief addition to Article 10 of the Statute of the European System of Central Banks and of the European Central Bank, allowing it to amend elements of its operation (as is explained below). *Article 6* made minor changes to the applicability of the Protocol on Privileges and Immunities of the European Communities to the ECJ and CFI.

Part II contained a further seven transitional and technical articles. The first four tidy up the changes to the Union's judicial provisions to take account of the expiry of the TECSC in 2002. Thus *Article 7* repeals the old Protocol containing the Statute of the ECJ and replaces it with a new one attached to the TEU as well as to the TEAEC and the TEC. Then, while *Article 8* eliminates judicial references in the TECSC, *Article 9* gives the ECJ continuing jurisdiction where necessary. *Article 10* repeals the 1988 Council Decision setting up the Court of First Instance which is now more firmly rooted in the treaties save, again, for ECSC matters.

The remaining articles provide for the treaty to last for an unlimited period (*Article 11*), for it to be ratified and implemented in the normal way (*Article 12*), and for all language variants to be authentic (*Article 13*). After the signatures this is followed by protocols, a final act and declarations. These are considered at greater length below. The *Official Journal* version appeared in hard copy in mid-March 2001, a few days after the electronic form was posted.

An Overview of the Treaty

What has interested most people, of course, is not the packaging but the substantive contents. And many were greatly disappointed by what was agreed, feeling it far too restricted. Others, notably in the UK, saw it as going far too far towards a 'superstate'. Yet despite this, what was actually agreed and documented in amending-treaty form at Nice as documented then has proved surprisingly hard to sum up. Indeed, many appreciations are simply long undifferentiated lists of changes. There are two reasons for this. One is that, as the Irish Attorney-General said after the June vote, it is probably neutral on most of the key issues. The other is that Nice was actually more far-reaching than initial federationist criticism suggested, and this in several ways, including in its considerable symbolic encouragement to enlargement.

Most attention has focused on the two other major dimensions of Nice, and it is to these which we turn first. The second major element of Nice was the way it underpinned the move to enlargement by making a series of alterations to institutional processes. However, although the IGC was described as dealing with 'institutional reform' it defined this in a restricted way, not looking at the broader questions which administrative scientists might expect but actually concentrating quite narrowly on questions of representation and decision-making. In doing this it was, of course, helping the Union to fulfil one of its self-imposed Copenhagen conditions for enlargement, that the EU would be ready to accept new members.

But there was a third element to the treaty: the way it also took on board the need for other improvements to the way the Union works. Some of these were partly linked to enlargement, others were responses to existing perceived problems. Taken together these two material elements of Nice meant a good deal of change to institutional representation and balance. And, at the same time as guiding the Union to implementing the proposed changes needed for efficiency and enlargement, Nice also opened the way towards further institutional changes. So it needs to be taken more seriously than many were originally prepared to do.

Providing the institutional underpinning for an enlarged Union was not easy because, for the first time, the EU had to try to anticipate a potentially different situation. It therefore came up with five sets of changes which unambiguously seek to address the likely problems of an enlarged Union. To begin with there are the nearly forty articles where, on a case-by-case basis, QMV replaces unanimity in whole or part. These relate to the nomination of officials, enhanced co-operation and some ten policy areas. Some of these are also subjected to co-decision on the grounds that they are routine matters where a single state should not be able to hold up developments in the larger Union.

Then come changes to the system of weighting of votes which moves from relatively simple figures into the three hundreds, more or less to the benefit of the larger states. When it comes to setting the thresholds for positive majorities, three criteria are introduced: a quota of votes, a majority of the states and, eventually and if challenged, 62% of the population. Blocking minorities are also adjusted to the benefit of larger states. Some doubt has been expressed as to whether all this will actually make decision-making easier in the enlarged Union.

The treaty also provides for reducing the size of the Commission in stages, first to one commissioner per member state and then, once the Union has more than 27 members, to no more than 26, provided there is an equitable rotation system. Lastly, the size of all the representative institutions is capped to prevent them becoming unmanageably large. Where the EP is concerned it will be allowed to go past not merely 700 but also past the new total of 732, whether to allow new entrants between elections or, perhaps, to reward existing member states. Once and seemingly for all, restrictions are also placed on the size of secondary bodies like the Committee of the Regions.

At the same time there are a related series of changes which look partly forward to enlargement and partly back to existing institutional difficulties. One of these is the enhanced stress on democracy and rights, including a yellow-card procedure for states which offend against established norms of democratic practice. Another is the very extensive changes to the provisions on closer (now 'enhanced') co-operation, which were rewritten in order to make them more usable than those established at Amsterdam. This was done mainly by reducing the number of states needed to start such a project and making it much more difficult for a single state to block them. It also involves extending it to political aspects of the CFSP. All this looks forward to an enlarged Union.

A third aspect of the TN lies in the changes it makes to the way in which the Union and Community are presently working. To some extent these are a reflection on Amsterdam, as in the replacement of the over-rigid flexibility provisions, the revision of the incomplete thinking on the size of the EP and on the EU's over-reliance on the WEU. However, they are also a response to longer standing problems such as the backlog of cases clogging up the courts. They can also reflect outside events.

Where the TEU is concerned, these improvements begin with a number of external relations changes, largely eliminating the WEU from the treaty (and transferring some of its responsibilities to the Political and Security Committee of the EU) and changing the way in which the Presidency can negotiate for the Union. A limited competence in external negotiations on services is also established for the EC. And a new external Title XXI is introduced into the TEC. There is also a change to Pillar III, where the Eurojust network is given treaty status. In all this there is a boost to the guiding role of the

European Council, the quintessential representative of the EU, and a body which will increasingly often meet in Brussels.

On the TEC side we need to note three sets of institutional changes. To begin with, the role of the Commission president has been strengthened in a number of ways while the Commission itself both gains and loses from some other changes. The EP has also gained a little, notably in its judicial rights. Finally, there are very major – and often overlooked – changes to the organization and working of the European Courts. These gain a new flexibility in deciding their own structure and working. The courts can now create lower-level panels for specialist matters and the Court of First Instance becomes the portal to the whole judicial process. Alongside this are a number of more general innovations: the addition of a Social Protection Committee, a new definition of the role of political parties and clarifications of the role of inter-institutional agreements. None the less, Nice was not a 'Christmas tree' treaty as Maastricht and Amsterdam had been. States refrained from hanging domestically attractive baubles on the treaty and concentrated on decision-making.

This was in line with the way Nice sought to continue some of the rationalizing approach of Amsterdam to treaty presentation. Thus it made contingency plans for the expiry of the TECSC, worked through general principles of representation and not through references to specific numbers of states, and swept up a number of non-treaty changes. All this, like the increasing stress on rights and values, gives things a more 'constitutional' feel. The same might also be said of the apparent willingness to consider changing the mode of treaty revision hinted at in the 'Declaration on the future of the Union' and urged by Gray and others. At the same time Nice moved clauses around, thus avoiding too many additions to the Amsterdam numbering. All the same, lower-case letters are back as part of the numbering system of the TEC even though, as we will see, this need not have been so. The desire for political emphasis took precedence over simplicity of management. Also returning are a few gaps where articles have been deleted.

Against all this must be set a number of complications. Nice has a significant preamble, as we have already noted. It also adds a number of protocols and declarations which cannot easily be assimilated to the constitutive treaties. These will have to be looked at every time a new state joins, thus giving the declarations a higher standing than is normally the case. However, Nice has far fewer protocols than Amsterdam and only about a third as many declarations. And it also provides for staged implementation of some of its provisions, while also opening the way for the addition of new parallel arrangements for enhanced co-operation. Hence Nice cannot be regarded as simply a window treaty. It is such, but it is also, to some extent, a separate construction and we will have to refer to it for some time to come, especially after the Irish referendum in 2001 which refocused attention on it as a package deal as well as, probably wrongly, querying its relevance to enlargement.

Protocols and Enlargement

The institutional changes on which so much attention was expended at the time were only part of the major encouragement Nice gives to enlargement. Yet this too has been rather played down even though doing this was the *raison d'être* of the whole IGC process. Nice actually encourages enlargement in ways which go beyond the details of the institutional changes which take up the bulk of the treaty. And the positive response of most candidate countries suggests that this has been appreciated outside the Union.

To begin, Nice helps enlargement through its preamble. This therefore has the negotiators:

RECALLING the historic importance of the ending of the division of the European continent,

DESIRING to complete the process started by the Treaty of Amsterdam of preparing the institutions of the European Union to function in an enlarged Union,

DETERMINED on this basis to press ahead with the accession negotiations in order to bring them to a successful conclusion, in accordance with the procedure laid down in the Treaty on European Union,

HAVE RESOLVED to amend the Treaty on European Union, the Treaties establishing the European Communities and certain related acts.

In other words, Nice is placed firmly in the context of the hard realities of ongoing European unification and expansion. The whole justification of the treaty is thus linked to enlargement, and this is very important. Had there been no agreement, the psychological damage to the wider Europe would have been immense.

At the same time Nice also removes the last internal barrier to enlargement. Indeed it claims in point 2 of the Declaration on the future of the Union that the specific changes made in the treaty mean that the Union has met its own Copenhagen criterion of institutional readiness for enlargement. While some may doubt this, the candidate states have accepted it at face value. And the Union is now committed to acting as if it were true. There can be no excuse for delay now until institutional changes have been completed. Indeed, in the declaration there is a formal commitment that the Union will not use the need for further institutional changes as an obstacle to enlargement.

The candidates could also take comfort in the Declaration on the enlargement of the European Union. This, which, like its predecessor, is printed below and not in relation to a specific treaty, made it plain that the candidate countries were expected to take their place in the EU institutions and were, give or take, to do so on equal terms with the existing member states. The fact that the declaration lays down their allocation of seats and votes appears to remove a possible cause of difficulty in accession negotiations. At the same time it provides an incentive to complete talks in time to take part in the 2004 IGC. There are further hints elsewhere in the treaty about participation in the next EP elections so we can say that there is something of a timetable for enlargement if not the absolute dates that some candidate countries wanted.

So Nice does give a major political impetus to enlargement. And this is reinforced by the ways and the languages it uses to do this. Much of the treaty's encouragement to enlargement is tied up with the protocol on the subject. This is an interesting approach since it could have been done in the treaty proper. But, because the question of institutional adaption was so technical, involved changes at varying times and phases, and affected so many treaties, to give it specific unity as an attached and binding document makes sense. For similar reasons we deal with them in part here and not only in the context of those parts of the TEU and TEC they altered. Not to do this would both reduce the impact of Nice as an 'enlargement' treaty and make it more difficult to assess its own inherent characteristics. In other words, it would obscure the fact that the treaty, and notably its Protocol on the enlargement of the European Union and the related declarations, will remain a substantive element of the treaty base. And since the language they use is often helpful to enlargement, it is worth assessing them and printing them in full here, as well as later in the *Guide* when talking about revised treaty articles.

As with the TA, the Treaty of Nice seemingly ends with the signatures which follow its general and final provisions. Yet, as Box 1 shows, the treaty also contains four legally binding protocols which appear immediately after the signatures. As we have already seen, protocols contain provisions which have the same legal standing as treaty articles. They must therefore be taken into consideration when reading the treaties.

Box 1 Protocols introduced by the TN

Protocol annexed to the *Treaty on European Union* and to the *Treaties establishing the European Communities* (see p. 169):

- **Protocol on the enlargement of the European Union**

Protocol annexed to the *Treaty on European Union*, to the *Treaty establishing the European Community* and to the *Treaty establishing the European Atomic Energy Community* (see pp. 493–504):

- **Protocol on the Statute of the Court of Justice**

Protocols annexed to the *Treaty establishing the European Community* (see pp. 539–40):

- **Protocol on the financial consequences of the expiry of the ECSC Treaty and on the Research Fund for Coal and Steel**
- **Protocol on Article 67 of the Treaty establishing the European Community**

Those protocols introduced by Nice are also of note for the reason that two of them establish a new role for protocols in so far as they contain either treaty amendments which will come into force at a specified future date or legally binding changes to how decisions are to be taken in specified areas in the future. The need for a further IGC is therefore by-passed. In other words, the Union has agreed both its negotiating stance at future accession treaties (implicitly requiring the candidates to accept this) and the way in which the Council is to implement the new changes when the time comes. They thus serve as a manual or code of conduct. All this is highly significant for enlargement.

The second of the four protocols adopted at Nice contains the revised Statute of the Court of Justice which replaces the existing Protocols on the Statute of the Court of Justice attached to the TEC and TEAEC as repealed by Article 7 TN. However, we should note that, in recognition of the growing competence of the ECJ to rule on matters within Pillars II and III of the EU, the new protocol is also attached to the TEU. It is therefore printed and commented on in conjunction with the TEC (see pp. 493–504). The protocol does not, however, replace that attached to the TECSC, although many of the latter's provisions were repealed at Nice (Article 8 TN). The protocol's provisions do apply, though, when the ECJ exercises its powers under the TECSC.

The third and fourth protocols introduced by Nice are both annexed to the TEC alone. The first deals with the financial consequences of the TECSC's expiry on 23 July 2002, providing for the transfer of all ECSC assets and liabilities to the EC on the following day and confirming that the revenue from the assets will be used to fund research in sectors related to the coal and steel industry. The final new protocol concerns changes to decision-making regarding Article 67 TEC originally destined for inclusion in a declaration. The upgrade to protocol status means that from 1 May 2004 the Council will act by QMV when adopting measures for administrative co-operation within the areas of freedom, security and justice provided for in Articles 61–69 TEC.

The remaining protocol, which is actually listed first of the four, relates to enlargement. Because the issue is so central to the nature and impact of the Treaty of Nice, it needs to be commented on and printed here. Understanding how this will work also requires us to take note not just of the preamble to Nice and the Declaration on the future of the Union already discussed, but also of three further declarations, as these contain the rules of implementation for the protocol. So these are printed here as well.

The enlargement protocol consists of four articles, most of them dealing with specific institutions. The first of the articles, however, repeals, with effect from the Treaty's coming into force, the Protocol on the institutions with the prospect of enlargement of the European Union. This, which was adopted at Amsterdam in 1997, goes because it has become redundant, Nice having addressed the issue of institutional reform. Indeed, it is to this issue that the remaining three articles are dedicated.

Thus Article 2 contains an amendment to Article 190(2) TEC on the allocation of seats in the EP to each of the existing 15 member states from 2004. Depending on how many candidate states the EU admits prior to 2004 the allocation of seats may be altered by the Council, presumably acting by unanimity. Article 3 then deals with the weighting of votes and voting thresholds in the Council in an enlarged EU providing for the introduction of various treaty amendments on 1 January 2005. Explicit reference is made to the Declaration on the enlargement of the European Union adopted at Nice (Declaration No. 20 TN). The final article contains amendments to be introduced to the TEC on 1 January 2005 and later when the EU consists of 27 member states. These establish the Commission's size, respectively, as one commissioner per member state and less than the number of member states, leaving the decision on size and rotation in an EU(27+) to the Council acting unanimously. The actual texts are as follows:

Protocol on the enlargement of the European Union

THE HIGH CONTRACTING PARTIES

HAVE AGREED UPON the following provisions, which shall be annexed to the Treaty on European Union and to the Treaties establishing the European Communities:

Article 1
Repeal of the Protocol on the institutions

The Protocol on the institutions with the prospect of enlargement of the European Union, annexed to the Treaty on European Union and to the Treaties establishing the European Communities, is hereby repealed.

Article 2
Provisions concerning the European Parliament

1. On 1 January 2004 and with effect from the start of the 2004–2009 term, in Article 190(2) of the Treaty establishing the European Community and in Article 108(2) of the Treaty establishing the European Atomic Energy Community, the first subparagraph shall be replaced by the following:

'The number of representatives elected in each Member State shall be as follows:

Belgium	22
Denmark	13
Germany	99
Greece	22
Spain	50
France	72
Ireland	12
Italy	72
Luxembourg	6
Netherlands	25
Austria	17
Portugal	22
Finland	13
Sweden	18
United Kingdom	72'

2. Subject to paragraph 3, the total number of representatives in the European Parliament for the 2004–2009 term shall be equal to the number of representatives specified in Article 190(2) of the Treaty establishing the European Community and in Article 108(2) of the Treaty establishing the European Atomic Energy Community plus the number of representatives of the new Member States resulting from the accession treaties signed by 1 January 2004 at the latest.

3. If the total number of members referred to in paragraph 2 is less than 732, a pro rata correction shall be applied to the number of representatives to be elected in each Member State, so that the total number is as close as possible to 732, without such a correction leading to the number of representatives to be elected in each Member State being higher than that provided for in Article 190(2) of the Treaty establishing the European Community and in Article 108(2) of the Treaty establishing the European Atomic Energy Community for the 1999–2004 term.
The Council shall adopt a decision to that effect.

4. By way of derogation from the second paragraph of Article 189 of the Treaty establishing the European Community and from the second paragraph of Article 107 of the Treaty establishing the European Atomic Energy Community, in the event of the entry into force of accession treaties after the adoption of the Council decision provided for in the second subparagraph of paragraph 3 of this Article, the number of members of the European Parliament may temporarily exceed 732 for the period for which that decision applies. The same correction as that referred to in the first subparagraph of paragraph 3 of this Article shall

be applied to the number of representatives to be elected in the Member States in question.

Article 3
Provisions concerning the weighting of votes in the Council

1. On 1 January 2005:

(a) in Article 205 of the Treaty establishing the European Community and in Article 118 of the Treaty establishing the European Atomic Energy Community:

(i) paragraph 2 shall be replaced by the following:

'2. Where the Council is required to act by a qualified majority, the votes of its members shall be weighted as follows:

Belgium	12
Denmark	7
Germany	29
Greece	12
Spain	27
France	29
Ireland	7
Italy	29
Luxembourg	4
Netherlands	13
Austria	10
Portugal	12
Finland	7
Sweden	10
United Kingdom	29

Acts of the Council shall require for their adoption at least 169 votes in favour cast by a majority of the members where this Treaty requires them to be adopted on a proposal from the Commission.
In other cases, for their adoption acts of the Council shall require at least 169 votes in favour, cast by at least two-thirds of the members.'

(ii) the following paragraph 4 shall be added:

'4. When a decision is to be adopted by the Council by a qualified majority, a member of the Council may request verification that the Member States constituting the qualified majority represent at least 62% of the total population of the Union. If that condition is shown not to have been met, the decision in question shall not be adopted.'

(b) In Article 23(2) of the Treaty on European Union, the third subparagraph shall be replaced by the following text:

'The votes of the members of the Council shall be weighted in accordance with Article 205(2) of the Treaty establishing the European Community. For their adoption, decisions shall require at least 169 votes in favour cast by at least two-thirds of the members. When a decision is to be adopted by the

Council by a qualified majority, a member of the Council may request verification that the Member States constituting the qualified majority represent at least 62% of the total population of the Union. If that condition is shown not to have been met, the decision in question shall not be adopted.'

(c) In Article 34 of the Treaty on European Union, paragraph 3 shall be replaced by the following:

'3. Where the Council is required to act by a qualified majority, the votes of its members shall be weighted as laid down in Article 205(2) of the Treaty establishing the European Community, and for their adoption acts of the Council shall require at least 169 votes in favour, cast by at least two-thirds of the members. When a decision is to be adopted by the Council by a qualified majority, a member of the Council may request verification that the Member States constituting the qualified majority represent at least 62% of the total population of the Union. If that condition is shown not to have been met, the decision in question shall not be adopted.'

2. At the time of each accession, the threshold referred to in the second subparagraph of Article 205(2) of the Treaty establishing the European Community and in the second subparagraph of Article 118(2) of the Treaty establishing the European Atomic Energy Community shall be calculated in such a way that the qualified majority threshold expressed in votes does not exceed the threshold resulting from the table in the Declaration on the enlargement of the European Union, included in the Final Act of the Conference which adopted the Treaty of Nice.

Article 4
Provisions concerning the Commission

1. On 1 January 2005 and with effect from when the first Commission following that date takes up its duties, Article 213(1) of the Treaty establishing the European Community and Article 126(1) of the Treaty establishing the European Atomic Energy Community shall be replaced by the following:

'1. The Members of the Commission shall be chosen on the grounds of their general competence and their independence shall be beyond doubt.
The Commission shall include one national of each of the Member States.
The number of Members of the Commission may be altered by the Council, acting unanimously.'

2. When the Union consists of 27 Member States, Article 213(1) of the Treaty establishing the European Community and Article 126(1) of the Treaty establishing the European Atomic Energy Community shall be replaced by the following:

'1. The Members of the Commission shall be chosen on the grounds of their general competence and their independence shall be beyond doubt.
The number of Members of the Commission shall be less than the number of Member States. The Members of the Commission shall be chosen according to a rotation system based on the principle of equality, the implementing arrangements for which shall be adopted by the Council, acting unanimously.

The number of Members of the Commission shall be set by the Council, acting unanimously.'

This amendment shall apply as from the date on which the first Commission following the date of accession of the twenty-seventh Member State of the Union takes up its duties.

3. The Council, acting unanimously after signing the treaty of accession of the twenty-seventh Member State of the Union, shall adopt:
– the number of Members of the Commission;
– the implementing arrangements for a rotation system based on the principle of equality containing all the criteria and rules necessary for determining the composition of successive colleges automatically on the basis of the following principles:
 (a) Member States shall be treated on a strictly equal footing as regards determination of the sequence of, and the time spent by, their nationals as Members of the Commission; consequently, the difference between the total number of terms of office held by nationals of any given pair of Member States may never be more than one;
 (b) subject to point (a), each successive college shall be so composed as to reflect satisfactorily the demographic and geographical range of all the Member States of the Union.

4. Any State which accedes to the Union shall be entitled, at the time of its accession, to have one of its nationals as a Member of the Commission until paragraph 2 applies.

As has become clear, the protocol is not self-sufficient. It mainly covers interim arrangements and lays down the principles of implementation. However, to work out how many seats a candidate country is to be given, notably in the EP, reference has to be made to the Declaration on the enlargement of the European Union (Declaration No. 20 TN). This specifies the exact number of EP, EcoSoc and CoR seats and Council votes each specific country is to be given. Even if this is technically provisional since the declaration is not legally binding, and there can be little doubt that the Czech Republic and Hungary will raise the question of their representation in the EP at the time of accession, there is also an element of take it or leave it to the decisions. The fact that this declaration as well as the one that follows (Declaration No. 21 TN) provide further guidance on future thresholds for QMV shows how sensitive the issue is. The final Declaration on the venue for future European Councils owes its existence to a COREPER-inspired attempt to win Belgian support during the final difficult hours of the Nice summit. However, it points in a more centralizing direction than many other of the changes made at Nice. Hence it adds to the unease expressed after the Irish vote on 7 June 2001. And it could cause difficulties with new member states who may well want to impress their own citizens by having a summit at home.

20. DECLARATION ON THE ENLARGEMENT OF THE EUROPEAN UNION*

The common position to be adopted by the Member States at the accession conferences, as regards the distribution of seats at the European Parliament, the weighting of votes in the Council, the composition of the Economic and Social Committee and the composition of the Committee of the Regions will correspond to the following tables for a Union of 27 Member States.

1. THE EUROPEAN PARLIAMENT

Member States	EP seats
Germany	99
United Kingdom	72
France	72
Italy	72
Spain	50
Poland	50
Romania	33
Netherlands	25
Greece	22
Czech Republic	20
Belgium	22
Hungary	20
Portugal	22
Sweden	18
Bulgaria	17
Austria	17
Slovakia	13
Denmark	13
Finland	13
Ireland	12
Lithuania	12
Latvia	8
Slovenia	7
Estonia	6
Cyprus	6
Luxembourg	6
Malta	5
Total	732

*The tables in this declaration take account only of those candidate countries with which accession negotiations have actually started. (Footnote appears in original of Declaration.)

2. THE WEIGHTING OF VOTES IN THE COUNCIL

Members of the Council	Weighted votes
Germany	29
United Kingdom	29
France	29
Italy	29
Spain	27
Poland	27
Romania	14
Netherlands	13
Greece	12
Czech Republic	12
Belgium	12
Hungary	12
Portugal	12
Sweden	10
Bulgaria	10
Austria	10
Slovakia	7
Denmark	7
Finland	7
Ireland	7
Lithuania	7
Latvia	4
Slovenia	4
Estonia	4
Cyprus	4
Luxembourg	4
Malta	3
Total	345

Acts of the Council shall require for their adoption at least 258 votes in favour, cast by a majority of members, where this Treaty requires them to be adopted on a proposal from the Commission.

In other cases, for their adoption acts of the Council shall require at least 258 votes in favour cast by at least two-thirds of the members.

When a decision is to be adopted by the Council by a qualified majority, a member of the Council may request verification that the Member States constituting the qualified majority represent at least 62% of the total population of the Union. If that condition is shown not to have been met, the decision in question shall not be adopted.

3. THE ECONOMIC AND SOCIAL COMMITTEE

Member States	Members
Germany	24
United Kingdom	24
France	24
Italy	24
Spain	21
Poland	21
Romania	15
Netherlands	12
Greece	12
Czech Republic	12
Belgium	12
Hungary	12
Portugal	12
Sweden	12
Bulgaria	12
Austria	12
Slovakia	9
Denmark	9
Finland	9
Ireland	9
Lithuania	9
Latvia	7
Slovenia	7
Estonia	7
Cyprus	6
Luxembourg	6
Malta	5
Total	344

4. THE COMMITTEE OF THE REGIONS

Member States	Members
Germany	24
United Kingdom	24
France	24
Italy	24
Spain	21
Poland	21
Romania	15
Netherlands	12
Greece	12
Czech Republic	12

Belgium	12
Hungary	12
Portugal	12
Sweden	12
Bulgaria	12
Austria	12
Slovakia	9
Denmark	9
Finland	9
Ireland	9
Lithuania	9
Latvia	7
Slovenia	7
Estonia	7
Cyprus	6
Luxembourg	6
Malta	5
Total	344

21.   DECLARATION ON THE QUALIFIED MAJORITY THRESHOLD AND THE NUMBER OF VOTES FOR A BLOCKING MINORITY IN AN ENLARGED UNION

Insofar as all the candidate countries listed in the Declaration on the enlargement of the European Union have not yet acceded to the Union when the new vote weightings take effect (1 January 2005), the threshold for a qualified majority will move, according to the pace of accessions, from a percentage below the current one to a maximum of 73.4%. When all the candidate countries mentioned above have acceded, the blocking minority, in a Union of 27, will be raised to 91 votes, and the qualified majority threshold resulting from the table given in the Declaration on enlargement of the European Union will be automatically adjusted accordingly.

22.   DECLARATION ON THE VENUE FOR EUROPEAN COUNCILS

As from 2002, one European Council meeting per Presidency will be held in Brussels. When the Union comprises 18 members, all European Council meetings will be held in Brussels.

Final Act, Declarations and Retrospect

Thereafter there is the final act listing what the IGC agreed as well as the numerous declarations which the IGC either adopted or noted. These are: the Treaty of Nice, the four protocols outlined above, 24 Declarations adopted by the IGC, and three declarations of which the IGC took note. Then annexed to the final act are all the declarations listed. They are printed later in the *Guide* and commented on in conjunction with the treaties to which they are attached. Unlike the final act associated with the Treaty of Amsterdam, however, there are no consolidated versions of the TEU and TEC attached, even for purely 'illustrative purposes'.

Following in the footsteps of the SEA, TEU and TA, Nice succeeds in furthering the declarationization of the treaties by annexing to the final act a total of twenty-seven declarations. As has been the case in the past, most of these (24) have been adopted by the IGC and thus accepted by all fifteen member states. A smaller number (3) are by one or more member states. Also, following earlier treaties, some declarations appear to enjoy a higher status being declarations by 'The High Contracting Parties' (Nos. 5 and 9) who formally signed the Treaty of Nice. Most are simply those of 'The Conference', although as was the case at Amsterdam a number have no identifiable ownership (Nos. 1, 20–23). This is somewhat puzzling and potentially of concern since these five contain some of the most significant declarations, dealing as they do with the development of the EU's security and defence policy, enlargement, the location of European Council meetings, and the future of the EU.

The majority of the adopted declarations annexed to the final act of the TN contain statements clarifying interpretations of specific articles. One relates to a provision in the TEU (No. 2). A further 15 relate to new or existing articles found in the TEC (Nos. 3–17). Other declarations refer specifically to the Court of Auditors (No. 18), the ESCB–ECB statute (No. 19) and the protocol concerning the expiry of the TECSC (No. 24). This leaves the 'unowned' declarations already noted, one of which (No. 20) is of considerable significance for member states and non-member states alike since it contains, albeit not in a legally binding form, the projected distribution of seats and votes in an EU of 27 member states which will form the basis for the member states' common position in accession negotiations. The other declaration of considerable note is that concerning the future of the EU (No. 23), which sets out an agenda and preparatory steps for a further IGC in 2004 (see pp. 644–51).

As regards the 'noted' declarations, the first is unilateral and confirms Alicante as the seat of the Board of Appeal of the Office for Harmonisation in the Internal Market. The remaining two owe their existence to last-minute changes to the wording of Article 161 TEC. Declaration No. 2n confirms Greek, Spanish and Portuguese understanding of 'multiannual' as meaning the financial perspective which the EU will adopt from 1 January 2007 while Declaration No. 3n contains the response of Denmark, Germany, the Netherlands and Austria countering this. For the text of the declarations, see pp. 73–6, 196–7 and 561–5.

FINAL ACT

The **CONFERENCE OF THE REPRESENTATIVES OF THE GOVERNMENTS OF THE MEMBER STATES** convened in Brussels on 14 February 2000 to adopt by common accord the amendments to be made to the Treaty on European Union, the Treaties establishing respectively the European Community, the European Atomic Energy Community and the European Coal and Steel Community and certain related Acts has adopted the following texts:

I. Treaty of Nice amending the Treaty on European Union, the Treaties establishing the European Communities and certain related Acts

II. Protocols

A. Protocol annexed to the Treaty on European Union and to the Treaties establishing the European Communities:
– Protocol on the enlargement of the European Union

B. Protocol annexed to the Treaty on European Union, to the Treaty establishing the European Community and to the Treaty establishing the European Atomic Energy Community:
 – Protocol on the Statute of the Court of Justice

C. Protocols annexed to the Treaty establishing the European Community:
 – Protocol on the financial consequences of the expiry of the ECSC Treaty and on the Research Fund for Coal and Steel
 – Protocol on Article 67 of the Treaty establishing the European Community

The Conference adopted the following declarations annexed to this Final Act:

1. Declaration on the European security and defence policy
2. Declaration on Article 31(2) of the Treaty on European Union
3. Declaration on Article 10 of the Treaty establishing the European Community
4. Declaration on the third paragraph of Article 21 of the Treaty establishing the European Community
5. Declaration on Article 67 of the Treaty establishing the European Community
6. Declaration on Article 100 of the Treaty establishing the European Community
7. Declaration on Article 111 of the Treaty establishing the European Community
8. Declaration on Article 137 of the Treaty establishing the European Community
9. Declaration on Article 175 of the Treaty establishing the European Community
10. Declaration on Article 181a of the Treaty establishing the European Community
11. Declaration on Article 191 of the Treaty establishing the European Community
12. Declaration on Article 225 of the Treaty establishing the European Community
13. Declaration on Article 225(2) and (3) of the Treaty establishing the European Community
14. Declaration on Article 225(2) and (3) of the Treaty establishing the European Community
15. Declaration on Article 225(3) of the Treaty establishing the European Community
16. Declaration on Article 225a of the Treaty establishing the European Community
17. Declaration on Article 229a of the Treaty establishing the European Community
18. Declaration on the Court of Auditors
19. Declaration on Article 10.6 of the Statute of the European System of Central Banks and of the European Central Bank
20. Declaration on the enlargement of the European Union
21. Declaration on the qualified majority threshold and the number of votes for a blocking minority in an enlarged Union
22. Declaration on the venue for European Councils

23. Declaration on the future of the Union
24. Declaration on Article 2 of the Protocol on the financial consequences of the expiry of the ECSC Treaty and on the Research Fund for Coal and Steel

The Conference took note of the following declarations annexed to this Final Act:

1. Declaration by Luxembourg
2. Declaration by Greece, Spain and Portugal on Article 161 of the Treaty establishing the European Community
3. Declaration by Denmark, Germany, the Netherlands and Austria on Article 161 of the Treaty establishing the European Community

Done at Nice this twenty-sixth day of February in the year two thousand and one.*

Despite all this, and what it has done for enlargement, Nice is clearly not a treaty based on a major project as was Maastricht. So it should not be seen as a failure of ambition. It had more limited, as well as more speculative, aims. And it succeeded. Nice was both a political deal, and one which was enshrined in a formal treaty document of an amending rather than a constitutive nature. And it gave a psychological boost to enlargement. In other words, Nice has a multiple personality.

Nice embodies a hard-fought compromise about combining efficiency with the defence of states' rights, something which emerges from the fact that it has been attacked by both extremes. However, those states emerged from the process bruised and often without their erstwhile allies. This is an interesting reflection on the first treaty to be seen through to negotiation by a large state presidency. In fact the divisions go beyond that between large and small states. At the same time Nice has also changed the balance between states as a whole and the institutions in complicated and often contradictory ways. Equally, the institutions have both gained and lost from the treaty. All of this means that Nice has probably changed the political dynamics of the Union. This uncertain new balance makes it hard to assess how effectively the actual changes agreed at Nice will work.

Substantively, of course, Nice is an attempt to keep the existing show on the road by trying to second guess the future working of the existing Union. Here despite the manifold abuse heaped on it in December 2000 there are, as Galloway and others have come to realize, good things about it, despite the defensive mode in which most states approached the negotiations. So it is not certain that some of the paper complications will actually hold things up. And it has the great advantage of having avoided the worse crisis of leaving destabilizing leftovers. None the less, a large number of items on many wish lists were set aside, such as: adding the Charter of Fundamental Rights to the treaties, ending the opt-outs, establishing a hierarchy of norms, giving the Union legal personality, making co-decision the standard legislative procedure, giving Parliament control of the executive and reforming the pillar structure. Yet, given the obvious fact that there was no real popular will for further major developments, as was to be made clear by some Irish voters on 7 June 2001, it was perhaps as well that Nice did not attempt to introduce these. To have done so could well have triggered even greater uproar.

---

*This phrase appears in each of the official languages of the member states (Spanish, Danish, German, Greek, English, French, Gaelic, Italian, Dutch, Portuguese, Finnish, Swedish) and is followed by the signatures of the member states' plenipotentiaries.

However, the treaty did leave open the possibility of further institutional clarification, if not of development. In the meantime Nice, assuming it will finally be ratified, has given the Union a service which should improve its working in the short term while it tries to cope with wider and deeper questions and the longer term. And it also offers it an MOT certificate for the next stage of its enlarged existence, always assuming that its limitations – exposed as they were after the Irish voted 'no' – do not, in the end, prevent its ratification. On the downside, it was yet another ambiguous, complicated and opaque package deal, as becomes apparent when we turn to the Treaty on European Union in its post-Nice form.

III The Treaty on European Union

In theory, the Treaty on European Union (TEU) is of the same legal standing as all the other European Treaties. Yet in practice it seems to be becoming more significant than the other constitutive treaties, even the TEC. There are three reasons for this. To begin with, the TEU, as a fundamental constitutive treaty, actually creates the Union as the quintessential European body. This is because the Union is established as a hat, or better a cloak, for the other pillars which, although it is loose and flowing, still means that there is no direct entry to the Community. Membership in the EC comes along as a free gift with entry to the Union. So, in position if not in status, the TEU seems to be a superior treaty. And Nice seems to have accepted this.

Secondly, as an amending as well as a constitutive treaty, the TEU when it was first applied made substantive changes to the TEC and the way the Community operates. Indeed, it went much further here than any other European Treaty, notably where EMU was concerned. This gives it particular technical importance. And, thirdly, it matters more politically and psychologically than other treaties such as the SEA. The original TEU proclaimed itself as marking 'a new stage in European integration'. Hence, as we have already seen, many critics regard 'Maastricht' as the symbol of an enforced rush to supra-national statehood. Even though others regard it in a very different light, such reactions are important and show us that 'Maastricht' has a symbolic status not matched by any other text. So the TEU is a starting point for understanding contemporary attitudes towards the whole integration enterprise.

This makes it important to look at the TEU ahead of the TEC, even though many think the latter is the heart of 'true' integration. So we now want to look at the TEU in its own right as a self-standing treaty rather than use it as a loose framework, as we did in our previous commentary. This is important for two reasons. The first is that the TEU is a somewhat more self-contained document than the TEC, needing less reference to ECJ case law. This is because the TEU largely excludes the ECJ from having jurisdiction. Moreover, it is still quite new and there has been less time for jurisprudence to develop. Equally, the treaty does not deal with those aspects of everyday life where legal conundrums are most likely to arise. In this sense the TEU is, as Beaumont and Weatherill say, a more political document, perhaps even a more constitutionalist one, than the TEC.

There is a second reason for seeing the TEU as important. This is because of the way that, as we have already noted, the changes made at Amsterdam subtly reinforced its position as one of the twin foundations of the European construction. Equally, this justifies our decision to disregard the argument that the two bodies should now be regarded as one. So, because of all this, we need to think first about the treaty as a whole.

This means looking at it as it was originally, as it developed following Amsterdam and as it should be after Nice is ratified. Then we can go on to print and comment in more detail on its various components from preamble, through principles, to protocols and beyond. Even after Amsterdam the TEU remained a variegated and ambiguous document, offering justification for a number of conflicting interpretations even if the TA did reinforce its standing, notably through the way it wrote general axioms for the whole enterprise into its articles. Nice, in some ways, accentuated this ambiguity, extending the treaty text, adding further nuances and generally emphasizing the guiding role of the TEU within the European enterprise.

i An Overview

If the TEU is now the key to understanding integration as a whole we need to see it as a whole. However, even if the Treaty of Amsterdam turned the TEU into more of a freestanding document, summarizing and appreciating it today is still very difficult. This is not only because of the political controversy surrounding 'Maastricht'. It is also because, as an amending treaty, the TEU now has a kind of gap where the changes it made to the TEC and the other constitutive treaties have been absorbed into the latter and are no longer easily distinguishable. Moreover, Amsterdam made significant changes to the treaty and the composition of the Union's pillars, showing that the TEU is an evolving treaty.

The difficulties are compounded by the way in which, when talking of what 'Maastricht' or 'Amsterdam' did, most commentators concentrate on the changes to the Union's material constitution and rarely distinguish between the TEU as a (now partly absorbed) amending document and as a constitutive treaty. Nor do they always discriminate between the TEU as such and the TEC. To be fair the complicated relationship between the Union and the Community, on which the former is founded, gives them every right to do so. None the less, the TEU is something with which we need to come to terms.

If we look at the actual TEU as a document, it is a complex text of somewhat variable tone and changing structure. None the less it does establish a limited if not wholly clear overarching structure for interaction: the European Union. This took the integration process beyond the Single Market into Economic and Monetary Union and diverse forms of closer political integration. In fact, as Dyson says, it was a Janus-faced treaty, revolutionary in its introduction of a sound money-based EMU and more cautiously gradualist in its political changes. Many of the policy and institutional elements amongst the latter were then improved and restructured at Amsterdam whereas Nice, apart from enhanced co-operation, made only limited changes. The TEU remains, however, a significant and complex text. Indeed, the jury is still out on its nature and impact.

The Structure and Style of the Treaty

The Treaty on European Union as it emerged from the two sets of negotiations leading to Maastricht was a single text with a clear overall structure. It began, in the conventional way, with a preamble, went on to a series of titles, and finished with a raft of protocols and declarations. Within the main body of the treaty there were only nineteen articles, which were not numbered but were distinguished by a capital letter so that they would not be confused with TEC articles. The preamble consisted of a dozen recitals which make the aims of the Union pretty clear.

Moreover, four of the seven original titles relate to the Union. None of these is internally subdivided. The first, following on the conclusion of the preamble, formally established the Union and then went on to spell out the new organization's objectives, institutional framework, direction and responsibilities. And it did this relatively briefly and clearly in the 'common provisions', so called because many of them relate to the Community pillar as well as the Union proper. This constitutive role is also visible in Title VIII – Final Provisions. This provided for the judicial enforcement, validation and amendment of the treaty. Prior to this Titles V and VI set up the Union's two semi-detached pillars: those concerned with the common foreign and security policy (CFSP) and justice and home affairs (JHA). In the case of the former this meant giving revised provisions governing European Political Co-operation (EPC) a more solid treaty standing.

The trouble was that most of this constitutive contribution was then obscured by the fact that three of the TEU's titles, covering articles G to I, were amendments to the three original European Treaties. As such they were immensely long, especially G, and could only be followed if one had a copy of the TEC, TECSC and TEAEC to hand. They accounted for 111 pages in the official version of the TEU out of the 141 given over to the treaty proper. The various protocols and declarations took up a further 108 pages. In fact the Union clauses proper were relatively slim, and made up no more than a tenth of the whole treaty. Many people have attacked the treaty for being too long, some 253 pages in the official version, containing 60,000 words in all. But it should be remembered that many pieces of national legislation are far longer. Thus, to invoke one contemporary of the TEU, the UK government's Finance Act of 1994 ran to 417 pages embracing 241 articles plus appendices and schedules.

Moreover, the amendments to the other European Treaties were much more complex, structurally and linguistically, than Titles I and VII because they were a consistent series of italicized amendments to other treaties. There were 86 of them in the case of the TEC, but though they followed the order of the TEC they lacked clear headings and thematic groupings. And, the references to the various chapters, sections and titles of the TEC were an added complication. Furthermore, the content of the amendments was much more technical and procedural than the principles laid out in Title I. It was really these amendments, and the way they had to be set out, that gave rise to the vociferous criticisms of the impenetrable language in which the treaties were written and the resulting lack of transparency which we have already noted.

Even though their removal leaves a hole, we need to remember that the changes contained in Article G (now 8) were of supreme political importance. They extended the EC's policy responsibilities, enhanced the powers of its institutions, made provisions for new principles like citizenship and subsidiarity and introduced EMU. Such changes were politically very sensitive so that attention was focused on them and made the text seem very complicated. In the consolidated versions, published in 1997, this is not really apparent since the amendment provisions are not actually printed, turning III, IV and V into ghost titles. Moreover, Amsterdam was to insert another title, not to mention rewriting one, only for Nice to rewrite the former. All this, as we will see, makes it hard to appreciate now what the TEU actually did as an amending treaty.

The Establishment of the Union

The essential constitutive role of the TEU was, as we have already seen, to create the Union as a singular, specific entity within the treaty base. With the TEU entering into force on 1 November 1993, no longer was European Union an aspiration or a process. Maastricht made it a reality albeit an ambiguous and unclear one. For, whatever everyday usages (or some academic arguments) are, legally the Union is something different from the Community. Its creation was justified by the desire to improve the lot of the peoples of Europe and carry forward the process of integration in the new circumstances of the post-1989 world. Its original objectives were to develop social conditions and to encourage co-operation among the member states, whose identities it is pledged to respect. Equally, it aimed to promote itself in the international arena.

So much is readily apparent. What is less clear is the Union's concrete structure. As an entity the Union is described in the TEU as being founded on the Community. But the EU also draws on inter-governmental action. And the TEU tends to see things in these terms rather than talking of three pillars as has since become the norm among practitioners and observers. So the Union has at least two modes of operation: Community-based and inter-governmental. All its decision-making is nevertheless supposed to be done openly and close to the people. There is also a good deal of overlap, with EC rules increasingly penetrating the inter-governmental elements and the latter prescribing action to the EC.

Operationally the Union works through a single institutional framework but under the guidance of the European Council which, paradoxically, is not part of that framework. This reflects the fact that although the Union has a slightly superior status it has neither internal legal personality nor its own means of action. Indeed, there was no way that the negotiators at Maastricht could have, or would have, changed the existing communities and their constitutive treaties to give the Union these powers. The idea was also largely rejected at Amsterdam, although Nice does talk of the institutions of the Union.

However, the Union is also rather variable in substance. This is a reflection partly of the different powers of the various pillars and partly of the various opt-outs within the Community pillar, notably concerning EMU. Indeed, the precise role of the member states is inconsistent and poorly articulated. The Union has to be regarded as an inchoate and uncertain construction, reflecting the way it was negotiated rather than any clear blueprint. Given all this it is not surprising that the structure of the Union has been described as closer to MFI than Montesquieu. Westlake has said that the concept becomes more amorphous the more it is used. In sum, the constitutive element of the TEU lacks clarity and is incomplete. Treating the whole shebang as the Union, for simplicity's sake, is thus quite understandable, even if technically inaccurate.

Amsterdam and the Union

Moreover, the Union is far from a finished creation. It is in evolution even if it has a long way to go to match the changes in the TEC. Amsterdam soon added a further complication to understanding and assessing the TEU. In its first article the final version of the TA made 15 changes to the TEU, and the changes made to the three original constitutive treaties also had implications for the Union as such. At the same time, some of the new protocols and declarations have also helped to redefine the Union.

In the first place, the TA widened the aims and objectives of the Union through changes to the preamble and the common provisions. The Union, as well as the Community, undertook to seek, on the one hand, the creation of an area of freedom, security and justice, greater consistency, a high level of employment, more sustainable development and, especially, the upholding of social and human rights. The last now includes setting up a mechanism for suspending the rights of states held to be in breach of their democratic responsibilities. On the other, it looked to the creation of a common defence policy and a common defence. All this helped to endow the Union with new characteristics, making it more democratic, more integrated and more open.

Secondly, the TA made considerable changes to the Union's pillars, all of which emerged consolidated in various ways. Thus the EC pillar was strengthened by the incorporation of both Schengen and much of the old third pillar together with the ending of the UK's Social Chapter opt-out. The CFSP was also subject to major change in an attempt both to make it more consistently effective and to make progress towards a common defence policy. However, it was not folded into the EC pillar as some had hoped, nor was the Western European Union (WEU) established as a fourth pillar. Equally the negotiators refused to give the Union legal personality although they did give the Council presidency and the European Council a larger role in negotiation and external policy-making. At the same time, they allowed the virtual reinstatement of the Luxembourg veto on decisions taken by QMV in pillars II and III. Hence Title V retains the same heading, but has been considerably reorganized. Title VI sees much of its material transferred to the EC pillar, so that both its heading and contents are significantly altered to give it the new concentration on police and judicial co-operation in criminal matters.

At the same time Amsterdam introduced provisions on flexibility, or 'closer co-operation' as it was formally known, which, if they were to be used, could introduce a new variability in the policy operation of the Union, perhaps even creating virtual pillars or opt-outs. This is despite the new commitments to increased member state co-operation, notably through constructive abstention in the CFSP. Title VII now contains overarching guidance on what should happen when a group of states try and go further than the existing level of integration. However, the changes also gave the ECJ and, to a lesser extent, the Commission new linking responsibilities, something which had been largely excluded in most areas of Union activity in 1992.

The last title, originally Title VII and now Title VIII, combines further basic statements about the judicial nature of the Union, with provisions for amendment, application and ratification. These changes meant that the structure of the treaty changed somewhat, as Box 2 shows. The working versions of the TA made available in 1997 omit amendments and additions, so that the structure stands out more clearly. The structure remains the same, albeit with the slimming down of Title VI and the addition of the new Title VII on closer co-operation. One major change, however, is that articles are now numbered sequentially. They have also lost the letter prefixes found in the original TEU.

Amsterdam added only one protocol specific to the TEU alone, that on Article 17 concerning enhanced co-operation with the WEU, which relates to the CFSP pillar. Five protocols on Schengen were annexed to the TEU as well as the TEC. A series of declarations was also accepted. None of this seriously changes the nature of the Union as such. Nor do the three new institutional protocols shared with the original founding treaties. However, the Greek-inspired declarations on the status of churches and the last-minute statement on the fight against fraud do underline some of the Union's new characteristics.

As well as changing the actual structure and operation of the Union and its components, thus bringing them closer together and, we hope, making it more effective, the TA does

Box 2   Outline structure of the TEU, as amended by the TA

Preamble

Title I	Common Provisions
Title II	Provisions amending the Treaty establishing the European Economic Community with a view to establishing the European Community
Title III	Provisions amending the Treaty establishing the European Coal and Steel Community
Title IV	Provisions amending the Treaty establishing the European Atomic Energy Community
Title V	Provisions on a Common Foreign and Security Policy
Title VI	*Provisions on Police and Judicial Co-operation in Criminal Matters*
Title VII	**Provisions on Closer Co-operation**
Title VIII	Final Provisions

Protocols
Final Act
Declarations

change the status of the TEU. Post-Amsterdam, the material Union has become more cohesive with slightly fewer opt-outs, more QMV and more linkages between the pillars. Indeed, as a document, the TEU seems to have become a tighter and more constitutive text thanks to the fact that Titles II–IV, having served their purpose, are no longer printed in full. Moreover, the key decisions for the Union and the Community are profiled in the TEU and not the TEC, whose preamble, significantly, does not change.

None the less, for many 'Maastricht' retains the iconic status it gained in the mid-1990s. And, despite its more consolidated form, no *Verfassungspatriotismus* (constitutional patriotism) has developed as a result of simplification, despite the hopes that Amsterdam had reinforced the legitimacy and popularity of the Union. The post-Amsterdam TEU therefore remains a complex and contradictory document.

Nice and the Union

As part of its moves to give the Union its pre-enlargement MOT, Nice gave the TEU a surprisingly extensive service. If it did not add anything structurally as Amsterdam had done (see the outline in Box 2), it made three main changes. Firstly, it reinforced the Treaty's stress on values, thus setting the tone for the enlarging Union as a whole. Secondly, it made a number of minor changes to the second and third pillars, reflecting a need to improve their working. And thirdly, for a mixture of reasons, it did a major rewrite of the 'flexibility' provisions in a now renamed Title VII to allow them to be used in the larger Union. Taken together this involved both the fifteen separate and immediate changes to the TEU listed in Article 1 of the TN and two further amendments once the Protocol on the Enlargement of the European Union begins to take effect. Out of this comes a general enhancement of the standing not just of the treaty as such but also of the Union and its main institution, the European Council.

Where values are concerned, Nice made a significant change to Article 7, allowing the

Union to take action where it anticipated a problem in the area of democracy and human rights. This reflected the problem thrown up by the arrival in government of the Austrian Freedom Party in 2000. And while Nice did not respond to suggestions that the new Charter of Fundamental Rights should be anchored in Article 6 it did include other references which strengthened the Union's concerns for values. Upholding the Union's values is thus an overt criterion for starting on enhanced co-operation under Article 27a and, by implication, in Article 43.

Where the two inter-governmental pillars are concerned, Nice started by strengthening the Union's role in defence matters. It did this by excising most references to the WEU, thus accepting that the Union is no longer a purely civilian body. This was reinforced by the transfer of responsibility for managing humanitarian military intervention to the EU's Political and Security Committee. Changes were then made to bring in two legal co-operation mechanisms, notably Eurojust, within the ambit of Pillar III. There is also talk of bringing Schengen into the Union framework.

The largest volume of changes to the TEU came in Title VI on what is now 'enhanced co-operation' or flexibility. Thanks to the addition of ten new articles, and the revision or replacement of others, a new code has been devised, clarifying the constraints, extent and procedures of the concept. It can now be triggered rather more easily and the European Council can only reflect on reservations among non-participating member states. In doing this the TEU sets the tone for enhanced co-operation not only in the second and third pillars but also for the Community.

This was one way in which the status of the TEU was quietly enhanced at Nice. Talk of 'Union policies' and 'Union institutions' is thus significant. The way in which Pillar II international agreements are made binding on the institutions also points in the same direction. Moreover, such changes will probably help to enhance the role of the European Council. The most significant changes to the status of the Union, however, are slightly outwith the TEU, as with new references to the Union in the preamble, the future changes to facilitate enlargement and in the amended TEC where Article 248 now attributes the *Official Journal* to the Union and not the Community. However, no formal decision to

Box 3   Outline structure of the TEU, as amended by the TN

Preamble	
Title I	Common Provisions
Title II	Provisions amending the Treaty establishing the European Economic Community with a view to establishing the European Community
Title III	Provisions amending the Treaty establishing the European Coal and Steel Community
Title IV	Provisions amending the Treaty establishing the European Atomic Energy Community
Title V	Provisions on a Common Foreign and Security Policy
Title VI	Provisions on Police and Judicial Co-operation in Criminal Matters
Title VII	Provisions on **Enhanced** Co-operation
Title VIII	Final Provisions
Protocols	
Final Act	
Declarations	

merge the Union with the Community was taken at Nice and, in some instances, the Community institutions do get new influence in the Union, notably where the Commission and enhanced co-operation are concerned. The outcome of Nice, like that of Amsterdam, was to increase the complexity of the TEU.

The TEU after Nice – an Outline

The treaty now has 63 articles rather than the 53 it had after Amsterdam. Yet it still starts with an emphatic preamble situating the treaty in its post-1989 context and setting out its motivation, its clear socially oriented objectives and its characteristics. It adds new aims to the Community enterprise. It also provides some guarantees for member states uneasy about the onward movement of integration. Most of this is then underlined in the Common Provisions which enshrine the ambivalence about the Union since their wording allows the EU to be understood as a kind of alliance and not an organizational structure or framework. It is also something which is in full continuity with the past although it builds high where human rights are concerned. In other words, the common provisions, as well as helping to create a 'chapeau' for the pillars, lay down a number of constitutional principles.

Lying at the heart of these is the European Council, the role of which is considerably expanded and underlined by the two most recent treaties although it remains a forum and not a single locus of power. And its powers are subject to the treaties, to the rule of law in general and to the will of the member states. Throughout the TEU there is a changing and uncertain balance between supra-nationalism and inter-governmentalism. The Union respects the identities of its member states and gives them space. Yet it also encourages them to work together in new ways and places them under various obligations with regard to closer co-operation and diplomacy, for instance. In other words, because the states are so central to the Union, the common provisions are somewhat inchoate.

The now ghostly heart of the TEU is the changes it makes to the TEC and the Community, bringing in new principles such as citizenship, proportionality and subsidiarity. Even more significantly, within this political cloak there is an economic wolf to be found in the form of EMU. There is also a widened range of other policies to be found. Some of these were developed at Amsterdam. This was particularly the case with Schengen and many aspects of Justice and Home Affairs which are slowly becoming Community responsibilities. And Nice has fine-tuned the decision-making procedures of the institutions.

In the second pillar the EU continues its slow evolution towards a military and defence dimension of its own, at the expense of the WEU, at least where humanitarian provision is concerned. The new provisions redefine the Union's external instruments. The CFSP involves the Union as such, because it is nominally self-contained and even after Nice the states have ways of bringing pressure to bear on more communal decision-making. However, at the same time the Union is closely inter-related with other aspects of EC external relations and the Nice changes accentuate this. It also emphasizes the role of the European Council. All this has contributed to its continuing difficulties. As a result the Union was given a thorough makeover at Amsterdam, being granted the capacity to negotiate international deals in the domains covered by the two inter-governmental pillars, a capacity extended at Nice.

The third pillar changed even more with Amsterdam, not just because it was slimmed down but because, as part of the 'Area of Freedom, Security and Justice', the Union is acquiring new responsibilities in the fields of border crossing and free movement, even if these have to be carried out for it by the EC. So the latter now deals with things like asylum and visas with the former providing a framework for co-operation in criminal affairs in the revamped third pillar. As with the CFSP the third pillar appears less distinct than it used to do thanks to the post-Amsterdam renumbering. There is also a strange kind of inter-governmentalism here in the way in which states can opt into the ECJ's jurisdiction.

This kind of variability shows up again in the new title on enhanced co-operation, which was originally a pragmatic solution to problems expected because of UK intransigence which did not, in the event, materialize after 1997. As a result the provisions were systematically overhauled and, perhaps, simplified at Nice. Conditions have been eased but remain quite stiff and may not prove as usable as some think.

The final provisions then tell us more about the Union: its increasing acceptance of ECJ scrutiny and its commitment to democracy and human rights, especially where new members are concerned. However, the discussion of the mode of treaty revision is no longer fully reflective of actual practice. Finally to all this are added a number of protocols relating to the institutional future of the Union and to the working of its inter-governmental pillars. And its unfinished and uncertain nature is emphasized by some of the declarations attached to the final act. In other words, the treaty not merely makes massive changes to the integration enterprise but gives many, often conflicting, hints about what the Union actually is.

Understanding the TEU

Given all this we have to conclude that the TEU is not easy to understand. It is a shifting, sometimes sloppily drafted and imperfectly articulated document. Even when we look at it, as we should, as a treaty *per se* and as the constitutive basis of the Union as an organization, it presents us with many unanswered questions. Despite claims from the likes of von Bogdandy and Nettesheim that the Union is really a united body, there are major confusions between its component systems. Thus, while the TEU probably does now enjoy a higher status than the TEC, this is contested by many. And there is no simple hierarchy. And arguments about the pillars and the relationship between the Community and the Union continue.

When it comes to assessing the nature and virtues of the TEU, its very complexity means that from the beginning there was evidence to substantiate most interpretations. And things have not been helped by the rapidity of changes to the Union and its founding treaty, even if Nice made far fewer changes to the TEU than did Amsterdam. In any case the treaty really dodges the essential questions of where authority lies and whether the Union is dominated by the member states or whether it represents a massive step towards a federal state. In fact, because it reflects multiple political imperatives, the fallibility of existing constitutional arrangements and a changing European context, it points in a whole variety of ways. But usually it only suggests and does not resolve. Thus even claims that EMU means inevitable political centralization are belied by the way in which the treaty provides no mechanism to force member-state governments to sing from the same hymn sheet. It is the result of pluralist bargaining and not of constitutional blueprints. Equally, it tends to emphasize objectives rather than structures and delivery, as the preamble makes clear. So it is really up to readers to assess these and make up their own mind what they think about the TEU and the Union itself. To assist in this process the *Guide* now turns to a more detailed presentation and discussion of the treaty's provisions.

ii Preamble

As we said in the Introduction, treaty preambles can be of some legal significance, despite their traditional brevity and often grandiose language. All Community legislation is, after all, required to state the reasons behind it. In the case of the TEU it would certainly be unwise to dismiss its preamble as mere scene-setting of no real importance, as did John Major and others in the United Kingdom at the time it was being ratified. They were prone to dismiss the Maastricht preamble as 'Eurobabble' or 'waffle' because it made high-sounding, but very imprecise, pronouncements which were drafted after the rest of the treaty and not at Maastricht itself. For this reason the House of Lords felt that the vague and, in its view, essentially political concept of 'subsidiarity' ought to be relegated to the preamble. Others, of course, overlooked the preamble altogether.

However, the UK was not wholly consistent in its attitude. Hence there was great objection to the idea of the Union having 'a federal vocation', a principle which would clearly have been 'trailed' in the preamble, ahead of the binding reference in Article 1. This led to it being replaced by a more ' UK friendly' reference to 'an ever closer union' marked by subsidiarity. This was clearly British inspired. If it had all been meaningless verbiage there would have been no call to change it. In fact it caused considerable dissent even though the phrase had been in the TEC from the beginning. Equally, the Danes sought to minimize the importance of the reference to the creation of the 'Union' in the preamble even though the ECJ has no remit to consider it.

In other words, even doubters accept that preambles matter to some extent even if they do not themselves always create rights. And in the European context, common sense suggests that preambles do have meaning. Given that the treaties are essentially a record of what the states are willing to do together, it is obvious that the TEU should start with a clear and concise statement of who is authorizing the changes, why and exactly what the amendments are. This is what is done in most ordinary EC legislation.

So there are two main elements in the preamble, one which formally establishes the authority of the treaty and another which sets out the rationale and purpose for the new treaty. The first gives the treaty full legitimacy since it is done in the name of the heads of state. Such listings can be interesting, as with the fact that Ireland is not formally described as a republic. However, for the ordinary reader the second element is the more important. This is because it makes clear, as Gormley says, what innovations have been introduced, as well as helping readers to situate new treaties, in other words serving as a kind of advertising flier. Equally, it gives us some hints about what the negotiators believed the Union to be.

The preamble printed below is essentially that written in 1992 since the TA merely amended it slightly and did not detract from its validity and Nice left it unchanged. Only if either treaty had replaced or repealed the TEU would a new preamble have been drafted. Equally, the fact that many of those who actually signed the 1992 treaty were not involved at Amsterdam is irrelevant. As it was, the TA merely enhanced the existing text. Interestingly, because the negotiators were working on a draft treaty, they took preambular changes into account from the beginning. Since the negotiations leading to Nice concentrated on changes to the institutional arrangements in the TEC, to the virtual exclusion of new tasks for the Union, the question of further changes did not really arise. In any case, as we have seen, Nice has its own preamble.

The TEU preamble starts with the formal listing of the heads of state, irrespective of their actual constitutional powers, underwriting the treaty at the time it was signed. The list does not include the heads of those states which subsequently joined the EU, who underwrite the treaty through their accession treaties. One interesting fact is that the president of Ireland is not described as the head of the Irish Republic because this description touched on the sensitive questions of the claim to sovereignty over the island as a whole which, until the peace process, was enshrined in the Irish Constitution. This caused some difficulties in the initial negotiations on entry.

In any case, the preamble ends by stating that, in view of what is said in the various recitals, they have decided to establish a European Union as a means of carrying forward the general process of integration. Being illustrious personages, however, heads of state do not travel to sign it themselves. They nominate politically responsible ministers to do this for them. Because of the TEU's dual financial and political origins, the signatories are both foreign ministers and finance ministers.

The reference to 'exchanging full powers' relates to their being able to prove that they are entitled to act for their country and its head of state. This is not just a traditionalist hangover from earlier times when such information was not flashed around the world by the media, and delegates needed assurance, in the form of parchment, that those with whom they were dealing were who, and what, they claimed to be. The proliferation of treaties makes having this increasingly important. In any case it all reinforces the view that, legally speaking, the TEU is an act of the states as such and not of the Union. And what they agree to is the treaty text, word for word.

In between these two formal statements are a series of staccato recitals which portray the heads of state as collectively sharing various feelings about what they wish to do and why. The aims are the dominant part in this and, as has been suggested, there should be a recital for every substantive element in the treaty. This does seem to be the case here since the preamble, after briefly setting out the context and motivation for the changes made, devotes most of its attention to spelling out the main innovations made at Maastricht: EMU, flanking policies, citizenship, the CFSP, institutional refinements, justice and home affairs and subsidiarity. It might be asked why the TEU preamble should talk about so many things which are in the TEC. The answer is that they were agreed at Maastricht and made up the amending part of the TEU rather than its constitutive side.

The first two recitals also provide the motivation for the treaty, in this case to signal that things have changed where integration is concerned. This is partly, but presumably not wholly, thanks to the end of the Cold War. The new context calls for adapting the process of integration. This evolutionary dimension is underscored both by the eleventh recital and the reference following to further steps. In other words, there is a strong stress on continuity.

The first three recitals also imply specific new aims: helping to complete the reunification and stabilization of Europe; creating structures which will serve in the future; and promoting fundamental political principles to which Europe in general and the existing member states are committed. This suggests that there is a democratic pressure behind this. However, the fifth recital limits the impact of this concern for closer ties by stressing that solidarity should not be at the expense of national characteristics, mainly in the west. The recital also links up to the concept of rights since it commits the Union to limiting centralization and respecting the identities of the various national populations, a point given fuller force first by the references to subsidiarity and decisions being taken closer to citizens in the twelfth recital and then in Article 6 TEU. This enhanced stress on rights and social concerns is important. Equally, subsidiarity is signalled here as a democratic characteristic of the Union as a whole and not just of the EC.

Much of this might possibly be provided through enlargement of the EU, although this was not really on the agenda in 1991-2 and the second recital is one of the few not to be picked up in the common provisions. However, the third recital's litany of political values can also be seen as related to this, certainly after Amsterdam. This, as we will see, gave a considerable new emphasis to concepts of democracy and human rights, greatly extending the latter into areas such as equality and expectations of good administrative practice, but because the principle was not changed the negotiators at Amsterdam presumably felt no need to change the preamble. The fourth recital reflects the UK's 1997 decision to accept the EC's Social Charter of 1989, thereby indirectly underlining the Union's commitment to fundamental rights. However, the prior reference is to the Council of Europe's Social Charter, which is rather wider in scope than that of the EC. The fact that this recital is entered here rather than in the TEC may say something about the Union's overarching responsibilities but it is more a reflection of the fact that this was an Amsterdam change to the TEU.

The next set of recitals are commitments to improve existing processes of integration: institutional, economic and social, the last being a counterbalance to the rigours of the Internal Market. Amsterdam also qualified the pledge to economic progress through a nod, if not more, to sustainable development. The references to the single institutional framework and to EMU are again significant where the nature of the Union is concerned since neither of these is, somewhat anomalously, now visibly contained in the consolidated TEU. And the common provisions (see below) provide only an echo of the ideas of social progress and monetary union.

The following recitals spell out some more of the elements either added to the integration process or reinforced as a result of the TEU: citizenship, the common foreign and security policy (CFSP) and provisions for free movement. The point that citizenship is only available to nationals of member states stands out clearly. The CFSP recital was altered at Amsterdam to extend the aim to military matters provided that the European Council so decides. In other words the mention of Article 17 is a sop to those who feared that the Union would be coerced into setting up its own armed forces.

In 1992 the eleventh recital contained a reference to the justice and home affairs provisions of the treaty which became redundant with the reconstruction of the third pillar at Amsterdam. It was then replaced by a more up-to-date phrase bringing in the new public relations concept of 'an area of freedom, security and justice'. However, the recital reminds us that the Treaty of Amsterdam as such also covers not merely the new provisions in this field but those of Schengen as well.

Finally, as we have already seen, the preamble comes back to the question of reconciling closer co-operation with popular concerns, if not with popular participation. The mention of 'creating an ever closer union among the peoples of Europe' caused some controversy after Maastricht. This was because many critics read it as meaning the eventual eclipse of individual national societies. However, as Weiler has pointed out, this is incorrect. The phrase clearly envisages the continuance of the peoples of Europe, and not their amalgamation into a single melting pot. No matter how close they get, they remain separate in his view. He sees this as a statement about the constitutional tolerance of the Union which accepts the basic humanity and rights of all those involved in the enterprise and does not seek imperialistically to transform and subjugate them.

In any case, the phrase was not added *de novo* to the treaty base in 1991. It is something which has been explicitly present throughout the life of the EC. All member states tacitly accepted this aim when they ratified the TEC in which it first appeared or acceded to the EC. Moreover, the preamble, with its reference to the establishment of the European Communities, its mention of continuing the process and, later, of taking further steps needed to advance European integration, points in the same direction.

It all implies that the Union is in full continuity with what has gone before and takes responsibilities for all its actions, present and future. At the same time, the preamble gives us something of steer on the nature both of the treaties and of the Union. And, given that the new 'enhanced co-operation' provisions have to be in conformity with the objectives of the Union, the preamble may have a further role to play. None the less, it already makes it clear, even if the UK did not always appreciate this, that the treaty is 'an act of the member states', and can be seen as offering them some defence against excessive integration, especially since it tries to balance their rights against the demands of solidarity and co-operation. The preamble also hints that the Union is where the buck now starts and stops.

Yet, at the same time it does not give the Union as such as much attention as we might expect, and it emphasizes its symbiotic relationship with the EC. Indeed, it can suggest that the Union is less a body politic than a framework whose main purpose is to provide a home for a disparate series of emphatic aims. However, to turn these latter into incontrovertibly binding obligations, the Union needs the reassuring constraint of formal treaty articles. These are to be found in the common provisions.

HIS MAJESTY THE KING OF THE BELGIANS, HER MAJESTY THE QUEEN OF DENMARK, THE PRESIDENT OF THE FEDERAL REPUBLIC OF GERMANY, THE PRESIDENT OF THE HELLENIC REPUBLIC, HIS MAJESTY THE KING OF SPAIN, THE PRESIDENT OF THE FRENCH REPUBLIC, THE PRESIDENT OF IRELAND, THE PRESIDENT OF THE ITALIAN REPUBLIC, HIS ROYAL HIGHNESS THE GRAND DUKE OF LUXEMBOURG, HER MAJESTY THE QUEEN OF THE NETHERLANDS, THE PRESIDENT OF THE PORTUGUESE REPUBLIC, HER MAJESTY THE QUEEN OF THE UNITED KINGDOM OF GREAT BRITAIN AND NORTHERN IRELAND,

RESOLVED to mark a new stage in the process of European integration undertaken with the establishment of the European Communities,

RECALLING the historic importance of the ending of the division of the European continent and the need to create firm bases for the construction of the future Europe,

CONFIRMING their attachment to the principles of liberty, democracy and respect for human rights and fundamental freedoms and of the rule of law,

CONFIRMING their attachment to fundamental social rights as defined in the European Social Charter signed at Turin on 18 October 1961 and in the 1989 Community Charter of the Fundamental Social Rights of Workers,

DESIRING to deepen the solidarity between their peoples while respecting their history, their culture and their traditions,

DESIRING to enhance further the democratic and efficient functioning of the institutions so as to enable them better to carry out, within a single institutional framework, the tasks entrusted to them,

RESOLVED to achieve the strengthening and the convergence of their economies and to establish an economic and monetary union including, in accordance with the provisions of this Treaty, a single and stable currency,

DETERMINED to promote economic and social progress for their peoples, taking into account the principle of sustainable development and within the context of the accomplishment of the internal market and of reinforced cohesion and environmental protection, and to implement policies ensuring that advances in economic integration are accompanied by parallel progress in other fields,

RESOLVED to establish a citizenship common to nationals of their countries,

RESOLVED to implement a common foreign and security policy including the **progressive** framing of a common defence policy, which *might lead* to a common defence **in accordance with the provisions of Article 17,** thereby reinforcing the European identity and its independence in order to promote peace, security and progress in Europe and in the world,

RESOLVED *to facilitate* the free movement of persons, while ensuring the safety and security of their peoples, by **establishing an area of freedom, security and justice, in accordance with the provisions of this Treaty,**

RESOLVED to continue the process of creating an ever closer union among the peoples of Europe, in which decisions are taken as closely as possible to the citizen in accordance with the principle of subsidiarity,

IN VIEW of further steps to be taken in order to advance European integration,

HAVE DECIDED to establish a European Union and to this end have designated as their Plenipotentiaries:

HIS MAJESTY THE KING OF THE BELGIANS:
Mark EYSKENS, Minister for Foreign Affairs,
Philippe MAYSTADT, Minister for Finance;

HER MAJESTY THE QUEEN OF DENMARK:
Uffe ELLEMANN-JENSEN, Minister for Foreign Affairs,
Anders FOGH RASMUSSEN, Minister for Economic Affairs;

THE PRESIDENT OF THE FEDERAL REPUBLIC OF GERMANY:
Hans-Dietrich GENSCHER, Federal Minister for Foreign Affairs,
Theodor WAIGEL, Federal Minister for Finance;

THE PRESIDENT OF THE HELLENIC REPUBLIC:
Antonios SAMARAS, Minister for Foreign Affairs,
Efthymios CHRISTODOULOU, Minister for Economic Affairs;

HIS MAJESTY THE KING OF SPAIN:
Francisco FERNÁNDEZ ORDÓÑEZ, Minister for Foreign Affairs,
Carlos SOLCHAGA CATALÁN, Minister for Economic Affairs and Finance;

THE PRESIDENT OF THE FRENCH REPUBLIC:
Roland DUMAS, Minister for Foreign Affairs,
Pierre BÉRÉGOVOY, Minister for Economic and Financial Affairs and the Budget;

THE PRESIDENT OF IRELAND:
Gerard COLLINS, Minister for Foreign Affairs,
Bertie AHERN, Minister for Finance;

THE PRESIDENT OF THE ITALIAN REPUBLIC:
Gianni DE MICHELIS, Minister for Foreign Affairs,
Guido CARLI, Minister for the Treasury;

HIS ROYAL HIGHNESS THE GRAND DUKE OF LUXEMBOURG:
Jacques F. POOS, Deputy Prime Minister, Minister for Foreign Affairs,
Jean-Claude JUNCKER, Minister for Finance;

HER MAJESTY THE QUEEN OF THE NETHERLANDS:
Hans VAN DEN BROEK, Minister for Foreign Affairs,
Willem KOK, Minister for Finance;

THE PRESIDENT OF THE PORTUGUESE REPUBLIC:
João de Deus PINHEIRO, Minister for Foreign Affairs,
Jorge BRAGA DE MACEDO, Minister for Finance;

HER MAJESTY THE QUEEN OF THE UNITED KINGDOM OF GREAT
BRITAIN AND NORTHERN IRELAND:
The Rt. Hon. Douglas HURD, Secretary of State for Foreign and Common-
wealth Affairs,
The Hon. Francis MAUDE, Financial Secretary to the Treasury;

WHO, having exchanged their full powers, found in good and due form, have
agreed as follows:

iii Common Provisions

The common provisions are closely linked to the preamble, to most of which they give
not merely indicative standing but incontrovertible and full legal status. Mention in the
common provisions makes the Union's aims both operational and justiciable. As we have
seen, one or two recitals are not actually followed up. However, the common provisions
deal more with the what and how than does the preamble. With Title VIII – Final
Provisions they are fundamental to the constitutive role of the TEU. They also carry
forward the scene-setting of the preamble by underlining objectives and establishing the
overall design and tone of the Union. Hence they are important.

The fact that the provisions of Title I are 'common' does not mean they are of low
status. Far from it. It simply indicates that they refer to all the various titles and, by
implication, to the institutions and bodies which implement its provisions, not to mention
the three Communities. Indeed Weyland and his colleagues (Cloos et al) refer to them as
the 'hat' or 'chapeau' of the Union since everything else in the Union is subject to them.
Their legal importance can, in fact, be gauged from the fact that, as we implied above,
the Danish government sought unsuccessfully, ahead of its second TEU referendum in
1993, to establish that not all the objectives should apply to them.

Despite this the common provisions do not seem to have been fully thought through.
As Weyland says, they followed on the initial decision to create inter-governmental pillars
for diplomacy and home affairs, which demanded some kind of pediment to hold the
pillars together. But, because there was no clear view of what the Union was meant to
be, the common provisions are not terribly well ordered. There is no clear logic to the
sequence in which the articles appear and, within articles, there can be rather varied and
unrelated items. Given that the initial Luxembourg draft was rather more organized we
must put this down to later haggling among the member states. So, whatever their origins,
there is no doubt that the common provisions, like the final provisions, offer us only an
inchoate and embryonic definition of the Union.

Article 1 (ex A) is really a corollary of the last statement of the preamble. It is included not just to establish continuity but also to implement the preamble's aim of making the creation of a Union the first and crucial achievement of the treaty. Indeed, the second paragraph has a rather 'preambular' ring about it. The insistence on the fact that the Union is established by a treaty points to the essential role of the member states in the process of closer integration. However, the acceptance that the process of integration is dynamic, suggests, as Demaret points out, that their relations with the Union can change over time.

Yet the treaty then talks of creating *a* Union, implying there can be more than one, even though this one then becomes *the* Union. But, rather than define the new body more precisely, as the Luxembourg draft had done, it goes on to talk, a trifle confusingly, about the treaty as such. Admittedly this can fairly be described as a stage in the process of ever closer union, but what we need to know is, 'What is the Union?' The phraseology of 'ever closer union' which is taken, as we have already seen, from the TEC, replaces a suggested commitment in the revised Dutch treaty draft to 'a process leading gradually to a Union with a federal goal'. This was rejected by the British as too threatening, although some authorities feel that, in fact, the revised formulation could actually be seen as more redolent of inexorable centralization. However, Weiler's reading is probably correct here.

This process of 'ever closer union' has specific political characteristics involving firstly, decision-making. In 1992 the text spoke of taking decisions 'as closely as possible to the citizen', this being the nearest the TEU got to accepting its ultimate reliance on popular sovereignty. After Amsterdam decisions are also to be taken 'openly'. This is probably not to be interpreted as making transparency a generalized constitutional principle since no general rules have yet emerged and the text only speaks of doing this 'as openly as possible' and not just 'openly'. In other words it is a pragmatic aspiration and not an enthusiastic commitment. And each institution does things its own way.

Secondly, according to the last paragraph of Article 1, the Union has a twofold structure, resting on the Community and on non-EC procedures. There is no mention of three pillars as such. And the Union is simply founded on the Community. It does not supersede it. This paragraph was put in to reassure those who feared fragmentation and renationalization that there was still really only one European enterprise. The same may also have been true of the references to solidarity and subsidiarity which, like the idea of a new stage in the integration process, take up points made in the preamble. Subsidiarity, for instance, is presumably one of the forms of co-operation referred to here.

The tasks of the Union are then said to be organizing relations between the member states and their peoples, which is not the way the Union is usually conceived. This formulation has been little noticed even though it is open to a variety of politically charged interpretations. This concern for tasks leads, in *Article 2* (ex B), to a fuller exposition of the Union's objectives as trailed in the preamble. As is common in treaties, this lists a series of sets of more precise aims. There are five of these, beginning with reinforcing economic freedom and progress through EMU and full employment, something added in part due to the intervention of the Jospin government at Amsterdam. In any case, the mention of EMU as part of 'this treaty' may now be read as saying something about the status of the Union as the overarching and controlling body even if, presumably, the reference was at first simply to the original TEU.

The second set of objectives is external: the creation of a more effective international presence, a purpose which was widened at Amsterdam to facilitate a move to a common defence. Because the question was so sensitive the article repeats the agreed formula laid down in the preamble including the reference to Article 17 TEU. None the less, by 1997 there was much less fear that this might lead to the militarization of the Union than there had been earlier in the decade, although the desire of some states that the post-1998 moves towards enhanced military organization in the Union be reflected in the treaty was not met.

The next two sets of objectives concern internal EU affairs, seeking to protect human rights, and – controversially – using citizenship as the means to do this. As we will see, reinforcing citizenship was a major concern in the mid-1990s. The set also includes co-operation on judicial and related affairs. This last was replaced after Amsterdam by a new undertaking, again meant to convince EU citizens that they would enjoy an area of freedom, security and justice in the domains specified. Interestingly this relates directly to the TEC yet is not mentioned in the list of EC activities in Article 3 TEC, which might again suggest that the treaties see the Union as the ultimately responsible framework.

The final aims are to maintain 'in full' and develop the *acquis communautaire*, that is to say the sum of the Community's past and present aspirations, actions and achievements in legislation, although there is no formal definition, as Weatherill notes. Interestingly, apart from the following reference in Article 3 TEU, this is the only mention of the *acquis communautaire* in either the TEU or, and perhaps more surprisingly, the TEC. This emphasis on maintaining and developing the *acquis communautaire* has been seen as making for rigidity, but it can equally be seen as stressing the continuity between the Union and the pre-TEU Community and this is certainly the way it was intended by the negotiators. It was included, according to Weyland, to show that the Union treaty would not mean any backsliding on what had been achieved. Equally, the acceptance that the new arrangements might have to be reviewed, something implicitly repeated in the last paragraph of the article, was put in to reassure those who felt that progress in CFSP and elsewhere might be jeopardized by the concessions being made to states, notably by the mention of subsidiarity as a principle to be upheld in future developments, something about which many supporters of increasing integration had doubts. However, the common provisions make it plain that this is not a universal principle but a narrowly applicable one, hence the reference to the relevant clause, in the event Article 5 TEC.

Overall, Article 2 rather suggests that the Union is a body set up to achieve certain policy ends, just as is the EC. This has to be set against the fact that some of these objectives are statelike. However, no change was made at Nice to reflect the new stress on rights. Equally, the Court of Justice has, in the *Grau Gomis* (1995) case, underlined the fact that it is debarred from ruling on the article.

The concern for the *acquis* appears again in *Article 3* (ex C) as a justification for the commitment to having one institutional framework, that is to say not creating new management bodies but continuing to use the existing EC institutions to hold the Union together, even sometimes in the inter-governmental pillars, for instance through the provisions in Articles 28 and 41 (ex J.11 and K.8). While this was initially seen by some as undermining the inter-governmental element of the Union it had to be included to assure the then Commission President Delors and others that the new arrangements were not a recipe for fragmentation. The renewed stress, introduced at Amsterdam, on consistency in the external field, following on those in the preamble and in Article 1 TEU, might also be seen as pointing in the same direction, although the legal limits on the institutions' powers are also noted. And nothing was done to bring the many streams of external policy together under one heading, let alone to give the Union as such legal personality. The Amsterdam addition suggests that those who, like Curtin, believed that the stress on respecting the *acquis*, on consistency and on the single framework, was belied by other elements of the treaty, including Article 46 TEU, were not wholly wrong.

Ambiguities about the nature of the Union recur in *Article 4* (ex D). The first and last clauses of this owe their existence to the TEU, while much of the second is taken directly from the SEA. The apparent innovation therefore is not the institutionalization of the European Council but the fact that this is recognized as having a linked motor and steering role within the Union, a role many felt belonged to the Commission. Prior to this Article 2 SEA had limited itself to the bland statement that, twice a year, the European Council brought together the heads of member-state governments, their foreign ministers and the two representatives of the Commission. It did not say what the European Council did or how it worked. And the way the contribution of the states has evolved has turned out to be somewhat different from what Monnet had originally envisaged. However, the 1983 Stuttgart Solemn Declaration, building on other non-treaty decisions in the late 1970s, had actually said much of what is now in the first clause of Article 4, although talking of impulsion rather than impetus. It also contained the dual requirements for reports. These are largely formal and do not imply any real accountability to the European Parliament.

In other words, the TEU really only confirms existing practice. This is also true of the reference to the chairmanship. However, the TEU changes are important partly for the new emphasis they gave the European Council and partly for what is said elsewhere about its relations with the Community pillar. And Amsterdam was to reinforce both tendencies.

What the TEU mainly does is to give the European Council real Union status in line with its media role. Indeed it is the only Union body and does not occur in the Community's list of institutions (see Article 7 TEC) although it is mentioned in Articles 11(2), 99(2), 113 (3) and 128 TEC. As such it is both important, being the overriding and dynamic force in the Union, and a symbol of the latter's ultimate inter-governmentalism. As Nicoll and Salmon say, it is therefore above scrutiny. Yet, somewhat ambiguously, the TEU does not pick up the Stuttgart reference to the European Council assuring coherence, a task which now falls specifically to the Council of the Union as Article 3 implies. The TEU also turned the European Council into a quasi-Community body since it had to meet – minus the Commission members – as the Council of Ministers to start off the move to the final stage of EMU. Declarations attached to the original TEU (Nos. 3 and 4) allow the presidency to bring in finance ministers when the Council and European Council deal with EMU matters. Amsterdam and Nice were to reinforce this legal ambiguity when they made the European Council responsible for action against member states suspected or guilty of breaches of human rights, as we shall see below when looking at Article 7 TEU.

The TEU gives little guidance as to how the European Council should work. In practice the latter is very flexible and has few rules. It meets both formally and informally, whether in plenary meetings, in restricted sessions, over meals or in bilateral discussions. Its agenda, which is simply laid out in a letter circulated by the presidency, is thus fairly fluid and can easily get side-tracked. This was one reason why at Nice an attempt was made to separate the normal summit from the IGC discussions.

Equally, since, apart from heads of government and foreign (or economics) ministers, there are very few advisers present, its discussions can be very free and frank. The address by the president of the EP, which precedes the gathering, is largely formal. However, large numbers of advisers are usually waiting outside the doors and, with the media circus which now accompanies the summits, there can be hundreds of people in the host town. Nice was believed to have attracted some 6,000 officials and observers, not to mention the demonstrators. Declaration No. 22 TN says that, from 2002, one European Council per presidency must be held in Brussels and, once the EU gets its eighteenth member, all summits must be there. This alleged bribe to Belgium may turn out to be a poisoned chalice.

For all these reasons the European Council, understandably, produces no minutes. A set of presidency conclusions, drawn up with the assistance of the Council and Commission secretariats is, however, issued at the end of formal meetings. In the case of more informal gatherings, such as that at Biarritz in October 2000, even this can be dispensed with, being replaced by a mere press conference by the presidency's head of state or government. However, since the 1999 Tampere summit, if not before, it has become something of a policy-making as well as a deliberative body. And this can inflate the conclusions so that they can serve for launching processes of policy development, as happened at Lisbon.

Elsewhere in the treaty, especially after Amsterdam, there is more indication of what providing impetus and guidelines really means. Certainly the European Council has a predominant role in formulating and enunciating foreign-policy strategy, which includes a special responsibility for defence matters, as Article 13 TEU shows. It can also now function as a court of peers on the questions of democratic performance (Article 7 TEU), constructive abstention (Article 23 TEU) and flexibility within the Community pillar (Article 11 TEC). Beyond this the Council, of course, now acts in practice as the accepted final stage in the treaty revision process even though this is not brought out in Article 48 TEU. Equally, albeit minus its Commission members, it acts as an electoral college for the President of the Commission and as a replacement for the Council.

Increasingly, and perhaps more significantly, it has been used to launch major programmes. This started with the creation of the EMS, was developed at Edinburgh in 1992, and has accelerated since 1997. Thus Amsterdam, Tampere and Lisbon all produced quasi-legislative determinations. The Lisbon process on employment, economic reform and social cohesion in particular is now seen as an essential Union concern. As a result of all this the European Council is very much the public face of the Union attracting far more media attention than the Community institutions.

So, while the European Council usually needs the three pillars to prompt it and turn its thoughts into action and precise legislation – acting by proxy as Nicoll and Salmon say – it is none the less the powerful and indispensable agency that Bulmer and others have called it. Indeed Eijsbouts says the Union could not survive without it. Only in the European Council can the political consensus necessary to drive the Union forward be generated. What the recent treaties have done is to give its role a loose but still significant legal foundation. And for some this has given the Union a more inter-governmental tone. Indeed some see the European Council as more of a process of ongoing inter-governmental discussion and negotiation, than as an institution as such. Controversially, some, like Blair, would like to build on this.

The detailed way in which the European Council, like the Union itself, depends on other bodies is then brought out in *Article 5* (ex E). This offers a way of ensuring that the main EC institutions, to which the Court of Auditors was added in 1999 reflecting its upgrading at Maastricht and Amsterdam courtesy of the need for greater financial control in the Union, are subject to the TEU and not just to the existing TEC, TECSC and TEAEC. It thus makes clear that they are all subject to the rule of law and are consequently very dependent on the treaties for their authority. This piece of liberal constitutionalism also says something about the status of the Union, since the EU is clearly able to redefine the Community's powers whereas the Community as such cannot do the same to the Union. Thus the Court of Justice, as the commentary on Article 46 TEU will show, is specifically excluded from ruling on certain parts of the treaty. Moreover, there are no real constraints on the Union's one institution, the European Council.

The two remaining articles in the common provisions, the second of which was added at Amsterdam with a view to eastwards enlargement, are mainly concerned with fundamental rights, which have become an increasingly important theme in the life of the Union. Hence, whereas after Maastricht leading legal authorities complained that the Union had no human-rights foundation, after Amsterdam McGoldrick could argue that the EU was now a 'human rights community'. This is probably fair comment. None the less, human rights get mixed up with other issues and there are some limitations to what the TEU now offers.

If we look at *Article 6* (ex F) we find that there are now four numbered paragraphs. The last of these has nothing to do with human rights but is an enabling clause, a little like Article 308 TEC, which can be used to allow new initiatives which come to be necessary as the EU develops. This is a sensible provision although inter-governmental critics were not happy about it. It was pushed by Spain, which was also unsuccessfully looking for a reference to adequate financial means, to ensure that the new arrangements did not stop existing transfers of funds to poorer states.

The present third paragraph is half of the old first paragraph, where respect was made dependent on the states remaining democratic, a concept which still figures in the present first paragraph. The reference to national identities represents a continuing need to reassure states that, in the post-1989 circumstances, the Union is not going to become a superstate. Given that some Europhobes like Holmes fear that the phrase is a threat since it might allow outsiders to decide what 'our' national identity actually is, it is perhaps wrong to dismiss it as 'verbal rhetoric' as von Bogdandy and others do. Others, like Berthu, are in fact alarmed because the commitment has slipped down the pecking order with the new stress on democratic rights, which refer as much to people as to states, in the new first paragraph. The fact that the Luxembourg idea of putting a reference to national parliaments at this point in the common provisions was rejected probably did not console either set of critics.

If talk of national identity is not wholly removed from the concept of fundamental rights the rest of Article 6 deals with the latter much more directly. The new first paragraph represents a considerable strengthening of the Union's commitment to four fundamental values: liberty, democracy, rights and the rule of law. But the wording makes it clear that these mainly arise from what is already in national legal systems and are not bestowed *d'haut en bas* by the Union itself. And there is no reference here to the new Charter of Fundamental Rights since this was resisted by the IGC. However, the member states have also signed up to the Council of Europe's 1950 Convention on Human Rights and its values also need to be recognized. This is particularly so since the ECJ has often been guided by the Convention in judgements such as *Nold* (1974), even though it was to rule in its 1996 opinion that the EU as such is not presently able to subscribe to it. Therefore, at least where the acts of institutions are concerned, the European Convention is now more or less justiciable. Moreover, Advocates-General of the Court have now begun to refer to the new Charter in their opinions.

The changes made to Article 6 by the TA were part of a general move towards recognizing and respecting human rights in the Union. This shows up in the fact that, as the final provisions show, the ECJ can now hear cases arising out of Article 6(2), which gives rights a new legal foundation. Equally, it now has oversight of the procedural elements of the revised Article 7. The paragraph here is essentially a restatement of the ECJ's existing practice but, because it allows the Court to decide on how it will use the European Convention, is of symbolic importance to Wachsmann and other authorities. The trend is also visible in the new clause on social rights, in references to rights in the second and third pillars (Article 11 TEU and, as we shall see later in the *Guide*, in Article 30 TEU) albeit to a much lesser extent than previously, and in the way that democracy and rights have been made a condition both of entry and of continuing full membership, as Article 7 makes clear. There are also declarations on churches (Nos. 11 and 8n TA), the death penalty (No. 1 TA) and transparency (No. 41 TA), all of which point in the same direction. These are discussed later in the *Guide*.

The reasons for this new emphasis included the awareness of racist attacks and the growing strength of far-right political forces behind them. Dissatisfaction at the fact that the original TEU merely ratified the existing state of affairs and did not reflect the Union's development into an increasingly important political organization also played a part. For many, European precedents mean that the new Union ought to defend human rights and democracy, a point made in 1993 by the German Constitutional Court and followed up by the institutions in a variety of ways. Concerns about the stability of potential member states also seem to have played a part.

It was clearly this last factor which led the Amsterdam negotiators to insert the original version of *Article 7*. This – which has been said to play the same role as Article 39 of the United Nations (UN) Charter – then allowed the heads of government, meeting as the Council, to hear accusations of 'serious and persistent breaches' of the principles of democracy, freedom, human rights, legality and liberty and, where appropriate, to exclude the offending state from decision-making. However, it gave no power to take action ahead of such a breach and this was what was felt to be needed when Austria formed a government including Haider's far-right Freedom Party. The fourteen governments, acting outside the European Council as such, were forced to impose a boycott of their own. This proved both ineffective and widely unpopular. So, after allowing a group of Wise Persons to dig them out of their hole, the states – led by Belgium – moved to improve and strengthen Article 7 so as to deal with risks as well as realities.

Nice therefore inserted a new paragraph 1 and renumbered the remaining five. The new paragraph allows a third of the member states, the Commission or the EP to propose to the Council that there is a risk of one of the member states offending against the values of the Union. The Council has then to hear the offending state, something which did not happen with Austria, much to Vienna's annoyance. If the state and, if necessary, an independent inquiry fail to satisfy the Council about the future, it can then rule that there is 'a clear risk of a serious breach' of the principles in Article 6(1). There are thus two implicit conditions here: the problem must be obvious and it must involve more than a minor infringement. In any case, such a ruling requires a four-fifths majority, currently twelve member states, and is to be accompanied by advice on future conduct. Having thus shown the offender the 'yellow card' the Council then continues to monitor the suspect state. Presumably, if it heeds the warning it can then be formally cleared. However, the treaty does not explicitly say this but the fact that the procedure copies what happened with Austria and accepts the need to work with the offending party makes it quite clear.

If, on the other hand, the state ignores the card and commits further 'fouls', then the original procedure, now paragraph 2, comes into play. This allows either the Commission or a third of the states to invite the European Council (sitting as the Council of the Union) to rule that a state is in a clear and continuing breach of its responsibilities to basic values. One view is that this means that a state would have to offend against at least two of the underlying values listed in Article 6(1) since Article 7 talks simply of offending against principles and not 'all the principles'. And again the offending party could submit a case in its own defence.

If this fails then the Council has two possible options, although it is not obligated to do anything. If it is unanimous the Council can, firstly, issue a formal 'red card' stating that there was a 'serious and persistent' breach of values. Here too there are two conditions to be fulfilled, which overlap in part with those in the 'yellow card' procedure. Thereafter, secondly, it can decide, by qualified majority, to take sanctions against the offending state. The Council cannot expel an offending member state which, a little ironically, remains bound to observe EU rules. All it can do is to suspend the state from some, or all, of the rights of membership, which presumably means taking part in the European Council, voting in the Council and perhaps enjoying financial and other benefits. Moreover, suspension is not meant to hurt ordinary people so a rash decision by the Council could leave it open to lawsuits. And the treaty does provide for the red card conditions to be changed or withdrawn. Presumably where a state had made some progress it could be encouraged to go further by a concession such as being allowed to receive funds again.

The Nice changes not only allow the EP a greater role but also bring the ECJ on to the margins of what is effectively a political process. The EP can now be proactive in signalling a possible problem, whereas it is excluded from doing so in suspension cases, although it can veto the issue of a card of either colour. Paragraph 6 has also been altered to require a two-thirds majority for this, the same majority as is required to dismiss the Commission. And whereas under Amsterdam the ECJ had no standing in the matter, it can now be asked to rule on whether the proper procedures have been followed. This too reflects the feeling that the way Austria was treated offended against natural justice.

Some thought that Amsterdam would be the beginning of forcing a state to forfeit its sovereignty or accept exclusion but the Austrian case showed that there was a real dislike of xenophobia in the Union. In any case, rather than being either as draconian as Robin Cook claimed, or the first example of differentiated integration in the TEU as Ehlermann suggests, the process is milder than that applied by the Council of Europe from whom it was originally copied. The fact that it is both spelled out in such detail and demands not merely a solid consensus (something demanded by the UK and others at Nice) but much consultation with the 'suspect' shows the uncertainties about the process even in an enlarged Union.

All this shows that the common provisions remain very hesitant about the mix of supra-nationalism and inter-governmentalism in the Union. States, especially under the TA, get many assurances about their integrity yet at the same time they are also subject to new rules and procedures. And guarantees are also offered that the interests of the common enterprise will not be abandoned. Hence, they do not provide a clear definition of either the nature or the structure of the Union. This, like the European Council, remains sketchy and unclear, still being as much process as organization. The text is, in fact, messy and ambiguous, reflecting both the present interdependence between the Union and the Community and the desire to square the creation of the Union with the maintenance of continuity in integration. And, although this part of the Treaty is devoted to general principles, the text rarely goes into details unless forced to do so by the states, as in Article 7. Hence it is hard to sum up the basic principles of the Union.

All this reflects the way the TEU was negotiated between 1991 and 2000. This was a triumph in that it reconciled the very different views of the member states, all of which had to be given reassurances if the overall package was to be approved. Unfortunately this resulted in an unwieldy and somewhat contradictory opening title in the treaty. However, the TEU makes it clear that the Union rests on its partition into what are widely described as the three pillars and it is to the first of these that the *Guide*, after reproducing the content of Title I, now turns.

TITLE I

COMMON PROVISIONS

Article 1 (ex A)

By this Treaty, the HIGH CONTRACTING PARTIES establish among themselves a EUROPEAN UNION, hereinafter called 'the Union'.

This Treaty marks a new stage in the process of creating an ever closer union among the peoples of Europe, in which decisions are taken **as openly as possible and** as closely as possible to the citizen.

The Union shall be founded on the European Communities, supplemented by the policies and forms of co-operation established by this Treaty. Its task shall be to organise, in a manner demonstrating consistency and solidarity, relations between the Member States and between their peoples.

Article 2 (ex B)

The Union shall set itself the following objectives:

– to promote economic and social progress **and a high level of employment and to achieve** *balanced and sustainable development*, in particular through the creation of an area without internal frontiers, through the strengthening of economic and social cohesion and through the establishment of economic and monetary union, ultimately including a single currency in accordance with the provisions of this Treaty;

– to assert its identity on the international scene, in particular through the implementation of a common foreign and security policy including the **progressive** framing of a common defence policy, which *might lead* to a common defence, **in accordance with the provisions of Article 17;**

– to strengthen the protection of the rights and interests of the nationals of its Member States through the introduction of a citizenship of the Union;

– **to maintain and develop the Union as an area of freedom, security and justice, in which the free movement of persons is assured in conjunction with appropriate measures with respect to external border controls, asylum, immigration and the prevention and combating of crime;**

– to maintain in full the *acquis communautaire* and build on it with a view to considering to what extent the policies and forms of co-operation introduced by this Treaty may need to be revised with the aim of ensuring the effectiveness of the mechanisms and the institutions of the Community.

The objectives of the Union shall be achieved as provided in this Treaty and in accordance with the conditions and the timetable set out therein while respecting the principle of subsidiarity as defined in Article 5 of the Treaty establishing the European Community.

Article 3 (ex C)

The Union shall be served by a single institutional framework which shall ensure the consistency and the continuity of the activities carried out in order to attain its objectives while respecting and building upon the *acquis communautaire*.

The Union shall in particular ensure the consistency of its external activities as a whole in the context of its external relations, security, economic and development policies. The Council and the Commission shall be responsible for ensuring such consistency **and shall co-operate to this end.** They shall ensure the implementation of these policies, each in accordance with its respective powers.

Article 4 (ex D)

The European Council shall provide the Union with the necessary impetus for its development and shall define the general political guidelines thereof.

The European Council shall bring together the Heads of State or Government of the Member States and the President of the Commission. They shall be assisted by the Ministers for Foreign Affairs of the Member States and by a Member of the Commission. The European Council shall meet at least twice a year, under the chairmanship of the Head of State or Government of the Member State which holds the Presidency of the Council.

The European Council shall submit to the European Parliament a report after each of its meetings and a yearly written report on the progress achieved by the Union.

Article 5 (ex E)

The European Parliament, the Council, the Commission, the Court of Justice **and the Court of Auditors** shall exercise their powers under the conditions and for the purposes provided for, on the one hand, by the provisions of the Treaties establishing the European Communities and of the subsequent Treaties and Acts modifying and supplementing them and, on the other hand, by the other provisions of this Treaty.

Article 6 (ex F)

1. **The Union is founded on the principles of liberty,** *democracy,* **respect for human rights and fundamental freedoms, and the rule of law, principles which are common to the Member States.**

2. The Union shall respect fundamental rights, as guaranteed by the European Convention for the Protection of Human Rights and Fundamental Freedoms signed in Rome on 4 November 1950 and as they result from the constitutional traditions common to the Member States, as general principles of Community law.

3. *The Union shall respect the national identities of its Member States.*

4. The Union shall provide itself with the means necessary to attain its objectives and carry through its policies.

Article 7 (new – TA)

1. On a reasoned proposal by one third of the Member States, by the European Parliament or by the Commission, the Council, acting by a majority of four-fifths of its members after obtaining the assent of the European Parliament, may determine that there is a clear risk of a serious breach by a Member State of principles mentioned in Article 6(1), and address appropriate recommendations to that State. Before making such a determination, the Council shall hear the Member State in question and, acting in accordance with the same procedure, may call on independent persons to submit within a reasonable time limit a report on the situation in the Member State in question.

The Council shall regularly verify that the grounds on which such a determination was made continue to apply.

2. The Council, meeting in the composition of the Heads of State or Government and acting by unanimity on a proposal by one third of the Member States or by the Commission and after obtaining the assent of the European Parliament, may determine the existence of a serious and persistent breach by a Member State of principles mentioned in Article 6(1), after inviting the government of the Member State in question to submit its observations.

3. Where such a determination *under paragraph 2* has been made, the Council, acting by a qualified majority, may decide to suspend certain of the rights deriving from the application of this Treaty to the Member State in question, including the voting rights of the representative of the government of that Member State in the Council. In doing so, the Council shall take into account the possible consequences of such a suspension on the rights and obligations of natural and legal persons.

The obligations of the Member State in question under this Treaty shall in any case continue to be binding on that State.

4. The Council, acting by a qualified majority, may decide subsequently to vary or revoke measures taken under *paragraph 3* in response to changes in the situation which led to their being imposed.

5. For the purposes of this Article, the Council shall act without taking into account the vote of the representative of the government of the Member State in question. Abstentions by members present in person or represented shall not prevent the adoption of decisions referred to in *paragraph 2*. A qualified majority shall be defined as the same proportion of the weighted votes of the members of the Council concerned as laid down in Article 205(2) of the Treaty establishing the European Community.

This paragraph shall also apply in the event of voting rights being suspended pursuant to *paragraph 3*.

6. For the purposes of *paragraphs 1 and 2*, the European Parliament shall act by a two-thirds majority of the votes cast, representing a majority of its members.

iv Amendments to Other Treaties

At this point the Treaty on European Union presents us with a problem because its next titles are, nowadays, empty, even ghostly. This is because they have become redundant and the material in them has been absorbed elsewhere in the European Treaties. Initially all amendments to the treaties establishing the European Community, the European Coal and Steel Community and Euratom were printed in full as Articles 8–10 of the TEU. However, once the latter came into effect these changes were inserted into the respective treaties. This meant that the instructions contained in the three titles had served their purpose and no longer needed to figure in the TEU. Hence, when Amsterdam was published, they were excluded from the printed version of the revised TEU. This precedent was followed by the consolidated versions used as the basis of the *Guide*.

Their exclusion is common sense since repeating them today would cause confusion. It could lead casual readers to think both that they were new and that the instructions they contain had still to be acted on. Equally their inclusion, especially after Nice, would have made the consolidated TEU far longer, much more complex and less user-friendly than it ought to be. As it is, the TEU is now a relatively compact treaty thanks to the way these three titles have become empty shells.

None the less, this does mean, as we have suggested, that there is something of a hole at the heart of the TEU. And the tendency not to reprint the protocols either exacerbates this sense of incompleteness. This too is done for understandable reasons of convenience, but it all makes it harder to see what the TEU actually involves. In other words, it is not so easy now to look at the full TEU as it was when the document was first drawn up.

So, although all that appears in the consolidated version is what we print below, we need to be aware that these now vanished elements are of considerable importance. Indeed, it is not unfair to say that both negotiators and the public have been more worried about the changes originally listed in Titles II–IV, especially EMU, than about what was in the Union parts of the TEU. This was because, as we have already argued, the TEU went far beyond the SEA in the extent of the changes it made to the Communities. And it was also the long series of amendments in these titles which were at the root of the complaints about the complexity and impenetrable nature of the 'Maastricht' text. Hence it is worth reminding ourselves what were the corporeal realities now reduced to phantom status.

TITLE II
PROVISIONS AMENDING THE TREATY ESTABLISHING THE EUROPEAN ECONOMIC COMMUNITY WITH A VIEW TO ESTABLISHING THE EUROPEAN COMMUNITY

Article 8 (ex G)

(not reproduced)

TITLE III
PROVISIONS AMENDING THE TREATY ESTABLISHING THE EUROPEAN COAL AND STEEL COMMUNITY

Article 9 (ex H)

(not reproduced)

TITLE IV
PROVISIONS AMENDING THE TREATY ESTABLISHING THE EUROPEAN ATOMIC ENERGY COMMUNITY

Article 10 (ex I)

(not reproduced)

The three sets of amendments originally contained in Titles II to IV made up almost half of the 61,351 words of the whole TEU. Each of them was a single article (originally G to I) containing a whole series of amendments, 136 in all. Of these the central elements were the 86 alterations to the TEC and thus to the Union's essential first pillar, the

European Community. These ranged very widely while Titles III and IV were largely confined to repeating the institutional changes made under Title II.

Article G on its own accounted for almost a third of the whole TEU so it was a very large-scale exercise in amendment and development. It was divided into seven lettered blocs. The first, listed as point A, was a general requirement that, throughout the treaty, the term 'European Economic Community' should be replaced by 'European Community', something which caused some fluttering in British Eurosceptic nests. The text did not specify exactly where this should be done, but it was. And it did make a symbolic change to the nature of the pillar.

The remaining blocs equated with the various parts of the TEC where more concrete alterations were made. Thus B made changes to the principles, objectives and activities, notably writing the ECB and subsidiarity into the former. It also renumbered a number of articles. Thereafter C authorized the insertion of a new Part Two to the TEC covering the then controversial subject of citizenship.

The largest element of Title II was that given over to bloc D. This ordered the amalgamation of the old Parts Two and Three into a new-style Part Three, dedicated to Community policies. This included 29 separate changes often deriving from adding the new decision-making mechanisms. More significant was amendment 25, which contained 27 new articles, divided into new chapters, dealing with EMU. The remaining elements of D were given over to inserting new policy competences bestowed on the Community at Maastricht: culture, public health, consumer protection, industry, cohesion, research and environment amongst them. Part Four on overseas territories was not touched.

Bloc E then went on to make 45 amendments to the institutional provisions of the TEC. These include references to political parties, the new co-decision arrangements, the extension of other decision-making procedures, the Ombudsman, the presidency, COREPER, the ECJ's new ability to fine recalcitrant states, the Committee of the Regions and new financial procedures, often directed against fraud. Most of these were fairly small changes textually but they none the less made up a substantial element of the treaty. Equally, they made considerable changes to the institutional density and practice of the Community. Finally, Blocs F and G contained single amendments to Annex III of the TEC and the EIB statute respectively. All told, these changes, which are indicated in Annex 2 of the *Guide*, altered the axioms by which the EC worked, extended its policy scope, refined its decision-making, provided it with new budgetary and legal constraints, and committed it to a single currency. So it is not surprising that they were the subject of so much controversy in the early and mid-1990s.

Because the TEU decided, as we have already seen, to give the Union a single institutional framework, it was also necessary to make consequential changes to the treaties governing the other Communities, especially as these still had a life of their own. This was nominally done at separate IGCs shortly before the official signing of the TEU in February 1992. Changes introduced to the ECSC and Euratom treaties were contained in two further single-article Titles. Title III thus listed 21 amendments to the TECSC. Most of these were institutional replications but new provisions on fraud, finance and the Faroes were also added. This was not the case with the 29 amendments to the TEAEC, since this was much closer in form to the TEC. None the less, references to COREPER, the ECJ and the Ombudsman had to be entered.

As a result there was exact consonance with the European Community, reflecting the realities on the ground. Such changes need to be remembered even though they have now been integrated with the respective treaties. The same is true of the amendments introduced by Amsterdam and Nice, although those relating to the TECSC obviously had only a limited lifespan, given the treaty's expiry in 2002. In reality, however, little attention is now paid to these changes, though Nice had to follow suit and made similar amendments to those negotiated for the Community itself. And there is no lack of interest when it comes to the changes made to the next three titles of the present-day TEU.

v Common Foreign and Security Policy

As we have just seen, looking at the Community pillar in the aftermath of the changes made by Title II of the TEU is not a straightforward matter. Fortunately assessing the new pillars added to the Union at Maastricht is somewhat easier. Nevertheless, Amsterdam did make extensive changes to Title V on the common foreign and security policy (CFSP). And while the Treaty of Nice, despite appearances, made relatively limited further alterations, these have their own complications.

Assessing the pillars is important because they reflect the clear desire of most member states to co-operate on their own terms and maintain ultimate control over the areas where they are willing to co-ordinate their activities. The creation of the Union in 1993 can thus be seen as an attempt to do this, notably in the external dimension in a more formal and mainstream way than in the Single European Act (SEA) back in the 1980s. This meant the creation of the CFSP within the full treaty framework of the Union. It was, in part, a response to critics like Delors who had railed against the fact that he was denounced by Nelson Mandela for the half-hearted 'European' response to sanctions in South Africa when this was the fault of the member states acting through so-called European political co-operation (EPC), and not a weak Community activity.

Even so an assessment is not without its difficulties because, in the case of the second and third pillars, there is a complication in the sense that both were systematically reordered and rewritten at Amsterdam. The changes made to the CFSP represented an attempt, foreshadowed in the old Article N TEU, to make the Union's external relations more coherent and less inter-governmental. This did not succeed and what happened involved no structural alterations, simply a thorough redefining of the existing pillar arrangements. Hence there continued to be a considerable, and ambiguous, overlap between the second pillar and the various external elements of the TEC and the Community's own activities. What the negotiators tried to do was to make the CFSP more effective and logical. In other words only further incremental improvements were introduced since, as Dashwood as well as Peterson and Sjursen rightly imply, this is the only likely option for the member states.

In any case, because there was so much change at Amsterdam, it is important before commenting on the present text to explain what was in the original CFSP. In particular, its main lines, the problems it encountered and the overall thrust of the Amsterdam changes need to be looked at. This will make the precise new formulations more comprehensible. What is clear, of course, is that the difficulties of creating an effective Union external policy are ongoing.

Improving the Union's international identity was a major aim of the 1991 IGC on Political Union. The post-SEA situation had not allowed the Community to act effectively and in a unified way as both the Gulf War and Yugoslavia showed. However, while the member states agreed on this they were divided on how it should be done, whether through multilateral action, under the NATO umbrella, or in a new, more autonomous way, using the Community and its methods, including majority voting. Not surprisingly, what emerged was a compromise. Maastricht agreed to repeal the old SEA provisions and in their place set up a more systematized system of inter-governmental co-operation, extended to security matters for the first time, within the Union but outside the Community. And, where relations with NATO were concerned, any European operations were not to be to its detriment. Europe's own defence alliance, the Western European Union (WEU) was therefore brought closer to the EU as a convenient channel for dealing with security questions, a move emphasized by a new protocol.

The original text of Title V thus began with a one-line article (J) which formally established the CFSP, subject to conditions laid down in the succeeding Articles J.1 to J.11 which made up the bulk of the title. The fivefold objectives of the policy were spelled out in Article J.1, along with the means to achieve them: systematic co-operation amongst the states, the adoption of common positions and the pursuit of joint actions. States collectively were required to support and work with this according to Articles J.1(4) and J.2. Article J.3 then defined joint actions at some length while Article J.4 noted that there was the potential for the development of a common defence policy, and even a common defence, and set out the new supporting role of the WEU in this domain. The next three articles indicated the roles to be played by the presidency, consular missions and the European Parliament in the CFSP, while that of the Commission was noted in Article J.9. Article J.8 made it clear that it was the European Council which laid down the guidelines for the policy, supported by a Council which, in the main, would decide by unanimity. Then, building on Article J.4, Article J.10 drew attention to the need for a future review of the process in 1996. The final article tried to establish the financial responsibilities of the pillar.

The insistence on looking again at the CFSP within a couple of years was symptomatic of the disillusion of those who wished to see the Union have a 'real' foreign policy, politically emphatic and with meaningful military back-up. Their doubts were intensified by the way things worked out after the TEU came into operation. Although the new structures were set up, and produced voluminous statements on world affairs, along with some joint actions and common positions, this did not make a real impact notably on the Bosnian situation where it was US military and political muscle which brought about the 1995 Dayton Accord. Hence people began to doubt whether the Maastricht changes were as big a step forward as had initially been hoped. They were seen as legally unclear, uncertain in nature and limited in scope. And, as commentators like Regelsberger and Wessels have noted, the member states generally lacked the political will to make best use of the TEU's provisions.

So the 1996 IGC found itself confronted with the challenge of increasing the Union's international capacity as one of its main themes. This proved to be less contentious than some other items and led, as we have already noted, to a large-scale tidying up of the TEU centring on greater consistency, greater effectiveness and more commitment to a military back-up. The lack of argument possibly reflected the absence of major external crises which might have constrained concessions and allowed a solution in which everybody got something and, as we have seen, an attempt was made to streamline the pillar and give it more clout. Hence a good deal of the text was amended, some articles relocated and some bits excised in order to create a more organized pillar, now running to 18 articles. This then meant changing the numbers within the title. Initially this was done by readjusting the J numbers. However, these were then given unlettered numbers in the consolidated version of the TEU published with the October 1997 version of the TA. This printed the altered J numbers in brackets, misleadingly implying a degree of continuity with the original Maastricht text.

Because this is confusing, Table 1 shows how the original provisions of the CFSP were moved about and renumbered. The 'new' numbers are those in the consolidated treaty. In our own printing of the title we also give the original pre-Amsterdam lettering in

Table 1 The destination of CFSP Provisions in the light of the Treaty of Amsterdam

Pre-TA	J.1(1)	J.1(2)	J.1(3)	J.1(4)	J.2(1)	J.2(2)	J.2(3)	J.3(1)	J.3(2)
Post-TA	J.1(1)	J.1(1)	J.2	J.1(2)	J.6	J.5	J.9(1)	J.3(1)	J.13(2)
New	11(1)	11(1)	12	11(2)	16	15	19(1)	13(1)	23(2)
Pre-TA	J.3(3)	J.3(4)	J.3(5)	J.3(6)	J.3(7)	J.4(1)	J.4(2)	J.4(4)	J.4(5)
Post-TA	J.4(2)	J.4(3)	J.4(5)	J.4(6)	J.4(7)	J.7(1)	J.7(1)	J.7(1)	J.7(4)
New	14(2)	14(3)	14(5)	14(6)	14(7)	17(1)	17(1)	17(1)	17(4)
Pre-TA	J.4(6)	J.5(1)	J.5(2)	J.5(3)	J.5(4)	J.6	J.7	J.8(1)	J.8(2)
Post-TA	J.7(5)	J.8(1)	J.8(2)	J.8(3)	J.9(2)	J.10	J.11	J.3(1)	J.3(3)
New	17(5)	18(1)	18(2)	18(3)	19(2)	20	21	13(1)	13(3)
Pre-TA	J.8(2)	J.8(3)	J.8(4)	J.8(5)	J.9	J.11(1)	J.11(2)	J.11(2)	J.11(2)
Post-TA	J.13(1)	J.12(1)	J.12(2)	J.15	J.17	J.18(1)	J.18(2)	J.18(2)	J.18(2)
New	23(1)	22(1)	22(2)	25	27	28(1)	28(2)	28(2)	28(2)

brackets. The five new articles on enhanced co-operation tacked on, with lower-case letters, to Article 27 are not included in the table, being unrelated to the original TEU provisions.

What this renumbering in search of the negotiators' new aims involved in practice was quite an extensive reworking of the CFSP. To begin with, the CFSP gained in visibility by being accepted as a given and not a new venture. More significantly, Amsterdam committed the Union not merely to a definite defence policy but also to a real defence should the member states so decide. The humanitarian tasks, known as the 'Petersberg' missions after the suburb of Bonn where they were agreed in 1992, were accepted as a Union responsibility. They involve military activity in humanitarian and rescue tasks, peacekeeping and crisis management, including peacemaking. And the WEU was temporarily brought much more into the EU's orbit and its tasks clarified through a series of protocols and declarations.

On a more mundane level, Amsterdam supported these initiatives through new structures: the High Representative, the Policy Planning and Early Warning Unit and a reformed 'troika'. At the same time the aims and instruments were rationalized giving the latter in particular a far more logical nature. The European Council was given an enhanced role in all this. Decision-making was also improved, partly through the idea of 'constructive abstention' which was designed to allow a majority of states to carry out external ventures. Beyond this there was a move towards QMV in implementation and allowance was made for the presidency to lead the Union in negotiating treaties.

However, none of this satisfied critics such as Bonvicini who were demanding a new 'Amsterdam' well before the TA was even ratified. This is a little unfair to what was a fairly fundamental attempt at developing the obligations laid down in Article 2 TEU. Amsterdam's amendments, in fact, sought to improve decision-making and links with the EC while maintaining the essentials of inter-governmentalism. As it was, the changes did mark a further stage towards both coherence and military capacity. And developments outside the treaties, notably involving the Kosovo crisis and Anglo-French initiatives, have meant that, despite the many obstacles, states did move on the military front and were therefore prepared to consider further moves at Nice.

Much of the response to Nice suggested that there had been major changes in the defence field. And reference in the presidency's conclusions to a common European security and defence policy (CESDP) implied that a significant renaming and reorientation of the CFSP, such as the Netherlands had wanted, was in hand. Yet while some defence-related changes were agreed at Nice, many of these, like the decisions on the CESDP and the European Rapid Reaction Force (ERRF), were the outcome of decisions taken not in the IGC as such but in the normal part of the European Council meeting. Hence they are not in the TN even though some states, like Benelux, had hoped to include them. Neutral members, in particular Ireland, with a possible referendum on ratification in mind, helped to ensure that this was not the case.

What the TN did was essentially fivefold. Firstly, it largely excised the WEU from the TEU. As a corollary of this, secondly, it made defence a clear EU responsibility, carried out by the renamed Political and Security Committee, sometimes known by its French acronym of COPS. Thirdly, it revised the provisions for presidency-led negotiation of international agreements. However, the fourth group of changes were the most extensive. These replaced the unused provision for constructive abstention by a set of provisions on enhanced co-operation in the non-military and non-defence fields. Fifthly, there was a minor extension of the use of QMV. None of this attracted much attention but it was a not insignificant tidying-up of the CFSP, even if it left decision-making less than crystal clear.

If we look at Title V in its post-Nice form we find a relatively coherent set of provisions for what is now a recognized and important element of the Union. Hence *Article 11* (ex J.1) omits the mention of formal establishment provided in the old Article J, thus demonstrating that the CFSP has become an accepted fixture. In other words, while the SEA hoped that a common external policy could be established and Maastricht showed that it could be, Amsterdam accepted that it had emerged but still needed clarification. Hence Article 11 commits the Union alone, rather than with the member states as at Maastricht. This may have been done to remove any suggestion that the Union has control of national foreign policies as such. However, it is more likely that this was done, as Dashwood suggests, to give more coherence since, when now acting as the EU, states do not have a separate existence as they did previously. They are the Union.

Paragraph 2 of Article 11, in fact, spells out the responsibilities of the states albeit in two semi-detached elements rather than in a wholly unified and specific way. The first – to support the CFSP actively and unreservedly in a spirit of loyalty and mutual solidarity – was inserted at Maastricht as was the last sentence of the second – refraining from action contrary to the interests of the EU and likely to impair its effectiveness in international relations. And this has been surprisingly effective where the new neutral members, who might have been expected to have difficulties with the CFSP, are concerned. This echoes Article 10 TEC which makes a similar point about internal state obligations to the EC.

What is new here is the requirement to improve on existing levels of co-operation and develop 'mutual political solidarity'. This not only reflects awareness of the weakness of the CFSP between 1993 and 1997 but also reinforces obligations in the light of the new elements concerning enhanced co-operation. It all seems to mean that states have three duties: to support; to do more together; and not to upset the apple cart. This could be read as suggesting that the CFSP is not just an inter-governmental forum but something more constraining, even if it is not subject to the Community method. All the same, there are exceptions.

Prior to this, the first paragraph of Article 11 also tells us that the policy to be implemented is to cover 'all areas of foreign and security policy'. This statement of the obvious, which commits the cardinal sin of trying to define something in terms of itself, has become a meaningless oddity because the TA cut out the 1992 reference to member states joining with the Union in establishing a CFSP so that the original suggestion was that the CFSP would deal with those areas covered by national foreign and security policies. Not adjusting the phrasing may also have been a hint from the Amsterdam negotiators that security is now more firmly in the frame and that the CFSP does not extend to external economic policy concerns. Equally, it may be a way of emphasizing that the scope of the CFSP is not limitless, as one reading of the treaty might imply, but is actually limited to the objectives in the next article. Whatever the truth it is a sloppy piece of drafting and saying that the policy should cover all aspects of foreign and security affairs might have been better.

The objectives of the policy are also now centred on the Union as such and not the Union and the member states. This is reinforced by the new reference to the 'integrity of the Union', which thus becomes not just a community of values but also a kind of territorial entity. Cameron has suggested that this supposedly puts the EU 'only one step away from a mutual defence guarantee'. The step is, however, arguably a long one given the still embryonic EU role in defence matters.

The TEU's emphasis is, nevertheless, on maintaining existing borders as the reference to the UN Charter, Helsinki Final Act and the Paris Charter testifies. By implication, this can also be seen as a statement that the EU does not have external territorial ambitions and, that, despite its move into the security arena, the EU accepts that frontiers can only be changed by consent. However, the negotiators did recognize that the Union now has sensitive external borders, a recognition deriving from both Greek concerns over Turkey and Macedonia and the addition of Finland and Austria. None less, the overwhelming stress remains on promoting good causes such as democracy, human rights and the rule of law and respect for human rights. Surprisingly there is no repetition of the concern for the Union's international identity mentioned in Article 2 TEU. Given the complexity and uncertainties of Article 11 it is not surprising that it is left to the European Council to define the principles and guidelines according to which the Union is to implement the CFSP (Article 13).

When it comes to putting the objectives into practice the new *Article 12* (ex J.1(3)) is a much clearer statement of means than the previous rather convoluted statements about what member states should do. The Union now has a simple list of five rather rationally ordered and more action-oriented means set out in hierarchical order. Of these only the common strategies are wholly new and suggest a more systematic attempt to work out exactly what Union interests in foreign and security affairs are. Strengthening co-operation among states is now portrayed as merely one of many ways of implementing Union aims and not a rather separate class of actions as was suggested by ex J.1(3). The precise meaning of these are then spelled out in the succeeding articles. However, Article 12 does not exhaust the means available since Article 24 introduced a now amended new provision for concluding formal agreements with other states. This was used in April 2001 to conclude an agreement with Yugoslavia about the EU monitoring mission there. Moreover, the reference in Article 13(3) to common strategies being implemented 'in particular' by adopting joint actions and common positions suggests, as Dashwood notes, that other instruments may also be used. Indeed, as Hillion points out, the common strategy with Russia, for example, has been implemented using measures adopted not just under Title V but also under provisions found in Title VI TEU and the TEC. *Sui generis* Council decisions are also possible under Article 13(2). This emphasizes the growing importance of the Union as an international actor. Indeed, Dashwood is of the opinion that the article does, effectively, give the Union legal personality.

The explanation given in *Article 13* (ex J.3 and J.8(1–2)) of the first instrument – guidelines – is very limited since it neither defines it nor establishes the relationship between principles and strategies. The former might include things like ensuring that Union interests are served, that the right means and resources are used and that particular countries or regions are treated in particular ways, but we do not know. All we are told is that the European Council shall define such principles, and the TA makes it clear that this extends to defence matters on which later articles give the European Council almost a monopoly. And their remit has, as Dashwood points out, been extended beyond joint actions to the full range of CFSP activities envisaged at Maastricht.

When it comes to common strategies the European Council is subject to a limitation. They can only be devised for areas where the member states have important interests in common. In other words, something of concern to a single state and which is considered unimportant in the overall scheme of things will not be the subject of a common strategy. Thus there are now common strategies on Russia and the Ukraine but not on the Spanish enclaves in Morocco. Common strategies have to be purposeful and organized according to Article 12(2). They also have to be consonant with general guidelines. Because they are umbrella provisions – and even here Solana and others have criticized them for being too broadly defined and lacking focus – they need more specific actions to implement them and this in turns means they need to be co-ordinated. Perhaps because of this, common positions and joint actions can, according to Article 23(2), be decided by QMV when they derive from common strategies.

Such duties fall on the Council, which can also suggest common strategies. However, it is not clear whether the European Council needs a recommendation in order to create a strategy. The answer is certainly yes in practical terms, if not in legal theory, even if the European Council did ignore the fact that the TA had not entered into force when first inviting the Council in December 1998 to prepare common strategies. Some authorities have, however, expressed concerns that all this makes decision-making unhealthily prominent and will make the European Council too much of a decision-making body, affecting the Union/Community border. The Council also has the task of ensuring the consistency with which the negotiators were so much concerned. However, this is no easy task given that the Community-based common commercial policy and development co-operation fall within the remit. Finally, the addition of the reference to defence in paragraph 1 points up the diversity of the Union's external relations.

When it comes to joint actions *Article 14* (ex J.3) offers a much clearer definition than previously. Joint actions are concrete ways of acting so as to implement common strategies and other aims. Again they have to be purposeful and organized. And while the Council can revoke them, until this is done they are binding on member states. The new reference to inviting submissions from the Commission recognizes the fact that very often the Commission will be caught up in a joint action, even though it cannot itself autonomously propose them off its own bat, and things are likely to work better if the Commission (given in particular its responsibilities under the EC pillar of the Union) is forewarned and forearmed. Similar thoughts underlie paragraphs 5 to 7, which reflect the fact that Union decision-making procedures are rarely consistent with the realities of foreign crises as experienced by member states. And paragraph 7 could be read as opening the way to a kind of differentiated integration, although the changes introduced by Nice make this unnecessary.

Although apparently ranking below joint actions in the treaty, common positions would seem to occupy a place above them in practice, since they are general approaches to problem areas or conditions, which one would expect to be subsets of common strategies, with joint actions then turning these middle-range approaches into concrete action. Because they are approaches, and not an action, they are not subject to the same requirements of rational planning as the other instruments of the CFSP. However, *Article 15* (ex J.2(2)) does now at least offer a clearer definition than was available in 1992. Some authorities believe that this means the common position will be the standard CFSP procedure, others that it remains a rather constraining and passive instrument. *Article 16* (ex J.2(1)) then defines what should be understood by systematic co-operation among member states. Whether states will behave in this public-spirited way is far from certain, especially as some, like Georges Berthu MEP, feel that Amsterdam's reattribution of influence from the states as a group to the Union as such is a threat.

Having detailed the foreign-policy part of the CFSP the TEU then goes on to consider security questions. *Article 17* (ex J.4), which was considerably amended at Nice, is a major advance on the previous situation in at least three ways. Firstly, it brings armaments into the purview of the Union. Secondly, it talks now both more definitely of having a defence policy and of allowing the European Council to recommend the creation of a common defence, should it ever decide to do so. And Declaration No. 1 TN requires a rapid move down this road, even before ratification. However, this still leaves the decision very much in the hands of the member states. And Amsterdam emphasized the links of some with NATO.

Thirdly, by eliminating both the second subparagraph and the first three subparagraphs of paragraph 3 which Amsterdam had inserted to spell out how the WEU, as 'an integral part of the EU', was to act, Nice leaves the Union as such in unchallenged charge of its developing defence interests. This does make the text easier to follow although it means that, having been brought much more closely into the mainstream, the WEU is now largely excised. However, it is not wholly removed from the treaties as Belgium and Italy would have liked. It is no longer either a means of access to military capacity or a means of elaborating military policy. And this has been done without major treaty amendment.

However, the WEU does retain a treaty basis, both through the reference to it as a subordinate framework for bilateral action in paragraph 4; and in the Protocol on Article J.7 [now 17] of the Treaty on European Union and two declarations, Nos. 2 and 3 TA. These followed an earlier declaration (No. 30 TEU) adopted at Maastricht and set out what Amsterdam expected its role to be. The WEU also has a concrete existence in the sense that it still provides (in Article 5 of the Brussels treaty) a binding military defence guarantee. The Union has yet to take this over. It has, however, installed its high representative (see below) as Secretary-General of the WEU and was expecting a residual WEU structure to take the defence guarantee on board by the summer of 2001. The WEU also has various agencies, missions and armaments groups which are not due to pass into EU control for a while.

In making these changes the TN reflects, firstly, the Marseilles decisions of 13 November 2000 which saw the WEU handing over its crisis-management responsibilities to the EU. As a result, ahead of any expiry of its founding treaty, the WEU was to wind up its dialogues and military staff provision. Its parliamentary side will probably pass to the EP. However, nothing is said about either its associate members, associate partners or observers or the Amsterdam provision – then contained in Article 17(3) – that all EU member states could take part in its ventures. At Nice, the European Council did, though, agree that European non-member states, including Russia and Ukraine, as well as other interested states such as Canada, could be invited to participate in EU-led operations.

Secondly, it reflects the concrete progress in equipping the Union with military provision. Building on a Council decision on the modalities of executing the Petersberg tasks, taken immediately following the TA's entry into force, meetings of defence ministers became common while there were a series of moves to accept and staff a rapid reaction force of 60,000 troops by 2004. One caveat to the apparent enthusiasm for the defence dimension: Article 6 of the Protocol on the Position of Denmark exempts the country from participation both in terms of EU guidelines and the common defence policy. None the less, all this allows the Union to deploy troops for the first time.

Against this there is stronger, if somewhat ambiguous, recognition of the commitment of many member states to NATO, a recognition reinforced by the Protocol on Article 17 introduced by the TA, even though this calls for closer EU–WEU co-operation. Indeed some, like Gourlay and Remacle, thought that in seeking to assuage UK and other fears about potential threats to NATO the TA actually strengthened the position of NATO. NATO thus retains the ability to act on its own, as indeed do member states under Article 17(4). And Article 17(5) makes it clear that, although review is envisaged, none of these limited moves can be changed without an IGC, thus giving uneasy member states a veto. Given the Eurosceptic opposition to the whole Nice package this is not likely to be easily conceded.

Equally, although the TEU now encourages member states to co-operate in the field of armaments so as to ensure that the Union has independent sources of equipment, this is both very voluntaristic and not much more than a ratification of existing practices. All in all, this is a long way from a European army and a supra-national defence policy. At best it is, as Peterson and Sjursen said of Amsterdam, a ratcheting-up of the defence and security dimensions of the CFSP.

Article 18 (ex J.5) then begins an exposition on how all this is to be made to work. The TA here responds to the call in Article 3 TEU for the EU to 'ensure consistency in its external activities as a whole' by strengthening the role of the presidency, allowing it to use both the Commission, in representation and implementation, and the wider range of services provided by the new high representative which would include, as *Article 26* shows, both planning and policy development and representation whether generally or in specific relationships. Nice allowed appointment of the high representative by QMV through its amendments to *Article 23(2)* (ex J.3(2)). In the pursuit of the former goal the high representative can also draw on the new, but relatively small, unit set up under Declaration No. 6 TA. Questions have been asked as to whether this will really get the sensitive information it needs from the member states even though Declaration No. 2 TA looks for this, as Lodge and Flynn have noted.

The presidency is not given any specific responsibility for consistency in all this, despite its close relations with the high representative who is so charged. *Article 19* (ex J.2(3) and J.5(4)) also invites member states who have major roles in international bodies such as the UN both to uphold EU stances and to inform other member states of what is going on. However, paragraph 2 rather implies that member states cannot be forced to lay aside their interests while sitting in international organizations. Member states can also propose policy measures and, like the presidency, call for emergency action.

The actual running of the Council Secretariat is now delegated to a new deputy Secretary General, a move which some see as ignoring the broader mediating role carried out by the Secretary General as such since the new Secretary General is likely to be fully occupied with foreign, security and defence affairs. Indeed, the TEU implicitly uses the high representative to replace the outgoing presidency state in what was formally the troika, the combination of previous, present and future Council presidencies used to represent the Union internationally. As for the practice of appointing special delegates for specific trouble spots such as Bosnia and the Middle East, this was also written in at Amsterdam. Later on, the TEU, in *Articles 21 and 24*, makes the presidency responsible for relations with the EP and, more importantly, for opening negotiations on behalf of the Union. This raises difficult questions about the standing of the Union in international affairs.

Beyond this, the unaltered *Article 20* (ex J.6) provides for co-operation between national and Commission diplomatic services to uphold EU policy, now including joint actions. The Commission is still described as fully associated with the representational and implementational sides of the CFSP although this might seem a little ambiguous given the new role of the high representative or 'Monsieur PESC' as the French nicknamed the office. That said, Chris Patten as Commissioner for External Relations has taken the place of the future presidency in troika visits. This is in line with both the broader formula in *Article 27* (ex J.9) and the Commission's responsibilities under Article 3 TEU to help the Council ensure consistency inside the CFSP. Its staff are likely, moreover, to work in the Policy Planning and Early Warning Unit, although it does not have the same rights of initiative that it does under the TEC. The Commission also has a reporting duty in the CFSP along with the right to request an urgent meeting under the unchanged *Articles 21 and 22* (ex J.7 and J.8(3–4)).

The first of these two articles continues to allow the EP a limited informational and monitoring role. After Nice the Parliament hoped to utilize its rights to try to establish some influence over the Petersberg tasks. It does, however, have a role in the financing of the CFSP under *Article 28* (ex J.11). This provides that administrative actions are carried by the EC budget over which the Parliament has statutory control. Operational costs are also charged to the EC budget except where, as already noted, the operations have military or defence implications or where the Council decides that military costs are to be borne by those member states participating in the action. Some member states feared that involving the EP would allow it to try to control foreign policy but this has not so far happened, even though the Parliament's supporters certainly welcomed this new 'power of the purse' when the TA was first published. The ECJ, on the other hand, does not even have the limited rights given it by Amsterdam in the third pillar.

The final mechanism is the Political and Security Committee, described in *Article 25* (ex J.8(5)), which has seen its role twice augmented. At Amsterdam, in line with Declaration No. 5 TA, it emerged as the Political Committee, a body of no formally defined membership but in practice consisting of senior civil servants, which is supposed to meet as soon as there is a crisis, its relations with the rather similar COREPER being regulated by arrangements envisaged in Declaration No. 28 TEU. At Nice the Committee, which first met in March 2000, had its title formally changed to include security while a new paragraph in Article 25 gave it both oversight of crisis management operations and the possibility of taking specific implementing decisions. This was done because otherwise there was no treaty base for such activities. The reformed Committee has, as Duke notes, been seen as a linchpin of a new and more co-ordinated security policy and an anchor for the EU's embryonic military staff which currently meets in an 'interim' European Union Military Committee (EUMC). Given this it is odd that no formal provision was made for the high representative to chair the Political and Security Committee (PSC).

All this makes it clear that the member states, acting through the European Council and the Council proper, are the key elements in the CFSP. Indeed, they seem to have emerged stronger from the Amsterdam revisions even if they have to draw on Commission support and the Commission has an implied veto on the CFSP's principles and guidelines and common strategies through its participation in the European Council. But the member states act as member states and not, as was once the case, as 'High Contracting Parties'. Indeed, as with the creation of the high representative and the enhanced role of the Commission, further changes introduced by the TA clearly reflect concerns about the appropriateness of a purely inter-governmental CFSP, especially where voting procedures and international negotiation are concerned.

On voting procedures, the first indent of *Article 23(1)* redefines unanimity, according to which the Council generally takes decisions under Title V, bringing this into line with practice within the Community pillar which disregards abstentions. There had been some feeling that the positive agreement of every state was necessary to authorize CFSP initiatives. This partial dilution of the idea of inter-governmental consensus was then built on in the next indent of the paragraph introducing the principle of 'constructive abstention', which first emerged in the Irish presidency's 1996 draft treaty. The idea was that, by standing aside, an abstaining state accepts the legitimacy of a Union action in which it does not want to be involved and, more importantly, avoids being bound by it and is free of any responsibility for its costs. In such cases, a 'spirit of mutual solidarity' supposedly prevails. Abstaining member states are obliged not to take any action which might compromise EU action.

In theory, despite the danger of too many states abstaining, or of one going beyond abstention to opposition, this should have facilitated the adoption of decisions. In practice the option was not used and, as we will see below, the clause may have been made redundant by the addition of the new enhanced co-operation articles. We might wonder why both this and the reference to the old-style voting weights and thresholds in indent 2 were not removed at Nice when the use of QMV was extended to electing the high representative. However the second subparagraph of Article 23(2), which the EP sees as a veto, means that a state could block such a nomination on grounds of principle although this seems a bit farfetched. Personalities are less likely to offend vital principles than joint actions.

None the less, the vast majority of decisions under the CFSP remain unanimous and there is a real possibility of a blockage, a way round which is still needed, even with enhanced co-operation. The same desire to preserve states' rights shows up in the fact that when the Council acts by QMV, the simple act of making a formal declaration of opposition means that the vote will not be taken according to Article 23(2). Then, if there is a qualified majority – calculated in accordance with the vote distribution in Article 205(2) TEC – the matter can be referred up to the European Council. The question then arises as to whether the other states would actually wish to deny an objecting state the right to 'an appeal'. The precedent of the Luxembourg Compromise suggests not where actions are concerned, though it might be different with a nomination.

Allen argues that the new principle might just as well be labelled 'destructive abstention'. Allowing member states to disassociate themselves from decisions in these ways would reveal divisions just when the Union wished to demonstrate its unity and firmness. It might also precipitate disagreements with states seeking, as Duke has suggested, to use abstention to avoid financial obligations. As Keatinge notes, the procedure is cumbersome and unlikely to be used for trivial matters. All the same, it is another reminder of the extent to which inter-governmentalism dominates the CFSP. Ultimately, no member state can be bound to a common policy against its will.

Moreover, if states controlling more than a third of the total of weighted votes take this option then the initiative would fall, undermining the idea of 'common' in the CFSP. The idea may well have been a gesture to the former neutrals. However, it is not dissimilar to the provisions for flexibility found elsewhere and builds on Declaration No. 27 TEU, if not on EPC. The declaration invited uneasy member states not to push things to a vote when it was clear that there was a majority in favour of the matter under discussion. A further declaration, No. 25 TEU, permits member states to act separately in the interests of such countries or territories without this affecting the EU's interests. These precedents were then followed up at Nice leaving the constructive abstention in place where ordinary QMV decisions are involved.

The new provisions on decision-making also extend to international agreements which may be concluded under *Article 24*. At Amsterdam the Council was allowed to authorize the presidency to negotiate international agreements. But not only was unanimity needed to open negotiations, the outcome would have to be accepted unanimously too. Moreover, member states with special constitutional requirements could effectively opt out, leaving other member states to apply the agreement provisionally, thus opening the way for a form of closer co-operation for those who initially opt in. This, as Ehlermann pointed out, would be applicable to third-pillar agreements too thanks to a final indent. This is a procedure which alarms both extremes of the political spectrum since Berthu sees the evasion of ratification as a major, and new, threat to the states while the EP resents its exclusion.

Nice made this even more complicated. While the revised Article 24(5) left the extension to Title VI and the constitutional opt-out in place, it added the possibility that the agreement would apply *pro tem*, even to states adducing difficulties. It did this by eliminating the phrase about decisions applying provisionally 'to them', that is to say only to those member states without constitutional difficulties. Certainly some Eurosceptics have seen this as a threat to their constitutional specificities. However, the text says only that the Council 'may' apply the agreement *pro tem*. It is not obliged to do so. And, although the TN brought in a limited amount of QMV, it also insists that where there is unanimity in internal decision-making this should apply externally. More significantly, it makes it clear that all such agreements are binding on the institutions, thus subjecting them to quasi-inter-governmental decisions in a slight twist on what had long been the case under Article 300(7) (ex 228) TEC. There is also an echo of the 1971 *AETR* judgment confirming the Community's powers to act externally where it has internal competence. However, Bonde argues that through this member states not in sympathy with such agreements could be forced to accept them, which seems unlikely. In any case, it all shows the ambiguity of the nature of CFSP decision-making.

While the adoption of decisions should also be facilitated by the extension of the use of qualified majority voting, particularly after Nice, there are again some caveats. Since the TA, QMV covers both the adoption of joint actions, common positions and 'other decisions' on the basis of a common strategy, and any decisions implementing a joint action or common position (Article 23(2)). By extension, 'one-off' positions and actions will remain a matter for unanimity as will all defence-related issues. While the member states may be willing to use EC voting norms within the CFSP, those powerful militarily are not willing to give away control to smaller states less likely to be involved in financing and staging military actions.

However, member states were also aware at Amsterdam of the downside of this insistence on their sovereignty. For some IGC delegations, one way round this was to endow the Union as such with legal personality, allowing it rather than the Community to sign treaties. However, two specific proposals for doing this, submitted by the Irish and Dutch presidencies, were ignored in favour of a curious half-way house between legal personality and inter-governmentalism. Thus Article 24 allows the Council, as we noted in the Introduction, to approve international agreements negotiated for it by the presidency on both diplomatic and criminal justice matters. As Dashwood points out, the agreement on the administration of Mostar, taken by the states acting within the framework of the Union, points in this direction even if it confuses the question of legal personality. As he says, it is unclear whether this is simply a convenient negotiating procedure or, as Aust assumes, a new treaty-making right for the Union. Declaration No. 4 TA leans heavily towards the former, stating that any agreements concluded 'shall not imply any transfer of competence for the Member States to the [EU]'. What international credibility such deals may have is uncertain, especially as states can make their acceptance dependent on domestic approval which could create a quasi-permanent opt-out. There is also the possibility that constructive abstention could be invoked.

At Nice a new dimension was added to the CFSP by the introduction of a new code of behaviour on enhanced co-operation. This is interposed with letter suffixes between Articles 27 and 28 since they represent a new decision-making process beyond those already established but something affected by the financing arrangements which end the title. *Article 27a* starts somewhat abruptly, assuming that enhanced co-operation has already been defined whereas it actually comes later in the TEU, and sets out the general requirements for enhanced co-operation in the CFSP. While theoretically allowing it to cover any area of the title, the article lays down specific conditions: that it fits in with the general drift of the CFSP; that it meets conditions of consistency; that it does not infringe either the rights of the EC or the provisions of Articles 43–45 TEU. This makes the point that Title VII sets the tone for enhanced co-operation in general. However, there is no provision for a delaying reference up to the European Council as there is elsewhere in the treaties since, as Articles 27c and 27d make clear, the member states are the key decision-makers in all this.

Two further constraints are imposed by *Article 27b*, which firstly limits enhanced co-operation to the implementation of specific instruments and secondly excludes all military and defence activities. The former means that there cannot be a partial 'common strategy' involving only a few member states, which seems only sensible. The latter is somewhat in contradiction with Article 27a but was enforced by the United Kingdom and two neutral states, Ireland and Sweden, for their own reasons although this only happened just before Nice, suggesting there was some willingness to consider the idea. Defence is still only partly a Union matter, it seems, despite the existence of a common European security and defence policy.

Having defined the parameters the new articles then go on to establish how to go about establishing enhanced co-operation within the CFSP. *Article 27c* allows states to approach the Council with a suggestion. The latter can only proceed after the Commission has given a formal opinion but this has to focus on the question of consistency with Union (and not Community as was originally suggested) policies. Some think that this means that the Commission position is a weak one. And it is not absolutely certain that the Council would have to accept its decision. It seems to have the authority to decide as it chooses, though, since it would want to utilize the Commission's services, it is unlikely that it would ignore a negative view. None the less, the Commission is less influential in this pillar than elsewhere in the TEU. This is also true of the Parliament, which only has a right of information, although it is partly compensated by a new and continuing obligation, established in *Article 27d*, on the high representative to report to them.

Other member states which decide not to take part in an enhanced co-operation activity when it starts can, according to *Article 27e*, apply to join later provided they get approval. The treaty now provides a new mechanism, which goes beyond the Amsterdam phraseology, and which is echoed in the third pillar at Article 40b. It also echoes the drift of Title VII, which is to encourage all members to take part by creating as few obstacles as possible. The mechanism is somewhat obscure. What is clear is that, once it decides that it wants to join an existing activity, the member state concerned has to notify the Council and inform – suggesting this is a formality – the Commission. The latter has three months to give its views and, no later than a month after it does, the Council must decide two things. One is to accept in principle and this it can do passively. It only needs to act by QMV if it decides not to accept the application there and then but to hold it over. And it then has to justify its decision and agree to re-examine it, making the rejection only temporary. The old QMV thresholds left behind in Article 23(2) are used here. However, presumably the Council could make a positive statement and vote to accept. The second thing is to decide if it itself (and not the Commission as in the first and third pillars) wishes to place any special conditions on the new participant. All this, which is underwritten in Title VII at Article 43b, shows that member-state interests weigh more heavily in the CFSP than elsewhere.

Whether the member states will actually take up the facility for enhanced co-operation remains uncertain. If they do it opens the same kind of risks as does constructive abstention. And it is potentially more cumbersome to establish, which suggests that constructive abstention could retain its appeal. None the less, both the failure to reconcile it with the latter and the possibility of differential participation mean that the title has lost some of its post-Amsterdam rational clarity. In other words, while the revised Title V services and fine-tunes the CFSP, moving it towards being a more effective Union-run policy, the very diverse nature of EU external relations, to which we will return later, means that there are still many difficulties, gaps and unanswered questions. These will only be answered by the practice of the CFSP, thus reinforcing its evolutionary nature. And much the same is probably true of the third pillar.

TITLE V

PROVISIONS ON A COMMON FOREIGN AND SECURITY POLICY

Article 11 (ex J.1)

1. The *Union shall* define and implement a common foreign and security *policy covering* all areas of foreign and security policy, *the objectives of which shall be*:
– to safeguard the common values, fundamental interests, independence **and integrity** of the Union **in conformity with the principles of the United Nations Charter**;
– to strengthen the security of the *Union* in all ways;
– to preserve peace and strengthen international security, in accordance with the principles of the United Nations Charter, as well as the principles of the Helsinki Final Act and the objectives of the Paris Charter, **including those on external borders**;
– to promote international co-operation;
– to develop and consolidate democracy and the rule of law, and respect for human rights and fundamental freedoms.

2. The Member States shall support the Union's external and security policy actively and unreservedly in a spirit of loyalty and mutual solidarity.

The Member States shall work together to enhance and develop their mutual political solidarity. They shall refrain from any action which is contrary to the interests of the Union or likely to impair its effectiveness as a cohesive force in international relations.

The Council shall ensure that these principles are complied with.

Article 12 (ex J.1(3))

The Union shall pursue *the objectives set out in Article 11 by*:
– **defining the principles of and general guidelines for the common foreign and security policy**;
– **deciding on common strategies**;
– adopting *joint actions;*
– **adopting common positions**;
– **strengthening** systematic co-operation between Member States in the conduct of policy.

Article 13 (ex J.8(1–2))

1. The European Council shall define the principles of and general guidelines for the common foreign and security policy, **including for matters with defence implications.**

2. **The European Council shall decide on common strategies to be implemented by the Union in areas where the Member States have important interests in common.**
Common strategies shall set out their objectives, duration and the means to be made available by the Union and the Member States.

3. The Council shall take the decisions necessary for defining and implementing the common foreign and security policy on the basis of the general guidelines defined by the European Council.

The Council shall recommend common strategies to the European Council and shall implement them, in particular by adopting joint actions and common positions.

The Council shall ensure the unity, consistency and effectiveness of action by the Union.

Article 14 (ex J.3)

1. The Council shall *adopt joint actions.* **Joint actions shall address specific situations where operational action by the Union is deemed to be required. They shall lay down** *their objectives, scope,* **the means to be made available to the Union,** if necessary *their duration, and* the conditions for their implementation.

2. If there is a change in circumstances having a substantial effect on a question subject to joint action, the Council shall review the principles and objectives of that action and take the necessary decisions. As long as the Council has not acted, the joint action shall stand.

3. Joint actions shall commit the Member States in the positions they adopt and in the conduct of their activity.

4. **The Council may request the Commission to submit to it any appropriate proposals relating to the common foreign and security policy to ensure the implementation of a joint action.**

5. Whenever there is any plan to adopt a national position or take national action pursuant to a joint action, information shall be provided in time to allow, if necessary, for prior consultations within the Council. The obligation to provide prior information shall not apply to measures which are merely a national transposition of Council decisions.

6. In cases of imperative need arising from changes in the situation and failing a Council decision, Member States may take the necessary measures as a matter of urgency having regard to the general objectives of the joint action. The Member State concerned shall inform the Council immediately of any such measures.

7. Should there be any major difficulties in implementing a joint action, a Member State shall refer them to the Council which shall discuss them and seek appropriate solutions. Such solutions shall not run counter to the objectives of the joint action or impair its effectiveness.

Article 15 (ex J.2(2))

The Council shall **adopt** common positions. **Common positions shall define the approach of the Union to a particular matter of a geographical or thematic nature.** Member States shall ensure that their national policies conform to the common positions.

Article 16 (ex J.2(1))

Member States shall inform and consult one another within the Council on any matter of foreign and security policy of general interest in order to ensure that **the Union's influence** is exerted as effectively as possible by means of concerted and convergent action.

Article 17 (ex J.4)

1. The common foreign and security policy shall include all questions relating to the security of the Union, including **the progressive** framing of a common defence *policy, which might lead* to a common defence, **should the European Council so decide. It shall in that case recommend to the Member States the adoption of such a decision in accordance with their respective constitutional requirements.**

The policy of the Union in accordance with this Article shall not prejudice the specific character of the security and defence policy of certain Member States and shall respect the obligations of certain Member States, which see their common defence realised in the North Atlantic Treaty Organisation (NATO), under the North Atlantic Treaty and be compatible with the common security and defence policy established within that framework.

The progressive framing of a common defence policy will be supported, as Member States consider appropriate, by co-operation between them in the field of armaments.

2. Questions referred to in this Article shall include humanitarian and rescue tasks, peacekeeping tasks and tasks of combat forces in crisis management, including peacemaking.

3. **Decisions having defence implications dealt with under this** *Article* **shall be taken without prejudice to the policies and obligations referred to in paragraph 1,** *second* **subparagraph.**

4. The provisions of this Article shall not prevent the development of closer co-operation between two or more Member States on a bilateral level, in the framework of the *Western European Union (WEU) and NATO,* provided such co-operation does not run counter to or impede that provided for in this Title.

5. With a view to furthering the objectives of this **Article, the** provisions of this Article **will be reviewed in accordance with** Article 48.

Article 18 (ex J.5)

1. The Presidency shall represent the Union in matters coming within the common foreign and security policy.

2. The Presidency shall be responsible for the implementation of **decisions taken under this Title;** in that capacity it shall in principle express the position of the Union in international organisations and international conferences.

3. The Presidency shall be assisted by the Secretary-General of the Council who shall exercise the function of High Representative for the common foreign and security policy.

4. The Commission shall be fully associated *in the tasks referred to in paragraphs 1 and 2*. The Presidency shall be assisted *in those tasks* if need be by the next Member **State** to hold the Presidency.

5. The Council may, whenever it deems it necessary, appoint a special representative with a mandate in relation to particular policy issues.

Article 19 (ex J.2(3) and J.5(4))

1. Member States shall co-ordinate their action in international organisations and at international conferences. They shall uphold the common positions in such fora.

In international organisations and at international conferences where not all the Member States participate, those which do take part shall uphold the common positions.

2. Without prejudice to *paragraph 1 and Article 14(3)*, Member States represented in international organisations or international conferences where not all the Member States participate shall keep the latter informed of any matter of common interest.

Member States which are also members of the United Nations Security Council will concert and keep the other Member States fully informed. Member States which are permanent members of the Security Council will, in the execution of their functions, ensure the defence of the positions and the interests of the Union, without prejudice to their responsibilities under the provisions of the United Nations Charter.

Article 20 (ex J.6)

The diplomatic and consular missions of the Member States and the Commission Delegations in third countries and international conferences, and their representations to international organisations, shall co-operate in ensuring that the common positions and **joint actions** adopted by the Council are complied with and implemented.

They shall step up co-operation by exchanging information, carrying out joint assessments and contributing to the implementation of the provisions referred to in Article 20 of the Treaty establishing the European Community.

Article 21 (ex J.7)

The Presidency shall consult the European Parliament on the main aspects and the basic choices of the common foreign and security policy and shall ensure that the views of the European Parliament are duly taken into consideration. The European Parliament shall be kept regularly informed by the Presidency and the Commission of the development of the Union's foreign and security policy.

The European Parliament may ask questions of the Council or make recommendations to it. It shall hold an annual debate on progress in implementing the common foreign and security policy.

Article 22 (ex J.8(3–4))

1. Any Member State or the Commission may refer to the Council any questions relating to the common foreign and security policy and may submit proposals to the Council.

2. In cases requiring a rapid decision, the Presidency, of its own motion, or at the request of the Commission or a Member State, shall convene an extraordinary Council meeting within forty-eight hours or, in an emergency, within a shorter period.

Article 23 (drawing on ex J.8(2) and J.3(2))

1. *Decisions under this Title shall be taken by the Council acting unanimously.* Abstentions by members present in person or represented shall not prevent the adoption of such decisions.

When abstaining in a vote, any member of the Council may qualify its abstention by making a formal declaration under the present subparagraph. In that case, it shall not be obliged to apply the decision, but shall accept that the decision commits the Union. In a spirit of mutual solidarity, the Member State concerned shall refrain from any action likely to conflict with or impede Union action based on that decision and the other Member States shall respect its position. If the members of the Council qualifying their abstention in this way represent more than one third of the votes weighted in accordance with Article 205(2) of the Treaty establishing the European Community, the decision shall not be adopted.

2. By derogation from the provisions of paragraph 1, the Council shall act by qualified majority:
– when adopting joint actions, common positions or taking any other decision on the basis of a common strategy;
– when adopting any decision implementing a joint action or a common position;
– when appointing a special representative in accordance with Article 18(5).

If a member of the Council declares that, for important and stated reasons of national policy, it intends to oppose the adoption of a decision to be taken by qualified majority, a vote shall not be taken. The Council may, acting by a qualified majority, request that the matter be referred to the European Council for decision by unanimity.

The votes of the members of the Council shall be weighted in accordance with Article 205(2) of the Treaty establishing the European Community. For their adoption, decisions shall require at least 62 votes in favour, cast by at least 10 members.

This paragraph shall not apply to decisions having military or defence implications.

3. *For procedural questions, the Council shall act by a majority of its members.*

Article 24 (new – TA)

1. When it is necessary to conclude an agreement with one or more States or international organisations in implementation of this Title, the Council may authorise the Presidency, assisted by the Commission as appropriate, to open negotiations to that effect. Such agreements shall be concluded by the Council on a recommendation from the Presidency.

2. The Council shall act unanimously when the agreement covers an issue for which unanimity is required for the adoption of internal decisions.

3. When the agreement is envisaged in order to implement a joint action or common position, the Council shall act by a qualified majority in accordance with Article 23(2).

4. *The provisions of this Article shall also apply to matters falling under Title VI. When the agreement covers an issue for which a qualified majority is required for the adoption of internal decisions or measures, the Council shall act by a qualified majority in accordance with Article 34(3).*

5. *No agreement shall be binding on a Member State whose representative in the Council states that it has to comply with the requirements of its own constitutional procedure; the other members of the Council may agree that the agreement shall nevertheless apply provisionally.*

6. Agreements concluded under the conditions set out by this Article shall be binding on the institutions of the Union.

Article 25 (ex J.8(5))

Without prejudice to Article 207 of the Treaty establishing the European Community, a Political **and Security** *Committee shall* monitor the international situation in the areas covered by the common foreign and security policy and contribute to the definition of policies by delivering opinions to the Council at the request of the Council or on its own initiative. It shall also monitor the implementation of agreed policies, without prejudice to the responsibility of the Presidency and the Commission.

Within the scope of this Title, this Committee shall exercise, under the responsibility of the Council, political control and strategic direction of crisis management operations.

The Council may authorise the Committee, for the purpose and for the duration of a crisis management operation, as determined by the Council, to take the relevant decisions concerning the political control and strategic direction of the operation, without prejudice to Article 47.

Article 26 (new – TA)

The Secretary-General of the Council, High Representative for the common foreign and security policy, shall assist the Council in matters coming within the scope of the common foreign and security policy, in particular through contributing to the formulation, preparation and implementation of policy decisions, and, when appropriate and acting on behalf of the Council at the request of the Presidency, through conducting political dialogue with third parties.

Article 27 (ex Article J.9)

The Commission shall be fully associated with the work carried out in the common foreign and security policy field.

Article 27a (new – TN)

1. Enhanced co-operation in any of the areas referred to in this Title shall be aimed at safeguarding the values and serving the interests of the Union as a whole by asserting its identity as a coherent force on the international scene. It shall respect:
– the principles, objectives, general guidelines and consistency of the common foreign and security policy and the decisions taken within the framework of that policy;
– the powers of the European Community, and
– consistency between all the Union's policies and its external activities.

2. Articles 11 to 27 and Articles 27b to 28 shall apply to the enhanced co-operation provided for in this Article, save as otherwise provided in Article 27c and Articles 43 to 45.

Article 27b (new – TN)

Enhanced co-operation pursuant to this Title shall relate to implementation of a joint action or a common position. It shall not relate to matters having military or defence implications.

Article 27c (new – TN)

Member States which intend to establish enhanced co-operation between themselves under Article 27b shall address a request to the Council to that effect.

The request shall be forwarded to the Commission and to the European Parliament for information. The Commission shall give its opinion particularly on whether the enhanced co-operation proposed is consistent with Union policies. Authorisation shall be granted by the Council, acting in accordance with the second and third subparagraphs of Article 23(2) and in compliance with Articles 43 to 45.

Article 27d (new – TN)

Without prejudice to the powers of the Presidency or of the Commission, the Secretary-General of the Council, High Representative for the common foreign and security policy, shall in particular ensure that the European Parliament and all members of the Council are kept fully informed of the implementation of enhanced co-operation in the field of the common foreign and security policy.

Article 27e (new – TN)

Any Member State which wishes to participate in enhanced co-operation established in accordance with Article 27c shall notify its intention to the Council and inform the Commission. The Commission shall give an opinion to the Council within three months of the date of receipt of that notification. Within four months of the date of receipt of that notification, the Council shall take a decision on the request and on such specific arrangements as it may deem necessary. The decision shall be deemed to be taken unless the Council, acting by a qualified majority within the same period, decides to hold it in abeyance;

in that case, the Council shall state the reasons for its decision and set a deadline for re-examining it.

For the purposes of this Article, the Council shall act by a qualified majority. The qualified majority shall be defined as the same proportion of the weighted votes and the same proportion of the number of the members of the Council concerned as those laid down in the third subparagraph of Article 23(2).

Article 28 (ex J.11)

1. Articles *189, 190, 196* to *199, 203, 204, 206* to *209, 213* to *219, 255* and *290* of the Treaty establishing the European Community shall apply to the provisions relating to the areas referred to in this Title.

2. Administrative expenditure which the provisions relating to the areas referred to in this Title entail for the institutions shall be charged to the budget of the European Communities.

3. *Operational expenditure to which the implementation of those provisions gives rise* shall also be charged to *the budget of the European Communities*, except for such expenditure arising from operations having military or defence implications and cases where the Council acting unanimously decides otherwise.

In cases where expenditure is not charged to the budget of the European Communities it shall be charged to the Member States in accordance with the gross national product scale, unless the Council acting unanimously decides otherwise. As for expenditure arising from operations having military or defence implications, Member States whose representatives in the Council have made a formal declaration under Article 23(1), second subparagraph, shall not be obliged to contribute to the financing thereof.

4. *The budgetary procedure laid down in the Treaty establishing the European Community shall apply to the expenditure charged to the budget of the European Communities.*

vi Police and Judicial Co-operation in Criminal Matters

Like the CFSP, the third pillar today is very different from what it was in 1992. Indeed it actually differs more, because Amsterdam did not merely rewrite what was then 'Co-operation in the fields of Justice and Home Affairs' (JHA), but restructured it by transferring some of its responsibilities to the TEC and giving it a new focus and a new name – 'Police and Judicial Co-operation in Criminal Matters' (PJCCM). Nice was to make only the most limited of adjustments to this. So, to start, we need to recall what the treaty originally prescribed for the third pillar. We can then move on to look at the present situation. What we find is the same kind of ambiguity about the status of the pillar as is visible in the CFSP.

When the third pillar was initially devised, it represented a distinct advance on the unsystematic arrangements for co-operation in justice and home affairs developed in the 1970s and 1980s involving the TREVI process and the ad hoc group on immigration mentioned in the SEA. It was also a response to promptings from Chancellor Kohl and others who, in mid-1991, called for provisions relating to rights of asylum, immigration and the establishment of a European Police Office to be included in the treaty then under negotiation. In effect, what actually emerged in the final document exceeded these demands. The original TEU wrote in a ten-clause title, beginning with a one-line clause formally recognizing that there would be co-operation in justice and home affairs subject to the provisions in Articles K.1 to K.9 which followed.

The provisions included a list of areas, such as immigration, combating drug-addiction and defeating fraud, which could be considered for such co-operation. Where police co-operation was concerned the possibility of an EU-wide Police Office (Europol) was canvassed. However, this was to be looked at in terms of both European human rights rules and member states' sovereign responsibility for internal security. As with the CFSP, two means were seen for doing this: co-ordination amongst the states as such and the unanimous adoption of specified measures (joint positions, joint action and conventions) by the Council of Ministers. The latter was to be assisted in this by a special co-ordinating committee (the so-called K.4 Committee) of officials and by the Commission, which also had limited powers of initiative. Proceedings within the pillar were to be reported to the EP.

On the other hand, member states were required to support common positions inside international organizations. But they were allowed, via Article K.7, to go further in bilateral co-operation within the field while also drawing on Community financing. Finally, Article K.9, a so-called *passerelle* clause, allowed them to transfer further elements of JHA policy to Community procedures without the need for a formal IGC but with member states having to ratify any decision. All this showed member-state uncertainties about acting collectively in such sensitive areas. It also demonstrated a desire to balance easier internal movement associated with the Single Market with higher external barriers.

In the event, not a great deal of use was made of all this before Amsterdam. Decision-making was slow, difficult and lacked transparency so member-state behaviour was not much affected by the outcomes. Only two conventions, those of Dublin on asylum and Europol, were adopted, the former having been in the pipeline before Maastricht, and no use was made of the *passerelle*. Concerns also existed over the lack of judicial and parliamentary supervision at both national and EU levels. Hence there was much talk of making the provisions more precise and effective. And a surprising amount of progress was made in the 1996 IGC, partly because of the difficulties in dealing with the increasing number of asylum seekers in the mid-1990s and the feeling that public opinion would therefore warm to measures which would balance the right of free movement with new controls on external border movements, crime and migration. It was therefore agreed to add further elements of the third pillar to the Community, along with Schengen, albeit in a staged way and while allowing the United Kingdom and Ireland to opt out. And, even though this was a radical development, it attracted surprisingly little criticism.

The Amsterdam Treaty, as is clear from the TEU's preamble and Article 2, in fact made the creation of what is called 'an area of freedom, security and justice' one of the Union's high-profile priorities. This was quite significant, if not quite on the scale of EMU. It involved a number of moves towards supra-nationalism, notably in the role given to the ECJ, but it still falls short of providing real policies in such areas as asylum and action remains dependent on member states' consent. Much of the implementation of this is provided for in Title IV (Articles 61–69) of the TEC to which much of the contents of the old Pillar III was transferred. In their place is a slimmed-down, extensively rewritten and reordered set of provisions relating specifically to criminal justice matters. In fact it is an ambiguous, complex and highly technical code of conduct for member states.

Although slimmed down, the actual scope of what is now Pillar III is larger than its

Table 2 The destination of JHA Provisions in the light of the Treaty of Amsterdam

Pre-TA	K.1(7)	K.1(9)	K.2(2)	K.3(1)	K.3(2)(c)	K.4(1)	K.4(2)	K.4(3)
Post-TA	K.1	K.1	K.5	K.6(1)	K.6(2)(d)	K.8(1)	K.8(2)	K.6(3)
New	29	29	33	34(1)	34(2)(d)	36(1)	36(2)	34(3)

Pre-TA	K.4(3)	K.5	K.6	K.6	K.7	K.8(1)	K.8(2)	K.9
Post-TA	K.6(4)	K.9	K.11(2)	K.11(3)	K.12(1)	K.13(1)	K.13(2)	K.14
New	34(4)	37	39(2)	39(3)	40(1)	41(1)	41(2)	42

title implies. In part, this is because it also covers the prevention and combating of racism and xenophobia (Article 29 TEU), although little is said about how this is to be done. Moreover, thanks to the Protocol Integrating the Schengen *Acquis* into the Framework of the European Union, elements of earlier Schengen co-operation not included in the *acquis* of Part Three, Title IV of the TEC fall within the activities of PJCCM. These include certain immigration and external border issues, most notably the Schengen Information System. A further general point to be made is that the TA renumbered all of Title VI thus removing the familiar K. prefix to its article numbers. Since this makes things hard to follow we provide Table 2 above showing the evolution of the various clauses.

Nice left this structure largely unchanged, which again suggests that the Amsterdam changes had garnered general support. In fact it made two sets of amendments. The first, and least far-reaching, was the way that it wrote pre-existing judicial linkages into the treaty, in line both with the acceptance of Amsterdam's rationalizing approach and the decisions of the 1999 Tampere Council at the start of what we have suggested might be the beginning of a new policy-making role. The second, more extensive, set of changes was the way it rewrote the pillar's enhanced co-operation provisions, inserting two new articles to do so, thus somewhat offsetting its attempt at rationalization. For the EP this did not go far enough, as it would have liked to have seen more change in this area, notably through the creation of a special prosecutor for fraud against the Union and further communitarization (including of Europol) so that there would be democratic and ECJ control of such police and judicial activities as were laid down in the title. Conversely, others of a more sceptical mind saw the first changes as a further threat to national legal and police autonomy. And the UK government has resisted some of the suggested implementing proposals which have followed Nice.

However, the IGC 2000 negotiators rejected both going any further towards communitarization and ideas of increasing the stress on rights. So the title retains most of its post-Amsterdam characteristics. Hence it does not now start with a general reference to the establishment of a home-affairs policy as it did when it first appeared in the TEU. Instead, in *Article 29* (ex K.1) it stresses the policy objectives of creating 'a high level of safety' for citizens through anti-racism activities and inter-state co-operation on criminal matters something which was extended to include law enforcement authorities and thus, as den Boer notes, to state intelligence services. However, the concern for combating racism and xenophobia seems somewhat cosmetic as the subject is not referred to elsewhere in the title. The same is true of the reference in Article 13 TEC to the EC taking 'appropriate action' although agreement at Amsterdam was accompanied by further progress towards the establishment of a European Monitoring Centre for Racism and Xenophobia in Vienna, a convenient development given that 1997 was the European Year against Racism and Xenophobia.

As for the old acknowledgement in Article K.2 that co-operation in this area should comply with the Council of Europe's Convention on Human Rights (ECHR) this is not repeated directly. Rather the emphasis is far more on the repression of a range of offences, extended by the TA to include the prevention and combating of trafficking in drugs and persons, offences against children, illicit arms trafficking and corruption. Actual use of drugs is not mentioned. And clearly this is to be done in conjunction with EC action.

Three inter-governmental means for doing this are indicated including the new possibility of approximation of rules on criminal matters. Nice added to the second of these a reference to the new European Judicial Co-operation Unit, or 'Eurojust', thus giving it more formal standing and moving the EU further in the direction of more institutionalized judicial co-operation which the EP has been seeking. As Declaration No. 2 TN makes clear, this unit consisting of national judicial officials was agreed at Tampere in October 1999. The wording comes directly from the Presidency Conclusions. The Unit's role is to co-ordinate national prosecutions and support investigations in organized crime, especially those involving Europol with which, thanks to French insistence, it is now on a legal par. Making sure that appeals for judicial assistance in such cases were speeded up was a major aim of the unit. This reflected difficulties experienced by the Italian 'clean hands' judges in getting rapid responses to 'letters rogatory' – requests from a court in one country to the court in another requesting testimony or documentation. This is followed up by further additions to Article 31.

Before this *Article 30*, rather than listing areas of common interest, talks of common action of two kinds as a way of creating the new area of security and justice. Firstly, there is a whole range of precise forms of existing police operations in which Europol is to have an enhanced role. The body is not, however, granted autonomy. Instead it retains its role of supporting the member states. National control is reflected in Declaration No. 7 TA which insists on national judicial accountability. Secondly, in a way that anticipates the provisions of Articles 61–63 TEC, the Council is required to take further initiatives over the five years beginning in May 1999, both to extend Europol's operational capacities and to create a cross-border information network. This is something of a constitutional innovation.

Common action, according to *Article 31*, is to be reinforced by such things as judicial co-operation, including facilitating, possibly within five years, minimum rules covering constituent elements of criminal acts and penalties in the areas of organized crime, terrorism and drug trafficking. These are the key objectives of the pillar as a whole. Nice took things further, adding a second paragraph setting out, to begin with, how the Council should utilize Eurojust; avoiding presenting obstacles to co-ordination; supporting it in cross-border criminal investigations – using the words of Tampere – and facilitating the Unit's relations with the European judicial network. This, as Declaration No. 2 TN reminds us, was the result of a JHA joint action of June 1998. The network is a series of formalized contacts between national judiciaries designed to help with both extradition and criminal investigations. Tampere looked to seeing working procedures for Eurojust established by the end of 2001 but some proposals made after Nice, which envisage a role for the Commission and a degree of control over national judiciaries, have met a cool response in Whitehall.

However, Declaration No. 8 TA states that no member state shall be obliged to introduce minimum sentences. Where this means the police or courts of one member state operating in the territory of another, whether in hot pursuit or in some other way, this is to be subject to rules established by the Council under the provisions of *Article 32*. If the Council does not lay down such conditions then it cannot happen. And *Article 33* (ex K.2(2)) continues to make it clear that such rules cannot detract from essential national sovereignty in these areas. Indeed the revised article cuts out the Maastricht reference to the role of the European Convention on Human Rights, strengthening the national position.

The title then moves on to establish how all this is to be done. On the one hand *Article 34(1)* (ex K.3(1)) provides that member states are required to consult, presumably bilaterally or multilaterally, on administrative co-ordination within the Council, which thus becomes a forum for organizing inter-governmental action. On the other hand, *Article 34(2)* (ex K.3(2)) allows the Council collectively to legislate in one of four new ways which are more substantial and clearly defined than those defined at Maastricht: common positions, framework decisions, decisions and conventions. In all cases, proposals may be made by the Council, a member state or the Commission. Equally the outcome can take the form of frameworks which some see as creating a kind of third pillar equivalent to directives in the first pillar.

Such legislative acts are, according to Declaration No. 9 TA, to be published in the *Official Journal* in the normal way. Moreover, only one of these – common positions – is not binding since they are general stances which states have to defend in international fora, a point underlined by *Article 37* (ex K.5). Monar has suggested – even though only a handful were adopted prior to Amsterdam – that these might become the preferred instrument under this pillar, something which could threaten the *acquis communautaire*.

Both framework and ordinary decisions are binding. The former replaces joint actions and is a version of the EC directive, allowing states to decide how to implement an agreed strategy. Equally, ordinary actions seem to need national implementing legislation since they do not have direct effect. The same is true for the fourth type of measure which may be adopted under Pillar III: conventions. These were first made available under Pillar III when the TEU entered into force in 1993. But few were drafted and even fewer were quickly ratified. Hence, the TA introduced time limits for the commencement of ratification procedures. Moreover, in a move more reminiscent of the US Constitution than the EU's treaty base, conventions now come into effect once two-thirds of the states – significantly described as 'contracting parties' rather than member states – adopt them. This 'rolling ratification' procedure clearly speeds up the implementation of conventions but, as den Boer observes, this may not encourage a coherent and intelligible application of the provisions. Generally all PJCCM instruments are to be adopted unanimously, even if the Commission can suggest them. And it is made clear that they are not to lead to harmonization of domestic criminal law.

None the less, there is a further significant innovation in *Article 35* which makes some of this subject to ECJ jurisdiction. The Court is allowed to give preliminary rulings on the three binding instruments and related implementing legislation. However, this is subject to strict conditions. The first is that member states have to opt in to its jurisdiction, an idea floated by EC lawyers like Curtin after seeing the difficulties which emerged over the establishment of Europol. Hence, according to Article 35(1), member states *may* accept preliminary rulings from the ECJ on the validity and interpretation of decisions, framework decisions, conventions and implementing measures. To do so, they must issue a formal notification, assumed to be non-revocable, of their acceptance of ECJ jurisdiction. Declaration No. 10 TA makes it incumbent on such states to ensure that their courts refer queries to the ECJ. This owes its origins to UK reservations.

At the time when the TA was signed, six notifications were noted. Austria, Belgium, Germany, Greece, Luxembourg and the Netherlands all declared that they would accept the jurisdiction of the ECJ. Other member states initially proved less keen on the idea, although Finland, Italy, Portugal, Spain and Sweden all made subsequent declarations. The hesitancy if not reluctance is perhaps because it opens the way to an unstated form of closer co-operation, as Ehlermann says. Consequently, ECJ jurisdiction in the areas noted is limited in terms of geographical scope. This could certainly undermine the uniformity of interpretation and application of the various measures adopted. Hence, as Monar points out, it could also create differences within the EC in terms of the judicial protection afforded to individuals.

There are also other limits to the ECJ's jurisdiction. It may not, for example, review the validity of any police operations or measures taken by a member state relating to the safeguarding of internal security (Article 35(5)). This has led Arnull to claim that the provision is 'iniquitous', designed to weaken judicial security and pose a serious threat to the uniform application of the law. Such matters are to be dealt with by national courts or the European Court of Human Rights in Strasbourg. The ECJ also cannot act without the Commission or one of the member states asking it to do so. By implication, the treaty seems to allow the possibility that a non-participating state could bring an action, although this seems unlikely. Also, where disputes arise between member states regarding the interpretation or application of measures adopted under Pillar III, the matter is first referred to the Council. Only if the Council fails to resolve the issue can the ECJ issue a ruling according to Article 35(7). Finally, looking momentarily to relevant provisions outside Title VI, the ECJ's competence to rule on the respect for human rights does not cover actions of the member states, just those of the institutions (see Article 46(d) TEU). The ECJ has, however, full jurisdiction to review the legality of ordinary decisions.

The next few articles largely deal with the involvement of other institutional actors. *Article 36* (ex K.4(1–2)) restates the role of the old K.4, now known as the Article 36 Committee, the pendant to the Political and Security Committee in the CFSP pillar. Since Maastricht this can now share in drafting as well as advising. As previously, the Commission is described as being fully associated with the pillar's work, a point underlined by the reference to Article 18 TEU in *Article 37* (ex K.5). It also gains limited rights of judicial and legislative initiative. As for the Council presidency, Article 37 also provides it with a role in representing the Union, as appropriate, in international fora. In these, in line with CFSP provisions, the member states are to defend common positions. This paves the way for a formal recognition via *Article 38* of the right of the presidency and the Council to negotiate international agreements in the area of police and judicial co-operation in criminal matters as provided in the second pillar.

Where the EP is concerned there is still only a limited consultative role for it in Pillar III. Thus it has the right to be consulted before legislation is actually passed and to be kept regularly informed of discussions within the Council and is required to hold an annual debate on the progress made within the pillar by *Article 39(2–3)* (ex K.6). However, this consultation is mandatory and not merely a voluntary matter of information. The TA did, however, upgrade the position of the EP by obliging the Council to consult it before adopting specific measures. Previously, the EP had simply been consulted on the 'principal activities' of JHA co-operation. Consultation covers decisions, framework decisions, conventions and the use of the *passerelle* in Article 42. Still, the EP remains a peripheral actor in Pillar III co-operation. For example, after being consulted the EP must issue its opinion within a time limit. Failure to do so leaves the Council free to proceed, so the EP cannot delay provisions which it does not like. Equally, consultation does not extend to common positions. It does, however, take place where closer co-operation under the new Article 40 is concerned, the EP seeing its role increase from simple notification at Amsterdam, to formal consultation at Nice (see Article 40a(2)).

The EP cannot, though, bring cases before the ECJ. That said, by making it the norm via *Article 41* (ex K.8) that operational, as well as administrative, expenditure concerning

PJCCM be charged to the EC budget, the TA did provide the EP with an additional opportunity to exert influence. The Council has to make a deliberate decision if it wishes to depart from this mode of financing. All the same, democratic control over Pillar III activities through the EP remains weak. That the TA made some limited concessions to national parliaments, as in Article 42, hardly changed the situation.

Yet although the EP's powers with regard to PJCCM remain weak, especially after Nice, the changes brought about by the TA do represent overall a partial communitarizing of the EU's second inter-governmental pillar. Hence, Fennelly has gone so far as to suggest that the TA brought about 'a significant shift to harmony between the two Treaties'. Such a shift could be followed by further communitarization, although this was not really the case at Nice unless the references to Eurojust and the Judicial Network are taken as being essentially supra-national. The *passerelle* clause in *Article 42* (ex K.9) allows the Council, acting unanimously and having consulted the EP, to shift PJCCM matters into Title IV of the TEC. The involvement of the EP was new at Amsterdam.

Although many expected the *passerelle* to be abolished, given that it had never been used, it was given a new lease of life at Amsterdam and was left in place at Nice. This facility and the precedent established by the TA suggest that the harmony between the treaties may be a prelude to an eventual further whittling down of the pillar, perhaps even to an eventual merger, always assuming there would be consensus on such moves. Indeed, Collins' view of the third pillar is that it has become 'a kind of laboratory for co-operation between member states'.

That said, the TA also enhanced links between the EU's two inter-governmental pillars. As already noted, certain CFSP mechanisms (Articles 18 and 19 TEU) are to be used to defend common positions in international fora (Article 37 TEU). In addition, PJCCM measures may be included in agreements concluded under the CFSP pillar with non-member states or international organizations (Article 38 TEU). However, Declaration No. 4 TA again makes it clear that such agreements cannot involve any transfer of power to the Union. So, although Amsterdam's partial communitarization of Pillar III may be welcomed by those keen to see more supra-national policy-making in the EU, inter-governmentalism is still strong.

The one remaining element of the title, dealing with enhanced co-operation, seems a trifle out of place at this point, rather as do the new clauses in Title V. None the less, it is significant after Nice which updated the element. At Amsterdam there had only been a single very long article. This laid down conditions for flexibility in the pillar, established both a procedure for invoking it and an appeal to the European Council against doing so, rules for late entry, and relationships with Title VII on 'closer co-operation'.

Nice, as part of its general spring-cleaning of flexibility, replaced this with three articles: a revised and shorter 40, 40a and 40b. The new *Article 40* begins by condensing paragraph 1 of its predecessor (ex K.7) making it clear that enhanced co-operation can only be undertaken in order to speed up the creation of the area of freedom, security and justice and the other aims of the title. Equally it must not undermine the EC. Its second and third paragraphs repeat the old paragraph 4 setting out first the relationship of police and judicial enhanced co-operation to the rest of Titles VI and VII and then what the authority of the ECJ actually is.

Article 40a also uses some of the wording of the previous article in order to set out a clearer procedure for actually starting an experiment in enhanced co-operation. This involves an application to the Commission which can set the wheels in motion. However, if the latter does not wish to proceed with the idea itself, all it can do is tell the aggrieved states. A minimum of eight states – as opposed to a majority before – can still go ahead, assuming that they can muster a qualified majority in the Council and have consulted the EP. The EP has to be consulted but obviously cannot block a move of which it disapproves.

Whereas in the previous version a state could, assuming there was a majority willing to allow this, invoke a kind of Luxembourg compromise arrangement and get the matter referred up to the European Council where it could veto the idea, the Nice variant replaces this with what appears to be a delaying mechanism. At the behest of the UK it is now open to a state, unhappy with the example of enhanced co-operation envisaged, to get it referred to the European Council. Only after the matter has been 'raised' in the latter may the Council proceed. Given that the European Council has no formal agenda, this suggests there has to be a discussion. However, there is no requirement for a decision and the text does not encourage any changes to the proposed joint venture. None the less, we must wonder whether, should the summit either express strong reservations about the principle or recommend alterations, the Council would actually persevere with its original intentions. As at a number of other points in the Nice changes, the text says only that the Council 'may' go ahead despite the reference, not that it must. Informally, if not legally, the UK view that this remains a brake could well prove correct. Certainly the wording does not, as others have suggested, clearly establish an automatic right to proceed.

Finally, *Article 40b* takes over paragraph 3 of the Amsterdam Article 40 to establish a mechanism for late entrants to an enhanced co-operation activity. The Commission, rather than the Council as in Pillar II, can suggest specific conditions to help incorporate the new entrant. However, the Council now seems free to disregard these with a clearer conscience than under the Amsterdam rules. Apart from this, the resulting text is almost identical to that laid down in Article 27e TEU although the voting procedure is not mentioned here as it is in Title V. But, as before, the last line of the article makes it clear that the rules laid down in Title VII take precedence although this merely ratifies the provisions of Article 40b.

What Nice has done, therefore, is to reduce the provisions on enhanced co-operation within the pillar to something more procedural than before. There are general requirements deriving from Title VII and mechanisms for starting and joining an activity. Reference to the Schengen protocol has been excised and duplication of the conditions has been largely eliminated. Although all this is logical enough we might query the decision to divide the provisions into three separate articles. Admittedly this avoids too long an article but it both forces an unnecessary change in the numbering of the TEU and gives the impression that there is more than one code of flexible practice. The changes made are also hard to read in terms of the balance of inter-governmentalism and supra-nationalism since they point in several directions.

TITLE VI

PROVISIONS ON POLICE AND JUDICIAL CO-OPERATION IN CRIMINAL MATTERS

Article 29 (drawing on ex K.1)

Without prejudice to the powers of the European Community, the Union's objective shall be to provide citizens with a high level of safety within an area of freedom, security and justice by developing common action among the Member States in the fields of police and judicial co-operation in criminal matters and by preventing and combating racism and xenophobia.

That objective shall be achieved by *preventing and combating crime, organised or otherwise, in particular terrorism,* trafficking in persons and offences against children, *illicit drug trafficking* and illicit arms trafficking, corruption *and fraud, through:*

– *closer co-operation between police forces, customs authorities* and other competent authorities in the Member States, *both directly and through the European Police Office (Europol),* in accordance with the provisions of Articles 30 and 32;
– *closer co-operation between judicial* and other competent authorities of the Member States including co-operation through the European Judicial Co-operation Unit ('Eurojust'), in accordance with the provisions of Articles 31 and 32;
– approximation, where necessary, of rules on criminal matters in the Member States, in accordance with the provisions of Article 31(e).

Article 30 (new – TA)

1. Common action in the field of police co-operation shall include:
(a) operational co-operation between the competent authorities, including the police, customs and other specialised law enforcement services of the Member States in relation to the prevention, detection and investigation of criminal offences;
(b) the collection, storage, processing, analysis and exchange of relevant information, including information held by law enforcement services on reports on suspicious financial transactions, in particular through Europol, subject to appropriate provisions on the protection of personal data;
(c) co-operation and joint initiatives in training, the exchange of liaison officers, secondments, the use of equipment, and forensic research;
(d) the common evaluation of particular investigative techniques in relation to the detection of serious forms of organised crime.

2. The Council shall promote co-operation through Europol and shall in particular, within a period of five years after the date of entry into force of the Treaty of Amsterdam:
(a) enable Europol to facilitate and support the preparation, and to encourage the co-ordination and carrying out, of specific investigative actions by the competent authorities of the Member States, including operational actions of joint teams comprising representatives of Europol in a support capacity;
(b) adopt measures allowing Europol to ask the competent authorities of the Member States to conduct and co-ordinate their investigations in specific cases and to develop specific expertise which may be put at the disposal of Member States to assist them in investigating cases of organised crime;
(c) promote liaison arrangements between prosecuting/investigating officials specialising in the fight against organised crime in close co-operation with Europol;
(d) establish a research, documentation and statistical network on cross-border crime.

Article 31 (new – TA)

1. Common action on judicial co-operation in criminal matters shall include:
(a) facilitating and accelerating co-operation between competent ministries and judicial or equivalent authorities of the Member States, including, where appropriate, co-operation through Eurojust, in relation to proceedings and the enforcement of decisions;
(b) facilitating extradition between Member States;
(c) ensuring compatibility in rules applicable in the Member States, as may be necessary to improve such co-operation;
(d) preventing conflicts of jurisdiction between Member States;
(e) progressively adopting measures establishing minimum rules relating to the constituent elements of criminal acts and to penalties in the fields of organised crime, terrorism and illicit drug trafficking.

2. The Council shall encourage co-operation through Eurojust by:
(a) enabling Eurojust to facilitate proper co-ordination between Member States' national prosecuting authorities;
(b) promoting support by Eurojust for criminal investigations in cases of serious cross-border crime, particularly in the case of organised crime, taking account, in particular, of analyses carried out by Europol;
(c) facilitating close co-operation between Eurojust and the European Judicial Network, particularly, in order to facilitate the execution of letters rogatory and the implementation of extradition requests.

Article 32 (new – TA)

The Council shall lay down the conditions and limitations under which the competent authorities referred to in Articles 30 and 31 may operate in the territory of another Member State in liaison and in agreement with the authorities of that State.

Article 33 (ex K.2(2))

This Title shall not affect the exercise of the responsibilities incumbent upon Member States with regard to the maintenance of law and order and the safeguarding of internal security.

Article 34 (ex K.3 and K.4(3))

1. In the areas referred to in this Title, Member States shall inform and consult one another within the Council with a view to co-ordinating their action. To that end, they shall establish collaboration between the relevant departments of their administrations.

2. The Council **shall take measures** *and promote co-operation*, using the appropriate form and procedures **as set out in this Title,** contributing to the pursuit of the objectives of the Union. *To that end, acting unanimously on the initiative of any Member State or of the Commission, the Council may:*
(a) adopt common positions defining the approach of the Union to a particular matter;
(b) adopt framework decisions for the purpose of approximation of the laws and regulations of the Member States. Framework decisions shall be binding upon the Member States as to the result to be achieved but shall leave to the national

authorities the choice of form and methods. They shall not entail direct effect;

(c) adopt decisions for any other purpose consistent with the objectives of this Title, excluding any approximation of the laws and regulations of the Member States. These decisions shall be binding and shall not entail direct effect; the Council, acting by a qualified majority, shall adopt measures necessary to implement those decisions at the level of the Union;

(d) establish conventions which it shall recommend to the Member States for adoption in accordance with their respective constitutional requirements. Member States shall begin the procedures applicable within a time limit to be set by the Council.

Unless they provide otherwise, conventions shall, once adopted by at least half of the Member States, enter into force for those Member States. Measures implementing conventions shall be adopted within the Council by a majority of two-thirds of the Contracting Parties.

3. Where the Council is required to act by a qualified majority, the votes of its members shall be weighted as laid down in Article 205(2) of the Treaty establishing the European Community, and for their adoption acts of the Council shall require at least 62 votes in favour, cast by at least 10 members.

4. *For procedural questions, the Council shall act* by a majority of its members.

Article 35 (new – TA)

1. The Court of Justice of the European Communities shall have jurisdiction, subject to the conditions laid down in this Article, to give preliminary rulings on the validity and interpretation of framework decisions, and decisions on the interpretation of conventions established under this Title and on the validity and interpretation of the measures implementing them.

2. By a declaration made at the time of signature of the Treaty of Amsterdam or at any time thereafter, any Member State shall be able to accept the jurisdiction of the Court of Justice to give preliminary rulings as specified in paragraph 1.

3. A Member State making a declaration pursuant to paragraph 2 shall specify that either:

(a) any court or tribunal of that State against whose decisions there is no judicial remedy under national law may request the Court of Justice to give a preliminary ruling on a question raised in a case pending before it and concerning the validity or interpretation of an act referred to in paragraph 1 if that court or tribunal considers that a decision on the question is necessary to enable it to give judgment, or

(b) any court or tribunal of that State may request the Court of Justice to give a preliminary ruling on a question raised in a case pending before it and concerning the validity or interpretation of an act referred to in paragraph 1 if that court or tribunal considers that a decision on the question is necessary to enable it to give judgment.

4. Any Member State, whether or not it has made a declaration pursuant to paragraph 2, shall be entitled to submit statements of case or written observations to the Court in cases which arise under paragraph 1.

5. The Court of Justice shall have no jurisdiction to review the validity or proportionality of operations carried out by the police or other law enforcement services of a Member State or the exercise of the responsibilities incumbent

upon Member States with regard to the maintenance of law and order and the safeguarding of internal security.

6. The Court of Justice shall have jurisdiction to review the legality of framework decisions and decisions in actions brought by a Member State or the Commission on grounds of lack of competence, infringement of an essential procedural requirement, infringement of this Treaty or of any rule of law relating to its application, or misuse of powers. The proceedings provided for in this paragraph shall be instituted within two months of the publication of the measure.

7. The Court of Justice shall have jurisdiction to rule on any dispute between Member States regarding the interpretation or the application of acts adopted under Article 34(2) whenever such dispute cannot be settled by the Council within six months of its being referred to the Council by one of its members. The Court shall also have jurisdiction to rule on any dispute between Member States and the Commission regarding the interpretation or the application of conventions established under Article 34(2)(d).

Article 36 (ex K.4(1–2))

1. A Co-ordinating Committee shall be set up consisting of senior officials. In addition to its co-ordinating role, it shall be the task of the Committee to:
– give opinions for the attention of the Council, either at the Council's request or on its own initiative;
– contribute, without prejudice to Article 207 of the Treaty establishing the European Community, to the preparation of the Council's discussions in the areas referred to in Article 29.

2. The Commission shall be fully associated with the work in the areas referred to in this Title.

Article 37 (ex K.5)

Within international organisations and at international conferences in which they take part, Member States shall defend the common positions adopted under the provisions of this Title.
Articles 18 and 19 shall apply as appropriate to matters falling under this Title.

Article 38 (new – TA)

Agreements referred to in Article 24 may cover matters falling under this Title.

Article 39 (ex K.6)

1. The Council shall consult the European Parliament before adopting any measure referred to in Article 34(2)(b), (c) and (d). The European Parliament shall deliver its opinion within a time-limit which the Council may lay down, which shall not be less than three months. In the absence of an opinion within that time-limit, the Council may act.

2. The Presidency and the Commission shall regularly inform the European Parliament of discussions in the areas covered by this Title.

3. The European Parliament may ask questions of the Council or make recommendations to it. Each year, it shall hold a debate on the progress made in the areas referred to in this Title.

Article 40 (new – TA)

1. **Enhanced** *co-operation in any of the areas referred to in this Title shall have the aim of enabling the Union to develop more rapidly into an area of freedom, security and justice, while respecting the powers of the European Community and the objectives laid down in this Title.*

2. Articles 29 to 39 and Articles 40a to 41 shall apply to the enhanced co-operation provided for by this Article, save as otherwise provided in Article 40a **and in Articles 43 to 45.**

3. *The provisions of the Treaty establishing the European Community concerning the powers of the Court of Justice and the exercise of those powers shall apply to this Article* **and to Articles 40a and 40b.**

Article 40a (new – TN)

1. *Member States which intend to establish* **enhanced** *co-operation between themselves* **under Article 40 shall address a request to the Commission, which may submit a proposal to the Council to that effect. In the event of the Commission not submitting a proposal, it shall inform the Member States concerned of the reasons for not doing so. Those Member States may then submit an initiative to the Council designed to obtain authorisation for the enhanced co-operation concerned.**

2. *The authorisation referred to in paragraph 1 shall be granted,* **in compliance with Articles 43 to 45,** *by the Council, acting by a qualified majority,* **on a proposal from the Commission or on the initiative of at least eight Member States, and after consulting the European Parliament.** *The votes of the members of the Council shall be weighted in accordance with Article 205(2) of the Treaty establishing the European Community.*

A member of the Council may request that the matter be referred to the European Council. After that matter has been raised before the European Council, the Council may act in accordance with the first subparagraph of this paragraph.

Article 40b (new – TN)

Any Member State which wishes to participate in **enhanced** *co-operation established in accordance with* **Article 40a** *shall notify its intention to the Council and to the Commission, which shall give an opinion to the Council within three months of the date of receipt of that notification, possibly accompanied by a recommendation for such specific arrangements as it may deem necessary for that Member State to become a party to the co-operation in question. The Council shall take a decision on the request within four months of the date of receipt of that notification. The decision shall be deemed to be taken unless the Council, acting by a qualified majority within the same period, decides to hold it in abeyance; in that case, the Council shall state the reasons for its decision and set a deadline for re-examining it.*

For the purposes of this Article, the Council shall act under the conditions set out in **Article 44(1).**

Article 41 (ex K.8)

1. *Articles 189, 190, 195, 196 to 199, 203, 204, 205(3), 206 to 209, 213 to 219, 255 and 290 of the Treaty establishing the European Community shall apply to the provisions relating to the areas referred to in this Title.*

2. Administrative expenditure which the provisions relating to the areas referred to in this Title entail for the institutions shall be charged to the budget of the European Communities.

3. *Operational expenditure to which the implementation of those provisions gives rise* **shall also be charged** to the budget of the European Communities, **except where the Council acting unanimously decides otherwise. In cases where expenditure is not charged to the budget of the European Communities it shall be charged to the Member States in accordance with the gross national product scale, unless the Council acting unanimously decides otherwise.**

4. *The budgetary procedure laid down in the Treaty establishing the European Community shall apply to the expenditure charged to the budget of the European Communities.*

Article 42 (ex K.9)

The Council, acting unanimously on the initiative of the Commission or a Member State, **and after consulting the European Parliament,** may decide *that action in areas referred to in Article 29 shall fall under* **Title IV** *of the Treaty establishing the European Community*, and at the same time determine the relevant voting conditions relating to it. It shall recommend the Member States to adopt that decision in accordance with their respective constitutional requirements.

vii Closer and Enhanced Co-operation

The one major structural change to the TEU introduced by the Treaty of Amsterdam was the addition of a new Title VII. This dealt with what had been known as 'flexibility' but which, come October 1997, was more formally described as 'closer co-operation'. This was felt to be a better description of what was intended. Three years or so later Nice changed the heading yet again, to 'enhanced co-operation' thus giving it more of an integrationist feel.

The name was initially changed because 'flexibility' was felt to be a vague and ill-defined term which covered all kinds of what has been called 'differentiated integration'. By this is meant a situation in which member states do not all take part in all aspects of formal European interaction. They can thus stand aloof permanently, delay their participation, go further than others or move at a different speed. And they can, as Stubb has pointed out, do this in different areas, by different legal means and at different times. What emerged from Amsterdam in October 1997 was one specific institutionalized form by which some states could embark on tighter and deeper forms of policy and political collaboration within the overall EU framework. By then too the title's three articles ceased to be an appendage to the K series of Pillar III and were given independent status by renumbering.

For many observers 'closer co-operation' was one of Amsterdam's few significant innovations. Its newness, however, was relative. What Amsterdam did, in fact, was to give it an institutionalized and judicial form. As Shaw remarks, it was not a separate pillar as such but an overarching framework for the development of closer co-operation. Yet, the irony is that, once agreed, it was not used. The reason for this is usually ascribed both to the rigidity and complexity of the conditions laid down for its implementation and to changing political conditions. Indeed, for some, the whole point had been to make sure that the idea was inoperable. For others, it was the triumph of political enthusiasm over common sense whether because the idea itself is unworkable or because, as Michael Spicer MP wrongly claimed, it amounted to 'the decommissioning of the national veto'.

Whatever the reason, although the idea often worried believers in a strict adherence to the Community method, it was a major issue on the agenda of the 2000 IGC as some states sought to make it more flexible, in the best senses of the word, and user-friendly. In the event, Nice almost completely rewrote the provisions of the title, linking them to changes not only in the two inter-governmental pillars but to alterations in the TEC. At the same time the title was given its new heading in an attempt to give the concept a more positive and pro-integration spin. This reflected underlying doubts about the meaning and virtues of the idea despite its longish history.

Although it is in the treaty and follows normal EU institutional processes, the concept of enhanced co-operation is, of course, an exceptionally political one. Not surprisingly, a good deal of ink has been spilt over what it means – which is not really made clear even after the Nice changes – and why it is there. To some extent, this is because the motives behind it were somewhat contradictory. It was also because it has taken many forms.

The idea of closer or enhanced co-operation goes back a long way. Something like it had been known in practice through similar processes such as the WEU, Schengen, and various kinds of opt-outs which meant that not all states were doing everything mentioned in the treaties. Similar possibilities have been in the treaties from the beginning since Article 306 (ex 233) TEC authorizes additional action by the Benelux countries where Community provision fails to measure up to their common objectives. More general ideas about differentiated integration were then floated by Willy Brandt and Leo Tindemans in the mid-1970s, leading to considerable theoretical debate.

More practical steps were then taken by the SEA and the TEU. The former, under Article 95(4) (ex 100a(4)) TEC, allowed member states to maintain justified additional levels of protection in areas subject to EC-wide harmonization. The latter went beyond this to allow not just opt-outs from but selective participation in EMU, which implied that there would be different monetary and legal systems within the Union. And while in the UK many saw the TEU as a move towards centralization, for others it represented a brutal recognition of diversity, reflecting the fact that many of the new policy areas have a history of selective involvement, as Missiroli observes.

This caused great concern among Community lawyers like Curtin who became very afraid of the possibilities of fragmentation. They felt that the whole idea of opt-outs was wrong and that the only way to prevent things getting out of hand was to constitutionalize, and thus channel, any resort to differentiation. As long as all member states were held within the same framework it would not matter too much if not all had the same rights. To this concern were added other worries in the run-up to Amsterdam. One was the likely impact of eastwards enlargement which could bring in states unable to meet all the requirements of the *acquis*. Another was the dissatisfaction with the way the two inter-governmental pillars had worked, which meant that little progress was made in making the Union an international force or a body which could collaborate effectively against societal threats. A third concern was that if only a few countries qualified for

EMU, they would need to be able to make special arrangements to hold Euroland together since the TEC framework would not be able to do this.

The third and most important concern came from the growing difficulties with the United Kingdom over the Social Chapter, EMU, the role of the ECJ and, especially, BSE. It was this which led the Major government to withdraw co-operation in 1995. Although the experiment was more farce than force, it was seen as something which could not be ignored, as any repetition could plunge the Union into inertia. One way of getting round this was to provide a means of by-passing an awkward state in the future. This led Kohl and Chirac in December 1995 to take up the idea of a 'hard core' Europe floated by Lamers and Schäuble of the CDU in 1994 and suggest that there could be not just a temporary arrangement but a permanent mechanism for some states to go farther and faster. This found some support in the Benelux countries and also in the Commission and EP both of which wanted to preserve the integrity of integration and to prevent any kind of à la carte Europe such as John Major appeared to espouse.

So the idea was taken up by the Turin Council in 1995 and went on to figure largely in the pre-Amsterdam negotiations. There was a good deal of debate about how this should be done, whether through overall 'enabling' clauses or through a series of special arrangements for different cases. There was thus much thought that the third pillar would be an ideal place to experiment whereas there was little enthusiasm for doing so in the CFSP. Even though countries such as Finland and Greece were against, the Irish got the Council Legal Service to draft one general clause and three specific exemplifications for each pillar. Further drafts then went on to decide how many states would be needed to trigger closer co-operation and what the voting arrangements should be.

However, the election of a more amenable UK government in May 1997 meant that the main political imperative for resorting to flexibility disappeared. And one technical justification was also removed by the agreement to merge Schengen into the Union's first and second pillars. None the less, the idea seemed to have developed a momentum of its own and it finished up on the agenda of the Amsterdam summit which dispatched it, according to legend, in under ten minutes. This was enough for Blair to exclude any real enabling clause in the CFSP and to write in the possibility of appealing upwards to the European Council, a 'brake' which foreign ministers had previously rejected. The Labour government in the UK was much less keen on the idea than its predecessors, fearing that flexibility would be used to demote it whereas the Tories claimed to be willing to trade the right for some states to forge ahead with their right to stand aloof from new rules. However, some more hostile elements of the party were more impressed by the threat implicit in letting others move to a more federal solution.

Unease in other quarters, including the Iberians and the institutions, ensured that what emerged was a very carefully defined set of enabling procedures divided into three articles: tight conditions, decision-making and parliamentary involvement. The idea is also trailed in earlier titles of the post-Amsterdam TEU, for instance in Article 17(4) in the CFSP. In other words, as Areilza said, the Amsterdam title was less a matter of principle than a set of supposedly practical procedures to deal with a possible political problem. The very term 'flexibility' went out the window as a result since, as Shaw says, it was felt to be too vague, too reminiscent of an à la carte Europe and too closely linked again to some of the wilder and more threatening ideas which had been circulating in the mid-90s. However, this did not completely end the terminological confusion about situations in which not all states go as far, as fast or in the same direction, to which Ehlermann and Stubb have drawn our attention.

In any case, the TA did not deliver real 'closer co-operation', even though the political problems which helped to produce the title had not gone away. As a result, the idea of revising what was seen as 'inflexible flexibility' emerged as an important theme in the 2000 IGC, even though initially a majority of member states opposed amendment. Faced with the prospects of renewed dissidence and large-scale expansion the argument was put forward that if the treaty-based process was not reformed then closer co-operation would start up outside the treaties, with unforeseeable effects. The Commission's Wise Men thus proposed relaxing the brake which allowed a state opposing closer co-operation to appeal up to the European Council. Others wanted to reduce the high threshold of states needed to trigger experiments and others still wanted to make the conditions less onerous. However, the UK, Finnish and Greek governments all expressed reservations, especially as the existing rules had not been used and no areas where it might be used had been identified. Conversely, the Conservative Party in Britain sought to make an overall flexibility clause, which would allow states to decide which rules beyond core SEM regulations they would adopt, a *sine qua non* for accepting any other changes. However, this return to what was actually the practice of the old communist Council for Mutual Economic Assistance (CMEA) had no echo either in the IGC or, when it was reiterated in their 2001 election manifesto, in other states. In any case, were it ever to be acted on it would constitute such a fundamental change to the nature of the Union that it could not be left in Title VII. It would require a major reworking of the preamble and Articles 3 and 6 of the TEU at the very least.

In fact, with the Benelux countries and Italy taking up this more limited view of flexibility, a reluctant Portuguese presidency held preliminary discussions at Sintra in mid-April 2000. Although this failed to suggest where revised proposals might be used, a certain momentum built up, encouraged by the linked ideas being floated by Joschka Fischer and Jacques Chirac about the long-term future of the Union which brought back to life all the various models of European integration identified by Junge. This led to the Portuguese recommending further consideration to the heads of government. Hence the Feira summit agreed that the question should be added to the IGC agenda but coupled this with the statement that any changes must respect cohesion and solidarity inside the Union.

Under the French a good deal of progress was made, even though, as Galloway notes, the IGC found itself in 'the realms of virtual reality', considering in a somewhat surreal manner treaty amendments to provisions which had never been used and considering situations which could not be clearly identified. The French started by asking general questions about conditions and the virtues of a uniform procedure across the pillars, this being a matter of pushing integration further. The last reflected concern about possible blockages in a wider Union. All this garnered reasonable support with the UK at one time, supported by Austria, being willing to move quite a long way on flexibility in the second pillar. This led the Spanish to propose an extension to the CFSP where constructive abstention had not proved helpful. Guidelines based on tailoring the procedures to the specific needs of different sectors were discussed in late August 2000. The idea was then given a major fillip in early October by a paper from the Germans and Italians arguing not for an à la carte EU but for a normal mechanism to help integration go further in a larger Union by removing the emergency brake, easing the trigger mechanism and increasing the role of the Commission. This was supported by a wordy text.

By late November a somewhat more circumspect and concise text had emerged, thanks to the Council Secretariat. This was to be adopted almost unchanged at Nice. By then the UK government had overcome its resistance to the idea. One addition which did gain acceptance was the idea that acts taken under enhanced co-operation should not become part of the *acquis*. None the less, there was a coherent package, especially in the initial version of the treaty.

It sits a little oddly here, given that the TEU has already set out conditions and procedures for flexibility in the earlier inter-governmental pillars. Equally, further provisions appear at Articles 11 and 11a TEC, but these provide only for specific operating procedures for the TEC. Generally, in fact, activating any form of enhanced co-operation will have to conform with the provisions set out in Title VII covering general conditions, decision-making rules and guarantees on financial and other effects. The clauses can be regarded as horizontal in that they apply across the whole Union. Observers will also have to be remembered in understanding the overall effect of the new flexibility provisions. They could mean that the whole concept remains too difficult to use.

What we have in Title VII to provide these overall guidelines are a new heading and six articles. The change in the title was inserted so as to signify that this was not a kind of opt-out, but something more positive, a means of allowing a vanguard of states to move forward, allowing others to join them later. The six articles compare to three at Amsterdam. Half of the former no longer have simple numbers but have acquired lower-case letter suffixes.

Article 43, as amended by Nice, starts not by defining what is meant by enhanced co-operation and why, logical though this would have been, but with a statement making the structures of the Union and Community available to those states who – apparently as an act of will – intend to embark on co-operation dependent on a range of conditions. Most of these, as Weatherill notes, loom forbiddingly. They are essentially negative 'keep off the grass' conditions: not offending the *acquis*, cohesion, free trade, the Internal Market, the powers of the Union, the rights of non-participating states, the Schengen provisions and the treaties, a formidable list which whittles down the possible areas for experiment. It omits only two of the original Amsterdam conditions – compliance with Articles 11 TEC and 40 TEU and use only as a last resort – and the second of these is simply relocated. Indeed, Nice is more restrictive than Amsterdam in that firstly indent (b) previously referred to the principles of the treaties, which created potential 'wriggle room', and secondly there is now, at (d), a self-denying ordinance which prevents any experiments where the Union has sole competence. The whole of the TEC and TEU apparently now have to be observed while experiments can only take place in grey areas of shared competence. All this is not merely limiting but makes the concept of enhanced co-operation as such harder to grasp.

At the same time enhanced co-operation has to demonstrate other more positive virtues: that it is in line with the objectives of the Union and Community (thus justifying the new heading of the title), involves at least eight states and is open to all states. The first of these is now wider than it was before since Amsterdam required closer co-operation only to respect Union objectives. The aim of this, which implies a cross-reference to objectives as defined in the preambles and Article 2 TEU and Articles 2 and 3 TEC, was clearly to prevent any kind of backsliding. In other words those states which wish to try enhancing co-operation will presumably have to show that doing so will take the Union deeper. Where the numerical requirement is concerned this is simpler and will in an enlarged EU be less constraining than the previous demand that a majority of states should be on board. By the time the EU reaches the fullest enlargement envisaged at Nice this would mean an unrealistic 14. The need to be open, cross-referenced to the idea of enhanced co-operation being a last resort, is a major theme of the title. The assumption seems to be that timing is all. Some states, possibly the present ones, will be ready earlier than latecomers, and can then prepare the next stage of integration for them, free from the restraints of treaty change.

However, the requirement that such experiments should only be tried as 'a last resort' is taken out of Article 43 and made a separate new *Article 43a*, thereby giving it more emphasis. This is particularly so given the Italo-German pressure to remove the reference and make enhanced co-operation a normal procedure. Moreover, such an assessment cannot be simply a whim. It has to be agreed by the Council that not merely has the aim of the experiment not been achieved by normal procedures, which could imply that an attempt has been made, exhausting the normal remedies, but that it is unlikely to be achieved in the foreseeable future, perhaps because one state did not like the idea. This is not wholly objective but it does set up clearer tests than did Amsterdam. But they are probably more rigorous in terms of time and benchmarks.

Article 43b, another new insertion, then makes it clear that there can be no cronyism either when an experiment is launched or later. Any state, even a would-be wrecker, can join at the start. However, once the experiment is up and running, a latecomer has to agree to be bound by its rules even though it had not helped to make them, in true Community fashion. The reservations about openness inserted at Amsterdam have been withdrawn. At the same time there is an obligation on the first-wave states and the Commission to encourage others to join. Here too it rather looks as if the assumption is that enhanced co-operation is really a means of starting a general project about which one or two states have doubts which may be overcome once it becomes clear that the sky has not fallen in.

None the less, this insistence on conditions and openness shows that there were real doubts about the idea. Had this not been so then these two elements could have been made paragraphs 2 and 3 of Article 43, perhaps with indent (j) and possibly (h) added to paragraph 3. This would have avoided a change to the consolidated renumbering. However, it would not have given the points quite so much stress, which is presumably why it was done.

Article 44 (ex K.16) then moves on to decision-making, but as it does so it implies that the concept of enhanced co-operation had been positively described in Article 43. It makes it clear that the specific rules laid down elsewhere in the treaties have to be observed, albeit with the exclusion of representatives of non-participating states from voting, notably when unanimity is required. Such ministers can take part in the debates, however, in line with the principles laid down in Articles 43a and 43b. This is also likely to have been one of the reasons for the addition of the final separate subparagraph of paragraph 1, making it clear that the results of such decision-making cannot be part of the *acquis*. This minimizes the extent of exclusion but argues against the idea of enhanced co-operation as something leading to EU-wide deepening.

Paragraph 2 is then taken over from the old Article 43 but with the addition of a statement that such acts are binding on those states that sign up to them. In other words, they are not to play at 'enhanced co-operation' or pay it mere lip service. The warning to other states not to obstruct the experiment is repeated unchanged. This suggests that, at Amsterdam, there was already some awareness of possible difficulties arising from enhanced co-operation.

This also appears to have been the case at Nice, given the amended *Article 45* which seems to hint at a possibility of fragmentation. This replaced an older clause requiring regular reports to the EP. It now makes the Council and Commission jointly responsible for ensuring that there is consistency between joint ventures and Union and Community policies. The treaty also spells out that they have to co-operate in doing this, suggesting that the Commission may have to be more involved, notably in monitoring joint ventures, than has previously been suggested.

Before the treaty gets to this, however, it has upgraded the old paragraph 2 of Article 44 to a separate *Article 44a* dealing with costs. Basically, expenditure from the joint venture is borne by the participating states. However, the Council can, unanimously, decide otherwise. And Nice added a phrase to make it clear that all members of the Council, and not just those from participating states, would have to be involved in the decision. Equally, the EP now has to be consulted, though nothing is said about whether all MEPs or only those from participating countries can discuss the matter. Both the addition and the creation of a new article, doing further damage to the clarity of the renumbering, would seem to testify to the need to reinforce the inclusiveness and the controls of the whole procedure.

All in all, despite the fact that the procedures were negotiated as a whole, a close reading of the text does not substantiate the generally held belief that this was one of Nice's better products. It shows that while the concept has been clarified, extended, notably to the CFSP where many had felt it would be most useful, the emergency brake eased, the role of the institutions fine-tuned and the critical mass necessary reduced, it is still subject to a whole string of conditions. Most notably, it cannot be a regular mechanism. It has to be exceptional, and shown to be so. And there are a whole range of procedural niceties to be observed. In other words, it seems to be something of a nuclear option when all else fails, if not a marketing device stimulated by the Fischer–Chirac debate. It needs a political crisis to justify it. At the same time, it clearly rests on conflicting strategies and political ambitions. So it is hardly surprising that it remains a very ill-defined concept.

Although some have feared it would be used too quickly (and possibly rashly so as to push forward integration at the expense of reticent member states and to get round the rigidities of the post-Nice QMV arrangements), this does not seem very likely. It may be a pragmatic way of reconciling disagreements without the rigidities of opt-outs, as Wessels and Shaw have argued, but there is a real possibility that it could remain a white elephant. This reflects the doubts in the EP, in some candidate countries such as Poland and of some Eurosceptics. For the latter it can be a way of ratcheting up integration and of rolling back the frontiers of Brussels interventionism as many UK Conservatives wish. But the remaining restrictions suggest that it will not become an accepted general strategy and a first step towards a permanent asymmetric, multi-perspectival polity.

Even if it is used, critics have rightly pointed out that it may raise problems of solidarity in the Union. Nor would it necessarily bring the Union closer to the people. And it would do little for transparency. The same, of course, might be said of the TEU's many protocols.

TITLE VII

PROVISIONS ON ENHANCED CO-OPERATION.

Article 43 (new – TA)

Member States which intend to establish enhanced co-operation between themselves may make use of the institutions, procedures and mechanisms laid down by this Treaty and by the Treaty establishing the European Community provided that the proposed co-operation:

(a) is aimed at furthering the objectives of the Union and of the Community, at protecting and serving *their* interests and at reinforcing their process of integration;

(b) respects *the said Treaties* and the single institutional framework of the Union;

(c) respects the *acquis communautaire* and the measures adopted under the other provisions of the said Treaties;

(d) remains within the limits of the powers of the Union or of the Community and does not concern the areas which fall within the exclusive competence of the Community;

(e) does not undermine the internal market as defined in Article 14(2) of the Treaty establishing the European Community, or the economic and social cohesion established in accordance with Title XVII of that Treaty;

(f) does not constitute a barrier to or discrimination in trade between the Member States and does not distort competition between them;

(g) involves a minimum of eight Member States;

(h) respects the competences, rights *and obligations* of those Member States which do not participate therein;

(i) does not affect the provisions of the Protocol integrating the Schengen *acquis* into the framework of the European Union;

(j) is open to all the Member States, in accordance with Article 43b.

Article 43a (new – TN)

Enhanced co-operation may be undertaken only *as a last resort,* when it has been established within the Council that the objectives of such co-operation cannot be attained within a reasonable period by applying the relevant provisions of the Treaties.

Article 43b (new – TN)

When enhanced co-operation is being established, it shall be open to all Member States. It shall also be open to them at any time, in accordance with Articles 27e and 40b of this Treaty and with Article 11a of the Treaty establishing the European Community, subject to compliance with the basic decision and with the decisions taken within that framework. The Commission and the Member States participating in enhanced co-operation shall ensure that as many Member States as possible are encouraged to take part.

Article 44 (new – TA)

1. For the purposes of the adoption of the acts and decisions necessary for the implementation of enhanced co-operation referred to in Article 43, the relevant institutional provisions of this Treaty and of the Treaty establishing the European Community shall apply. However, while all members of the Council shall be able to take part in the deliberations, only those representing Member States participating in enhanced co-operation shall take part in the adoption of decisions. The qualified majority shall be defined as the same proportion of the weighted votes and the same proportion of the number of the Council members concerned as laid down in Article 205(2) of the Treaty establishing the European Community, and in the second and third subparagraphs of Article 23(2) of this Treaty as regards enhanced co-operation established on the basis of Article 27c. Unanimity shall be constituted by only those Council members concerned.

Such acts and decisions shall not form part of the Union *acquis.*

2. *Member States shall apply, as far as they are concerned, the acts and decisions adopted for the implementation of the enhanced co-operation in which they participate.* Such acts and decisions shall be binding only on those Member States which participate in such co-operation and, as appropriate, shall be directly applicable only in those States. *Member States which do not participate*

*in such co-operation shall not impede the implementation thereof by the partici-
pating Member States.*

Article 44a (new – TN)

Expenditure resulting from implementation of **enhanced** *co-operation, other than
administrative costs entailed for the institutions, shall be borne by the participating
Member States, unless* **all members of** *the Council, acting unanimously* **after
consulting the European Parliament,** *decide otherwise.*

Article 45 (new – TA)

The Council and the Commission shall ensure the consistency of activities
undertaken on the basis of this Title and the consistency of such activities with
the policies of the Union and the Community, and shall co-operate to that end.

viii   Final Provisions

This last title of the treaty proper takes us back to the kind of general constitutive
questions raised in the common provisions as part of pulling the Union together. The
purpose of the title was, according to one negotiator, to show that the Union is indeed a
whole. Hence, one of its tasks is to offer further interesting hints about the Union's
nature, mainly in its first four articles. One of these was slightly changed at Nice, which
otherwise left the title alone.

At the same time the title, which changed its number at Amsterdam because of the
insertion of the arrangements for what was then 'closer co-operation', plays a second
role: it arranges for the TEU and the Union itself to come into effect. All treaties have
provisions about amending, applying, ratifying and validating their contents. Those in
the last four articles of the TEU both parallel and draw on those in the TEC.

The first of these two tasks is the more sensitive one. Hence at Maastricht the title went
through a whole series of changes in drafting, with new bits being added, or indeed taken
away in the case of a further reference to a 'federal character', up to the last moment.
This chequered history left a number of uncertainties about the nature of the Union.
These were only partly addressed at Amsterdam, which made only limited changes,
essentially to the judicial status of the TEU. The contribution of Nice was to complicate
this somewhat.

The title's first provision, *Article 46* (ex L), was one of the late additions at Maastricht.
Essentially it is an elaboration on the reference to a single institutional framework in
Article 3 TEU. It does this by largely excluding the ECJ from the two new inter-
governmental pillars and from the common provisions of the Union. In other words, its
jurisdiction is defined by the treaties and not by its own actions. Initially this exclusion
was almost total, meaning that the Court could rule neither on the institutional arrangements of the Union nor directly on the rights of member states and individuals laid down
in Article 6. This was a matter of great concern to many who believe in the importance
of the rule of law in the Union. They did not like the ECJ's exclusion from the inter-
governmental pillars save in questions of finance or where the third pillar *passerelle* was
invoked.

However, since Amsterdam the Court has gained in four ways. To begin with it can now adjudicate on Article 6(2) where acts of the institutions are concerned. This is a symbolic extension of the Court's human rights jurisdiction, especially where the European Convention for the Protection of Human Rights and Fundamental Freedoms is involved. Secondly, it has seen its influence in Title VI extended through the right of states to opt into its orbit where the meaning of conventions and other acts are concerned. And some states did this prior to the TA's ratification. Thirdly, it has gained a voice in considering the legality of authorization of, and accession to, operations involving closer co-operation. These Amsterdam changes have been seen as a significant extension of ECJ authority over the states by some Eurosceptics.

Beyond this, the ECJ retains the right to adjudicate on the final provisions including, perhaps oddly, this listing of the limits on its own powers. The changes do mean therefore that the Union is slightly more caught up in Community law than was the case before despite the implications of Union sovereignty in Article 46. The ECJ also made clear in *Airport Transit Visas* (1998) its view that it has a duty to ensure that acts under the second pillar do not encroach on the Community. All this reflects the ambiguities of the Union, especially those caused by maintaining the EC within the Union but without the power itself to alter its own arrangements. And when Nice demoted indent (e) to (f) and replaced it with a new clause allowing the ECJ to adjudicate on the question of whether due process has been followed in any 'prosecutions' under Article 7, it added to the confusion by offering the ECJ a fourth increase in its jurisdiction. The clause was included in order to reassure member states that the rules would be followed and that irregularities would invalidate any decisions wrongly taken under Article 7. In other words, there is not to be a kangaroo-style judgment such as that which Austria felt it had had imposed on it in 2000.

One other implication of the article is that the Union has the ability, and right, to alter the TEC. This accounts for the insertion at Maastricht of *Article 47* (ex M), which reassures the Community that it will not be subverted by the inter-governmentalism of the other two pillars. However, while the article very clearly upholds the integrity of the constitutive treaties, by virtue of Article 46 TEU the ECJ still has the power, as Lenaerts and van Nuffel note, to pronounce on any institutional or member-state action alleged to constitute an infringement of EC law even if the action is taken under the CFSP or PJCCM pillar. The validity of the constitutive treaties thus remains, save as specified elsewhere.

The same cannot be said for those parts of the Merger Treaty and the Single European Act which are formally repealed in *Article 50* (ex P). The articles of the former, relating to the Council and Commission, which had appeared as *de facto* Treaty of Rome provisions in previous quasi-official versions of the TEC, had already been revised by Article 8 of the TEU. Perhaps the drafters thought they were like Dracula and could only be permanently quietened by a further stake. Much the same is true of the changes made to the SEA which replace the reference to the European Council and wind up EPC. However, the fact that the TEU underwrites the TEC says something about their respective statuses and leaves open the possibility that the Union could, at some stage, change its mind and alter the standing of the Community's founding documents.

Article 48 (ex N) figures logically here since any sensible treaty or constitution must make allowances for revision before it concludes. The present text was largely transferred from Article 236 of the pre-Maastricht TEC which was then repealed. However, Article 48 makes three significant changes. The first is that it now allows for revision of all the founding treaties, including the TEU. So, as we noted above, amendment of the TEC is normally only possible as part of a change to the Union. It is worth noting, however, that certain provisions found in the European Treaties (e.g. Articles 22, 190(4) and 269 TEC,

Article 42 TEU, Article 95 TECSC, and Articles 76, 85 and 90 TEAEC) allow for the procedure in Article 48 to be by-passed. Secondly, the ECB is given a consultative voice on changes relating to EMU provisions in the TEC. Prior to Amsterdam this was not used since the negotiators were desperate not to touch EMU in case it opened a Pandora's box of political change. The ECB was, however, consulted as part of the 2000 IGC and issued its opinion on proposed amendments relating to EMU shortly before the Nice European Council. The third change at Amsterdam was the elimination of the reference to calling a new IGC in 1996, which was out of line with the attempts to tidy up the treaty. This means, of course, that beyond preambular references to 'ever closer union', hints about the evolutive nature of the Union and its objectives have been removed from the treaties, except where Article 17(5) TEU, dealing with defence and the CFSP, is concerned.

The mechanism of revision of the treaties remains strictly inter-governmental. This was queried after 1993 by the European Movement, by the Lamers–Schäuble paper and subsequently by many others. The call was usually for the EP to be given rights to draft treaty amendments or, at least, to give its formal assent to them. This was often linked to demands that the treaties should be replaced by a fully fledged constitution which would demand a different approach to revision. Such demands were, however, passed over in silence by the negotiators in 1996, save to the extent to which they agreed to tidy up the texts. Hence they came back in the run-up to Nice linked to the idea of splitting the treaties into two, a set of basic principles which could only be changed by an IGC and a separate set of policy prescriptions which could be changed more easily. This too was rejected for reasons we explore in Annex 3. However, as discussed in Division V below, Nice was to open the question of treaty revision with its talk, in the Declaration on the Future of the Union (No. 23 TN), of a wide public debate and other ways of carrying things forward.

As it is, in practice the process of revision has already changed somewhat. The TEU gives the impression that amendment comes about somewhat contingent upon when a single state or the Commission has a mind to change things. In reality there has been an increasing tendency for one IGC to mandate another. There were hints of this in the SEA. Then in 1992 there was a formal commitment to holding one in 1996. And, although Amsterdam did not do this directly, the Protocol on the Institutions with the Prospect of Enlargement of the European Union talked of a comprehensive review conference on all existing institutional arrangements, which seems to be an IGC with a slightly different remit. In any event, as we have seen, this process was speeded up and compressed as a result of the pressures of enlargement. Hence the Cologne Council agreed, as a collective act, to call a narrow IGC in 2000. Moreover, even before Nice there was talk, notably from Germany, of having yet another, wider ranging, IGC in 2004. Political horse trading at Nice ensured that this was accepted and a further commitment to a new IGC was made, again rendering somewhat nugatory the provisions of Article 48.

All of this might seem to render the article superfluous. However, without it there would be immense uncertainty about revision procedures and decisions such as those taken at Cologne and Nice might not be possible. The fact that the provisions remain in the treaty and have not been revised in order to bring them into line with actual practice means that some types of treaty change are ruled out. Thus the British Conservative Party's hopes, if elected, of holding an IGC over the weekend of the June 2001 Gothenburg summit would be ruled out, unless the EP was standing by at the same time to consider the idea. Conversely, as the run up to the SEA showed, a simple majority can be enough to enable the Council to deliver its opinion in favour of calling an IGC.

Next comes *Article 49* (ex O). This, in its pre-Amsterdam form, transposed into the TEU the old Article 237 TEC on the accession of new members, as amended by the SEA, which had added the requirement for EP assent. By moving the accession clause into the TEU the negotiators forced new states to accept the inter-governmental pillars and their *acquis* by removing the possibility of their joining the EC alone. Membership of the EC now comes as part of the Union package which, again, says something about the status of the two bodies and their founding treaties. By extension this presumably rules out present member states transferring back from the Union to the EC. However, although the article does not make this clear, new applicants will also have to continue to sign up to Euratom and the ECSC at the same time as they join the Union, assuming that there is enlargement before the TECSC lapses in the summer of 2002. Thereafter they will have to sign up to the EC and Euratom, unless the simplification process envisaged for 2004 leads to the latter being folded into the European Community.

The only change made at Amsterdam to the conditions for application, set out formally in Article 49, was to add a political condition to the geographic condition – that a state be European – for application. Applicant states, through the reference to Article 6(1) TEU, have to respect democracy, freedom, human rights, liberty and the rule of law if they are to be acceptable. Arguably this condition has always existed, implicitly at least, through the call in the TEC's preamble to 'peoples of Europe who share their ideal' to join. The reference to Article 6(1) TEU could be read as implying that these values have to be demonstrated both by conformity with the ECHR and with general practice in the existing member states, something which is open to interpretation in a way which a formal decision by the Council of Europe that a state was in breach of the Convention would not be. Although there is no reference to Article 7 TEU it would seem to follow that this would very much apply to new entrants. And the Charter of Fundamental Rights was not evoked in this context at Nice.

In any case enlargement also needs an *avis* from the Commission, unanimous support in the Council and the backing of presently 314 MEPs, not to mention the endorsement of all national parliaments, always assuming that a referendum was not thought necessary as it was in France in 1972 at the time of the EC's first enlargement. Indeed, in the run-up to Nice fears were expressed that Austria might do this, while an unguarded and supposedly misconstrued remark from Commissioner Verheugen seemed to suggest that Germany ought to vote on enlargement. In the event, Nice did not alter the provisions here either.

The remaining four clauses are more technical and say little about the nature of the Union. Because, as we have seen before, all the European Treaties retain their legal validity, the Maastricht negotiators had to include *Article 50* (ex P) in order to repeal certain of them. Articles 2–6 of the Merger Treaty had provided details on the presidency, the meetings and procedures of the Council of Ministers, COREPER, and voting on ECJ salaries while Articles 10–18 had dealt with the composition, nomination, resignation, officers and procedures of the Commission. The last two articles in each sequence repealed previous provisions on these subjects in the three Community treaties. Where the SEA is concerned the TEU repealed its provisions both on the European Council and on EPC, especially the detailed Title III. In both cases the TEU had, as we have seen, already upgraded their status. The reference to two signings of the SEA reflects the fact that national difficulties made it impossible for some member states to meet the initial deadline.

The question arises as to why this clause was not eliminated in the course of consolidation at Amsterdam. This is especially the case where the Merger Treaty is concerned since this was wholly repealed by Article 9(1) TA. Leaving Article 50 in the text may provide legal certainty but it also reinforces the complexity of the TEU and its relation to previous treaties. The reason seems to be that the 1996 IGC did not wish to extend simplification to the TEU since this was new and still politically sensitive. It could, however, figure on the simplification agenda in 2004.

All the last three articles, *Articles 51–53* (ex Q–S), replicate provisions originally found in the TEC and still partly paralleled there. The first makes the Union a body of equally unlimited duration, a point seized on by the Court in *Costa* v. *ENEL* to rule that the member states in establishing the TEC intended to create a new legal order which was binding on individuals and themselves. To some, the fact that the TEU is, like the TEC and TEAEC, concluded for an unlimited period sits oddly with the existence within it of some arrangements which are legally and practically transitory. Also, it suggests that once a state has accepted the treaty it cannot withdraw from the Union, a point underlined by the absence of any provision for secession although authorities on both sides of the political spectrum have argued that such an arrangement is needed. Alternatively, it can be argued that Article 48 on treaty revision would suffice. It might be asked why there is no reference here to the TECSC. This is because it was some way off when the article was drafted. In any case the additions to the Treaty of Nice were more or less to clear this up.

Article 52 (ex R) largely follows ex Article 247 TEC and, through paragraph 1, leaves ratification purely and solely in the hands of national authorities. This reflects the importance of the national element in the European Treaties. Ratification can involve either parliamentary approval or a referendum vote. The latter are playing an increasingly important political role particularly after the Irish 'no' in line with Roberts-Thompson's assessment. They give those states which have such votes a disproportionate influence, reflected in criticisms of 'surrendering our sovereignty to Dublin' in the Commons debate on Nice.

A popular reading is that if a country votes 'no' then the whole treaty falls. But this is not what the treaty actually says. As the 7 June 2001 referendum in Ireland was to emphasize, large political issues lie hidden behind its deceptively simple wording. Hence, for all its apparent simplicity and obvious brevity, Article 52, like its TEC counterpart, is highly significant politically and constitutionally. It demands that all original parties to the treaty must ratify it for it to become operative. In other words, once a state has agreed to a text as a 'High Contracting Party' it is bound to seek ratification. And it does so in its own way and not according to rules laid down by the TEU or TEC as such. There are clear implications here that the member states, or more precisely the six original member states, are prior to the Community. Later entrants indicate their acceptance of this status by accession treaties. And there is nothing about qualifying ratification or placing a time limit on it.

However, as 1992 had made clear, there is no mechanism for proceeding if not all states ratify the treaty or amendments to it. This silence can be seen either as giving flexibility or as ruling out any change not duly approved by all states involved. It is thus a very delicate matter politically. And while member states may find the requirement for unanimity annoying, leading to instability as it does, they do not really wish to lose this sign of their 'mastership' of the treaties much as some pro-integration forces would like to happen. Hence, neither Amsterdam nor Nice went down this road. Despite the problems caused by demanding unanimous ratification, this is likely to remain the case even though the EP has, since the early 1990s, been seeking a share in ratification and removal of the reference to member states' own 'constitutional requirements'. To change it would suggest all too clearly that only big battalions matter. And such a change would itself require unanimous approval.

In fact, the Danish precedent suggests that where a single state is involved (especially if a small one and on the basis of only small percentages of votes) it can be 'encouraged' to think again. This certainly seems to be so in the Irish case. If more than one state objected then it would certainly mean going 'back to the drawing board'. And while this has been attacked as undemocratic, there is also a case for saying that, given the inter-governmental nature of the treaty process, true democracy requires that the rights of all ratifying assemblies and electorates be equally recognized.

In any case, when ratification is complete the formal documents detailing the process and the fact that the state has ratified are then handed over to the Italian government since, as we explained in the Introduction, it has acquired the safekeeping of the Treaties. It has the duty of checking that the due processes have been completed and, under Article 53, of certifying the official copy of the agreed texts. It is for the Italians then to inform the rest of the Community that this has happened. None of this confers any special powers on Italy. The instrument of ratification, such as that which was handed by the British ambassador in Rome on 2 August 1993 once Lord Rees-Mogg had decided not to appeal against the rejection of his application for a judicial review, is a vellum document, detailing the ratification procedures, the treaties ratified and the authority to ratify. To it is appended the national seal in good medieval fashion.

The second paragraph of Article 52 provides a mechanism for the original TEU to come into force. Again, we might think that this could have been eliminated during consolidation since it now seems a bit dated and inaccurate given that the TEU actually only came into effect on 1 November 1993. However, as with Article 50, the aim was not to rock the boat. Here again opinions might vary in 2004.

The aim of the delay after the deposit of the last act of ratification described here was to give a breathing space to get the new arrangements organized. However, in practice much preparation had already been done and some of the treaty's provisions had already been anticipated. The fact that the precise date remains in the text is because the Union is a new body and we need to know when it became operative. The Treaties of Amsterdam and Nice made no mention of a specific date.

Finally, *Article 53* (ex S) lays down the standard provisions for authenticating and confirming ratification. These were updated at Amsterdam to take account of the 1995 enlargement to the EFTA states and their languages. Austria, being a German-speaking country, did not need a specific mention. Nice had no reason to make any changes to this which is slightly different from the similar provisions in the TEC.

The fact that all versions are of equal standing is more significant symbolically than practically. It again reinforces the point that the states are 'the masters of the treaties'. This is both wise and democratic, but it can cause problems of interpretation of the Treaty as it can with Community legislation and law. There are cases when the language variants do not absolutely cohere.

There then follow two formal sentences stressing the validity of the document, where it was done, and the sovereign right of the signatories to sign it on behalf of their states. The two representatives of each state, one foreign minister and one finance minister, given the nature of the 1991 IGCs, then sign to signify their state's acceptance of the treaty agreements. However, this is not the end of affairs since the legally binding texts also include the various protocols. And beyond this there is the final act and the various declarations annexed to it.

TITLE VIII (ex Title VII) FINAL PROVISIONS

Article 46 (ex Article L)

The provisions of the Treaty establishing the European Community, the Treaty establishing the European Coal and Steel Community and the Treaty establishing the European Atomic Energy Community concerning the powers of the Court of Justice of the European Communities and the exercise of those powers shall apply only to the following provisions of this Treaty:

(a) provisions amending the Treaty establishing the European Economic Community with a view to establishing the European Community, the Treaty establishing the European Coal and Steel Community and the Treaty establishing the European Atomic Energy Community;

(b) **provisions of Title VI, under the conditions provided for by Article 35;**

(c) **provisions of Title VII, under the conditions provided for by Article 11 of the Treaty establishing the European Community and Article 40 of this Treaty;**

(d) **Article 6(2) with regard to action of the institutions, insofar as the Court has jurisdiction under the Treaties establishing the European Communities and under this Treaty;**

(e) **the purely procedural stipulations in Article 7, with the Court acting at the request of the Member State concerned within one month from the date of the determination by the Council provided for in that Article;**

(f) Articles 46 to 53.

Article 47 (ex Article M)

Subject to the provisions amending the Treaty establishing the European Economic Community with a view to establishing the European Community, the Treaty establishing the European Coal and Steel Community and the Treaty establishing the European Atomic Energy Community, and to these final provisions, nothing in this Treaty shall affect the Treaties establishing the European Communities or the subsequent Treaties and Acts modifying or supplementing them.

Article 48 (ex Article N)

The government of any Member State or the Commission may submit to the Council proposals for the amendment of the Treaties on which the Union is founded.

If the Council, after consulting the European Parliament and, where appropriate, the Commission, delivers an opinion in favour of calling a conference of representatives of the governments of the Member States, the conference shall be convened by the President of the Council for the purpose of determining by common accord the amendments to be made to those Treaties. The European Central Bank shall also be consulted in the case of institutional changes in the monetary area.

The amendments shall enter into force after being ratified by all the Member States in accordance with their respective constitutional requirements.

Article 49 (ex Article O)

Any European State **which respects the principles set out in Article 6(1)** may apply to become a member of the Union. It shall address its application to the Council, which shall act unanimously after consulting the Commission and after receiving the assent of the European Parliament, which shall act by an absolute majority of its component members.

The conditions of admission and the adjustments to the Treaties on which the Union is founded which such admission entails shall be the subject of an agreement between the Member States and the applicant State. This agreement shall be submitted for ratification by all the contracting States in accordance with their respective constitutional requirements.

Article 50 (ex Article P)

1. Articles 2 to 7 and 10 to 19 of the Treaty establishing a single Council and a single Commission of the European Communities, signed in Brussels on 8 April 1965, are hereby repealed.

2. Article 2, Article 3(2) and Title III of the Single European Act signed in Luxembourg on 17 February 1986 and in The Hague on 28 February 1986 are hereby repealed.

Article 51 (ex Article Q)

This Treaty is concluded for an unlimited period.

Article 52 (ex Article R)

1. This Treaty shall be ratified by the High Contracting Parties in accordance with their respective constitutional requirements. The instruments of ratification shall be deposited with the Government of the Italian Republic.

2. This Treaty shall enter into force on 1 January 1993, provided that all the instruments of ratification have been deposited, or, failing that, on the first day of the month following the deposit of the instrument of ratification by the last signatory State to take this step.

Article 53 (ex Article S)

This Treaty, drawn up in a single original in the Danish, Dutch, English, French, German, Greek, Irish, Italian, Portuguese and Spanish languages, the texts in each of these languages being equally authentic, shall be deposited in the archives of the government of the Italian Republic, which will transmit a certified copy to each of the governments of the other signatory States.

Pursuant to the Accession Treaty of 1994, the Finnish and Swedish versions of this Treaty shall also be authentic.

IN WITNESS WHEREOF the undersigned Plenipotentiaries have signed this Treaty.

Done at Maastricht on the seventh day of February in the year one thousand nine hundred and ninety-two.

Mark EYSKENS
Philippe MAYSTADT
Uffe ELLEMANN-JENSEN
Anders FOGH RASMUSSEN

Hans-Dietrich GENSCHER
Theodor WAIGEL
Antonios SAMARAS
Efthymios CHRISTODOULOU
Francisco FERNÁNDEZ ORDÓÑEZ
Carlos SOLCHAGA CATALÁN
Roland DUMAS
Pierre BÉRÉGOVOY
Gerard COLLINS
Bertie AHERN
Gianni DE MICHELIS
Guido CARLI
Jacques F. POOS
Jean-Claude JUNCKER
Hans VAN DEN BROEK
Willem KOK
João de Deus PINHEIRO
Jorge BRAGA DE MACEDO
Douglas HURD
Francis MAUDE

ix   Protocols

Legally speaking, the full TEU is made up not just of the preamble and the 63 articles we have already examined. It also includes a whole raft of protocols. These, as we have seen, are formal documents which contain material which add and expand treaty provisions, whether those of the TEU as such or other treaties amended by it and of which they form an integral part in legal terms if not where their position is concerned. Their function is essentially to elucidate certain elements of the treaties to which they relate. Hence, they often contain lengthy and detailed provisions on a specific topic or institution which, if contained in the treaty proper, would make it more cumbersome to read. They are therefore slightly separate from the treaty proper because they are listed in and under-written by the IGC's final acts in which formal decisions are taken to annex them to the appropriate treaties.

The provisions contained within the protocols are legally binding on the member states of the Union and must be applied in conjunction with the treaty provisions to which they relate, which opens the way to legal effect and judicial protection. They are subject to ratification by member states who, as the 'High Contracting Parties', agreed them as they did the eight titles which precede them. Hence they are a largely binding part of normal international law, since they to some extent modify or supplement the treaty proper. And they can help to define the Union. However, they have no force outside the treaty.

In the case of the TEU, only one protocol was originally annexed to the treaty itself. Yet the TEU did annex a further sixteen protocols to the TEC, as Box 4 shows. As we saw earlier in the *Guide*, a further eight were added to the TEU at Amsterdam (see Box 5 on p. 159). One of these, the Protocol on Article J.7 [now 17] of the Treaty on European Union (1), was attached to the TEU alone, whereas the others were shared with the TEC. These were those integrating the Schengen *acquis* into the framework of the European

Union (2); the two protocols on related UK and Irish aspects of this (3) and (4); and a similar one on Denmark (5). The TEU also had a third share in three others: on the institutions with the prospect of enlargement of the European Union (11); on the location of the seats of the institutions (12); and on the role of national parliaments in the European Union (13). Amsterdam also repealed three of the protocols annexed by the TEU to the TEC back in 1992: those amending the protocol on the privileges and immunities of the European Communities (7); on the Social Chapter (14); and on the shared administration of the CoR and EcoSoc (16).

Later on, at Nice, as we have already seen, one Protocol was added and one repealed. The addition was the new improved statute for the ECJ discussed further below. However, it is worth noting here that attaching the statute to the TEU helps both to reinforce the importance of the Union and to hint that European law is no longer just EC law, a point also discussed below. In fact the statute makes it clear that it derives from the TEU as well as from the Community treaties. It also makes special arrangements for dealing with

---

Box 4   Protocols introduced by the TEU (1992)

Protocols annexed to the TEC (see pp. 475–544)
1. Protocol on the Acquisition of Property in Denmark
2. Protocol Concerning Article 141 [ex 119] of the Treaty Establishing the European Community
3. Protocol on the Statute of the European System of Central Banks and of the European Central Bank
4. Protocol on the Statute of the European Monetary Institute
5. Protocol on the Excessive Deficit Procedure
6. Protocol on the Convergence Criteria Referred to in Article 121 [ex 109j] of the Treaty Establishing the European Community
7. Protocol Amending the Protocol on the Privileges and Immunities of the European Communities (repealed by TA)
8. Protocol on Denmark
9. Protocol on Portugal
10. Protocol on the Transition to the Third Stage of Economic and Monetary Union
11. Protocol on Certain Provisions Relating to the United Kingdom of Great Britain and Northern Ireland
12. Protocol on Certain Provisions Relating to Denmark
13. Protocol on France
14. Protocol on Social Policy, to which is Annexed an Agreement Concluded between the Member States of the European Community with the Exception of the United Kingdom of Great Britain and Northern Ireland, to which two Declarations are Attached (repealed by TA)
15. Protocol on Economic and Social Cohesion
16. Protocol on the Economic and Social Committee and the Committee of the Regions (repealed by TA)

Protocols annexed to the TEU and to the Treaties Establishing the European Communities

17. Protocol Annexed to the Treaty on European Union and to the Treaties Establishing the European Communities [relating to Article 40.3.3 of the Irish Constitution]

preliminary rulings on migration and related problems arising from those states which opt into its jurisdiction under Article 35 TEU.

The Amsterdam Protocol on the Institutions with the Prospect of Enlargement of the European Union was repealed by Article 1 of its replacement, the Protocol on the Enlargement of the European Union, which has been printed on pp. 68–72. Given the importance of the former it is included below. Nice made no other changes to the TEU's protocols although it did add two to the TEC. All told there are currently 23 protocols associated with the TEU: 13 which it annexed to the TEC, and 10 which are annexed to the TEU.

The first batch, as Box 4 shows, contain provisions relating almost exclusively to the EC in its post-TEU form and were formally annexed to the amended TEC at Maastricht. They are therefore examined in IV xxxi and at other points in the *Guide*. Although their length precludes the same level of analysis given to the articles of the European Treaties proper, they are still significant and tell us something about the 1992 TEU. For not only do they show the TEU to be an amending as well as a constitutive treaty, they can also provide long-term exemptions from EC projects such as EMU. This made them helpful to governments but a worry to legal commentators concerned for the integrity of the Community, its law and *acquis*. Such fears were another reason why doubts were expressed about the proliferation of protocols even though, had the detailed statutes of the various financial bodies been included in the treaty proper, the complaints would probably have been even more vociferous.

The final protocol (17), that relating to Ireland's anti-abortion legislation, is actually annexed both to the TEU and to the Treaties establishing the European Communities. It states that nothing in any of the four treaties to which it is annexed may affect the application in Ireland of Article 40.3.3 of the Irish Constitution which enshrines the right to life of the unborn child. This then had to be changed when the rule was challenged as an infringement of EC rules on free movement after a court case about a ban on an Irish girl seeking an abortion in Britain. The Irish government failed to secure an amendment to the protocol to make it clear that it was not imposing such a ban but its sentiments are recorded in the Declaration of the High Contracting Parties to the Treaty on European Union adopted on 1 May 1992, which also allows for a revision of the protocol in the light of constitutional change in the Irish Republic. When adopted, Curtin viewed the protocol as setting a precedent for the application of specific national constitutional provisions to be exempt from EC law. Such fears have not necessarily been borne out, at least not in terms of similar protocols being adopted.

The 'Irish' protocol underlines the TEU's status as a constitutive act since it relates to areas of activity within the EU which the TEU itself establishes. This constitutive role was reinforced by the TA which, as already mentioned and as restated in Box 5, spawned a further 13 protocols, eight of which are annexed to the TEU whether alone or in conjunction with other treaties. Only the first of these is exclusive to the TEU and concerns the enhancement of EU–WEU co-operation as already noted on p. 110. This follows a formal statement of member states' commitments to NATO, giving it somewhat the status of a declaration.

The protocols annexed to both the TEU and the TEC deal with some of the major structural policy shifts made at Amsterdam and their implications for peripheral states. These relate to the free movement of people and the integration of the Schengen *acquis* into the framework of the EU. They also contain various opt-outs/opt-ins concerning the positions of Denmark, Ireland and the United Kingdom. Several provisions (italicized in the treaty extract below) in the Protocol on the Position of Denmark, notably concerning defence, are taken directly from the Decision on Denmark adopted at the 1992 Edinburgh European Council following the country's first referendum on the TEU. The decision, the legal status of which was ambiguous, was designed to clarify Danish commitments resulting from the TEU and assuage popular fears about the future direction of the EU. By placing some of its key provisions in a protocol, their legally binding nature is assured, at least as far as the commitments concerning the common defence policy and a common defence are concerned.

Box 5   Protocols introduced by the TA (1997)

Protocol annexed to the Treaty on European Union:

1. Protocol on Article J.7 [now 17] of the Treaty on European Union

Protocols annexed to the Treaty on European Union and to the Treaty establishing the European Community:

2. Protocol Integrating the Schengen *Acquis* into the Framework of the European Union
3. Protocol on the application of certain aspects of Article 7a [now 14] of the Treaty Establishing the European Community to the United Kingdom and to Ireland
4. Protocol on the Position of the United Kingdom and Ireland
5. Protocol on the Position of Denmark

Protocols annexed to the Treaty on European Union and to the Treaties establishing the European Community, the European Coal and Steel Community and the European Atomic Energy Community:

11. Protocol on the Institutions with the Prospect of Enlargement of the European Union (repealed by TN)
12. Protocol on the Location of the Seats of the Institutions and of Certain Bodies and Departments of the European Communities and of Europol
13. Protocol on the Role of National Parliaments in the European Union

---

The next three protocols, like that concerning the Irish Constitution, are annexed not only to the TEU, but also to the TEC, TECSC and TEAEC. The first, now repealed, concerns enlargement and proposed reforms to the size of the Commission and to the distribution of votes within the Council for when the EU's next enlargement takes place. A commitment to a comprehensive review of the composition and functioning of the institutions prior to an expansion of the EU beyond 20 member states was also made. This was, essentially, a reflection of the fact that there was insufficient political will (and time) to come to a substantive agreement at Amsterdam and the need for a concession to disappointed states. However, although it played a part in launching the 2000 IGC it was overtaken by events, as noted elsewhere, and formally set aside at Nice.

The next protocols confirm the geographical location of institutions, stating at the insistence of the French government, and to the chagrin of the EP, that the EP shall have its seat in Strasbourg and hold its monthly plenary sessions there. The disillusion was the greater for the fact that the protocol seems to have been slipped through at the last moment when other heads of government were not paying attention. The last protocol upgrades Declaration No. 13 TEU and details more precisely the role of national parliaments in the EU in an attempt to reassure citizens that their national representatives are involved in the EU process and can make recommendations. An enhanced role was also given to the standing conference of their European Affairs Committees (known as COSAC from the French).

The reason that all these protocols are attached to the TEU is that they alter the pillar structure and the position of member states within it. They also give additional emphasis to some of the decisions taken at Amsterdam. Equally, because the Union has a single institutional framework, the TEU must be cognizant of major changes to the latter. And, like some of the declarations, they are needed to give it guidance on its own workings. Given this, however, we might ask why the protocol on subsidiarity is not also attached to the TEU. None the less, the protocols contain important provisions concerning the EU.

In fact, the protocols attached to the TEU fulfil five functions. First, they can clarify a member state's obligations under the TEU and the relationship between the TEU and a member state's own constitution. Second, as with the protocols relating to the institutions, they can give greater politico-legal force to existing political agreements. Third, protocols can contain political statements designed to guide the development of the EU. Fourth, there are protocols which contain opt-outs from and opt-ins to specific policy areas. As such they establish and detail the extent of variable geometry within the EU. Finally, in the case of the protocols attached to some of the other treaties, they provide detailed instructions for institutions or pillars, whether now or, increasingly after Nice, in the future.

Their legal standing, however, is a little less clear when compared to that of the protocols attached to the TEC since no explicit statement on their status is included in the TEU. We can assume, however, that they occupy a similar status to the protocols attached to the other European Treaties in so far as their provisions should be viewed as forming an integral part of the TEU. Indeed, it is difficult to ignore the protocols since they often contain significant provisions concerning, in particular, procedural matters. It cannot be assumed, however, that the protocols are legally binding in the same way as those attached to the TEC. In terms of EC law, they are not. Only a limited number of provisions in the TEU fall under the jurisdiction of the ECJ (see Article 46 TEU) and none of the protocols annexed to the treaty relate to these. Hence, as with other TEU provisions over which the ECJ has no jurisdiction, any obligation a member state feels towards adherence is essentially political.

Reference to the International Court of Justice (ICJ) is, in theory, possible since the TEU creates treaty obligations binding in international law. The failure of member states so far to take EU matters to the ICJ suggests that recourse to ensure implementation of a protocol in the future is unlikely. To date there has been no obvious need since protocols have either been implemented or, as we have seen in the case of the protocol concerning enlargement, been overtaken by events.

Protocol Annexed to the TEU and to the EC, ECSC and EAEC Treaties by the TEU

PROTOCOL ANNEXED TO THE TREATY ON EUROPEAN UNION AND TO THE TREATIES ESTABLISHING THE EUROPEAN COMMUNITIES

THE HIGH CONTRACTING PARTIES,

HAVE AGREED upon the following provision, which shall be annexed to the Treaty on European Union and to the Treaties establishing the European Communities:

Nothing in the Treaty on European Union, or in the Treaties establishing the European Communities, or in the Treaties or Acts modifying or supplementing those Treaties, shall affect the application in Ireland of Article 40.3.3 of the Constitution of Ireland.

Protocol Annexed to the TEU by the Treaty of Amsterdam

PROTOCOL ON ARTICLE 17 [ex J.7] OF THE TREATY ON EUROPEAN UNION

THE HIGH CONTRACTING PARTIES,

BEARING IN MIND the need to implement fully the provisions of Article 17(1) [ex J.7(1)], second subparagraph, and (3) of the Treaty on European Union,

BEARING IN MIND that the policy of the Union in accordance with Article 17 [ex J.7] shall not prejudice the specific character of the security and defence policy of certain Member States and shall respect the obligations of certain Member States, which see their common defence realised in NATO, under the North Atlantic Treaty and be compatible with the common security and defence policy established within that framework,

HAVE AGREED UPON the following provision, which is annexed to the Treaty on European Union,

The European Union shall draw up, together with the Western European Union, arrangements for enhanced co-operation between them, within a year from the entry into force of the Treaty of Amsterdam.

Protocols Annexed to the TEU and the EC Treaty by the Treaty of Amsterdam

PROTOCOL INTEGRATING THE SCHENGEN *ACQUIS* INTO THE FRAMEWORK OF THE EUROPEAN UNION

THE HIGH CONTRACTING PARTIES,

NOTING that the Agreements on the gradual abolition of checks at common borders signed by some Member States of the European Union in Schengen on 14 June 1985 and on 19 June 1990, as well as related agreements and the rules adopted on the basis of these agreements, are aimed at enhancing European integration and, in particular, at enabling the European Union to develop more rapidly into an area of freedom, security and justice,

DESIRING to incorporate the abovementioned agreements and rules into the framework of the European Union,

CONFIRMING that the provisions of the Schengen *acquis* are applicable only if and as far as they are compatible with the European Union and Community law,

TAKING INTO ACCOUNT the special position of Denmark,

TAKING INTO ACCOUNT the fact that Ireland and the United Kingdom of Great Britain and Northern Ireland are not parties to and have not signed the abovementioned agreements; that provision should, however, be made to allow those Member States to accept some or all of the provisions thereof,

RECOGNISING that, as a consequence, it is necessary to make use of the provisions of the Treaty on European Union and of the Treaty establishing the European Community concerning closer co-operation between some Member States and that those provisions should only be used as a last resort,

TAKING INTO ACCOUNT the need to maintain a special relationship with the Republic of Iceland and the Kingdom of Norway, both States having confirmed their intention to become bound by the provisions mentioned above, on the basis of the Agreement signed in Luxembourg on 19 December 1996,

HAVE AGREED UPON the following provisions, which shall be annexed to the Treaty on European Union and to the Treaty establishing the European Community,

Article 1.

The Kingdom of Belgium, the Kingdom of Denmark, the Federal Republic of Germany, the Hellenic Republic, the Kingdom of Spain, the French Republic, the Italian Republic, the Grand Duchy of Luxembourg, the Kingdom of the Netherlands, the Republic of Austria, the Portuguese Republic, the Republic of Finland and the Kingdom of Sweden, signatories to the Schengen agreements, are authorised to establish closer co-operation among themselves within the scope of those agreements and related provisions, as they are listed in the Annex to this Protocol, hereinafter referred to as the 'Schengen *acquis*'. This co-operation shall be conducted within the institutional and legal framework of the European Union and with respect for the relevant provisions of the Treaty on European Union and of the Treaty establishing the European Community.

Article 2.

1. From the date of entry into force of the Treaty of Amsterdam, the Schengen *acquis*, including the decisions of the Executive Committee established by the Schengen agreements which have been adopted before this date, shall immediately apply to the thirteen Member States referred to in Article 1, without prejudice to the provisions of paragraph 2 of this Article. From the same date, the Council will substitute itself for the said Executive Committee.

The Council, acting by the unanimity of its Members referred to in Article 1, shall take any measure necessary for the implementation of this paragraph. The Council, acting unanimously, shall determine, in conformity with the relevant provisions of the Treaties, the legal basis for each of the provisions or decisions which constitute the Schengen *acquis*.

With regard to such provisions and decisions and in accordance with that determination, the Court of Justice of the European Communities shall exercise the powers conferred upon it by the relevant applicable provisions of the Treaties. In any event, the Court of Justice shall have no jurisdiction on measures or decisions relating to the maintenance of law and order and the safeguarding of internal security.

As long as the measures referred to above have not been taken and without prejudice to Article 5(2), the provisions or decisions which constitute the Schengen *acquis* shall be regarded as acts based on Title VI of the Treaty on European Union.

2. The provisions of paragraph 1 shall apply to the Member States which have signed accession protocols to the Schengen agreements, from the dates decided by the Council, acting with the unanimity of its Members mentioned in Article 1, unless the conditions for the accession of any of those States to the Schengen *acquis* are met before the date of the entry into force of the Treaty of Amsterdam.

Article 3.

Following the determination referred to in Article 2(1), second subparagraph, Denmark shall maintain the same rights and obligations in relation to the other signatories to the Schengen agreements, as before the said determination with regard to those parts of the Schengen *acquis* that are determined to have a legal basis in Title IV [ex IIIa] of the Treaty establishing the European Community.

With regard to those parts of the Schengen *acquis* that are determined to have legal base in Title VI of the Treaty on European Union, Denmark shall continue to have the same rights and obligations as the other signatories to the Schengen agreements.

Article 4.

Ireland and the United Kingdom of Great Britain and Northern Ireland, which are not bound by the Schengen *acquis*, may at any time request to take part in some or all of the provisions of this *acquis*.

The Council shall decide on the request with the unanimity of its members referred to in Article 1 and of the representative of the Government of the State concerned.

Article 5.

1. Proposals and initiatives to build upon the Schengen *acquis* shall be subject to the relevant provisions of the Treaties.

In this context, where either Ireland or the United Kingdom or both have not notified the President of the Council in writing within a reasonable period that they wish to take part, the authorisation referred to in Article 11 [ex 5a] of the Treaty establishing the European Community or Article 40 [ex K.12] of the Treaty on European Union shall be deemed to have been granted to the Member States referred to in Article 1 and to Ireland or the United Kingdom where either of them wishes to take part in the areas of co-operation in question.*

---

*The reference to Article K.12 is to the new Article 40 (ex K. 12) inserted into the TEU by the TA.

2. The relevant provisions of the Treaties referred to in the first subparagraph of paragraph 1 shall apply even if the Council has not adopted the measures referred to in Article 2(1), second subparagraph.

Article 6.

The Republic of Iceland and the Kingdom of Norway shall be associated with the implementation of the Schengen *acquis* and its further development on the basis of the Agreement signed in Luxembourg on 19 December 1996. Appropriate procedures shall be agreed to that effect in an Agreement to be concluded with those States by the Council, acting by the unanimity of its members mentioned in Article 1. Such Agreement shall include provisions on the contribution of Iceland and Norway to any financial consequences resulting from the implementation of this Protocol.

A separate Agreement shall be concluded with Iceland and Norway by the Council, acting unanimously, for the establishment of rights and obligations between Ireland and the United Kingdom of Great Britain and Northern Ireland on the one hand, and Iceland and Norway on the other, in domains of the Schengen *acquis* which apply to these States.

Article 7.

The Council shall, acting by a qualified majority, adopt the detailed arrangements for the integration of the Schengen Secretariat into the General Secretariat of the Council.

Article 8.

For the purposes of the negotiations for the admission of new Member States into the European Union, the Schengen *acquis* and further measures taken by the institutions within its scope shall be regarded as an *acquis* which must be accepted in full by all States candidates for admission.

Annex–Schengen *Acquis*

1. The Agreement, signed in Schengen on 14 June 1985, between the Governments of the States of the Benelux Economic Union, the Federal Republic of Germany and the French Republic on the gradual abolition of checks at their common borders.

2. The Convention, signed in Schengen on 19 June 1990, between the Kingdom of Belgium, the Federal Republic of Germany, the French Republic, the Grand Duchy of Luxembourg and the Kingdom of the Netherlands, implementing the Agreement on the gradual abolition of checks at their common borders, signed in Schengen on 14 June 1985, with related Final Act and common declarations.

3. The Accession Protocols and Agreements to the 1985 Agreement and the 1990 Implementation Convention with Italy (signed in Paris on 27 November 1990), Spain and Portugal (signed in Bonn on 25 June 1991), Greece (signed in Madrid on 6 November 1992), Austria (signed in Brussels on 28 April 1995) and Denmark, Finland and Sweden (signed in Luxembourg on 19 December 1996), with related Final Acts and declarations.

4. Decisions and declarations adopted by the Executive Committee established by the 1990 Implementation Convention, as well as acts adopted for the implementation of the Convention by the organs upon which the Executive Committee has conferred decision making powers.

PROTOCOL ON THE APPLICATION OF CERTAIN ASPECTS OF ARTICLE 14 [ex 7a] OF THE TREATY ESTABLISHING THE EUROPEAN COMMUNITY TO THE UNITED KINGDOM AND TO IRELAND

THE HIGH CONTRACTING PARTIES,

DESIRING to settle certain questions relating to the United Kingdom and Ireland,

HAVING REGARD to the existence for many years of special travel arrangements between the United Kingdom and Ireland,

HAVE AGREED UPON the following provisions, which shall be annexed to the Treaty establishing the European Community and to the Treaty on European Union,

Article 1.

The United Kingdom shall be entitled, notwithstanding Article 14 [ex 7a] of the Treaty establishing the European Community, any other provision of that Treaty or of the Treaty on European Union, any measure adopted under those Treaties, or any international agreement concluded by the Community or by the Community and its Member States with one or more third States, to exercise at its frontiers with other Member States such controls on persons seeking to enter the United Kingdom as it may consider necessary for the purpose:

(a) of verifying the right to enter the United Kingdom of citizens of States which are Contracting Parties to the Agreement on the European Economic Area and of their dependants exercising rights conferred by Community law, as well as citizens of other States on whom such rights have been conferred by an agreement by which the United Kingdom is bound; and

(b) of determining whether or not to grant other persons permission to enter the United Kingdom.

Nothing in Article 14 [ex 7a] of the Treaty establishing the European Community or in any other provision of that Treaty or of the Treaty on European Union or in any measure adopted under them shall prejudice the right of the United Kingdom to adopt or exercise any such controls. References to the United Kingdom in this Article shall include territories for whose external relations the United Kingdom is responsible.

Article 2.

The United Kingdom and Ireland may continue to make arrangements between themselves relating to the movement of persons between their territories ('the Common Travel Area'), while fully respecting the rights of persons referred to in Article 1, first paragraph, point (a) of this Protocol. Accordingly, as long as they maintain such arrangements, the provisions of Article 1 of this Protocol shall apply to Ireland under the same terms and conditions as for the United Kingdom. Nothing in Article 14 [ex 7a] of the Treaty establishing the European Community, in any other provision of that Treaty or of the Treaty on European Union or in any measure adopted under them, shall affect any such arrangements.

Article 3.

The other Member States shall be entitled to exercise at their frontiers or at any point of entry into their territory such controls on persons seeking to enter their territory from the United Kingdom or any territories whose external relations are under its responsibility for the same purposes stated in Article 1 of this Protocol, or from Ireland as long as the provisions of Article 1 of this Protocol apply to Ireland.

Nothing in Article 14 [ex 7a] of the Treaty establishing the European Community or in any other provision of that Treaty or of the Treaty on European Union or in any measure adopted under them shall prejudice the right of the other Member States to adopt or exercise any such controls.

PROTOCOL ON THE POSITION OF THE UNITED KINGDOM AND IRELAND

THE HIGH CONTRACTING PARTIES,

DESIRING to settle certain questions relating to the United Kingdom and Ireland,

HAVING REGARD to the Protocol on the application of certain aspects of Article 14 [ex 7a] of the Treaty establishing the European Community to the United Kingdom and to Ireland,

HAVE AGREED UPON the following provisions which shall be annexed to the Treaty establishing the European Community and to the Treaty on European Union,

Article 1.

Subject to Article 3, the United Kingdom and Ireland shall not take part in the adoption by the Council of proposed measures pursuant to Title IV [ex IIIa] of the Treaty establishing the European Community. By way of derogation from Article 205(2) [ex 148(2)] of the Treaty establishing the European Community, a qualified majority shall be defined as the same proportion of the weighted votes of the members of the Council concerned as laid down in the said Article 205(2) [ex 148(2)]. The unanimity of the members of the Council, with the exception of the representatives of the government of the United Kingdom and Ireland, shall be necessary for decisions of the Council which must be adopted unanimously.

Article 2.

In consequence of Article 1 and subject to Articles 3, 4 and 6, none of the provisions of Title IV [ex IIIa] of the Treaty establishing the European Community, no measure adopted pursuant to that Title, no provision of any international agreement concluded by the Community pursuant to that Title, and no decision of the Court of Justice interpreting any such provision or measure shall be binding upon or applicable in the United Kingdom or Ireland; and no such provision, measure or decision shall in any way affect the competences, rights and obligations of those States; and no such provision, measure or decision shall in any way affect the *acquis communautaire* nor form part of Community law as they apply to the United Kingdom or Ireland.

Article 3.

1. The United Kingdom or Ireland may notify the President of the Council in writing, within three months after a proposal or initiative has been presented to the Council pursuant to Title IV [ex IIIa] of the Treaty establishing the European Community, that it wishes to take part in the adoption and application of any such proposed measure, whereupon that State shall be entitled to do so. By way of derogation from Article 205(2) [ex 148(2)] of the Treaty establishing the European Community, a qualified majority shall be defined as the same proportion

of the weighted votes of the members of the Council concerned as laid down in the said Article 205(2) [ex 148(2)].

The unanimity of the members of the Council, with the exception of a member which has not made such a notification, shall be necessary for decisions of the Council which must be adopted unanimously. A measure adopted under this paragraph shall be binding upon all Member States which took part in its adoption.

2. If after a reasonable period of time a measure referred to in paragraph 1 cannot be adopted with the United Kingdom or Ireland taking part, the Council may adopt such measure in accordance with Article 1 without the participation of the United Kingdom or Ireland. In that case Article 2 applies.

Article 4.

The United Kingdom or Ireland may at any time after the adoption of a measure by the Council pursuant to Title IV [ex IIIa] of the Treaty establishing the European Community notify its intention to the Council and to the Commission that it wishes to accept that measure. In that case, the procedure provided for in Article 11(3) [ex 5a(3)] of the Treaty establishing the European Community shall apply *mutatis mutandis.**

Article 5.

A Member State which is not bound by a measure adopted pursuant to Title IV (ex IIIa) of the Treaty establishing the European Community shall bear no financial consequences of that measure other than administrative costs entailed for the institutions.

Article 6.

Where, in cases referred to in this Protocol, the United Kingdom or Ireland is bound by a measure adopted by the Council pursuant to Title IV [ex IIIa] of the Treaty establishing the European Community, the relevant provisions of that Treaty, including Article 68 [ex 73p], shall apply to that State in relation to that measure.

Article 7.

Articles 3 and 4 shall be without prejudice to the Protocol integrating the Schengen *acquis* into the framework of the European Union.

Article 8.

Ireland may notify the President of the Council in writing that it no longer wishes to be covered by the terms of this Protocol. In that case, the normal treaty provisions will apply to Ireland.

PROTOCOL ON THE POSITION OF DENMARK

THE HIGH CONTRACTING PARTIES,

RECALLING the Decision of the Heads of State or Government, meeting within the European Council at Edinburgh on 12 December 1992, concerning certain problems raised by Denmark on the Treaty on European Union,

HAVING NOTED the position of Denmark with regard to Citizenship, Economic and Monetary Union, Defence Policy and Justice and Home Affairs as laid down in the Edinburgh Decision,

---

*The reference to Article 5a(3) is to the new Article 11(3) inserted into the TEC by the TA.

BEARING IN MIND Article 3 of the Protocol integrating the Schengen *acquis* into the framework of the European Union,

HAVE AGREED UPON the following provisions, which shall be annexed to the Treaty establishing the European Community and to the Treaty on European Union,

PART I

Article 1.

Denmark shall not take part in the adoption by the Council of proposed measures pursuant to Title IV [ex IIIa] of the Treaty establishing the European Community.* By way of derogation from Article 205(2) [ex 148(2)] of the Treaty establishing the European Community, a qualified majority shall be defined as the same proportion of the weighted votes of the members of the Council concerned as laid down in the said Article 205(2) [ex 148(2)]. The unanimity of the members of the Council, with the exception of the representative of the government of Denmark, shall be necessary for the decisions of the Council which must be adopted unanimously.

Article 2.

None of the provisions of Title IV [ex IIIa] of the Treaty establishing the European Community, no measure adopted pursuant to that Title, no provision of any international agreement concluded by the Community pursuant to that Title, and no decision of the Court of Justice interpreting any such provision or measure shall be binding upon or applicable in Denmark; and no such provision, measure or decision shall in any way affect the competences, rights and obligations of Denmark; and no such provision, measure or decision shall in any way affect the *acquis communautaire* nor form part of Community law as they apply to Denmark.

Article 3.

Denmark shall bear no financial consequences of measures referred to in Article 1, other than administrative costs entailed for the institutions.

Article 4.

Articles 1, 2 and 3 shall not apply to measures determining the third countries whose nationals must be in possession of a visa when crossing the external borders of the Member States, or measures relating to a uniform format for visas.

Article 5.

1. Denmark shall decide within a period of 6 months after the Council has decided on a proposal or initiative to build upon the Schengen *acquis* under the provisions of Title IV [ex IIIa] of the Treaty establishing the European Community, whether it will implement this decision in its national law. If it decides to do so, this decision will create an obligation under international law between Denmark and the other Member States referred to in Article 1 of the Protocol integrating the Schengen *acquis* into the framework of the European Union as well as Ireland or the United Kingdom if those Member States take part in the areas of co-operation in question.

2. If Denmark decides not to implement a decision of the Council as referred to in paragraph 1, the Member States referred to in Article 1 of the Protocol integrating

---

*The reference in this protocol to Title IIIA is the Title IIIA inserted into the TEU by the TA.

the Schengen *acquis* into the framework of the European Union will consider appropriate measures to be taken.

PART II

Article 6.

With regard to measures adopted by the Council in the field of Articles 13(1) [ex J.3(1)] and 17 [ex J.7] of the Treaty on European Union, *Denmark does not participate in the elaboration and the implementation of decisions and actions of the Union which have defence implications, but will not prevent the development of closer co-operation between Member States in this area.* * Therefore Denmark shall not participate in their adoption. Denmark shall not be obliged to contribute to the financing of operational expenditure arising from such measures.

PART III

Article 7.

At any time Denmark may, in accordance with its constitutional requirements, inform the other Member States that it no longer wishes to avail itself of all or part of this Protocol. *In that event, Denmark will apply in full all relevant measures then in force taken within the framework of the European Union.*

PROTOCOL ON THE INSTITUTIONS WITH THE PROSPECT OF ENLARGEMENT OF THE EUROPEAN UNION†

THE HIGH CONTRACTING PARTIES,

HAVE AGREED UPON the following provisions, which shall be annexed to the Treaty on European Union and to the Treaties establishing the European Communities,

Article 1

At the date of entry into force of the first enlargement of the Union, notwithstanding Article 213(1) [ex 157(1)] of the Treaty establishing the European Community, Article 9(1) of the Treaty establishing the European Coal and Steel Community and Article 126(1) of the Treaty establishing the European Atomic Energy Community, the Commission shall comprise one national of each of the Member States, provided that, by that date, the weighting of the votes in the Council has been modified, whether by reweighting of the votes or by dual majority, in a manner acceptable to all Member States, taking into account all relevant elements, notably compensating those Member States which give up the possibility of nominating a second member of the Commission.

Article 2

At least one year before the membership of the European Union exceeds twenty, a conference of representatives of the governments of the Member States shall be convened in order to carry out a comprehensive review of the provisions of the Treaties on the composition and functioning of the institutions.

---

*The reference to Article J.7 is to the restructured Article 17 [ex J.7] created by the TA.
†To be repealed on the entry into force of the Treaty of Nice.

PROTOCOL ON THE LOCATION OF THE SEATS OF THE INSTITUTIONS AND OF CERTAIN BODIES AND DEPARTMENTS OF THE EUROPEAN COMMUNITIES AND OF EUROPOL

THE REPRESENTATIVES OF THE GOVERNMENTS OF THE MEMBER STATES,

HAVING REGARD to Article 289 [ex 216] of the Treaty establishing the European Community, Article 77 of the Treaty establishing the European Coal and Steel Community and Article 189 of the Treaty establishing the European Atomic Energy Community,

HAVING REGARD to the Treaty on European Union,

RECALLING AND CONFIRMING the Decision of 8 April 1965, and without prejudice to the decisions concerning the seat of future institutions, bodies and departments,

HAVE AGREED UPON the following provisions, which shall be annexed to the Treaty on European Union and the Treaties establishing the European Communities,

Sole Article

(a) The European Parliament shall have its seat in Strasbourg where the 12 periods of monthly plenary sessions, including the budget session, shall be held. The periods of additional plenary sessions shall be held in Brussels. The committees of the European Parliament shall meet in Brussels. The General Secretariat of the European Parliament and its departments shall remain in Luxembourg.

(b) The Council shall have its seat in Brussels. During the months of April, June and October, the Council shall hold its meetings in Luxembourg.

(c) The Commission shall have its seat in Brussels. The departments listed in Articles 7, 8 and 9 of the Decision of 8 April 1965 shall be established in Luxembourg.

(d) The Court of Justice and the Court of First Instance shall have their seats in Luxembourg.

(e) The Court of Auditors shall have its seat in Luxembourg.

(f) The Economic and Social Committee shall have its seat in Brussels.

(g) The Committee of the Regions shall have its seat in Brussels.

(h) The European Investment Bank shall have its seat in Luxembourg.

(i) The European Monetary Institute and the European Central Bank shall have their seat in Frankfurt.

(j) The European Police Office (Europol) shall have its seat in The Hague.

PROTOCOL ON THE ROLE OF NATIONAL PARLIAMENTS IN THE EUROPEAN UNION

THE HIGH CONTRACTING PARTIES,

RECALLING that scrutiny by individual national parliaments of their own government in relation to the activities of the Union is a matter for the particular constitutional organisation and practice of each Member State,

DESIRING, however, to encourage greater involvement of national parliaments in the activities of the European Union and to enhance their ability to express their views on matters which may be of particular interest to them,

HAVE AGREED UPON the following provisions, which shall be annexed to the Treaty on European Union and the Treaties establishing the European Communities,

I. Information for national parliaments of Member States

1. All Commission consultation documents (green and white papers and communications) shall be promptly forwarded to national parliaments of the Member States.

2. Commission proposals for legislation as defined by the Council in accordance with Article 207(3) [ex 151(3)] of the Treaty establishing the European Community, shall be made available in good time so that the government of each Member State may ensure that its own national parliament receives them as appropriate.

3. A six-week period shall elapse between a legislative proposal or a proposal for a measure to be adopted under Title VI of the Treaty on European Union being made available in all languages to the European Parliament and the Council by the Commission and the date when it is placed on a Council agenda for decision either for the adoption of an act or for adoption of a common position pursuant to Article 251 [ex 189b] or 252 [ex 189c] of the Treaty establishing the European Community, subject to exceptions on grounds of urgency, the reasons for which shall be stated in the act or common position.

II. The Conference of European Affairs Committees

4. The Conference of European Affairs Committees, hereinafter referred to as COSAC, established in Paris on 16–17 November 1989, may make any contribution it deems appropriate for the attention of the institutions of the European Union, in particular on the basis of draft legal texts which representatives of governments of the Member States may decide by common accord to forward to it, in view of the nature of their subject matter.

5. COSAC may examine any legislative proposal or initiative in relation to the establishment of an area of freedom, security and justice which might have a direct bearing on the rights and freedoms of individuals. The European Parliament, the Council and the Commission shall be informed of any contribution made by COSAC under this point.

6. COSAC may address to the European Parliament, the Council and the Commission any contribution which it deems appropriate on the legislative activities of the Union, notably in relation to the application of the principle of subsidiarity, the area of freedom, security and justice as well as questions regarding fundamental rights.

7. Contributions made by COSAC shall in no way bind national parliaments or prejudge their position.

Protocol Annexed to the TEU and to the TEC, TECSC and TEAEC by the Treaty of Nice

Protocol on the Enlargement of the European Union (see above pp. 68–72)

Protocol Annexed to the TEU and to the TEC and TEAEC by the Treaty of Nice

Protocol on the Statute of the Court of Justice (see below pp. 493–504)

x   Final Act and Declarations

As we have just seen, protocols are kept somewhat apart from the rest of the TEU because of their length. Hence, as well as being printed after the main body of the text, they are mentioned again in the last part of the treaty structure, the so-called final act. Although this is a rather formal and unappealing document, it needs to be remembered. So do the many declarations which figure in it, and nowhere else. These too have something to tell us about the Union and the thinking of the people who set it up.

As a result, this subdivision of the *Guide* looks first, and in brief, at the final act as such. It then goes on to consider the range of declarations. We also give some attention to those found in the TA final act which are especially relevant to the Union. However, such is their number and technical nature that we cannot comment on them all, let alone at length.

Final Act

The final act which follows the TEU carries out two main functions. First, it records in brief the purpose of the four IGCs which drafted the TEU, the work of which it concludes. It reminds us of an overlooked fact, that the two IGCs that were convened in December 1990 were not the only ones involved in drafting the TEU. Two were convened on 3 February 1992, four days before the TEU was finally signed, to amend certain institutional provisions contained in the ECSC and Euratom treaties following amendments to the Treaty of Rome. At the same time it makes the point that there was unanimous agreement among the member states in amending the existing treaties.

Secondly, it summarizes the texts which the IGCs adopted. Hence, the Maastricht final act notes the TEU (without expanding on its contents); lists the protocols adopted, indicating clearly the treaty or treaties to which they are to be annexed; and provides a list of the declarations adopted by the IGC. These are then presented as unnumbered annexes to the final act. Contrary to Amsterdam, these are in one continuous listing since none of them was a unilateral statement. They were all adopted by the conference as a whole.

In the official version of the TEU, the signatures of all those accepting the treaty for their states are again appended. This presumably shows that they agree not just to the purposes of the negotiations, as set out in the preamble, but also to their outcome. And they also give them the chance to append last-minute thoughts in the form of declarations. The latter thus have a real legal significance and deserve printing here.

TREATY ON EUROPEAN UNION – FINAL ACT

1. The Conferences of the Representatives of the Governments of the Member States convened in Rome on 15 December 1990 to adopt by common accord the amendments to be made to the Treaty establishing the European Economic Community with a view to the achievement of political union and with a view to the final stages of economic and monetary union, and those convened in Brussels on 3 February 1992 with a view to amending the Treaties establishing respectively the European Coal and Steel Community and the European Atomic Energy Community as a result of the amendments envisaged for the Treaty establishing the European Economic Community have adopted the following texts:

I   the Treaty on European Union

II   Protocols

1. Protocol on the acquisition of property in Denmark
2. Protocol concerning Article 141 [ex 119] of the Treaty establishing the European Community
3. Protocol on the Statute of the European System of Central Banks and of the European Central Bank
4. Protocol on the Statute of the European Monetary Institute
5. Protocol on the excessive deficit procedure
6. Protocol on the convergence criteria referred to in Article 121 [ex 109j] of the Treaty establishing the European Community
7. Protocol amending the Protocol on the privileges and immunities of the European Communities
8. Protocol on Denmark
9. Protocol on Portugal
10. Protocol on the transition to the third stage of economic and monetary union
11. Protocol on certain provisions relating to the United Kingdom of Great Britain and Northern Ireland
12. Protocol on certain provisions relating to Denmark
13. Protocol on France
14. Protocol on social policy, to which is annexed an agreement concluded between the Member States of the European Community with the exception of the United Kingdom of Great Britain and Northern Ireland, to which two declarations are attached
15. Protocol on economic and social cohesion
16. Protocol on the Economic and Social Committee and the Committee of the Regions
17. Protocol annexed to the Treaty on European Union and to the Treaties establishing the European Communities

The Conferences agreed that the Protocols referred to in 1 to 16 above will be annexed to the Treaty establishing the European Community and that the Protocol referred to in 17 above will be annexed to the Treaty on European Union and to the Treaties establishing the European Communities.

2. At the time of signature of these texts, the Conferences adopted the declarations listed below and annexed to this Final Act:

III Declarations

1. Declaration on civil protection, energy and tourism
2. Declaration on nationality of a Member State
3. Declaration on Part Three, Titles III and VII [ex VI], of the Treaty establishing the European Community
4. Declaration on Part Three, Title VII [ex VI], of the Treaty establishing the European Community
5. Declaration on monetary co-operation with non-Community countries
6. Declaration on monetary relations with the Republic of San Marino, the Vatican City and the Principality of Monaco
7. Declaration on Article 158 [ex 73d] of the Treaty establishing the European Community
8. Declaration on Article 111 [ex 109] of the Treaty establishing the European Community
9. Declaration on Part Three, Title XIX [ex XVI], of the Treaty establishing the European Community
10. Declaration on Articles 111 [ex 109], 174 [ex 130r] and 181 [ex 130y] of the Treaty establishing the European Community
11. Declaration on the Directive of 24 November 1988 (Emissions)
12. Declaration on the European Development Fund
13. Declaration on the role of national parliaments in the European Union
14. Declaration on the Conference of the Parliaments
15. Declaration on the number of members of the Commission and of the European Parliament
16. Declaration on the hierarchy of Community Acts
17. Declaration on the right of access to information
18. Declaration on estimated costs under Commission proposals
19. Declaration on the implementation of Community law
20. Declaration on assessment of the environmental impact of Community measures
21. Declaration on the Court of Auditors
22. Declaration on the Economic and Social Committee
23. Declaration on co-operation with charitable associations
24. Declaration on the protection of animals
25. Declaration on the representation of the interests of the overseas countries and territories referred to in Article 299(3) and (6)(a) and (b) [ex 227(3) and (5)(a) and (b)] of the Treaty establishing the European Community
26. Declaration on the outermost regions of the Community
27. Declaration on voting in the field of the common foreign and security policy
28. Declaration on practical arrangements in the field of the common foreign and security policy
29. Declaration on the use of languages in the field of the common foreign and security policy
30. Declaration on Western European Union
31. Declaration on asylum
32. Declaration on police co-operation
33. Declaration on disputes between the ECB and the EMI and their servants

Done at Maastricht this seventh day of February in the year one thousand nine hundred and ninety-two.

Declarations

As is the case with most of the EU's other constitutive and amending treaties, the final act associated with the TEU has annexed to it a variety of declarations, many of them very specifically national. Most of these are the product of the initial signing of the TEU. Others relating to the TEU's provisions have since been added by Amsterdam and Nice to the mass of such declarations surrounding the European Treaties. However, declarations are less likely than protocols to be allocated to a named treaty although this does happen. And then, as already suggested, they can have a special quasi-constitutive importance.

Unlike most of the protocols noted in the previous subdivision, declarations are not legally binding and are neither subject to the jurisdiction of the ECJ nor regarded as creating any meaningful obligations on any of the member states or Community institutions. Rather, as we showed in our earlier discussion of the declarations either adopted or noted by the IGC which drafted the TA (see pp. 50–51), they tend either to provide clarification of specific provisions or contain statements of intent. But whereas at Amsterdam some at least were attached by one or more strong-minded states, those discussed here were all collectively adopted by the four IGCs which drew up the TEU. Hence most of the 1992 declarations begin with the statements which show the commitment of the conference to whatever is being said. Again, unlike Amsterdam, none are related to protocols.

Of the 33 declarations, the majority contain statements of intent. These include the declarations on future treaty amendments (1 and 16), both of which were, in the event, effectively ignored, EMU (4–6), the environment (9 and 20), the role of national parliaments (13 and 14), the composition, status, roles and effectiveness of institutions (15, 21, 22, 28 and 33), transparency (17), estimated costs of legislation (18), implementation of EC law (19), co-operation with charitable associations (23), the protection of animals (24), overseas countries and territories and outermost regions (25 and 26), the CFSP (27–29), WEU (30), asylum (31) and police co-operation (32). The remaining declarations either affirm the rights of member states to take certain decisions (e.g. regarding nationality (2) and tax law (7)) or to retain derogations (11) or clarify provisions found in the TEC (e.g. on EMU (3 and 8), treaty-making power (10)). Most of these declarations are referred to elsewhere in the *Guide*. A thirty-fourth declaration was added in May 1992 to help get the Irish government out of its little local difficulty on abortion.

This does not exhaust the list of declarations associated with the TEU. Amsterdam (see especially Division II above) agreed five which refer specifically to the revised TEU. It also noted two more added by individual states. To reinforce what has already been said about them, they are further commented on and then printed below. Of the first group, one deals with the abolition of the death penalty (No. 1 TA) making the point that it is not effectively in force and implying that new states should not practise it, thus underlining the human rights concerns of the Union. The next two deal with the WEU (Nos. 2 and 3 TA). The second of these is actually more akin to a protocol than to the average declaration since it lays down a comprehensive code of conduct for the WEU. However, since it was agreed by the WEU and not the IGC, it can only be noted by the latter and not given binding status. The same might also be said about the Declaration on the establishment of a policy planning and early warning unit (No. 6 TA). The fourth one makes it clear that, in authorizing the presidency to negotiate on the Union's behalf, the member states did not intend to give the Union new powers (No. 4 TA). The workings of the new CFSP are also clarified by Declaration No. 5 TA.

These are followed by a series of declarations spelling out the conference's understanding of the legal status of the new third pillar (Nos. 7–10 TA), again emphasizing states' rights. They also provide reassurance to states which feared being forced to accept centrally defined sentences in state prosecutions. This is followed by a further endorsement of fundamental rights, relating this time to churches and to secular freedom of thought (No. 11 TA). In turn this leads on to a Greek-sponsored declaration noted by the conference (No. 8n TA). Some of these provisions obviously have implications for the TEC as well. These are printed below.

Finally, a number of the declarations merely noted by the conference ought to be mentioned. These deal with understandings of the way in which the member states concerned would deal with the incorporation of Schengen, and its opt-outs, into the TEC (Nos. 2n, 4n and 7n TA). More important is the Belgian-sponsored Declaration No. 5n TA which was an implied threat to the whole process of enlargement, arising from frustration at the lack of institutional progress at Amsterdam. Finally, as we have already seen, at the time of signature of Amsterdam, a number of states signified their willingness to accept ECJ jurisdiction where co-operation in criminal matters was concerned.

At Nice, as already demonstrated, further declarations were added to the treaty base, though not specifically to the TEU final act. As well as those on enlargement (Nos. 20 and 21 TN), which seem to have a greater status than most (see pp. 72–6), we should also note two others which are printed below (Nos. 1 and 2 TN). Such declarations seem to matter more than most since they have to be used in the process of enlargement, always assuming that they are not set aside. They both tell us something about the shape of the enlarging Union and remind us that the Union is an ambiguous affair, not just a still-complex treaty but, since 1992, an organized body. And as such it rests not just on the two inter-governmental pillars but on the Community, which forms its ever changing first pillar. And it can also help to define the Union. Declaration 23 on the future of the European Union is also relevant (see pp. 564–5).

All these things help to give a different cast to the Union and need to be remembered here. Indeed, for all that they can add to the underlying ambiguity of the TEU, such additions are a sign of the growing importance of the TEU. Even though it was less affected by Nice it has to be seen as the equal of the TEC, if not as its superior. The Belgian declaration (No. 6n TA) is in fact a good example of the way in which the TEU increasingly provides axioms for the whole enterprise. Hence, much discussion of the Community, to which the *Guide* moves next, is often cast in terms of the Union.

Declarations Attached to the Final Act Associated with the TEU

1.   DECLARATION ON CIVIL PROTECTION, ENERGY AND TOURISM

The Conference declares that the question of introducing into the Treaty establishing the European Community Titles relating to the spheres referred to in Article 3(u) [ex 3(t)] of that Treaty will be examined, in accordance with the procedure laid down in Article N(2) [now deleted] of the Treaty on European Union, on the basis of a report which the Commission will submit to the Council by 1996 at the latest. The Commission declares that Community action in those spheres will be pursued on the basis of the present provisions of the Treaties establishing the European Communities.

2. DECLARATION ON NATIONALITY OF A MEMBER STATE

The Conference declares that, wherever in the Treaty establishing the European Community reference is made to nationals of the Member States, the question whether an individual possesses the nationality of a Member State shall be settled solely by reference to the national law of the Member State concerned. Member States may declare, for information, who are to be considered their nationals for Community purposes by way of declaration lodged with the Presidency and may amend any such declarations when necessary.

3. DECLARATION ON PART THREE, TITLES III AND VII [ex VI], OF THE TREATY ESTABLISHING THE EUROPEAN COMMUNITY

The Conference affirms that, for the purposes of applying the provisions set out in Part Three, Title III, Chapter 4 on capital and payments, and Title VII [ex VI] on economic and monetary policy, of this Treaty, the usual practice, according to which the Council meets in the composition of Economic and Finance Ministers, shall be continued, without prejudice to Article 121(2) to (4) [ex 109j(2) to (4)] and Article 122(2) [ex 109k(2)].

4. DECLARATION ON PART THREE, TITLE VII [ex VI], OF THE TREATY ESTABLISHING THE EUROPEAN COMMUNITY

The Conference affirms that the President of the European Council shall invite the Economic and Finance Ministers to participate in European Council meetings when the European Council is discussing matters relating to Economic and Monetary Union.

5. DECLARATION ON MONETARY CO-OPERATION WITH NON-COMMUNITY COUNTRIES

The Conference affirms that the Community shall aim to contribute to stable international monetary relations. To this end the Community shall be prepared to co-operate with other European countries and with those non-European countries with which the Community has close economic ties.

6. DECLARATION ON MONETARY RELATIONS WITH THE REPUBLIC OF SAN MARINO, THE VATICAN CITY AND THE PRINCIPALITY OF MONACO

The Conference agrees that the existing monetary relations between Italy and San Marino and the Vatican City and between France and Monaco remain unaffected by the Treaty establishing the European Community until the introduction of the ECU as the single currency of the Community.
The Community undertakes to facilitate such renegotiations of existing arrangements as might become necessary as a result of the introduction of the ECU as a single currency.

7.   DECLARATION ON ARTICLE 58 [ex 73d] OF THE TREATY ESTABLISHING THE EUROPEAN COMMUNITY

The Conference affirms that the right of Member States to apply the relevant provisions of their tax law as referred to in Article 58(1)(a) [ex 73d(1)(a)] of this Treaty will apply only with respect to the relevant provisions which exist at the end of 1993. However, this Declaration shall apply only to capital movements between Member States and to payments effected between Member States.

8.   DECLARATION ON ARTICLE 111 [ex 109] OF THE TREATY ESTABLISHING THE EUROPEAN COMMUNITY

The Conference emphasizes that use of the term 'formal agreements' in Article 111 (1) [ex 109(1)] is not intended to create a new category of international agreement within the meaning of Community law.

9.   DECLARATION ON PART THREE, TITLE XIX [ex XVI], OF THE TREATY ESTABLISHING THE EUROPEAN COMMUNITY

The Conference considers that, in view of the increasing importance of nature conservation at national, Community and international level, the Community should, in exercising its powers under the provisions of Part Three, Title XIX [ex XVI], take account of the specific requirements of this area.

10.   DECLARATION ON ARTICLES 111 [ex 109], 174 [ex 130r] and 181 [ex 130y] OF THE TREATY ESTABLISHING THE EUROPEAN COMMUNITY

The Conference considers that the provisions of Article 111(5) [ex 109(5)], Article 174(4) [ex 130r(4)], second subparagraph, and Article 181 [ex 130y] do not affect the principles resulting from the judgement handed down by the Court of Justice in the *AETR* case.*

11.   DECLARATION ON THE DIRECTIVE OF 24 NOVEMBER 1988 (Emissions)

The Conference declares that changes in Community legislation cannot undermine the derogations granted to Spain and Portugal until 31 December 1999 under the Council Directive of 24 November 1988 on the limitation of emissions of certain pollutants into the air from large combustion plants.

12.   DECLARATION ON THE EUROPEAN DEVELOPMENT FUND

The Conference agrees that the European Development Fund will continue to be financed by national contributions in accordance with the current provisions.

---

*In the *AETR* case the ECJ ruled that where the Community has an explicit internal competence it has a parallel external competence. In such areas, member states may not therefore act independently of the Community. Furthermore where a member state does enter into an obligation under an international agreement which conflicts with EC law, the latter overrides any such obligation.

13. DECLARATION ON THE ROLE OF NATIONAL PARLIAMENTS IN THE EUROPEAN UNION

The Conference considers that it is important to encourage greater involvement of national parliaments in the activities of the European Union.

To this end, the exchange of information between the national parliaments and the European Parliament should be stepped up. In this context, the governments of the Member States will ensure, *inter alia*, that national parliaments receive Commission proposals for legislation in good time for information or possible examination.

Similarly, the Conference considers that it is important for contacts between the national parliaments and the European Parliament to be stepped up, in particular through the granting of appropriate reciprocal facilities and regular meetings between members of Parliament interested in the same issues.

14. DECLARATION ON THE CONFERENCE OF THE PARLIAMENTS

The Conference invites the European Parliament and the national parliaments to meet as necessary as a Conference of the Parliaments (or 'assises').

The Conference of the parliaments will be consulted on the main features of the European Union, without prejudice to the powers of the European Parliament and the rights of the national parliaments. The President of the European Council and the President of the Commission will report to each session of the Conference of the Parliaments on the state of the Union.

15. DECLARATION ON THE NUMBER OF MEMBERS OF THE COMMISSION AND OF THE EUROPEAN PARLIAMENT

The Conference agrees that the Member States will examine the questions relating to the number of members of the Commission and the number of members of the European Parliament no later than at the end of 1992, with a view to reaching an agreement which will permit the establishment of the necessary legal basis for fixing the number of members of the European Parliament in good time for the 1994 elections. The decisions will be taken in the light, *inter alia*, of the need to establish the overall size of the European Parliament in an enlarged Community.

16. DECLARATION ON THE HIERARCHY OF COMMUNITY ACTS

The Conference agrees that the Intergovernmental Conference to be convened in 1996 will examine to what extent it might be possible to review the classification of Community acts with a view to establishing an appropriate hierarchy between the different categories of act.

17. DECLARATION ON THE RIGHT OF ACCESS TO INFORMATION

The Conference considers that transparency of the decision-making process strengthens the democratic nature of the institutions and the public's confidence in the administration. The Conference accordingly recommends that the Commission submit to the Council no later than 1993 a report on measures designed to improve public access to the information available to the institutions.

18.   DECLARATION ON ESTIMATED COSTS UNDER COMMISSION PROPOSALS

The Conference notes that the Commission undertakes, by basing itself where appropriate on any consultations it considers necessary and by strengthening its system for evaluating Community legislation, to take account in its legislative proposals of costs and benefits to the Member States' public authorities and all the parties concerned.

19.   DECLARATION ON THE IMPLEMENTATION OF COMMUNITY LAW

1. The Conference stresses that it is central to the coherence and unity of the process of European construction that each Member State should fully and accurately transpose into national law the Community Directives addressed to it within the deadlines laid down therein.

Moreover, the Conference, while recognizing that it must be for each Member State to determine how the provisions of Community law can best be enforced in the light of its own particular institutions, legal system and other circumstances, but in any event in compliance with Article 249 [ex 189] of the Treaty establishing the European Community, considers it essential for the proper functioning of the Community that the measures taken by the different Member States should result in Community law being applied with the same effectiveness and rigour as in the application of their national law.

2. The Conference calls on the Commission to ensure, in exercising its powers under Article 211 [ex 155] of this Treaty, that Member States fulfil their obligations. It asks the Commission to publish periodically a full report for the Member States and the European Parliament.

20.   DECLARATION ON ASSESSMENT OF THE ENVIRONMENTAL IMPACT OF COMMUNITY MEASURES

The Conference notes that the Commission undertakes in its proposals, and that the Member States undertake in implementing those proposals, to take full account of their environmental impact and of the principle of sustainable growth.

21.   DECLARATION ON THE COURT OF AUDITORS

The Conference emphasizes the special importance it attaches to the task assigned to the Court of Auditors by Articles 246 [ex 188a], 247 [ex 188b], 248 [ex 188c] and 275 [ex 206] of the Treaty establishing the European Community.

It requests the other Community institutions to consider, together with the Court of Auditors, all appropriate ways of enhancing the effectiveness of its work.

22. DECLARATION ON THE ECONOMIC AND SOCIAL COMMITTEE

The Conference agrees that the Economic and Social Committee will enjoy the same independence with regard to its budget and staff management as the Court of Auditors has enjoyed hitherto.

23. DECLARATION ON CO-OPERATION WITH CHARITABLE ASSOCIATIONS

The Conference stresses the importance, in pursuing the objectives of Article 136 [ex 117] of the Treaty establishing the European Community, of co-operation between the latter and charitable associations and foundations as institutions responsible for social welfare establishments and services.

24. DECLARATION ON THE PROTECTION OF ANIMALS

The Conference calls upon the European Parliament, the Council and the Commission, as well as the Member States, when drafting and implementing Community legislation on the common agricultural policy, transport, the internal market and research, to pay full regard to the welfare requirements of animals.

25. DECLARATION ON THE REPRESENTATION OF THE INTERESTS OF THE OVERSEAS COUNTRIES AND TERRITORIES REFERRED TO IN ARTICLE 299(3) AND (6)(A) AND (B) [EX 227(3) AND (5)(A) AND (B)] OF THE TREATY ESTABLISHING THE EUROPEAN COMMUNITY

The Conference, noting that in exceptional circumstances divergences may arise between the interests of the Union and those of the overseas countries and territories referred to in Article 299(3) and (6)(a) and (b) [ex 227(3) and (5)(a) and (b)], agrees that the Council will seek to reach a solution which accords with the position of the Union. However, in the event that this proves impossible, the Conference agrees that the Member State concerned may act separately in the interests of the said overseas countries and territories, without this affecting the Community's interests. The Member State concerned will give notice to the Council and the Commission where such a divergence of interests is likely to occur and, when separate action proves unavoidable, make it clear that it is acting in the interests of an overseas territory mentioned above.

This declaration also applies to Macao and East Timor.

26. DECLARATION ON THE OUTERMOST REGIONS OF THE COMMUNITY

The Conference acknowledges that the outermost regions of the Community (the French overseas departments, Azores and Madeira and Canary Islands) suffer from major structural backwardness compounded by several phenomena (remoteness, island status, small size, difficult topography and climate, economic dependence on a few products), the permanence and combination of which severely restrain their economic and social development.

It considers that, while the provisions of the Treaty establishing the European Community and secondary legislation apply automatically to outermost regions, it is nonetheless possible to adopt specific measures to assist them inasmuch and as long as there is an objective need to take such measures with a view to the economic and social development of those regions. Such measures should have as their aim both the completion of the internal market and a recognition of the regional reality to enable the outermost regions to achieve the average economic and social level of the Community.

27. DECLARATION ON VOTING IN THE FIELD OF THE COMMON FOREIGN AND SECURITY POLICY

The Conference agrees that, with regard to Council decisions requiring unanimity, Member States will, to the extent possible, avoid preventing a unanimous decision where a qualified majority exists in favour of that decision.

28. DECLARATION ON PRACTICAL ARRANGEMENTS IN THE FIELD OF THE COMMON FOREIGN AND SECURITY POLICY

The Conference agrees that the division of work between the Political Committee and the Committee of Permanent Representatives will be examined at a later stage, as will the practical arrangements for merging the Political Co-operation Secretariat with the General Secretariat of the Council and for co-operation between the latter and the Commission.

29. DECLARATION ON THE USE OF LANGUAGES IN THE FIELD OF THE COMMON FOREIGN AND SECURITY POLICY

The Conference agrees that the use of languages shall be in accordance with the rules of the European Communities.

For COREU communications, the current practice of European political co-operation will serve as a guide for the time being.

All common foreign and security policy texts which are submitted to or adopted at meetings of the European Council and of the Council as well as all texts which are to be published are immediately and simultaneously translated into all the official Community languages.

30. DECLARATION ON WESTERN EUROPEAN UNION

The Conference notes the following declarations:

I. DECLARATION

by Belgium, Germany, Spain, France, Italy, Luxembourg, the Netherlands, Portugal and the United Kingdom of Great Britain and Northern Ireland, which are members of the Western European Union and also members of the European Union on

THE ROLE OF THE WESTERN EUROPEAN UNION AND ITS RELATIONS WITH THE EUROPEAN UNION AND WITH THE ATLANTIC ALLIANCE

Introduction

1. WEU Member States agree on the need to develop a genuine European security

and defence identity and a greater European responsibility on defence matters. This identity will be pursued through a gradual process involving successive phases. WEU will form an integral part of the process of the development of the European Union and will enhance its contribution to solidarity within the Atlantic Alliance. WEU Member States agree to strengthen the role of WEU, in the longer term perspective of a common defence policy within the European Union which might in time lead to common defence, compatible with that of the Atlantic Alliance.

2. WEU will be developed as the defence component of the European Union and as a means to strengthen the European pillar of the Atlantic Alliance. To this end, it will formulate common European defence policy and carry forward its concrete implementation through the further development of its own operational role.

WEU Member States take note of Article J.4 relating to the common foreign and security policy of the Treaty on European Union which reads as follows:

1. *The common foreign and security policy shall include all questions relating to the security of the Union, including the eventual framing of a common defence policy, which might in time lead to a common defence.*

2. *The Union requests the Western European Union (WEU), which is an integral part of the development of the Union, to elaborate and implement decisions and actions of the Union which have defence implications. The Council shall, in agreement with the institutions of the WEU, adopt the necessary practical arrangements.*

3. *Issues having defence implications dealt with under this Article shall not be subject to the procedures set out in Article J.3.*

4. *The policy of the Union in accordance with this Article shall not prejudice the specific character of the security and defence policy of certain Member States and shall respect the obligations of certain Member States under the North Atlantic Treaty and be compatible with the common security and defence policy established within that framework.*

5. *The provisions of this Article shall not prevent the development of closer co-operation between two or more Member States on a bilateral level, in the framework of the WEU and the Atlantic Alliance, provided such co-operation does not run counter to or impede that provided for in this Title.*

6. *With a view to furthering the objectives of this Treaty, and having in view the date of 1998 in the context of Article XII of the Brussels Treaty, the provisions of this Article may be revised as provided for in Article N(2) on the basis of a report to be presented in 1996 by the Council to the European Council, which shall include an evaluation of the progress made and the experience gained until then.*

A. WEU's relations with the European Union

3. The objective is to build up WEU in stages as the defence component of the European Union. To this end, WEU is prepared, at the request of the European Union, to elaborate and implement decisions and actions of the Union which have defence implications.

To this end, WEU will take the following measures to develop a close working relationship with the Union:

– as appropriate, synchronization of the dates and venues of meetings and harmonization of working methods;

– establishment of close co-operation between the Council and Secretariat-General of WEU on the one hand, and the Council of the Union and General Secretariat of the Council on the other;

– consideration of the harmonization of the sequence and duration of the respective Presidencies;

– arranging for appropriate modalities so as to ensure that the Commission of the European Communities is regularly informed and, as appropriate, consulted on WEU activities in accordance with the role of the Commission in the common foreign and security policy as defined in the Treaty on European Union;

– encouragement of closer co-operation between the Parliamentary Assembly of WEU and the European Parliament.

The WEU Council shall, in agreement with the competent bodies of the European Union, adopt the necessary practical arrangements.

B. WEU's relations with the Atlantic Alliance

4. The objective is to develop WEU as a means to strengthen the European pillar of the Atlantic Alliance. Accordingly WEU is prepared to develop further the close working links between WEU and the Alliance and to strengthen the role, responsibilities and contributions of WEU Member States in the Alliance. This will be undertaken on the basis of the necessary transparency and complementarity between the emerging European security and defence identity and the Alliance. WEU will act in conformity with the positions adopted in the Atlantic Alliance.

– WEU Member States will intensify their co-ordination on Alliance issues which represent an important common interest with the aim of introducing joint positions agreed in WEU into the process of consultation in the Alliance which will remain the essential forum for consultation among its members and the venue for agreement on policies bearing on the security and defence commitments of Allies under the North Atlantic Treaty.

– Where necessary, dates and venues of meetings will be synchronized and working methods harmonized.

– Close co-operation will be established between the Secretariats-General of WEU and NATO.

C. Operational role of WEU

5. WEU's operational role will be strengthened by examining and defining appropriate missions, structures and means, covering in particular:

– WEU planning cell;

– closer military co-operation complementary to the Alliance in particular in the fields of logistics, transport, training and strategic surveillance;

– meetings of WEU Chiefs of Defence Staff;

– military units answerable to WEU.

Other proposals will be examined further, including:

– enhanced co-operation in the field of armaments with the aim of creating a European armaments agency;

– development of the WEU Institute into a European Security and Defence Academy.

Arrangements aimed at giving WEU a stronger operational role will be fully compatible with the military dispositions necessary to ensure the collective defence of all Allies.

D. Other measures

6. As a consequence of the measures set out above, and in order to facilitate the strengthening of WEU's role, the seat of the WEU Council and Secretariat will be transferred to Brussels.

7. Representation of the WEU Council must be such that the Council is able to exercise its functions continuously in accordance with Article VIII of the modified Brussels Treaty. Member States may draw on a double-hatting formula, to be worked out, consisting of their representatives to the Alliance and to the European Union.

8. WEU notes that, in accordance with the provisions of Article J.4(6) concerning the common foreign and security policy of the Treaty on European Union, the Union will decide to review the provisions of this Article with a view to furthering the objective to be set by it in accordance with the procedure defined. The WEU will re-examine the present provisions in 1996. This re-examination will take account of the progress and experience acquired and will extend to relations between WEU and the Atlantic Alliance.

II. DECLARATION

by Belgium, Germany, Spain, France, Italy, Luxembourg, the Netherlands, Portugal and the United Kingdom of Great Britain and Northern Ireland which are members of the Western European Union.

'The Member States of WEU welcome the development of the European security and defence identity. They are determined, taking into account the role of WEU as the defence component of the European Union and as the means to strengthen the European pillar of the Atlantic Alliance, to put the relationship between WEU and the other European States on a new basis for the sake of stability and security in Europe. In this spirit, they propose the following:

States which are members of the European Union are invited to accede to WEU on conditions to be agreed in accordance with Article XI of the modified Brussels Treaty, or to become observers if they so wish. Simultaneously, other European Member States of NATO are invited to become associate members of WEU in a way which will give them the possibility of participating fully in the activities of WEU.

The Member States of WEU assume that treaties and agreements corresponding with the above proposals will be concluded before 31 December 1992.'

31. DECLARATION ON ASYLUM

1. The Conference agrees that, in the context of the proceedings provided for in Articles K.1 and K.3 of the provisions on co-operation in the fields of justice and home affairs, the Council will consider as a matter of priority questions concerning Member States' asylum policies, with the aim of adopting by the beginning of 1993 common action to harmonize aspects of them, in the light of the work programme and timetable contained in the report on asylum drawn up at the request of the European Council meeting in Luxembourg on 28 and 29 June 1991.*

2. In this connection, the Council will also consider, by the end of 1993, on the basis of a report, the possibility of applying Article 42 [ex K.9] to such matters.

---

*The areas to which this Declaration refers were subsequently transferred to the TEC by the TA.

32.   DECLARATION ON POLICE CO-OPERATION

The Conference confirms the agreement of the Member States on the objectives underlying the German delegation's proposals at the European Council meeting in Luxembourg on 28 and 29 June 1991.

For the present, the Member States agree to examine as a matter of priority the drafts submitted to them, on the basis of the work programme and timetable agreed upon in the report drawn up at the request of the Luxembourg European Council, and they are willing to envisage the adoption of practical measures in areas such as those suggested by the German delegation, relating to the following functions in the exchange of information and experience:
- support for national criminal investigation and security authorities, in particular in the co-ordination of investigations and search operations;
- creation of databases;
- central analysis and assessment of information in order to take stock of the situation and identify investigative approaches;
- collection and analysis of national prevention programmes for forwarding to Member States and for drawing up Europe-wide prevention strategies;
- measures relating to further training, research, forensic matters and criminal records departments.

Member States agree to consider on the basis of a report, during 1994 at the latest, whether the scope of such co-operation should be extended.

33.   DECLARATION ON DISPUTES BETWEEN THE ECB AND THE EMI AND THEIR SERVANTS

The Conference considers it proper that the Court of First Instance should hear this class of action in accordance with Article 224 [ex 168a] of the Treaty establishing the European Community. The Conference therefore invites the institutions to adapt the relevant rules accordingly.

34.   DECLARATION OF THE HIGH CONTRACTING PARTIES TO THE TREATY ON EUROPEAN UNION [Guimarães, 1 May 1992]

The High Contracting Parties to the Treaty on European Union signed at Maastricht on the seventh day of February 1992,

Having considered the terms of Protocol No. 17 to the said Treaty on European Union which is annexed to that Treaty and to the Treaties establishing the European Communities,

Hereby give the following legal interpretation:

That it was and is their intention that the Protocol shall not limit freedom to travel between Member States or, in accordance with conditions which may be laid down, in conformity with Community law, by Irish legislation, to obtain or make available in Ireland information relating to services lawfully available in Member States.

At the same time the High Contracting Parties solemnly declare that, in the event of a future constitutional amendment in Ireland which concerns the subject matter of Article 40.3.3 of the Constitution of Ireland and which does not conflict with the intention of the High Contracting Parties hereinbefore expressed, they will, following the entry into force of the Treaty on European Union, be favourably disposed to amending the said Protocol so as to extend its application to such constitutional amendment if Ireland so requests.

Declarations Relating to the TEU Annexed to the Final Act Associated with the Treaty of Amsterdam

1. DECLARATION ON THE ABOLITION OF THE DEATH PENALTY

With reference to Article F(2) [now 6(2)] of the Treaty on European Union, the Conference recalls that Protocol No. 6 to the European Convention for the Protection of Human Rights and Fundamental Freedoms signed in Rome on 4 November 1950, and which has been signed and ratified by a large majority of Member States, provides for the abolition of the death penalty.

In this context, the Conference notes the fact that since the signature of the above-mentioned Protocol on 28 April 1983, the death penalty has been abolished in most of the Member States of the Union and has not been applied in any of them.

2. DECLARATION ON ENHANCED CO-OPERATION BETWEEN THE EUROPEAN UNION AND THE WESTERN EUROPEAN UNION

With a view to enhanced co-operation between the European Union and the Western European Union, the Conference invites the Council to seek the early adoption of appropriate arrangements for the security clearance of the personnel of the General Secretariat of the Council.

3. DECLARATION RELATING TO WESTERN EUROPEAN UNION

The Conference notes the following Declaration, adopted by the Council of Ministers of the Western European Union on 22 July 1997

'DECLARATION OF WESTERN EUROPEAN UNION ON THE ROLE OF WESTERN EUROPEAN UNION AND ITS RELATIONS WITH THE EUROPEAN UNION AND WITH THE ATLANTIC ALLIANCE

INTRODUCTION

1. The Western European Union (WEU) Member States agreed at Maastricht in 1991 on the need to develop a genuine European Security and Defence Identity (ESDI) and to assume a greater European responsibility for defence matters. In the light of the Treaty of Amsterdam, they reaffirm the importance of continuing and strengthening these efforts. WEU is an integral part of the development of the European Union (EU) providing the Union with access to an operational capability, notably in the context of the Petersberg tasks and is an essential element of the development of the ESDI within the Atlantic Alliance in accordance with the Paris Declaration and with the decisions taken by NATO ministers in Berlin.

2. Today the WEU Council brings together all the Member States of the European Union and all the European Members of the Atlantic Alliance in accordance with

their respective status. The Council also brings together those States with the Central and Eastern European States linked to the European Union by an Association Agreement and that are applicants for accession to both the European Union and the Atlantic Alliance. WEU is thus establishing itself as a genuine framework for dialogue and co-operation among Europeans on wider European security and defence issues.

3. In this context, WEU takes note of Title V of the Treaty on European Union regarding the EU's common foreign and security policy, in particular Articles J.3(1) [now 13(1)], J.7 [now 17] and the Protocol to Article J.7 [now 17], which read as follows:*

Article J.3(1) [now 13(1)]

1. The European Council shall define the principles of and general guidelines for the common foreign and security policy, including for matters with defence implications.

Article J.7 [now 17]

1. The common foreign and security policy shall include all questions relating to the security of the Union, including the progressive framing of a common defence policy, in accordance with the second subparagraph, which might lead to a common defence, should the European Council so decide. It shall in that case recommend to the Member States the adoption of such a decision in accordance with their respective constitutional requirements.

The Western European Union (WEU) is an integral part of the development of the Union providing the Union with access to an operational capability notably in the context of paragraph 2. It supports the Union in framing the defence aspects of the common foreign and security policy as set out in this Article. The Union shall accordingly foster closer institutional relations with the WEU with a view to the possibility of the integration of the WEU into the Union, should the European Council so decide. It shall in that case recommend to the Member States the adoption of such a decision in accordance with their respective constitutional requirements.

The policy of the Union in accordance with this Article shall not prejudice the specific character of the security and defence policy of certain Member States and shall respect the obligations of certain Member States, which see their common defence realised in the North Atlantic Treaty Organisation (NATO), under the North Atlantic Treaty and be compatible with the common security and defence policy established within that framework.

The progressive framing of a common defence policy will be supported, as Member States consider appropriate, by co-operation between them in the field of armaments.

2. Questions referred to in this Article shall include humanitarian and rescue tasks, peacekeeping tasks and tasks of combat forces in crisis management, including peacemaking.

3. The Union will avail itself of the WEU to elaborate and implement decisions and actions of the Union which have defence implications.

The competence of the European Council to establish guidelines in accordance

---

*The text which follows is that introduced by the TA. It does not contain the amendments contained in the TN.

with Article J.13 [now 13] shall also obtain in respect of the WEU for those matters for which the Union avails itself of the WEU.

When the Union avails itself of the WEU to elaborate and implement decisions of the Union on the tasks referred to in paragraph 2, all Member States of the Union shall be entitled to participate fully in the tasks in question. The Council, in agreement with the institutions of the WEU, shall adopt the necessary practical arrangements to allow all Member States contributing to the tasks in question to participate fully and on an equal footing in planning and decision-taking in the WEU.

Decisions having defence implications dealt with under this paragraph shall be taken without prejudice to the policies and obligations referred to in paragraph 1, third subparagraph.

4. The provisions of this Article shall not prevent the development of closer co-operation between two or more Member States on a bilateral level, in the framework of the WEU and the Atlantic Alliance, provided such co-operation does not run counter to or impede that provided for in this Title.

5. With a view to furthering the objectives of this Article, the provisions of this Article will be reviewed in accordance with Article N [now 48].

Protocol on Article J.7 (see p. 161)

A. WEU's RELATIONS WITH THE EUROPEAN UNION: ACCOMPANYING THE IMPLEMENTATION OF THE TREATY OF AMSTERDAM

4. In the 'Declaration on the Role of the Western European Union and its Relations with the European Union and with the Atlantic Alliance' of 10 December 1991, WEU Member States set as their objective 'to build up WEU in stages as the defence component of the European Union'. They today reaffirm this aim as developed by the Treaty of Amsterdam.

5. When the Union avails itself of WEU, WEU will elaborate and implement decisions and actions of the EU which have defence implications.

In elaborating and implementing decisions and actions of the EU for which the Union avails itself of WEU, WEU will act consistently with guidelines established by the European Council.

WEU supports the Union in framing the defence aspects of the European Union Common Foreign and Security Policy as set out in Article J.7 [now 17] of the Treaty on European Union.

6. WEU confirms that when the European Union avails itself of WEU to elaborate and implement decisions of the Union on the tasks referred to in Article J.7(2) [now 17(2)] of the Treaty on European Union, all Member States of the Union shall be entitled to participate fully in the tasks in question in accordance with Article J.7(3) [now 17(3)] of the Treaty on European Union.

WEU will develop the role of the Observers in WEU in line with provisions contained in Article J.7(3) [now 17(3)] and will adopt the necessary practical arrangements to allow all Member States of the EU contributing to the tasks undertaken by WEU at the request of the EU to participate fully and on an equal footing in planning and decision-taking in the WEU.

7. Consistent with the Protocol on Article J.7 [now 17] of the Treaty on European Union, WEU shall draw up, together with the European Union, arrangements for

enhanced co-operation between them. In this regard, a range of measures, on some of which work is already in hand in WEU, can be taken forward now, such as:

– arrangements for improving the co-ordination of the consultation and decision-making processes of the respective Organisations, in particular in crisis situations;
– holding of joint meetings of the relevant bodies of the two Organisations;
– harmonisation as much as possible of the sequence of the Presidencies of WEU and the EU, as well as the administrative rules and practices of the two Organisations;
– close co-ordination of the work of the staff of the Secretariat-General of the WEU and the General Secretariat of the Council of the EU, including through the exchange and secondment of personnel;
– arrangements to allow the relevant bodies of the EU, including its Policy Planning and Early Warning Unit, to draw on the resources of WEU's Planning Cell, Situation Centre and Satellite Centre;
– co-operation in the field of armaments, as appropriate, within the framework of the Western European Armaments Group (WEAG), as the European forum for armaments co-operation, the EU and WEU in the context of rationalisation of the European armaments market and the establishment of a European Armaments Agency;
– practical arrangements for ensuring co-operation with the European Commission reflecting its role in the CFSP as defined in the revised Treaty on European Union;
– improved security arrangements with the European Union.

B.   RELATIONS BETWEEN WEU AND NATO IN THE FRAMEWORK OF THE DEVELOPMENT OF AN ESDI WITHIN THE ATLANTIC ALLIANCE

8. The Atlantic Alliance continues to be the basis of collective defence under the North Atlantic Treaty. It remains the essential forum for consultation among Allies and the framework in which they agree on policies bearing on their security and defence commitments under the Washington Treaty. The Alliance has embarked on a process of adaptation and reform so that it can more effectively carry out the full range of its missions. This process is aimed at strengthening and renewing the transatlantic partnership, including building an ESDI within the Alliance.

9. WEU is an essential element of the development of the European Security and Defence Identity within the Atlantic Alliance and will accordingly continue its efforts to strengthen institutional and practical co-operation with NATO.

10. In addition to its support for the common defence enshrined in Article 5 of the Washington Treaty and Article V of the modified Brussels Treaty, WEU takes an active role in conflict prevention and crisis management as provided for in the Petersberg Declaration. In this context, WEU undertakes to perform its role to the full, respecting the full transparency and complementarity between the two Organisations.

11. WEU affirms that this identity will be grounded on sound military principles and supported by appropriate military planning and will permit the creation of militarily coherent and effective forces capable of operating under the political control and strategic direction of WEU.

12. To this end, WEU will develop its co-operation with NATO, in particular in the following fields:
– mechanisms for consultation between WEU and NATO in the context of a crisis;
– WEU's active involvement in the NATO defence planning process;
– operational links between WEU and NATO for the planning, preparation and conduct of operations using NATO assets and capabilities under the political control and strategic direction of WEU, including:
  • military planning, conducted by NATO in co-ordination with WEU, and exercises;
  • a framework agreement on the transfer, monitoring and return of NATO assets and capabilities;
  • liaison between WEU and NATO in the context of European command arrangements.

This co-operation will continue to evolve, also taking account of the adaptation of the Alliance.

C.   WEU's OPERATIONAL ROLE IN THE DEVELOPMENT OF THE ESDI

13. WEU will develop its role as the European politico-military body for crisis management, by using the assets and capabilities made available by WEU nations on a national or multinational basis, and having recourse, when appropriate, to NATO's assets and capabilities under arrangements being worked out. In this context, WEU will also support the UN and OSCE in their crisis management tasks.

WEU will contribute, in the framework of Article J.7 [now 17] of the Treaty on European Union, to the progressive framing of a common defence policy and carry forward its concrete implementation through the further development of its own operational role.

14. To this end, WEU will take forward work in the following fields:
– WEU has developed crisis management mechanisms and procedures which will be updated as WEU gains experience through exercises and operations. The implementation of Petersberg missions calls for flexible modes of action geared to the diversity of crisis situations and making optimum use of the available capabilities including through recourse to national headquarters, which might be one provided by a framework nation, or to a multinational headquarters answerable to WEU or to NATO assets and capabilities;
– WEU has already worked out Preliminary Conclusions on the Formulation of a Common European Defence Policy which is an initial contribution on the objectives, scope and means of a common European defence policy.

WEU will continue this work on the basis in particular of the Paris Declaration and taking account of the relevant elements of the decisions of WEU and NATO summits and ministerial meetings since Birmingham. It will focus on the following fields:
  • definition of principles for the use of armed forces of the WEU States for WEU Petersberg operations in pursuit of common European security interests;
  • organisation of operational means for Petersberg tasks, such as generic and contingency planning and exercising, preparation and interoperability of forces,

including through participation in the NATO defence planning process, as appropriate;
  • strategic mobility on the basis of its current work;
  • defence intelligence, through its Planning Cell, Situation Centre and Satellite Centre;
– WEU has adopted many measures to strengthen its operational role (Planning Cell, Situation Centre, Satellite Centre). The improvement of the functioning of the military components at WEU Headquarters and the establishment, under the Council's authority, of a military committee will represent a further enhancement of structures which are important for the successful preparation and conduct of WEU operations;
– with the aim of opening participation in all its operations to Associate Members and Observer States, WEU will also examine the necessary modalities to allow Associate Members and Observer States to participate fully in accordance with their status in all operations undertaken by WEU;
– WEU recalls that Associate Members take part on the same basis as full members in operations to which they contribute, as well as in relevant exercises and planning. WEU will also examine the question of participation of the Observers as fully as possible in accordance with their status in planning and decision-taking within WEU in all operations to which they contribute;
– WEU will, in consultation where appropriate with the relevant bodies, examine the possibilities for maximum participation in its activities by Associate Members and Observer States in accordance with their status. It will address in particular activities in the fields of armaments, space and military studies;
– WEU will examine how to strengthen the Associate Partners' participation in an increasing number of activities.'

4. DECLARATION ON ARTICLES J.14 [now 24] AND K.10 [now 38] OF THE TREATY ON EUROPEAN UNION

The provisions of Articles J.14 [now 24] and K.10 [now 38] of the Treaty on European Union and any agreements resulting from them shall not imply any transfer of competence from the Member States to the European Union.

5. DECLARATION ON ARTICLE J.15 [now 25] OF THE TREATY ON EUROPEAN UNION

The Conference agrees that Member States shall ensure that the Political Committee referred to in Article J.15 [now 25] of the Treaty on European Union is able to meet at any time, in the event of international crises or other urgent matters, at very short notice at Political Director or deputy level.

6. DECLARATION ON THE ESTABLISHMENT OF A POLICY PLANNING AND EARLY WARNING UNIT

The Conference agrees that:

1. A policy planning and early warning unit shall be established in the General Secretariat of the Council under the responsibility of its Secretary-General, High Representative for the CFSP. Appropriate co-operation shall be established with the Commission in order to ensure full coherence with the Union's external economic and development policies.

2. The tasks of the unit shall include the following:

(a) monitoring and analysing developments in areas relevant to the CFSP;

(b) providing assessments of the Union's foreign and security policy interests and identifying areas where the CFSP could focus in future;

(c) providing timely assessments and early warning of events or situations which may have significant repercussions for the Union's foreign and security policy, including potential political crises;

(d) producing, at the request of either the Council or the Presidency or on its own initiative, argued policy options papers to be presented under the responsibility of the Presidency as a contribution to policy formulation in the Council, and which may contain analyses, recommendations and strategies for the CFSP.

3. The unit shall consist of personnel drawn from the General Secretariat, the Member States, the Commission and the WEU.

4. Any Member State or the Commission may make suggestions to the unit for work to be undertaken.

5. Member States and the Commission shall assist the policy planning process by providing, to the fullest extent possible, relevant information, including confidential information.

7. DECLARATION ON ARTICLE K.2 [now 30] OF THE TREATY ON EUROPEAN UNION

Action in the field of police co-operation under Article K.2 [now 30] of the Treaty on European Union, including activities of Europol, shall be subject to appropriate judicial review by the competent national authorities in accordance with rules applicable in each Member State.

8. DECLARATION ON ARTICLE K.3(e) [now 31(e)] OF THE TREATY ON EUROPEAN UNION

The Conference agrees that the provisions of Article K.3(e) [now 31(e)] of the Treaty on European Union shall not have the consequence of obliging a Member State whose legal system does not provide for minimum sentences to adopt them.

9. DECLARATION ON ARTICLE K.6(2) [now 34(2)] OF THE TREATY ON EUROPEAN UNION

The Conference agrees that initiatives for measures referred to in Article K.6(2) [now 34(2)] of the Treaty on European Union and acts adopted by the Council thereunder shall be published in the *Official Journal of the European Communities,* in accordance with the relevant Rules of Procedure of the Council and the Commission.

10. DECLARATION ON ARTICLE K.7 [now 35] OF THE TREATY ON EUROPEAN UNION

The Conference notes that Member States may, when making a declaration pursuant to Article K.7(2) [now 35(2)] of the Treaty on European Union, reserve the right to make provisions in their national law to the effect that, where a question relating to the validity or interpretation of an act referred to in Article K.7(1) [now 35(1)] is raised in a case pending before a national court or tribunal against whose decision there is no judicial remedy under national law, that court or tribunal will be required to refer the matter to the Court of Justice.

11. DECLARATION ON THE STATUS OF CHURCHES AND NON-CONFESSIONAL ORGANISATIONS

The European Union respects and does not prejudice the status under national law of churches and religious associations or communities in the Member States.

The European Union equally respects the status of philosophical and non-confessional organisations.

42. DECLARATION ON THE CONSOLIDATION OF THE TREATIES

The High Contracting Parties agreed that the technical work begun during the course of this Intergovernmental Conference shall continue as speedily as possible with the aim of drafting a consolidation of all the relevant Treaties, including the Treaty on European Union.

They agreed that the final results of this technical work, which shall be made public for illustrative purposes under the responsibility of the Secretary-General of the Council, shall have no legal value.

2n. DECLARATION BY DENMARK ON ARTICLE K.14 [now 42] OF THE TREATY ON EUROPEAN UNION

Article K.14 [now 42] of the Treaty on European Union requires the unanimity of all members of the Council of the European Union, i.e. all Member States, for the adoption of any decision to apply the provisions of Title IIIa (now IV) of the Treaty establishing the European Community on visas, asylum, immigration and other policies related to free movement of persons to action in areas referred to in Article K.1 [now 29]. Moreover, any unanimous decision of the Council, before coming into force, will have to be adopted in each Member State, in accordance with its constitutional requirements. In Denmark, such adoption will, in the case of a transfer of sovereignty, as defined in the Danish constitution, require either a majority of five sixths of members of the Folketing or both a majority of the members of the Folketing and a majority of voters in a referendum.

4n. DECLARATION BY IRELAND ON ARTICLE 3 OF THE PROTOCOL ON THE POSITION OF THE UNITED KINGDOM AND IRELAND

Ireland declares that it intends to exercise its right under Article 3 of the Protocol on the position of the United Kingdom and Ireland to take part in the adoption of measures pursuant to Title IIIa (now IV) of the Treaty establishing the European Community to the maximum extent compatible with the maintenance of its Common Travel Area with the United Kingdom. Ireland recalls that its participation in the Protocol on the application of certain aspects of Article 7a [now 14] of the Treaty establishing the European Community reflects its wish to maintain its Common Travel Area with the United Kingdom in order to maximise freedom of movement into and out of Ireland.

6n. DECLARATION BY BELGIUM, FRANCE AND ITALY ON THE PROTOCOL ON THE INSTITUTIONS WITH THE PROSPECT OF ENLARGEMENT OF THE EUROPEAN UNION

Belgium, France and Italy observe that, on the basis of the results of the Intergovernmental Conference, the Treaty of Amsterdam does not meet the need, reaffirmed at the Madrid European Council, for substantial progress towards reinforcing the institutions.

Those countries consider that such reinforcement is an indispensable condition for the conclusion of the first accession negotiations. They are determined to give the fullest effect appropriate to the Protocol as regards the composition of the Commission and the weighting of votes and consider that a significant extension of recourse to qualified majority voting forms part of the relevant factors which should be taken into account.

7n. DECLARATION BY FRANCE CONCERNING THE SITUATION OF THE OVERSEAS DEPARTMENTS IN THE LIGHT OF THE PROTOCOL INTEGRATING THE SCHENGEN *ACQUIS* INTO THE FRAMEWORK OF THE EUROPEAN UNION

France considers that the implementation of the Protocol integrating the Schengen *acquis* into the framework of the European Union does not affect the geographical scope of the Convention implementing the Schengen Agreement of 14 June 1985 signed in Schengen on 19 June 1990, as it is defined by Article 138, first paragraph, of that Convention.

8n. DECLARATION BY GREECE CONCERNING THE DECLARATION ON THE STATUS OF CHURCHES AND NON-CONFESSIONAL ORGANISATIONS

With reference to the Declaration on the status of churches and non-confessional organisations, Greece recalls the Joint Declaration on Mount Athos annexed to the Final Act of the Treaty of Accession of Greece to the European Communities.*

---

*Mount Athos is a self-governing community of monasteries on the Chalidice peninsula. Its autonomous status was recognized by the Greek government in 1926 and is enshrined in the Greek Constitution. The 1979 declaration reads:

Recognizing that the special status granted to Mount Athos, as guaranteed by Article 105 of the Hellenic Constitution, is justified exclusively on grounds of a spiritual and religious nature, the Community will ensure that this status is taken into account in the application and subsequent preparation of provisions of Community law, in particular in relation to customs privileges, tax exemptions and the right of establishment.

Declarations Relating to the TEU Received on the Occasion of the Signing of the Treaty of Amsterdam

DECLARATIONS ON ARTICLE K.7 [now 35] OF THE TREATY ON EUROPEAN UNION AS AMENDED BY THE TREATY OF AMSTERDAM

On the occasion of the signing of the Treaty of Amsterdam on 2 October 1997 the Italian Republic, the depositary of the Treaty, received, pursuant to Article K.7 [now 35] of the Treaty on European Union as amended by the Treaty of Amsterdam, the following declarations:

'On the signing of the Treaty of Amsterdam the following Member States stated that they accepted the jurisdiction of the Court of Justice of the European Communities in accordance with the procedure laid down in Article K.7(2) and (3) [now 35(2) and (3)]:

the Kingdom of Belgium, the Federal Republic of Germany, the Hellenic Republic, the Grand Duchy of Luxembourg and the Republic of Austria, in accordance with the procedure laid down in paragraph 3(b).

When making the above declaration, the Kingdom of Belgium, the Federal Republic of Germany, the Grand Duchy of Luxembourg and the Republic of Austria reserved the right to make provisions in their national law to the effect that, where a question relating to the validity or interpretation of an act referred to in Article K.7(1) [now 35(1)] is raised in a case pending before a national court or tribunal against whose decision there is no judicial remedy under national law, that court or tribunal will be required to refer the matter to the Court of Justice.'

In addition, the Kingdom of the Netherlands declared that the Netherlands would accept the jurisdiction of the Court of Justice of the European Communities as laid down in the aforementioned Article K.7 [now 35]; its government was still considering whether, under Article K.7(3) [now 35(3)], the option of bringing a matter before the Court could be granted to courts or tribunals other than those against whose decisions there is no remedy.

Declarations Relating to the TEU Annexed to the Final Act Associated with the Treaty of Nice

1. DECLARATION ON THE EUROPEAN SECURITY AND DEFENCE POLICY

In accordance with the texts approved by the European Council in Nice concerning the European security and defence policy (Presidency report and Annexes), the objective for the European Union is for that policy to become operational quickly. A decision to that end will be taken by the European Council as soon as possible in 2001 and no later than at its meeting in Laeken/Brussels, on the basis of the existing provisions of the Treaty on European Union. Consequently, the entry into force of the Treaty of Nice does not constitute a precondition.

2. DECLARATION ON ARTICLE 31(2) OF THE TREATY ON EUROPEAN UNION

The Conference recalls that:
– the decision to set up a unit composed of national prosecutors, magistrates or police officers of equivalent competence, detached from each Member State (Eurojust), having the task of facilitating proper co-ordination between national prosecuting authorities and of supporting criminal investigations in organised crime cases, was provided for in the Presidency conclusions of the European Council at Tampere on 15 and 16 October 1999;
– the European Judicial Network was set up by Joint Action 98/428/JHA adopted by the Council on 29 June 1998 (OJ L 191, 7.7.1998, p. 4).

IV The Treaty Establishing the European Community

Although everyday usage increasingly privileges the term 'Union' to describe the European integration project and therefore, like recent treaties, stresses the Treaty on European Union as the basis of integration, it would be wrong to ignore or undervalue the Treaty establishing the European Community (TEC). Admittedly, the Federal Trust does argue that it can be overlooked in the process of simplification but not everyone would agree with them. Many would accept that the TEC remains a key European Treaty. In fact it is vitally important both to integration in general and to the Union in particular.

There are at least five reasons for this. Firstly, it is the ultimate founding treaty which underpins the whole European enterprise. It was the document which gave the post-war integration process its second and more general wind. It has attracted great enthusiasm and loyalty over the years and has a not-to-be-derided psychological importance. This links to a second factor, the way in which the TEC creates the institutions which embody the ambitions of those who believe in the European project. The institutions exemplify the supra-national decision-making method and the aspirations of European integration. Because of this, the Community, its institutions, processes and structures attract a great deal of political support. There is thus a desire that the TEC should not be 'polluted' by the inter-governmentalism of the EU's other pillars.

Thirdly, it is the TEC which gives the EU its legal right to act, both domestically and externally. This is because, domestically, it is the TEC which is the essential basis of what has generally been called 'Community law'. Indeed, looking at the TEC means considering the contribution of ECJ judgments to the meaning and understanding of the treaty in a way which, as the 1995 *Grau Gomis* ruling made clear, cannot be done for the TEU. Externally it is the TEC which gives the Community 'legal personality', the recognized right to take international decisions. Without this it could not function.

Fourthly, it is in the TEC that we find the key policies which make up the *acquis communautaire*. Together they give the Union its regulatory dimension and thus make most impact on ordinary people. And for many these policies are the Union's greatest achievement. They can be regarded as principles and not just as applications.

Lastly, the provisions of the TEC in turn have a considerable impact on the Union, reflecting the way the TEU often looks to the TEC to carry out tasks for it as with citizenship. The symbiotic relationship between the two can also be seen in the TEU in articles such as 7(5), 20, 23(1), 23(2), 25, 28(1), 34(3), 36(1), 40a(2), 41, 43(e), 43b, 44(1) and 46.

Not surprisingly, when the European University Institute sought to split the treaties it found that it could not really do away with the TEC. It was too closely involved with the

overall enterprise. Indeed, all attempts at simplification come up against the same problem. And, as things stand, any changes or entry to the Union requires either the ratification
or the acceptance of the TEC. In other words, treating the TEC separately in the *Guide*
recognizes its innate importance. It also justifies our decision not to regard the Union and
the Community as one and the same.

Hence, in this division of the *Guide* we start by trying to introduce and characterize
the treaty as a whole so as to emphasize this importance. After this preliminary analysis
we go on to comment upon and to print the whole of the treaty, from its preamble to its
final act and the attached declarations. This will, we hope, bring out the range, importance
and complexity of the Community provisions. It will also reflect the fact that the TEC
has changed greatly over the years.

i An Overview

The TEU is complex more because of the overlapping pillar structure it creates than
because of its nature as a treaty. The TEC, on the other hand, is structurally more or less
unitary but as a treaty it is much more complicated than the TEU. To some extent this is
because it is much older than the TEU and has therefore changed more over the years,
not so much in its overall structure but in its detailed contents. So looking at the treaty
as it is today does not tell us everything about it. We need to look not only at its structure
and style, but also at its evolution, its contents and its meaning.

All told, the TEC has become a relatively full document, setting out key principles, a
growing set of policy objectives and the institutions and decision-making processes to
help achieve them. Hence it remains quite a complex and lengthy document, despite the
fact that it has become cleaner and clearer since Amsterdam removed timetable clauses
and the confusing numbering. The TEC is, of course, heavily dependent on some of the
statutes contained in the protocols for the establishment of institutional processes. What
this suggests is that the TEC needs to be understood, not as a constitution, but as an
inter-governmental arrangement. None the less, it has a life of its own and should not be
overlooked.

The Structure and Style of the Treaty

As we have said, the TEC is a complex document. At present, in its post-Amsterdam
consolidated form, it consists of 314 articles. This will rise to 318 if Nice is ratified. It is
divided not into titles, as is the case with the TEU but, as Box 6 shows, into six parts
plus final provisions. This choice was made because of the relative length of the TEC,
which meant that it needed to be sectionalized in a way which the TEU does not. It also
has inherited 4 annexes, nearly 30 protocols, 4 conventions and 9 declarations, to which
Amsterdam and Nice made further contributions. In its present form it runs to seven
times as many pages as the TEU.

The structure is important not just because of size but because of the order of the parts.
Contrary to many national constitutions they start with principles and, especially, policies
and only bring institutions in afterwards as a way of achieving the objectives set out
earlier. This says something about the nature of the treaty and the Community. Because
it is really the original and basic founding or constitutive treaty, the TEC itself has never

Box 6   The structure of the Contemporary TEC

Preamble

Part One   Principles
Part Two   Citizenship of the Union
Part Three   Community Policies
Part Four   Associations of the Overseas Countries and Territories
Part Five   Institutions of the Community
Part Six   General and Final Provisions
Final Provisions

Annexes

Protocols
Final Act
Declarations

amended any other treaty. It is always amended by other agreements drawn up by IGCs. In other words, it enshrines the key commitments made by member states about what they are prepared to do together and how they are prepared to do it.

It is sometimes said that, because of this, the TEC is simply a framework treaty, laying down the broad outlines and leaving it to the future, and the institutions, to work out the details. This is something of a simplification. The treaty is certainly indicative, emphasizing aims, overall strategies and tactical targets. But these things cannot be explored in any way people choose. Thus the treaty also sets out many of the means, whether procedures or policy measures, which states and institutions have to utilize. Very often there are special parameters and conditions, not to mention exceptions. And so, while there are many succinct constitutional-type provisions, these are not always sparse or simple. The treaty is often very sophisticated and specific, making the 'where' and the 'what' of its policy prescriptions very clear. It also adds many complicating caveats, reinforcing its legalistic tone. But, for the most part, it is not over detailed, especially in Part Five.

A purely framework treaty was and remains almost impossible given the complexity of the issues and the reservations of the member states about losing autonomy. Equally, the treaty has to set out the obligations into which the member states have entered and by which they have agreed to be bound. Hence, in order to operationalize its underlying idea of sharing resources and sovereignty, the treaty sets up a series of stately quadrilles involving the member states and the EC as such and its institutions. And, as time has gone on, it has become more wordy, specific and complex, reflecting the way that integration has become more pervasive and sensitive as member states have sought to hammer out agreements and defend their positions. As a result the TEC has become a more uneven document than the TEU, going from parsimonious principle to detailed regulation. None the less, the treaty is not an exclusive and exhaustive guide to the way the Community actually works.

The actual structure begins with a preamble indicating the mainly economic overall drift of the treaty and the means by which these are to be achieved. Its main commitments are then set out in more binding form in the principles. The two have to be seen as two sides of the same aspiration. The principles, like Part Two on citizenship of the Union, which is inserted here and not in the TEU to ensure that it would be justiciable, are relatively short both in terms of the number of articles and the length of the text. Neither part is internally subdivided. In fact there are only sixteen articles for the principles and six, somewhat more terse, articles on citizenship.

Thereafter the treaty sets out the policies agreed in order to meet the main economic commitments, including economic and monetary union (EMU). This is, significantly, by far the longest part, running to nearly 160 articles and virtually half the whole document. After Nice it will be divided basically into twenty-one titles. Many of these are shorter than those in the TEU, particularly the more recent ones. These new policy responsibilities often only manage a single article. Some, like those covering agriculture and transport, are unitary titles. Provisions on the common market, free movement and EMU and social policy are all divided into chapters. The EMU provisions include the largest number of articles and are probably the longest and most detailed. The provisions on competition, even though they include only nine medium-length articles, are divided not only into chapters but into sections as well.

Part Four is a historical curiosity with its assumption that colonies could be a subordinate part of the Community established by their metropolitan masters. The institutional and decision-making procedures to make all this work then follow in Part Five. This is the second longest element with nearly 90 articles, most of them surprisingly brief. Because the first title of Part Five deals with institutions, its main chapter is divided into five subsections, one for each institution established under Article 7 TEC. There is, however, no space for the European Central Bank. These are followed by the chapters on, first, the shared decision-making 'common provisions', and then by chapters on the consultative institutions. Part Five ends with the financial arrangements needed to fund the institutions set out in Title II, often emphasizing the need for financial probity and security. The fact that the TEC looks at policies ahead of institutions, giving the former almost twice as much space as the latter, is significant. This is not the order we normally find in national constitutions – or in the TECSC – where institutions appear early on as an expression of state sovereignty. Again it says something about the inter-governmental purposes of the founding fathers.

The last element of the TEC, Part Six, deals partly with external questions and partly with technical questions. However, it is actually undivided because it runs to only 30 relatively brief articles, set out without a great deal of logic. Most of these cover questions of legal applicability and status but others look to slightly random aspects of the Community's external relations. The last two articles of these are specifically designated as final provisions in a kind of coda to the treaty proper touching on its coming into effect.

All these are then followed by the various supplementary elements of the treaty. Some of these, like the statute of the ECJ, are dense and important. And, assuming Nice is ratified, the contents of the various protocols and declarations relating to enlargement will have a major role to play in shaping the way the EC works. In fact it is impossible, as we shall see, to consider Part Five without them.

The Establishment of the TEC

This is part of the way in which the TEC has filled out over the years. Originally, it was a shorter document of 248 articles. Structurally it was a little different with six slightly differently focused parts. Principles were as now but Part Two was given over to foundations, covering basic activities such as free movement, the customs union, agriculture and transport, each with its own title, making it clear that these were the fundamental concerns. Only the two titles on free movement were further subdivided.

Part Three was headed policy in the singular and comprised titles on common rules, economic policy and social affairs, in other words the flanking policies. Each title was divided into chapters but only Chapter 1 of the common rules, covering competition, was divided in sections. The structure of Parts Four to Six on association, institutional provisions and general and final provisions was much as now. And if, overall, the presentation was relatively clear, because of Pierre Uri's style and the fact that the articles were shorter and numbered consecutively, we have to remember that the treaty was accompanied by a major 'Convention on Certain Institutions' which filled out a good deal of detail about the shared organs.

Thereafter there were, at first, relatively few changes to this as Annex 2 shows. Neither the 1967 Merger Treaty nor the changes of the 1970s made much difference. However, the Certain Financial Provisions Treaty did add three articles and the withdrawal of Greenland added another. Otherwise only minor alterations were made by accession treaties (to the numbers of representatives in the various institutions) and the 1976 Act on Direct Elections.

As we have already seen it was the Single European Act (SEA) which was the first amending treaty to have a major impact on the TEC. Through the 25 articles of the second chapter of its Part Two, dedicated to the Community treaties, it actually added three new titles to the original Part Two, covering cohesion, environment and research and technological development together with a new chapter to Title II on economic policy. This involved 'supplementing' the TEC, as the SEA put it, with 27 new articles, each with a lower-case letter. These covered the internal market, social matters and decision-making, as did many of the other changes to existing articles. This took the TEC to nearly 280 articles and gave it a more policy-oriented feel. On the other hand, the SEA also ratified the way the term 'Parliament' had replaced the original reference to the European 'Assembly'.

The TEU built on this in three ways. To begin with it involved a notable restructuring, with the addition of a new Part Two and the rolling over of the two policy-oriented parts into a new Part Three on Community policies. This suggests that the original distinction between foundations and flanking policies had been lost sight of by then. The headings and numbers of many titles were changed at the same time, often upgrading earlier chapters as in the case of the common commercial policy. New titles were also created within this part, so as to accommodate new policy responsibilities including culture, public health and trans-European networks.

Secondly, all this involved the addition of nearly 50 new articles. The largest number of these, and both the longest and most explosive, were those in the new title on EMU in Part Three. Moreover, the TEU 'inserted', as it now chose to say in a way revealing the downgrading of the TEC, articles on co-decision, the ECB and institutional adaption. Some articles were also rewritten and a few renumbered. And, thirdly, for the first time some articles were repealed, six in all.

Minor changes were also made to one annex and one protocol. New protocols were of course tacked on, notably on social policy, thanks to the UK's insistence on not taking part. All this was brought about by the 86 detailed amendments to the TEC set out in Article G TEU. At the same time, all, by then obsolete, references to the 'European Economic Community' were replaced by the term 'European Community'. Taken all together this made the TEC longer, denser and more explicit on policy. For some it made it more authoritative even though it was now subject to the TEU and was full of statements upholding member-state rights.

Amsterdam and the TEC

Most of these changes were commented on in the first variant of the *Guide*. However, the process of evolution within the TEC did not stop with Maastricht. Responding to new pressures from domestic politics, to changes in the continental context and to a growing concern that the EU's workings needed to be rationalized, a whole variety of changes were introduced. In fact, through its 59 separate amendments, Amsterdam made significant changes in three directions: structure; policy and institutional adaptation; and simplification. As a result, the TEC emerged in a cleaner and clearer form on paper. It also acquired refined responsibilities and working practices. In all this it often acted to make possible changes ordained in the revisions to the TEU, notably in what was then Article 236 TEC.

Initially, in structural terms, the TA's entry into force in 1999 saw three new titles added to Part Three. The main one here was the transfer of provisions on asylum and visas from the then JHA pillar of the TEU. This meant the insertion of a new Title IIIa on 'Visa, Asylum, Immigration and Other Policies Related to Free Movement of Persons', briefly numbered 73i–73q. Provision was also made for the integration of the Schengen *acquis*, albeit in undefined ways, into the framework of the Union. This was, of course, subject to new protocolar derogations for Denmark, Ireland and the UK. The new Title VIa on employment was numbered 109n–109s while the new article on customs co-operation became Title VIIa. At the same time more than 20 new articles were also added, notably by bringing in much of the old Social Chapter into the treaty proper. Articles were also repealed as were two protocols on social policy and EcoSoc and the Committee of the Regions. None the less, Amsterdam added to the Community's policy responsibilities even if not in such a dramatic and public way as had been the case in 1991.

Secondly, it made a number of significant adaptations to the principles and practices of the existing treaty. It added provisions on closer co-operation, sustainable development and a new stress on rights and resistance to discrimination to the Community's principles. Three clarifications were also made to citizenship. A number of small changes to existing policy provisions were also made. There were a number of institutional changes as well: fixing the size of the EP, changing the powers of the Commission president and altering the leadership of the Council Secretariat. In procedural terms Amsterdam also improved rules on audit and transparency, increased co-decision (using a simplified Article 189b procedure), and extended both the use of QMV and consultation of the advisory organs.

Beyond this, as we have already noted, Amsterdam gave the treaty its first ever makeover. Simplification sharpened up the text after its somewhat haphazard development. Amsterdam eliminated outdated elements, slightly reordered it and, most significantly, endowed it with a more logical and consistent enumeration. However, as Annex 3 shows, this did not have the impact it deserved. As a result Amsterdam left the feeling that legitimacy, efficiency and readiness for enlargement still needed addressing.

The TEC and Nice

Nice made quantitatively limited but qualitatively important changes to the TEC. Structurally its only change was to add a single article title to Part Two to cover technical assistance to third countries. It only added four new articles: Article 11a revising the rules for enhanced co-operation, Article 181a on technical assistance, Article 225a on the creation of new judicial panels and Article 229a on intellectual property. There were also minor changes to protocols. Declaration No. 3 TN giving the go-ahead to inter-institutional agreements ought also to be noted both for itself and as an example of Nice's innovative (if excessive) use of declarations.

Alongside this Nice, as overwhelmingly an amending treaty, changed a whole range of articles in Parts Two and Five to bring in QMV decision-making and sometimes co-decision. It also added a number of changes to policy provisions and their implementation. Thus flexibility was revised as 'enhanced co-operation', a new interest was shown in social protection with the creation of a committee and a new concern was shown for limiting social exclusion and enhancing citizenship and responsiveness. There was also a significant addition to Article 133 on international negotiations in the field of intellectual property.

More significant was the large-scale rewriting of the articles on the ECJ which were fundamentally reorganized structurally and procedurally. This led to the replacement and reattachment of the statute of the ECJ. These were one of a number of changes to institutional arrangements to bring them into line with the needs of enlargement, generally fixing the principles of composition and ceilings instead of giving numbers related to the actual states involved. However, where the EP was concerned the numbers were actually increased in a somewhat doubtful way. At the same time changes were made in the Commission and the way it is controlled by its president.

One of the interesting things about Nice where the institutional provisions are concerned is that there are several versions of these. Basic principles are laid down in the TEC proper but these have to be read, firstly, in conjunction with the figures given in the Protocol on the enlargement of the European Union. These cover the short term. Secondly, however, they also have to be read in conjunction with Declarations Nos. 20 and 21 TN which spell out what is anticipated will happen as and when enlargement takes place. There are also controversial new rules about thresholds and venues. These are set out in the following subdivisions as well as above (see pp. 68–76).

Although such changes may mean that enlargement has been made possible institutionally, there is a downside. The result of this, assuming that the treaty is ratified, will be that the TEC becomes slightly longer and certainly more complicated. Not merely is the numbering less tidy but it is anything but clear where we should find answers. Equally, some of the changes in decision-making are far from transparent. And the proliferation of decision-making procedures remains. None the less, Nice has added the final touches to the treaty as it now is.

The Contents of the TEC: An Introduction

For most people the technical adjustments are of much less interest than the actual changes they make to the Community's material constitution. What we potentially have in the TEC is a complex set of provisions. The preamble sets the treaty in context, states its economic, social and solidarity aims and establishes pooling of resources and sovereignty as its fundamental support and method. These are then built on in the principles which outline specific policies, rules of procedure (often highlighting restraints), institutional bases, treaty obligations and values such as anti-discrimination and cohesion. They also involve a potentially significant innovation in the introduction of subsidiarity. This is one of the ways in which the treaty lays down how the EC should work, making it ultimately dependent on such meta-decisions by the member states, even if, as with subsidiarity, it also looks to the TEC to carry out its tasks for it.

This, like citizenship, set out in Part Two, is a provision of constitutional significance.

It is dependent on member-state status and essentially turns on free movement. To make this work EU citizens have the right to vote in national and European elections in their country of residence. Equally there are some generic rights such as ease of dealing with the Community institutions. For some this gives the Community more the air of a polity, though this is only hinted at and, even so, is greatly contested.

Part Three lists the things that the Community is set to do while seeking to apply these principles and aims. The real foundations of the Community, although the term is no longer used, remain essentially a market resting on the four freedoms: the free movement of goods, people, capital and services. However, they have substantially increased beyond the core areas. And in so doing the part helps to flesh out the Community's concern for rights. This leads to the flanking policies needed to make these work, notably competition. What we have is a series of indicative statements, leaving it up to the institutional arrangements to build on them. Thus in transport the treaty limits itself to setting out parameters. In other words the EC's policy competences vary as between sectors. Very few of them are 'exclusive' powers in fact. Moreover, the Community does not always utilize all the policy possibilities opened up by the treaty.

Competition is a major concern, despite the talk of the EC being *dirigiste*. It is here that EMU fits in with its convergence conditions. Although this is the longest and most dense element of the TEC, in practice it has proved less prescriptive than critics claim. The part also contains now redundant articles on the European Monetary Institute and provisions on the common commercial policy which might have had a more logical home alongside some of the other externally directed clauses. There has also been an increasing stress on what is loosely called social policy in the treaty.

Many of the policy provisions set out in Part Three are seen as joint ventures between the EC as such and the member states. This is very much the case with the employment title added at Amsterdam. Equally, many of the later policy aims at the end of the part are highly targeted and subject to many limitations. In the case of the environment – concern for which is one of a number of cross-sectoral or horizontal provisions in the TEC – member states can, in any case, go beyond TEC norms. None the less, along with Part One, Part Three goes a long way towards justifying the TEC's role as the provider of the *acquis* to the Union.

If Part Four has no great relevance today thanks to the ending of many formal colonial links, Part Five has become an increasingly important element of the TEC. Yet it is surprisingly parsimonious in its expression. It sets out basic aims, procedures and responsibilities for the institutions, which are all subject to the treaty. It does not give them a free hand. Even the EP, recognized as democratically legitimated, has to look elsewhere in the treaty for its exact rights. Its own section of Chapter 1, like those given over to other institutions, does not tell us everything. The powers of the Council, which are primordial, disguise the fact that it is a very diverse and fragmented body. And it is a Union body and not simply a diet of ministerial ambassadors. Equally, the Commission's powers are highly specified. The judicial provisions also do not always tell the whole story though the two Courts – of Justice and of First Instance – are now more of a fully fledged judiciary and not just a single tribunal. However, crucial doctrines like direct effect, loyalty and pre-emption are not fully documented in the treaty.

The TEC also circumscribes the forms that the EC's legal output can take and ensures that these emerge through strictly regulated procedures. In fact the TEC specifies in considerable detail how the formal stages of policy-making should be organized. And in doing this they also have to respect data privacy. The financial provisions then set out both the principles underlying the budget and the fact that this essentially involves providing the necessary monies for carrying out the tasks agreed earlier in the treaty.

Own resources are therefore barely mentioned whereas the budgetary process is regulated, including what happens if the EP rejects the budget. There is also stress on the need to maintain effective and honest financial management. In all these arrangements, what stands out is the interdependence of the main institutions and their need to work together, despite representing conflicting legitimacies. It also highlights the fact that they do not fit neatly into standard functional categories such as executive and legislature.

Part Six on general and final provisions seeks to clarify the Community's status, staffing and liability, though it does not do this in a wholly logical way. At Article 308, for instance, is the crucial 'catch all' policy clause that has allowed the Community to act in domains where there is no explicit treaty provision. The part also indicates the extent of the TEC's applicability, both territorially and where member states are concerned. There are also some rather fragmentary rules about external relations. So Part Six is far from insignificant.

This is all built on by the many protocols and declarations attached to the treaty. As Nice shows, these are often of considerable importance. There are also some dated annexes of agricultural products affected by Article 32 and qualifying territories. In sum, what we have is a set of agreements, arrived at individually over time by the member states and not always fully consistent and co-ordinated. There is a wide gap between this and a fully fledged European polity, let alone a 'superstate'.

Understanding the TEC

However, today's TEC is not an easy thing to appraise. It has somewhat changed over time from being the basic treaty to being a subordinate text. As a result it has lost a little of its supra-national tone and has become both more and less constitutional. It is more constitutional in the way in which Nice has altered some of its style. But it is less so in the way it has been subordinated to the TEU and the way it is dependent on protocols, declarations and extra-treaty operations, including ECJ judgments.

None the less, it remains a wide-ranging and sophisticated document and one which sets the fundamental economic basis of the European enterprise. It is still a treaty which seeks political aims through economic and policy means. And it sets up workable institutions with both considerable powers and a life of their own. But, at the same time, it surrounds their operation with many caveats and conditions reflecting the fact that they are essentially treaty creations, whatever their supporters and critics might think.

Although it has achieved many of its ends, it remains an unfinished treaty. There are no agreed and timelessly valid solutions for the Community. The TEC remains in evolution. And although some of its changes can emerge outside the treaty, major alterations depend on an IGC. Nice made this all too clear. Even if Nice is ratified, the TEC is likely to change again in the future. This means that it does need to be taken seriously along with the TEU. Since much of its essential nature is enshrined in its preamble and the related principles, it is to these that the *Guide* now turns.

ii Preamble

Like most classic international agreements the Treaty establishing the European Community starts with a preamble stating its strategic direction. Because the TEC remains an important treaty and one which is more than a mere framework its preamble similarly continues to be effective and deserving of attention, despite the coming of the TEU. This is not only because it is politically and legally significant. It is because its contents tell us a good deal about the TEC as a whole. And, although most of it dates from the past, it is still in evolution, as Amsterdam showed.

Although much recent dispute about preambles has focused on that to the TEU, that to the TEC also remains politically important. It is, after all, the source of the reference to 'an ever closer Union' which, as we have already seen, caused so much controversy at Maastricht. And some critics would still like to see it excised. This is because of its political symbolism and the way it gives a very clear steer as to what the whole enterprise is about. As a result the TEC preamble remains controversial. For some it threatens oppressive centralization and for others it is a solemn endorsement of twin commitments: to democracy and integration based on a common market. And, for today's candidate countries, the invitation to like-minded countries to join is rightly seen as a moral undertaking and one which is taken very seriously.

Legally the TEC preamble matters in a way that the introduction to the TEU does not. Normally it is printed as part of the 'text' of the TEC, given the expectation that there should be a recital for every substantive element of the treaty. This is why preambles can often be drawn up after the main text of the treaty has been agreed to ensure that there is full coverage. Here Constantinescu and his colleagues argue that it is not a good introduction to the principles which follow. Indeed they suggest it is simply the first part of a wider definition of axioms for the Community.

In line with precedents from international law, the ECJ has made use of the preamble, notably in *Van Gend en Loos* (1963) to justify its beliefs that the TEC created a new legal order and in *Defrenne* (1976) to justify a commitment to social progress by curbing discrimination based on gender. However, the Court – and even more so the Commission – has been cautious in its use of the preamble so, generally, its legal effect is illustrative and strategic, not directly binding and detailed. As Weiler says, the TEC preamble is part of Community hermeneutics.

In terms of style and content, the TEC preamble is less ambitious and flamboyant than that of the TECSC but more general and less policy-oriented than that to the TEU. The preamble to the TECSC, which draws on the Schuman Declaration of 1950, talks in flowery tones of historic conflicts and divisions giving way to peace and solidarity (see p. 568). It is more downbeat and focused on practical actions. Indeed, the context of the treaty, a normal element of preambles, appears only implicitly in its mention of liberty and trade barriers. The motivation for the enterprise can be said to be a trifle understated.

The preamble to the TEC dwells mainly on the intentions of the drafters: the aims they sought to achieve and the means by which they would seek to do this. Of the original nine recitals, the first three deal with the aims of the proposed construction amongst the Six. These are, firstly, to create 'an ever closer union' which caused no discussion until inserted in the TEU. At the time the TEC was drafted it was a vague aspiration and one which, for Constantinescu, merely thought in terms of a growing tissue of relations between people, laws and institutions, not the creation of a state. Given references to it, especially in the 1983 Stuttgart Declaration, it has since sometimes been read by critics as presaging ever increasing pressure on member states because it makes no reference to nations as such. The creation of a body called a Union may have encouraged such views.

Others have claimed it as a statement not merely that the Community is based on its peoples but that their wishes are paramount. In other words, it is a symbol of the Community's democratic credentials. Both views are slightly exaggerated. The reference to the 'foundations' makes it clear that the Community is a means of creating and sustaining exchange among ordinary people.

Secondly, the preamble commits the EC to achieving economic and social progress within the countries of the peoples of Europe. It also brings in here the first means: the reduction of barriers between states. This cannot safely be read as suggesting the abolition of the latter. Indeed, the third aim is to secure better living and working conditions of the peoples of the participating countries. Interestingly this does not mention growth as such. It reflects the social aspirations of the post-1945 era and the fact that the Community was initially more concerned with peoples as constituents of working economies and societies than as political actors. Later on the preamble also canvasses a number of external aims: liberalizing world trade, maintaining colonial ties and spreading peace throughout Europe. The eighth recital also mentions liberty although it is unclear whether this means in Soviet Europe or inside the Community. If the latter then the recital can be seen as a statement about the EC's concern for fundamental rights and freedoms.

However, there is even more stress on the means by which these things are to be done, and it is here that the preamble shows its innovativeness. Domestically, the second and fourth recitals make it clear that common action is needed to reduce barriers and achieve progress in areas such as competition. The fifth recital points to the development of social and regional policies as a means of facilitating economic unification. What is now the tenth recital further sees the pooling of resources as a means of achieving wider political goals in Europe and not, as we might now expect, of securing better macro-economic policy. Where external means are concerned, the preamble looks to a liberalizing common commercial policy (CCP), to an undefined solidarity with overseas countries and to utilizing the principles of the UN Charter. Because the treaty retains Part Four on association, and there is still a sense of obligation to the ex-colonies, the preambular reference has not been removed even though it now means much less than it did in 1958.

Both internal and external aims are, of course, to be achieved by the creation of the Community itself which is the ultimate means to the ends sought by the founding fathers. Interestingly, there is no specific reference to the Common Market or to free movement as such, though there are hints. Equally, the reference to the CCP is the only specific reference to policy in the preamble, which prefers to talk of removing obstacles and taking various kinds of action without indicating what form they should take. As a result the TEC preamble can be said to be a slightly incomplete prologue to the treaty itself. It points directly, in the seventh recital, to Part Four, in most of its recitals to the contents of the old Part Two but rather less to policies. And there is no mention of Part Five on the institutions at all while the preamble's international references are not really sustained by the contents of Part Six. In this it falls short of the norms later established by the TEU.

In this the preamble to the TEC reflects the caution of the times. Those who drafted it did not know how it would develop. So it describes aspirations, not established structures. However, it clearly was hoped that the treaty would prove an initial stage in an ongoing process, one that would overcome the various divisions in Europe. This explains the invitations to other states – both western and eastern, no doubt – to join. The preamble was not changed by the SEA which has its own rather more wordy and policy-oriented preamble. The TEU preamble, as we have already seen, spelled out the tasks required by a new phase of integration.

Amsterdam did not really have a preamble of its own but it did for the first time make one change to the preamble of the TEC. This was to write in a new ninth recital stressing the EC's commitment to promoting the 'education society'. This was to be achieved by the development of knowledge 'to the highest possible level' through wide access to basic and continuing education. Berthu rightly asks why this was done given that education is not a mainstream competence of the Union and Amsterdam did not change the details of the relevant treaty articles although it did strengthen environmental concerns and recognition of the national role in cultural policy. The answer is probably that the drafters wanted to encourage popular identification and point towards what many, like Tony Blair, see as the *sine qua non* of economic modernization and competitiveness. It may also have been seen as supporting the idea of citizenship, which needs education. Whatever the reason the addition does not really change the overall feel or balance of the preamble. Nice, of course, made no changes at all here.

Hence the TEC preamble remains mainly focused on economic matters, but there is also a clear social message as well as a broad political concern, while the economic references themselves are relatively general. However, its prophetic hints about enlargement have rarely been noticed. In any case, it does not really justify those who like to see the initial EEC as purely a free-trade area. The statesmen of the time clearly had broader intentions than this. What is now the tenth recital implies that the creation of the Community is a means of achieving the diplomatic, political and social aims already mentioned as well as the more strictly economic objectives.

The original twelve signatories then testify to all these commitments. Interestingly, only one of them, the Belgian Snoy, then held a clearly economic office. Most were either career diplomats or foreign ministers, although three were heads of government. Some of them like Bech, Hallstein and Spaak are very much among the founding fathers of the Community, even though they acted in the name of their formal heads of state.

The twelve indicated their endorsement of the Community and its objectives firstly by appending their signatures to the treaties, to signify, in the absence of their heads of state, that their countries legitimated the treaty. These signatures remain with us, however, because they actually accompanied the original document. It is in the accession treaties that we find the signatures of later entrants, while the amending treaties carry the member states' approval of subsequent amendments. Secondly, they formally agreed not just the broad aims of the preamble but the detailed contents of the treaty proper. And it is to the amended TEC that we now turn.

TREATY ESTABLISHING THE EUROPEAN COMMUNITY

HIS MAJESTY THE KING OF THE BELGIANS, THE PRESIDENT OF THE FEDERAL REPUBLIC OF GERMANY, THE PRESIDENT OF THE FRENCH REPUBLIC, THE PRESIDENT OF THE ITALIAN REPUBLIC, HER ROYAL HIGHNESS THE GRAND DUCHESS OF LUXEMBOURG, HER MAJESTY THE QUEEN OF THE NETHERLANDS,*

DETERMINED to lay the foundations of an ever closer union among the peoples of Europe,

RESOLVED to ensure the economic and social progress of their countries by common action to eliminate the barriers which divide Europe,

AFFIRMING as the essential objective of their efforts the constant improvements of the living and working conditions of their peoples,

---

*The Kingdom of Denmark, the Hellenic Republic, the Kingdom of Spain, Ireland, the Republic of Austria, the Portugese Republic, the Republic of Finland, the Kingdom of Sweden and the United Kingdom of Great Britain and Northern Ireland have since become members of the European Community.

RECOGNISING that the removal of existing obstacles calls for concerted action in order to guarantee steady expansion, balanced trade and fair competition,

ANXIOUS to strengthen the unity of their economies and to ensure their harmonious development by reducing the differences existing between the various regions and the backwardness of the less-favoured regions,

DESIRING to contribute, by means of a common commercial policy, to the progressive abolition of restrictions on international trade,

INTENDING to confirm the solidarity which binds Europe and the overseas countries and desiring to ensure the development of their prosperity, in accordance with the principles of the Charter of the United Nations,

RESOLVED by thus pooling their resources to preserve and strengthen peace and liberty, and calling upon the other peoples of Europe who share their ideal to join in their efforts,

DETERMINED to promote the development of the highest possible level of knowledge for their peoples through a wide access to education and through its continuous updating,

HAVE DECIDED to create a EUROPEAN COMMUNITY and to this end have designated as their Plenipotentiaries:

HIS MAJESTY THE KING OF THE BELGIANS:
Mr Paul Henri SPAAK, Minister for Foreign Affairs,
Baron J. Ch. SNOY ET D'OPPUERS, Secretary-General of the Ministry of Economic Affairs, Head of the Belgian Delegation to the Intergovernmental Conference;

THE PRESIDENT OF THE FEDERAL REPUBLIC OF GERMANY:
Dr. Konrad ADENAUER, Federal Chancellor,
Professor Dr. Walter HALLSTEIN, State Secretary of the Federal Foreign Office;

THE PRESIDENT OF THE FRENCH REPUBLIC:
Mr Christian PINEAU, Minister for Foreign Affairs,
Mr Maurice FAURE, Under-Secretary of State for Foreign Affairs;

THE PRESIDENT OF THE ITALIAN REPUBLIC:
Mr Antonio SEGNI, President of the Council of Ministers,
Professor Gaetano MARTINO, Minister for Foreign Affairs;

HER ROYAL HIGHNESS THE GRAND DUCHESS OF LUXEMBOURG:
Mr Joseph BECH, President of the Government, Minister for Foreign Affairs,
Mr Lambert SCHAUS, Ambassador, Head of the Luxembourg Delegation to the Intergovernmental Conference;

HER MAJESTY THE QUEEN OF THE NETHERLANDS:
Mr Joseph LUNS, Minister for Foreign Affairs,
Mr. J. LINTHORST HOMAN, Head of the Netherlands Delegation to the Intergovernmental Conference;

WHO, having exchanged their full powers, found in good and due form, have agreed as follows.

iii Principles

The first two parts of the Treaty establishing the European Community are among its most constitutional in tone, given that they set out general principles and basic provisions on citizenship. Not merely have they, especially the former, played an important part in the evolution of the EC but they now make up an important element of the Union's overall axioms. As its heading suggests, Part One lays down the objectives and rules for the Community, preparing the way initially for the technical foundations (Part Two) and, since Maastricht, for Part Three on policies. However, the norms it contains are no longer self-contained because they have to be read in conjunction with articles in the TEU which, to some extent, parallel some of the provisions of the TEC's Part One. Equally, the latter ranges more widely than the Community as such although it does fill in many of the lacunae in the preamble with which, as we have seen, it is often paired.

Essentially what Part One does as it seeks to set out the Community's targets is to clarify what the EC actually does, under what conditions and by what means. Since Amsterdam it has done this rather more crisply, simply and transparently, thanks to the elimination of the timetable articles and the confusing numbering. Part One, in fact, is one of the places where the simplification process was most effective, giving the text a slightly more 'constitutional' feel.

Looking more closely we can see Part Two as comprising three sections, each with a specific role, and the following commentary looks at the text in this way. To begin with, Articles 1–4 specify, and sometimes justify, the Community and its tasks. Secondly, in Articles 5 and 6 (and to a lesser extent Article 16) the legal conditions which must be met when carrying out these tasks are laid down. Finally, Articles 7–15 indicate the means by which these tasks are to be performed. And some of the articles in the second and third sections can be seen as indicating some of the rights which the Union recognizes.

Though many of the points raised here are dealt with more thoroughly later in the treaties, without such an initial statement of general provisions and axioms the rest of the treaty would be both hard to understand and somewhat imperfect in itself. These principles can also be used to query existing or proposed Community legislation. However, although they specify the practical objectives and institutional obligations of the Community they do not constitute a clear-cut and complete code of constitutional principles and policy responsibilities. Many of these have to be found elsewhere in the TEC or, like direct effect and pre-emption, in ECJ interpretation. None the less, the principles of Part One remain an essential starting point for understanding not just the Community but much about the whole integration process.

The Community and its Tasks

The first thing which Part One does is to see the Community formally established and its *raison d'être* spelled out. This is done in one of the few articles not to change its numbering after Amsterdam. In fact it starts in *Article 1* by virtually repeating the last recital of the preamble with the addition that establishment of the Community is a matter between the High Contracting Parties. This rather suggests the EC is an association of states, and, of course, until Maastricht, it was denominated as the European Economic Community. The change has removed the question as to how widely 'economic' should be interpreted, something which occasionally worried the ECJ as seen in *Mr and Mrs F.* v. *Belgian State*

(1975). But it does not define the Community any more clearly, since even the concept 'European' is not wholly clear. On the one hand, it is *a* Community and not *the* Community, implying that there are more than one. On the other, it is not specified whether the Community is simply an amalgam of the EEC, Euratom and the ECSC or whether it is something more, an organic entity in other words. At least Article 1 does all this in a somewhat simpler way than the comparable articles of the TEU, which set the Union out in more detail and in a clearer context.

The next two articles, in attempting to make clear what the Community is to do, tell us more about what the EC is, even though neither of them is clearly focused. Both also keep their old numbers. *Article 2* builds on the preamble's references to concerted action and economic unification. It shows that the Community is a purposive association. It is not created to 'be' but to 'do'.

The article also talks of an apparently single task but is not able to sum it up in a single phrase. We might see this as the amelioration of social and economic conditions within a coherent and converging body of countries but the article actually talks of a whole variety of forms of promotion: of competitiveness, of equality, of jobs, of living standards and of social solidarity, even though not everyone would accept that these were all mutually compatible. Nor should we regard this as an exclusive list of what the Community actually does. In practice it does much more, so that the article must to some extent be regarded as indicative.

Moreover, the article accepts that this one task of unifying the member states could be seen either as a separate task or as a further means by which amelioration is to be achieved. In its post-Maastricht and Amsterdam form the TEC sets out three main means to be used to achieve the economic and social goals set out in the preamble and the rest of the article: the common market, Economic and Monetary Union (EMU) and common activities and policies between the member states. In other words, the EC cannot go about meeting its objectives as it chooses. It has to follow the prescribed strategy. Conversely, creating policies can be seen as an obligation on the member states.

The mention of development suggests that the notion of the economic is understood in a broad way. Hence, the common market is, in a way, somewhat instrumental as Chalmers says. It is not an end in itself. Nor is it something which is either divorced from wider considerations or has no implications for member states' economic management, as Eurosceptics claim was once the case.

Even though they are not comprehensive, the goals are much wider and more specific than was originally the case in 1957 when they were restricted to increasing growth and prosperity. The addition of these new and broader targets may reflect what the Community has, over the years, decided that it wants to do but it also creates a partial overlap with Article 3, which was not there in 1957. Moreover, not all the targets are fully consistent. The original text was shorter and more clearly aspirational and definitional. It more clearly set out a rationale for the Community than it did a list of policies. Equally, bringing states together then appeared as a side-effect of growth and less an end in itself, as now seems to be the case.

Today, because of the way new targets have been added to Article 2, both it and Article 3 have to be looked at to establish the range and legal base of most of the EC's legislative activity. *Article 3*, of course, does indicate what should be done and does not really say what should not be done. However, Article 2 is more likely to be cited by the ECJ since it often seeks not technical support but an indication of what the ultimate ends of the Community, or its '*finalités*' are. Regional policy thus owes its origins to this rather than the next article. To sum up using the language of quality assessment, Article 2 now represents the aims and Article 3 the objectives of the EC.

Article 3 does, in fact, build on its predecessor by specifying the activities of the Community. It thus lists 21 concrete actions to help the Community meet its underlying aims and tasks. This is almost twice as many as had been envisaged in 1957 and some have described it as more of a shopping list, or a declaration of political intentions, than a strict definition of competences. However, the items on the list are not all of the same type or standing. Two tirets are negative, banning member states from imposing levies (a) and obstacles on economic relations with other member states (c). Six require the establishment of a formal policy, presumably involving legislation. Three of these, (b), (e) and (f), are designated as common policies covering trade, agriculture, fisheries and transport, thereby giving them an enhanced status, albeit of an undefined kind. This compares with the ordinary policies – social, environmental and development co-operation – required by the other three (j), (l) and (r).

Nine more require unspecified forms of action, not necessarily involving policy legislation. These are free movement of persons; competition; approximation of laws; employment co-ordination; cohesion; competitiveness; promotion of research and technological development; association; and energy, civil protection and tourism. In practice several of these have led to the creation of clear-cut policies, notably competition. However, this does not mean that the EC has exclusive competence in all these areas.*

In fact, the provisions of the four tirets (o), (p), (q) and (t) covering trans-European networks, health protection, education, training, culture and consumer protection make it clear that the EC is only to act in a limited or supportive way. Harmonization is thus only allowed where required by the working of the common market. And, where employment is concerned, even though this was written into the treaties at Amsterdam largely at French behest, the EC is denied a lead role. Moreover, not all of the objectives point to specific treaty articles, the prime examples being energy, civil protection and tourism (u). And this is despite the intentions expressed in Declaration No. 1 TEU.

However, activities (a) to (d) clearly operate to help the creation of a common market whereas (e) to (l) relate to policies and their co-ordination. Objectives (m) to (u) can be regarded as spelling out the broader and more practical measures or activities the EC is to engage in. The reasons for the differences are not always clear. At the outset the reason was that they were trying to specify general action rather than processes, but since then there has been less willingness to entrust new legislative powers to the Community so looser forms of words are used. This is most obviously the case with (i), which was added by Amsterdam. For historic reasons no objectives are listed for EMU.

Paragraph 2 on gender equality, also added in 1997, has the appearance of being tacked on since it does not fall into any of the aforementioned categories and is to be a concern in all EC activities. In other words, it is as much a condition as an aim although Berthu sees it as a way of extending EC competence under the guise of protecting rights. Despite these vagaries, listing things in this way might suggest that the powers of the Community are limited to those mentioned here, but this is not the case. Other powers are created elsewhere in Part One and in the TEC in general. Moreover, beyond these conferred powers, Article 308 TEC allows for further action where the purposes of Articles 2 and 3 have not been met. All this provides more, albeit somewhat conflicting, evidence about the definition of the Community suggesting that, in complex modern societies, even single tasks have to take on a multi-faceted appearance in practice.

The final set of objectives appears in *Article 4* (ex 3a), which was added at Maastricht. It goes into detail on Economic and Monetary Union, which was not envisaged when most of the elements of Article 3 were drawn up. Adding references to EMU to Article 3

---

*This is discussed further in the introduction to Part Three of the TEC below, pp. 234–6.

would have made this even longer and less digestible. It would also have somewhat obscured the actual significance of monetary union in the 1990s. A separate article for its objectives helps to mark it out.

The first paragraph partly returns to the original formulation of Article 2 by talking of co-ordinating member state economic policies. This becomes a new base for the EC's economic strategy along with the Internal Market and common activities. The addition is a not unhelpful updating of the reference in Article 2. However, there is a condition attached to this: such activities must have a free-market nature.

This is also true of monetary union, the outlines of which are then summed up in the second paragraph. The article emphasizes the concern for controlling inflation although it also allows that EMU policies can support not only growth but also the other economic policies of the Community. What these are is not made wholly clear.

On the one hand, the article can be read as elevating price stability over the solidarity and social progress referred to in the preamble, Article 3 and the TEU. Equally, there is no reference here to the objectives of maintaining employment and increasing standards of living set out in Article 2. The EP pushed for mention of these things prior to Amsterdam but without success.

On the other hand, the third subparagraph talks of 'activities' – by which fixing exchange rates, co-ordinating national policies and defining objectives and policies are presumably meant – fitting in with stable prices, budgetary rectitude and balanced current accounts. Such obligations again clearly fall on member states as such along with the EC as a whole. All this gives real emphasis to the ideas of monetary policy enshrined in the TEC via Maastricht at the expense of the other goals of the Union and does not reconcile them. It also begins to lay down conditions to be observed by the Community in seeking to achieve its targets.

Conditions to be Met

Although the main tasks of the Community are economic, we have already seen a number of constraints on its freedom of action. Some rules thus apply only to relations between member states, harmonization has to be functionally necessary and, in some areas, the EC can only act in a supporting role. At the same time policies and other measures have to respect both gender equality and the freedom of the market.

These restraints are reinforced, according to *Article 6* (ex 3c), by environmental concerns, especially where the use of finite natural resources is involved. The EC is obliged to integrate environmental protection requirements into the definition and implementation of policies with specific emphasis placed on promoting sustainable development. Doubts have, however, been expressed about how binding this will prove. We might also think that both avoiding discrimination, as in Articles 12 and 13, and assisting services of general economic interest, as defined in Article 16, might also be seen as further restraints as well as objectives. Unfortunately the treaty is not set out in such a way as to make clear whether this is so.

However, it is *Article 5* (ex 3b) which goes furthest in laying down conditions for EC action, and in this case they are much more political than economic. These so-called 'subsidiarity' provisions were immensely controversial at the time of the ratification of the TEU. They were cited by both John Major and the Danish government as a sign that national interests were not being overruled by Brussels. And the working out of a code of practice to implement the article played some part in helping to reassure Danish opinion in 1992–3 in advance of the second referendum on the TEU. However, many were sceptical about the reality of the concept, it being seen by some Eurosceptics as a spur to 'centralizing federalism' and not a barrier to it. Other articles, like Articles 10 and 308 as they now are, were held to rob it of both actual and legal effect. None the less, it became a major theme of debates on EU governance and the perceived need to bring the Union closer to its citizens. Hence it was reformulated in the Protocol on the application of the principles of subsidiarity and proportionality attached to the TEC at Amsterdam. This in turn was accompanied by Declaration No. 43 TA.

The idea of subsidiarity goes back to Calvinist and Catholic political thought, as we showed in *European Union and European Community*, but it emerged from the 1970s in the context of the EU. It was then increasingly used during the 1980s to answer regional and state fears about the growing influence of the EC but without raising the spectre of a centralized federation. Hence at Maastricht it was inserted into the TEC rather than into the TEU. This was not because the idea applies only to the Community, since both the preamble and the first two articles of the TEU specifically refer to subsidiarity as a characteristic of the Union and the way it works. Indeed, the TEU makes it clear that Article 5 TEC defines the concept for the EU as a whole. So, its insertion at this point in the TEC seems to reflect, on the one hand, the role of the TEC as a support of the Union and, on the other, the need for the concept to be judicially enforceable.

Although the TEU implies that Article 5 provides a full account of subsidiarity, and only that, this is not what we actually find. For, although it is apparently a short and succinct article it is actually a complex and multi-level provision, and each of its three elements raise as many questions as they answer. The first paragraph deals with the attribution of competence and is copied from Article 4 of the EP's 1984 Draft Treaty on European Union. It provides a very emphatic statement of the fact that the Community is not an autonomous and uncontrolled body but that it is subject to the treaties in two ways: that what it does must be in line with what has been set out; and that in doing these things it has to respect the kinds of legal restraints later set out in Article 7 TEC. Hence the EC's authority is limited in line with the best tenets of Western constitutionalism. None of this is new, since it is reinforcing the principle of conferred powers already inserted into the treaty in what is now Article 7, but was no doubt inserted to reassure worried member states.

The second paragraph, the authorship of which was claimed by Douglas Hurd, deals in part with the necessity for EC action. It applies only to those areas where the EC does not have exclusive authority. Where it does, then the Community is required to act as necessary to fulfil its treaty obligations, although no more than this. However, there is no absolute certainty as to which fields these are. This is partly because the TEC is not written in terms of clear attribution of powers and partly because of the way that member-state and Community responsibilities can be intertwined. Moreover, there is some argument as to whether the Community actually has to exercise an authority in order to lay claim to it.

In any case, in those areas where it does not have exclusive authority, it has to observe not specific rules of distribution of power as in federal constitutions, but the 'principle' of subsidiarity. This is not defined as we might expect a principle to be defined, in a terse but generally applicable way, such as 'decisions should always be taken at the lowest possible level'. This was done in Articles 1 and 6 of the TEU with their talk of decisions being taken as close to the people as possible and respecting national identities, but here there is a more opaque formulation. The assumption seems to be that 'everybody knows what subsidiarity means'. Yet, this is not so in practice. Thus, under Major, the UK government refused to treat subsidiarity as a general constitutional principle applicable to subnational levels of government as the Austrians, Belgians and Germans saw it in Declaration No. 3n TA. The Conservative government in the UK saw subsidiarity purely as a matter of transferring responsibilities back to Westminster, much to the annoyance of the Scots and others at home.

Moreover, the treaty actually ducks not merely the job of defining the principle as such but also that of spelling out exactly what its application might mean in practice. It provides only partial indicators of the circumstances where the principle might come into play. These are when member states cannot achieve a task on their own – a clause added at the last moment in 1991 to reassure Germany that the ability of member states to undertake policy initiatives was not being excluded – and if there is evidence that community action would produce 'added value'. This is subjective and leaves open questions such as whether member states have to experiment first or whether an abstract decision can be made. Equally it can be read both as a new restraint on Brussels and as a justification for further interventionism. And, in any case, the treaties are not clear whether subsidiarity is an overriding principle or not.

The third paragraph then goes on to raise what is actually a separate question, and one which the TEU does not lead us to expect. This is the issue of 'proportionality', or of the extent, intensity and nature of Community action, whether in areas of exclusive competence or elsewhere. This liberal constitutionalist principle comes from German law and argues, albeit perhaps not so bluntly, that 'sledgehammers should not be used to crack nuts'. In other words, when the Community acts it should do so with moderation and use only those powers which are sufficient to achieve the desired end. This is in line with the use of the term 'insofar' in paragraph 2. An example might be when seeking to resolve a merger case involving large Danish and Swedish firms, the Community would not seek new powers to regulate all mergers throughout the EU involving more than €1,000 million market capitalization. Another might be not using full legislation when a code of conduct might secure the same results. This is still somewhat vague and the concept is only partly reconciled with the idea of subsidiarity as such.

What we have, then, is a partial code of practice for a sensible but underdefined and imperfectly operationalized principle. Moreover, there is not much indication of who is to operate it. Nor is there great certainty about its justiciability. As a new general principle of the Union it is implicitly under the jurisdiction of the ECJ. And this is reinforced by the fact that the guidelines are not merely in the TEC but are written in legal rather than general style. Some supporters of integration have therefore seen it as opening the way to challenges to such cherished concepts as Article 308. Unfortunately, the vagueness and political sensitivity of the concept, and the lack of preparedness of the Commission and EP to police the principle, have meant that the ECJ has not shown much enthusiasm for acting on the article, let alone fully defining subsidiarity. Nevertheless, it has generally refused to accept subsidiarity as a reason for overruling questions of rights. The European Council has also declared that the principle does not have direct effect.

Partly because of these uncertainties, subsidiarity has become very political. It is in fact a contested concept. Some critics of the EC see the idea as meaningless, if not a smoke-screen for further integration given that it presupposes a rigid legal framework and not member-state autonomy. Others, with a different view of integration, worry about its potential for preventing policy co-ordination and perhaps even for breaking up the Union. As a result, limited use has been made of it even though Amsterdam sought to clarify and operationalize the concept.

Since Maastricht the Commission has issued regular reports on the application of the principle and has both recast some acts and refrained from introducing some proposed new legislation. The preambles of many new acts now justify the legislation in terms of subsidiarity. However there has been no real culling of laws. The idea has also been a minor element in the debate on governance in the EU started by the Commission. Member states have been ambiguous in their attitudes, often upholding the principle but avoiding it in practice when it suited their interests to have things done at Community level.

Prior to this subsidiarity had been used to help win the Danes round. The Birmingham summit in 1992 equated 'subsidiarity' with 'nearness', which, as already suggested, would not be accepted by all defenders of the former. However, the UK presidency's ideas were rejected as too negative, while the Commission's own proposals were immensely detailed and obscure. None the less, an agreement was reached at Edinburgh in an annex to the Presidency Conclusions which gave enhanced emphasis to the standing of the concept and spelled out what it was supposed to do and on what conditions.

While the Danes accepted these clarifications, the status of the new rules was somewhat uncertain. Hence at Amsterdam many of them were written into the TEC as a Protocol on the application of the principles of subsidiarity and proportionality. These were made binding principles and had to be obeyed in all legislation. New enactments would therefore have both to justify themselves and to meet three criteria: that the legislation dealt with transnational matters; that action by member states alone would conflict with the treaties; and that co-ordinated action would bring added value. Legislation would also have to be simple, to be based on consultation and to leave room for member states' participation And the whole thing would be subject to evaluation, review and reconsideration. Indeed, the European Councils of Portschach, Vienna and Helsinki in 1998 and 1999 did follow it up.

However, it was also made clear that the subsidiarity principle did not relieve member states of their obligations under the TEC. Hence doubts about the extent to which it can protect member states have continued. These were reinforced by the fears expressed by the Commission in Agenda 2000. As a result less has been heard of it of late. So it remains a technically limited aspiration, somewhat tied to the circumstances of the early 1990s, rather than a crisp and generally applicable constitutional practice. Paradoxically it seems to emphasize both the binding nature of the treaties and their failure to take on a clear federationist dimension.

Community Methods

Having set out the aims and objectives of the Community and some of the conditions to be observed in meeting them, Part One moves on to specify the ways in which this might be done. In other words, targets are not supposed to be fulfilled without positive action. Fulfilling them involves, firstly, setting up institutions within the Community and, secondly, a series of working procedures, often involving the member states. And many of these provisions are of significant constitutional importance.

This might not be immediately obvious with *Article 7* (ex 4) which looks a very simple and straightforward list of institutions but actually has tremendous implications in several directions. To begin with it sets out the institutional embodiment of the Community and, in so doing, details the single institutional framework mentioned by Article 3 TEU. This is partly why the five institutions – the EP, Council, Commission, ECJ and Court of Auditors – are listed here ahead of the fuller discussion in Part Five TEC. The latter really assumes the existence of Article 7 but specifying them here also makes it clear that the Community does not have the autonomy to set up any such institutions it wants. They are there for a purpose, and not as of right. In fact institutions only exist to enable the

Community to carry out the functions allocated to it. In other words they are subject to specific limitations even if they have *de facto* and *de jure* independence, something which member states are expected to recognize. None of them is described as supra-national, as was the Commission's forerunner under the TECSC, the High Authority.

This constitutionalist tone is carried on by the final phrase of the first paragraph, which now reinforces the idea of conferred powers. Originally this was first mentioned here whereas, since Amsterdam, it follows on the same provision in Article 5. In any case this phrase makes it very clear that all institutional power is conferred by the treaty and the institutions cannot arrogate powers to themselves. Everything they do must be justified by something in the TEC; a legal base, in other words. Equally, they are required to do everything which the treaties ask of them and cannot evade their responsibilities, as shown by the ECJ in *European Parliament* v. *Council* (1985) concerning transport policy. Article 7 can thus be seen as a statement that the Community is subject to the rule of law, a very fundamental principle the effects of which stretch well beyond the institutions alone.

At the same time the TEC creates a kind of hierarchy of institutions. Despite the attacks on the bureaucracy of Brussels, the treaty understands institutions not as bureaucratic administrations but in a legal sense. What counts here are the formal rights of Community bodies. Those, described here as 'institutions', have considerable powers whereas the Economic and Social Committee and the Committee of the Regions have far less authority. Because these consultative bodies are, in common-sense terms, also institutions, the former are often known as 'full' institutions. Beyond this, of course, there are many other organs in the Community that lack treaty-based status.

There is some uncertainty about what the rights of full institutions are, partly because the article itself is largely silent on the matter. However, they have, to begin with, a limited autonomy so that they can, subject to due process, act in order to fulfil the EC's tasks. And this means taking decisions which are usually binding, including on member states. As a result such decisions are subject to judicial review by the ECJ. Equally, full institutions have wide authority to bring cases before the Court in order to defend their rights and seek annulment, as *European Parliament* v. *Council* (1985) shows. They also have the right to fix their own operations without reference to others and the financial resources to support them.

All this amounts to enjoying considerable precedence within the Union. Their very existence gives the Community much of its identity and independence. And this, in turn, rubs off on them. Because of this, other bodies have sought promotion to the status of full institution in order to gain the standing and prerogatives which this brings. Only the Court of Auditors has been successful, as its addition to the Article 7 list through the TEU shows. For some authorities, moreover, the precise configuration of institutions suggests the embryo of a European Federation, although to say this is to assume a rigid and structure-based view of what a federal system is. Moreover, there is a subtle balance between the institutions which involves, as Bieber says, competition as well as co-operation. None the less, according to the Advocate-General in *European Parliament* v. *Council* (1990), the division of competences in Article 7 provides a framework within which institutional development takes place so that this is a dynamic and not a static arrangement.

The other bodies mentioned in paragraph 2 not only play a supporting role but an advisory one. And until Nice they could only advise the Commission and Council. However, there is clearly an obligation on the latter to consult them. None the less, both Committees have sought upgrading from what they feel is a demeaning situation which fails to recognize their legitimacy. But they have not been allowed to follow the Court of Auditors in its upwards march.

This brings us to *Article 8* (ex 4a), which provides a statutory reference to the two institutional arrangements set up to run EMU: the network of national banks known as the European System of Central Banks (ESCB) and the European Central Bank (ECB). Perhaps because all this is newer, and the product of more uncertain times, Article 8 makes reference to the treaty as controlling not just the way the two work but also their establishment. Equally, the article establishes the legitimacy of the detailed statute governing their operation contained in the Protocol on the Statute of the European System of Central Banks and of the European Central Bank. In doing so, it echoes the long-standing reference to the European Investment Bank (EIB) now found at *Article 9* (ex 4b). Here, too, the subordination of the Bank to the TEC is emphasized, although the EIB does have legal personality. This is not apparent from Article 9 but results from provisions contained in the Protocol on the Statute of the European Investment Bank. All of this makes it clear that the institutions are, at least on paper, subject to the treaties and are not fully self-governing. This is an important constitutional point.

So too is the next article, on the relations between member states and the Community. Although the original member states created the Community, and now sustain it with the newcomers, this does not mean that they retain total freedom. They have to agree to accept the rules they have themselves adopted in order to help the Community carry out its agreed tasks. Hence *Article 10* (ex 5) is the first of six articles that lay out key procedures for helping the EC to achieve its aims and objectives. It deals with what is referred to as the duty of loyal or sincere co-operation with the Community. This is a formal statement that the member states, like the institutions, have obligations towards the EC. As German speakers would say, they have to be *Bundestreu*, faithful to the larger entity, a point made in relation to external activity in Article 11(2) TEU. However, it is not a statement of subordination as such. Rather it is a reminder that member states are expected to live up to what they have promised in signing or acceding to the treaty.

Article 10 is, however, cast in terms neither of principle nor of passive acquiescence but of purposive action. Member states are told that they must take all appropriate measures in three directions: obeying the treaty's specific prescriptions for participating member states; following up the decisions taken by the institutions; and generally working to help the EC to achieve its ends. In other words, member states are required to be proactive and aware of what the EC is seeking to do. This requirement is reinforced by a final sentence which warns member states against creating obstacles for the onward development of the Community. All this adds up to a clear statement of the fact that the member states are jointly responsible for making the EC work. By implication they are answerable for their actions.

The impact of Article 10 is thus not a simple matter of technical implementation. It is much wider both politically and legally. As Temple Lang observes, the ECJ has vigorously deduced specific duties from the relatively general and vague wording of the article and extended its meaning. Member states are thus now required to refrain from acting in areas where the Community has full competence, unless specifically authorized by the EC. They must also set aside their own laws even if Community action breaches the former. They must do this as soon as a law is passed even though it has not been implemented. And all national authorities are subject to EC influence. So Article 10 places considerable political restraints on member states.

This obviously has legal implications. In fact the legal ramifications go beyond this in at least two ways. Firstly, national courts are very much involved in following up EC law and ensuring that its protection is extended to ordinary citizens, for instance in matters of gender equality. Secondly, as already noted, member states are accountable for their actions. And, where they misapply or fail to implement EC law, and this disadvantages individuals, the latter have a right to compensation. This was established in the 1992 *Francovich* case.

The duty of loyal co-operation has, however, been extended by the *Zwartveld* (1990) judgment of the ECJ to the institutions. They are legally required to help member states as they seek to carry out their duties under Article 10. Institutions are not allowed to obstruct the member states. And Declaration No. 3 TN reinforces this by encouraging inter-institutional agreements to help them be more supportive. Equally, the declaration stresses the importance of member-state loyalty to the Union. All this makes it clear that Article 10 now contains a major constitutional principle and one which can be constraining for member states. Hence, its relation to opt-outs and flexibility deserve more attention than they have so far received.

Flexibility is now, in fact, the subject of the next two articles. This reflects the fact that Nice made major changes to the Amsterdam provisions. It slimmed down and divided the existing long Article 11. In so doing Nice made it clear that the articles are a means of implementing the provisions of Title VII TEU and not a separate code of practice. This means that the TEC's provisions on enhanced co-operation are simpler and more straightforward. This is one reason why they are perhaps more likely to be used than their predecessors.

At Amsterdam, where closer co-operation was first introduced to the TEC, the article had five paragraphs. The first laid down five conditions for embarking on experiments in flexibility. It then went on to establish that authorization would normally be given by a qualified majority of the Council following a formal request and opinions from the Commission. However, other member states were able to appeal against this to the European Council. Since this body acts by unanimity this meant there was a veto whereas the ECJ was excluded. The third paragraph set out how other member states could apply at a later stage. The last two paragraphs established that any experiments in flexibility would be subject to the TEC, to the provisions of Title VII TEU and to the rules on Schengen.

As we have seen the complexity and stringency of all this meant that there were no experiments. Hence it was reconsidered during the 2000 IGC, which looked at the idea as a whole rather than in terms of the TEC alone. And although when a text emerged in November a separate set of conditions for the first pillar was still being considered, this did not make it to the final drafts.

What Nice decided on essentially was a shorter, three-paragraph *Article 11* (ex 5a). The first paragraph is a largely procedural one setting out how member states who want to experiment should go about applying to the Commission. This is phrased in much the same way as the TEU has it for the third pillar in Article 40a TEU. The Commission has the option of forwarding this to the Council and does not have to consult the EP at this stage. The reference up from Council now changes. It was originally to the Council of Ministers meeting in the composition of heads of government and states. With Nice the reference is to European Council, implying formal Commission involvement in deliberations. As before there is no sanction on the former if it rejects the proposal, merely a duty of explanation. The paragraph does lay down a kind of condition since a proposal has to relate to one of the policy fields found in the TEC.

Paragraph 2 makes it clear that authorization can only be given if there is wide institutional approval. Not merely does the Commission have to make a proposal but the EP has to be consulted or give its assent, depending on whether the policy field is governed by co-decision. This gives the EP a possible veto. Equally, the Council has both to find a majority and to satisfy itself that the requirements of Title VII TEU have been met. Only if these provide otherwise will the TEC not apply. The idea of EP assent is a new insertion, as is the next subparagraph which provides for the same facility for a reference up to the European Council as in Article 40a TEU. This apparent removal of the 'emergency brake' in important policy areas has worried some UK Eurosceptics. On the other hand, the third subparagraph, the old fourth paragraph of Article 11, reinforces the fact that enhanced co-operation must be within the powers conferred by the treaties.

Article 11a then takes up the previous third paragraph of Article 11. This deals with a later application to join an enhanced co-operation operation. It is no doubt because this is seen as very different from the initial establishment of an experiment that it has been made a separate article, showing that the articles are very much procedural. It is also a matter of highlighting the openness of the new enhanced co-operation procedure as laid down in the TEU. The transferred text continues to make the Commission responsible for advising the Council on whether to accept an application and, if so, how to implement it.

Technically, all this is a clear improvement on the previous complications and inflexibility. However, while most opinion has welcomed the improvements, and believes that the provisions both will be used and will have a significant effect on the EU, there are doubters. Some Eurosceptics see it as a means of going further and not of reining the EC back. Moreover, some of the leaders of the Irish 'no' campaign singled the clauses out for criticism because they were seen as a way of letting larger member states further exploit smaller ones, a reading out of line with the overall drift of the provisions.

In any case, having set out these methods, Part One goes on to build on this by listing a number of things which the Community is to do when carrying out its tasks. Together they make up a set of rights. *Article 12* (ex 6) is a long-standing and very basic provision and linked to the idea of free movement, banning discrimination on grounds of nationality. This was inserted in the original TEC in order to make sure that the common market was not distorted by national preferences, for instance customs levies. It is a somewhat negative rule, however, seeking to ban rather than to introduce positive changes. None the less, it conditions how the EC goes about its tasks by requiring it to treat all member-state nationals the same, even if there has to be a cross-border element for the rule to apply. Member states too are bound to treat nationals of other member states in the same way as they treat their own.

Moreover, it is a provision with direct effect, save where the TEC makes special provision, a fact made clear in *Costa* v. *ENEL* (1964). The second subparagraph allows the Council to adopt rules against national discrimination, using co-decision. Beyond this the ECJ has used Article 12 to create a general doctrine of equality by ensuring that non-nationals in a member state enjoy the same privileges as nationals. This includes special rules on intellectual property even where this is close to national identity. It has also led to the extension of national educational rights to others. This is despite the fact that the text does not specifically mention individuals and even though such discrimination is now fairly rare. And it does not have implications for citizenship as such, as the *Gilly* (1998) ruling shows.

For many, however, such provisions did not go far enough in recognizing that there was a wider and more specifically Community dimension to upholding basic rights against discrimination. This showed up in ECJ jurisprudence, in member-state feelings and the 1989 Social Charter, in the TEU's citizenship provisions and in Commission and EP proposals, notably to combat racism. Hence it figured on the 1996 IGC agenda and led to the Irish presidency tabling a general clause using almost the same language as that in Article 12. This, however, went too far for most member states so what Amsterdam finished up with was more restricted and not directly effective. Moreover, as Whittle and others have pointed out, it does not prohibit discrimination.

Rather, *Article 13* (ex 6a) allows the Community to take 'appropriate action' to combat a variety of forms of discrimination. These include both sex discrimination, which was also written into Article 2 TEC, thus making it a key principle of Community legislation, and accompanied by a revision to Article 141(3) TEC, and discrimination on the grounds of disability, which some commentators felt had been unfairly overlooked. Declaration No. 22 TA makes it incumbent on the institutions to take this into account. Among the other areas are discrimination on the basis of age, religion or belief and sexual orientation.

However, the list does not specifically include colour, language or social origin. The first two are presumably felt to be covered by the 'racial and ethnic origin' reference and the latter, though actually reflecting concerns for the Roma, may have been felt too capable of misinterpretation. In any case, it still establishes a new condition for EC action if not exactly a new means as Bell and other commentators note. For Barnard it also reinforces the substance of citizenship even if it does not create full rights to equality being essentially a matter of non-discrimination. Lenaerts suggests that it might also provide the ideal foundation upon which to build a comprehensive fundamental rights policy, presumably drawing on the Charter of Fundamental Rights proclaimed at Nice.

The wording differs somewhat from that in Article 12 as is required by its non-binding nature. It begins by recognizing that action against discrimination can be taken under other TEC articles, goes on to insist on unanimity in decision-making (because of the sensitive nature of the field) and then circumscribes the legislative measures which can be taken. It does not ban discrimination but seeks pre-emptive strategies to dissuade people from discrimination. In other words, the idea of 'combating' discrimination – which is not defined – is focused on society and not just on member states. And all this is to be done within the limits of powers conferred by the Treaty. This contrasts, as Toggenburg notes, with the wider 'scope of application' of the TEC found in Article 12.

Nice then allowed the use of co-decision and QMV when adopting measures in support of member-state action against discrimination. And it is made clear that such measures cannot replace or harmonize national legislation on the subject, although Eurosceptic opinion has been inclined to see the provision as a threat. Legal commentators such as Flynn have been uncertain about what areas, content and forms of legislation may actually come from it. The concept of appropriateness is not very clear. Despite this, Article 13 has been seen as entrenching generally applicable civil values in the TEC. However, it does this in a less far-reaching way than in the TEU since it only applies where the EC has power through other treaty articles. Indeed, the article is not fully freestanding because of the influence of Article 6 TEU. None the less, it means that such privileges are not restricted to workers as such and there is a treaty base for future action.

Article 14 (ex 7a) then reverts more directly to questions of methods. This, thanks to simplification, brings together elements of the old Articles 7a and 7b to maintain the commitment to the Single Market both as principle and practice. It now leaves out the complicated timetables of the past but notes the symbolic '1992' deadline. The reference to other treaty articles points towards the need for consistency of interpretation. Paragraph 2 then takes up the classic definition of the internal market first advanced in the SEA. Finally, paragraph 3 is taken over from the old Article 7b to specify the decision-making procedures to be used in Single Market matters, implicitly making the point that the market is still not complete.

However, although the Single Market normally takes precedence over everything else including state sovereignty – and the *Commission* v. *France* (1997) case shows that this means that member states are required to uphold free movement even against rioting peasants – there are exceptions. *Article 15* (ex 7c) thus recognizes that some member states can have structural problems in adjusting to the rigours of the Single Market.

Hence they can propose temporary measures to help them through, which presupposes that the Community as such will have to approve them, assuming the Commission so recommends. But this is a structural matter involving less developed economies, and not an escape clause for cyclical crisis situations in the generality of member states. This, which echoes other provisions in the treaties, may be of significance to new member states from central and eastern Europe.

Finally, *Article 16* (ex 7d) goes some way towards recognizing the French belief that some economic activities do not fit wholly comfortably into a free-market context. This was a point on which the 1996 Reflection Group picked up. However, the article is both imprecise and restricted, as Pernice and others have observed. It talks only vaguely of 'general economic interest' and not of public services, though the ECJ has interpreted the former as covering telecommunications, postal services, transport, and other utilities such as electricity. This is reflected in the reference to public services in Declaration No. 13 TA and the need for implementation of Article 16 to respect in full the ECJ's relevant jurisprudence. Indeed, Ross argues that Article 16 codifies the existing case law. Some treaty-based clarity has also been provided through the annexing of the Protocol on the system of public broadcasting in the Member States to the TEC by Amsterdam. All the same the precise effects of the article are uncertain. It does not, for instance, provide a clear-cut justification for state aids.

Equally, while it recognizes the contribution of such services to people at large, in line with thinking on the European social model, it emphasizes the limitations within which support for them can be given. The fact that it is not mentioned in Article 3 is also significant. The reference to principles rather than to precise rules makes it even more opaque. The stress on the role of member states as well as treaty limitations narrows its effects down further since the situation in the member states is often very dissimilar.

So, even though Declaration No. 16 TA foresees a role for the ECJ in enforcing it, this will not be easy. None the less, the article was introduced for a purpose. It now reminds us that the Community is more than just a cut-throat market even if it does the reminding in a symbolic rather than a substantive way, and was perhaps intended as a gesture to ordinary citizens.

This uncertainty is a continuing characteristic of Part One of the TEC. Despite the way it has been tidied up after Amsterdam, it clearly remains a somewhat unco-ordinated list of provisions. Nice did not really affect this fact. None the less, the provisions do point us in a number of directions. To begin with, they leave the common market as a central, indeed an enhanced, concern of the Community. Secondly, they maintain the latter as a body with wide objectives. Thirdly, they make the principles more specific, more cross-referenced and, perhaps, even a little simpler in expression if not in status. Fourthly, they tend to treat the treaty and the Community more as part of a wider enterprise and not as a self-contained operation. Finally, they leave the member states in a somewhat ambiguous state. They are both gainers and losers from the changes made at Amsterdam and Nice.

Equally, the status and significance of its discussion of rights remain unclear. Certainly the conditions for the tasks point towards a growing recognition of rights within the EC. But they are still ultimately derived from economic considerations and not formulated in a way reminiscent of a bill of rights. None the less, this aspect of Part One points the way to the idea of citizenship to which the *Guide* turns next.

PART ONE   PRINCIPLES

Article 1 (ex Article 1)

By this Treaty, the HIGH CONTRACTING PARTIES establish among themselves a EUROPEAN COMMUNITY.

Article 2 (ex Article 2)

The Community shall have as its task, by establishing a common market and an economic and monetary union and by implementing common policies or activities referred to in Articles 3 and 4, to promote throughout the Community a harmonious, balanced **and sustainable** development of economic activities, *a high level of employment and of social protection*, **equality between men and women,** sustainable and non-inflationary growth, a high degree **of competitiveness and** convergence of economic performance, **a high level of protection and improvement of the quality of the environment,** the raising of the standard of living and quality of life, and economic and social cohesion and solidarity among Member States.

Article 3 (ex Article 3 simplified)

1. For the purposes set out in Article 2, the activities of the Community shall include, as provided in this Treaty and in accordance with the timetable set out therein:
(a) the *prohibition*, as between Member States, of customs duties and quantitative restrictions on the import and export of goods, and of all other measures having equivalent effect;
(b) a common commercial policy;
(c) an internal market characterised by the abolition, as between Member States, of obstacles to the free movement of goods, persons, services and capital;
(d) measures concerning the entry and movement of persons as provided for in **Title IV**;
(e) a common policy in the sphere of agriculture and fisheries;
(f) a common policy in the sphere of transport;
(g) a system ensuring that competition in the internal market is not distorted;
(h) the approximation of the laws of Member States to the extent required for the functioning of the common market;
(i) **the promotion of co-ordination between employment policies of the Member States with a view to enhancing their effectiveness by developing a co-ordinated strategy for employment;**
(j) a policy in the social sphere comprising a European Social Fund;
(k) the strengthening of economic and social cohesion;
(l) a policy in the sphere of the environment;
(m) the strengthening of the competitiveness of Community industry;
(n) the promotion of research and technological development;
(o) encouragement for the establishment and development of trans-European networks;
(p) a contribution to the attainment of a high level of health protection;
(q) a contribution to education and training of quality and to the flowering of the cultures of the Member States;
(r) a policy in the sphere of development co-operation;

(s) the association of the overseas countries and territories in order to increase trade and promote jointly economic and social development;

(t) a contribution to the strengthening of consumer protection;

(u) measures in the spheres of energy, civil protection and tourism.

2. In all the activities referred to in this Article, the Community shall aim to eliminate inequalities, and to promote equality, between men and women.

Article 4 (ex Article 3a)

1. For the purposes set out in Article 2, the activities of the Member States and the Community shall include, as provided in this Treaty and in accordance with the timetable set out therein, the adoption of an economic policy which is based on the close co-ordination of Member States' economic policies, on the internal market and on the definition of common objectives, and conducted in accordance with the principle of an open market economy with free competition.

2. Concurrently with the foregoing, and as provided in this Treaty and in accordance with the timetable and the procedures set out therein, these activities shall include the irrevocable fixing of exchange rates leading to the introduction of a single currency, the ECU, and the definition and conduct of a single monetary policy and exchange-rate policy the primary objective of both of which shall be to maintain price stability and, without prejudice to this objective, to support the general economic policies in the Community, in accordance with the principle of an open market economy with free competition.

3. These activities of the Member States and the Community shall entail compliance with the following guiding principles: stable prices, sound public finances and monetary conditions and a sustainable balance of payments.

Article 5 (ex Article 3b)

The Community shall act within the limits of the powers conferred upon it by this Treaty and of the objectives assigned to it therein.

In areas which do not fall within its exclusive competence, the Community shall take action, in accordance with the principle of subsidiarity, only if and insofar as the objectives of the proposed action cannot be sufficiently achieved by the Member States and can therefore, by reason of the scale or effects of the proposed action, be better achieved by the Community.

Any action by the Community shall not go beyond what is necessary to achieve the objectives of this Treaty.

Article 6 (new – TA, drawing on ex Article 130r(2))

Environmental protection requirements must be integrated into the definition and implementation of the Community policies and activities referred to in Article 3, in particular with a view to promoting sustainable development.

Article 7 (ex Article 4)

1. The tasks entrusted to the Community shall be carried out by the following institutions:

    a EUROPEAN PARLIAMENT,

    a COUNCIL,

a COMMISSION,
a COURT OF JUSTICE,
a COURT OF AUDITORS.

Each institution shall act within the limits of the powers conferred upon it by this Treaty.

2. The Council and the Commission shall be assisted by an Economic and Social Committee and a Committee of the Regions acting in an advisory capacity.

Article 8 (ex Article 4a)

A European System of Central Banks (hereinafter referred to as 'ESCB') and a European Central Bank (hereinafter referred to as 'ECB') shall be established in accordance with the procedures laid down in this Treaty; they shall act within the limits of the powers conferred upon them by this Treaty and by the Statute of the ESCB and of the ECB (hereinafter referred to as 'Statute of the ESCB') annexed thereto.

Article 9 (ex Article 4b)

A European Investment Bank is hereby established, which shall act within the limits of the powers conferred upon it by this Treaty and the Statute annexed thereto.

Article 10 (ex Article 5)

Member States shall take all appropriate measures, whether general or particular, to ensure fulfilment of the obligations arising out of this Treaty or resulting from action taken by the institutions of the Community. They shall facilitate the achievement of the Community's tasks.

They shall abstain from any measure which could jeopardise the attainment of the objectives of this Treaty.

Article 11 (new – TA)

1. Member States which intend to establish enhanced co-operation between themselves in one of the areas referred to in this Treaty shall address a request to the Commission, which may submit a proposal to the Council to that effect. In the event of the Commission not submitting a proposal, it shall inform the Member States concerned of the reasons for not doing so.

2. Authorisation to *establish* enhanced *co-operation as* referred to in paragraph 1 shall be granted, *in compliance with Articles 43 to 45 of the Treaty on European Union,* by the Council, acting by a qualified majority on a proposal from the Commission and after consulting the European Parliament. When enhanced co-operation relates to an area covered by the procedure referred to in Article 251 of this Treaty, the assent of the European Parliament shall be required.

A member of the Council may request that the matter be referred to the European Council. After that matter has been raised before the European Council, the Council may act in accordance with the first subparagraph of this paragraph.

3. *The acts and decisions necessary for the implementation of* enhanced *co-operation activities shall be subject to all the relevant provisions of this Treaty, save as otherwise provided in this Article and in Articles 43 to 45 of the Treaty on European Union.*

Article 11a (new – TN)

Any Member State which wishes to *participate in* enhanced co-operation *established in accordance with Article 11* shall notify its intention to the Council and to the Commission, which shall give an opinion to the Council within three months of the date of receipt of that notification. Within four months of the date *of receipt* of that notification, the Commission shall *take a decision* on it, and on such specific arrangements as it may deem necessary.

Article 12 (ex Article 6)

Within the scope of application of this Treaty, and without prejudice to any special provisions contained therein, any discrimination on grounds of nationality shall be prohibited.

The Council, acting in accordance with the procedure referred to in **Article 251**, may adopt rules designed to prohibit such discrimination.

Article 13 (new – TA)

1. Without prejudice to the other provisions of this Treaty and within the limits of the powers conferred by it upon the Community, the Council, acting unanimously on a proposal from the Commission and after consulting the European Parliament, may take appropriate action to combat discrimination based on sex, racial or ethnic origin, religion or belief, disability, age or sexual orientation.

2. By way of derogation from paragraph 1, when the Council adopts Community incentive measures, excluding any harmonisation of the laws and regulations of the Member States, to support action taken by the Member States in order to contribute to the achievement of the objectives referred to in paragraph 1, it shall act in accordance with the procedure referred to in Article 251.

Article 14 (ex Article 7a simplified, drawing too on ex Article 7b)

1. The Community shall adopt measures with the aim of progressively establishing the internal market over a period expiring on 31 December 1992, in accordance with the provisions of this Article and of Articles 15, 26, 47(2), 49, 80, 93 *and* 95 and without prejudice to the other provisions of this Treaty.

2. The internal market shall comprise an area without internal frontiers in which the free movement of goods, persons, services and capital is ensured in accordance with the provisions of this Treaty.

3. *The Council, acting by a qualified majority on a proposal from the Commission, shall determine the guidelines and conditions necessary to ensure balanced progress in all the sectors concerned.*

Article 15 (ex Article 7c)

When drawing up its proposals with a view to achieving the objectives set out in Article 14, the Commission shall take into account the extent of the effort that certain economies showing differences in development will have to sustain during the period of establishment of the internal market and it may propose appropriate provisions.

If these provisions take the form of derogations, they must be of a temporary nature and must cause the least possible disturbance to the functioning of the common market.

Article 16 (new – TA)

Without prejudice to Articles 73, 86 and 87, and given the place occupied by services of general economic interest in the shared values of the Union as well as their role in promoting social and territorial cohesion, the Community and the Member States, each within their respective powers and within the scope of application of this Treaty, shall take care that such services operate on the basis of principles and conditions which enable them to fulfil their missions.

iv Citizenship of the Union

Having set out the bases of the Community and, in doing so, hinted at a number of rights for individuals and others which need to be observed, the TEC builds on this, thanks to the TEU, by establishing a form of citizenship. This reflected an underlying trend in the Community in the years running up to Maastricht to take people and rights more seriously. Hence the new provisions were agreed in 1991. They were then consolidated by Amsterdam, which made relations between the Union and its citizens one of its main themes. Nice made only minor changes to these provisions.

What has emerged from this is what many see as still a somewhat limited set of rights. None the less, they proved controversial during the ratification of the TEU. In practice, however, the new Part Two did not lead to immediate or great change and it has largely become accepted. However, the provisions are not without dynamism and have given rise to a good deal of academic debate.

The idea of citizenship did not come out of the blue in 1991. Initially it drew on the fact that the original TEC did create certain rights for individuals, including free movement, while also banning discrimination on grounds of nationality. Moreover, it established access to the ECJ in these areas. Such rights derived essentially from those economic activities with which the treaty was concerned. They were strengthened by ECJ jurisprudence which, from *Van Gend en Loos* (1963) onward, sought to empower and involve individuals in Community affairs and increasingly developed a rights-based view of the EC. Such considerations began to appear on the agendas of European summits in the early 1970s partly because of German pressures and, in the 1980s following the 1985 Adonnino Report, they widened into the beginnings of a policy on a 'people's Europe'. The aim was to make the EC more attractive to ordinary people. However, the approach was something of a ragbag of ideas and it did not address either the needs for democratic legitimacy for the Community or the perceived need to do something political to offset the effects of economic rationalization brought about by the 1992 programme.

The concept of citizenship was therefore taken up by President Mitterrand and others during the run-up to the 1991 IGCs. In the autumn of 1990 the Spanish government submitted a considered plea for a statement of the rights, freedoms and obligations of citizens in the new Community, things which it believed were implicit in the Single Market project. The Spanish envisaged this as a further pillar of the new Union. The idea was supported by the Commission and agreed in principle in December 1990.

The provisions thereafter agreed on were seen, according to Article 2 TEU, as a way of strengthening the rights and interests of the nationals of member states. In other words, they were meant to offer people something to make them think more warmly of the European enterprise and not to create a brand-new set of rights as such. None the less, as Meehan says, this does move things beyond citizenship as simply something to do with being a worker. In fact, as Moxon-Browne points out, the provisions reflected an ongoing Europeanization of rights and largely made *de jure* what already existed *de facto*. Putting them into a part of the TEC on their own, rather than adding them to the principles, gave them a showcase to encourage people to esteem and use them. Equally, talk of EU citizenship may have been an attempt to rally popular support for the new organization.

However, the way this was done created a technical anomaly because, despite being described as 'citizenship of the Union', the provisions were not put in the TEU but in the TEC. This hardly served to make them more comprehensible to the general public. Yet there were three reasons for doing this. Firstly, because the Union does not have a legal personality, the provisions could not be judicially enforced there. Indeed, the provisions provide no protection in the two inter-governmental pillars. So they had to go in the Community pillar and by implication the TEC. Secondly, because the rights were not really new but came largely from existing EC economic rights, it made more sense to add them to the TEC. Thirdly, had they gone into the TEU as such, this might have made the Union seem a more threatening and political body than its creators wished, given that citizenship is often seen as essential to both statehood and constitution-making. As part of the existing and familiar Community they might prove more acceptable.

None the less, there was much resistance to the proposals, partly because the text was read by some, notably in Denmark, as replacing national citizenship. This had to be clarified by the European Council at Edinburgh in 1992. Despite such reservations the idea remained very significant after Maastricht because it was so relevant to the need to end the popular alienation from the Union revealed by reactions to ratification. So it was taken up by the Westendorp Reflection Group in 1995. And though this failed to get new rights such as transparency and access to documents entered into Part Two of the TEC, Amsterdam did develop the concern for 'the Union and its citizens'. As well as trying to package such policies as consumer protection, employment and social balance as 'people related', reflecting a new social concern and a desire to make policy more relevant to the citizen, it did both clarify and extend civic rights. On the first it made it clear that Union citizenship was complementary to national citizenship. On the second, it talked in Article 1 TEU of taking decisions more openly as well as more closely to citizens. Equally, it stressed the need to educate citizens and give them access to data, information and language support. The idea of an 'area of freedom, security and justice' also pointed in this direction, as has already been suggested. This built on the existing availability of rights in education, property and social security.

In all, Amsterdam gave the whole concept of rights and citizenship a new prominence suitable to its more 'constitutional' tone. This was in line with a growing academic debate on the subject. There was a good deal of analysis of what was now being provided, what its weaknesses actually were and how it could, and should, be developed. And, although the idea lost political prominence thereafter despite academic stress on the fact that reviews of the concept could have led to EU provisions overtaking national citizenship, Nice gave it a new and evolutionary twist. Thus it changed the decision-making procedures as well as implicitly, and guardedly, linking citizenship to questions of passports and social security.

What has come out of all this is a set of six relatively brief articles. The first, *Article 17* (ex 8) formally creates the status in its initial paragraph. In line with Article 2 TEU, it makes citizenship an objective and not, as Welsh has pointed out, just a derivative of other treaty articles. It is not explicitly defined here although the following reference to national citizenship might be taken to imply that it is more a matter of nationality than of formal, EU-wide rights.

The second sentence, in fact, shows that EU citizenship is not self-contained or directly enjoyed but comes as a consequence of national citizenship. Acceptance of ultimate national sovereignty in this area was underlined by Declaration No. 2 TEU which, in an unsuccessful attempt to allay nationalist fears, reaffirmed the sole right of states to decide questions of nationality and citizenship even though the creation of citizenship might imply that the EU was a full state. However, Union citizenship applies automatically and cannot be rejected by unwilling national citizens. This suggests that it is accepted as an element of national provision. Yet, if states can decide who should have EU citizenship, they are not given unilateral power to determine its content. This has led many critics to attack the concept because it directly excludes many millions of people resident in the Union who do not, and cannot, possess the nationality of their host country, thus increasing the impression of a 'fortress Europe'.

Because these formulations did not satisfy Danish and other critics, Amsterdam took note of what was agreed at Edinburgh and added a new sentence underlining the secondary status of EU citizenship. There is also a hint in the reference to not replacing national citizenship that EU citizenship will never be allowed to become superior even if Article 22 might seem to leave open such a possibility. Yet even this did not satisfy Berthu, who saw it as a snide suggestion that national citizenship was, in practice, incomplete because it needed this sort of addition. He would have preferred to see it described as 'subordinate'.

The second paragraph of Article 17 places a further restraint on EU citizenship by making it plain that its rights derive from the EC Treaty alone, despite its Union links. In other words, citizenship is another example of conferred powers, though what the rights in question actually are is left to later articles to make clear. There is neither the full list some would have liked nor a cross-reference to the citations in Part One. Even less light is cast on what constitutes the duties of citizenship referred to here, suggesting that the mention is a rather ritualistic affair. It is doubtful whether the ECJ would wish to condemn citizens for failing to meet such vague obligations.

Article 18 (ex 8a) begins the process of defining and specifying the nature of EU citizenship and its rights. Significantly it does this by restating in its first paragraph the basic economic right to move and reside within the member states. Here, although there is a clear continuity with the Single Market as defined in the TEC, there is also an innovation. Article 18 provides an autonomous right of circulation and establishment. This had only existed in restricted form in the jurisprudence deriving from the EC Treaty. Yet, as Bourrinet says, it is a prerequisite for the efficient working of the Single Market, at least where ordinary individuals are concerned, although the right may not be immediately available to nationals of the candidate countries, showing that even the TEC is subject to subsequent accession or other treaties.

Generally the aim of the article was simply to add a new dimension to the rights already enjoyed by citizens of member states. It sought to add nothing and certainly not to take anything away. However, in *Gallagher* (1995) the ECJ suggests that if it does not actually prevent the member states from using security grounds to restrict free movement it does mean that this can only be done if non-nationals are not singled out. Moreover, the institutions can intervene to maintain and develop these economic rights and the way they are exercised. Timetables for doing this and confirming civic rights are laid down in Articles 19 onward.

None the less, rights are subject not merely to the conditions laid down by the TEC but to any relevant secondary legislation. In other words, it is a formal creation and one related to residence rather than a basic, inherent and untrammelled human right. Paragraphs 2 and 3 of Article 18, respectively revised and added by Nice, then provide for the Community to fill out any gaps in the treaty's provision for citizenship by co-decision rather than unanimity as had originally been the case. The fact that QMV now applies to this worries people like Bonde as does the potential for exploitation by the ECJ. However, Nice did bar EC action from touching on passports, identity cards, residence permits and provisions concerning social security and social protection. While this is intended to defend sensitive areas like passports and benefits against interference, it does implicitly link them to EU citizenship even if states remain the only bodies which can issue the documents which prove eligibility for the privileges of EU citizenship.

Moreover, it is incumbent on proposers of any new legislation to demonstrate that there is a real gap. None the less, the article does not provide a full legal basis for civil rights even if it moves somewhat away from the idea of the citizen as worker and raises the idea of free movement to a higher plane. It also leaves unanswered some difficult questions such as what is the balance between political and market derived rights, although it has been used by the ECJ, in *Bickel and Franz* (1998), to derive the right to have dealings in their own language and not just that of the host state. The ECJ has been less keen on using the article in cases of discrimination.

Article 19 (ex 8b), the longest of the six articles in Part Two, brings in the first political element of citizenship by allowing limited voting rights. These do include the right to actually stand for elections, which is perhaps more important. Some commentators see all this as highly significant despite the limitations. However, voting in local elections is only possible for those EU citizens resident in another member state. Decisions on this are very much a matter for member states, the role of the EP being nominal, even though the first paragraph allows member states with difficulties to delay introducing the rules. This probably refers to Luxembourg, where some villages could be swamped by the number of resident Portuguese workers if they all chose to vote. Indeed, one of the little ironies of integration is that this has proved harder to implement in pro-integration countries than it has in sceptical states like the UK, where Irish voting has long been accepted. Implementing paragraph 2 on EP elections, which is a clear reflection of the wider horizons of EU citizenship, has been less problematic even though the same decision-making rules are provided. Rules were adapted in 1993.

Part Two then abruptly shifts its focus from inside to outside the EC. Hence *Article 20* (ex 8c) lays down rules for allowing otherwise unrepresented citizens to seek consular assistance from another member state. Given that there are only five non-EU states where all 15 are represented and 17 where there were as few as two member states present, this could be useful. Interestingly, the way this is to be done is decided by states among themselves and not in a formal EU framework, since this is a very inter-governmental matter.

Thereafter Part Two reverts to domestic concerns and, in *Article 21* (ex 8d), offers a kind of judicial protection to EU citizens by restating their right to petition the EP and to lay their grievances before the Ombudsman. However, the details of this are established in Articles 194–5 TEC and elsewhere. Where citizens are communicating with the EU institutions there is, since Amsterdam, a right to do so in their own languages. Declaration No. 4 TN suggests that replies ought to come in a 'reasonable' time, whatever this might mean. There is some ambiguity about which institutions are meant to be covered by this, depending on whether the reference is to full institutions in Article 7 or all the bodies mentioned there, including EcoSoc and the Committee of the Regions.

Finally, there is provision for some forward movement in citizenship. According to

Article 22 this can come in two inter-related ways. One is through Commission monitoring of the way the provisions are working, something which is clearly expected to lead to further changes in line with the way the Union itself changes, a somewhat subjective approach. Given that the Commission thinks that citizenship is a mobilizing concept its reports are likely to play up its importance and the need for development. The second way forward would then follow on from this through new measures. These can only enhance citizenship and not reduce it, something that alarms Eurosceptics. However, what seems to be envisaged is not ordinary legislation but treaty amendments since the measures have to be both passed unanimously and formally ratified by national acts.

Basically, this rather suggests that Part Two is more a matter of codifying existing practice than of being essentially a catalyst. And the codification is untidy, problematic and restricted. Thus it offers very limited, and secondary, political rights and some economic ones. At present these do not constitute a full endowment of primary political rights, partly because they can be legally withheld in certain circumstances. None the less, they were controversial in 1992 and it does not seem that citizenship is likely to expand in the near future even though so far it does not seem either to have led to much activity or to have enjoyed much success in developing public sympathy and support for the EU. Weiler's belief that EU citizenship would lead to a new democratic legitimacy for the Union sounds equally unlikely. This may be because EU citizenship is a somewhat top-down matter and cannot be chosen positively. Equally, it does not seem to have done much for developing rights since this has happened outside citizenship.

PART TWO   CITIZENSHIP OF THE UNION

Article 17 (ex Article 8)

1. Citizenship of the Union is hereby established. Every person holding the nationality of a Member State shall be a citizen of the Union. **Citizenship of the Union shall complement and not replace national citizenship.**

2. Citizens of the Union shall enjoy the rights conferred by this Treaty and shall be subject to the duties imposed thereby.

Article 18 (ex Article 8a)

1. Every citizen of the Union shall have the right to move and reside freely within the territory of the Member States, subject to the limitations and conditions laid down in this Treaty and by the measures adopted to give it effect.

2. **If action by the Community should prove necessary to attain this objective and this Treaty has not provided the necessary powers,** *the Council may adopt provisions with a view to facilitating the exercise of the rights referred to in paragraph 1. The Council shall act in accordance with the procedure referred to in Article 251.*

3. **Paragraph 2 shall not apply to provisions on passports, identity cards, residence permits or any other such document or to provisions on social security or social protection.**

Article 19 (ex Article 8b)

1. Every citizen of the Union residing in a Member State of which he is not a national shall have the right to vote and to stand as a candidate at municipal elections in the Member State in which he resides, under the same conditions as

nationals of that State. This right shall be exercised subject to detailed arrangements *adopted* by the Council, acting unanimously on a proposal from the Commission and after consulting the European Parliament; these arrangements may provide for derogations where warranted by problems specific to a Member State.

2. Without prejudice to Article *190(4)* and to the provisions adopted for its implementation, every citizen of the Union residing in a Member State of which he is not a national shall have the right to vote and to stand as a candidate in elections to the European Parliament in the Member State in which he resides, under the same conditions as nationals of that State. This right shall be exercised subject to detailed arrangements *adopted* by the Council, acting unanimously on a proposal from the Commission and after consulting the European Parliament; these arrangements may provide for derogations where warranted by problems specific to a Member State.

Article 20 (ex Article 8c)

Every citizen of the Union shall, in the territory of a third country in which the Member State of which he is a national is not represented, be entitled to protection by the diplomatic or consular authorities of any Member State, on the same conditions as the nationals of that State. *Member States shall establish* the necessary rules among themselves and start the international negotiations required to secure this protection.

Article 21 (ex Article 8d)

Every citizen of the Union shall have the right to petition the European Parliament in accordance with Article *194*.

Every citizen of the Union may apply to the Ombudsman established in accordance with Article *195*.

Every citizen of the Union may write to any of the institutions or bodies referred to in this Article or in Article 7 in one of the languages mentioned in Article 314 and have an answer in the same language.

Article 22 (ex Article 8e)

The Commission shall report to the European Parliament, to the Council and to the Economic and Social Committee *every three years* on the application of the provisions of this Part. This report shall take account of the development of the Union.

On this basis, and without prejudice to the other provisions of this Treaty, the Council, acting unanimously on a proposal from the Commission and after consulting the European Parliament, may adopt provisions to strengthen or to add to the rights laid down in this Part, which it shall recommend to the Member States for adoption in accordance with their respective constitutional requirements.

Community Policies

The *Guide* now moves on to the longest of the TEC's six 'Parts', Part Three. This now comprises a total of 160 articles (Articles 23–181a (ex 9–130t)) brought together under the general rubric of 'Community Policies'. The heading is slightly misleading since Part Three includes provisions governing the Single Market's four freedoms, themselves principles as opposed to policies. This was clear in the way in which the TEC was organized prior to the TEU when the current Part Three comprised Part Two, 'Foundations of the Community', and Part Three, 'Policy of the Community', of the treaty. It is thus preferable to consider the part as covering those areas in which the Community, as opposed to the Union, has a formal competence to act. This is reflected in the 21 named 'titles' into which it is divided. These cover an array of areas of EC regulatory and redistributive action ranging from 'Free Movement of Goods' and 'Economic and Monetary Union' to 'Economic and Social Cohesion' and 'Development Co-operation'. The first two of these when extended to include the free movement of capital and services as well as economic and monetary union create what can be viewed as the economic constitution of the EU.

Few of the policy competences contained in Part Three date back to when the TEC was signed in 1957. Then only seven policy titles existed. The SEA and TEU added three and seven titles respectively and, in the process, expanded and amended others. The EC's policy competences were thus increased. The TEU also placed all the policy titles in the current Part Three under the generic title 'Community Policies'. More recently, the TA increased the number of titles by inserting a further three: one on 'Visas, Asylum, Immigration and Other Policies Related to Free Movement of Persons', which sees the transfer and therefore the 'communitarization', albeit incomplete as Wessels argues, of competences previously found in Pillar III of the Union; a second on 'Employment'; and a third on 'Customs Co-operation'. The TA also introduced amendments to a further 13 titles. Nice's impact was less substantial, adding only Title XXI on 'Economic, Financial and Technical Co-operation with Third Countries' – which consists of a single article – and amending only 11 articles spread across seven titles.

The insertion by the SEA and TEU of new titles and thus new articles into the treaty resulted in many article numbers carrying letter suffixes (e.g. 73g). More than two-thirds of the 27 articles governing Economic and Monetary Union (Articles 103a–109m) fell into this category. While such a system of numbering may have appeared rather messy, it soon became familiar. All this changed with Amsterdam. As a consequence of consolidation, all suffixes were removed and all Part Three articles, with the sole exception of Article 105, were assigned new numbers. Also, the simplification process saw 37 articles amended in some form and a further 43 by then obsolete articles deleted. A slight blemish did appear in Amsterdam's tidying up of Part Three with Nice's introduction of Article 181a, which saw the reintroduction of letter suffixes. Slimmed down by Amsterdam from 180 to 159 articles, Part Three none the less remains the longest subdivision of the TEC.

With the expansion of what is now Part Three of the TEC, the formal policy competences of the EC have been substantially increased. They have been extended beyond the core economic activities of the original common market, such as the free movement of goods (including agriculture) and competition, to include, in Pollack's words, 'almost every conceivable area of political, economic and social life'. Before exploring these formal competences in more detail, several points concerning the link between EC competence and EC activity should be noted. First, competences in the treaty differ in terms of the authority which they give the EC. In certain cases, such as competition and the free movement of goods, services, capital and workers, the EC is granted regulatory powers and can adopt legislation which is binding on all member states. This tends to reflect how central the area is to the economic principles on which the EU is based, in this case the Single Market. In other areas the regulatory capacity of the EC is weak. Dehousse, for example, describes health, vocational training and culture as 'limited competences without regulatory meaning'. And in cases such as employment, the EC's role is limited to the co-ordination of best practice. In others, the EC acts through recommendations, thus creating what is often referred to as 'soft law'.

This leads to two further points. Second, the EC rarely enjoys exclusive competence. Generally, the competence to legislate is shared with the member states, a point underlined by the Treaty of Nice's amendments to the EC's treaty-making power under Article 133 on commercial policy. Indeed, the EC's role is often limited to supporting the actions of the member states. Third, the nature of competences is often a reflection of the political and economic climate when the provisions were agreed. This is certainly the case with Title II on agriculture. And returning to the employment title, when it was agreed at Amsterdam, the member states were keen to respond to popular concerns about unemployment. Yet the prevailing emphasis on deregulation meant that EC competences would be limited, particularly given popular opposition to increasing the EU's regulatory powers further.

Fourth, there are many policy areas for which the EC originally had no explicit competence yet where it has nevertheless acted and only afterwards gained an explicit competence to act. This is due to two provisions. On the one hand, the so-called 'catch-all' Article 308 (ex 235) has, in the absence of explicit provisions, empowered the EC since 1958 to adopt by unanimity 'appropriate measures' to achieve an objective of the TEC. The opportunities thus created have been seized with the EC becoming active in promoting legislation and policy initiatives in the environmental sphere long before an explicit competence for action on the environment was inserted into the treaty by the SEA. On the other hand there is Article 95 (ex 100a) which, since the SEA, has allowed the EC to adopt by a qualified majority unspecified measures, subject to certain restrictions, necessary to complete the Single Market. Consequently, there are several titles, notably the shorter ones, where the arrival of policy competences post-dates EC action. In amending the treaty, member states have often been formalizing existing implicit competences rather than introducing substantial new powers. Or in the words of Buchan, treaty amendment has, in some instances, been 'a case of making new bottles into which to pour old wine so as to make it more drinkable'. In other cases, member states have actually used IGCs to insert explicit treaty provisions and adopt protocols either to restrict recourse to specific articles, notably Article 95, or to limit interpretations of competences. Both the TEU and Amsterdam, for example, delimited areas where the harmonization of national laws and regulations is prohibited (see Articles 129, 149–152). Nice, meanwhile, bars the EC from adopting measures relating to taxation in certain areas (see Article 157).

Fifth, the presence of a policy competence within the TEC does not guarantee activity at the EC level. This was most obviously the case in the 1960s and 1970s when certain so-called 'common' policies, notably transport, and key economic freedoms such as the free movement of services, capital and workers either failed to emerge or were developed only slowly despite the existence of treaty provisions. This changed in the late 1980s when the EC's legislative programme underwent unprecedented expansion. The increase in decision-making in Brussels raised concerns at the popular level and among regional governments, notably in Germany, over what was perceived as an excessive centralization of power in the hands of the EC. As a result, subsidiarity and proportionality were promoted as key principles in determining whether action should be pursued at the EC level. Decision-making at the EC level was therefore being constrained, a process reinforced by the EC's supra-national institutions' public support for the decentralization of policy-making. Furthermore, EC activity has often depended on the financial resources available. With the period since the mid-1990s being characterized by greater budgetary and fiscal austerity within the EU, the EC's role in promoting distributive and redistributive policies is, as Pollack argues, likely to be further constrained in the future.

A sixth point concerns responsibility for exercising competences at the EC. Traditionally, the Commission always had the sole right of initiative and the Council, increasingly in collaboration with the EP, adopted decisions. Since the TEU, this has changed. With regard to EMU, for example, much responsibility for the exercise of competences lies with the European Central Bank. In other areas, such as Title IV, 'Visas, Asylum, Immigration and Other Policies Related to the Free Movement of Persons', the so-called 'community-method' is introduced only over time. And then there is the jurisdiction of the ECJ. Prior to Amsterdam, it had jurisdiction over all areas of activity governed by the provisions of the TEC. Since then, limits have accompanied the introduction of some new competences (see Article 68).

Finally, although Part Three consists of what seem at first glance to be 21 titles dedicated to discrete policy areas, there is overlap, notably where Title VI is concerned. Once again, mention should be made of Article 95 and, more generally, the TEC's provisions for the approximation of legislation. Use of these has on many occasions led to disputes on the appropriate legal base for action. In many instances, the matter has only been resolved through recourse to the ECJ (see, for example, *Germany v. European Parliament and Council*, 2000). Moreover, not only is there overlap between titles in terms of competence, there are various provisions having so-called 'horizontal' application. We have come across one of these already, Article 6 TEC on the integration of environmental protection requirements into the definition and implementation of EC policies. Within Part Three, there are a further five similar provisions requiring the EC's objectives with regard to employment (Article 127(2)), health protection (Article 152(1)), consumer protection (Article 153(2)), economic and social cohesion (Article 159) and development co-operation (Article 178) to be taken into consideration in the policy-making process.

What all this means is that in Part Three we are confronted by a considerable range of provisions, some old, some new, which vary in terms of detail, length and the extent to which they ascribe powers to the EC. Many have remained unchanged since they first appeared in the treaty, others have undergone significant amendment or revision. Some have been forgotten, some are the focus of almost daily attention. Many are provisions which people have never heard of, others are well known. Some are marginal to the EC's core activities. Some, like those with which Part Three commences, provide the underpinnings of the EC if not the Union.

v Free Movement of Goods

The first title of Part Three is dedicated to the most fundamental of the economic principles underpinning the Community – the free movement of goods. This is emphasized not just by its continued presence as the first-mentioned policy in Part Three, but also by the prominence given to the establishment of the common market and to the prohibition of barriers to the free movement of goods in Articles 2 and 3(1)(a) TEC. The emphasis on 'prohibition' in the latter is reflected in the content and revised wording of Title I.

Since Amsterdam it is a much slimmer title, having been shorn of its many obsolete provisions concerning the establishment of the EC's customs union in the 1960s. Today it contains only nine articles (Articles 23–31), substantially fewer than the original 29 (ex Articles 9–37). Moreover, the emphasis now is firmly on the 'prohibition' rather than 'elimination' of barriers to the free movement of goods.

The first two articles in the title act as an introduction to the provisions which follow. The first, *Article 23* (ex 9), establishes the customs union as the basis of the Community before defining its scope and nature. Thus, the customs union covers 'all trade in goods', meaning 'manufactured and material objects', and involves the prohibition of customs duties and measures having equivalent effect on all trade between member states, including goods imported into the EC, thereby creating a free-trade area. Furthermore, it involves the adoption of a common customs tariff to be imposed on trade with third countries, thus turning the free-trade area into a customs union. Interestingly, in this respect, reference is made to 'products' as opposed to 'goods', although given the consistent use in other language versions of the treaty (e.g. *Waren* in the German version), there is no difference in meaning. *Article 24* (ex 10) then underlines the emphasis on the free movement of goods within the EC by providing for the free circulation of goods originating from a third country provided import formalities have been complied with. There are, however, some exceptions as the 1957 Protocol on goods originating in and coming from certain countries and enjoying special treatment when imported into a Member State makes clear.

The remainder of the title is split into two chapters. The first of these is dedicated to the customs union. Originally it was subdivided into two sections dealing with the elimination of customs duties between the member states and the setting up of the common customs tariff (CCT). Amsterdam dispensed with the subdivisions, however, having repealed all but three of the original 18 articles. The first of the remaining provisions, *Article 25* (ex 12), is a statement prohibiting customs duties, including those of a fiscal nature, and measures having equivalent effect on imports and exports. Second, *Article 26* (ex 28) provides for the Council to fix the duties comprising the CCT by a qualified majority on a proposal from the Commission. Note that the EP is excluded from the process. And third, *Article 27* (ex 29) sets out the principles which are to guide the Commission when proposing the level of CCT duties. These include the need to promote trade with non-member states and an expansion of consumption, as well as four principles which empower the EC to adopt potentially protectionist and preferential measures. Hence the Commission must seek to improve the competitive position of undertakings within the EC, ensure supplies of raw materials and semi-finished goods, avoid serious disturbances in the economies of the member states and ensure the rational development of production. Among the repealed provisions is ex Article 25 which allowed exceptions to be made in the Community-wide application of the CCT.

The second chapter concerns the prohibition of quantitative restrictions between the member states. Such prohibition is emphasized in *Article 28* (ex 30) which bans quantitative restrictions (i.e. quotas) and 'measures having equivalent effect' on imports between member states. As the ECJ noted in *Commission* v. *France* (1997), this makes Article 28 'an indispensable instrument' for the realization of the Internal Market. The same can also be said of *Article 29* (ex 34), which bans quantitative restrictions and measures having equivalent effect on exports between member states.

This brings us to the question of what should be understood by 'measures having equivalent effect'. A list of such measures was issued in 1969 in Directive 70/50 and includes any price-fixing, administrative formalities, and commercial, promotional activities of a discriminatory nature. The list has been extended through the case law of the

ECJ, notably in the 1974 *Dassonville* ruling, which held that 'any measure which is capable of directly or indirectly, actually or potentially, hindering intra-Community trade constitutes a measure having equivalent effect to a quantitative restriction'. Since then, the ECJ in *Keck* (1993) has re-examined and sought to 'clarify' its case law on the meaning of 'measures having equivalent effect' and adopted a more restrictive interpretation than that in *Dassonville*. Finally, mention should be made of the 1979 *Cassis de Dijon* ruling which established the principle of mutual recognition seized on by the Commission in drawing up the programme of legislative proposals for the completion of the Internal Market by 1992. To some, the *Cassis de Dijon* ruling played an instrumental role in assisting in the revival of the EC in the 1980s.

Moving on, even according to the treaty the prohibition of restrictions on the movement of goods is not absolute. Under *Article 30* (ex 36), imports, exports and goods in transit may be restricted or even prohibited on various grounds including public morality, public policy, public security, the protection of human, animal or plant health and the protection of national treasures. In the eyes of the ECJ, this list is exhaustive. As for the treaty, it confirms that any restrictions can only be adopted if they do not constitute arbitrary discrimination or a disguised restriction on trade. Moreover, they cannot be adopted if an EC-wide minimum standard is in place. This has not prevented member states from using Article 30, particularly with regard to public morality for the banning of pornographic materials (see *Regina* v. *Henn and Darby* (1979)) and to public health. However, the ECJ has been very cautious in accepting use of Article 30 exemptions, often discovering that protectionist motives as opposed to overriding concerns for public health, for example, have been behind a ban (see, for example, *Commission* v. *France* (1983)). Very few restrictions have been introduced on the grounds of public policy, public security or the protection of national treasures, as Steiner notes. Where they have, the ECJ has interpreted the latter narrowly.

One last point here concerns the Protocol on protection of welfare of Animals. This was introduced at Amsterdam to placate the UK government in the light of domestic opposition to the export of live animals. It stresses the need for the welfare requirements to be taken into consideration in the development of relevant policies but only in general terms. Hence, soon after it had been adopted Dodd *et al.* were doubting whether the protocol could be relied on to restrict live exports. Such doubts were borne out by the ECJ in *Compassion in World Farming* (1996) where it ruled that Article 36 could not be used to prevent live exports.

Finally, *Article 31* (ex 37) addresses the position of state monopolies within the customs union. State monopolies do not include those limited to domestic products, as the ECJ ruled in *Pubblico Ministero* v. *Manghera* (1976). Moreover, as the ECJ confirmed in *Sacchi* (1974), Article 31 applies only to goods and not to services. Hence, it needs to be read alongside Article 28 TEC. Furthermore, in considering the significance of Article 31, attention should also be paid to Article 86 on state monopolies and services.

In terms of its provisions, Article 31 requires state monopolies of a commercial character to be adjusted so that no discrimination on the basis of nationality exists with regard to the procurement or marketing of goods. In effect this bans state monopolies from having exclusive rights to import. The Commission has therefore been able to draw on the article to promote the liberalization of electricity supply markets within the EC. Article 31 does not, however, prevent the existence of state monopolies. Rules on ownership within member states are the preserve of national governments (see Article 295).

The significance of the articles in Title I lies in the contribution they have made to the establishment of the free movement of goods within the EC. The fact that many of the provisions found in the title when it first appeared in the treaty in 1957 have now been repealed is testament to the fact that they have been successfully implemented and that the customs union and the principle of the free movement of goods is firmly established. Indeed, the EC has moved on since the customs union was established on 1 July 1968 to the completion of the internal market in which the free movement of goods is taken to involve more than simply the removal of tariffs, quantitative restrictions and measures having equivalent effect. Attention switched in the 1980s and 1990s to the removal of so-called non-tariff barriers. Hence, in understanding the 'free movement of goods' within the context of the EC, it is necessary to consider the role played by other provisions in the treaty, notably Articles 39–60 on the free movement of persons, services and capital, and Article 95 on the approximation of laws. Moreover, the free movement of goods forms only one element of the customs union and only one element of the common market which the original six member states set out to create in the 1950s. The customs union has its external trade policy dimension – the common commercial policy (Articles 131–134), while a common market needs common rules, not least on competition and tax (Articles 81–93). In the case of the EC it was also to involve the establishment of common policies. The first and most ambitious of these is the common agricultural policy (Articles 32–38) to which the *Guide* next turns.

PART THREE   COMMUNITY POLICIES

TITLE I

FREE MOVEMENT OF GOODS

Article 23 (ex Article 9)

1. The Community shall be based upon a customs union which shall cover all trade in goods and which shall involve the prohibition between Member States of customs duties on imports and exports and of all charges having equivalent effect, and the adoption of a common customs tariff in their relations with third countries.

2. The provisions of *Article 25* and of Chapter 2 of this Title shall apply to products originating in Member States and to products coming from third countries which are in free circulation in Member States.

Article 24 (ex Article 10 simplified)

Products coming from a third country shall be considered to be in free circulation in a Member State if the import formalities have been complied with and any customs duties or charges having equivalent effect which are payable have been levied in that Member State, and if they have not benefited from a total or partial drawback of such duties or charges.

Chapter 1   The customs union

Article 25 (ex Article 12 simplified)

Customs duties on imports and exports and charges having equivalent effect *shall be prohibited* between Member States. *This prohibition shall also apply to customs duties of a fiscal nature.*

Article 26 (ex Article 28 simplified)

Common Customs Tariff duties shall be fixed by the Council acting by a qualified majority on a proposal from the Commission.

Article 27 (ex Article 29 simplified)

In carrying out the tasks entrusted to it under this *Chapter* the Commission shall be guided by:
(a) the need to promote trade between Member States and third countries;
(b) developments in conditions of competition within the Community insofar as they lead to an improvement in the competitive capacity of undertakings;
(c) the requirements of the Community as regards the supply of raw materials and semi-finished goods; in this connection the Commission shall take care to avoid distorting conditions of competition between Member States in respect of finished goods;
(d) the need to avoid serious disturbances in the economies of Member States and to ensure rational development of production and an expansion of consumption within the Community.

Chapter 2   *Prohibition* of quantitative restrictions between Member States

Article 28 (ex Article 30 simplified)

Quantitative restrictions on imports and all measures having equivalent effect shall be prohibited between Member States.

Article 29 (ex Article 34, simplified)

Quantitative restrictions on exports, and all measures having equivalent effect, shall be prohibited between Member States.

Article 30 (ex Article 36 simplified)

The provisions of Articles 28 and 29 shall not preclude prohibitions or restrictions on imports, exports or goods in transit justified on grounds of public morality, public policy or public security; the protection of health and life of humans, animals or plants; the protection of national treasures possessing artistic, historic or archaeological value; or the protection of industrial and commercial property. Such prohibitions or restrictions shall not, however, constitute a means of arbitrary discrimination or a disguised restriction on trade between Member States.

Article 31 (ex Article 37, simplified)

1. Member States *shall adjust* any State monopolies of a commercial character so as to ensure *that no* discrimination regarding the conditions under which goods are procured and marketed exists between nationals of Member States.

The provisions of this Article shall apply to any body through which a Member State, in law or in fact, either directly or indirectly supervises, determines or appreciably influences imports or exports between Member States. These provisions shall likewise apply to monopolies delegated by the State to others.

2. Member States shall refrain from introducing any new measure which is contrary to the principles laid down in paragraph 1 or which restricts the scope of the

Articles dealing with the *prohibition* of customs duties and quantitative restrictions between Member States.

3. If a State monopoly of a commercial character has rules which are designed to make it easier to dispose of agricultural products or obtain for them the best return, steps should be taken in applying the rules contained in this Article to ensure equivalent safeguards for the employment and standard of living of the producers concerned.

vi Agriculture

The second title of Part Three deals with agriculture and is the legal home of the most famous if not notorious of EC policies, the common agricultural policy (CAP). As in the case of the free movement of goods in Title I, the prominence given to agriculture by placing it early on in the main body of the TEC underlines the importance that the original six member states attached to it as a vital area of economic activity. Indeed, not only does agriculture appear immediately after the provisions relating to the customs union, it also appears before the remaining three freedoms – the free movement of persons, services and capital – which today, along with EMU, provide the fundamental economic underpinnings of the EC. Whether agriculture would occupy such a prominent position if the treaty were to be drafted today is very much open to question. With the agricultural sector employing less than 5.5% of the EU's workforce and accounting for little more than 1.8% of GDP within the EU in 1999, the case for special attention would be almost impossible to make. The provisions governing agriculture are therefore very much a product of the time when the TEC was drafted. France, for example, would not have agreed to the treaty had they not been included. Yet despite widespread criticism of the CAP and seemingly universal dissatisfaction with its costs, its provisions remain in the treaty. Not only do they remain present, they remain essentially unamended.

The title governing agriculture consists of seven articles (Articles 32–38, ex 38–47) following Amsterdam's repeal of three articles (ex 44, 45 and 47). These dealt with the period prior to the establishment of the customs union and the CAP and the organization of the Economic and Social Committee. The first two were obsolete, although Declaration No. 14 TA confirms that the repeal does not call into question the case law deriving from ex Article 44. The third article was repealed so as to give the EcoSoc greater flexibility in its internal organization. Of the articles that remain, the first, *Article 32* (ex 38), declares that agriculture is part of the common market. Subject to the provisions in the title, therefore, TEC provisions governing free movement and competition apply to agriculture. Article 32 also sets out the EC's definition of agriculture which includes not only products 'of the soil' and 'of stockfarming', but also 'fisheries'. The products are then listed in Annex I to the treaty. Any goods not listed (e.g. manufactured goods) are subject to general TEC provisions governing free movement. The list is amended using Article 308 TEC.

The wording of Article 32 means that Title II provides the legal basis for not just the CAP but also the common fisheries policy (CFP), even if, as Churchill notes, not all the objectives laid down for agriculture – increased productivity, for example – can easily be applied. That Title II applies to fisheries was confirmed in Article 100 of the 1972 Act of Accession which the ECJ in *Kramer* (1976) subsequently interpreted as conferring on the

EC exclusive competence to determine conditions for fishing with a view to ensuring the protection of fishing grounds and the conservation of stocks. It was then explicitly acknowledged by the TEU, which expanded the reference in Article 3(1)(d) TEC so that the EC has listed among its activities 'a common policy in the sphere of agriculture and fisheries'. All this, and a desire to preserve fish stocks, has resulted in a policy based on 'total allowable catches' (TACs) and some structural funding for the fishing industry. Also of significance for the CFP are the TEC's provisions on the right of establishment (Articles 43–48) and it is these which have caused so much anguish for UK governments since they undermine notions of 'national waters' and open up access to TACs to 'foreign' fishing vessels registered in the UK, resulting in so-called 'quota-hopping'. This was most evident in the 1991 *Factortame* ruling of the ECJ which forced amendments to the UK Merchant Fishing Act of 1988. Opposition in the 1990s to quota-hopping led the UK government during the 1996 IGC to push, without success, for a protocol restricting such practices.

That the EC is obliged to develop a common policy for agriculture is stated in Article 32(4). Yet although the treaty provides for the CAP and the CFP, it does not detail how either is to operate. This is left to the Commission and Council to decide. In the case of agriculture, some guidance is provided. *Article 33* (ex 39) lists five objectives for the policy, most of which reflect the desire of the EC's founder members to become self-sufficient in agricultural production by maintaining and developing the agricultural sector within the economy. The first two objectives require that the policy promotes increased agricultural productivity and ensures a fair standard of living for the agricultural community, while the third and fourth objectives prioritize the stabilization of markets and the guaranteed availability of supplies. The fifth objective relates more to the consumer in that the common policy is to ensure that agricultural products are available at reasonable prices. Any adjustments to agriculture are to be taken 'by degrees', thus avoiding swift radical change, and with due appreciation being given to the significance of agriculture for the economy as a whole. In addition, agricultural policy must take into consideration other TEC objectives, notably concerning the environment, public health and economic and social cohesion (see Articles 6, 152 and 158–159 TEC, respectively).

As Snyder and others have pointed out, the objectives are inherently contradictory, and in the words of the Commission's first president, Walter Hallstein, constitute 'nothing less than an encyclopaedia of economic problems'. Unsurprisingly the ECJ has seen fit to comment on this, holding in *Beus* (1968) that not all the objectives need necessarily be simultaneously and fully attained. In practice this has certainly been the case, as complaints about the cost of agricultural produce within the EC testify.

The wording of Article 33 clearly implies advocacy of a significantly different approach towards agriculture compared to the more liberal, free-market approach adopted with regard to goods generally. Title II advocates a common policy which is interventionist. This is underlined by the provisions in *Article 36* (ex 42) empowering the Council to limit the applicability of EC competition rules (Articles 81–89) to agricultural products. Indeed, the authorization of state aid by the Council is actively encouraged where it maintains or furthers the economic development of businesses involved in the agricultural sector.

Further guidance on how the EC market for agriculture is to be organized is provided in *Article 34* (ex 40), where three forms are suggested: common rules on competition, compulsory co-ordination of national market organizations and a European market organization. It then proposes that price regulation, production and marketing aids, storage arrangements and a mechanism for stabilizing trade with third countries all be part of the common organization. Provision is also made for the establishment of one or more guidance and guarantee funds to help the EC achieve the objectives set out in

Article 32. Furthermore, *Article 35* (ex 41) proposes for inclusion in the CAP measures for the co-ordination of vocational training programmes, research into agricultural production and the promotion of consumer consumption. And *Article 38* (ex 46) helps to ensure fair competition between producers in different member states in the absence of common organization. Many of the provisions in Title II are very vague. This reflects the distinct lack of consensus in 1957 on what form a common policy should take. Not surprisingly, the vagueness of the TEC provisions helped to ensure that efforts to elaborate the CAP in the 1950s and 1960s often became bogged down in heated political arguments on how to proceed.

Having set out the principles and suggestions for the CAP, the title turns to implementing the common policy. Despite Amsterdam's simplification of the treaty, *Article 37* (ex 43) retains the now seemingly redundant references to the procedure and timetable for the CAP's formulation and initial development. Retaining the reference to the original 1958 Stresa conference, which elaborated on the TEC's provisions and helped prepare the way for the CAP, is of advantage to supporters of the policy since it in effect confers on the established principles a special, entrenched and historic status. The article still has relevance, though, since it details how the policy is to be implemented. Hence, tucked away in the third subparagraph of paragraph 2 is a phrase in which the Council is charged, on the basis of proposals from the Commission, with making regulations, issuing directives and taking decisions by a qualified majority. The Council's preparatory work is carried out by a Special Committee on Agriculture, although this is not apparent from the TEC. Despite advances generally in its legislative role, the EP has limited influence over the CAP, given that it is only consulted. And despite proposals, Nice did not change the situation. The EP has nevertheless threatened, albeit on only a handful of occasions, to withhold its opinion, thus obstructing the adoption of proposals in the hope of influencing reform.

The EP is not alone in seeking to see the CAP reformed. And there can be little doubt that it does need reform, particularly as the EU maintains its commitment to expand, mainly eastwards, to include the ten candidate countries and eventually even Turkey. Moreover, there are demands from further afield for the EC to reduce the price subsidies which form such a key element of the CAP. International trade talks within GATT and WTO frameworks often see the EC coming under intense pressure to reform the CAP. Some reforms have been introduced, most notably in 1992 (the so-called MacSharry reforms) and again in 1999 as part of the Agenda 2000 package of reforms to prepare the EU for enlargement. All the same, many of the CAP's early mechanisms remain and it is these which provide the focus for much of the criticism which is levelled against the EC's most developed policy.

In a Europe where free trade, declining state intervention and an emphasis on competition have become central to the economic consensus, the CAP is an anomaly. Its success in meeting most of the objectives laid down in Article 33 (ex 39) – there are generally doubts as to whether it has achieved reasonable prices to the consumer – has come as a result of a common EC-wide system based on guaranteed prices and Community preference which emerged in the 1960s and remains today. This led to increased production, stable markets, generally acceptable standards of living for the agricultural community and assured supplies. The productivist principles of the CAP did lead, however, to overproduction in the 1980s and 1990s. And with guaranteed prices helping the CAP account for up to three-quarters of the EC budget, there was open criticism, particularly from member states such as the United Kingdom whose farmers received comparatively little from the CAP, that the policy was too costly and that there were other more legitimate demands on the EC's budgetary resources.

Moreover, the CAP has been heavily criticized for its lack of concern for environmental protection, a factor which led to the SEA and later Amsterdam (see Article 6 TEC) emphasizing the need for environmental consideration to be shown when developing policies. At the same time, there have clearly been major concerns raised about the quality of agricultural produce, most notably with the increasing evidence of BSE in cattle seemingly throughout the EC. And the animal rights lobby has had some success in ensuring animal welfare is taken into account in policy development, Maastricht adopting a declaration (No. 24 TEU) and the TA introducing a protocol on the subject. Given environmental and health concerns, coupled with incidences of fraud, the size of agricultural sectors in many candidate countries and international pressure for reform, the nature and operation of the CAP is unlikely to remain unchanged. Indeed, reform negotiations are scheduled for 2006 and there is German pressure for the CAP to be considered as part of the 2004 IGC. It might be too much to expect, however, that the TEC's provisions, even to increase the role of the EP, would ever be substantially changed. Proposals to this effect have been made by Grant and Corbett, yet no IGC has ever seriously addressed the issue.

TITLE II

AGRICULTURE

Article 32 (ex Article 38, simplified)

1. The common market shall extend to agriculture and trade in agricultural products. 'Agricultural products' means the products of the soil, of stockfarming and of fisheries and products of first-stage processing directly related to these products.

2. Save as otherwise provided in Articles 33 to 38, the rules laid down for the establishment of the common market shall apply to agricultural products.

3. The products subject to the provisions of Articles 33 to 38 are listed in Annex I to this Treaty.

4. The operation and development of the common market for agricultural products must be accompanied by the establishment of a common agricultural policy.

Article 33 (ex Article 39)

1. The objectives of the common agricultural policy shall be:
(a) to increase agricultural productivity by promoting technical progress and by ensuring the rational development of agricultural production and the optimum utilisation of the factors of production, in particular labour;
(b) thus to ensure a fair standard of living for the agricultural community, in particular by increasing the individual earnings of persons engaged in agriculture;
(c) to stabilise markets;
(d) to assure the availability of supplies;
(e) to ensure that supplies reach consumers at reasonable prices.

2. In working out the common agricultural policy and the special methods for its application, account shall be taken of:
(a) the particular nature of agricultural activity, which results from the social structure of agriculture and from structural and natural disparities between the various agricultural regions;

(b) the need to effect the appropriate adjustments by degrees;

(c) the fact that in the Member States agriculture constitutes a sector closely linked with the economy as a whole.

Article 34 (ex Article 40, simplified)

1. In order to attain the objectives set out in Article 33, a common organisation of agricultural markets shall be established.

This organisation shall take one of the following forms, depending on the product concerned:

(a) common rules on competition;

(b) compulsory co-ordination of the various national market organisations;

(c) a European market organisation.

2. The common organisation established in accordance with paragraph 1 may include all measures required to attain the objectives set out in Article 33, in particular regulation of prices, aids for the production and marketing of the various products, storage and carryover arrangements and common machinery for stabilising imports or exports.

The common organisation shall be limited to pursuit of the objectives set out in Article 33 and shall exclude any discrimination between producers or consumers within the Community.

Any common price policy shall be based on common criteria and uniform methods of calculation.

3. In order to enable the common organisation referred to in paragraph 1 to attain its objectives, one or more agricultural guidance and guarantee funds may be set up.

Article 35 (ex Article 41)

To enable the objectives set out in Article 33 to be attained, provision may be made within the framework of the common agricultural policy for measures such as:

(a) an effective co-ordination of efforts in the spheres of vocational training, of research and of the dissemination of agricultural knowledge; this may include joint financing of projects or institutions;

(b) joint measures to promote consumption of certain products.

Article 36 (ex Article 42)

The provisions of the Chapter relating to rules on competition shall apply to production of and trade in agricultural products only to the extent determined by the Council within the framework of Article 37(2) and (3) and in accordance with the procedure laid down therein, account being taken of the objectives set out in Article 33.

The Council may, in particular, authorise the granting of aid:

(a) for the protection of enterprises handicapped by structural or natural conditions;

(b) within the framework of economic development programmes.

Article 37 (ex Article 43, simplified)

1. In order to evolve the broad lines of a common agricultural policy, the Commission shall, immediately this Treaty enters into force, convene a conference of the Member States with a view to making a comparison of their agricultural policies, in particular by producing a statement of their resources and needs.

2. Having taken into account the work of the Conference provided for in paragraph 1, after consulting the Economic and Social Committee and within two years of the entry into force of this Treaty, the Commission shall submit proposals for working out and implementing the common agricultural policy, including the replacement of the national organisations by one of the forms of common organisation provided for in Article 34(1), and for implementing the measures specified in this Title.

These proposals shall take account of the interdependence of the agricultural matters mentioned in this Title.

The Council shall, on a proposal from the Commission and after consulting the European Parliament, *acting by a qualified majority,* make regulations, issue directives, or take decisions, without prejudice to any recommendations it may also make.

3. The Council may, acting by a qualified majority and in accordance with paragraph 2, replace the national market organisations by the common organisation provided for in Article 34(1) if:
(a) the common organisation offers Member States which are opposed to this measure and which have an organisation of their own for the production in question equivalent safeguards for the employment and standard of living of the producers concerned, account being taken of the adjustments that will be possible and the specialisation that will be needed with the passage of time;
(b) such an organisation ensures conditions for trade within the Community similar to those existing in a national market.

4. If a common organisation for certain raw materials is established before a common organisation exists for the corresponding processed products, such raw materials as are used for processed products intended for export to third countries may be imported from outside the Community.

Article 38 (ex Article 46)

Where in a Member State a product is subject to a national market organisation or to internal rules having equivalent effect which affect the competitive position of similar production in another Member State, a countervailing charge shall be applied by Member States to imports of this product coming from the Member State where such organisation or rules exist, unless that State applies a countervailing charge on export.

The Commission shall fix the amount of these charges at the level required to redress the balance; it may also authorise other measures, the conditions and details of which it shall determine.

vii   Free Movement of Persons, Services and Capital

Having dealt with agriculture, Part Three of the TEC turns its attention once again to provisions governing the freedoms which underpin the Single Market. In Title III, which consists of 22 articles, we find most of the provisions governing the remaining three freedoms: the free movement of persons, the free movement of services and the free movement of capital, the abolition of obstacles to which features prominently in the principles of the EC (see Article 3(1)(c)). Other key provisions can be found in Title I (Articles 23–31) and Title VI, Chapter 3 (Article 95). Attention should also be drawn to Article 16 TEC which emphasizes a general presumption in favour of the freedom of establishment and the right to provide services within the EC and the provisions of Title IV concerning the establishment of an area of freedom, security and justice which builds on existing EC efforts to realize the free movement of people. Both Article 16 and Title IV were introduced to the TEC by Amsterdam.

Title III is divided into four chapters. The first of these covers Articles 39–42 and concerns workers. Hence, the reference to 'persons' in the title of Title III might appear misleading. Indeed, for a more complete picture of TEC provisions on the free movement of people, we must also look elsewhere in the treaty, notably to Article 18(1) which declares the right, albeit subject to limitations, of all EU citizens 'to move and to reside freely within the territories of the Members States', and to Title IV on the EU as an 'area of freedom, security and justice'. The interpretation of 'workers' by the ECJ has, however, led to rights conferred under Chapter 1 being extended more widely than the term might imply. Generous judicial interpretations of the provisions in Chapter 2 on the right of establishment within the EC (Articles 43–48) and in Chapter 3 dealing with the free movement of services (Articles 49–55) have had a similar effect, extending rights beyond strict readings of the treaty provisions. Chapter 4 deals with the free movement of capital and payments (Articles 56–60).

Since the TEC was signed it is Chapter 4 which has experienced most change, the TEU providing for all existing articles to be replaced from 1 January 1994 to reflect the start of Stage II of EMU. In the other chapters, changes introduced by the SEA and TEU related solely to decision-making and, except in the case of services, a move away from unanimity within the Council to QMV and co-decision with the EP. Amsterdam impact was more wide-ranging. First, it extended the use of co-decision, albeit with the Council generally acting by unanimity, to Articles 42 and 47(2). Second, it repealed 12 obsolete articles (ex 53, 62, 67–73a, 73e, 73h), most of which related to transitional periods. Others were revised with Amsterdam's third impact: the simplification of various articles (i.e. ex 48(1), 49, 52, 54, 59, 61(2), 63, 64) to reflect the prohibition of restrictions on the freedom of establishment and on the movement of services. Such simplification also entailed the removal or rewording of various provisions from a further eight articles. Finally, Amsterdam renumbered all the articles. The Treaty of Nice, by comparison, had no impact on the title, although some revisions were contemplated as noted below.

Such changes mean that today Title III is much shorter than in the past. This does not mean, however, that the provisions are necessarily clear in terms of meaning or that decision-making is uniform. On the former, a detailed understanding of the provisions contained in the first three chapters is possible only through recourse to both secondary legislation and the case law of the ECJ. As regards the latter, there is no uniformity of procedure. It is clear, though, that member states are sensitive about sharing decision-making power with regard to services and the movement of capital. Here, in Chapters 3 and 4, the EP is at best consulted on the adoption of measures. This is not to say that the

EP has no role in the adoption of legislation governing the three freedoms of the Single Market covered in Title III. For decision-making governing the establishment of the Single Market is as much determined by the provisions of Article 95 as it is by those in the discussion which follows. Moreover, awareness of the provisions governing EMU is also necessary, the Economic and Financial Committee being responsible for assisting the Council with preparing its decisions under Articles 59 and 60. Hence, as with many other areas of the treaty, those in Title III should not be read in isolation

The Free Movement of Workers

The shortest of the four chapters in Title III is Chapter 1, 'Workers'. As noted, this contrasts with the reference to 'persons' in the title of Title III something which was recognized during the 2000 IGC in a proposal, in the end unsuccessful, to alter the title to 'Workers and Persons Treated as Such'. As much would have given a truer reflection of the content of the chapter.

The first article of Chapter 1, *Article 39* (ex 48), states that the free movement of workers within the EC shall be secured through the abolition of discrimination based on nationality with regard to employment, pay and working conditions. It then lists workers' rights in this respect: to accept offers of employment and move freely anywhere in the EC, to stay in a member state for the purpose of finding employment and to remain in a member state having been employed there. As such, the article, in the view of the Council and the ECJ (see *Levin* (1982) and *Royer* (1976), for example), confers on EU citizens fundamental rights, rights which following ECJ rulings extend not just to full-time workers but also those in part-time work and those actively seeking work. The rights also cover the dependants of workers and extend beyond periods of employment and into retirement. Hence, migrant workers enjoy the same tax and social benefits as nationals. In addition, the ECJ takes into consideration relevant provisions of the European Convention on Human Rights when interpreting the provisions of this chapter.

Rights may, however, be limited, as Article 39(3) provides, on the grounds of public policy, public health or public security. The same grounds can be invoked to restrict rights of establishment under Article 56. The grounds are, however, rather vague. Hence Council Directive 64/221 was adopted to provide greater substance. This has not prevented numerous cases coming before the ECJ. In dealing with these, the Court has tended to adopt strict interpretations of public policy and public security, terms which are used interchangeably. Cases of note include *Van Duyn* (1964) and *Bouchereau* (1977). The ECJ has also interpreted public health narrowly, as in its rulings in *Commission* v. *Netherlands* (1991).

Moreover, there are restrictions on the type of employment which migrant workers can undertake. Article 39(4) states that employment in the 'public services' is not covered. The ECJ has, however, interpreted this narrowly noting, for example, that 'public services' cannot be taken to mean any employment offered by the state (see *Sotgiu* v. *Deutsche Bundespost* (1974)). It is the nature of the employment which is the determining factor. Also, as O'Keefe notes, the provision introduced by the TEU allowing non-nationals to stand as local councillors creates the possibility of non-nationals supervising the functioning of services from which they are excluded from becoming employed.

How the EC is to bring about the free movement of workers is addressed in the chapter's remaining three articles. First, as *Article 40* (ex 49) provides, there are legislative means regarding access to labour markets. Directives and regulations may be adopted with particular emphasis on promoting co-operation between national employment services, abolishing administrative restrictions on qualifying periods for and on the choice of employment for workers from other member states and establishing mechanisms for making information regarding employment opportunities available throughout the EC. Any legislative measures here are to be adopted by the Council using the co-decision procedure and after consulting EcoSoc. Second, under *Article 41* (ex 50), there is encouragement for joint programmes between member states to promote the exchange of young workers, a mechanism supported in Article 150 TEC with provisions for vocational and youth training. The role of the Community is not, however, made explicit.

The chapter's final article, *Article 42* (ex 51), brings us into the area of social security, requiring the EC to adopt measures relating to the aggregation and transferability of benefits between member states for migrant workers. This has proved a difficult task given the complexity of diverse national schemes and the sensitivities surrounding 'immigration' in domestic politics in many member states. Nevertheless, regulations have been adopted despite the need for the Council to act unanimously. Pressure has often mounted for a shift to QMV, yet although Amsterdam saw the upgrading of the EP's role from non-involvement to co-decision, the Council continues to act by unanimity. UK opposition to QMV has been the main cause of the block here. Its rejection of a proposed shift at Nice also put paid to a consultative role for EcoSoc and the Committee of the Regions.

TITLE III

FREE MOVEMENT OF PERSONS, SERVICES AND CAPITAL

Chapter 1   Workers

Article 39 (ex Article 48 simplified)

1. Freedom of movement for workers shall be secured within the Community.

2. Such freedom of movement shall entail the abolition of any discrimination based on nationality between workers of the Member States as regards employment, remuneration and other conditions of work and employment.

3. It shall entail the right, subject to limitations justified on grounds of public policy, public security or public health:

(a) to accept offers of employment actually made;

(b) to move freely within the territory of Member States for this purpose;

(c) to stay in a Member State for the purpose of employment in accordance with the provisions governing the employment of nationals of that State laid down by law, regulation or administrative action;

(d) to remain in the territory of a Member State after having been employed in that State, subject to conditions which shall be embodied in implementing regulations to be drawn up by the Commission.

4. The provisions of this Article shall not apply to employment in the public service.

Article 40 (ex Article 49 simplified)

The Council shall, acting in accordance with the procedure referred to in Article 251 and after consulting the Economic and Social Committee, issue directives or make regulations setting out the measures required to bring about freedom of movement for workers, as defined in Article 39, in particular:

(a) by ensuring close co-operation between national employment services;
(b) *by abolishing* those administrative procedures and practices and those qualifying periods in respect of eligibility for available employment, whether resulting from national legislation or from agreements previously concluded between Member States, the maintenance of which would form an obstacle to liberalisation of the movement of workers;
(c) *by abolishing* all such qualifying periods and other restrictions provided for either under national legislation or under agreements previously concluded between Member States as imposed on workers of other Member States conditions regarding the free choice of employment other than those imposed on workers of the State concerned;
(d) by setting up appropriate machinery to bring offers of employment into touch with applications for employment and to facilitate the achievement of a balance between supply and demand in the employment market in such a way as to avoid serious threats to the standard of living and level of employment in the various regions and industries.

Article 41 (ex Article 50)

Member States shall, within the framework of a joint programme, encourage the exchange of young workers.

Article 42 (ex Article 51)

The Council shall, **acting in accordance with the procedure referred to in Article 251,** adopt such measures in the field of social security as are necessary to provide freedom of movement for workers; to this end, it shall make arrangements to secure for migrant workers and their dependants:

(a) aggregation, for the purpose of acquiring and retaining the right to benefit and of calculating the amount of benefit, of all periods taken into account under the laws of the several countries;
(b) payment of benefits to persons resident in the territories of Member States.

The Council shall act unanimously throughout the procedure referred to in Article 251.

The Right of Establishment

Chapter 2 of Title III takes the idea of free movement further by providing for the right of establishment. Shortened by Amsterdam from seven to six articles (Articles 43–48, ex 52–58), it deals not only with the rights within the EC of companies and firms legally established within a member state but also with those of self-employed nationals of a member state who are not covered by the provisions of the previous chapter on the free movement of workers (see *Article 48*, ex 58). The aim of the EC is to guarantee to nationals of member states the freedom of establishment, interpreted by the ECJ as 'the actual pursuit of an economic activity through a fixed "establishment" for an indefinite period'. This is achieved through the prohibition of restrictions on the establishment of undertakings within the EC provided for in *Article 43* (ex 52). The emphasis is clearly on nationals of the member states. The TEC offers, however, no definition of what is to be understood by a 'national'. Instead, as confirmed in Declaration No. 2 TEU, this is left to the member states, something which has considerable significance for the concept of EU citizenship (see Articles 17–22 TEC). It is also worth noting that Articles 45–48 apply to services too (see Article 55).

Freedom of establishment is to be achieved through directives which fulfil the objectives listed in *Article 44(2)* (ex 54(3)). These include the development of trade and production, the guaranteeing of certain rights for self-employed workers, the abolition of restrictive administrative procedures, the enabling of nationals from one member state to acquire and use land and buildings situated in another member state, the enabling of companies to establish branches in other EC countries, the co-ordination of safeguards required of companies and firms and fair competition. The list is extensive. Directives are to adopted by the Council via co-decision and after consulting EcoSoc.

Not all activities are subject to the provisions of such directives, as *Article 45* (ex 55) tells us. The exercise of 'official authority' – left undefined in the treaty but narrowly construed by the ECJ in *Reyners* v. *Belgian State* (1974) and *Thijssen* (1993), for example – is exempted. Likewise, the Council may, acting by QMV on a proposal from the Commission, exempt other areas. Moreover, *Article 46* (ex 56) permits exemptions from the provisions contained in Chapter 2 on the grounds of public policy, public security and public health. Such grounds, as noted in the earlier discussion of Article 39(3) TEC, are narrowly defined. Article 46 also calls on the Council to issue directives via the co-decision procedure for the co-ordination of national provisions governing the treatment of foreign nationals on the grounds listed.

Finally, Chapter 2 seeks in *Article 47* (ex 57) to promote the free movement of self-employed persons through the mutual recognition of diplomas and other formal qualifications, the co-ordination of national measures governing the self-employed and the co-ordination of national training requirements for the professions. Directives aimed at achieving these are to be adopted using the co-decision procedure, the latter being introduced by Amsterdam. Previously, at least following the SEA, the co-operation procedure had been used. Where, however, the directive involves a member state amending existing principles laid down by law in relation to professional training requirements and conditions of access the Council must act unanimously. Proposals during the 2000 IGC to remove this derogation and use QMV instead were rejected. Finally, special attention is drawn in paragraph 3 to the medical and allied and pharmaceutical professions, where the removal of restrictions on the freedom of establishment is conditional on the co-ordination of the national conditions for the exercise of these professions. This has entailed the co-ordination of study curricula.

Chapter 2   Right of Establishment

Article 43 (ex Article 52 simplified)

Within the framework of the provisions set out below, restrictions on the freedom of establishment of nationals of a Member State in the territory of another Member State shall be *prohibited*. Such *prohibition* shall also apply to restrictions on the setting-up of agencies, branches or subsidiaries by nationals of any Member State established in the territory of any Member State.

Freedom of establishment shall include the right to take up and pursue activities as self-employed persons and to set up and manage undertakings, in particular companies or firms within the meaning of the second paragraph of Article 48, under the conditions laid down for its own nationals by the law of the country where such establishment is effected, subject to the provisions of the Chapter relating to capital.

Article 44 (ex Article 54 simplified)

1. In order to *attain* freedom of establishment as regards a particular activity, the Council, acting in accordance with the procedure referred to in Article 251 and after consulting the Economic and Social Committee, shall act by means of directives.

2. The Council and the Commission shall carry out the duties devolving upon them under the preceding provisions, in particular:

(a) by according, as a general rule, priority treatment to activities where freedom of establishment makes a particularly valuable contribution to the development of production and trade;

(b) by ensuring close co-operation between the competent authorities in the Member States in order to ascertain the particular situation within the Community of the various activities concerned;

(c) by abolishing those administrative procedures and practices, whether resulting from national legislation or from agreements previously concluded between Member States, the maintenance of which would form an obstacle to freedom of establishment;

(d) by ensuring that workers of one Member State employed in the territory of another Member State may remain in that territory for the purpose of taking up activities therein as self-employed persons, where they satisfy the conditions which they would be required to satisfy if they were entering that State at the time when they intended to take up such activities;

(e) by enabling a national of one Member State to acquire and use land and buildings situated in the territory of another Member State, insofar as this does not conflict with the principles laid down in Article 33(2);

(f) by effecting the progressive abolition of restrictions on freedom of establishment in every branch of activity under consideration, both as regards the conditions for setting up agencies, branches or subsidiaries in the territory of a Member State and as regards the subsidiaries in the territory of a Member State and as regards the conditions governing the entry of personnel belonging to the main establishment into managerial or supervisory posts in such agencies, branches or subsidiaries;

(g) by co-ordinating to the necessary extent the safeguards which, for the protection of the interests of members and other, are required by Member States of companies or firms within the meaning of the second paragraph of Article 48 with a view to making such safeguards equivalent throughout the Community;

(h) by satisfying themselves that the conditions of establishment are not distorted by aids granted by Member States.

Article 45 (ex Article 55)

The provisions of this Chapter shall not apply, so far as any given Member State is concerned, to activities which in that State are connected, even occasionally, with the exercise of official authority.

The Council may, acting by a qualified majority on a proposal from the Commission, rule that the provisions of this Chapter shall not apply to certain activities.

Article 46 (ex Article 56)

1. The provisions of this Chapter and measures taken in pursuance thereof shall not prejudice the applicability of provisions laid down by law, regulation or administrative action providing for special treatment for foreign nationals on grounds of public policy, public security or public health.

2. *The Council shall, acting in accordance with the procedure referred to in Article 251, issue directives for the co-ordination of the abovementioned provisions.*

Article 47 (ex Article 57)

1. In order to make it easier for persons to take up and pursue activities as self-employed persons, the Council shall, acting in accordance with the procedure referred to in Article 251, issue directives for the mutual recognition of diplomas, certificates and other evidence of formal qualifications.

2. For the same purpose, the Council shall, **acting in accordance with the procedure referred to in Article 251,** issue directives for the co-ordination of the provisions laid down by law, regulation or administrative action in Member States concerning the taking-up and pursuit of activities as self-employed persons. The Council, acting unanimously **throughout the procedure referred to in Article 251,** shall decide on directives the implementation of which involves in at least one Member State amendment of the existing principles laid down by law governing the professions with respect to training and conditions of access for natural persons. In other cases the Council shall act *by qualified majority.*

3. In the case of the medical and allied and pharmaceutical professions, the progressive abolition of restrictions shall be dependent upon co-ordination of the conditions for their exercise in the various Member States.

Article 48 (ex Article 58)

Companies or firms formed in accordance with the law of a Member State and having their registered office, central administration or principal place of business within the Community shall, for the purposes of this Chapter, be treated in the same way as natural persons who are nationals of Member States.

'Companies or firms' means companies or firms constituted under civil or commercial law, including cooperative societies, and other legal persons governed by public or private law, save for those which are non-profit-making.

The Free Movement of Services

Having dealt with the free movement of workers and rights of establishment, Title III turns in Chapter 3 to the free movement of services within the EC (Articles 49–55, ex 59–66). The meaning of 'services' here is defined in *Article 50* (ex 60) as activities for remuneration and those not covered by provisions governing the free movement of goods, capital and persons. The definition is thus broad. Certain activities are singled out as 'services': industrial and commercial activities as well as those of craftspeople and the professions. The list is, however, by no means exhaustive. And all 'services' are also subject to Articles 45–48 contained in the previous chapter on the right of establishment. This follows, the latter being a logical extension of the cross-border provision of services. As *Article 51* (ex 61) states, Chapter 3 does not cover transport, this being the focus of Articles 70–80 in Title V. Furthermore, liberalization of banking and insurance services connected with the movement of capital is to take place in line with liberalization of capital movements governed by Chapter 4 (Articles 56–69).

As *Article 49* (ex 59) provides, the basic principle governing services is that restrictions on their provision, and, through the case law of the ECJ (see *Luisi* (1984)), their receipt, are prohibited. This is certainly the case where a national of a member state is providing or receiving the service. For some countries, this is problematic. Ireland, for example, has a constitutional ban on abortion. Hence the rather bland-sounding Protocol annexed to the Treaty on European Union and to the Treaties establishing the European Communities confirms the primacy of the Irish Constitution's provisions where abortion is concerned. However, in line with the Declaration of the High Contracting Parties to the Treaty on European Union adopted on 1 May 1992, Irish citizens are permitted to avail themselves of such services in other member states.

Returning to the TEC proper, the second paragraph of Article 49 empowers the Council to extend by QMV the coverage of Chapter 3 to nationals of third countries. All the same, as *Article 54* (ex 65) reveals, restrictions are not automatically prohibited, member states being allowed to apply restrictions which have not been abolished provided they do so without discrimination on the basis of nationality or residence.

The thrust therefore of EC activity is liberalization, as confirmed in *Article 52* (ex 63) which calls on the Council in consultation with the EP and EcoSoc to issue directives by QMV for the purpose of liberalizing specific services. Priority is to be given to measures which affect production or help to promote trade. And, under *Article 53* (ex 64), member states commit themselves to undertake liberalization beyond this, subject to the situation in the economic sector concerned. The proviso is important since it can be invoked to prevent liberalization. Also under Article 53, the Commission is charged with making recommendations.

Chapter 3   Services

Article 49 (ex Article 59 simplified)

Within the framework of the provisions set out below, restrictions on freedom to provide services within the Community shall be *prohibited* in respect of nationals of Member States who are established in a State of the Community other than that of the person for whom the services are intended.

The Council may, acting by a qualified majority on a proposal from the Commission, extend the provisions of the Chapter to nationals of a third country who provide services and who are established within the Community.

Article 50 (ex Article 60)

Services shall be considered to be 'services' within the meaning of this Treaty where they are normally provided for remuneration, insofar as they are not governed by the provisions relating to freedom of movement for goods, capital and persons.

'Services' shall in particular include:
(a) activities of an industrial character;
(b) activities of a commercial character;
(c) activities of craftsmen;
(d) activities of the professions.

Without prejudice to the provisions of the Chapter relating to the right of establishment, the person providing a service may, in order to do so, temporarily pursue his activity in the State where the service is provided, under the same conditions as are imposed by that State on its own nationals.

Article 51 (ex Article 61 simplified)

1. Freedom to provide services in the field of transport shall be governed by the provisions of the Title relating to transport.

2. The liberalisation of banking and insurance services connected with movements of capital shall be effected in step with *the liberalisation* of movement of capital.

Article 52 (ex Article 63 simplified)

1. In order to *achieve* the liberalisation of a specific service, the Council shall, on a proposal from the Commission and after consulting the Economic and Social Committee and the European Parliament, issue directives *acting by a qualified majority.*

2. As regards *the directives referred to in paragraph 1,* priority shall as a general rule be given to those services which directly affect production costs or the liberalisation of which helps to promote trade in goods.

Article 53 (ex Article 64 simplified)

The Member States declare their readiness to undertake the liberalisation of services beyond the extent required by the directives issued pursuant to Article *52(1),* if their general economic situation and the situation of the economic sector concerned so permit.

To this end, the Commission shall make recommendations to the Member States concerned.

Article 54 (ex Article 65)

As long as restrictions on freedom to provide services have not been abolished, each Member State shall apply such restrictions without distinction on grounds of nationality or residence to all persons providing services within the meaning of the first paragraph of Article 49.

Article 55 (ex Article 66)

The provisions of Articles 45 to 48 shall apply to the matters covered by this Chapter.

The Free Movement of Capital and Payments

Chapter 4 contains the most heavily revised provisions found in Title III. Indeed, none of those originally found in the title survive today. All were replaced, as envisaged in the TEU, with the launch of Stage II of EMU in 1994. Hence, articles envisaging the progressive abolition of restrictions on the movement of capital and payments within the EC, the progressive co-ordination of exchange rates and remedies for disturbances from capital movements have all now gone. In their place we find the EC's commitment to the prohibition of all restrictions on the movement of capital and on payments (*Article 56*, ex 73b). This is a fundamental requirement of both the Single Market and Economic and Monetary Union and one for which member states were obliged to make the necessary preparations before 1 January 1994 (see Article 116(2)(1)). However, one notable exemption does exist. The Protocol on the acquisition of property in Denmark annexed to the TEC by the TEU confirms that existing Danish legislation restricting the purchase of second homes by non-nationals can be retained. At the time of writing, similar protocols were being sought by some of the candidate countries negotiating accession of the EU in 2001.

The prohibition of restrictions on the movement of capital does not automatically apply, however, to the movement of capital to or from non-member states, although the EC is committed under *Article 57* (ex 73c) to liberalize movement in this area. Moreover, *Article 58* (ex 73d) allows member states to differentiate in their tax law between taxpayers based on place of residence and where their tax is invested. Member states may also take appropriate measures to combat tax evasion. However, no measures may be used in a discriminatory fashion or constitute a disguised restriction. And, according to Declaration No. 7 TEU, the first paragraph of Article 58 only applies to provisions governing capital movements and payments effected between member states in place on 31 December 1993 (i.e. prior to the second stage of EMU being launched). Finally, the provisions of Chapter 4 may not prejudice the applicability of restrictions on the right of establishment.

So, in principle, capital is to move freely within the EC. The exception is capital going to or coming from non-member states, where free movement is not automatic. Indeed, *Article 59* (ex 73f) allows the Council, acting by QMV on a Commission proposal and after consulting the ECB, to take safeguard measures where such capital movements cause or threaten to cause serious difficulties for the operation of EMU. Measures can last a maximum of six months and may be adopted only if 'strictly necessary'. Similarly, the Council may by the same mechanism, albeit without consultation of the ECB, regulate as well as liberalize the movement of capital to or from non-member states. If, however, a proposed measure represents 'a step back' with regard to liberalization, the Council under Article 57(2) must act by unanimity. Finally, *Article 60* (ex 73g) empowers the Council to take, by QMV, urgent measures regarding capital movements as part of any EC sanctions against a non-member state under Article 301. In the absence of such measures, a member state may act unilaterally. Its actions may, however, be subsequently amended or overturned by the Council, acting by QMV. Clearly the emphasis is on pursuing a common EC position.

Chapter 4   Capital and Payments

Article 56 (ex Article 73b)

1. Within the framework of the provisions set out in this Chapter, all restrictions on the movement of capital between Member States and between Member States and third countries shall be prohibited.

2. Within the framework of the provisions set out in this Chapter, all restrictions on payments between Member States and between Member States and third countries shall be prohibited.

Article 57 (ex Article 73c)

1. The provisions of Article 56 shall be without prejudice to the application to third countries of any restrictions which exist on 31 December 1993 under national or Community law adopted in respect of the movement of capital to or from third countries involving direct investment – including in real estate – establishment, the provision of financial services or the admission of securities to capital markets.

2. Whilst endeavouring to achieve the objective of free movement of capital between Member States and third countries to the greatest extent possible and without prejudice to the other Chapters of this Treaty, the Council may, acting by a qualified majority on a proposal from the Commission, adopt measures on the movement of capital to or from third countries involving direct investment – including investment in real estate – establishment, the provision of financial services or the admission of securities to capital markets. Unanimity shall be required for measures under this paragraph which constitute a step back in Community law as regards the liberalisation of the movement of capital to or from third countries.

Article 58 (ex Article 73d)

1. The provisions of Article 56 shall be without prejudice to the right of Member States:
(a) to apply the relevant provisions of their tax law which distinguish between taxpayers who are not in the same situation with regard to their place of residence or with regard to the place where their capital is invested;
(b) to take all requisite measures to prevent infringements of national law and regulations, in particular in the field of taxation and the prudential supervision of financial institutions, or to lay down procedures for the declaration of capital movements for purposes of administrative or statistical information, or to take measures which are justified on grounds of public policy or public security.

2. The provisions of this Chapter shall be without prejudice to the applicability of restrictions on the right of establishment which are compatible with this Treaty.

3. The measures and procedures referred to in paragraphs 1 and 2 shall not constitute a means of arbitrary discrimination or a disguised restriction on the free movement of capital and payments as defined in Article 56.

Article 59 (ex Article 73f)

Where, in exceptional circumstances, movements of capital to or from third countries cause, or threaten to cause, serious difficulties for the operation of economic and monetary union, the Council, acting by a qualified majority on a proposal from the Commission and after consulting the ECB, may take safeguard measures with regard to third countries for a period not exceeding six months if such measures are strictly necessary.

Article 60 (ex Article 73g)

1. If, in the cases envisaged in Article *301*, action by the Community is deemed necessary, the Council may, in accordance with the procedure provided for in Article *301*, take the necessary urgent measures on the movement of capital and on payments as regards the third countries concerned.

2. Without prejudice to Article 297 and as long as the Council has not taken measures pursuant to paragraph 1, a Member State may, for serious political reasons and on grounds of urgency, take unilateral measures against a third country with regard to capital movements and payments. The Commission and the other Member States shall be informed of such measures by the date of their entry into force at the latest.

The Council may, acting by a qualified majority on a proposal from the Commission, decide that the Member State concerned shall amend or abolish such measures. The President of the Council shall inform the European Parliament of any such decision taken by the Council.

viii Visas, Asylum, Immigration and Other Policies Related to Free Movement of Persons

Part Three's fourth title is a relative newcomer to the TEC, being inserted by the Treaty of Amsterdam in 1999. It owes its existence to the revamping of treaty provisions governing internal security within the EU, previously contained in Pillar III on justice and home affairs (JHA) and in Article 100c TEC, as well as a desire to build on existing proposals and co-operation designed to realize the free movement of people within the EU. Three key changes – or surgical operations, as den Boer prefers – were undertaken at Amsterdam. These were the creation of 'an area of freedom, security and justice'; the slimming down and renaming of the EU's third pillar (see Articles 29–42 TEU); and the incorporation of the Schengen *acquis* into the TEU. It is the first and the third of these which concern us here, although there are obviously overlaps with the TEU provisions as the treaty text itself confirms.

Title IV of Part Three of the TEC contains nine articles (Articles 61–69) which provide the basis for the progressive establishment of 'an area of freedom, security and justice' (*Article 61*) in line with the EU's objectives as laid down in Article 2 TEU and the new eleventh recital of the TEU's preamble. Such an explicit goal is new to the EU and involves the EC seeking to make further progress in realizing genuine free movement of people in line with Article 14 TEC. Interestingly though, there is no reference to 'an area of freedom, security and justice' in the list of EC activities set out in Article 3. All that is mentioned is that the EC shall adopt 'measures concerning the entry and movement of persons as provided for in Title IV'. This helps to explain the thrust of Title IV. It does not, however, cast much light on what is meant by 'an area of freedom, security and justice', not that this is an easy task. As Smith and Wallace point out, there are inherent tensions: security as an objective does not fit easily with freedom and justice. Some guidance is provided in Article 2 TEU, which states that the area is one in which 'the free movement of persons is assured in conjunction with appropriate measures with respect to external border controls, asylum, immigration and the prevention and combating of crime'. Bearing this in mind, it should come as no surprise that the title draws heavily on some of the existing JHA activities of the EU initially carried out under Pillar III. These have now been partially 'communitarized' and appear here in Title IV.

Moreover, the new title integrates much of the co-operation which existing member states except Ireland and the United Kingdom have been pursuing within the so-called Schengen framework. This accounts, in part, for the fact these two member states plus Denmark have 'opt-outs' from Title IV. It also helps explain the unusually large number of protocols and declarations relating to the title, a reflection of the differing views among member states concerning how to achieve the desired 'area of freedom, security and justice'. As den Boer notes, the area is 'bogged down by compromise'. It is difficult to disagree given the extremely labyrinthine provisions produced at Amsterdam and then later complicated by Nice. All the same, the provisions do have their supporters. Among these are Monar and O'Keefe, the latter declaring Title IV to be 'one of the outstanding achievements of the Amsterdam negotiations'.

In order to establish the 'area of freedom, security and justice', *Article 61(a)* requires the EC to adopt measures in a variety of areas and with differing degrees of urgency. Within five years of Amsterdam's entry into force (i.e. before 1 May 2004) and not by 1 January 2001 as some had proposed, measures are to be adopted which aim to ensure the free movement of people within the EC. These are to be accompanied by so-called flanking measures covering the strengthening of external EU border controls, asylum, immigration, and, within Pillar III of the EU (see Articles 29–42 TEU), the prevention and combating of crime. Also, within the five years stated, internal EC border controls on people are to be removed, rules on short-stay visas for nationals from non-member states (taking into account foreign policy matters) are to be agreed (Declaration No. 16 TA), standards and procedures for external border checks are to be adopted and the right of nationals from non-member states to move freely within the EC for a limited period of three months is to be upheld (*Article 62*). Under *Article 63*, however, member states retain the right to conclude agreements with non-member states concerning border controls thanks to the Protocol on external relations of the Member States with regard to the crossing of external borders adopted at Amsterdam. Furthermore, EC measures on asylum concerning minimum, as opposed to high-level substantive, standards for asylum procedures, burden sharing regarding refugees and displaced people and immigration policy issues are to be adopted by 1 May 2004. These, as anticipated, are to be in line with the 1951 Geneva Convention and 1967 Protocol concerning refugees.

On asylum policy matters, consultations are to be held with the United Nations High Commissioner for Refugees as well as other agencies (Declaration No. 17 TA). And where immigration policy is concerned, member states retain the right to conclude agreements with non-member states provided these agreements comply with EC law (Declaration No. 18 TA). While member states will be bound to all decisions taken under Title IV, *Article 64(2)* does permit them to take emergency measures when faced with a sudden influx of nationals from non-member states and allows the Council by QMV to adopt measures to assist the member state concerned. Also on asylum, the TEC's provisions govern only non-nationals of member states. This is made clear in the Protocol on asylum for nationals of Member States of the European Union introduced by the TA at Spain's behest to stop terrorists seeking asylum in another member state. This notes that member states are generally to be treated as 'safe' countries for asylum purposes and appears to confer a lesser status on nationals of member states, particularly since the area of freedom, security and justice is yet to be established. Belgium, the country which Spain had in mind when advocating the protocol, has nevertheless stated in a declaration (No. 5n TA) that it will continue to examine each application from a national of a member state. Further declarations relating to asylum note that member states will take the organizational measures necessary to fulfil their obligations under the 1951 Geneva Convention relating to the status of refugees (No. 48 TA) and confirm intentions to review procedures for dealing with 'manifestly unfounded' asylum applications (No. 49 TA).

In addition to the matters laid down in the temporal clauses noted so far, Title IV through *Article 61(b–d)* envisages other measures being adopted, albeit not within any strict time limit, regarding asylum, immigration, the rights of nationals of non-member states, judicial co-operation in civil matters, the strengthening of administrative co-operation and police and judicial co-operation in criminal matters (under Pillar III). In addition, *Article 65* provides for judicial co-operation in civil matters with cross-border implications, albeit without affecting national constitutional rules on the freedom of the press and freedom of expression (Declaration No. 20 TA), and for national adminis-trations to co-operate with one another and with the Commission as *Article 66* makes clear. It should be noted, however, that *Article 64(1)* (ex 100c(5)) confirms the primacy of member states' own internal measures where the maintenance of law and order is concerned. Here, foreign policy considerations may be taken into account when adopting measures (Declaration No. 19 TA).

All this signals more intense co-operation between the member states and the emergence of an embryonic EC-based immigration and asylum policy. And this has been reflected in the raft of measures contained in the action plan adopted at the Vienna European Council in December 1998 and the more than 200 legislative proposals made in the build-up to the Tampere European Council in October 1999. This suggests a clear desire on the part of the EU to realize the 'area of freedom, security and justice'. Indeed, Monar has argued that the ambitiousness of the proposals and intensity of negotiations suggest a volume of activity comparable to that which preceded the launch of the Single Market programme in the mid-1980s. This is reflected in the decision-making structures which have been developed to deal with the array of issues covered under the rubric of justice and home affairs. Yet there are significant criticisms of the way in which the EU is realizing its area of freedom, security and justice. Most notable among these are those levelled against the increasing control being exercised over external borders and entry into the EU – often referred to as the 'fortress Europe' approach – and the increasing amount of law-enforcement measures being introduced on citizens within the EU. Monar adds two others: the development of common aims in the area of immigration policy and the social integration of asylum seekers and immigrants, noting too that the commitment to burden sharing is weaker than Germany would like.

All the areas listed for action in Title IV were originally the proposed subject of co-operation within the inter-governmental JHA pillar of the EU. Only a few matters concerning visas were covered by the EC pillar. Others could have been transferred to the EC pillar via the so-called *passerelle* clause. In fact, Declaration No. 31 TEU envisaged consideration of areas of asylum policy being transferred to the EC by the end of 1993. No transfers ever took place. Consequently, Amsterdam could be seen to have brought about a communitarization of the pillar by bringing many, if not all of them (customs co-operation in criminal matters and the fight against fraud generally remain in Pillar III) into Title IV. The communitarization – or Amsterdamization as it is sometimes known

– is, however, staged. Therefore a rather messy process of competence shifts will be taking place during the first five years of the title's existence. This can be seen by looking at how decision-making is to be carried out.

First, there is the question of where initiative lies. During the 1999–2004 period, as provided for in *Article 67(1)*, both the Commission and the member states may initiate proposals. Only after this 'transitional period' is the procedure communitarized with the sole right of initiative conferred on the Commission. Even then, the Commission is obliged to consider any requests from member states.

Second, the involvement of the EP is generally limited to consultation both during and after the transitional period. At Amsterdam, it was agreed in *Article 67(4)* that co-decision would be introduced automatically only after the five years for two minor areas: the procedures and conditions for issuing visas by member states and rules on a uniform visa. Other areas could be the subject of co-decision only with the unanimous agreement of the Council. Although the TEC does not state when or even if a decision will be taken, a declaration adopted at Amsterdam and developments at Nice (see below) imply that the Council will act before the end of the transitional period, this being 1 May 2004 (Declaration No. 21 TA). All the same, the EP was highly critical of the arrangements inserted by the TA. Commentators such as Boeles also criticized the lack of overall parliamentary scrutiny of Title IV decisions. Hence, against such a background and a professed desire to facilitate decision-making, it was agreed at Nice to extend the co-decision procedure to more areas. The outcome was, however, limited and fell short of EP wishes. Co-decision will now be used for measures concerning judicial co-operation in civil matters except where these involve family law, and asylum and some refugee matters, albeit provided that the Council under *Article 67(5)* has already agreed 'common rules and basic principles' in these areas. Hence, the majority of provisions will, unless agreed otherwise, remain subject to Council decision and EP consultation. All the same, with the shift of competence to the EC pillar, decision-making has at least become more transparent with increased EP and public access to documents and proposals. And the EP will be able to exercise some influence over the title, given its budgetary powers.

Third, there is the matter of how the Council decides. Both during and after the transitional period, *Article 67(1)* declares that decisions are to be taken by unanimity except in those areas where co-decision applies. Here the Council acts by QMV. Although consideration was given to extending the use of QMV at Nice, the member states proved reluctant to endorse significant changes, at least in the short-term. The Protocol on Article 67 of the TEC requires QMV to be used for measures on administrative co-operation under Article 66 from the end of the transitional period (1 May 2004). It does not, however, provide for increased EP involvement through co-decision. The consultation procedure still applies. As for the extension of QMV in other areas, this is deferred. In Declaration No. 5 TN it was agreed that a Council decision would be taken before the end of the transitional period (i.e. by 1 May 2004) to extend co-decision to Article 62(3) on the conditions under which nationals of non-member states can travel freely within the EU, Article 63(3)(b) on burden-sharing with regard to receiving refugees and Article 62(2)(a) for standards and procedures for external border checks provided agreement has been reached on the scope of measures concerning the crossing by people of member states' external borders. The member states also committed the Council to endeavouring to extend the application of co-decision. The declaration is, however, merely a political statement and has no binding legal force. Moreover, there is no indication as to when any changes will apply. Indeed, when tidying up the agreements reached at Nice, a reference to 1 May 2004 was deleted. Changes to decision-making under Title IV will depend on the detail of the Council decision whenever it comes.

Fourth, regarding communitarization, is the position of the ECJ. Although most of Title IV falls under its jurisdiction, the ECJ, according to *Article 68*, has no jurisdiction over any measure or decision relating to the maintenance of law and order or internal security in a member state taken on the basis of Article 62(1). Similarly, echoing Article 33 TEU, it has no jurisdiction over the legality of national measures taken in order to maintain law and order and internal security as referred to in Article 64, although O'Keefe argues that the ECJ is competent to determine the limits of its jurisdiction in this area. According to *Article 67(2)*, a unanimous Council decision is necessary to alter the jurisdiction. Also, no ECJ ruling may be applied to a judgment by a national court or tribunal which has become *res judicata* (i.e. a matter already adjudicated upon that cannot be raised again). The role of national courts is further emphasized by the fact that only courts of last resort may seek a ruling from the ECJ on matters covered by Articles 61–69, a restriction which, according to Langrish, was designed to reduce the risk of the ECJ becoming overloaded with cases. Added to this, the semi-detached relationship which Denmark has with Title IV activities (see below) involves its actions falling outside the jurisdiction of the ECJ. Also, with the UK and Ireland not automatically participating in Title IV measures, legal homogeneity within the EC is further constrained. As Fennelly argues, all this makes the ECJ's position highly complex.

The approach adopted to communitarization in Title IV clearly departs from established EC practice and makes the title unique within the treaty. Its uniqueness is underlined by Article 69, which draws attention to three protocols relating to the title. The explicit reference is arguably unjustified, given that Article 311 TEC declares all annexed protocols to be an integral part of the treaty. The first two protocols, the Protocol on the position of the United Kingdom and Ireland and the Protocol on the position of Denmark, provide all three countries with what, at first glance, appear to be complete opt-outs from the provisions of, measures adopted under, and ECJ rulings relating to Title IV. They are also exempt from any financial consequences of Title IV measures. This reflects political pragmatism on the part of Denmark in the light of popular concerns about integration and follows the decision adopted at the Edinburgh European Council in December 1992 limiting Denmark's involvement in JHA matters. By contrast, it is rigid adherence to principle on the part of the United Kingdom that accounts for its opt-out. Ireland, meanwhile, finds itself semi-detached from Title IV owing to its desire to retain the common travel area with the United Kingdom and, in particular, the open frontier with Northern Ireland, as Hedemann-Robinson and others have noted. Hence, the 'area of freedom, security and justice' does not fully cover all the EU.

Yet, the protocols are not straightforward opt-outs. They should be viewed more as 'opt-in' arrangements. Denmark, for example, has agreed to adopt measures covering visa requirements and visa formats and may, within six months of an extension of the Schengen *acquis*, decide to implement any decision adopted. In what Monar views as one of the most peculiar arrangements introduced by Amsterdam, any decision implemented creates obligations under only international law and not that of the EC. As far as Ireland and the United Kingdom are concerned, they may on notification to the Council Presidency participate in the adoption of measures under Title IV and implement measures already adopted. Also, Ireland, along with Denmark but not the United Kingdom, has the right at any time to inform the other member states that it no longer wishes its protocol to apply. In the case of the United Kingdom, it is widely held that treaty amendment would be necessary before it could accede fully to Title IV.

The third protocol, the Protocol on the application of certain aspects of Article 14 of the Treaty establishing the European Community to the United Kingdom and to Ireland, while not relating directly to Title IV, nevertheless underlines the limited involvement of the two countries in the 'area of freedom, security and justice'. According to the protocol, the United Kingdom is entitled to retain 'such controls . . . as it may consider necessary' on people entering its territory. The free movement of people is not therefore to entail the disbanding of UK border controls. Moreover, the protocol allows the United Kingdom and Ireland to maintain the common travel area which allows passport-free travel between the two countries. It is for the sake of maintaining this arrangement that Ireland is covered by the protocol. Hence, for as long as such an arrangement is in place, Ireland will be able to maintain controls on people entering the country. Officially, though, the Irish government supports the abolition of border controls and full participation in Title IV activities, expressing at Amsterdam its desire to participate in Title IV decisions provided they are compatible with the common travel area (Declaration No. 4n TA). There is a downside for UK and Irish nationals. While, in the case of the former at least, the retention of border controls may be domestically popular, the *quid pro quo* is that the other EU member states retain the right to subject UK and Irish nationals to controls when entering their territories. Of significance is the fact that the protocol covers all territories for which the United Kingdom is responsible. Hence, the Spanish authorities will be able to refer to it in justifying frontier controls in relation to Gibraltar.

On the one hand, the existence of the three protocols promotes confusion, fragmentation and inequity, as Hedemann-Robinson notes. It is also likely to lead to differentiated case law. Barents has been particularly critical of the arrangements concerning Denmark's position while Toth expresses deep concerns generally about the impact of the protocols on the nature of EC law, arguing that they sound the death-knell for all the major principles which have formed the foundation of the EC's legal order: the unitary nature of EC law; uniform interpretation and application of rules; and the maintenance of the *acquis communautaire*. On the other hand, by accommodating reservations about, if not outright opposition to, integration in politically sensitive areas such as border controls, immigration and asylum, the protocols have paved the way for existing Schengen co-operation being placed on the more solid foundation of the EU. Had not the three protocols been agreed it is unlikely that a fourth protocol, complete with its opt-in arrangements for the United Kingdom and Ireland, would have been adopted at Amsterdam.

The protocol in question is the Dutch-inspired Protocol integrating the Schengen *acquis* into the framework of the European Union. This envisages the partial communitarization of a further body of measures – estimated at around 3,000 pages of secondary legislation – adopted by the 13 EU member states which have been involved in so-called Schengen co-operation. The measures apply automatically to all member states except Ireland and the United Kingdom, although a unilateral declaration (No. 7n TA) does restrict application in the case of France to exclude the country's overseas territories. Ireland and the United Kingdom may seek to opt-in to arrangements. Any opt-in is subject, however, to unanimous agreement among the other member states, a more stringent requirement compared to Title IV measures generally, where approval is granted by QMV, and one which, as the UK government has acknowledged, allows Spain to veto UK participation over the Gibraltar dispute. The UK government had originally assumed that decisions would require QMV.

Schengen co-operation was initiated outside the framework of the EC in the 1980s in response to the desire of the Benelux, French and German governments to remove internal border controls as part of efforts to realize the free movement of people. Other EU member states except the UK and Ireland gradually joined them. What the protocol adopted at Amsterdam does is to call for each element of the so-called Schengen *acquis*, identified as best possible in an annex, to be allocated a formal legal base in either Part Three, Title IV of the TEC or Title VI of the TEU. A French-inspired declaration (No. 15

TA) requires the said levels in the context of the abolition of border controls to be maintained. The deadline envisaged was the date on which the Treaty of Amsterdam entered into force (Declaration No. 44 TA), the provisions of the protocol therefore necessitating implementation before they had been formally ratified! As it turned out, the process took slightly longer, not least because there was no firm agreement on what constituted the *acquis* and not all texts had been published. Eventually the Council took the necessary decisions on 20 May 1999. As Kuijper, Peers and den Boer all record, most elements of the Schengen *acquis* were allocated a firm legal base in either the TEC, the TEU, or the TEC and the TEU, the major exception being those governing the Schengen Information System (SIS) which were provisionally allocated, as envisaged in the protocol, to the PJCCM pillar of the EU. This was no mean achievement, although questions have been raised, for example by Smith and Wallace, about the democratic legitimacy and transparency of the process employed. Amsterdam was ratified without national parliaments knowing exactly what constituted the Schengen *acquis* or what is implied by it.

So, even though it is relatively new, Title IV almost from its inception has provided the legal basis for a substantial body of legislation. None of this initially applied to either the UK or Ireland, although the UK government almost immediately exercised its option to opt-in to participate in measures covering law enforcement and criminal judicial cooperation, including the SIS. The Irish government soon followed with the Council moving to obtain, as envisaged, the opinion of the Commission (see Declaration No. 45 TA). Such involvement as well as that announced subsequently clearly implied that the United Kingdom had no intention of remaining wholly outside Title IV co-operation. It also provided the other member states with the opportunity to show their commitment to facilitating UK and Irish involvement as envisaged in Declaration No. 46 TA. In fact, Ireland would have become a full participant had it not been for the common travel area with the United Kingdom. The protocols nevertheless emphasize the à la carte nature of UK (and Irish) participation. This contrasts with the position of two non-member states, Iceland and Norway, which had become associated with Schengen arrangements in the mid-1990s so as to ensure the continued functioning of the Nordic Passport Union. At Amsterdam, agreement was reached on arranging for their continued involvement. Hence, in line with Article 6 of the Schengen *acquis* protocol and an associated declaration (No. 47 TA), a formal agreement was concluded in May 1999. And in future, all new members will be full participants in Schengen activities, the protocol implying that there will be no future opt-outs. Whether a shift from differentiated to universal participation will take place, as de Zwaan and Vrouenraets suggest might be the case, remains to be seen.

TITLE IV

VISAS, ASYLUM, IMMIGRATION AND OTHER POLICIES RELATED TO FREE MOVEMENT OF PERSONS

Article 61 (new – TA)

In order to establish progressively an area of freedom, security and justice, the Council shall adopt:

(a) within a period of five years after the entry into force of the Treaty of Amsterdam, measures aimed at ensuring the free movement of persons in accordance with Article 14, in conjunction with directly related flanking measures with respect to external border controls, asylum and immigration, in accordance with the provisions of Article 62(2) and (3) and Article 63(1)(a) and (2)(a), and measures to prevent and combat crime in accordance with the provisions of Article 31(e) of the Treaty on European Union;

(b) other measures in the fields of asylum, immigration and safeguarding the rights of nationals of third countries, in accordance with the provisions of Article 63;

(c) measures in the field of judicial co-operation in civil matters as provided for in Article 65;

(d) appropriate measures to encourage and strengthen administrative co-operation, as provided for in Article 66;

(e) measures in the field of police and judicial co-operation in criminal matters aimed at a high level of security by preventing and combating crime within the Union in accordance with the provisions of the Treaty on European Union.

Article 62 (new – TA)

The Council, acting in accordance with the procedure referred to in Article 67, shall, within a period of five years after the entry into force of the Treaty of Amsterdam, adopt:

(1) measures with a view to ensuring, in compliance with Article 14, the absence of any controls on persons, be they citizens of the Union or nationals of third countries, when crossing internal borders;

(2) measures on the crossing of the external borders of the Member States which shall establish:

(a) standards and procedures to be followed by Member States in carrying out checks on persons at such borders;

(b) rules on visas for intended stays of no more than three months, including:

(i) *the list of third countries whose nationals must be in possession of visas when crossing the external borders* and those whose nationals are exempt from that requirement;

(ii) the procedures and conditions for issuing visas by Member States;

(iii) *a uniform format for visas;*

(iv) rules on a uniform visa;

(3) measures setting out the conditions under which nationals of third countries shall have the freedom to travel within the territory of the Member States during a period of no more than three months.

Article 63 (new – TA)

The Council, acting in accordance with the procedure referred to in Article 67, shall, within a period of five years after the entry into force of the Treaty of Amsterdam, adopt:

(1) measures on asylum, in accordance with the Geneva Convention of 28 July 1951 and the Protocol of 31 January 1967 relating to the status of refugees and other relevant treaties, within the following areas:

(a) criteria and mechanisms for determining which Member State is responsible for considering an application for asylum submitted by a national of a third country in one of the Member States,

(b) minimum standards on the reception of asylum seekers in Member States,

(c) minimum standards with respect to the qualification of nationals of third countries as refugees,

(d) minimum standards on procedures in Member States for granting or withdrawing refugee status;

(2) measures on refugees and displaced persons within the following areas:

(a) minimum standards for giving temporary protection to displaced persons from third countries who cannot return to their country of origin and for persons who otherwise need international protection,

(b) promoting a balance of effort between Member States in receiving and bearing the consequences of receiving refugees and displaced persons;

(3) measures on immigration policy within the following areas:

(a) conditions of entry and residence, and standards on procedures for the issue by Member States of long term visas and residence permits, including those for the purpose of family reunion,

(b) illegal immigration and illegal residence, including repatriation of illegal residents;

(4) measures defining the rights and conditions under which nationals of third countries who are legally resident in a Member State may reside in other Member States.

Measures adopted by the Council pursuant to points 3 and 4 shall not prevent any Member State from maintaining or introducing in the areas concerned national provisions which are compatible with this Treaty and with international agreements.

Measures to be adopted pursuant to points 2(b), 3(a) and 4 shall not be subject to the five year period referred to above.

Article 64 (new – TA, drawing on ex Article 100c (2) and (5))

1. This Title shall not affect the exercise of the responsibilities incumbent upon Member States with regard to the maintenance of law and order and the safeguarding of internal security.

2. In the event of one or more Member States being confronted with an emergency situation characterised by a sudden inflow of nationals of third countries and without prejudice to paragraph 1, the Council may, acting by qualified majority on a proposal from the Commission, adopt provisional measures of a duration not exceeding six months for the benefit of the Member States concerned.

Article 65 (new – TA)

Measures in the field of judicial co-operation in civil matters having cross-border implications, to be taken in accordance with Article 67 and insofar as necessary for the proper functioning of the internal market, shall include:

(a) improving and simplifying:

– the system for cross-border service of judicial and extrajudicial documents;

– co-operation in the taking of evidence;

– the recognition and enforcement of decisions in civil and commercial cases, including decisions in extrajudicial cases;

(b) promoting the compatibility of the rules applicable in the Member States concerning the conflict of laws and of jurisdiction;

(c) eliminating obstacles to the good functioning of civil proceedings, if necessary by promoting the compatibility of the rules on civil procedure applicable in the Member States.

Article 66 (new – TA)

The Council, acting in accordance with the procedure referred to in Article 67, shall take measures to ensure co-operation between the relevant departments of the administrations of the Member States in the areas covered by this Title, as well as between those departments and the Commission.

Article 67 (new – TA)

1. During a transitional period of five years following the entry into force of the Treaty of Amsterdam, the Council shall act unanimously on a proposal from the Commission or on the initiative of a Member State and after consulting the European Parliament.

2. After this period of five years:
– the Council shall act on proposals from the Commission; the Commission shall examine any request made by a Member State that it submit a proposal to the Council;
– the Council, acting unanimously after consulting the European Parliament, shall take a decision with a view to providing for all or parts of the areas covered by this Title to be governed by the procedure referred to in Article 251 and adapting the provisions relating to the powers of the Court of Justice.

3. By derogation from paragraphs 1 and 2, measures referred to in Article 62(2)(b) (i) and (iii) shall, from the entry into force of the Treaty of Amsterdam, be adopted by the Council acting by a qualified majority on a proposal from the Commission and after consulting the European Parliament.

4. By derogation from paragraph 2, measures referred to in Article 62(2)(b) (ii) and (iv) shall, after a period of five years following the entry into force of the Treaty of Amsterdam, be adopted by the Council acting in accordance with the procedure referred to in Article 251.

5. By derogation from paragraph 1, the Council shall adopt, in accordance with the procedure provided in Article 251:
– the measures provided for in Article 63(1) and (2)(a) provided that the Council has previously adopted, in accordance with the provisions of paragraph 1 of this Article, Community legislation defining the common rules and basic principles governing these issues.
– the measures provided for in Article 65 with the exception of aspects relating to family law.

Article 68 (new – TA)

1. Article 234 shall apply to this Title under the following circumstances and conditions: where a question on the interpretation of this Title or on the validity or interpretation of acts of the institutions of the Community based on this Title is raised in a case pending before a court or a tribunal of a Member State against whose decisions there is no judicial remedy under national law, that court or tribunal shall, if it considers that a decision on the question is necessary to enable it to give judgment, request the Court of Justice to give a ruling thereon.

2. In any event, the Court of Justice shall not have jurisdiction to rule on any measure or decision taken pursuant to Article 62(1) relating to the maintenance of law and order and the safeguarding of internal security.

3. The Council, the Commission or a Member State may request the Court of Justice to give a ruling on a question of interpretation of this Title or of acts of the institutions of the Community based on this Title. The ruling given by the Court of Justice in response to such a request shall not apply to judgments of courts or tribunals of the Member States which have become *res judicata*.

Article 69 (new – TA)

The application of this Title shall be subject to the provisions of the Protocol on the position of the United Kingdom and Ireland and to the Protocol on the position of Denmark and without prejudice to the Protocol on the application of certain aspects of Article 14 of the Treaty establishing the European Community to the United Kingdom and to Ireland.

ix Transport

Whereas the provisions of Title IV are relative newcomers to the TEC – having been inserted by Amsterdam – those in the next title on transport date back to when the treaty was signed in the 1950s. Half of the articles in Title V have since been amended either to bring about changes in decision-making (Article 71(1)) or following the simplification of the treaty base introduced at Amsterdam (Articles 71(2), 72, 75(1), 75(2), 76(1), 79, 80(2)). And all were renumbered when the TA entered into force in 1999. The Treaty of Nice had no direct impact on the provisions.

The EC's aim with regard to transport is similar to that for agriculture: to establish a common policy (Article 3(1)(f) and *Article 70*, ex 74). Transport therefore enjoys special treatment within the treaty, a point underlined by Article 51(1) which exempts transport from the earlier provisions of Title III, Chapter 3 on services. For many years this exemption, combined with the reference in *Article 71(1)* (ex 75(1)) to the 'distinctive features of transport' allowed the Council to argue that transport was not subject to the general rules of the treaty, notably those relating to the application of the competition rules, freedom of establishment and freedom to provide services. One by one, from 1974 onwards, these contentions were demolished by the ECJ, which established the position that the purpose of the separate transport title was to allow the Council to take account of the distinctive features of transport in applying the general rules of the treaty, but not to deny their application altogether. Finally, in *Parliament* v. *Council* (1985), the Court ruled that although the Council could not be said to be in breach of its obligations under the treaty to develop a common transport policy (CTP), since the content of such a policy was not sufficiently defined for such a case to stand up, it was in breach on grounds of failure to lay down the common rules specified in Article 71(1)(a) and 71(1)(b). A year later the *Nouvelles Frontières* (1986) judgment confirmed that the Council's obligation to formulate a policy applied just as much to air (and by implication to sea) transport as it did to inland transport. Moreover, only when rules were laid down in the Council could member states' airlines be protected from the direct application of the treaty competition rules. Between 1985 and 1992 these judgments, combined with the political impetus of the Single Market programme, led the Council to establish, mode by mode, the foundations of an essentially liberal market in transport services. Even so, the continued reference to 1 January 1958 as well as accession dates within *Article 72* (ex 76) – unique save for Article 307 TEC – allows member states to maintain their existing national rules until common rules have been laid down under Article 71(1) and reflects the limited progress which the EC has made even now in developing the common transport policy.

The scope of the common transport policy is defined in *Article 80* (ex 84) which states that the policy is to cover rail, road and inland waterway transport. Sea and air transport are not automatically covered. This is because, as Greaves notes, they are closely linked to national defence and have traditionally been viewed as symbols of statehood. Originally, the Council could extend the CTP to these areas via unanimous decision, although few efforts were made to do so during the first 25 years of the EC. From 1986, achieving agreement in the Council was facilitated under the SEA by amending Article 80(2) to allow QMV to be applied to sea and air transport.

The substance of EC transport policy is set out, but only in very broad terms, in *Article 71* (ex 75). The first indent of its first paragraph is the basis for rules governing transport between the member states, whilst the second indent is the basis for rules allowing the carriers of one member state to operate services within another (cabotage). In addition the TEU introduced at the third indent a reference to transport safety, relegating the long-standing reference to 'any other appropriate provisions' to the fourth and final indent. This catch-all clause has been widely used to balance liberalization of market access with harmonization of competitive conditions, for example through common provisions for the licensing of carriers, common working conditions for staff, or common technical specifications for vehicles. The TEU also added provisions on trans-European networks (Articles 154–156), which establish a specific basis for Community action to facilitate the development of transport infrastructure. This has been accompanied by increased emphasis on the environmental impact of both infrastructure and services, whilst the Protocol on Protection and Welfare of Animals, introduced at Amsterdam, brings all 'sentient beings' within the ambit of welfare considerations.

The TEU also introduced changes to the decision-making procedure. The Council would continue to act by QMV but was now obliged to use the co-operation procedure rather than just consult the EP, as well as EcoSoc, as had been the case. Amsterdam went further by replacing co-operation with co-decision and adding consultation of the Committee of the Regions (Article 71(1)). There are, however, exceptions to this rule, despite proposals in the 2000 IGC to have them removed. If a measure is likely to have serious effects on the standard of living and employment in particular areas of the EC, the Council is required under Article 71(2) to act unanimously and only in consultation with the EP and EcoSoc.

Furthermore, *Article 75* (ex 79) requires the Council, acting by QMV, and having consulted only EcoSoc (and not the EP!), to lay down measures for abolishing discrimination with regard to differential charges on national and non-national carriers. The Commission is provided with an investigative role to ensure that the discrimination is abolished. Also, as provided for in *Article 76* (ex 80), free competition is to be promoted through the prohibition of charges or conditions favourable to one or more undertakings, except where the charges are fixed to 'meet competition'. Provision is then made in *Article 77* (ex 81) for the Commission to recommend measures to assist member states in their 'endeavour' to reduce charges, already limited to 'a reasonable level', imposed for border crossings. In these and other cases under Title V the Commission may consult the special advisory committee for transport provided for in *Article* 79 (ex 93). The committee is made up of experts designated by member state governments.

The emphasis on non-discrimination and freer competition in Articles 75–77 should not mislead readers into believing that there is the same emphasis on liberalization in Title V as there is in other areas of the TEC. Indeed, when the TEC was concluded a large part of the transport industries was, and in many countries still is, in public ownership. This explains a bias among governments towards protection of the interests of transport providers, something which is reflected in Title V. Hence, *Article* 74 (ex 78) requires that any measures concerning transport rates and conditions shall take account of the economic circumstances of carriers, while *Article* 73 (ex 77) allows member states to grant state aid for transport co-ordination and for the discharge of public service obligations. Furthermore, *Article* 76 (ex 80) makes provision for the Commission to authorize tariffs designed to protect particular undertakings or industries on grounds of regional economic or social policy. In the same spirit there is a special dispensation for Germany in *Article* 78 (ex 82), to permit the implementation of measures designed to redress the economic disadvantages caused to certain regions affected by the division of the country. While seemingly anomalous following German reunification in 1990, the provision has been retained despite proposals to remove it in the IGC, which led to the TEU. The same is true of Article 87(2)(c) concerning state aids.

One area where Title V is silent is external relations, particularly those between the EC and other international transport organizations. It therefore stands in sharp contrast to Title IX governing the common commercial policy, lacking an equivalent of Article 133 on the conclusion of trade agreements. However, the need to manage relations with many other inter-governmental organizations set up long before 1958 to facilitate international transport beyond the borders of the Community, was bound to prove contentious, and has in fact given rise to a number of important judgments by the ECJ, including the seminal 1971 *AETR* ruling in which the Court ruled that the EC has competence to conclude international agreements in areas where it has an internal competence to act.

TITLE V (ex Title IV)

TRANSPORT

Article 70 (ex Article 74)

The objectives of this Treaty shall, in matters governed by this Title, be pursued by Member States within the framework of a common transport policy.

Article 71 (ex Article 75 simplified)

1. For the purpose of implementing Article 70, and taking into account the distinctive features of transport, the Council shall, **acting in accordance with the procedure referred to in Article 251** and after consulting the Economic and Social Committee **and the Committee of the Regions,** lay down:
   (a) common rules applicable to international transport to or from the territory of a Member State or passing across the territory of one or more Member States;
   (b) the conditions under which non-resident carriers may operate transport services within a Member State;
   (c) measures to improve transport safety;
   (d) any other appropriate provisions.

2. *By way of derogation from the procedure provided for in paragraph 1, where the application of provisions concerning the principles of the regulatory system for transport would be liable to have a serious effect on the standard of living and on employment in certain areas and on the operation of transport facilities, they shall be laid down by the Council acting unanimously on a proposal from the Commission, after consulting the European Parliament and the Economic and Social Committee. In so doing, the Council shall take into account the need for adaptation to the economic development which will result from establishing the common market.*

Article 72 (ex Article 76 simplified)

Until the provisions referred to in Article 71(1) have been laid down, no Member State may, without the unanimous approval of the Council, make the various provisions governing the subject *on 1 January 1958 or, for acceding States, the date of their accession* less favourable in their direct or indirect effect on carriers of other Member States as compared with carriers who are nationals of that State.

Article 73 (ex Article 77)

Aids shall be compatible with this Treaty if they meet the needs of co-ordination of transport or if they represent reimbursement for the discharge of certain obligations inherent in the concept of a public service.

Article 74 (ex Article 78)

Any measures taken within the framework of this Treaty in respect of transport rates and conditions shall take account of the economic circumstances of carriers.

Article 75 (ex Article 79 simplified)

1. In the case of transport within the Community, discrimination which takes the form of carriers charging different rates and imposing different conditions for the carriage of the same goods over the same transport links on grounds of the country of origin or of destination of the goods in question shall be abolished.

2. Paragraph 1 shall not prevent the Council from adopting other measures in pursuance of Article 71(1).

3. *The Council shall,* acting by a qualified majority on a proposal from the Commission and after consulting the Economic and Social Committee, lay down rules for implementing the provisions of paragraph 1.

The Council may in particular lay down the provisions needed to enable the institutions of the Community to secure compliance with the rule laid down in paragraph 1 and to ensure that users benefit from it to the full.

4. The Commission shall, acting on its own initiative or on application by a Member State, investigate any cases of discrimination falling within paragraph 1 and, after consulting any Member State concerned, shall take the necessary decisions within the framework of the rules laid down in accordance with the provisions of paragraph 3.

Article 76 (ex Article 80 simplified)

1. The imposition by a Member State, in respect of transport operations carried out within the Community, of rates and conditions involving any element of support or protection in the interest of one or more particular undertakings or industries shall be *prohibited, unless* authorised by the Commission.

2. The Commission shall, acting on its own initiative or on application by a Member State, examine the rates and conditions referred to in paragraph 1, taking account in particular of the requirements of an appropriate regional economic policy, the needs of underdeveloped areas and the problems of areas seriously affected by political circumstances on the one hand, and of the effects of such rates and conditions on competition between the different modes of transport on the other.

After consulting each Member State concerned, the Commission shall take the necessary decisions.

3. The prohibition provided for in paragraph 1 shall not apply to tariffs fixed to meet competition.

Article 77 (ex Article 81)

Charges or dues in respect of the crossing of frontiers which are charged by a carrier in addition to the transport rates shall not exceed a reasonable level after taking the costs actually incurred thereby into account.

Member States shall endeavour to reduce these costs progressively.

The Commission may make recommendations to Member States for the application of this Article.

Article 78 (ex Article 82)

The provisions of this Title shall not form an obstacle to the application of measures taken in the Federal Republic of Germany to the extent that such measures are required in order to compensate for the economic disadvantages caused by the division of Germany to the economy of certain areas of the Federal Republic affected by that division.

Article 79 (ex Article 83 simplified)

An Advisory Committee consisting of experts designated by the governments of Member States shall be attached to the Commission. The Commission, whenever it considers it desirable, shall consult the Committee on transport matters without prejudice to the *powers of* the Economic and Social Committee.

Article 80 (ex Article 84 simplified)

1. The provisions of this Title shall apply to transport by rail, road and inland waterway.

2. The Council may, acting by a qualified majority, decide whether, to what extent and by what procedure appropriate provisions may be laid down for sea and air transport.

The procedural provisions of Article 71 shall apply.

x Common Rules on Competition, Taxation and Approximation of Laws

Title VI of Part Three of the amended EC Treaty contains, under a new and more accurate heading, the provisions previously found in Title I of Part Three on common rules. These rules, unless otherwise specified, relate to all areas of Community activity provided for in the TEC. However, as the TEU-inspired renaming indicates, the common rules fall into three distinct categories, each of which has its own chapter heading within the title. These appear in the treaty in what might be regarded as a descending order of importance with regard to the customs union and the Internal Market. The first chapter of the title contains extensive rules governing competition between undertakings within the EC and state aids (Articles 81–89). The second chapter then addresses the framework in which undertakings operate by providing for the harmonization of taxation (Articles 90–93). The final chapter provides a general set of rules for the approximation of laws in all areas not covered elsewhere in the treaty, notably with regard to the Internal Market (Articles 94–97). Provisions on visa policy inserted by the TEU were revised and incorporated into Title IV by the TA.

Amsterdam also affected the title in five other ways. First, it amended what was Article 100a (now 95) on establishing the Internal Market. Second, it deleted obsolete provisions on dumping and renumbered the sections of Chapter 1 accordingly. Third, former Articles 97 and 100b were repealed. Fourth, five articles were amended as part of the simplification process. And finally, all provisions in the title were renumbered. By contrast, Nice had no direct impact at all despite various proposals to alter provisions governing tax harmonization.

Competition

Title VI's first chapter is dedicated to rules governing competition within the EC. These are of fundamental importance to the operation of the Internal Market and provide the basis for one of the best examples of a truly supra-national policy. This is not to say that the rules apply to all areas of economic activity. Agricultural products listed in Annex I to the TEC are not, for example, covered. Similarly, where governed by the provisions of Title V, transport services are exempt. This does not detract from the significance of the rules which the TEC establishes in the two sections. The first of these comprises rules applying to undertakings, while the second contains provisions governing the use of state aids.

As stated in the principles at the beginning of the TEC, one task of the EC is the establishment of 'a system ensuring that competition in the internal market is not distorted' (Article 3(1)(g)). Article 4(1) TEC helps clarify what type of system is envisaged, noting that economic policy within the EC is to be conducted 'in accordance with the principle of an open market economy with free competition'. The same principle also underpins the role which EMU is to play in supporting the general economic policies of the EC (Article 4(2) TEC). How the principle is to be implemented is determined in the main by the provisions in the two sections of Title VI, Chapter 1.

The first of these sections – rules applying to undertakings – consists of six articles, all of which date back to 1957. While inspired by those contained in the TECSC, they are watered-down versions of these even though their scope is much wider. They cover restrictive practices, monopolies and the public sector, and provide the Commission with overall responsibility for their application.

The section opens with *Article 81* (ex 85) which provides the backbone of the EC's competition regime by listing the restrictive practices (cartels) prohibited as incompatible with the common market – agreements, decisions or concerted practices between undertakings which may prevent, restrict or distort trade between member states. It then provides a non-exhaustive list of such practices which includes price fixing, production control and market-sharing arrangements. Such agreements or decisions are declared automatically void, although in establishing in 1969 the *de minimis* principle the ECJ excluded all agreements which have only an insignificant impact on the market. There are also exemptions laid down in Article 81(3). These are agreements, decisions or concerted practices that contribute to improving the production or distribution of goods or promoting technical or economic progress. In all cases, the consumers must be permitted 'a fair share of the resulting benefit'. Such agreements, decisions and concerted practices are subject to two provisos. They may neither impose restrictions which are not indispensable to the attainment of the objectives mentioned nor create opportunities for competition to be eliminated. Finally, it should be noted that it is not just undertakings from member states which are affected by the prohibition on restrictive practices. Those from non-member states economically active in the EC are affected too, as Damro notes and as any foray into the decisions of the Commission will reveal.

Having addressed restrictive practices, attention is turned in *Article 82* (ex 86) to monopolies. Here, the TEC prohibits the abuse by one or more undertakings of a dominant position within the common market albeit only 'insofar as it may affect trade between Member States'. Guidance on what is understood by abuse is then provided with particular emphasis being placed on the imposition of unfair purchasing or selling prices, limiting production, applying dissimilar conditions to equivalent transactions, and making the conclusion of contracts subject to the acceptance of supplementary and unconnected obligations. There are, unlike in Article 81, no exemptions from the prohibition. This places great importance on how 'abuse' is interpreted and the market defined, a job primarily, as indicated below, for the Commission.

With these principles of competition policy established, a simplified *Article 83* (ex 87) requires that the Council give effect to them through appropriate regulations and directives. Good examples include the various regulations creating block exemptions from the provisions of Article 81. These are adopted by the Council by QMV and in consultation with the EP with emphasis being placed on the Council adopting regulations and directives which provide for fines and periodic penalty payments to ensure compliance, ensure effective supervision, define the scope of Article 81 and 82, define the respective functions of the ECJ and Commission and determine the relationship between national laws, Articles 81–86 TEC and legislation resulting from these. What this means, in effect, is that policy and procedures regarding competition depend very much on secondary legislation and not the TEC itself. Here, Regulation 17/62 is of particular note, as are the various regulations containing 'block exemptions' from Article 81. These placed responsibility for enforcing competition on the Commission with the ECJ providing judicial review. Also of note are the regulations and decisions governing the EC's merger policy. No explicit provision for this is contained in the TEC. Instead merger policy exists thanks to the Commission's endeavours and the ECJ's generous interpretation of the scope of Articles 81 and 86 in the *Continental Can* (1972) and *British American Tobacco* (1987) rulings. Significant reforms are, however, in the pipeline as Goldschmidt and Lanz discuss.

Returning to what is actually in the TEC, we find *Article 84* (ex 88) which deals with review prior to the adoption of regulations and directives in accordance with Article 83. During this period, it is the authorities in the member states that are responsible for ruling on the admissibility of agreements, decisions or concerted practices. In practice, however, the Commission plays the dominant role in competition matters, something envisaged by *Article 85* (ex 89) which charges the Commission with ensuring the application of the principles set out in Articles 81 and 82. Hence, it is responsible for investigating, either on its own initiative or in response to an application from a member state, cases of suspected infringement. Here it is to be assisted by the relevant national authorities, although these cannot grant exemptions since Article 81(3) does not have direct effect.

Throughout the history of the EC the Commission has indeed played a key role in developing and enforcing competition policy. This, however, is due more to the provisions of Regulation 17/62 than to the provisions of Article 85. Indeed, the latter have direct relevance for only a limited number of areas. Hence, the Commission rarely makes use of the infringement procedures detailed in it, using instead, those set out in Regulation 17/62. Moreover, thanks to Regulation 17/62, the Commission enjoys the roles of investigating officer, judge and jury with regard to suspected breaches of Articles 81 and 82. And where breaches are formally established, the Commission may require that restrictive practices or monopolies be terminated and fine undertakings up to €1 million or 10 per cent of their annual worldwide turnover, whichever is higher. Concerns have, however, been expressed over how the Commission has exercised its powers leading to strong German support prior to Amsterdam for establishing an independent European cartel office along the lines of the German *Bundeskartellamt*. The idea found little support among the other member states even though a decision attached to the 1965 Merger Treaty had envisaged such an office.

Finally in Section 1, *Article 86* (ex 90) turns our attention, initially at least, to public-sector undertakings, thus acknowledging that state ownership is not incompatible with the TEC despite references elsewhere to free-market principles. This is later confirmed in Article 295 TEC. In addition, Article 86 covers undertakings to which member states grant special or exclusive rights. Neither these nor 'public undertakings' are defined in the treaty, leaving it to secondary legislation (see Directives 80/723 and 90/388). What the TEC does is prohibit member states from either enacting or maintaining in force any rules governing the undertakings mentioned which are contrary to the TEC's provisions governing either competition (Articles 81–89) or discrimination on grounds of nationality (Article 12). There are no exemptions.

The article then requires that competition rules be applied to national monopolies and undertakings – either public or private – which provide services of 'general economic interest', a term which, as Lane notes, is a creation of the treaty and not one which comes from any of the member states. It nevertheless enjoys favour with those responsible for drafting treaty amendments, featuring as it does in Article 16 TEC. Guidance on its meaning has, however, been provided by the ECJ, which has interpreted it broadly to include, *inter alia*, utilities, postal services, public telephone systems, the maintenance of non-commercially viable air routes, supplementary pension schemes and national public broadcasting services.

Although competition rules must be applied, exemption is possible: competition rules must not obstruct the undertaking from carrying out the tasks entrusted to it. Prior to the 1990s, interpretations of 'obstruct' were restrictive and hence there were no instances where the ECJ found that the conditions of the proviso were met. Since then, as Lane notes, the ECJ has adopted more generous interpretations. Moreover, the Commission has accepted the argument of the German *Länder* that public credit institutions in

Germany are generally exempt, a point noted in Declaration 37 TA and which, according to both von Kyaw and Hrbek, the German government vigorously defended in the 2000 IGC but failed to have inserted into the treaty as the *Länder* representatives wished. Austria and Luxembourg also consider that the declaration applies to the credit institutions in their countries (Declaration No. 1n TA). Clearly this first exemption clause has attracted much attention. The same cannot be said for the second: that the development of trade not be affected to such an extent 'as would be contrary to the interests of the Community'. Indeed, virtually no case law exists on this.

Responsibility for ensuring the application of Article 86 lies unsurprisingly with the Commission, which is empowered by the TEC to address, where necessary, appropriate directives and decisions to the member states. The fact that such a move may involve the Commission in sensitive issues of national policy means that it is used only with caution. Indeed, as Flynn notes, Article 86 generally was 'very much a sleeping provision' of the TEC until the 1990s. And when it was used by the Commission, the legality of most directives and decisions was challenged, albeit usually unsuccessfully, by member states. Caution has also characterized the Commission's handling of its responsibilities under the second section of Chapter 1.

Section 2 deals with state aids and consists of three articles. The first of these, *Article 87* (ex 92), deems all forms of state aid which distort or threaten to distort competition by favouring certain undertakings or the production of certain goods to be incompatible with the Internal Market insofar as they affect trade between member states. This does not mean that the TEC takes a dim view of all state aid. Certain categories are acceptable, as is evident in the various exemptions from the treaty's rules listed in Article 87. First, there are those provided for elsewhere in the TEC, for example in Article 73 on aspects of transport and Article 86(2) on public undertakings. Second, there are those listed in Article 87(2) which are expressly compatible with the Internal Market. Essentially these are aid of a social character granted to individual consumers, aid to repair damage caused by natural disasters and exceptional occurrences and aid granted to Germany to help compensate for the economic disadvantages caused by the division of the country after 1949. The last of these would appear to be rather anomalous, given German unification in 1990, and indeed proposals were made to repeal the provision at Maastricht. The German government objected, however, on the grounds that the economic disadvantages would persist beyond unification. The provision also survived simplification at Amsterdam as did a similar reference in Article 78 TEC.

In addition to these express exemptions from the prohibition contained in paragraph 1, Article 87(3) lists forms of aid which may be considered compatible with the common market. These discretionary exemptions cover a variety of areas: aid to promote economic development, aid to promote the execution of important projects, aid to remedy serious disturbances in the economy of a member state, aid to facilitate the development of 'certain economic activities or certain economic areas', and aid to promote culture and heritage conservation (added by the TEU). In addition, there is a more general provision allowing for the exemption of 'such other categories of aid as may be specified'. It is the responsibility of the Council, acting by QMV, to specify these on a proposal from the Commission.

With such a long list of vaguely defined exemptions, the treaty provides, as Cini and McGowan as well as others note, room not only for flexibility when enforcing policy, but also scope for a good measure of ambiguity. This brings us to *Article 88* (ex 93) which charges the Commission, in co-operation with the member states, with keeping under constant review all systems of state aid existing in the member states. Here, the Commission is required to propose 'appropriate measures' in line with the progressive development and functioning of the common market. In other words, an approved state aid may in time be deemed incompatible with the common market. In such cases and where the Commission finds that a state aid is incompatible with the latter or is being misused, the state is required to abolish or alter the aid within a timeframe determined by the Commission. Of significance here is the centrality of the Commission to the enforcement of the TEC's provisions.

The flexibility with regard to the application of the TEC's provisions on state aid is also seen in the next subparagraph of Article 88(2). This allows the Council, acting by unanimity, to decide on application from a member state that a state aid be considered compatible with the common market provided that it is justified by 'exceptional circumstances'. This rarely used provision can lead to a politicization, as it did in 2002, of the enforcement of state aid policy since any Commission investigation into the compatibility of a state aid with the TEC is automatically suspended. If, however, the Council fails to act within three months of the exemption application, the decision reverts to the Commission.

The centrality of the Commission to state aid policy is underlined in the final paragraph of Article 88, which requires states to notify it of any plans to grant or alter aid. This is not something that the member states have traditionally done with much enthusiasm and remains a major problem for the Commission in implementing state aid policy. The reasons behind the reluctance of member states to notify are many and include not least the fact that state aid is often used to promote domestic political objectives. Moreover, the implications of notification are not always welcome, for the Commission is obliged to judge whether the planned aid is compatible with the common market. Where plans are considered incompatible the Commission is required to initiate immediately the procedures laid down in Article 88(2). At the same time, the affected state is obliged not to put into effect the plans until the Commission has issued its decision.

This brings us to the final competition provision, *Article 89* (ex 94), which calls on the Council to agree via regulations, by QMV, detailed rules governing the application of Articles 87 and 88. Particular emphasis is placed on the Council determining the conditions in which Article 88(3) will apply and the categories of aid exempted from the notification procedure laid down therein. As is usual under the TEC, the Council acts on a proposal from the Commission. Also, since the TEU, it adopts regulations in consultation with the EP. Prior to this amendment to the treaty, the EP had been excluded from decision-making under the competition chapter of Title VI. This should not have caused the EP any undue concern since the first Article 89 regulation was only adopted in 1998. In effect what this means in the light of the other provisions of this section is that state aid policy, as Cini and McGowan argue, is very much a Commission policy and one that, traditionally at least, has been developed independent of the Council and EP.

TITLE *VI* (ex Title V)

COMMON RULES ON COMPETITION, TAXATION AND APPROXIMATION OF LAWS

Chapter 1   Rules on competition

Section 1   Rules applying to undertakings

Article 81 (ex Article 85)

1. The following shall be prohibited as incompatible with the common market: all

agreements between undertakings, decisions by associations of undertakings and concerted practices which may affect trade between Member States and which have as their object or effect the prevention, restriction or distortion of competition within the common market, and in particular those which:

(a) directly or indirectly fix purchase or selling prices or any other trading conditions;

(b) limit or control production, markets, technical development, or investment;

(c) share markets or sources of supply;

(d) apply dissimilar conditions to equivalent transactions with other trading parties, thereby placing them at a competitive disadvantage;

(e) make the conclusion of contracts subject to acceptance by the other parties of supplementary obligations which, by their nature or according to commercial usage, have no connection with the subject of such contracts.

2. Any agreements or decisions prohibited pursuant to this Article shall be automatically void.

3. The provisions of paragraph 1 may, however, be declared inapplicable in the case of:

– any agreement or category of agreements between undertakings;

– any decision or category of decisions by associations of undertakings;

– any concerted practice or category of concerted practices, which contributes to improving the production or distribution of goods or to promoting technical or economic progress, while allowing consumers a fair share of the resulting benefit, and which does not:

(a) impose on the undertakings concerned restrictions which are not indispensable to the attainment of these objectives;

(b) afford such undertakings the possibility of eliminating competition in respect of a substantial part of the products in question.

Article 82 (ex Article 86)

Any abuse by one or more undertakings of a dominant position within the common market or in a substantial part of it shall be prohibited as incompatible with the common market insofar as it may affect trade between Member States.

Such abuse may, in particular, consist in:

(a) directly or indirectly imposing unfair purchase or selling prices or other unfair trading conditions;

(b) limiting production, markets or technical development to the prejudice of consumers;

(c) applying dissimilar conditions to equivalent transactions with other trading parties, thereby placing them at a competitive disadvantage;

(d) making the conclusion of contracts subject to acceptance by the other parties of supplementary obligations which, by their nature or according to commercial usage, have no connection with the subject of such contracts.

Article 83 (ex Article 87 simplified)

1. *The appropriate regulations or directives to give effect to the principles set out in Articles 81 and 82 shall be laid down by the Council, acting by a qualified majority on a proposal from the Commission and after consulting the European Parliament.*

2. The regulations or directives referred to in paragraph 1 shall be designed in particular:

(a) to ensure compliance with the prohibitions laid down in Article 81(1) and in Article 82 by making provision for fines and periodic penalty payments;
(b) to lay down detailed rules for the application of Article 81(3), taking into account the need to ensure effective supervision on the one hand, and to simplify administration to the greatest possible extent on the other;
(c) to define, if need be, in the various branches of the economy, the scope of the provisions of Articles 81 and 82;
(d) to define the respective functions of the Commission and of the Court of Justice in applying the provisions laid down in this paragraph;
(e) to determine the relationship between national laws and the provisions contained in this Section or adopted pursuant to this Article.

Article 84 (ex Article 88)

Until the entry into force of the provisions adopted in pursuance of Article 83, the authorities in Member States shall rule on the admissibility of agreements, decisions and concerted practices and on abuse of a dominant position in the common market in accordance with the law of their country and with the provisions of Article 81, in particular paragraph 3, and of Article 82.

Article 85 (ex Article 89 simplified)

1. Without prejudice to Article 84, the Commission *shall ensure* the application of the principles laid down in Articles 81 and 82. On application by a Member State or on its own initiative, and in co-operation with the competent authorities in the Member States, who shall give it their assistance, the Commission shall investigate cases of suspected infringement of these principles. If it finds that there has been an infringement, it shall propose appropriate measures to bring it to an end.

2. If the infringement is not brought to an end, the Commission shall record such infringement of the principles in a reasoned decision. The Commission may publish its decision and authorise Member States to take the measures, the conditions and details of which it shall determine, needed to remedy the situation.

Article 86 (ex Article 90)

1. In the case of public undertakings and undertakings to which Member States grant special or exclusive rights, Member States shall neither enact nor maintain in force any measure contrary to the rules contained in this Treaty, in particular to those rules provided for in Article 12 and Articles 81 to 89.

2. Undertakings entrusted with the operation of services of general economic interest or having the character of a revenue-producing monopoly shall be subject to the rules contained in this Treaty, in particular to the rules on competition, insofar as the application of such rules does not obstruct the performance, in law or in fact, of the particular tasks assigned to them. The development of trade must not be affected to such an extent as would be contrary to the interests of the Community.

3. The Commission shall ensure the application of the provisions of this Article and shall, where necessary, address appropriate directives or decisions to Member States.

Section 2   Aids granted by States

Article 87 (ex Article 92 simplified)

1. Save as otherwise provided in this Treaty, any aid granted by a Member State or through State resources in any form whatsoever which distorts or threatens to distort competition by favouring certain undertakings or the production of certain goods shall, insofar as it affects trade between Member States, be incompatible with the common market.

2. The following shall be compatible with the common market:

(a) aid having a social character, granted to individual consumers, provided that such aid is granted without discrimination related to the origin of the products concerned;

(b) aid to make good the damage caused by natural disasters or exceptional occurrences;

(c) aid granted to the economy of certain areas of the Federal Republic of Germany affected by the division of Germany, insofar as such aid is required in order to compensate for the economic disadvantages caused by that division.

3. The following may be considered to be compatible with the common market:

(a) aid to promote the economic development of areas where the standard of living is abnormally low or where there is serious underemployment;

(b) aid to promote the execution of an important project of common European interest or to remedy a serious disturbance in the economy of a Member State;

(c) aid to facilitate the development of certain economic activities or of certain economic areas, where such aid does not adversely affect trading conditions to an extent contrary to the common interest;

(d) aid to promote culture and heritage conservation where such aid does not affect trading conditions and competition in the Community to an extent that is contrary to the common interest;

(e) such other categories of aid as may be specified by decision of the Council acting by a qualified majority on a proposal from the Commission.

Article 88 (ex Article 93)

1. The Commission shall, in co-operation with Member States, keep under constant review all systems of aid existing in those States. It shall propose to the latter any appropriate measures required by the progressive development or by the functioning of the common market.

2. If, after giving notice to the parties concerned to submit their comments, the Commission finds that aid granted by a State or through State resources is not compatible with the common market having regard to Article 87, or that such aid is being misused, it shall decide that the State concerned shall abolish or alter such aid within a period of time to be determined by the Commission.

If the State concerned does not comply with this decision within the prescribed time, the Commission or any other interested State may, in derogation from the provisions of Articles 226 and 227, refer the matter to the Court of Justice direct.

On application by a Member State, the Council may, acting unanimously, decide that aid which that State is granting or intends to grant shall be considered to be compatible with the common market, in derogation from the provisions of Article 87 or from the regulations provided for in Article 89, if such a decision is justified by exceptional circumstances. If, as regards the aid in question, the Commission has already initiated the procedure provided for in the first subparagraph of this paragraph, the fact that the State concerned has made its application to the Council shall have the effect of suspending that procedure until the Council has made its attitude known.

If, however, the Council has not made its attitude known within three months of the said application being made, the Commission shall give its decision on the case.

3. The Commission shall be informed, in sufficient time to enable it to submit its comments, of any plans to grant or alter aid. If it considers that any such plan is not compatible with the common market having regard to Article 87, it shall without delay initiate the procedure provided for in paragraph 2. The Member State concerned shall not put its proposed measures into effect until this procedure has resulted in a final decision.

Article 89 (ex Article 94)

The Council, acting by a qualified majority on a proposal from the Commission and after consulting the European Parliament, may make any appropriate regulations for the application of Articles 87 and 88 and may in particular determine the conditions in which Article 88(3) shall apply and the categories of aid exempted from this procedure.

Taxation

The second chapter of Title VI currently contains four articles relating to taxation (Articles 90–93, ex 95–99). Originally there were five articles, but thanks to simplification at Amsterdam an obsolete one on turnover taxes was repealed. Amsterdam also simplified Article 90 (ex 95). Prior to this ex Article 99 (now 93) had been replaced under the SEA then undergone a minor change to facilitate EcoSoc consultation at Maastricht. Had the Commission and most member-state governments had their way at the 2000 IGC, then Article 93 would have undergone significant reform and a protocol to the TEC added to allow for more QMV and an extension of its coverage to direct taxation. Resolute opposition from the Irish, Luxembourg and UK governments ensured that no changes were eventually introduced at Nice. Chapter 2 today is therefore identical to how it was once Amsterdam came into force.

The aim of the chapter's provisions is to promote fair competition within the EC by eliminating as far as possible discrimination against goods imported from other member states due to differences in national regimes covering indirect taxation (e.g. VAT, excise duty, registration charges, road taxes etc.). They thus complement the provisions governing the free movement of goods, notably Article 25 (ex 12). This is no more true than in the case of *Article 90* (ex 95) which prevents member states from abusing national tax-raising powers to discriminate against imports from other member states. Any internal taxation may not be in excess of that imposed directly or indirectly on similar domestic products. Reverse discrimination – where internal taxation on domestic products is higher than imported products – is not, however, ruled out. Furthermore, no internal taxation creating indirect protection on products from other member states may be imposed.

Having established what is barred, the provisions of *Article 91* (ex 96) require that the repayment of excess internal taxation does not exceed that imposed. This is to counter disguised export subsidies. As Weatherill and Beaumont note, however, this is as far as the TEC goes with regard to special domestic provisions for exports since Article 90 does not explicitly cover these. In its rulings, the ECJ has tended though to extend the application of Article 90 to exports, arguing that imposing higher indirect taxes on exports discourages free trade and cannot be permitted. The use of tax disincentives to prevent the export of scarce commodities is therefore contrary to EC law.

Then, *Article 92* (ex 98) prohibits the granting of remissions and repayments in respect of exports where indirect taxation, with the exception of turnover taxes, is concerned. Furthermore, the imposition of countervailing charges, unless approved for a limited period by the Council acting by QMV, is prohibited.

This leaves us with the most contentious provisions of Chapter 2, those in *Article 93* (ex 99) concerning the harmonization of indirect taxation. These as noted above received much attention at Nice as a majority of member states sought to move from the existing unanimity requirement to QMV for the adoption of relevant measures. What Article 93 does is to empower the Council on a Commission proposal to adopt 'provisions' for the harmonization of national legislation concerning turnover taxes, excise duties and 'other forms of indirect taxation'. All provisions are to be adopted by unanimity and following consultation of the EP and EcoSoc. Moreover, provisions can only be adopted to the extent that harmonization is 'necessary to ensure the establishment and functioning of the internal market within the time limit laid down in Article 14'.

In other words, the harmonization of indirect taxes is not regarded as automatic but rests on essentially political and economic considerations. With member states each having a veto, whether harmonization is 'necessary' is a matter of interpretation for each national government. All the same, pressure for harmonization has been increasing, not least because the time limit referred to – 31 December 1992 – has long passed. Retaining the reference, which some say should have been deleted with simplification at Amsterdam, helps to reinforce arguments that the harmonization of indirect taxes is integral to the realization of the free movement of goods and services and is long overdue. Such arguments have been behind efforts to simplify decision-making rules.

However, tax harmonization is undoubtedly one of the most sensitive areas of integration, as the lead-up to Nice showed. Even those open to a shift to QMV were generally willing to see unanimity abandoned only in a very limited number of well-defined areas. Moreover, reflecting sensitivities about EC involvement on taxation issues, Nice actually introduced one provision – Article 157(3) on industry – which expressly forbids the introduction of measures containing tax provisions. Yet concerns persist about the incompleteness of the Internal Market, particularly in the light of the launch of EMU in 1999. Hence, debates over whether QMV should be used for tax harmonization will continue. And as some commentators have argued, the determination of some member states to avoid the EC adopting rules on tax harmonization may see others resorting to enhanced co-operation to overcome persistent national vetoes.

Chapter 2   Tax provisions

Article 90 (ex Article 95 simplified)

No Member State shall impose, directly or indirectly, on the products of other Member States any internal taxation of any kind in excess of that imposed directly or indirectly on similar domestic products.

Furthermore, no Member State shall impose on the products of other Member States any internal taxation of such a nature as to afford indirect protection to other products.

Article 91 (ex Article 96)

Where products are exported to the territory of any Member State, any repayment of internal taxation shall not exceed the internal taxation imposed on them whether directly or indirectly.

Article 92 (ex Article 98)

In the case of charges other than turnover taxes, excise duties and other forms of indirect taxation, remissions and repayments in respect of exports to other Member States may not be granted and countervailing charges in respect of imports from Member States may not be imposed unless the measures contemplated have been previously approved for a limited period by the Council acting by a qualified majority on a proposal from the Commission.

Article 93 (ex Article 99)

The Council shall, acting unanimously on a proposal from the Commission and after consulting the European Parliament and the Economic and Social Committee, adopt provisions for the harmonisation of legislation concerning turnover taxes, excise duties and other forms of indirect taxation to the extent that such harmonisation is necessary to ensure the establishment and the functioning of the internal market within the time-limit laid down in Article 14.

The Approximation of Laws

The purpose of Title VI, Chapter 3 is to provide for the approximation, where deemed necessary for the functioning of both the common market and the Internal Market and not provided for elsewhere in the treaty, of the laws of the member states. It therefore supplements provisions on approximation and harmonization found elsewhere in the TEC, notably where the free movement of goods, services, capital and workers is concerned. Understandably, the provisions contained in the chapter have been of considerable significance for the development of the EC. Their use has also attracted much attention among Eurosceptics and member states reluctant to entertain the harmonization and approximation of national legislation.

Today, the chapter consists of only four Articles (Articles 94–97, ex 100–102) as compared to three originally and seven following insertions by the SEA and the TEU specifying new areas for the approximation of laws, such as the Internal Market and visas. Since then, Amsterdam has repealed three articles, two (ex Articles 100c and 100d) as a consequence of the new provisions covering the area of freedom, security and justice in Title IV, and one (ex Article 100b) through simplification. Amsterdam also amended Article 95 (ex 100a). Nice, meanwhile, had no impact, although for much of the 2000 IGC Article 94 appeared set for repeal in the light of proposed changes to Article 93. These were eventually abandoned.

The purpose of *Article 94* (ex 100) is to provide the EC with an express competence to approximate the 'laws, regulations or administrative provisions' of the member states where these directly affect the establishment or functioning of the common market. Any approximation is to be carried out through directives proposed by the Commission and adopted by the Council acting unanimously. Since the TEU, the Council has been obliged to consult the EP and EcoSoc in all cases. In the past, Article 94 was heavily used, for example to adopt the 1975 directive on the equal treatment of men and women. However, with the insertion into the TEC over time of more policy-specific articles, use has decreased, with the EC generally adopting approximating measures under the new articles. This, according to Moravscik, has come in spite of opposition from the Commission, which views the dedicated titles as providing implicit or not explicit constraints on EC action. One set of noticeable exceptions are the directives on the European works councils and parental leave adopted under the Social Chapter in 1994 and 1996, respectively. Article 100 was used to apply them to the United Kingdom when it agreed to the repeal of the Protocol on social policy at Amsterdam.

By contrast, extensive use is still made of *Article 95* (ex 100a), which first appeared in the TEC thanks to the SEA. To Weiler this was the single most important provision of the SEA, to Bradley it was the 'star feature' providing the basis for harmonizing legislation facilitating the completion of the Internal Market on the basis of QMV. Others such as Streit and Müssler have been less enthusiastic, viewing it as heralding 'a breakthrough for integration by intervention'.

The article has since been amended both by the TEU and, more extensively, by Amsterdam. In its first paragraph we have provisions governing its purpose: to provide a derogation from Article 94 where measures concerning the establishment and functioning of the Internal Market, as Article 14 TEC notes, are concerned. The derogation involves the Council adopting measures – in other words, not just directives but also regulations – by QMV and through co-decision with the EP. EcoSoc is also consulted. In formulating and implementing proposals full regard is to be paid to the welfare requirements of animals thanks to the UK-inspired Protocol on protection and welfare of animals adopted at Amsterdam. Declaration No. 22 TA also requires the needs of persons with a disability to be taken into consideration.

There are limits to the application of Article 95. As paragraph 2 makes clear, it may not apply to fiscal measures, measures concerning the free movement of people and measures relating to the rights and interests of employed persons. Such measures can be adopted under Article 94, although harmonization of certain aspects of each is possible under other TEC provisions: indirect taxation (Article 93), free movement of workers (Articles 40, 42, 44, 46, 47 and 52) and social policy (Article 137).

In adopting measures under Article 95, the Commission must ensure that proposals assume a high level of protection where they cover health, safety, environmental protection and consumer protection. Such a provision complements statements found elsewhere in the TEC on these matters (see Articles 6, 152 and 153). For some member states this did not go far enough. Hence, at Amsterdam reference was added to the need for the Commission to take into account any new developments based on scientific facts. Furthermore, the EP and the Council were also required to play a role in ensuring high levels of protection.

Amsterdam also introduced changes to paragraph 4 which concerns the maintenance of higher national levels of protection once a harmonization measure has been adopted. It also added four new paragraphs (5–8) in an attempt, as McDonagh notes, to strike a delicate balance between the right of member states to maintain higher standards and the need to ensure that these do not constitute a means of arbitrary discrimination or a disguised restriction on trade. Moreover, the changes represented an attempt to overcome some of the poor initial drafting of the article which had so confused lawyers. Basically, where a state – often one outvoted in Council – wishes to maintain national provisions for reasons concerning the environment or working environment or on grounds of major need in accordance with Article 30 TEC (e.g. public morality, public policy, public security, health, protection of national treasures), it may do so provided it notifies the Commission of the reasons. Interestingly, there is no reference to consumer protection. Likewise, a member state may introduce national provisions provided they are based on 'new' scientific evidence and are notified to the Commission.

On receipt of notifications the Commission has six months – although this can normally be extended for a further period of six months by the Commission – to either approve or reject the national provisions on the grounds that they represent arbitrary or disguised restrictions to trade or constitute an obstacle to the functioning of the Internal Market. It can also decide to propose an adaptation to the measure. As Langrish notes, this qualifies somewhat the relaxation of Internal Market rules in favour of protecting the environment. If no Commission decision is forthcoming, the measures are deemed to have been approved. Finally, where a member state raises a specific problem related to public health, the Commission is required to consider immediately whether 'appropriate' measures should be proposed. As Ehlermann notes, this rules out unilateral action by member states with regard to public health.

The remaining two paragraphs of Article 95 then return to provisions originally inserted into ex Article 100a by the SEA. The first allows for the Commission or a member state, where it suspects that a member state is making improper use of the previous provisions, to bring the matter before the ECJ. The second then calls for harmonization measures, where appropriate, to include safeguard clauses permitting member states to take 'provisional measures', albeit subject to EC overview, on non-economic grounds covered by Article 30 TEC.

This brings us to *Article 96* (ex 101) concerning distortions to competition in the common market resulting from different national laws, regulations or administrative actions. Here, where the Commission believes that such distortion needs to be eliminated, it is required to consult the relevant member states. If such consultation does not lead to an agreement eliminating the distortion the matter is passed to the Council which, on a Commission proposal, issues necessary directives by QMV. The Commission and Council may also take other appropriate measures provided for in the TEC. The tendency of the Commission, however, is to refer national measures impeding trade in goods to the ECJ.

Finally, we have *Article 97* (ex 102) which deals with potential distortion to competition resulting from the adoption or amendment of a national law, regulation or administrative action. Where the member state believes distortion may result it is required to consult with the Commission which will then recommend measures to avoid distortion. If the member state fails to comply with the recommendation, then the other member states are not obliged to amend their own national provisions in order to eliminate distortion. Moreover, Article 96 will not apply where the distortion affects only the member state which has ignored the Commission's recommendation.

Chapter 3   Approximation of laws

Article 94 (ex Article 100)

The Council shall, acting unanimously on a proposal from the Commission and after consulting the European Parliament and the Economic and Social Committee, issue directives for the approximation of such laws, regulations or administrative provisions of the Member States as directly affect the establishment or functioning of the common market.

Article 95 (ex Article 100a)

1. By way of derogation from Article 94 and save where otherwise provided in this Treaty, the following provisions shall apply for the achievement of the objectives set out in Article 14. The Council shall, acting in accordance with the procedure referred to in Article 251 and after consulting the Economic and Social Committee, adopt the measures for the approximation of the provisions laid down by law, regulation or administrative action in Member States which have as their object the establishment and functioning of the internal market.

2. Paragraph 1 shall not apply to fiscal provisions, to those relating to the free movement of persons nor to those relating to the rights and interests of employed persons.

3. The Commission, in its proposals envisaged in paragraph 1 concerning health, safety, environmental protection and consumer protection, will take as a base a high level of protection, **taking account in particular of any new development based on scientific facts. Within their respective powers, the European Parliament and the Council will also seek to achieve this objective.**

4. If, after the adoption *by the Council* or by the Commission *of a harmonisation measure*, a Member State deems it necessary to **maintain** national provisions on grounds of major needs referred to in Article 30, or relating to the protection of the environment or the working environment, it shall notify the Commission of these provisions **as well as the grounds for maintaining them.**

5. **Moreover, without prejudice to paragraph 4, if, after the adoption by the Council or by the Commission of a harmonisation measure, a Member State deems it necessary to introduce national provisions based on new scientific evidence relating to the protection of the environment or the working environment on grounds of a problem specific to that Member State arising after the adoption of the harmonisation measure, it shall notify the Commission of the envisaged provisions as well as the grounds for introducing them.**

6. The Commission shall, **within six months of the notifications as referred to in paragraphs 4 and 5, approve or reject the national provisions involved** after having verified *whether or not* they are a means of arbitrary discrimination or a disguised restriction on trade between Member States **and whether or not they shall constitute an obstacle to the functioning of the internal market.**

In the absence of a decision by the Commission within this period the national provisions referred to in paragraphs 4 and 5 shall be deemed to have been approved.

When justified by the complexity of the matter and in the absence of danger for human health, the Commission may notify the Member State concerned that the period referred to in this paragraph may be extended for a further period of up to six months.

7. **When, pursuant to paragraph 6, a Member State is authorised to maintain or introduce national provisions derogating from a harmonisation measure, the Commission shall immediately examine whether to propose an adaptation to that measure.**

8. When a Member State raises a specific problem on public health in a field which has been the subject of prior harmonisation measures, it shall bring it to the attention of the Commission which shall immediately examine whether to propose appropriate measures to the Council.

9. By way of derogation from the procedure laid down in Articles 226 and 227, the Commission and any Member State may bring the matter directly before the Court of Justice if it considers that another Member State is making improper use of the powers provided for in this Article.

10. The harmonisation measures referred to above shall, in appropriate cases, include a safeguard clause authorising the Member States to take, for one or more of the non-economic reasons referred to in Article 30, provisional measures subject to a Community control procedure.

Article 96 (ex Article 101 simplified)

Where the Commission finds that a difference between the provisions laid down by law, regulation or administrative action in Member States is distorting the conditions of competition in the common market and that the resultant distortion needs to be eliminated, it shall consult the Member States concerned.

If such consultation does not result in an agreement eliminating the distortion in question, the Council shall, on a proposal from the Commission, *acting by a qualified majority*, issue the necessary directives. The Commission and the Council may take any other appropriate measures provided for in this Treaty.

Article 97 (ex Article 102)

1. Where there is a reason to fear that the adoption or amendment of a provision laid down by law, regulation or administrative action may cause distortion within the meaning of Article 96, a Member State desiring to proceed therewith shall consult the Commission. After consulting the Member States, the Commission shall recommend to the States concerned such measures as may be appropriate to avoid the distortion in question.

2. If a State desiring to introduce or amend its own provisions does not comply with the recommendation addressed to it by the Commission, other Member States shall not be required, in pursuance of Article 96, to amend their own provisions in order to eliminate such distortion. If the Member State which has ignored the recommendation of the Commission causes distortion detrimental only to itself, the provisions of Article 96 shall not apply.

xi Economic and Monetary Union

The TEU's most significant impact on the EC was to make the establishment of Economic and Monetary Union (EMU) a key objective. To this end, EMU was not only promoted as a major means for achieving the EU's objectives (Article 2 TEU), but was also declared a foundation of the EC (Article 2 TEC). The commitment to EMU was further underlined by the insertion of 24 new articles, into the TEC. These appear in Title VII and govern not just economic and monetary policy within the EC but also preparations both for

EMU and for its operation. Moreover, they contain the timetable used for establishing EMU on 1 January 1999 and provisions setting up key institutions such as the European Central Bank (ECB) and the European System of Central Banks (ESCB).

And this is not all. The enormity and complexity of the whole EMU operation is reflected in the fact that the TEU introduced 11 new protocols and seven declarations related to the project. Thankfully, Amsterdam failed to add to these, although it did of course renumber all but one of the provisions as well as the Title, formerly Title VI. But interestingly, although the name of the single currency – the euro (€) – had been agreed, it was not inserted into the TEC in place of the existing 'ECU'. Nor did Nice venture to change this, by now, obvious anomaly in the treaty. Likewise, it did not delete any of the provisions governing the period prior to EMU's launch on 1 January 1999 many of which were now technically redundant. Nice did, however, introduce some changes to decision-making, along with three related declarations and an addition to a statute.

In Title VII we find, therefore, provisions (Articles 98–124) which for the most part are relative newcomers to the TEC and which in most cases were the product of extensive negotiation, primarily at Maastricht, as Dyson and Featherstone show. This explains in part their complexity. We should also bear in mind that in providing for EMU the TEU created new institutions, all of which required detailed provisions particularly given the important roles they were being assigned. And then there were those member states – Denmark and the United Kingdom – which were unwilling to be bound by any obligation to participate in EMU. They needed derogations written into the treaty. Consequently, in Title VII we have at almost 7,500 words, by far the longest title found in the TEC. Comprising chapters covering policy, institutions and transitional provisions, the title is to many readers also one of the treaty's most confusing. Indeed, it does not lend itself to the approach generally adopted in the *Guide* of article-by-article commentary. Hence, in discussing Title VII we adopt for ease of comprehension a more thematic approach reflecting not just the fact that EMU is up and running, but also that not all provisions apply to all member states.

First, though, it is worth recalling that not all the EMU provisions owe their existence to the TEU. Some actually date back, at least in part, to when the TEC was signed in 1957, although as Middlemas notes, the articles on monetary integration and co-operation at the time were essentially 'rather pale and dim'. These were contained in a title on economic policy. What remains of these concern: the principle that EC member states should regard their economic policies as a matter of common concern and co-ordinate them (*Article 99(1)*, ex 103(1) and originally 6(1)); the establishment and some tasks of the now defunct Monetary Committee (*Article 114*, ex 109c(1), originally 105(2) TEC); direct intervention where severe difficulties arise (*Article 100*, ex 103(1), originally 103(2) and (4) TEC); and remedial action in the case of balance of payments difficulties (*Articles 119–120*, ex 109h–109i, originally Articles 108–109 TEC). Other provisions find their origins in the Single European Act (SEA) which established in the TEC the first-ever reference to 'economic and monetary union' by placing the words in brackets as part of the pre-TEU title of Title II, Chapter 1, 'Co-operation in Economic and Monetary Policy'. Due at least in part to this, the ECJ in *Opinion 1/91* (1991) inferred that EMU was a *de facto* objective of the EC.

The impact of the SEA can also be seen in the reference to the European Monetary System (EMS) in *Article 124* (ex 109m, originally 102a(1) TEC). However, the SEA did not go so far as to integrate the 1979 statute governing the EMS into the TEC either fully or as an annex. The treaty base regarding EMU matters remained small, leaving it to the TEU to introduce the overwhelming majority of provisions. In doing so, the TEU also provided for a fundamental restructuring of the original title dedicated to economic policy.

Title VII, 'Economic and Monetary Policy', is, in its current form, divided into four chapters. The first of these consists of seven articles dealing with economic policy within the EC (Articles 98–104). The three remaining chapters – 'Monetary Policy', 'Institutional Provisions' and 'Transitional Provisions' – are devoted to monetary matters (Articles 105–124). This apparent imbalance in treaty space, dedicated on the one hand to economic policy and on the other to monetary matters, is a reflection of how misleading the notion is of the EC as an economic and monetary union. For although the idea of economic union is implied in the commitment to the establishment of EMU, the EC is far from being a full economic union as such. The TEU provided for monetary union in the sense of a single currency, a European Central Bank and a single monetary policy, but was far more restrained in the powers which it conferred on the EC for the conduct of economic policy. To some, transferring to the supra-national EC economic policy-making competence would have required the granting of independent budgetary authority and by implication tax-raising and increased legislative powers. This was simply too much for the member states. Hence, the actual conduct of economic policy remains in the hands of the member states. As Seidel notes, the provisions on economic union may restrict the sovereignty of the member states, but they do not create a sovereign power at the EC level.

Also of particular note with regard to Title VII is the complexity of what results from its provisions. Owing to the existence of opt-out protocols and the fact that member states can only participate fully in EMU if they meet various entry criteria, not all provisions apply to all member states. In other words, we are faced with an area of EC activity in which there is so-called 'flexibility'. At a basic level, the difference is between those 12 member states currently participating fully in EMU and those which are outside the so-called 'eurozone': Denmark, Sweden and the United Kingdom. These in treaty language are referred to as 'member states with a derogation'. This group can be further divided though into those which have formal opt-outs from full EMU (Denmark and the United Kingdom), and those which have failed to meet the criteria for participation. At present, only Sweden is in such a position. Come enlargement, however, it can be anticipated that most, if not all, acceding states will find themselves, initially at least, in this notionally transitional category. Approaching Title VII with these three groups in mind facilitates an understanding of the treaty's EMU provisions.

Before turning to the first of these three groups, we need to consider those provisions of Title VII which apply to all member states irrespective of their status within the EMU process. The first set of these can be found in Chapter 1 on economic policy. As already noted, much of the responsibility for action here remains with the member states. They are, however, obliged to pursue policy with a view to contributing to the achievement of the EC's objectives as defined in Article 2 (see *Article 98*, ex 102a). There is also a clear emphasis on mutual co-ordination and adherence to broad guidelines adopted by the Council by QMV (Declaration No. 3 TEU). Such guidelines are adopted following agreement reached by the European Council with economic and finance (ECOFIN) ministers in attendance (*Article 99(1–2)*, ex 103(1–2), also Declaration No. 4 TEU).

Moreover, as provided for in *Article 99(3–5)* (ex 103(3–5)), economic convergence and member states' compliance with the guidelines are to be regularly monitored by the Council with reports being presented to the EP. Indeed, where a member state's economic policy is considered by the Commission to be inconsistent with the Council's guidelines, the Council may, by QMV, make and publicize a non-legally binding recommendation to the member state concerned. The aim of this process of peer review – the mechanisms of which are adopted via the co-operation procedure – is to compel member states not only to meet their obligations with regard to the EU's economic objectives if they are part of the eurozone, but also in preparing for EMU. Commitment to the process was underlined in 1997 with the adoption of the Stability and Growth Pact requiring member states to prove annually that their budgetary situation provides the basis for price stability and sustainable growth (see V v). Failure to meet obligations first led to a reprimand in February 2001 when Ireland was criticized for cutting taxes and sharply increasing public spending, a public warning designed to promote the international credibility of the euro and the EMU set-up.

The economic objectives of the EU and the economic policy tasks which the EC is to fulfil are not specifically mentioned in Chapter 1. Instead, the former are to be found in Article 2 (ex B) TEU which lists them, post-Amsterdam, as promoting 'economic and social progress and a high level of employment' and achieving 'balanced and sustainable development'. EMU, alongside the Internal Market and the strengthening of economic and social cohesion, is seen as a key means to these ends, a point underlined in Article 2 TEC which sets as the EC's tasks, *inter alia*, the promotion of 'a harmonious, balanced and sustainable development of economic activities . . . sustainable and non-inflationary growth, a high degree of competitiveness and convergence of economic performance'. In pursuing these tasks, the EC is required to act in accordance with certain principles. These are laid down in *Article 98* (ex 102a) and Article 4 TEC and include stable prices, sound public finances and monetary conditions, a sustainable balance of payments, an efficient allocation of resources, and the principle of an open market economy with free competition. Article 4 TEC also declares that economic policy is to be based on 'the close co-ordination of Member States' economic policies, on the internal market and on the definition of common objectives'.

More specifically, the first paragraph of *Article 104* (ex 104c) obliges member states to avoid excessive government deficits. One member state, however, is exempt from this. Under *Article 116(4)* (ex 109e(4)), the United Kingdom as part of its opt-out is only obliged to 'endeavour' to avoid such deficits. The emphasis on budgetary discipline is also reflected in the powers of the Commission to monitor member states' performance.

In doing so, it proceeds on the basis of the reference values contained in the Protocol on excessive deficit procedure as noted in Article 104(2). The protocol has since been supplemented, but not replaced as envisaged in Article 104(14), by a Council regulation. This was adopted as part of the Stability and Growth Pact in 1997. Hence, planned or actual government deficit is to be no greater than 3%, and total government debt should not exceed 60% of the member state's GDP. If a member state fails, or risks failing, to fulfil one or both of these criteria, the Commission produces a report and forwards it to the Economic and Financial Committee provided for in Article 114(2) for an opinion. The Commission can then forward an opinion to the Council which, if it decides that an excessive deficit exists, may, acting by QMV and without the affected state participating, make recommendations to the member state concerned to rectify the situation (see Article 104(3–7 and 12)). If the member state fails to reduce its budget deficit sufficiently, the Council may under Article 104(8) make its original recommendations public. However, the member state concerned may not be referred to the Court of Justice under either Article 169 or 170 as a result of non-compliance (see Article 104(10)). Persistent failure to address the deficit can, though, lead to the Council specifying, except in the case of the United Kingdom, deficit reduction measures under Article 104(9). And for as long as the member state concerned does not comply with the Council's requirements, Article 104(11) provides for additional measures including fines to be imposed. All decisions are communicated to the EP. As for how decisions are reached within the Council in respect of Article 104, a two-thirds weighted majority without the affected state participating is required (see Article 104(13)).

The strong emphasis on budgetary discipline is underlined by other provisions of Chapter 1. *Article 101* (ex 104) thus prohibits national central banks and the European Central Bank from extending overdraft facilities to EC institutions, governments and public authorities. Only publicly owned credit institutions are exempt. Furthermore, except where based on 'prudential considerations', privileged access to financial institutions is also prohibited (*Article 102*, ex 104a), although the Azores and Madeira are allowed to benefit from an interest-free credit facility with the Banco de Portugal (see Protocol on Portugal). And then there is *Article 103* (ex 104b), which removes EC and member-state liability for the assumption of financial commitments of government or public bodies, except where these commitments involve the joint execution of specific projects. This constitutes the so-called 'no-bail-out' rule. Definitions for the application of the article are adopted using the co-operation procedure and thus involve the EP, whose role was briefly under threat during the 2000 IGC when consideration was given to abandoning the co-operation procedure and replacing it with the Council simply consulting the EP. The proposal was not taken up.

Finally with regard to Chapter 1 and economic policy, we have *Article 100* (ex 103a), which allows the Council to decide on measures to be adopted, including direct financial assistance, where a member state is in economic difficulties arising either from the supply of certain products or from exceptional circumstances beyond its control. Originally the Council always acted unanimously except when using QMV where the circumstances were caused by natural disasters. Nice extended QMV to all decisions covered by the article. Thanks to the insistence of the UK government, it also confirmed that decisions must comply with the financial perspectives of the EU and inter-institutional agreements on budgetary discipline (Declaration No. 6 TN), thus ensuring that any financial assistance is compatible with the 'no-bail-out' rule in Article 103.

With the economic policy provisions of Title VII discussed, we can now turn to monetary policy as it applies to all member states irrespective of whether they are participating fully in EMU or not. A first provision applicable would appear to be *Article 114(1)* (ex 109c(1)) governing the Monetary Committee. This committee was established in 1958 and charged with promoting monetary policy co-ordination 'to the full extent necessary for the functioning of the common market' and advising on the monetary and financial situation in the EC. However, it ceased operations at the end of 1998 and was replaced by the Economic and Financial Committee (EFC) provided for in *Article 114(2–4)* (ex 109c(2–4)). Its role is very similar to that of its predecessor: issuing opinions; keeping under review the economic situation (as opposed to the monetary situation, which is now the responsibility of the ECB and ESCB) and the financial situation in the member states; reporting regularly to the Council and Commission; assisting in preparations for ECOFIN councils; and examining at least annually the situation regarding capital movements and the freedom of payments. In practice, it also oversees the Stability and Growth Pact and prepares meetings of the Eurogroup (see below). After the ECB's Governing Council, it is probably the second most powerful unelected committee in the EU. Similarities with the Monetary Committee can also be found in the EFC's composition – no more than two appointees per member state and from the Commission – except that up to two appointees of the ECB now participate. Detailed provisions on the composition are to be adopted by the Council after consulting the ECB and EFC. Finally, the EFC assumes earlier monitoring roles of the Monetary Committee with regard to the monetary and financial situation in those member states outside the eurozone.

Beyond these institutional provisions, all member states are obliged to observe the provisions governing the first two stages of the process which led to EMU on 1 January 1999. The first stage actually predated the TEU beginning on 1 July 1990 and involved obligations then based on other TEC articles and Council Decisions and now laid down in: *Article 116(2)* (ex 109e(2)) on the free movement of capital within the EC, the removal of all restrictions on payments, and the adoption by member states of multiannual programmes designed to promote the lasting economic convergence with a view to economic and monetary union, paying particular attention to the maintenance of price stability and sound public finances; *Article 114(1)* (ex 109c(1)) on the promotion of policy co-ordination among the member states' policies in these and other areas necessary for the effective functioning of the Internal Market; and *Article 124* (ex 109m) on member states treating their exchange rate policies, as they had been obliged to do so since the SEA, as a matter of common concern, taking into account co-operation within the EMS. The TEU also tightened up surveillance procedures. Hence, under *Article 116(2)* (ex 109e(2)) the Council was charged with assessing progress made towards achieving economic and monetary convergence and in the implementation of EC law relating to the completion of the Internal Market. Finally during Stage I, *Article 119* (ex 109h) and *Article 120* (ex 109i), both of which, as noted above, date back to 1957, allow member states with balance of payments difficulties to be offered assistance. The member state concerned may also take necessary protective measures.

All the obligations of Stage I still apply to 'member states with derogations'. These states, unless expressly exempted, are also obliged to adhere to the requirements of Stage II which began on 1 January 1994 in line with *Article 116(1–2)* (ex 109e(1–2)) and which involved intensified preparations for EMU. Hence, national central banks were to be independent (see *Article 109*, ex 108 and *Article 116(5)*, ex 109e(5)) and states other than those with opt-outs had to pursue policies with a view to meeting the so-called convergence criteria (see below).

So, now to the provisions regulating those states which are full members of EMU, that is to say those eleven states which established the single currency area, the 'eurozone', when the single currency, the euro (€), was launched on 1 January 1999, plus Greece which joined on 1 January 2001. For these twelve states, the policy provisions of Chapter 2 on monetary policy and the institutional provisions of Chapter 3 are those which primarily apply. As far as policy is concerned, the eurozone-12 in entering the final stage of EMU irrevocably fixed their exchange rates and committed themselves to the rapid introduction of a single currency. Early decisions on the latter were taken on the basis of unanimity in accordance with *Article 123(4)* (ex 109l(4)) and included the decision to move from participating national currencies to the single currency as from 1 January 2002. Nice altered the unanimity requirement to a two-thirds majority.

According to the Treaty, and in the absence of agreement on a more attractive name at Maastricht, the single currency is to be the 'ECU', the abbreviation of the European Currency Unit, which existed as part of EMU's precursor, the European Monetary System (EMS) established 1979.* However, it was agreed in December 1995, and very much at Germany's insistence, to drop 'ECU' and call the single currency

---

*This depends very much on which version of the TEU is read. Most versions, including those which have appeared in the *Official Journal*, use 'ECU'. That issued jointly by the Council and Commission in February 1992 mistakenly uses 'ecu' although a list of corrigenda was later provided. More significant, however, was the use of 'écu' in the French government's versions of the TEU distributed countrywide in advance of the referendum in September 1992. An 'écu', it should be recalled, was an old French coin.

the euro.* Subsequently the symbol of the euro – €– was adopted, though no amendments have been made to the TEC to reflect this change. What the treaty is clear on, though, is that the value of the currency is irrevocably fixed (*Article 118* (ex 109g)). Devaluation cannot take place. Similarly, there is no provision for a member state to withdraw from the euro.

The euro is managed by the European System of Central Banks (ESCB), a body which has full legal personality according to *Article 107(1–3)* (ex 106(1–3)) and which the Commission originally proposed should be called the 'Eurofed'. It consists of the European Central Bank (ECB) and national central banks. The latter act in accordance with the guidelines and instructions of the ECB since it is the decision-making bodies of the ECB – the Governing Council and Executive Board – which govern the ESCB. All this is expanded upon in a statute contained in the Protocol on the Statute of the European System of Central Banks and of the European Central Bank. And, seeing as it creates a new configuration in the EU's own institutional structure, Featherstone has argued that EMU in many respects constitutes a fourth pillar of the Union.

The main role of the ESCB, as laid down in the TEC in *Article 105(1)*, is to maintain price stability (i.e. low inflation) and to act in accordance with the principles of a market economy with free competition as well as those set out in Article 4 TEC and noted above. Moreover, through *Article 105(2–3)*, the eurozone-12 have transferred to the ESCB competence for defining and implementing EC monetary policy, holding and managing their official foreign reserves (excluding working balances), conducting foreign exchange operations and promoting the smooth operation of payment systems. Finally, the ESCB under *Article 105(5)* contributes to the 'smooth' conduct of policies relating to the prudential supervision of credit institutions and the stability of the financial system.

Significant powers are therefore vested in the ECB as the key decision-making institution within the ESCB. The ECB is situated in Frankfurt thanks to an agreement reached in 1993 but not mentioned in the treaties until confirmed in the Protocol on the location of the seats of the institutions and of certain bodies and departments of the European Communities and of Europol adopted at Amsterdam. It then came into operation on 1 July 1998 once the decision to launch the final stage of EMU in 1999 had been taken, and replaced the European Monetary Institute (EMI) which had been instrumental in preparing the ground for full EMU. The EMI, as provided for in *Article 117* (ex 109f) and the Protocol on the Statute of the European Monetary Institute, had in turn replaced the Committee of Central Bank Governors set up in 1964 to promote co-operation between member states' central banks.

Modelled on the German Bundesbank, if not being the Bundesbank writ large, the ECB has legal personality thanks to *Article 107(2)* (ex 106(2)) and, like the ESCB is fully independent and forbidden from taking instructions from any member state government or other EC institution (see *Article 108* (ex 107)). Its independence from political interference – a German prerequisite for participation in EMU – is thus guaranteed. Neither the Council nor the Commission nor the EP is directly involved in decisions taken by the ECB. Provision is made, however, for the Council and the Commission to be represented, without having the right to vote, at meetings of the Governing Council. These, however, take place only every six months. In addition, the ECB must present an annual report to the EC institutions. Its president as well as other members of the executive board may appear before the competent committees of the EP when requested

---

*One reason for Germany's insistence on change was that use of ECU would have led to derisory remarks about the new currency for 'one ECU' in German translates as 'ein ECU' which sounds remarkably similar to 'Eine Kuh' meaning 'a cow'!

(*Article 113*, ex 109b). As Haan and Eijffinger note, all this has raised concerns about the democratic accountability of the ECB, concerns which have been reduced in part, though not fully, by the practice of the Bank.

In terms of structure, the organization of the ECB is set out in detail in the Protocol on the Statute of the European System of Central Banks and of the European Central Bank. The first paragraph of *Article 112* (ex 109a) does, however, note that it is headed by a Governing Council comprising the governors of the national central banks of all member states and the members of the Executive Board of the ECB. How the Governing Council votes is set out in Article 10 of the protocol, which originally could not be altered without a formal treaty amendment. Nice changed this by inserting an enabling provision allowing EU heads of state or government to amend the provisions by unanimity without the need for an IGC. The change was accompanied by Declaration No. 19 TN, which anticipated a recommendation 'as soon as possible' although the ECB in welcoming the new clause did not expect the need for any adjustment in the near future.

Turning to the second paragraph of Article 112 and the Executive Board, this consists of six professional bankers or monetary experts appointed by the governments of those member states participating in the euro. Appointments are, according to the treaty, for a single term of eight years. In practice, the terms of office of the members of the first Executive Board range from four to eight years. The significance of this is that from 2002 onwards one member will need to be replaced each year, possibly by a *de facto* UK appointee were the United Kingdom to join the euro. Also worth noting is that when appointing the Executive Board's first president, Wim Duisenberg, in May 1998, an 'understanding' was reached that Duisenberg would only serve half of his scheduled eight-year term and step down in 2002 in favour of Jean-Claude Trichet, the heavily championed candidate of the French government and president. Returning to the TEC, the Protocol amending the Protocol on the privileges and immunities of the European Communities extends the latter to cover the ECB while Declaration No. 33 TEU confers on the Court of First Instance responsibility to deal with staff disputes.

The powers and tasks of the ECB are highly significant and are summarized in *Article 106(1)* (ex 105a(1)). It essentially controls the single currency, having exclusive responsibility for authorizing the issue of euro banknotes. In practice, national central banks will issue the notes and these notes will be the only such notes to have legal tender in the eurozone. Only in the case of France and its overseas territories will a member state retain the privilege of monetary emission (Protocol on France). As for coins, although these will be issued, thanks to *Article 106(2)* (ex 105a(2)), by the member states – thus allowing them to control the design on one side – the volume to be issued is subject to the approval of the ECB.

The tasks ascribed to the ECB also extend into the realm of policy-making. Hence, according to Article 3 of the Statute of the European System of Central Banks and of the European Central Bank, the ECB through the ESCB defines and implements monetary policy for the eurozone. Despite French, Italian and Commission efforts to include unemployment and growth targets, the key principle underpinning policy is low inflation. This has meant a considerable transfer of power from member states to the EC since the ECB has responsibility for setting interest rates for the eurozone. Also, under *Article 110* (ex 108a), the ECB conducts foreign-exchange operations concerning the euro, holds and manages the official reserves of those participating states, and makes legally binding and directly applicable regulations on the minimum level of reserves to be held by national central banks, on the efficiency of clearing and payment systems and on the supervision of credit institutions. And, where an undertaking fails to comply with an ECB regulation or decision, the Bank may impose a fine. Finally, *Article 105(4)* provides for the ECB to be consulted by other EC institutions and national authorities on matters within its competences. It may also issue opinions.

The creation of new institutions with key roles in the operation and management of EMU might suggest that the likes of the Council, Commission and EP play far lesser roles in the project than in other areas of EC policy-making. This is arguably the case. The Commission clearly does not enjoy the same managerial and administrative status with regard to EMU as it does in other areas of EC activity. Where it does have the right of initiative it is often shared with the ECB (i.e. under Articles 107(5), 107(6), 111(1) and 111(2)). Also, it is obliged when called upon by the Council to issue a recommendation or make a proposal to act 'without delay' (see *Article 115*, ex 109d). As for the EP, its involvement in policy-making is for the most part limited to consultation and the receipt of information. Only in a few areas – those governing multilateral surveillance of member states' economic policy under *Article 99(5)* (ex 103(5)); the ban on privileged access to financial institutions under *Article 102(2)* (ex 104a(2)); and the 'no-bail-out' rule in *Article 103(2)* (ex 104b(2)) – does the co-operation procedure apply. Despite pressure, no agreement was reached at Nice on replacing these last remaining provisions for co-operation with either co-decision as the EP wanted or consultation as French drafts proposed. The provisions on EMU do, however, contain two areas where the EP is required to give its assent – amendments to the Statute of the ESCB provided for in *Article 107(5)* (ex 106(5)) and the conferral on the ECB of specific supervisory tasks governing credit and other financial institutions except insurance undertakings under *Article 105(6)*. The first of these actually allows an IGC to be by-passed for certain articles, although to date no use of the provision has been made.

This brings us to the Council. Given the powers vested in the ECB, the Council clearly plays less of a leading role with regard to the eurozone than it does in other areas of EU activity. *Article 111(1–4)* (ex 109(1–4)) does, however, provide it with a central role in the conclusion of formal agreements on an exchange-rate system for the euro in relation to non-EC currencies, one mechanism through which the EC is supposed to contribute to stable international monetary relations (see Declarations Nos. 5 and 6 TEU). It is the Council, acting by unanimous decision of the eurozone member states, which concludes such agreements and which, by QMV, can adopt, adjust or abandon central rates within the system. It is also within the remit of the Council, acting by QMV, to: formulate general orientations for exchange-rate policy in relation to non-EC currencies; decide arrangements for the negotiation and conclusion of binding agreements concerning monetary or foreign-exchange regime matters; determine the position of the EC at international level with regard to EMU-related matters; and take decisions regarding representation at international level. On the last of these, the importance of all eurozone members participating fully in preparing EC positions was stressed at Nice (Declaration No. 7 TN). All such powers are normally exercised on the basis of either a Commission proposal and in consultation with the ECB or simply an ECB recommendation. Only rarely is the EP consulted. All this extends the EC's treaty-making powers, although no new category of international agreement is formally established and existing principles remained unaffected (see Declarations Nos. 8 and 10 TEU). It should be noted, however, that *Article 111(5)* (ex 109(5)), like Articles 174(4), 181 and 181a(3) later in the TEC, confirms the right of member states to negotiate in international bodies and conclude international agreements. Beyond external relations, the Council is charged in *Article 106(2)* (ex 105a(2)) with adopting, via the co-operation procedure and having consulted the ECB, measures necessary for the harmonization of denominations of coins. While technically such measures were adopted in advance of the euro's introduction, further measures will still require Council approval.

Finally regarding the Council, any discussion of the TEC provisions on EMU is not complete without reference to the informal Eurogroup which comprises ministers from the member states participating in the eurozone and which held its first meeting in June 1998. Technically, this Eurogroup (originally known as the Euro-11 Council) has no treaty base. Instead, as with the Stability and Growth Pact, it has emerged as a result of political pressure from certain member states, notably France, keen to ensure that policy-making on EMU remains as far as possible the preserve of participants only. This can be seen in the way in which meetings take place on the fringes of ECOFIN Council meetings and do not include ministers from Denmark, Sweden and the United Kingdom. Whether this is the reason or not, it is arguable that the treaty provisions have neither created a satisfactory general political structure for working with the ECB nor established the position of the Eurogroup in particular. The predominance of bankers in the drafting committee may well have helped to create the present dilemmas.

Having dealt with the treaty provisions governing the eurozone-12, we turn to the position of the so-called 'member states with a derogation' – those member states which have either not qualified for Stage III of EMU as provided for in *Article 122(1)* (ex 109k(1)) or have opted out (see below). Although *Article 122(3)* (ex 109k(3)) states that certain articles will not apply to them once Stage III of EMU has been launched, the states still have obligations under Title VII. These include all those contained in Chapter 1 except those regarding measures to remedy an excessive deficit under *Article 104(9)* (ex 104c(9)). Hence, they are exempt from being fined for non-compliance with Council recommendations under *Article 104(11)* (ex 104c(11)). With regard to monetary matters, the provisions of Articles 105, 106, 110 and 111 concerning the tasks and responsibilities of the ESCB, ECB and Council are not applicable. These exempt the states from the EC monetary policy defined and implemented through the ESCB, any act of the ECB, and exchange-rate arrangements with non-member state currencies. The states are, however, required under *Article 124* (ex 109m) to treat their exchange-rate policy as a matter of common interest to the EC and in doing so take account of the experiences gained through the European Monetary System (EMS).

The *quid pro quo* for fewer obligations, however, is significant. Member states with a derogation are excluded from Council decisions relating to the articles listed, the rights and obligations of the ESCB and the appointment of members to the Executive Board of the ECB. Also, as already noted, they obviously do not participate in the deliberations of the Eurogroup. Moreover, national central banks of member states with derogations do not participate in the most important decision-making procedures of the ECB and ESCB (see *Article 122(3–6)*, ex 109k(3–6)). Article 43 of the ESCB and ECB statute provide further exclusions and exemptions. This does not mean to say that the treaty excludes these states and their national central banks totally from decision-making on EMU. As provided in *Article 123(3)* (ex 109l(3)), they do participate in the work of the ECB's General Council. Its roles are though relatively minor and generally limited to data collection and ECB staffing. As Usher notes, all this renders awkward notions of common policies and a single institutional structure at the EC level and offers a taste of the realities of 'enhanced co-operation'. A first practical example of exclusion occurred in 1998 when the composition of the Executive Board was decided at a Council meeting during the UK presidency but which Austria chaired. Later, in 2001, the Belgian finance minister chaired meetings of the Eurogroup during the Swedish presidency of the Council.

This brings us to the provisions which enable 'member states with a derogation' to divest themselves of the untidy and rather derogatory tag and participate fully in EMU. *Article 122(2)* (ex 109k(2)) calls on the Commission and the ECB to report, at least every two years or at the request of a member state, on the extent to which the 'states with a derogation' meet the so-called convergence criteria which current eurozone participants had to meet before they could participate in Stage III. These are outlined in *Article 121(1)* (ex 109j(1)) and given more detail in the Protocol on the excessive deficit procedure and the Protocol on the convergence criteria referred to in Article 121 (ex 109j) of the Treaty Establishing the European Community. If we accept Tsoukalis's line, these are arguably mechanistic, arbitrary and perhaps even superfluous since in economic terms they can provide at best only a very rough indication of economic stability. Nevertheless, German insistence in the face of opposition from the Commission, Greece, Ireland, Portugal and Spain meant that they featured prominently in the TEU. Opposition to them continued in the lead-up to Stage III of EMU. They were therefore the focus of much criticism, particularly from those who were critical of either their restrictiveness or the absence of any broader economic criteria such as growth rates and unemployment. Any concerns were overlooked and the criteria remain unchanged for states wishing to become members of the eurozone. This is not to say they were rigidly adhered to when the decision was made in 1998 on which member states would participate in Stage III. It is widely held that the criteria were 'fudged' both to facilitate as large a eurozone as possible and to avoid the political fallout of excluding the likes of Italy in particular. This once again shows that strict adherence to the rules of the TEC can easily be compromised in favour of political expediency.

In short, to participate in Stage III of EMU a member state must have a sustainable rate of inflation which is no greater than 1.5 percentage points above that of the three lowest rates in the EC; its currency must have maintained its position within the narrow band of the Exchange Rate Mechanism for at least two years without a devaluation; average long-term interest rates in the country must not have exceeded the level of the three lowest rates in the EC by more than two percentage points over a period of at least one year; the government budget deficit must be less than 3% of the country's GDP; and the overall public debt of the member state must not exceed 60% of its GDP. The reference values indicated concerning debt are not, however, fixed. It is left to the Council under *Article 104(6)* (ex 104c(6)) to decide exactly what constitutes an 'excessive deficit'. In addition to assessing whether member states meet the convergence criteria, Commission reports are also to consider the development of the euro, the results of the integration of markets, balance of payments, and the development of various price indices such as unit labour costs. Finally, a state must demonstrate the independence of its national central bank in accordance with *Article 109* (ex 108).

Once the Commission–ECB assessment has been completed the Council, meeting as heads of government or state, can then, by QMV and having consulted the EP, decide to abrogate derogations. This having been done, the rate at which the currency of the state(s) concerned will be replaced by the euro is decided by the Council acting unanimously and without states still with a derogation voting (see *Article 123(5)*, ex 109l(5)). Preparations are then completed for the now derogation-less state(s) to adopt the euro from an agreed date. Up to now, the procedure has only been applied in the case of Greece, although the biennial assessment in 2000 covered Sweden too.

This leaves us with the two member states with opt-outs: the United Kingdom and Denmark. Their obligations are set out in dedicated protocols attached to the TEC and not in a generalized opt-out provision which, as Forster notes, the UK and other member-state governments sought during the Maastricht negotiations. The first, the Protocol on certain provisions relating to the United Kingdom of Great Britain and Northern Ireland, automatically reserves to the UK government and Parliament the decision to participate in Stage III and the adoption of the single currency. Hence, even if the United Kingdom does meet the convergence criteria it is not obliged, as other states with the exception of Denmark technically are, to join the eurozone. Moreover, the protocol exempts the United Kingdom from adopting measures in preparation for Stage III. Consequently, there is no obligation on the UK government to grant the Bank of England its independence in line with Article 108, even though the incoming Labour government in 1997 did so. The protocol also makes explicit that the United Kingdom shall retain its powers in the field of monetary policy in line with national law. Moreover, under *Article 116(4)* (ex 109e(4)), it is only obliged to 'endeavour' to avoid an excessive government deficit. The United Kingdom must, though, contribute to the operating expenses of the ECB.

The overall situation regarding Denmark is slightly different. According to the Protocol on certain provisions relating to Denmark, Denmark is bound to participate in Stage III unless it notifies the Council of its intention to exempt itself. In fact, such notification was made in December 1992 following the 'no' vote in the national referendum six months earlier and almost a year before the TEU entered into force. Hence, once Stage III was launched, Denmark became a 'member state with a derogation' and assumed the right to decide alone whether it would seek to abrogate the exemption. Efforts in this direction were made by the government in 2000 when it held a referendum on adopting the euro. The outcome was a victory for the 'no' campaigners, leaving Denmark alongside the United Kingdom and Sweden outside the eurozone. One final point concerning Denmark is that its national bank retains the right to carry out existing tasks regarding parts of the country (i.e. Greenland) that are not part of the EC (see Protocol on Denmark).

With the TEC provisions governing 'member states with a derogation' discussed, the *Guide* has covered all currently applicable provisions of the TEC regarding EMU. This leaves only those which became redundant with the launch of Stage III of EMU at the start of 1999. Of these, those on the European Monetary Institute (EMI), which have already been noted, were 'liquidated' in line with Article 123(2). As a consequence, *Article 117* (ex 109f) and the Protocol on the Statute of the European Monetary Institute cease to serve any purpose. The same is true of *Article 121(2–4)* (ex 109j(2–4)) determining the procedure for launching Stage III of EMU, *Article 123(1)* (ex 109l(1)) on establishing the ESCB and ECB and the Protocol on the transition to the third stage of Economic and Monetary Union, which confirmed the political commitment of the member states to see EMU established. All these were the focus of much heated discussion in the negotiations which led to the TEU. Today they are of no significance to the functioning of EMU.

So, with the *Guide* having commented on the provisions in Title VII, it can now turn to a more recent set of provisions, those on employment, which were inserted into the TEC by Amsterdam. Before doing so, it is worth noting several observations concerning the position of EMU within the European Treaties. First, the TEC's provisions occupy, as we have already noted, a considerable amount of space. Including the various protocols, they account for more than 20,000 words. Second, they confer on the EC, and in particular the ECB, significant powers which have traditionally remained the preserve of national governments. As such, the writing of the EMU provisions into the TEC represents a hitherto unequalled transfer of formal sovereign powers, by 12 member states at least, to supra-national institutions. Third, the significance of the provisions for the political economy of the EU and its member states is considerable. Economic principles of low inflation and price stability have become firmly embedded in the *de facto* material constitution of the EU. While the TEC also talks, as we will now see, of the EC contributing to a high level of employment, such an attractive goal ranks constitutionally within the European Treaties well below the principles of sound money which so evidently underpin EMU.

TITLE *VII* (ex Title VI)

ECONOMIC AND MONETARY POLICY

Chapter 1   Economic policy

Article 98 (ex Article 102a)

Member States shall conduct their economic policies with a view to contributing to the achievement of the objectives of the Community, as defined in Article 2, and in the context of the broad guidelines referred to in Article 99(2). The Member States and the Community shall act in accordance with the principle of an open market economy with free competition, favouring an efficient allocation of resources, and in compliance with the principles set out in Article 4.

Article 99 (ex Article 103)

1. Member States shall regard their economic policies as a matter of common concern and shall co-ordinate them within the Council, in accordance with the provisions of Article 98.

2. The Council shall, acting by a qualified majority on a recommendation from the Commission, formulate a draft for the broad guidelines of the economic policies of the Member States and of the Community, and shall report its findings to the European Council.

The European Council shall, acting on the basis of the report from the Council, discuss a conclusion on the broad guidelines of the economic policies of the Member States and of the Community.

On the basis of this conclusion, the Council shall, acting by a qualified majority, adopt a recommendation setting out these broad guidelines. The Council shall inform the European Parliament of its recommendation.

3. In order to ensure closer co-ordination of economic policies and sustained convergence of the economic performances of the Member States, the Council shall, on the basis of reports submitted by the Commission, monitor economic developments in each of the Member States and in the Community as well as the consistency of economic policies with the broad guidelines referred to in paragraph 2, and regularly carry out an overall assessment.

For the purpose of this multilateral surveillance, Member States shall forward information to the Commission about important measures taken by them in the field of their economic policy and such other information as they deem necessary.

4. Where it is established, under the procedure referred to in paragraph 3, that the economic policies of a Member State are not consistent with the broad guidelines referred to in paragraph 2 or that they risk jeopardising the proper functioning of economic and monetary union, the Council may, acting by a qualified majority on a recommendation from the Commission, make the necessary recommendations to the Member State concerned. The Council may, acting by a qualified majority on a proposal from the Commission, decide to make its recommendations public.

The President of the Council and the Commission shall report to the European Parliament on the results of multilateral surveillance. The President of the Council may be invited to appear before the competent committee of the European Parliament if the Council has made its recommendations public.

5. The Council, acting in accordance with the procedure referred to in Article 252, may adopt detailed rules for the multilateral surveillance procedure referred to in paragraphs 3 and 4 of this Article.

Article 100 (ex Article 103a)

1. Without prejudice to any other procedures provided for in this Treaty, the Council may, acting **by a qualified majority** on a proposal from the Commission, decide upon the measures appropriate to the economic situation, in particular if severe difficulties arise in the supply of certain products.

2. Where a Member State is in difficulties or is seriously threatened with severe difficulties caused by **natural disasters or** exceptional occurrences beyond its control, the Council, *acting* **by a qualified majority** on a proposal from the Commission, *may* grant, under certain conditions, Community financial assistance to the Member State concerned. The President of the Council shall inform the European Parliament of the decision taken.

Article 101 (ex Article 104)

1. Overdraft facilities or any other type of credit facility with the ECB or with the central banks of the Member States (hereinafter referred to as 'national central banks') in favour of Community institutions or bodies, central governments, regional, local or other public authorities, other bodies governed by public law, or public undertakings of Member States shall be prohibited, as shall the purchase directly from them by the ECB or national central banks of debt instruments.

2. Paragraph 1 shall not apply to publicly owned credit institutions which, in the context of the supply of reserves by central banks, shall be given the same treatment by national central banks and the ECB as private credit institutions.

Article 102 (ex Article 104a)

1. Any measure, not based on prudential considerations, establishing privileged access by Community institutions or bodies, central governments, regional, local or other public authorities, other bodies governed by public law, or public undertakings of Member States to financial institutions, shall be prohibited.

2. The Council, acting in accordance with the procedure referred to in Article 252, shall, before 1 January 1994, specify definitions for the application of the prohibition referred to in paragraph 1.

Article 103 (ex Article 104b)

1. The Community shall not be liable for or assume the commitments of central governments, regional, local or other public authorities, other bodies governed by public law, or public undertakings of any Member State, without prejudice to mutual financial guarantees for the joint execution of a specific project. A Member State shall not be liable for or assume the commitments of central governments, regional, local or other public authorities, other bodies governed by public law,

or public undertakings of another Member State, without prejudice to mutual financial guarantees for the joint execution of a specific project.

2. If necessary, the Council, acting in accordance with the procedure referred to in Article 252, may specify definitions for the application of the prohibition referred to in Article 101 and in this Article.

Article 104 (ex Article 104c)

1. Member States shall avoid excessive government deficits.

2. The Commission shall monitor the development of the budgetary situation and of the stock of government debt in the Member States with a view to identifying gross errors. In particular it shall examine compliance with budgetary discipline on the basis of the following two criteria:
(a) whether the ratio of the planned or actual government deficit to gross domestic product exceeds a reference value, unless:
   – either the ratio has declined substantially and continuously and reached a level that comes close to the reference value;
   – or, alternatively, the excess over the reference value is only exceptional and temporary and the ratio remains close to the reference value;
(b) whether the ratio of government debt to gross domestic product exceeds a reference value, unless the ratio is sufficiently diminishing and approaching the reference value at a satisfactory pace.

The reference values are specified in the Protocol on the excessive deficit procedure annexed to this Treaty.

3. If a Member State does not fulfil the requirements under one or both of these criteria, the Commission shall prepare a report. The report of the Commission shall also take into account whether the government deficit exceeds government investment expenditure and take into account all other relevant factors, including the medium-term economic and budgetary position of the Member State.

The Commission may also prepare a report if, notwithstanding the fulfilment of the requirements under the criteria, it is of the opinion that there is a risk of an excessive deficit in a Member State.

4. The Committee provided for in Article 114 shall formulate an opinion on the report of the Commission.

5. If the Commission considers that an excessive deficit in a Member State exists or may occur, the Commission shall address an opinion to the Council.

6. The Council shall, acting by a qualified majority on a recommendation from the Commission, and having considered any observations which the Member State concerned may wish to make, decide after an overall assessment whether an excessive deficit exists.

7. Where the existence of an excessive deficit is decided according to paragraph 6, the Council shall make recommendations to the Member State concerned with a view to bringing that situation to an end within a given period. Subject to the provisions of paragraph 8, these recommendations shall not be made public.

8. Where it establishes that there has been no effective action in response to its recommendations within the period laid down, the Council may make its recommendations public.

9. If a Member State persists in failing to put into practice the recommendations

of the Council, the Council may decide to give notice to the Member State to take, within a specified time-limit, measures for the deficit reduction which is judged necessary by the Council in order to remedy the situation.

In such a case, the Council may request the Member State concerned to submit reports in accordance with a specific timetable in order to examine the adjustment efforts of that Member State.

10. The rights to bring actions provided for in Articles 226 and 227 may not be exercised within the framework of paragraphs 1 to 9 of this Article.

11. As long as a Member State fails to comply with a decision taken in accordance with paragraph 9, the Council may decide to apply or, as the case may be, intensify one or more of the following measures:
– to require the Member State concerned to publish additional information, to be specified by the Council, before issuing bonds and securities;
– to invite the European Investment Bank to reconsider its lending policy towards the Member State concerned;
– to require the Member State concerned to make a non-interest-bearing deposit of an appropriate size with the Community until the excessive deficit has, in the view of the Council, been corrected;
– to impose fines of an appropriate size.

The President of the Council shall inform the European Parliament of the decisions taken.

12. The Council shall abrogate some or all of its decisions referred to in paragraphs 6 to 9 and 11 to the extent that the excessive deficit in the Member State concerned has, in the view of the Council, been corrected. If the Council has previously made public recommendations, it shall, as soon as the decision under paragraph 8 has been abrogated, make a public statement that an excessive deficit in the Member State concerned no longer exists.

13. When taking the decisions referred to in paragraphs 7 to 9, 11 and 12, the Council shall act on a recommendation from the Commission by a majority of two-thirds of the votes of its members weighted in accordance with Article 205(2), excluding the votes of the representative of the Member State concerned.

14. Further provisions relating to the implementation of the procedure described in this Article are set out in the Protocol on the excessive deficit procedure annexed to this Treaty.

The Council shall, acting unanimously on a proposal from the Commission and after consulting the European Parliament and the ECB, adopt the appropriate provisions which shall then replace the said Protocol.

Subject to the other provisions of this paragraph, the Council shall, before 1 January 1994, acting by a qualified majority on a proposal from the Commission and after consulting the European Parliament, lay down detailed rules and definitions for the application of the provisions of the said Protocol.

Chapter 2   Monetary policy

Article 105

1. The primary objective of the ESCB shall be to maintain price stability. Without prejudice to the objective of price stability, the ESCB shall support the general

economic policies in the Community with a view to contributing to the achievement of the objectives of the Community as laid down in Article 2. The ESCB shall act in accordance with the principle of an open market economy with free competition, favouring an efficient allocation of resources, and in compliance with the principles set out in Article 4.

2. The basic tasks to be carried out through the ESCB shall be:
– to define and implement the monetary policy of the Community;
– to conduct foreign exchange operations consistent with the provisions of Article 111;
– to hold and manage the official foreign reserves of the Member States;
– to promote the smooth operation of payment systems.

3. The third indent of paragraph 2 shall be without prejudice to the holding and management by the governments of Member States of foreign-exchange working balances.

4. The ECB shall be consulted:
– on any proposed Community act in its fields of competence;
– by national authorities regarding any draft legislative provision in its fields of competence, but within the limits and under the conditions set out by the Council in accordance with the procedure laid down in Article 107(6).

The ECB may submit opinions to the appropriate Community institutions or bodies or to national authorities on matters in its fields of competence.

5. The ESCB shall contribute to the smooth conduct of policies pursued by the competent authorities relating to the prudential supervision of credit institutions and the stability of the financial system.

6. The Council may, acting unanimously on a proposal from the Commission and after consulting the ECB and after receiving the assent of the European Parliament, confer upon the ECB specific tasks concerning policies relating to the prudential supervision of credit institutions and other financial institutions with the exception of insurance undertakings.

Article 106 (ex Article 105a)

1. The ECB shall have the exclusive right to authorise the issue of banknotes within the Community. The ECB and the national central banks may issue such notes. The banknotes issued by the ECB and the national central banks shall be the only such notes to have the status of legal tender within the Community.

2. Member States may issue coins subject to approval by the ECB of the volume of the issue. The Council may, acting in accordance with the procedure referred to in Article 252 and after consulting the ECB, adopt measures to harmonise the denominations and technical specifications of all coins intended for circulation to the extent necessary to permit their smooth circulation within the Community.

Article 107 (ex Article 106)

1. The ESCB shall be composed of the ECB and of the national central banks.

2. The ECB shall have legal personality.

3. The ESCB shall be governed by the decision-making bodies of the ECB which shall be the Governing Council and the Executive Board.

4. The Statute of the ESCB is laid down in a Protocol annexed to this Treaty.

5. Articles 5.1, 5.2, 5.3, 17, 18, 19.1, 22, 23, 24, 26, 32.2, 32.3, 32.4, 32.6, 33.1(a) and 36 of the Statute of the ESCB may be amended by the Council, acting either by a qualified majority on a recommendation from the ECB and after consulting the Commission or unanimously on a proposal from the Commission and after consulting the ECB. In either case, the assent of the European Parliament shall be required.

6. The Council, acting by a qualified majority either on a proposal from the Commission and after consulting the European Parliament and the ECB or on a recommendation from the ECB and after consulting the European Parliament and the Commission, shall adopt the provisions referred to in Articles 4, 5.4, 19.2, 20, 28.1, 29.2, 30.4 and 34.3 of the Statute of the ESCB.

Article 108 (ex Article 107)

When exercising the powers and carrying out the tasks and duties conferred upon them by this Treaty and the Statute of the ESCB, neither the ECB, nor a national central bank, nor any member of their decision-making bodies shall seek or take instructions from Community institutions or bodies, from any government of a Member State or from any other body. The Community institutions and bodies and the governments of the Member States undertake to respect this principle and not to seek to influence the members of the decision-making bodies of the ECB or of the national central banks in the performance of their tasks.

Article 109 (ex Article 108)

Each Member State shall ensure, at the latest at the date of the establishment of the ESCB, that its national legislation including the statutes of its national central bank is compatible with this Treaty and the Statute of the ESCB.

Article 110 (ex Article 108a)

1. In order to carry out the tasks entrusted to the ESCB, the ECB shall, in accordance with the provisions of this Treaty and under the conditions laid down in the Statute of the ESCB:
– make regulations to the extent necessary to implement the tasks defined in Article 3.1, first indent, Articles 19.1, 22 and 25.2 of the Statute of the ESCB and in cases which shall be laid down in the acts of the Council referred to in Article 107(6);
– take decisions necessary for carrying out the tasks entrusted to the ESCB under this Treaty and the Statute of the ESCB;
– make recommendations and deliver opinions.

2. A regulation shall have general application. It shall be binding in its entirety and directly applicable in all Member States.

Recommendations and opinions shall have no binding force.

A decision shall be binding in its entirety upon those to whom it is addressed.

Articles 253 to 256 shall apply to regulations and decisions adopted by the ECB.

The ECB may decide to publish its decisions, recommendations and opinions.

3. Within the limits and under the conditions adopted by the Council under the procedure laid down in Article 107(6), the ECB shall be entitled to impose fines or periodic penalty payments on undertakings for failure to comply with obligations under its regulations and decisions.

Article 111 (Article 109)

1. By way of derogation from Article 300, the Council may, acting unanimously on a recommendation from the ECB or from the Commission, and after consulting the ECB in an endeavour to reach a consensus consistent with the objective of price stability, after consulting the European Parliament, in accordance with the procedure in paragraph 3 for determining the arrangements, conclude formal agreements on an exchange-rate system for the ECU in relation to non-Community currencies. The Council may, acting by a qualified majority on a recommendation from the ECB or from the Commission, and after consulting the ECB in an endeavour to reach a consensus consistent with the objective of price stability, adopt, adjust or abandon the central rates of the ECU within the exchange-rate system. The President of the Council shall inform the European Parliament of the adoption, adjustment or abandonment of the ECU central rates.

2. In the absence of an exchange-rate system in relation to one or more non-Community currencies as referred to in paragraph 1, the Council, acting by a qualified majority either on a recommendation from the Commission and after consulting the ECB or on a recommendation from the ECB, may formulate general orientations for exchange-rate policy in relation to these currencies. These general orientations shall be without prejudice to the primary objective of the ESCB to maintain price stability.

3. By way of derogation from Article 300, where agreements concerning monetary or foreign exchange regime matters need to be negotiated by the Community with one or more States or international organisations, the Council, acting by a qualified majority on a recommendation from the Commission and after consulting the ECB, shall decide the arrangements for the negotiation and for the conclusion of such agreements. These arrangements shall ensure that the Community expresses a single position. The Commission shall be fully associated with the negotiations.
Agreements concluded in accordance with this paragraph shall be binding on the institutions of the Community, on the ECB and on Member States.

4. Subject to paragraph 1, the **Council, acting by a qualified majority on a proposal from the Commission and after consulting the ECB, shall** decide on the position of the Community at international level as regards issues of particular relevance to economic and monetary union **and on** its representation in compliance with the allocation of powers laid down in Articles 99 and 105.

5. Without prejudice to Community competence and Community agreements as regards economic and monetary union, Member States may negotiate in international bodies and conclude international agreements.

Chapter 3   Institutional provisions

Article 112 (ex Article 109a)

1. The Governing Council of the ECB shall comprise the members of the Executive Board of the ECB and the Governors of the national central banks.

2.(a) The Executive Board shall comprise the President, the Vice-President and four other members.
(b) The President, the Vice-President and the other members of the Executive Board shall be appointed from among persons of recognised standing and

professional experience in monetary or banking matters by common accord of the governments of the Member States at the level of Heads of State or Government, on a recommendation from the Council, after it has consulted the European Parliament and the Governing Council of the ECB.

Their term of office shall be eight years and shall not be renewable.

Only nationals of Member States may be members of the Executive Board.

Article 113 (ex Article 109b)

1. The President of the Council and a member of the Commission may participate, without having the right to vote, in meetings of the Governing Council of the ECB. The President of the Council may submit a motion for deliberation to the Governing Council of the ECB.

2. The President of the ECB shall be invited to participate in Council meetings when the Council is discussing matters relating to the objectives and tasks of the ESCB.

3. The ECB shall address an annual report on the activities of the ESCB and on the monetary policy of both the previous and current year to the European Parliament, the Council and the Commission, and also to the European Council. The President of the ECB shall present this report to the Council and to the European Parliament, which may hold a general debate on that basis.

The President of the ECB and the other members of the Executive Board may, at the request of the European Parliament or on their own initiative, be heard by the competent committees of the European Parliament.

Article 114 (ex Article 109c)

1. In order to promote co-ordination of the policies of Member States to the full extent needed for the functioning of the internal market, a Monetary Committee with advisory status is hereby set up.

It shall have the following tasks:

– to keep under review the monetary and financial situation of the Member States and of the Community and the general payments system of the Member States and to report regularly thereon to the Council and to the Commission;

– to deliver opinions at the request of the Council or of the Commission, or on its own initiative for submission to those institutions;

– without prejudice to Article 207, to contribute to the preparation of the work of the Council referred to in Articles 59, 60, 99(2), (3), (4) and (5), 100, 102, 103, 104, 116(2), 117(6), 119, 120, 121(2) and 122(1);

– to examine, at least once a year, the situation regarding the movement of capital and the freedom of payments, as they result from the application of this Treaty and of measures adopted by the Council; the examination shall cover all measures relating to capital movements and payments; the Committee shall report to the Commission and to the Council on the outcome of this examination.

The Member States and the Commission shall each appoint two members of the Monetary Committee.

2. At the start of the third stage, an Economic and Financial Committee shall be set up. The Monetary Committee provided for in paragraph 1 shall be dissolved.

The Economic and Financial Committee shall have the following tasks:

- to deliver opinions at the request of the Council or of the Commission, or on its own initiative for submission to those institutions;
- to keep under review the economic and financial situation of the Member States and of the Community and to report regularly thereon to the Council and to the Commission, in particular on financial relations with third countries and international institutions;
- without prejudice to Article 207, to contribute to the preparation of the work of the Council referred to in Articles 59, 60, 99(2), (3), (4) and (5), 100, 102, 103, 104, 105(6), 106(2), 107(5) and (6), 111, 119, 120(2) and (3), 122(2), 123(4) and (5), and to carry out other advisory and preparatory tasks assigned to it by the Council;
- to examine, at least once a year, the situation regarding the movement of capital and the freedom of payments, as they result from the application of this Treaty and of measures adopted by the Council; the examination shall cover all measures relating to capital movements and payments; the Committee shall report to the Commission and to the Council on the outcome of this examination.

The Member States, the Commission and the ECB shall each appoint no more than two members of the Committee.

3. The Council shall, acting by a qualified majority on a proposal from the Commission and after consulting the ECB and the Committee referred to in this Article, lay down detailed provisions concerning the composition of the Economic and Financial Committee. The President of the Council shall inform the European Parliament of such a decision.

4. In addition to the tasks set out in paragraph 2, if and as long as there are Member States with a derogation as referred to in Articles 122 and 123, the Committee shall keep under review the monetary and financial situation and the general payments system of those Member States and report regularly thereon to the Council and to the Commission.

Article 115 (ex Article 109d)

For matters within the scope of Articles 99(4), 104 with the exception of paragraph 14, 111, 121, 122 and 123(4) and (5), the Council or a Member State may request the Commission to make a recommendation or a proposal, as appropriate. The Commission shall examine this request and submit its conclusions to the Council without delay.

Chapter 4   Transitional provisions

Article 116 (ex Article 109e simplified)

1. The second stage for achieving economic and monetary union shall begin on 1 January 1994.

2. Before that date:
(a) each Member State shall:
   - adopt, where necessary, appropriate measures to comply with the prohibitions laid down in Article 56 and in Articles 101 and 102(1);
   - adopt, if necessary, with a view to permitting the assessment provided for in subparagraph (b), multiannual programmes intended to ensure the lasting

convergence necessary for the achievement of economic and monetary union, in particular with regard to price stability and sound public finances;

(b) the Council shall, on the basis of a report from the Commission, assess the progress made with regard to economic and monetary convergence, in particular with regard to price stability and sound public finances, and the progress made with the implementation of Community law concerning the internal market.

3. The provisions of Articles *101*, *102*(1), *103*(1), and *104* with the exception of paragraphs 1, 9, 11 and 14 shall apply from the beginning of the second stage.

The provisions of Articles *100*(2), *104*(1), (9) and (11), *105*, *106*, *108*, *111*, *112*, *113* and *114*(2) and (4) shall apply from the beginning of the third stage.

4. In the second stage, Member States shall endeavour to avoid excessive government deficits.

5. During the second stage, each Member State shall, as appropriate, start the process leading to the independence of its central bank, in accordance with Article *109*.

Article 117 (ex Article 109f simplified)

1. At the start of the second stage, a European Monetary Institute (hereinafter referred to as 'EMI') shall be established and take up its duties; it shall have legal personality and be directed and managed by a Council, consisting of a President and the Governors of the national central banks, one of whom shall be Vice-President.

The President shall be appointed by common accord of the governments of the Member States at the level of Heads of State or Government, on a recommendation *from the* Council of the EMI, and after consulting the European Parliament and the Council. The President shall be selected from among persons of recognised standing and professional experience in monetary or banking matters. Only nationals of Member States may be President of the EMI. The Council of the EMI shall appoint the Vice-President. The Statute of the EMI is laid down in a Protocol annexed to this Treaty.

2. The EMI shall:
- strengthen co-operation between the national central banks;
- strengthen the co-ordination of the monetary policies of the Member States, with the aim of ensuring price stability;
- monitor the functioning of the European Monetary System;
- hold consultations concerning issues falling within the competence of the national central banks and affecting the stability of financial institutions and markets;
- take over the tasks of the European Monetary Co-operation Fund, which shall be dissolved; the modalities of dissolution are laid down in the Statute of the EMI;
- facilitate the use of the ECU and oversee its development, including the smooth functioning of the ECU clearing system.

3. For the preparation of the third stage, the EMI shall:
- prepare the instruments and the procedures necessary for carrying out a single monetary policy in the third stage;
- promote the harmonisation, where necessary, of the rules and practices governing the collection, compilation and distribution of statistics in the areas within its field of competence;
- prepare the rules for operations to be undertaken by the national central banks within the framework of the ESCB;

– promote the efficiency of cross-border payments;
– supervise the technical preparation of ECU banknotes.

At the latest by 31 December 1996, the EMI shall specify the regulatory, organisational and logistical framework necessary for the ESCB to perform its tasks in the third stage. This framework shall be submitted for decision to the ECB at the date of its establishment.

4. The EMI, acting by a majority of two thirds of the members of its Council, may:
– formulate opinions or recommendations on the overall orientation of monetary policy and exchange-rate policy as well as on related measures introduced in each Member State;
– submit opinions or recommendations to governments and to the Council on policies which might affect the internal or external monetary situation in the Community and, in particular, the functioning of the European Monetary System;
– make recommendations to the monetary authorities of the Member States concerning the conduct of their monetary policy.

5. The EMI, acting unanimously, may decide to publish its opinions and its recommendations.

6. The EMI shall be consulted by the Council regarding any proposed Community act within its field of competence.

Within the limits and under the conditions set out by the Council, acting by a qualified majority on a proposal from the Commission and after consulting the European Parliament and the EMI, the EMI shall be consulted by the authorities of the Member States on any draft legislative provision within its field of competence.

7. The Council may, acting unanimously on a proposal from the Commission and after consulting the European Parliament and the EMI, confer upon the EMI other tasks for the preparation of the third stage.

8. Where this Treaty provides for a consultative role for the ECB, references to the ECB shall be read as referring to the EMI before the establishment of the ECB.

9. During the second stage, the term 'ECB' used in Articles 230, 232, 233, 234, 237 and 288 shall be read as referring to the EMI.

Article 118 (ex Article 109g)

The currency composition of the ECU basket shall not be changed.

From the start of the third stage, the value of the ECU shall be irrevocably fixed in accordance with Article 123(4).

Article 119 (ex Article 109h)

1. Where a Member State is in difficulties or is seriously threatened with difficulties as regards its balance of payments either as a result of an overall disequilibrium in its balance of payments, or as a result of the type of currency at its disposal, and where such difficulties are liable in particular to jeopardise the functioning of the common market or the progressive implementation of the common commercial policy, the Commission shall immediately investigate the position of the State in question and the action which, making use of all the means at its disposal, that State has taken or may take in accordance with the provisions of this Treaty. The Commission shall state what measures it recommends the State concerned to take.

If the action taken by a Member State and the measures suggested by the Commission do not prove sufficient to overcome the difficulties which have arisen or which threaten, the Commission shall, after consulting the Committee referred to in Article 114, recommend to the Council the granting of mutual assistance and appropriate methods therefor.

The Commission shall keep the Council regularly informed of the situation and of how it is developing.

2. The Council, acting by a qualified majority, shall grant such mutual assistance; it shall adopt directives or decisions laying down the conditions and details of such assistance, which may take such forms as:

(a) a concerted approach to or within any other international organisations to which Member States may have recourse;

(b) measures needed to avoid deflection of trade where the State which is in difficulties maintains or reintroduces quantitative restrictions against third countries;

(c) the granting of limited credits by other Member States, subject to their agreement.

3. If the mutual assistance recommended by the Commission is not granted by the Council or if the mutual assistance granted and the measures taken are insufficient, the Commission shall authorise the State which is in difficulties to take protective measures, the conditions and details of which the Commission shall determine.

Such authorisation may be revoked and such conditions and details may be changed by the Council acting by a qualified majority.

4. Subject to Article 122(6), this Article shall cease to apply from the beginning of the third stage.

Article 120 (ex Article 109i)

1. Where a sudden crisis in the balance of payments occurs and a decision within the meaning of Article 119(2) is not immediately taken, the Member State concerned may, as a precaution, take the necessary protective measures. Such measures must cause the least possible disturbance in the functioning of the common market and must not be wider in scope than is strictly necessary to remedy the sudden difficulties which have arisen.

2. The Commission and the other Member States shall be informed of such protective measures not later than when they enter into force. The Commission may recommend to the Council the granting of mutual assistance under Article 119.

3. After the Commission has delivered an opinion and the Committee referred to in Article 114 has been consulted, the Council may, acting by a qualified majority, decide that the State concerned shall amend, suspend or abolish the protective measures referred to above.

4. Subject to Article 122(6), this Article shall cease to apply from the beginning of the third stage.

Article 121 (ex Article 109j)

1. The Commission and the EMI shall report to the Council on the progress made in the fulfilment by the Member States of their obligations regarding the achievement of economic and monetary union. These reports shall include an

examination of the compatibility between each Member State's national legislation, including the statutes of its national central bank, and Articles *108* and *109* of this Treaty and the Statute of the ESCB. The reports shall also examine the achievement of a high degree of sustainable convergence by reference to the fulfilment by each Member State of the following criteria:

– the achievement of a high degree of price stability; this will be apparent from a rate of inflation which is close to that of, at most, the three best performing Member States in terms of price stability;
– the sustainability of the government financial position; this will be apparent from having achieved a government budgetary position without a deficit that is excessive as determined in accordance with Article *104(6)*;
– the observance of the normal fluctuation margins provided for by the exchange-rate mechanism of the European Monetary System, for at least two years, without devaluing against the currency of any other Member State;
– the durability of convergence achieved by the Member State and of its participation in the exchange-rate mechanism of the European Monetary System being reflected in the long-term interest-rate levels.

The four criteria mentioned in this paragraph and the relevant periods over which they are to be respected are developed further in a Protocol annexed to this Treaty. The reports of the Commission and the EMI shall also take account of the development of the ECU, the results of the integration of markets, the situation and development of the balances of payments on current account and an examination of the development of unit labour costs and other price indices.

2. On the basis of these reports, the Council, acting by a qualified majority on a recommendation from the Commission, shall assess:

– for each Member State, whether it fulfils the necessary conditions for the adoption of a single currency;
– whether a majority of the Member States fulfil the necessary conditions for the adoption of a single currency,

and recommend its findings to the Council, meeting in the composition of the Heads of State or Government. The European Parliament shall be consulted and forward its opinion to the Council, meeting in the composition of the Heads of State or Government.

3. Taking due account of the reports referred to in paragraph 1 and the opinion of the European Parliament referred to in paragraph 2, the Council, meeting in the composition of the Heads of State or Government, shall, acting by a qualified majority, not later than 31 December 1996:

– decide, on the basis of the recommendations of the Council referred to in paragraph 2, whether a majority of the Member States fulfil the necessary conditions for the adoption of a single currency;
– decide whether it is appropriate for the Community to enter the third stage, and if so:
– set the date for the beginning of the third stage.

4. If by the end of 1997 the date for the beginning of the third stage has not been set, the third stage shall start on 1 January 1999. Before 1 July 1998, the Council, meeting in the composition of the Heads of State or Government, after a repetition of the procedure provided for in paragraphs 1 and 2, with the exception of the second indent of paragraph 2, taking into account the reports referred to in paragraph 1 and the opinion of the European Parliament, shall, acting by a

qualified majority and on the basis of the recommendations of the Council referred to in paragraph 2, confirm which Member States fulfil the necessary conditions for the adoption of a single currency.

Article 122 (ex Article 109k)

1. If the decision has been taken to set the date in accordance with Article $121(3)$, the Council shall, on the basis of its recommendations referred to in Article $121(2)$, acting by a qualified majority on a recommendation from the Commission, decide whether any, and if so which, Member States shall have a derogation as defined in paragraph 3 of this Article. Such Member States shall in this Treaty be referred to as 'Member States with a derogation'.

If the Council has confirmed which Member States fulfil the necessary conditions for the adoption of a single currency, in accordance with Article $121(4)$, those Member States which do not fulfil the conditions shall have a derogation as defined in paragraph 3 of this Article. Such Member States shall in this Treaty be referred to as 'Member States with a derogation'.

2. At least once every two years, or at the request of a Member State with a derogation, the Commission and the ECB shall report to the Council in accordance with the procedure laid down in Article $121(1)$. After consulting the European Parliament and after discussion in the Council, meeting in the composition of the Heads of State or Government, the Council shall, acting by a qualified majority on a proposal from the Commission, decide which Member States with a derogation fulfil the necessary conditions on the basis of the criteria set out in Article $121(1)$, and abrogate the derogations of the Member States concerned.

3. A derogation referred to in paragraph 1 shall entail that the following Articles do not apply to the Member State concerned: Articles $104(9)$ and (11), $105(1)$, (2), (3) and (5), 106, 110, 111 and $112(2)(b)$. The exclusion of such a Member State and its national central bank from rights and obligations within the ESCB is laid down in Chapter IX of the Statute of the ESCB.

4. In Articles $105(1)$, (2) and (3), 106, 110, 111 and $112(2)(b)$, 'Member States' shall be read as 'Member States without a derogation'.

5. The voting rights of Member States with a derogation shall be suspended for the Council decisions referred to in the Articles of this Treaty mentioned in paragraph 3. In that case, by way of derogation from Articles 205 and $250(1)$, a qualified majority shall be defined as two-thirds of the votes of the representatives of the Member States without a derogation weighted in accordance with Article $205(2)$, and unanimity of those Member States shall be required for an act requiring unanimity.

6. Articles 119 and 120 shall continue to apply to a Member State with a derogation.

Article 123 (ex Article 109l)

1. Immediately after the decision on the date for the beginning of the third stage has been taken in accordance with Article $121(3)$, or, as the case may be, immediately after 1 July 1998:
– the Council shall adopt the provisions referred to in Article $107(6)$;
– the governments of the Member States without a derogation shall appoint, in

accordance with the procedure set out in Article 50 of the Statute of the ESCB, the President, the Vice-President and the other members of the Executive Board of the ECB. If there are Member States with a derogation, the number of members of the Executive Board may be smaller than provided for in Article 11.1 of the Statute of the ESCB, but in no circumstances shall it be less than four.

As soon as the Executive Board is appointed, the ESCB and the ECB shall be established and shall prepare for their full operation as described in this Treaty and the Statute of the ESCB. The full exercise of their powers shall start from the first day of the third stage.

2. As soon as the ECB is established, it shall, if necessary, take over tasks of the EMI. The EMI shall go into liquidation upon the establishment of the ECB; the modalities of liquidation are laid down in the Statute of the EMI.

3. If and as long as there are Member States with a derogation, and without prejudice to Article 107(3) of this Treaty, the General Council of the ECB referred to in Article 45 of the Statute of the ESCB shall be constituted as a third decision-making body of the ECB.

4. At the starting date of the third stage, the Council shall, acting with the unanimity of the Member States without a derogation, on a proposal from the Commission and after consulting the ECB, adopt the conversion rates at which their currencies shall be irrevocably fixed and at which irrevocably fixed rate the ECU shall be substituted for these currencies, and the ECU will become a currency in its own right. This measure shall by itself not modify the external value of the ECU. The Council, **acting by a qualified majority of the said Member States, on a proposal from the Commission and after consulting the ECB**, shall take the other measures necessary for the rapid introduction of the ECU as the single currency of those Member States. **The second sentence of Article 122(5) shall apply.**

5. If it is decided, according to the procedure set out in Article 122(2), to abrogate a derogation, the Council shall, acting with the unanimity of the Member States without a derogation and the Member State concerned, on a proposal from the Commission and after consulting the ECB, adopt the rate at which the ECU shall be substituted for the currency of the Member State concerned, and take the other measures necessary for the introduction of the ECU as the single currency in the Member State concerned.

Article 124 (ex Article 109m)

1. Until the beginning of the third stage, each Member State shall treat its exchange-rate policy as a matter of common interest. In so doing, Member States shall take account of the experience acquired in co-operation within the framework of the European Monetary System (EMS) and in developing the ECU, and shall respect existing powers in this field.

2. From the beginning of the third stage and for as long as a Member State has a derogation, paragraph 1 shall apply by analogy to the exchange-rate policy of that Member State.

xii Employment

Title VIII is one of the newest in the treaty, having been inserted by the TA. Focusing as it does on employment, it is one of the additions which leads Pollack to argue that Amsterdam was very much a 'Blairite' treaty, one which, through its provisions on employment, social policy, rights and the environment, represented a 'weak left turn' for the EU away from neo-liberalism to regulated capitalism. Others such as Dehousse go further, arguing that it might one day become the technical basis for a revival of Keynesianism. This is, of course, a matter for speculation. It is fair to say that Amsterdam did raise the profile of employment, adding not just Title VIII but also, as already noted, 'the promotion of co-ordination between employment policies of the Member States' as a task of the EC in Article 3(1)(i); the aim of such co-ordination is to enhance the effectiveness of policies by developing a co-ordinated strategy for employment.

All this should not lead us to think that employment was not a concern of the EC prior to Amsterdam which also inserted a reference to 'the promotion of employment' into Article 136 TEC concerning social policy. The TEU, for example, inserted a reference to 'a high level of employment' in Article 2 TEC and 'lasting high employment' in Article 1 of the Social Chapter to which all member states except the United Kingdom were signatories. Article B (now 2) TEU also referred to 'a high level of employment' as an objective of the Union. While the latter was obviously new, the reference in Article 2 TEC, despite the contention of Cloos and others that it merely rectified an omission at the time the SEA was drafted, very much reflected a desire to retain in the TEC the reference which was originally contained in Article 104, the content of which the TEU deleted. And this was not the only reference to employment to be found in the TEC when signed in 1957. Article 140 called on the Commission to encourage co-operation and the co-ordination of member-state action regarding employment. Moreover, the treaty has long contained other established references to employment in the context of agricultural and related sectors (Articles 31(3), 37(3)(a)) and transport (Article 71(2)), the free movement of workers and the abolition of discrimination based on nationality (Articles 39 and 40), the granting of state aids (Article 87(3)(a)), the role of the European Social Fund (Article 146), and of course the employees of EC institutions and bodies (Articles 236, 283 and 288).

What the introduction of Title VIII did, therefore, was to build on original TEC provisions concerning certain employment issues and flesh out the reference to a high level of employment established as an EC task by the TEU. It also provided a treaty base for the increasing activity of the EC with regard to employment. For much of the 1990s, in the face of high levels of unemployment, normally above 10% of the workforce, and a tightening of public expenditure as member states prepared for EMU, the Commission had been pushing for EC action to promote employment initiatives. This led to the European Council adopting the so-called 'Essen Strategy' in December 1994 and The Jobs Challenge: The Dublin Declaration on Employment two years later. As O'Riordan notes, it also helped to sustain the growing interest in providing a firm treaty foundation for employment initiatives. Despite outright opposition from the Major government in the United Kingdom and significant disagreements late on over content between Blair and Jospin, Amsterdam was to deliver precisely this, even if it failed to amend the reference to 'high employment' to 'full employment' as the Swedish government and the European Trade Union Confederation wished. The German government, while sceptical of the title, accepted it to secure opposition Social Democrat support domestically for ratification.

Amsterdam provided a firm treaty base for employment initiatives through six articles

(Articles 125–130), all of which were later left untouched by Nice and which, in line with a French-inspired resolution on employment and growth adopted at Amsterdam, were to be implemented immediately and therefore before the TA had been ratified. The first, *Article 125*, builds on Article 3(1)(i) TEC by asserting the intention of the EC and the member states not only to develop a co-ordinated strategy for employment but also to promote 'a skilled, trained and adaptable workforce and labour markets responsive to economic change'. This, it is noted, will assist in achieving the aims of both Article 2 TEC and Article 2 TEU. *Article 126* then links employment to economic policy, by requiring that member states, when seeking to achieve the EC's objectives, act in a manner consistent with the broad economic policy guidelines adopted by the Council under Article 99(2) TEC, a point underlined later in Article 128(2). In a second paragraph, the article requires the member states to regard employment promotion as a matter of common concern and to co-ordinate their action, noting that national practices on the responsibilities of the social partners – management and labour – differ. As for the EC's contribution, this is spelt out in *Article 127* as involving the encouragement, support and complementing of co-operation between member states. Moreover, as is the case with environmental protection requirements under Article 6 TEC, the objective of a high level of employment is to be taken into consideration in the formulation and development of EC policies and activities.*

Turning to institutional responsibilities and decision-making, we find in *Article 128* mechanisms which, as both Langrish and Kenner note, shadow those used for adopting economic policy guidelines under Article 99 TEC. Each year the European Council, acting on a joint annual report from the Council and Commission, considers the employment situation in the EC and adopts conclusions, something which the specially-convened 'jobs summit' of the European Council in Luxembourg in October 1997 did when adopting a job-creation strategy based on employability, entrepreneurship, adaptability and equal opportunities. This was followed in 1999 by the Lisbon European Council which set a target of 70% employment within the EU by 2010.

The conclusions then form the basis for Council guidelines, adopted by QMV and in consultation with the EP, EcoSoc and the Committee of the Regions, which member states are obliged to take into account in their employment policies. A review of national policies is then carried out each year with the Council examining implementation records and potentially issuing, by QMV, recommendations to member states. Although the Commission also receives the annual national reports, it has no power to issue recommendations. Instead it forwards, jointly with the Council, an annual report on employment in the EC and implementation of policy guidelines to the European Council. The only body to have a formal input into Council deliberations is the Employment Committee provided for in Article 130 and discussed below.

Where the Commission does have more of a role to play is under *Article 129*, which provides for incentive measures designed to encourage and support co-operation among member states to be adopted by the EC using the co-decision procedure. The Commission thus assumes its traditional policy-initiator role. The incentive measures which may be adopted may not, however, involve any harmonization of national laws and regulations, being limited to initiatives, possibly involving pilot projects, designed to develop the exchange of information and best practices, provide comparative analysis and advice,

---

*In the English language version of the TEC, reference in Article 6 TEC is to 'definition and implementation of the Community policies' compared to 'formulation and implementation of Community policies and activities' in Article 127(1). This contrasts with other language versions where the wording in the two provisions is identical.

and promote innovative approaches and evaluating experiences. Declaration No. 23 TA states that the grounds for incentive measures as well as their duration and maximum funding should always be specified. Any funding is to be financed under Heading 3 (Internal Policies) of the EU budget (Declaration No. 24 TA). Clearly, the provisions do not provide any scope for EC legislation. So-called 'soft law' – or the more open method of co-ordination – is the focus.

This leaves us with the final article of Title VIII, *Article 130*, which provides for the establishment of an Employment Committee consisting of members drawn from each member state and the Commission. In effect, Article 130 does not provide for a new committee. Rather, it allows the Council to upgrade, as it did in January 2000, the status of the existing Employment and Labour Market Committee established in 1997 and rename it the Employment Committee as part of the EC's increased activity with regard to employment. Despite the upgrade, the Committee's role remains advisory. It monitors the national employment policies and employment situation in the EC, consults with management and labour, issues opinions and contributes to Council preparations regarding the annual examination of employment policies under Article 128.

With the six articles inserted at Amsterdam the EC gained a clearly identifiable legal framework for pursuing EC action regarding employment. The provisions may, as Kenner argues, be extremely pliable and thus create the capacity for a flexible approach to policy-making in the light of often conflicting policy demands. Yet, it is clearly the case that Title VIII on employment does not enjoy the same status and force within the TEC as, for example, the provisions on Economic and Monetary Union. As Sciarra notes, the institutional framework is comparatively weak and there is no legally meaningful outcome from the procedures provided for. Padoan maintains, however, that member states will be under pressure to adapt national employment policies, in part to ensure their competitiveness and in part to gain leverage in design and implementation of EC policies in general. And then there is the significance of peer pressure.

Beyond this there is the question of where employment ranks among the priorities of the EC and EU. Certainly at present one would be hard pushed to suggest that it enjoyed greater prominence than macro-economic policy inspired by the ECB and the efficiency of the Internal Market. The TEC may have gained a title dedicated to employment at Amsterdam, but this in no way heralds the advent of a concerted EC policy on the matter. Unlike Title IX, Common Commercial Policy, Title VIII does not represent a significant shift in policy competence to the EC level.

TITLE VIII

EMPLOYMENT (new – TA)

Article 125 (new – TA)

Member States and the Community shall, in accordance with this Title, work towards developing a co-ordinated strategy for employment and particularly for promoting a skilled, trained and adaptable workforce and labour markets responsive to economic change with a view to achieving the objectives defined in Article 2 of the Treaty on European Union and in Article 2 of this Treaty.

Article 126 (new – TA)

1. Member States, through their employment policies, shall contribute to the achievement of the objectives referred to in Article 125 in a way consistent with

the broad guidelines of the economic policies of the Member States and of the Community adopted pursuant to Article 99(2).

2. Member States, having regard to national practices related to the responsibilities of management and labour, shall regard promoting employment as a matter of common concern and shall co-ordinate their action in this respect within the Council, in accordance with the provisions of Article 128.

Article 127 (new – TA)

1. The Community shall contribute to a high level of employment by encouraging co-operation between Member States and by supporting and, if necessary, complementing their action. In doing so, the competences of the Member States shall be respected.

2. The objective of a high level of employment shall be taken into consideration in the formulation and implementation of Community policies and activities.

Article 128 (new – TA)

1. The European Council shall each year consider the employment situation in the Community and adopt conclusions thereon, on the basis of a joint annual report by the Council and the Commission.

2. On the basis of the conclusions of the European Council, the Council, acting by a qualified majority on a proposal from the Commission and after consulting the European Parliament, the Economic and Social Committee, the Committee of the Regions and the Employment Committee referred to in Article 130, shall each year draw up guidelines which the Member States shall take into account in their employment policies. These guidelines shall be consistent with the broad guidelines adopted pursuant to Article 99(2).

3. Each Member State shall provide the Council and the Commission with an annual report on the principal measures taken to implement its employment policy in the light of the guidelines for employment as referred to in paragraph 2.

4. The Council, on the basis of the reports referred to in paragraph 3 and having received the views of the Employment Committee, shall each year carry out an examination of the implementation of the employment policies of the Member States in the light of the guidelines for employment. The Council, acting by a qualified majority on a recommendation from the Commission, may, if it considers it appropriate in the light of that examination, make recommendations to Member States.

5. On the basis of the results of that examination, the Council and the Commission shall make a joint annual report to the European Council on the employment situation in the Community and on the implementation of the guidelines for employment.

Article 129 (new – TA)

The Council, acting in accordance with the procedure referred to in Article 251 and after consulting the Economic and Social Committee and the Committee of the Regions, may adopt incentive measures designed to encourage co-operation between Member States and to support their action in the field of employment through initiatives aimed at developing exchanges of information and best practices, providing comparative analysis and advice as well as promoting innovative approaches and evaluating experiences, in particular by recourse to pilot projects.

Those measures shall not include harmonisation of the laws and regulations of the Member States.

Article 130 (new – TA)

The Council, after consulting the European Parliament, shall establish an Employment Committee with advisory status to promote co-ordination between Member States on employment and labour market policies. The tasks of the Committee shall be:
– to monitor the employment situation and employment policies in the Member States and the Community;
– without prejudice to Article 207, to formulate opinions at the request of either the Council or the Commission or on its own initiative, and to contribute to the preparation of the Council proceedings referred to in Article 128.

In fulfilling its mandate, the Committee shall consult management and labour.

Each Member State and the Commission shall appoint two members of the Committee.

xiii   Common Commercial Policy

To readers of the treaty today it is somewhat odd that, stuck in the middle of the 21 titles in Part Three, the overwhelming majority of which concern internal EC matters, we now find provisions dedicated to the common commercial policy (CCP) and the EC's trade relations with non-member states. The reason for this is that almost all the policy provisions added to the treaty since the 1950s have been inserted after the titles concerning the four freedoms, agriculture, common rules and economic policy. And since the CCP was originally tucked away in Chapter 4 of the economic policy title and was never moved it now finds itself sandwiched between a host of domestic policy provisions. This does not mean that it has remained untouched by the process of treaty reform. Thanks to Maastricht, the original CCP chapter was upgraded to a title.

Moreover, and offering a foretaste of what was to happen generally at Amsterdam with simplification, the TEU removed two articles (ex Articles 111 and 114) relating to the transitional period as well as other redundant provisions found elsewhere in the title. The then Article 116 calling on member states to co-ordinate their positions in international fora was also deleted since the necessary co-ordination was now provided for under the CFSP (see Article 19(1), ex J.2(3) TEU). Despite Commission efforts, however, Maastricht did not, as Devuyst notes, substantially alter the CCP's scope. The same was true of Amsterdam, which only simplified one article before renumbering all in the title. Nice had a greater impact.

Today Title IX consists of just four articles (Articles 131–134). These provide the basis for the CCP noted in the preamble to the TEC. The policy is also listed prominently as an area of EC activity in Article 3(1)(b) TEC, in part because it is a natural complement to the customs union on which the EC is based. Indeed, it is under the provisions governing the customs union (Articles 25–27 TEC) that the common customs tariff which forms the basis of the CCP is set. In these too we find a set of principles, prominent among which is 'the need to promote trade', which by implication are supposed to inform the content, direction and operation of the CCP. And alongside these there are references in the preamble of the TEC to the EC contributing to 'the progressive abolition of restrictions on international trade'.

Such a desire is reflected in the aims of the CCP as laid down in *Article 131* (ex 110), the only article in the title which retains its original wording. The text, as Loth has noted, is bursting with compromise formulas. On the one hand, the member states aim to contribute to the 'harmonious' development of world trade through the abolition of trade barriers, an aim which was reinforced by a similar statement found, prior to its repeal at Amsterdam, in ex Article 18 TEC. At the same time, the abolition is to be 'progressive' and reflect the 'common interest' of the member states. The cautious embrace of freer international trade evident here is also reflected in the article's second paragraph, which seeks to balance the enthusiasm of some of the EC's founder members for international trade liberalization with the more protectionist inclinations of others. Hence, while perceived to be 'favourable', it is only accepted that the effects of opening up the EC market to imports 'may' increase the competitive strength of domestic undertakings.

Whatever the views of the founding members on the principles underpinning the CCP, such a policy does exist. Its scope is, however, restricted essentially to trade in goods, and even here there are exceptions, agricultural trade for example being regulated by the CAP. Nevertheless, the *Combined Nomenclature*, published annually by the Commission, contains over 16,000 tariff headings for which the EC is responsible in operating a trade policy common to all its member states. Hence, the CCP is one of the most highly integrated of EC policies, a point underlined by the array of trade and trade-based agreements which the EC has concluded with non-member states. All of these must, however, be compatible with the rules of the World Trade Organization (WTO) and the General Agreement on Tariffs and Trade (GATT), although as the likes of Peers and McMahon show with regard to bananas, the EC has not always been the most compliant member.

Before Title IX provides further details on the CCP's content and operation, *Article 132* (ex 112) calls on the member states progressively to harmonize national systems regarding export grants, thereby creating a level playing field for domestic undertakings. Directives for this purpose, albeit subject to the restrictions laid down in paragraph 2, are to be adopted by the Council using QMV. As with decision-making elsewhere in the title, there is no formal involvement of the EP.

Turning to *Article 133* (ex 113) we come to the core provisions regarding the CCP. Despite, as Young observes, substantial changes in the international economic environment and the trade agenda of GATT and the WTO, these had undergone only limited change prior to Nice. The article begins by declaring that the policy is to be based on uniform principles without setting these out. It then proceeds to identify the main elements of the CCP, although the list is not exhaustive: changes in tariff rates, the conclusion of tariff and trade agreements, trade liberalization, export policy and anti-dumping measures. Proposals for implementing the CCP are to be submitted to the Council by the Commission.

This brings us to paragraph 3 and trade agreements, a highly significant set of provisions since these confirm the fact that the EC has legal personality and is empowered to enter into legally binding arrangements with third parties, or in the case of Article 133, 'one or more States or international organizations', the latter being added at Maastricht to confirm the EC's competence to be a signatory to GATT agreements. What this all means is that the EC has so-called 'treaty-making power' with regard to trade in goods and cross-border services. And this power is exclusive to the EC. Member states cannot act on their own. Other areas of EC treaty-making power, whether exclusive or shared with the member states, can be found in Articles 71(1)(a), 111(3), 170, 174(4), 181 and 310 while Articles 149(3), 150(3), 151(3), 152(3), 155(3), 303 and 304 TEC also mandate the EC to pursue co-operation at the international level.

How agreements are to be negotiated is then explained. The Commission makes recommendations to the Council which can then authorize the opening negotiations. These are then conducted by the Commission. However, the Commission does not have free rein when negotiating. According to the treaty, it is obliged to conduct negotiations 'in consultation' with the so-called 'Article 133 Committee' of member state officials and operate within mandates issued by the Council. Nice has since added further requirements, the Commission having to report regularly to the Article 133 Committee and the Commission and Council having to ensure that any agreements negotiated are compatible with internal EC policies and rules. Both of these represent an attempt by the member states to ensure maximum control over negotiations and the content of agreements – even if they did not adopt a protocol on EU participation in WTO proceedings proposed during the 2000 IGC – and can be explained in part by the extensions in the scope of the CCP agreed at Nice as noted below.

Once the Commission has negotiated an agreement under Article 133, the Council may formally conclude it by QMV. Once again, there is no mention of the EP being involved in the conclusion process, even though the Luns–Westerterp process does provide for the EP to be informed about the negotiations. This is confirmed when the relevant provisions of Article 300 TEC, to which the final sentence of paragraph 3 directs us, are read. These do, however, allow the Council to authorize the Commission to approve minor modifications to the agreement. They also allow any agreement to be referred to the ECJ to test its compatibility with the TEC and for the TEC itself to be amended to facilitate the lawful conclusion of the agreement. Once concluded and in force the agreement is binding on the member states and institutions.

Returning to Article 133, we find in paragraphs 5 and 6 new provisions introduced by Nice to build on those added at Amsterdam empowering the Council to extend the scope of the EC's treaty-making powers under Article 133 to cover services and intellectual property. Such powers had long been considered, featuring as they did during the Maastricht and Amsterdam negotiations as Cloos et al. and McDonagh note. However, at no point could unanimous agreement be reached on including them within the scope of Article 113 even though, in the light of the ECJ's Opinion 1/94, it was clear that there were limits to the EC's exclusive competence and that a coherent CCP and effective participation in the World Trade Organization necessitated change. At Nice too, despite the urgings of the Finnish government in particular, support for extending the scope of the CCP was far from total, leaving what Monar refers to as a 'tortuous compromise': provisions which are both confusing and less clear than before. Indeed, attempts to clarify the provisions made by the jurist-linguists tidying up Nice between December 2000 and its signing in February 2001 came to nothing, COREPER and the member states returning to them the draft text untouched, mainly owing to Danish reservations, fearful of the whole compromise unravelling. Precise interpretation will be left to the ECJ.

As IGC watchers have noted, Article 133 saw the greatest number of options, redrafts and new proposals during the 2000 IGC with the final text being agreed only late on the last evening of the Nice European Council. What emerged in paragraph 5 is an agreed extension of paragraphs 1–4 to the conclusion of agreements covering trade in services and commercial aspects of intellectual property, although when acting the Council will do so by unanimity where the EC acts internally by unanimity, where the EC has yet to act and where horizontal agreements in limited areas, as opposed to all areas, as the French had supposedly sought, are concerned. Moreover, member states reserve the right to maintain and conclude their own agreements with non-member states and international organizations. Nice does not therefore confer on the EC exclusive competence regarding trade in services and commercial aspects of intellectual property. Moreover, through paragraph 6, further restrictions are imposed. First, no agreement may be concluded if it goes beyond the EC's internal powers, particularly where legal harmonization is concerned. Second, certain areas are excluded from being the subject of EC agreements. Trade in cultural, audiovisual, educational, social and human health services are, at France's insistence, declared to be of shared EC and member state competence and therefore agreements covering them must be concluded by both. Agreements concerning transport are, as paragraph 6 reminds us, already provided for under Articles 70–80 and 300 TEC.

What this all means is that, as Galloway argues, four types of agreement are possible under Article 133: agreements falling entirely within the scope of exclusive EC competence – concluded by QMV as is presently the case; agreements extending beyond the areas where the EC had exclusive competence before Nice and including areas in which the EC has exercised its powers internally – concluded by QMV or unanimity depending on the content of the agreement; agreements covering matters which extend into areas where internal powers have been conferred on the EC, but where the EC has not yet exercised those powers – concluded unanimously; and so-called 'mixed' agreements covering areas under both EC and member state competence – concluded by both the EC and the member states.

On the one hand this does not make for a particularly clear understanding of EC treaty-making powers with regard to the CCP. Political compromise at Nice, as has so often been the case with IGCs, has not always contributed to greater clarity in the TEC. On the other hand, the changes to Article 133 introduced by Nice have extended the potential scope of the CCP and increased the potential use of QMV with regard to trade in services and the commercial aspects of intellectual property. As for other aspects of the latter, application of paragraphs 1–4 can still be extended thanks to a revised version of the Amsterdam addition now found in paragraph 7.

So, finally, to *Article 134* which begins by providing for co-operation between member states in implementing the CCP so as to avoid trade deflection. The value of such action is not disputed. The same cannot be said with regard to what follows in so far as provisions are made for the Commission, in certain instances, to authorize member states to take protective measures by introducing import restrictions against other member states. To many this provision should have been repealed at Maastricht along with Articles 111, 114 and 116, as the Commission argued at the time, since it is incompatible with the Single Market. It was, however, retained, if not given 'authentic confirmation' as Bourgeois argues, through amendments introduced by the TEU requiring member states in urgent cases to seek authorization from the Commission, as opposed to acting unilaterally, to take measures deemed necessary to reduce any economic difficulties resulting from application of the CCP. The Commission may decide, however, that measures be adopted, amended or abolished. In selecting appropriate measures, priority is to be given to those which cause least disturbance to the functioning of, somewhat surprisingly given simplification at Amsterdam, the 'common market' and not the 'internal market'.

TITLE *IX* (ex Title VII)

COMMON COMMERCIAL POLICY

Article 131 (ex Article 110)

By establishing a customs union between themselves Member States aim to contribute, in the common interest, to the harmonious development of world trade, the progressive abolition of restrictions on international trade and the lowering of customs barriers.

The common commercial policy shall take into account the favourable effect which the abolition of customs duties between Member States may have on the increase in the competitive strength of undertakings in those States.

Article 132 (ex Article 112 simplified)

1. Without prejudice to obligations undertaken by them within the framework of other international organisations, Member States shall *progressively harmonise* the systems whereby they grant aid for exports to third countries, to the extent necessary to ensure that competition between undertakings of the Community is not distorted.

On a proposal from the Commission, the Council shall, *acting by a qualified majority,* issue any directives needed for this purpose.

2. The preceding provisions shall not apply to such a drawback of customs duties or charges having equivalent effect nor to such a repayment of indirect taxation including turnover taxes, excise duties and other indirect taxes as is allowed when goods are exported from a Member State to a third country, insofar as such a drawback or repayment does not exceed the amount imposed, directly or indirectly, on the products exported.

Article 133 (ex Article 113)

1. The common commercial policy shall be based on uniform principles, particularly in regard to changes in tariff rates, the conclusion of tariff and trade agreements, the achievement of uniformity in measures of liberalisation, export policy and measures to protect trade such as those to be taken in the event of dumping or subsidies.

2. The Commission shall submit proposals to the Council for implementing the common commercial policy.

3. Where agreements with one or more States or international organisations need to be negotiated, the Commission shall make recommendations to the Council, which shall authorise the Commission to open the necessary negotiations. **The Council and the Commission shall be responsible for ensuring that the agreements negotiated are compatible with internal Community policies and rules.**

The Commission shall conduct these negotiations in consultation with a special committee appointed by the Council to assist the Commission in this task and within the framework of such directives as the Council may issue to it. **The Commission shall report regularly to the special committee on the progress of negotiations.**

The relevant provisions of Article 300 shall apply.

4. In exercising the powers conferred upon it by this Article, the Council shall act by a qualified majority.

5. Paragraphs 1 to 4 shall also apply to the negotiation and conclusion of agreements in the fields of trade in services and the commercial aspects of intellectual property, insofar as those agreements are not covered by the said paragraphs and without prejudice to paragraph 6.

By way of derogation from paragraph 4, the Council shall act unanimously when negotiating and concluding an agreement in one of the fields referred to in the first subparagraph, where that agreement includes provisions for which unanimity is required for the adoption of internal rules or where it relates to a field in which the Community has not yet exercised the powers conferred upon it by this Treaty by adopting internal rules.

The Council shall act unanimously with respect to the negotiation and conclusion of a horizontal agreement insofar as it also concerns the preceding subparagraph or the second subparagraph of paragraph 6.

This paragraph shall not affect the right of the Member States to maintain and conclude agreements with third countries or international organisations insofar as such agreements comply with Community law and other relevant international agreements.

6. An agreement may not be concluded by the Council if it includes provisions which would go beyond the Community's internal powers, in particular by leading to harmonisation of the laws or regulations of the Member States in an area for which this Treaty rules out such harmonisation.

In this regard, by way of derogation from the first subparagraph of paragraph 5, agreements relating to trade in cultural and audiovisual services, educational services, and social and human health services, shall fall within the shared competence of the Community and its Member States. Consequently, in addition to a Community decision taken in accordance with the relevant provisions of Article 300, the negotiation of such agreements shall require the common accord of the Member States. Agreements thus negotiated shall be concluded jointly by the Community and the Member States.

The negotiation and conclusion of international agreements in the field of transport shall continue to be governed by the provisions of Title V and Article 300.

7. Without prejudice to the first subparagraph of paragraph 6, *the Council, acting unanimously on a proposal from the Commission and after consulting the European Parliament, may extend the application of paragraphs 1 to 4 to international negotiations and agreements on Intellectual property insofar as they are not covered by paragraph 5.*

Article 134 (ex Article 115)

In order to ensure that the execution of measures of commercial policy taken in accordance with this Treaty by any Member State is not obstructed by deflection of trade, or where differences between such measures lead to economic difficulties in one or more Member States, the Commission shall recommend the methods for the requisite co-operation between Member States. Failing this, the Commission may authorise Member States to take the necessary protective measures, the conditions and details of which it shall determine.

In case of urgency, Member States shall request authorisation to take the necessary measures themselves from the Commission, which shall take a decision as soon as possible; the Member States concerned shall then notify the measures to the other Member States. The Commission may decide at any time that the Member States concerned shall amend or abolish the measures in question.

In the selection of such measures, priority shall be given to those which cause the least disturbance of the functioning of the common market.

xiv   Customs Co-operation

Having briefly concerned itself with the outside world through the provisions on the common commercial policy, the TEC in Title X turns its attention once again to essentially internal matters. The title, which was inserted by the TA, consists of a single article, *Article 135*, providing for increased customs co-operation between the member states and between the member states and the Commission, measures being adopted using the co-decision procedure.

This is not to say that customs co-operation is a relatively new item on the EC's agenda. Co-operation dates back to the 1960s with bodies such as the Mutual Assistance Group '92 (MAG '92 – customs) being set up from the mid-1980s onwards to promote greater co-operation among the member states. And then at Maastricht, a provision similar to that in Article 135 was included in Title VI of the TEU with customs co-operation being slated for possible transfer to the EC pillar via the *passerelle* clause then found in Article K.9 TEU. What Amsterdam did therefore was to communitarize most aspects of customs co-operation, shifting competence from the JHA pillar of the Union to the EC. As Duff points out, this made sense given the EC's responsibilities for creating an area of freedom, security and justice. However, co-operation concerning criminal matters affecting national judicial systems is expressly excluded from the remit of Article 135, remaining instead the subject of inter-governmental co-operation in Pillar III under Articles 29 and 30(1)(a) TEU. The presence of the inter-governmental pillar is also felt in practice since customs co-operation matters are still dealt with by the Article 36 Committee.

TITLE X (new – TA)

CUSTOMS CO-OPERATION

Article 135 (new – TA)

Within the scope of application of this Treaty, the Council, acting in accordance with the procedure referred to in Article 251, shall take measures in order to strengthen customs co-operation between Member States and between the latter and the Commission. These measures shall not concern the application of national criminal law or the national administration of justice.

xv Social Policy, Education, Vocational Training and Youth

Having addressed trade matters and customs co-operation, the TEC turns over the next few titles to what might loosely be termed 'social matters'. In the first, Title XI (ex VIII), it deals with a variety of policy areas under the heading Social Policy, Education, Vocational Training and Youth and gives substance to the EC's stated task of promoting 'a high level of employment and social protection, equality between men and women . . . [and] the raising of the standard of living and quality of life' (Article 2 TEC) and of pursuing 'a policy in the social sphere' (Article 3(1)(j) TEC). The title consists of 15 articles divided among three chapters, dedicated to Social Provisions (Articles 136–145, ex 117–122), the European Social Fund (Articles 146–148, ex 123–125), and Education, Vocational Training and Youth (Articles 149 and 150, ex 126 and 127), the latter being added by the TEU. Few of the articles are as they were when the TEC was signed. Indeed, the majority have either been inserted or amended at some point. Here the TA had a significant impact and not simply because it renumbered them all and supplemented the provisions with Title VIII on employment discussed earlier in the *Guide*. As for Nice, its contribution was to amend two articles, mainly in terms of presentation and with regard to decision-making procedures, and insert a third on the Social Protection Committee.

Social Provisions

Turning to Chapter 1, 'Social provisions', this is by far the most amended of the three chapters in Title XI, containing only one article, *Article 145* (ex 122), which has remained unaltered since 1958. It obliges the Commission to report annually on social developments and where invited to by the EP. As for the rest of the articles in the chapter, although three underwent amendment as a result of Nice, most owe either their existence or current shape to Amsterdam. This is because, following New Labour's first victory in the 1997 UK general election, provisions contained in the so-called 'Social Chapter' agreed at Maastricht in 1991 which allowed the UK government to opt out of new social policy measures were belatedly inserted into the TEC.*

The first article in Chapter 1, *Article 136* (ex 117), sets out the objectives of the EC with regard to social policy and requires the EC, when pursuing them, to bear in mind the social rights set out in the European Social Charter agreed in Turin in 1961 by members of the Council of Europe and the EC's own Charter of Fundamental Social Rights of Workers adopted by 11 member states in 1989. These references, which also appear in the preamble to the TEC, as revised by the TA, are significant since they signal a broader context for social policy than that defined by the provisions of the TEC itself. Being inserted by Amsterdam, they also reflect EC efforts to give social policy a higher profile and greater substance, something which is also reflected in the policy objectives. These, following Maastricht and Amsterdam, are: the promotion of employment,

*The Social Chapter, formally known as the Protocol on Social Policy, to which is Annexed an Agreement, concluded between the member states of the European Community with the exception of the United Kingdom of Great Britain and Northern Ireland, to which two declarations are attached, is reproduced in *OJ* C224, 31 August 1992, pp. 126–129.

improved living and working conditions, proper social protection, dialogue between management and labour, the developing of human resources, and the combating of exclusion.

Clearly, social policy in the EC context is somewhat removed from what is often understood to be social policy in most domestic contexts. It is far from being about the totality of welfare provision and evidently excludes healthcare, pension and education provision. That said, the objectives of the EC have increased beyond the promotion of improved working conditions and an improved standard of living for workers as originally contained in ex Article 117. This expansion has caused concern in some quarters leading the UK government, for example, to argue strongly and successfully at Nice for a guarantee that social policy measures will neither affect the right of member states to define the fundamental principles of their own social security systems nor significantly affect the financial equilibrium of such systems (Article 137(4)).

In order to achieve the objectives, the EC, according to *Article 136* (ex 117), is to work alongside the member states in adopting implementing measures which take into account diversities in national practices with particular attention being drawn to 'contractual relations', and the need to maintain the competitiveness of the EC economy. In line with Declaration 23 TEU, the EC is to co-operate with charitable associations too. The measures adopted, it is believed, will result from the functioning of the common market which in turn will favour the harmonization of social systems. They will also come about as a result of the approximation of national laws, regulations and administrative action.

How the above objectives are to be achieved is set out in *Article 137* (ex 118), as amended and restructured for the purpose of clarity by the Treaty of Nice. Here it is clearly noted that the EC's role is to support and complement the activities of the member states, underlining the fact that social policy is not an area of exclusive EC competence. Where the EC and member states are to act is then spelt out in a list of 11 areas, several of which can be traced back to the original TEC. Others, such as the social protection of workers and the representation and collective defence of the interests of workers and employers, date to either the Social Chapter or, in the case of social exclusion, to the TA. Only the modernization of social protection systems is a recent addition agreed at Nice. Certain areas, such as pay and the right to strike, are explicitly excluded as areas from EC action (Article 137(5)). According to Declarations Nos. 25 TA and 8 TN, any expenditure under Article 137 is to fall under heading 3 (Internal Policies) of the EU budget.

The types of measures which the EC can adopt are set out in Article 137(2) along with the decision-making procedures to be followed. Thus, so-called 'soft' measures excluding any harmonization of laws or regulations and designed to encourage co-operation in terms of information exchange and improved knowledge may be adopted using the co-decision procedure and in consultation with EcoSoc and the Committee of the Regions. Directives containing minimum requirements for gradual implementation may also be adopted in all areas listed in Article 137(1) except the Nice additions, although Declaration No. 26 TA does commit the member states to avoid health and safety measures which will discriminate against small- and medium-sized enterprises. The emphasis, though, is on minimum standards, leaving member states free, as in other areas such as the environment, to maintain and introduce more stringent protective measures provided they are compatible with the TEC (Article 137(4)).

As for how directives are adopted, in most instances the Council will act under the co-decision procedure. However, directives in some areas – that is those concerning social security, the social protection of workers, the protection of workers where their employment contract is terminated, the representation and collective defence of workers and the conditions of employment for third-country nationals legally employed in the EC – are all to be adopted by the Council acting unanimously and after consultation with the EP, EcoSoc and the Committee of the Regions. At Nice, various member states wished to extend co-decision and, by implication, QMV to these matters. They failed, and co-decision was only extended to measures modernizing social protection schemes. What was agreed, however, was that the Council, by unanimous vote, can apply the co-decision procedure to the adoption of measures in all remaining areas except social security and social protection of workers. Whether this 'switchover' clause or *passerelle* will ever be activated is open to question. As Galloway notes, experience to date suggests that without automaticity such clauses are never used.

As for the implementation of measures, this is normally the responsibility of the member states. Article 137(3) does, however, allow for management and labour to be entrusted with implementation where there is a joint request to do so. In such cases, the member state concerned has to ensure that it can guarantee the results imposed by any directive. Such involvement of management and labour is a novel development and one which is also reflected in the provisions of *Articles 138* and *139*, the first of which calls on the Commission to promote consultation and dialogue between the two at the EC level and consult them both when considering and submitting proposals in the social policy sphere. Moreover, where management and labour so wish they may seek to conclude contractual relations and agreements under Article 139. Negotiations on any agreement should not normally last more than nine months before being concluded and implemented, where necessary by Council decision. What, in effect, is provided for here is the establishment at EC level of labour and management as 'formal co-actors' in the decision-making process governing social policy. As Falkner argues, policy procedures therefore 'fit the classic formula for corporatist concertation' with policy being decided in a 'corporatist policy community'. This is a radical development and interestingly, as Szyszczak notes, one that excludes the EP from decision-making. It also suggests a minor role for the member states, although in Declaration No. 27 TA they absolve themselves of any obligation to apply agreements directly and assert the primacy of national legislation. Yet how much use will be made of the 'social dialogue' created is open to question. Employers in the past have been reluctant partners.

In addition to measures adopted by the Council and the 'social partners', Chapter 1 also contains provisions for Commission-sponsored studies and co-ordination of member state action 'in all social policy fields', but in particular in the following areas: employment, labour law and working conditions, basic and advanced vocational training, social security, the prevention of occupational accidents and diseases, occupational hygiene and the right of association and collective bargaining between employers and workers. Before delivering any opinions, the Commission is obliged to consult EcoSoc, but not the EP (*Article 140*, ex 118). Such action is not particularly contested. The same cannot be said for what has emanated from the next set of social policy provisions.

For the EC, one of the most dynamic and politically contentious areas of case law has been that concerning equal pay between men and women. It has its origins in the first two paragraphs of the French-inspired *Article 141* (ex 119). The first of these is one of several TEC articles outlawing discrimination in some form, laying down that the member states shall 'ensure the principle of equal pay for male and female workers for equal work or work of equal value is applied'. Amsterdam added 'or work of equal value' thus recognizing that discrimination can arise when exact comparisons cannot always be made. The second paragraph then provides definitions of 'pay' and 'equal pay'. At first glance, the definitions may appear straightforward and comprehensive. However, the ECJ has tended to interpret these broadly, extending 'pay' to include, for example, pensions. In terms of the European Treaties, this has had an interesting impact. For as a consequence of the ECJ's ambiguous 1990 ruling in *Barber* v. *Guardian Royal Exchange*, the member states sought to clarify whether indeed the principle of equal pay in Article 141 should be applied to pensions covering the period prior to the date of the ruling. Unsurprisingly given the potential costs involved – estimated at up to £40 billion in the case of UK industry alone – the member states opted for a restrictive interpretation. To ensure its legal standing it was inserted in a legally binding protocol – the Protocol concerning Article 119 of the Treaty establishing the European Union. As Hervey noted at the time, this so-called 'Barber Protocol' was legally and politically contentious since its existence appeared to many to undermine the ECJ's monopoly on interpretative competence and the separation of powers within the EC. Nevertheless, the ECJ has had no choice but to accept the protocol's provisions.

Returning to the provisions of Article 141, paragraph 3 states that the Council acting in accordance with the co-decision procedure – and without consulting the social partners – may adopt measures to ensure the application of the principle of equal opportunities and equal treatment of men and women in employment and occupational matters, notably regarding equal pay for equal work. This paragraph was inserted into the TEC by Amsterdam and clearly enhances the EC's role in promoting equal opportunities and, alongside Article 13 TEC, in challenging discrimination. The imprecise wording of the new provision leads the likes of Szyszczak to argue that it has the potential to provide the focus for exploring just how far the constitutional boundaries of sex discrimination go within EC law.

This all suggests that Article 141 will continue to attract much controversy, an argument strengthened by consideration of paragraph 4 which has its origins in the Social Chapter and, as Arnull notes, a desire to reverse the ECJ's 1995 ruling in *Kalanke* v. *Bremen* precluding positive discrimination. It allows member states to take positive action measures to ensure that 'the under-represented sex' (as opposed to 'women' originally) may pursue vocational activities and to prevent or compensate him/her for disadvantages in professional careers. Although the neutering of the provision may have disappointed many, Declaration No. 28 TA does call, in the first instance, for measures aimed at improving the position of women in working life to be adopted.

Moving on, *Article 142* (ex 120) requires that member states endeavour to maintain the existing equivalence between paid holiday schemes. The innocuous provision, in the TEC at France's behest yet only invoked once in 1995 as the basis for a Council recommendation, is then followed by an addition to the treaty, *Article 143*, inserted by the TA which calls on the Commission to produce an annual report for the Council, EP and EcoSoc on the demographic situation in the Community and the EC's record in achieving the social policy objectives set out in Article 136. The Commission can also be called upon by the EP to report on 'particular problems concerning the social situation'. *Article 145*, which has required the Commission since the EC was founded to include a separate chapter on social developments in its annual report to the EP, also permits the EP to call on the Commission to report on 'particular problems concerning social conditions'.

This leaves us with *Article 144*, a totally new article inserted into the treaty by Nice following a proposal from the Irish government. It provides for a Social Protection Committee modelled on the Employment Committee (see Article 130). Hence, composed of appointees from the member states and the Commission, it has only an advisory function in promoting co-operation between the member states on social protection. Also, the Committee is not new; Article 44 simply provides a legal base for a committee which already exists. As Galloway notes, this may place the Committee on a firmer legal footing, but it also reflects a 'worrying' trend towards increasing compartmentalization of work within the Council. This, it is argued, runs counter to the desire to enhance the overall coherence of work in the Council by limiting the number of Council formations and strengthening the role of COREPER. Such concerns aside, the upgrading of the Committee has been welcomed as signalling a more positive future involvement of the EC in promoting good practice.

TITLE XI (ex Title VIII)

SOCIAL POLICY, EDUCATION, VOCATIONAL TRAINING AND YOUTH

Chapter 1   Social Provisions

Article 136 (ex Article 117)

The Community *and the Member States,* **having in mind fundamental social rights such as those set out in the European Social Charter signed at Turin on 18 October 1961 and in the 1989 Community Charter of the Fundamental Social Rights of Workers,** *shall have as their objectives the promotion of employment, improved living and working conditions,* so as to make possible their harmonisation while the improvement is being maintained, *proper social protection, dialogue between management and labour, the development of human resources with a view to lasting high employment and the combating of exclusion.*

To this end the Community and the Member States shall implement measures which take account of the diverse forms of national practices, in particular in the field of contractual relations, and the need to maintain the competitiveness of the Community economy.

They believe that such a development will ensue not only from the functioning of the common market, which will favour the harmonisation of social systems, but also from the procedures provided for in this Treaty and from the approximation of provisions laid down by law, regulation or administrative action.

Article 137 (ex Article 118a)

1. With a view to achieving the objectives of Article 136, the Community shall support and complement the activities of the Member States in the following fields:
(a) improvement in particular of the working environment to protect workers' health and safety;
(b) working conditions;
(c) social security and social protection of workers;
(d) protection of workers where their employment contract is terminated;
(e) the information and consultation of workers;
(f) representation and collective defence of the interests of workers and employers, including co-determination, subject to paragraph 5;
(g) conditions of employment for third-country nationals legally residing in Community territory;
(h) the integration of persons excluded from the labour market, without prejudice to Article 150;
(i) equality between men and women with regard to labour market opportunities and treatment at work;

(j) the combating of social exclusion;

(k) the modernisation of social protection systems without prejudice to point (c).

2. To this end, the Council:

(a) *may adopt measures designed to encourage co-operation between Member States through initiatives aimed at improving knowledge, developing exchanges of information and best practices, promoting innovative approaches and evaluating experiences,* excluding any harmonisation of the laws and regulations of the Member States;

(b) may adopt, in the fields referred to in paragraph 1(a) to (i), *by means of directives, minimum requirements for gradual implementation, having regard to the conditions and technical rules obtaining in each of the Member States. Such directives shall avoid imposing administrative, financial and legal constraints in a way which would hold back the creation and development of small and medium-sized undertakings.*

The Council shall act in accordance with the procedure referred to in Article 251 after consulting the Economic and Social Committee and the Committee of the Regions, except in the fields referred to in paragraph 19(c), (d), (f) and (g) of this Article, where the Council shall act unanimously on a proposal from the Commission, after consulting the European Parliament and the said Committees. The Council, acting unanimously on a proposal from the Commission, after consulting the European Parliament, may decide to render the procedure referred to in Article 251 applicable to paragraph 1(d), (f) and (g) of this Article.

3. *A Member State may entrust management and labour, at their joint request, with the implementation of directives adopted pursuant to* paragraph 2.

In this case, it shall ensure that, no later than the date on which a directive must be transposed in accordance with Article 249, management and labour have introduced the necessary measures by agreement, the Member State concerned being required to take any necessary measure enabling it at any time to be in a position to guarantee the results imposed by that directive.

4. *The provisions adopted pursuant to this Article:*

– shall not affect the right of Member States to define the fundamental principles of their social security systems and must not significantly affect the financial equilibrium thereof;

– *shall not prevent any Member State from maintaining or introducing more stringent protective measures compatible with this Treaty.*

5. *The provisions of this Article shall not apply to pay, the right of association, the right to strike or the right to impose lock-outs.*

Article 138

1. *The Commission shall have the task of promoting the consultation of management and labour at Community level and shall take any relevant measure to facilitate their dialogue by ensuring balanced support for the parties.*

2. *To this end, before submitting proposals in the social policy field, the Commission shall consult management and labour on the possible direction of Community action.*

3. *If, after such consultation, the Commission considers Community action advisable, it shall consult management and labour on the content of the envisaged*

proposal. Management and labour shall forward to the Commission an opinion or, where appropriate, a recommendation.

4. On the occasion of such consultation, management and labour may inform the Commission of their wish to initiate the process provided for in Article 139. The duration of the procedure shall not exceed nine months, unless the management and labour concerned and the Commission decide jointly to extend it.

Article 139 (ex Article 118b)

1. Should management and labour so desire, the dialogue between them at Community level may lead to contractual relations, including agreements.

2. Agreements concluded at Community level shall be implemented either in accordance with the procedures and practices specific to management and labour and the Member States or, in matters covered by Article 137, at the joint request of the signatory parties, by a Council decision on a proposal from the Commission.

The Council shall act by qualified majority, except where the agreement in question contains one or more provisions relating to one of the areas **for which unanimity is required pursuant to Article 137(2),** *in which case it shall act unanimously.*

Article 140 (ex Article 118)

With a view to achieving the objectives of Article 136 and without prejudice to the other provisions of this Treaty, the Commission shall encourage co-operation between the Member States and facilitate the co-ordination of their action in all social policy fields *under this chapter*, particularly in matters relating to:
– employment;
– labour law and working conditions;
– basic and advanced vocational training;
– social security;
– prevention of occupational accidents and diseases;
– occupational hygiene;
– the right of association and collective bargaining between employers and workers.

To this end, the Commission shall act in close contact with Member States by making studies, delivering opinions and arranging consultations both on problems arising at national level and on those of concern to international organisations.

Before delivering the opinions provided for in this Article, the Commission shall consult the Economic and Social Committee.

Article 141 (ex Article 119)

1. Each Member State shall ensure that the principle of equal pay for male and female workers for equal work **or work of equal value** *is applied.*

2. For the purpose of this Article, 'pay' means the ordinary basic or minimum wage or salary and any other consideration, whether in cash or in kind, which the worker receives directly or indirectly, in respect of his employment, from his employer.

Equal pay without discrimination based on sex means:
(a) that pay for the same work at piece rates shall be calculated on the basis of the same unit of measurement;

(b) that pay for work at time rates shall be the same for the same job.

3. The Council, acting in accordance with the procedure referred to in Article 251, and after consulting the Economic and Social Committee, shall adopt measures to ensure the application of the principle of equal opportunities and equal treatment of men and women in matters of employment and occupation, including the principle of equal pay for equal work or work of equal value.

4. With a view to ensuring full equality in practice between men and women in working life, the principle of equal treatment *shall not prevent any Member State from maintaining or adopting measures providing for specific advantages in order to make it easier for* the under-represented sex *to pursue a vocational activity or to prevent or compensate for disadvantages in professional careers.*

Article 142 (ex Article 120)

Member States shall endeavour to maintain the existing equivalence between paid holiday schemes.

Article 143

The Commission shall draw up a report each year on progress in achieving the objectives of Article 136, including the demographic situation in the Community. It shall forward the report to the European Parliament, the Council and the Economic and Social Committee.

The European Parliament may invite the Commission to draw up reports on particular problems concerning the social situation.

Article 144 (new – TN)

The Council, after consulting the European Parliament, shall establish a Social Protection Committee with advisory status to promote co-operation on social protection policies between Member States and with the Commission. The tasks of the Committee shall be:
– to monitor the social situation and the development of social protection policies in the Member States and the Community;
– to promote exchanges of information, experience and good practice between Member States and with the Commission;
– without prejudice to Article 207, to prepare reports, formulate opinions or undertake other work within its fields of competence, at the request of either the Council or the Commission or on its own initiative.
In fulfilling its mandate, the Committee shall establish appropriate contacts with management and labour.
Each Member State and the Commission shall appoint two members of the Committee.

Article 145 (ex Article 122)

The Commission shall include a separate chapter on social developments within the Community in its annual report to the European Parliament.

The European Parliament may invite the Commission to draw up reports on any particular problems concerning social conditions.

The European Social Fund

The second chapter in Title XI contains three articles (Articles 146–148, ex 123–125) which relate to the establishment, tasks and operation of the European Social Fund (ESF). The first of these establishes the ESF, an event which took place in the late 1950s, and spells out its aim, this being to improve employment opportunities for workers and thereby raise standards of living. This is to be done primarily through increasing labour mobility, although the TEU was responsible for adding a reference to facilitating adaption to industrial change through vocational training and retraining (*Article 146*, ex 123). Today, therefore, the activities of the ESF complement, if not support, those of the EC under Articles 125–130 on employment and Article 150 (ex 127) on vocational training. In recent years the ESF has been responsible for funding of over €4.5 million worth of projects annually within the EU.

Who runs the ESF is set out in *Article 147* (ex 124). This places responsibility for administration in the hands of the Commission which is assisted by a committee of governmental, trade union and employers' representatives. As for what the ESF actually does, this is determined under *Article 148* (ex 125) by the Council using, thanks to the TA, the co-decision procedure. Amsterdam was also responsible for involving the Committee of the Regions as a consultative body alongside EcoSoc in deliberations on implementing decisions.

Chapter 2   The European Social Fund

Article 146 (ex Article 123)

In order to improve employment opportunities for workers in the internal market and to contribute thereby to raising the standard of living, a European Social Fund is hereby established in accordance with the provisions set out below; it shall aim to render the employment of workers easier and to increase their geographical and occupational mobility within the Community, and to facilitate their adaptation to industrial changes and to changes in production systems, in particular through vocational training and retraining.

Article 147 (ex Article 124)

The Fund shall be administered by the Commission.
The Commission shall be assisted in this task by a Committee presided over by a Member of the Commission and composed of representatives of governments, trade unions and employers' organisations.

Article 148 (ex Article 125)

The Council, acting in accordance with the procedure referred to in Article 251 and after consulting the Economic and Social Committee **and the Committee of the Regions,** shall adopt implementing decisions relating to the European Social Fund.

Education, Vocational Training and Youth

This brings us to the final chapter in Title XI, Chapter 3, 'Education, vocational training and youth', which consists of two articles: Article 149 (ex 126) on education and Article 150 (ex 127) on vocational training. These provide the main legal bases for pursuing the only goal of the member states added to the TEC's preamble by Amsterdam: 'the development of the highest possible level of knowledge for their peoples through a wide access to education and though continuous updating'. For Shaw this confers on education a constitutional status within the EC/EU. The preambular reference is then followed by Article 3(1)(q) TEC which notes that the EC is to be active in contributing to 'education and training of quality' in the member states. However, despite the title of Chapter 3, no reference is made to 'youth'. Moreover, Chapter 3 contains no dedicated article to the issue. Its inclusion does signify, though, the priority the EC gives to youth in implementing measures under the title.

The first article was introduced to the TEC by the TEU and appeared to be providing the EC with a new policy competence. In fact, the EC had already been active in many areas covered by the article as programmes such as ERASMUS (European Action Scheme for the Mobility of University Students), LINGUA (Action Programme to Promote Foreign Language Competence in the Community) and COMETT (Programme of the Community in Education and Training for Technologies) testified. These had been adopted using various treaty bases including Article 308 (ex 235) and had led to various challenges in the ECJ over the question of EC competence to act, notably in the *ERASMUS* and *Gravier* cases. In the light of these and disputes over procedure the member states sought to define more closely where the EC could act through the introduction of *Article 149* (ex 126) by the TEU. It calls on the EC to encourage co-operation among the member states in developing what is referred to as 'quality education'. In addition, it permits the EC to support and supplement member state action, although great emphasis is placed on respecting member states' responsibility for their national educational policies. The EC is, for example, allowed neither to impinge on the content and organization of education systems nor to undermine their linguistic and cultural diversity (Article 149(1), ex 126(1)). Such constraints would appear to narrow down exactly what the EC can actually do. As Shaw notes, the provisions, alongside those in Article 150 (ex 127), can clearly be regarded as a reassertion of member state control after the Commission had arguably been 'running wild' in terms of promoting education initiatives.

The limits on EC action can also be seen in paragraph 2, which sets out the aims of EC action and indicates how some of them can be achieved. Thus the EC is to develop the 'European dimension' in education through language teaching and dissemination, and encourage staff and student mobility by encouraging the academic recognition of diplomas and periods of study, something which, as noted, has been under way since the mid-1980s with the ERASMUS, LINGUA, COMETT and now the LEONARDO and SOCRATES programmes. The EC is also to encourage co-operation among educational establishments; the development of information exchange among the member states on common issues concerning education; development of youth exchanges as well as those of instructors; and the development of distance learning. As paragraph 3 implies, such activities are not restricted to the member states: co-operation on educational matters is to be fostered with non-member states and international organizations too, notably the Council of Europe.

The mechanisms through which all this is to be realized are contained in the final paragraph of Article 149 (ex 126). First, incentive measures may be adopted provided they do not entail any harmonization of national laws or regulations. Such measures are to be agreed by the Council using the co-decision procedure and in consultation with the EcoSoc and Committee of the Regions, consultation of the latter acknowledging the role which the German *Länder* play in policy-making on education. Second, the Council may adopt recommendations. This it simply does on the basis of a Commission proposal without formally consulting any other institution or committee.

Having addressed co-operation on selected educational matters, Chapter 3 turns to vocational training in *Article 150* (ex 127). Paragraph 1 authorizes the EC to implement a dedicated policy in support of the actions of the member states. As with education, the EC is to fully respect the organization and content of national policies. Unlike education, however, explicit competences to act with regard to vocational training have always been in the TEC and indeed some of the original ones are still present (for example: Article 35 (ex 41), the reference to the exchange of young workers in Article 41 (ex 50) and Article 57(2) (ex 47(2))). And on the basis of these a set of principles for a Community vocational policy was formulated as early as 1963. Few significant policy initiatives were taken, however, until the 1970s when various action plans were adopted and a European Centre for the Development of Vocational Training (CEDEFOP) was set up in 1975 to advise the Commission when formulating EC policy. The present TEC provisions date back to the TEU and define more precisely the EC's role, even if they do remove the reference originally found in Article 128 to a 'common vocational policy'. According to paragraph 2, EC action should facilitate adaption to industrial change through vocational training and retraining; improve initial and continuing vocational training so as to facilitate integration into labour markets; facilitate access to vocational training; stimulate co-operation among institutions and firms; and develop information and experience exchange.

As with EC educational initiatives, co-operation with non-member states and international organizations is to be pursued. The means by which EC action is to be achieved do differ in that they are less specific. With regard to vocational policy, the Council may adopt 'measures'. This it does using the co-decision procedure, as opposed to the co-operation procedure prior to Amsterdam, and in consultation with EcoSoc and the Committee of the Regions. Such measures may not entail any harmonization of national laws or regulations. To some this might seem odd given that legislation in the area of the mutual recognition of diplomas and other qualifications is a form of harmonization. Such legislation is, however, adopted on the basis of TEC provisions governing the Single Market (e.g. Article 95, ex 100a). As with so many areas of EC activity, action in a given policy area is rarely based simply on a dedicated title or chapter in the treaty.

Chapter 3   Education, vocational training and youth

Article 149 (ex Article 126)

1. The Community shall contribute to the development of quality education by encouraging co-operation between Member States and, if necessary, by supporting and supplementing their action, while fully respecting the responsibility of the Member States for the content of teaching and the organisation of education systems and their cultural and linguistic diversity.

2. Community action shall be aimed at:
– developing the European dimension in education, particularly through the teaching and dissemination of the languages of the Member States;
– encouraging mobility of students and teachers, *inter alia* by encouraging the academic recognition of diplomas and periods of study;

– promoting co-operation between educational establishments;
– developing exchanges of information and experience on issues common to the education systems of the Member States;
– encouraging the development of youth exchanges and of exchanges of socio-educational instructors;
– encouraging the development of distance education.

3. The Community and the Member States shall foster co-operation with third countries and the competent international organisations in the field of education, in particular the Council of Europe.

4. In order to contribute to the achievement of the objectives referred to in this Article, the Council:
– acting in accordance with the procedure referred to in Article 251, after consulting the Economic and Social Committee and the Committee of the Regions, shall adopt incentive measures, excluding any harmonisation of the laws and regulations of the Member States;
– acting by a qualified majority on a proposal from the Commission, shall adopt recommendations.

Article 150 (ex Article 127)

1. The Community shall implement a vocational training policy which shall support and supplement the action of the Member States, while fully respecting the responsibility of the Member States for the content and organisation of vocational training.

2. Community action shall aim to:
– facilitate adaptation to industrial changes, in particular through vocational training and retraining;
– improve initial and continuing vocational training in order to facilitate vocational integration and reintegration into the labour market;
– facilitate access to vocational training and encourage mobility of instructors and trainees and particularly young people;
– stimulate co-operation on training between educational or training establishments and firms;
– develop exchanges of information and experience on issues common to the training systems of the Member States.

3. The Community and the Member States shall foster co-operation with third countries and the competent international organisations in the sphere of vocational training.

4. The Council, acting in accordance with the procedure referred to in Article 251 and after consulting the Economic and Social Committee **and the Committee of the Regions,** shall adopt measures to contribute to the achievement of the objectives referred to in this Article, excluding any harmonisation of the laws and regulations of the Member States.

xvi Culture

As with many other titles found in Part Three of the TEC, Title XII on culture is of comparatively recent origin, being introduced in 1993 by the TEU. Similarly, its insertion did not signal a wholly new departure for the EC in terms of policy competence. As Granturco argues, EC action can be traced back to the 1970s with the Copenhagen summit of the European Council in 1973 adopting a 'Declaration on European Identity' and the Commission issuing a communication on Community action in the cultural sector in 1977. In addition, member states had long been able to invoke cultural heritage under Article 36 (now 30) to restrict the movement of goods in protection of national treasures possessing artistic, historic or archaeological value. Later, in the 1980s, the Commission was instrumental in launching the idea of a European Cultural Area and programmes such as the European City of Culture and MEDIA directed at supporting audiovisual projects.

All of this took place without a specific competence for EC action. It also raised concerns among some member states that the EC was encroaching too far into an area of national sovereignty. Hence, and with concerns that inappropriate use was being made of Article 95 (ex 100a) to impact on cultural matters via the Single Market programme, the TEU introduced Title XII and its sole provision, Article 151 (ex 128). This was not the only reference to culture in the revised TEC. The TEU also amended Article 3 TEC to include 'a contribution ... to the flowering of the cultures of the Member States' among the activities of the EC. This was followed by a new exemption from the state aid rules under Article 87(2)(a) (ex 92(2)(a)) for 'aid to promote culture and heritage conservation' and the reference under Article 149(1) (ex 126(1)) to respecting cultural diversity when promoting co-operation on education matters.

The insertion of *Article 151* (ex 128) into the TEC did not really signal, however, an empowerment of the EC with regard to culture. In many respects, its provisions tend to impose explicit constraints on the EC, a point also implicit in the reference to the member states 'desiring to deepen the solidarity between their peoples while respecting their history, their culture and their traditions' in the preamble of the TEU and in the reference to the EU respecting the national identities of its member states in Article 6(3) TEU as amended by Amsterdam. This is underlined in paragraph 1 of Article 151, which confirms the EC's role as contributing to 'the flowering of cultures of the Member States while respecting their national and regional diversity'. Admittedly, the EC is also to bring to the fore, 'the common cultural heritage', but the emphasis is clearly on promoting national cultures, thus maintaining cultural diversity. The introduction of 'culture' to the TEC should not be seen as portending the imposition of cultural homogeneity on its members by the EC.

Moving on, Article 151 lists in paragraph 2 the general aims of EC action in the cultural sphere. Essentially, these involve encouraging co-operation among the member states in improving people's cultural awareness, safeguarding Europe's cultural heritage, promoting creativity and facilitating cultural exchanges. Following on from this, the article makes provision for the EC and its member states to foster cultural links with third countries and international organizations. It also requires the EC to take cultural aspects into account when pursuing action in other areas in which it is competent. The Treaty of Amsterdam took this further, noting the primary purpose as being 'to respect and promote the diversity of . . . [the EC's] cultures'.

The final paragraph of the article then describes the decision-making procedures for adopting so-called 'incentive measures' and recommendations through which EC action

is to be implemented. These reflect those in Article 149 (ex 12
only in consultation with the Committee of the Regions, is
a Council decision is required for recommendations. Here,
German *Länder*, which have exclusive competence for cultu
means that the TEC requires that all Council decisions be
posals were made during the 2000 IGC to move to QMV
BBC commentator predicted would see Nice being remen
introducing subsidized folk dancing. National sensitivities, re
position granted to 'trade in cultural services' in the revised Ar
meaning that the Council must continue to act by unanimit
past, such a requirement, given the emphasis on supporting c
and the prominent standing of the subsidiarity principle, must
of excessive sensitivity to the demands of national sovereignty

TITLE *XII* (ex Title IX)

CULTURE

Article 151 (ex Article 128)

1. The Community shall contribute to the flowering of the cultures of the Member States, while respecting their national and regional diversity and at the same time bringing the common cultural heritage to the fore.

2. Action by the Community shall be aimed at encouraging co-operation between Member States and, if necessary, supporting and supplementing their action in the following areas:
– improvement of the knowledge and dissemination of the culture and history of the European peoples;
– conservation and safeguarding of cultural heritage of European significance;
– non-commercial cultural exchanges;
– artistic and literary creation, including in the audiovisual sector.

3. The Community and the Member States shall foster co-operation with third countries and the competent international organisations in the sphere of culture, in particular the Council of Europe.

4. The Community shall take cultural aspects into account in its action under other provisions of this Treaty, **in particular in order to respect and to promote the diversity of its cultures.**

5. In order to contribute to the achievement of the objectives referred to in this Article, the Council:
– acting in accordance with the procedure referred to in Article 251 and after consulting the Committee of the Regions, shall adopt incentive measures, excluding any harmonisation of the laws and regulations of the Member States. The Council shall act unanimously throughout the procedure referred to in Article 251;
– acting unanimously on a proposal from the Commission, shall adopt recommendations.

xvii Public Health

As with the previous title, Title XIII consists of only a single article introduced by the TEU and amended by Amsterdam. It sets out in a much-amended and almost entirely rephrased Article 152 (ex 129) – originally the home of provisions governing the European Investment Bank (EIB) now found in Article 266 (ex 198d) – EC competences relating to public health. In doing so, it provides a legal basis for EC action in an area where, since 1977, the national health ministers have met in the Council of Ministers, and since the SEA, the EC has been active, notably through its social, environmental and R&D policy provisions and Articles 95 and 308 (ex 100a and 235). Among the measures adopted were ones promoting health and safety in the workplace as part of its social policy, improved living and working conditions through tighter controls over environmental pollution, medical and health research, the funding of extensive public awareness campaigns on AIDS and cancer and legislation on public health matters, most controversially on banning tobacco advertising. Public health considerations had also featured in actions by member states to limit imports, the movement of workers and the right of establishment under Articles 30, 39 and 46 (ex 36, 48 and 56).

For the most part, the initiatives mentioned were ad hoc and not part of any overall strategy for public health, although shortly before the Maastricht summit in December 1991 the Council did make several declarations and resolutions regarding EC action on, among other things, health policy choices, health and the environment and drug abuse. These followed various proposals to the 1991 IGC on including provision for health policy in the TEC which, in turn, led to the insertion of what is now, following Amsterdam's renumbering of the Treaty, *Article 152* as well as reference in Article 3(1)(p) (ex 3(o)) to the EC contributing to 'the attainment of a high level of health protection'. This aim was originally repeated at the start of Article 152 with a later reference – to Randall one whose human resource and methodological ramifications had not been fully thought through – to health protection being a constituent part of other EC policies.

With the TA, however, the status of 'a high level of health protection' was raised so that it is now to be ensured in the definition and implementation of all EC policies and activities. Such a development came in the light of Belgian proposals and followed outbreaks of bovine spongiform encephalopathy (BSE) and Creutzfeldt–Jakob disease (CJD) and concerns that public health considerations needed to inform policy, notably with regard to agriculture, something which also contributed to the insertion of paragraph 8 into Article 95 allowing member states to call on the Commission to re-examine an existing single-market measure on public health grounds. It can, however, lead to tension with other policy areas. One good example is with the CAP, where health policy objectives and subsidies to tobacco producers do not sit well together.

Article 152(1) then continues to outline the areas which EC action may cover, noting that it is to complement national policies thus reflecting the principle of subsidiarity. Following Amsterdam the list is more extensive and specific, bringing in references to improving public health, preventing human illness and disease and obviating sources of danger to human health. That EC action in addition to that of the member states is reinforced in paragraph 2, which allows the EC to lend support to member state initiatives and requires the member states with Commission support to co-ordinate national policies and action. This is then followed in paragraph 3 by a call to the EC and the member states to foster co-operation with non-member states and competent international organizations.

The mechanisms which the EC may deploy are set out in Article 152(4). Thus the

Council, via the co-decision procedure and after consulting EcoSoc and the Committee of the Regions, may adopt measures setting high standards of quality and safety for 'substances of human origin' such as organs and blood, albeit without affecting national provisions on their donation or medical use, as well as measures in the veterinary and phytosanitary fields. Such measures, unlike prior to the TA, may include the harmonization of national laws. Hence, although competence for the administration of public health remains firmly in the hands of the individual member states, a point emphasized in paragraph 5, the changes introduced by Amsterdam do, as Dehousse observes, increase the regulatory role of the EC. However, it is made clear that EC measures, as is the case with regard to social, consumer protection and environmental policy (see Articles 138(5), 153(5) and 176), may not prevent member states from maintaining or introducing more stringent measures.

In addition to such measures, Article 152(4) calls on the EC and member states, as originally envisaged in the TEU, to adopt incentive measures to improve human health (but excluding any legislative harmonization) and recommendations. While the former are adopted using the co-decision procedure and in consultation with EcoSoc and the Committee of the Regions, recommendations simply require the Council to act by QMV on a Commission proposal.

TITLE *XIII* (ex Title X)

PUBLIC HEALTH

Article 152 (ex Article 129)

1. *A high level of human health protection* shall be ensured in the definition and implementation of all Community policies and activities.

Community action, which shall complement national policies, shall be directed towards *improving public health, preventing human illness and diseases, and obviating sources of danger to human health. Such action shall cover the fight against the* major health scourges, by promoting research into their causes, their transmission and their prevention, as well as health information and education.

The Community shall complement the Member States' action in reducing drugs-related health damage, including information and prevention.

2. *The Community shall encourage co-operation between the Member States in the areas referred to in this Article and, if necessary, lend support to their action.*

Member States shall, in liaison with the Commission, co-ordinate among themselves their policies and programmes in the areas referred to in paragraph 1. The Commission may, in close contact with the Member States, take any useful initiative to promote such co-ordination.

3. The Community and the Member States shall foster co-operation with third countries and the competent international organisations in the sphere of public health.

4. *The Council, acting in accordance with the procedure referred to in Article 251 and after consulting the Economic and Social Committee and the Committee of the Regions, shall contribute to the achievement of the objectives referred to in this Article through adopting:*
(a) measures setting high standards of quality and safety of organs and substances of human origin, blood and blood derivatives; these measures shall not prevent

> any Member State from maintaining or introducing more stringent protective measures;
> (b) by way of derogation from Article 37, measures in the veterinary and phytosanitary fields which have as their direct objective the protection of public health;
> (c) incentive measures *designed to protect and improve human health*, excluding any harmonisation of the laws and regulations of the Member States.
>
> *The Council,* acting by a qualified majority on a proposal from the Commission, *may also adopt recommendations for the purposes set out in this Article.*
>
> *5. Community action in the field of public health shall fully respect the responsibilities of the Member States for the organisation and delivery of health services and medical care. In particular, measures referred to in paragraph 4(a) shall not affect national provisions on the donation or medical use of organs and blood.*

xviii Consumer Protection

Title XIV, like the two titles preceding it, consists of a single article. Article 153 contains provisions for consumer protection which were originally inserted into the TEC by the TEU. They have since been amended and enhanced by Amsterdam on the basis of Finnish, Danish and Belgian proposals and partly in response to the outcry over BSE, but left untouched by Nice. As in so many other cases, the relative youth of the provisions does not mean that, when it was inserted, the article provided the EC with a wholly new competence. In fact, the consumer had been written into the TEC from the outset, gaining mention in the original Articles 39(1)(e), 40(3), 85(3) and 86 (now 33(1)(e), 34(2), 81(3) and 82, respectively). Yet no formal basis existed for an EC policy, even though various 'soft law' initiatives were launched from 1972 onwards and in 1987 the SEA in inserting the forerunner to what is now Article 95(3) included a specific reference to consumer protection in the TEC as part of the drive towards establishing the Internal Market.

This certainly helped to facilitate the adoption of measures so that by the time Maastricht inserted a dedicated title on consumer protection into the TEC there already existed a block of binding legislation covering, *inter alia,* product safety, advertising, consumer credit and the liability of service providers. Consequently, as Weatherill observes, Maastricht did not represent a watershed in the development of EC consumer policy. Indeed, the title was very much underused as scepticism towards EC regulation rose and greater emphasis was placed on subsidiarity. Maastricht cannot, though, be overlooked. It did, after all, result in the EC gaining a more high profile and formal competence to 'contribute to the attainment of a high level of consumer protection'.

A significant feature of the article which is now found in the TEC, *Article 153* (ex 129a), is that it extends the EC's competence to pursue a high level of consumer protection beyond solely the context of Internal Market legislation as provided for under the SEA, a development furthered by Amsterdam. Indeed, since the TA, paragraph 1 sets out the purpose of EC action as promoting the interests of consumers and ensuring a high level of consumer protection. It thus echoes the intention of the EC, noted in Article 3(1)(t) (ex 3(s)), to contribute to a strengthening of consumer protection. There then follows a list of objectives: protecting the health, safety and economic interests of consumers, and, since Amsterdam, promoting their new rights to information, education and to organize themselves to safeguard their consumer interests.

How these objectives are to be achieved is laid down in paragraph 3, a revised version of the original first paragraph. First, measures are to be adopted, as was already the case, under Article 95 as part of the Internal Market legislation. Second, the EC is to adopt 'measures', as opposed to 'specific action' prior to Amsterdam, which support, supplement and, once again following the TA, monitor member-state policies. These, as noted in the next paragraph, are to be adopted by the Council using the co-decision procedure having consulted EcoSoc, a consultation which has gained more formal importance since Nice revised the membership of EcoSoc to include consumers (see Article 257). The change to paragraph 2 is significant since, prior to the TA, the EC's competence to pursue measures such as a ban on tobacco advertising under the then Article 100a (now 95) was questionable. The amendment to Article 153(3)(b) helps to fill the gaps in a previously inadequate article.

Beyond specific consumer protection measures, paragraph 2 requires that consumer protection requirements are taken into account in the definition and implementation of EC policies. This horizontal provision, like that concerning employment in Article 127(2), dates back to Amsterdam. However, no matter what specific measures are adopted, member states cannot be prevented under paragraph 5 from taking more stringent protective measures so long as these are compatible with the TEC and the Commission is informed. This is also the case with social policy, aspects of public health policy and environmental policy – see Articles 138(5), 152(4)(a) and 176.

What all this means, particularly since Amsterdam, is that the position of the consumer has gained greater prominence in the activities of the EC. Not only is consumer protection to be promoted, it is also recognized as a horizontal policy objective, even if it does not enjoy core task status in Article 2 TEC as the Danes and Belgians had wanted at Amsterdam. Moreover, with Amsterdam, consumers have been given certain rights and the EC now monitors member-state policies. Whether all this really means that, as Stuyck argues, EC consumer law has come of age, remains to be seen. Looking at the treaty base, it is clear that provisions exist for consumer protection to feature far more prominently in the EC's activities than has traditionally been the case.

TITLE *XIV* (ex Title XI)

CONSUMER PROTECTION

Article 153 (ex Article 129a)

1. *In order* to promote the interests of consumers and *to ensure a high level of consumer protection, the Community shall contribute to protecting the health, safety and economic interests of consumers,* as well as to promoting their right to information, education and to organise themselves in order to safeguard their interests.

2. Consumer protection requirements shall be taken into account in defining and implementing other Community policies and activities.

3. The Community shall contribute to the attainment of the objectives *referred to in paragraph 1* through:
(a) measures adopted pursuant to Article 95 in the context of the completion of the internal market;
(b) measures *which support, supplement* and monitor the policy pursued by the Member States.

4. The Council, acting in accordance with the procedure referred to in Article 251

and after consulting the Economic and Social Committee, shall adopt the measures referred to in paragraph 3(b).

5. **Measures** adopted pursuant to paragraph 4 shall not prevent any Member State from maintaining or introducing more stringent protective measures. Such measures must be compatible with this Treaty. The Commission shall be notified of them.

xix Trans-European Networks

As with the three preceding titles, Title XV on Trans-European Networks (TENs) was inserted into the TEC by Maastricht. It consists of three articles (Articles 154–156) which set out the means by which the EC is to establish and develop TENs covering transport, telecommunications and energy, something encouraged in Article 3(1)(o) (ex 3(o)) TEC. The three articles as well as the title (formerly Title XII) were all renumbered at Amsterdam with two of the articles attracting amendments through the TA too. Nice, however, left all three untouched.

As *Article 154* (ex 129b) notes, the EC is to contribute to the establishment and development of TENs involving the interconnection and interoperability of national transport, telecommunications and energy infrastructures in order to achieve a variety of objectives. These include those explicitly listed, these being assisting EU citizens, economic operators and regional and local communities to derive 'full benefits' from the Internal Market, as well as those contained in Articles 14 and 158 TEC covering respectively the completion of the Internal Market and the strengthening of economic and social cohesion. In pursuing these objectives, particular attention is to be paid to linking peripheral, landlocked and island regions with central regions of the EC. The fact that the EC is to 'contribute' means that it will not be working alone but in co-operation with the member states.

The objectives of TENs provide a clear indication as to the reason for the inclusion of Title XV in the TEC. In 1991 the Commission argued strongly that completion of the Internal Market required not just deregulation and liberalization but also structural measures. The member states tended to agree even if, as Cloos *et al.* note, the final wording did not reflect all individual preferences, and no explicit link was established with economic policy in Article 98 TEC.

In order to facilitate the establishment of TENs, *Article 155* (ex 129c) makes the EC responsible for identifying the necessary infrastructure projects of common interest and for ensuring the interoperability of national networks. In particular, it is to establish guidelines covering objectives and priorities and implement necessary measures – including harmonization – in the field of technical standardization. With regard to the first of these, the EC was originally allowed to support the efforts of member states in financing transport infrastructure projects. The TA amended the wording of the third indent of paragraph 1 so that the EC has a more general role in supporting projects supported by the member states. All the same, the definition of support remains unchanged. Projects of common interest may receive EC support via, in particular, feasibility studies, loan guarantees and interest rate subsidies. In practice this involves the European Investment Bank (EIB). Also, the Cohesion Fund may be used to support projects in individual member states. In all cases, the EC's activities are to take into account the economic viability of all projects.

Beyond the financing of projects, member states, in liaison with the Commission, are required to co-ordinate national infrastructure projects that are likely to have an impact on the creation of TENs. Finally, provision is made for co-operation with third countries in the promotion of projects of mutual interest and in ensuring the interoperability of their networks with those of the EC. Hence, the notion of 'trans-European' clearly involves going beyond the EU's borders, something which project proposals and funding reflect. In addition to projects involving only member states such as that covering electricity supply between Greece and Italy, others include non-members. Good examples include the 'Nordic Triangle' rail project connecting the Norwegian, Swedish and Danish capitals, and the various infrastructure programmes involving central and eastern European countries.

As far as decision-making regarding TENs is concerned, *Article 156* (ex 129d) provides that all guidelines and measures are to be adopted in accordance with the co-decision procedure. Prior to Amsterdam, measures aimed at ensuring interoperability and providing financial assistance were adopted via the co-operation procedure. In all cases the Council is required to consult both EcoSoc and the Committee of the Regions before making its final decision. Similarly, where the guidelines or a project relate to the territory of a member state, guidelines and measures must have the approval of the member state concerned.

TITLE *XV* (ex Title XII)

TRANS-EUROPEAN NETWORKS

Article 154 (ex Article 129b)

1. To help achieve the objectives referred to in Articles *14* and *158* and to enable citizens of the Union, economic operators and regional and local communities to derive full benefit from the setting-up of an area without internal frontiers, the Community shall contribute to the establishment and development of trans-European networks in the areas of transport, telecommunications and energy infrastructures.

2. Within the framework of a system of open and competitive markets, action by the Community shall aim at promoting the interconnection and interoperability of national networks as well as access to such networks. It shall take account in particular of the need to link island, landlocked and peripheral regions with the central regions of the Community.

Article 155 (ex Article 129c simplified)

1. In order to achieve the objectives referred to in Article *154*, the Community:
– shall establish a series of guidelines covering the objectives, priorities and broad lines of measures envisaged in the sphere of trans-European networks; these guidelines shall identify projects of common interest;
– shall implement any measures that may prove necessary to ensure the interoperability of the networks, in particular in the field of technical standardisation;
– may support **projects of common interest supported by Member States**, which are identified in the framework of the guidelines referred to in the first indent, particularly through feasibility studies, loan guarantees or interest-rate subsidies; the Community may also contribute, through the Cohesion Fund *set up* pursuant to Article *161*, to the financing of specific projects in Member States in the area of transport infrastructure.

The Community's activities shall take into account the potential economic viability of the projects.

2. Member States shall, in liaison with the Commission, co-ordinate among themselves the policies pursued at national level which may have a significant impact on the achievement of the objectives referred to in Article 154. The Commission may, in close co-operation with the Member State, take any useful initiative to promote such co-ordination.

3. The Community may decide to co-operate with third countries to promote projects of mutual interest and to ensure the interoperability of networks.

Article 156 (ex Article 129d)

The guidelines **and other measures** referred to in Article 155(1) shall be adopted by the Council, acting in accordance with the procedure referred to in Article 251 and after consulting the Economic and Social Committee and the Committee of the Regions.

Guidelines and projects of common interest which relate to the territory of a Member State shall require the approval of the Member State concerned.

xx Industry

In Title XVI, Industry, we have the fourth title in Part Three to consist of only a single article. *Article 157* (ex 130) was introduced to the TEC by the TEU. Left untouched by Amsterdam, the article did undergo some amendment at Nice as discussed below. Its presence in the TEC owes much to the determination of some governments, as McGowan notes, to 'trump competition policy' and the restrictions on state aid in Articles 87 and 88 TEC and provide a counterbalance to the market liberalization thrust of the Internal Market programme. Most keen were the Belgian and French governments, which in the lead-up to Maastricht sought the insertion of a reference to industrial policy into the treaty. Despite objections from other member states, their desire to see the legitimacy of industrial policy recognized and the EC equipped with explicit powers to promote the competitiveness of European industry prevailed, although the final wording of the article fell well short of what they were advocating at the time. It is, as with so many provisions, a compromise, something which is reflected too in the title of Title XVI: 'Industry' as opposed to 'Industrial Policy'. Moreover, the insertion of Title XVI (then Title XIII) did not herald a new departure for the EC. Already in 1990 the Council of Ministers had approved a Commission communication on industrial policy. Its content, however, reflected many of the differences of opinion which dominated debates on the wording of Article 157 in the Maastricht negotiations.

Although the traditionally more interventionist member states succeeded in getting Title XVI inserted into the TEC, they arguably lost the debate over its content, which reflects very much the dominant view at the time – and indeed since – that liberalization and deregulation as opposed to intervention are the way forward in promoting industrial competitiveness. As much is apparent too in the wording of Article 3(1)(m), which refers to the EC 'strengthening the competitiveness of Community industry'. All the same, fears existed that Title XVI would herald an interventionist policy. Streit and Müssler, for example, argued that along with the new provisions concerning research and development, cohesion, culture, public health, consumer protection and trans-European networks, the content of Title XVI brought about a profound change in the economic constitution of the EC. No longer would the principle of undistorted competition enjoy primacy. Instead, the TEU was promoting an interventionist industrial policy which threatened to undermine competition.

In reality, no such shift took place. And given the content of Article 157, coupled with prevailing consensus on limited government intervention and the limited financial resources and political support which the EC has at its disposal to intervene, none should have been anticipated. For as the first paragraph notes, 'open and competitive markets' are given prominence and EC and member-state action is limited to four areas, none of which contains any reference to the maintenance of traditional industries or heavy government involvement in industry. In addition, it is made explicitly clear in the final paragraph of the article that no measure may be introduced on the basis of Article 157 that could lead to the distortion of competition. Nice went further in ruling out any measures which contain either tax provisions or relate to employees' rights and interests. Instead, the four areas for action stress the speeding-up of the adjustment of industry to structural change, initiative, small- and medium-sized enterprises, co-operation between undertakings and innovation and research and technological development (RTD). There are therefore overlaps with EC competences in other areas, notably economic and social cohesion and RTD. And the emphasis on competition means that Title XVI generally complements rather than competes with the TEC's long-standing competition provisions found in Articles 81–93.

The creation of conditions promoting the competitiveness of European industry to which Title XVI is dedicated is not a matter solely for the EC to pursue. Rather, the onus is placed on the member states to proceed by way of consultations with one another and only where necessary to co-ordinate their action. Furthermore, where the EC as a whole is to contribute to the achievement of the objectives set out in paragraph 1, it is to do so through policies pursued under other provisions in the treaty. The only decisions the EC may take on the basis of Article 157 are specific measures designed to support action taken in the member states. Such decisions, while originally to be taken on the basis of unanimity within the Council with only a consultative role for the EP and EcoSoc, are since Nice to be adopted under the co-decision procedure with EcoSoc being consulted.

TITLE *XVI* (ex Title XIII)

INDUSTRY

Article 157 (ex Article 130)

1. The Community and the Member States shall ensure that the conditions necessary for the competitiveness of the Community's industry exist.

For that purpose, in accordance with a system of open and competitive markets, their action shall be aimed at:
– speeding up the adjustment of industry to structural changes;
– encouraging an environment favourable to initiative and to the development of undertakings throughout the Community, particularly small and medium-sized undertakings;
– encouraging an environment favourable to co-operation between undertakings;
– fostering better exploitation of the industrial potential of policies of innovation, research and technological development.

2. The Member States shall consult each other in liaison with the Commission and, where necessary, shall co-ordinate their action. The Commission may take any useful initiative to promote such co-ordination.

3. The Community shall contribute to the achievement of the objectives set out in paragraph 1 through the policies and activities it pursues under other provisions of this Treaty. The Council, acting **in accordance with the procedure referred to in Article 251** *and after consulting* the Economic and Social Committee, may decide on specific measures in support of action taken in the Member States to achieve the objectives set out in paragraph 1.

This Title shall not provide a basis for the introduction by the Community of any measure which could lead to a distortion of competition **or contains tax provisions or provisions relating to the rights and interests of employed persons.**

xxi Economic and Social Cohesion

Part Three's next title, Title XVII, is slightly older than the five preceding it. The title, which consists of five articles (Articles 158–161), is dedicated to economic and social cohesion and was inserted into the TEC as Part Three, Title V by the SEA. The TEU then moved the provisions to Title XIV and in terms of substance replaced provisions in the existing, yet by then defunct, Article 130d calling on the EC to clarify and rationalize the tasks of the Structural Funds with new provisions. It also added two new paragraphs to Article 130b and gave added recognition to the strengthening of economic and social cohesion by including it not just as an explicit area of EC activity in Article 2 and ex Article 3(k) (now 3(1)(k)) TEC but also as an EU objective in ex Article B (now 2) TEU. Mention was also made of 'reinforced cohesion' in the preamble to the TEU. Furthermore, the preamble as well as ex Article A (now 1) TEU gave prominence to the principle of 'solidarity' between the member states with a similar reference being inserted into Article 2 TEC. Such developments in the absence of any corresponding references to competition have led Frazer and others to suggest that cohesion now has primacy over competition within the EC. This is a matter of debate.

Apart from giving the articles their present numbers, tidying up the wording in Article 161 and renumbering the Title XVII, the impact of Amsterdam on the title was limited to the insertion of 'or islands' alongside regions in Article 158 and a change in the decision-making procedure to be applied under Article 162. As Pollack argues, the fact that cohesion received only limited attention can be explained by the absence of any core neo-liberal project in the TA. Hence, there were no demands from the likes of Spain as there had been with the SEA and TEU for additional spending on cohesion policies. Moreover, it was accepted that the real debate over policy reform and funding would occur in 1999 with the adoption of the EU's financial perspective for 2000–2006. Similar arguments can be used to explain the limited impact which Nice too had on Title XVII. This amended Article 159 and added a new third paragraph to Article 161. The wording of the latter did, however, prove contentious and led, as discussed below, to two declarations being noted by the 2000 IGC.

The insertion of Articles 158–162 into the TEC reflected concerns within the EC that without assistance its less-developed regions would not be well placed to cope with competitive pressures released by the completion of the Internal Market. Concerns for less-developed regions had been expressed earlier, although generally they failed to make their presence felt in the TEC. There were some exceptions. Germany succeeded in gaining special recognition in what are now Articles 78 and 87(2)(c) for those *Länder* affected by the division of the country. And provisions in Article 87(3)(c) do allow for regional aid to be exempted from prohibitions on state aid. Moreover, the 1957 Protocol on Italy draws attention to the Rome government's efforts to provide an infrastructure for the less developed areas of the country.

The limited interest which the TEC originally showed in regional development generally changed, however, with the SEA. It inserted provisions setting out the means by which the EC would attempt to strengthen economic and social cohesion or, in other words, reduce the economic and social disparities which existed between its various regions. This is made clear in *Article 158* (ex 130a). As such, the insertion of Title XVII, along with a commitment to double budgetary expenditure on promoting cohesion, represented a concession by the richer to the less-developed member states (Greece, Ireland, Portugal and Spain) for acceptance of the Internal Market programme. A similar trade-off occurred with respect to the TEU. Here, the richer member states agreed to the creation of a Cohesion Fund in *Article 161* (ex 130e) in exchange for the poorer member states' acceptance of the provisions relating to EMU. The purpose of the fund is to provide financial assistance for projects involving the environment, transport infrastructure and TENs. Eligibility details are set out in the Protocol on economic and social cohesion annexed to the TEC by the TEU.

The means by which the goal of economic and social cohesion is to be achieved are described in *Article 159* (ex 130b). They include the co-ordination of member states' economic policies and action taken through the three Structural Funds – the European Agricultural Guidance and Guarantee Fund, Guidance Section (EAGGF), the European Social Fund (ESF) and the European Regional Development Fund (ERDF) – and the European Investment Bank (EIB) as well as 'other existing financial mechanisms' such as the Financial Instrument for Fisheries Guidance. Moreover, and thanks to an Irish initiative at Maastricht, the objectives set out in Article 158 are to be taken into account in the formulation and implementation of EC policies as well as the completion of the Internal Market. The prominence given to economic and social cohesion is therefore slightly greater than that given to other objectives such as consumer protection (Article 153(2)) and human health protection (Article 152(1)), although it does not enjoy as much prominence as environmental protection (Article 6).

As a result of amendments introduced by the TEU, progress in attaining the objectives set out in *Article 158* is to be monitored by the Commission. Where necessary a triennial report is to be accompanied by a list of appropriate proposals to improve the situation. Essentially, such proposals are to be implemented through the Structural Funds, although provision is made for specific action to be taken independently of them. In such instances, the Council used to act by unanimity and after consulting the EP, EcoSoc and the Committee of the Regions. Since Nice the co-decision procedure has been used with EcoSoc and the Committee of the Regions retaining their consultative role.

This brings us to *Article 160* (ex 130c) which deals with the only Structural Fund not provided for earlier in the TEC – the European Regional Development Fund – the others being covered by Articles 37 (EAGGF) and 148 (ESF). Originally not provided for in the TEC, this was established in 1975 on the basis of ex Article 235 (now 308) TEC and gained formal recognition through amendments to the treaty introduced by the SEA. Its purpose was and remains to assist in redressing regional imbalances in the EC. This is done by participating in the development and adjustment of regions whose development is deemed to be lagging, and the conversion of regions affected by industrial decline.

Implementing decisions relating to the ERDF are taken in accordance with *Article 162* (ex 130e) which since the TEU has seen the Council acting under the co-decision procedure and after consulting EcoSoc and the Committee of the Regions. Previously the co-operation procedure was used.

The only provisions of Title XVII left to discuss are the first and last provisions of *Article 161* (ex 130d). These lay down the procedure by which not only the tasks, priority objectives, organization and general rules of the three Structural Funds are to be defined but also how their effectiveness and co-ordination are to be ensured. The significance of the provision cannot be overstated since decisions taken on the basis of Article 161 currently impact on annual expenditure of approximately €31,000 million or 30% of the EU budget, figures which are set to rise to €41,250 million and 39% of the EU budget for an enlarged EU by 2006.

According to Article 161, decisions governing the Structural Funds have traditionally been taken by the Council acting unanimously on the basis of a Commission proposal. Initially, the EP was involved through the co-operation procedure but since the TEU the assent procedure has been used with EcoSoc and the Committee of the Regions being consulted. Nice, however, signalled a shift to QMV within the Council from 1 January 2007, a procedural change which was widely regarded as essential if decisions on the Structural Funds are to be reached in an enlarged EU. Not all member states were supportive of the move. Hence, at the insistence of the Spanish government, a proviso was included in the new third paragraph: if, by the beginning of January 2007, the EU has not adopted its next 'multiannual financial perspective' and a corresponding inter-institutional agreement then unanimity will be retained until these things are finally agreed.

What this means is that each member state will keep its veto over allocations to the Structural Funds when negotiating the next EU budget package, something which analyses in candidate countries have obviously noted. There are, however, differences over what is meant by 'multiannual'. The Spanish, Greek and Portuguese governments understand it as meaning of the same duration (i.e. 7 years to 2013) as the current financial perspective (Declaration No. 2n TN) while in a retaliatory Declaration No. 3n TN the Danish, German, Dutch and Austrian governments adhere to the view that the length should not be predetermined and that it is the Commission's prerogative to propose a shorter duration for the next budget. Evidently, with the prospect of EU enlargement and declining net receipts the Mediterranean trio are seeking to retain as much control over Structural Funds as possible. Whether this will be enough to prevent what Forthergill predicts might be the premature death of cohesion policy remains to be seen.

The two declarations noted at Nice are not the only statements found outside the main body of the TEC that affect the provisions of Title XVII. There are three further declarations which deserve mention. The first (Declaration No. 9 TEU) requires the EC to consider nature conservation in promoting economic and social cohesion while Declaration No. 30 TA acknowledges the need to take account of the structural handicaps which island regions face in developing legislation. The third declaration (No. 26 TEU) relates specifically to new provisions inserted at Maastricht into Article 227(2) requiring attention to be paid to the structural problems of the French overseas *départements*, the Azores, Madeira and the Canary Islands. Also of note is the Protocol on Economic and Social Cohesion annexed to the TEC as a compromise solution to Spanish demands that changes to the Structural Funds agreed at Maastricht be given a firm legal basis, ideally in the TEC. The protocol simply provides for the political decisions to be implemented via secondary legislation.

TITLE *XVII* (ex Title XIV)

ECONOMIC AND SOCIAL COHESION

Article 158 (ex Article 130a)

In order to promote its overall harmonious development, the Community shall develop and pursue its actions leading to the strengthening of its economic and social cohesion.

In particular, the Community shall aim at reducing disparities between the levels of development of the various regions and the backwardness of the least favoured regions or islands, including rural areas.

Article 159 (ex Article 130b)

Member States shall conduct their economic policies and shall co-ordinate them in such a way as, in addition, to attain the objectives set out in Article *158*. The formulation and implementation of the Community's policies and actions and the implementation of the internal market shall take into account the objectives set out in Article *158* and shall contribute to their achievement. The Community shall also support the achievement of these objectives by the action it takes through the Structural Funds (European Agricultural Guidance and Guarantee Fund, Guidance Section; European Social Fund; European Regional Development Fund), the European Investment Bank and the other existing financial instruments.

The Commission shall submit a report to the European Parliament, the Council, the Economic and Social Committee and the Committee of the Regions every three years on the progress made towards achieving economic and social cohesion and on the manner in which the various means provided for in this Article have contributed to it. This report shall, if necessary, be accompanied by appropriate proposals.

If specific actions prove necessary outside the Funds and without prejudice to the measures decided upon within the framework of the other Community policies, such actions may be adopted by the Council acting **in accordance with the procedure referred to in Article 251** and after consulting the Economic and Social Committee and the Committee of the Regions.

Article 160 (ex Article 130c)

The European Regional Development Fund is intended to help to redress the main regional imbalances in the Community through participation in the development and structural adjustment of regions whose development is lagging behind and in the conversion of declining industrial regions.

Article 161 (ex Article 130d simplified)

Without prejudice to Article *162*, the Council, acting unanimously on a proposal from the Commission and after obtaining the assent of the European Parliament and consulting the Economic and Social Committee and the Committee of the Regions, shall define the tasks, priority objectives and the organisation of the Structural Funds, which may involve grouping the Funds. The Council, acting by the same procedure, shall also define the general rules applicable to them and the provisions necessary to ensure their effectiveness and the co-ordination of the Funds with one another and with the other existing financial instruments.

A Cohesion Fund set up by the Council in accordance with the same procedure shall provide a financial contribution to projects in the fields of environment and trans-European networks in the area of transport infrastructure.

From 1 January 2007, the Council shall act by a qualified majority on a proposal from the Commission after obtaining the assent of the European Parliament and after consulting the Economic and Social Committee and the Committee of the Regions if, by that date, the multiannual financial perspective applicable from 1 January 2007 and the Interinstitutional Agreement relating thereto have been adopted. If such is not the case, the procedure laid down by this paragraph shall apply from the date of their adoption.

Article 162 (ex Article 130e)

Implementing decisions relating to the European Regional Development Fund shall be taken by the Council, acting in accordance with the procedure referred to in Article 251 and after consulting the Economic and Social Committee and the Committee of the Regions.

With regard to the European Agricultural Guidance and Guarantee Fund, Guidance Section, and the European Social Fund, Articles 37 and 148 respectively shall continue to apply.

xxii Research and Technological Development

As with most titles in Part Three of the TEC, Title XVIII, Research and Technological Development (RTD), is not an original feature of the treaty. Instead, it owes its existence to the SEA which inserted 11 articles on RTD into the TEC. The reason for doing this was to enhance the EC's role in assisting with the modernization of European industry deemed vital if Europe were to compete successfully with the USA and Japan on world markets. The new title, then Title VI, was subsequently renumbered, reworded and amended by the TEU to give a more coherent approach to RTD activity. The TEU also raised the status of EC responsibility for RTD by including it as an area of EC activity singled out in what is now Article 3(1)(n). Amsterdam has since amended the decision-making procedures used and renumbered the title (now Title XVIII) as well as its provisions. Nice had no impact here.

The main objective of EC activity regarding RTD is set out in *Article 163* (ex 130f) and is to strengthen the scientific and technological bases of EC industry and encourage it to become more competitive at internal level, an objective which echoes the purpose of EC action regarding industry set out in Title XVI. In addition, the EC is charged more generally with promoting 'all the research activities deemed necessary by virtue of the Chapters of this Treaty'. The reference to chapters is rather misleading, since a strict interpretation would confine EC activity to the identifiable 'chapters' found in Titles I, III, VI, VII and XI of Part Three of the TEC. Instead, the reference should be read as meaning 'titles', hence covering all activities falling under the treaty's Part Three – Community Policies.

In pursuing its objective, the EC is required to encourage research *per se* as well as research co-operation between companies and research bodies and opening up opportunities in the Internal Market. In essence, therefore, despite a rewording of the provisions, the objectives of the EC remain unchanged following the amendments introduced by the TEU. However, a subtle change was introduced in that, where previously the EC had concerned itself with the scientific and technological base of '*European*' industry, as a result of the TEU it now contents itself solely with that of '*Community*' industry. This has not prevented non-member states participating in EC programmes, though. A more noticeable change to Article 163 brought about by the TEU was the replacement of the existing paragraph 3 concerning RTD and the Internal Market, with a provision for all RTD activities pursued under the Treaty to be adopted in accordance with the provisions now laid down in Title XVIII.

According to *Article 164* (ex 130g), EC action in the area of RTD is to complement the activities of the member states in promoting research co-operation, the dissemination of the results of such research and the mobility and training of researchers. As in other areas of EC activity, co-operation is not restricted to within the Community. It is also to be pursued with non-member states and international organizations. How RTD objectives are to be achieved is set out in *Article 165* (ex 130h) and *Article 166* (ex 130i). The first of these requires member states and the EC to co-ordinate their RTD activities so that they are mutually consistent. The Commission is to promote co-ordination in close co-operation with the member states. The second means is through the adoption of a multiannual framework programme setting out the objectives and broad lines of RTD activity and the maximum financial contribution to be made by the EC. Such a programme, which may be adapted or supplemented, is to be adopted by the Council, having consulted EcoSoc, in accordance with the co-decision procedure. Prior to Maastricht, the EP was only consulted. And thanks to Amsterdam the need for unanimity within the Council has now gone, being replaced by QMV. The actual implementation of the framework programmes is to be carried out through specific programmes adopted by the Council, in consultation with the EP and EcoSoc, on the basis of QMV. As a result of the TEU, the funding required may not exceed that of the framework programme overall. Moreover, thanks to the Protocol on protection and welfare of animals introduced at Amsterdam the welfare requirements of all 'sentient beings' and not just humans are to be taken into account when formulating and implementing RTD policies.

Further provisions regarding the implementation of the framework programme are found in the title's next six articles. The first of these, *Article 167* (ex 130j) requires the Council to agree rules governing participation in the framework programmes and the dissemination of research results. *Article 168* (ex 130k) then provides for so-called supplementary programmes. These do not cover all member states and hence do not automatically attract EC funding although Community participation is possible, as confirmed by *Article 169* (ex 130l), and it is the Council which decides rules applicable to supplementary programmes, notably regarding the dissemination of results.

Returning specifically to the multiannual framework programme, *Article 170* (130m) provides for co-operation with third countries and competent international organizations. This is to be regulated by an agreement concluded on the basis of Article 300. How programmes are to be implemented is picked up on in *Article 171* (ex 130n), which allows the EC to establish joint undertakings or any other necessary structures. The form of these is determined by the Council which, according to *Article 172* (ex 130o), acts in consultation with the EP and EcoSoc using QMV. Prior to Amsterdam unanimity had been required. Other acts of the Council provided for under Articles 167–169 are adopted using the co-decision procedure with EcoSoc being consulted. Originally, prior again to

Amsterdam, the co-operation procedure was used. This leaves us with Article 173 (ex 130p) which, having been introduced by the TEU, requires the Commission to present an annual report to the EP and the Council on RTD activities.

TITLE *XVIII* (ex Title XV)

RESEARCH AND TECHNOLOGICAL DEVELOPMENT

Article 163 (ex Article 130f)

1. The Community shall have the objective of strengthening the scientific and technological bases of Community industry and encouraging it to become more competitive at international level, while promoting all the research activities deemed necessary by virtue of other Chapters of this Treaty.

2. For this purpose the Community shall, throughout the Community, encourage undertakings, including small and medium-sized undertakings, research centres and universities in their research and technological development activities of high quality; it shall support their efforts to co-operate with one another, aiming, notably, at enabling undertakings to exploit the internal market potential to the full, in particular through the opening-up of national public contracts, the definition of common standards and the removal of legal and fiscal obstacles to that co-operation.

3. All Community activities under this Treaty in the area of research and technological development, including demonstration projects, shall be decided on and implemented in accordance with the provisions of this Title.

Article 164 (ex Article 130g)

In pursuing these objectives, the Community shall carry out the following activities, complementing the activities carried out in the Member States:
(a) implementation of research, technological development and demonstration programmes, by promoting co-operation with and between undertakings, research centres and universities;
(b) promotion of co-operation in the field of Community research, technological development and demonstration with third countries and international organisations;
(c) dissemination and optimisation of the results of activities in Community research, technological development and demonstration;
(d) stimulation of the training and mobility of researchers in the Community.

Article 165 (ex Article 130h)

1. The Community and the Member States shall co-ordinate their research and technological development activities so as to ensure that national policies and Community policy are mutually consistent.

2. In close co-operation with the Member States, the Commission may take any useful initiative to promote the co-ordination referred to in paragraph 1.

Article 166 (ex Article 130i)

1. *A multiannual framework programme, setting out all the activities of the Community, shall be adopted by the Council, acting in accordance with the*

procedure referred to in Article 251 after consulting the Economic and Social Committee.

The framework programme shall:
– establish the scientific and technological objectives to be achieved by the activities provided for in Article 164 and fix the relevant priorities;
– indicate the broad lines of such activities;
– fix the maximum overall amount and the detailed rules for Community financial participation in the framework programme and the respective shares in each of the activities provided for.

2. The framework programme shall be adapted or supplemented as the situation changes.

3. The framework programme shall be implemented through specific programmes developed within each activity. Each specific programme shall define the detailed rules for implementing it, fix its duration and provide for the means deemed necessary. The sum of the amounts deemed necessary, fixed in the specific programmes, may not exceed the overall maximum amount fixed for the framework programme and each activity.

4. The Council, acting by a qualified majority on a proposal from the Commission and after consulting the European Parliament and the Economic and Social Committee, shall adopt the specific programmes.

Article 167 (ex Article 130j)

For the implementation of the multiannual framework programme the Council shall:
– determine the rules for the participation of undertakings, research centres and universities;
– lay down the rules governing the dissemination of research results.

Article 168 (ex Article 130k)

In implementing the multiannual framework programme, supplementary programmes may be decided on involving the participation of certain Member States only, which shall finance them subject to possible Community participation.

The Council shall adopt the rules applicable to supplementary programmes, particularly as regards the dissemination of knowledge and access by other Member States.

Article 169 (ex Article 130l)

In implementing the multiannual framework programme the Community may make provision, in agreement with the Member States concerned, for participation in research and development programmes undertaken by several Member States, including participation in the structures created for the execution of those programmes.

Article 170 (ex Article 130m)

In implementing the multiannual framework programme the Community may make provision for co-operation in Community research, technological development and demonstration with third countries or international organisations.

The detailed arrangements for such co-operation may be the subject of agreements between the Community and the third parties concerned, which shall be negotiated and concluded in accordance with Article *300*.

Article *171* (ex Article *130n*)

The Community may set up joint undertakings or any other structure necessary for the efficient execution of Community research, technological development and demonstration programmes.

Article *172* (ex Article *130o*)

The Council, acting **by qualified majority** on a proposal from the Commission and after consulting the European Parliament and the Economic and Social Committee, shall adopt the provisions referred to in Article *171*.

The Council, acting in accordance with the procedure referred to in Article *251* and after consulting the Economic and Social Committee, shall adopt the provisions referred to in Articles *167*, *168* and *169*. Adoption of the supplementary programmes shall require the agreement of the Member States concerned.

Article *173* (ex Article *130p*)

At the beginning of each year the Commission shall send a report to the European Parliament and the Council. The report shall include information on research and technological development activities and the dissemination of results during the previous year, and the work programme for the current year.

xxiii Environment

The provisions on the environment contained within Title XIX, like many of the provisions printed in the *Guide*, are relative if not total newcomers to the TEC. Indeed, although the EC became active on the environment from the early 1970s, adopting for example legislation to combat and control pollution and protect endangered species and laying down principles regarding its action, it was not until after the fourth Environmental Action Programme had been adopted that the SEA inserted what is now Title XIX into the treaty and the EC gained any formal competences for action on environmental matters. Prior to this, it relied heavily and not without controversy on, as Burchell and Lightfoot note, Articles 94 (ex 100) and 308 (ex 235) TEC as well as some favourable rulings from the ECJ.

Since the SEA, almost all of the treaty provisions on the environment have been amended. The TEU extending the EC's competences both qualitatively and quantitatively was followed by Amsterdam promoting the importance of the environment within EC policy-making generally and increasing the decision-making role of the Committee of the Regions. As for Nice, its impact was rather limited, thanks mainly to the UK and Irish governments blocking moves to extend QMV to eco-taxes, and simply results in the removal of some ambiguities in the text of the treaty.

As with most other policy areas the TEC's provisions governing the environment are not contained solely within the dedicated title. Indeed, the environment is noted as early as Article 2, where 'improvement of the quality of the environment' is established as a task of the EC, and Article 3(1)(l) (ex 3(k)), where it declares 'a policy in the sphere of the environment' as an EC activity. The first of these references dates back to Amsterdam, which upgraded the reference to 'respecting the environment' inserted by the TEU, thus further 'greening' the treaty. The second was inserted by the TEU promoting EC activity from 'action' as called for under the SEA's amendments to the TEC to 'policy', thus underlining the emphasis which the EC wished to place on the environment. Such emphasis was accompanied by references elsewhere in the TEC to taking as a base high levels of environmental protection when adopting single market legislation (Article 100a(3), now 95(3)). The status of environmental protection within EC policy-making has since, thanks to the TA, risen further to assume first rank status. First, the TA inserted into Article 2 (ex B) TEU reference to 'balanced and sustainable development' as an objective of the EU. Second, it moved provisions demanding that environmental protection requirements be integrated into the definition and implementation of all EC policy areas, previously found in Article 130r(2) and echoed in Declaration No. 20 TEU, to Article 6 in the principles of the TEC. And third, the TA enhanced Article 6 TEC by adding a reference to the promotion of sustainable development.

So even before the treaty reaches the dedicated title, it is clear that environmental protection as a principle enjoys considerable prominence in the EU's treaty base. However, as Macrory and others have noted, interpretations of the TEC tend to favour economic over environmental interests. And, although welcome, Article 6 is essentially consolation for those member states, such as Sweden, Denmark and Austria, who sought at Amsterdam to insert express references regarding the environment into the treaty provisions for each sectoral policy provision and restructure the economic and political hierarchies in the TEC. Hence, Amsterdam's additions are arguably more of symbolic and political value than legal significance. All the same, they signal a further development of the treaty base with regard to the environment.

Title XIX consists of three articles, the first of which is *Article 174* (ex 130r). This sets out clearly the role of environmental policy as contributing to the pursuit of four objectives: preserving, protecting and improving the quality of the environment; protecting human health; prudent and rational utilization of natural resources; and promoting measures at international level to deal with regional or worldwide environmental problems. EC environmental policy is thus wide-ranging and extends not only to all existing policy areas but also, thanks to the fourth objective which was added by the TEU, geographically beyond the territory of the EU. In its second paragraph, Article 174 expands on these objectives by emphasizing the goal of a high level of protection, albeit 'taking into account the diversity of situations' in the EC's various regions. It then proceeds to list the principles underpinning policy. The first of these – the precautionary principle – was introduced by the TEU. The remaining three – preventive action, the principle that environmental damage should be rectified at source, and the principle of the polluter pays – date back to the SEA and indeed to the principles developed in the 1970s. Having set out the principles, Article 174 provides a first reference to harmonization measures as a means by which the EC may pursue environmental protection. The need to accommodate diversity within the EC is evident, though, in the provision for safeguard clauses allowing member states, for non-economic reasons and subject to inspection, to take provisional measures exempting themselves from full harmonization.

Having set out the role, aims and principles of environmental policy, Article 174 proceeds to list those matters which are to be taken into consideration when preparing policy. These concern scientific and technical data, regional variations in environmental conditions, the potential costs and benefits of action or a lack thereof and the economic and social development of the EC. The final paragraph picks up the theme of pursuing environmental co-operation beyond the EU's borders by obliging the EC to co-operate with non-member states and international organizations and providing for the conclusion, albeit while recalling member states' own competences to negotiate, of agreements via Article 300 (ex 228). The desire to ensure that the EU plays an international role in promoting environmental protection was also emphasized at Nice, where the member states expressed their determination to see the EU take a lead in promoting environmental protection in the Union and internationally by making full use of all possibilities offered by the TEC (Declaration No. 9 TN). This is not to say that the EC has been inactive internationally. Since the mid-1970s it has been a signatory to various conventions and has been represented at both the 1992 Rio conference on the environment and development and the 1997 Kyoto conference on climate change.

Article 175 (ex 130s) lays down the procedures by which action is to be taken and measures are to be adopted. Given that the environment is an EC competence, it is the Commission that draws up legislative proposals. In doing so, it is committed, although not obliged, to undertake an environmental impact assessment (Declaration No. 12 TA). Once the Commission's proposal is on the table it is the Council that plays the main role in adopting environmental legislation. Under the SEA, it normally acted on the basis of unanimity following consultation with the EP and EcoSoc. Following the TEU, the EP became more involved in decision-making through the use of the co-operation procedure, albeit only for certain measures. Since then, co-decision has been introduced by Amsterdam and the Committee of the Regions given a consultative role (Article 175(1)). However, it is still the case that not all decisions are adopted via the co-decision procedure. Consultation is still used for those measures listed in Article 175(2), a list which Nice partly rephrased in order to iron out some of the ambiguities. It includes measures 'primarily' of a fiscal nature, measures affecting town and country planning, the quantitative management and availability of water resources, land use with the exception of waste management and measures significantly affecting energy supply in a given member state. The Council may, by unanimity, decide to adopt measures by QMV.

In other areas, the Commission may propose general action programmes containing priority objectives. These are adopted using the co-decision procedure with appropriate implementing measures then being adopted according to either Article 175(1) or Article 175(2) depending on their coverage. As for funding and implementing environmental policy, both are the responsibility of the member states. There are, however, exceptions regarding the former. Some aspects of environmental policy are covered by the EU budget. Moreover, where the costs to a public authority of implementing a measure are deemed disproportionate, a member state may be granted a derogation or receive financial support through the Cohesion Fund. This is specifically aimed at assisting the less-developed regions of the EC in coping with the costs of EC policy.

So, to the final provision of Title XIX. This is Article 176 (ex 130t) which allows member states to maintain or indeed introduce measures concerning environmental protection which are more stringent than those adopted under Article 175 provided they are compatible with the TEC and are notified to the Commission. As Macrory and others note, this contradicts the concept of a single market with harmonized standards, even though it is supported by the revised provisions of Article 95. There is little likelihood of the provisions or the principle being repealed. For the more environmentally minded member states its retention is often of considerable political importance, at least domestically.

TITLE *XIX* (ex Title XVI)

ENVIRONMENT

Article 174 (ex Article 130r)

1. Community policy on the environment shall contribute to pursuit of the following objectives:
– preserving, protecting and improving the quality of the environment;
– protecting human health;
– prudent and rational utilisation of natural resources;
– promoting measures at international level to deal with regional or worldwide environmental problems.

2. Community policy on the environment shall aim at a high level of protection taking into account the diversity of situations in the various regions of the Community. It shall be based on the precautionary principle and on the principles that preventive action should be taken, that environmental damage should as a priority be rectified at source and that the polluter should pay.

In this context, harmonisation measures answering environmental protection requirements shall include, where appropriate, a safeguard clause allowing Member States to take provisional measures, for non-economic environmental reasons, subject to a Community inspection procedure.

3. In preparing its policy on the environment, the Community shall take account of:
– available scientific and technical data;
– environmental conditions in the various regions of the Community;
– the potential benefits and costs of action or lack of action;
– the economic and social development of the Community as a whole and the balanced development of its regions.

4. Within their respective spheres of competence, the Community and the Member States shall co-operate with third countries and with the competent international organisations. The arrangements for Community co-operation may be the subject of agreements between the Community and the third parties concerned, which shall be negotiated and concluded in accordance with Article 300.

The previous subparagraph shall be without prejudice to Member States' competence to negotiate in international bodies and to conclude international agreements.

Article 175 (ex Article 130s simplified)

1. The Council, acting in accordance with the procedure referred to in Article 251 and after consulting the Economic and Social Committee **and the Committee of the Regions**, shall decide what action is to be taken by the Community in order to achieve the objectives referred to in Article 174.

2. By way of derogation from the decision-making procedure provided for in paragraph 1 and without prejudice to Article 95, the Council, acting unanimously on a proposal from the Commission and after consulting the European Parliament, the Economic and Social Committee **and the Committee of the Regions**, shall adopt:
(a) provisions primarily of a fiscal nature;

(b) measures *affecting:*
   – town and country planning;
   – **quantitative** management of water resources **or affecting, directly or indirectly, the availability of those resources;**
   – *land use, with the exception of waste management;*
(c) measures significantly affecting a Member State's choice between different energy sources and the general structure of its energy supply.

The Council may, under the conditions laid down in the *first* subparagraph, define those matters referred to in this paragraph on which decisions are to be taken by a qualified majority.

3. In other areas, general action programmes setting out priority objectives to be attained shall be adopted by the Council, acting in accordance with the procedure referred to in Article 251 and after consulting the Economic and Social Committee **and the Committee of the Regions.**

The Council, acting under the terms of paragraph 1 or paragraph 2 according to the case, shall adopt the measures necessary for the implementation of these programmes.

4. Without prejudice to certain measures of a Community nature, the Member States shall finance and implement the environment policy.

5. Without prejudice to the principle that the polluter should pay, if a measure based on the provisions of paragraph 1 involves costs deemed disproportionate for the public authorities of a Member State, the Council shall, in the act adopting that measure, lay down appropriate provisions in the form of:
– temporary derogations, and/or
– financial support from the *Cohesion Fund set up pursuant to Article 161.*

Article 176 (ex Article 130t)

The protective measures adopted pursuant to Article 175 shall not prevent any Member State from maintaining or introducing more stringent protective measures. Such measures must be compatible with this Treaty. They shall be notified to the Commission.

xxiv Development Co-operation

The penultimate title of Part Three, Title XX, shifts the focus of the TEC once more to the external relations of the EC, this time explicitly with developing countries. The title and its five articles (Articles 177–181) are by no means vintage provisions, being inserted into the treaty by the TEU only in 1993. This is not to say that the EC has not traditionally been interested in the developing world. In fact it has long-established relations with such countries, often inspired by the TEC's provisions in Part Four on association, as Grilli and others have noted. Moreover, declarations adopted at the time the TEC was negotiated in the 1950s called on the EU to develop ties with certain less-developed countries. Agreements that have since been concluded have tended to be based on Articles 308 and 310, the TEC's 'catch-all' and association provisions, both of which require unanimity, and not an explicit treaty base for relations with developing countries. Dutch efforts to have the SEA remedy the situation failed. At Maastricht they proved more successful, leaving Amsterdam little to do other than alter the decision-making procedure for EC measures.

The first of the five articles dedicated to development co-operation, *Article 177* (ex 130u), outlines the threefold purpose of EC policy: to foster sustained economic and social development in developing countries, particularly in the disadvantaged countries of the world, to promote the smooth and gradual integration of these countries into the world economy and to campaign against poverty. These goals are to be pursued through policies which complement those of the member states. In other words, the EC does not enjoy exclusive competence. Moreover, the EC is to help develop and consolidate democracy and the rule of law and contribute to the general objective of respecting human rights and fundamental freedoms. All this implies a degree of conditionality characterizing development co-operation which is also to be pursued while complying with international commitments, such as those entered into within the framework of the United Nations.

Much of what Article 177 provides for had, as implied above, already been going on before the TEU inserted Title XX (then XVII) into the TEC. Due recognition is provided in the final paragraph of *Article 179* (ex 130w) which notes, seemingly innocently, that any measures adopted by the EC shall not affect existing co-operation with the African, Caribbean and Pacific (ACP) countries within the framework of the 1989 ACP–EC Convention. The convention, more commonly referred to as Lomé IV, has since expired and been replaced by the ACP–EC Partnership Agreement signed in Cotonou, Benin, in June 2000. Article 179(3) does, however, have a more meaningful purpose. As Declaration No. 12 TEU reminds us, the European Development Fund, which is dedicated to the ACP countries, is funded by national contributions and not as one might expect out of the EC budget. As Cloos *et al.* note, the desire of the French and UK governments to keep it so explains the reference to the ACP–EC Convention.

Returning to the initial provisions of Article 179, we find that the Council is empowered to adopt 'necessary measures', including multiannual programmes, to achieve the EC's objectives regarding development co-operation. These are not all that it can adopt. The caveat 'without prejudice to the other provisions of this Treaty' leaves the Council free to use other TEC provisions (e.g. Article 133) as the basis for action. Where it does use Article 179, the necessary measures are to be adopted using the co-decision procedure. Prior to Amsterdam the co-operation procedure was used.

With regard to implementation, provision exists for the European Investment Bank (EIB) to assist. *Article 180* (ex 130x) then reinforces the principle that EC policy should complement that of the member states by requiring the co-ordination of national and EC aid programmes. To this end the Commission is authorized to take 'any useful initiative'. Moreover, the EC and the member states are obliged to consult with one another generally, as well as in international fora, on their aid programmes. Mention is also made of the EC and the member states taking 'joint action' and the latter assisting in the implementation of EC aid programmes.

These last two points are followed in *Article 181* (ex 130y) with a call for the EC and the member states to co-operate with non-member states and international organizations with regard to development policy. Provision also exists for the co-operation to be formalized though agreements concluded on the basis of Article 300. However, it is made clear, just as in Articles 111(5), 174(4) and 181a(3), that the conclusion of such agreements shall not encroach on member states' competence to negotiate in international bodies and conclude international agreements.

Finally, as is now quite common in the TEC, *Article 178* (ex 130v) requires that the EC's objectives regarding development policy be taken into account when implementing other relevant EC policies. Good examples are the CCP and the CAP.

TITLE XX (ex Title XVII)

DEVELOPMENT CO-OPERATION

Article 177 (ex Article 130u)

1. Community policy in the sphere of development co-operation, which shall be complementary to the policies pursued by the Member States, shall foster:
– the sustainable economic and social development of the developing countries, and more particularly the most disadvantaged among them;
– the smooth and gradual integration of the developing countries into the world economy;
– the campaign against poverty in the developing countries.
2. Community policy in this area shall contribute to the general objective of developing and consolidating democracy and the rule of law, and to that of respecting human rights and fundamental freedoms.
3. The Community and the Member States shall comply with the commitments and take account of the objectives they have approved in the context of the United Nations and other competent international organisations.

Article 178 (ex Article 130v)

The Community shall take account of the objectives referred to in Article 177 in the policies that it implements which are likely to affect developing countries.

Article 179 (ex Article 130w simplified)

1. Without prejudice to the other provisions of this Treaty, the Council, acting in accordance with the procedure referred to in Article 251, shall adopt the measures necessary to further the objectives referred to in Article 177. Such measures may take the form of multiannual programmes.
2. The European Investment Bank shall contribute, under the terms laid down in its Statute, to the implementation of the measures referred to in paragraph 1.
3. The provisions of this Article shall not affect co-operation with the African, Caribbean and Pacific countries in the framework of the ACP-EC Convention.

Article 180 (ex Article 130x)

1. The Community and the Member States shall co-ordinate their policies on development co-operation and shall consult each other on their aid programmes, including in international organisations and during international conferences. They may undertake joint action. Member States shall contribute if necessary to the implementation of Community aid programmes.
2. The Commission may take any useful initiative to promote the co-ordination referred to in paragraph 1.

Article 181 (ex Article 130y)

Within their respective spheres of competence, the Community and the Member States shall co-operate with third countries and with the competent international organisations. The arrangements for Community co-operation may be the subject of agreements between the Community and the third parties concerned, which shall be negotiated and concluded in accordance with Article 300.

The previous paragraph shall be without prejudice to Member States' competence to negotiate in international bodies and to conclude international agreements.

xxv   Economic, Financial and Technical Co-operation with Third Countries

So to the final and indeed youngest of the titles in Part Three of the TEC: Title XXI. This was inserted by the Treaty of Nice in response to proposals that agreements with non-member states on economic, financial and technical co-operation should be concluded using QMV. Hitherto, such agreements, for example the TACIS programme for the successor states to the Soviet Union, had been concluded on the basis of unanimity under the 'catch-all' Article 308. With few, if any, member states willing to contemplate QMV for Article 308, the idea of a separate title gained support.

The title consists of just one wholly new Article, *Article 181a*. This, incidentally, is one of only three TEC articles currently including a letter suffix in its number. Its first paragraph empowers the EC, within its competences, to carry out economic, financial and technical co-operation measures with non-member states. Such measures, which as Declaration No. 10 TN notes do not include balance of payment support, are to complement those carried out by the member states and, following a late addition to the article, be consistent with the EC's development policy. Furthermore, and using wording almost identical to that found in Article 177(2) TEC, policy is to contribute to the general objectives of developing and consolidating democracy and the rule of law and to the objective of respecting human rights and fundamental freedoms. In many respects, this is not new, but simply a reflection of existing practice, particularly since the early 1990s, where assistance for and co-operation with non-member states has had such political conditions attached.

Paragraph 2 then outlines how co-operation measures are to be adopted. Not surprisingly the Council is to act by QMV. It is somewhat odd, however, that co-decision is not used, as with development co-operation under Article 179(1). For Dashwood, this defies rational explanation. The Council simply consults the EP. Moreover, QMV is not used in all cases. There are exceptions: association agreements and 'agreements to be concluded with the States which are candidates for accession to the Union' will require unanimity. Knowing that the exceptions were inserted late in the day at the insistence of the Greek government, it should come as no surprise that the wording reflects a clear if decidedly narrow-minded desire to maintain a veto over as much as possible of the EC's relations with Turkey, notably financial assistance.

This brings us to the final paragraph which, with one slight procedural alteration, reproduces Article 174(4) on co-operation with third countries and competent international organizations. Here, arrangements for EC co-operation may be the subject of agreements concluded under Article 300. Any agreement may not, however, encroach on the competences of the member states to negotiate in international bodies and conclude international agreements.

TITLE XXI (new – TN)

ECONOMIC, FINANCIAL AND TECHNICAL CO-OPERATION WITH THIRD COUNTRIES

Article 181a (new – TN)

1. Without prejudice to the other provisions of this Treaty, and in particular those of Title XX, the Community shall carry out, within its spheres of competence, economic, financial and technical co-operation measures with third countries. Such measures shall be complementary to those carried out by the Member States and consistent with the development policy of the Community.

Community policy in this area shall contribute to the general objective of developing and consolidating democracy and the rule of law, and to the objective of respecting human rights and fundamental freedoms.

2. The Council, acting by a qualified majority on a proposal from the Commission and after consulting the European Parliament, shall adopt the measures neces-sary for the implementation of paragraph 1. The Council shall act unanimously for the association agreements referred to in Article 310 and for the agreements to be concluded with the States which are candidates for accession to the Union.

3. Within their respective spheres of competence, the Community and the Member States shall co-operate with third countries and the competent international organisations. The arrangements for Community co-operation may be the subject of agreements between the Community and the third parties concerned, which shall be negotiated and concluded in accordance with Article 300.

The first subparagraph shall be without prejudice to the Member States' competence to negotiate in international bodies and to conclude international agreements.

xxvi Association of the Overseas Countries and Territories

Having dealt with the longest of the TEC's Parts, the *Guide* now turns its attention to one of its shortest, Part Four on the Association of the Overseas Countries and Territories (OCTs). This dates back to 1957 and French insistence that, as Küsters argues, the other member states commit themselves to assist France with her colonial obligations as a way of ensuring French ratification of the TEC. What emerged was a collection of six articles (now Articles 182–187) dedicated to the association of mainly French OCTs. These were listed in an Annex IV to the TEC which has since undergone various amendments being renumbered Annex II, tidied up and updated at Amsterdam to produce the current list of 20 OCTs covering 900,000 people.* Prior to this, Part Four had gained an extra Article

---

*Greenland, New Caledonia and Dependencies, French Polynesia, French Southern and Antarctic Territories, Wallis and Futuna Islands, Mayotte, Saint Pierre and Miquelon, Aruba, Netherlands Antilles (Bonaire, Curaçao, Saba, Sint Eustatius, Sint Maarten), Anguilla, Cayman Islands, Falkland Islands, South Georgia and the South Sandwich Islands, Montserrat, Pitcairn, Saint Helena and Dependencies, British Antarctic Territory, British Indian Ocean Territory, Turks and Caicos Islands, British Virgin Islands, Bermuda.

(now *Article 188*) applying its provisions to Greenland on the latter's departure from the EC in 1985. Since then, Amsterdam has simplified three articles. It also saw the adoption of a declaration. Nice left Part Four untouched.

The purpose of association is first signalled in the TEC in the preamble, which in its seventh recital notes the intention of the member states to 'confirm the solidarity which binds Europe and the overseas countries'. It goes on to note the desire of the former to ensure the development of the OCTs' prosperity in accordance with the United Nations Charter. After this in Article 3(1)(s) association of the OCTs with the EC is singled out as a task of the Community. The purpose of this is to increase trade and promote jointly economic and social development.

As implied already and indeed confirmed in *Article 182* (ex 131), association under Part Four is restricted to non-European countries and territories. Moreover, eligibility requires them to have 'special relations' with one of four member states: Denmark, France, the Netherlands and the United Kingdom. Prior to Amsterdam, Belgium and Italy were also mentioned. Their removal from Article 182 reflects changes in the list of OCTs eligible for association as contained in Annex II. This no longer includes any Italian and Belgian OCTs since these, along with others, have gained independence and established their own relations with the EC, often through one of the various Lomé Conventions concluded using Article 310 TEC. The list in Annex II has, however, gained additions, most obviously as a result of the United Kingdom's accession to the EC in 1973. This is not to say that Part Four covers all the territories for which the member states are responsible. As Article 299 notes, several of them are excluded from the geographical application of the TEC.

Having established which OCTs are eligible for Part Four association, Article 182 continues by establishing the purpose of association: to promote the economic and social development of the OCTs and to establish close economic relations between them and the EC. Moreover, association is to serve primarily to further the interests and prosperity of the inhabitants of the OCTs 'in order to lead them to the economic, social and cultural development to which they aspire'. Interestingly, we find here, in the third paragraph of Article 182, the only explicit reference found in the TEC to its preamble and the principles contained therein.

The objectives of association are then laid down in *Article 183* (ex 132) and include equal trade status to member states; member state and EC financed investment in the OCTs; equal right to participate in tenders and supplies for investment financed by the EC; and equal rights of establishment as laid down in the TEC. *Article 184* (ex 133) then clarifies trade arrangements by prohibiting customs duties on trade between the OCTs and the EC. The OCTs may, however, levy customs duties, up to a limit, which meet the needs of their development and industrialization or produce revenue for their budgets. Also of relevance here is the Protocol concerning imports into the European Community of petroleum products refined in the Netherlands Antilles. Finally, the introduction or alteration of any customs duties on imports to the OCTs should not give rise to any direct or indirect discrimination between imports from the various member states. Where trade deflection to the detriment of an EC member state does occur, the Commission under *Article 185* (ex 134) may be called upon to propose measures to remedy the situation.

Finally, *Article 186* (ex 135) envisages the free movement of workers between the EC and the OCTs. This is to be achieved, subject to provisions relating to public health, public security and public policy, through agreements concluded by the Council acting unanimously. Also acting by unanimity, although proposals were made at Nice to move to QMV, the Council is empowered under *Article 187* (ex 136) to lay down provisions detailing the rules and procedures for the association of the OCTs. In doing so, it is obliged to draw on experiences of the association. In contrast to what is usual under the TEC, the Council acts on its own initiative and is not required to proceed on the basis of a Commission proposal. As with all other aspects of Part Four associations there is no provision for the involvement of the EP. Despite the prominence which the TEC gives to the OCTs, relations between them and the member states remain very much the preserve of the latter.

This does not mean to say that the OCTs do not feature in EC policy-making. As Bainbridge notes, the EC takes care to ensure that their position with regard to aid and trade, for example, is no less advantageous than that granted to the ACP countries. Moreover, differences over rights of establishment and the free movement of persons persist, not least because agreements on the latter envisaged in Article 135 have still to be adopted. They are likely to feature in the future too thanks to the creation of EU citizenship. Citizens of the Danish, Dutch and French OCTs as well as Falkland Islanders are all nationals of the respective member states. They are therefore EU citizens.

That the OCTs cannot and should not be ignored was confirmed at Amsterdam with the adoption of Declaration No. 36 TA dedicated to them. In this, member states 'solemnly' restated that the purpose of association under Part Four had not changed but recognized that the special arrangements conceived in 1957 could no longer deal with the development challenges which the OCTs posed. Hence, in line with Article 136, the Council (and not the Commission) was called on to review association arrangements by February 2000. The purpose of the review, as well as to confirm the member states' commitment to the OCTs, was fourfold: to provide more effective promotion of economic and social development; to develop OCT–EU relations further; to take more account of the diversity of the OCTs; and to ensure improved effectiveness of financial assistance.

PART FOUR ASSOCIATION OF THE OVERSEAS COUNTRIES AND TERRITORIES

Article 182 (ex Article 131 simplified)

The Member States agree to associate with the Community the non-European countries and territories which have special relations with *Denmark, France, the Netherlands and the United Kingdom*. These countries and territories (hereinafter called the 'countries and territories') are listed in Annex *II* to this Treaty.

The purpose of association shall be to promote the economic and social development of the countries and territories and to establish close economic relations between them and the Community as a whole.

In accordance with the principles set out in the Preamble to this Treaty, association shall serve primarily to further the interests and prosperity of the inhabitants of these countries and territories in order to lead them to the economic, social and cultural development to which they aspire.

Article 183 (ex Article 132)

Association shall have the following objectives.

(1) Member States shall apply to their trade with the countries and territories the same treatment as they accord each other pursuant to this Treaty.

(2) Each country or territory shall apply to its trade with Member States and with the other countries and territories the same treatment as that which it applies to the European State with which is has special relations.

(3) The Member States shall contribute to the investments required for the progressive development of these countries and territories.

(4) For investments financed by the Community, participation in tenders and supplies shall be open on equal terms to all natural and legal persons who are nationals of a Member State or of one of the countries and territories.

(5) In relations between Member States and the countries and territories the right of establishment of nationals and companies or firms shall be regulated in accordance with the provisions and procedures laid down in the Chapter relating to the right of establishment and on a non-discriminatory basis, subject to any special provisions laid down pursuant to Article *187*.

Article 184 (ex Article 133 simplified)

1. Customs duties on imports into the Member States of goods originating in the countries and territories shall be *prohibited* in conformity with the *prohibition* of customs duties between Member States in accordance with the provisions of this Treaty.

2. Customs duties on imports into each country or territory from Member States or from the other countries or territories shall be *prohibited* in accordance with the provisions of *Article 25*.

3. The countries and territories may, however, levy customs duties which meet the needs of their development and industrialisation or produce revenue for their budgets.

The duties referred to in the preceding subparagraph *may not exceed* the level of those imposed on imports of products from the Member State with which each country or territory has special relations.

4. Paragraph 2 shall not apply to countries and territories which, by reason of the particular international obligations by which they are bound, already apply a non-discriminatory customs tariff.

5. The introduction of or any change in customs duties imposed on goods imported into the countries and territories shall not, either in law or in fact, give rise to any direct or indirect discrimination between imports from the various Member States.

Article 185 (ex Article 134)

If the level of the duties applicable to goods from a third country on entry into a country or territory is liable, when the provisions of Article *184(1)* have been applied, to cause deflections of trade to the detriment of any Member State, the latter may request the Commission to propose to the other Member States the measures needed to remedy the situation.

Article 186 (ex Article 135)

Subject to the provisions relating to public health, public security or public policy, freedom of movement within Member States for workers from the countries and territories, and within the countries and territories for workers from Member States, shall be governed by agreements to be concluded subsequently with the unanimous approval of Member States.

Article 187 (ex Article 136 simplified)

The Council, acting unanimously, shall, on the basis of the experience acquired under the association of the countries and territories with the Community and of the principles set out in this Treaty, lay down provisions as regards the detailed rules and the procedure for the association of the countries and territories with the Community.

Article 188 (ex Article 136a)

The provisions of Articles *182 to 187* shall apply to Greenland, subject to the specific provisions for Greenland set out in the Protocol on special arrangements for Greenland, annexed to this Treaty.

xxvii Institutions of the Community

After dealing with the Community's erstwhile links with the overseas countries and territories of some of its member states, the TEC turns to the more significant matter of 'institutions'. However, we should note that it mainly takes a rather narrow view of what these actually are, defining them in terms of the list contained in Article 7 TEC.* Essentially, institutions within the treaty are arrangements for political decision-making and not administrative infrastructures even though it is at this lower level that many of the Community's recent institutional problems have arisen. In any case, the TEC only introduces them once policies have been elaborated. It thus rather implies that what really matters are the functions which member states have agreed to carry out in common so that institutions are simply a means to carry them out.

The reality is more complex. The Union and the Community are held together by the 'single institutional framework' set out in Part Five of the TEC. Apart from the European Council, the EU has no institutions of its own, even though the preamble to the Treaty of Nice refers to 'the institutions of the European Union', and has to borrow those of the Community. Because the latter's institutions have already been listed as such in Article 7 TEC, Part Five does not have formally to create the institutions. It assumes them even though they have not really been defined in Part One. What we have in Part Five is twofold. First, there are further details on the institutions themselves, their competences, their ground rules and something of their procedures. However, this does not include the European Central Bank, partly because it was a late addition to the TEC and partly because it is an independent body with its own statute.

Secondly, Part Five makes it clear what the 'framework' of the institutions actually is, the carefully defined and interdependent decision-making arrangements within which they have to work. Hence, although much of Part Five is set out as blocks of articles on specific institutions, this is misleading in three ways. To begin with, each block shows the close relations between the institutions and the checks and balances imposed on them by the treaty negotiators. Furthermore, they have to work within generally applicable – or common – decision-making procedures. And, finally, much of what they do is decided not within these blocks but within other parts of the treaties, in relation to specific policy provisions. Because of this enhanced interdependence the single institutional framework

---

*Article 288 TEC can be seen as having a wider view. See *SGECM* v. *EIB* (1992).

is a complex one, even though the TEC presently fails to involve the ECB fully in it. And it also means that we cannot see any of the institutions as playing straightforward and simple roles as executive, judiciary and legislature. Most of the institutions in fact play crossover roles.

Partly because of this, the Community's institutions are key to an understanding of the Union in general. They are strategically important as a group and they also play distinctive tactical roles of their own. These are often complex and they can be conflictual as well as co-operative. Hence their balance, and particularly that between the inter-governmental Council and the more supra-national Commission, ECJ and CFI, and the EP, is seen as critical to the nature and development of the Union.

Although the treaty does not really develop this aspect of things, it does emerge both from the way the institutions give strategic substance to the Union and the Community and from the nature of the roles ascribed to specific institutions. Institutions are significant in a number of ways, in fact. To begin with, they distinguish the EC from the many inter-governmental organizations which do not have such institutions. Moreover, they give it a certain degree of legitimation. Pescatore and others see the major institutions as each representing a different legitimacy: the EP expressing the popular democratic will; the Council representing the member states as such; the Commission defending the 'European interest'; and the ECJ establishing the rule of law. More recently, the Court of Auditors has sought to bring in the legitimacy of financial probity.

The balance between the institutions points to the importance of the various interests inside the Community, whether inter-governmental or supra-national. Their competences and rules, notably in finance and Council voting procedures, exemplify the balance of power between the Union and its member states. So, finally, partly because of this, the Commission, Council and EP are seen as forming an interest of their own in decision-making, seeking not merely to fill in gaps and carry out the will of the member states but to extend their own powers and their own view of the Union. It is these two factors, along with the actual policy-making powers of the Union, which make the institutions so controversial, especially among Eurosceptics. They would prefer the institutions to be merely an arena in which member state preferences can be reconciled while for many federationists the institutions are the essence of the 'integration project'.

The political salience of the institutions appears clearly in the controversy over the changes made to them at Amsterdam and, even more, at Nice. Amsterdam was thus attacked both for whittling down national rights and for failing to develop sustainable federal institutions despite the many changes it made. Nice, of course, was the end of an IGC on 'institutional reform', with no real remit to change policy provisions. And it made many very important changes to the Part Five arrangements even if it did not write them all in. Indeed, it is here that the detailed provisions of the Protocol on the enlargement of the Union and the related declarations have to be taken into account most carefully. Without them the future of Part Five cannot be properly understood. This is because they introduced staged changes to the size of institutions and, above all, to voting weights and procedures in the Council.*

If we look briefly at the changes made by these two most recent amending treaties we find that, whereas at Amsterdam the EP was the great gainer with an extension of a simplified form of co-decision and the eclipse of co-operation, it did less well out of Nice,

---

*See also the Protocol on the institutions with the prospect of enlargement of the European Union adopted at Amsterdam (and later repealed by Nice) which provided that, by the time of the next enlargement, the Commission would be reduced to one national per member state provided those states surrendering a seat had been properly compensated by a reweighting of votes in the Council.

which made less wide-ranging moves to QMV and co-decision than the EP wished. It also undid the capping agreed at Nice and subjected it to new controls by the Council. Conversely, the Council of Ministers gained in both and, assuming Nice is ratified, will see its working practices change greatly with a reweighting of member state votes, new threshold rules and new powers. It also saw a significant change to its secretarial arrangements.

On both occasions attempts were made to strengthen the Commission and its president and to cap its size. This was one of the issues bequeathed by Amsterdam to Nice. And the latter partly ducked the challenge, despite the fall of the Santer Commission. Hence some, like Neunreither, see it as being forced into a role closer to that of the UN Secretariat.

Where the ECJ was concerned it saw a modest extension to its powers with Amsterdam whereas Nice offers it a major structural overhaul to help it cope with such new powers and with the ever-increasing workload. Concern over fraud also saw new changes to the powers and organization of the Court of Auditors. While decision-making procedures were tightened up at Amsterdam their overall style remained untouched. Minor changes were, however, made to the advisory bodies, notably at Amsterdam. One of the problems about these changes was that, as we have seen, they tended to be very institution-specific and left broader questions of inter-relationships and the balance of power untouched.

However, such changes did not add greatly to the length of Part Five. The institutional provisions remain slimmer and less numerous than those which have occupied previous divisions of the *Guide*. There are in fact only about 90 articles on the institutions compared to some 160 on policies. They are divided between two titles, the first and longest dealing with the institutions as such and the second with financial matters. The former is then divided into five chapters, the first of which is further split into five sections dealing, in due order, with the institutions established through Article 7 TEC. The others deal with decision-making and the advisory bodies. The financial provisions bring up the rear, to be followed by Part Six containing external, legal and ratification clauses.

This may sound as though everything is cut and dried. Not so. Like many constitutions, the TEC just indicates the outlines of the institutions rather than spelling out the last 'jot and tittle' of the way they are to function. And these do not cohere directly with the traditional 'division of powers'. Many questions are therefore left unanswered or are resolved outside the Treaty.

None the less, all this should remind us that bodies like the Community cannot just have 'powers' or 'policies'. Laws and other kinds of rules are not self-implementing. They need something to exercise and apply them, especially in a body whose range of members and policies is expanding in the way those of the Community are. It is here that the institutions, of all types and not just the canonical ones of Article 7 TEC, come into play. In other words, the institutions make a reality of the Union and help to hold it together. As Monnet said, institutions are the means for turning men's ideas into permanent reality, so, while 'nothing is possible without men. Nothing is lasting without institutions.' And much recent theorizing sees institutions, broadly interpreted, as the key to the dynamic of politics in Europe.

The European Parliament

Like the TECSC before it the TEC starts its institutional provisions with the European Parliament (EP). This is the first institution not because it is the most powerful but because it symbolizes the popular sovereignty on which the Community is supposed to rest, as it does in most Western countries. Thus it derives a nominal primacy from the essential democratic role of parliaments in Western societies and from the EP's specific claim to represent the people of Europe. In reality, of course, it has had to fight to make itself felt, and only slowly has it come to enjoy the status of a 'Parliament' rather than an 'Assembly' and also to play an active part in decision-making. As we have seen, Amsterdam was very helpful to it since the changes to the co-decision procedure extended the range and intensity of its involvement in legislation. Nice helped too, Wessels noting calculations that the EP is involved in 66% of all decisions under the TEC. Its growing influence helped it to force the resignation of the Santer Commission in 1999. However, it was not rewarded for this either by turnout in the subsequent elections or by the negotiators a year later. So it remains, especially after Nice, dissatisfied with its lot.

The TEC does not begin by creating the EP because this has already been done by Article 7 TEC. In fact *Article 189* (ex 137) offers a definition of the EP, no longer as an assembly but as a Parliament. However, it is still composed of the representatives, not of the citizens of the Union as the Germans had suggested in 1991, but of the peoples of the member states. The article then defines the EP's powers, which are not organic and inherent but derived from specific treaty empowerment. For the TEC the EP matters as much because it has specific tasks as because it is there.

These tasks, of course, are no longer limited to the advisory and supervisory as was the case before Maastricht upgraded the EP. They extend as far as the treaty specifies. However, they are not gathered together here and there is no equivalent to Article 250 on legislative acts which lists the Parliament's forms of influence in decision-making. Two, co-decision and co-operation, are set out at Articles 251 and 252 but assent, consultation and information are not defined here.* Even so, compared to Articles 202 and 211, there is a hint that the EP is there to be as much as to do.

One of Amsterdam's main innovations was to add to Article 189 a cap on the size of the EP. Prior to this it had, like the UK House of Commons, been allowed to grow unchecked as new states joined, with no thought for either efficiency or logistics. But the prospect of enlargement, noted in Declaration No. 15 TEU, encouraged the negotiators to fix the size of the assembly at 700 to prevent it becoming too much like the old Supreme Soviet of the USSR. If this had not been done, in other words, it was felt that it would have become purely ceremonial and unable to exercise any effective influence. It could also outgrow the capacity of any building likely to be available to it in Brussels or Strasbourg.

However, in order to cope with the transition from the present number of MEPs to a reduced number, and to provide rewards for negotiating sacrifices elsewhere, Nice had to change this. Thus it increases the cap to 732. And this could rise further after accession treaties are signed, given that Hungary and the Czech Republic were denied the extra

---

*Assent gives the EP a veto on things such as association and enlargement under Articles 49, 161, 190 and 300 TEC. It was extended at Nice to Article 7 TEU and Articles 11 and 161 TEC. Consultation means that the EP's opinion must be both sought and noted, even if not acted upon. This was widened at Nice to include Articles 37, 67, 83, 181a and 279 TEC. Information means simply that the EP has to listen and cannot formally respond.

seats needed to give them parity with other member states in the same size band. The new cap was related to the decisions made on allocating seats. At present these are a historic settlement (and one challenged in 1976). So in revising them the 2000 IGC had to take two principles into account: the principle of 'appropriateness' laid down in Article 190 and the desire of some small member states to prevent the larger ones getting a second reward, in the shape of EP seats, on top of benefits from the reweighting of votes in the Council.

The IGC was presented with two main possibilities for reallocating: a linear and proportionate reduction of present allocations (with a basic allowance to help micro states) and a distribution more closely linked to population. Both had slightly different effects, as Galloway details, the first helping the smallest member states and introducing a set of bands, while the second produced more diversity, overall cuts (save for Germany) and markedly fewer seats for small member states. In the end the IGC opted for a compromise which used a linear reduction for smaller member states and applied more population-related figures at the top while generally sticking to a 'banding' approach. Because this left anomalies and dissent, further inducements to conclude were found by raising the ceiling. Then the actual figures agreed for the existing 15 member states after 2004 were included in the Protocol on enlargement of the European Union while the overall allocations for a 27-strong Union were printed in declaration No. 20 TN on the enlargement of the European Union. For convenience we have added the revised figures for the existing member states in brackets at Article 190.

However, the changes will not come into effect for some time, for two reasons. Firstly, between 2004 and 2009 the protocol provides that the number of seats will be the new allocation of 535 plus any seats resulting from states who sign accession treaties by 1 January 2004.* And, if the resulting total should prove to be less than 732, then the states involved will be given bonus seats, providing that their total shares (for those existing members) are no higher than in the present 626 house. The decision on the bonuses will be wholly in the hands of the Council acting by simple majority.

Secondly, as the number of member states rises, Article 2(4) of the Protocol on enlargement of the European Union allows the number of MEPs temporarily to rise above 732 in order to avoid ejecting sitting members during a session. Corrections will be made at the next election. The wording also seems to suggest that if numbers then are still below 732 a further bonus can be allocated, again by a decision in Council. However, if no states enter before 2004 and the EP size was set at 732 in 2004, and thereafter several states were to join before 2009, as could happen, the EP could inflate significantly. This would be a very brief inflation, before the 2009 adjustment came in. In other words, the overall new allocations might not be effective until 2014, or even after, depending on the pace of accessions.

The whole thing is remarkably badly drafted and the EP is right to describe it as 'complex, possibly uncertain and not free of risks'. Exactly how many MEPs there will be at any given time cannot be known for some time yet. And the possibilities of challenge and EU enlargement beyond 27 could complicate things further. All this clearly shows that the EP does not enjoy the esteem that its place in the TEC suggests it should. Not surprisingly, the EP was hurt and angry at the way its size was used by the French presidency, without consultation, to provide negotiating '*douceurs*' for recalcitrant member states at Nice.

---

*Declaration No. 20 TN allocates seats to applicant states as follows: Poland 50; Romania 33; Czech Republic 20; Hungary 20; Bulgaria 17; Slovakia 13; Lithuania 12; Latvia 8; Slovenia 7; Estonia and Cyprus 6 each; and Malta 5.

Article 190 (ex 138), which derives from the 1976 Act concerning the election of the representatives of the Assembly by direct universal suffrage, then develops this in two ways. However, it first, in paragraph 1, repeats the definition of the EP, and underlines the legitimacy of its members (MEPs) by insisting on direct universal suffrage for their election. Nomination by national parliaments is thus excluded. However, the article leaves details of how MEPs should be elected till later.

The first development on Article 189 comes in paragraph 2 which sets out the existing allocation of seats. Secondly it adds to this a caveat, inserted at Amsterdam, requiring that any changes to the list must provide appropriate representation for the member states involved. In other words any new allocation must be acceptable rather than absolutely fair and proportionate. Because the package deal at Nice was accepted, albeit grudgingly, we can accept it as appropriate for the existing member states, especially for Germany and Luxembourg, which are the only member states not scheduled to lose seats in 2004. Whether the overall allocation for the future is fair and proportionate, especially for some of the candidates, is less certain. There will still be a factor of ten difference in the number of people served by MEPs, from over 800,000 in the case of the largest member states to no more than 70,000 in the smallest, with an average of some 570,000. Partly because of the unwillingness to grade Hungary and the Czech Republic, new entrants come off worst here with a slightly higher than average load for their MEPs.

The article then goes on to specify a five-year term for MEPs, although without reference to the starting date of 1979 for calculating this. Paragraph 4 then reverts to the question of the nature of the electoral process. And since Amsterdam it offers the possibility not of an absolutely identical electoral process but of the drafting of one based simply on common principles, looking for processes which were similar but not identical, thus allowing a certain amount of national choice. However, even though in 1999 the UK shifted to a system based on proportional representation it has not been possible to get agreement on such a shared system even though proposals have been made in the EP. Whenever it is secured, of course, it will be for a unanimous Council to pass the appropriate rules, providing firstly that the EP generates a majority of all its members, whether actually present at the session when the vote is taken or not. This idea was introduced at Maastricht for quasi-constitutional decisions and may reflect unease at low levels of attendance in the EP. Secondly, moreover, the member states must be willing to ratify any deal. Progress on this seems likely to be slow as a result. The paragraph also gives us the nearest thing there is to a definition of what 'assent' requires.

Paragraph 5, which was changed at Nice to replace unanimity by QMV, was inserted at Amsterdam in order to regularize the status of MEPs. This responded to concerns for the way they sometimes carried out their duties. Here the EP is allowed to draw up rules for its own members but whereas before 1999 it had full control, the Commission now has a voice and the Council a veto. Moreover, any changes to the tax regime for MEPs will be subject to unanimity, something insisted on to prevent creating a precedent for general tax harmonization by QMV. In any case, internal EP opposition to changing the existing allowances system has slowed up the process of devising a statute for MEPs.

Article 191 (ex 138a), which was also introduced at Maastricht, recognizes the roles which political parties can and should play within the Union, and by implication in the EP. What is meant by integration here is not fully specified but it appears to mean increased public awareness of, and involvement in, the politics of the Union. However, the citizens cannot do this directly but only through political parties. The addition made at Nice has added to Eurosceptic fears that the purpose of such regulations, to be adopted using the co-decision procedure, is to exclude 'critical' parties from funding and full participation. Equally the phrase 'political parties at European level' can be seen as excluding single-nation formations. This explains Declaration No. 11 TN which meets this fear by providing that all political forces represented in the EP must be treated equally. It also makes two other points; that no EU money granted under this heading must find its way to national parties and that the article must not be read as giving the EU any extra powers. Nor can it be invoked against national constitutional rules.

While Declaration No. 11 TN answers two sets of concerns about funding for parties, it does not say anything at all about political groups in the EP itself. These are extremely important in the way the EP now works. Yet there is not even a mention of their external contacts and relations with national parties. Moreover, the involvement of Council in Article 191 can be seen as another example of the limitations on the EP's autonomy.

This also appears in *Article 192* (ex 138b), since the act of specifying the EP's legislative roles – in order to make clear what are the treaty-based powers mentioned in Article 189 – can be seen as restricting its democratic rights. And those rights differ according to the procedures listed. It might also be argued that alongside assent, co-decision, co-operation and consultation (still among the most numerous), the EP also has a right to be informed under other articles as Chalmers and Galloway both discuss. The brevity of these provisions suggests that the EP has not always been thought of as essentially a legislator.

The second paragraph points slightly in the other direction since, by allowing the EP to request Commission proposals on matters of its choice, it gains a pale reflection of the right of initiative that it has long wanted. The EP wants to be a full legislature with the right to propose the laws it wants, even though in most parliaments such things are increasingly controlled by governments. However, the Commission does not have to agree to the request although, in fact, it often encourages the EP to make such requests so that it does not seem too activist itself. This, of course, leaves no trace in the Treaty.

Alongside this share in the EC's decision-making process, the EP is given another power by *Article 193* (ex 138c). Since Maastricht this allows a substantial body of opinion in the EP to request the establishment of a Committee of Inquiry to look into alleged abuses in the implementation of EC law, provided that these are not *sub judice*. However, it cannot be a standing committee and rules governing its operation have to be jointly agreed with the Commission and the Council. None the less, this power can be seen as one which the EP exercises in defence of the Union's citizens.

The next two articles tell us something more about the EP's concerns for public grievances. Since Maastricht *Article 194* (ex 138d) enshrines the *de facto* right of petition to the EP which, in the view of Chalmers, has existed since 1953. It is, however, a circumscribed right. It can only lead to action where an individual or a body has been personally disadvantaged by EC action. Generalized complaints about what the Union is and does will not be acted on under this rubric, though there is nothing to stop such criticisms being publicly directed at the EP.

Though the EP can directly take up such grievances itself, *Article 195* (ex 138e) provides a more convenient way of doing it. This is the Ombudsman, who can hear complaints of maladministration by bodies other than the ECJ and CFI, whether referred directly – provided they are from member state nationals – or through the EP. However, the article – which was fleshed out by Council Decision 94/262 – makes it clear that while the Ombudsman emerges from the EP, as the regular elections show, and follows the Scandinavian parliamentary style of the office, the Ombudsman is completely independent of the EP and cannot be dictated to by it. In practice this has been very much the case and the Ombudsman has been an active force in bringing pressure on institutions to provide information and look to the way they carry out their duties, often using the office's right to mount 'own initiative' investigations. In fact, Bonnor argues that the Ombudsman's achievement is more to make soft law than to remedy citizens' grievances as such.

The four remaining articles of Section 1 deal with questions of organization. According to *Article 196* (ex 139) the EP thus has to hold at least one session per year. Implicitly this suggests a short period in the spring, but in practice the EP meets in a series of cycles throughout the year allowing for committee, group and plenary meetings. However, the length of session is important since, while the EP is formally sitting, its members enjoy legal immunity. The provision for special sessions echoes those in some national constitutions but have rarely been invoked.

Article 197 (ex 140) does two things. One is to empower the EP to elect a president who, the ECJ has accepted, in *Council* v. *Parliament* (1986), can act for the EP, and other officials. The president is therefore politically influential and certainly more than a simple chairperson. Indeed the presidency is closer to the role of the Speaker in Stuart times, when the post very much led, and spoke for, the English Parliament. Details of officials are set out in the EP's Rules of Procedure because they are not defined here. Presently the EP is guided by a Bureau consisting mainly of the heads of political groups, while its housekeeping is in the hands of MEPs known as Questors. It is also assisted by a professional staff of administrators, lawyers and technical advisers. The treaty, furthermore, says nothing either about the various committees of the EP or about its working procedures.

The second function of Article 197 is to establish some form of accountability to the EP. Thus commissioners can be observers and have a right to be heard should they ask to be. Equally the Commission must respond to written or verbal enquiries from MEPs whereas the Council can decide for itself how it shall be heard, thus showing that there is limited accountability. Usually this is actually done through the Council presidency which reports regularly. In any case, the EP cannot refuse to hear the Council suggesting that the latter wishes to give direction rather than rendering account of its own executive activities.

Normally when the EP votes, *Article 198* (ex 141) requires a majority of those present and voting even though elsewhere, as we have seen, the treaty does require an absolute or enhanced majority. Also, there has to be a minimum number of MEPs present, currently a third or 209. The Rules of Procedure which specify this (and also provide that the minimum is only operative if actually challenged) are given legal status by *Article 199* (ex 142). As regards the Rules of Procedure themselves, the EP has full autonomy in drafting them and has used them to ensure that it uses all the possibilities for exercising influence.

Article 200 (ex 143) partly goes back to accountability by requiring from the Commission a yearly overall report on its activities. The same is not asked of the Council. Chalmers argues that this is to show that the EP has more control over the Commission than over the Council. However, while the EP has to consider the Commission's report publicly, it is not required to come to a decision on it and, in fact, MEPs normally pay more attention to the outline of the Commission's programme at the start of the year. Moreover, the Council usually does report via the presidency while Article 4 TEU calls for written and oral reports from the European Council. Equally the Council has answered oral questions from MEPs since 1983.

Finally, *Article 201* (ex 144), draws attention to what has been shown to be one of the EP's key powers, that of censuring the Commission. The nature of the censure is implicitly defined quite narrowly. A mere warning is not possible, only total dismissal. A carefully defined timetable is laid down for doing this. Ultimately an enhanced majority is required not actually to dismiss the Commission but to force it collectively to resign, which is a strange way of implementing what is, effectively, the 'nuclear' option where Commission accountability is concerned. Indeed, there is no provision for dismissing individual members, something which would have been very useful in 1999 and for which the EP has long called.

All this tells us only a limited amount about the EP. Indeed, even though the TEC is here serving as a framework document, it is one of the more unrevealing passages. There is no emphatic statement about the EP's significance and authority, no real indication of the way it actually works and no full list of its rights. These are, of course, scattered throughout the treaties. And the informal activities of the EP, including its unceasing search for more authority, are also understandably absent.

The EP tends to highlight its lack of legislative powers, complaining about the absence of a right of initiative and the limited scope of co-decision, and seeing this as the essence of the democratic deficit. None the less, it is a more effective transformative parliament than many, with a good record in amending legislation. To this should be added its limited legitimizing role since assent extends only to such areas as association, the budget, enhanced co-operation and enlargement. The EP is largely excluded from treaty revision.

In fact the section throws up other functional weaknesses which are perhaps even more important. These include the EP's limited and indirect representativeness which can produce a lack of connection with the peoples of Europe. Equally, its role as a scrutinizer of the rest of the Union is limited, self-generated and not publicly esteemed. As the section makes clear, the EP is very much part of the EU system, intimately related with the other institutions, and not clearly demarcated as the voice of the public. Nor is it really the arena where the great questions of the day are thrashed out. Hence its educational and informational roles are limited and patchy.

The fact that it plays only a small part in providing the executive leaders of the Union may also influence this. In fact it can often be a paddock for ex-leaders put out to grass. So too can the fact that the EP, even after Amsterdam, has somewhat uncertain and underdeveloped relations with national parliaments.* Legally, the EP has to be consulted and actually listened to, as the *Roquette Frères* v. *Council (Isoglucose)* (1980) case showed, but as the section suggests, it is still somewhat a controlled Parliament, despite its prominent place in the treaty's pecking order.

PART FIVE   INSTITUTIONS OF THE COMMUNITY

TITLE I

PROVISIONS GOVERNING THE INSTITUTIONS

Chapter 1   The Institutions

Section 1   The European Parliament

Article 189 (ex Article 137)

The European Parliament, which shall consist of representatives of the peoples of the States brought together in the Community, shall exercise the powers conferred upon it by this Treaty.

The number of Members of the European Parliament shall not exceed 732.

---

*Declarations Nos. 13 and 14 TEU and the Protocol on the Role of National Parliaments in the European Union adopted at Amsterdam on relations with national parliaments and their European Affairs Committees have failed to resolve this question. Hence the place of national parliaments in the political architecture of the Union is one of the four key issues on the agenda for the 2004 debate and IGC.

Article 190 (new)

1. *The representatives in the European Parliament of the peoples of the States brought together in the Community shall be elected by direct universal suffrage.*

2. *The number of representatives elected in each Member State shall be as follows:* *

Belgium	25	(22)
Denmark	16	(13)
Germany	99	(99)
Greece	25	(22)
Spain	64	(50)
France	87	(72)
Ireland	15	(12)
Italy	87	(72)
Luxembourg	6	(6)
Netherlands	31	(25)
Austria	21	(17)
Portugal	25	(22)
Finland	16	(13)
Sweden	22	(18)
United Kingdom	87	(72)

In the event of amendments to this paragraph, the number of representatives elected in each Member State must ensure appropriate representation of the peoples of the States brought together in the Community.

3. *Representatives shall be elected for a term of five years.*

4. *The European Parliament shall draw up a proposal for elections by direct universal suffrage in accordance with a uniform procedure in all Member States or in accordance with principles common to all Member States.*

The Council shall, acting unanimously after obtaining the assent of the European Parliament, which shall act by a majority of its component members, lay down the appropriate provisions, which it shall recommend to Member States for adoption in accordance with their respective constitutional requirements.

5. **The European Parliament, *after* seeking an opinion from the Commission and with the approval of the Council acting, by a qualified majority, *shall* lay down the regulations and general conditions governing the performance of the duties of its Members. All rules or conditions relating to the taxation of Members or former Members shall require unanimity within the Council.**

Article 191 (ex Article 138a)

Political parties at European level are important as a factor for integration within the Union. They contribute to forming a European awareness and to expressing the political will of the citizens of the Union.

The Council, acting in accordance with the procedure referred to in Article 251, shall lay down the regulations governing political parties at European level and in particular the rules regarding their funding.

---

*Article 2.1 of the Protocol on Enlargement of the European Union provides that these figures be scaled back to 535 with effect from 1 January 2004 so that they will be operative from the beginning of the next Parliament. The new figures are therefore printed in brackets here.

Article 192 (ex Article 138b)

Insofar as provided in this Treaty, the European Parliament shall participate in the process leading up to the adoption of Community acts by exercising its powers under the procedures laid down in Articles 251 and 252 and by giving its assent or delivering advisory opinions.

The European Parliament may, acting by a majority of its Members, request the Commission to submit any appropriate proposal on matters on which it considers that a Community act is required for the purpose of implementing this Treaty.

Article 193 (ex Article 138c)

In the course of its duties, the European Parliament may, at the request of a quarter of its Members, set up a temporary Committee of Inquiry to investigate, without prejudice to the powers conferred by this Treaty on other institutions or bodies, alleged contraventions or maladministration in the implementation of Community law, except where the alleged facts are being examined before a court and while the case is still subject to legal proceedings.

The temporary Committee of Inquiry shall cease to exist on the submission of its report.

The detailed provisions governing the exercise of the right of inquiry shall be determined by common accord of the European Parliament, the Council and the Commission.

Article 194 (ex Article 138d)

Any citizen of the Union, and any natural or legal person residing or having its registered office in a Member State, shall have the right to address, individually or in association with other citizens or persons, a petition to the European Parliament on a matter which comes within the Community's fields of activity and which affects him, her or it directly.

Article 195 (ex Article 138e)

1. The European Parliament shall appoint an Ombudsman empowered to receive complaints from any citizen of the Union or any natural or legal person residing or having its registered office in a Member State concerning instances of maladministration in the activities of the Community institutions or bodies, with the exception of the Court of Justice and the Court of First Instance acting in their judicial role.

In accordance with his duties, the Ombudsman shall conduct inquiries for which he finds grounds, either on his own initiative or on the basis of complaints submitted to him direct or through a Member of the European Parliament, except where the alleged facts are or have been the subject of legal proceedings. Where the Ombudsman establishes an instance of maladministration, he shall refer the matter to the institution concerned, which shall have a period of three months in which to inform him of its views. The Ombudsman shall then forward a report to the European Parliament and the institution concerned. The person lodging the complaint shall be informed of the outcome of such inquiries.

The Ombudsman shall submit an annual report to the European Parliament on the outcome of his inquiries.

2. The Ombudsman shall be appointed after each election of the European Parliament for the duration of its term of office. The Ombudsman shall be eligible for reappointment.

The Ombudsman may be dismissed by the Court of Justice at the request of the European Parliament if he no longer fulfils the conditions required for the performance of his duties or if he is guilty of serious misconduct.

3. The Ombudsman shall be completely independent in the performance of his duties. In the performance of those duties he shall neither seek nor take instructions from any body. The Ombudsman may not, during his term of office, engage in any other occupation, whether gainful or not.

4. The European Parliament shall, after seeking an opinion from the Commission and with the approval of the Council acting by a qualified majority, lay down the regulations and general conditions governing the performance of the Ombudsman's duties.

Article 196 (ex Article 139)

The European Parliament shall hold an annual session. It shall meet, without requiring to be convened, on the second Tuesday in March.

The European Parliament may meet in extraordinary session at the request of a majority of its Members or at the request of the Council or of the Commission.

Article 197 (ex Article 140)

The European Parliament shall elect its President and its officers from among its Members.

Members of the Commission may attend all meetings and shall, at their request, be heard on behalf of the Commission.

The Commission shall reply orally or in writing to questions put to it by the European Parliament or by its Members.

The Council shall be heard by the European Parliament in accordance with the conditions laid down by the Council in its Rules of Procedure.

Article 198 (ex Article 141)

Save as otherwise provided in this Treaty, the European Parliament shall act by an absolute majority of the votes cast.

The Rules of Procedure shall determine the quorum.

Article 199 (ex Article 142)

The European Parliament shall adopt its Rules of Procedure, acting by a majority of its Members.

The proceedings of the European Parliament shall be published in the manner laid down in its Rules of Procedure.

Article 200 (ex Article 143)

The European Parliament shall discuss in open session the annual general report submitted to it by the Commission.

Article 201 (ex Article 144)

If a motion of censure on the activities of the Commission is tabled before it, the European Parliament shall not vote thereon until at least three days after the motion has been tabled and only by open vote.

If the motion of censure is carried by a two-thirds majority of the votes cast, representing a majority of the Members of the European Parliament, the Members of the Commission shall resign as a body. They shall continue to deal with current business until they are replaced in accordance with Article 214. In this case, the term of office of the Members of the Commission appointed to replace them shall expire on the date on which the term of office of the Members of the Commission obliged to resign as a body would have expired.

The Council

Compared to the EP, the Council of Ministers has an apparently less elevated position in the hierarchy but, probably, more power. Indeed, it has been hailed as the representative and guardian of the member states and their governments. Yet the TEC actually says very little about this dimension of its nature. Indeed, it is arguable that what emerges from the treaty is as much another Community institution as a purely inter-governmental one. Interestingly the treaty still refers to it simply as the Council and not as either the Council of the Union, which is how it styles itself, or even as the Council of Ministers. Equally, the treaty obscures the multiple nature of the Council.

In other words, Section 2 confirms Hayes-Renshaw and Wallace's view of the Council as the most important but also the most misunderstood of all the EC institutions. This is partly because the treaty gives us only a limited insight into its actual complexities. And it has to be said that the changes to reweighting and voting thresholds made at Nice do nothing to make it easier to understand. This remains true even after the long and head-scratching analysis for which they call.

The treaty discussion of the Council begins in a very low-key introductory way, not by defining the Council, presumably because this has been created in Article 7, but by stressing in *Article 202* (ex 145) that it exists to ensure that the objectives of the TEC are attained. Not only does it not specifically say that it represents the member states but its powers do not amount to a complete right for member states to do what they like. Their authority is limited firstly by the treaty and secondly by the way the article specifies the ways its responsibility must be exercised. However, the Council's duties are actually spelled out quite broadly here. We need to look to other places in the TEC and not to mention in the two inter-governmental pillars to get a more precise idea of what they are. And, in any case, there is no clear delimitation of tasks as between the Council and other institutions.

In fact, the article accords the Council three types of role: ensuring co-ordination of member states' economic policies; taking decisions; and conferring power on the Commission to act. Of these, the first has been a relatively minor element until recently. With the development of EMU it has become increasingly significant, as we have made clear earlier in the *Guide*, although the fact that not all member states are, or will be, inside the eurozone means that there is a problem in reconciling the role of the Council in its ECOFIN composition with that of the ministerial grouping of the Eurogroup.

Taking decisions – in ways specified elsewhere in the section and the TEC at large – is a very bluntly and elliptically expressed duty but it is probably the most important. It is interesting that the treaty here does not refer to legislating. This is made clearer in Chapter 2 of Part Five. So, in reality there can be no Community legislation without Council approval. This can involve laying down broad guidelines, turning the general ideas of the European Council into legally viable forms, and issuing a whole range of opinions.

The third indent is long and somewhat obscure. It allows the Council not just to get the Commission to implement the decisions which emerge from it but to specify how this should be done. A Council decision of 1987, scheduled for updating in line with Declaration No. 31 TA, spelled all this out and the ECJ has accepted that it can be done in general terms and does not need minute specification. It happens in such areas as agriculture, competition and external relations. The fact that the Council does this suggests that, given its transient and variable nature, it is not in a good position to implement its own acts even if, as the Commission complains, it does not delegate enough. However, this delegation also requires a motion from the Commission – assuming that the procedures referred to here are those of implementation and the conditions related to it – to do this, which seems somewhat perverse.

In any case, many authorities would argue, as do Hayes-Renshaw and Wallace, that the Council's actual roles go beyond this. For them it is an executive body, a source of legislation, a permanent negotiating forum, part of a dialogue with the Commission and the representative of the member states. Others would add that the Council has the ability to control finance, to scrutinize other institutions, to request reports and studies and to act externally. It also has to respond to the EP and other institutions. Only some of these tasks are actually mentioned in Section 2, the rest appearing in a host of other TEC provisions. And many are also to be found in the TEU since the Council is very active in the other pillars. The Treaty of Nice makes this range of activities very clear since it adds or amends a raft of appointments, legislative involvement and other measures. The last includes deciding how to change voting thresholds in line with enlargement and ensuring consistency both on EU policies in general and in cases of enhanced co-operation. More than ever after Nice the Council appears as a multi-tasked body. And this has implications for its composition.

Article 203 (ex 146) starts to define the Council by specifying its normal membership. Since Maastricht this has, in order to assist decentralized member states like Belgium and Germany, been phrased carefully so as to allow regional ministers to represent the member state. This demands the member state conferring decision-making powers on them, something which can also be done to ambassadors when no ministers are available for a meeting. Hence ministers are more the mandatees of government than representatives in the Burkean sense. They thus often attend with large numbers of advisers so that the Council can in practice be a fairly large body especially as the Commission usually has representatives present as observers and honest brokers. Even though recent treaty reforms have increased the number of occasions on which the Council meets in the composition of heads of government or of state there is no reference to this since premiers and presidents are covered by the existing wording, being more able than most ministers to commit their states.

Next the article talks of who should hold the presidency, though without fully defining what the office actually entails, despite its significance both to the Union and to domestic politics. This may be because it was inserted into the TEC by the Merger Treaty. Implicitly the presidency is portrayed as the means by which the member states can steer the Union, a position of responsibility without power as Constantinescu and his colleagues observe. The fact that the member state holding the presidency normally has two seats at Council meetings is not mentioned. In the article tenure of the presidency is now phrased in terms of constitutional principle rather than listing the order of member states as was previously the case.

However, there is no mention here either of the composition of the Council or of its support services. The treaty, in fact, speaks throughout of the Council as a single body. In reality, of course, it is multiple as befits its range of interests and responsibilities. The single Council has been a legal fiction since at least the mid-1960s. The Council, like the French Council of Ministers under the *ancien régime*, can take a variety of forms depending on the subjects it is discussing, while yet remaining 'the Council'. There is thus a lot of difference between the Education Council, the General Affairs Council and the Transport Council, for instance. Tensions between formations have been known, as between ECOFIN and Agriculture in the early 1980s. Consolidating the Council is therefore one of the aims of institutional reformers.

Where supports such as standing committees and working groups are concerned there is no mention. Secretarial services are only brought in at Article 207. Before then *Article 204 (ex 147)* sets out when and why the Council should meet. This implies both that the presidency can decide when to call it and that it has to accede to a request for it to be summoned. In fact the calendar of meetings is not a matter of infrequent gatherings called at will, but is fixed well in advance and agreed by common accord. There can be the best part of a hundred meetings every year.

Having outlined the main tasks and procedures of the Council, Section 2 next turns to voting arrangements. These are of fundamental importance for the distribution of power in the Council and beyond. Only recently have voting records even been published, along with the explanations sometimes attached to votes. And it is on these questions of voting that Nice will, assuming it is ratified, make significant changes. This is because of their innate complications and sensitivity, something which requires a longer exposition than for virtually any other article of the treaties. Yet, without setting them out in detail, neither Nice nor the overall distribution of power in the enlarging Union can be understood, always assuming the changes are comprehensible in the first place.

Article 205 (ex 148) starts by suggesting that the normal mode of decision-making is by simple majority, that is by eight to seven at present. In fact simple majority decisions are the exception, even more so now than they used to be.* They are avoided because they can be seen as favouring small member states too much and normally relate to procedural matters. In other words, the treaty normally does 'provide otherwise'. Unanimity is not actually mentioned here until paragraph 3 which makes it clear that unanimity can actually be described as '*nem con*' since abstentions do not prevent a 'unanimous' vote. What matters is that nobody formally objects. Indeed, as Hayes-Renshaw and Wallace say, theoretically an act could be passed by Luxembourg alone if all the others abstained. In practice a third of the member states have been known to stand aside in a vote. In any case, the wording set down here has been written into other parts of the European Treaties, notably in the inter-governmental pillars, so as to ensure consistency in Council decision-making procedures.

Paragraph 2 suggests that the main voting procedure is QMV. Because member states are so different in size simple majority has always been unacceptable on grounds of equity, political acceptability and the need for decisions to have a clear legitimacy. Some other means had to be found. Hence, as in the TECSC, the TEC, perhaps influenced by some historic German precedents, gave each member state not the traditional single vote

---

*Articles 208 and 209 are still subject to simple majority, as are 251(7), 252(g) and 284 along with the much more significant Article 48 TEU on the calling of an IGC. Some policy areas, like training, used to be subject to the same rule in the past.

but a multiple vote, roughly relating to its population. It also laid down rules for obtaining majorities using these.

The question of which articles should be decided by QMV has been a matter of increasing controversy. The EP and others believe that it is vital for effective decision-making and pushed for it at Amsterdam. They gained some of what they wanted but pressures on Kohl prevented this going as far as it might have done. Nice made further limited changes and, as in 1997, encouraged complaints that national rights were being trampled underfoot.*

The original weights, as such, were a bargain among the original six member states and one which was generous to smaller member states. Because the weightings took the form not of individually crafted awards but of a series of 'bands' giving member states of roughly the same population the same number of votes, the system was easily extended to other member states as they joined, save perhaps in the case of Spain. This accounts for the figures printed below. However, the likely impact of enlargement to many more small member states meant that the larger member states demanded a recalculation in their favour, especially if they were to surrender a commissioner as they had hinted at Amsterdam that they might do. But getting agreement on new figures bedevilled the Nice summit, taking up two-thirds of the discussions. Comparative standings and the desire to try to control the future evolution of the Union seem to have made member states so unwilling to compromise, even when this threw clarity to the winds.

None the less, Nice made three sets of changes to the existing rules, beginning with new weightings. The initial result here was the new figures in Article 3 of the Protocol on enlargement of the European Union. These are to replace the existing text with effect from 1 January 2005 and are printed below in brackets for convenience. Owing to the French refusal to concede symbolic primacy to Germany, the new allocation sticks to bands save where the Netherlands is concerned. It was conceded an extra vote in last-minute haggling. The failure to recognize Germany's weight meant that other member states saw no reason why they should accept more accurate reweightings in their case either. In the end, large member states got roughly three times their present allocation and smaller ones double. The new figures mean that, in an EU of 15, Germany will have 21.86% of the votes and the UK 15.79%. These shares represent a gain for the moment but will of course go down as enlargement takes place. In an EU of 27 member states they will be 17.09% and 12.34%, respectively.

Beyond this, Declaration No. 20 TN also proposes similar allocations to all the candidate countries.† So, by the time the EU reaches 27 members, a German vote will represent some 2.8 million people, one from the UK just over 2 million while those of Luxembourg and Malta will cover only about 100,000. The overall average will be 1,390,000 souls per vote. However, because the candidates' allocations are only set out in a declaration they are open to challenge and alteration in a way the figures for the 15, enshrined in a protocol, are not.

---

*The French identified some 70 possible instances which might be changed, but in fact only about 30 were actually agreed thanks to national 'red lines in the sand'. Assessments of the number involved change depending on whether one counts by article or part of article. Articles 23 and 24 TEU and 13, 18, 62, 63, 65, 66, 100, 111, 114, 123, 133, 137, 157, 159, 161, 181a, 190, 191, 207, 214, 215, 223, 224, 247, 258, 263 and 279 are among those affected, although not all of them immediately. Some MEPs have their eyes on at least a further 25 cases.

†Declaration No. 20 TN allocates votes to applicant states as follows: Poland 27; Romania 14; Czech Republic 12; Hungary 12; Bulgaria 10; Slovakia and Lithuania 7 each; Latvia, Slovenia, Estonia and Cyprus 4 each; Malta 3. This makes a grand total of 345 in an EU of 27 member states. Unlike the distribution of EP seats, the list contains no obvious anomalies.

While the figures as such are straightforward, albeit inflated and more difficult to calculate mentally, the same cannot be said of the second set of changes proposed at Nice. These affect the calculation of majorities and minorities. They cover three hypothetical situations: after 2005 assuming no enlargement; during the expansion period; and when the Union finally reaches 27. Unfortunately these are complex, contested and contradictory.

The present situation on majorities and minorities, as set out below in Article 205, is twofold. Where the Council requires a Commission proposal for an act, the threshold for a qualified majority is set at 62 votes of 87. This level, which is equivalent to 71.26% of the vote, means that the large member states need several allies to push legislation through. The minimum is eight member states and would normally represent 58.16% of the population, somewhat less than was originally the case.

It also means that a minority of 26 votes (29.89%) can block the passage of an act. The blocking minority is normally calculated by deducting the threshold from the total and then adding one. To achieve this level at present can require at least three member states, assuming two large ones plus Spain, representing 12% of the population. Conversely this would require, at least, two large member states and either Spain or two small member states other than Luxembourg to oppose legislation. The present blocking minority, which dates from 1995, has been controversial. Hence, under the 1994 Ioannina compromise where member states with 23–25 votes indicate their likely opposition, steps have to be taken to find 'within a reasonable time' a 'satisfactory solution', although this has rarely been necessary.

Where a Commission proposal is not needed, at least 10 member states have to be in favour (this in addition to the 62-vote minimum). The aim of this is presumably to show greater support where decisions are taken by governmental representatives somewhat outside the normal Community legislative modes. However, we should note that the provision also applies to cases where the Commission merely recommends or other institutions request action. In any case, the same weightings and thresholds apply as where a Commission proposal is involved. Academic discussion rarely singles out this mode for special attention but it is relevant to some articles of the TEC as well as to the inter-governmental pillars. Among the former are provisions such as Article 187 on relations with OCTs, Article 119(2) on granting emergency financial aid to member states in balance of payments difficulties and Article 221 on the number of ECJ judges. In the latter case, as with any ESCB call for action versus a national bank, a request from the institution is required for the Council to act.

Nice proposed several not wholly consistent changes to these rules.* To begin from 2005 and assuming there is no enlargement by then, the threshold for an act based on a Commission proposal will be 169 votes out of 237 (71.73%). However, these votes still have to be cast by a majority of member states. This request for eight member states, irrespective of their votes, will still largely be irrelevant then since the largest seven member states can only muster 168 votes, making a numerical majority of member states necessary for a qualified majority of votes in any case. In other modes of decision-making, where a Commission proposal is not involved, 10 member states will have to be involved in the 169 votes. This means one more member state will be needed than the numbers alone require.

*In fact, as noted earlier and discussed by Neunreither, COREPER had to change the treaty text to eliminate one glaring inconsistency which arose because the tables of votes were not updated when the final declarations were agreed. This discussion uses the altered figures, although there is still a discrepancy between the protocol and the correction in the declaration.

In both procedures the blocking minority, using the normal calculation, becomes 69 (29.11%), a figure which can be reached by two larger member states plus one of the member states with 12 votes or more. The combination would represent a minimum of 30.08% of the population. It is also one more than the votes of existing southern member states, which may be significant in financial contexts. However, it can also be reached by the eight smallest member states representing 13.79% of the population. This may make it harder generally to block acts though making it easier for larger member states to do so. If there is an accession before 2005, which now seems likely, either the new member state will have to be accommodated inside the existing weightings or the new ones will have to be brought forward through the accession treaty.

Moreover, thanks to the third change made at Nice, in either case it is open to a member state, under what from January 2005 will be paragraph 4 of the article, to query a vote on the basis that the votes do not emanate from member states representing at least 62% of the total population of the Union. This is presently 376 million and will rise to 482 million. If this is demonstrated the act will fall. In other words, this population verification is not automatic and an act can get through without such demographic backing if nobody challenges it. This provision is in line with the way the Council treats abstentions. Opinions are divided as to whether the demographic challenge will be ignored or regularly invoked by disgruntled member states. Galloway thinks that it will not be used because the Community does not really work in this way.

This safety-net procedure works very much to the advantage of Germany, which is why it was introduced. Spain, the Netherlands and Greece are estimated to be the main losers. Because under the rule 38% of the population can block decisions, Germany (with 22% of the present population and 17% of the final) presently needs only three other larger member states to defeat an act. Without Germany four large member states and several small ones would be needed. With 27 member states the biggest five and any other, excepting the three smallest, would suffice to block decisions. Although all this was done to compensate Germany for the refusal, deriving from French beliefs and *amour propre*, to give it the additional basic votes, calculations by Ludlow and others suggest that the safety net is the equivalent of giving Germany four extra votes. This may, as Felsenthal and Machover say, be more equitable than actually increasing the weightings but it was probably more than Germany would have expected anyway, given the Dutch and Spanish precedents. In any case it will make much less difference once the Union enlarges.

Returning to the second set of changes made by Nice for the period of enlargement up to and including 26 member states, paragraph 2 of Article 2 of the Protocol on enlargement of the European Union comes into play. This provides that, at each accession, the QMV threshold shall be calculated to ensure that it does not exceed the figures which can be deduced from the table already mentioned and set out in Point 2 of Declaration No. 20 TN. This declaration also says, implicitly referring to a Union of 27, that the threshold shall be 258 votes (74.78%). The parallel requirements for a majority and two-thirds of member states being in favour, depending on whether a Commission proposal was required, remain, as does the demographic challenge already mentioned. The numerical majority provision is superfluous since the 13 largest member states can only muster 256 votes. None the less, it will become significant demographically, as we suggest below. And the two-thirds rule could make a difference since it would require five extra member states beyond the 13 largest.

The figure of 258 gives a blocking minority, again implicitly in a Union of 27, of 88 (25.52%). However, Declaration 21 – which was added late on to resolve uncertainties – calls this into question by giving an explanation, of sorts, of what is to happen between

2005 and the accession of the twenty-seventh member state. The wording is obscure but the EP has to be right in saying that the declaration can only apply to the period during which the sixteenth to the twenty-sixth member states join. In any case, in the course of this process the threshold is to move from a percentage below the existing one (of 71.26%) to a maximum of 73.4%. The decimal places may seem gratuitous, but they are necessary in order to ensure that member states do not get offered fractions of votes. They have been given, and will want to keep, whole-number votes.

The reference to reducing the existing percentages was apparently inserted to cover the eventuality that some patterns of enlargement might marginally reduce the threshold. The insertion gives the treaty insurance cover in case of complaint. The maximum threshold during this period would work out at between 233 and 250, depending on whether the last entrant is the largest or smallest of the candidates. The blocking minority would therefore be between 102 and 86. The negotiators seem to have assumed that the latter was the more likely scenario since Declaration No. 21 TN does not talk of lowering the figure.

The Declaration, in fact, completes the Treaty's provisions on majorities and minorities by also saying that the blocking minority, which is here specifically mentioned for almost the first time, will in turn have to be adjusted once the EU reaches 27 member states. And it specifies how this is to be done: by further raising the hurdle to 91 votes (26.38%). This in turn requires a further adjustment to the threshold. Using the normal calculations this means 255 (73.91%) of the votes (involving a minimum of 58.39% of the population).* In concrete terms this means both that more than 14 member states will continue to be needed for a majority and that three large member states plus one other will be able to block legislation. The blocking minority of 91 will require a minimum of four member states, excluding Malta, representing 36.62% of the population. It would take the fifteen smallest member states to pass the bar.

It is in this context that the requirement for a majority of member states becomes important. This is because the 14 smallest member states, alone representing 11.62% of the population, could conceivably block a decision with more than enough votes behind it if they all objected. The EP calls this 'the member state safety net'. Certainly it is one point at which the complexities of Nice cannot, as the Irish 'no' campaigners claim, be read simply as favouring the larger member states. As the House of Commons Library Paper on Nice points out, over time the relative importance of large member states is bound to reduce, even allowing for the effects of Nice.

According to Article 3(2) of the protocol, making all these changes, both during enlargement and once there are 27 states in the Union, will be done by Council decision at every enlargement. Some changes may also need to be confirmed in accession treaties. Given that the requirement that 'the votes do not exceed the limits in the Declaration' is not wholly clear and, more importantly, the fact that majorities and minorities symbolize the balance of power among member states, this could open the way to debates and

---

*However, this causes two problems. One is that this is more than is allowed during the transitional period up to and including when the twenty-sixth member joins, when the limit is said to be 73.4%. The other is that the protocol seems, as Felsenthal and Machover say, to have fixed the final threshold at 258 not 255. It has been suggested both that 258 can be regarded as a maximum rather than a target or that there is an error based on the fact that inconsistent documents were being used at the time. If this means that the declaration takes precedence over the protocol this is at variance with normal legal assumptions. Hence Bonde argues that the protocol will have to be changed because it cannot be overridden by a non-binding declaration. However, the informed view is that the protocol figure is wrong – springing from a last-minute drafting error – and that the declaration decision does over-rule it.

alterations. And the latter could heighten the chance that court cases might be launched over the Nice rules. However, since the mathematical margin for manoeuvre is quite small it may prove possible to set the quotas to general satisfaction.

All this remains mind-numbingly complicated and opaque. More worryingly, it is also imprecise, inconsistent and uncertain in its operation. Indeed, some of the assumptions made about how it will work out do not derive solely from what is said in the Treaty of Nice. One of the problems is that the declarations are only political statements or, as Yataganas notes, 'gentlemen's agreements', which try to define negotiating positions in coming accession negotiations. Whether this excuses their inconsistency is a moot point. In any case a change to figures mentioned in the wording of the protocol might have helped to resolve it.

Although the EP has become less concerned about this, the arrangements are likely to hamper decision-making in the eyes of many, including the EP. Felsenthal and Machover have argued that while changes for the existing 15 represent an improvement, the various provisions for an EU of 27 do not. Their view is that they will make it four to five times as hard to get agreement, especially with the deliberate jump when membership of the EU reaches 27. It would have been better to have lowered the bar ahead of enlargement, perhaps to 207 or 60%. In other words Nice will make enlargement hard but, in turn, enlargement will make it harder to change the rules even though this would be advisable in the view of Peel and others. For the Centre for Economic Policy Research the chances of an act getting through will fall from 1 in 12 to 1 in 20.

Suggestions of a majority of weighted votes plus a majority of the population or of proportional or square-root systems would clearly have been simpler to operate and understand, even if they have their problems. However, concerns for power and fear of the future carried the day. It all shows that state selfishness matters more than super-statism. And there can be no confidence that any new negotiations would produce a better result.

Where member state interests are less engaged, as in the rest of Section 2 which is less concerned with power indices, the treaty becomes simpler and less in need of detailed exegesis. Thus the third and presently final paragraph of Article 205, which as we have seen regulates what should be done about abstentions in cases of unanimity, also leads to *Article 206* (ex 150). The latter allows one member state to cast a proxy vote on behalf of one, and only one, other member state. Doing it for more could be abusive. The article probably caters for situations when a minister is *empeché* (prevented), presumably for a shortish period only. Illness, travel problems or double booking could be possible reasons. So, in theory, could answering a call of nature. However, the Council's Rules of Procedure suggests this is not what is in mind since they allow for instructions to be given by the absent member state, though what the sanctions for disobedience are is not clear. However, it seems to be a very uncommon practice even though Article 206(3) caters for it when specifying how unanimity is defined.

The next four articles go back to questions of organization. *Article 207* (ex 151) thus first recognizes the existence of the Committee of Permanent Representatives (COREPER). This, composed of ambassadors to the EU, is vitally important because of the spasmodic nature of the actual Council. Meeting at two levels it provides continuity. And, at Amsterdam, it was authorized to take formal decisions as a result. Paragraph 2 was also inserted at Amsterdam and amended at Nice. The former took over the Secretary Generalship and used it to create a spokesperson for the CFSP, leaving a new post of Deputy Secretary General to oversee the day-to-day working of the actual Secretariat, although its structures and working arrangements are the responsibility of the Council as a whole. This is a rather offhand form of legitimation of the Secretariat (and especially its Legal Service), which is a very significant body even if it is not capable of implementation and monitoring. Nice, of course, allowed both major posts to be elected by QMV.

Paragraph 3 then makes it clear that the Council has the freedom to draft its own working rules and does not have to submit them to anyone else for approval. However, since Amsterdam it is obliged to write them so as to provide public access to its documents and to ensure that reasons are given for its legislative decisions. But it can decide which documents are affected. And many would say that, despite the reference to the co-decision procedure, it has adopted a very restrictive approach to allowing the public to see its papers.

Article 208 (ex 152) shows that the Council is not dependent on its own resources but can call those of the Commission into play. The article gives it a kind of right of initiative through the facility of directing the Commission to investigate and report on questions referred to it. This the Council does all the time. Generally the Commission acts as requested but, in the aftermath of the Prodi–Kinnock reforms, it may be that the Commission will be forced to decline such invitations if it does not have the resources to carry them out. Under *Article 209* (ex 153), the Council can also set up committees. These can be bodies such as the Special Committee on Agriculture. It can also refer to committees set up to oversee implementation by the Commission, whether advisory (or consultative), management or regulatory. Use of such bodies, often described as 'comitology', derives in part from the provisions of the third indent of Article 202 thus, to some extent, partially excluding the EP. The Council also proceeds through a large number of working parties of its own, which examine the proposals submitted by the Commission. Finally, at *Article 210* (ex 154) the Section allows the Council to set the salaries of the main Court officials. Nice extended these to the Court of First Instance. To an extent this gives the Council a certain 'power of the purse'. The fact that QMV applied to this was often used in UK debates on Nice to make the point that little of substance had been given away by agreeing to extend QMV.

All this shows the complexity of the Council as an institution, a complexity which has increased over time. Nice has merely amplified the problem, albeit in a confusing way. The treaty also makes clear that the Council is very much a Community institution. It is an inter-governmental forum whose decisions can pass into national law. So, in theory, it has to take the Community interest into account and not just seek the lowest common denominator. In other words, it is both European and national, as Hayes-Renshaw and Wallace say, something that probably militates against it being turned into a simple second legislative chamber as some would wish.

Section 2   The Council

Article 202 (ex Article 145)

To ensure that the objectives set out in this Treaty are attained the Council shall, in accordance with the provisions of this Treaty:
– ensure co-ordination of the general economic policies of the Member States;
– have power to take decisions;
– confer on the Commission, in the acts which the Council adopts, powers for the
  implementation of the rules which the Council lays down. The Council may
  impose certain requirements in respect of the exercise of these powers. The
  Council may also reserve the right, in specific cases, to exercise directly implementing powers itself. The procedures referred to above must be consonant
  with principles and rules to be laid down in advance by the Council, acting

unanimously on a proposal from the Commission and after obtaining the Opinion of the European Parliament.

Article 203 (ex Article 146)

The Council shall consist of a representative of each Member State at ministerial level, authorised to commit the government of that Member State.

The office of President shall be held in turn by each Member State in the Council for a term of six months in the order decided by the Council acting unanimously.*

Article 204 (ex Article 147)

The Council shall meet when convened by its President on his own initiative or at the request of one of its members or of the Commission.

Article 205 (ex Article 148) (to 31.12.2004)

1. Save as otherwise provided in this Treaty, the Council shall act by a majority of its members.

2. Where the Council is required to act by a qualified majority, the votes of its members shall be weighted as follows:

Belgium	5
Denmark	3
Germany	10
Greece	5
Spain	8
France	10
Ireland	3
Italy	10
Luxembourg	2
Netherlands	5
Austria	4
Portugal	5
Finland	3
Sweden	4
United Kingdom	10

For their adoption, acts of the Council shall require at least:

– 62 votes in favour where this Treaty requires them to be adopted on a proposal from the Commission,

– 62 votes in favour, cast by at least 10 members, in other cases.

3. Abstentions by members present in person or represented shall not prevent the adoption by the Council of acts which require unanimity.

---

*Prior to the EU's 1995 enlargement, the order was contained in the article itself. The most recent Council decision has the presidency being held in the following order: 2001 Sweden, Belgium; 2002 Spain, Denmark; 2003 Greece, Italy; 2004 Ireland, Netherlands; 2005 Luxembourg, United Kingdom; 2006 Austria, Germany. The last is now seeking to exchange with Finland.

Article 205 (ex Article 148) (from 1.1.2005)*

1. Save as otherwise provided in this Treaty, the Council shall act by a majority of its members.

2. Where the Council is required to act by a qualified majority, the votes of its members shall be weighted as follows:

Belgium	12
Denmark	7
Germany	29
Greece	12
Spain	27
France	29
Ireland	7
Italy	29
Luxembourg	4
Netherlands	13
Austria	10
Portugal	12
Finland	7
Sweden	10
United Kingdom	29

Acts of the Council shall require for their adoption at least **169** *votes in favour* **cast by a majority of the members** *where this Treaty requires them to be adopted on a proposal from the Commission. In other cases, for their adoption acts of the Council shall require at least* **169** *votes in favour, cast by at least* **two-thirds** *of the members.*

3. Abstentions by members present in person or represented shall not prevent the adoption by the Council of acts which require unanimity.

4. When a decision is to be adopted by the Council by a qualified majority, a member of the Council may request verification that the Member States constituting the qualified majority represent at least 62% of the total population of the Union. If that condition is shown not to have been met, the decision in question shall not be adopted.

Article 206 (ex Article 150)

Where a vote is taken, any member of the Council may also act on behalf of not more than one other member.

Article 207 (ex Article 151)

1. A committee consisting of the Permanent Representatives of the Member States shall be responsible for preparing the work of the Council and for carrying out the tasks assigned to it by the Council. **The Committee may adopt procedural decisions in cases provided for in the Council's Rules of Procedure.**

2. The Council shall be assisted by a General Secretariat, under the **responsibility**

---

*As already noted, the wording of Article 205 from 1.1.2005 comes from the Protocol on the Enlargement of the European Union and is inserted here for convenience. It does not appear in this way in published versions of the treaty. For the full text of the protocol see above pp. 68–72.

of a Secretary-General, **High Representative for the common foreign and security policy, who shall be assisted by a Deputy Secretary-General responsible for the running of the General Secretariat.** The Secretary-General and the Deputy Secretary-General shall be appointed by the Council **acting by a qualified majority. The Council shall decide on the organisation of the General Secretariat.**

3. The Council shall adopt its Rules of Procedure.
For the purpose of applying Article 255(3), the Council shall elaborate in these Rules the conditions under which the public shall have access to Council documents. For the purpose of this paragraph, the Council shall define the cases in which it is to be regarded as acting in its legislative capacity, with a view to allowing greater access to documents in those cases, while at the same time preserving the effectiveness of its decision-making process. In any event, when the Council acts in its legislative capacity, the results of votes and explanations of votes as well as statements in the minutes shall be made public.

Article 208 (ex Article 152)

The Council may request the Commission to undertake any studies the Council considers desirable for the attainment of the common objectives, and to submit to it any appropriate proposals.

Article 209 (ex Article 153)

The Council shall, after receiving an opinion from the Commission, determine the rules governing the committees provided for in this Treaty.

Article 210 (ex Article 154)

The Council shall, acting by a qualified majority, determine the salaries, allowances and pensions of the President and Members of the Commission, and of the President, Judges, Advocates-General and Registrar of the Court of Justice, **and of the Members and Registrar of the Court of First Instance.** It shall also, again by a qualified majority, determine any payment to be made instead of remuneration.

The Commission

Nice had a somewhat more benign effect on the Commission than it did on the Council. In fact, it succeeded where Amsterdam had failed in establishing clearer and more effective lines of control over commissioners and Commission staff. However, Nice was not without its surprises either. And, even after revision, the TEC tells us very little about the actual working of this most significant and controversial institution despite the fact that weaknesses in its management capacity underlay the crisis of 1998–9 and, for Metcalfe, will be the key to its future

As well as giving the Commission new powers, Amsterdam had sought to curb its size ahead of enlargement. But there was no consensus on how to do this so a weak proposal contained in the Protocol on the institutions with the prospect of enlargement of the European Union to look at it later was all that emerged. Even this depended on finding compensation elsewhere for those member states which might lose out in a reduction of the size of the Commission. Hence the Commission became one of the Amsterdam leftovers on which the 2000 IGC had to concentrate.

Amsterdam was only a little more successful in its attempts to strengthen the president of the Commission and to encourage necessary reforms. The office was formally given overall political control over the Commission in 1999. Yet following hostility from the EP and a damning independent report on the way the Commission handled appointments, funding and programme supervision, the president could not force the two most exposed members of his Commission, Edith Cresson and Manuel Marin, to resign in order to save the whole College of Commissioners, as it is known. The College as a whole therefore had to resign, ahead of an EP vote. In any case the provision was probably too little as well as too late. This was true both of its effectiveness and its focus, which ignored the Commission's infrastructure.

Amsterdam's other ideas of Commission reform, floated by Declaration No. 32 TA, were also overtaken by these events and what they showed about the depth and location of the Commission's problems. The declaration had noted that a reorganization of tasks and departments was in train and that, to encourage this, the president should be able to dispose of portfolios, and to appoint vice-presidents, including one for external relations. Responsibility for this was then shared among six commissioners with a consequent lack of policy coherence. However, the revelations of internal financial and managerial weaknesses in the Santer Commission went far beyond this. So, the new president, Romano Prodi, was encouraged to push ahead with a much more radical infrastructural reform, led by Vice-President Neil Kinnock. This status, along with the new political climate and the fact that Kinnock comes from one of the more critical member states, gave him more leverage than his predecessors. The reform programme started before the 2000 IGC concluded and is still ongoing.

Nice was, indirectly, to legitimate this process. It was also to give the president formal powers, so clearly lacking in 1998, to discipline failing colleagues. At the same time Nice gave the Commission new responsibilities under Article 7 TEU, in enhanced co-operation and for the ECJ statute. However, it left the TEC provisions on the Commission still relatively exiguous. They are not much more than a bare framework. None the less, they do make it clear that the Commission is not the 'mere civil service' some Eurosceptics believe it once was and ought still to be. Its treaty obligations make its decision-making and political potential clear.

In fact the treaty is decidedly cavalier about its treatment of the Commission as a bureaucracy. Even after Nice, Section 3 only hints at its existence in Article 217 and elsewhere. Indeed, the TEC does not say very much about the role of the College, and even less about its services, and spends most of its time talking about the hiring and firing of Commissioners. Given the problem of the management and implementation deficits recently revealed by Stevens and Stevens, among others, this seems unwise.

Section 3, like its immediate predecessors, starts by assuming that Article 7 TEC had called the Commission into existence. So the surprisingly terse *Article 211* (ex 155) says what it does, not what it is. The rationale given for the Commission is to make sure that the Single Market develops and functions effectively. This is somewhat narrower than the remit given to the Council in Article 202 and might be thought to justify a narrow reading of its powers and role. However, the precise ways provided for doing this go wider than either this or what is said about the Council.

The first of these ways is to act as the 'guardian of the treaty' and ensure that the whole of the TEC (but not related treaties apparently) is obeyed and that the institutions neither ignore it nor fail to act on it. This role means that the Commission is involved in the ECJ's preliminary ruling cases under Article 234. Moreover, the reference to 'measures taken . . . pursuant' to the treaties can be seen as making the Commission responsible for guarding the *acquis* in general and not just the treaties. In any case, fulfilling this role requires both a monitoring activity and an enforcement role, whether through persuasion or through prosecution under Articles 226–230 TEC.

As a result the Commission can, secondly, make its views clear on anything touched on by the treaty. The two terms used are significant since 'recommendations' can prescribe conduct in a way that an opinion cannot, though neither are necessarily 'proposals' in the sense used by the treaty's decision-making provisions such as Article 205. The former are directly related to the provisions of Article 208. The latter enshrines an advisory role. This, like monitoring, requires the Commission to develop a research capacity for which it can draw both on Article 284 TEC and on its rights of consultation with other EC institutions.

In all this the treaty gives the Commission a free hand in interpreting what the TEC actually covers, which is why it is often seen as embodying 'the Community interest', a phrase which first appeared in the original Article 9 TECSC and is now in Article 213 TEC. Because of this many also see the Commission as the defender of smaller member states. This is because their over-representation is part of the basic settlement. Equally, they need protecting against the bigger battalions. In any case, these two roles of guardianship and policy-making are normally seen as the key ones, obscuring the Commission's important management tasks and hence overlooking the weaknesses in the way they are carried out. These tasks spring in part from other elements of the treaty and in part from the third means the TEC provides for the Commission to fulfil its strategic purpose.

This is specified in Article 211, which allows the Commission both to take decisions of its own and also to take part in the co-operative inter-institutional decision-making procedures established by the treaties, for instance at Articles 251 and 252 TEC. The former can outnumber the latter by a factor of ten. Examples are anti-dumping, merger control, abuse of dominant position and agricultural market legislation decisions. Finally, the Commission can exercise the powers delegated to it under Article 202. Unfortunately, the Commission's own ambitions, and its sense of obligation, has led it to take on too many jobs, many of them at the behest of a Council which failed to give the Commission the resources needed to do it properly. This mismatch has been seen as one of the main causes of the Commission's administrative failures and has led Kinnock to seek a better match between programmes and the allocation of resources, with the barely concealed threat that the Commission might refuse to carry out a Council suggestion if it does not have the means to do it properly.

For many people, in any case, all this is a very incomplete account of the roles the Commission actually still plays, even though these are less emphatic than those of the old High Authority of the ECSC and have come under pressure in recent years. Very often the Commission is referred to as the 'Community executive'. This is a partial truth. Article 211 says very little about execution, except in so far as the Commission is involved in decision-making and implementation. It does not make it clear how important the Commission is in terms of enforcement. And while its legislative role can be deduced from Article 211, the essential constitutional principle of the Commission's monopoly of legislative initiative is not clearly and explicitly stated here. As Beaumont and Weatherill argue, this is contained in a series of articles throughout the treaty, including Article 308.

At the same time the Commission's quasi-judicial activities are hidden, though they are partly implicit in Article 282. This makes it clear that the Commission is the Community's sole legal representative. Equally, the Commission's managerial work, both administrative and financial, is not mentioned here. This, like the Commission's external representational role, has also to be deduced from other parts of the treaty. There is also a set of residual roles played by the Commission – as counsellor, receptionist, troubleshooter – many of which are not based on specific treaty articles. In other words, the article offers only a blurred sketch of the Commission's real-life face. And in doing so it obscures the administrative warts.

Article 212 on the presentation of a retrospective report can be regarded as a further means by which the Commission is to ensure the working of the treaty and the common market. The report is general in two ways, one in that it embraces all the Community's activities and not just those of the Commission, and the other in that it is widely available. In other words, although its publication is linked to the EP's calendar, thus symbolizing a form of accountability in line with Article 200, the report is not specifically to the EP. It can be considered to be addressed to the broader Community audience as well. This is why the *Annual Report* is debated without a formal resolution being passed. In other words the Commission cannot fairly be made to answer for what is essentially a description of what has happened throughout the Community. Conversely, the speech on prospective activities from the Commission president which accompanies the report is more focused on Commission activities and MEPs' views. In any case, it is a rather formal matter which does not address the major gaps in Section 3's specification of the Commission's functions.

In fact, having briefly set out the tasks of the Commission, the section devotes almost all the rest of its articles to questions of officers and structures, mostly relating to the College of Commissioners as such. The first definition of what the Commission actually is comes in *Article 213* (ex 157). This presently specifies the number of members and lays down broad qualifications necessary to hold the post. At the time of writing 10 member states have a single Commissioner and the five largest have two each, thus making up the 20. At the moment this could be taken as implying that the president would have a casting vote since there is no automatic majority as required by Article 219 and which is provided for in the Court of Justice.

The prospect of eastward enlargement has called the numbers involved into question. Previously the assumption has been that this allocation would be applied to new entrants, which would mean 33 commissioners in a Union of 27 member states. Most felt that this was too large for effectiveness, especially if the Union did not extend its policy competences. It could also encourage those with limited portfolios to invent work for themselves. However, Amsterdam failed to resolve this, partly because of the desire of the smaller member states to have a commissioner of their own to defend their needs. So the TA finished up by simply canvassing the surrender of the larger member states' second commissioner providing compensation was forthcoming.

As already suggested, Nice was more successful in dealing with the matter although it did not produce either the streamlined Commission or the rapid transition wished for by the French presidency. Article 4 of the Protocol on the enlargement of the European Union thus lays down a three-stage process of adaption beginning with no change till 2004, always assuming there is no enlargement before then. Secondly, an initial alteration to Article 213(1) provides that, from 2005, when the new compensatory weightings and thresholds kick in, the size of the Commission will fall to one commissioner per member state. The EU will then follow this principle until, and including, accession of the twenty-sixth member state. Changes required by accessions can be made under the authority of the third indent of Article 231(1). The third and most radical changes, however, have to wait. Only later will the third stage come into play.

In fact, at the first renewal of the Commission following the entry of the twenty-seventh member state a further revision of Article 213(1) comes into force. This, like its predecessor, is printed below for convenience. This provides that the number of commissioners shall be fewer than the number of member states, that is no more than 26. The exact number is not specified and has to be fixed by the Council acting unanimously thus avoiding the need for an IGC.

So how big might it be? Ever since Monnet some member states have wanted a small Commission, no larger than 12, but this argument was lost by the French presidency prior to Nice. The likelihood is that the Commission will not be much different from what it is today, perhaps 21 or even 25. Indeed, discussions in the light of the Irish 'no' to Nice in summer 2001 suggested that the number of commissioners could be set at one fewer than the number of member states (i.e. 26 in an EU of 27) with the post of Attorney-General being created to ensure that all member states had a national present at Commission meetings. This would certainly make the implementation of the other new conditions easier. It would also avoid causing too much pain to individual member states.

Whatever their number, the most radical change is likely to be the origin of the commissioners and the criteria for their selection. In fact, the new commissioners are to be chosen by a rotation system based on the principle of equality. The Commission document explaining Nice to its citizens talks of it being 'absolutely fair'. What this means is partly spelled out in paragraph 3, which demands equal treatment in terms of timing and sequence. To show that this has been achieved the formula is suggested that no member state of any pair will ever enjoy more than one term more than the other in a given period. This is not a luminous formulation but it is, at least, less opaque than the QMV threshold rules.

Furthermore, the College must be a fair reflection of the demographic and geographic mix of the member states. This suggests, firstly, that there must always be some large, some medium and some small member states. Working out which is which is easy enough, although Spain, Poland, Romania and the Netherlands could be close as borderline cases. The precise balance will be difficult to decide, so will pairings of member states. And amalgamating this with geographical considerations would seem almost impossible.

Secondly, it calls for geographical criteria which do not presently exist. Agreed sub-regions will have to be defined both for the transition period and for the 27-member EU. This could be problematic, given tensions between neighbouring states. One possible geographical division might be into south-western, Benelux, central (including Germany, Austria, the Czech Republic and Hungary), Nordic and south-eastern. The problem cases would appear to be Poland on the one hand and the UK and Ireland on the other. Is the former 'Nordic' or should it be part of a separate 'north-eastern' grouping? The latter could form a group, which might not go down well in Dublin which might prefer to be in the south-western group. Equally, the UK might not appreciate being bracketed with France and the Benelux countries. Clearly the idea could open up a can of worms as lively as that of Nice. At the very least, resolving the problem will be difficult for an organism which does not have the experience of the Swiss in balancing cultural, political and geographical interests.

Assuming agreement on the principles, how is all this to be put into effect? The Protocol on the enlargement of the European Union provides that the Council, acting unanimously, has to decide the system and adopt the implementing arrangements. However, on the first, the issue is so sensitive that the likelihood must be that the decision will be taken by heads of government either at a European Council summit or meeting as the Council of the Union. The fact that the Council is also required to 'set' the numbers and to determine the formation of colleges 'automatically' rather reinforces this view.

Finally paragraph 4 of Article 4 of the protocol provides that any acceding state should be entitled to have a commissioner on joining prior to the final implementation of the new system. This would seem to mean that, assuming there was a gap between the accession treaty of the twenty-seventh member state and the installation of the next Commission, the last member state would, briefly, get a commissioner. The provision prevents a latecomer being treated worse than earlier entrants. It may also be seen as throwing a sop to those candidate countries which did not warm to the idea of rotation and which feared that not having a commissioner might adversely affect their public's opinion. The revisions made at Nice also seem to have resulted in the formal elimination of the third sentence of Article 213(1), which specifies that only nationals of member states may become commissioners. However, the protocol makes it clear that this is still the assumption since it is mentioned in discussing equal representation.

Article 213(2), which was not changed at Nice, reinforces the requirement for Commission members' demonstrable independence. This, like competence, is necessary for the Commission to defend the general interest. Alignment with member states or lobbies would make this much harder. There then follows two longish paragraphs of definition of what this independence means in practice: taking no orders, behaving appropriately and not taking on any other posts which might compromise their independence. These requirements are underlined by the taking of an oath on acceding to office and can be enforced by the ECJ. The sanctions include the loss of pensions, privileges and immunities. Equally, member states are required to refrain from doing anything to undermine the independence of commissioners.

Beyond this, of course, there is the possibility of enforced resignation under Article 201. And, as we have seen, in 1999 the threat of this forced the Santer Commission to step down *en bloc* when individual members refused to resign. This, as is implied by Article 189, is part of a general supervisory power of the EP. However, this does not mean that the Commission has to accept guidance from the EP. This too would be contrary to the requirement not to take instructions.

This stress on independence is a little hard to reconcile with the desire of smaller member states to maintain their presence in the College. In fact, as Lequesne says, commissioners can and do make clear the financial needs and special circumstances of their states. Being present at the very beginning of the policy process means that their needs can be borne in mind in policy development. This is really why they, and particularly the candidate states, are so keen on representation in the Commission. Existing 'Western' commissioners are unlikely to be familiar with the situation of, say, the Baltic states or the Mediterranean islands. At the same time, rather than seeking to use the Commission to make illicit gains for their states, they wish to ensure that they are not overwhelmed by large member-state concerns and what might be seen at home as 'imposed' legislation. Equally, involvement in the policy-initiation process will help to legitimatize EU membership at home. Interestingly, pushing national interests was not one of the main complaints directed against the Santer Commission. Indeed, one complaint from Margaret Thatcher was the opposite: that commissioners had 'gone native'. In reality, what we usually find is a 'decent neutrality', although this too does not mean that commissioners are mere civil servants.

Article 214 goes on to set out how the commissioners, wherever they come from, should be appointed. Their term of office is to be five years unless dismissed by censure motion. Since Maastricht the terms have coincided with EP elections, increasing the impression of accountability to the EP. And, although the TEC will continue to read that they are not limited to one term, the halving of larger member states' entitlement and the introduction of rotation makes this much less likely. This could have implications for continuity and effectiveness as Neunreither argues. However, others believe it was a good move where enlargement was concerned.

Paragraph 2 of Article 214 was changed in two ways to reflect what has become known as the 'lex Prodi'. At Amsterdam this had been revised so as to give the EP more say in the appointment of the president of the Commission, to the annoyance of Berthu and other defenders of national parliaments. The office is mentioned in Article 210 apropos of his or her salary, but until now it has not been referred to in Section 3. Previously the EP had been consulted on the nomination but now it has a right of approval. Even if this is only a quasi-veto in practice, it may well make the leaders more conscious of what the EP wants, especially if it has allies among the heads of government. This could influence their choice of political orientation and views on integration as well as the nationality of the nominee. The president in turn was also given a right of veto rather than merely being consulted on the choice of the other members of the College.

Following the practical precedents established after the fall of the Santer Commission, Nice took this process of strengthening the presidency three steps further. Firstly it transferred nomination from the governments as such to the Council, composed of heads of government and state, and, thanks to a late agreement, decided that they would act by QMV, a new experience for the collected premiers and presidents. The latter obviously decided that full legitimacy was less important than convenience and the avoidance of a blockage such as that of the 1994 UK blocking of Dehaene's nomination. It was this which led to the choice of the hapless Santer. Despite this the change has not been universally welcomed in the United Kingdom.

Secondly, Nice agreed that the Council, presumably in its normal composition, should adopt the list of nominees for the Commission, again by QMV. This means that, while the president can query such nominations, national selections could be voted down if some nominations do not carry enough credibility. What is not clear is whether this vote is to be an en bloc one or a series of ad persona votes. It must be that the president would be asked to agree each nomination individually but the Council might prefer to avoid damaging rejections of specific favourite sons or daughters, especially as the vote is part of a quite formal investiture process.

Thus, thirdly, while the overall nominations then have to be approved by the EP en bloc (rather than merely registered at the end of the process), the Council, in an unspecified format, has then to give them a final endorsement. This too is done through QMV. Whether this second investiture could be used to change nominations approved by the EP is not clear, although failure to find a majority would certainly send them all back to the beginning of the process. However, since the changes have generally prevented such blackballing this may be too cynical a reading.

Nice also changed aspects of Article 215 (ex 159) which covers leaving office. Where a Commissioner dies, is excluded or resigns, the Council can decide, without even consulting the EP, whether or not to fill the post for the remainder of the five-year term. Nice allows a replacement to be appointed by QMV whereas a decision not to fill the post needs unanimity. The reason for this difference is presumably that the member state losing a post has to be seen to approve, thus avoiding charges of victimization. One can imagine that if a Commissioner died shortly before a general renewal there would be little point in shoehorning in a newcomer, especially after rotation was in place. However, it seems that there is no such discretion where the president is concerned. There has to be one and the formal process just described would have to be invoked, even for a short tenure.

In the case of resignation a commissioner would, according to the last line of Article 215, normally carry on dealing with day-to-day affairs until physically replaced. This must be true of the president as well, although it is not actually stated. However, Article 216 (ex 160) shows that, where a commissioner is either incapacitated or is found guilty of major misdemeanours, both the Commission as a whole and the Council can apply to the ECJ to have him or her compulsorily retired. This happened in 1974 when Commissioner Borschette fell into a coma.

Article 217 (ex 161) represents one of the major changes at Nice. From Maastricht the article had simply allowed the appointment of two vice-presidents, replacing the manifold appointments made up till then. This is still presently the case with the sensitive tasks of rebuilding confidence in the political credibility and, especially, the administrative reliability of the Commission being given to vice-presidencies rather than external relations. In 2000 the issue of vice-presidents resurfaced because it was seen as a way either of creating a necessary core within a large Commission or as a cynical device for demoting commissioners from small member states. In the event the issue was swept up into a new Article 217, which also inherited an element of Article 219.

The revised article thus reasserts the point that the Commission has to accept the president's political leadership. This makes it clear that the Commission is a political rather than a merely administrative body. What guidance means is not made clear. Declaration No. 32 TA talked of 'broad discretion' so it can probably be regarded as the right to indicate the overall direction of the Commission, if not to set compulsory guidelines. Equally, it does not mean taking all key day-to-day decisions but it must mean having the last word in cases of policy dispute. Given the emerging debate about what the Union's overall economic strategy should be, this is significant.

But the article goes beyond this and makes major strides in strengthening the president's control of the College. To begin with the president is given formal control of the internal organization of the Commission, something which had been lacking under Delors and Santer, and is also given a mandate to ensure consistency and efficiency. Paragraph 2 then makes it plain that this extends to deciding on the administrative structure of the Commission as a whole. This, which can be seen as an underwriting of the ongoing reforms, is the nearest Section 3 comes to recognizing the Commission's infrastructure although it is somewhat tangential, as is the less-convincing reference in Article 218.

Secondly, Paragraph 2, drawing on Declaration No. 32 TA, also allows the president to allocate portfolios and reshuffle them if needed during his or her term of office. This limits the possibility of interference, whether from member state governments or, more significantly, from personal recalcitrance. Indeed, commissioners are obliged to follow the president's leadership and orders. Moreover, paragraph 4 gives them no possibility of staying in office if the president wishes them to go. This is a response to the impasse in which Santer had found himself in 1999. Prodi initially circumvented this by requiring his team to give him a signed but undated letter of resignation on taking up their post. The Nice revisions make this ploy unnecessary by giving the president complete control and thus resolving the question of the 'personal responsibility of commissioners', as it had become known.

Thirdly, paragraph 3 lets the president, as opposed to the Commission, appoint such vice-presidents as he feels fit with none of the restrictions of the past. This represents an abrupt reversal in thinking. It probably reflects the fact that, since capping the Commission was being delayed, the threat of demotion was less than the obvious need for authority in the Commission. Equally, the Commission's wish that the treaty should allow specific tasks to be devolved to vice-presidents had been rejected. Unease was also offset by the provision that the College as such has to approve nominations. None the less, the right may well be useful come enlargement.

So, if all this means that future incumbents should be in a far better position to direct and control both College and administration, the president is not omnipotent. Paragraph 1 insists on collegiality in the College, something which is probably necessary, given the way member states regard 'their' representatives. Equally, the College as a whole has to approve the decision to request a resignation as well as the appointment of vice-presidents. The former seems the most sensitive point and was probably inserted to avoid vendettas. A dismissal with the backing of the rest of the College would clearly carry more legitimacy, limiting if not eliminating the feeling that 'our man' was being victimized. Furthermore, as implied earlier, normally the president only has one vote. To this extent, then, the idea of the president as simply *primus inter pares* remains. Again, the fact that member states nominate commissioners makes such caution understandable.

Article 218 (ex 162) and *Article 219* (ex 163), the last of Section 3, provide the only real guidance on how the Commission actually works. They make clear that, while the Commission is self-organizing and can decide how it acts, it must co-operate with the Council on mutually acceptable terms. However, the article makes it clear that they are separate bodies. When it comes to voting there is automatic majority, which requires an uneven number of members, as the IGC rejected the Commission's request for a presidential casting vote to be statutorily written in. Nice therefore seems to have overlooked the fact that, after enlargement or in January 2005, Article 213 will not actually specify how many members there are in the Commission. The quorum, presently a majority of the Commission, may also have to be regularly reset over the next few years.

In any case, neither article says much about the various procedures by which the College actually works, any more than the new Article 217 makes clear what the internal structure of the Commission staff actually is. The former are set out in the Rules of Procedure as, to some extent, is the latter. The demand that the Rules of Procedure themselves be published can be taken to symbolize a recognition that the Commission needs to be publicly accountable. The reference to departments here is significant, a confirmation of the fact that the Commission is an administration and not just a College. This is partly followed up in Articles 283 and 288, although the staff regulations have to be approved by the Council. However, there is no mention of the Secretary General as there is for the Council. Indeed, it is here that the TEC's framework approach appears strongly. While entering details of directorates-general, staff hierarchies or detailed procedures would be too constricting, the experience of 1999 might have suggested the wisdom of inserting a brief article on the management expectations of the Commission administration.

As a result the Commission emerges as a somewhat shadowy body from the TEC despite its clear importance. What it is there for is not wholly clear from Section 3 but, incontrovertibly, it matters both because of its specific roles and because it has become the workhorse, or *'cheville ouvrière'* of the EU. This reminds us that the Commission cannot be just an executive, let alone a civil service. It is a politico-administrative body which crosses the normal boundaries of the separation of powers, straying into the legislative and the judicial as well as the executive. Whether the Nice reforms will overcome its political difficulties and allow it to become the more independent and supra-national force the EP believes it to be remains to be seen. But its nature and its ongoing governance and management reforms ensure that it will remain controversial.

Section 3   The Commission

Article 211 (ex Article 155)

In order to ensure the proper functioning and development of the common market, the Commission shall:

– ensure that the provisions of this Treaty and the measures taken by the institutions pursuant thereto are applied;
– formulate recommendations or deliver opinions on matters dealt with in this Treaty, if it expressly so provides or if the Commission considers it necessary;
– have its own power of decision and participate in the shaping of measures taken by the Council and by the European Parliament in the manner provided for in this Treaty;
– exercise the powers conferred on it by the Council for the implementation of the rules laid down by the latter.

Article 212 (ex Article 156)

The Commission shall publish annually, not later than one month before the opening of the session of the European Parliament, a general report on the activities of the Community.

Article 213 (ex Article 157) (to 31.12.2004)

1. The Commission shall consist of 20 Members, who shall be chosen on the grounds of their general competence and whose independence is beyond doubt.

The number of Members of the Commission may be altered by the Council, acting unanimously.
Only nationals of Member States may be Members of the Commission.

The Commission must include at least one national of each of the Member States, but may not include more than two Members having the nationality of the same State.

2. The Members of the Commission shall, in the general interest of the Community, be completely independent in the performance of their duties.

In the performance of these duties, they shall neither seek nor take instructions from any government or from any other body. They shall refrain from any action incompatible with their duties. Each Member State undertakes to respect this principle and not to seek to influence the Members of the Commission in the performance of their tasks.

The Members of the Commission may not, during their term of office, engage in any other occupation, whether gainful or not. When entering upon their duties they shall give a solemn undertaking that, both during and after their term of office, they will respect the obligations arising therefrom and in particular their duty to behave with integrity and discretion as regards the acceptance, after they have ceased to hold office, of certain appointments or benefits. In the event of any breach of these obligations, the Court of Justice may, on application by the Council or the Commission, rule that the Member concerned be, according to the circumstances, either compulsorily retired in accordance with Article 216 or deprived of his right to a pension or other benefits in its stead.

Article 213 (ex Article 157) (from 1.1.2005)

1. The *Members of the* Commission shall be chosen on the grounds of their general competence and *their* independence shall be beyond doubt.

The Commission shall include one national of each of the Member States.

The number of Members of the Commission may be altered by the Council, acting unanimously.

2. The Members of the Commission shall, in the general interest of the Community, be completely independent in the performance of their duties.

In the performance of these duties, they shall neither seek nor take instructions from any government or from any other body. They shall refrain from any action incompatible with their duties. Each Member State undertakes to respect this principle and not to seek to influence the Members of the Commission in the performance of their tasks.

The Members of the Commission may not, during their term of office, engage in any other occupation, whether gainful or not. When entering upon their duties they shall give a solemn undertaking that, both during and after their term of office, they will respect the obligations arising therefrom and in particular their duty to behave with integrity and discretion as regards the acceptance, after they have ceased to hold office, of certain appointments or benefits. In the event of any breach of these obligations, the Court of Justice may, on application by the Council or the Commission, rule that the Member concerned be, according to the circumstances, either compulsorily retired in accordance with Article 216 or deprived of his right to a pension or other benefits in its stead.

Article 213 (ex Article 157) (from when the EU consists of 27 or more member states)

1. The *Members of the* Commission shall be chosen on the grounds of their general competence and *their* independence shall be beyond doubt.

The number of Members of the Commission shall be less than the number of Member States. The Members of the Commission shall be chosen according to a rotation system based on the principle of equality, the implementing arrangements for which shall be adopted by the Council, acting unanimously.

The number of Members of the Commission shall be set by the Council, acting unanimously.

2. The Members of the Commission shall, in the general interest of the Community, be completely independent in the performance of their duties.

In the performance of these duties, they shall neither seek nor take instructions from any government or from any other body. They shall refrain from any action incompatible with their duties. Each Member State undertakes to respect this principle and not to seek to influence the Members of the Commission in the performance of their tasks.

The Members of the Commission may not, during their term of office, engage in any other occupation, whether gainful or not. When entering upon their duties they shall give a solemn undertaking that, both during and after their term of office, they will respect the obligations arising therefrom and in particular their duty to behave with integrity and discretion as regards the acceptance, after they have ceased to hold office, of certain appointments or benefits. In the event of any breach of these obligations, the Court of Justice may, on application by the Council or the Commission, rule that the Member concerned be, according to the circumstances, either compulsorily retired in accordance with Article 216 or deprived of his right to a pension or other benefits in its stead.

Article 214 (ex Article 158, simplified)

1. The Members of the Commission shall be appointed, in accordance with the procedure referred to in paragraph 2, for a period of five years, subject, if need be, to Article 201.
Their term of office shall be renewable.

2. **The Council, meeting in the composition of Heads of State or Government and acting by a qualified majority,** *shall nominate the person it intends to appoint as President of the Commission;* **the nomination shall be approved by the European Parliament.**

The Council, acting by a qualified majority and by common accord with the nominee for President, shall adopt the list of the other persons whom it intends to appoint as Members of the Commission, drawn up in accordance with the proposals made by each Member State.

The President and the other Members of the Commission thus nominated shall be subject as a body to a vote of approval by the European Parliament. After approval by the European Parliament, the President and the other Members of the Commission shall be appointed by **the Council, acting by a qualified majority.**

Article 215 (ex Article 159)

Apart from normal replacement, or death, the duties of a Member of the Commission shall end when he resigns or is compulsorily retired.

A vacancy caused by resignation, compulsory retirement or death shall be filled for the remainder of the Member's term of office by a new Member appointed **by the Council, acting by a qualified majority.** The Council may, acting unanimously, decide that such a vacancy need not be filled.

In the event of resignation, compulsory retirement or death, the President shall be replaced for the remainder of his term of office. The procedure laid down in Article 214(2) shall be applicable for the replacement of the President.

Save in the case of compulsory retirement under Article 216, Members of the Commission shall remain in office until they have been replaced **or until the Council has decided that the vacancy need not be filled, as provided for in the second paragraph of this Article.**

Article 216 (ex Article 160)

If any Member of the Commission no longer fulfils the conditions required for the performance of his duties or if he has been guilty of serious misconduct, the Court of Justice may, on application by the Council or the Commission, compulsorily retire him.

Article 217 **(new – TN)**

1. *The Commission shall work under the political guidance of its President,* **who shall decide on its internal organisation in order to ensure that it acts consistently, efficiently and on the basis of collegiality.**

2. **The responsibilities incumbent upon the Commission shall be structured and allocated among its Members by its President. The President may reshuffle the allocation of those responsibilities during the Commission's term of office. The**

Members of the Commission shall carry out the duties devolved upon them by the President under his authority.

3. After obtaining the approval of the College, the President shall appoint Vice-Presidents from among its Members.

4. A Member of the Commission shall resign if the President so requests, after obtaining the approval of the College.

Article 218 (ex Article 162)

1. The Council and the Commission shall consult each other and shall settle by common accord their methods of co-operation.

2. The Commission shall adopt its Rules of Procedure so as to ensure that both it and its departments operate in accordance with the provisions of this Treaty. It shall ensure that these rules are published.

Article 219 (ex Article 163)

The Commission shall act by a majority of the number of Members provided for in Article 213.

A meeting of the Commission shall be valid only if the number of Members laid down in its Rules of Procedure is present.

The Court of Justice

The European Court of Justice (ECJ) represents the fourth legitimacy of the Community: its dependence on the rule of law. This would be important in any western European democratic structure. It is particularly important in the Union context because of the need both to control supra-national institutions and to hold the member states together. With no police or army to enforce its acts, the ECJ was the only body available to give final rulings on treaty obligations, meanings and disputes. Indeed, it has been said that without the Court and a legally enforceable framework European integration could have broken up. Certainly the existence of European law, as well as being necessary so that the EC can sue and be sued, differentiates the Community from other international organizations. In other words, it gives life and substance to the Community even though it is nowhere fully defined in the treaty.

As well as symbolizing both the 'law' in general and the emerging corpus of European law in particular, the ECJ has come to play an equally important role in social life. Its rulings and principles have already made a major impact on ordinary life beyond the constitutional effects of the treaties. Not merely has its role grown organically over the years but its remit was widened by treaty amendment, most recently at Amsterdam, despite grumbles from the UK and other member states about its influence and the effects of its judgments. Indeed, both supporters and critics have seen the ECJ as being a significant political actor in its own right within the Union.

The coming into effect in 1999 of its Amsterdam powers was, however, to increase the already mounting overload on the Courts. This was a problem which Nice had to address. It did so with surprising but little remarked effectiveness. As a result the TEC now provides a more flexible account of both the structures of the Courts and their specific forms and modes of jurisdiction. Even so, the treaty still gives a very pale impression of the importance of the judicial elements of the European Treaties and the Union at large.

The Court has its roots in the ECSC Court, which was introduced to control the powerful High Authority. Rather than complicate matters by creating separate jurisdictions for the two new Communities, the 1957 Convention on Certain Institutions merged them with the ECSC Court. The amalgamated body went on to develop an increasingly authoritative body of case law which turned EC law into a code which was both superior to national law and binding on individuals. This and enlargement increased its workload and in 1989, using the facilities granted by the SEA, the Council created a lower tribunal, the Court of First Instance (CFI), to help reduce a growing backlog of cases. However, the TEU then went on to give the Courts new tasks of enforcement, new organizational facilities and new areas of responsibility. The rights of institutions to bring cases before it were also extended. The jurisdiction of the Courts was not, however, extended to include all the EU's activities, as is clear from Article 46 TEU.

This was not to be the end of the Courts' development. In fact, at Amsterdam, despite a certain UK reticence which helped to exclude the ECJ in a number of instances, the treaty still extended the Courts' jurisdiction. Amsterdam gave the Courts new, albeit limited, roles vis-à-vis the Court of Auditors, in migration questions, in human rights, in closer co-operation, in environment, in simplification and in the revised third pillar under Article 35 TEU where member states could opt into its jurisdiction. However, while it made no further changes to the structure of the Courts it did deliberately enhance the status of law. Hence it began to talk of EU as well as EC law, according to the preamble of the Protocol Integrating the Schengen acquis into the framework of the European Union. Thus it insisted on the maintenance of legal integrity in policy, in public services and in subsidiarity.

For many lawyers these new roles and recognition had a sting in their tail. This was because the new facilities threatened to increase the pressure on the Courts. Even with the creation of the CFI and some procedural changes the number of cases pending in 2000 was about 1,650, far higher than in 1990. This was despite the fact that the Courts were clearing about two-thirds as many cases every year by the end of the decade as they had at the beginning. The backlog sprang essentially from a doubling in the number of new cases coming before the Courts, especially for preliminary rulings. This in turn reflected the way the new lower Court bedded down and the way public acceptance of the EC legal dimension also grew. As a result, rather than dealing more rapidly with cases, the time between submission and resolution had risen to virtually two years. Hence, early in 1999 the Court warned of a structural imbalance, threatening to undermine both its role as the arbiter of EC law and its public standing.

The coming into effect of Amsterdam promised to make things even worse, promising more cases. It was also expected that the enhanced audit provisions, the development of EMU and trademark disputes were all likely to deluge the Courts with new work. And, beyond this there was the matter of enlargement to a wide range of new member states with less familiarity with EU legal norms, which could produce a further wave of cases of different sorts. Hence a good deal of thought was given to judicial reform. The Courts and the Commission made submissions of their own, as did some of the member states. The Commission drew on a study group it set up under former ECJ president Ole Due. Ideas of restrictively filtering appeals and referrals, setting up national or flying courts, more flexible working practices, sharing tasks more effectively with the CFI (perhaps turning the ECJ into a clear Supreme Constitutional Court) and creating specialized panels for routine cases were all canvassed. These were considered by a special technical group, the Friends of the Presidency, and their recommendations were accepted without much change by the IGC proper, as was a much revised statute for the ECJ which partly filled out the indications of the TEC proper.

In the event Nice, as well as opening a possible way to ECJ jurisdiction on both intellectual property questions and the procedural element of the suspension of a member state under Article 7 TEU, achieved five major changes in the legal organization of the Community and Union largely embodied in a revised statute (see pp. 493–504). To begin with, it made a number of structural changes, adding specialized judicial panels to the CFI and creating a new element inside the ECJ itself: the Grand Chamber. Both of these are to help speed up legal proceedings. Secondly, and equally important, the CFI was upgraded into a position consonant with its name. It is now to become the main common law judge in the EC dealing with most direct actions.* Hence, most cases will indeed now start there. Logically enough, therefore, it was made easier to increase its allocation of judges should the workload demand it. However, the CFI is not made an institution in its own right.

Thirdly, the working practices of the Courts are changed, reducing the need for Advocate-General's opinions and introducing emergency review procedures. Fourthly, the basis of membership is changed ahead of enlargement, ensuring that all the legal systems of the candidate countries will have an input. Finally, the Courts have been given more freedom to change their own rules of procedure, since these now only need QMV approval in Council. Whether these changes will remedy the problems already identified remains to be seen. They may do, but they seem also to have given rise to some new inconsistencies.

Despite these changes, Section 4, Chapter 1, of Part Five retains its original form. It falls, as already suggested, into two distinct parts, the first dealing with structures and the second with the types of actions possible. The first half begins with *Article 220* (ex 164) which assumes the existence of the Courts. Thus its first paragraph extends to the CFI the ECJ's continuing duty to ensure that 'the law' is observed in the interpretation and application of the treaty. This suggests, as Hartley observes, that the law must be regarded as something superior to, and wider than, treaty-based law, ample though this is.† In other words, the treaties have to be in line with general principles of law. However, in *Opinion 1991/1* on the possibility of an EEA Court, the ECJ made it clear that this did not mean the ECJ could accept direction from outside because of the legal autonomy of the Community. Indeed the 1971 *AETR* judgment had already stated that the internal powers of the Union give it rights of external action. Conversely, the reference to the treaty has also been taken to mean that the ECJ can only act within the powers allowed it by the TEC. Hence, while it is the Community's supreme judicial authority, the ECJ does not have the kind of general powers enjoyed by the International Court of Justice in The Hague.

In any case, the Court is given two interrelated functions here. One is ensuring that there is a clear view on what the treaties actually mean in the first place. The other is ensuring that this meaning is followed through in the working of the treaty, overseeing the way national courts actually apply the rules. To put it another way, the article creates obligations on national courts, as the 1990 *Zwartveld* ruling shows.

---

*A direct action is an action begun in the Community courts, not in a national court as is a preliminary ruling case, and resolved in the former normally without appeal. Most of these actions are established by the treaties, although parties may themselves refer matters to the ECJ directly in certain, rarely invoked, circumstances. Indirect actions include preliminary rulings, staff cases and arbitration.

†The sources of EC law here are primarily the acts of member states such as the treaties and subsidiary conventions and secondarily derived legislation (regulations and the like), case law, some international agreements and the general tradition of European law. This includes concepts such as equality, fundamental rights, legal certainty, non-discrimination, proportionality, the right to a hearing and legal professional privilege.

The second paragraph then introduces the new technical panels, albeit in a subordinate category. This is made clear by the use of the term 'in addition', by the statement that their competence was treaty-based and strictly conditioned and the mention of being 'attached' to the CFI. This was the wording used, prior to Nice, to define the CFI's links to the ECJ. By being attached, the CFI automatically shared the privileges of the ECJ and was regarded as simply another dimension of the basic Court. However, the term might suggest an inferior position, which is why it will no longer be used. Indeed, the first paragraph of Article 220 talks of 'each within its jurisdiction', implying that the two are now essentially equal in line with the general upgrading of the CFI. In other words, the CFI is to be regarded as another manifestation of the ECJ and not a separate legal forum. However, the fact that there are possibilities of both appeal and review suggests that there is a continuing element of hierarchy between the two. Whether the CFI becomes the element which applies the law leaving the ECJ as the reflective dimension remains to be seen. Much will depend on how the division of preliminary ruling jurisdiction works out in practice.

Article 221 (ex 165) now replaces a simple statement of how many judges there are, previously 15 but with no indication of whence they should come, by the entrenched principle that there should be one judge per member state. This is important because it guarantees to candidate countries that their place, and their legal traditions, will be present inside an enlarged Union. So, rather than accede to German desires for a very small 'constitutional' court, the EU has made it clear that it wants to have people who know national as well as EU law involved. Given this there is probably no need to say that judges should be 'nationals' of the member states as is now to be done for the Court of Auditors, although not doing so could conceivably offer a useful flexibility to new member states with weak and under-prepared judiciaries. It may also be that this wording says something more about the independence of the judges and, indeed, there is no mention of nationality in the revised statute. Equally, the Council loses the possibility of increasing the number of judges.

The second paragraph then lays down that the ECJ will meet in chambers or small teams of judges. These are normally composed of three or five judges, or in a new formation, the 'Grand Chamber', a direct if somewhat clumsy translation of the French *'grande chambre'*. This replicates what was informally known as the 'Small Plenum'. It will, according to the statute, be composed of the president, the presidents of the two larger chambers and eight others. Given that, as requested by the Court, the presidents will serve for at least three years this has given rise to fears that this could be the beginnings of two tiers of judges. Perhaps a total of 15 judges might have been better as it would be well over half the enlarged Court. However, Article 221 also allows for a full meeting of the Court, although this has a low quorum. A 'plenary' hearing, as it is known, will still be necessary, according to the statute, for actions such as the dismissal of an auditor, a commissioner or the Ombudsman. Suggestions that the Grand Chamber should decide whether there should be a full hearing were rejected, as was the old right of member states to require this in cases affecting them.

One of the innovations made to Community legal practice by the TEC then occurs in *Article 222* (ex 166). This provides that, alongside the judges, there should be a second body of judicial officers: the advocates-general. This office is not found in UK law although it resembles the public prosecutor or government commissioner found in continental legal systems. The advocates-general are members of the ECJ with similar privileges to the judges, but they fulfil a different role. Rather than being referees they are more consultants. They exist to brief the Court, relating them to national and relevant European law. They can also propose solutions and verdicts. And, finally they can also indicate how these solutions might affect future cases. So, to some extent their 'reasoned submissions' or 'opinions' – now mentioned explicitly in the TEC – make up for the facts that neither are there the lower 'federal' courts found in the American judicial system nor do ECJ judgments offer dissenting opinions. This has been felt as a lack by the Dutch and common law countries and has helped to preserve the advocates-general because they help to develop the law and offer points of comparison in the way minority opinions can do. A good example is the way in which they have started to utilize the Charter of Fundamental Rights in their submissions. Similarly, their ideas are not binding but are made public and are usually followed by the judges. Hence they have been described as the 'embodied conscience of the ECJ'.

None the less, the advocates-general had been under attack prior to Nice on the grounds that they helped to drag cases out. And, following on a change to Article 222, Article 20 of the statute will allow the ECJ to dispense with a written submission from an advocate-general if the latter, at the oral hearing, believes there is no substantive point of law involved in the case. None the less, they were maintained although their numbers are, for the medium-term, to stay at eight, unless the ECJ decides otherwise and requests the Council to appoint more. Moreover, Article 224 says that the Court itself can, if it chooses, appoint advocates-general to the CFI. Given that the CFI's new duties include giving preliminary rulings, it is not surprising that the idea of having such preparatory submissions was inserted into the treaty. This suggests that the Court, which did not greatly defer to advocate-generals' views before the 1980s, now sees them as worthwhile. The omission of the second reference to 'assisting' the Court may also suggest that their value is seen as being as much to the legal system as to the Court itself.

Moreover, the posts can also serve a useful training role as many advocates-general go on to be judges. Each advocate-general in turn functions as first advocate-general, a post which is likely to grow in importance.* Normally each of the large member states, including Spain, nominates one, leaving the smaller member states to appoint the others in rotation. This approach will require review with enlargement.

Article 223 (ex 167, 168, 188) contains a series of statements about qualifications, officers and appointments. Less logically, since Nice it also deals with the Rules of Procedure. As before judges and advocates-general are expected to be both neutral and qualified in the law, although this does not necessarily mean court practitioners. They can be academics, legal experts in ministries or barristers, as well as judges *per se*. In any event, they are the only officials now appointed by 'common accord' of the member-state governments, although nominations are rarely challenged. The EP has not been successful in gaining a foothold in the process and its idea of one non-renewable term for judges has not been acted upon. President, judges and advocates-general can still all be reappointed at the expiry of their term. No maximum number of terms is specified.

Nice has also simplified the provisions for replacement. In order to ensure continuity and consistency of approach, which is important for legal certainty, provision is made for a partial renewal every three years. The details of this were originally spelled out in the treaty but have now been left to the Statute, although Article 9 of the latter will also need updating as enlargement gets under way. The article also allows the judges to select their president, who acts as the steer of the Court, and the head of their extensive administrative services, the registrar. Their appointment is transferred from the old Article 224. Perhaps because of the mention of rules, the old Article 245 reference to the Rules of Procedure – the detailed guide to the way the Court works – has been transferred here too. What is more important

---

*Although the treaty does not specify this, each judge and advocate-general is assisted by one or more legal secretaries or referendaires. These are personal legal advisers. Such posts can also serve as a springboard for a higher position in the ECJ.

is that these can now be approved by QMV within the Council and not unanimity. This was a compromise since the negotiators did not want to give the ECJ full freedom to change its rules, even though the European Court of Human Rights has this power.

Nice made even more changes to *Article 224* in order to entrench the upgrading of the Court of First Instance. To an extent it also replaces the previous Article 225 which set it up. The Court is now assumed and Article 224 starts by defining its membership, which is to be at least equivalent to the number of member states, thus establishing an enlargement-friendly principle. Equally, the wording leaves the door open to further appointments via the ECJ statute, thus allowing the CFI to respond relatively rapidly to any future increase in its caseload. This is also true of the already mentioned potentiality of having advocates-general. And Article 50 of the statute allows it to sit with single judges as well as in chambers and a Grand Chamber. The assumption seems to be that it will normally sit in chambers.

The article also lays down slightly less demanding qualifications, and seems to weaken the national requirement. Rules on terms of office, renewals and officers are all identical to those of the ECJ. However, when it comes to the Rules of Procedure these have also to be agreed by the ECJ. This would seem to be a matter of uniformity rather than hierarchy. The final sentence of the article, insisting that the two differ only where the treaty says so, reinforces this view.

Article 225 (ex 168a) then updates the existing limited provisions on the jurisdiction of the CFI. In doing this it makes use of some of the phrasing of the Court's own rather wordy suggested redraft. The CFI's remit is now to be at least threefold. Firstly, it is now, as we suggested in the first version of the *Guide* it might become, the main court for most direct actions, whether for annulment, failure to act, contractual damages, staff disputes or arbitration. The real exception is infringement cases under Article 226. And even this omission can be changed via the ECJ statute. Secondly, it is to hear appeals from the judicial panels mentioned in Article 220. However, in order to ensure consistency there is provision for a further review by the ECJ itself. Thirdly, the CFI may, and probably will, be able to hear preliminary ruling cases if the statute so provides, thus reversing the clear ban previously in force. Barents suggests, however, that this would unnecessarily overburden the CFI further.

A series of declarations also throw light on the relation between the CFI and the ECJ. Indeed, Declaration No. 12 TN invites Commission and Court to start work on refining the two jurisdictions in direct actions so that a more precise delimitation can be considered as soon as Nice comes into effect. The Court must also, according to Declaration No. 13 TN, clarify through the statute the rules for handling the review process mentioned in Article 225(2) and then, according to Declaration No. 14 TN, rapidly evaluate their working. The aim of this is to ensure speed and consistency of judgment. At present the statute deals only with the status quo, although it does provide a means of redirecting suits which are addressed to the wrong court in its Article 54. Finally, Declaration No. 15 TN makes it plain that preliminary rulings will definitely be transmitted to the CFI by requiring an ultra-rapid response to any CFI decision to refer any special problems they present to the ECJ. Indeed, given the weight of business these involve, little would be gained in terms of speeding up proceedings if some were not transferred.

Article 225a is an invention of Nice and allows the creation of lower-level judicial panels. Their establishment can be suggested by the Commission or required by the ECJ, albeit after consultation. The act setting them up has to specify their powers and procedures, though the panels themselves can draw up their own rules subject to ECJ and Council approval. The assumption seems to be that, because of their very different subject matter, they will not all be of the same type. Declaration No. 16 TN instructs the ECJ to set up a staff tribunal as soon as possible as this would take a lot of pressure off the main courts. And the conference also 'took note' of a Luxembourg declaration (No. 1n TN) which says that it would not seek to use its prerogative to house the courts to force the removal of the Trade Mark body from Alicante, should this, as seems likely, be reconstituted as a panel.

Procedures involving the judicial panels can include an appeal to the CFI either on a point of law or a matter of fact, depending on what the treaty says. Even though membership of the panels requires more specialist qualifications they still have to be accepted unanimously by the Council. The final element of the article stresses the need for uniformity. This rather suggests that a considerable burden is being put on the panels as a way of handling many low-level, routine technical cases. This ends the structural element of Section 4.

The following articles, which make up a numerical though not a quantitative majority, are concerned with who should bring cases before the Courts, the kind of cases to be heard by the Courts and with the way they should be heard. The first of these, set out in *Article 226* (ex 169) are what are known as 'infringement' proceedings relating to a member state failing to meet its obligations and thereby 'infringing' treaty requirements. This is the main legal channel for acting against member states within the EU and might be seen as providing a mechanism for enforcing the requirement for loyalty to the Union set out in Article 10 TEC. Indeed French legal usage is to talk of cases brought under this article as dealing with 'default on treaty obligations', which is a broader and more telling description than infringement.

In any case, the article here makes the Commission responsible both for monitoring member states' implementation of Community rules and for delivering a preliminary warning. Where a member state does not heed the latter, the Commission can bring proceedings before the Court but does not have to do so. The sanctions open to the ECJ are spelled out in Article 228. However, the process can lead to references to the EP's Committee on Petitions and the Ombudsman, depending on the complainant. Article 88 (ex 93) TEC provides another and simpler procedure for bringing member states before the Court, at least where state aids are concerned.

Member states are also allowed to sue each other for non-compliance providing the Commission's early warning procedure has been invoked first. In practice member states have been reluctant to do this. It is easier and cheaper to let the Commission act. However, their right to do so is still asserted in *Article 227* (ex 170) and, as *France* v. *UK* (1979) shows, it has been used. The assumption would also be that if they did bring a case, which the Commission then rejected, they would be likely to drop it. Both articles raise the question of how a member state is to be defined. Case law suggests that, on the one hand, judicial acts are excluded here and, on the other, non-governmental bodies like universities can be taken to be representatives of the member state. However, because of the sensitivity of cases brought against member states, these will remain reserved to the ECJ as such, as will EIB and ECB cases under Article 237.

Article 228 (ex 171) builds, as already suggested, on Article 226. Once an infringement charge has been levelled the Court can find against the member state involved. In the past there were no sanctions to this but, at UK prompting, Maastricht wrote in the possibility of fining defaulting member states if the Commission so recommends. The Court does not have to follow this but the Commission would be in a good position to estimate likely costs. *Article 229* (ex 172) allows the EP and Council to give the Court the widest discretion in fixing fines, something which came to worry the Major government. In any case, before this the Commission has to go through a set process but can suggest the level of the penalty. Member states can still mount their own challenges notwithstanding.

Nice next inserts a new provision at *Article 229a* to allow judgment in the case of disputes on EU patent rights. This is the only extension in ECJ competence within the

TEC made in the TN. However, as well as going through the normal Community decision-making procedure, the provisions will have to be ratified nationally as well. This is another response to likely increases in workload. It is a task which could be devolved to a specialist panel, a possibility which is hinted at in Declaration No. 17 TN.

Article 230 (ex 173) introduces a new form of case procedure, that leading to annulment. This is based on a general power for the Court to reconsider binding acts, essentially those which have gone through the normal EC decision-making processes, when these are brought to its attention by member states, institutions or private interests. Their complaints in fact form the largest body of cases heard by the ECJ. In the first instance the EP seemed to stand outside this but, on the one hand, *Les Verts* (1986) brought its administrative acts within the purview of those which could be reviewed. Then, on the other hand, Nice allows the EP to bring issues of principle itself and not just cases needed to defend its own political rights. This is also reflected in changes to Article 300(6). Previous to this Amsterdam had given the Court of Auditors the right to bring defence of privileges cases. In all cases, however, there is a cut-off point after which such cases cannot be brought.

If the Court considers the claim justified, it may under *Article 231* (ex 174) annul the act. However, doing this could be a destabilizing nuclear option. Hence the article allows the ECJ to rule out only certain elements of a regulation, thereby assuring legal certainty by allowing the status quo to continue where possible. Directives would be more likely to be struck down *in toto*. In any case, *Article 232* (ex 175) builds on this and on Article 230 to ensure institutions act not only within but also on the law. It creates a procedure for bringing claims for 'failure to act' which, as it points out, is itself an 'infringement' of the treaty, albeit of a narrower kind than that envisaged in Article 226. As a result of the article, providing due process has been followed, and complainants specify which measures have not been taken, legal and administrative inaction can be challenged. A classic example of this was *European Parliament* v. *Council* (1985), in which the ECJ ruled that the Council had failed to create the transport policy which the treaty required it to do. The code of annulment is completed by *Article 233* (ex 176), which requires member states to remedy their inactivity, although without directly specifying sanctions. However, damages are not excluded.

Thereafter Section 4 moves on to indirect action, the all-important matter of preliminary rulings. These have been both the most numerous and the most significant, legally speaking. They involve a judgment by the Court on what an article or legislative act means and how it relates to EC law as a whole, something which means trying to define the EC and its law more systematically than the treaties can do. Their significance springs from the fact that it is through these rulings that the ECJ has both developed EC law, often through crucial and controversial rulings which have created legal doctrines of direct effect and supremacy, and, in conjunction with national courts, ensured its uniform application.*

---

*Direct effect means that the law is immediately binding on individual citizens of member states both in terms of constraints and of access to the ECJ as supreme court. National courts have to recognize these rights. In other words, direct effect allows individuals to use EC law, whether against states or other individuals, even though the treaties do not specifically say this. Moreover many EC acts apply directly as soon as they are passed and do not need domestic action to enact them. Equally, although there are no supremacy clauses as such in the treaty, it does take precedence. EC law must be fully applied and *Simmenthal* (1979) provides both for this and for striking down any decisions which contradict EC law. Thus EC law cannot be overridden by national law. We should note that the term is often equated with being directly applicable which, strictly speaking, means that an EC act goes straight into operation once agreed by the EC institutions and normally needs no national action to operationalize it.

This is because, most importantly, the article in question, now numbered *Article 234* (ex 177), empowers the ECJ to interpret the treaty. This it has done creatively, emphatically and frequently. Moreover, the Court has adopted a wide view of what is meant by an act of the Community in the terms of tiret (b), extending it to association and other external agreements. Article 234 also allows it to quash acts. Tiret (c) is, conversely, of limited significance, referring as it does to the interpretation of the procedural ground rules of some bodies which have been endorsed by the Council.

Where national courts are concerned they all have discretion to refer cases. And they, especially lower-level courts, have made considerable and growing use of it. Where there is no appeal against a court decision domestically, reference becomes obligatory. This has raised the question of what constitutes a court for the purposes of Article 234. In the view of Advocate-General Colomer, commenting in *de Coster* v. *Collège des Bourg-mestres* (2001), the case law has been casuistic and vague. He argues that it needs clarification after Amsterdam's changes to preliminary rulings and ahead of enlargement. He suggests that a 'court' has to be defined as an independent body within a national judicial system with the power to state the law and render judgments. If this is followed it may restrict the number of referrals.

In any case, in responding the ECJ pronounces only on the law and not on the facts of the case. All this has helped to develop close links between the ECJ and national judiciaries. Furthermore, this has helped to lead member states to accept controversial rulings about which they may not always be too happy. In turn this has assisted in the establishment of EC law as a force for integration.

The load such references generated, despite the absence of pleadings, led the Due Committee and the Commission to recommend a tightening up of the procedure during the 2000 IGC. They wanted to encourage national courts to resolve matters and to explain their references better. Often it was not clear to the ECJ why things were being referred to them. But the IGC refused to go along with these changes.* Hence the article remains as it was. Of course the Court cannot, in virtue of either this or Article 230, strike down rulings by national courts.

The next five articles extend the ECJ's remit beyond such constitutional-type cases. *Article 235* (ex 178) allows the ECJ to hear contractual cases in which individuals allegedly suffer loss because of the EU and seek compensation. In this it makes an appeal to the general law of the member states as Community law clearly cannot diverge too far from this. *Article 236* (ex 179) gives rise to perhaps a twelfth of all cases but little of the procedure is spelled out here since the article merely points to more detailed rules in the Staff Regulations. In fact the latter require staff to exhaust administrative remedies before going to the Court. Moreover, given the volume of work responsibility was transferred to the CFI at Amsterdam. Yet it, in turn, found itself forced to set up one-judge hearings as a result. With Nice, other articles and declarations make it clear that the bulk of the work will now go to a new panel and not the appeal board suggested by the ECJ. Appeals will only be possible on points of law and not of fact.

Although *Article 237* (ex 180) is much longer it is no more significant than its predecessors. It is a symbol that the EU's banking organs are subject to the rule of law, a point made apropos of the EIB in tirets (b) and (c). Tirets (a) and (d) allow the EIB directors and ECB board to act in the same way as the Commission in bringing infringe-

---

*The IGC thus rejected the Court's suggestion that national courts should be required to consult the ECJ when it proposes not to apply a Community act on the grounds of invalidity, a procedure consecrated in practice by the *Firm Foto Frost* (1987) ruling.

ment cases in its sphere. Thereafter, tiret (d) also allows the ECB to take national banks to court and seek remedial measures.

Article 238 (ex 181) grants the ECJ a limited role in domestic law where this is called for by arbitration clauses in EC contracts. These can specify which legal code should apply. This interrelates with *Article 240* (ex 183), which makes the point that national courts can hear EC cases unless specifically debarred by the TEC. This also reinforces the fact that EC law is national law and, in a sense, national courts are EC courts. Then *Article 239* (ex 182) permits the ECJ to hear treaty-based disputes between member states. It also points the way to Article 292, which forbids member-state use of other forms of dispute settlement. However, it has yet to be used.

Article 241 (ex 184) supplements Article 230. According to Beaumont and Weatherill this is a complex technical device to assist ordinary actors to challenge the effects of a regulation when the time for challenging under Article 230 has gone by. In other words, when an illegal act has been properly implemented, but to the disadvantage of the citizen or firm, they can use this to query the original act. The Court has allowed this secondary facility to be extended beyond regulations.

There then follow three articles on aspects of putting ECJ judgments into effect. *Article 242* (ex 185) allows the Court to freeze the operation of a regulation while it is considering a case. This would only arise with a direct action. *Article 243* (ex 186) also allows the ECJ to suggest ways to regulate affairs during such consideration or, more likely, when moving to an annulment. This would be to help legal certainty. Then, when Court judgments are applied, *Article 244* (ex 187) assimilates them to legislative acts. In this the EC differs very much from other international bodies.

The final article in the section, *Article 245* (ex 188), goes back to organizational questions. It was upgraded at Nice, but not quite as the Court itself had suggested. The statute is still given treaty status by being enshrined in a protocol, now attached to three treaties. The revised text of this was included in the Nice agreement. The statute can now be changed by QMV. This should make it easier. However, in the past, on the one hand, only the Court could request such a revision. Now the Commission can also do so. On the other hand, in the past the revisions could only deal with procedures. Now they can extend to the whole statute save for the initial provisions on the independence of judges.

What all this amounts to is a considerable structural change, to the benefit of the Court of First Instance. The question must be whether the Nice amendments will achieve their aims given the slight uncertainties about the relationship of the two courts. The precise role of the ECJ is a little hard to define at present while the statute needs to be considered alongside the treaty proper.* Whether the changes to the preliminary rulings will be effective and maintain the integrationist drive of EC law remains to be seen. Equally important, will they succeed in reducing the time taken to render judgments and therefore the backlog of cases? Failure here could have implications for the ECJ's legitimacy, especially given fears in the United Kingdom that moves to bring Eurojust into the treaty and reinforce the fight against fraud through the *corpus juris* threaten the common law.†

---

*The Statute is presently divided into five titles: Judges, Organization, Procedures, CFI and Final Provisions. Although it is longer than its predecessor it is still a somewhat terse document. It sets out much of the way that cases run but still needs to be supplemented by the Rules of Procedure.

†*Corpus juris* is a proposal stimulated by the need to do more to counteract budgetary fraud in the EU, which is hard to prosecute because of the lack of legal uniformity among the member states. The proposal was that there should be a common 'body' of definitions of financial fraud, of standards of evidence and of uniform procedures of investigation. The latter implies a transnational prosecution service. It was this which worried sceptics in the UK.

Opinions are, not surprisingly, somewhat divided on these issues, especially ahead of the implementation of Nice.

Section 4   The Court of Justice

Article 220 (ex Article 164)

The Court of Justice **and the Court of First instance, each within its jurisdiction,** shall ensure that in the interpretation and application of this Treaty the law is observed.

In addition, judicial panels may be attached to the Court of First Instance under the conditions laid down in Article 225a in order to exercise, in certain specific areas, the judicial competence laid down in this Treaty.

Article 221 (ex Article 165)

The Court of Justice shall consist of **one judge per Member State.**

The Court of Justice shall sit in chambers or in a Grand Chamber, in accordance with the rules laid down for that purpose in the Statute of the Court of Justice. When provided for in the Statute, the Court of Justice may also sit as a full Court.

Article 222 (ex Article 166)

The Court of Justice shall be assisted by eight Advocates-General. *Should the Court of Justice so request, the Council, acting unanimously, may increase the number of Advocates-General.*

It shall be the duty of the Advocate-General, acting with complete impartiality and independence, to make, in open court, reasoned submissions on cases **which, in accordance with the Statute of the Court of Justice, require his involvement.**

Article 223 (ex Articles 167, 168, 188)

The Judges and Advocates-General *of the Court of Justice* shall be chosen from persons whose independence is beyond doubt and who possess the qualifications required for appointment to the highest judicial offices in their respective countries or who are jurisconsults of recognised competence; they shall be appointed by common accord of the governments of the Member States for a term of six years.

Every three years there shall be a partial replacement of the Judges *and Advocates-General,* **in accordance with the conditions laid down in the Statute of the Court of Justice.**

The Judges shall elect the President of the Court of Justice from among their number for a term of three years. He may be re-elected.

Retiring Judges and Advocates-General *may be reappointed.*

The Court of Justice shall appoint its Registrar and lay down the rules governing his service.

The Court of Justice shall establish *its Rules of Procedure. Those Rules shall require the approval of the Council,* **acting by a qualified majority.**

Article 224 (new – TN)

The Court of First instance shall comprise at least one judge per Member State. The number of Judges shall be determined by the Statute of the Court of Justice. The Statute may provide for the Court of First Instance to be assisted by Advocates-General.

The members of the Court of First Instance shall be chosen from persons whose independence is beyond doubt and who possess the ability required for appointment to high judicial office. They shall be appointed by common accord of the governments of the Member States for a term of six years. The membership shall be partially renewed every three years. Retiring members shall be eligible for reappointment.

The Judges shall elect the President of the Court of First Instance from among their number for a term of three years. He may be re-elected.

The Court of First Instance shall appoint its Registrar and lay down the rules governing his service.

The Court of First Instance shall establish its Rules of Procedure in agreement with the Court of Justice. Those Rules shall require the approval of the Council, acting by a qualified majority.

Unless the Statute of the Court of Justice provides otherwise, the provisions of this Treaty relating to the Court of Justice shall apply to the Court of First Instance.

Article 225 (ex Article 168a)

1. The Court of First Instance shall *have jurisdiction to hear and determine at first instance actions or proceedings referred to in* Articles 230, 232, 235, 236 and 238, with the exception of those assigned to a judicial panel and those reserved in the Statute for the Court of Justice. The Statute may provide for the Court of First Instance to have jurisdiction for other classes of action or proceeding.

Decisions given by the Court of First Instance under this paragraph may be subject to a right of appeal to the Court of Justice on points of law only, under the conditions and within the limits laid down by the Statute.

2. The Court of First Instance shall have jurisdiction to hear and determine actions or proceedings brought against decisions of the judicial panels set up under Article 225a.

Decisions given by the Court of First Instance under this paragraph may exceptionally be subject to review by the Court of Justice, under the conditions and within the limits laid down by the Statute, where there is a serious risk of the unity or consistency of Community law being affected.

3. The Court of First Instance shall have jurisdiction to hear and determine questions referred for preliminary ruling under Article 234, in specific areas laid down by the Statute.

Where the Court of First Instance considers that the case requires a decision of principle likely to affect the unity or consistency of Community law, it may refer the case to the Court of Justice for a ruling.

Decisions given by the Court of First Instance on questions referred for a preliminary ruling may exceptionally be subject to review by the Court of Justice, under the conditions and within the limits laid down by the Statute, where there is a serious risk of the unity or consistency of Community law being affected.

Article 225a (new – TN)

The Council, acting unanimously on a proposal from the Commission and after consulting the European Parliament and the Court of Justice or at the request of the Court of Justice and after consulting the European Parliament and the Commission, may create judicial panels to hear and determine at first instance certain classes of action or proceeding brought in specific areas.

The decision establishing a judicial panel shall lay down the rules on the organisation of the panel and the extent of the jurisdiction conferred upon it.

Decisions given by judicial panels may be subject to a right of appeal on points of law only or, when provided for in the decision establishing the panel, a right of appeal also on matters of fact, before the Court of First Instance.

The members of the judicial panels shall be chosen from persons whose independence is beyond doubt and who possess the ability required for appointment to judicial office. They shall be appointed by the Council, acting unanimously.

The judicial panels shall establish their Rules of Procedure in agreement with the Court of Justice.

Those Rules shall require the approval of the Council, acting by a qualified majority.

Unless the decision establishing the judicial panel provides otherwise, the provisions of this Treaty relating to the Court of Justice and the provisions of the Statute of the Court of Justice shall apply to the judicial panels.

Article 226 (ex Article 169)

If the Commission considers that a Member State has failed to fulfil an obligation under this Treaty, it shall deliver a reasoned opinion on the matter after giving the State concerned the opportunity to submit its observations.

If the State concerned does not comply with the opinion within the period laid down by the Commission, the latter may bring the matter before the Court of Justice.

Article 227 (ex Article 170)

A Member State which considers that another Member State has failed to fulfil an obligation under this Treaty may bring the matter before the Court of Justice.

Before a Member State brings an action against another Member State for an alleged infringement of an obligation under this Treaty, it shall bring the matter before the Commission.

The Commission shall deliver a reasoned opinion after each of the States concerned has been given the opportunity to submit its own case and its observations on the other party's case both orally and in writing.

If the Commission has not delivered an opinion within three months of the date on which the matter was brought before it, the absence of such opinion shall not prevent the matter from being brought before the Court of Justice.

Article 228 (ex Article 171)

1. If the Court of Justice finds that a Member State has failed to fulfil an obligation under this Treaty, the State shall be required to take the necessary measures to comply with the judgment of the Court of Justice.

2. If the Commission considers that the Member State concerned has not taken such measures it shall, after giving that State the opportunity to submit its observations, issue a reasoned opinion specifying the points on which the Member State concerned has not complied with the judgment of the Court of Justice.

If the Member State concerned fails to take the necessary measures to comply with the Court's judgment within the time-limit laid down by the Commission, the latter may bring the case before the Court of Justice.

In so doing it shall specify the amount of the lump sum or penalty payment to be paid by the Member State concerned which it considers appropriate in the circumstances.

If the Court of Justice finds that the Member State concerned has not complied with its judgment it may impose a lump sum or penalty payment on it.

This procedure shall be without prejudice to Article 227.

Article 229 (ex Article 172)

Regulations adopted jointly by the European Parliament and the Council, and by the Council, pursuant to the provisions of this Treaty, may give the Court of Justice unlimited jurisdiction with regard to the penalties provided for in such regulations.

Article 229a **(new – TN)**

Without prejudice to the other provisions of this Treaty, the Council, acting unanimously on a proposal from the Commission and after consulting the European Parliament, may adopt provisions to confer jurisdiction, to the extent that it shall determine, on the Court of Justice in disputes relating to the application of acts adopted on the basis of this Treaty which create Community industrial property rights. The Council shall recommend those provisions to the Member States for adoption in accordance with their respective constitutional requirements.

Article 230 (ex Article 173)

The Court of Justice shall review the legality of acts adopted jointly by the European Parliament and the Council, of acts of the Council, of the Commission and of the ECB, other than recommendations and opinions, and of acts of the European Parliament intended to produce legal effects vis-à-vis third parties.

It shall for this purpose have jurisdiction in actions brought by a Member State, **the European Parliament,** the Council or the Commission on grounds of lack of competence, infringement of an essential procedural requirement, infringement of this Treaty or of any rule of law relating to its application, or misuse of powers.

The Court of Justice shall have jurisdiction under the same conditions in actions brought by the **Court of Auditors** and by the ECB for the purpose of protecting their prerogatives.

Any natural or legal person may, under the same conditions, institute proceedings against a decision addressed to that person or against a decision which, although in the form of a regulation or a decision addressed to another person, is of direct and individual concern to the former.

The proceedings provided for in this Article shall be instituted within two months of the publication of the measure, or of its notification to the plaintiff, or, in the absence thereof, of the day on which it came to the knowledge of the latter, as the case may be.

Article 231 (ex Article 174)

If the action is well founded, the Court of Justice shall declare the act concerned to be void.

In the case of a regulation, however, the Court of Justice shall, if it considers this necessary, state which of the effects of the regulation which it has declared void shall be considered as definitive.

Article 232 (ex Article 175)

Should the European Parliament, the Council or the Commission, in infringement of this Treaty, fail to act, the Member States and the other institutions of the Community may bring an action before the Court of Justice to have the infringement established.

The action shall be admissible only if the institution concerned has first been called upon to act. If, within two months of being so called upon, the institution concerned has not defined its position, the action may be brought within a further period of two months.

Any natural or legal person may, under the conditions laid down in the preceding paragraphs, complain to the Court of Justice that an institution of the Community has failed to address to that person any act other than a recommendation or an opinion.

The Court of Justice shall have jurisdiction, under the same conditions, in actions or proceedings brought by the ECB in the areas falling within the latter's field of competence and in actions or proceedings brought against the latter.

Article 233 (ex Article 176)

The institution or institutions whose act has been declared void or whose failure to act has been declared contrary to this Treaty shall be required to take the necessary measures to comply with the judgment of the Court of Justice.

This obligation shall not affect any obligation which may result from the application of the second paragraph of Article 288.

This Article shall also apply to the ECB.

Article 234 (ex Article 177)

The Court of Justice shall have jurisdiction to give preliminary rulings concerning:
(a) the interpretation of this Treaty;
(b) the validity and interpretation of acts of the institutions of the Community and of the ECB;

(c) the interpretation of the statutes of bodies established by an act of the Council, where those statutes so provide.

Where such a question is raised before any court or tribunal of a Member State, that court or tribunal may, if it considers that a decision on the question is necessary to enable it to give judgement, request the Court of Justice to give a ruling thereon.

Where any such question is raised in a case pending before a court or tribunal of a Member State against whose decisions there is no judicial remedy under national law, that court or tribunal shall bring the matter before the Court of Justice.

Article 235 (ex Article 178)

The Court of Justice shall have jurisdiction in disputes relating to compensation for damage provided for in the second paragraph of Article 288.

Article 236 (ex Article 179)

The Court of Justice shall have jurisdiction in any dispute between the Community and its servants within the limits and under the conditions laid down in the Staff Regulations or the Conditions of Employment.

Article 237 (ex Article 180)

The Court of Justice shall, within the limits hereinafter laid down, have jurisdiction in disputes concerning:
(a) the fulfilment by Member States of obligations under the Statute of the European Investment Bank. In this connection, the Board of Directors of the Bank shall enjoy the powers conferred upon the Commission by Article 226;
(b) measures adopted by the Board of Governors of the European Investment Bank. In this connection, any Member State, the Commission or the Board of Directors of the Bank may institute proceedings under the conditions laid down in Article 230;
(c) measures adopted by the Board of Directors of the European Investment Bank. Proceedings against such measures may be instituted only by Member States or by the Commission, under the conditions laid down in Article 230, and solely on the grounds of non-compliance with the procedure provided for in Article 21(2), (5), (6) and (7) of the Statute of the Bank;
(d) the fulfilment by national central banks of obligations under this Treaty and the Statute of the ESCB. In this connection the powers of the Council of the ECB in respect of national central banks shall be the same as those conferred upon the Commission in respect of Member States by Article 226. If the Court of Justice finds that a national central bank has failed to fulfil an obligation under this Treaty, that bank shall be required to take the necessary measures to comply with the judgment of the Court of Justice.

Article 238 (ex Article 181)

The Court of Justice shall have jurisdiction to give judgement pursuant to any arbitration clause contained in a contract concluded by or on behalf of the Community, whether that contract be governed by public or private law.

Article 239 (ex Article 182)

The Court of Justice shall have jurisdiction in any dispute between Member States which relates to the subject matter of this Treaty if the dispute is submitted to it under a special agreement between the parties.

Article 240 (ex Article 183)

Save where jurisdiction is conferred on the Court of Justice by this Treaty, disputes to which the Community is a party shall not on that ground be excluded from the jurisdiction of the courts or tribunals of the Member States.

Article 241 (ex Article 184)

Notwithstanding the expiry of the period laid down in the fifth paragraph of Article 230, any party may, in proceedings in which a regulation adopted jointly by the European Parliament and the Council, or a regulation of the Council, of the Commission, or of the ECB is at issue, plead the grounds specified in the second paragraph of Article 230 in order to invoke before the Court of Justice the inapplicability of that regulation.

Article 242 (ex Article 185)

Actions brought before the Court of Justice shall not have suspensory effect. The Court of Justice may, however, if it considers that circumstances so require, order that application of the contested act be suspended.

Article 243 (ex Article 186)

The Court of Justice may in any cases before it prescribe any necessary interim measures.

Article 244 (ex Article 187)

The judgements of the Court of Justice shall be enforceable under the conditions laid down in Article 256.

Article 245 (ex Article 188)

The Statute of the Court of Justice is laid down in a separate Protocol.

The Council, acting unanimously at the request of the Court of Justice and after consulting *the European Parliament and the Commission,* **or at the request of the Commission and after consulting the European Parliament and the Court of Justice,** *may amend the provisions of the Statute,* **with the exception of Title I.**

The Court of Auditors

Mention of fighting fraud leads to consideration of the last of the EC's five institutions listed in Article 7 TEC. Because of concern about financial mismanagement the auditors have gained increasing status and significance within the Union, and therefore the treaty, over the last decade. Amsterdam and Nice were no exception to this. So although there are only three articles in the section, they are long and quite important.

The Court (CoA) began life as two audit boards for the EC and Euratom. These were then merged in 1966 and then, in 1975, upgraded to the status of a court – the term used in France for a similar body. The CoA was set up not as a small expert unit but on a normal EC national representation basis. The elevation reflected the widening range of Community expenditure to things like Lomé and the CAP. When it became operative after 1977 the Court actually found some difficulty both in getting itself organized and in asserting itself *vis-à-vis* other institutions, notably the Commission. The TEU aided its progress by giving it the status of a Community institution and requesting, through Declaration No. 21 TEU, that the other institutions assist in enhancing the effectiveness of its work. Maastricht brought it in from the cold, as Laffan puts it, in recognition of the growing need for enhanced financial control and the feeling that the Court had not had the resources or standing to provide this in the past. The TEU also wrote into the treaty the acceptance of budgetary discipline, a commitment to sound financial management and an attack on fraud. Most importantly the CoA was asked to provide what was known as a Statement of Assurance (SoA) certifying that the accounts it assessed were reliable, something it had not previously had to do.

Yet this too proved insufficient and, again at UK behest, Amsterdam extended its remit to the administrative aspects of Pillars II and III as well as to other agencies including the EIB. This overcame the latter's resistance to scrutiny. It also allowed the Court to take legal action to defend its own privileges while encouraging institutions and member states to work with it. At the same time it gained new rights of consultation, information and reporting.

This had some impact on the Commission, which set out to improve its own financial performance and relations with the Court. However, the 1999 revelations of grave irregularities in the Santer Commission showed that overall financial control needed yet further strengthening. This need was also revealed by the difficulties the Court had in scrutinizing member states' use of EU monies. All this led to thoughts of further treaty changes for the Court ahead of the 2000 IGC. The Commission believed that cutting the size of the CoA to 12 was the answer (possibly with a Council-like rotation scheme), although the Court itself felt this would be counter-productive, politically and technically. Like the ECJ it needed to be in touch with all national audit systems. So it came out in favour of having one, more independent, member for each member state along with a rationalized internal structure so that all decisions did not have to be taken by all members together with some new policy changes.

It was partly successful because Nice made a number of changes. It agreed to allow one seat per member state and accepted the creation of chambers. It also went some way towards giving the Court's members more independence by allowing them to draft their own Rules of Procedure and increasing the range of their statements of assurance. However, it did not accept either the desire for a nomination procedure like that of the judges of the ECJ or the suggestions for changes to Articles 271–279.

So what we now have in Section 5 are three articles dealing with roles, structures and operations respectively. In *Article 246* (ex 188a), as with the ECJ, the section starts with a broad statement of the obligations of the Court of Auditors. This is almost too lapidary and offhand, since it raises the question of what is '*the* audit', implying that there is only one operation. In fact the rest of the section suggests that there is some uncertainty as to whether what is being described are ongoing processes or one single, albeit annual, inquiry into Community accounts carried out at a given time. Nor does 'carry out' imply much in the way of enforcement, which is out of line with the growing concern over financial rectitude and effectiveness. The French version tells us that the Court 'ensures' that accounts are audited and something on these lines might have been preferable. In any event, the article can be taken as establishing that EC accounts have to be audited and that the Court is the body entrusted with the duty of doing this.

What the Court actually consists of is then set out in *Article 247* (ex 188b). Following Nice it is now described as a body of one 'national' from each member state, a slightly more restrictive formulation than for judges. However, like the latter, the auditors have to be suitably qualified in national terms. The reference to 'external' might suggest 'foreign' but should be taken to mean not 'in-house' accountants but stand-alone financial-control services used to audit firms and organizations. Equally, they have to be clearly independent. What this means for the way they behave, if not in terms of their qualifications, is indicated later in Article 247(4–5).

They serve for six years, again a longish time to ensure that they develop and deploy experience. They can be reappointed, although the Court itself had hoped before Nice for one single non-renewable term of 12 years. They are appointed by QMV even though, again, the Court would have preferred 'by common accord'. However, the reference to adopting the list suggests that the Council really only has formally to endorse member-state nominations. The EP is still only consulted – in order to ensure independence – although it would have liked more influence. Despite this, it has been able to force member states to change their nominees. The rules for the presidency are identical to those of the ECJ and, indeed, the two posts have a similar role.

The article goes on to spell out in some detail provisions for the standing, replacement and rights of the members of the Court. To begin with the requirements of independence are clarified. They involve rejecting bias, whether national or sectoral, and maintaining personal financial integrity. Paragraph 5 adds two procedural riders to this: that, like commissioners, auditors must be full-timers and take an oath to obey those conditions to which the TEC subjects them. In particular they are not to take up lucrative positions on leaving office. This presumably is to ensure that confidential information is not leaked.

Secondly, there are two paragraphs setting down the normal kind of EU institutional procedures for leaving office. These allow a resigning auditor to stay on until a replacement takes up the post. More significantly, paragraph 7 provides a due process for dismissal. Only incapacity or breach of undertakings on independence are allowable as grounds for this. Thirdly and lastly, the Council is required to set salaries and emoluments. Paragraph 9 also bestows on members of the Court the same legal and diplomatic protection as other high EU appointees.

Finally, *Article 248* (ex 188c), which was significantly amended both by Maastricht and Nice, deals with the Court's operation, extent, process and reporting. Its first paragraph makes it clear that, unless otherwise specified, the Court's remit extends to all EU bodies. And, by inference from the following paragraph, it extends to all income and expenditure. It also, since Nice, not only requires a general SoA but allows the Court to go into more detail on particular areas. This was something which it felt it had not had the powers or resources to do in the past but which was necessary to help it monitor what was going on and decide whether the overall accounts gave a truly accurate picture and rested on appropriate procedures. This gives the Court new powers of inquiry and leverage.

Paragraphs 2 and 3 then offer further definitions of what auditing means. It involves assessing two areas: the procedural propriety of income and expenditure records and the way the monies are actually managed while they are in Community hands. Amsterdam made it obligatory for the Court to report on irregularities and not just on wrongdoing.

The text then moves to talk of 'the' audit. In the case of income and payments it covers both nominal and real sums and the actual act does not have to wait till the end of the financial year. Paragraph 3 gives more details of the actual act of audit, which can involve site visits as well as working from records submitted by bodies such as the Commission.

The former springs from the CoA's pressing need to follow the paper trail into member states where many EU monies are raised and disbursed. It needs co-operation with national audit offices. And while this often happens, there can be difficulties. Because Amsterdam had not sorted these out Declaration No. 18 TN suggests that there should be a contact committee between the Court and the national services. In the rest of the paragraph institutions along with national services are placed under an obligation to provide information although apparently only for 'the' audit. Since Amsterdam even the EIB has had to move in this direction, although co-operation with the CoA and the Commission had already been taking place, as Declaration No. 33 TA notes.

Paragraph 4 was revised at Nice. It continues to require an annual report and this is published, along with institutional responses, thus putting the latter under further pressure and scrutiny as the reports get wide and often critical coverage. On the basis of this regularly trenchant appraisal, which has to be submitted by the end of November, the EP has to decide by 30 April whether to endorse the Commission's handling of the budget and give it a formal 'discharge', which it does not always do. The Court can also decide, of its own volition, to produce special audits to highlight what it sees as particular problems. These can cover aspects of the audit process, ideas on proposed legislation and the need for further financial regulations. It produces about three of each every year. They can be requested by other bodies, notably the Council and the EP, to whom the CoA has a special duty because of their budgetary responsibilities. This is further spelled out in Article 183, which requires the CoA to be heard and whose decisions will, as a result of Nice, be subject to QMV after 2007 once the next cohesion-linked financial perspectives have been agreed.

Beyond this, Nice added two new elements. On the one hand it allowed the CoA to set up a formal internal structure, so as to avoid having to do everything in a nearly 30-strong formation and allowing it to improve its work rate as enlargement draws on. On the other hand, what these are and what they are to produce is to be laid down in the Court's Rules of Procedure. These had not previously been mentioned but now can be drawn up (rather than adopted) by the Court itself, like those of the ECJ, and then passed on to the Council for approval by QMV.

Again, whether these changes will give the Court more muscle and allow it to get on top of Community finances and the way they are managed remains to be seen. Nice, after all, failed to establish the special prosecutor required by the *corpus juris* to act against fraud involving Community finances. However, there is no doubt that these questions have become an increasing concern in recent years and the treaty bears the marks of it. Obviously they are closely related to the Community's budgetary provisions. However, before going on to deal with these the TEC next moves to consider its decision-making procedures and the other advisory institutions.

Section 5   The Court of Auditors

Article 246 (ex Article 188a)

The Court of Auditors shall carry out the audit.

Article 247 (ex Article 188b, simplified)

1. The Court of Auditors shall consist of **one national from each Member State.**

2. The Members of the Court of Auditors shall be chosen from among persons who belong or have belonged in their respective countries to external audit bodies or who are especially qualified for this office. Their independence must be beyond doubt.

3. The Members of the Court of Auditors shall be appointed for a term of six years. *The Council, acting by a qualified majority after consulting the European Parliament,* **shall adopt the list of Members drawn up in accordance with the proposals made by each Member State.** *The term of office of the Members of the Court of Auditors shall be renewable.*

They shall elect the President of the Court of Auditors from among their number for a term of three years. The President may be re-elected.

4. The Members of the Court of Auditors shall, in the general interest of the Community, be completely independent in the performance of their duties.

In the performance of these duties, they shall neither seek nor take instructions from any government or from any other body. They shall refrain from any action incompatible with their duties.

5. The Members of the Court of Auditors may not, during their term of office, engage in any other occupation, whether gainful or not. When entering upon their duties they shall give a solemn undertaking that, both during and after their term of office, they will respect the obligations arising therefrom and in particular their duty to behave with integrity and discretion as regards the acceptance, after they have ceased to hold office, of certain appointments or benefits.

6. Apart from normal replacement, or death, the duties of a Member of the Court of Auditors shall end when he resigns, or is compulsorily retired by a ruling of the Court of Justice pursuant to paragraph 7.

The vacancy thus caused shall be filled for the remainder of the Member's term of office.

Save in the case of compulsory retirement, Members of the Court of Auditors shall remain in office until they have been replaced.

7. A Member of the Court of Auditors may be deprived of his office or of his right to a pension or other benefits in its stead only if the Court of Justice, at the request of the Court of Auditors, finds that he no longer fulfils the requisite conditions or meets the obligations arising from his office.

8. The Council, acting by a qualified majority, shall determine the conditions of employment of the President and the Members of the Court of Auditors and in particular their salaries, allowances and pensions. It shall also, by the same majority, determine any payment to be made instead of remuneration.

9. The provisions of the Protocol on the privileges and immunities of the European Communities applicable to the Judges of the Court of Justice shall also apply to the Members of the Court of Auditors.

Article 248 (ex Article 188c)

1. The Court of Auditors shall examine the accounts of all revenue and expenditure of the Community. It shall also examine the accounts of all revenue and expenditure of all bodies set up by the Community insofar as the relevant constituent instrument does not preclude such examination.

The Court of Auditors shall provide the European Parliament and the Council with a statement of assurance as to the reliability of the accounts and the legality and regularity of the underlying transactions **which shall be published in the** *Official Journal of the European* **Union. This statement may be supplemented by specific assessments for each major area of Community activity.**

2. The Court of Auditors shall examine whether all revenue has been received and all expenditure incurred in a lawful and regular manner and whether the financial management has been sound. **In doing so, it shall report in particular on any cases of irregularity.**

The audit of revenue shall be carried out on the basis both of the amounts established as due and the amounts actually paid to the Community.

The audit of expenditure shall be carried out on the basis both of commitments undertaken and payments made.

These audits may be carried out before the closure of accounts for the financial year in question.

3. The audit shall be based on records and, if necessary, performed on the spot in *the* other institutions of the Community, **on the premises of any body which manages revenue or expenditure on behalf of the Community and in the Member States, including on the premises of any natural or legal person in receipt of payments from the budget.** In the Member States the audit shall be carried out in liaison with national audit bodies or, if these do not have the necessary powers, with the competent national departments. **The Court of Auditors and the national audit bodies of the Member States shall co-operate in a spirit of trust while maintaining their independence.** These bodies or departments shall inform the Court of Auditors whether they intend to take part in the audit.

The other institutions of the Community, **any bodies managing revenue or expenditure on behalf of the Community, any natural or legal person in receipt of payments from the budget,** and the national audit bodies or, if these do not have the necessary powers, the competent national departments, shall forward to the Court of Auditors, at its request, any document or information necessary to carry out its task.

In respect of the European Investment Bank's activity in managing Community expenditure and revenue, the Court's rights of access to information held by the Bank shall be governed by an agreement between the Court, the Bank and the Commission. In the absence of an agreement, the Court shall nevertheless have access to information necessary for the audit of Community expenditure and revenue managed by the Bank.

4. The Court of Auditors shall draw up an annual report after the close of each financial year. It shall be forwarded to the other institutions of the Community and shall be published, together with the replies of these institutions to the observations of the Court of Auditors, in the *Official Journal of the European* **Union.**

The Court of Auditors may also, at any time, submit observations, particularly in the form of special reports, on specific questions and deliver opinions at the request of one of the other institutions of the Community.

It shall adopt its annual reports, special reports or opinions by a majority of its Members. **However, it may establish internal chambers in order to adopt certain categories of reports or opinions under the conditions laid down by its Rules of Procedure.**

It shall assist the European Parliament and the Council in exercising their powers of control over the implementation of the budget.

The Court of Auditors shall draw up its Rules of Procedure. Those rules shall require the approval of the Council, acting by a qualified majority.

Provisions Common to Several Institutions: Decision-making

Having introduced the key decision-making institutions, the TEC now moves on to link them more closely together. It does this by setting out the parameters within which they are to interrelate when fulfilling the tasks set them by the European Treaties. In other words Chapter 2 of Title I, Provisions common to several institutions, is more significant than its description might suggest. 'Common provisions' conveys an impression of an unimportant miscellany. In reality these are vitally important rules because they deal essentially with decision-making and hence with power, whether that of the institutions or that of the member states.

The chapter is also more focused than might be thought. It provides what, perhaps a little overenthusiastically, has been called a 'legislative code'. But there is no single, general legislative power, only a list of specific acts, and even this is not comprehensive. Other parts of the TEC have implications for the legislative process just as much as those in this chapter. None the less, it shows what the institutions are intended to produce in the way of legislative output, what their working mechanisms for legislating are, and how they should interrelate. And it makes clear that the institutions, including the member states collectively in the Council, have to work within the rules and do only what the treaty lets them do.

Over time, the chapter has undergone various changes, the SEA and TEU introducing provisions governing the co-operation and co-decision procedures, respectively. More recently, Amsterdam simplified and streamlined co-decision. Thanks to changes elsewhere in the TEC, in theory inspired by a now deleted call then contained in ex Article 189b(8) for extending the use of co-decision, use of the procedure was extended to new areas, thereby again increasing the EP's influence in policy-making. The EP gained rather less at Nice, in part because the moves towards co-decision were inconsistent, limited and highly controversial since they involved more QMV, which was seen as the epitome of 'superstatism' in some cases. However, Nice made no substantive changes to the text. As a result, the chapter remains as it was after Amsterdam: complex and at the centre of debates about where power does, and should, lie in the Union.

The text of the chapter begins by laying out, in *Article 249* (ex 189), the authority under which the EC acts and the forms which those acts should take. This gives shape and substance to the specific powers already mentioned at earlier points in the treaty. The wording makes clear both the fact that this authority is not a general or inherent norm but a function of the tasks incumbent on the Community, as indicated in Articles 2 and 3 TEC, and is further limited by the necessity for conformity with the treaty's overall rules.

At present the Community's legislative output can take five forms, the effects if not the nature of which are defined here. Taken together they help to differentiate the EC from other international organizations while the ECJ has used the article to establish the primacy of EC law. However, they are not presented in absolute rank order, a fact which has led to continuing but wholly unsuccessful pressure for a proper hierarchy of norms.

This would distinguish between organic (or superior) laws, ordinary laws and executive orders etc., as is done in many continental constitutions. Despite Declaration No. 16 TEU and some discussion in 1996 things have been left as they are. And, in any case, the list of acts here is not exclusive since it omits soft-law acts and inter-institutional agreements, although these were given a cautious and limited mention in Declaration No. 3 TN.

The first of the five forms of act, the regulation, might seem to have a higher status than the others since the English text talks of them being 'made' rather than 'issued', although the French version uses *'arrêter'* – which means decides or decrees – for both regulations and directives. In any case, a regulation is defined as an act, all of which applies to the Community as a whole, and is directly applicable. By this should be meant that it is legally binding as soon as it is published in the *Official Journal* and does not need any national intervention or reception to make it operative. This is unless the regulation in question requires national implementation, as did that on the tachograph. And this is an obligation as was highlighted in *Commission* v. *United Kingdom* (1979). Declaration No. 19 TEU also points in this direction and emphasizes state obligations to treat EC law with the same commitment as national legislation. However, the term is often conflated with 'direct effect', the principle that EC law is binding on and usable by ordinary citizens, whether or not it comes from a directly applicable regulation or an indirectly generated directive. The ECJ has made it clear that all regulations are directly applicable but not all are directly effective.

As well as not normally being able to change the nature of the regulation, member states cannot decide when a regulation should be applied. The TEC specifies the use of regulations in only a limited number of cases, particularly those where uniformity is a prime requirement such as in agriculture, the free movement of workers, competition, state aid, EMU, the budget and staffing (see Articles 37(3), 40, 83, 89, 110, 279 and 283 TEC). The Commission often uses the form in is own legislative output.

The second form, the directive, is binding on the overall aim but leaves it to member states to decide how to achieve the aim. Their use is required in areas of EC activity such as those covered by Articles 44, 46, 47, 52, 94, 96, 133(3) and 137(2) TEC. Although a directive need not cover all member states it must be specifically addressed to at least one. In other words it is a two-stage kind of legislation. As a result it is only recently that directives themselves have had to be published. Where they emerge from co-decision this is now the case. Typically a deadline is laid down for member states to do this and league tables are kept of member-state success in meeting their obligations. Failure to transpose directives into national law can lead to criticism and court cases. All this suggests that a directive should be a broad framework. In fact some directives are more detailed than the text implies, so the distinction has become a little blurred in practice although it has implications for legal rights under Article 234. None the less, with the rise of ideas of subsidiarity, the directive has become the key form of legislation.

Decisions are of less importance. They are used to indicate legislative acts which are binding on specific member states. These are common in the agricultural field in line with Article 37.* The German text distinguishes between these *'Entscheidungen'* and mere administrative decisions or *'Beschlüsse'*. Although recommendations and opinions are not binding they too can be important. The first, often issued by the Commission to assist in national policy development especially in fields where the Community has shared

---

*Other articles which provide for decisions include 75(4), 85(2), 86(3), 87(3)(e), 88(2), 100, 104, 110(1), 119(2), 120(3), 148 and 162.

responsibility, often can provide useful guidelines for action.* Equally, the second, especially when used by the ECJ, can set out broad conceptions of law which can have significant long-term political and general effects. We have already seen this with reference to Opinion 2/94 on EU accession to the European Convention on Human Rights.

Article 250 (ex 189a) gives implicit guidance on how the choice between these forms should be made, when it is not prescribed by specific treaty articles. The logic of saying, in paragraph 1, that the Council needs unanimity to overturn a Commission proposal is that the Commission chooses the form of legislation involved. This can be seen as giving some legal definition to what a 'proposal' actually entails. Unanimity is also an important constraint since, although it suggests that member-state decision-making is still seen as the norm, the reality is that gaining this is harder now than it used to be. A further sign of the Commission's freedom of action is in paragraph 2 which allows it to change its proposal at any time before the Council has acted on a Community act, save in a Conciliation Committee under Article 251(4).

Having set out the various types of Community act, Chapter 2 goes on to give details of two specific decision-making procedures involving the EP: co-operation and co-decision. However, these labels are now nowhere used in the treaty, although the former was mentioned between 1987 and 1993. Today they are coyly described as either 'the procedure referred to in Article 251' or 'the procedure referred to in Article 252'. However, thanks to renumbering they are a little more easily identifiable than used to be the case when they were Articles 189b and 189c respectively.

In any case, the second of these is now largely redundant since it was eliminated at Amsterdam save where EMU is concerned (see Articles 99(5), 102(2), 103(2) and 106(2) TEC). These were left untouched in order to avoid any risk of destabilizing the euro. Nice came close to excising these but decided not to do so after ECOFIN ministers pointed out that, since the procedure would be replaced by mere consultation, the change would weaken the EP's influence. This reminds us that there is no mention in Chapter 2 of consultation or of other forms of interaction with the EP such as assent and information. Nor is there any indication of the wider political process involved in all this.

Article 251 (ex 189b) was introduced at Maastricht to give the EP for the first time an ability both to shape the detail of legislation and to share in deciding whether or not a proposal as a whole goes forward or not. Hence the term co-decision or, less commonly nowadays, 'negative assent'. The second element, in other words, is a blocking power, an ability to prevent an act proceeding. The EP has not been offered, let along given, the power to insist that an act becomes law. As with its right to amend it has to discuss everything with the Council, with the Commission watching on the sidelines. Moreover, the procedure only applies to those articles of the treaty which make specific reference to its use. None the less, Articles 249 and 254 make it clear that the EP is part of the legislative process. The original process, set out at Maastricht, was complex and lengthy. It involved four points at which an act could pass or fail.† It began with a Commission proposal submitted to the Council and the EP. Thereafter the former agreed a common position by QMV and put this to the EP, which could allow it to pass by inaction. It could also reject or amend it. In the first case the Council could either acquiesce and kill

---

*Recommendations are required by the treaty under various articles such as Articles 53, 77, 97, 99, 104(7), 119(1), 128(4), 149(4) and 151(5).

†For a diagrammatic exposition of these and the co-operation procedure, see Church and Phinnemore (1995, pp. 299 and 301). A diagram of the revised process can be found in Nicoll and Salmon (2000, p. 103).

the act or resort to optional conciliation. If this worked then both parties had a further chance to kill or cure it.

If the Council accepted the amendments they could go through. If it rejected them then conciliation followed. If an agreed text emerged and both parties ratified it the act passed. If it did not, the Council could, in a third reading, either give way or revert to its original common position. In both cases the agreement of the two bodies was still needed for it to pass. Neither could force it through on its own. All this made it a very long drawn-out, overcomplicated and slightly uncertain process, although it was regularly and often successfully used between 1993 and 1999.

Acting on what was then Article N(2) TEU, Amsterdam sought to rectify these weaknesses by making five main changes. To begin with it made agreement on the first reading possible, doing away with the 'intention to reject' and thus eliminating the first Conciliation Committee. Secondly, it imposed tighter timetables. Thirdly, it cut things short by stopping the Council continuing consideration after an EP rejection. Fourthly, it forced the Conciliation Committee to focus on the EP's amendments. And, lastly, it made conciliation more authoritative. This is because, if there is no agreement, then the act fails there and then. There is, in other words, no third reading, and this provides the EP with extra leverage on the Council in the Conciliation Committee.

What we now find in the new slimmed-down text is therefore a three-stage process which starts with a Commission proposal. This is then given a first parliamentary reading at which the EP can approve the draft or amend by simple majority. The text of the treaty does not fully make clear that an opinion is not a simple yes or no matter but a reflective appraisal with suggested changes. If the EP approves, the Council at its first reading can then directly adopt the act. If the EP takes no action then, again, similarly it can pass.

If the EP chooses to make amendments and the Council does not like them a second stage is triggered. The Council then has to adopt a common position by QMV. This is not a rejection of EP amendments as such and may involve accepting some but not all the suggested changes. The Council has, in fact, to tell the EP in detail what it has done and why. A second EP reading then follows. This, in turn gives the EP one chance to reject the act and two to keep moving forward. Thus, if it can generate an absolute majority to reject the common position unchanged, the act fails.

One way to move forward is to take no action so that, after a 12-week delay, the act can pass. The other, is to again amend the draft act, now by an absolute majority, which may, of course, produce a different outcome from that at the first reading. The requirement is inserted to ensure that the EP is really committed to its changes and was not merely 'trying it on'. In any case the amended act goes back from the EP to the Commission, which has to advise the Council on the new revisions. Faced with the Commission's revised draft, the Council has its own second reading. If it accepts the revised amended draft unaltered, the act can go through. However, if the Council wishes to accept some amendments which the Commission has rejected, it needs unanimity to do so in line with Article 250.

If it rejects some of the new amendments put forward by the EP, then the third stage, of conciliation proper, follows, assuming that both sides are willing to negotiate. The bargaining takes place in a Conciliation Committee which is an assembly of delegates, drawn equally from the EP and the Council and therefore quite large. It has to work from the EP's amendment and not the original draft. If the Committee is successful in agreeing a compromise text then the act can go through, although it needs formal approval, by QMV in Council and absolute majority in the EP. And the text leaves open the possibility that one or both of the institutions could reject what their negotiators had agreed for them. Furthermore, if there is no agreed text from the Conciliation Committee then the act is killed off. So the Conciliation Committee is the crucial phase and there is great pressure on the parties to agree and get a 'result', even an unsatisfactory one. None the less, although it allows the EP an ability to influence the content of legislation as well as to decide on its overall acceptability, the process remains drawn out, especially as Article 251 still allows the two partners to extend the timetable. Declaration No. 34 TA does, though, urge that extension be avoided. The procedure also remains somewhat complex and is not always easy to follow.

As well as seeking to streamline the process itself, Amsterdam went on to extend its usage, partly to replace co-operation but also partly to bring it into new areas. It virtually doubled its use as a result.* Nice came under great pressure to take this further and make co-decision the automatic decision-making mode, at least where QMV decisions were concerned. However, the IGC chose not to go down this road. This was partly because Amsterdam was too recent for there to be any enthusiasm for starting again. It was also partly because the IGC was so taken up with other concerns and conflicts. So, although it did extend the use of co-decision it did not do so on the basis of any clear principle, such as to particular classes of act or on all instances of QMV. It reacted in a very pragmatic way, making six changes but often only allowing it in parts of an article.† And only three of the new QMV provisions were coupled with co-decision. This was to cause intense annoyance in EP and reformist circles, which saw Nice as a retrograde step, one going back on the gains of Amsterdam.

The co-operation procedure set out in *Article 252* (ex 189c) is a much more limited affair in two ways. One is that, as already noted, it now does not apply outside EMU and even there it is not greatly used. To the likes of Dashwood, it has outlived its usefulness. The other is that the procedure merely offers the EP a greater, but still uncertain, chance of getting its ideas accepted. And this only happens if the Council agrees to co-operate in a complicated process involving two readings. In other words it is a decision-shaping facility and not a decision-taking one.

The first opportunity for legislation to emerge from the co-operation procedure comes after the EP has received a reasoned draft act. If the EP either accepts or ignores this it goes through anyway. In this first reading, the EP simply offers its opinion on the draft act. If the EP chooses it can by absolute majority propose amendments. These can be absorbed by the Commission and then resubmitted to the Council, along with any it prefers not to accept. The Council then requires only QMV to accept this but unanimity to overrule it and substitute a version of its own. In other words, the barrier for rejecting the EP's contribution is raised but not eliminated. And, unless acting by simple majority it agrees to extend the time, the Council can kill a revised bill by inaction. This was better than consultation although it offers the EP far less than does co-decision. So few tears were shed after Amsterdam upgraded most areas requiring the use of co-operation to co-decision.

The next two articles then return Chapter 2 to the mechanisms and forms of legislation. The first, *Article 253* (ex 190), established the manner in which Community acts (whoever originates them) have to be published. By requiring all acts to be accompanied by a

---

*Amsterdam extended co-decision to a number of existing provisions: 12, 18, 42, 46(2), 47, 71(1), 80, 148, 150(4), 156, 162, 172, 175 and 179. It also coupled it with various new provisions: 11, 129; 135, 141(3), 255; 280(4), 284 and 285.
†Co-decision at Nice was thus immediately extended to the following TEC articles: 13, 18, 65, 157, 159 and 191. It applies along with unanimity in the Council in Articles 42 and 151. Deferred co-decision and QMV articles are 62(2)(a), 62(3), 63(3)(b) and 67. The fact that an article is subject to co-decision also has implications for enhanced co-operation since, according to Article 11 TEC, the assent of the EP is needed to approve an experiment.

statement of reasons the article is not asking simply for a legalistic technicality but making an important constitutional point. This is that legislation cannot be based on whim or bureaucratic inertia but must have a specified motive and a factual context. It must have taken into account any obligatory consultations required by the TEC, such as those from the two consultative committees discussed below. Implicitly, this gives the ECJ the right to strike down acts which do not satisfy these criteria and in which the reasons behind an act are vague, inadequate or even totally absent. For some this is the beginning of a commitment to transparency, one emphasized at Maastricht by Declaration No. 17 TEU and at Amsterdam by the introduction of Article 255 and Declaration No. 39 TA on the quality of the drafting of legislation. Others are less certain, especially as Article 253 does not apply to member-state acts, even those in Community spheres of activity. In any case, it explains why so much EC legislation starts rather tediously by listing treaty articles, previous decisions and inputs from other bodies.

This is followed in *Article 254* (ex 191) by rules on where and how the final version of an act, and its rationale, have to be published. All co-decision acts have to be signed by the presidents of the Council and the EP, symbolizing the dual legitimacy of such acts. There is also implicit reference to the procedure used to adopt the act in question. Once signed they are then published in the *Official Journal* and here Nice has made its only change to the chapter, replacing 'Community' by 'Union' in the *Official Journal*'s title. This, which has already been trailed where the auditors are concerned, reinforces our contention that everyday usage is increasingly using 'Union' to describe the whole integration process. Now, irrespective of the actual source of the legislation and other material involved, it all comes out under the Union's umbrella.

Publication of most kinds of act, as paragraph 2 shows, can also often trigger automatic implementation thanks to the timetable contained here. However, legislation can propose a staggered timetable for activation in order to make things easier for national administrations. Publication in the *Official Journal* for generally applicable acts or by direct notification is thus required. Other provisions cover the enforcement of acts which are binding on member states. So paragraph 3 explains why some directives have not been published in the past.

At this point Amsterdam, in a further attempt to respond to post-Maastricht concerns for public understanding of the Union in general and to ECJ cases such as *Carvel* v. *Council* (1995) in particular, interposes a new *Article 255* on transparency. Paragraph 1 sets out a general, albeit conditional, privilege of access to institutional documents for individuals and corporate bodies. However, non-EU citizens and bodies, even though resident in the Union, are excluded. The Council was given until May 2001 to draw up a code of practice for this, agreed by co-decision. However, each institution can add riders of its own, sometimes in Rules of Procedure, which further limits the generosity of the concession. And, under Declaration No. 35 TA, a member state may request that a document originating in it is not released. Hence in practice access is still conceded somewhat grudgingly and the article is a long way short of US-style absolute rights of information.

Thereafter *Article 256* (ex 192) ends the chapter by providing for enforcement of Community acts. This is a complicated legal complement to Article 249 spelling out what happens when such acts impose financial obligations. It deals with acts which apply to individuals or corporate bodies, and brings their enforcement into line with national and EC law. Having thus clarified the legal status of Community acts, Part Five does not resolve some of the obscurities of Chapter 2 caused by its dyarchic patterns of decision-making. What it does do is to move on to clear up some institutional loose ends before considering the financing of the Community's activities. In any case, apparently technical matters such as co-decision do count. They can show where power lies and shape inter-institutional relations. And the density of these proposals are unparalleled among international organizations.

Chapter 2   Provisions common to several institutions

Article 249 (ex Article 189)

In order to carry out their task and in accordance with the provisions of this Treaty, the European Parliament acting jointly with the Council, the Council and the Commission shall make regulations and issue directives, take decisions, make recommendations or deliver opinions.

A regulation shall have general application. It shall be binding in its entirety and directly applicable in all Member States.

A directive shall be binding, as to the result to be achieved, upon each Member State to which it is addressed, but shall leave to the national authorities the choice of form and methods.

A decision shall be binding in its entirety upon those to whom it is addressed.

Recommendations and opinions shall have no binding force.

Article 250 (ex Article 189a)

1. Where, in pursuance of this Treaty, the Council acts on a proposal from the Commission, unanimity shall be required for an act constituting an amendment to that proposal, subject to Article 251(4) and (5).

2. As long as the Council has not acted, the Commission may alter its proposal at any time during the procedures leading to the adoption of a Community act.

Article 251 (ex Article 189b)

1. Where reference is made in this Treaty to this Article for the adoption of an act, the following procedure shall apply.

2. The Commission shall submit a proposal to the European Parliament and the Council.

The Council, acting by a qualified majority after obtaining the opinion of the European Parliament,
- if it approves all the amendments contained in the European Parliament's opinion, may adopt the proposed act thus amended;
- if the European Parliament does not propose any amendments, may adopt the proposed act;
- shall otherwise adopt a common position *and communicate it to the European Parliament*. The Council shall inform the European Parliament fully of the reasons which led it to adopt its common position. The Commission shall inform the European Parliament fully of its position.

If, within three months of such communication, the European Parliament:
(a) approves the common position *or has not taken a decision*, the act in question shall be deemed to have been adopted in accordance with that common position;
(b) rejects, *by an absolute majority of its component members, the common position, the proposed act shall be deemed not to have been adopted;*

(c) proposes amendments to the common position by an absolute majority of its component members, the amended text shall be forwarded to the Council and to the Commission, which shall deliver an opinion on those amendments.

3. If, within three months of the matter being referred to it, the Council, acting by a qualified majority, approves all the amendments of the European Parliament, **the act in question shall be deemed to have been adopted in the form of the common position thus amended;** however, the Council shall act unanimously on the amendments on which the Commission has delivered a negative opinion. If the Council does not approve **all the amendments,** the President of the Council, in agreement with the President of the European Parliament, shall **within six weeks** convene a meeting of the Conciliation Committee.

4. The Conciliation Committee, which shall be composed of the members of the Council or their representatives and an equal number of representatives of the European Parliament, shall have the task of reaching agreement on a joint text, by a qualified majority of the members of the Council or their representatives and by a majority of the representatives of the European Parliament. The Commission shall take part in the Conciliation Committee's proceedings and shall take all the necessary initiatives with a view to reconciling the positions of the European Parliament and the Council. **In fulfilling this task, the Conciliation Committee shall address the common position on the basis of the amendments proposed by the European Parliament.**

5. If, within six weeks of its being convened, the Conciliation Committee approves a joint text, the European Parliament, acting by an absolute majority of the votes cast, and the Council, acting by a qualified majority, shall **each** have a period of six weeks from that approval in which to adopt the act in question in accordance with the joint text. If either of the two institutions fails to approve the proposed act within that period, it shall be deemed not to have been adopted.

6. Where the Conciliation Committee does not approve a joint text, **the proposed act shall be deemed not to have been adopted.**

7. The periods of three months and six weeks referred to in this Article **shall** be extended by a maximum of one month and two weeks respectively **at the initiative** of the European Parliament **or** the Council.

Article 252 (ex Article 189c)

Where reference is made in this Treaty to this Article for the adoption of an act, the following procedure shall apply:

(a) The Council, acting by a qualified majority on a proposal from the Commission and after obtaining the opinion of the European Parliament, shall adopt a common position.

(b) The Council's common position shall be communicated to the European Parliament. The Council and the Commission shall inform the European Parliament fully of the reasons which led the Council to adopt its common position and also of the Commission's position.

If, within three months of such communication, the European Parliament approves this common position or has not taken a decision within that period, the Council shall definitively adopt the act in question in accordance with the common position.

(c) The European Parliament may, within the period of three months referred to in point (b), by an absolute majority of its component Members, propose amendments to the Council's common position. The European Parliament may also, by the same majority, reject the Council's common position. The result of the proceedings shall be transmitted to the Council and the Commission.

If the European Parliament has rejected the Council's common position, unanimity shall be required for the Council to act on a second reading.

(d) The Commission shall, within a period of one month, re-examine the proposal on the basis of which the Council adopted its common position, by taking into account the amendments proposed by the European Parliament.

The Commission shall forward to the Council, at the same time as its re-examined proposal, the amendments of the European Parliament which it has not accepted, and shall express its opinion on them. The Council may adopt these amendments unanimously.

(e) The Council, acting by a qualified majority, shall adopt the proposal as re-examined by the Commission. Unanimity shall be required for the Council to amend the proposal as re-examined by the Commission.

(f) In the cases referred to in points (c), (d) and (e), the Council shall be required to act within a period of three months. If no decision is taken within this period, the Commission proposal shall be deemed not to have been adopted.

(g) The periods referred to in points (b) and (f) may be extended by a maximum of one month by common accord between the Council and the European Parliament.

Article 253 (ex Article 190)

Regulations, directives and decisions adopted jointly by the European Parliament and the Council, and such acts adopted by the Council or the Commission, shall state the reasons on which they are based and shall refer to any proposals or opinions which were required to be obtained pursuant to this Treaty.

Article 254 (ex Article 191)

1. Regulations, directives and decisions adopted in accordance with the procedure referred to in Article 251 shall be signed by the President of the European Parliament and by the President of the Council and published in the *Official Journal of the European* **Union**. They shall enter into force on the date specified in them or, in the absence thereof, on the twentieth day following that of their publication.

2. Regulations of the Council and of the Commission, as well as directives of those institutions which are addressed to all Member States, shall be published in the *Official Journal of the European* **Union**. They shall enter into force on the date specified in them or, in the absence thereof, on the twentieth day following that of their publication.

3. Other directives, and decisions, shall be notified to those to whom they are addressed and shall take effect upon such notification.

Article 255 (new – TA)

1. Any citizen of the Union, and any natural or legal person residing or having its registered office in a Member State, shall have a right of access to European Parliament, Council and Commission documents, subject to the principles and the conditions to be defined in accordance with paragraphs 2 and 3.

2. General principles and limits on grounds of public or private interest governing this right of access to documents shall be determined by the Council, acting in accordance with the procedure referred to in Article 251 within two years of the entry into force of the Treaty of Amsterdam.

3. Each institution referred to above shall elaborate in its own Rules of Procedure specific provisions regarding access to its documents.

Article 256 (ex Article 192)

Decisions of the Council or of the Commission which impose a pecuniary obligation on persons other than States, shall be enforceable.

Enforcement shall be governed by the rules of civil procedure in force in the State in the territory of which it is carried out. The order for its enforcement shall be appended to the decision, without other formality than verification of the authenticity of the decision, by the national authority which the government of each Member State shall designate for this purpose and shall make known to the Commission and to the Court of Justice.

When these formalities have been completed on application by the party concerned, the latter may proceed to enforcement in accordance with the national law, by bringing the matter directly before the competent authority.

Enforcement may be suspended only by a decision of the Court of Justice. However, the courts of the country concerned shall have jurisdiction over complaints that enforcement is being carried out in an irregular manner.

Other Institutions

After dealing then with the main Community institutions and the way they interact to make decisions, the TEC goes on to signal the existence of three other organs which take up the last three chapters of Title I of Part Five. Two of these bodies are long established, the Economic and Social Committee (EcoSoc) dating back to the ECSC, and the European Investment Bank (EIB) due to Italian promptings at the time the TEC was originally being negotiated. The Committee of the Regions (CoR) is an upgrading of an earlier informal gathering formalized through the TEU. Two of them – EcoSoc and CoR – are advisory bodies and were set up ostensibly to assist the main institutions. Hence their position here is a further reminder that they are not of the same standing and influence as the 'big five' dealt with in Chapter 1. This part of the treaty also serves as a convenient place into which to fit the EIB. A more detached and technical body than the others, it was previously mentioned among the policies but because it is a functioning organ it was, logically enough, transferred here. And beyond this, there are a range of other agencies set up by the Community under powers bestowed by the treaties – examples including the European Environment Agency and the European Centre for the Development of Vocational Training – but not thought worthy of specific mention themselves.

In any case, the symbolism of this positioning has not always been welcomed by the three auxiliary bodies themselves. Indeed, all of them have sought to maintain and even increase their status in one way or another. This has led both to a certain tension and to a number of changes, notably to the Committee of the Regions, at Amsterdam and Nice. Here both the advisory committees also had their size recalibrated ahead of enlargement.

None the less, the individual chapters are relatively short while the provisions within them remain relatively limited and do not tell us a great deal about the actual workings and roles of the institutions. In fact they all have a part to play in EC politics and decision-making even if they have little place in the remaining structures of the Union.

The Economic and Social Committee

EcoSoc dates back to 1957, when it was introduced to represent what were seen, in the days of post-war consensus, as the forces which needed to be brought together to assist in building a new European order free of the class conflicts of the inter-war years. It echoes similar provisions in the constitutions of Benelux, France, Italy and, since 1973, Ireland. At first it exercised a certain influence but it was then eclipsed by the EP. Critics can therefore see it as either redundant or as an unwelcome reminder of corporatism which gives interest groups an unhealthy institutionalized influence. Supporters believe it provides both a valuable contact with the non-political world and a means of improving the drafting of EU legislation. The latter view seems to have carried the day, just.

Because it has survived and sometimes prospered, EcoSoc was given new rights of consultation at Amsterdam although not, as it wished, on employment and monetary matters. Prior to Nice the Commission saw it as a way of increasing the influence of civil society and suggested both capping its size ahead of enlargement, at perhaps 244, and of changing its basis of membership to get away from strict categories and member-state domination. Equally it wanted it to have more freedom to pronounce on relevant matters.

In the event the IGC only went some way towards satisfying such aspirations. To begin with it decided to cap the membership at a much higher level than the Commission suggested so as to avoid requiring further sacrifices of the existing member states. The latter were allowed to keep their present allocations, which many already found a little constricting given the need equally to represent the Committee's three broad constituencies. Similar proportions were followed in suggested allocations to candidate countries. Moreover, there was a feeling that if major changes were made to EcoSoc the same concessions would have to be made to the more assertive Committee of the Regions, thereby disturbing the existing political balances. All this meant that no change was made to the basis of selection except that alternate nominations were done away with. And although the Committee's rights of consultation were slightly extended in the social field, it found itself faced with a new rival in the new Social Protection Committee.

What we now find in Chapter 4 is a relatively brief series of articles dealing with status, membership, organization and rights, but not much else. *Article 257* (ex 193) begins by requiring the establishment of EcoSoc, as if it were a novelty and irrespective of the reference to it in Article 7(2). More significantly, the article reasserts EcoSoc's consultative nature. However, this is slightly qualified elsewhere as in Article 198, where consultation is made mandatory.*

The article then goes on to specify the kind of socio-economic and other interests EcoSoc is supposed to represent. Since Nice the reference to members coming from various 'activities' has been replaced by a reference to their being drawn not just from

---

*Consultation was previously required in Articles 40, 44, 52, 71, 80, 93, 94, 95, 128, 129, 137, 140, 141, 144, 148, 149, 150, 152, 153, 156, 157, 159, 161, 162, 166, 172 and 175. The precise extent of coverage was then changed at Nice in Articles 137, 157, 159, 161 and 175.

'civil society' but from its 'organized' elements. This latter insertion would seem to underline the rights of employers' organizations, professional bodies and unions at the expense of ordinary society. Moreover, as well as maintaining the rather old-fashioned descriptions of 'dealers' and 'carriers' the Nice revisions replace 'representatives of the general public' by the 'general interest'. And even though this apparent disdain for the grass roots might be thought to be offset by the addition of consumers, this probably refers to office holders in consumer organizations rather than the average shopper. In fact tradition rather than law has it that the membership is divided equally among three broad constituencies: employers, workers, and other economic actors, including agriculture and the professions. Consumers would presumably fit into the third group. In practice half the employers come from industry and most of the workers' representatives from trade unions.

The next two articles go further into membership by specifying national quotas, most of which are divisible by three so as to allow equal representation of the triad of socio-economic categories already mentioned.* *Article 258* (ex 194) introduces a new paragraph setting an upper limit of 350 on the size of the committee. This is less than half that of the EP, whereas it had been suggested earlier in 2000 that a third would be a more appropriate size. In the event the proposed allocations will only come to 344, which may be inside the new cap but is a figure which, like that of the Committee of the Regions, may easily become confused with the Council's 345 votes.

The final element of the article was not changed at Nice and continues to insist on the fact that member states and organized interests are not to give their representatives orders which prevent them from saying what they think. While in line with democratic practice, and the 'general interest of the Community', we might still ask what the use of trade unionists or farmers who do not speak for their constituencies might be. This is particularly so when we remember that this replaced a statement that members were there simply in a personal capacity. The reference to a general interest reinforces the argument that EcoSoc does represent the 'live social forces' of the Community. This may suggest an acceptance that the Community is not just a matter of states. Hence, although members are part-time they can be paid expenses and compensation for loss of earnings. The article's previous reference to terms of office was transferred at Nice to the following clause.

Article 259 (ex 195) was, in fact, altered drastically at Nice. It now starts by specifying the term of office and making it clear that member states propose names. However, there is now no reference to asking member states to provide a list of twice as many 'nationals' as the member state had places, which had been done to allow for full representation if nominal representatives were otherwise engaged. Equally the obligation of consulting the Commission and European organizations if it so wished (which it rarely did), is also dropped. Nor is there any reference to ensuring equal representation of the various interests. Having somewhat widened the scope of membership the old rigid divisions may no longer have seemed appropriate. Yet, while this gives the member states a bit more freedom of choice, they now could face a potential obstacle to the acceptance of their choices. This is because the Council will now act by QMV not unanimity in adopting the collective lists of names. As before, terms of office can be extended without apparent limitation.

---

*This is not wholly true of the allocations proposed in Declaration No. 20 TN, point 3. These will give Poland 21, Romania 15, Bulgaria, the Czech Republic and Hungary 12 each, Slovakia and Lithuania 9 apiece and Cyprus 6, but the luckless Slovenes, Latvians and Estonians (7 each), and Malta (5) will have to deny one lobby an equal share of seats.

This is followed by another pair of articles, this time dealing with the organization of EcoSoc and neither of which was changed at Nice. *Article 260* (ex 196) allows the committee to appoint a chairman and officers, which may suggest a wish to limit its aspirations. Certainly it is much more limp and vague than the French phrasing, which uses the more usual title of president and talks of a 'bureau', which is a collective organism, or steering committee, and not just a set of individual office holders. Thanks to Maastricht, details of this can be decided by EcoSoc on its own. Equally, the right to meet without being instructed to do so by someone else is symbolically important, even though either the Council or Commission could summon it should they ever choose so to do. Meeting on its own initiative is the normal way.

Moreover, since Amsterdam EcoSoc is no longer bound by the requirement to have agricultural and transport subsections. It still has to have appropriate specialist sections – past examples including energy and nuclear, economy and finance, industry and commerce, social questions, external relations, regional development, environment, and health and consumer affairs – to prepare draft opinions for consideration by the whole Committee (Article 261). The nature of these subsections, as well as other such bodies, can be laid down autonomously through the Rules of Procedure. This facility could well prove useful now that Nice has opened up membership of the Committee. Subcommittees can also be similarly established and, although they cannot take unilateral action, their views have to be laid before the Council and Commission. By implication the full EcoSoc has to approve what is said on its behalf or, at least, not object to it. Given the fuss about the shared Secretariat with the Committee of the Regions it is surprising that there is no mention of such administrative services, either here or, even more surprisingly, in Chapter 4. This is out of line with the provisions made for the five key institutions. It may, therefore, be a silent symbol of the lesser status of the two committees.

Finally, *Article 262* (ex 198) specifies the importance of EcoSoc's consultative opinions. In some cases these are specified by the TEC but the Council and Commission are also free to ask for a view if they so choose. Amsterdam gave the EP the same right, as the last paragraph of the article shows. However, the Council and the Commission can set a deadline for a reply and can also proceed if the Committee does not produce its advice in time. It is unclear that the EP can yet do the same. This betrays the fact that the Committee was originally envisaged as a means of providing the Council and the Commission with helpful advice.

More significantly, the right to produce own-initiative opinions is recognized here. This allows the Committee to comment on things which it thinks important even if the other institutions do not want to know. The wording of the paragraph suggests that they cannot resist an 'own-initiative' report as this has to be laid before them, even if they do not act on it. In practice many of the Committee's reports, of which it produces between 150 and 200 each year, whether mandatory or optional, are ignored. The Committee also provides information, liaises with other bodies, promotes sectional understanding and publicizes the views of the interests it represents.

Despite all this, and despite some outside support, EcoSoc has never succeeded in forcing itself into the inner decision-making triangle, notwithstanding Declaration No. 22 TEU. Its role, in other words, is somewhat ritualistic. And its likely expansion may make it more representative but not more effective. Hence its rivalry with the Committee of the Regions, to which the treaty now turns, may well continue.

Chapter 3   The Economic and Social Committee

Article 257 (ex Article 193)

An Economic and Social Committee is hereby established. It shall have advisory status.

The Committee shall consist of representatives of the various **economic and social components of organised civil society,** and in particular representatives of producers, farmers, carriers, workers, dealers, craftsmen, professional occupations, **consumers and the general interest.**

Article 258 (ex Article 194)

The number of members of the Economic and Social Committee shall not exceed 350.

The number of members of the Committee shall be as follows:

Belgium	12
Denmark	9
Germany	24
Greece	12
Spain	21
France	24
Ireland	9
Italy	24
Luxembourg	6
Netherlands	12
Austria	12
Portugal	12
Finland	9
Sweden	12
United Kingdom	24

The members of the Committee may not be bound by any mandatory instructions. They shall be completely independent in the performance of their duties, in the general interest of the Community.

The Council, acting by a qualified majority, shall determine the allowances of members of the Committee.

Article 259 (ex Article 195)

1. *The members of the Committee shall be appointed for four years,* **on proposals from the Member States. The Council, acting by a qualified majority, shall adopt the list of members drawn up in accordance with the proposals made by each Member State.** *The term of office of the members of the Committee shall be renewable.*

2. The Council shall consult the Commission. It may obtain the opinion of European bodies which are representatives of the various economic and social sectors to which the activities of the Community are of concern.

Article 260 (ex Article 196)

The Committee shall elect its chairman and officers from among its members for a term of two years. It shall adopt its Rules of Procedure.

The Committee shall be convened by its chairman at the request of the Council or of the Commission. It may also meet on its own initiative.

Article 261 (ex Article 197, simplified)

The Committee shall include specialised sections for the principal fields covered by this Treaty.

These specialised sections shall operate within the general terms of reference of the Committee. They may not be consulted independently of the Committee.

Subcommittees may also be established within the Committee to prepare on specific questions or in specific fields, draft opinions to be submitted to the Committee for its consideration.

The Rules of Procedure shall lay down the methods of composition and the terms of reference of the specialised sections and of the subcommittees.

Article 262 (ex Article 198)

The Committee must be consulted by the Council or by the Commission where this Treaty so provides. The Committee may be consulted by these institutions in all cases in which they consider it appropriate. It may issue an opinion on its own initiative in cases in which it considers such action appropriate.

The Council or the Commission shall, if it considers it necessary, set the Committee, for the submission of its opinion, a time-limit which may not be less than one month from the date on which the chairman receives notification to this effect. Upon expiry of the time-limit, the absence of an opinion shall not prevent further action.

The opinion of the Committee and that of the specialised section, together with a record of the proceedings, shall be forwarded to the Council and to the Commission.

The Committee may be consulted by the European Parliament.

The Committee of the Regions

Although the Committee of the Regions appears in the treaty as virtually the twin of EcoSoc, in practice there has been plenty of sibling rivalry between them. This reflects the fact that the former is one of the newest EU bodies and it is certainly among the most assertive, for all that it is only consultative. The CoR was set up as an unofficial body by the Commission in the 1980s and then, thanks to the rise of the growing influence of subnational political forces in western Europe, was formalized at Maastricht. It was made a separate body rather than a subsection of EcoSoc as had once been considered, but its autonomy was limited by being forced to share administrative services with the older body. This caused tension.

This was due, in part, to the fact that the CoR symbolized for many a possible move to a 'Europe of the Regions' and a new form of democratic representation. Hence there has been talk of the CoR becoming a second parliamentary chamber speaking for new political forces. Ahead of Nice, the Commission canvassed the idea of calculating its membership on a similar basis to that of the EP. In practice it was able to exploit such feelings as well as its own dynamism. Hence, it was able to overcome UK ideas of nominating ministers with regional responsibilities to it. Equally, it was able to establish its case for its administrative independence from EcoSoc, especially in its administrative provisions. This was conceded by the 1996 IGC.

Amsterdam in the event gave the CoR only some of what it had wanted, a cause of some disappointment. For instance there was no recognition of its elective basis. None the less, it did gain the right to its own Secretariat, saw dual membership with the EP ruled out and was allowed to adopt its own Rules of Procedure. Equally, it gained extra rights of consultation. But neither in 1997 nor in 2000 did it receive full institutional status, which was a very urgent claim. In 1997 this was to an extent because the German *Länder* were by then more interested in using domestic and other EU channels to achieve their ends. However, Nice was more sympathetic to the CoR, writing in the need for an elective mandate, changing the nature of its appointment system and further extending its consultative role. At the same time the CoR, like EcoSoc, saw its size altered ahead of enlargement. However, these changes were not quite what the Commission and the CoR had wanted. And, in any case, textually the CoR provisions remain very much modelled on those of EcoSoc.

Article 263 (ex 198a) formally establishes the CoR and gives it a name and status. This is despite the fact that these things were done in 1993 and are consecrated in Article 7(2) TEC. Presumably the repetition of its advisory status is meant as something of a warning. However, since Nice there is now a requirement that members must have been elected to subnational office or enjoy similar status. This means that their basic salaries are paid by their authorities rather than the Union. And, later in the fourth paragraph, it is made clear that as soon as members lose their elected seat, they have to give up their place on the Committee. This can be seen as a gesture towards the democratic deficit but it also gives the Committee a bargaining chip in its search for extra power. It allows the CoR to claim that it represents an important democratic interest within the Community. No guidance is given on what the split between local and regional representation should be, even though this has caused some tensions inside the Committee since leaders of big regions like Catalonia have a very different standing and very different interests from communal councillors for instance.

Following on the EcoSoc provisions, the article now lays down an absolute ceiling on membership of 350 and Point 4 of Declaration No. 20 TN makes it clear that the actual figure will be 344. Whether this will dilute its claim to institutional promotion is not clear. Within these targets, the same allocations already noted apply, although the argument that they need to be divisible by three is not applicable. There was no response to Commission views that the Committee really needed a different basis because the regional structure of Europe was so different from that of society.

When it comes to appointments member states still have to present two lists to ensure that stand-ins are available should domestic obligations prevent attendance. This used to be the case with EcoSoc but after Nice is not so. Whether this means that the negotiators implicitly accepted the CoR's claims and saw subnational posts as more demanding than those of trade union leaders and business executives is unclear. In any case, what happens is that member states make proposals, these are then amalgamated and the resulting list is approved by QMV. This is presumably in line with changes elsewhere. Some authorities think that member states have, none the less, forfeited their ability to query lists from other member states because of the new formulation.

In any case, names proposed on the lists cannot be MEPs for democratic reasons. The term is, again, for four years but can be renewed. Where members lose their seats after electoral defeat at home the basic selection process would seem to have to be invoked rather than allowing alternates to serve out the term. The article ends by insisting on the independence of members but, again, justifies this in terms of the general Community interest. This too could be read as implying a recognition of the fact that the Union is made up not only of member states but of other territorial interests.

This is followed by a brief *Article 264* (ex 198b) which sets out rules for the operation and leadership of the Committee. This, in the English version, is again to be led by a chairman and officers. Equally, it too can adopt its Rules of Procedure without reference to the Council. However, the latter also shares with the Commission the right to summon it, as is the case with EcoSoc. The two-year term, with no mention of re-election, has one advantage over its fellow Committee, allowing the post to be shared between regional and local representatives over the four-year term. Also, there is no mention of internal sections although these now exist, as do loose political groupings.

Finally, *Article 265* (ex 198c) deals with the CoR's consultative role. It requires that Council and Commission must consult the CoR where the treaty directs, as well as when they consider it appropriate.* Amsterdam highlighted the need to consult on cross-border questions but not, as some would have liked, on subsidiarity. It also has a right to comment on matters referred to EcoSoc, a reflection of its concern for its status. At the same time Amsterdam wrote in the right of the EP to consult it. Nice extended its rights of consultation to social exclusion and social protection.

Beyond formal consultation, the CoR can also issue an opinion when it feels there are regional issues involved in matters referred to EcoSoc. All its opinions are forwarded to Council and Commission in just the same way as those of EcoSoc. It remains to be seen, however, whether the former make more use of them than they have done in the past. For all the changes made at Nice the willingness of the other institutions to allow the CoR to become a meaningful part of the real decision-making process remains to be proved. So there is no certainty that the CoR will in the future either replace EcoSoc or gain institutional and political promotion.

Chapter 4   The Committee of the Regions

Article 263 (ex Article 198a)

A Committee, *hereinafter referred to as the 'Committee of the Regions', consisting of representatives of regional and local bodies* who either hold a regional or local authority electoral mandate or are politically accountable to an elected assembly, is hereby established with advisory status.

The number of members of the Committee of the Regions shall not exceed 350.

The number of members of the Committee shall be as follows:

Belgium	12
Denmark	9
Germany	24
Greece	12
Spain	21

*Previously the treaty provided for the CoR to be consulted under Articles 128, 129, 137, 148, 149, 150, 151, 152, 156, 159, 161, 162 and 175. Nice slightly altered the Committee's rights under articles 137, 159, 161 and 175.

France	24
Ireland	9
Italy	24
Luxembourg	6
Netherlands	12
Austria	12
Portugal	12
Finland	9
Sweden	12
United Kingdom	24

The members of the Committee and an equal number of alternate members shall be appointed for four years on proposals from the respective Member States. Their term of office shall be renewable. **The Council, acting by a qualified majority, shall adopt the list of members and alternate members drawn up in accordance with the proposals made by each Member State. When the mandate referred to in the first paragraph on the basis of which they were proposed comes to an end, the term of office of members of the Committee shall terminate automatically and they shall then be replaced for the remainder of the said term of office in accordance with the same procedure. No member of the Committee shall at the same time be a Member of the European Parliament.**

The members of the Committee may not be bound by any mandatory instructions. They shall be completely independent in the performance of their duties, in the general interest of the Community.

Article 264 (ex Article 198b)

The Committee of the Regions shall elect its chairman and officers from among its members for a term of two years.

It shall adopt its Rules of Procedure.

The Committee shall be convened by its chairman at the request of the Council or of the Commission. It may also meet on its own initiative.

Article 265 (ex Article 198c)

The Committee of the Regions shall be consulted by the Council or by the Commission where this Treaty so provides and in all other cases, **in particular those which concern cross-border co-operation,** in which one of these two institutions considers it appropriate.

The Council or the Commission shall, if it considers it necessary, set the Committee, for the submission of its opinion, a time-limit which may not be less than one month from the date on which the chairman receives notification to this effect. Upon expiry of the time-limit, the absence of an opinion shall not prevent further action.

Where the Economic and Social Committee is consulted pursuant to Article 262, the Committee of the Regions shall be informed by the Council or the Commission of the request for an opinion. Where it considers that specific regional interests are involved, the Committee of the Regions may issue an opinion on the matter.

The Committee of the Regions may be consulted by the European Parliament.

It may issue an opinion on its own initiative in cases in which it considers such action appropriate.

The opinion of the Committee, together with a record of the proceedings, shall be forwarded to the Council and to the Commission.

The European Investment Bank

The European Investment Bank (EIB) is a very different kind of body from EcoSoc and the CoR, and one only recently inserted in Part Five. The move has not affected its status for, while it is picked out as a body in its own right, it is separated from the other monetary organs. Nor does it have a close relationship to mainstream decision-making processes. It thus remains a largely autonomous and freestanding body dedicated to carrying out developmental investment within less favoured regions of the Community and abroad, both in central and eastern Europe and in the developing world. This is in line with indications in the preamble and Article 3 TEC.

The Bank has always been insistent on its freedom of action although it is very clearly subject to the treaty. However, Amsterdam and Nice have brought it a little closer into the overall institutional pattern of the EU. Thus the former required it in Article 248(3) to come to a multilateral agreement about supplying information to the Court of Auditors. If it failed to negotiate this the Court could simply requisition the details it needed. Otherwise it looks to its own external audit since its dealings are often confidential and reflect its own judgments and not those of the Community institutions.

Article 266 (ex 198d) does not actually create the Bank since this has been done in Article 9 TEC which, like Article 266, also draws attention to the provisions governing its activities contained in the Protocol on the Statute of the European Investment Bank. Instead it gives it legal personality even though the Union as such does not have this. However, without this right to make legally binding and internationally respected acts, the Bank could not safely conduct its business. It has to be able to enter into contracts and to pursue those who default on their loans. When the article talks of the member states being 'members' of the Bank it means that they are the investors although, in fact, most of the EIB's funds are not donated but raised on the capital markets since the Bank has the very high credit rating of AAA.

Nice provided a further reminder of the Bank's long-established statute. In seeking flexibility ahead of enlargement, it allowed the Bank, or the Commission, to propose changes to the decision-making provisions of the statute. However, this remains subject to unanimous approval by the Council after consultation. Otherwise the wording is the same as was agreed for changes to the ECJ statute. The statute provides for a board of governors, drawn from national finance ministers, which lays down broad targets and guidelines for lending; a board of nationally nominated part-time directors who make individual decisions on lending; and a supervisory management committee which handles day-to-day matters. Normally these are decided by simple majority vote but this might not be appropriate in the future. The expectation is that the Bank will come forward with suggestions for change once Nice is ratified.

Article 267 (ex 198e) then provides a threefold rationale for the bank: assisting less developed regions (which was its original purpose); helping to modernize the Community economy (notably in communications, environment and industrial competitiveness); and supporting projects which are of interest to more than one country. This last has allowed it to move into financing projects outside the existing member states. Two means are specified for achieving these aims: making loans and guaranteeing other investments. In other words, it can give the backing of its high credit rating to other people's investments, as it did with the Channel Tunnel. Indeed, it never lends more than half of a project's costs, a fact which may help to explain why it is also required to co-operate with other relevant EC funds and policies. This points us to the budgetary regulations which follow Chapter 5.

Chapter 5   The European Investment Bank

Article 266 (ex Article 198d)

The European Investment Bank shall have legal personality.

The members of the European Investment Bank shall be the Member States.

The Statute of the European Investment Bank is laid down in a Protocol annexed to this Treaty. **The Council, acting unanimously, at the request of the European Investment Bank and after consulting the European Parliament and the Commission, or at the request of the Commission and after consulting the European Parliament and the European Investment Bank, may amend Articles 4, 11 and 12 and Article 18(5) of the Statute of the Bank.**

Article 267 (ex Article 198e)

The task of the European Investment Bank shall be to contribute, by having recourse to the capital market and utilising its own resources, to the balanced and steady development of the common market in the interest of the Community. For this purpose the Bank shall, operating on a non-profit-making basis, grant loans and give guarantees which facilitate the financing of the following projects in all sectors of the economy:

(a) projects for developing less-developed regions;
(b) projects for modernising or converting undertakings or for developing fresh activities called for by the progressive establishment of the common market, where these projects are of such a size or nature that they cannot be entirely financed by the various means available in the individual Member States;
(c) projects of common interest to several Member States which are of such a size or nature that they cannot be entirely financed by the various means available in the individual Member States.

In carrying out its task, the Bank shall facilitate the financing of investment programmes in conjunction with assistance from the Structural Funds and other Community financial instruments.

xxviii   Financial Provisions

Institutions, like policies, need money to make sure they work. Hence the TEC has always had a financial element. And, because money matters, it is rewarded with a separate title. The financial arrangements of the Community matter in at least three ways. To begin with, they say much about the nature of the Community as an organism. What we find is a means of providing monies for agreed activities. The Community budget, in other words, does not really play the wider social and economic roles that national budgets do. Secondly, financing arrangements indicate the major policy objectives of the Community and its member states. And, although the treaty does not make this clear, spending priorities are still skewed. Thirdly, control of Community financing is a major area of conflict both among the member states and between the member states as a whole and the institutions, and notably the EP. The scale of contributions is a matter of real concern for the member states. The EP, as Nicoll and Salmon say, does not vote 'supply' as is the case in representative national democracies but is only consulted on aspects of expenditure. This has always galled it.

However, although quite detailed, Title II does not tell us everything we need to know about Community financing. What the treaty offers are definitions of the budget, the procedures by which it is to be agreed and the forms of accountability which it requires. Important though these are, they leave aside some of the major elements of actual Community financing. These have developed out of some of the difficulties arising from the treaty provisions. Because of the reticences of the member states these have yet to be added to the treaty. So neither Amsterdam nor Nice made major changes to the extensive reworking agreed at Maastricht.

The first four articles of the title make it clear what the Community budget is supposed to be. They thus offer us a kind of definition. *Article 268* (ex 199) begins by indicating the scope and nature of the budget. By doing this it makes the point that Community financing is subject to the rule of law and has to be accounted for. Implicitly there are, as Laffan and others point out, five basic budgetary principles: universality, unity, annuality, specificity and equilibrium. Of these the last is perhaps the most revealing of the nature of the Community and its financing.

Initially, the article provides that all Community finances have to be included in the estimates. In other words, the budget is to be 'universal'. This point is reinforced firstly by the mention of European Social Fund expenditure and secondly by the Maastricht addition of references to the administrative costs of the two inter-governmental pillars. Operational expenditure is then given a formal opt-out from the principle of universality. Interestingly neither the drafters nor the simplifiers of Amsterdam thought fit to amend the reference to 'co-operation in the fields of justice and home affairs' to bring this into line with the changes then made to the third pillar. However, universality is not as complete as this might suggest since, in practice, ECSC finances, the funding of Europol, capital provision for the EIB and member-state aid and other payments to third world countries are all excluded. The EP believes that the budget should be all-inclusive.

The article also speaks of one set of estimates, making it clear that there is one Community budget and not a series of forms of financing by institution or sector. This 'unity' makes estimation much easier. And, according to the treaty, these estimates have to be annual. In other words, decisions have to be made every year and the Community is not granted ongoing, uncontrolled, rights of revenue raising and expenditure. In this the TEC reflects the normal practice in Western democracies. However, the bitter arguments that purely annual budgets generated in periods of financial stringency and argument over the UK contribution led the EC to go outside the treaty provisions and move away from over-reliance on annual financing.

So today practice is different. In fact, since 1988 there have been a series of multiannual financial frameworks, known as 'perspectives' and agreed by the member states collectively and implemented in part by inter-institutional agreements. Although the latter have not always worked nor given the EP all it wanted, overall the system has, from the 1990s, created what Laffan has described as 'budgetary peace'. The first two of these perspectives, in 1988 and 1992, were known as the Delors I and Delors II packages while the third was agreed at Berlin in spring 2000 following the Commission's Agenda 2000 paper. It runs until 2006 and makes the first allowances for the costs of enlargement.

Financial perspectives lay down monetary ceilings and targets for varying forms of expenditure and the annual budget has to be established within these guidelines. This seems somewhat unconstitutional and there was pressure at Maastricht to write them into the treaty.* However, this was rejected since nobody wanted to complicate an already tense situation with bitter arguments about money, especially as the first package was so new and experimental. Like their successors at Amsterdam the negotiators preferred to leave monetary questions for separate solution at the due time, in this case under the German presidency in early 2000.

The fourth principle, 'specification' means that all sums must be spent on identified purposes and not vaguely appropriated. Equally, the idea that expenditure must derive from a legal base is implicit in the article. Since 1982, in fact, there has been no spending without legal authority. This has given rise to what are known as 'budgetary lines', specifying that monies can legally be spent in given areas.

Finally, the article also requires the budget to be balanced. This 'equilibrium' provision, which is becoming fashionable in member-state financing, means that the Community must run neither at a profit nor at a loss. It must only have enough incoming finance to ensure that agreed activities can be carried out. In other words, the term is used here to indicate that the budget is essentially concerned with funding the agreed expenditures of the Union. Indeed, as we will see, facilities which potentially go beyond this, such as what have become known as 'own resources', were only introduced to help balance the budget when existing inputs failed, and not to achieve other goals.

In other words, the Community budget is not a full budget in the classic sense. Thus the EC has no fiscal policy, no borrowing rights and no social and economic management roles. Its purpose is therefore not really to redistribute resources across the Union, though the cohesion policy does do a little of this, nor is it intended to make up the incomes of less fortunate social groups. Similarly, it is not a tool for stabilizing the European economies, damping them down when they are in danger of overheating or stimulating them when they are falling into recession. Though many would like to see this, the budget is too small and too constrained to be able to carry out such tasks openly and effectively.

While the budget does have wider implications, in conception the treaty sees it as essentially an agreed statement that monies will be made available to meet the expenditure necessary to achieve the Community's ends. Or, as Westlake puts it, the EC budget is the reverse of a national budget. This is because it starts with expenditure and then finds revenue for it. Such facts show how far the Community is from being an autonomous state. Indeed, at first, it was funded simply by *ex gratia* payments from the member states.

This proved to be neither terribly efficient nor in keeping with growing EC ambitions. It was felt that the Community should have more reliable revenue. Hence from 1970 the

---

*It is worth noting that Declaration No. 8 TN (relating to Article 137) specifically refers to the perspectives, giving it a kind of treaty base. There are other precedents for this.

treaty was altered to give the EC its 'own resources'. And *Article 269* (ex 201) provides the legal basis for this form of financial support. However, they are only partly the Community's 'own' in the sense that these are monies which the member states agree to transfer permanently to the EC even though they originate in, and are collected by, the member states. This fact lay behind Mrs Thatcher's demands to 'give us our money back'. In other words, the Community does not have its own tax-raising powers, although the Belgian presidency somewhat unsuccessfully tried to float the idea in the second half of 2001.

Since 1970 therefore, when the initial system of funding by member-state donations was ended, the treaty has made clear that all expenditure must be met from funds which have been made over to the EC. This rules out reliance on handouts from rich member states which might thus gain leverage over policy-making even though it is the member states who actually collect and pass on the revenues agreed. However, to give the Community some freedom of manoeuvre the exact form of 'own resources' is not specified. This proved wise since, in the 1980s the Community found it extremely hard to keep the budget in balance and had to resort to a number of stratagems to do so. These included using what was known as a 'negative reserve', changing the rates of growth figures and postponing expenditure.

Even this was not enough and the member states had to put their hands in their pockets on occasions. This helped Mrs Thatcher in her battle to get a rebate on the UK budgetary contribution but in the end it forced the Community to invent a new GDP-related payment. It also promoted an increasing concern for budgetary discipline so as to ensure that this sort of thing did not happen again. And, in fact, since the late 1980s, the Community has rarely spent its full allowance, a fact which has encouraged the budgetary peace.

At present the 'own resources' consist of the product of levies on imported agricultural produce, customs duties charged under the CCT, a small share of VAT and the GDP-based contribution, in ascending order of importance. In fact the last mentioned now accounts for almost half the EC's income, having replaced VAT as the main contributor in recent years. The reference to other revenues is to take account of the fact that the Community does receive miscellaneous payments over and above those actually agreed and helps to maintain the principles of universality and specificity.

Decisions about own resources are made by the member states in Council. Because of the importance of money they both decide unanimously and seek national ratification. The EP is merely consulted, giving it little influence whereas national parliaments normally provide government revenue or 'vote supply' as it is technically known. This means that it has less control over spending than its national counterparts, a fact the treaty makes very clear. In other words, as has often been pointed out, the EC has representation without taxation.

Thereafter *Article 270* (ex 201a) writes in the guarantees of budgetary discipline and balance agreed in 1988. It does this by requiring the Commission to ensure that there is room in the budget (whether annual or, presumably, medium-term) for any new or altered proposals. Equally, Declaration 18 TEU notes the Commission's acceptance that it should assess the impact of its proposals on the public finances and economies of the member states. All this ties in with the developing concern for sound financial management much championed by the United Kingdom.

Finally, in this first element of the title, *Article 271* (ex 202) continues to regulate the expenditure side of the budget by emphasizing annuality. However, the reference to rules made under Article 279 – rather than Article 269 because this is a matter of financial control rather than revenue raising – provides some legal cover for the financial perspectives. Equally, save where salaries are concerned, the Community is allowed to carry forward any unspent balances. We should also note that money can be formally committed in one year but actually spent in another since it is not always possible to spend credits at once. Institutions and programmes cannot always physically absorb the amounts of money to which they are entitled.

The article also outlines the heads of expenditure, which are in part determined by the institutions which incur them as well as by function. Although there is no mention of the crucial distinction between compulsory expenditure (CE) and non-compulsory expenditure (NCE) the implication is, again, that there must be a legal basis for all expenditure, normally in the form of a policy decision under Part Four of the TEC. The two forms of expenditure differ politically, as Bainbridge points out. Compulsory spending is decided on by the Council and is deemed, by a 1982 agreement, to be that which is necessary to meet the EC's formal obligations both external and internal, including having an agricultural policy.

In the past this fact, which is supported by the more agrarian member states, fatally skewed the budget. In 1980 80% of the Community's spending went on CE, mostly on agriculture. It now amounts to about half the EC's outgoings leaving the EP with the last word on the rest of spending. This too has now become much more diverse involving external affairs, minor domestic policies and research spending. Administrative costs are, in comparison, relatively small. The question of whether the Community can move monies allocated for one purpose to another, known as the right of virement, is dealt with in Article 274. However, it cannot transfer monies from CE to NCE purposes.

While these first articles defining the budget are relatively brief, those on the budgetary process are much longer, albeit fewer in number. This is because the member states wished to control the way the money their taxpayers and consumers helped to raise was actually spent. In fact *Article* 272 (ex 203), which sets out the timetable and stages, takes up almost a third of Title II by itself. Even so, it can be said to be a somewhat approximate and legalistic guide to the financial decision-making process. The remaining two articles deal with the questions of what happens if the process breaks down and how, assuming this is not the case, the budget process is then actually put into action.

The first paragraph lays down that the EC's financial year is the calender year, thus avoiding favouring any more eccentric national precedents. The second, which starts the process as such, makes it clear that each institution has to take responsibility for its own expenditure needs. However, it is the Commission which turns these claims into a preliminary draft budget (PDB), where they are set against potential revenues. And it can call institutional claims into question by proposals of its own.

Paragraph 3 then sets out the timetable. The PDB has to be laid before the Council no later than 1 September. In fact, this does not give nearly enough time to get agreement by 31 December, so the Commission usually starts work in the early part of one year and submits its proposed draft budget to the Budget Council in May or June, recognizing that Brussels tends to shut down in August. The latter, after consulting the EP through what are known as concertation sessions, then produces a revised (and usually slimmed down) draft in July. However, it has to inform its institutional partners if it intends to diverge from the PDB. The revised budget, now a full draft budget (DB), is then submitted to the EP's Budget Committee and thence to a plenary meeting in October.

In coming to its decisions, the EP has to remember that it has authority over non-compulsory expenditure, but not over compulsory expenditures such as those on the CAP. It presently needs 314 votes to propose amendments to the first but only a majority of those voting to query the second. The difference is explained by the need to have a convincing mandate for any increase in NCE, a requirement perhaps somewhat at odds with normal national budgetary powers of parliaments. And the treaty gives it an incentive to make amendments since if it does not, the draft budget will anyway go into effect after some six weeks' delay.

The Council then has to reconsider the amended budget and requires a qualified majority to rule on EP amendments. It can accept expenditure-neutral amendments simply by not taking a vote whereas if it does the same to those changes which would increase expenditure, inaction leads to their rejection. Modification of EP amendments means that the resulting draft then returns to the EP for final approval in December. Within a fortnight it has either to vote by an enhanced majority of three-fifths of those voting to accept or, if it has a good case, it can reject it and ask for a new budget to be presented. The December session gives the EP another chance to press for higher NCE in further inter-institutional discussions. However, *Council* v. *European Parliament* (1992) suggests that the EP has to exercise its right to amend the revenue provisions carefully, keeping on the right side both of the law and the Council's own powers. Moreover, CE cannot be challenged at the second reading. Once agreement has been reached the EP's president formally announces that the budget is approved, in a ceremony known as 'signing off the budget', thus giving it a nominal democratic legitimacy.

Article 272(9) goes off on a slightly different tack since it concerns a ceiling on increases in NCE which the Commission has to set according to technical criteria before 1 May. These days this is rarely done though it was important in the 1980s when there were serious clashes between the EP and the Council. Since then, inter-institutional agreements, adopted within the context of the medium-term budgetary perspectives already noted, have taken the heat out of the situation. This is because the negotiation of inter-institutional agreements brings the parties together to agree on what is NCE and what the rate of growth should be. Once agreed these tend to be adhered to. Finally, in the tenth paragraph, all institutions are reminded of their duty to abide by the TEC and its strictures on equilibrium.

Because the budgetary process allows for rejection – something which happened on three occasions in the 1980s, including once over a supplementary budget – *Article 273* (ex 204) has since 1970 been needed to establish what happens when the budget is turned down. Otherwise there would be total inertia and crisis. The solution found is to allow the Community to spend for each month of the new year when there is no budget, one-twelfth of the previous year's expenditure. This prevents any escape from budgetary cuts. All this is provided both that such sums are not greater than what was proposed in the draft budget and that the Council does not expressly authorize extra spending. The EP is allowed to query such authorizations. As Nicoll points out, the system of twelfths can be constraining since expenditure varies throughout the year and the Commission could find itself with either too little or too much to see it through. In any case, because the EP's powers of amendment have grown in the 1990s it has become much less likely to reject the budget, since to do so would jeopardize its own spending priorities. This has made the budget less contentious in some ways although the EP would still like to have the ultimate control over all spending which it believes national parliaments have.

Passing the budget is of course not the end of the process. Once agreed it has to be put into effect. This, as *Article 274* (ex 205) makes clear, is up to the Commission. The latter is responsible for implementing, rather than managing the budget, the TEU adding a new caveat about doing this in a spirit of sound financial management. Both facts limit the Commission's ability to use its budgetary responsibilities for political purposes. Generally the Commission is made accountable for implementing the budget correctly and within the legal and policy frameworks laid down for it. These allow it to vire monies from one heading to another, reflecting the fact that the Community does not always spend up to the limits specified in the budget. However, all the other institutions also have to conform to such rules.

Mention of the Commission's own responsibility and the principles of sound financial management lead the title towards considerations of broader financial accountability and probity. This, which takes up the rest of Title II, is something that has become of increasing importance since the late 1970s. Hence, *Article 275* (ex 205a) requires an annual report to the Council and the EP on the way the budget was implemented. Since the budget has implications for the overall financial health of the Community the Commission also has to report on the Community's assets and liabilities. This it normally does as part of its regular financial report.

Although tersely and generally phrased, the article gives the EP what it has long desired, the oversight of budgetary outturns, something which most national parliaments enjoy. How it exercises it is made clear in *Article 276* (ex 206). To begin with it does so in conjunction with the Council and, since Amsterdam, with the Court of Auditors. Secondly, it can seek further information from the Commission, whether written or oral. On the basis of this it can give the Commission a discharge, that is to say a legitimizing statement that the budget has been properly and efficiently put into effect. This is now done on a sounder basis than in the past. It also means that there is more in the way of independent scrutiny of Community spending as both the United Kingdom and the EP have wanted. However, the text does not specify what happens if the EP refuses to grant a discharge.

The third paragraph then looks at what happens after discharge is given. The Commission is, in fact, required to act on recommendations made in the process of discharge. It can also, since Maastricht, be required to report formally on how it has responded to the criticisms made to it and what it did to ensure that other institutions did their duty. This means that there is double pressure on the Commission both in its own management and in its monitoring of the rest of the EC. The fact that such reports have to go before the auditors ensures that the pressure can be maintained.

Article 277 (ex 207) and *Article 278* (ex 208) next lay down rules for the way in which monies are actually paid to the Community. The former requires that the budget is denominated in 'units of account' rather than specifically either the ECU or, more importantly now, the euro. Using such units can be authorized by general financial regulations. The latter, which relates to surpluses generated by investments and the operational need to have funds available in different member states, is also now heading for virtual obsolescence given that since 2002 there are few member-state currencies into which the Commission may want to move funds. However, there could be a residual need for the article to cope with holdings of kroner, sterling, and possibly the currencies of acceding states in the future. Article 278 also makes it hard for the Commission to by-pass national treasuries in any such dealings.

The two final articles go back directly to questions of probity. *Article 279* (ex 209), which was amended at Nice, provides the basis for passing the more detailed financial regulations which have been invoked on several occasions in the title. Under the revised paragraph 1 the Council, after consulting the EP and the Court of Auditors, can issue rules on implementing, and reporting upon, the budget. The Council can also specify the responsibilities of budget holders and make provision for inspection of their accounts. All this is further testimony to growing concern for sound financial management, notably among the UK government. And, from 2007, such rules can be decided by QMV.

Nice also turned a previous subparagraph of the original article into a separate second numbered paragraph. This allows a unanimous Council to control exactly how monies are made available to the Commission, so as to ensure its cash flow. The revisions thus again point towards a desire to enhance financial probity. This was something championed by the Major government.

To underline this, at Amsterdam a revision was made to strengthen the old general invocation about combating fraud against the Community with the same vigour as if it were perpetrated against their own finances. *Article 280* (ex 209a) now, thanks to UK suggestions, requires not only specific national deterrent measures but also co-operation among national anti-fraud authorities. This comes on top of the more general provision on combating fraud contained in Article 29 TEU. At the same time the Community has, since Amsterdam, gained a new power to use co-decision to lay down measures which would ensure the same level of protection against fraud found within member states. However, these are not to infringe national practices and there has been no movement on the idea of creating a transnational EC prosecution service to deal with fraud. This is despite the way that the aftermath of the resignation of the Santer Commission in 1999 revealed the existence of major financial weaknesses in the Community. Probity, in other words, comes second to sovereignty.

Paragraph 5 does, however, make the Commission and the member states jointly responsible for monitoring and implementing the fight against fraud. Given this hesitation it is not surprising that there are still problems with fraud and, especially, with financial management. It remains to be seen how far the Kinnock reforms, launched in 2000, will be successful in dealing with this. These propose much clearer rules and responsibilities for Commission budget holders, of whom much more will be expected.

It also shows that the budget remains very much a matter of supporting EC expenditure and is not really a tool of wider social goals. It falls well short of the level of distribution felt necessary to address the real divergences between member states. In any case, the EC still spends less than many of its member states, even small ones like Denmark. However, it has implications for the type and range of economic policies pursued. And, although it is less dominated by the CAP than it used to be, the contrast between the Community's wider ambitions and its historically derived and sectorally supported patterns of spending remains problematic.

Hence, the budget remains a politically sensitive matter in a number of ways. It causes conflict between institutions with the EP seeking to increase its budgetary control and legitimacy. It can also cause discord between institutions and member states (notably on how far to use the budget to increase integration) and among the member states themselves. This depends on whether they are net contributors or not. Those that are, and they are an increasing number, wish to see some relief whereas those who have been beneficiaries wish to remain so. Hence there was great controversy when the 1998 report on 'Financing the Union' spelled out for the first time who the gainers and the losers really were. Arguments over this will intensify after enlargement in line with the prescriptions of Agenda 2000. The 'no' campaign in Ireland was well aware of this, despite its disclaimers, and Spanish reservations about cohesion funding, as already noted, reinforce this concern.

Given that, irrespective of its impact on existing member states, enlargement will have very severe implications for the budget, especially where agricultural and structural spending is concerned, arguments about financial arrangements could easily intensify in future. Money will continue to matter in a Union of 27, albeit in changing ways. So the budget is likely to remain a difficult area of the TEC. And it is not the last, since the final rounding off element of the TEC also has a few surprises of its own.

TITLE II

FINANCIAL PROVISIONS

Article 268 (ex Article 199)

All items of revenue and expenditure of the Community, including those relating to the European Social Fund, shall be included in estimates to be drawn up for each financial year and shall be shown in the budget.

Administrative expenditure occasioned for the institutions by the provisions of the Treaty on European Union relating to common foreign and security policy and to co-operation in the fields of justice and home affairs shall be charged to the budget. The operational expenditure occasioned by the implementation of the said provisions may, under the conditions referred to therein, be charged to the budget.

The revenue and expenditure shown in the budget shall be in balance.

Article 269 (ex Article 201)

Without prejudice to other revenue, the budget shall be financed wholly from own resources.

The Council, acting unanimously on a proposal from the Commission and after consulting the European Parliament, shall lay down provisions relating to the system of own resources of the Community, which it shall recommend to the Member States for adoption in accordance with their respective constitutional requirements.

Article 270 (ex Article 201a)

With a view to maintaining budgetary discipline, the Commission shall not make any proposal for a Community act, or alter its proposals, or adopt any implementing measure which is likely to have appreciable implications for the budget without providing the assurance that that proposal or that measure is capable of being financed within the limit of the Community's own resources arising under provisions laid down by the Council pursuant to Article 269.

Article 271 (ex Article 202)

The expenditure shown in the budget shall be authorised for one financial year, unless the regulations made pursuant to Article 279 provide otherwise.

In accordance with conditions to be laid down pursuant to Article 279, any appropriations, other than those relating to staff expenditure, that are unexpended at the end of the financial year may be carried forward to the next financial year only.

Appropriations shall be classified under different chapters grouping items of expenditure according to their nature or purpose and subdivided, as far as may be necessary, in accordance with the regulations made pursuant to Article 279.

The expenditure of the European Parliament, the Council, the Commission and the Court of Justice shall be set out in separate parts of the budget, without prejudice to special arrangements for certain common items of expenditure.

Article 272 (ex Article 203)

1. The financial year shall run from 1 January to 31 December.

2. Each institution of the Community shall, before 1 July, draw up estimates of its expenditure. The Commission shall consolidate these estimates in a preliminary draft budget. It shall attach thereto an opinion which may contain different estimates.

The preliminary draft budget shall contain an estimate of revenue and an estimate of expenditure.

3. The Commission shall place the preliminary draft budget before the Council not later than 1 September of the year preceding that in which the budget is to be implemented.

The Council shall consult the Commission and, where appropriate, the other institutions concerned whenever it intends to depart from the preliminary draft budget.

The Council, acting by a qualified majority, shall establish the draft budget and forward it to the European Parliament.

4. The draft budget shall be placed before the European Parliament not later than 5 October of the year preceding that in which the budget is to be implemented.

The European Parliament shall have the right to amend the draft budget, acting by a majority of its Members, and to propose to the Council, acting by an absolute majority of the votes cast, modifications to the draft budget relating to expenditure necessarily resulting from this Treaty or from acts adopted in accordance therewith.

If, within 45 days of the draft budget being placed before it, the European Parliament has given its approval, the budget shall stand as finally adopted. If within this period the European Parliament has not amended the draft budget nor proposed any modifications thereto, the budget shall be deemed to be finally adopted.

If within this period the European Parliament has adopted amendments or proposed modifications, the draft budget together with the amendments or proposed modifications shall be forwarded to the Council.

5. After discussing the draft budget with the Commission and, where appropriate, with the other institutions concerned, the Council shall act under the following conditions:

(a) the Council may, acting by a qualified majority, modify any of the amendments adopted by the European Parliament;

(b) with regard to the proposed modifications:

– where a modification proposed by the European Parliament does not have the effect of increasing the total amount of the expenditure of an institution, owing in particular to the fact that the increase in expenditure which it would involve would be expressly compensated by one or more proposed modifications correspondingly reducing expenditure, the Council may, acting by a qualified majority, reject the proposed modification. In the absence of a decision to reject it, the proposed modification shall stand as accepted;

– where a modification proposed by the European Parliament has the effect of increasing the total amount of the expenditure of an institution, the Council may, acting by a qualified majority, accept this proposed modification. In the absence of a decision to accept it, the proposed modification shall stand as rejected;

– where, in pursuance of one of the two preceding subparagraphs, the Council has rejected a proposed modification, it may, acting by a qualified majority, either retain the amount shown in the draft budget or fix another amount.

The draft budget shall be modified on the basis of the proposed modifications accepted by the Council. If, within 15 days of the draft being placed before it, the Council has not modified any of the amendments adopted by the European Parliament and if the modifications proposed by the latter have been accepted, the budget shall be deemed to be finally adopted. The Council shall inform the European Parliament that it has not modified any of the amendments and that the proposed modifications have been accepted.

If within this period the Council has modified one or more of the amendments adopted by the European Parliament or if the modifications proposed by the latter have been rejected or modified, the modified draft budget shall again be forwarded to the European Parliament. The Council shall inform the European Parliament of the results of its deliberations.

6. Within 15 days of the draft budget being placed before it, the European Parliament, which shall have been notified of the action taken on its proposed modifications, may, acting by a majority of its Members and three-fifths of the votes cast, amend or reject the modifications to its amendments made by the Council and shall adopt the budget accordingly. If within this period the European Parliament has not acted, the budget shall be deemed to be finally adopted.

7. When the procedure provided for in this Article has been completed, the President of the European Parliament shall declare that the budget has been finally adopted.

8. However, the European Parliament, acting by a majority of its Members and two-thirds of the votes cast, may, if there are important reasons, reject the draft budget and ask for a new draft to be submitted to it.

9. A maximum rate of increase in relation to the expenditure of the same type to be incurred during the current year shall be fixed annually for the total expenditure other than that necessarily resulting from this Treaty or from acts adopted in accordance therewith.

The Commission shall, after consulting the Economic Policy Committee, declare what this maximum rate is as it results from:

– the trend, in terms of volume, of the gross national product within the Community;
– the average variation in the budgets of the Member States;
and
– the trend of the cost of living during the preceding financial year.

The maximum rate shall be communicated, before 1 May, to all the institutions of the Community. The latter shall be required to conform to this during the budgetary procedure, subject to the provisions of the fourth and fifth subparagraphs of this paragraph.

If, in respect of expenditure other than that necessarily resulting from this Treaty or from acts adopted in accordance therewith, the actual rate of increase in the draft budget established by the Council is over half the maximum rate, the European Parliament may, exercising its right of amendment, further increase the total amount of that expenditure to a limit not exceeding half the maximum rate.

Where the European Parliament, the Council or the Commission consider that the activities of the Communities require that the rate determined according to the procedure laid down in this paragraph should be exceeded, another rate may be fixed by agreement between the Council, acting by a qualified majority, and the European Parliament, acting by a majority of its Members and three-fifths of the votes cast.

10. Each institution shall exercise the powers conferred upon it by this Article, with due regard for the provisions of the Treaty and for acts adopted in accordance therewith, in particular those relating to the Community's own resources and to the balance between revenue and expenditure.

Article 273 (ex Article 204)

If, at the beginning of a financial year, the budget has not yet been voted, a sum equivalent to not more than one-twelfth of the budget appropriations for the preceding financial year may be spent each month in respect of any chapter or other subdivision of the budget in accordance with the provisions of the Regulations made pursuant to Article 279; this arrangement shall not, however, have the effect of placing at the disposal of the Commission appropriations in excess of one-twelfth of those provided for in the draft budget in course of preparation.

The Council may, acting by a qualified majority, provided that the other conditions laid down in the first subparagraph are observed, authorise expenditure in excess of one-twelfth.

If the decision relates to expenditure which does not necessarily result from this Treaty or from acts adopted in accordance therewith, the Council shall forward it immediately to the European Parliament; within 30 days the European Parliament, acting by a majority of its Members and three-fifths of the votes cast, may adopt a different decision on the expenditure in excess of the one-twelfth referred to in the first subparagraph. This part of the decision of the Council shall be suspended until the European Parliament has taken its decision. If within the said period the European Parliament has not taken a decision which differs from the decision of the Council, the latter shall be deemed to be finally adopted.

The decisions referred to in the second and third subparagraphs shall lay down the necessary measures relating to resources to ensure application of this Article.

Article 274 (ex Article 205)

The Commission shall implement the budget, in accordance with the provisions of the regulations made pursuant to Article 279, on its own responsibility and within the limits of the appropriations, having regard to the principles of sound financial management. **Member States shall co-operate with the Commission to ensure that the appropriations are used in accordance with the principles of sound financial management.**

The regulations shall lay down detailed rules for each institution concerning its part in effecting its own expenditure.

Within the budget, the Commission may, subject to the limits and conditions laid down in the regulations made pursuant to Article 279, transfer appropriations from one chapter to another or from one subdivision to another.

Article 275 (ex Article 205a)

The Commission shall submit annually to the Council and to the European Parliament the accounts of the preceding financial year relating to the implementation of the budget. The Commission shall also forward to them a financial statement of the assets and liabilities of the Community.

Article 276 (ex Article 206)

1. The European Parliament, acting on a recommendation from the Council which shall act by a qualified majority, shall give a discharge to the Commission in respect of the implementation of the budget. To this end, the Council and the European Parliament in turn shall examine the accounts and the financial statement referred to in Article 275, the annual report by the Court of Auditors together with the replies of the institutions under audit to the observations of the Court of Auditors, **the statement of assurance referred to in Article 248(1), second subparagraph** and any relevant special reports by the Court of Auditors.

2. Before giving a discharge to the Commission, or for any other purpose in connection with the exercise of its powers over the implementation of the budget, the European Parliament may ask to hear the Commission give evidence with regard to the execution of expenditure or the operation of financial control systems. The Commission shall submit any necessary information to the European Parliament at the latter's request.

3. The Commission shall take all appropriate steps to act on the observations in the decisions giving discharge and on other observations by the European Parliament relating to the execution of expenditure, as well as on comments accompanying the recommendations on discharge adopted by the Council.

At the request of the European Parliament or the Council, the Commission shall report on the measures taken in the light of these observations and comments and in particular on the instructions given to the departments which are responsible for the implementation of the budget. These reports shall also be forwarded to the Court of Auditors.

Article 277 (ex Article 207, simplified)

The budget shall be drawn up in the unit of account determined in accordance with the provisions of the regulations made pursuant to Article 279.

Article 278 (ex Article 208)

The Commission may, provided it notifies the competent authorities of the Member States concerned, transfer into the currency of one of the Member States its holdings in the currency of another Member State, to the extent necessary to enable them to be used for purposes which come within the scope of this Treaty. The Commission shall as far as possible avoid making such transfers if it possesses cash or liquid assets in the currencies which it needs.

The Commission shall deal with each Member State through the authority designated by the State concerned. In carrying out financial operations the Commission shall employ the services of the bank of issue of the Member State concerned or of any other financial institution approved by that State.

Article 279 (ex Article 209)

1. The Council, acting unanimously on a proposal from the Commission and after consulting the European Parliament and obtaining the opinion of the Court of Auditors, shall:
(a) make Financial Regulations specifying in particular the procedure to be adopted for establishing and implementing the budget and for presenting and auditing accounts;
(b) *lay down rules concerning the responsibility of financial controllers, authorising officers and accounting officers, and concerning appropriate arrangements for inspection.*
From 1 January 2007, the Council shall act by a qualified majority on a proposal from the Commission and after consulting the European Parliament and obtaining the opinion of the Court of Auditors.

2. *The Council, acting unanimously on a proposal from the Commission and after consulting the European Parliament and obtaining the opinion of the Court of Auditors, shall determine the methods and procedure whereby the budget revenue provided under the arrangements relating to the Community's own resources shall be made available to the Commission, and determine the measures to be applied, if need be, to meet cash requirements.*

Article 280 (ex Article 209a)

1. The Community and the Member States shall counter fraud and any other illegal activities affecting the financial interests of the Community through measures to be taken in accordance with this Article, which shall act as a deterrent and be such as to afford effective protection in the Member States.

2. Member States shall take the same measures to counter fraud affecting the financial interests of the Community as they take to counter fraud affecting their own financial interests.

3. Without prejudice to other provisions of this Treaty, the Member States shall co-ordinate their action aimed at protecting the financial interests of the Community against fraud. To this end they shall organise, together with the Commission, close and regular co-operation between the competent authorities.

4. The Council, acting in accordance with the procedure referred to in Article 251, after consulting the Court of Auditors, shall adopt the necessary measures in the fields of the prevention of and fight against fraud affecting the financial interests of the Community with a view to affording effective and equivalent protection in the Member States. These measures shall not concern the application of national criminal law or the national administration of justice.

5. The Commission, in co-operation with Member States, shall each year submit to the European Parliament and to the Council a report on the measures taken for the implementation of this Article.

xxix General and Final Provisions

Whereas previous parts of the TEC have a degree of coherence, this is not really the case with its sixth and final part. In fact, its diversity is even greater than its denomination suggests. Part Six actually falls into two subdivisions, a short final one with its own subheading of 'Final Provisions' embracing only Articles 313 and 314, and a longer initial one with no heading. Prior to Amsterdam a third subdivision entitled 'Setting up the Institutions' and consisting of six articles existed. These, along with a further article relating to the transitional period, were repealed as part of the TA's simplification process.

The first of the two remaining subdivisions is itself mainly an amalgam of two kinds of articles: those dealing with the legal status of the Community and the TEC as such and, a smaller number, dealing with some aspects of the EC's external relations. However, these are a long way from being a full statement on the EC's external relations. Beyond this there are some articles which, like Article 286, do not really fall into either category. Yet this diversity does not mean that the Part Six articles are insignificant. Some of them, like Article 308, are extremely important and have played significant roles in and during the development of the EC. So the part deserves to be taken seriously. Moreover, it rounds off the treaty by specifying the conditions of its applicability, legally and externally. However, these 'General and Final Provisions' should not be confused with the Final Act of the treaty, which is discussed later in the *Guide*.

The first clause in Part Six, *Article 281* (ex 210), illustrates this significance very well. It is very brief but far-reaching and highly influential in itself. It also paves the way for a set of articles on the legal status and powers of the EC. By stating that the Community shall have 'legal personality', it makes clear that the EC can act with legal authority, domestically and externally. Hence the Community as a body can act in law like an ordinary individual or firm. It thus has the autonomy and authority to bear rights and duties. These include owning property, entering into legally binding agreements, suing and being sued. And its legal personality is distinct from that of the member states. However, whereas the latter have this as an inherent right, the Community's legal personality is bestowed by the member states through the TEC. It must therefore be exercised within the limits of the treaty. None the less, it allows the Community and its institutions, which normally act for it, to carry out its functions and objectives in a legally binding way. This is important in such matters as contracts, employment and, of course, external relations.

The TECSC actually specified that its authority was external but this was not felt necessary for the EC. And since then the *AETR* judgment in 1971 has made it clear that the Community, through the doctrine of 'parallelism', has external jurisdiction wherever it has internal competence. In any case the claim has been accepted by international law, as has the fact that legal personality is exercised for the Community by its institutions. None the less, it is somewhat odd for the Union to have to rely on the Community as such to take external action. Prior to Amsterdam, the suggestion was made that the power of legal personality should be conferred on the Union. This was rejected by the IGC since it would have meant a major change in the nature and relationships of the two bodies. However, Article 24 TEU was altered to allow the EU some international activity and this was underwritten by Nice.

The nature and extent of the Community's domestic personality is then defined by *Article 282* (ex 211) allowing it freely to buy, sell and plead before national courts. Equally, judgments can be enforced against it. In all this it has as full powers as national laws provide for any other corporate body. Implicitly the member states are required to recognize its rights in relevant fields. Such rights are subject to national property law. The Commission has the key role here and generally under Article 282, although the other institutions can, and do, own buildings.

Thereafter *Article 283* (ex 212) begins the definition of the status of the employees of the Communities or 'servants' as English law still likes to call them. Given the importance of the institutions, as the means by which the Community acts, it is important that the Community as such can control its staff. They are to form one administration and be subject to staff regulations. This is the way that civil services are normally regulated in continental Europe. These are now being revised as part of the administrative reform of the Commission led by Commission vice-president Neil Kinnock. Staff matters are presently justiciable in the Court of First Instance but, once Nice is approved, a special staff panel is likely to be set up. Staff are also subject to the rules on confidentiality laid down in Article 287, which is the nearest the EC gets to an Official Secrets Act. Recent controversies, such as that surrounding Bernard Connolly, have shown that this is a sensitive area.

One reason for this is that the Commission is privy to a good deal of confidential information and, according to *Article 284* (ex 213), has a right to gather it subject to treaty rules and Council monitoring. The phrasing of the article is less specific than that in the TECSC but allows it to inquire, inform and verify. This might not seem very important but, given that the EC is not a federal state with its own field agencies, it relies on this right of information to follow the way that member states implement EC decisions. Without such a right the Commission and its staff – who are clearly affected by the provision as Article 287 below makes clear – could be excluded by national rules and interests.

The next two articles build on this interest in data. Both were inserted at Amsterdam. *Article 285* allows the Community to collect statistics provided that these meet basic standards. This provides a treaty base for Eurostat the Community's well-respected statistical service. Measures for the production of statistics are to be adopted via co-decision. Moreover, in a second paragraph principles governing the production of statistics are spelt out. This brings us to *Article 286*, which can be seen as a partial response to post-Maastricht criticisms that the Commission was oppressive since it gives people guarantees that information on them will be properly protected and sets up a new agency to do this. Co-decision means that the EP has a say in enforcing the guarantees. *Article 287* (ex 214) then offers firms and other interests the assurance that confidential information supplied to the Community will remain confidential. Disclosure is only accepted by the ECJ when there is a convincing reason for it and the *Stanley Adams* case (1985) was a significant example where the Commission fell down on its obligations. Former Commissioner Bangemann also ran into trouble when his intention of taking up a position with a Spanish communications company was seen to threaten misuse of commercially sensitive information. Equally, firms and others are expected to preserve the secrecy of information to which they may become privy in their dealings with the Commission save when otherwise directed by national courts.

Part Six then reverts to an aspect of the Community legal standing. One of the essential elements of having legal personality is the ability to enter into contracts with third parties, contracts being widely interpreted. *Article 288* (ex 215) therefore establishes the EC's liability to normal national laws of contract. Thus a contract concluded with a Danish furniture company for desks would be governed by Danish law as well as by EC law. Normally contracts contain a clause indicating which law will cover it. The ECJ can hold a watching brief in such cases. About one EC case in 12 involves such contractual matters although the Community is rarely successfully prosecuted.

The second subparagraph goes on to set out the Community's obligation to make good losses suffered by third parties in their business dealings with the EC. There has to be a major breach for this to be operative and the *Brasserie du Pêcheur and Factortame* case (1996) has established that the member states are covered by the Community's obligations, and are thus open to open-ended claims for damages caused by misimplementation of EC law. According to the ECJ in *Marshall* (1993) this is seen as effectively a matter of human rights and there has been academic debate on whether this may not be a way forward for the protection of the individual within the Union. At present cases have to be brought within five years of loss being suffered. The third subparagraph further makes it plain that the Community is responsible for mistakes by its agents both where the rules they have to operate are faulty and where gaps in the rules force them to take damaging actions.

Having set out the legal authority of the Community and its servants, Part Six then goes off on another tack entirely and sets out some basic rules for the way the Community and its institutions should work. *Article 289* (ex 216) on the seats of the institutions is obviously related to staffing since the institutions do not function effectively if they are peripatetic, as the travails of the EP show. However, it raises rather different questions. The institutions referred to here are implicitly those bodies listed in Article 7 TEC and not the broader range of administrative agencies, although the latter are usually parcelled up among the states so that everybody gets something. This shows that the term 'the seat' is not understood as being one single capital site.

Locations are decided essentially by a strengthened form of unanimity, but involving governments as a whole rather than the Council *per se*. Hence the most recent decisions, which went against the wishes of bodies like the EP, were the First Decision on the Seats of the Institutions agreed in 1992 at the Edinburgh European Council and the Protocol on the location of the seats of the institutions and of certain bodies and departments of the European Communities and of Europol introduced by Amsterdam. Both largely endorsed the present nonsensical status quo about the EP. The ECJ, as in *France* v. *European Parliament* (1997), has generally ruled in favour of the member states and against the EP on this issue. Helpfully the first of the declarations of which the Conference took note at Nice (Declaration No. 1n TN) shows Luxembourg agreeing not to demand the trademark panel, which had previously been allocated to Spain, even though the new panels, being courts, as such are meant to be in Luxembourg city.

Questions which go beyond mere administration are also raised by *Article 290* (ex 217) on the languages to be used in the institutions. Language is a sensitive matter, hence the requirement for unanimity so as to satisfy national interests. For reasons of efficiency the ECJ is allowed to make its own arrangements. Prior to Nice the reference to language was in the Rules of Procedure but it is now in clause 64 of the revised statute agreed in 2000. In practice institutions often decide for themselves. Almost all published documents are translated into the 11 official languages, as is the Union's *Official Journal* itself, and no one version has precedence. However, not all working documents are translated and the working languages of the Community tend to be English and French. The languages issue has caused much friction in recent years and is set to increase with enlargement.

Article 291 returns Part Six to questions of status and rights by conferring quasi-diplomatic immunity on the Community as such within the member states. Normally this sort of thing is decided by inter-governmental agreement, so this is an innovative and not insignificant provision. The exact privileges and immunities are set out in a protocol. This was originally annexed to the TEC, but in 1967 was replaced by the Protocol on privileges and immunities of the European Communities annexed to the Merger Treaty. The protocol also provides for the inviolability of Community premises, papers and messengers. Envoys accredited to the Community also have quasi-diplomatic status. Such questions of status are particularly relevant in matters of external relations. The effect of the Merger Treaty was to repeal Article 291's predecessor, the original Article 218. The resulting gap in the TEC was then filled by Amsterdam, as part of its simplification process, using the wording of the Merger Treaty as a replacement in Article 218. This was also amended to include reference to the ESCB and ECB. The reason for all this was that the Merger Treaty was being repealed. Nice makes a minor change to the protocol to cope with the changes made to the Community's legal structure.

The next set of articles, although not given a heading of their own, set out some ground rules which member states have to follow as members of the Community. *Article 292* (ex 219) thus prevents them from trying to resolve a dispute about the TEC either in an ad hoc bilateral way or by taking the case before any other internal juris-diction, for example the European Court of Human Rights or the International Court of Justice. This makes two points: that EC law is distinct from international law and that the member states have to accept that they are subject to a supra-national constraint, reflecting the argument of Article 239. In other words, this provides both a further statement on the autonomy of EC law and a guarantee of good behaviour by the member states.

The next articles extend and clarify this undertaking by providing guidelines on the legal treatment to be accorded foreign individuals, businesses and courts within the Community context. So the treaty does let member states resolve some problems bilater-ally thanks to *Article 293* (ex 220). This allows such deals where there is a good reason in areas related both to the Single Market and to individual needs. But there is no obligation to do so. In other words there is a safety-catch on such deals. Acceptable areas for such deals include civic rights, double taxation and mutual recognition of firms. This is reinforced by *Article 294* (ex 221), which makes it clear that the principle of non-discrimination applies to firms as well as to individuals.

While these can be decided bilaterally many questions about the enforcement of a court order from one member state in another, raised in the last indent of Article 293, are regulated by the 1968 Brussels Convention. This allows the ECJ an oversight in such matters and is rated as being on the same level as the treaty as the *Kleinwort Benson* (1995) case shows. However, *Article 295* (ex 222) does give member states a guarantee that the TEC does not affect domestic property law. This has caused problems where intellectual property is concerned, as in *Collins* v. *Imtrat Handelsgesellschaft GmbH* (1993), in part because the article specifically extends to the TEC as a whole and not just to specific articles. It can be seen as a way of showing that the EC, in this field, does not impose new rules on the states. Moreover, and thanks to what Beaumont and Weatherill refer to as its agnosticism, Article 295 is understood not to preclude state ownership of property.

The article can also be considered as one of four which offer states a guarantee of their independence, especially in time of crisis. Thus the first paragraph of *Article 296* (ex 223) makes it plain that disclosure of information, presumably under Article 284, does not extend to the national security of the member states. This can include economic infor-mation as well as military matters. While there are no such provisions in the TECSC and

TEAEC there are similar clauses on capital movements in the TEC and on CFSP questions elsewhere in the TEU. However, the provision for taking sectoral measures in the transitional period, which had attracted interest from neutral states, was eliminated by simplification at Amsterdam. However, pressure from the EP and the Commission to remove this infringement of the market, which has hindered the development of transnational armament firms, has not been successful since states like the discretion available under what is, as Eikenberg points out, an ambiguous article. Hence the Council has never bothered to revise its now somewhat out-of-date list of war goods and has only recently addressed the question of arms exports.

The paragraph also allows states limited derogation from the rules of the Single Market, including those on free movement. This allows them to take specific measures, of their own choosing and without consulting the EP, on the materials of war. However, all this is providing that these do not spill over into the rest of the market and providing that only products mutually agreed in 1958 are involved. The ECJ has, in the *Campus Oil* case (1984), defined what should be understood by a security threat. It does this more widely than the appropriate Geneva Convention. However, generally there has not been much of a problem.

Moreover, to avoid such a spillover *Article 297* (ex 224) requires that, in critical circumstances, states consult with each other. The non-involved states do not, however, have a right of veto. Hence, traditional views of the article present it as a reserve of member-state sovereignty although Koutrakos challenges this. All the same, should action by a member state under Article 297 distort competition within the common market, the Commission has a duty under *Article 298* (ex 225) to try and resolve the problem. There is a fallback procedure in the second paragraph, explained in detail by Stefanou and Xanthaki, which allows a case to be brought against a member state felt to be abusing the derogation. Because such issues would be very sensitive the ECJ hears them in private. As yet, the procedure has only been invoked once, in *Commission* v. *Greece* (1996). An *in camera* session of the ECJ did not take place since the Commission dropped proceedings.

Part Six now returns to legal formalities and, in so doing, begins to move towards questions of external action. The application of the TEC to the member states, as well as its geographical coverage, is restated by *Article 299* (ex 227). This changes with every enlargement. Its inclusion is for legal certainty and should not be understood as a statement of Community superiority. It is also mainly economic in scope, hence the exclusion of UK bases in Cyprus, which are not economic areas.

In any case, Article 299 is now a very long article thanks to additions at Amsterdam inspired by Declaration No. 26 TEU and the desire of some member states to overcome the *Legros* (1992) and *Lancry* (1994) rulings of the ECJ limiting the power of the Council to adapt EC law. Paragraph 1 makes it clear that the TEC applies to the metropolitan territory of all member states. Metropolitan territory is to be understood as including air space, continental shelf, plus planes and vessels under member state control. The next paragraphs go on, in the main, to specify which dependencies are covered by it, excluding some UK dependencies, the Faeroes and only in part the Channel Islands and the Isle of Man. This means, for example, that full free movement does not apply there after a ruling in *Rui Alberta Pereira Roque* (1995). The ECJ, in *Government of Gibraltar* v. *Council and Commission* (1993) has also excluded Gibraltar.

Paragraph 2 now allows special measures to be adopted by QMV to help particularly peripheral islands. The Åland Islands reference in paragraph 5 derives from the 1994 accession treaty. There is also a vestigial reference to Part Four, Association. Finally,

Declaration No. 25 TEU allows member states to act in the interests of certain overseas countries and territories where their interests diverge from those of the EC.

Such special arrangements for distant places raises the question of how the Community as such relates to the rest of the wider world as they make plain that the EC enjoys the right and capacity to act outside the home territories of the member states. The next six articles introduce some of the relevant issues and there is a further reference at Article 310. These deal with procedures for foreign relations, specific international relationships, obligations and association agreements. The articles also spill over into questions of a broader application which ought not to be overlooked. However, there is little in the way of general principles of policy. So as a guide to EU/EC external relations this is very limited. Only recently have any references to the CFSP been included and these only because the support of the EC is needed and not on grounds of logical principle.

Moreover, Part Six does not provide a comprehensive guide to what is actually in the TEC on the subject. Details are scattered throughout the TEC, as with Article 133. This, as we have seen, is now somewhat cut off from other relevant articles. In fact, even after Amsterdam, the treaty does not reveal very much about the aims, implementation or structure of the EC's external relations, partly because so much of this has developed as day-to-day practice and not as a constitutional strategy. It is also partly because this is not what the treaty is trying to do. Part Six is there, as we have already suggested, to make it clear how far the applicability of the substantive elements actually goes.

The articles here are so placed, in other words, because they are the logical extension of the idea of legal personality established in Article 281. The latter is an accumulation of attributes which show that the entity concerned is a subject of national law and has the legal right, and the capability, to pursue its international rights and duties by bringing legal claims, for example. These include the abilities to send and receive envoys and, especially here, to enter into binding foreign treaty agreements in its own right. To this extent the EC does not act in virtue of the powers of the member states, but on its own authority and this is recognized by international law. Such agreements can also have internal effects.

Given that the principle of Community external relations is already established, *Article 300* (ex 228) first supplies the internal mechanisms and codes of procedure for making, not policy in general, but specific one-off deals. Always a long article, it has been expanded and complicated by Amsterdam and Nice. Paragraph 1 makes it clear that ultimate responsibility lies with the Council, provided there is a treaty-based justification. As with Article 133 the Commission suggests a negotiation and draws up the brief, known as the 'mandate', but it is subject both to the control of specific Council guidance and to monitoring by an inter-governmental committee. And, despite the provision for the Commission to be given extra responsibility for changes in agreements, the overall impression is that the Commission has been put on an increasingly short leash.

As paragraph 2 makes clear, decisions are normally taken by QMV and this includes actually deciding to sign an agreement. As Dashwood says, signing thus becomes a distinct act and one which has implications for when the agreement comes into force, as it may be needed before the often long drawn-out ratification procedures have been concluded or where suspension takes place because of human rights abuses. This was one of the changes made at Amsterdam to help fill out the gaps in external provisions. However, in fields where unanimity applies in internal decision-making, decisions must be taken unanimously. This is also the case where agreements are to be suspended or the Community needs to change its negotiating position within a joint committee or some other such forum set up by an agreement. Nice widened the scope of this so that it now applies generally and not only to association agreements concluded under Article 310. The EP has only to be informed of such changes whereas paragraph 3 writes in consultation for many deals but not commercial agreements signed under Article 133 and some others, even where co-decision would be required internally. Moreover, the EP is obliged to act rapidly and, if it does not do so, then the act goes through anyway. Informal understandings can also be brought under this procedure.

However, the EP is given a right of assent on association and similar agreements, on agreements which involve changes in decisions taken by co-decision and on deals with major financial implications. Nice also strengthened the EP's position by adding it to the list of those able to ask for an ECJ ruling on whether a proposed agreement is in conformity with the treaty. This was not something which all member states explicitly supported, but was allegedly viewed as necessary to obtain the EP's political support for Nice. Shaw, however, views this as the logical corollary of the change made to Article 230. Where the ECJ rules an agreement incompatible with the TEC, the agreement can only be applied after a treaty amendment is adopted. The same thing applies, according to paragraph 4, when the Council knowingly seeks an agreement outside the treaty. Given the difficulty of amending the treaties, this has never happened. Once an agreement is passed in due form, the institutions have to accept (paragraph 7), again reinforcing member state influence.

Having set up the mechanisms by which decisions can be taken – albeit at the risk of a severe strain on language as Dashwood puts it – the next five articles provide more concise specifications of where they can be taken. Thus *Article 301* (ex 228a) provides justification for suspending deals where it is necessary to deploy sanctions in support of the CFSP. For Szyszcak this opens the way to the ECJ pronouncing on CFSP policies. Then *Article 302* (ex 229) makes it clear that the UN is covered by this. It is for the Commission to implement the relations necessitated by the preambular reference to working within the principles of the UN, whether directly or in bodies like UNESCO. The Commission is also told to conduct relations with other international bodies such as the ILO and, especially the WTO. This is because it is a body with more continuity and administrative resources than the other EC institutions. However, there is no mention of the aims or motives to guide the Commission when it does all this.

Article 303 (ex 230) seems to read as if the Community has not had relations with the Council of Europe whereas the reality is there was an initial exchange of letters in 1959. Since then there have been a large number of agreements on co-operation, so that 'maintaining' might have been a better term. The fact that the Community as a whole undertakes to co-operate on a wide front with the Council of Europe (CoE) and the Organization for Economic Co-operation and Development (OECD) (see Article 304, ex 231) probably reflects past difficulties. At one stage both bodies were rivals to the Community and so leaving things to the Commission alone might not, therefore, have been well received. Deals with the economically significant OECD also need unanimous backing from the member states. In fact the EC sorted out its relations in 1961 and enjoys a special status inside the OECD.

At this point the treaty partly changes direction again back to legal matters, albeit ones partly related to obligations arising from external relations, reflecting the fact that agreements impinge on national sovereignty. *Article 305* (ex 232) clarifies the continuing legal authority and effectiveness of the other two Community treaties. The phraseology is different because the TECSC, pre-dating the TEC as it does, might be thought to have been superseded by it in a way that the TEAEC itself signed at Rome could not be. By implication both treaties have external effects of their own.

Article 306 (ex 233) next establishes both that there is no problem with the Benelux Union and that this will continue, even though many of its aims are now pursued by the Community. Then *Article 307* (ex 234), which was simplified by Amsterdam, establishes the general principle behind this, which is that previous accords concluded by member states are not rendered void by EC membership. Indeed, the EC as a whole can be bound by some of these accords and cannot, in other words, make unilateral changes to the acts of nation-states. Conversely, the wording does not imply that states can use this to renounce other treaty obligations. The text reinforces this by establishing a requirement to eliminate any difficulties which may arise from prior accords. It also argues that states have a duty to consider such accords a general benefit and one which has to be extended to the supra-national institutions. The ECJ has also ruled that member states are constrained by the TEC only in so far as this is necessary to safeguard EC policies. There is no general infringement of their sovereignty.

When it comes to *Article 308* (ex 235) we are on even more controversial ground. This key 'catch-all' provision allows the Community to do needful things not otherwise specified in the treaty. This is of general application and only a minority of the many hundreds of times the article has been evoked relate to external matters. It is therefore a useful residual power, included and retained in the TEC, to offset the rigidities of conferred powers. Weiler refers to it as the EC's 'elastic clause', its 'necessary and proper' provision.

Despite the fact that there are conditions for its use, involving, on the one hand, unanimity and, on the other, the need to comply with treaty objectives, an unassailably clear need and an obvious gap, Article 308 has been vigorously attacked as an example of the Community's overweening ambitions and appetite. This is despite the fact that the EP and ECJ play only minor roles. The fact that it poses no limitations of scope, apart from preventing the creation of wholly new powers, and can help to create new rights through gap filling, as Chalmers says, has encouraged accusations of 'creeping competence'. Indeed, according to Moravscik, there was some thought of amending this prior to the SEA but German reluctance prevented it.

In any case, much less use is made of Article 308 today than in its heyday – the 1970s and early 1980s – when early narrow interpretations of the provisions gave way to more creative and expansive readings of its scope, as Weiler notes. This is because of changes to the TEC. First, the EC has been granted more explicit competences to act thanks to the SEA, Maastricht, Amsterdam and, to a much lesser extent, Nice. Second, certain additions to the TEC such as the ban on legislative harmonization in areas such as education, culture and public health, have meant that some activities previously pursued or contemplated under Article 308 are now effectively 'off limits'.

Article 309 was inserted at Amsterdam to amplify Article 7(2) TEU and overcome the EC/EU divide. By making it clear that suspension of rights applies in the EC pillar it prevents an offending state from claiming that the charges against it only affected the inter-governmental pillars. In fact, it imposes a double whammy since not merely would an offending state lose voting rights but it would be required to go on meeting its financial and other obligations. And paragraph 4 ensures that the offending state cannot use the voting rules to obstruct a hostile decision. Nice did not alter this to take account of the 'yellow card' procedure.

This brings us to *Article 310* (ex 238) and back to external relations again. What the TEC provides for here is the establishment of vaguely defined association agreements with individual states, groups of states or international organizations. Originally designed with closer relations between the then EEC and the UK in mind, the provisions have been put to various uses. Indeed, extensive use was made of Article 310 in the 1990s to enhance relations with European non-member states although the resulting agreements were of a somewhat one-sided nature, as Phinnemore has shown. Its application, however, is not confined to Europe. It has therefore provided the basis for various agreements, notable among these being those such as Lomé and Cotonou with the ACP countries.

Article 311 (ex 239) has far fewer implications for external relations. Indeed, it is a basic legal statement which could have been located in the final provisions. It is a clear statement that protocols are a full part of the treaty, endorsed by all the signatories, and not, as some think, a means of undermining the treaty through inter-governmental whim. And, should anyone doubt this, they would find that violating the protocols was the same as violating the treaty. This is not the case with declarations, as the *Guide* has already noted.

Finally *Article 312* (ex 240) through an apparently harmless statement makes a vital political point. For not only is the treaty meant to run and run but it is meant to be irreversible and thereby committed to continuing constitutional development, thus emphasizing the significance of the steps taken in Rome in 1957. Hence there are no provisions for reservations or, more importantly, secession (although a way round this was found for Greenland to leave in 1985). None the less, the article encapsulates the ambitions, initial and continuing, to make the Community a significant and influential body. But it does nothing to resolve the messy nature of its provisions on external relations. Nor does the treaty end on this emphatic note since arrangements have to be made for ratification and the validity of the various language versions. This is done in the final provisions element of Part Six.

PART SIX   GENERAL AND FINAL PROVISIONS

Article 281 (ex Article 210)

The Community shall have legal personality.

Article 282 (ex Article 211)

In each of the Member States, the Community shall enjoy the most extensive legal capacity accorded to legal persons under their laws; it may, in particular, acquire or dispose of movable and immovable property and may be a party to legal proceedings. To this end, the Community shall be represented by the Commission.

Article 283*

The Council shall, acting by a qualified majority on a proposal from the Commission and after consulting the other institutions concerned, lay down the Staff Regulations of officials of the European Communities and the Conditions of Employment of other servants of those Communities.

Article 284 (ex Article 213)

The Commission may, within the limits and under conditions laid down by the Council in accordance with the provisions of this Treaty, collect any information and carry out any checks required for the performance of the tasks entrusted to it.

Article 285 (new – TA)

1. Without prejudice to Article 5 of the Protocol on the Statute of the European System of Central Banks and of the European Central Bank, the Council, acting in accordance with the procedure referred to in Article 251, shall adopt measures for the production of statistics where necessary for the performance of the activities of the Community.

2. The production of Community statistics shall conform to impartiality, reliability, objectivity, scientific independence, cost-effectiveness and statistical confidentiality; it shall not entail excessive burdens on economic operators.

Article 286 (new – TA)

1. From 1 January 1999, Community acts on the protection of individuals with regard to the processing of personal data and the free movement of such data shall apply to the institutions and bodies set up by, or on the basis of, this Treaty.

2. Before the date referred to in paragraph 1, the Council, acting in accordance with the procedure referred to in Article 251, shall establish an independent supervisory body responsible for monitoring the application of such Community acts to Community institutions and bodies and shall adopt any other relevant provisions as appropriate.

Article 287 (ex Article 214)

The members of the institutions of the Community, the members of committees, and the officials and other servants of the Community shall be required, even after their duties have ceased, not to disclose information of the kind covered by the obligation of professional secrecy, in particular information about undertakings, their business relations or their cost components.

Article 288 (ex Article 215)

The contractual liability of the Community shall be governed by the law applicable to the contract in question.

---

*Prior to the Treaty of Amsterdam's simplification process, these provisions were contained in Article 24(1), second subparagraph of the Treaty Establishing a Single Council and a Single Commission of the European Communities, the so-called Merger Treaty, of 8 April 1965. In various published versions of the Treaty of Rome, they appeared as Article 212.

In the case of non-contractual liability, the Community shall, in accordance with the general principles common to the laws of the Member States, make good any damage caused by its institutions or by its servants in the performance of their duties.

The preceding paragraph shall apply under the same conditions to damage caused by the ECB or by its servants in the performance of their duties.

The personal liability of its servants towards the Community shall be governed by the provisions laid down in their Staff Regulations or in the Conditions of Employment applicable to them.

Article 289 (ex Article 216)

The seat of the institutions of the Community shall be determined by common accord of the Governments of the Member States.

Article 290 (ex Article 217)

The rules governing the languages of the institutions of the Community shall, without prejudice to the provisions contained in the **Statute** of the Court of Justice, be determined by the Council, acting unanimously.

Article 291

The Community shall enjoy in the territories of the Member States such privileges and immunities as are necessary for the performance of its tasks, under the conditions laid down in the Protocol of 8 April 1965 on the privileges and immunities of the European Communities. *The same shall apply to* the European Central Bank, the European Monetary Institute, and *the European Investment Bank*.

Article 292 (ex Article 219)

Member States undertake not to submit a dispute concerning the interpretation or application of this Treaty to any method of settlement other than those provided for therein.

Article 293 (ex Article 220)

Member States shall, so far as is necessary, enter into negotiations with each other with a view to securing for the benefit of their nationals:
– the protection of persons and the enjoyment and protection of rights under the same conditions as those accorded by each State to its own nationals;
– the abolition of double taxation within the Community;
– the mutual recognition of companies or firms within the meaning of the second paragraph of Article 48, the retention of legal personality in the event of transfer of their seat from one country to another, and the possibility of mergers between companies or firms governed by the laws of different countries;
– the simplification of formalities governing the reciprocal recognition and enforcement of judgments of courts or tribunals and of arbitration awards.

Article 294 (ex Article 221, simplified)

Member States shall accord nationals of the other Member States the same treatment as their own nationals as regards participation in the capital of companies or firms within the meaning of Article 48, without prejudice to the application of the other provisions of this Treaty.

Article 295 (ex Article 222)

This Treaty shall in no way prejudice the rules in Member States governing the system of property ownership.

Article 296 (ex Article 223)

1. The provisions of this Treaty shall not preclude the application of the following rules:
(a) no Member State shall be obliged to supply information the disclosure of which it considers contrary to the essential interests of its security;
(b) any Member State may take such measures as it considers necessary for the protection of the essential interests of its security which are connected with the production of or trade in arms, munitions and war material; such measures shall not adversely affect the conditions of competition in the common market regarding products which are not intended for specifically military purposes.

2. *The Council may, acting unanimously on a proposal from the Commission, make changes to the list, which it drew up on 15 April 1958, of the products to which the provisions of paragraph 1(b) apply.*

Article 297 (ex Article 224)

Member States shall consult each other with a view to taking together the steps needed to prevent the functioning of the common market being affected by measures which a Member State may be called upon to take in the event of serious internal disturbances affecting the maintenance of law and order, in the event of war, serious international tension constituting a threat of war, or in order to carry out obligations it has accepted for the purpose of maintaining peace and international security.

Article 298 (ex Article 225)

If measures taken in the circumstances referred to in Articles 296 and 297 have the effect of distorting the conditions of competition in the common market, the Commission shall, together with the State concerned, examine how these measures can be adjusted to the rules laid down in the Treaty.

By way of derogation from the procedure laid down in Articles 226 and 227, the Commission or any Member State may bring the matter directly before the Court of Justice if it considers that another Member State is making improper use of the powers provided for in Articles 296 and 297. The Court of Justice shall give its ruling *in camera*.

Article 299 (ex Article 227, simplified)*

1. This Treaty shall apply to the Kingdom of Belgium, the Kingdom of Denmark, the Federal Republic of Germany, the Hellenic Republic, the Kingdom of Spain, the French Republic, Ireland, the Italian Republic, the Grand Duchy of Luxembourg, the Kingdom of the Netherlands, the Republic of Austria, the Portuguese Republic, the Republic of Finland, the Kingdom of Sweden and the United Kingdom of Great Britain and Northern Ireland.

2. *The provisions of this Treaty shall apply to the French overseas departments, the Azores, Madeira and the Canary Islands.*

However, taking account of the structural social and economic situation of the French overseas departments, the Azores, Madeira and the Canary Islands, which is compounded by their remoteness, insularity, small size, difficult topography and climate, economic dependence on a few products, the permanence and combination of which severely restrain their development, the Council, acting by a qualified majority on a proposal from the Commission and after consulting the European Parliament, shall adopt specific measures aimed, in particular, at laying down the conditions of application of the present Treaty to those regions, including common policies.

The Council shall, when adopting the relevant measures referred to in the second subparagraph, take into account areas such as customs and trade policies, fiscal policy, free zones, agriculture and fisheries policies, conditions for supply of raw materials and essential consumer goods, State aids and conditions of access to Structural Funds and to horizontal Community programmes.

The Council shall adopt the measures referred to in the second subparagraph taking into account the special characteristics and constraints of the outermost regions without undermining the integrity and the coherence of the Community legal order, including the internal market and common policies.

3. The special arrangements for association set out in Part Four of this Treaty shall apply to the overseas countries and territories listed in Annex *II* to this Treaty.

This Treaty shall not apply to those overseas countries and territories having special relations with the United Kingdom of Great Britain and Northern Ireland which are not included in the aforementioned list.

4. The provisions of this Treaty shall apply to the European territories for whose external relations a Member State is responsible.

5. *The provisions of this Treaty shall apply to the Åland Islands in accordance with the provisions set out in Protocol No. 2 to the Act concerning the conditions of accession of the Republic of Austria, the Republic of Finland and the Kingdom of Sweden.*

6. Notwithstanding the preceding paragraphs:
(a) this Treaty shall not apply to the Faeroe Islands;
(b) this Treaty shall not apply to the Sovereign Base Areas of the United Kingdom of Great Britain and Northern Ireland in Cyprus;
(c) this Treaty shall apply to the Channel Islands and the Isle of Man only to the extent necessary to ensure the implementation of the arrangements for those islands set out in the Treaty concerning the accession of new Member States

---

*The new wording of paragraph 2 draws on the Declaration on the Outermost Regions of the Community adopted at the time the TEU was signed.

to the European Economic Community and to the European Atomic Energy Community signed on 22 January 1972.

Article 300 (ex Article 228)

1. Where this Treaty provides for the conclusion of agreements between the Community and one or more States or international organisations, the Commission shall make recommendations to the Council, which shall authorise the Commission to open the necessary negotiations. The Commission shall conduct these negotiations in consultation with special committees appointed by the Council to assist it in this task and within the framework of such directives as the Council may issue to it.

In exercising the powers conferred upon it by this paragraph, the Council shall act by a qualified majority, except in the cases *where the first subparagraph of paragraph 2 provides that the Council shall act unanimously.*

2. Subject to the powers vested in the Commission in this field, **the signing, which may be accompanied by a decision on provisional application before entry into force, and the conclusion of the agreements shall be decided on** by the Council, acting by a qualified majority on a proposal from the Commission. The Council shall act unanimously when the agreement covers a field for which unanimity is required for the adoption of internal rules and for the agreements referred to in Article *310*.

By way of derogation from the rules laid down in paragraph 3, the same procedures shall apply for a decision to suspend the application of an agreement, and for the purpose of establishing the positions to be adopted on behalf of the Community in a body set up by *an agreement, when* **that body is called upon to adopt decisions having legal effects, with the exception of decisions supplementing or amending the institutional framework of the agreement.**

The European Parliament shall be immediately and fully informed of any decision under this paragraph concerning the provisional application or the suspension of agreements, or the establishment of the Community position in a body *set up by an agreement.*

3. The Council shall conclude agreements after consulting the European Parliament, except for the agreements referred to in Article *133(3)*, including cases where the agreement covers a field for which the procedure referred to in Article *251* or that referred to in Article *252* is required for the adoption of internal rules. The European Parliament shall deliver its opinion within a time-limit which the Council may lay down according to the urgency of the matter. In the absence of an opinion within that time-limit, the Council may act.

By way of derogation from the previous subparagraph, agreements referred to in Article *310*, other agreements establishing a specific institutional framework by organising co-operation procedures, agreements having important budgetary implications for the Community and agreements entailing amendment of an act adopted under the procedure referred to in Article *251* shall be concluded after the assent of the European Parliament has been obtained.

The Council and the European Parliament may, in an urgent situation, agree upon a time-limit for the assent.

4. When concluding an agreement, the Council may, by way of derogation from paragraph 2, authorise the Commission to approve modifications on behalf of the

Community where the agreement provides for them to be adopted by a simplified procedure or by a body set up by the agreement; it may attach specific conditions to such authorisation.

5. When the Council envisages concluding an agreement which calls for amendments to this Treaty, the amendments must first be adopted in accordance with the procedure laid down in Article 48 of the Treaty on European Union.

6. The **European Parliament,** the Council, the Commission or a Member State may obtain the opinion of the Court of Justice as to whether an agreement envisaged is compatible with the provisions of this Treaty. Where the opinion of the Court of Justice is adverse, the agreement may enter into force only in accordance with Article 48 of the Treaty on European Union.

7. Agreements concluded under the conditions set out in this Article shall be binding on the institutions of the Community and on Member States.

Article 301 (ex Article 228a)

Where it is provided, in a common position or in a joint action adopted according to the provisions of the Treaty on European Union relating to the common foreign and security policy, for an action by the Community to interrupt or to reduce, in part or completely, economic relations with one or more third countries, the Council shall take the necessary urgent measures. The Council shall act by a qualified majority on a proposal from the Commission.

Article 302 (ex Article 229, simplified)

It shall be for the Commission to ensure the maintenance of all appropriate relations with the organs of the United Nations and of its specialised agencies.

The Commission shall also maintain such relations as are appropriate with all international organisations.

Article 303 (ex Article 230)

The Community shall establish all appropriate forms of co-operation with the Council of Europe.

Article 304 (ex Article 231)

The Community shall establish close co-operation with the Organisation for Economic Co-operation and Development, the details of which shall be determined by common accord.

Article 305 (ex Article 232)

1. The provisions of this Treaty shall not affect the provisions of the Treaty establishing the European Coal and Steel Community, in particular as regards the rights and obligations of Member States, the powers of the institutions of that Community and the rules laid down by that Treaty for the functioning of the common market in coal and steel.

2. The provisions of this Treaty shall not derogate from those of the Treaty establishing the European Atomic Energy Community.

Article 306 (ex Article 233)

The provisions of this Treaty shall not preclude the existence or completion of regional unions between Belgium and Luxembourg, or between Belgium, Luxembourg and the Netherlands, to the extent that the objectives of these regional unions are not attained by application of this Treaty.

Article 307 (ex Article 234)

The rights and obligations arising from agreements concluded before *1 January 1958 or, for acceding States, before the date of their accession,* between one or more Member States on the one hand, and one or more third countries on the other, shall not be affected by the provisions of this Treaty.

To the extent that such agreements are not compatible with this Treaty, the Member State or States concerned shall take all appropriate steps to eliminate the incompatibilities established. Member States shall, where necessary, assist each other to this end and shall, where appropriate, adopt a common attitude. In applying the agreements referred to in the first paragraph, Member States shall take into account the fact that the advantages accorded under this Treaty by each Member State form an integral part of the establishment of the Community and are thereby inseparably linked with the creation of common institutions, the conferring of powers upon them and the granting of the same advantages by all the other Member States.

Article 308 (ex Article 235)

If action by the Community should prove necessary to attain, in the course of the operation of the common market, one of the objectives of the Community and this Treaty has not provided the necessary powers, the Council shall, acting unanimously on a proposal from the Commission and after consulting the European Parliament, take the appropriate measures.

Article 309 (ex Article 236)

1. Where a decision has been taken to suspend the voting rights of the representative of the government of a Member State in accordance with Article 7(3) of the Treaty on European Union, these voting rights shall also be suspended with regard to this Treaty.

2. Moreover, where the existence of a serious and persistent breach by a Member State of principles mentioned in Article 6(1) of the Treaty on European Union has been determined in accordance with Article 7(2) of that Treaty, the Council, acting by a qualified majority, may decide to suspend certain of the rights deriving from the application of this Treaty to the Member State in question. In doing so, the Council shall take into account the possible consequences of such a suspension on the rights and obligations of natural and legal persons.

The obligations of the Member State in question under this Treaty shall in any case continue to be binding on that State.

3. The Council, acting by a qualified majority, may decide subsequently to vary or revoke measures taken in accordance with paragraph 2 in response to changes in the situation which led to their being imposed.

4. When taking decisions referred to in paragraphs 2 and 3, the Council shall act

without taking into account the votes of the representative of the government of the Member State in question. By way of derogation from Article 205(2) a qualified majority shall be defined as the same proportion of the weighted votes of the members of the Council concerned as laid down in Article 205(2).

This paragraph shall also apply in the event of voting rights being suspended in accordance with paragraph 1. In such cases, a decision requiring unanimity shall be taken without the vote of the representative of the government of the Member State in question.

Article 310 (ex Article 238)

The Community may conclude with one or more States or international organisations agreements establishing an association involving reciprocal rights and obligations, common action and special procedures.

Article 311 (ex Article 239)

The protocols annexed to this Treaty by common accord of the Member States shall form an integral part thereof.

Article 312 (ex Article 240)

This Treaty is concluded for an unlimited period.

xxx Final Provisions

The final element of the TEC proper is a very brief one, embracing just two articles to complete the rounding-off process started earlier in Part Six. The element is also unusual, for structural reasons, as well as because of its brevity. Thus the final provisions is virtually the only separate subelement of the TEC which is not described as a chapter, section or the equivalent. It has only a heading and not a number. There is probably no real constitutional significance in this. It is merely a reflection of the fact that the two last items in the General and Final Provisions, Articles 313 and 314, are a clear coda to Part Six. Their function is to set out quasi-transitional arrangements for the coming into force of the original treaty. Hence they are not an undifferentiated strand in a bigger title, as is the case with the TEU whose Title VIII contains articles with virtually the same wording.

All this may seem very technical. However, as we have seen, this is politically very sensitive because of the way people read *Article 313* (ex 247) and it raises major questions about the Union and its future. Moreover, although these articles are very formal, they also remind us that the overall enterprise is based on both the TEU and the TEC. In other words, change in contents or acceptance cannot just be done through the TEU. Amending and accession treaties have to deal with both and failure to ratify the former would mean that either the state involved would fail to join the Union and the Community or that all changes to the two key European treaties would fall. Thus by rejecting the Treaty of Nice Irish voters affected the TEC as well as the TEU. However, such a rejection of a treaty amending the TEC does not deprive the existing TEC of its validity.

The nature of the ratification document and the procedures for ratification are identical to those specified in Article 52 TEU. Indeed, the latter merely echoed this earlier wording. Because the TEC was signed in Rome, formal documents of ratification have to be deposited there. And, if this is not done before the middle of a month, six weeks have to elapse between the last ratification and the treaty coming into effect. This applies to the original document and to later revisions. Otherwise only a fortnight need pass before a treaty becomes operative.

However, there is one slight difference between the second item in the final provisions, *Article 314* (ex 248), and its counterpart, Article 53, in the TEU. This, however, is a matter of implementation and not of principle. The former, reflecting the fact that the TEC was signed by only six states, records that the TEC was drawn up in a single original in four languages. The TEU has 10 languages listed. The second subparagraph of Article 314 TEC lists the eight other authentic language versions of the TEC which exist thanks to subsequent accession treaties, and not just the two, those in Swedish and Finnish, referred to in the TEU. The reference to accession treaties in the plural also points to the fact that the TEC and the TEU are only two among the many European Treaties.

The TEC then ends with signatures, emphasizing the fact that it remains a treaty and not a constitution. And the signatures are of those who actually originally signed the treaty in 1957. The accession treaties carry the signatures of those who committed the states which joined the Community later and, in order to do so, ratified the TEC. However, before looking at the accession treaties and other aspects of the treaty base, the *Guide* needs to consider the remaining elements of the TEC, the protocols and declarations.

FINAL PROVISIONS

Article 313 (ex Article 247)

This Treaty shall be ratified by the High Contracting Parties in accordance with their respective constitutional requirements. The instruments of ratification shall be deposited with the Government of the Italian Republic.

This Treaty shall enter into force on the first day of the month following the deposit of the instrument of ratification by the last signatory State to take this step. If, however, such deposit is made less than 15 days before the beginning of the following month, this Treaty shall not enter into force until the first day of the second month after the date of such deposit.

Article 314 (ex Article 248)

This Treaty, drawn up in a single original in the Dutch, French, German, and Italian languages, all four texts being equally authentic, shall be deposited in the archives of the Government of the Italian Republic, which shall transmit a certified copy to each of the Governments of the other signatory States.

Pursuant to the Accession Treaties, the Danish, English, Finnish, Greek, Irish, Portuguese, Spanish and Swedish versions of this Treaty shall also be authentic.

IN WITNESS WHEREOF, the undersigned Plenipotentiaries have signed this Treaty.

Done at Rome this twenty-fifth day of March in the year one thousand nine hundred and fifty-seven.

P. H. SPAAK,	J. Ch. SNOY ET D'OPPUERS
ADENAUER	HALLSTEIN
PINEAU	M. FAURE
Antonio SEGNI	Gaetano MARTINO
BECH	Lambert SCHAUS
J. LUNS	J. LINTHORST HOMAN

xxxi Protocols

Although the signatures following Article 314 imply that this is where the treaty proper ends, the first set of 'related instruments' which follow – the protocols – form an 'integral part' of the TEC and have the same legal standing as the numbered provisions of the treaty. This is not only stated in Article 311 TEC, but also implicit in the wording of many of the protocols themselves. Several make reference to articles 'of this Treaty'. This clearly means that the protocols cannot be ignored. As Curtin points out, the protocols 'must be considered as if belonging to the Treaty itself with all the consequences that entails in terms of judicial protection and legal effect'. Thus, the provisions contained in the protocols are legally binding on the member states and must be applied in conjunction with the treaty provisions to which they relate. The same is true of protocols attached to the TECSC and TEAEC (see V i and V ii). The importance of the protocols is underlined by the significance they have for the operation of key EC institutions, notably the EIB and ECB, and the fact that some cover major areas of EC activity, notably EMU and Schengen co-operation. Most protocols are, however, very detailed documents and by no means the most accessible of treaty texts. Problems surrounding their accessibility to readers are compounded by the proliferation of protocols since the TEC was signed.

Originally, the TEC had annexed to it a total of 10 protocols, each of which, unlike more recent protocols, was individually signed by the signatories to the TEC. In most cases these original protocols contained either transitional provisions relating to quotas or provisions clarifying the application of the TEC in certain areas of particular interest to individual member states (see Box 7 on p. 480). The one exception was the protocol containing the statute of the EIB. Its existence resulted from the requirement originally contained in Article 266 (ex 198d, previously 129) TEC that the statute be contained in a protocol annexed to the treaty. In addition, there were two protocols concerning imports of bananas and raw coffee which were annexed to the Implementing Convention on the Association of the Overseas Countries and Territories with the Community concluded at the same time as the TEC. Since then, the number of protocols annexed to the TEC has more than trebled, leading to what is referred to as the 'protocolarization' of the TEC. Changes brought about by the TA have seen the repeal of several protocols. Even so, this has hardly brought an end to the protocolarization: the TA itself introduced 12 new protocols to the TEC. Nice added a further four.

The increase in the number of protocols annexed to the TEC can be traced back to April 1957 when, within a month of the TEC being signed, agreement was reached, as required by Article 245 (ex 188) and as noted in the final act, on the *Protocol on the Statute of the Court of Justice of the European Community* (1957). This contained details of the ECJ's organization and procedures. Soon thereafter, and as envisaged in the original Article 218 and in the final act, a *Protocol on the privileges and immunities of the European Economic Community* (1957) was also agreed. This was later repealed and replaced with a single *Protocol on privileges and immunities of the European Communities* annexed to the Merger Treaty (1965). This covers those who are members of or work for the institutions of the EC, ECSC and EAEC. These include MEPs, representatives of the member states taking part in the work of the institutions, officials and servants of the Commission, and those involved in the work of the ECB and ECJ. Two further protocols were annexed to the TEC prior to the TEU. The first, the *Protocol concerning imports into the European Community of petroleum products refined in the Netherlands Antilles*, dates from 1962. The second is the *Protocol on special arrangements for Greenland*. This was annexed to the TEC in 1984 following Greenland's departure from the EC.*

The first time, however, that the TEC experienced a significant increase in the number of its protocols was with the entry into force of the TEU. It introduced 17 new protocols, 16 of which were attached exclusively to the TEC. The seventeenth protocol was annexed to the TEC as well as the TEU, TECSC and TEAEC (see III ix). This doubling of the number of protocols annexed to the TEC heralded the protocolarization of the EU's treaties. It also saw protocols put to new uses. For the most part, those protocols agreed in the 1950s and 1960s were essentially either explanatory in nature or contained detailed statutes governing one or more institutions. Some of those annexed to the TEC by the TEU perform similar functions.

However, the TEU did introduce two more types of protocol. The first were the two declaratory protocols. Both these concern EMU. The first, the *Protocol on the transition to the third stage of economic and monetary union*, declares the irreversible character of the EC's movement to Stage III and requires all member states to respect the will of the EC to proceed towards this goal. It thus acts as a counter to the opt-outs from EMU discussed below. The second protocol, the *Protocol on economic and social cohesion*, reaffirms the EC's aim to compensate its poorer members for the possible economic impact of EMU on their economies through a strengthening of economic and social cohesion among member states.

The second new category of protocol introduced by the TEU includes those containing so-called 'opt-outs' from certain areas of EC integration. Three such protocols were adopted at the time of the TEU. Two – the *Protocol on certain provisions relating to Denmark* and the *Protocol on certain provisions relating to the United Kingdom of Great Britain and Northern Ireland* – provide Denmark and the United Kingdom with permanent opt-outs from Stage III of EMU, while the third – the *Protocol on social policy* – granted the United Kingdom an opt-out from new areas of social policy. It was repealed by the TA. A fourth protocol, the *Protocol on the acquisition of property in Denmark*, also contains an exemption of sorts from Article 49 (ex 59) TEC since it allows for the retention of existing Danish legislation.† Granting such opt-outs clearly runs counter to the express objective of the Union, laid down in Article 2 (ex B) TEU, of maintaining in full the *acquis communautaire* and of building on it. As a result, commentators have accused the TEU of 'hijacking' the *acquis* and of undermining the general application of EC law. As Curtin points out, opt-outs appear to institutionalize, contrary to the provisions of the TEC, the possibility of the differentiated application of EC law. It thus undermines the concept of developing the *acquis*. It also brings into question whether the EC can maintain clear and coherent legal structures. It thus raises

---

*See Article 3(2) of the Treaty amending, with regard to Greenland, the Treaties establishing the European Communities, *OJ* L29, 1 February 1985.

†Greece sought an identical protocol, but the request was rejected on the basis that it was made too late.

similar questions to those concerning the impact of the flexibility clauses introduced by the TA (see III viii). Moreover, the introduction of opt-outs sets a precedent for future IGCs.

Two further protocols introduced by the TEU also raise questions about the coherence of the EC's legal order. The first is the so-called Barber Protocol, formally titled *Protocol concerning Article 119 [now 141] of the Treaty establishing the European Community*. This restricts the definition of remuneration under Article 141 (ex 119) TEC. While seemingly straightforward, the protocol, as both Curtin and Hervey note, effectively undermines the ECJ's ability to clarify its own judgments by inserting into EC law a politically acceptable and financially convenient interpretation of a given treaty provision. The second protocol is the *Protocol annexed to the Treaty on European Union and to the Treaties establishing the European Communities*. It grants the anti-abortion provisions in the Irish Constitution special status. Thus nothing in any of the four treaties noted may affect the application in Ireland of Article 40.3.3. of the Irish Constitution. The implication of this protocol is that it sets a precedent for the application of specific national constitutional provisions to be exempt from EC law. Given the concerns voiced during the ratification debate over constitutional guarantees being undermined by the TEU, notably in Germany, the protocol was seen by Curtin and others as setting a precedent which could prove highly damaging to the integrative efforts of the EC and EU, and to the uniform application of EC law. In the event, the opposite seems to have been the case and, judging by the June 2001 referendum campaign, in Ireland at least the protection offered by this to local autonomies and sensitivities was not felt to be sufficient.

Turning to the remaining and arguably less contentious protocols introduced by the TEU, most concern aspects of EMU. Of these, two relate to the criteria which member states must meet if they are to proceed to Stage III. The first of these, the *Protocol on the excessive deficit procedure*, defines various terms to be used in assessing whether a member state has an excessive government deficit as referred to in Article 104 (ex 104c) TEC. This was supposed to have been replaced in accordance with Article 104(14) TEC. It has not. The second, the *Protocol on the convergence criteria referred to in Article 109j [now 121] of the Treaty establishing the European Community*, clarifies the provisions regarding the convergence criteria. Two further protocols concern EMU. The first of these is *Protocol on the Statute of the European System of Central Banks and of the European Central Bank* and covers, *inter alia*, the constitution of the ESCB; its objectives, tasks, organization, monetary functions and operations; prudential supervision; the bank's financial provisions; general provisions; the procedure for amending the statute; and various transitional and other provisions. The second protocol is the *Protocol on the Statute of the European Monetary Institute*. Technically this is now defunct since the EMI ceased operations on 31 December 1998. The two protocols fulfil an identical function to earlier protocols on the EIB and the ECJ, although the former is unique within the context of the European Treaties in that it contains provisions, as yet unused, for its own revision.* Other EMU-related protocols concern the Bank of Denmark's right to carry out its existing responsibilities with regard to Greenland and the Faeroe Islands (*Protocol on Denmark*); the interest-free credit facility which Portugal provides the Azores and Madeira (*Protocol on Portugal*); France's right to maintain monetary control over its overseas territories (*Protocol on France*); and the extension of the protocol

---

*The provisions, contained in Article 41, detail a 'simplified amendment procedure' whereby selected articles may be amended by the Council acting only by QMV provided the recommendation comes from the ECB. If the amendment is urged by the Commission, then unanimity must be used. In both cases EP assent is required.

concerning the privileges and immunities of the European Communities to the EMI and ESCB (*Protocol amending the Protocol on the privileges and immunities of the European Communities*). A final protocol, the *Protocol on the Economic and Social Committee and the Committee of the Regions*, stated that the Committee of the Regions and EcoSoc will share a common organizational structure. It has since been repealed by the TA, much to the relief of the regional interest.

If the effect of the TEU was to herald the protocolarization of the EU's treaties and raise questions over the coherence of the EC's legal structures, the impact of the TA was essentially to exacerbate the situation. Admittedly, the TA does repeal 12 protocols. Amendments to the TEC resulted in the *Protocol on social policy*, which contained the UK opt-out, and the *Protocol on the Economic and Social Committee and the Committee of the Regions* being repealed. Simplification also saw the repeal of a further nine protocols. These were the *Protocol amending the Protocol on the privileges and immunities of the European Communities* and eight of the original 13 protocols (see Box 7). A second impact which the TA had was to amend eight protocols. In most cases this involved no more than deleting lists of signatories. Other amendments meant changes in article numbers (e.g. to the *Protocol on Italy*),* updating miscellaneous provisions in the light of other deletions, and repealing Article 3 of the *Protocol on special arrangements for Greenland*. Only in the *Protocol on the Statute of the Court of Justice of the European Economic Community* was a change of note introduced. A reference to the applicability of the *Protocol on Privileges and Immunities of the European Communities* to key officials of the ECJ was inserted.

The TA's contribution to the protocolarization of the TEC came with the annexing of 12 new protocols to the treaty. Five are annexed to the TEC alone. A further four are annexed to the TEU and the TEC, while three more are annexed to the TEU as well as the TEC, TECSC and TEAEC. Of the five protocols which the TA annexes solely to the TEC, two clarify for all member states the meaning of important articles in the TEC. The first of these, the *Protocol on asylum for nationals of Member States of the European Union*, outlines the exceptional instances when a member-state national may seek asylum in another EU member state. The second protocol, the *Protocol on the application of the principles of subsidiarity and proportionality* gives full legal standing to earlier European Council statements (Birmingham and Edinburgh in 1992) and the inter-institutional agreement of 28 October 1993 on subsidiarity. Hence, the principle should be easier to implement in the future and be more easily justiciable. The relevance to all member states of the remaining three protocols is less apparent. Indeed, their presence in the TA arguably reflects the need to meet the demands of specific states since resistances ensured that the provisions were contained in protocols and not in the treaty proper.

Thus the third new protocol, the *Protocol on external relations of the Member States with regard to the crossing of external borders*, confirms the rights of member states to negotiate and conclude with third countries agreements regarding procedures at border crossings, provided they are compatible with EC law. The fourth protocol attached to the TEC, the *Protocol on the system of public broadcasting in the Member States*, contains opaque provisions affirming the right of member states to fund public-service broadcasting. This was inserted following pressure from the German *Länder*. Finally, the *Protocol on protection and welfare of animals* stands out as a model of negotiated fudge.

---

*The change in the numbering in the protocol appears to be redundant. Simplification led to the updating of references to Articles 108 and 109 so that the protocol referred to Articles 109h and 109i (now 119 and 120 respectively). Yet, owing to Italian participation in Stage III of EMU from 1 January 1999, these two articles no longer apply to Italy.

Its presence reflects the need to respond to demands from the United Kingdom, for domestic consumption reasons, for the provisions of the Declaration on the protection of animals (No. 24 TEU) to be strengthened and for the welfare of animals to be taken into full consideration when formulating and implementing key EC policies. The wording of the provisions and the fact that they appear only in a protocol and are not inserted into the treaty proper are a reflection of the resistance offered by the likes of France and Spain. Hence, although full regard is to be paid to the welfare requirements of animals, full respect is also to be given to the customs and traditions practised in the member states.

In numerical terms, the impact of Nice on the protocols attached to the TEC was limited. Two new ones were annexed to the TEC alone, one was repealed and one amended. Two further protocols – that on enlargement and that containing the new statute of the Court of Justice – were annexed to the TEC as well as other treaties. Of those protocols annexed exclusively to the TEC, the first, the *Protocol on the financial consequences of the expiry of the ECSC Treaty and on the Research Fund for Coal and Steel*, transfers all ECSC assets and liabilities, as they exist on 23 July 2002, to the EC. All revenue from the assets is to be used to finance a 'Research Fund for Coal and Steel'. The second protocol, the *Protocol on Article 67 of the Treaty establishing the European Community*, is one of the shortest annexed to the TEC. It consists of a single article, originally proposed for inclusion in a declaration, confirming that from 1 May 2004 the Council will act by QMV when adopting measures for administrative co-operation within the areas of freedom, security and justice provided for in Articles 61–69 TEC. Why such a provision is contained in a protocol and not instated into the treaty text itself is unclear.

This leaves the two protocols attached to other treaties in addition to the TEC. As noted earlier in the *Guide*, the first, the *Protocol on the enlargement of the European Union*, concerns staged institutional reforms necessary for enlargement. Therefore, in addition to repealing the *Protocol on the institutions with the prospect of enlargement of the European Union*, it impacts directly on provisions of the TEC, providing for staged reforms to the EP, Council and Commission as the EU expands its membership. The second protocol, the *Protocol on the Statute of the Court of Justice*, is also of considerable significance since, as its title indicates, it contains the revised statute of the ECJ. Unlike its predecessor, which the TN repealed, the new protocol is annexed to the TEU as well as the TEC. It is therefore discussed above in the context of both Articles 220–245 TEC and TEU protocols (see pp. 157–8 and 404–11).

Finally, mention should be made of the two protocols reproduced below which were amended by Nice. The first, the *Protocol on the Statute of the European System of Central Banks and of the European Central Bank*, saw a new article added allowing for amendments via the Council and national ratification – a *de facto* mini-IGC – to certain rules concerning the Governing Council of the ECB. The second protocol amended by the TN is not technically annexed to the TEC. Rather, the *Protocol on privileges and immunities of the European Communities* is annexed to the 1965 Merger Treaty. The amendment extends application of certain provisions to the registrar and judges of the Court of First Instance.

Box 7   Protocols annexed to the TEC and the Impact of the TA and TN

	Date	TA	TN
Protocol on the Statute of the European Investment Bank*	1957	simplified	
Protocol on German internal trade and connected problems	1957	repealed	
Protocol on certain provisions relating to France	1957	repealed	
Protocol on Italy*	1957	simplified	
Protocol on the Grand Duchy of Luxembourg	1957	repealed	
Protocol on goods originating in and coming from certain countries and enjoying special treatment when imported into a member state*	1957	simplified	
Protocol on the treatment to be applied to products within the province of the European Coal and Steel Community in respect of Algeria and the Overseas Departments of the French Republic	1957	repealed	
Protocol on mineral oils and certain of their derivatives	1957	repealed	
Protocol on the application of the Treaty establishing the European Economic Community to the non-European parts of the Kingdom of the Netherlands	1957	repealed	
Protocol on the tariff quota for imports of raw coffee	1957	repealed	
Protocol on the tariff quota for imports of bananas	1957	repealed	
Protocol on the Statute of the Court of Justice of the European Community	1957	simplified	repealed
Protocol concerning imports into the European Community of petroleum products refined in the Netherlands Antilles*	1962	simplified	
Protocol on special arrangements for Greenland*	1984	simplified	
Protocol on the acquisition of property in Denmark*	1992		
Protocol concerning Article 119 [now 141] of the Treaty establishing the European Community*	1992		
Protocol on the Statute of the European System of Central Banks and of the European Central Bank*	1992	simplified	amended
Protocol on the Statute of the European Monetary Institute*	1992	simplified	
Protocol on the excessive deficit procedure*	1992		
Protocol on the convergence criteria referred to in Article 109j [now 121] of the Treaty establishing the European Community*	1992		
Protocol amending the Protocol on the privileges and immunities of the European Communities	1992	repealed	
Protocol on Denmark*	1992		
Protocol on Portugal*	1992		
Protocol on the transition to the third stage of economic and monetary union*	1992		

Protocol on certain provisions relating to the United Kingdom of Great Britain and Northern Ireland*	1992		
Protocol on certain provisions relating to Denmark*	1992		
Protocol on France*	1992		
Protocol on Social Policy (. . .) (*Social Chapter*)	1992	repealed	
Protocol on economic and social cohesion*	1992		
Protocol on the Economic and Social Committee and the Committee of the Regions	1992	repealed	
Protocol annexed to the Treaty on European Union and to the Treaties establishing the European Communities	1992		
Protocol on asylum for nationals of Member States of the European Union*	1997	new	
Protocol on the application of the principles of subsidiarity and proportionality*	1997	new	
Protocol on external relations of the Member States with regard to the crossing of external borders*	1997	new	
Protocol on the system of public broadcasting in the Member States*	1997	new	
Protocol on protection and welfare of animals*	1997	new	
Protocol on the financial consequences of the expiry of the ECSC Treaty and on the Research Fund for Coal and Steel*	2001		new
Protocol on Article 67 of the Treaty establishing the European Community*	2001		new
Protocols annexed to the Merger Treaty			
Protocol on privileges and immunities of the European Communities*	1965	amended	amended
Protocols annexed to TEC and TEU			
Protocol integrating the Schengen *acquis* into the framework of the European Union**	1997	new	
Protocol on the application of certain aspects of Article 7a [now 14] of the Treaty establishing the European Community to the United Kingdom and to Ireland**	1997	new	
Protocol on the position of the United Kingdom and Ireland**	1997	new	
Protocol on the position of Denmark**	1997	new	
Protocols annexed to TEC, TEU, TECSC and TEAEC			
Protocol annexed to the Treaty on European Union and to the Treaties establishing the European Communities**	1992		
Protocol on the institutions with the prospect of enlargement of the European Union**	1997	new	repealed
Protocol on the location of the seats of the institutions and of certain bodies and departments of the European Communities and of Europol**	1997	new	

Protocol on the role of national parliaments in the European Union**	1997	new	
Protocol on the enlargement of the European Union	2001		new
Protocols also annexed to TEC, TEU and TEAEC			
Protocol on the Statute of the Court of Justice*	2001		new

* Denotes that the Protocol is reproduced below.

** Denotes that the Protocol is reproduced above on pp. 161–71.

NB The text of the remaining Protocols can be found in *Treaties establishing the European Communities (Luxembourg: OOPEC, 1973).*

PROTOCOL ON THE STATUTE OF THE EUROPEAN INVESTMENT BANK (1957)

THE HIGH CONTRACTING PARTIES

DESIRING to lay down the Statute of the European Investment Bank provided for in Article 266 of this Treaty.

HAVE AGREED upon the following provisions, which shall be annexed to this Treaty:

Article 1. The European Investment Bank established by Article 266 of this Treaty (hereinafter called the 'Bank') is hereby constituted; it shall perform its functions and carry on its activities in accordance with the provisions of this Treaty and of this Statute.

The seat of the Bank shall be determined by common accord of the Governments of the Member States.

Article 2. The task of the Bank shall be that defined in Article 267 of this Treaty.

Article 3. In accordance with Article 266 of this Treaty, the following shall be members of the Bank: [here follow the names of the member states]

Article 4.1. The capital of the Bank shall be one hundred billion (100 000 000 000) euro, subscribed by the Member States as follows:*

Germany	17 766 355 000	France	17 766 355 000
Italy	17 766 355 000	United Kingdom	17 766 355 000
Spain	6 530 656 000	Belgium	4 924 710 000
Netherlands	4 924 710 000	Sweden	3 267 057 000
Denmark	2 493 522 000	Austria	2 444 649 000
Finland	1 404 544 000	Greece	1 335 817 000
Portugal	860 858 000	Ireland	623 380 000
Luxembourg	124 677 000		

The unit of account shall be defined as being the euro used by the European Communities. The Board of Governors, acting unanimously on a proposal from the Board of Directors, may alter the definition of the unit of account.

The Member States shall be liable only up to the amount of their share of the capital subscribed and not paid up.

---

*As amended by the EIB Board of Governors on 5 June 1998. See *OJ* c247, 31 August 1999, p. 6.

2. The admission of a new member shall entail an increase in the subscribed capital corresponding to the capital brought in by the new member.

3. The Board of Governors may, acting unanimously, decide to increase the subscribed capital.

4. The share of a member in the subscribed capital may not be transferred, pledged or attached.

Article 5.1. The subscribed capital shall be paid in by Member States to the extent of 6% on average of the amounts laid down in Article 4(1).

2. In the event of an increase in the subscribed capital, the Board of Governors, acting unanimously, shall fix the percentage to be paid up and the arrangements for payment.

3. The Board of Directors may require payment of the balance of the subscribed capital, to such extent as may be required for the Bank to meet its obligations towards those who have made loans to it.

Each Member State shall make this payment in proportion to its share of the subscribed capital in the currencies required by the Bank to meet these obligations.

Article 6.1. The Board of Governors may, acting by a qualified majority on a proposal from the Board of Directors, decide that Member States shall grant the Bank special interest bearing loans if and to the extent that the Bank requires such loans to finance specific projects and the Board of Directors shows that the Bank is unable to obtain the necessary funds on the capital markets on terms appropriate to the nature and purpose of the projects to be financed.

2. Special loans may not be called for until the beginning of the fourth year after the entry into force of this Treaty. They shall not exceed 400 million units of account in the aggregate or 100 million units of account per annum.

3. The term of special loans shall be related to the term of the loans or guarantees which the Bank proposes to grant by means of the special loans; it shall not exceed twenty years. The Board of Governors may, acting by a qualified majority on a proposal from the Board of Directors, decide upon the prior repayment of special loans.

4. Special loans shall bear interest at 4% per annum, unless the Board of Governors, taking into account the trend and level of interest rates on the capital markets, decides to fix a different rate.

5. Special loans shall be granted by Member States in proportion to their share in the subscribed capital; payment shall be made in national currency within six months of such loans being called for.

6. Should the Bank go into liquidation, special loans granted by Member States shall be repaid only after the other debts of the Bank have been settled.

Article 7.1. Should the value of the currency of a Member State in relation to the unit of account defined in Article 4 be reduced, that State shall adjust the amount of its capital share paid in its own currency in proportion to the change in value by making a supplementary payment to the Bank.

2. Should the value of currency of a Member State in relation to the unit of account defined in Article 4 be increased, the Bank shall adjust the amount of the capital share paid in by that State in its own currency in proportion to the change in value by making a repayment to that State.

3. For the purpose of this Article, the value of the currency of a Member State in

relation to the unit of account, defined in Article 4, shall correspond to the rate for converting the unit of account into this currency and vice versa based on market rates.

4. The Board of Governors, acting unanimously on a proposal from the Board of Directors, may alter the method of converting sums expressed in units of account into national currencies and vice versa.

Furthermore, acting unanimously on a proposal from the Board of Directors, it may define the method for adjusting the capital referred to in paragraphs 1 and 2 of this Article; adjustment payments must be made at least once a year.

Article 8. The Bank shall be directed and managed by a Board of Governors, a Board of Directors and a Management Committee.

Article 9.1. The Board of Governors shall consist of the Ministers designated by the Member States.

2. The Board of Governors shall lay down general directives for the credit policy of the Bank, with particular reference to the objectives to be pursued as progress is made in the attainment of the common market.

The board of Governors shall ensure that these directives are implemented.

3. The Board of Governors shall in addition:
(a) decide whether to increase the subscribed capital in accordance with Article 4(3) and Article 5(2);
(b) exercise the powers provided in Article 6 in respect of special loans;
(c) exercise the powers provided in Articles 11 and 13 in respect of the appointment and the compulsory retirement of the members of the Board of Directors and the Management Committee, and those powers provided in the second subparagraph of Article 13(1);
(d) authorise the derogation provided for in Article 18(1);
(e) approve the annual report of the Board of Directors;
(f) approve the annual balance sheet and profit and loss account;
(g) exercise the powers and functions provided in Articles 4, 7, 14, 17, 26 and 27;
(h) approve the rules of procedure of the Bank.

4. Within the framework of this Treaty and this Statute, the Board of Governors shall be competent to take, acting unanimously, any decision concerning the suspension of the operations of the Bank and, should the event arise, its liquidation.

Article 10. Save as otherwise provided in this Statute, decisions of the Board of Governors shall be taken by a majority of its members. This majority must represent at least 50% of the subscribed capital. Voting by the Board of Governors shall be in accordance with the provisions of Article 205 of this Treaty.

Article 11.1. The Board of Directors shall have sole power to take decisions in respect of granting loans and guarantees and raising loans; it shall fix the interest rates on loans granted and the commission on guarantees; it shall see that the Bank is properly run; it shall ensure that the Bank is managed in accordance with the provisions of this Treaty and of this Statute and with the general directives laid down by the Board of Governors.

At the end of the financial year the Board of Directors shall submit a report to the Board of Governors and shall publish it when approved.

2. The Board of Directors shall consist of 25 directors and 13 alternates.

The directors shall be appointed by the Board of Governors for five years as shown below:
– three directors nominated by the Federal Republic of Germany,
– three directors nominated by the French Republic,
– three directors nominated by the Italian Republic,
– three directors nominated by the United Kingdom of Great Britain and Northern Ireland,
– two directors nominated by the Kingdom of Spain,
– one director nominated by the Kingdom of Belgium,
– one director nominated by the Kingdom of Denmark,
– one director nominated by the Hellenic Republic,
– one director nominated by Ireland,
– one director nominated by the Grand Duchy of Luxembourg,
– one director nominated by the Kingdom of the Netherlands,
– one director nominated by the Republic of Austria,
– one director nominated by the Portuguese Republic,
– one director nominated by the Republic of Finland,
– one director nominated by the Kingdom of Sweden,
– one director nominated by the Commission.

The alternates shall be appointed by the Board of Governors for five years as shown below:
– two alternates nominated by the Federal Republic of Germany,
– two alternates nominated by the French Republic,
– two alternates nominated by the Italian Republic,
– two alternates nominated by the United Kingdom of Great Britain and Northern Ireland,
– one alternate nominated by common accord of the Kingdom of Spain and the Portuguese Republic,
– one alternate nominated by common accord of the Benelux countries,
– one alternate nominated by common accord of the Kingdom of Denmark, the Hellenic Republic and Ireland,
– one alternate nominated by common accord of the Republic of Austria, the Republic of Finland and the Kingdom of Sweden,
– one alternate nominated by the Commission.

The appointments of the directors and the alternates shall be renewable.

Alternates may take part in the meetings of the Board of Directors. Alternates nominated by a State, or by common accord of several States, or by the Commission, may replace directors nominated by that State, by one of those States or by the Commission respectively. Alternates shall have no right of vote except where they replace one director or more than one director or where they have been delegated for this purpose in accordance with Article 12(1).

The President of the Management Committee or, in his absence, one of the Vice-Presidents, shall preside over meetings of the Board of Directors but shall not vote.

Members of the Board of Directors shall be chosen from persons whose independence and competence are beyond doubt; they shall be responsible only to the Bank.

3. A director may be compulsorily retired by the Board of Governors only if he no longer fulfils the conditions required for the performance of his duties; the Board must act by a qualified majority.

If the annual report is not approved, the Board of Directors shall resign.

4. Any vacancy arising as a result of death, voluntary resignation, compulsory retirement or collective resignation shall be filled in accordance with paragraph 2. A member shall be replaced for the remainder of his term of office, save where the entire Board of Directors is being replaced.

5. The Board of Governors shall determine the remuneration of members of the Board of Directors. The Board of Governors shall, acting unanimously, lay down what activities are incompatible with the duties of a director or an alternate.

Article 12.1. Each director shall have one vote on the Board of Directors. He may delegate his vote in all cases, according to procedures to be laid down in the Rules of Procedure of the Bank.

2. Save as otherwise provided in this Statute, decisions of the Board of Directors shall be taken by a simple majority of the members entitled to vote. A qualified majority shall require 17 votes in favour. The Rules of Procedure of the Bank shall lay down how many members of the Board of Directors constitute the quorum needed for the adoption of decisions.

Article 13.1. The Management Committee shall consist of a President and six Vice-Presidents appointed for a period of six years by the Board of Governors on a proposal from the Board of Directors. Their appointments shall be renewable.

The Board of Governors acting unanimously, may vary the number of members on the Management Committee.

2. On a proposal from the Board of Directors adopted by a qualified majority, the Board of Governors may, acting in its turn by a qualified majority, compulsorily retire a member of the Management Committee.

3. The Management Committee shall be responsible for the current business of the Bank, under the authority of the President and the supervision of the Board of Directors.

It shall prepare the decisions of the Board of Directors, in particular decisions on the raising of loans and the granting of loans and guarantees; it shall ensure that these decisions are implemented.

4. The Management Committee shall act by a majority when delivering opinions on proposals for raising loans or granting loans and guarantees.

5. The Board of Governors shall determine the remuneration of members of the Management Committee and shall lay down what activities are incompatible with their duties.

6. The President or, if he is prevented, a Vice-President shall represent the Bank in judicial and other matters.

7. The officials and other employees of the Bank shall be under the authority of the President. They shall be engaged and discharged by him. In the selection of staff, account shall be taken not only of personal ability and qualifications but also of an equitable representation of nationals of Member States.

8. The Management Committee and the staff of the Bank shall be responsible only to the Bank and shall be completely independent in the performance of their duties.

Article 14.1. A Committee consisting of three members, appointed on the grounds of their competence by the Board of Governors, shall annually verify that the operations of the Bank have been conducted and its books kept in a proper manner.

2. The Committee shall confirm that the balance sheet and profit and loss account are in agreement with the accounts and faithfully reflect the position of the Bank in respect of its assets and liabilities.

Article 15. The Bank shall deal with each Member State through the authority designated by that State. In the conduct of financial operations the Bank shall have recourse to the bank of issue of the Member State concerned or to other financial institutions approved by that State.

Article 16.1. The Bank shall co-operate with all international organisations active in fields similar to its own.

2. The Bank shall seek to establish all appropriate contacts in the interests of co-operation with banking and financial institutions in the countries to which its operations extend.

Article 17. At the request of a Member State or of the Commission, or on its own initiative, the Board of Governors, shall, in accordance with the same provisions as governed their adoption, interpret or supplement the directives laid down by it under Article 9 of this Statute.

Article 18.1. Within the framework of the task set out in Article 267 of this Treaty, the Bank shall grant loans to its members or to private or public undertakings for investment projects to be carried out in the European territories of Member States, to the extent that funds are not available from other sources on reasonable terms.

However, by way of derogation authorised by the Board of Governors, acting unanimously on a proposal from the Board of Directors, the Bank may grant loans for investment projects to be carried out, in whole or in part, outside the European territories of Member States.

2. As far as possible, loans shall be granted only on condition that other sources of finance are also used.

3. When granting a loan to an undertaking or to a body other than a Member State, the Bank shall make the loan conditional either on a guarantee from the Member State in whose territory the project will be carried out or on other adequate guarantees.

4. The Bank may guarantee loans contracted by public or private undertakings or other bodies for the purpose of carrying out projects provided for in Article 267 of this Treaty.

5. The aggregate amount outstanding at any time of loans and guarantees granted by the Bank shall not exceed 250% of its subscribed capital.

6. The Bank shall protect itself against exchange risks by including in contracts for loans and guarantees such clauses as it considers appropriate.

Article 19.1. Interest rates on loans to be granted by the Bank and commission on guarantees shall be adjusted to conditions prevailing on the capital market and shall be calculated in such a way that the income therefrom shall enable the Bank to meet its obligations, to cover its expenses and to build up a reserve fund as provided for in Article 24.

2. The Bank shall not grant any reduction in interest rates. Where a reduction in the interest rate appears desirable in view of the nature of the project to be financed, the Member State concerned or some other agency may grant aid towards the payment of interest to the extent that this is compatible with Article 87 of this Treaty.

Article 20. In its loan and guarantee operations, the Bank shall observe the following principles:

1. It shall ensure that its funds are employed as rationally as possible in the interests of the Community.

It may grant loans or guarantees only:

(a) where, in the case of projects carried out by undertakings in the production sector, interest and amortisation payments are covered out of operating profits, or, in other cases, either by a commitment entered into by the State in which the project is carried out or by some other means; and

(b) where the execution of the project contributes to an increase in economic productivity in general and promotes the attainment of the common market.

2. It shall neither acquire any interest in an undertaking nor assume any responsibility in its management unless this is required to safeguard the rights of the Bank in ensuring recovery of funds lent.

3. It may dispose of its claims on the capital market and may, to this end, require its debtors to issue bonds or other securities.

4. Neither the Bank nor the Member States shall impose conditions requiring funds lent by the Bank to be spent within a specified Member State.

5. The Bank may make its loan conditional on international invitations to tender being arranged.

6. The Bank shall not finance, in whole or in part, any project opposed by the Member State in whose territory it is to be carried out.

Article 21.1. Applications for loans or guarantees may be made to the Bank either through the Commission or through the Member State in whose territory the project will be carried out. An undertaking may also apply direct to the Bank for a loan or guarantee.

2. Applications made through the Commission shall be submitted for an opinion to the Member State in whose territory the project will be carried out. Applications made through a Member State shall be submitted to the Commission for an opinion.

Applications made direct by an undertaking shall be submitted to the Member State concerned and to the Commission.

The Member State concerned and the Commission shall deliver their opinions within two months. If no reply is received within this period, the Bank may assume that there is no objection to the project in question.

3. The Board of Directors shall rule on applications for loans or guarantees submitted to it by the Management Committee.

4. The Management Committee shall examine whether applications for loans or guarantees submitted to it comply with the provisions of this Statute, in particular with Article 20. Where the Management Committee is in favour of granting the loan or guarantee, it shall submit the draft contract to the Board of Directors; the Committee may make its favourable opinion subject to such conditions as it considers essential. Where the Management Committee is against granting the loan or guarantee, it shall submit the relevant documents together with its opinion to the Board of Directors.

5. Where the Management Committee delivers an unfavourable opinion, the Board of Directors may not grant the loan or guarantee concerned unless its decision is unanimous.

6. Where the Commission delivers an unfavourable opinion, the Board of Directors may not grant the loan or guarantee concerned unless its decision is unanimous, the director nominated by the Commission abstaining.

7. Where both the Management Committee and the Commission deliver an unfavourable opinion, the Board of Directors may not grant the loan or guarantee.

Article 22.1. The Bank shall borrow on the international capital markets the funds necessary for the performance of its tasks.

2. The Bank may borrow on the capital market of a Member State either in accordance with the legal provisions applying to the internal issues, or, if there are no such provisions in a Member State, after the Bank and the Member State concerned have conferred together and reached agreement on the proposed loan.

The competent authorities in the Member State concerned may refuse to give their assent only if there is reason to fear serious disturbances on the capital market of that State.

Article 23.1. The Bank may employ any available funds which it does not immediately require to meet its obligations in the following ways:
(a) it may invest on the money markets;
(b) it may, subject to the provisions of Article 20(2), buy and sell securities issued by itself or by those who have borrowed from it;
(c) it may carry out any other financial operation linked with its objectives.

2. Without prejudice to the provisions of Article 25, the Bank shall not, in managing its investments engage in any currency arbitrage not directly required to carry out its lending operations or fulfil commitments arising out of loans raised or guarantees granted by it.

3. The Bank shall, in the fields covered by this Article, act in agreement with the competent authorities or with the bank of issue of the Member State concerned.

Article 24.1. A reserve fund of up to 10% of the subscribed capital shall be built up progressively. If the state of the liabilities of the Bank should so justify, the Board of Directors may decide to set aside additional reserves. Until such times as the reserve fund has been fully built up, it shall be fed by:
(a) interest received on loans granted by the Bank out of sums to be paid up by the Member States pursuant to Article 5;
(b) interest received on loans granted by the Bank out of funds derived from repayment of the loans referred to in (a);
to the extent that this income is not required to meet the obligations of the Bank or to cover its expenses.

2. The resources of the reserve fund shall be so invested as to be available at any time to meet the purpose of the fund.

Article 25.1. The Bank shall at all times be entitled to transfer its assets in the currency of one Member State into the currency of another Member State in order to carry out financial operations corresponding to the task set out in Article 267 of this Treaty, taking into account the provisions of Article 23 of this Statute. The Bank shall, as far as possible, avoid making such transfers if it has cash or liquid assets in the currency required.

2. The Bank may not convert its assets in the currency of a Member State into the currency of a third country without the agreement of the Member State concerned.

3. The Bank may freely dispose of that part of its capital which is paid up in gold

or convertible currency and of any currency borrowed on markets outside the Community.

4. The Member States undertake to make available to the debtors of the Bank the currency needed to repay the capital and pay the interest on loans or commissions on guarantees granted by the Bank for projects to be carried out in their territory.

Article 26. If a Member State fails to meet the obligations of membership arising from this Statute, in particular the obligation to pay its share of the subscribed capital, to grant its special loans or to service its borrowings, the granting of loans or guarantees to that Member State or its nationals may be suspended by a decision of the Board of Governors, acting by a qualified majority.

Such decision shall not release either the State or its nationals from their obligations towards the Bank.

Article 27.1. If the Board of Governors decides to suspend the operations of the Bank, all its activities shall cease forthwith, except those required to ensure the due realisation, protection and preservation of its assets and the settlement of its liabilities.

2. In the event of liquidation, the Board of Governors shall appoint the liquidators and give them instructions for carrying out the liquidation.

Article 28.1. In each of the Member States, the Bank shall enjoy the most extensive legal capacity accorded to legal persons under their laws; it may, in particular, acquire or dispose of movable or immovable property and may be a party to legal proceedings.

2. The property of the Bank shall be exempt from all forms of requisition or expropriation.

Article 29. Disputes between the Bank on the one hand, and its creditors, debtors or any other person on the other, shall be decided by the competent national courts, save where jurisdiction has been conferred on the Court of Justice.

The Bank shall have an address for service in each Member State. It may, however, in any contract, specify a particular address for service or provide for arbitration.

The property and assets of the Bank shall not be liable to attachment or to seizure by way of execution except by decision of a court.

Article 30*

1. The Board of Governors may, acting unanimously, decide to establish a European Investment Fund, which shall have legal personality and financial autonomy, and of which the Bank shall be a founding member.

2. The Board of Governors shall establish the Statute of the European Investment Fund by unanimous decision. The Statute shall define, in particular, its objectives, structure, capital, membership, financial resources, means of intervention and auditing arrangements, as well as the relationship between the organs of the Bank and those of the Fund.

3. Notwithstanding the provisions of Article 20(2), the Bank shall be entitled to participate in the management of the Fund and contribute to its subscribed capital up to the amount determined by the Board of Governors acting unanimously.

*As inserted by the Act of 25 March 1993 amending the Protocol on the Statute of the European Investment Bank empowering the Board of Governors to establish a European Investment Fund; this amendment came into force on 1 May 1994.

4. The European Community may become a member of the Fund and contribute to its subscribed capital. Financial institutions with an interest in the objectives of the Fund may be invited to become members.

5. The Protocol on the privileges and immunities of the European Communities shall apply to the Fund, to the members of its organs in the performance of their duties as such and to its staff.

The Fund shall in addition be exempt from any form of taxation or imposition of a like nature on the occasion of any increase in its capital and from the various formalities which may be connected therewith in the State where the Fund has its seat. Similarly, its dissolution or liquidation shall not give rise to any imposition. Finally, the activities of the Fund and of its organs carried out in accordance with its Statute shall not be subject to any turnover tax.

Those dividends, capital gains or other forms of revenue stemming from the Fund to which the members, other than the European Community and the Bank, are entitled, shall however remain subject to the fiscal provisions of the applicable legislation.

6. The Court of Justice shall, within the limits hereinafter laid down, have jurisdiction in disputes concerning measures adopted by organs of the Fund. Proceedings against such measures may be instituted by any member of the Fund in its capacity as such or by Member States under the conditions laid down in Article 230 of this Treaty.

PROTOCOL ON ITALY (1957)

THE HIGH CONTRACTING PARTIES,
DESIRING to settle certain particular problems relating to Italy,
HAVE AGREED upon the following provisions, which shall be annexed to this Treaty:

The MEMBER STATES OF THE COMMUNITY
TAKE NOTE of the fact that the Italian Government is carrying out a 10 year programme of economic expansion designed to rectify the disequilibria in the structure of the Italian economy, in particular by providing an infrastructure for the less developed areas in southern Italy and in the Italian islands and by creating new jobs in order to eliminate unemployment;
RECALL that the principles and objectives of this programme of the Italian Government have been considered and approved by organizations for international co-operation of which the Member States are members;
RECOGNIZE that it is in their common interest that the objectives of the Italian programme should be attained;
AGREE, in order to facilitate the accomplishment of this task by the Italian Government, to recommend to the institutions of the Community that they should employ all the methods and procedures provided in this Treaty and, in particular, make appropriate use of the resources of the European Investment Bank and the European Social Fund;
ARE OF THE OPINION that the institutions of the Community should, in applying this Treaty, take account of the sustained effort to be made by the Italian economy in the coming years and of the desirability of avoiding dangerous stresses

in particular within the balance of payments or the level of employment, which might jeopardize the application of this Treaty in Italy;

RECOGNIZE that in the event of Articles *119* and *120* being applied it will be necessary to take care that any measures required of the Italian Government do not prejudice the completion of its programme for economic expansion and for raising the standard of living of the population.

DONE at Rome this twenty-fifth day of March in the year one thousand nine hundred and fifty-seven.

PROTOCOL ON GOODS ORIGINATING IN AND COMING FROM CERTAIN COUNTRIES AND ENJOYING SPECIAL TREATMENT WHEN IMPORTED INTO A MEMBER STATE (1957)*

THE HIGH CONTRACTING PARTIES,

DESIRING to define in greater detail the application of this Treaty to certain goods originating in and coming from certain countries and enjoying special treatment when imported into a Member State,

HAVE AGREED upon the following provisions, which shall be annexed to this Treaty:

1. The application of the Treaty establishing the European Community shall not require any alteration in the customs treatment applicable *on 1 January 1958, to imports into the Benelux countries of goods originating in and coming from Surinam or the Netherlands Antilles.*

2. Goods imported into a Member State and benefiting from the treatment referred to above shall not be considered to be in free circulation in that State within the meaning of Article 24 of this Treaty when re-exported to another Member State.

3. *Member States shall* communicate to the Commission and to the other Member States their rules governing the special treatment referred to in this Protocol, together with a list of the goods entitled to such treatment.

They shall also inform the Commission and the other Member States of any changes subsequently made to those lists or in the treatment.

4. The Commission shall ensure that the application of these rules cannot be prejudicial to other Member States; to this end it may take any appropriate measures as regards relations between Member States.

DONE at Rome this twenty-fifth day of March in the year one thousand nine hundred and fifty-seven.

---

*The TA's simplification of the protocol resulted in the removal of references to goods imported into France from Morocco, Tunisia, Vietnam, Cambodia, Laos and French settlements in the New Hebrides, and into Italy from Libya and Somaliland. It also saw the deletion, as with all of the surviving protocols from 1957, of the list of signatories.

PROTOCOL ON THE STATUTE OF THE COURT OF JUSTICE (2001)*

THE HIGH CONTRACTING PARTIES

DESIRING to lay down the Statute of the Court of Justice provided for in Article 245 of the Treaty establishing the European Community and in Article 160 of the Treaty establishing the European Atomic Energy Community,

HAVE AGREED upon the following provisions, which shall be annexed to the **Treaty on European Union,** the Treaty establishing the European Community *and the Treaty establishing the European Atomic Energy Community:*

Article 1 (ex Article 1)

The Court **of Justice** shall be constituted and shall function in accordance with the provisions of **the Treaty on European Union (EU Treaty),** *of the Treaty establishing the European Community (EC Treaty), of the Treaty establishing the European Atomic Energy Community (EAEC Treaty)* and of this Statute.

TITLE I   JUDGES AND ADVOCATES-GENERAL

Article 2 (ex Article 2)

Before taking up his duties each Judge shall, in open court, take an oath to perform his duties impartially and conscientiously and to preserve the secrecy of the deliberations of the Court.

Article 3 (ex Article 3)

The Judges shall be immune from legal proceedings. After they have ceased to hold office, they shall continue to enjoy immunity in respect of acts performed by them in their official capacity, including words spoken or written.

The Court, sitting **as a full Court,** may waive the immunity.

Where immunity has been waived and criminal proceedings are instituted against a Judge, he shall be tried, in any of the Member States, only by the court competent to judge the members of the highest national judiciary.

Articles 12 to 15 and Article 18 of the Protocol on the privileges and immunities of the European Communities shall apply to the Judges, Advocates-General, Registrar and Assistant Rapporteurs *of the Court,* without prejudice to the provisions relating to immunity from legal proceedings of Judges which are set out in the preceding paragraphs.

Article 4 (ex Article 4)

The Judges may not hold any political or administrative office.

They may not engage in any occupation, whether gainful or not, unless exemption is exceptionally granted by the Council.

When taking up their duties, they shall give a solemn undertaking that, both during and after their term of office, they will respect the obligations arising therefrom, in particular the duty to behave with integrity and discretion as regards the acceptance, after they have ceased to hold office, of certain appointments or benefits.

Any doubt on this point shall be settled by decision of the Court.

*Unemphasized text originates from the Protocol on the Statute of the Court of Justice of the European Community, which was repealed by Nice and which the current protocol replaces.

Article 5 (ex Article 5)

Apart from normal replacement, or death, the duties of a Judge shall end when he resigns.

Where a Judge resigns, his letter of resignation shall be addressed to the President of the Court for transmission to the President of the Council. Upon this notification a vacancy shall arise on the bench.

Save where Article 6 applies, a Judge shall continue to hold office until his successor takes up his duties.

Article 6 (ex Article 6)

A Judge may be deprived of his office or of his right to a pension or other benefits in its stead only if, in the unanimous opinion of the Judges and Advocates-General of the Court, he no longer fulfils the requisite conditions or meets the obligations arising from his office.

The Judge concerned shall not take part in any such deliberations.

The Registrar of the Court shall communicate the decision of the Court to the President of the European Parliament and to the President of the Commission and shall notify it to the President of the Council.

In the case of a decision depriving a Judge of his office, a vacancy shall arise on the bench upon this latter notification.

Article 7 (ex Article 7)

A Judge who is to replace a member of the Court whose term of office has not expired shall be appointed for the remainder of his predecessor's term.

Article 8 (ex Article 8)

The provisions of Articles 2 to 7 shall apply to the Advocates-General.

TITLE II   ORGANISATION

Article 9 (new – TN)

When, every three years, the Judges are partially replaced, eight and seven Judges shall be replaced alternately.

When, every three years, the Advocates-General are partially replaced, four Advocates-General shall be replaced on each occasion.

Article 10 (ex Article 9)

The Registrar shall take an oath before the Court to perform his duties impartially and conscientiously and to preserve the secrecy of the deliberations of the Court.

Article 11 (ex Article 10)

The Court shall arrange for replacement of the Registrar on occasions when he is prevented from attending the Court.

Article 12 (ex Article 11)

Officials and other servants shall be attached to the Court to enable it to function. They shall be responsible to the Registrar under the authority of the President.

Article 13 (ex Article 12)

On a proposal from the Court, the Council may, acting unanimously, provide for the appointment of Assistant Rapporteurs and lay down the rules governing their service. The Assistant Rapporteurs may be required, under conditions laid down in the Rules of Procedure, to participate in preparatory inquiries in cases pending before the Court and to co-operate with the Judge who acts as Rapporteur.

The Assistant Rapporteurs shall be chosen from persons whose independence is beyond doubt and who possess the necessary legal qualifications; they shall be appointed by the Council.

They shall take an oath before the Court to perform their duties impartially and conscientiously and to preserve the secrecy of the deliberations of the Court.

Article 14 (ex Article 13)

The Judges, the Advocates-General and the Registrar shall be required to reside at the place where the Court has its seat.

Article 15 (ex Article 14)

The Court shall remain permanently in session. The duration of the judicial vacations shall be determined by the Court with due regard to the needs of its business.

Article 16 (new – TN)

The Court shall form chambers consisting of three and five Judges. The Judges shall elect the Presidents of the chambers from among their number. The Presidents of the chambers of five Judges shall be elected for three years. They may be re-elected once.

The Grand Chamber shall consist of eleven Judges. It shall be presided over by the President of the Court. The Presidents of the chambers of five Judges and other Judges appointed in accordance with the conditions laid down in the Rules of Procedure shall also form part of the Grand Chamber.

The Court shall sit in a Grand Chamber when a Member State or an institution of the Communities that is party to the proceedings so requests.

The Court shall sit as a full Court where cases are brought before it pursuant to Article 195(2), Article 213(2), Article 216 or Article 247(7) of the EC Treaty or Article 107d(2), Article 126(2), Article 129 or Article 160b(7) of the EAEC Treaty.

Moreover, where it considers that a case before it is of exceptional importance, the Court may decide, after hearing the Advocate-General, to refer the case to the full Court.

Article 17 (ex Article 15)

Decisions of the Court shall be valid only when an uneven number of its members is sitting in the deliberations.

Decisions of the chambers consisting of either three or five Judges shall be valid only if they are taken by three Judges.

Decisions of the Grand Chamber shall be valid only if nine Judges are sitting.

Decisions of the full Court shall be valid only if eleven Judges are sitting.

In the event of one of the Judges of a chamber being prevented from attending, a Judge of another chamber may be called upon to sit in accordance with conditions laid down in the Rules of Procedure.

Article 18 (ex Article 16)

No Judge or Advocate-General may take part in the disposal of any case in which he has previously taken part as agent or adviser or has acted for one of the parties, or in which he has been called upon to pronounce as a member of a court or tribunal, of a commission of inquiry or in any other capacity.

If, for some special reason, any Judge or Advocate-General considers that he should not take part in the judgment or examination of a particular case, he shall so inform the President. If, for some special reason, the President considers that any Judge or Advocate-General should not sit or make submissions in a particular case, he shall notify him accordingly.

Any difficulty arising as to the application of this Article shall be settled by decision of the Court.

A party may not apply for a change in the composition of the Court or of one of its chambers on the grounds of either the nationality of a Judge or the absence from the Court or from the chamber of a Judge of the nationality of that party.

TITLE III   PROCEDURE

Article 19 (ex Article 17)

The **Member** States and the institutions of the Communities shall be represented before the Court by an agent appointed for each case; the agent may be assisted *by an adviser or by a lawyer.*

The States, other than the Member States, which are parties to the Agreement on the European Economic Area and also the EFTA Surveillance Authority referred to in that Agreement shall be represented in same manner.

Other parties must be represented *by a lawyer.*

Only a lawyer authorised to practise before a court of a Member State or of another State which is a party to the Agreement on the European Economic Area may represent or assist a party before the Court.

Such agents, advisers and lawyers shall, when they appear before the Court, enjoy the rights and immunities necessary to the independent exercise of their duties, under conditions laid down in the Rules of Procedure.

As regards such advisers and lawyers who appear before it, the Court shall have the powers normally accorded to courts of law, under conditions laid down in the Rules of Procedure.

University teachers being nationals of a Member State whose law accords them a right of audience shall have the same rights before the Court as are accorded by this Article *to lawyers.*

Article 20 (ex Article 18)

The procedure before the Court shall consist of two parts: written and oral.

The written procedure shall consist of the communication to the parties and to the institutions of the *Communities* whose decisions are in dispute, of applications, statements of case, defences and observations, and of replies, if any, as well as of all papers and documents in support or of certified copies of them.

Communications shall be made by the Registrar in the order and within the time laid down in the Rules of Procedure.

The oral procedure shall consist of the reading of the report presented by a Judge acting as Rapporteur, the hearing by the Court of agents, advisers and lawyers and of the submissions of the Advocate-General, as well as the hearing, if any, of witnesses and experts.

Where it considers that the case raises no new point of law, the Court may decide, after hearing the Advocate-General, that the case shall be determined without a submission from the Advocate-General.

Article 21 (ex Article 19)

A case shall be brought before the Court by a written application addressed to the Registrar. The application shall contain the applicant's name and permanent address and the description of the signatory, the name of the party *or names of the parties* against whom the application is made, the subject-matter of the dispute, the form of order sought and a brief statement of the **pleas in law** on which the application is based.

The application shall be accompanied, where appropriate, by the measure the annulment of which is sought or, in the circumstances referred to in Article 232 of *the EC* Treaty *and Article 148 of the EAEC Treaty,* by documentary evidence of the date on which an institution was, in accordance with *those Articles,* requested to act. If the documents are not submitted with the application, the Registrar shall ask the party concerned to produce them within a reasonable period, but in that event the rights of the party shall not lapse even if such documents are produced after the time-limit for bringing proceedings.

Article 22*

A case governed by Article 18 of the EAEC Treaty shall be brought before the Court by an appeal addressed to the Registrar. The appeal shall contain the name and permanent address of the applicant and the description of the signatory, a reference to the decision against which the appeal is brought, the names of the respondents, the subject-matter of the dispute, the submissions and a brief statement of the grounds on which the appeal is based.

The appeal shall be accompanied by a certified copy of the decision of the Arbitration Committee which is contested.

If the Court rejects the appeal, the decision of the Arbitration Committee shall become final.

If the Court annuls the decision of the Arbitration Committee, the matter may be re-opened, where appropriate, on the initiative of one of the parties in the case, before the Arbitration Committee. The latter shall conform to any decisions on points of law given by the Court.

Article 23 (ex Article 20)

In the cases governed by *Article 35(1) of the EU Treaty,* by Article 234 of *the EC* Treaty *and by Article 150 of the EAEC Treaty*, the decision of the court or tribunal of a Member State which suspends its proceedings and refers a case to the Court shall be notified to the Court by the court or tribunal concerned. The decision shall then be notified by the Registrar of the Court to the parties, to the Member States and to the Commission, and also to the Council **or to the European Central Bank** if the act the validity or interpretation of which is in dispute originates from **one of them, and to the European Parliament and the Council if the act the validity or interpretation of which is in dispute was adopted jointly by those two institutions.**

Within two months of this notification, the parties, the Member States, the Commission, and, where appropriate, **the European Parliament,** the Council **and the European Central Bank** shall be entitled to submit statements of case or written observations to the Court.

---

*The provision was originally found in Article 20 of the Protocol on the Statute of the Court of Justice of the European Atomic Energy Community.

In the cases governed by Article 234 of the EC Treaty, the decision of the national court or tribunal shall, moreover, be notified by the Registrar of the Court to the States, other than the Member States, which are parties to the Agreement on the European Economic Area and also to the EFTA Surveillance Authority referred to in that Agreement which may, within two months of notification, where one of the fields of application of that Agreement is concerned, submit statements of case or written observations to the Court.

Article 24 (ex Article 21)

The Court may require the parties to produce all documents and to supply all information which the Court considers desirable. Formal note shall be taken of any refusal.

The Court may also require the Member States and institutions not being parties to the case to supply all information which the Court considers necessary for the proceedings.

Article 25 (ex Article 22)

The Court may at any time entrust any individual, body, authority, committee or other organisation it chooses with the task of giving an expert opinion.

Article 26 (ex Article 23)

Witnesses may be heard under conditions laid down in the Rules of Procedure.

Article 27 (ex Article 24)

With respect to defaulting witnesses the Court shall have the powers generally granted to courts and tribunals and may impose pecuniary penalties under conditions laid down in the Rules of Procedure.

Article 28 (ex Article 25)

Witnesses and experts may be heard on oath taken in the form laid down in the Rules of Procedure or in the manner laid down by the law of the country of the witness or expert.

Article 29 (ex Article 26)

The Court may order that a witness or expert be heard by the judicial authority of his place of permanent residence.

The order shall be sent for implementation to the competent judicial authority under conditions laid down in the Rules of Procedure. The documents drawn up in compliance with the letters rogatory shall be returned to the Court under the same conditions.

The Court shall defray the expenses, without prejudice to the right to charge them, where appropriate, to the parties.

Article 30 (ex Article 27)

A Member State shall treat any violation of an oath by a witness or expert in the same manner as if the offence had been committed before one of its courts with jurisdiction in civil proceedings. At the instance of the Court, the Member State concerned shall prosecute the offender before its competent court.

Article 31 (ex Article 28)

The hearing in court shall be public, unless the Court, of its own motion or on application by the parties, decides otherwise for serious reasons.

Article 32 (ex Article 29)

During the hearings the Court may examine the experts, the witnesses and the parties themselves. The latter, however, may address the Court only through their representatives.

Article 33 (ex Article 30)

Minutes shall be made of each hearing and signed by the President and the Registrar.

Article 34 (ex Article 31)

The case list shall be established by the President.

Article 35 (ex Article 32)

The deliberations of the Court shall be and shall remain secret.

Article 36 (ex Article 33)

Judgments shall state the reasons on which they are based. They shall contain the names of the Judges who took part in the deliberations.

Article 37 (ex Article 34)

Judgments shall be signed by the President and the Registrar. They shall be read in open court.

Article 38 (ex Article 35)

The Court shall adjudicate upon costs.

Article 39 (ex Article 36)

The President of the Court may, by way of summary procedure, which may, in so far as necessary, differ from some of the rules contained in this Statute and which shall be laid down in the Rules of Procedure, adjudicate upon applications to suspend execution, as provided for in Article 242 of *the EC* Treaty *and Article 157 of the EAEC Treaty,* or to prescribe interim measures in pursuance of Article 243 of **the EC** Treaty *or Article 158 of the EAEC Treaty,* or to suspend enforcement in accordance with the *fourth* paragraph of Article 256 of *the EC Treaty or the third paragraph of Article 164 of the EAEC Treaty.*

Should the President be prevented from attending, his place shall be taken by another Judge under conditions laid down in the Rules of Procedure.

The ruling of the President or of the Judge replacing him shall be provisional and shall in no way prejudice the decision of the Court on the substance of the case.

Article 40 (ex Article 37)

Member States and institutions of the Communities may intervene in cases before the Court.

The same right shall be open to any other person establishing an interest in the result of any case submitted to the Court, save in cases between Member States, between institutions of the *Communities* or between Member States and institutions of the *Communities.*

Without prejudice to the second paragraph, the States, other than the Member States, which are parties to the Agreement on the European Economic Area, and also the EFTA Surveillance Authority referred to in that Agreement, may intervene in cases before the Court where one of the fields of application [of] that Agreement is concerned.

An application to intervene shall be limited to supporting the *form of order sought* by one of the parties.

Article 41 (ex Article 38)

Where the defending party, after having been duly summoned, fails to file written submissions in defence, judgment shall be given against that party by default. An objection may be lodged against the judgment within one month of it being notified. The objection shall not have the effect of staying enforcement of the judgment by default unless the Court decides otherwise.

Article 42 (ex Article 39)

Member States, institutions of the Communities and any other natural or legal persons may, in cases and under conditions to be determined by the Rules of Procedure, institute third-party proceedings to contest a judgment rendered without their being heard, where the judgment is prejudicial to their rights.

Article 43 (ex Article 40)

If the meaning or scope of a judgment is in doubt, the Court shall construe it on application by any party or any institution of the Communities establishing an interest therein.

Article 44 (ex Article 41)

An application for revision of a judgment may be made to the Court only on discovery of a fact which is of such a nature as to be a decisive factor, and which, when the judgment was given, was unknown to the Court and to the party claiming the revision.

The revision shall be opened by a judgment of the Court expressly recording the existence of a new fact, recognising that it is of such a character as to lay the case open to revision and declaring the application admissible on this ground.

No application for revision may be made after the lapse of 10 years from the date of the judgment.

Article 45 (ex Article 42)

Periods of grace based on considerations of distance shall be determined by the Rules of Procedure.

No right shall be prejudiced in consequence of the expiry of a time-limit if the party concerned proves the existence of unforeseeable circumstances or of *force majeure*.

Article 46 (ex Article 43)

Proceedings against the Communities in matters arising from non-contractual liability shall be barred after a period of five years from the occurrence of the event giving rise thereto. The period of limitation shall be interrupted if proceedings are instituted before the Court or if prior to such proceedings an application is made by the aggrieved party to the relevant institution of the Communities. In the latter event the proceedings must be instituted within the period of two months provided for in Article 230 of the EC Treaty *and Article 146 of the EAEC Treaty*; the provisions of the second paragraph of Article 232 of the EC Treaty *and the second paragraph of Article 148 of the EAEC Treaty, respectively*, shall apply where appropriate.

TITLE IV   THE COURT OF FIRST INSTANCE OF THE EUROPEAN COMMUNITIES

Article 47 (ex Article 44)

Articles 2 to 8, Articles *14 and 15, the first, second, fourth and fifth paragraphs of Article 17 and Article 18* shall apply to the Court of First Instance and its members. The oath referred to in Article 2 shall be taken before the Court of Justice and the decisions referred to in Articles 3, 4 and 6 shall be adopted by that Court after hearing the Court of First Instance.

The fourth paragraph of Article 3 and Articles 10, 11 and 14 shall apply to the Registrar of the Court of First Instance *mutatis mutandis*.

Article 48 (new – TN)

The Court of First Instance shall consist of 15 Judges.

Article 49 (new – TN)

The members of the Court of First Instance may be called upon to perform the task of an Advocate-General.

It shall be the duty of the Advocate-General, acting with complete impartiality and independence, to make, in open court, reasoned submissions on certain cases brought before the Court of First Instance in order to assist the Court of First Instance in the performance of its task.

The criteria for selecting such cases, as well as the procedures for designating the Advocates-General, shall be laid down in the Rules of Procedure of the Court of First Instance.

A member called upon to perform the task of Advocate-General in a case may not take part in the judgment of the case.

Article 50 (new – TN)

The Court of First Instance shall sit in chambers of three or five Judges. The Judges shall elect the Presidents of the chambers from among their number. The Presidents of the chambers of five Judges shall be elected for three years. They may be re-elected once. The composition of the chambers and the assignment of cases to them shall be governed by the Rules of Procedure. In certain cases governed by the Rules of Procedure, the Court of First Instance may sit as a full court or be constituted by a single Judge.

The Rules of Procedure may also provide that the Court of First Instance may sit in a Grand Chamber in cases and under the conditions specified therein.

Article 51 (new – TN)

By way of exception to the rule laid down in Article 225(1) of the EC Treaty and Article 140a(1) of the EAEC Treaty, the Court of Justice shall have jurisdiction in actions brought by the Member States, by the institutions of the Communities and by the European Central Bank.

Article 52 (ex Article 45)

The President of the Court of Justice and the President of the Court of First Instance shall determine, by common accord, the conditions under which officials and other servants attached to the Court of Justice shall render their services to the Court of First Instance to enable it to function. Certain officials or other servants shall be responsible to the Registrar of the Court of First Instance under the authority of the President of the Court of First Instance.

Article 53 (ex Article 46)

The procedure before the Court of First Instance shall be governed by Title III.

Such further and more detailed provisions as may be necessary shall be laid down in its Rules of Procedure. The Rules of Procedure may derogate from the fourth paragraph of Article 40 and from Article 41 in order to take account of the specific features of litigation in the field of intellectual property.

Notwithstanding the fourth paragraph of *Article 20*, the Advocate-General may make his reasoned submissions in writing.

Article 54 (ex Article 47)

Where an application or other procedural document addressed to the Court of First Instance is lodged by mistake with the Registrar of the Court of Justice, it shall be transmitted immediately by that Registrar to the Registrar of the Court of First Instance; likewise, where an application or other procedural document addressed to the Court of Justice is lodged by mistake with the Registrar of the Court of First Instance, it shall be transmitted immediately by that Registrar to the Registrar of the Court of Justice.

Where the Court of First Instance finds that it does not have jurisdiction to hear and determine an action in respect of which the Court of Justice has jurisdiction, it shall refer that action to the Court of Justice; likewise, where the Court of Justice finds that an action falls within the jurisdiction of the Court of First Instance, it shall refer that action to the Court of First Instance, whereupon that Court may not decline jurisdiction.

Where the Court of Justice and the Court of First Instance are seised of cases in which the same relief is sought, the same issue of interpretation is raised or the validity of the same act is called in question, the Court of First Instance may, after hearing the parties, stay the proceedings before it until such time as the Court of Justice shall have delivered judgment. Where applications are made for the same act to be declared void, the Court of First Instance may also decline jurisdiction in order that the Court of Justice may rule on such applications. In the cases referred to in this paragraph, the Court of Justice may also decide to stay the proceedings before it; in that event, the proceedings before the Court of First Instance shall continue.

Article 55 (ex Article 48)

Final decisions of the Court of First Instance, decisions disposing of the substantive issues in part only or disposing of a procedural issue concerning a plea of lack of competence or inadmissibility, shall be notified by the Registrar of the Court of First Instance to all parties as well as all Member States and the institutions of the Communities even if they did not intervene in the case before the Court of First Instance.

Article 56 (ex Article 49)

An appeal may be brought before the Court of Justice, within two months of the notification of the decision appealed against, against final decisions of the Court of First Instance and decisions of that Court disposing of the substantive issues in part only or disposing of a procedural issue concerning a plea of lack of competence or inadmissibility.

Such an appeal may be brought by any party which has been unsuccessful, in whole or in part, in its submissions. However, interveners other than the Member States and the institutions of the Communities may bring such an appeal only where the decision of the Court of First Instance directly affects them.

With the exception of cases relating to disputes between the Communities and their servants, an appeal may also be brought by Member States and institutions of the Communities which did not intervene in the proceedings before the Court of First Instance. Such Member States and institutions shall be in the same position as Member States or institutions which intervened at first instance.

Article 57 (ex Article 50)

Any person whose application to intervene has been dismissed by the Court of First Instance may appeal to the Court of Justice within two weeks from the notification of the decision dismissing the application.

The parties to the proceedings may appeal to the Court of Justice against any decision of the Court of First Instance made pursuant to Article 242 or Article 243 or the fourth paragraph of Article 256 of the *EC* Treaty *or Article 157 or Article 158 or the third paragraph of Article 164 of the EAEC Treaty* within two months from their notification.

The appeal referred to in the first two paragraphs of this Article shall be heard and determined under the procedure referred to in *Article 39*.

Article 58 (ex Article 51)

An appeal to the Court of Justice shall be limited to points of law. It shall lie on the grounds of lack of competence of the Court of First Instance, a breach of procedure before it which adversely affects the interests of the appellant as well as the infringement of Community law by the Court of First Instance.

No appeal shall lie regarding only the amount of the costs or the party ordered to pay them.

Article 59 (ex Article 52)

Where an appeal is brought against a decision of the Court of First Instance, the procedure before the Court of Justice shall consist of a written part and an oral part. In accordance with conditions laid down in the Rules of Procedure, the Court of Justice, having heard the Advocate-General and the parties, may dispense with the oral procedure.

Article 60 (ex Article 53)

Without prejudice to Articles 242 and 243 of *the EC* Treaty *or Articles 157 and 158 of the EAEC Treaty*, an appeal shall not have suspensory effect.

By way of derogation from Article 244 of *the EC* Treaty *and Article 159 of the EAEC Treaty*, decisions of the Court of First Instance declaring a regulation to be void shall take effect only as from the date of expiry of the period referred to in the first paragraph of *Article 56* of this Statute or, if an appeal shall have been brought within that period, as from the date of dismissal of the appeal, without prejudice, however, to the right of a party to apply to the Court of Justice, pursuant to Articles 242 and 243 of *the EC* Treaty *or Articles 157 and 158 of the EAEC Treaty*, for the suspension of the effects of the regulation which has been declared void or for the prescription of any other interim measure.

Article 61 (ex Article 54)

If the appeal is well founded, the Court of Justice shall quash the decision of the Court of First Instance. It may itself give final judgment in the matter, where the state of the proceedings so permits, or refer the case back to the Court of First Instance for judgment.

Where a case is referred back to the Court of First Instance, that Court shall be bound by the decision of the Court of Justice on points of law.

When an appeal brought by a Member State or *an institution of the Communities*, which did not intervene in the proceedings before the Court of First Instance, is well founded, the Court of Justice may, if it considers this necessary, state which of the effects of the decision of the Court of First Instance which has been quashed shall be considered as definitive in respect of the parties to the litigation.

Article 62 (new – TN)

In the cases provided for in Article 225(2) and (3) of the EC Treaty and Article 140a(2) and (3) of the EAEC Treaty, where the First Advocate-General considers that there is a serious risk of the unity or consistency of Community law being affected, he may propose that the Court of Justice review the decision of the Court of First Instance.

The proposal must be made within one month of delivery of the decision by the Court of First Instance. Within one month of receiving the proposal made by the First Advocate-General, the Court of Justice shall decide whether or not the decision should be reviewed.

TITLE V   FINAL PROVISIONS

Article 63 (ex Article 55)

The Rules of Procedure of *the Court of Justice* and of the Court of First Instance shall contain *any provisions* necessary for applying and, where required, supplementing this Statute.

Article 64 (new – TN)

Until the rules governing the language arrangements applicable at the Court of Justice and the Court of First Instance have been adopted in this Statute, the provisions of the Rules of Procedure of the Court of Justice and of the Rules of Procedure of the Court of First Instance governing language arrangements shall continue to apply. Those provisions may only be amended or repealed in accordance with the procedure laid down for amending this Statute.

PROTOCOL CONCERNING IMPORTS INTO THE EUROPEAN COMMUNITY OF PETROLEUM PRODUCTS REFINED IN THE NETHERLANDS ANTILLES (1962)

THE HIGH CONTRACTING PARTIES,

BEING DESIROUS of giving fuller details about the system of trade applicable to imports into the European Community of petroleum products refined in the Netherlands Antilles,

HAVE AGREED on the following provisions to be appended to that Treaty:

Article 1. This protocol is applicable to petroleum products coming under the Brussels Nomenclature numbers 27.10, 27.11, 27.12, ex 27.13 (paraffin wax, petroleum or shale wax and paraffin residues) and 27.14, imported for use in Member States.

Article 2. Member States shall undertake to grant petroleum products refined in the Netherlands Antilles the tariff preferences resulting from the Association of the latter with the Community, under the conditions provided for in this Protocol. These provisions shall hold good whatever may be the rules of origin applied by the Member States.

Article 3.1. When the Commission at the request of a Member State or on its own initiative, establishes that imports into the Community of petroleum products refined in the Netherlands Antilles under the system provided for in Article 2 above are giving rise to real difficulties on the market of one or more Member

States, it shall decide that Customs duties on the said imports shall be introduced, increased or re-introduced by the Member States in question, to such an extent and for such a period as may be necessary to meet that situation. The rates of the Customs duties thus introduced, increased or reintroduced may not exceed the Customs duties applicable to third countries for these same products.

2. The provisions of paragraph 1 can in any case be applied when imports into the Community of petroleum products refined in the Netherlands Antilles reach two million metric tons a year.

3. The Council shall be informed of decisions taken by the Commission in pursuance of paragraphs 1 and 2, including those directed at rejecting the request of a Member State. The Council shall, at the request of any Member State, assume responsibility for the matter and may at any time amend or revoke them by a decision taken by a qualified majority.

Article 4.1. If a Member State considers that imports of petroleum products refined in the Netherlands Antilles, made either directly or through another Member State under the system provided for in Article 2 above, are giving rise to real difficulties on its market and that immediate action is necessary to meet them, it may on its own initiative decide to apply Customs duties applicable to such imports, the rate of which may not exceed those of the Customs duties applicable to third countries in respect of the same products. It shall notify its decision to the Commission which shall decide within one month whether the measures taken by the State should be maintained or must be amended or cancelled. The provisions of Article 3(3) shall be applicable to such decision of the Commission.

2. When quantities of petroleum products refined in the Netherlands Antilles imported either directly or through another Member State, under the system provided for in Article 2 above, into a Member State or States of the EC exceed during a calendar year the tonnage shown in the Annex to this Protocol, the measures taken in pursuance of paragraph 1 by that or those Member States for the current year shall be considered to be justified; the Commission shall, after assuring itself that the tonnage fixed has been reached, formally record the measures taken. In such a case the other Member States shall abstain from formally placing the matter before the Council.

Article 5. If the Community decides to apply quantitative restrictions to petroleum products, no matter whence they are imported, these restrictions may also be applied to imports of such products from the Netherlands Antilles. In such a case preferential treatment shall be granted to the Netherlands Antilles as compared with third countries.

Article 6.1. The provisions of Articles 2–5 shall be reviewed by the Council by unanimous decision, after consulting the European Parliament and the Commission, when a common definition of origin for petroleum products from third countries and Associated countries is adopted, or when decisions are taken within the framework of a common commercial policy for the products in question or when a common energy policy is established.

2. When such revision is made, however, equivalent preferences must in any case be maintained in favour of the Netherlands Antilles in a suitable form and for a minimum quantity of $2\frac{1}{2}$ million metric tons of petroleum products.

3. The Community's commitments in regard to equivalent preferences as mentioned in paragraph 2 of this Article may, if necessary, be broken down country

by country taking into account the tonnage indicated in the Annex to this Protocol.

Article 7. For the implementation of this Protocol, the Commission is responsible for following the pattern of imports into the Member States of petroleum products refined in the Netherlands Antilles. Member States shall communicate to the Commission, which shall see that it is circulated, all useful information to that end in accordance with the administrative conditions recommended by it.

Done at Brussels, the thirteenth day of November, one thousand nine hundred and sixty-two.

Annex to the Protocol:

For the implementation of Article 4(2) of the Protocol concerning imports into the European Community of petroleum products refined in the Netherlands Antilles, the High Contracting Parties have decided that the quantity of 2 million metric tons of petroleum products from the Antilles shall be allocated among the Member States as follows:

Germany	625 000 metric tons
Belgo-Luxembourg Economic Union	200 000 metric tons
France	75 000 metric tons
Italy	100 000 metric tons
Netherlands	1 000 000 metric tons.

PROTOCOL ON SPECIAL ARRANGEMENTS FOR GREENLAND (1984)

Article 1.1. The treatment on import into the Community of products subject to the common organization of the market in fishery products, originating in Greenland, shall, while complying with the mechanisms of the common market organization, involve exemption from customs duties and charges having equivalent effect and the absence of quantitative restrictions or measures having equivalent effect if the possibilities for access to Greenland fishing zones granted to the Community pursuant to an agreement between the Community and the authority responsible for Greenland are satisfactory to the Community.

2. All measures relating to the import arrangements for such products, including those relating to the adoption of such measures, shall be adopted in accordance with the procedure laid down in Article 37 of the Treaty establishing the European Community.

Article 2. The Commission shall make proposals to the Council, which shall act by a qualified majority, for the transitional measures which it considers necessary, by reason of the entry into force of the new arrangements, with regard to the maintenance of rights acquired by natural or legal persons during the period when Greenland was part of the Community and the regularization of the situation with regard to financial assistance granted by the Community to Greenland during that period.

PROTOCOL ON THE ACQUISITION OF PROPERTY IN DENMARK (1992)

THE HIGH CONTRACTING PARTIES,

DESIRING to settle certain particular problems relating to Denmark,

HAVE AGREED UPON the following provision, which shall be annexed to the Treaty establishing the European Community:

Notwithstanding the provisions of this Treaty, Denmark may maintain the existing legislation on the acquisition of second homes.

PROTOCOL CONCERNING ARTICLE *141* [EX 119] OF THE TREATY ESTABLISHING THE EUROPEAN COMMUNITY (1992)

THE HIGH CONTRACTING PARTIES,
HAVE AGREED UPON the following provision, which shall be annexed to the Treaty establishing the European Community:

For the purposes of Article *141* of this Treaty, benefits under occupational social security schemes shall not be considered as remuneration if and in so far as they are attributable to periods of employment prior to 17 May 1990, except in the case of workers or those claiming under them who have before that date initiated legal proceedings or introduced an equivalent claim under the applicable national law.

PROTOCOL ON THE STATUTE OF THE EUROPEAN SYSTEM OF CENTRAL BANKS AND OF THE EUROPEAN CENTRAL BANK (1992)

THE HIGH CONTRACTING PARTIES,
DESIRING to lay down the Statute of the European System of Central Banks and of the European Central Bank provided for in Article *8* of the Treaty establishing the European Community,
HAVE AGREED upon the following provisions, which shall be annexed to the Treaty establishing the European Community:

Chapter I   Constitution of the ESCB
Article 1. The European System of Central Banks

1.1. The European System of Central Banks (ESCB) and the European Central Bank (ECB) shall be established in accordance with Article *8* of this Treaty; they shall perform their tasks and carry on their activities in accordance with the provisions of this Treaty and of this Statute.

1.2. In accordance with Article *107*(1) of this Treaty, the ESCB shall be composed of the ECB and of the central banks of the Member States ('national central banks'). The Institut monétaire luxembourgeois will be the central bank of Luxembourg.

Chapter II   Objectives and Tasks of the ESCB
Article 2. Objectives
In accordance with Article *105*(1) of this Treaty, the primary objective of the ESCB shall be to maintain price stability. Without prejudice to the objective of price stability, it shall support the general economic policies in the Community with a view to contributing to the achievement of the objectives of the Community as laid down in Article *2* of this Treaty. The ESCB shall act in accordance with the principle of an open market economy with free competition, favouring an efficient allocation of resources, and in compliance with the principles set out in Article *4* of this Treaty.

Article 3. Tasks

3.1. In accordance with Article 105(2) of this Treaty, the basic tasks to be carried out through the ESCB shall be:
– to define and implement the monetary policy of the Community;
– to conduct foreign exchange operations consistent with the provisions of Article 111 of this Treaty;
– to hold and manage the official foreign reserves of the Member States;
– to promote the smooth operation of payment systems.

3.2. In accordance with Article 105(3) of this Treaty, the third indent of Article 3.1 shall be without prejudice to the holding and management by the governments of Member States of foreign exchange working balances.

3.3. In accordance with Article 105(5) of this Treaty, the ESCB shall contribute to the smooth conduct of policies pursued by the competent authorities relating to the prudential supervision of credit institutions and the stability of the financial system.

Article 4. Advisory functions

In accordance with Article 105(4) of this Treaty:
(a) the ECB shall be consulted:
    – on any proposed Community act in its fields of competence;
    – by national authorities regarding any draft legislative provision in its fields of competence, but within the limits and under the conditions set out by the Council in accordance with the procedure laid down in Article 42;
(b) the ECB may submit opinions to the appropriate Community institutions or bodies or to national authorities on matters in its fields of competence.

Article 5. Collection of statistical information

5.1. In order to undertake the tasks of the ESCB, the ECB, assisted by the national central banks, shall collect the necessary statistical information either from the competent national authorities or directly from economic agents. For these purposes it shall co-operate with the Community institutions or bodies and with the competent authorities of the Member States or third countries and with international organizations.

5.2. The national central banks shall carry out, to the extent possible, the tasks described in Article 5.1.

5.3. The ECB shall contribute to the harmonization, where necessary, of the rules and practices governing the collection, compilation and distribution of statistics in the areas within its fields of competence.

5.4. The Council, in accordance with the procedure laid down in Article 42, shall define the natural and legal persons subject to reporting requirements, the confidentiality regime and the appropriate provisions for enforcement.

Article 6. International co-operation

6.1. In the field of international co-operation involving the tasks entrusted to the ESCB, the ECB shall decide how the ESCB shall be represented.

6.2. The ECB and, subject to its approval, the national central banks may participate in international monetary institutions.

6.3. Articles 6.1 and 6.2 shall be without prejudice to Article 111(4) of this Treaty.

Chapter III   Organization of the ESCB

Article 7. Independence

In accordance with Article 108 of this Treaty, when exercising the powers and carrying out the tasks and duties conferred upon them by this Treaty and this Statute, neither the ECB, nor a national central bank, nor any member of their decision-making bodies shall seek or take instructions from Community institutions or bodies, from any government of a Member State or from any other body. The Community institutions and bodies and the governments of the Member States undertake to respect this principle and not to seek to influence the members of the decision-making bodies of the ECB or of the national central banks in the performance of their tasks.

Article 8. General principle

The ESCB shall be governed by the decision-making bodies of the ECB.

Article 9. The European Central Bank

9.1. The ECB which, in accordance with Article 107(2) of this Treaty, shall have legal personality, shall enjoy in each of the Member States the most extensive legal capacity accorded to legal persons under its law; it may, in particular, acquire or dispose of movable and immovable property and may be a party to legal proceedings.

9.2. The ECB shall ensure that the tasks conferred upon the ESCB under Article 105(2), (3) and (5) of this Treaty are implemented either by its own activities pursuant to this Statute or through the national central bank pursuant to Articles 12.1 and 14.

9.3. In accordance with Article 107(3) of this Treaty, the decision-making bodies of the ECB shall be the Governing Council and the Executive Board.

Article 10. The Governing Council

10.1. In accordance with Article 112(1) of this Treaty, the Governing Council shall comprise the members of the Executive Board of the ECB and the Governors of the national central banks.

10.2. Subject to Article 10.3, only members of the Governing Council present in person shall have the right to vote. By way of derogation from this rule, the Rules of Procedure referred to in Article 12.3 may lay down that members of the Governing Council may cast their vote by means of teleconferencing. These rules shall also provide that a member of the Governing Council who is prevented from voting for a prolonged period may appoint an alternate as a member of the Governing Council.

Subject to Articles 10.3 and 11.3, each member of the Governing Council shall have one vote. Save as otherwise provided for in this Statute, the Governing Council shall act by a simple majority. In the event of a tie the President shall have the casting vote.

In order for the Governing Council to vote, there shall be a quorum of two-thirds of the members. If the quorum is not met, the President may convene an extraordinary meeting at which decisions may be taken without regard to the quorum.

10.3. For any decisions to be taken under Articles 28, 29, 30, 32, 33 and 51, the votes in the Governing Council shall be weighted according to the national central banks' shares in the subscribed capital of the ECB. The weight of the votes of the members of the Executive Board shall be zero. A decision requiring a qualified majority shall be adopted if the votes cast in favour represent at least two thirds of the subscribed capital of the ECB and represent at least half of the shareholders. If a Governor is unable to be present, he may nominate an alternate to cast his weighted vote.

10.4. The proceedings of the meetings shall be confidential. The Governing Council may decide to make the outcome of its deliberations public.

10.5. The Governing Council shall meet at least ten times a year.

10.6 Article 10.2 may be amended by the Council meeting in the composition of the Heads of State or Government, acting unanimously either on a recommendation from the ECB and after consulting the European Parliament and the Commission, or on a recommendation from the Commission and after consulting the European Parliament and the ECB. The Council shall recommend such amendments to the Member States for adoption. These amendments shall enter into force after having been ratified by all the Member States in accordance with their respective constitutional requirements.

A recommendation made by the ECB under this paragraph shall require a decision by the Governing Council acting unanimously.

Article 11. The Executive Board

11.1. In accordance with Article 112(2)(a) of this Treaty, the Executive Board shall comprise the President, the Vice-President and four other members.

The members shall perform their duties on a full-time basis. No member shall engage in any occupation, whether gainful or not, unless exemption is exceptionally granted by the Governing Council.

11.2. In accordance with Article 112(2)(b) of this Treaty, the President, the Vice-President and the other Members of the Executive Board shall be appointed from among persons of recognized standing and professional experience in monetary or banking matters by common accord of the governments of the Member States at the level of the Heads of State or of Government, on a recommendation from the Council after it has consulted the European Parliament and the Governing Council.

Their term of office shall be 8 years and shall not be renewable.

Only nationals of Member States may be members of the Executive Board.

11.3. The terms and conditions of employment of the members of the Executive Board, in particular their salaries, pensions and other social security benefits shall be the subject of contracts with the ECB and shall be fixed by the Governing Council on a proposal from a Committee comprising three members appointed by the Governing Council and three members appointed by the Council. The members of the Executive Board shall not have the right to vote on matters referred to in this paragraph.

11.4. If a member of the Executive Board no longer fulfils the conditions required for the performance of his duties or if he has been guilty of serious misconduct, the Court of Justice may, on application by the Governing Council or the Executive Board, compulsorily retire him.

11.5. Each member of the Executive Board present in person shall have the right to vote and shall have, for that purpose, one vote. Save as otherwise provided, the Executive Board shall act by a simple majority of the votes cast. In the event of a tie, the President shall have the casting vote. The voting arrangements shall be specified in the Rules of Procedure referred to in Article 12.3.

11.6. The Executive Board shall be responsible for the current business of the ECB.

11.7. Any vacancy on the Executive Board shall be filled by the appointment of a new member in accordance with Article 11.2.

Article 12. Responsibilities of the decision-making bodies

12.1. The Governing Council shall adopt the guidelines and take the decisions necessary to ensure the performance of the tasks entrusted to the ESCB under this Treaty and this Statute. The Governing Council shall formulate the monetary policy of the Community including, as appropriate, decisions relating to intermediate monetary objectives, key interest rates and the supply of reserves in the ESCB and shall establish the necessary guidelines for their implementation.

The Executive Board shall implement monetary policy in accordance with the guidelines and decisions laid down by the Governing Council. In doing so the Executive Board shall give the necessary instructions to national central banks. In addition the Executive Board may have certain powers delegated to it where the Governing Council so decides.

To the extent deemed possible and appropriate and without prejudice to the provisions of this Article, the ECB shall have recourse to the national central banks to carry out operations which form part of the tasks of the ESCB.

12.2. The Executive Board shall have the responsibility for the preparation of meetings of the Governing Council.

12.3. The Governing Council shall adopt Rules of Procedure which determine the internal organization of the ECB and its decision-making bodies.

12.4. The Governing Council shall exercise the advisory functions referred to in Article 4.

12.5. The Governing Council shall take the decisions referred to in Article 6.

Article 13. The President

13.1. The President or, in his absence, the Vice-President shall chair the governing Council and the Executive Board of the ECB.

13.2. Without prejudice to Article 39, the President or his nominee shall represent the ECB externally.

Article 14. National central banks

14.1. In accordance with Article 109 of this Treaty, each Member State shall ensure, at the latest at the date of the establishment of the ESCB, that its national legislation, including the statutes of its national central bank, is compatible with this Treaty and this Statute.

14.2. The Statutes of the national central banks shall, in particular, provide that the term of office of a Governor of a national central bank shall be no less than 5 years.

A Governor may be relieved from office only if he no longer fulfils the conditions required for the performance of his duties or if he has been guilty of serious misconduct. A decision to this effect may be referred to the Court of Justice by the Governor concerned or the Governing Council on grounds of infringement of this Treaty or of any rule of law relating to its application. Such proceedings shall be instituted within two months of the publication of the decision or of its notification to the plaintiff or, in the absence thereof, of the day on which it came to knowledge of the latter, as the case may be.

14.3. The national central banks are an integral part of the ESCB and shall act in accordance with the guidelines and instructions of the ECB. The Governing Council shall take the necessary steps to ensure compliance with the guidelines and instructions of the ECB, and shall require that any necessary information be given to it.

14.4 National central banks may perform functions other than those specified in this Statute unless the Governing Council finds, by a majority of two thirds of the votes cast, that these interfere with the objectives and tasks of the ESCB. Such functions shall be performed on the responsibility and liability of national central banks and shall not be regarded as being part of the functions of the ESCB.

Article 15. Reporting commitments

15.1. The ECB shall draw up and publish reports on the activities of the ESCB at least quarterly.

15.2. A consolidated financial statement of the ESCB shall be published each week.

15.3. In accordance with Article 113(3) of this Treaty, the ECB shall address an annual report on the activities of the ESCB and on the monetary policy of both the previous and the current year to the European Parliament, the Council and the Commission, and also the European Council.

15.4. The reports and statements referred to in this Article shall be made available to interested parties free of charge.

Article 16. Bank notes

In accordance with Article 106(1) of this Treaty, the Governing Council shall have the exclusive right to authorize the issue of bank notes within the Community. The ECB and the national central banks may issue such notes. The bank notes issued by the ECB and the national central banks shall be the only such notes to have the status of legal tender within the Community.

The ECB shall respect as far as possible existing practices regarding the issue and design of bank notes.

Chapter IV   Monetary Functions and Operations of the ESCB

Article 17. Accounts with the ECB and the national central banks

In order to conduct their operations, the ECB and the national central banks may open accounts for credit institutions, public entities and other market participants and accept assets, including book-entry securities, as collateral.

Article 18. Open market and credit operations

18.1. In order to achieve the objectives of the ESCB and to carry out its tasks, the ECB and the national central banks may:
– operate in the financial markets by buying and selling outright (spot or forward) or under repurchase agreement and by lending or borrowing claims and market-able instruments, whether in Community or in non-Community currencies, as well as precious metals;
– conduct credit operations with credit institutions and other market participants, with lending being based on adequate collateral.

18.2. The ECB shall establish general principles for open market and credit oper-ations carried out by itself or the national central banks, including for the announce-ment of conditions under which they stand ready to enter into such transactions.

Article 19. Minimum reserves

19.1. Subject to Article 2, the ECB may require credit institutions established in Member States to hold minimum reserves on accounts with the ECB and national central banks in pursuance of monetary policy objectives. Regulations concerning the calculation and determination of the required minimum reserves may be established by the Governing Council. In cases of non-compliance the ECB shall be entitled to levy penalty interest and to impose other sanctions with comparable effect.

19.2. For the application of this Article, the Council shall, in accordance with the procedure laid down in Article 42, define the basis for minimum reserves and the maximum reserves and the maximum permissible ratios between those reserves and their basis, as well as the appropriate sanctions in cases of non-compliance.

Article 20. Other instruments of monetary control

The Governing Council may, by a majority of two thirds of the votes cast, decide upon the use of such other operational methods of monetary control as it sees fit, respecting Article 2.

The Council shall, in accordance with the procedure laid down in Article 42, define the scope of such methods if they impose obligations on third parties.

Article 21. Operations with public entities

21.1. In accordance with Article 101 of this Treaty, overdrafts or any other type of credit facility with the ECB or with the national central banks in favour of Community institutions or bodies, central governments, regional, local or other public authorities, other bodies governed by public law, or public undertakings of Member States shall be prohibited, as shall the purchase directly from them by the ECB or national central banks of debt instruments.

21.2. The ECB and national central banks may act as fiscal agents for the entities referred to in 21.1.

21.3. The provisions of this Article shall not apply to publicly-owned credit institutions which, in the context of the supply of reserves by central banks, shall be given the same treatment by national central banks and the ECB as private credit institutions.

Article 22. Clearing and payment systems

The ECB and national central banks may provide facilities, and the ECB may make regulations, to ensure efficient and sound clearing and payment systems within the Community and with other countries.

Article 23. External operations

The ECB and national central banks may:
– establish relations with central banks and financial institutions in other countries and, where appropriate, with international organizations;
– acquire and sell spot and forward all types of foreign exchange assets and precious metals; the term 'foreign exchange asset' shall include securities and all other assets in the currency of any country or units of account in whatever form held;
– hold and manage the assets referred to in this Article;
– conduct all types of banking transactions in relations with third countries and international organizations, including borrowing and lending operations.

Article 24. Other operations

In addition to operations arising from their tasks, the ECB and national central banks may enter into operations for their administrative purposes or for their staff.

Chapter V   Prudential Supervision

Article 25. Prudential supervision

25.1. The ECB may offer advice to and be consulted by the Council, the Commission and the competent authorities of the Member States on the scope and implementation of Community legislation relating to the prudential supervision of credit institutions and to the stability of the financial system.

25.2. In accordance with any decision of the Council under Article 105(6) of this Treaty, the ECB may perform specific tasks concerning policies relating to the prudential supervision of credit institutions and other financial institutions with the exception of insurance undertakings.

Chapter VI   Financial Provisions of the ESCB

Article 26. Financial accounts

26.1. The financial year of the ESCB and national central banks shall begin on the first day of January and end on the last day of December.

26.2. The annual accounts of the ECB shall be drawn up by the Executive Board, in accordance with the principles established by the Governing Council. The accounts shall be approved by the Governing Council and shall thereafter be published.

26.3. For analytic and operational purposes, the Executive Board shall draw up a consolidated balance sheet of the ESCB, comprising those assets and liabilities of the national central banks that fall within the ESCB.

26.4. For the application of this Article, the Governing Council shall establish the necessary rules for standardizing the accounting and reporting of operations undertaken by the national central banks.

Article 27. Auditing

27.1. The accounts of the ECB and national central banks shall be audited by independent external auditors recommended by the Governing Council and approved by the Council. The auditors shall have full power to examine all books and accounts of the ECB and national central banks and obtain full information about their transactions.

27.2. The provisions of Article 248 of this Treaty shall only apply to an examination of the operational efficiency of the management of the ECB.

Article 28. Capital of the ECB

28.1. The capital of the ECB, which shall become operational upon its establishment, shall be ECU 5 000 million. The capital may be increased by such amounts as may be decided by the Governing Council acting by the qualified majority provided for in Article 10.3, within the limits and under the conditions set by the Council under the procedure laid down in Article 42.

28.2. The national central banks shall be the sole subscribers to and holders of the capital of the ECB. The subscription of capital shall be according to the key established in accordance with Article 29.

28.3. The Governing Council, acting by the qualified majority provided for in Article 10.3, shall determine the extent to which and the form in which the capital shall be paid up.

28.4. Subject to Article 28.5, the shares of the national central banks in the subscribed capital of the ECB may not be transferred, pledged or attached.

28.5. If the key referred to in Article 29 is adjusted, the national central banks shall transfer among themselves capital shares to the extent necessary to ensure that the distribution of capital shares corresponds to the adjusted key. The Governing Council shall determine the terms and conditions of such transfers.

Article 29. Key for capital subscription

29.1. When in accordance with the procedure referred to in Article 123(1) of this Treaty the ESCB and the ECB have been established, the key for subscription of the ECB's capital shall be established. Each national central bank shall be assigned a weighting in this key which shall be equal to the sum of:

- 50% of the share of its respective Member State in the population of the Community in the penultimate year preceding the establishment of the ESCB;
- 50% of the share of its respective Member State in the gross domestic product at market prices of the Community as recorded in the last five years preceding the penultimate year before the establishment of the ESCB.

The percentages shall be rounded up to the nearest multiple 0.05 percentage points.

29.2. The statistical data to be used for the application of this Article shall be provided by the Commission in accordance with the rules adopted by the Council under the procedure provided for in Article 42.

29.3. The weighting assigned to the national central banks shall be adjusted every five years after the establishment of the ESCB by analogy with the provisions laid down in Article 29.1. The adjusted key shall apply with effect from the first day of the following year.

29.4. The Governing Council shall take all other measures necessary for the application of this Article.

Article 30. Transfer of foreign reserve assets to the ECB

30.1. Without prejudice to Article 28, the ECB shall be provided by the national central banks with foreign reserve assets, other than Member States' currencies, ECUs, IMF reserve positions and SDRs, up to an amount equivalent to ECU 50 000 million. The Governing Council shall decide upon the proportion to be called up by the ECB following its establishment and the amounts called up at later dates. The ECB shall have the full right to hold and manage the foreign reserves that are transferred to it and to use them for the purposes set out in this Statute.

30.2. The contributions of each national central bank shall be fixed in proportion to its share in the subscribed capital of the ECB.

30.3. Each national central bank shall be credited by the ECB with a claim equivalent to its contribution. The Governing Council shall determine the denomination and remuneration of such claims.

30.4. Further calls of foreign reserve assets beyond the limit set in Article 30.1 may be effected by the ECB, in accordance with Article 30.2, within the limits and under the conditions set by the Council in accordance with the procedure laid down in Article 42.

30.5. The ECB may hold and manage IMF reserve positions and SDRs and provide for the pooling of such assets.

30.6. The Governing Council shall take all other measures necessary for the application of this Article.

Article 31. Foreign reserve assets held by national central banks

31.1. The national central banks shall be allowed to perform transactions in fulfilment of their obligations towards international organizations in accordance with Article 23.

31.2. All other operations in foreign reserve assets remaining with the national central banks after the transfers referred to in Article 30, and Member States' transactions with their foreign exchange working balances shall, above a certain limit to be established within the framework of Article 31.3, be subject to approval by the ECB in order to ensure consistency with the exchange rate and monetary policies of the Community.

31.3. The Governing Council shall issue guidelines with a view to facilitating such operations.

Article 32. Allocation of monetary income of national central banks

32.1. The income accruing to the national central banks in the performance of the ESCB's monetary policy function (hereinafter referred to as 'monetary income') shall be allocated at the end of each financial year in accordance with the provisions of this Article.

32.2. Subject to Article 32.3, the amount of each national central bank's monetary income shall be equal to its annual income derived from its assets held against notes in circulation and deposit liabilities to credit institutions. These assets shall be earmarked by national central banks in accordance with guidelines to be established by the Governing Council.

32.3. If, after the start of the third stage, the balance sheet structures of the national central banks do not, in the judgment of the Governing Council, permit the application of Article 32.2, the Governing Council, acting by a qualified majority, may decide that, by way of derogation from Article 32.2, monetary income shall be measured according to an alternative method for a period of not more than five years.

32.4. The amount of each national central bank's monetary income shall be reduced by an amount equivalent to any interest paid by that central bank on its deposit liabilities to credit institutions in accordance with Article 19.

The Governing Council may decide that national central banks shall be indemnified against costs incurred in connection with the issue of bank notes or in exceptional circumstances for specific losses arising from monetary policy operations undertaken for the ESCB. Indemnification shall be in a form deemed appropriate in the judgment of the Governing Council; these amounts may be offset against the national central banks' monetary income.

32.5. The sum of the national central banks' monetary income shall be allocated to the national central banks in proportion to their paid-up shares in the capital of the ECB, subject to any decision taken by the Governing Council pursuant to Article 33.2.

32.6. The clearing and settlement of the balances arising from the allocation of monetary income shall be carried out by the ECB in accordance with guidelines established by the Governing Council.

32.7. The Governing Council shall take all other measures necessary for the application of this Article.

Article 33. Allocation of net profits and losses of the ECB

33.1. The net profit of the ECB shall be transferred in the following order:

(a) an amount to be determined by the Governing Council, which may not exceed 20% of the net profit, shall be transferred to the general reserve fund subject to a limit equal to 100% of the capital;

(b) the remaining net profit shall be distributed to the shareholders of the ECB in proportion to their paid-up shares.

33.2. In the event of a loss incurred by the ECB, the shortfall may be offset against the general reserve fund of the ECB and, if necessary, following a decision by the Governing Council, against the monetary income of the relevant financial year in proportion and up to the amounts allocated to the national central banks in accordance with Article 32.5.

Chapter VII   General Provisions

Article 34. Legal acts

34.1. In accordance with Article *110* of this Treaty, the ECB shall:
– make regulations to the extent necessary to implement the tasks defined in Article 3.1, first indent, Articles 19.1, 22 or 25.2 and in cases which shall be laid down in the acts of the Council referred to in Article 42;
– take decisions necessary for carrying out the tasks entrusted to the ESCB under this Treaty and this Statute;
– make recommendations and deliver opinions.

34.2. A regulation shall have general application. It shall be binding in its entirety and directly applicable in all Member States.

Recommendations and opinions shall have no binding force.

A decision shall be binding in its entirety upon those to whom it is addressed.

Articles *253* to *256* of this Treaty shall apply to regulations and decisions adopted by the ECB.*

The ECB may decide to publish its decisions, recommendations and opinions.

34.3. Within the limits and under the conditions adopted by the Council under the procedure laid down in Article 42, the ECB shall be entitled to impose fines or periodic penalty payments on undertakings for failure to comply with obligations under its regulations and decisions.

Article 35. Judicial control and related matters

35.1. The acts or omissions of the ECB shall be open to review or interpretation by the Court of Justice in the cases and under the conditions laid down in this Treaty. The ECB may institute proceedings in the cases and under the conditions laid down in this Treaty.

35.2. Disputes between the ECB, on the one hand, and its creditors, debtors or any other person, on the other, shall be decided by the competent national courts, save where jurisdiction has been conferred upon the Court of Justice.

35.3. The ECB shall be subject to the liability regime provided for in Article *288* of this Treaty. The national central banks shall be liable according to their respective national laws.

35.4. The Court of Justice shall have jurisdiction to give judgment pursuant to any arbitration clause contained in a contract concluded by or on behalf of the ECB, whether that contract be governed by public or private law.

35.5. A decision of the ECB to bring an action before the Court of Justice shall be taken by the Governing Council.

35.6. The Court of Justice shall have jurisdiction in disputes concerning the fulfilment by a national central bank of obligations under this Statute. If the ECB

---

*In the absence of a corresponding change here, the new Article 255 inserted by the TA into the TEC on the enforcement of pecuniary obligations would appear to apply even though the ECB does not, however, possess the competence to impose such obligations. Published versions of the Protocol now refer to Articles '253, 254 and 256'.

considers that a national central bank has failed to fulfil an obligation under this Statute, it shall deliver a reasoned opinion on the matter after giving the national central bank concerned the opportunity to submit its observations. If the national central bank concerned does not comply with the opinion within the period laid down by the ECB, the latter may bring the matter before the Court of Justice.

Article 36. Staff

36.1. The Governing Council, on a proposal from the Executive Board, shall lay down the conditions of employment of the staff of the ECB.

36.2. The Court of Justice shall have jurisdiction in any dispute between the ECB and its servants within the limits and under the conditions laid down in the conditions of employment.

Article 37. Seat

Before the end of 1992, the decision as to where the seat of the ECB will be established shall be taken by common accord of the governments of the Member States at the level of Heads of State or of Government.

Article 38. Professional secrecy

38.1. Members of the governing bodies and the staff of the ECB and the national central banks shall be required, even after their duties have ceased, not to disclose information of the kind covered by the obligation of professional secrecy.

38.2. Persons having access to data covered by Community legislation imposing an obligation of secrecy shall be subject to such legislation.

Article 39. Signatories

The ECB shall be legally committed to third parties by the President or by two members of the Executive Board or by the signatures of two members of the staff of the ECB who have been duly authorized by the President to sign on behalf of the ECB.

Article 40. Privileges and immunities

The ECB shall enjoy in the territories of the Member States such privileges and immunities as are necessary for the performance of its tasks, under the conditions laid down in the Protocol on the privileges and immunities of the European Communities.*

Chapter VIII   Amendment of the Statute and Complementary Legislation

Article 41. Simplified amendment procedure

41.1. In accordance with Article 107(5) of this Treaty, Articles 5.1, 5.2, 5.3, 17, 18, 19.1, 22, 23, 24, 26, 32.2, 32.3, 32.4, 32.6, 33.1(a) and 36 of this Statute may be amended by the Council, acting either by a qualified majority on a recommendation from the ECB and after consulting the Commission, or unanimously on a proposal from the Commission and after consulting the ECB. In either case the assent of the European Parliament shall be required.

41.2. A recommendation made by the ECB under this Article shall require a unanimous decision by the Governing Council.

Article 42. Complementary legislation

In accordance with Article 107(6) of this Treaty, immediately after the decision

---

*The TA deletes the words 'annexed to the Treaty establishing a Single Council and a Single Commission of the European Communities'.

on the date for the beginning of the third stage, the Council, acting by a qualified majority either on a proposal from the Commission and after consulting the European Parliament and the ECB or on a recommendation from the ECB and after consulting the European Parliament and the Commission, shall adopt the provisions referred to in Articles 4, 5.4, 19.2, 20, 28.1, 29.2, 30.4, and 34.3 of this Statute.

Chapter IX   Transitional and Other Provisions for the ESCB

Article 43. General Provisions

43.1. A derogation as referred to in Article 122(1) of this Treaty shall entail that the following Articles of this Statue shall not confer any rights or impose any obligations on the Member State concerned: 3, 6, 9.2, 12.1, 14.3, 16, 18, 19, 20, 22, 23, 26.2, 27, 30, 31, 32, 33, 34, 50 and 52.

43.2. The central banks of Member States with a derogation as specified in Article 122(1) of this Treaty shall retain their powers in the field of monetary policy according to national law.

43.3. In accordance with Article 122(4) of this Treaty, 'Member States' shall be read as 'Member States without a derogation' in the following Articles of this Statute: 3, 11.2, 19, 34.2 and 50.

43.4 'National central banks' shall be read as 'central banks of Member States without a derogation' in the following Articles of this Statute: 9.2, 10.1, 10.3, 12.1, 16, 17, 18, 22, 23, 27, 30, 31, 32, 33.2 and 52.

43.5. 'Shareholders' shall be read as 'central banks of Member States without a derogation' in Articles 10.3 and 33.1.

43.6. 'Subscribed capital of the ECB' shall be read as 'capital of the ECB subscribed by the central banks of Member States without a derogation' in Articles 10.3 and 30.2.

Article 44. Transitional tasks of the ECB

The ECB shall take over those tasks of the EMI which, because of the derogations of one or more Member States, still have to be performed in the third stage.

The ECB shall give advice in the preparations for the abrogation of the derogations specified in Article 122 of this Treaty.

Article 45. The General Council of the ECB

45.1. Without prejudice to Article 107(3) of this Treaty, the General Council shall be constituted as a third decision-making body of the ECB.

45.2. The General Council shall comprise the President and Vice-President of the ECB and the Governors of the national central banks. The other members of the Executive Board may participate, without having the right to vote, in meetings of the General Council.

45.3. The responsibilities of the General Council are listed in full in Article 47 of this Statute.

Article 46. Rules of procedure of the General Council

46.1. The President or, in his absence, the Vice-President of the ECB shall chair the General Council of the ECB.

46.2. The President of the Council and a member of the Commission may participate, without having the right to vote, in meetings of the General Council.

46.3. The President shall prepare the meetings of the General Council.

46.4. By way of a derogation from Article 12.3, the General Council shall adopt its Rules of Procedure.

46.5. The Secretariat of the General Council shall be provided by the ECB.

Article 47. Responsibilities of the General Council

47.1. The General Council shall:
– perform the tasks referred to in Article 44;
– contribute to the advisory functions referred to in Articles 4 and 25.1.

47.2. The General Council shall contribute to:
– the collection of statistical information as referred to in Article 5;
– the reporting activities of the ECB as referred to in Article 15;
– the establishment of the necessary rules for the application of Article 26 as referred to in Article 26.4;
– the taking of all other measures necessary for the application of Article 29 as referred to in Article 29.4;
– the laying down of the conditions of employment of the staff of the ECB as referred to in Article 36.

47.3. The General Council shall contribute to the necessary preparations for irrevocably fixing the exchange rates of the currencies of Member States with a derogation against the currencies, or the single currency, of the Member States without a derogation, as referred to in Article 123(5) of this Treaty.

47.4. The General Council shall be informed by the President of the ECB of decisions of the Governing Council.

Article 48. Transitional provisions for the capital of the ECB

In accordance with Article 29.1 each national central bank shall be assigned a weighting in the key for subscription of the ECB's capital. By way of derogation from Article 28.3, central banks of Member States with a derogation shall not pay up their subscribed capital unless the General Council, acting by a majority representing at least two thirds of the subscribed capital of the ECB and at least half of the shareholders, decides that a minimal percentage has to be paid up as a contribution to the operational costs of the ECB.

Article 49. Deferred payment of capital, reserves and provisions of the ECB

49.1. The central bank of a Member State whose derogation has been abrogated shall pay up its subscribed share of the capital of the ECB to the same extent as the central banks of other Member States without a derogation, and shall transfer to the ECB foreign reserve assets in accordance with Article 30.1. The sum to be transferred shall be determined by multiplying the ECU value at current exchange rates of the foreign reserve assets which have already been transferred to the ECB in accordance with Article 30.1, by the ratio between the number of shares subscribed by the national central bank concerned and the number of shares already paid up by the other national central banks.

49.2. In addition to the payment to be made in accordance with Article 49.1, the central bank concerned shall contribute to the reserves of the ECB, to those provisions equivalent to reserves, and to the amount still to be appropriated to the reserves and provisions corresponding to the balance of the profit and loss account as at 31 December of the year prior to the abrogation of the derogation. The sum to be contributed shall be determined by multiplying the amount of reserves, as defined above and as stated in the approved balance sheet of the ECB, by the ratio between the number of shares subscribed by the central bank concerned and the number of shares already paid up by the other central banks.

Article 50. Initial appointment of the members of the Executive Board

When the Executive Board of the ECB is being established, the President, the Vice-President and the other members of the Executive Board shall be appointed by common accord of the governments of the Member States at the level of Heads of State or of Government, on a recommendation from the Council and after consulting the European Parliament and the Council of the EMI. The President of the Executive Board shall be appointed for 8 years. By way of derogation from Article 11.2, the Vice-President shall be appointed for 4 years and the other members of the Executive Board for terms of office of between 5 and 8 years. No term of office shall be renewable. The number of members of the Executive Board may be smaller than provided for in Article 11.1, but in no circumstance shall it be less than four.

Article 51. Derogation from Article 32

51.1. If, after the start of the third stage, the Governing Council decides that the application of Article 32 results in significant changes in national central banks' relative income positions, the amount of income to be allocated pursuant to Article 32 shall be reduced by a uniform percentage which shall not exceed 60% in the first financial year after the start of the third stage and which shall decrease by at least 12 percentage points in each subsequent financial year.

51.2. Article 51.1 shall be applicable for not more than five financial years after the start of the third stage.

Article 52. Exchange of bank notes in Community currencies

Following the irrevocable fixing of exchange rates, the Governing Council shall take the necessary measures to ensure that bank notes denominated in currencies with irrevocably fixed exchange rates are exchanged by the national central banks at their respective par values.

Article 53. Applicability of the transitional provisions

If and as long as there are Member States with a derogation Articles 43 to 48 shall be applicable.

PROTOCOL ON THE STATUTE OF THE EUROPEAN MONETARY INSTITUTE (1992)

THE HIGH CONTRACTING PARTIES,
DESIRING to lay down the Statute of the European Monetary Institute,
HAVE AGREED upon the following provisions, which shall be annexed to the Treaty establishing the European Community;

Article 1. Constitution and name

1.1. The European Monetary Institute (EMI) shall be established in accordance with Article 117 of this Treaty; it shall perform its functions and carry out its activities in accordance with the provisions of this Treaty and of this Statute.

1.2. The members of the EMI shall be the central banks of the Member States ('national central banks'). For the purposes of this Statute, the Institut monétaire luxembourgeois shall be regarded as the central bank of Luxembourg.

1.3. Pursuant to Article 117 of this Treaty, both the Committee of Governors and the European Monetary Co-operation Fund (EMCF) shall be dissolved. All assets and liabilities of the EMCF shall pass automatically to the EMI.

Article 2. Objectives

The EMI shall contribute to the realization of the conditions necessary for the transition to the third stage of Economic and Monetary Union, in particular by:
– strengthening the co-ordination of monetary policies with a view to ensuring price stability;
– making the preparations required for the establishment of the European System of Central Banks (ESCB), and for the conduct of a single monetary policy and the creation of a single currency in the third stage;
– overseeing the development of the ECU.

Article 3. General principles

3.1. The EMI shall carry out the tasks and functions conferred upon it by this Treaty and this Statute without prejudice to the responsibility of the competent authorities for the conduct of the monetary policy within the respective Member States.

3.2. The EMI shall act in accordance with the objectives and principles stated in Article 2 of the Statute of the ESCB.

Article 4. Primary tasks

4.1. In accordance with Article 117(2) of this Treaty, the EMI shall:
– strengthen co-operation between the national central banks;
– strengthen the co-ordination of the monetary policies of the Member States with the aim of ensuring price stability;
– monitor the functioning of the European Monetary System (EMS);
– hold consultations concerning issues falling within the competence of the national central banks and affecting the stability of financial institutions and markets;
– take over the tasks of the EMCF; in particular it shall perform the functions referred to in Articles 6.1, 6.2 and 6.3;
– facilitate the use of the ECU and oversee its development, including the smooth functioning of the ECU clearing system.

The EMI shall also:
– hold regular consultations concerning the course of monetary policies and the use of monetary policy instruments;
– normally be consulted by the national monetary authorities before they take decisions on the course of monetary policy in the context of the common framework for *ex ante* co-ordination.

4.2. At the latest by 31 December 1996, the EMI shall specify the regulatory, organizational and logistical framework necessary for the ESCB to perform its tasks in the third stage, in accordance with the principle of an open market economy with free competition. This framework shall be submitted by the Council of the EMI for decision to the ECB at the date of its establishment.

In accordance with Article 117(3) of this Treaty, the EMI shall in particular:
– prepare the instruments and the procedures necessary for carrying out a single monetary policy in the third stage;
– promote the harmonization, where necessary, of the rules and practices governing the collection, compilation and distribution of statistics in the areas within its field of competence;

– prepare the rules for operations to be undertaken by the national central banks in the framework of the ESCB;
– promote the efficiency of cross-border payments;
– supervise the technical preparation of ECU bank notes.

Article 5. Advisory functions

5.1. In accordance with Article 117(4) of this Treaty, the Council of the EMI may formulate opinions or recommendations on the overall orientation of monetary policy and exchange rate policy as well as on related measures introduced in each Member State. The EMI may submit opinions or recommendations to governments and to the Council on policies which might affect the internal or external monetary situation in the Community and, in particular, the functioning of the EMS.

5.2. The Council of the EMI may also make recommendations to the monetary authorities of the Member States concerning the conduct of their monetary policy.

5.3. In accordance with Article 117(6) of this Treaty, the EMI shall be consulted by the Council regarding any proposed Community act within its field of competence.

Within the limits and under the conditions set out by the Council acting by a qualified majority on a proposal from the Commission and after consulting the European Parliament and the EMI, the EMI shall be consulted by the authorities of the Member States on any draft legislative provision within its field of competence, in particular with regard to Article 4.2.

5.4. In accordance with Article 117(5) of this Treaty, the EMI may decide to publish its opinions and its recommendations.

Article 6. Operational and technical functions

6.1. The EMI shall:
– provide for the multilateralization of positions resulting from interventions by the national central banks in Community currencies and the multilateralization of intra-Community settlements;
– administer the very short-term financing mechanism provided for by the Agreement of 13 March 1979 between the central banks of the Member States of the European Economic Community laying down the operating procedures for the European Monetary System (hereinafter referred to as 'EMS Agreement') and the short-term monetary support mechanism provided for in the Agreement between the central banks of the Member States of the European Economic Community of 9 February 1970, as amended;
– perform the functions referred to in Article 11 of Council Regulation (EEC) No. 1969/88 of 24 June 1988 establishing a single facility providing medium-term financial assistance for Member States' balances of payments.

6.2. The EMI may receive monetary reserves from the national central banks and issue ECUs against such assets for the purpose of implementing the EMS Agreement. These ECUs may be used by the EMI and the national central banks as a means of settlement and for transactions between them and the EMI. The EMI shall take the necessary administrative measures for the implementation of this paragraph.

6.3. The EMI may grant to the monetary authorities of third countries and to international monetary institutions the status of 'Other Holders' of ECUs and fix the terms and conditions under which such ECUs may be acquired, held or used by Other Holders.

6.4. The EMI shall be entitled to hold and manage foreign exchange reserves as an agent for and at the request of national central banks. Profits and losses regarding these reserves shall be for the account of the national central bank depositing the reserves. The EMI shall perform this function on the basis of bilateral contracts in accordance with rules laid down in a decision of the EMI. These rules shall ensure that transactions with these reserves shall not interfere with the monetary policy and exchange rate policy of the competent monetary authority of any Member State and shall be consistent with the objectives of the EMI and the proper functioning of the Exchange Rate Mechanism of the EMS.

Article 7. Other tasks

7.1. Once a year the EMI shall address a report to the Council on the state of the preparations for the third stage. These reports shall include an assessment of the progress towards convergence in the Community, and cover in particular the adaptation of monetary policy instruments and the preparation of the procedures necessary for carrying out a single monetary policy in the third stage, as well as the statutory requirements to be fulfilled for national central banks to become an integral part of the ESCB.

7.2. In accordance with the Council decisions referred to in Article 117(7) of this Treaty, the EMI may perform other tasks for the preparation of the third stage.

Article 8. Independence

The members of the Council of the EMI who are the representatives of their institutions shall, with respect to their activities, act according to their own responsibilities. In exercising the powers and performing the tasks and duties conferred upon them by this Treaty and this Statute, the Council of the EMI may not seek or take any instructions from Community institutions or bodies or governments of Member States. The Community institutions and bodies as well as the governments of the Member States undertake to respect this principle and not seek to influence the Council of the EMI in the performance of its tasks.

Article 9. Administration

9.1. In accordance with Article 117(1) of this Treaty, the EMI shall be directed and managed by the Council of the EMI.

9.2. The Council of the EMI shall consist of a President and the Governors of the national central banks, one of whom shall be Vice-President. If a Governor is prevented from attending a meeting, he may nominate another representative of his institution.

9.3. The President shall be appointed by common accord of the governments of the Member States at the level of Heads of State or of Government, on a recommendation from, as the case may be, the Committee of Governors or the Council of the EMI, and after consulting the European Parliament and the Council. The President shall be selected from among persons of recognized standing and professional experience in monetary or banking matters. Only nationals of Member States may be President of the EMI. The Council of the EMI shall appoint the Vice-President. The President and Vice-President shall be appointed for a period of three years.

9.4. The President shall perform his duties on a full-time basis. He shall not engage in any occupation, whether gainful or not, unless exemption is exceptionally granted by the Council of the EMI.

9.5. The President shall:
– prepare and chair meetings of the Council of the EMI;

– without prejudice to Article 22, present the views of the EMI externally;

– be responsible for the day-to-day management of the EMI.

In the absence of the President, his duties shall be performed by the Vice-President.

9.6. The terms and conditions of employment of the President, in particular his salary, pension and other social security benefits, shall be the subject of a contract with the EMI and shall be fixed by the Council of the EMI on a proposal from a Committee comprising three members appointed by the Committee of Governors or the Council of the EMI, as the case may be, and three members appointed by the Council. The President shall not have the right to vote on matters referred to in this paragraph.

9.7. If the President no longer fulfils the conditions required for the performance of his duties or if he has been guilty of serious misconduct, the Court of Justice may, on application by the Council of the EMI, compulsorily retire him.

9.8. The Rules of Procedure of the EMI shall be adopted by the Council of the EMI.

Article 10. Meetings of the Council of the EMI and voting procedures

10.1. The Council of the EMI shall meet at least ten times a year. The proceedings of Council meetings shall be confidential. The Council of the EMI may, acting unanimously, decide to make the outcome of its deliberations public.

10.2. Each member of the Council of the EMI or his nominee shall have one vote.

10.3. Save as otherwise provided for in this Statute, the Council of the EMI shall act by a simple majority of its members.

10.4. Decisions to be taken in the context of Articles 4.2, 5.4, 6.2 and 6.3 shall require unanimity of the members of the Council of the EMI.

The adoption of opinions and recommendations under Articles 5.1 and 5.2, the adoption of decisions under Articles 6.4, 16 and 23.6 and the adoption of guidelines under Article 15.3 shall require a qualified majority of two thirds of the members of the Council of the EMI.

Article 11. Interinstitutional co-operation and reporting requirements

11.1. The President of the Council and a member of the Commission may participate, without having the right to vote, in meetings of the Council of the EMI.

11.2. The President of the EMI shall be invited to participate in Council meetings when the Council is discussing matters relating to the objectives and tasks of the EMI.

11.3. At a date to be established in the Rules of Procedure, the EMI shall prepare an annual report on its activities and on monetary and financial conditions in the Community. The annual report, together with the annual accounts of the EMI, shall be addressed to the European Parliament, the Council and the Commission and also to the European Council.

The President of the EMI may, at the request of the European Parliament or on his own initiative, be heard by the competent Committees of the European Parliament.

11.4. Reports published by the EMI shall be made available to interested parties free of charge.

Article 12. Currency denomination

The operations of the EMI shall be expressed in ECUs.

Article 13. Seat

Before the end of 1992, the decision as to where the seat of the EMI will be established shall be taken by common accord of the governments of the Member States at the level of Heads of State or of Government.

Article 14. Legal capacity

The EMI, which in accordance with Article 117(1) of this Treaty shall have legal personality, shall enjoy in each of the Member States the most extensive legal capacity accorded to legal persons under their law; it may, in particular, acquire or dispose of movable or immovable property and may be a party to legal proceedings.

Article 15. Legal acts

15.1. In the performance of its tasks, and under the conditions laid down in this Statute, the EMI shall:
– deliver opinions;
– make recommendations;
– adopt guidelines, and take decisions, which shall be addressed to the national central banks.

15.2. Opinions and recommendations of the EMI shall have no binding force.

15.3. The Council of the EMI may adopt guidelines laying down the methods for the implementation of the conditions necessary for the ESCB to perform its functions in the third stage. EMI guidelines shall have no binding force; they shall be submitted for decision to the ECB.

15.4. Without prejudice to Article 3.1, a decision of the EMI shall be binding in its entirety upon those to whom it is addressed. Articles 253 and 254 of this Treaty shall apply to these decisions.

Article 16. Financial resources

16.1. The EMI shall be endowed with its own resources. The size of the resources of the EMI shall be determined by the Council of the EMI with a view to ensuring the income deemed necessary to cover the administrative expenditure incurred in the performance of the tasks and functions of the EMI.

16.2. The resources of the EMI determined in accordance with Article 16.1 shall be provided out of contributions by the national central banks in accordance with the key referred to in Article 29.1 of the Statute of the ESCB and be paid up at the establishment of the EMI. For this purpose, the statistical data to be used for the determination of the key shall be provided by the Commission, in accordance with the rules adopted by the Council, acting by a qualified majority on a proposal from the Commission and after consulting the European Parliament, the Committee of Governors and the Committee referred to in Article 114 of this Treaty.

16.3. The Council of the EMI shall determine the form in which contributions shall be paid up.

Article 17. Annual accounts and auditing

17.1. The financial year of the EMI shall begin on the first day of January and end on the last day of December.

17.2. The Council of the EMI shall adopt an annual budget before the beginning of each financial year.

17.3. The annual accounts shall be drawn up in accordance with the principles established by the Council of the EMI. The annual accounts shall be approved by the Council of the EMI and shall thereafter be published.

17.4. The annual accounts shall be audited by independent external auditors approved by the Council of the EMI. The auditors shall have full power to examine all books and accounts of the EMI and to obtain full information about its transactions.

The provisions of Article 248 of this Treaty shall only apply to an examination of the operational efficiency of the management of the EMI.

17.5. Any surplus of the EMI shall be transferred in the following order:
(a) an amount to be determined by the Council of the EMI shall be transferred to the general reserve fund of the EMI;
(b) any remaining surplus shall be distributed to the national central banks in accordance with the key referred to in Article 16.2.

17.6. In the event of a loss incurred by the EMI, the shortfall shall be offset against the general reserve fund of the EMI. Any remaining shortfall shall be made good by contributions from the national central banks, in accordance with the key as referred to in Article 16.2.

Article 18. Staff

18.1. The Council of the EMI shall lay down the conditions of employment of the staff of the EMI.

18.2. The Court of Justice shall have jurisdiction in any dispute between the EMI and its servants within the limits and under the conditions laid down in the conditions of employment.

Article 19. Judicial control and related matters

19.1. The acts or omissions of the EMI shall be open to review or interpretation by the Court of Justice in the cases and under the conditions laid down in this Treaty. The EMI may institute proceedings in the cases and under the conditions laid down in this Treaty.

19.2. Disputes between the EMI, on the one hand, and its creditors, debtors or any other person, on the other, shall fall within the jurisdiction of the competent national courts, save where jurisdiction has been conferred upon the Court of Justice.

19.3. The EMI shall be subject to the liability regime provided for in Article 288 of this Treaty.

19.4. The Court of Justice shall have jurisdiction to give judgment pursuant to any arbitration clause contained in a contract concluded by or on behalf of the EMI, whether that contract be governed by public or private law.

19.5. A decision of the EMI to bring an action before the Court of Justice shall be taken by the Council of the EMI.

Article 20. Professional Secrecy

20.1. Members of the Council of the EMI and the staff of the EMI shall be required, even after their duties have ceased, not to disclose information of the kind covered by the obligation of professional secrecy.

20.2. Persons having access to data covered by Community legislation imposing an obligation of secrecy shall be subject to such legislation.

Article 21. Privileges and immunities

The EMI shall enjoy in the territories of the Member States such privileges and immunities as are necessary for the performance of its tasks, under the conditions laid down in the Protocol on the privileges and immunities of the European Communities.*

Article 22. Signatories

The EMI shall be legally committed to third parties by the President or the Vice-President or by the signatures of two members of the staff of the EMI who have been duly authorized by the President to sign on behalf of the EMI.

Article 23. Liquidation of the EMI

23.1. In accordance with Article 123 of this Treaty, the EMI shall go into liquidation on the establishment of the ECB. All assets and liabilities of the EMI shall then pass automatically to the ECB. The latter shall liquidate the EMI according to the provisions of this Article. The liquidation shall be completed by the beginning of the third stage.

23.2. The mechanism for the creation of ECUs against gold and US dollars as provided for by Article 17 of the EMS agreement shall be unwound by the first day of the third stage in accordance with Article 20 of the said Agreement.

23.3. All claims and liabilities arising from the very short-term financing mechanism and the short-term monetary support mechanism, under the Agreements referred to in Article 6.1, shall be settled by the first day of the third stage.

23.4. All remaining assets of the EMI shall be disposed of and all remaining liabilities of the EMI shall be settled.

23.5. The proceeds of the liquidation described in Article 23.4 shall be distributed to the national central banks in accordance with the key referred to in Article 16.2.

23.6. The Council of the EMI may take the measures necessary for the application of Articles 23.4 and 23.5.

23.7. Upon the establishment of the ECB, the President of the EMI shall relinquish his office.

PROTOCOL ON THE EXCESSIVE DEFICIT PROCEDURE (1992)

THE HIGH CONTRACTING PARTIES,

DESIRING to lay down the details of the excessive deficit procedure referred to in Article 104 of the Treaty establishing the European Community,
HAVE AGREED upon the following provisions, which shall be annexed to the Treaty establishing the European Community:

Article 1. The reference values referred to in Article 104(2) of this Treaty are:
– 3% for the ratio of the planned or actual government deficit to gross domestic product at market prices;
– 60% for the ratio of government debt to gross domestic product at market prices.

Article 2. In Article 104 of this Treaty and in this Protocol:
– government means general government, that is central government, regional or local government and social security funds, to the exclusion of commercial operations, as defined in the European System of Integrated Economic Accounts;

---

*The TA deletes the words 'annexed to the Treaty establishing a Single Council and a Single Commission of the European Communities'.

– deficit means net borrowing as defined in the European System of Integrated Economic Accounts;
– investment means gross fixed capital formation as defined in the European System of Integrated Economic Accounts;
– debt means total gross debt at nominal value outstanding at the end of the year and consolidated between and within the sectors of general government as defined in the first indent.

Article 3. In order to ensure the effectiveness of the excessive deficit procedure, the governments of the Member States shall be responsible under this procedure for the deficits of general government as defined in the first indent of Article 2. The Member States shall ensure that national procedures in the Budgetary area enable them to meet their obligations in this area deriving from this Treaty. The Member States shall report their planned and actual deficits and the levels of their debt promptly and regularly to the Commission.

Article 4. The statistical data to be used for the application of this Protocol shall be provided by the Commission.

PROTOCOL ON THE CONVERGENCE CRITERIA REFERRED TO IN ARTICLE *121* [EX 109J] OF THE TREATY ESTABLISHING THE EUROPEAN COMMUNITY (1992)

THE HIGH CONTRACTING PARTIES,
DESIRING to lay down the details of the convergence criteria which shall guide the Community in taking decisions on the passage to the third stage of economic and monetary union, referred to in Article *121*(1) of this Treaty,
HAVE AGREED upon the following provisions, which shall be annexed to the Treaty establishing the European Community:

Article 1. The criterion on price stability referred to in the first indent of Article *121*(1) of this Treaty shall mean that a Member State has a price performance that is sustainable and an average rate of inflation, observed over a period of one year before the examination, that does not exceed by more than 1½ percentage points that of, at most, the three best performing Member States in terms of price stability. Inflation shall be measured by means of the consumer price index on a comparable basis, taking into account differences in national definitions.

Article 2. The criterion on the government budgetary position referred to in the second indent of Article *121*(1) of this treaty shall mean that at the time of the examination the Member State is not the subject of a Council decision under Article *104*(6) of this Treaty that an excessive deficit exists.

Article 3. The criterion on participation in the Exchange Rate Mechanism of the European Monetary System referred to in the third indent of Article *121*(1) of this Treaty shall mean that a Member State has respected the normal fluctuation margins provided for by the Exchange Rate Mechanism of the European Monetary System without severe tensions for at least the last two years before the examination. In particular, the Member State shall not have devalued its currency's bilateral central rate against any other Member State's currency on its own initiative for the same period.

Article 4. The criterion on the convergence of interest rates referred to in the fourth indent of Article *121*(1) of this Treaty shall mean that, observed over a period of one year before the examination, a Member State has had an average nominal long-term interest rate that does not exceed by more than 2 percentage points that of, at most, the three best performing Member States in terms of price stability. Interest rates shall be measured on the basis of long term government bonds or comparable securities, taking into account differences in national definitions.

Article 5. The statistical data to be used for the application of this Protocol shall be provided by the Commission.

Article 6. The Council shall, acting unanimously on a proposal from the Commission and after consulting the European Parliament, the EMI or the ECB as the case may be, and the Committee referred to in Article 114, adopt appropriate provisions to lay down the details of the convergence criteria referred to Article 121 of this Treaty, which shall then replace this Protocol.

PROTOCOL ON DENMARK (1992)

THE HIGH CONTRACTING PARTIES,
DESIRING to settle certain particular problems relating to Denmark,
HAVE AGREED UPON the following provisions, which shall be annexed to the Treaty establishing the European Community:

The provisions of Article 14 of the Protocol on the Statute of the European System of Central Banks and of the European Central Bank shall not affect the right of the National Bank of Denmark to carry out its existing tasks concerning those parts of the Kingdom of Denmark which are not part of the Community.

PROTOCOL ON PORTUGAL (1992)

THE HIGH CONTRACTING PARTIES,
DESIRING to settle certain particular problems relating to Portugal,
HAVE AGREED upon the following provisions, which shall be annexed to the Treaty establishing the European Community:

1. Portugal is hereby authorized to maintain the facility afforded to the Autonomous Regions of Azores and Madeira to benefit from an interest-free credit facility with the Banco de Portugal under the terms established by existing Portuguese law.

2. Portugal commits itself to pursue its best endeavours in order to put an end to the above mentioned facility as soon as possible.

PROTOCOL ON THE TRANSITION TO THE THIRD STAGE OF ECONOMIC AND MONETARY UNION (1992)

THE HIGH CONTRACTING PARTIES,
Declare the irreversible character of the Community's movement to the third stage of economic and monetary union by signing the new Treaty provisions on economic and monetary union.

Therefore all Member States shall, whether they fulfil the necessary conditions for the adoption of a single currency or not, respect the will for the Community to enter swiftly into the third stage, and therefore no Member State shall prevent the entering into the third stage.

If by the end of 1997 the date of the beginning of the third stage has not been set, the Member States concerned, the Community institutions and other bodies involved shall expedite all preparatory work during 1998, in order to enable the Community to enter the third stage irrevocably on 1 January 1999 and to enable the ECB and ESCB to start their full functioning from this date.

This Protocol shall be annexed to the Treaty establishing the European Community.

PROTOCOL ON CERTAIN PROVISIONS RELATING TO THE UNITED KINGDOM OF GREAT BRITAIN AND NORTHERN IRELAND (1992)

THE HIGH CONTRACTING PARTIES,

RECOGNIZING that the United Kingdom shall not be obliged or committed to move to the third stage of economic and monetary union without a separate decision to do so by its government and Parliament,

NOTING the practice of the government of the United Kingdom to fund its borrowing requirement by the sale of debt to the private sector,

HAVE AGREED the following provisions, which shall be annexed to the Treaty establishing the European Community:

1. The United Kingdom shall notify the Council whether it intends to move to the third stage before the Council makes its assessment under Article 121(2) of this Treaty.

Unless the United Kingdom notifies the Council that it intends to move to the third stage, it shall be under no obligation to do so.

If no date is set for the beginning of the third stage under Article 121(3) of this Treaty, the United Kingdom may notify its intention to move to the third stage before 1 January 1998.

2. Paragraphs 3 to 9 shall have effect if the United Kingdom notifies the Council that it does not intend to move to the third stage.

3. The United Kingdom shall not be included among the majority of Member States which fulfil the necessary conditions referred to in the second indent of Article 121(2) and the first indent of Article 121(3) of this Treaty.

4. The United Kingdom shall retain its powers in the field of monetary policy according to national law.

5. Articles 4(2), 104(1), (9) and (11), 105(1) to (5), 106, 108, 109, 110, 111, 112(1) and (2)(b) and 123(4) and (5) of this Treaty shall not apply to the United Kingdom. In these provisions references to the Community or the Member States shall not include the United Kingdom and references to national central banks shall not include the Bank of England.

6. Articles 116(4) and 119 and 120 of this Treaty shall continue to apply to the United Kingdom. Articles 114(4) and 124 shall apply to the United Kingdom as if it had a derogation.

7. The voting rights of the United Kingdom shall be suspended in respect of acts of the Council referred to in Articles listed in paragraph 5. For this purpose the weighted votes of the United Kingdom shall be excluded from any calculation of a qualified majority under Article 122(5) of this Treaty.

The United Kingdom shall also have no right to participate in the appointment of the President, the Vice-President and the other members of the Executive Board of the ECB under Articles 112(2)(b) and 123(1) of this Treaty.

8. Articles 3, 4, 6, 7, 9.2, 10.1, 10.3, 11.2, 12.1, 14, 16, 18 to 20, 22, 23, 26, 27, 30 to 34, 50 and 52 of the Protocol on the Statute of the European System of Central Banks and of the European Central Bank ('the Statute') shall not apply to the United Kingdom.

In those Articles, references to the Community or the Member States shall not include the United Kingdom and references to national central banks or shareholders shall not include the Bank of England.

References in Articles 10.3 and 30.2 of the Statute to 'subscribed capital of the ECB' shall not include capital subscribed by the Bank of England.

9. Article 123(3) of this Treaty and Articles 44 to 48 of the Statute shall have effect, whether or not there is any Member State with a derogation, subject to the following amendments:

(a) References in Article 44 to the tasks of the ECB and the EMI shall include those tasks that still need to be performed in the third stage owing to any decision of the United Kingdom not to move to that Stage.

(b) In addition to the tasks referred to in Article 47 the ECB shall also give advice in relation to and contribute to the preparation of any decision of the Council with regard to the United Kingdom taken in accordance with paragraphs 10(a) and 10(c).

(c) The Bank of England shall pay up its subscription to the capital of the ECB as a contribution of its operational costs on the same basis as national central banks of Member States with a derogation.

10. If the United Kingdom does not move to the third stage, it may change its notification at any time after the beginning of that stage. In that event:

(a) The United Kingdom shall have the right to move to the third stage provided only that it satisfies the necessary conditions. The Council, acting at the request of the United Kingdom and under the conditions and in accordance with the procedure laid down in Article 122(2) of this Treaty, shall decide whether it fulfils the necessary conditions.

(b) The Bank of England shall pay up its subscribed capital, transfer to the ECB foreign reserve assets and contribute to its reserves on the same basis as the national central bank of a Member State whose derogation has been abrogated.

(c) The Council, acting under the conditions and in accordance with the procedure laid down in Article 123(5) of this Treaty, shall take all other necessary decisions to enable the United Kingdom to move to the third stage.

If the United Kingdom moves to the third stage pursuant to the provisions of this protocol, paragraphs 3 to 9 shall cease to have effect.

11. Notwithstanding Articles 101 and 116(3) of this Treaty and Article 21.1 of the Statute, the government of the United Kingdom may maintain its 'ways and means' facility with the Bank of England if and so long as the United Kingdom does not move to the third stage.

PROTOCOL ON CERTAIN PROVISIONS RELATING TO DENMARK (1992)

THE HIGH CONTRACTING PARTIES,
DESIRING to settle, in accordance with the general objectives of the Treaty establishing the European Community, certain particular problems existing at the present time,
TAKING INTO ACCOUNT that the Danish Constitution contains provisions which may imply a referendum in Denmark prior to Danish participation in the third stage of economic and monetary union,
HAVE AGREED on the following provisions, which shall be annexed to the Treaty establishing the European Community:

1. The Danish Government shall notify the Council of its position concerning participation in the third stage before the Council makes its assessment under Article 121(2) of this Treaty.

2. In the event of a notification that Denmark will not participate in the third stage, Denmark shall have an exemption. The effect of the exemption shall be that all Articles and provisions of this Treaty and the Statute of the ESCB referring to a derogation shall be applicable to Denmark.

3. In such case, Denmark shall not be included among the majority of Member States which fulfil the necessary conditions referred to in the second indent of Article 121(2) and the first indent of Article 121(3) of this Treaty.

4. As for the abrogation of the exemption, the procedure referred to in Article 122(2) shall only be initiated at the request of Denmark.

5. In the event of abrogation of the exemption status, the provisions of this Protocol shall cease to apply.

PROTOCOL ON FRANCE (1992)

THE HIGH CONTRACTING PARTIES,
DESIRING to take into account a particular point relating to France,
HAVE AGREED upon the following provisions, which shall be annexed to the Treaty establishing the European Community:

France will keep the privilege of monetary emission in its overseas territories under the terms established by its national laws, and will be solely entitled to determine the parity of the CFP franc.

PROTOCOL ON ECONOMIC AND SOCIAL COHESION (1992)

THE HIGH CONTRACTING PARTIES,
RECALLING that the Union has set itself the objective of promoting economic and social progress, *inter alia*, through the strengthening of economic and social cohesion,
RECALLING that Article 2 of the Treaty establishing the European Community includes the task of promoting economic and social cohesion and solidarity between Member States and that the strengthening of economic and social cohesion figures among the activities of the Community listed in Article 3,
RECALLING that the provisions of Part Three, Title *XVII*, on economic and

social cohesion as a whole provide the legal basis for consolidating and further developing the Community's action in the field of economic and social cohesion, including the creation of a new fund,

RECALLING that the provisions of Part Three, Title *XV* on trans-European networks and Title *XIX* on environment envisage a Cohesion Fund to be set up before 31 December 1993,

STATING their belief that progress towards economic and monetary union will contribute to the economic growth of all Member States,

NOTING that the Community's Structural Funds are being doubled in real terms between 1987 and 1993, implying large transfers, especially as a proportion of GDP of the less prosperous Member States,

NOTING that the European Investment Bank is lending large and increasing amounts for the benefit of the poorer regions,

NOTING the desire for greater flexibility in the arrangements for allocation from the Structural Funds,

NOTING the desire for modulation of the levels of Community participation in programmes and projects in certain countries,

NOTING the proposal to take greater account of the relative prosperity of Member States in the system of own resources,

REAFFIRM that the promotion of economic and social cohesion is vital to the full development and enduring success of the Community, and underline the importance of the inclusion of economic and social cohesion in Articles 2 and 3 of this Treaty,

REAFFIRM their conviction that the Structural Funds should continue to play a considerable part in the achievement of Community objectives in the field of cohesion,

REAFFIRM their conviction that the European Investment Bank should continue to devote the majority of its resources to the promotion of economic and social cohesion, and declare their willingness to review the capital needs of the European Investment Bank as soon as this is necessary for that purpose,

REAFFIRM the need for a thorough evaluation of the operation and effectiveness of the Structural Funds in 1992, and the need to review, on that occasion, the appropriate size of these Funds in the light of the tasks of the Community in the area of economic and social cohesion,

AGREE that the Cohesion Fund to be set up before 31 December 1993 will provide Community financial contributions to projects in the fields of environment and trans-European networks in Member States with a per capita GNP of less than 90% of the Community average which have a programme leading to the fulfilment of the conditions of economic convergence as set out in Article *104*,

DECLARE their intention of allowing a greater margin of flexibility in allocating financing from the Structural Funds to specific needs not covered under the present Structural Funds regulations,

DECLARE their willingness to modulate the levels of Community participation in the context of programmes and projects of the Structural Funds, with a view to avoiding excessive increases in budgetary expenditure in the less prosperous Member States,

RECOGNIZE the need to monitor regularly the progress made towards achieving economic and social cohesion and state their willingness to study all necessary measures in this respect,

DECLARE their intention of taking greater account of the contributive capacity of individual Member States in the system of own resources, and of examining means of correcting, for the less prosperous Member States, regressive elements existing in the present own resources system,

AGREE to annex this Protocol to the Treaty establishing the European Community.

PROTOCOL ON ASYLUM FOR NATIONALS OF MEMBER STATES OF THE EUROPEAN UNION (1997)

THE HIGH CONTRACTING PARTIES;

WHEREAS pursuant to the provisions of Article 6(2) of the Treaty on European Union the Union shall respect fundamental rights as guaranteed by the European Convention for the Protection of Human Rights and Fundamental Freedoms signed in Rome on 4 November 1950;

WHEREAS the Court of Justice of the European Communities has jurisdiction to ensure that in the interpretation and application of Article 6(2) of the Treaty on European Union the law is observed by the European Community;

WHEREAS pursuant to Article 49 of the Treaty on European Union any European State, when applying to become a Member of the Union, must respect the principles set out in Article 6(1) of the Treaty on European Union;

BEARING IN MIND that Article 309 of the Treaty establishing the European Community establishes a mechanism for the suspension of certain rights in the event of a serious and persistent breach by a Member State of those principles;

RECALLING that each national of a Member State, as a citizen of the Union, enjoys a special status and protection which shall be guaranteed by the Member States in accordance with the provisions of Part Two of the Treaty establishing the European Community;

BEARING IN MIND that the Treaty establishing the European Community establishes an area without internal frontiers and grants every citizen of the Union the right to move and reside freely within the territory of the Member States;

RECALLING that the question of extradition of nationals of Member States of the Union is addressed in the European Convention on Extradition of 13 December 1957 and the Convention of 27 September 1996 drawn up on the basis of Article 31 of the Treaty on European Union relating to extradition between the Member States of the European Union;

WISHING to prevent the institution of asylum being resorted to for purposes alien to those for which it is intended;

WHEREAS this Protocol respects the finality and the objectives of the Geneva Convention of 28 July 1951 relating to the status of refugees;

HAVE AGREED UPON the following provisions which shall be annexed to the Treaty establishing the European Community,

SOLE ARTICLE
Given the level of protection of fundamental rights and freedoms by the Member States of the European Union, Member States shall be regarded as constituting safe countries of origin in respect of each other for all legal and practical purposes in relation to asylum matters. Accordingly, any application for asylum made by a national of a Member State may be taken into consideration or declared admissible for processing by another Member State only in the following cases:

(a) if the Member State of which the applicant is a national proceeds after the entry into force of the Treaty of Amsterdam, availing itself of the provisions of Article 15 of the Convention for the Protection of Human Rights and Fundamental Freedoms, to take measures derogating in its territory from its obligations under that Convention;

(b) if the procedure referred to in Article 7(1) of the Treaty on European Union has been initiated and until the Council takes a decision in respect thereof;

(c) if the Council, acting on the basis of Article 7(1) of the Treaty on European Union, has determined, in respect of the Member State of which the applicant is a national, the existence of a serious and persistent breach by that Member State of principles mentioned in Article 6(1);

(d) if a Member State should so decide unilaterally in respect of the application of a national of another Member State; in that case the Council shall be immediately informed; the application shall be dealt with on the basis of the presumption that it is manifestly unfounded without affecting in any way, whatever the cases may be, the decision-making power of the Member State.

PROTOCOL ON THE APPLICATION OF THE PRINCIPLES OF SUBSIDIARITY AND PROPORTIONALITY (1997)

THE HIGH CONTRACTING PARTIES,

DETERMINED to establish the conditions for the application of the principles of subsidiarity and proportionality enshrined in Article 5 of the Treaty establishing the European Community with a view to defining more precisely the criteria for applying them and to ensure their strict observance and consistent implementation by all institutions;

WISHING to ensure that decisions are taken as closely as possible to the citizens of the Union;

TAKING ACCOUNT of the Interinstitutional Agreement of 25 October 1993 between the European Parliament, the Council and the Commission on procedures for implementing the principle of subsidiarity;

HAVE CONFIRMED that the conclusions of the Birmingham European Council on 16 October 1992 and the overall approach to the application of the subsidiarity principle agreed by the European Council meeting in Edinburgh on 11–12 December 1992 will continue to guide the action of the Union's institutions as well as the development of the application of the principle of subsidiarity, and, for this purpose,

HAVE AGREED UPON the following provisions which shall be annexed to the Treaty establishing the European Community:

1. In exercising the powers conferred on it, each institution shall ensure that the principle of subsidiarity is complied with. It shall also ensure compliance with the principle of proportionality, according to which any action by the Community shall not go beyond what is necessary to achieve the objectives of the Treaty.

2. The application of the principles of subsidiarity and proportionality shall respect the general provisions and the objectives of the Treaty, particularly as regards the maintaining in full of the *acquis communautaire* and the institutional balance; it shall not affect the principles developed by the Court of Justice regarding the relationship between national and Community law, and it should take into account Article 6(4) of the Treaty on European Union, according to which 'the Union shall provide itself with the means necessary to attain its objectives and carry through its policies'.

3. The principle of subsidiarity does not call into question the powers conferred on the European Community by the Treaty, as interpreted by the Court of Justice. The criteria referred to in the second paragraph of Article 5 of the Treaty shall relate to areas for which the Community does not have exclusive competence. The principle of subsidiarity provides a guide as to how those powers are to be exercised at the Community level. Subsidiarity is a dynamic concept and should be applied in the light of the objectives set out in the Treaty. It allows Community action within the limits of its powers to be expanded where circumstances so require, and conversely, to be restricted or discontinued where it is no longer justified.

4. For any proposed Community legislation, the reasons on which it is based shall be stated with a view to justifying its compliance with the principles of subsidiarity and proportionality; the reasons for concluding that a Community objective can be better achieved by the Community must be substantiated by qualitative or, wherever possible, quantitative indicators.

5. For Community action to be justified, both aspects of the subsidiarity principle shall be met: the objectives of the proposed action cannot be sufficiently achieved by Member States' action in the framework of their national constitutional system and can therefore be better achieved by action on the part of the Community.

The following guidelines should be used in examining whether the abovementioned condition is fulfilled:
– the issue under consideration has transnational aspects which cannot be satisfactorily regulated by action by Member States;
– actions by Member States alone or lack of Community action would conflict with the requirements of the Treaty (such as the need to correct distortion of competition or avoid disguised restrictions on trade or strengthen economic and social cohesion) or would otherwise significantly damage Member States' interests;
– action at Community level would produce clear benefits by reason of its scale or effects compared with action at the level of the Member States.

6. The form of Community action shall be as simple as possible, consistent with satisfactory achievement of the objective of the measure and the need for effective enforcement. The Community shall legislate only to the extent necessary. Other things being equal, directives should be preferred to regulations and framework directives to detailed measures. Directives as provided for in Article 249 of the Treaty, while binding upon each Member State to which they are addressed as to the result to be achieved, shall leave to the national authorities the choice of form and methods.

7. Regarding the nature and the extent of Community action, Community measures should leave as much scope for national decision as possible, consistent with securing the aim of the measure and observing the requirements of the Treaty. While respecting Community law, care should be taken to respect well established national arrangements and the organisation and working of Member States' legal systems. Where appropriate and subject to the need for proper enforcement, Community measures should provide Member States with alternative ways to achieve the objectives of the measures.

8. Where the application of the principle of subsidiarity leads to no action being taken by the Community, Member States are required in their action to comply with the general rules laid down in Article 5 of the Treaty, by taking all appropriate

measures to ensure fulfilment of their obligations under the Treaty and by abstaining from any measure which could jeopardise the attainment of the objectives of the Treaty.

9. Without prejudice to its right of initiative, the Commission should:
– except in cases of particular urgency or confidentiality, consult widely before proposing legislation and, wherever appropriate, publish consultation documents;
– justify the relevance of its proposals with regard to the principle of subsidiarity; whenever necessary, the explanatory memorandum accompanying a proposal will give details in this respect. The financing of Community action in whole or in part from the Community budget shall require an explanation;
– take duly into account the need for any burden, whether financial or administrative, falling upon the Community, national governments, local authorities, economic operators and citizens, to be minimised and proportionate to the objective to be achieved;
– submit an annual report to the European Council, the European Parliament and the Council on the application of Article 5 of the Treaty. This annual report shall also be sent to the Committee of the Regions and to the Economic and Social Committee.

10. The European Council shall take account of the Commission report referred to in the fourth indent of point 9 within the report on the progress achieved by the Union which it is required to submit to the European Parliament in accordance with Article 4 of the Treaty on European Union.

11. While fully observing the procedures applicable, the European Parliament and the Council shall, as an integral part of the overall examination of Commission proposals, consider their consistency with Article 5 of the Treaty. This concerns the original Commission proposal as well as amendments which the European Parliament and the Council envisage making to the proposal.

12. In the course of the procedures referred to in Articles 251 and 252 of the Treaty, the European Parliament shall be informed of the Council's position on the application of Article 5 of the Treaty, by way of a statement of the reasons which led the Council to adopt its common position. The Council shall inform the European Parliament of the reasons on the basis of which all or part of a Commission proposal is deemed to be inconsistent with Article 5 of the Treaty.

13. Compliance with the principle of subsidiarity shall be reviewed in accordance with the rules laid down by the Treaty.

PROTOCOL ON EXTERNAL RELATIONS OF THE MEMBER STATES WITH REGARD TO THE CROSSING OF EXTERNAL BORDERS (1997)

THE HIGH CONTRACTING PARTIES,
TAKING INTO ACCOUNT the need of the Member States to ensure effective controls at their external borders, in co-operation with third countries where appropriate,
HAVE AGREED UPON the following provision, which shall be annexed to the Treaty establishing the European Community,

The provisions on the measures on the crossing of external borders included in Article 62(2)(a) of Title IV of the Treaty shall be without prejudice to the competence of Member States to negotiate or conclude agreements with third countries as long as they respect Community law and other relevant international agreements.

PROTOCOL ON THE SYSTEM OF PUBLIC BROADCASTING IN THE MEMBER STATES (1997)

THE HIGH CONTRACTING PARTIES,

CONSIDERING that the system of public broadcasting in the Member States is directly related to the democratic, social and cultural needs of each society and to the need to preserve media pluralism;

HAVE AGREED UPON the following interpretative provisions, which shall be annexed to the Treaty establishing the European Community,

The provisions of the Treaty establishing the European Community shall be without prejudice to the competence of Member States to provide for the funding of public service broadcasting insofar as such funding is granted to broadcasting organisations for the fulfilment of the public service remit as conferred, defined and organised by each Member State, and insofar as such funding does not affect trading conditions and competition in the Community to an extent which would be contrary to the common interest, while the realisation of the remit of that public service shall be taken into account.

PROTOCOL ON PROTECTION AND WELFARE OF ANIMALS (1997)

THE HIGH CONTRACTING PARTIES,

DESIRING to ensure improved protection and respect for the welfare of animals as sentient beings;

HAVE AGREED UPON the following provision which shall be annexed to the Treaty establishing the European Community,

In formulating and implementing the Community's agriculture, transport, internal market and research policies, the Community and the Member States shall pay full regard to the welfare requirements of animals, while respecting the legislative or administrative provisions and customs of the Member States relating in particular to religious rites, cultural traditions and regional heritage.

PROTOCOL ON THE FINANCIAL CONSEQUENCES OF THE EXPIRY OF THE ECSC TREATY AND ON THE RESEARCH FUND FOR COAL AND STEEL (2001)

THE HIGH CONTRACTING PARTIES,

DESIRING to settle certain questions relating to the expiry of the Treaty establishing the European Coal and Steel Community (ECSC);

WISHING to confer ownership of the ECSC funds on the European Community;

TAKING ACCOUNT of the desire to use these funds for research in sectors related to the coal and steel industry and therefore the necessity to provide for certain special rules in this regard;

HAVE AGREED UPON the following provisions, which shall be annexed to the Treaty establishing the European Community:

Article 1

1. All assets and liabilities of the ECSC, as they exist on 23 July 2002, shall be transferred to the European Community on 24 July 2002.

2. The net worth of these assets and liabilities, as they appear in the balance sheet of the ECSC of 23 July 2002, subject to any increase or decrease which may occur as a result of the liquidation operations, shall be considered as assets intended for research in the sectors related to the coal and steel industry, referred to as the 'ECSC in liquidation'. On completion of the liquidation they shall be referred to as the 'Assets of the Research Fund for Coal and Steel'.

3. The revenue from these assets, referred to as the 'Research Fund for Coal and Steel', shall be used exclusively for research, outside the research framework programme, in the sectors related to the coal and steel industry in accordance with the provisions of this Protocol and of acts adopted on the basis hereof.

Article 2

The Council, acting unanimously on a proposal from the Commission and after consulting the European Parliament, shall adopt all the necessary provisions for the implementation of this Protocol, including essential principles and proper decision-making procedures, in particular for the adoption of multiannual financial guidelines for managing the assets of the Research Fund for Coal and Steel and technical guidelines for the research programme of the Research Fund for Coal and Steel.

Article 3

Except as otherwise provided in this Protocol and in the acts adopted on the basis hereof, the provisions of the Treaty establishing the European Community shall apply.

Article 4

This Protocol shall apply from 24 July 2002.

PROTOCOL ON ARTICLE 67 OF THE TREATY ESTABLISHING THE EUROPEAN COMMUNITY (2001)

THE HIGH CONTRACTING PARTIES,
HAVE AGREED UPON the following provision, which shall be annexed to the Treaty establishing the European Community:

Sole Article

From 1 May 2004, the Council shall act by a qualified majority, on a proposal from the Commission and after consulting the European Parliament, in order to adopt the measures referred to in Article 66 of the Treaty establishing the European Community.

PROTOCOL ON PRIVILEGES AND IMMUNITIES OF THE EUROPEAN COMMUNITIES (1965) (annexed to the 1965 Merger Treaty)

THE HIGH CONTRACTING PARTIES,
CONSIDERING that, in accordance with Article 28 of the Treaty establishing a Single Council and a Single Commission of the European Communities, these

Communities and the European Investment Bank shall enjoy in the territories of the Member States such privileges and immunities as are necessary for the performance of their tasks,

HAVE AGREED upon the following provisions, which shall be annexed to this Treaty:

Chapter I: Property, Funds, Assets and Operations of the European Communities

Article 1. The premises and buildings of the Communities shall be inviolable. They shall be exempt from search, requisition, confiscation or expropriation. The property and assets of the Communities shall not be the subject of any administrative or legal measure of constraint without the authorisation of the Court of Justice.

Article 2. The archives of the Communities shall be inviolable.

Article 3. The Communities, their assets, revenues and other property shall be exempt from all direct taxes.

The governments of the Member States shall, wherever possible, take the appropriate measures to remit or refund the amount of indirect taxes or sales taxes included in the price of movable or immovable property, where the Communities make, for their official use, substantial purchases the price of which includes taxes of this kind. These provisions shall not be applied, however, so as to have the effect of distorting competition within the Communities.

No exemption shall be granted in respect of taxes and dues which amount merely to charges for public utility services.

Article 4. The Communities shall be exempt from all customs duties, prohibitions and restrictions on imports and exports in respect of articles intended for their official use; articles so imported shall not be disposed of, whether or not in return for payment, in the territory of the country into which they have been imported, except under conditions approved by the Government of that country.

The Communities shall also be exempt from any customs duties and any prohibitions and restrictions on imports and exports in respect of their publications.

Article 5. The European Coal and Steel Community may hold currency of any kind and operate accounts in any currency.

Chapter II. Communications and *Laissez-passer*

Article 6. For their official communications and the transmission of all their documents, the institutions of the Communities shall enjoy in the territory of each Member State the treatment accorded by that State to diplomatic missions.

Official correspondence and other official communications of the institutions of the Communities shall not be subject to censorship.

Article 7. 1. *Laissez-passer* in a form to be prescribed by the Council, which shall be recognised as valid travel documents by the authorities of the Members States, may be issued to members and servants of the institutions of the Communities by the Presidents of these institutions. These *laissez-passer* shall be issued to officials and other servants under conditions laid down in the Staff Regulations of officials and the Conditions of Employment of other servants of the Communities.

The Commission may conclude agreements for these *laissez-passer* to be recognised as valid travel documents within the territory of third countries.

2. The provisions of Article 6 of the Protocol on the privileges and immunities of

the European Coal and Steel Community shall, however, remain applicable to members and servants of the institutions who are at the date of entry into force of this Treaty in possession of the *laissez-passer* provided for in that Article, until the provisions of paragraph 1 of this Article are applied.

Chapter III. Members of the European Parliament

Article 8. No administrative or other restrictions shall be imposed on the free movement of members of the European Parliament travelling to or from the place of meeting of the European Parliament.

Members of the European Parliament shall, in respect of customs and exchange control, be accorded:

a) by their own government, the same facilities as those accorded to senior officials travelling abroad on temporary official missions;

b) by the governments of other Member States, the same facilities as those accorded to representatives of foreign governments on temporary official missions.

Article 9. Members of the European Parliament shall not be subject to any form of inquiry, detention or legal proceedings in respect of opinions expressed or votes cast by them in the performance of their duties.

Article 10. During the sessions of the European Parliament, its members shall enjoy:

a) in the territory of their own State, the immunities accorded to members of their parliament;

b) in the territory of any other Member State, immunity from any measure of detention and from legal proceedings.

Immunity shall likewise apply to members while they are travelling to and from the place of meeting of the European Parliament.

Immunity cannot be claimed when a member is found in the act of committing an offence and shall not prevent the European Parliament from exercising its right to waive the immunity of one of its members.

Chapter IV. Representatives of Member States taking part in the Work of the Institutions of the European Communities

Article 11. Representatives of Member States taking part in the work of the institutions of the Communities, their advisers and technical experts shall, in the performance of their duties and during their travel to and from the place of meeting, enjoy the customary privileges, immunities and facilities.

This Article shall also apply to members of the advisory bodies of the Communities.

Chapter V. Official and other Servants of the European Communities

Article 12. In the territory of each Member State and whatever their nationality, officials and other servants of the Communities shall:

a) subject to the provisions of the Treaties relating, on the one hand, to the rules on the liability of officials and other servants towards the Communities and, on the other hand, to the jurisdiction of the Court in disputes between the Communities and their officials and other servants, be immune from legal proceedings in respect of acts performed by them in their official capacity, including their words spoken or written. They shall continue to enjoy this immunity after they have ceased to hold office;

b) together with their spouses and dependent members of their families, not be subject to immigration restrictions or to formalities for registration of aliens;

c) in respect of currency or exchange regulations, be accorded the same facilities as are customarily accorded to officials of international organisations;

d) enjoy the right to import free of duty their furniture and effects at the time of first taking up their post in the country concerned, and the right to re-export free of duty their furniture and effects, on termination of their duties in that country, subject in either case to the conditions considered to be necessary by the government of the country in which this right is exercised;

e) have the right to import free of duty a motor car for their personal use, acquired either in the country of their last residence or in the country of which they are nationals on the terms ruling in the home market in that country, and to re-export it free of duty, subject in either case to the conditions considered to be necessary by the government of the country concerned.

Article 13. Officials and other servants of the Communities shall be liable to a tax for the benefit of the Communities on salaries, wages and emoluments paid to them by the Communities, in accordance with the conditions and procedure laid down by the Council, acting on a proposal from the Commission.

They shall be exempt from national taxes on salaries, wages and emoluments paid by the Communities.

Article 14. In the application of income tax, wealth tax and death duties and in the application of conventions on the avoidance of double taxation concluded between Members States of the Communities, officials and other servants of the Communities who, solely by reason of the performance of their duties in the service of the Communities, establish their residence in the territory of a Member State other than their country of domicile for tax purposes at the time of entering the service of the Communities, shall be considered, both in the country of their actual residence and in the country of domicile for tax purposes, as having maintained their domicile in the latter country provided that it is a member of the Communities. This provision shall also apply to a spouse, to the extent that the latter is not separately engaged in a gainful occupation, and to children dependent on and in the care of the persons referred to in this Article.

Movable property belonging to persons referred to in the first paragraph and situated in the territory of the country where they are staying shall be exempt from death duties in that country; such property shall, for the assessment of such duty, be considered as being in the country of domicile for tax purposes, subject to the rights of third countries and to the possible application of provisions of international conventions on double taxation.

Any domicile acquired solely by reason of the performance of duties in the service of other international organisations shall not be taken into consideration in applying the provisions of this Article.

Article 15. The Council shall, acting unanimously on a proposal from the Commission, lay down the scheme of social security benefits for officials and other servants of the Communities.

Article 16. The Council shall, acting on a proposal from the Commission and after consulting the other institutions concerned, determine the categories of officials and other servants of the Communities to whom the provisions of Article 12, the second paragraph of Article 13, and Article 14 shall apply, in whole or in part.

The names, grades and addresses of officials and other servants included in such categories shall be communicated periodically to the governments of the Member States.

Chapter VI. Privileges and Immunities of Missions of Third Countries Accredited to the European Communities

Article 17. The Member State in whose territory the Communities have their seat shall accord the customary diplomatic immunities and privileges to missions of third countries accredited to the Communities.

Chapter VII. General Provisions

Article 18. Privileges, immunities and facilities shall be accorded to officials and other servants of the Communities solely in the interests of the Communities.

Each institution of the Communities shall be required to waive the immunity accorded to an official or other servant wherever that institution considers that the waiver of such immunity is not contrary to the interests of the Communities.

Article 19. The institutions of the Communities shall, for the purpose of applying this Protocol, co-operate with the responsible authorities of the Member States concerned.

Article 20. Articles 12 to 15 and Article 18 shall apply to members of the Commission.

Article 21. Articles 12 to 15 and Article 18 shall apply to the Judges, the Advocates-General, the Registrar and the Assistant Rapporteurs of the Court of Justice **and to the Members of and Registrar of the Court of First Instance,** without prejudice to the provisions of Article 3 of the *Protocol* on the Statute of the Court of Justice *relating to* immunity from legal proceedings of Judges and Advocates-General.

Article 22. The Protocol shall also apply to the European Investment Bank, to the members of its organs, to its staff and to the representatives of the Member States taking part in its activities, without prejudice to the provisions of the Protocol on the Statute of the Bank.

The European Investment Bank shall in addition be exempt from any form of taxation or imposition of a like nature on the occasion of any increase in its capital and from the various formalities which may be connected therewith in the State where the Bank has its seat. Similarly, its dissolution or liquidation shall not give rise to any imposition. Finally, the activities of the Bank and of its organs carried on it accordance with its Statute shall not be subject to any turnover tax.

Article 23. *This Protocol shall also apply to the European Central Bank, to the members of its organs and to its staff, without prejudice to the provisions of the Protocol on the Statute of the European System of Central Banks and the European Central Bank.*

The European Central Bank shall, in addition, be exempt from any taxation or imposition of a like nature on the occasion of any increase in its capital and from the various formalities which may be connected therewith in the State where the Bank has its seat. The activities of the Bank and of its organs carried on in accordance with the Statute of the European System of Central Banks and the European Central Bank shall not be subject to any turnover tax.

The above provisions shall also apply to the European Monetary Institute. Its dissolution or liquidation shall not give rise to any imposition. *

---

*Article 23 was inserted as a result of the Protocol Amending the Protocol on the Privileges and Immunities of the European Communities introduced by the TEU. This protocol was repealed by the TA.

xxxii Final Act and Declarations

Final Act

Technically, the final act is not part of the TEC. Rather, it is the final act of the IGC which drafted it, a point underlined in the first instance by the brief record which it provides of the IGC. Second, the final act covers two treaties, the TEAEC as well as the TEC. Hence, it summarizes the texts which the IGC adopted, noting not only the TEC and the eleven protocols and the Implementing Convention on the Association of the Overseas Countries and Territories with the Community annexed to it, but also the TEAEC and its one protocol. It then proceeds to note the Convention on Certain Institutions Common to the European Communities, repealed by the TA, before listing six declarations adopted by the IGC and three which it simply noted. These declarations are then annexed to the final act. A record is also included of the four protocols which the IGC would be drawing up at a later date and to which treaty they would be annexed. The final act is then dated and signed by the plenipotentiaries of the heads of state identified in the preamble to the treaty. As record of events and a list of documents, the final act has no legal force. It is little more than an agreed statement of what has taken place within the IGC. It does provide, however, a repository for the various declarations which the IGC has either adopted or noted. And here we have followed the same strategy by adding the Declarations recently added to the TEC.

> The INTERGOVERNMENTAL CONFERENCE ON THE COMMON MARKET AND EURATOM, convened in Venice on 29 May 1956 by the Ministers for Foreign Affairs of the Kingdom of Belgium, the Federal Republic of Germany, the French Republic, the Italian Republic, the Grand Duchy of Luxembourg and the Kingdom of the Netherlands, having continued its deliberations in Brussels and having, on concluding them, met in Rome on 25 March 1957, has adopted the following texts.
>
> I
>
> 1. THE TREATY establishing the European Economic Community, and the Annexes thereto,
> 2. The Protocol on the Statute of the European Investment Bank,
> 3. The Protocol on German internal trade and connected problems,
> 4. The Protocol on certain provisions relating to France,
> 5. The Protocol on Italy,
> 6. The Protocol on the Grand Duchy of Luxembourg,
> 7. The Protocol on goods originating in and coming from certain countries and enjoying special treatment when imported into a Member State,
> 8. The Protocol on the treatment to be applied to products within the province of the European Coal and Steel Community in respect of Algeria and the overseas departments of the French Republic,
> 9. The Protocol on mineral oils and certain of their derivatives,
> 10. The Protocol on the application of the Treaty establishing the European Economic Community to the non-European parts of the Kingdom of the Netherlands,
> 11. The Implementing Convention on the Association of the Overseas Countries and Territories with the Community, and the Annexes thereto,

12. The Protocol on the tariff quota for imports of bananas,
13. The Protocol on the tariff quota for imports of raw coffee.

II

1. THE TREATY establishing the European Atomic Energy Community, and the Annexes thereto,
2. The Protocol on the application of the Treaty establishing the European Atomic Energy Community to the non-European parts of the Kingdom of the Netherlands.

III

THE CONVENTION on certain institutions common to the European Communities.

At the time of signature of these texts, the Conference adopted the declarations listed below and annexed to this Act:

1. Joint Declaration on co-operation with the States Members of international organizations,
2. Joint Declaration on Berlin,
3. Declaration of intent on the association of the independent countries of the franc area with the European Economic Community,
4. Declaration of intent on the association of the Kingdom of Libya with the European Economic Community,
5. Declaration of intent on the Trust Territory of Somaliland currently under the administration of the Italian Republic,
6. Declaration of intent on the association of Surinam and the Netherlands Antilles with the European Economic Community.

The Conference further took note of the declarations listed below and annexed to this Act:

1. Declaration by the Government of the Federal Republic of Germany on the definition of the expression 'German national',
2. Declaration by the Government of the Federal Republic of Germany on the application of the Treaties to Berlin,
3. Declaration by the Government of the French Republic on applications for patents covering information to be kept secret for defence reasons.

Finally, the Conference decided to draw up at a later date:

1. The Protocol on the Statute of the Court of Justice of the European Economic Community,
2. The Protocol on the privileges and immunities of the European Economic Community,
3. The Protocol on the Statute of the Court of Justice of the European Atomic Energy Community,
4. The Protocol on the privileges and immunities of the European Atomic Energy Community.

Protocols 1 and 2 shall be annexed to the Treaty establishing the European Economic Community;
Protocols 3 and 4 shall be annexed to the Treaty establishing the European Atomic Energy Community.

IN WITNESS WHEREOF, the undersigned Plenipotentiaries have signed this Final Act.

Done at Rome this twenty-fifth day of March in the year one thousand nine hundred and fifty-seven.

P.H. SPAAK	J. Ch. SNOY et d'OPPUERS
ADENAUER	HALLSTEIN
PINEAU	M. FAURE
Antonio SEGNI	Gaetano MARTINO
BECH	Lambert SCHAUS
J. LUNS	J. LINTHORST HOMAN

Declarations

The final act to the TEC lists nine declarations (see Box 8). These differ from protocols in so far as they are neither legally binding nor formally part of the TEC. Of the nine declarations, six were formally adopted by the IGC which drafted the TEC. The others were unilateral declarations by individual governments. Events since 1957 have meant that most of the declarations are of little relevance to the TEC today. Omitting them from the *Guide* would, however, render the presentation of the TEC incomplete. Declarations relating to the TEC added at Nice are, as already implied, discussed and printed below.

Of the six original declarations adopted by all six signatories, two are joint declarations. The first of these concerns co-operation with member states of international organizations generally, but was clearly designed to reassure other members of the Organization for European Economic Co-operation that the Six were intent on promoting freer trade throughout western Europe. The *Joint declaration on Berlin* recognizes the special position of the divided city located as it was within the Soviet bloc and confirms the solidarity of the EC member states for the people of Berlin. The declaration's reference to the 'free world' is one of only a few statements in or directly associated with the European Treaties which reflect the Cold War rhetoric of the early years of European integration.* The four remaining declarations are also geographically specific, containing statements of intent regarding the rapid establishment of economic associations with countries which were former colonies of individual member states: the Franc area, Libya, Somaliland, Surinam and the Netherlands Antilles (see IV xxv).

Rather than being formally 'adopted', the three unilateral declarations which follow were simply noted by the TEC's signatories. Two are declarations by the German government. The first extends through reference to the country's constitution, the *Grundgesetz* (basic law), the definition of 'German national' to include primarily Germans living in lands which constituted the German Reich at the end of 1937 (e.g. those in the German Democratic Republic created in 1949). In the second declaration the German government reserved the right to declare on ratification that the TEC and TEAEC would apply to Berlin, which prior to 1990 was formally administered by the Allied powers. Officially, these were the only written declarations issued by the German government.

---

*See also, the reference to 'the Russian Zone of Occupation' (i.e. the German Democratic Republic) in Section 22 of the Convention Containing the Transitional Provisions which was signed alongside the TECSC.

Box 8   Declarations annexed to the Final Act of the TEC and TEAEC

Joint declaration on co-operation with the states members of international organizations

Joint declaration on Berlin

Declaration of intent on the association of the independent countries of the Franc area
with the European Economic Community

Declaration of intent on the association of the Kingdom of Libya with the European
Economic Community

Declaration of intent on the Trust Territory of Somaliland currently under the administration of the Italian Republic

Declaration of intent on the association of Surinam and the Netherlands Antilles with
the European Economic Community

Declaration by the government of the Federal Republic of Germany on the definition
of the expression 'German national'

Declaration by the government of the Federal Republic of Germany on the application
of the treaties to Berlin

Declaration by the government of the French Republic on applications for patents
covering information to be kept secret for defence reasons

As Lippert and Stevens-Ströhmann note, a further verbal declaration was, however, made
by the German signatories (Adenauer and Hallstein) stating their assumption that a
re-evaluation of the TEC would be possible in the event of German unification. Even
though the TEU was negotiated shortly after German unification in 1990, it did not
involve the re-evaluation envisaged back in 1957. Finally, there is the third unilateral
declaration issued by the French government. This acts as a reminder that the final act to
which the declarations are attached also covers the EAEC. The declaration concerns the
granting of patents under the TEAEC.

With just nine declarations annexed to the final act, the TEC appears to be relatively
free of declarations compared with the TEU and TA. This is misleading since the IGCs
which drew up the various amending and accession treaties signed since 1957 have
adopted declarations which concern either provisions in the TEC or the EC as an
organization. For example, the final act to the SEA adopted nine (Nos. 1–9) and noted
a further eight (Nos. 1n–8n) declarations relating to the EC (see V iii). A further 27
declarations (Nos. 1–26 and 33) adopted as a result of the TEU also concern either the
TEC or the EC directly (see III x). This 'declarationization' of the TEC was furthered by
the TA and TN. Annexed to the former's final acts are 40 relevant declarations (Nos. 1,
11–39, 41–50) which relate either to provisions of the TEC or to the EC generally. In
addition, there is one declaration (No. 40) concerning the TECSE and the eight declarations concerning the position of one or more member states noted by the IGC (see
below). In the main these, as pointed out above, cover member state rights and concerns:
on confidentiality, foreign policy, industrial relations, media, public services, territories
and voluntary services. However, there are also a number of important institutional,
including financial, adjustments and a number of procedural guidelines, notably on
Schengen-related matters and subsidiarity.

The declarations adopted at Nice (Nos. 3–19, 23–24) also show strong signs of
reinforcing national reserves. They do this in three areas, in financial matters, notably on
the 'no-bail-out' clause; the adaptations needed from other institutions such as the ECJ

and the Auditors; and the importance of clarifying the respective powers of the EC and the member states. This is one of the key elements of the Declaration on the Future of Europe (see below, pp. 564–5) that started the IGC 2004 process. This shows the importance that declarations can actually have.

Finally, each of the accession treaties has introduced a variety of declarations relating to the EC (see V iv). Consequently, there are almost 200 Declarations either adopted or noted by IGCs which refer either directly or indirectly to the EC. None of these has ever been deleted, although changes to the TEC and developments within the EU have obviously made many redundant. This is certainly the case with those found attached to the final act associated with the TEC.

Declarations Attached to the Final Act Associated with the TEC and TEAEC

JOINT DECLARATION ON CO-OPERATION WITH THE STATES MEMBERS OF INTERNATIONAL ORGANIZATIONS

THE GOVERNMENTS OF THE KINGDOM OF BELGIUM, THE FEDERAL REPUBLIC OF GERMANY, THE FRENCH REPUBLIC, THE ITALIAN REPUBLIC, THE GRAND DUCHY OF LUXEMBOURG AND THE KINGDOM OF THE NETHERLANDS,

AT THE TIME of signature of the Treaties establishing the European Economic Community and the European Atomic Energy Community,

CONSCIOUS of the responsibilities which they are assuming for the future of Europe by combining their markets, bringing their economies closer together and laying down the principles and details of a common policy in this field,

RECOGNISING that, by setting up a customs union and working closely together on the peaceful development of nuclear energy, they will be ensuring economic and social progress and thus contributing not only to their own prosperity but also to that of other countries,

ANXIOUS that these countries should share in the prospects of expansion afforded thereby,

DECLARE THEIR READINESS to conclude, as soon as these Treaties enter into force, agreements with other countries, particularly within the framework of the international organisations to which they belong, in order to attain these objectives of common interest and to ensure the harmonious development of trade in general.

JOINT DECLARATION ON BERLIN

THE GOVERNMENTS OF THE KINGDOM OF BELGIUM, THE FEDERAL REPUBLIC OF GERMANY, THE FRENCH REPUBLIC, THE ITALIAN REPUBLIC, THE GRAND DUCHY OF LUXEMBOURG AND THE KINGDOM OF THE NETHERLANDS,

HAVING REGARD to the special position of Berlin and the need to afford it the support of the free world,

ANXIOUS to confirm their solidarity with the people of Berlin,

WILL USE THEIR GOOD OFFICES within the Community in order that all necessary measures may be taken to ease the economic and social situation of Berlin, to promote its development and to ensure its economic stability.

DECLARATION OF INTENT ON THE ASSOCIATION OF THE INDEPENDENT COUNTRIES OF THE FRANC AREA WITH THE EUROPEAN ECONOMIC COMMUNITY

THE GOVERNMENTS OF THE KINGDOM OF BELGIUM, THE FEDERAL REPUBLIC OF GERMANY, THE FRENCH REPUBLIC, THE ITALIAN REPUBLIC, THE GRAND DUCHY OF LUXEMBOURG AND THE KINGDOM OF THE NETHERLANDS,
TAKING INTO CONSIDERATION the economic, financial and monetary agreements and conventions concluded between France and the other independent countries of the franc area,
ANXIOUS to maintain and intensify the traditional trade flows between the Member States of the European Economic Community and these independent countries and to contribute to the economic and social development of the latter,
DECLARE THEIR READINESS, as soon as this Treaty enters into force, to propose to these countries the opening of negotiations with a view to concluding conventions for economic association with the Community.

DECLARATION OF INTENT ON THE ASSOCIATION OF THE KINGDOM OF LIBYA WITH THE EUROPEAN ECONOMIC COMMUNITY

THE GOVERNMENTS OF THE KINGDOM OF BELGIUM, THE FEDERAL REPUBLIC OF GERMANY, THE FRENCH REPUBLIC, THE ITALIAN REPUBLIC, THE GRAND DUCHY OF LUXEMBOURG AND THE KINGDOM OF THE NETHERLANDS,
TAKING INTO CONSIDERATION the economic links between Italy and the Kingdom of Libya,
ANXIOUS to maintain and intensify the traditional trade flows between the Member States of the Community and the Kingdom of Libya, and to contribute to the economic and social development of Libya,
DECLARE THEIR READINESS, as soon as this Treaty enters into force, to propose to the Kingdom of Libya the opening of negotiations with a view to concluding conventions for economic association with the Community.

DECLARATION OF INTENT ON THE TRUST TERRITORY OF SOMALILAND CURRENTLY UNDER THE ADMINISTRATION OF THE ITALIAN REPUBLIC

THE GOVERNMENTS OF THE KINGDOM OF BELGIUM, THE FEDERAL REPUBLIC OF GERMANY, THE FRENCH REPUBLIC, THE ITALIAN REPUBLIC, THE GRAND DUCHY OF LUXEMBOURG AND THE KINGDOM OF THE NETHERLANDS,
ANXIOUS, at the time of signature of the Treaty establishing the European Economic Community, to define the exact scope of Articles 182 [ex 131] and

299 [ex 227] of this Treaty, in view of the fact that under Article 24 of the
Trusteeship Agreement with respect to the trust Territory of Somaliland the
Italian administration of that Territory will end on 2 December 1960,
HAVE AGREED to give the authorities who will after that date be responsible
for the external relations of Somaliland the option of confirming the association
of the territory with the Community, and declare their readiness to propose, if
need be, to these authorities the opening of negotiations with a view to concluding conventions for economic association with the Community.

DECLARATION OF INTENT ON THE ASSOCIATION OF SURINAM AND THE NETHERLANDS ANTILLES WITH THE EUROPEAN ECONOMIC COMMUNITY

THE GOVERNMENTS OF THE KINGDOM OF BELGIUM, THE FED-
ERAL REPUBLIC OF GERMANY, THE FRENCH REPUBLIC, THE
ITALIAN REPUBLIC, THE GRAND DUCHY OF LUXEMBOURG AND
THE KINGDOM OF THE NETHERLANDS,
TAKING INTO CONSIDERATION the close ties which unite the several
parts of the Kingdom of the Netherlands,
ANXIOUS to maintain and intensify the traditional trade flows between the
Member States of the European Economic Community on the one hand and
Surinam and the Netherlands Antilles on the other, and to contribute to the
economic and social development of these countries,
DECLARE THEIR READINESS, as soon as this Treaty enters into force, to
open negotiations at the request of the Kingdom of the Netherlands, with a view
to concluding conventions for the economic association of Surinam and the
Netherlands Antilles with the Community.

DECLARATION BY THE GOVERNMENT OF THE FEDERAL REPUBLIC OF GERMANY ON THE DEFINITION OF THE EXPRESSION 'GERMAN NATIONAL'

At the time of signature of the Treaties establishing the European Economic
Community and the European Atomic Energy Community, the Government of
the Federal Republic of Germany makes the following declaration:
'All Germans as defined in the Basic Law for the Federal Republic of Germany
shall be considered nationals of the Federal Republic of Germany'.

DECLARATION BY THE GOVERNMENT OF THE FEDERAL REPUBLIC OF GERMANY ON THE APPLICATION OF THE TREATIES TO BERLIN

The Government of the Federal Republic of Germany reserves the right to
declare, when depositing its instruments of ratification, that the Treaty establishing the European Economic Community and the Treaty establishing the
European Atomic Energy Community shall equally apply to Land Berlin.

DECLARATION BY THE GOVERNMENT OF THE FRENCH REPUBLIC ON APPLICATIONS FOR PATENTS COVERING INFORMATION TO BE KEPT SECRET FOR DEFENCE REASONS

The Government of the French Republic,
Taking into account the provisions of Articles 17 and 25(2) of the Treaty establishing the European Atomic Energy Community,

Declares its readiness to take such administrative measures and to propose to the French Parliament such legislative measures as may be necessary to ensure that, as soon as this Treaty enters into force, applications for patents covering secret information result, following the normal procedure, in the grant of patents subject to temporary prohibition of publication.

Declarations Relating to the TEC Annexed to the Final Act Associated with the Treaty of Amsterdam

12. DECLARATION ON ENVIRONMENTAL IMPACT ASSESSMENTS

The Conference notes that the Commission undertakes to prepare environmental impact assessment studies when making proposals which may have significant environmental implications.

13. DECLARATION ON ARTICLE 7d [now 16] OF THE TREATY ESTABLISHING THE EUROPEAN COMMUNITY

The provisions of Article 7d [now 16] of the Treaty establishing the European Community on public services shall be implemented with full respect for the jurisprudence of the Court of Justice, *inter alia* as regards the principles of equality of treatment, quality and continuity of such services.

14. DECLARATION ON THE REPEAL OF ARTICLE 44 OF THE TREATY ESTABLISHING THE EUROPEAN COMMUNITY

The repeal of Article 44 of the Treaty establishing the European Community, which contains a reference to a natural preference between Member States in the context of fixing minimum prices during the transitional period, has no effect on the principle of Community preference as defined by the case law of the Court of Justice.

15. DECLARATION ON THE PRESERVATION OF THE LEVEL OF PROTECTION AND SECURITY PROVIDED BY THE SCHENGEN *ACQUIS*

The Conference agrees that measures to be adopted by the Council, which will have the effect of replacing provisions on the abolition of checks at common borders contained in the 1990 Schengen Convention, should provide at least the same level of protection and security as under the aforementioned provisions of the Schengen Convention.

16. DECLARATION ON ARTICLE 73j(2)(b) [now 62(2)(b)] OF THE TREATY ESTABLISHING THE EUROPEAN COMMUNITY

The Conference agrees that foreign policy considerations of the Union and the Member States shall be taken into account in the application of Article 73j(2)(b) [now 62(2)(b)] of the Treaty establishing the European Community.

17. DECLARATION ON ARTICLE 73k [now 63] OF THE TREATY ESTABLISHING THE EUROPEAN COMMUNITY

Consultations shall be established with the United Nations High Commissioner for Refugees and other relevant international organisations on matters relating to asylum policy.

18. DECLARATION ON ARTICLE 73k(3)(a) [now 63(3)(a)] OF THE TREATY ESTABLISHING THE EUROPEAN COMMUNITY

The Conference agrees that Member States may negotiate and conclude agreements with third countries in the domains covered by Article 73k(3)(a) [now 63(3)(a)] of the Treaty establishing the European Community as long as such agreements respect Community law.

19. DECLARATION ON ARTICLE 73l(1) [now 64(1)] OF THE TREATY ESTABLISHING THE EUROPEAN COMMUNITY

The Conference agrees that Member States may take into account foreign policy considerations when exercising their responsibilities under Article 73l(1) [now 64(1)] of the Treaty establishing the European Community.

20. DECLARATION ON ARTICLE 73m [now 65] OF THE TREATY ESTABLISHING THE EUROPEAN COMMUNITY

Measures adopted pursuant to Article 73m [now 65] of the Treaty establishing the European Community shall not prevent any Member State from applying its constitutional rules relating to freedom of the press and freedom of expression in other media.

21. DECLARATION ON ARTICLE 73o [now 67] OF THE TREATY ESTABLISHING THE EUROPEAN COMMUNITY

The Conference agrees that the Council will examine the elements of the decision referred to in Article 73o(2) [now 67(2)], second indent, of the Treaty establishing the European Community before the end of the five year period referred to in

Article 730 [now 67] with a view to taking and applying this decision immediately after the end of that period.

22. DECLARATION REGARDING PERSONS WITH A DISABILITY

The Conference agrees that, in drawing up measures under Article 100a [now 95] of the Treaty establishing the European Community, the institutions of the Community shall take account of the needs of persons with a disability.

23. DECLARATION ON INCENTIVE MEASURES REFERRED TO IN ARTICLE 109r [now 129] OF THE TREATY ESTABLISHING THE EUROPEAN COMMUNITY

The Conference agrees that the incentive measures referred to in Article 109r [now 129] of the Treaty establishing the European Community should always specify the following:
- the grounds for taking them based on an objective assessment of their need and the existence of an added value at Community level;
- their duration, which should not exceed five years;
- the maximum amount for their financing, which should reflect the incentive nature of such measures.

24. DECLARATION ON ARTICLE 109r [now 129] OF THE TREATY ESTABLISHING THE EUROPEAN COMMUNITY

It is understood that any expenditure under Article 109r [now 129] of the Treaty establishing the European Community will fall within Heading 3 of the financial perspectives.

25. DECLARATION ON ARTICLE 118 [now 137] OF THE TREATY ESTABLISHING THE EUROPEAN COMMUNITY

It is understood that any expenditure under Article 118 [now 137] of the Treaty establishing the European Community will fall within Heading 3 of the financial perspectives.

26. DECLARATION ON ARTICLE 118(2) [now 137(2)] OF THE TREATY ESTABLISHING THE EUROPEAN COMMUNITY

The High Contracting Parties note that in the discussions on Article 118(2) [now 137(2)] of the Treaty establishing the European Community it was agreed that the Community does not intend, in laying down minimum requirements for the protection of the safety and health of employees, to discriminate in a manner unjustified by the circumstances against employees in small and medium-sized undertakings.

27. DECLARATION ON ARTICLE 118b(2) [now 139(2)] OF THE TREATY ESTABLISHING THE EUROPEAN COMMUNITY

The High Contracting Parties declare that the first of the arrangements for application of the agreements between management and labour at Community level – referred to in Article 118b(2) [now 139(2)] of the Treaty establishing the European

Community – will consist in developing, by collective bargaining according to the rules of each Member State, the content of the agreements, and that consequently this arrangement implies no obligation on the Member States to apply the agreements directly or to work out rules for their transposition, nor any obligation to amend national legislation in force to facilitate their implementation.

28. DECLARATION ON ARTICLE 119(4) [now 141(4)] OF THE TREATY ESTABLISHING THE EUROPEAN COMMUNITY

When adopting measures referred to in Article 119(4) [now 141(4)] of the Treaty establishing the European Community, Member States should, in the first instance, aim at improving the situation of women in working life.

29. DECLARATION ON SPORT

The Conference emphasises the social significance of sport, in particular its role in forging identity and bringing people together. The Conference therefore calls on the bodies of the European Union to listen to sports associations when important questions affecting sport are at issue. In this connection, special consideration should be given to the particular characteristics of amateur sport.

30. DECLARATION ON ISLAND REGIONS

The Conference recognises that island regions suffer from structural handicaps linked to their island status, the permanence of which impairs their economic and social development.

The Conference accordingly acknowledges that Community legislation must take account of these handicaps and that specific measures may be taken, where justified, in favour of these regions in order to integrate them better into the internal market on fair conditions.

31. DECLARATION RELATING TO THE COUNCIL DECISION OF 13 JULY 1987

The Conference calls on the Commission to submit to the Council by the end of 1998 at the latest a proposal to amend the Council decision of 13 July 1987 laying down the procedures for the exercise of implementing powers conferred on the Commission.

32. DECLARATION ON THE ORGANISATION AND FUNCTIONING OF THE COMMISSION

The Conference notes the Commission's intention to prepare a reorganisation of tasks within the college in good time for the Commission which will take up office in 2000, in order to ensure an optimum division between conventional portfolios and specific tasks.

In this context, it considers that the President of the Commission must enjoy broad discretion in the allocation of tasks within the College, as well as in any reshuffling of those tasks during a Commission's term of office.

The Conference also notes the Commission's intention to undertake in parallel a corresponding reorganisation of its departments. It notes in particular the desirability of bringing external relations under the responsibility of a Vice-President.

33. DECLARATION ON ARTICLE 188c(3) [now 248(3)] OF THE TREATY ESTABLISHING THE EUROPEAN COMMUNITY

The Conference invites the Court of Auditors, the European Investment Bank and the Commission to maintain in force the present Tripartite Agreement. If a succeeding or amending text is required by any party, they shall endeavour to reach agreement on such a text having regard to their respective interests.

34. DECLARATION ON RESPECT FOR TIME LIMITS UNDER THE CO-DECISION PROCEDURE

The Conference calls on the European Parliament, the Council and the Commission to make every effort to ensure that the co-decision procedure operates as expeditiously as possible. It recalls the importance of strict respect for the deadlines set out in Article 189b [now 251] of the Treaty establishing the European Community and confirms that recourse, provided for in paragraph 7 of that Article, to extension of the periods in question should be considered only when strictly necessary. In no case should the actual period between the second reading by the European Parliament and the outcome of the Conciliation Committee exceed nine months.

35. DECLARATION ON ARTICLE 191a(1) [now 255(1)] OF THE TREATY ESTABLISHING THE EUROPEAN COMMUNITY

The Conference agrees that the principles and conditions referred to in Article 191a(1) [now 255(1)] of the Treaty establishing the European Community will allow a Member State to request the Commission or the Council not to communicate to third parties a document originating from that State without its prior agreement.

36. DECLARATION ON THE OVERSEAS COUNTRIES AND TERRITORIES

The Conference recognises that the special arrangements for the association of the overseas countries and territories (OCTs) under Part Four of the Treaty establishing the European Community were designed for countries and territories that were numerous, covered vast areas and had large populations. The arrangements have changed little since 1957.

The Conference notes that there are today only 20 OCTs and that they are extremely scattered island territories with a total population of approximately 900 000. Moreover, most OCTs lag far behind in structural terms, a fact linked to their particularly severe geographical and economic handicaps. In these circumstances, the special arrangements for association as they were conceived in 1957 can no longer deal effectively with the challenges of OCT development.

The Conference solemnly restates that the purpose of association is to promote the economic and social development of the countries and territories and to establish close economic relations between them and the Community as a whole.

The Conference invites the Council, acting in accordance with the provisions of

Article 136 [now 187] of the Treaty establishing the European Community, to review the association arrangements by February 2000, with the fourfold objective of:
– promoting the economic and social development of the OCTs more effectively;
– developing economic relations between the OCTs and the European Union;
– taking greater account of the diversity and specific characteristics of the individual OCTs, including aspects relating to freedom of establishment;
– ensuring that the effectiveness of the financial instrument is improved.

37. DECLARATION ON PUBLIC CREDIT INSTITUTIONS IN GERMANY

The Conference notes the Commission's opinion to the effect that the Community's existing competition rules allow services of general economic interest provided by public credit institutions existing in Germany and the facilities granted to them to compensate for the costs connected with such services to be taken into account in full. In this context, the way in which Germany enables local authorities to carry out their task of making available in their regions a comprehensive and efficient financial infrastructure is a matter for the organisation of that Member State. Such facilities may not adversely affect the conditions of competition to an extent beyond that required in order to perform these particular tasks and which is contrary to the interests of the Community.

The Conference recalls that the European Council has invited the Commission to examine whether similar cases exist in the other Member States, to apply as appropriate the same standards on similar cases and to inform the Council in its ECOFIN formation.

38. DECLARATION ON VOLUNTARY SERVICE ACTIVITIES

The Conference recognises the important contribution made by voluntary service activities to developing social solidarity.

The Community will encourage the European dimension of voluntary organisations with particular emphasis on the exchange of information and experiences as well as on the participation of the young and the elderly in voluntary work.

39. DECLARATION ON THE QUALITY OF THE DRAFTING OF COMMUNITY LEGISLATION

The Conference notes that the quality of the drafting of Community legislation is crucial if it is to be properly implemented by the competent national authorities and better understood by the public and in business circles. It recalls the conclusions on this subject reached by the Presidency of the European Council in Edinburgh on 11 and 12 December 1992, as well as the Council Resolution on the quality of drafting of Community legislation adopted on 8 June 1993 (*Official Journal of the European Communities*, No. C 166, 17.6.1993, p. 1).

The Conference considers that the three institutions involved in the procedure for adopting Community legislation, the European Parliament, the Council and the Commission, should lay down guidelines on the quality of drafting of the said legislation. It also stresses that Community legislation should be made more accessible and welcomes in this regard the adoption and first implementation of an accelerated working method for official codification of legislative texts, established by the Inter-instutional Agreement of 20 December 1994 (*Official Journal of the European Communities*, No. C 102, 4.4.1996, p. 2).

Therefore, the Conference declares that the European Parliament, the Council and the Commission ought to:
– establish by common accord guidelines for improving the quality of the drafting of Community legislation and follow those guidelines when considering proposals for Community legislation or draft legislation, taking the internal organisational measures they deem necessary to ensure that these guidelines are properly applied;
– make their best efforts to accelerate the codification of legislative texts.

40. DECLARATION CONCERNING THE PROCEDURE FOR CONCLUDING INTERNATIONAL AGREEMENTS BY THE EUROPEAN COAL AND STEEL COMMUNITY

The repeal of Article 14 of the Convention on the Transitional Provisions annexed to the Treaty establishing the European Coal and Steel Community does not alter existing practice concerning the procedure for the conclusion of international agreements by the European Coal and Steel Community.

41. DECLARATION ON THE PROVISIONS RELATING TO TRANSPARENCY, ACCESS TO DOCUMENTS AND THE FIGHT AGAINST FRAUD

The Conference considers that the European Parliament, the Council and the Commission, when they act in pursuance of the Treaty establishing the European Coal and Steel Community and the Treaty establishing the European Atomic Energy Community, should draw guidance from the provisions relating to transparency, access to documents and the fight against fraud in force within the framework of the Treaty establishing the European Community.

43. DECLARATION RELATING TO THE PROTOCOL ON THE APPLICATION OF THE PRINCIPLES OF SUBSIDIARITY AND PROPORTIONALITY

The High Contracting Parties confirm, on the one hand, the Declaration on the implementation of Community law annexed to the Final Act of the Treaty on European Union and, on the other, the conclusions of the Essen European Council stating that the administrative implementation of Community law shall in principle be the responsibility of the Member States in accordance with their constitutional arrangements. This shall not affect the supervisory, monitoring and implementing powers of the Community Institutions as provided under Articles 145 [now 202] and 155 [now 211] of the Treaty establishing the European Community.

44. DECLARATION ON ARTICLE 2 OF THE PROTOCOL INTEGRATING THE SCHENGEN *ACQUIS* INTO THE FRAMEWORK OF THE EUROPEAN UNION

The High Contracting Parties agree that the Council shall adopt all the necessary measures referred to in Article 2 of the Protocol integrating the Schengen *acquis* into the framework of the European Union upon the date of entry into force of the Treaty of Amsterdam. To that end, the necessary preparatory work shall be undertaken in due time in order to be completed prior to that date.

45. DECLARATION ON ARTICLE 4 OF THE PROTOCOL INTEGRATING THE SCHENGEN *ACQUIS* INTO THE FRAMEWORK OF THE EUROPEAN UNION

The High Contracting Parties invite the Council to seek the opinion of the Commission before it decides on a request under Article 4 of the Protocol integrating the Schengen *acquis* into the framework of the European Union by Ireland or the United Kingdom of Great Britain and Northern Ireland to take part in some or all of the provisions of the Schengen *acquis*.

They also undertake to make their best efforts with a view to allowing Ireland or the United Kingdom of Great Britain and Northern Ireland, if they so wish, to use the provisions of Article 4 of the said Protocol so that the Council may be in a position to take the decisions referred to in that Article upon the date of entry into force of that Protocol or at any time thereafter.

46. DECLARATION ON ARTICLE 5 OF THE PROTOCOL INTEGRATING THE SCHENGEN *ACQUIS* INTO THE FRAMEWORK OF THE EUROPEAN UNION

The High Contracting Parties undertake to make all efforts in order to make action among all Member States possible in the domains of the Schengen *acquis*, in particular whenever Ireland and the United Kingdom of Great Britain and Northern Ireland have accepted some or all of the provisions of that *acquis* in accordance with Article 4 of the Protocol integrating the Schengen *acquis* into the framework of the European Union.

47. DECLARATION ON ARTICLE 6 OF THE PROTOCOL INTEGRATING THE SCHENGEN *ACQUIS* INTO THE FRAMEWORK OF THE EUROPEAN UNION

The High Contracting Parties agree to take all necessary steps so that the Agreements referred to in Article 6 of the Protocol integrating the Schengen *acquis* into the framework of the European Union may enter into force on the same date as the date of entry into force of the Treaty of Amsterdam.

48. DECLARATION RELATING TO THE PROTOCOL ON ASYLUM FOR NATIONALS OF MEMBER STATES OF THE EUROPEAN UNION

The Protocol on asylum for nationals of Member States of the European Union does not prejudice the right of each Member State to take the organisational measures it deems necessary to fulfil its obligations under the Geneva Convention of 28 July 1951 relating to the status of refugees.

49. DECLARATION RELATING TO SUBPARAGRAPH (d) OF THE SOLE ARTICLE OF THE PROTOCOL ON ASYLUM FOR NATIONALS OF MEMBER STATES OF THE EUROPEAN UNION

The Conference declares that, while recognising the importance of the Resolution of the Ministers of the Member States of the European Communities responsible for immigration of 30 November/1 December 1992 on manifestly unfounded applications for asylum and of the Resolution of the Council of 20 June 1995 on minimum guarantees for asylum procedures, the question of abuse of asylum procedures and appropriate rapid procedures to dispense with manifestly unfounded applications for asylum should be further examined with a view to introducing new improvements in order to accelerate these procedures.

50. DECLARATION RELATING TO THE PROTOCOL ON THE INSTITUTIONS WITH THE PROSPECT OF ENLARGEMENT OF THE EUROPEAN UNION

Until the entry into force of the first enlargement it is agreed that the decision of the Council of 29 March 1994 ('the Ioannina Compromise') will be extended and, by that date, a solution for the special case of Spain will be found.

1n. DECLARATION BY AUSTRIA AND LUXEMBOURG ON CREDIT INSTITUTIONS

Austria and Luxembourg consider that the Declaration on public credit institutions in Germany also applies to credit institutions in Austria and Luxembourg with a comparable organisational structure.

3n. DECLARATION BY GERMANY, AUSTRIA AND BELGIUM ON SUBSIDIARITY

It is taken for granted by the German, Austrian and Belgian governments that action by the European Community in accordance with the principle of subsidiarity not only concerns the Member States but also their entities to the extent that they have their own law-making powers conferred on them under national constitutional law.

5n. DECLARATION BY BELGIUM ON THE PROTOCOL ON ASYLUM FOR NATIONALS OF MEMBER STATES OF THE EUROPEAN UNION

In approving the Protocol on asylum for nationals of Member States of the European Union, Belgium declares that, in accordance with its obligations under the 1951 Geneva Convention and the 1967 New York Protocol, it shall, in accordance with the provision set out in point (d) of the sole Article of that Protocol, carry out an individual examination of any asylum request made by a national of another Member State.

Declarations Relating to the TEC Annexed to the Final Act Associated with the Treaty of Nice

3. DECLARATION ON ARTICLE 10 OF THE TREATY ESTABLISHING THE EUROPEAN COMMUNITY

The Conference recalls that the duty of sincere co-operation which derives from Article 10 of the Treaty establishing the European Community and governs relations between the Member States and the Community institutions also governs relations between the Community institutions themselves. In relations between those institutions, when it proves necessary, in the context of that duty of sincere co-operation, to facilitate the application of the provisions of the Treaty establishing the European Community, the European Parliament, the Council and the Commission may conclude interinstutional agreements. Such agreements may not amend or supplement the provisions of the Treaty and may be concluded only with the agreement of these three institutions.

4. DECLARATION ON THE THIRD PARAGRAPH OF ARTICLE 21 OF THE TREATY ESTABLISHING THE EUROPEAN COMMUNITY

The Conference calls upon the institutions and bodies referred to in the third paragraph of Article 21 or in Article 7 to ensure that the reply to any written request by a citizen of the Union is made within a reasonable period.

5. DECLARATION ON ARTICLE 67 OF THE TREATY ESTABLISHING THE EUROPEAN COMMUNITY

The High Contracting Parties agree that the Council, in the decision it is required to take pursuant to the second indent of Article 67(2):
- will decide, from 1 May 2004, to act in accordance with the procedure referred to in Article 251 in order to adopt the measures referred to in Article 62(3) and Article 63(3)(b);
- will decide to act in accordance with the procedure referred to in Article 251 in order to adopt the measures referred to in Article 62(2)(a) from the date on which agreement is reached on the scope of the measures concerning the crossing by persons of the external borders of the Member States.

The Council will, moreover, endeavour to make the procedure referred to in Article 251 applicable from 1 May 2004 or as soon as possible thereafter to the other areas covered by Title IV or to parts of them.

6. DECLARATION ON ARTICLE 100 OF THE TREATY ESTABLISHING THE EUROPEAN COMMUNITY

The Conference recalls that decisions regarding financial assistance, such as are provided for in Article 100 and are compatible with the 'no-bail-out' rule laid down in Article 103, must comply with the 2000–2006 financial perspective, and in particular paragraph 11 of the Interinstutional Agreement of 6 May 1999 between the European Parliament, the Council and the Commission on budgetary discipline and improvement of the budgetary procedure, and with the corresponding provisions of future interinstutional agreements and financial perspectives.

7. DECLARATION ON ARTICLE 111 OF THE TREATY ESTABLISHING THE EUROPEAN COMMUNITY

The Conference agrees that procedures shall be such as to enable all the Member States in the euro area to be fully involved in each stage of preparing the position of the Community at international level as regards issues of particular relevance to economic and monetary union.

8. DECLARATION ON ARTICLE 137 OF THE TREATY ESTABLISHING THE EUROPEAN COMMUNITY

The Conference agrees that any expenditure incurred by virtue of Article 137 is to be charged to heading 3 of the financial perspective.

9. DECLARATION ON ARTICLE 175 OF THE TREATY ESTABLISHING THE EUROPEAN COMMUNITY

The High Contracting Parties are determined to see the European Union play a leading role in promoting environmental protection in the Union and in international efforts pursuing the same objective at global level. Full use should be made of all possibilities offered by the Treaty with a view to pursuing this objective, including the use of incentives and instruments which are market-oriented and intended to promote sustainable development.

10. DECLARATION ON ARTICLE 181a OF THE TREATY ESTABLISHING THE EUROPEAN COMMUNITY

The Conference confirms that, without prejudice to other provisions of the Treaty establishing the European Community, balance-of-payments aid to third countries falls outside the scope of Article 181a.

11. DECLARATION ON ARTICLE 191 OF THE TREATY ESTABLISHING THE EUROPEAN COMMUNITY

The Conference recalls that the provisions of Article 191 do not imply any transfer of powers to the European Community and do not affect the application of the relevant national constitutional rules.

The funding for political parties at European level provided out of the budget of the European Communities may not be used to fund, either directly or indirectly, political parties at national level.

The provisions on the funding for political parties shall apply, on the same basis, to all the political forces represented in the European Parliament.

12. DECLARATION ON ARTICLE 225 OF THE TREATY ESTABLISHING THE EUROPEAN COMMUNITY

The Conference calls on the Court of Justice and the Commission to give overall consideration as soon as possible to the division of jurisdiction between the Court of Justice and the Court of First Instance, in particular in the area of direct actions, and to submit suitable proposals for examination by the competent bodies as soon as the Treaty of Nice enters into force.

13. DECLARATION ON ARTICLE 225(2) AND (3) OF THE TREATY ESTABLISHING THE EUROPEAN COMMUNITY

The Conference considers that the essential provisions of the review procedure in Article 225(2) and (3) should be defined in the Statute of the Court of Justice. Those provisions should in particular specify:
- the role of the parties in proceedings before the Court of Justice, in order to safeguard their rights;
- the effect of the review procedure on the enforceability of the decision of the Court of First Instance;
- the effect of the Court of Justice decision on the dispute between the parties.

14. DECLARATION ON ARTICLE 225(2) AND (3) OF THE TREATY ESTABLISHING THE EUROPEAN COMMUNITY

The Conference considers that when the Council adopts the provisions of the Statute which are necessary to implement Article 225(2) and (3), it should put a procedure in place to ensure that the practical operation of those provisions is evaluated no later than three years after the entry into force of the Treaty of Nice.

15. DECLARATION ON ARTICLE 225(3) OF THE TREATY ESTABLISHING THE EUROPEAN COMMUNITY

The Conference considers that, in exceptional cases in which the Court of Justice decides to review a decision of the Court of First Instance on a question referred for a preliminary ruling, it should act under an emergency procedure.

16. DECLARATION ON ARTICLE 225a OF THE TREATY ESTABLISHING THE EUROPEAN COMMUNITY

The Conference asks the Court of Justice and the Commission to prepare as swiftly as possible a draft decision establishing a judicial panel which has jurisdiction to deliver judgements at first instance on disputes between the Community and its servants.

17. DECLARATION ON ARTICLE 229a OF THE TREATY ESTABLISHING THE EUROPEAN COMMUNITY

The Conference considers that Article 229a does not prejudice the choice of the judicial framework which may be set up to deal with disputes relating to the application of acts adopted on the basis of the Treaty establishing the European Community which create Community industrial property rights.

18. DECLARATION ON THE COURT OF AUDITORS

The Conference invites the Court of Auditors and the national audit institutions to improve the framework and conditions for co-operation between them, while maintaining the autonomy of each.

To that end, the President of the Court of Auditors may set up a contact committee with the chairmen of the national audit institutions.

19. DECLARATION ON ARTICLE 10.6 OF THE STATUTE OF THE EUROPEAN SYSTEM OF CENTRAL BANKS AND OF THE EUROPEAN CENTRAL BANK

The Conference expects that a recommendation within the meaning of Article 10.6 of the Statute of the European System of Central Banks and of the European Central Bank will be presented as soon as possible.

23. DECLARATION ON THE FUTURE OF THE UNION

1. Important reforms have been decided in Nice. The Conference welcomes the successful conclusion of the Conference of Representatives of the Governments of the Member States and commits the Member States to pursue the early ratification of the Treaty of Nice.

2. It agrees that the conclusion of the Conference of Representatives of the Governments of the Member States opens the way for enlargement of the European Union and underlines that, with ratification of the Treaty of Nice, the European Union will have completed the institutional changes necessary for the accession of new Member States.

3. Having thus opened the way to enlargement, the Conference calls for a deeper and wider debate about the future of the European Union. In 2001, the Swedish and Belgian Presidencies, in co-operation with the Commission and involving the European Parliament, will encourage wide-ranging discussions with all interested parties: representatives of national parliaments and all those reflecting public opinion, namely political, economic and university circles, representatives of civil society, etc.

The candidate States will be associated with this process in ways to be defined.

4. Following a report to be drawn up for the European Council in Göteborg in June 2001, the European Council, at its meeting in Laeken/Brussels in December 2001, will agree on a declaration containing appropriate initiatives for the continuation of this process.

5. The process should address, *inter alia*, the following questions:
– how to establish and monitor a more precise delimitation of powers between the European Union and the Member States, reflecting the principle of subsidiarity;
– the status of the Charter of Fundamental Rights of the European Union, proclaimed in Nice, in accordance with the conclusions of the European Council in Cologne;
– a simplification of the Treaties with a view to making them clearer and better understood without changing their meaning;
– the role of national parliaments in the European architecture.

6. Addressing the above mentioned issues, the Conference recognises the need to improve and to monitor the democratic legitimacy and transparency of the Union and its institutions, in order to bring them closer to the citizens of the Member States.

7. After these preparatory steps, the Conference agrees that a new Conference

of the Representatives of the Governments of the Member States will be convened in 2004, to address the above-mentioned items with a view to making corresponding changes to the Treaties.

8. The Conference of Member States shall not constitute any form of obstacle or pre-condition to the enlargement process. Moreover, those candidate States which have concluded accession negotiations with the Union will be invited to participate in the Conference. Those candidate States which have not concluded their accession negotiations will be invited as observers.

24. DECLARATION ON ARTICLE 2 OF THE PROTOCOL ON THE FINANCIAL CONSEQUENCES OF THE EXPIRY OF THE ECSC TREATY AND ON THE RESEARCH FUND FOR COAL AND STEEL

The Conference invites the Council to ensure, under Article 2 of the Protocol, the prolongation of the ECSC statistics system after the expiry of the ECSC Treaty until 21 December 2002 and to invite the Commission to make appropriate recommendations.

1n. DECLARATION BY LUXEMBOURG

Without prejudice to the Decision of 8 April 1965 and the provisions and possibilities contained therein regarding the seats of institutions, bodies and departments to be set up, the Luxembourg Government undertakes not to claim the seat of the Boards of Appeal of the Office for Harmonisation in the Internal Market (trade marks and designs), which will remain in Alicante, even if those Boards were to become judicial panels within the meaning of Article 220 of the Treaty establishing the European Community.

2n. DECLARATION BY GREECE, SPAIN AND PORTUGAL ON ARTICLE 161 OF THE TREATY ESTABLISHING THE EUROPEAN COMMUNITY

Greece, Spain and Portugal have agreed to the move to a qualified majority in Article 161 of the Treaty establishing the European Community on the basis that the word 'multiannual' in the third paragraph means that the financial perspective applicable from 1 January 2007 and the Inter-instutional Agreement relating thereto will have the same duration as the current financial perspective.

3n. DECLARATION BY DENMARK, GERMANY, THE NETHERLANDS AND AUSTRIA ON ARTICLE 161 OF THE TREATY ESTABLISHING THE EUROPEAN COMMUNITY

With regard to the Declaration by Greece, Spain and Portugal on Article 161 of the Treaty establishing the European Community, Denmark, Germany, the Netherlands and Austria declare that that Declaration is without prejudice to actions of the European Commission, in particular with respect to its right of initiative.

V Other Treaties and Related Documents

At the outset to the *Guide* we differentiated between two main types of European treaty: the constitutive and the amending. So far, the *Guide* has concentrated on the main treaties as examples of both categories. Detailed examination of the TEU and the TEC as constitutive treaties has been undertaken, complete with an analysis of the amendments introduced by the TEU, TA and TN. This division of the *Guide* concentrates on less prominent documents embraced by our understanding of the European Treaties. First, we have the 'original' constitutive European Treaty, the Treaty establishing the European Coal and Steel Community (TECSC) which dates back to 1951 and which is the only European Treaty with a limited shelf life. It expired on 23 July 2002 and will not be replaced. Second, the *Guide* examines the least known of the constitutive European Treaties, the Treaty establishing the European Atomic Energy Community (TEAEC). This was negotiated and signed alongside the TEC in 1957. At the time, it was anticipated that the resulting EAEC, often referred to as Euratom, would be the main focus of integration. Since then, however, it has been a rather marginal organization. The TEAEC is nevertheless important since it creates one of the three supra-national communities which have made up the first pillar of the EU.

The third treaty to be examined here is the Single European Act of 1987. This was the first major addition to the European Treaties concluded in the 1950s. As such, and despite its small size, it carried out significant amending and constitutive functions. It may now be little more than an historical document since its constitutive function has been supplanted by the TEU. Yet it retains great symbolic importance because of the role it played in revitalizing the EC in the 1980s. Moreover, it was the SEA which effectively initiated what has now become a regular feature of the EU's development – treaty reform.

In addition to the three treaties already mentioned, brief reference is made to accession treaties. These need to be remembered because they have a place in the treaty base. However, they are not reproduced, nor are they commented on in detail. Rather, the *Guide* outlines their general content and discusses their significance for the rest of the European Treaties.

We then go on to consider some more recent documents, which make up the European Treaties. The *Guide* therefore presents and discusses in brief first the 1997 Stability and Growth Pact concerning EMU, which seeks to complement the TEC in determining the conduct of EMU, and, second, the Charter of Fundamental Rights of the European Union proclaimed at Nice in December 2000. Finally, the division tries to pull the threads of all this together by asking what we have learned about the European Treaties and where they may go in the future, given the uncertainties of the post-Nice era.

i Treaty Establishing the European Coal and Steel Community

The Treaty establishing the European Coal and Steel Community (TECSC) is the original European Treaty. That its days have always been numbered was underlined by the TA, which replaced the original provision stating that the TECSC would expire 50 years after its entry into force with a firm date for its demise. Article 97 now states clearly that the TECSC 'shall expire on 23 July 2002'. Hence the TECSC is mainly of interest only to historians.* This does not mean that its contents will lose all relevance. Its preamble, apparently written only 10 days before the treaty was signed, retains political resonance since it outlines the early justification for supra-national integration within Europe. All the same, the recent expiry of the TECSC means that there is little value in reproducing it here. Instead, the *Guide* presents an outline of its structure and discusses the changes introduced by the TA before moving on to consider the implications of the treaty's expiry.

The TECSC consists of a preamble, four titles, three annexes and six protocols (see Box 9). In all, there are 117 articles. The preamble, as in other treaties, sets out the rationale for the ECSC, albeit with greater reference than most to its historical context. Thus, and drawing on the language used in the Schuman Declaration, it notes the member states' desire to overcome 'age-old rivalries', to provide 'the basis for a broader and deeper community among peoples long divided by bloody conflicts, and to lay the

Box 9   Structure and content of the TECSC post-TA

Preamble		
Title I	The European Coal and Steel Community	Articles 1–6
Title II	The Institutions of the Community	Articles 7–45
Chapter I	The Commission	Articles 8–19
Chapter II	The European Parliament	Articles 20–25
Chapter III	The Council	Articles 26–30
Chapter IV	The Court	Articles 31–45
Title III	Economic and Social Provisions	Articles 46–75
Chapter I	General provisions	Articles 46–48
Chapter II	Financial provisions	Articles 49–53
Chapter III	Investment and financial aid	Articles 54–56
Chapter IV	Production	Articles 57–59
Chapter V	Prices	Articles 60–64
Chapter VI	Agreements and concentrations	Articles 65–66
Chapter VII	Interference with conditions of competition	Article 67

*There was some debate on when expiry would occur, since there is some doubt as to when the last instrument of ratification was deposited with the French government as required under Article 99: 22 or 26 July 1952. The treaty's entry into force was set to be the following day with expiry 50 years later. Confusion continues to exist, Gormley arguing that the treaty expires at midnight on 24 July 2002.

foundations for institutions which will give direction to a destiny henceforward shared'. These references to historical differences are used to justify not only the ECSC's establishment but also integration beyond the economic sectors identified. Indeed, the absence from the preamble of the words 'coal' and 'steel', except in the title of the Community created, serves to highlight the broader intentions of the ECSC's original member states in concluding the treaty. The political ambitions associated with the treaty cannot easily be ignored when reading the preamble:

> THE PRESIDENT OF THE FEDERAL REPUBLIC OF GERMANY, HIS ROYAL HIGHNESS THE PRINCE ROYAL OF BELGIUM, THE PRESIDENT OF THE FRENCH REPUBLIC, THE PRESIDENT OF THE ITALIAN REPUBLIC, HER ROYAL HIGHNESS THE GRAND DUCHESS OF LUXEMBOURG, HER MAJESTY THE QUEEN OF THE NETHERLANDS,
>
> CONSIDERING that world peace can be safeguarded only by creative efforts commensurate with the dangers that threaten it,
>
> CONVINCED that the contribution which an organized and vital Europe can make to civilization is indispensable to the maintenance of peaceful relations,
>
> RECOGNIZING that Europe can be built only through practical achievements which will first of all create real solidarity, and through the establishment of common bases for economic development,
>
> ANXIOUS to help, by expanding their basic production, to raise the standard of living and further the works of peace,
>
> RESOLVED to substitute for age old rivalries the merging of their essential interests; to create, by establishing an economic community, the basis for a broader and deeper community among peoples long divided by bloody conflicts; and to lay the foundations for institutions which will give direction to a destiny henceforward shared,
>
> HAVE DECIDED to create a EUROPEAN COAL AND STEEL COMMUNITY and to this end have designated as their Plenipotentiaries:

Turning to the text of the treaty, the provisions soon focus on coal and steel with Title I identifying in some detail the tasks of the ECSC. The political and indeed legal significance of the new supra-national Community is, however, given prominence in the first title, Article 6 proclaiming that the ECSC has legal personality. In the other Community treaties, the assertion is left to Article 281 TEC and Article 184 TEAEC found in the general and final provisions towards the end. The supra-national and political nature of the ECSC is further underlined in Title II. Unlike the TEC and TEAC, which note the institutions and then move quickly on to policy provisions, the TECSC turns straight to the detail concerning the nature and roles of the institutions. Furthermore, in what can be seen as a clear attempt to signal the supra-national over the inter-governmental, the first set of institutional provisions concern the supra-national Commission and the European Parliament (originally referred to as the 'High Authority' and 'Assembly' respectively). The Council is dealt with third followed by the ECJ.

The provisions found in Title II are those which have seen most amendment since the TECSC was signed in 1951. These were introduced by the Convention on Certain Institutions Common to the European Communities (1957); the Merger Treaty (1965), which incidentally removed the only explicit references to 'supra-national' found in the European Treaties – from what was then Article 9, which bound the signatory states to respect the supra-national character of the High Authority; the Treaty amending certain budgetary provisions of the Treaties establishing the European Communities and of the Treaty establishing a single council and a single commission of the European Communities (1970); a Council decision of 26 November 1974; the Act concerning the election of the representatives of the EP (1976); the Treaty amending certain financial provisions (1975); the four acts of accession; the SEA; and the TEU. The most recent amendments were introduced by the TA and TN and mirrored amendments to the TEC concerning the appointment of the Commission; the powers of the Commission president; the duties and election of MEPs; the size of the EP; the organization of the Council Secretariat; reform of the ECJ; and the extension of ECJ jurisdiction to and the role of the Court of Auditors (see Box 10). Indeed, previous amendments to the TECSC have tended to bring its institutional provisions in line with those governing the EC and EAEC (see Annex 4). Simplification via the TA also affected six articles.

Far fewer changes have ever been introduced to Title III, which contains economic and social provisions. These cover most but not all areas of economic activity concerning the coal and steel industries. They do, however, grant the Commission greater executive and, in conjunction with Article 14, legislative powers than do the TEC and TECSC. Such powers remained almost unchanged after 1951. Indeed, only one amendment was made, and that in 1960 using the TECSC's procedures for minor revisions found in Article 95 to add a second paragraph to Article 56 on financial assistance. Since then three articles have been simplified by the TA (see Box 10).

A greater number of changes were introduced to Title IV containing general provisions. Most were concerned with the budget (Articles 78–78h) with other amendments altering, in the light of accessions, the territorial application of the treaty (Article 79) and treaty amendment procedures (Article 95).* The TEU also had an impact, removing

---

*Article 95 TECSC provides a unique example in the European Treaties of a treaty amendment involving a majority vote within the Council and the assent of the EP. Amendments may only adapt the rules for the Commission's exercise of its powers provided they do not conflict with the provisions of Articles 2, 3 and 4 or interfere with the relationship between the powers of the Commission and those of the other institutions. They are to be proposed jointly by the Commission and the Council, acting by a twelve-fifteenths majority, submitted to the ECJ for its opinion, forwarded to the EP before entering into force if approved by a majority of three-quarters of the votes cast and two-thirds of MEPs. This procedure was used to amend Article 56 TECSC in 1960.

Box 10   Impact of the TA and TN on the TECSC

Article	Impact of TA and TN (in *italic*)	Content of affected provisions
Amendments		
10(2)	new provision, as Article 214(2) (ex 158(2)) TEC	appointment of Commission
10(2)	*amendment, as to Article 214(2) TEC*	*appointment of Commission*
11	*amendment, as to Article 217 TEC*	*organization of Commission*
12	*amendment, as to Article 215 TEC*	*replacement of Commission*
13	new provision, as Article 219 (ex 163) TEC	organization of Commission
13	*deletion of first paragraph, 219 TEC*	*organization of Commission*
20	new provision, as Article 189 (ex 137) TEC	limit on size of EP
20	*amendment, as to Article 189 TEC*	*size of EP*
21(4)	new provision, as Article 190(4) (new) TEC	election of MEPs
21(5)	new provision, as Article 190(5) (new) TEC	duties of MEPs
21(5)	*amendment, as to Article 190(5) TEC*	*duties of MEPs*
30	new provision, as Article 207 (ex 151) TEC	Council Secretariat
30(2)	*amendment, as to Article 207 (2) TEC*	*Council Secretariat*
31	*amendment, as to Article 220 TEC*	*jurisdiction of Courts*
32	*amendment, as to Article 221 TEC*	*size of ECJ*
32a	*amendment, as to Article 222 TEC*	*advocates-general*
32b	*amendment, as to Article 223 TEC*	*appointments to ECJ*
32c	*amendment, as to Article 224 TEC*	*organization of CFI*
32d	*amendment, as to Article 225 TEC*	*jurisdiction of CFI*
32e	*amendment, as to Article 225a TEC*	*creation of judicial panels*
33	new provision, as Article 230 (ex 173) TEC	extension of ECJ power to CoA
33	*amendment, similar to Article 230 TEC*	*infringement proceedings*
45	*amendment, as to Article 245 TEC*	*ECJ statute*
45b	*amendment, as to Article 247 TEC*	*appointments to CoA*
45c	new provisions, as Article 248 (ex 188c) TEC	role of CoA
45c	*amendment, as to Article 248 TEC*	*role of CoA*
78c	new provisions, as Article 276 (ex Article 206) TEC	implementation of budget
78g(1)	new provision, as Article 274 (ex Article 205) TEC	discharge of budget
96	new provision, as Article 309 (new) TEC	suspension of voting rights
96	*amendment, as Article 309 TEC*	*suspension of voting rights*
Simplification		
2	simplified	deletion of 'progressively'	ECSC tasks
4	simplified	deletion of 'abolished and'	common market for coal and steel
7	amended	updating of institutions' names	Commission, EP, Council

10(3)	deleted	application of 10(1–2) in 1995–9	new commissioners' terms of office
16	simplified	repeal of transitional provisions	organization of Commission
21	amended	insertion of Article 14 EP Act	MEPs
32a	simplified	change to deadline	number of advocates-general
45b(3)	simplified	deletion of second subparagraph	Court of Auditors: term of office
50	amended	insertion of Article 28 of Merger Treaty	budget
52	repealed	repeal of outdated provision	transfer of funds to budget
76	amended	insertion of Article 20 of Merger Treaty	privileges and immunities
79	amended	deletions and additions	territorial application of treaty
84	simplified	removal of reference to 1951 convention	meaning of 'this Treaty'
85	repealed	repeal of transitional provision	location of transitional measures
93	simplified	updating to OECD	OEEC
95	simplified	removal of reference to transitional period	Convention on Transitional Provisions
97	simplified	insertion of specific date	expiry of ECSC Treaty
Annex III	simplified	removal of initials of plenipotentiaries	special steels
Protocol	simplified	removal of transitional provisions and list	ECJ (amended by TN)
Protocol	simplified	removal of transitional provisions and list	Council of Europe

Articles 96 and 98 on treaty revision and accession in favour of Articles 48 (ex N) and 49 (ex O) TEU. The TA's impact concerned the budget, amending Articles 78g(1) and 78c. Second, it introduced a new Article 96 on the suspension of a member state's voting rights which mirrors the new Article 309 TEC. Furthermore, the TA simplified a number of articles, notably Article 97 on the expiry of the TECSC (see above).

Beyond the text of the treaty, there are three original annexes and six protocols, only two of which date back to 1951. The latter, as the ECJ noted in *Industries Sidérurigiques Luxembourgeoises* (1956), are legally binding. When signed, there was also an Exchange of Letters Between the Government of the Federal Republic of Germany and the Government of the French Republic Concerning the Saar and a Protocol on the Privileges and Immunities of the Community. These were repealed by the TA's simplification process and the Merger Treaty (1965), respectively, the latter being replaced by the Protocol on the privileges and immunities of the European Communities. Unlike most other European Treaties there is no final act associated with the TECSC and no declarations as such. There was, at least until repealed by the TA, a Convention on the Transitional Provisions which contained a series of provisions governing the so-called preparatory and transitional periods of the ECSC. Many of these were similar to declarations in purpose but carried greater legal force since the Convention, being signed by state representatives, was in effect an international treaty. Following its repeal by the TA, the convention has little value today, although Declaration No. 40 TA notes that repeal does not alter existing practice concerning the procedure for the conclusion of international agreements by the ECSC. The TA also had an impact on the two remaining original protocols, the Protocol on the Statute of the Court of Justice, which is almost identical to the Protocol on the Statute of the Court of Justice of the European Community,* and the Protocol on relations with the Council of Europe. Both were simplified along with one of the annexes.

After 1951 a further five protocols were annexed to the TECSC as well as the TEU, the TEC and TEAEC (see Box 11). The first is the Protocol annexed to the Treaty on European Union and to the Treaties Establishing the European Communities, which was annexed to the TECSC by the TEU and which grants the anti-abortion provisions in the Irish Constitution special status within EC law. Of the remaining protocols three were

Box 11   Protocols and other acts annexed to the TECSC

Protocols annexed to the TECSC	Date	Impact of TA	Impact of TN
Protocol on the Statute of the Court of Justice	1951	amended	
Protocol on relations with the Council of Europe	1951	amended	
Protocol on the privileges and immunities of the Community	1951	*	
Convention on the transitional provisions	1951	repealed	
Exchange of letters between the government of the Federal Republic of Germany and the government of the French Republic concerning the Saar	1951	repealed	
Protocols also annexed to TEAEC, TEU, TEC and TECSC			
Protocol annexed to the Treaty on European Union and to the Treaties establishing the European Communities**	1992		
Protocol on the institutions with the prospect of enlargement of the European Union**	1997	new	repealed
Protocol on the location of the seats of the institutions and of certain bodies and departments of the European Communities and of Europol**	1997	new	
Protocol on the role of national parliaments in the European Union**	1997	new	
Protocol on the enlargement of the European Union**	2001		new

* repealed by the Merger Treaty (1965) and replaced in 1967 by the Protocol on the privileges and immunities of the European Communities attached to the Merger Treaty (see pp. 540–44).
** denotes that the protocol is reproduced above on pp. 68–72.

*Differences exist whether in substance or in wording with regard to the representation of and assistance to parties before the ECJ, stages of procedures, applications, the transmission of documents, preparatory inquiries, hearings, intervention, judgment by default, third-party proceedings, time limits, periods of limitation, special rules relating to disputes between member states and proceedings by third parties.

introduced by the TA: the Protocol on the Institutions with the prospect of enlargement of the European Union; the Protocol on the location of the seats of the institutions and of certain bodies and departments of the European Communities and of Europol; and the Protocol on the role of national parliaments in the European Union. In addition to repealing the first of these, Nice annexed the Protocol on the Enlargement of the European Union to the TECSC. All five protocols have been discussed earlier in the *Guide*.

This expiry of the TECSC on 23 July 2002 naturally raises questions concerning how coal and steel policy will operate in the future. In April 1991 agreement was reached among the member states that the treaty would be allowed to expire and that in the interim policy convergence between the ECSC and EC would be pursued. Hence, certain ECSC practices were subsequently phased out. Among these were the pricing controls permissible under Article 60 since these ran counter to the principles of the free market. In other areas, the levy provided for in Article 49 to fund the ECSC was set at 0% and effectively abandoned in 1999; the Commission ceased borrowing and lending activities in 1994; the codes for exemption from the absolute prohibition on state aid allowed under Article 95 were set to expire in 2002; and aid activities were subsumed under the Structural Funds. In the areas of competition policy, merger control, aid for retraining, and trade policy, the Commission set about alignment with EC practice. For example, a new competition act adopted by the ECSC in 2000 directed regulators to EC law and jurisprudence. Such convergence cannot guarantee a problem-free transition to the post-ECSC era. Certainly, there will be issues concerning the applicability and validity over time of the *lex specialis* which is ECSC case law.

The transfer of responsibility for coal and steel policy to the EC has caused few problems so far. In part this is due to the convergence drive. It also reflects the fact the EC has long had a role to play in these areas. This is because the TECSC does not provide a comprehensive framework for policy. Article 81 employs a restrictive definition of 'coal' and 'steel' and does not cover all categories used by producers. Moreover, the definition of an undertaking in Article 80 excludes small- and medium-sized distributors. Consequently some activities associated with coal and steel have long been dealt with under the TEC. And where matters concerning coal and steel are not covered by the provisions in the TECSC, the ECJ has ruled in *Deutsche Babcock* (1987) that the TEC and its provisions can apply. All the same, the passing of the TECSC will not be without impact. The Commission, for example, will see its powers of investigation, legislation and intervention reduced, and the ECSC Consultative Committee will cease to exist. Also, the assets of the ECSC will have to be disposed of. These include financial reserves of 1.3 billion euros as well as other assets which will be transferred to the EC for investment with the annual interest being used exclusively for research and development in coal and steel sectors.*

All the above developments have occurred without any treaty changes. The TEC, for example, has not been amended to accommodate the expiry of the TECSC. This is regrettable since without explicit references to coal and steel, for example in Article 3 TEC or in a dedicated title, the treaty lacks a firm statement of the EC's competences. Arguably, though, the declining economic significance of the coal and steel industries means that they no longer merit any special status. What would be welcome, however, is an amendment to Article 305 (ex 232) TEC. This currently states that nothing in the TEC will affect the TECSC. A simple amendment could tidy up the article and confirm

---

*Legally, Article 6 TECSC provides for the ECSC to dispose of its own property, but Article 305 (ex 232) TEC implies that the EC is the beneficiary. International law suggests that the assets be handed to the member states.

the status of the TECSC as an expired, and therefore no longer legally binding, treaty after 23 July 2002.

Much of this could have been done in the 2000 IGC. It was not. Instead, all that Nice does is to annex a new Protocol on the financial consequences of the Expiry of the ECSC Treaty on the Research Fund for Coal and Steel to the TEC. This protocol applies from 24 July 2002, the date on which it provides for the transfer of all the ECSC's assets and liabilities to the EC. The revenue from the assets is to be used to fund a Research Fund for Coal and Steel which will operate as a distinct fund outside any framework programmes for research which the EC adopts. Decisions relating to the implementation of the protocol are to be taken by the Council acting by unanimity and in consultation with the EP. In addition to the Council needing to take decisions relating to the Research Fund, Declaration No. 24 TN calls on the Council to prolong the ECSC statistics system until 31 December 2002.

ii Treaty Establishing the European Atomic Energy Community

The Treaty establishing the European Atomic Energy Community (TEAEC) was signed in Rome in 1957 at the same time as the TEC. As with TECSC, it rarely receives much attention even though its drafters thought it the more important of the two 'Rome' treaties and had great hopes that the EAEC would become the main vehicle for European integration. This was not to be as the EC became the most dynamic of the three communities and the EAEC failed to create the single atomic-energy market that was envisaged. Ever since, the activities of the EAEC (often referred to as Euratom) have become rather peripheral to the mainstream of integration activity within the EU. All the same, there are a few voices advocating the disbanding of this community. Indeed, the fact that the TEAEC is concluded for an unlimited period means that it is unlikely to follow, at least for the foreseeable future, the TECSC into the historical archives of the EU. Even so, the limited attention which is paid to the treaty means there is little point reproducing the entire text here and providing a detailed commentary. Instead, the *Guide* outlines its structure and discusses the changes introduced by the TA.

The TEAEC consists of a preamble, five titles, four annexes and five protocols (see Box 12). In all, there are 215 articles. Yet unlike the renumbered TEC, these do not follow a consistent sequential numerical order. Twelve articles combine numbers and letters (e.g. 107a). In other instances, there are numerical gaps in the treaty, a logical expectation given the final provisions are contained in Article 225! In fact, there are no Articles 94, 95, 100, 133, 180, 205 or 209–223. This does not mean that there are any major lacunae in the text. It is just that, over time, amendments have been made which have resulted in the repeal of some articles (see Annex 4).

One element of the treaty, which has remained unaltered since 1957 is the preamble. As in other constitutive treaties, it sets out the rationale for the body which it establishes. Very much reflecting the optimism of the time, it focuses on the major role anticipated for nuclear energy within industry and the need for states to join forces in realizing the development of a powerful nuclear industry which will provide extensive energy resources and general prosperity. This is to be done with due regard to health and safety and in co-operation with international organizations. Beyond such aspirations, the preamble

Box 12   Structure and content of the TEAEC post-TA

Preamble		
Title I	The Tasks of the Community	Articles 1–3
Title II	Provisions for the Encouragement of Progress in the Field of Nuclear Energy	Articles 4–106
Chapter I	Promotion of Research	Articles 4–11
Chapter II	Dissemination of Information	Articles 12–29
Chapter III	Health and Safety	Articles 30–39
Chapter IV	Investment	Articles 40–44
Chapter V	Joint Undertakings	Articles 45–51
Chapter VI	Supplies	Articles 52–76
Chapter VII	Safeguards	Articles 77–85
Chapter VIII	Property Ownership	Articles 86–91
Chapter IX	The Nuclear Common Market	Articles 92–99
Chapter X	External Relations	Articles 101–106
Title III	Provisions Governing the Institutions	Articles 107–170
Chapter I	The Institutions of the Community	Articles 107–160c
Chapter II	Provisions Common to Several Institutions	Articles 161–164
Chapter III	The Economic and Social Committee	Articles 165–170
Title IV	Financial Provisions	Articles 171–183a
Title V	General Provisions	Articles 184–208
	Final Provisions	Articles 224–225
Annex I	Fields of Research Concerning Nuclear Energy Referred to in Article 4 of this Treaty	
Annex II	Industrial Activities Referred to in Article 41 of this Treaty	
Annex III	Advantages which may be Conferred on Joint Undertakings under Article 48 of this Treaty	
Annex IV	List of Goods and Products Subject to the Provisions of Chapter IX on the Nuclear Common Market under Article 48 of this Treaty	

Protocol annexed to the Treaty on European Union and to the Treaties establishing the European Communities

Protocol on the location of the seats of the institutions and of certain bodies and departments of the European Communities and of Europol

Protocol on the role of national parliaments in the European Union

Protocol on the enlargement of the European Union

Protocol on the Statute of the Court of Justice

contains little, and certainly less in terms of political ambition than do the preambles to the TECSC and to the TEC. While the 'advancement of peace' is noted, reference to a determination to 'lay the foundations of an ever closer union among the peoples of Europe', so prominent in the TEC's preamble, is wholly absent.

HIS MAJESTY THE KING OF THE BELGIANS, THE PRESIDENT OF THE FEDERAL REPUBLIC OF GERMANY, THE PRESIDENT OF THE FRENCH REPUBLIC, THE PRESIDENT OF THE ITALIAN REPUBLIC, HER ROYAL HIGHNESS THE GRAND DUCHESS OF LUXEMBOURG, HER MAJESTY THE QUEEN OF THE NETHERLANDS,

RECOGNIZING that nuclear energy represents an essential resource for the development and invigoration of industry and will permit the advancement of the cause of peace,

CONVINCED that only a joint effort undertaken without delay can offer the prospect of achievements commensurate with the creative capacities of their countries,

RESOLVED to create the conditions necessary for the development of a powerful nuclear industry which will provide extensive energy resources, lead to the modernization of technical processes and contribute, through its many other applications, to the prosperity of their peoples,

ANXIOUS to create the conditions of safety necessary to eliminate hazards to the life and health of the public,

DESIRING to associate other countries with their work and to co-operate with international organizations concerned with the peaceful development of atomic energy,

HAVE DECIDED to create a EUROPEAN ATOMIC ENERGY COMMUNITY (EURATOM) and to this end have designated as their Plenipotentiaries:

Turning to the text of the treaty, the first title confirms the EAEC's establishment and notes as its task 'to contribute to the raising of the standard of living in the Member States and to the development of relations with the other countries by creating the conditions necessary for the speedy establishment and growth of nuclear industries'. Article 2 then lists how the EAEC is to achieve these: by promoting research and the dissemination of technical information; establishing uniform safety standards to protect the health of workers and of the general public; facilitating investment and ensuring the establishment of the basic installations necessary for the development of nuclear energy in the Community; ensuring a regular and equitable supply of ores and nuclear fuels; making certain that nuclear materials are not diverted to purposes other than those for which they are intended; exercising the right of ownership conferred upon it with respect to special fissile materials; creating a common market in specialized materials and equipment; ensuring the free movement of capital for investment; establishing freedom of employment for specialists; and establishing with other countries and international organizations such relations as will foster progress in the peaceful uses of nuclear energy. The title concludes with a list of the EAEC's institutions: EP, Council, Commission and ECJ. EcoSoc is also noted.

Title II then details the EAEC's competences with regard to the areas of activity listed in Article 2. The vast majority of these provisions read just as they did when the TEAEC was signed in 1957. Very few changes, other than through the TA's simplification procedure, have been made. The same cannot be said for Title III, which has three chapters concerning the institutions and decision-making. Many of the provisions mirror those found in the TEC and, to a lesser extent, the TECSC. Indeed, 76 of the 86 articles in the title (Articles 107–183) are identical in spirit if not in word to articles appearing

Box 13 Amendments to the TEAEC: Corresponding Articles in the TEC

TEAEC	107	107a	107b	107c	107d	108	109	110	111	112	113
TEC	189	192*	193	194	195	190	196	197	198	199	200

TEAEC	114	115	116	117	118	119	120	121	122	123	124
TEC	201	–	203	204	205	250	206	207	208	210	–

TEAEC	125	126	127	128	129	130	131	132	134	135	136
TEC	212	213	214	215	216	217	218	219	–	–	220

TEAEC	137	138	139	140	140a	140b	141	142	143	144	145
TEC	221	222	223	224	225	225a	226	227	228	–	–

TEAEC	146	147	148	149	150	151	152	153	154	155	156
TEC	230	231	232	233	234	235	236	238	239	240	241

TEAEC	157	158	159	160	160a	160b	160c	161	162	163	164
TEC	242	243	244	245	246	247	248	249	253	254	256

TEAEC	165	166	167	168	169	170	171	172	173	173a	174
TEC	257	258	259	260	261	262	–	–	269	270	–

TEAEC	175	176	177	178	179	179a	180b	181	182	183	183a
TEC	271	–	272	273	274	275	276	277	278	279	280

TEAEC	184	185	186†	187	188	189	190	191	192	193	194
TEC	281	282	283	284	288	289	290	291	10	292	–

TEAEC	195	196	197	198	199	200	201	202	203	204	206
TEC	–	–	–	299	302	303	304	306	308	309	310

TEAEC	207	208	224	225
TEC	311	312	313	314

in the TEC (see Box 13), a fact strengthened by the 1965 Merger Treaty which had a marked impact on some provisions (see Annex 4). This helps to explain why almost all of the TEAEC articles affected by amendments introduced by the TA can be found in Title III: the amendments follow those introduced to TEC provisions governing the institutions. The same is true of the amendments introduced by Nice. Almost all other changes affecting the TEAEC are a result of simplification. And the majority of these affect transitional provisions originally found in Title VI which was repealed by the TA (see Box 14). With most provisions in Title IV, Financial Provisions, and in Title V, General Provisions, having counterparts in the TEC too, amendments here are not unique. They reflect amendments to the TEC concerning the budget and suspension of a member state's voting rights. Likewise, simplification's impact on the final provisions is limited to an updating of the list of languages in which authentic versions of the treaty exist. Hence, in the TEAEC we have a treaty which, except for Title II, makes provision

*Second paragraph only.
†Technically, the provisions found in Article 186 are those of Article 24(1) of the Merger Treaty. Their formal insertion into the TEAEC appears to have been overlooked by both the TEU and the TA.

Box 14   Impact of the TA and TN on the TEAEC

Article	Impact of TA and TN (in *italic*) Explanation	Content of affected provisions
Amendments		
107	new provision, as Article 189 (ex 137) TEC	limit on size of EP
107	*amendment, as Article 189 TEC*	*size of EP*
108(3)	new provision, as Article 190(4) (new) TEC	election of MEPs
108(4)	new provision, as Article 190(4) (new) TEC	duties of MEPs
108(5)	*amendment, as Article 190(5) TEC*	*duties of MEPs*
121	new provision, as Article 207 (ex 151) TEC	Council Secretariat
121(2)	*amendment, as Article 207(2) TEC*	*Council Secretariat*
127(2)	new provision, as Article 214(2) (ex 158(2)) TEC	appointment of Commission
127(2)	*amendment, as Article 214(2) TEC*	*appointment of Commission*
128	*amendment, as Article 215 TEC*	*replacement of Commission*
130	*amendment, as Article 217 TEC*	*organization of Commission*
132	new provision, as Article 219 (ex 163) TEC	organization of Commission
132	*amendment, as Article 219 TEC*	*organization of Commission*
136	*amendment, as Article 220 TEC*	*jurisdiction of Courts*
137	*amendment, as Article 221 TEC*	*size of ECJ*
138	*amendment, as Article 222 TEC*	*advocates-general*
139	*amendment, as Article 223 TEC*	*appointments to ECJ*
140	*amendment, as Article 224 TEC*	*organization of CFI*
140a	*amendment, as Article 225 TEC*	*jurisdiction of CFI*
140b	*amendment, as Article 225a TEC*	*creation of judicial panels*
146	new provision, as Article 230 (ex 173) TEC	extension of ECJ power to CoA
146	*amendment, as Article 230 TEC*	*infringement proceedings*
160	*amendment, as Article 245 TEC*	*ECJ statute*
160b	*amendment, as Article 247 TEC*	*appointments to CoA*
160c	new provisions, as Article 248 (ex 188c) TEC	role of CoA
160c	*amendment, as Article 248 TEC*	*role of CoA*
163	*amendment, as Article 254(1) TEC*	*publication in Official Journal*
165	*amendment, as Article 257 TEC*	*organization of EcoSoc*
166	*amendment, as Article 258 TEC*	*organization of EcoSoc*
167(1)	*amendment, as Article 259(1) TEC*	*appointment to EcoSoc*
170	new provision, as Article 265 (ex 198c) TEC	consultation of EcoSoc
179	new provision, as Article 276 (ex Article 206) TEC	implementation of budget
180b(1)	new provision, as Article 274 (ex Article 205) TEC	discharge of budget
183	*amendment, as Article 279 TEC*	*budget*
190	*amendment, as Article 290 TEC*	*languages*
204	new provision, as Article 309 (new) TEC	suspension of voting rights
204	*amendment, as Article 309 TEC*	*suspension of voting rights*

Simplification

76	simplified	'entry into force' to '1 January 1958'	shortages
93	simplified	'abolish' to 'prohibit'	tariffs and QRs
94	repealed	repeal of transitional provision	establishment of CCT
95	repealed	repeal of transitional provision	establishment of CCT
98	simplified	deletion of deadline	insurance contracts
100	repealed	repeal of transitional provision	payments
104	amended	changes to deadlines	agreements with third parties
105	amended	changes to deadlines	agreements with third parties
106	simplified	change to deadline	agreements with third parties
108	amended	insertion of Article 14 EP Act	MEPs
127(3)	deleted	application of Article 127(1–2) in 1995–9	Commission's term of office
138	simplified	change to deadline	number of advocates-general
160b(3)	simplified	deletion of second subparagraph	Court of Auditors: term of office
181	simplified	deletion of three paragraphs	budget
191	new article	insertion on Article 128 Merger Treaty	privileges and immunities
198	amended	clarification	application of treaty
199	simplified	updating to World Trade Organization	GATT
209	repealed	repeal of transitional provision	first Council meeting
210	repealed	repeal of transitional provision	establishment of EcoSoc
211	repealed	repeal of transitional provision	first Assembly (EP) meeting
212	repealed	repeal of transitional provision	establishment of ECJ
213	repealed	repeal of transitional provision	establishment of Commission
214	repealed	repeal of transitional provision	first financial year
215	repealed	repeal of transitional provision	initial programmes
216	repealed	repeal of transitional provision	Article 9 – university
217	repealed	repeal of transitional provision	Article 24 – security gradings
218	repealed	repeal of transitional provision	Article 31 – basic standards
219	repealed	repeal of transitional provision	Article 33 – health and safety
220	repealed	repeal of transitional provision	Article 54 – agency
221	repealed	repeal of transitional provision	patents
222	repealed	repeal of transitional provision	supply contracts
223	repealed	repeal of transitional provision	Article 60 – reactors
225	amended	addition of languages	authenticity of treaty texts
Annex V	deleted	repeal of transitional provisions	Article 215 – initial programmes

for a Community structured, governed and administered in a manner very similar to the EC.

Parallels with the TEC are also reflected in the protocols annexed to the TEAEC and in the final act. When originally signed the treaty had annexed to it only one protocol, the Protocol on the Application of the Treaty establishing the European Atomic Energy Community to the non-European Parts of the Kingdom of the Netherlands. This concerned the application of the treaty to Surinam and Netherlands Antilles and, like protocols annexed to the TEC and TECSC, was legally binding (see Article 207). Long since redundant, it was repealed by the TA (see Box 15). Soon after the TEAEC was signed, however, two further protocols were added in line with the expectations laid down in the final act which the treaty shares with the TEC. These were the Protocol on the Statute of the Court of Justice of the European Atomic Energy Community (1957), since repealed by Nice, and the Protocol on the privileges and immunities of the European Atomic Energy Community (1957). The former was almost identical to the Protocol on the Statute of the Court of Justice of the European Community and underwent some simplification by the TA, being replaced later at Nice by the Protocol on the Statute of the Court of Justice. The latter protocol covering privileges and immunities was repealed and replaced in 1965 with a single Protocol on privileges and immunities of the European Communities annexed to the Merger Treaty which obviously covers the TEC too.

Box 15   Protocols annexed to the TEAEC

Protocols annexed to the TEAEC	Date	Impact of TA	Impact of TN
Protocol on the application of the Treaty establishing the European Atomic Energy Community to the non-European parts of the Kingdom of the Netherlands	1957	repealed	
Protocol on the privileges and immunities of the European Atomic Energy Community	1957	*	
Protocol on the Statute of the Court of Justice of the European Atomic Energy Community	1957	simplified	repealed
Protocols also annexed to the TEAEC, TEU, TEC and TECSC			
Protocol annexed to the Treaty on European Union and to the Treaties establishing the European Communities**	1992		
Protocol on the institutions with the prospect of enlargement of the European Union**	1997	new	repealed
Protocol on the location of the seats of the institutions and of certain bodies and departments of the European Communities and of Europol**	1997	new	
Protocol on the role of national parliaments in the European Union**	1997	new	
Protocol on the enlargement of the European Union**	2001		new
Protocols also annexed to the TEAEC and TEU and TEC			
Protocol on the Statute of the Court of Justice**	2001		new

* repealed by the Merger Treaty (1965) and replaced in 1967 by the Protocol on the privileges and immunities of the European Communities attached to the Merger Treaty (see pp. 540–44).
** denotes that the Protocol is reproduced in the *Guide*.

Since then, the TEAEC has had annexed to it a total of six protocols. The first four of these were introduced by the TA and are discussed above. They are the Protocol annexed to the Treaty on European Union and to the Treaties establishing the European Communities which grants the anti-abortion provisions in the Irish Constitution special status within EC law and was introduced by the TEU; the Protocol on the Institutions with the prospect of enlargement of the European Union which was subsequently repealed by Nice; the Protocol on the location of the seats of the institutions and of certain bodies and departments of the European Communities and of Europol; and the Protocol on the role of national parliaments in the European Union. All four of these the TEAEC shares or shared with the TEC as well as the TECSC and TEU. The same is true of the fifth, more recent protocol, the Protocol on the enlargement of the European Union annexed by Nice. Finally, as mentioned, Nice also annexed to the TEAEC the new Protocol on the Statute of the Court of Justice.

iii Single European Act

The Single European Act (SEA) is something of a vanishing treaty. The decisions which it took have now either been absorbed into the TEC or, where European Political Co-operation is concerned, superseded by the TEU. None the less, it remains a significant treaty and one whose preamble, general provisions and additional materials can often be cited. Hence, it is worth while saying something about it here.

It was signed in February 1986, entering into force 17 months later.* At the time it consisted of four titles and a total of 34 articles. As noted in the Introduction to the *Guide*, it performed both constitutive and amending functions. On the former, Article 30 formalized mechanisms for European Political Co-operation (EPC). Beyond EPC, 24 of the SEA's articles contained amendments to the existing European Treaties. The provisions contained in these 24 articles have since become part of the relevant treaties and in some cases (e.g. ex Articles 8b and 100b TEC) subsequently been repealed by the TA. Of the remaining provisions, those contained in Articles 2, 3(2) and 30 SEA were repealed by the TEU. Such developments mean that today there is little left of the SEA (see Box 16). Indeed, beyond the preamble, only seven articles worth reproducing remain. Legally speaking, the provisions which amend the European Treaties are still valid since there are no legally valid consolidated versions of either the TECSC or the TEAEC, and the consolidated versions of the TEC produced after the TEU and annexed to the final act associated with the TA are 'for illustrative purposes' only.

In terms of what does remain of the SEA, we have the declaratory preamble setting out the purpose of the provisions that follow. Thus, the SEA seeks to continue the work of the European Treaties in turning relations between the member states into a European Union. Here, as elsewhere in the preamble, reference is made to earlier declaratory statements of the European Council. In addition, the member states express their determination to promote democracy and fundamental rights, and to improve the economic and social situation within the EC. With regard to the first of these, reference is made to the role played by the EP. Later, and although the SEA hardly addresses the means by which it can be achieved, the progressive realization of Economic and Monetary

---

*The full text of the SEA can be found in *OJ* L169, 29 June 1987. It is also reproduced in *Bulletin of the European Communities*, Supplement 2/86.

Box 16   Structure and fate of the Single European Act

Content	Current Status
Preamble	
Title I – Common Provisions	
1 objectives and treaty bases for EC and EPC	
2 structure and meetings of European Council	repealed by TEU
3 powers and jurisdiction of EC and EPC bodies	para. 2 repealed by TEU
Title II – Provisions Amending the Treaties Establishing the European Communities	
Chapter I – Provisions amending the Treaty Establishing the European Coal and Steel Community	
4 new Article 32d on Court of First Instance	addition made to TECSC
5 supplement to Article 45 on Statute of ECJ	amendments made to TECSC
Chapter II – Provisions amending the Treaty Establishing the European Community	
Section 1 – Institutional Provisions	
6 provisions covered by new co-operation procedure	amendments made to TEC
7 new Article 149 – co-operation procedure	addition made to TEC
8 amendment to Article 237 on accession to EC	amendment made to TEC
9 amendment to Article 238 on association with EC	amendment made to TEC
10 supplement to Article 145 on Council powers	amendment made to TEC
11 new Article 168a on Court of First Instance	addition made to TEC
12 supplement to Article 188 on statute of ECJ	amendment made to TEC
Section 2 – Provisions relating to the foundations and the policy of the Community	
Subsection I – Internal Market	
13 new Article 8a on scope of Internal Market	addition made to TEC
14 new Article 8b on progress towards Internal Market	addition made to TEC
15 new Article 8c on accommodating economic differences	addition made to TEC
16 new and amended articles extending QMV	amendments made to TEC
17 new Article 99 on legislative harmonization	amendment made to TEC
18 new Article 100a on legislative harmonization using QMV	addition made to TEC
19 new Article 100b on inventory of Article 100a legislation	addition made to TEC
Subsection II – Monetary Capacity	
20 new Article 102a on co-operation	addition made to TEC
Subsection III – Social Policy	
21 new Article 118a on health and safety in workplace	addition made to TEC
22 new Article 118b on management–labour dialogue	addition made to TEC
Subsection IV – Economic and Social Cohesion	
23 new Title V with Articles 130a–130d on cohesion	addition made to TEC
Subsection V – Research and Development	
24 new Title VI with Articles 130f–130q on R&D	addition made to TEC
Subsection VI – Environment	
25 new Title VII with Articles 130r–130t on environment	addition made to TEC
Chapter III – Provisions amending the Treaty Establishing the European Atomic Energy Community	

Union is given notable prominence. Also the member states declare their desire for a smoother functioning of the EC institutions and an EC which can speak increasingly with one voice and promote international peace and security. In a bold display of enthusiasm the member states express too their conviction that the 'European idea', integration and 'further developments' correspond to the wishes of the peoples of Europe.

HIS MAJESTY THE KING OF THE BELGIANS, HER MAJESTY THE QUEEN OF DENMARK, THE PRESIDENT OF THE FEDERAL REPUBLIC OF GERMANY, THE PRESIDENT OF THE HELLENIC REPUBLIC, HIS MAJESTY THE KING OF SPAIN, THE PRESIDENT OF THE FRENCH REPUBLIC, THE PRESIDENT OF IRELAND, THE PRESIDENT OF THE ITALIAN REPUBLIC, HIS ROYAL HIGHNESS THE GRAND DUKE OF LUXEMBOURG, HER MAJESTY THE QUEEN OF THE NETHERLANDS, THE PRESIDENT OF THE PORTUGUESE REPUBLIC, HER MAJESTY THE QUEEN OF THE UNITED KINGDOM OF GREAT BRITAIN AND NORTHERN IRELAND,

MOVED by the will to continue the work undertaken on the basis of the Treaties establishing the European Communities and to transform relations as a whole among their States into a European Union, in accordance with the Solemn Declaration of Stuttgart of 19 June 1983,

RESOLVED to implement this European Union on the basis, firstly, of the Communities operating in accordance with their own rules and, secondly, of European co-operation among the signatory States in the sphere of foreign policy and to invest this Union with the necessary means of action,

DETERMINED to work together to promote democracy on the basis of the fundamental rights recognized in the constitutions and laws of the Member States, in the Convention for the Protection of Human Rights and Fundamental Freedoms and the European Social Charter, notably freedom, equality and social justice,

CONVINCED that the European idea, the results achieved in the fields of economic integration and political co-operation, and the need for new developments correspond to the wishes of the democratic peoples of Europe, for whom the European Parliament, elected by universal suffrage, is an indispensable means of expression,

AWARE of the responsibility incumbent upon Europe to aim at speaking ever increasingly with one voice and to act with consistency and solidarity in order more effectively to protect its common interests and independence, in particular to display the principles of democracy and compliance with the law and with human rights to which they are attached, so that together they may make their own contribution to the preservation of international peace and security in accordance with the undertaking entered into by them within the framework of the United Nations Charter,

DETERMINED to improve the economic and social situation by extending common policies and pursuing new objectives, and to ensure a smoother functioning of the Communities by enabling the institutions to exercise their powers under conditions most in keeping with Community interests,

WHEREAS at their Conference in Paris from 19 to 21 October 1972 the Heads of State or Government approved the objective of the progressive realization of economic and monetary union,

HAVING REGARD to the Annex to the conclusions of the Presidency of the European Council in Bremen on 6 and 7 July 1978 and the resolution of the European Council in Brussels on 5 December 1978 on the introduction of the European Monetary System (EMS) and related questions, and noting that in accordance with that resolution, the Community and the central banks of the Member States have taken a number of measures intended to implement monetary co-operation,

Turning to the seven articles whose provisions have neither been repealed nor inserted into another treaty or decision, the first two are to be found in Title I under the heading 'Common Provisions'. Despite their prominence, neither of these falls within the jurisdiction of the ECJ, as Article 31 SEA notes. Hence, their legal status is similar to most provisions in the TEU. Article 1 confirms the objective of the European Communities and EPC as contributing 'to making concrete progress towards European unity'. It then affirms that the former are founded on the European Treaties while EPC is governed by Title III SEA. References to EPC remain, despite their redundancy following EPC's replacement by CFSP, owing to the fact that the simplification of the European Treaties introduced by the TA did not extend to the SEA. As regards the second remaining article in Title I, the amended Article 3(1) deals with the powers and jurisdiction of the Communities' institutions, firmly implying that these will change through the adoption of further amending treaties.

Four of the remaining five articles reproduced below are found in Title IV containing general and final provisions. They are preceded, however, by Article 28, which declares that nothing in the SEA will be without prejudice to the provisions governing Spanish and Portuguese accession to the EU which coincided with the adoption of the SEA. Article 31 then sets out the jurisdiction of the ECJ, limiting it to the amendments to the European Treaties contained in Title II and to Article 32, which in turn declares that nothing in the SEA will affect either past or future European Treaties. Article 33 then deals with ratification in a manner similar to Article 313 TEC and is followed by a standard statement on the authenticity of the various official-language versions of the SEA. Confirmation in each official language of when the act was drawn up – unlike other European Treaties, two dates are given here because some signatories were held up by domestic factors – precedes the concluding signatures.

TITLE I Common provisions

Article 1. The European Communities and European political co-operation shall have as their objective to contribute together to making concrete progress towards European unity.

The European Communities shall be founded on the Treaties establishing the European Coal and Steel Community, the European Economic Community, the European Atomic Energy Community and on the subsequent treaties and acts modifying or supplementing them.

Political co-operation shall be governed by Title III. The provisions of that Title shall confirm and supplement the procedures agreed in the reports of Luxembourg (1970), Copenhagen (1973), London (1981), the Solemn Declaration on European Union (1983) and the practices gradually established among the Member States.

. . .

Article 3.1. The institutions of the European Communities, henceforth designated as referred to hereafter, shall exercise their powers and jurisdiction under the conditions and for the purposes provided for by the Treaties establishing the Communities and by the subsequent treaties and acts modifying or supplementing them and by the provisions of Title II.

. . .

TITLE II Provisions amending the Treaties Establishing the European Communities

Chapter IV – General provisions

Article 28. The provisions of this Act shall be without prejudice to the provisions of the instruments of Accession of the Kingdom of Spain and the Portuguese Republic to the European Communities.

. . .

TITLE IV General and final provisions

Article 31. The provisions of the Treaty establishing the European Coal and Steel Community, the Treaty establishing the European Economic Community and the Treaty establishing the European Atomic Energy Community concerning the powers of the Court of Justice of the European Communities and the exercise of those powers shall apply only to the provisions of Title II and to Article 32; they shall apply to those provisions under the same conditions as for the provisions of the said Treaties.

Article 32. Subject to Article 3(1), to Title II and to Article 31, nothing in this Act shall affect the Treaties establishing the European Communities or any subsequent treaties and acts modifying or supplementing them.

Article 33.1. This Act will be ratified by the High Contracting Parties in accordance with their respective constitutional requirements. The instruments of ratification will be deposited with the Government of the Italian Republic.

2. This Act will enter into force on the first day of the month following that in which the instrument of ratification is deposited of the last signatory State to fulfil that formality.

Article 34. This Act, drawn up in a single original in the Danish, Dutch, English, French, German, Greek, Irish, Italian, Portuguese and Spanish languages, the texts in each of these languages being equally authentic, will be deposited in the archives of the Government of the Italian Republic, which will remit a certified copy to each of the governments of the other signatory States.

IN WITNESS WHEREOF, the undersigned Plenipotentiaries have signed this Single European Act.

Done at Luxembourg on the seventeenth day of February in the year one thousand nine hundred and eighty-six and at The Hague on the twenty-eighth day of February in the year one thousand nine hundred and eighty-six.

[Signatures and names of plenipotentiaries]

As with most of the other European Treaties, these signatures do not signal the end of all that was agreed in concluding the SEA. This is left to the Final Act which follows and which lists exactly what the IGC agreed (see Box 17). Here, this is relatively straightforward with the final act recording the adoption of the SEA and 11 declarations. The IGC's noting of a further 9 declarations is also recorded. The 20 declarations are then annexed to the Final Act.

As with the TA, the difference between the adopted and the noted declarations is that the former are the expression of all participants in the IGC while the latter are declarations by one or more participants. With the SEA, as with the TEU, TA and TN, some of the 'adopted' declarations (Nos. 1, 2, 3, 5, 7, 8, 9 and 11) are in the name of the

Box 17 Final Act associated with the Single European Act

FINAL ACT

The Conference of the Representatives of the Governments of the Member States convened at Luxembourg on 9 September 1985, which carried on its discussions in Luxembourg and Brussels and adopted the following text:

I   Single European Act

II   At the time of signing this text, the Conference adopted the declarations listed hereinafter and annexed to this Final Act:

1. Declaration on the powers of implementation of the Commission
2. Declaration on the Court of Justice
3. Declaration on Article 8a [now 14] of the EC Treaty
4. Declaration on Article 100a [now 95] of the EC Treaty
5. Declaration on Article 100b [repealed by TA] of the EC Treaty
6. General Declaration on Articles 13 to 19 of the Single European Act
7. Declaration on Article 118a(2) [now 138(2)] of the EC Treaty
8. Declaration on Article 130d [now 161] of the EC Treaty
9. Declaration on Article 130r [now 174] of the EC Treaty
10. Declaration by the High Contracting Parties on Title III [repealed by TA] of the Single European Act
11. Declaration on Article 30(10)(g) [repealed by TA] of the Single European Act

The Conference also notes the declarations listed hereinafter and annexed to this Final Act:

1. Declaration by the Presidency on the time limit within which the Council will give its opinion following a first reading (Article 149(2) [now 252] of the EC Treaty)
2. Political Declaration by the Governments of the Member States on the free movement of persons
3. Declaration by the Government of the Hellenic Republic on Article 8a [now 14] of the EC Treaty
4. Declaration by the Commission on Article 28 [now 26] of the EC Treaty
5. Declaration by the Government of Ireland on Article 57(2) [now 47(2)] of the EC Treaty
6. Declaration by the Government of the Portuguese Republic on Articles 59 [now 49], second paragraph, and 84 [now 80] of the EC Treaty
7. Declaration by the Government of the Kingdom of Denmark on Article 100a [now 95] of the EC Treaty
8. Declaration by the Presidency and the Commission on the monetary capacity of the Community
9. Declaration by the Government of the Kingdom of Denmark on European Political Co-operation

Done at Luxembourg on the seventeenth day of February in the year one thousand nine hundred and eighty-six and at The Hague on the twenty-eighth day of February in the year one thousand nine hundred and eighty-six.

Leo TINDEMANS	Peter BARRY
Uffe ELLEMANN JENSEN	Giulio ANDREOTTI
Hans Dietrich GENSCHER	Robert GOEBBELS
Karolos PAPOULIAS	Hans VAN DEN BROEK
Francisco FERNÁNDEZ ORDÓÑEZ	Pedro PIRES DE MIRANDA
Roland DUMAS	Lynda CHALKER

'Conference' while others (here only No. 10) express the views of the 'High Contracting Parties'. Others (Nos. 4 and 6) have no explicit reference as to who has adopted them. With regard to the 'noted' declarations, these differ from those associated with other European Treaties in so far as they are not simply declarations of one or several member states. While this is true of some (Nos. 3, 5, 6, 7 and 9), others are declarations by either the Commission (No. 4), the presidency (No. 1) or both (No. 8). Moreover, one declaration (No. 2) is only 'noted' even though it is by all the governments of the member states. The explanation seems to lie in the fact that it is labelled a 'political' declaration although this sits oddly with the generally accepted view that all declarations are little more than political since they have no legal force.

As regards the content of the 'adopted' declarations, five (Nos. 1 and 3–6) concern the establishment of the Internal Market. Hence a call is made to enhance the implementation powers of the Commission and boost the 'advisory committee procedure' more commonly referred to as 'comitology'; the completion of the Internal Market by 31 December 1992 declared a political objective; the use of directives for the harmonization of legislation encouraged; the taking into consideration of member states' economic situation when promoting completion of the Internal Market; and the right of member states to adopt measures to combat illegal trade and terrorism. Other declarations cover the amendments to the jurisdiction of the ECJ (No. 2); health and safety in small and medium-sized enterprises (No. 7); an increase in the size of the Structural Funds (No. 8); the pursuit of action on the environment (No. 9); links between EPC and democratic non-member European countries (No. 10); and the siting of the EPC Secretariat in Brussels (No. 11). Of further note is that all declarations refer to specific articles in either the amended TEC or the SEA, thus pre-empting both political and judicial interpretations of the respective treaty provisions.

Attempts to use declarations for such a purpose are also evident in the 'noted' declarations (Nos. 3 and 5–7) by the Greek, Irish, Portuguese and Danish governments on legislation concerning sensitive sectors of the economy in the case of the first three and more stringent national provisions governing the workplace and the environment in the case of Denmark. Other 'noted' declarations by member states concern the promotion of co-operation to combat terrorism and international crime (No. 2) and Denmark's position in Nordic co-operation remaining unaffected by EPC (No. 9). The 'noted' declarations made by the presidency refer to measures to improve decision-making (No. 1) and, with the Commission, the possibility of further developments concerning the EC's monetary capacity not being prejudiced by SEA provisions (No. 8). The declaration made by the Commission concerns the impact of amendments to what is now Article 26 TEC on procedures for alterations to the Common Commercial Tariff (No. 4).

Adopted Declarations

[1] DECLARATION ON THE POWERS OF IMPLEMENTATION OF THE COMMISSION

The Conference asks the Community authorities to adopt, before the Act enters into force, the principles and rules on the basis of which the Commission's powers of implementation will be defined in each case. In this connection the Conference requests the Council to give the Advisory Committee procedure in particular a predominant place in the interests of speed and efficiency in the decision-making process, for the exercise of the powers of implementation conferred on the Commission within the field of Article 95 [ex 100a] of the EC Treaty.

[2] DECLARATION ON THE COURT OF JUSTICE

The Conference agrees that the provisions of Article 32d(1) of the ECSC Treaty, Article 225(1) [ex 168a(1)] of the EC Treaty and Article 140a(1) of the EAEC Treaty do not prejudge any conferral of judicial competence likely to be provided for in the context of agreements concluded between the Member States.

[3] DECLARATION ON ARTICLE 8a [now 14] OF THE EC TREATY

The Conference wishes by means of the provisions in Article 14 to express its firm political will to take before 1 January 1993 the decisions necessary to complete the internal market defined in those provisions, and more particularly the decisions necessary to implement the Commission's programme described in the White Paper on the internal market.

Setting the date of 31 December 1992 does not create an automatic legal effect.

[4] DECLARATION ON ARTICLE 100a [now 95] OF THE *EC* TREATY

In its proposals pursuant to Article 95(1) the Commission shall give precedence to the use of the instrument of a directive if harmonization involves the amendment of legislative provisions in one or more Member States.

[5] DECLARATION ON ARTICLE 100b [now repealed by TA] OF THE *EC* TREATY

The Conference considers that, since Article 15 [ex 8c] of the *EC* Treaty is of general application, it also applies to the proposals which the Commission is required to make under Article 100b [now repealed] of that Treaty.

[6] GENERAL DECLARATION ON ARTICLES 13 TO 19 OF THE SINGLE EUROPEAN ACT*

Nothing in these provisions shall affect the right of Member States to take such measures as they consider necessary for the purpose of controlling immigration from third countries, and to combat terrorism, crime, the traffic in drugs and illicit trading in works of art and antiques.

[7] DECLARATION ON ARTICLE 118a(2) [now 138(2)] OF THE *EC* TREATY

The Conference notes that in the discussions on Article 138(2) of the *EC* Treaty it was agreed that the Community does not intend, in laying down minimum requirements for the protection of the safety and health of employees, to discriminate in a manner unjustified by the circumstances against employees in small and medium sized undertakings.

[8] DECLARATION ON ARTICLE 130d [now 161] OF THE *EC* TREATY

In this context the Conference refers to the conclusions of the European Council in Brussels in March 1984, which read as follows:
'The financial resources allocated to aid from the Funds, having regard to the IMPs, will be significantly increased in real terms within the limits of financing possibilities.'

---

*These cover TEC articles concerning the establishment of the Internal Market. Post-TEU they were Articles 7a, 7b, 7c, 28, 57(2) (amended), 70(1), 84, 99 (amended), 100a (amended) and 100b. Articles 7b, 70(1) and 100b have since been repealed by the TA with the remainder being renumbered as Articles 14 (simplified), 15 (simplified), 26 (simplified), 47(2) (amended), 80 (simplified), 93 and 95 (amended).

[9] DECLARATION ON ARTICLE 130r [now 174] OF THE *EC* TREATY

Re paragraph 1, third indent:
The Conference confirms that the Community's activities in the sphere of the environment may not interfere with national policies regarding the exploitation of energy resources.

Re paragraph 5, second subparagraph:
The Conference considers that the provisions of Article 174(4), second subparagraph, do not affect the principles resulting from the judgment handed down by the Court of Justice in the AETR case.

[10] DECLARATION BY THE HIGH CONTRACTING PARTIES ON TITLE III [repealed by TA] OF THE SINGLE EUROPEAN ACT

The High Contracting Parties to Title III on European political co-operation reaffirm their openness to other European nations which share the same ideals and objectives. They agree in particular to strengthen their links with the member countries of the Council of Europe and with other democratic European countries with which they have friendly relations and close co-operation.

[11] DECLARATION ON ARTICLE 30(10)(g) [repealed by TA] OF THE SINGLE EUROPEAN ACT

The Conference considers that the provisions of Article 30(10)(g) do not affect the provisions of the Decision of the Representatives of the Governments of the Member States of 8 April 1965 on the provisional location of certain institutions and departments of the Communities.

Declarations 'Noted' by the Conference

[1n] DECLARATION BY THE PRESIDENCY ON THE TIME LIMIT WITHIN WHICH THE COUNCIL WILL GIVE ITS OPINION FOLLOWING A FIRST READING (ARTICLE 149(2) [now 252] OF THE *EC* TREATY)

As regards the declaration by the European Council in Milan, to the effect that the Council must seek ways of improving its decision-making procedures, the Presidency states its intention of completing the work in question as soon as possible.

[2n] POLITICAL DECLARATION BY THE GOVERNMENTS OF THE MEMBER STATES ON THE FREE MOVEMENT OF PERSONS

In order to promote the free movement of persons, the Member States shall co-operate, without prejudice to the powers of the Community, in particular as regards the entry, movement and residence of nationals of third countries. They shall also co-operate in the combating of terrorism, crime, the traffic in drugs and illicit trading in works of art and antiques.

[3n] DECLARATION BY THE GOVERNMENT OF THE HELLENIC REPUBLIC ON ARTICLE 8a [now 14] OF THE *EC* TREATY

Greece considers that the development of Community policies and actions, and the adoption of measures on the basis of Articles 70(1) [repealed by the TA] and 80 [ex 84], must both take place in such a way as not to harm sensitive sectors of Member States' economies.

[4n] DECLARATION BY THE COMMISSION ON ARTICLE 28 [now 26] OF THE *EC* TREATY

With regard to its own internal procedures, the Commission will ensure that the changes resulting from the amendment of Article 26 *EC* will not lead to delays in responding to urgent requests for the alteration or suspension of Common Customs Tariff duties.

[5n] DECLARATION BY THE GOVERNMENT OF IRELAND ON ARTICLE 57(2) [now 47(2)] OF THE *EC* TREATY

Ireland, in confirming its agreement to qualified majority voting under Article 47(2), wishes to recall that the insurance industry in Ireland is a particularly sensitive one and that special arrangements have had to be made by the Government of Ireland for the protection of insurance policy holders and third parties. In relation to harmonization of legislation on insurance, the Government of Ireland would expect to be able to rely on a sympathetic attitude from the Commission and from the other Member States of the Community should Ireland later find itself in a situation where the Government of Ireland considers it necessary to have special provision made for the position of the industry in Ireland.

[6n] DECLARATION BY THE GOVERNMENT OF THE PORTUGUESE REPUBLIC ON ARTICLES 59 [now 49], SECOND PARAGRAPH, AND 84 [now 80] OF THE *EC* TREATY

Portugal considers that as the change from unanimous to qualified majority voting in Articles 49, second paragraph, and 80 was not contemplated in the negotiations for the accession of Portugal to the Community and substantially alters the Community *acquis*, it must not damage sensitive and vital sectors of the Portuguese economy, and, wherever necessary, appropriate and specific transitional measures should be introduced to forestall the adverse consequences that could ensue for these sectors.

[7n] DECLARATION BY THE GOVERNMENT OF THE KINGDOM OF DENMARK ON ARTICLE 100a [now 95] OF THE *EC* TREATY

The Danish Government notes that in cases where a Member State is of the opinion that measures adopted under Article 95 do not safeguard higher requirements concerning the working environment, the protection of the environment or the needs referred to in Article 30 [ex 36], the provisions of Article 95(4) guarantee that the Member State in question can apply national provisions. Such national provisions are to be taken to fulfil the above-mentioned aim and may not entail hidden protectionism.

[8n] DECLARATION BY THE PRESIDENCY AND THE COMMISSION ON THE MONETARY CAPACITY OF THE COMMUNITY

The Presidency and the Commission consider that the provisions inserted in the *EC* Treaty with reference to the Community's monetary capacity are without prejudice to the possibility of further development within the framework of the existing powers.

[9n] DECLARATION BY THE GOVERNMENT OF THE KINGDOM OF DENMARK ON EUROPEAN POLITICAL CO-OPERATION

The Danish Government states that the conclusion of Title III on European political co-operation in the sphere of foreign policy does not affect Denmark's participation in Nordic co-operation in the sphere of foreign policy.

iv   Accession Treaties

As the Introduction to the *Guide* noted, accession treaties need to be considered as European Treaties since they introduce changes to the original. Indeed, Article 49 TEU on accession provides for 'adjustments' to be made. And it is certain that there will be further such treaties to cater for eastern enlargement within the lifetime of this *Guide*. Their reproduction in full is not justified since the amendments have all been incorporated into the text of the TEU and TEC reproduced above. It is worth noting, however, the general format of accession treaties and of the acts concerning the conditions of accession, since the latter form an integral part of the former and contain numerous protocols and declarations whose provisions often have long-lasting significance. Note, for example, the declaration introduced at the time of Amsterdam in 1997 by the Greek government which recalls the Joint Declaration concerning Mount Athos adopted back in 1979.

There have been four accession treaties concluded at the time of writing, one for each of the enlargements which have taken place. Each treaty follows a similar format consisting of a preamble and three articles (see Box 18).* The preamble performs a dual function. First it affirms the signatories' commitment to the objectives of the Union and to constructing on existing foundations the goal of an 'ever closer union among the peoples of Europe'. It thus emphasizes the dynamic nature of integration in a manner similar to other amending treaties. Second, the preamble notes the mechanism for and accepted desirability of the envisaged accession. This is underlined by the final recital's

---

*Prior to the establishment of the EU, states acceded to each Community. Technically the treaty of accession covered only the EC and EAEC. Accession to the ECSC was by a Council decision structured similarly to the treaty of accession.

Box 18   Format of Accession Treaties (based on 1994 Accession Treaty)

Treaty between [*names of the existing member states*], (Member States of the European Union) and [*names of the acceding states*] concerning the accession of [*names of the acceding states*] to the European Union

[*List of heads of state*]

UNITED in their desire to pursue the attainment of the objectives of the Treaties on which the European Union is founded;

DETERMINED in the spirit of those Treaties to construct an ever closer union among the peoples of Europe on the foundations already laid;

CONSIDERING that Article 49 of the Treaty on European Union affords European states the opportunity of becoming members of the Union;

CONSIDERING that the [*names of acceding states*] have applied to become members of the Union;

CONSIDERING that the Council of the European Union, after having obtained the opinion of the Commission and the assent of the European Parliament, has declared itself in favour of the admission of these States,

HAVE DECIDED to establish by common agreement the conditions and the adjustment to be made to the treaties on which the European Union is founded, and to this end have designated as their Plenipotentiaries

[*List of plenipotentiaries*]

WHO, having exchanged their full powers in good and due form,

HAVE AGREED AS FOLLOWS:

Article 1. 1. [*Names of the acceding states*] hereby become members of the European Union and parties to the Treaties on which the Union is founded as amended and supplemented.

2. The conditions of admission and the adjustments to the Treaties on which the Union is founded, entailed by such admission, are set out in the Act annexed to this Treaty. The Provisions of that Act shall form an integral part of this Treaty.

3. The provisions concerning the rights and obligations of the Member States and the powers and jurisdiction of the institutions of the Union as set out in the Treaties referred to in paragraph 1 shall apply in respect of this Treaty.

Article 2. 1. This Treaty shall be ratified by the High Contracting Parties in accordance with their respective constitutional requirements. The instruments of ratification shall be deposited with the Government of the Italian Republic by [*agreed date*] at the latest.

2. The Treaty shall enter into force on [*agreed date*] provided that all the instruments of ratification have been deposited before that date.

If, however, the States referred to in Article 1(1) have not all deposited their instruments of ratification in due time, the Treaty shall enter into force for those States that have deposited their instruments. In this case the Council of the European Union, acting unanimously, shall decide immediately upon such adjustments as have become indispensable to Article 3 of this Treaty and to [*list of relevant articles in Act of Accession, Annexes and Protocols*]; acting unanimously it may also declare that those provisions of the aforementioned Act [*of Accession*], including its Annexes and Protocols, which refer expressly to a State which has not deposited its instruments of ratification have lapsed, or it may adjust them.

3. Notwithstanding paragraph 3, the institutions of the Union may adopt before accession the measures referred to in [*relevant Articles*] of the Act of Accession [*etc*]. These measures shall enter into force only subject to and on the date of entry into force of this Treaty.

Article 3. This Treaty, drawn up in a single original in the [*languages of member and acceding states*], the . . . texts all being authentic, shall be deposited in the archives of the Government of the Italian Republic which will transmit a certified copy to each of the Governments of the other signatory states.

IN WITNESS WHEREOF the undersigned Plenipotentiaries have signed this Treaty,

Done at [*place*] on [*date*],

[*Signatures and names of plenipotentiaries*]

declaration that the respective heads of state agree to determine the conditions for accession.

The text of the treaty is surprisingly short. The detail concerning the conditions and adjustments relating to the accession are contained in an act of accession annexed to the treaty. The three articles in the treaty are, however, important. This is particularly the case with Article 1, which states that the acceding state is a member of the EU or EEC, depending on when the accession treaty was signed. Reference is then made to the act of accession containing the conditions of admission. Article 2 then details ratification provisions, noting that where more than one state is acceding to the EU non-ratification within an agreed time-frame will result in adjustments to the act of accession and Article 3 to exclude the non-ratifying state. The existence of such a provision has proved to be of use on two occasions: in 1972 and in 1994 when Norway failed to ratify the accession treaty. In both instances the Council swiftly adopted amending decisions. What would happen if an existing member state failed to ratify is not stated. Presumably, the treaty would simply fall, although given what happened with Maastricht in Denmark and Nice in Ireland, the relevant member state might be encouraged to 'try again' as we will shortly discuss. Finally, Article 3 confirms the authenticity of each of the language versions of the treaty and, by extension, of the act of accession. The treaty is then dated and signed by the plenipotentiaries.

This leads us to the act of accession and the detailed provisions governing the conditions of accession and the amendments to the EU's treaty base (see Box 19). Once again these follow a similar format beginning with Part One on principles before moving on to Part Two, which deals with adjustments to the treaties. Here much of the emphasis is on the institutional provisions contained in the European Treaties. Adjustments are also made to the geographical applicability of the treaties. The third part then details adaptations to acts adopted by EC institutions. Part Four, transitional measures, follows with individual titles governing each acceding state. The first title of Part Five contains provisions relating to the implementation of the act of accession, before concluding with Title II's final provisions on acceding states receiving certified copies of all the European Treaties and international agreements to which the EU and EC are party. Legally binding annexes and protocols then follow before a final act summarizes the documents adopted. These include the accession treaty, the act of accession complete with annexes and protocols and the texts of the European Treaties in the languages of the acceding states. Also included are exchanges of letters and non-binding declarations. Those which are 'adopted'

Box 19 Format of Acts of Accession (based on 1994 Act of Accession)

Act concerning the conditions of accession of [*names of the acceding member states*] and the adjustments to the Treaties on which the European Union is founded

Part One	Principles
Part Two	**Adjustments to the Treaties**
Title I	Provisions Governing the Institutions
Chapter 1	*The European Parliament*
Chapter 2	*The Council*
Chapter 3	*The Commission*
Chapter 4	*The Court of Justice*
Chapter 5	*The Court of Auditors*
Chapter 6	*The Economic and Social Committee*
Chapter 7	*The Committee of the Regions*
Chapter 8	*The ECSC Consultative Committee*
Chapter 9	*The Scientific and Technical Committee*
Title II	Other Adjustments
Part Three	**Adaptations to Acts Adopted by the Institutions**
Part Four	**Transitional Measures**
Title I	Institutional Provisions
Title II	*Deleted owing to Norway's non-ratification of Accession Treaty*
Title III	Transitional Measures Concerning Austria
Chapter 1	*Free movement of goods*
Chapter 2	*Free movement of persons, services and capital*
Chapter 3	*Competition Policy*
Chapter 4	*External Relations including Customs Union*
Chapter 5	*Financial and Budgetary Provisions*
Title IV	Transitional Measures Concerning Finland
Chapter 1	*Free movement of goods*
Chapter 2	*Free movement of persons, services and capital*
Chapter 3	*Fisheries*
Chapter 4	*External Relations including Customs Union*
Chapter 5	*Financial and Budgetary Provisions*
Title V	Transitional Measures Concerning Sweden
Chapter 1	*Free movement of goods*
Chapter 2	*Free movement of persons, services and capital*
Chapter 3	*Fisheries*
Chapter 4	*External Relations including Customs Union*
Chapter 5	*Financial and Budgetary Provisions*
Title VI	Agriculture
Chapter 1	*Provisions concerning national aids*
Chapter 2	*Other provisions*
Title VII	Other Provisions
Part Five	**Provisions Relating to the Implementation of this Act**
Title I	Setting up of the Institutions and Bodies
Title II	Applicability of the Acts of the Institutions
Title III	Final Provisions
Annexes	
Protocols	

reflect the views of all the signatories to the act of accession and are usually 'joint declarations'. Others contain the views of one or more signatories and are therefore either 'noted' by the plenipotentiaries or simply recorded as being 'made'. All declarations are annexed to the final act. In the case of the 1986 accession, the whole set of documents amounted to more than 480 pages.

The acts of accession are clearly significant treaties in so far as they govern the accession of states to the EU. For the most part, however, their provisions relating to the European Treaties are amendments and simply incorporated into the latter when accession takes place, and in the case of all but the most recent accessions have been superseded. Hence, there is little point in reproducing them here. What is reproduced, however, is a specimen model, since these remain distinct documents to which the acceding member states on occasion still refer. We also provide lists of the annexes, protocols, exchanges of letters and declarations associated with each accession. However, for reasons of space and the highly technical nature of many of these, we publish only the title of such documents and not their full text.

Annexes, Protocols, Exchanges of Letters and Declarations associated with the Accession of Denmark, Ireland and the United Kingdom to the EC in 1973*

Annexes

I	List referred to in Article 29 of the Act of Accession
II	List referred to in Article 30 of the Act of Accession
III	List of products referred to in Articles 32, 36 and 39 of the Act of Accession
IV	List of products referred to in Article 32 of the Act of Accession
V	List referred to in Article 107 of the Act of Accession
VI	List of countries referred to in Article 109 of the Act of Accession and in Protocol 22
VII	List referred to in Article 133 of the Act of Accession
VIII	List referred to in Article 148(1) of the Act of Accession
IX	List referred to in Article 148(2) of the Act of Accession
X	List referred to in Article 150 of the Act of Accession
XI	List referred to in Article 152 of the Act of Accession

Protocols

Protocol No. 1	on the Statute of the European Investment Bank [amended]
Protocol No. 2	on the Faroe Islands
Protocol No. 3	on the Channel Islands and the Isle of Man
Protocol No. 6	on certain quantitative restrictions relating to Ireland and Norway [amended]

*The list does not include those texts deleted by the Adaptation Decision (*OJ* L2, 1 January 1973) following Norway's non-ratification of the accession treaty. The full text of the annexes, protocols and declarations, as amended by Adaptation Decision 95/1 on 1 January 1973, can be found in *Documents Concerning the Accessions to the European Communities of the Kingdom of Denmark, Ireland and the United Kingdom of Great Britain and Northern Ireland, the Hellenic Republic, the Kingdom of Spain and the Portuguese Republic* (Luxembourg: OOPEC, 1987).

Exchanges of Letters

Exchange of Letters on Monetary Questions

Declarations *adopted* and annexed to the Final Act

1. Joint declaration on the Court of Justice
2. Joint declaration on the Sovereign Base Areas of the United Kingdom of Great Britain and Northern Ireland in Cyprus
3. Joint declaration on the fisheries sector

4. Joint declaration of intent on the development of trade relations with Ceylon, India, Malaysia, Pakistan and Singapore
5. Joint declaration on the free movement of workers

Declarations *noted* and annexed to the Final Act

Declaration by the Government of the Federal Republic of Germany on the application to Berlin of the Decision concerning Accession to the European Coal and Steel Community and the Treaty of Accession to the European Economic Community and the European Atomic Energy Community

Declarations *made* and annexed to the Final Act

1. Declaration by the Government of the United Kingdom of Great Britain and Northern Ireland on the definition of the term 'nationals' [Replaced on 1 January 1983, see *OJ* C23, 28 January 1983]
2. Declaration on the economic and industrial development of Ireland
3. Declarations on liquid milk, pigmeat and eggs
4. Declaration on the system of fixing Community farm prices
5. Declarations on hill farming

Annexes, Protocols and Declarations associated with the Accession of Greece to the EC in 1981*

Annexes

I	List referred to in Article 2 of the Act of Accession
II	List referred to in Article 22 of the Act of Accession
III	List of products referred to in Article 36(1) and (2) of the Act of Accession (Euratom)
IV	List of products referred to in Article 114 of the Act of Accession
V	List referred to in Article 115(1) of the Act of Accession
VI	List referred to in Article 115(3) of the Act of Accession
VII	List referred to in Article 117(1) of the Act of Accession
VIII	List referred to in Article 128 of the Act of Accession
IX	List referred to in Article 142(1) of the Act of Accession
X	List referred to in Article 142(2) of the Act of Accession
XI	List referred to in Article 144 of the Act of Accession
XII	List referred to in Article 145 of the Act of Accession

Protocols

Protocol No. 1   on the Statute of the European Investment Bank
Protocol No. 2   on the definition of the basic duty for matches falling within heading No. 36.06 of the Common Customs Tariff
Protocol No. 3   on the granting by the Hellenic Republic of exemption of customs duties on the import of certain products

*The full text of these can be found in *Documents Concerning the Accessions to the European Communities of the Kingdom of Denmark, Ireland and the United Kingdom of Great Britain and Northern Ireland, the Hellenic Republic, the Kingdom of Spain and the Portuguese Republic* (Luxembourg: OOPEC, 1987).

Protocol No. 4   on cotton
Protocol No. 5   on the participation of the Hellenic Republic in the funds of the
                 European Coal and Steel Community
Protocol No. 6   on the exchange of information with the Hellenic Republic in
                 the field of nuclear energy
Protocol No. 7   on the economic and industrial development of Greece

Declarations *adopted* and annexed to the Final Act

1. Joint declaration on the free movement of workers
2. Joint declaration on particular transitional measures which might be required
   in relations between Greece and Spain and Portugal after accession of the latter
   states
3. Joint declaration concerning Protocols to be concluded with certain third countries according to Article 118
4. Joint declaration on Mount Athos
5. Joint declaration on the procedure for the joint examination of national aids
   granted by the Hellenic Republic in the field of agriculture during the period
   prior to accession
6. Joint declaration on the joint examination procedure of the annual change in
   prices of agricultural products in Greece during the period prior to accession
7. Joint declaration on sugar, milk products, olive oil and products processed from
   fruit and vegetables
8. Joint declaration concerning the First Council Directive of 12 December 1977
   on the co-ordination of laws, regulations and administrative provisions relating
   to the taking up and pursuit of the business of credit institutions

Declarations *noted* and annexed to the Final Act

Declaration by the Government of the Federal Republic of Germany on the
application to Berlin of the Decision concerning Accession to the European Coal
and Steel Community and the Treaty of Accession to the European Economic
Community and the European Atomic Energy Community

Declaration by the Government of the Federal Republic of Germany on the
definition of the term 'nationals'

Declarations *made* and annexed to the Final Act

1. Declaration by the European Economic Community on Greek workers taking
   up and pursuing paid employment in the present Member States
2. Declaration by the European Economic Community on the European Regional
   Development Fund
3. Declaration by the Hellenic Republic on monetary questions

Annexes, Protocols and Declarations associated with the Accession of Spain and Portugal to the EC in 1986*

Annexes

I	List provided for in Article 26 of the Act of Accession
II	List provided for in Article 27 of the Act of Accession
III	List provided for in Article 43(1) first indent of the Act of Accession
IV	List provided for in Article 43(1) second indent of the Act of Accession
V	List provided for in Article 48(3) of the Act of Accession
VI	List provided for in Article 48(4) of the Act of Accession
VII	List provided for in Article 53 of the Act of Accession
VIII	List provided for in Article 75(3) of the Act of Accession
IX	List provided for in Article 158(1) of the Act of Accession
X	List provided for in Article 158(3) of the Act of Accession
XI	Technical procedures referred to in Article 163(3) of the Act of Accession
XII	List provided for in Article 168(4) of the Act of Accession
XIII	List provided for in Article 174 of the Act of Accession
XIV	List provided for in Article 176 of the Act of Accession
XV	List provided for in Article 177(3) of the Act of Accession
XVI	List provided for in Article 177(5) of the Act of Accession
XVII	List provided for in Article 178 of the Act of Accession
XVIII	List provided for in Article 200 of the Act of Accession
XIX	List provided for in Article 213 of the Act of Accession
XX	List provided for in Article 243(2) of the Act of Accession
XXI	List provided for in Article 245(1) of the Act of Accession
XXII	List provided for in Article 249(2) of the Act of Accession
XXIII	List provided for in Article 269(2) of the Act of Accession
XXIV	List provided for in Article 273(2) of the Act of Accession
XXV	List provided for in Article 278(1) of the Act of Accession
XXVI	List provided for in Article 280 of the Act of Accession
XXVII	List provided for in Article 355(3) of the Act of Accession
XXVIII	List provided for in Article 361 of the Act of Accession
XXIX	List provided for in Article 363 of the Act of Accession
XXX	List provided for in Article 364(3) of the Act of Accession
XXXI	List provided for in Article 365 of the Act of Accession
XXXII	List provided for in Article 378 of the Act of Accession
XXXIII	List provided for in Article 391(1) of the Act of Accession
XXXIV	List provided for in Article 391(2) of the Act of Accession
XXXV	List provided for in Article 393 of the Act of Accession
XXXVI	List provided for in Article 395 of the Act of Accession

Protocols

Protocol No. 1	on the Statute of the European Investment Bank
Protocol No. 2	concerning the Canary islands and Ceuta and Melilla

*The full text of these can be found in *Documents Concerning the Accessions to the European Communities of the Kingdom of Denmark, Ireland and the United Kingdom of Great Britain and Northern Ireland, the Hellenic Republic, the Kingdom of Spain and the Portuguese Republic* (Luxembourg: OOPEC, 1987).

Protocol No. 3   concerning the exchange of goods between Spain and Portugal for the period during which the transitional measures are applied

Protocol No. 4   Mechanism for additional responsibilities within the framework of Fisheries Agreements concluded by the Community with third countries

Protocol No. 5   on the participation of the new Member States in the funds of the European Coal and Steel Community

Protocol No. 6   concerning annual Spanish tariff quotas on the import of motor vehicles falling within subheading No. 87.02 A I b of the Common Customs Tariff referred to in Article 34 of the Act of Accession

Protocol No. 7   on Spanish quantitative quotas

Protocol No. 8   on Spanish patents

Protocol No. 9   on trade in textile products between Spain and the Community as at present constituted

Protocol No. 10   on the restructuring of the Spanish iron and steel industry

Protocol No. 11   on pricing rules

Protocol No. 12   on the regional development of Spain

Protocol No. 13   on the exchange of information with the Kingdom of Spain in the field of nuclear energy

Protocol No. 14   on cotton

Protocol No. 15   on the definition of the Portuguese basic duties for certain products

Protocol No. 16   on the granting by the Portuguese Republic of exemption from customs duties on the import of certain goods

Protocol No. 17   on trade in textile products between Portugal and the other Member States of the Community

Protocol No. 18   on the arrangements for the import of motor vehicles coming from other Member States

Protocol No. 19   on Portuguese patents

Protocol No. 20   on the restructuring of the Portuguese iron and steel industry

Protocol No. 21   on the economic and industrial development of Portugal

Protocol No. 22   on the exchange of information with the Portuguese Republic in the field of nuclear energy

Protocol No. 23   on the arrangements for the import into Portugal of motor vehicles coming from third countries

Protocol No. 24   on agricultural structures in Portugal

Protocol No. 25   on the application to Portugal of production disciplines introduced under the common agricultural policy

Declarations *adopted* and annexed to the Final Act

1. Joint declaration of intent on the development and intensification of relations with the countries of Latin America
2. Joint declaration concerning the economic and social development of the autonomous regions of the Azores and Madeira
3. Joint declaration on the free movement of workers
4. Joint declaration relating to workers from the present Member States established in Spain or Portugal and to Spanish and Portuguese workers established in the Community and members of their families

5. Joint declaration on the elimination of monopolies existing in the new Member States in the sphere of agriculture
6. Joint declaration on the adjustment of the 'acquis communautaire' in the vegetable oils and fats sector
7. Joint declaration on the arrangements applicable to trade in agricultural products between the Kingdom of Spain and the Portuguese Republic
8. Joint declaration on imports from third countries of products subject to the STM
9. Joint declaration on the application of the regulatory amount to table wines
10. Joint declaration on the STM in the cereals sector
11. Joint declaration on Protocol No. 2 concerning the Canary Islands and Ceuta and Melilla
12. Joint declaration on Protocol No. 2
13. Joint declaration on Article 9 of Protocol No. 2
14. Joint declaration concerning fisheries relations with third countries
15. Joint declaration concerning Protocols to be concluded with certain third countries
16. Joint declaration on the inclusion of the peseta and escudo in the ECU

Declarations *noted* and annexed to the Final Act

Declaration by the Government of the Federal Republic of Germany on the application to Berlin of the Decision concerning Accession to the European Coal and Steel Community and the Treaty of Accession to the European Economic Community and the European Atomic Energy Community

Declaration by the Government of the Federal Republic of Germany on the definition of the term 'nationals'

Declarations *made* and annexed to the Final Act

A. Joint Declarations: Community as at present constituted/Kingdom of Spain
  1. Joint declaration on the Spanish iron and steel industry
  2. Joint declaration on the prices of agricultural products in Spain
  3. Joint declaration on Spanish quality wines produced in specified regions
  4. Joint declaration on certain transitional measures and certain data of an agricultural nature with regard to Spain
  5. Joint declaration on the action programme to be drawn up for the verification of convergence phase in the fruit and vegetable sector with regard to Spain
  6. Joint declaration on the incidence in trade with the other Member States of national aid maintained on a transitional basis by the Kingdom of Spain
  7. Joint declaration on the application in Spain of Community socio-structural measures in the wine sector and provisions enabling the origin to be determined and the commercial movements of Spanish wine to be followed
  8. Joint declaration on future trade arrangements with Andorra

B. Joint Declarations: Community as at present constituted/Portuguese Republic
  1. Joint declaration concerning access to the Portuguese oil market
  2. Joint declaration on the Portuguese iron and steel industry
  3. Joint declaration concerning the First Council Directive of 12 December 1977 on the co-ordination of laws, regulations and administrative provisions relating to the taking up and pursuit of the business of credit institutions

4. Joint declaration on the prices of agricultural products in Portugal
5. Joint declaration on the action programme for the first stage of transition to be drawn up for the products subject to transition by stages with regard to Portugal
6. Joint declaration on certain transitional measures and certain data of an agricultural nature with regard to Portugal
7. Joint declaration on wine in Portugal
8. Joint declaration on supplies to the sugar refining industry in Portugal
9. Joint declaration concerning the introduction of the common system of value-added tax in Portugal

C. Declarations by the European Economic Community
1. Declaration by the European Economic Community on Spanish and Portuguese workers taking up and pursuing paid employment in the present Member States
2. Declaration by the European Economic Community on the participation of Spain and Portugal in the benefits derived from the resources of the European Social Fund
3. Declaration by the European Economic Community on the participation of Spain and Portugal in the benefits derived from the resources of the European Regional Development Fund
4. Declaration by the European Economic Community on supplies to the sugar refining industry in Portugal
5. Declaration by the European Economic Community on Community aid for monitoring and supervising the waters
6. Declaration by the European Economic Community on the adaptation and modernization of the Portuguese economy
7. Declaration by the European Economic Community on the application of the Community loan mechanism in favour of Portugal
8. Declaration by the European Economic Community on the application of the regulatory amount

D. Declarations by the Kingdom of Spain
1. Declaration by the Kingdom of Spain: CECAF zone
2. Declaration by the Kingdom of Spain on Latin America
3. Declaration by the Kingdom of Spain on Euratom

E. Declarations by the Portuguese Republic
1. Declaration by the Portuguese Republic on compensatory indemnities referred to in Article 358
2. Declaration by the Portuguese Republic: CECAF zone
3. Declaration by the Portuguese Republic on monetary questions

Annexes, Protocols, Exchanges of Letters and Declarations associated with the Accession of Austria, Finland and Sweden to the EC in 1995*

Annexes

I   List provided for in Article 29 of the Act of Accession [replaced]
II   List provided for in Article 30 of the Act of Accession [amended]
VI   List provided for in Articles 53, 73, 97 and 126 of the Act of Accession [amended]
VIII Provisions referred to in Article 69 of the Act of Accession
IX   List provided for in Article 71(2) of the Act of Accession
X   Provisions referred to in Article 84 of the Act of Accession
XI   List provided for in Article 99 of the Act of Accession
XII   Provisions referred to in Article 112 of the Act of Accession
XIII List provided for in Article 138(5) of the Act of Accession [amended]
XIV   List provided for in Article 140 of the Act of Accession [amended]
XV   List provided for in Article 151 of the Act of Accession [amended]
XVI   List provided for in Article 165(1) of the Act of Accession
XVII List provided for in Article 165(2) of the Act of Accession
XVIII List provided for in Article 167 of the Act of Accession [amended]
XIX   List provided for in Article 168 of the Act of Accession

Protocols

Protocol No. 1   on the Statute of the European Investment Bank [amended]
Protocol No. 2   on the Åland islands
Protocol No. 3   on the Sami people [amended]
Protocol No. 5   on the participation of the new Member States in the funds of the European Coal and Steel Community [amended]
Protocol No. 6   on special provisions for Objective 6 in the framework of the Structural Funds in Finland and Sweden [amended]
Protocol No. 8   on elections to the European Parliament in certain Member States during the interim period
Protocol No. 9   on road, rail and combined transport in Austria
Protocol No. 10   on the use of specific Austrian terms of the German language in the framework of the European Union

Declarations *adopted* and annexed to the Final Act

1. Joint Declaration on Common Foreign and Security Policy
2. Joint Declaration on Article 157(4) of the Act of Accession
3. Joint Declaration on the Court of Justice of the European Communities
4. Joint Declaration on the application of the Euratom Treaty
5. Joint Declaration on secondary residences

---

*The list does not include those texts deleted by Decision 95/1/ EC, Euratom, ECSC (*OJ* L1, 1 January 1995) following Norway's non-ratification of the accession treaty. The full text of the protocols and declarations, as amended by Decision 95/1 on 1 January 1995, can be found in *Documents Concerning the Accession of the Republic of Austria, the Republic of Finland, and the Kingdom of Sweden to the European Union* (Luxembourg: OOPEC, 1995). The annexes in the pre-Adaptation Decision form appear in *OJ* L73 (27 March 1972).

6. Joint Declaration on standards for the protection of the environment, health and product safety
7. Joint Declaration on Articles 32, 69, 84 and 112 of the Act of Accession
8. Joint Declaration on the institutional procedures of the Accession Treaty
9. Joint Declaration on Article 172 of the Act of Accession

Exchanges of Letters

Exchange of Letters between the European Union and the . . . [acceding states] on an information and consultation procedure for the adoption of certain decisions and other measures to be taken during the period preceding accession

Declarations *made* and annexed to the Final Act

A. Joint Declarations: The present Member States/Kingdom of Norway
10. Joint Declaration on the management of fisheries in waters north of 62° N
11. Joint Declaration on the 12-mile limit
12. Joint Declaration on ownership of fishing vessels
13. Joint Declaration on the supply of raw material for the fish processing industry in northern Norway
14. Declaration on Article 147 on the Norwegian food processing industry
15. Joint Declaration on Svalbard

B. Joint Declarations: The present Member States/Republic of Austria
16. Joint Declaration on the free movement of workers
17. Joint Declaration on safeguard measures under the agreements with countries of Central and Eastern Europe
18. Joint Declaration on the resolution of outstanding technical questions in the transport field
19. Joint Declaration on weights and dimensions for road transport vehicles
20. Joint Declaration on the Brenner base tunnel
21. Joint Declaration on Articles 6 and 76 of the Act of Accession

C. Joint Declarations: The present Member States/Republic of Finland
22. Joint Declaration on safeguarding Finland's transport links
23. Joint Declaration on the shipment of radioactive waste
24. Joint Declaration on the Non-Proliferation Treaty

D. Joint Declarations: The present Member States/Kingdom of Sweden
25. Joint Declaration on the Non-Proliferation Treaty
26. Joint Declaration on Article 127 of the Act of Accession

E. Joint Declarations: The present Member States/Various new Member States
27. Joint Declaration: Norway, Austria, Sweden: on PCB/PCT
28. Joint Declaration on Nordic co-operation
29. Joint Declaration on the number of animals eligible for the suckler-cow premium for Norway and Finland
30. Joint Declaration: Finland, Sweden: on the fishing possibilities in the Baltic Sea
31. Declaration on the processing industry in Austria and Finland

v Related Documents

Having dealt with the lesser known European Treaties, the *Guide* now turns briefly to consider some further documents which affect the operation of the EU. The first is the Stability and Growth Pact launched at Amsterdam in June 1997. The second, is the Charter of Fundamental Rights which was 'proclaimed' at Nice in December 2000. Like the Stability and Growth Pact, it sits in the shadows of the European Treaties. This is due to the fact that it is legally binding on neither the institutions nor the member states of the EU. It does nevertheless enjoy a privileged status among the wealth of documents which surround the European Treaties since not only is there pressure to draw up an EU

Constitution based in part on it, but the ECJ has already begun to take note of the Charter in its deliberations. The Stability and Growth Pact too enjoys a privileged status with two of its elements consisting of binding regulations at the core of economic policy within the EU.

Stability and Growth Pact

The Stability and Growth Pact emerged out of discussions, initiated by Germany in 1995, aimed at ensuring that member states respect their obligations under the TEC to avoid an excessive deficit. The idea behind the pact was that strong commitment to maintaining fiscal discipline would help bolster the international credibility of Economic and Monetary Union. This rightly implied, as Snyder notes, much greater emphasis on stability as opposed to growth and is reflected in both the content and the wording of the pact's three main elements, the first of which is the Resolution of the European Council on the Stability and Growth Pact adopted by the Amsterdam European Council.

The resolution provides, however, only 'political guidance' and is not legally binding. To implement it two regulations have been adopted: Council Regulation (EC) No. 1466/97 of 7 July 1997 on the strengthening of the surveillance of budgetary positions and the surveillance and co-ordination of economic policies and Council Regulation (EC) No. 1467/97 of 7 July 1997 on speeding up and clarifying the implementation of the excessive deficit procedure. These most definitely place legal obligations on the member states and are discussed by Hahn. The same cannot be said for the final element of the pact, the Resolution on Growth and Employment. This too was adopted at Amsterdam and was the result of French pressure to ensure that a clearer balance would exist within EMU between budgetary discipline and employment policy. While, politically, adoption of the resolution was important, the fact that it has not been followed by any implementing regulations means that its position within the Stability and Growth Pact is essentially secondary.

Resolution of the European Council on the Stability and Growth Pact

Amsterdam, 17 June 1997

I. Meeting in Madrid in December 1995, the European Council confirmed the crucial importance of securing budgetary discipline in stage three of economic and monetary union (EMU). In Florence, six months later, the European Council reiterated this view and in Dublin, in December 1996, it reached an agreement on the main elements of the Stability and Growth Pact. In stage three of EMU, Member States shall avoid excessive general government deficits: this is a clear Treaty obligation.* The European Council underlines the importance of safeguarding sound government finances as a means to strengthening the conditions for price stability and for strong sustainable growth conducive to employment creation. It is also necessary to ensure that national budgetary policies support stability oriented monetary policies. Adherence to the objective of sound budgetary positions close to balance or in surplus will allow all Member States to deal with

*Under Article 5 of Protocol 11, this obligation does not apply to the United Kingdom unless it moves to the third stage; the obligation under Article 116(4) of the Treaty establishing the European Community to endeavour to avoid excessive deficits shall continue to apply to the United Kingdom.

normal cyclical fluctuations while keeping the government deficit within the reference value of 3% of GDP.

II. Meeting in Dublin in December 1996, the European Council requested the preparation of a Stability and Growth Pact to be achieved in accordance with the principles and procedures of the Treaty. This Stability and Growth Pact in no way changes the requirements for participation in stage three of EMU, either in the first group or at a later date. Member States remain responsible for their national budgetary policies, subject to the provisions of the Treaty; they will take the necessary measures in order to meet their responsibilities in accordance with those provisions.

III. The Stability and Growth Pact, which provides both for prevention and deterrence, consists of this Resolution and two Council Regulations, one on the strengthening of the surveillance of budgetary positions and the surveillance and co-ordination of economic policies and another on speeding up and clarifying the implementation of the excessive deficit procedure.

IV. The European Council solemnly invites all parties, namely the Member States, the Council of the European Union and the Commission of the European Communities, to implement the Treaty and the Stability and Growth Pact in a strict and timely manner. This Resolution provides firm political guidance to the parties who will implement the Stability and Growth Pact. To this end, the European Council has agreed upon the following guidelines:

THE MEMBER STATES

1. commit themselves to respect the medium-term budgetary objective of positions close to balance or in surplus set out in their stability or convergence programmes and to take the corrective budgetary action they deem necessary to meet the objectives of their stability or convergence programmes, whenever they have information indicating actual or expected significant divergence from those objectives;

2. are invited to make public, on their own initiative, the Council recommendations made to them in accordance with Article 99(4);

3. commit themselves to take the corrective budgetary action they deem necessary to meet the objectives of their stability or convergence programmes once they receive an early warning in the form of a Council recommendation issued under Article 99(4);

4. will launch the corrective budgetary adjustments they deem necessary without delay on receiving information indicating the risk of an excessive deficit;

5. will correct excessive deficits as quickly as possible after their emergence; this correction should be completed no later than the year following the identification of the excessive deficit, unless there are special circumstances;

6. are invited to make public, on their own initiative, recommendations made in accordance with Article 104(7);

7. commit themselves not to invoke the benefit of Article 2(3) of the Council Regulation on speeding up and clarifying the excessive deficit procedure unless they are in severe recession; in evaluating whether the economic downturn is severe, the Member States will, as a rule, take as a reference point an annual fall in real GDP of at least 0.75%.

THE COMMISSION

1. will exercise its right of initiative under the Treaty in a manner that facilitates the strict, timely and effective functioning of the Stability and Growth Pact;

2. will present, without delay, the necessary reports, opinions and recommendations to enable the Council to adopt decisions under Article 99 and Article 104; this will facilitate the effective functioning of the early warning system and the rapid launch and strict application of the excessive deficit procedure;

3. commits itself to prepare a report under Article 104(3) whenever there is the risk of an excessive deficit or whenever the planned or actual government deficit exceeds the reference value of 3% of GDP, thereby triggering the procedure under Article 104(3);

4. commits itself, in the event that the Commission considers that a deficit exceeding 3% of GDP is not excessive and this opinion differs from that of the Economic and Financial Committee, to present in writing to the Council the reasons for its position;

5. commits itself, following a request from the Council under Article 115, to make, as a rule, a recommendation for a Council decision on whether an excessive deficit exists under Article 104(6).

THE COUNCIL

1. is committed to a rigorous and timely implementation of all elements of the Stability and Growth Pact in its competence; it will take the necessary decisions under Article 99 and Article 104 as is practicable;

2. is urged to regard the deadlines for the application of the excessive deficit procedure as upper limits; in particular, the Council, acting under Article 104(7), shall recommend that excessive deficits be corrected as quickly as possible after their emergence, no later than the year following their identification, unless there are special circumstances;

3. is invited always to impose sanctions if a participating Member State fails to take the necessary steps to bring the excessive deficit situation to an end as recommended by the Council;

4. is urged always to require a non-interest bearing deposit, whenever the Council decides to impose sanctions on a participating Member State in accordance with Article 104(11);

5. is urged always to convert a deposit into a fine after two years of the decision to impose sanctions in accordance with Article 104(11), unless the excessive deficit has in the view of the Council been corrected;

6. is invited always to state in writing the reasons which justify a decision not to act if at any stage of the excessive deficit or surveillance of budgetary positions procedures the Council did not act on a Commission recommendation and, in such a case, to make public the votes cast by each Member State.

Council Regulation (EC) No. 1466/97 of 7 July 1997 on the strengthening of the surveillance of budgetary positions and the surveillance and co-ordination of economic policies (*OJ* L 209, 2 August 1997)

THE COUNCIL OF THE EUROPEAN UNION,

Having regard to the Treaty establishing the European Community, and in particular Article 99(5) thereof,

Having regard to the proposal from the Commission,*

Acting in accordance with the procedure referred to in Article 252 of the Treaty,†

(1) Whereas the Stability and Growth Pact is based on the objective of sound government finances as a means of strengthening the conditions for price stability and for strong sustainable growth conducive to employment creation;

(2) Whereas the Stability and Growth Pact consists of this Regulation which aims to strengthen the surveillance of budgetary positions and the surveillance and co-ordination of economic policies, of Council Regulation (EC) No. 1467/97‡ which aims to speed up and to clarify the implementation of the excessive deficit procedure and of the Resolution of the European Council of 17 June 1997 on the Stability and Growth Pact,§ in which, in accordance with Article 4 of the Treaty on European Union, firm political guidelines are issued in order to implement the Stability and Growth Pact in a strict and timely manner and in particular to adhere to the medium-term objective of budgetary positions of close to balance or in surplus, to which all Member States are committed, and to take the corrective budgetary action they deem necessary to meet the objectives of their stability and convergence programmes, whenever they have information indicating actual or expected significant divergence from the medium-term budgetary objective;

(3) Whereas in stage three of economic and monetary union (EMU) the Member States are, according to Article *104* of the Treaty, under a clear Treaty obligation to avoid excessive general government deficits; whereas under Article 5 of Protocol (No. 11) on certain provisions relating to the United Kingdom of Great Britain and Northern Ireland to the Treaty, Article *104*(1) does not apply to the United Kingdom unless it moves to the third stage; whereas the obligation under Article *116*(4) to endeavour to avoid excessive deficits will continue to apply to the United Kingdom;

(4) Whereas adherence to the medium-term objective of budgetary positions close to balance or in surplus will allow Member States to deal with normal cyclical fluctuations while keeping the government deficit within the 3 % of GDP reference value;

(5) Whereas it is appropriate to complement the multilateral surveillance procedure of Article 99(3) and (4) with an early warning system, under which the Council will alert a Member State at an early stage to the need to take the necessary budgetary corrective action in order to prevent a government deficit becoming excessive;

OJ C 368, 6.12.1996, p. 9.

†Opinion of the European Parliament of 28 November 1996 (*OJ* C 380, 16.12.1996, p. 28), Council Common Position of 14 April 1997 (*OJ* C 146, 30.5.1997, p. 26) and Decision of the European Parliament of 29 May 1997 (*OJ* C 182, 16.6.1997).

‡*OJ* L 209, 2.8.1997, p. 6. See above, pp. 616–23.

§*OJ* C 236, 2.8.1997, p. 1. See above, pp. 607–9.

(6) Whereas the multilateral surveillance procedure of Article 99(3) and (4) should furthermore continue to monitor the full range of economic developments in each of the Member States and in the Community as well as the consistency of economic policies with the broad economic guidelines referred to in Article 99(2); whereas for the monitoring of these developments, the presentation of information in the form of stability and convergence programmes is appropriate;

(7) Whereas there is a need to build upon the useful experience gained during the first two stages of economic and monetary union with convergence programmes;

(8) Whereas the Member States adopting the single currency, hereafter referred to as 'participating Member States', will, in accordance with Article 121, have achieved a high degree of sustainable convergence and in particular a sustainable government financial position; whereas the maintenance of sound budgetary positions in these Member States will be necessary to support price stability and to strengthen the conditions for the sustained growth of output and employment; whereas it is necessary that participating Member States submit medium-term programmes, hereafter referred to as 'stability programmes'; whereas it is necessary to define the principal contents of such programmes;

(9) Whereas the Member States not adopting the single currency, hereafter referred to as 'non-participating Member States', will need to pursue policies aimed at a high degree of sustainable convergence; whereas it is necessary that these Member States submit medium-term programmes, hereafter referred to as 'convergence programmes'; whereas it is necessary to define the principal contents of such convergence programmes;

(10) Whereas in its Resolution of 16 June 1997 on the establishment of an exchange-rate mechanism in the third stage of economic and monetary union, the European Council issued firm political guidelines in accordance with which an exchange-rate mechanism is established in the third stage of EMU, hereafter referred to as 'ERM2'; whereas the currencies of non-participating Member States joining ERM2 will have a central rate vis-à-vis the euro, thereby providing a reference point for judging the adequacy of their policies; whereas the ERM2 will also help to protect them and the Member States adopting the euro from unwarranted pressures in the foreign-exchange markets; whereas, so as to enable appropriate surveillance in the Council, non-participating Member States not joining ERM2 will nevertheless present policies in their convergence programmes oriented to stability thus avoiding real exchange rate misalignments and excessive nominal exchange rate fluctuations;

(11) Whereas lasting convergence of economic fundamentals is a prerequisite for sustainable exchange rate stability;

(12) Whereas it is necessary to lay down a timetable for the submission of stability programmes and convergence programmes and their updates;

(13) Whereas in the interest of transparency and informed public debate it is necessary that Member States make public their stability programmes and their convergence programmes;

(14) Whereas the Council, when examining and monitoring the stability programmes and the convergence programmes and in particular their medium-term budgetary objective or the targeted adjustment path towards this objective, should take into account the relevant cyclical and structural characteristics of the economy of each Member State;

(15) Whereas in this context particular attention should be given to significant divergences of budgetary positions from the budgetary objectives of being close to balance or in surplus; whereas it is appropriate for the Council to give an early warning in order to prevent a government deficit in a Member State becoming excessive; whereas in the event of persistent budgetary slippage it will be appropriate for the Council to reinforce its recommendation and make it public; whereas for non-participating Member States the Council may make recommendations on action to be taken to give effect to their convergence programmes;

(16) Whereas both convergence and stability programmes lead to the fulfilment of the conditions of economic convergence referred to in Article *104*,

HAS ADOPTED THIS REGULATION:

SECTION 1   PURPOSE AND DEFINITIONS

Article 1

This Regulation sets out the rules covering the content, the submission, the examination and the monitoring of stability programmes and convergence programmes as part of multilateral surveillance by the Council so as to prevent, at an early stage, the occurrence of excessive general government deficits and to promote the surveillance and co-ordination of economic policies.

Article 2

For the purpose of this Regulation 'participating Member States' shall mean those Member States which adopt the single currency in accordance with the Treaty and 'non-participating Member States' shall mean those which have not adopted the single currency.

SECTION 2   STABILITY PROGRAMMES

Article 3

1. Each participating Member State shall submit to the Council and Commission information necessary for the purpose of multilateral surveillance at regular intervals under Article 99 of the Treaty in the form of a stability programme, which provides an essential basis for price stability and for strong sustainable growth conducive to employment creation.

2. A stability programme shall present the following information:
    (a) the medium-term objective for the budgetary position of close to balance or in surplus and the adjustment path towards this objective for the general government surplus/deficit and the expected path of the general government debt ratio;
    (b) the main assumptions about expected economic developments and important economic variables which are relevant to the realization of the stability programme such as government investment expenditure, real gross domestic product (GDP) growth, employment and inflation;
    (c) a description of budgetary and other economic policy measures being taken and/or proposed to achieve the objectives of the programme, and, in the case of the main budgetary measures, an assessment of their quantitative effects on the budget;
    (d) an analysis of how changes in the main economic assumptions would affect the budgetary and debt position.

3. The information about paths for the general government surplus/deficit ratio and debt ratio and the main economic assumptions referred to in paragraph 2(a) and (b) shall be on an annual basis and shall cover, as well as the current and preceding year, at least the following three years.

Article 4

1. Stability programmes shall be submitted before 1 March 1999. Thereafter, updated programmes shall be submitted annually. Member States adopting the single currency at a later stage shall submit a stability programme within six months of the Council Decision on its participation in the single currency.

2. Member States shall make public their stability programmes and updated programmes.

Article 5

1. Based on assessments by the Commission and the Committee set up by Article 114 of the Treaty, the Council shall, within the framework of multilateral surveillance under Article 99, examine whether the medium-term budget objective in the stability programme provides for a safety margin to ensure the avoidance of an excessive deficit, whether the economic assumptions on which the programme is based are realistic and whether the measures being taken and/or proposed are sufficient to achieve the targeted adjustment path towards the medium-term budgetary objective.

The Council shall furthermore examine whether the contents of the stability programme facilitate the closer co-ordination of economic policies and whether the economic policies of the Member State concerned are consistent with the broad economic policy guidelines.

2. The Council shall carry out the examination of the stability programme referred to in paragraph 1 within at most two months of the submission of the programme. The Council, on a recommendation from the Commission and after consulting the Committee set up by Article 114, shall deliver an opinion on the programme. Where the Council, in accordance with Article 99, considers that the objectives and contents of a programme should be strengthened, the Council shall, in its opinion, invite the Member State concerned to adjust its programme.

3. Updated stability programmes shall be examined by the Committee set up by Article 114 on the basis of assessments by the Commission; if necessary, updated programmes may also be examined by the Council in accordance with the procedure set out in paragraphs 1 and 2 of this Article.

Article 6

1. As part of multilateral surveillance in accordance with Article 99(3), the Council shall monitor the implementation of stability programmes, on the basis of information provided by participating Member States and of assessments by the Commission and the Committee set up by Article 114, in particular with a view to identifying actual or expected significant divergence of the budgetary position from the medium-term budgetary objective, or the adjustment path towards it, as set in the programme for the government surplus/deficit.

2. In the event that the Council identifies significant divergence of the budgetary position from the medium-term budgetary objective, or the adjustment path towards it, it shall, with a view to giving early warning in order to prevent the occurrence of an excessive deficit, address, in accordance with Article 99(4), a

recommendation to the Member State concerned to take the necessary adjustment measures.

3. In the event that the Council in its subsequent monitoring judges that the divergence of the budgetary position from the medium-term budgetary objective, or the adjustment path towards it, is persisting or worsening, the Council shall, in accordance with Article 99(4), make a recommendation to the Member State concerned to take prompt corrective measures and may, as provides in that Article, make its recommendation public.

SECTION 3   CONVERGENCE PROGRAMMES

Article 7

1. Each non-participating Member State shall submit to the Council and the Commission information necessary for the purpose of multilateral surveillance of regular intervals under Article 99 in the form of a convergence programme, which provides an essential basis for price stability and for strong sustainable growth conducive to employment creation.

2. A convergence programme shall present the following information in particular on variables related to convergence:

  (a) the medium-term objective for the budgetary position of close to balance or in surplus and the adjustment path towards this objective for the general government surplus/deficit; the expected path for the general government debt ratio; the medium-term monetary policy objectives; the relationship of those objectives to price and exchange rate stability;

  (b) the main assumptions about expected economic developments and important economic variables which are relevant to the realization of the convergence programme, such as government investment expenditure, real GDP growth, employment and inflation;

  (c) a description of budgetary and other economic policy measures being taken and/or proposed to achieve the objectives of the programme, and, in the case of the main budgetary measures, an assessment of their quantitative effects on the budget;

  (d) an analysis of how changes in the main economic assumptions would affect the budgetary and debt position.

3. The information about paths for the general government surplus/deficit ratio, debt ratio and the main economic assumptions referred to in paragraph 2(a) and (b) shall be on an annual basis and shall cover, as well as the current and preceding year, at least the following three years.

Article 8

1. Convergence programmes shall be submitted before 1 March 1999. Thereafter, updated programmes shall be submitted annually.

2. Member States shall make public their convergence programmes and updated programmes.

Article 9

1. Based on assessments by the Commission and the Committee set up by Article 114 of the Treaty, the Council shall, within the framework of multilateral surveillance under Article 99, examine whether the medium-term budget objective in the

convergence programme provides for a safety margin to ensure the avoidance of an excessive deficit, whether the economic assumptions on which the programme is based are realistic and whether the measures being taken and/or proposed are sufficient to achieve the targeted adjustment path towards the medium-term objective and to achieve sustained convergence.

The Council shall furthermore examine whether the contents of the convergence programme facilitate the closer co-ordination of economic policies and whether the economic policies of the Member State concerned are consistent with the broad economic policy guidelines.

2. The Council shall carry out the examination of the convergence programme referred to in paragraph 1 within at most two months of the submission of the programme. The Council, on a recommendation from the Commission and after consulting the Committee set up by Article 114, shall deliver an opinion on the programme. Where the Council, in accordance with Article 99, considers that the objectives and contents of a programme should be strengthened, the Council shall, in its opinion, invite the Member State concerned to adjust its programme.

3. Updated convergence programmes shall be examined by the Committee set up by Article 114 on the basis of assessments by the Commission; if necessary, updated programmes may also be examined by the Council in accordance with the procedure set out in paragraphs 1 and 2 of this Article.

Article 10

1. As part of multilateral surveillance in accordance with Article 99(3), the Council shall monitor the implementation of convergence programmes on the basis of information provided by non-participating Member States in accordance with Article 7(2)(a) of this Regulation and of assessments by the Commission and the Committee set up by Article 114 of the Treaty, in particular with a view to identifying actual or expected significant divergence of the budgetary position from the medium-term budgetary objective, or the adjustment path towards it, as set in the programme for the government surplus/deficit.

In addition, the Council shall monitor the economic policies of non-participating Member States in the light of convergence programme objectives with a view to ensure that their policies are geared to stability and thus to avoid real exchange rate misalignments and excessive nominal exchange rate fluctuations.

2. In the event that the Council identifies significant divergence of the budgetary position from the medium-term budgetary objective, or the adjustment path towards it, it shall, with a view to giving early warning in order to prevent the occurrence of an excessive deficit, address in accordance with Article 99(4), a recommendation to the Member State concerned to take the necessary adjustment measures.

3. In the event that the Council in its subsequent monitoring judges that the divergence of the budgetary position from the medium-term budgetary objective, or the adjustment path towards it, is persisting or worsening, the Council shall, in accordance with Article 99(4), make a recommendation to the Member State concerned to take prompt corrective measures and may, as provided in that Article, make its recommendation public.

SECTION 4   COMMON PROVISIONS

Article 11

As part of the multilateral surveillance described in this Regulation, the Council shall carry out the overall assessment described in Article 99(3).

Article 12

In accordance with the second subparagraph of Article 99(4) the President of the Council and the Commission shall include in their report to the European Parliament the results of the multilateral surveillance carried out under this Regulation.

Article 13

This Regulation shall enter into force on 1 July 1998.
This Regulation shall be binding in its entirety and directly applicable in all Member States.
Done at Brussels, 7 July 1997.

Council Regulation (EC) No. 1467/97 of 7 July 1997 on speeding up and clarifying the implementation of the excessive deficit procedure (OJ L 209, 2 August 1997)

THE COUNCIL OF THE EUROPEAN UNION,

Having regard to the Treaty establishing the European Community, and in particular the second subparagraph of Article 104(14) thereof,
Having regard to the proposal from the Commission,*
Having regard to the opinion of the European Parliament,†
Having regard to the opinion of the European Monetary Institute,

(1) Whereas it is necessary to speed up and to clarify the excessive deficit procedure set out in Article *104* of the Treaty in order to deter excessive general government deficits and, if they occur, to further their prompt correction; whereas the provisions of this Regulation, which are to the above effect and adopted under Article *104*(14) second subparagraph, constitute, together with those of Protocol (No. 5) to the Treaty, a new integrated set of rules for the application of Article *104*;

(2) Whereas the Stability and Growth Pact is based on the objective of sound government finances as a means of strengthening the conditions for price stability and for strong sustainable growth conducive to employment creation;

(3) Whereas the Stability and Growth Pact consists of this Regulation, of Council Regulation (EC) No. 1466/97‡ which aims to strengthen the surveillance of budgetary positions and the surveillance and co-ordination of economic policies and of the Resolution of the European Council of 17 June 1997 on the Stability and Growth Pact,§ in which, in accordance with Article 4 of the Treaty on European Union, firm political guidelines are issued in order to implement the Stability and Growth Pact in a strict and timely manner and in particular to adhere to the medium-term objective for budgetary positions of close to balance or in

---

*OJ C 368, 6.12.1996, p. 12.
†OJ C 380, 16.12.1996, p. 29.
‡OJ L 209, 2.8.1997, p. 1. See above, pp. 610–16.
§OJ C 236, 2.8.1997, p. 1. See above, pp. 607–9.

surplus, to which all Member States are committed, and to take the corrective budgetary action they deem necessary to meet the objectives of their stability and convergence programmes, whenever they have information indicating actual or expected significant divergence from the medium-term budgetary objective;

(4) Whereas in stage three of economic and monetary union (EMU) the Member States are, according to Article 104 of the Treaty, under a clear Treaty obligation to avoid excessive government deficits; whereas under Article 5 of Protocol (No. 11) to the Treaty, paragraphs 1, 9 and 11 of Article 104 do not apply to the United Kingdom unless it moves to the third stage; whereas the obligation under Article 116(4) to endeavour to avoid excessive deficits will continue to apply to the United Kingdom;

(5) Whereas Denmark, referring to paragraph 1 of Protocol (No. 12) to the Treaty has notified, in the context of the Edinburgh decision of 12 December 1992, that it will not participate in the third stage; whereas, therefore, in accordance with paragraph 2 of the said Protocol, paragraphs 9 and 11 of Article 104 shall not apply to Denmark;

(6) Whereas in stage three of EMU Member States remain responsible for their national budgetary policies, subject to the provisions of the Treaty; whereas the Member States will take the necessary measures in order to meet their responsibilities in accordance with the provisions of the Treaty;

(7) Whereas adherence to the medium-term objective of budgetary positions close to balance or in surplus to which all Member States are committed, contributes to the creation of the appropriate conditions for price stability and for sustained growth conducive to employment creation in all Member States and will allow them to deal with normal cyclical fluctuations while keeping the government deficit within the 3% of GDP reference value;

(8) Whereas for EMU to function properly, it is necessary that convergence of economic and budgetary performances of Member States which have adopted the single currency, hereafter referred to as 'participating Member States', proves stable and durable; whereas budgetary discipline is necessary in stage three of EMU to safeguard price stability;

(9) Whereas according to Article 122(3) Articles 104(9) and (11) only apply to participating Member States;

(10) Whereas it is necessary to define the concept of an exceptional and temporary excess over the reference value as referred to in Article 104(2)(a); whereas the Council should in this context, *inter alia*, take account of the pluriannual budgetary forecasts provided by the Commission;

(11) Whereas a Commission report in accordance with Article 104(3) is also to take into account whether the government deficit exceeds government investment expenditure and take into account all other relevant factors, including the medium-term economic and budgetary position of the Member State;

(12) Whereas there is a need to establish deadlines for the implementation of the excessive deficit procedure in order to ensure its expeditious and effective implementation; whereas it is necessary in this context to take account of the fact that the budgetary year of the United Kingdom does not coincide with the calendar year;

(13) Whereas there is a need to specify how the sanctions provided for in Article

104 could be imposed in order to ensure the effective implementation of the excessive deficit procedure;

(14) Whereas reinforced surveillance under the Council Regulation (EC) No. 1466/97 together with the Commission's monitoring of budgetary positions in accordance with paragraph 2 of Article *104* should facilitate the effective and rapid implementation of the excessive deficit procedure;

(15) Whereas in the light of the above, in the event that a participating Member State fails to take effective action to correct an excessive deficit, an overall maximum period of ten months from the reporting date of the figures indicating the existence of an excessive deficit until the decision to impose sanctions, if necessary, seems both feasible and appropriate in order to exert pressure on the participating Member State concerned to take such action; in this event, and if the procedure starts in March, this would lead to sanctions being imposed within the calendar year in which the procedure had been started;

(16) Whereas the Council recommendation for the correction of an excessive deficit or the later steps of the excessive deficit procedure, should have been anticipated by the Member State concerned, which would have had an early warning; whereas the seriousness of an excessive deficit in stage three should call for urgent action from all those involved;

(17) Whereas it is appropriate to hold the excessive deficit procedure in abeyance if the Member State concerned takes appropriate action in response to a recommendation under Article *104*(7) or a notice issued under Article *104*(9) in order to provide an incentive to Member States to act accordingly; whereas the time period during which the procedure would be held in abeyance should not be included in the maximum period of ten months between the reporting date indicating the existence of an excessive deficit and the imposition of sanctions; whereas it is appropriate to resume the procedure immediately if the envisaged action is not being implemented or if the implemented action is proving to be inadequate;

(18) Whereas, in order to ensure that the excessive deficit procedure has a sufficient deterrent effect, a non-interest-bearing deposit of an appropriate size should be required from the participating Member State concerned, whenever the Council decides to impose a sanction;

(19) Whereas the definition of sanctions on a prescribed scale is conducive to legal certainty; whereas it is appropriate to relate the amount of the deposit to the GDP of the participating Member State concerned;

(20) Whereas, whenever the imposition of a non-interest-bearing deposit does not induce the participating Member State concerned to correct its excessive deficit in due time, it is appropriate to intensify the sanctions; whereas it is then appropriate to transform the deposit into a fine;

(21) Whereas appropriate action by the participating Member State concerned in order to correct its excessive deficit is the first step towards abrogation of sanctions; whereas significant progress in correcting the excessive deficit should allow for the lifting of sanctions in accordance with paragraph 12 of Article *104*; whereas the abrogation of all outstanding sanctions should only occur once the excessive deficit has been totally corrected;

(22) Whereas Council Regulation (EC) No. 3605/93 of 22 November 1993 on the application of the Protocol on the excessive deficit procedure annexed to the

Treaty establishing the European Community* contains detailed rules for the reporting of budgetary data by Member States;

(23) Whereas, according to Article 117(8), where the Treaty provides for a consultative role for the European Central Bank (ECB), references to the ECB shall be read as referring to the European Monetary Institute before the establishment of the ECB,

HAS ADOPTED THIS REGULATION:

SECTION 1   DEFINITIONS AND ASSESSMENTS

Article 1

1. This Regulation sets out the provisions to speed up and clarify the excessive deficit procedure, having as its objective to deter excessive general government deficits and, if they occur, to further their prompt correction.

2. For the purpose of this Regulation 'participating Member States' shall mean those Member States which adopt the single currency in accordance with the Treaty and 'non-participating Member States' shall mean those which have not adopted the single currency.

Article 2

1. The excess of a government deficit over the reference value shall be considered exceptional and temporary, in accordance with Article 104(2)(a), second indent, when resulting from an unusual event outside the control of the Member State concerned and which has a major impact on the financial position of the general government, or when resulting from a severe economic downturn.

In addition, the excess over the reference value shall be considered temporary if budgetary forecasts as provided by the Commission indicate that the deficit will fall below the reference value following the end of the unusual event or the severe economic downturn.

2. The Commission when preparing a report under Article 104(3) shall, as a rule, consider an excess over the reference value resulting from a severe economic downturn to be exceptional only if there is an annual fall of real GDP of at least 2%.

3. The Council when deciding, according to Article 104(6), whether an excessive deficit exists, shall in its overall assessment take into account any observations made by the Member State showing that an annual fall of real GDP of less than 2% is nevertheless exceptional in the light of further supporting evidence, in particular on the abruptness of the downturn or on the accumulated loss of output relative to past trends.

SECTION 2   SPEEDING UP THE EXCESSIVE DEFICIT PROCEDURE

Article 3

1. Within two weeks of the adoption by the Commission of a report issued in accordance with Article 104(3), the Economic and Financial Committee shall formulate an opinion in accordance with Article 104(4).

*OJ L 332, 31.12.1993, p. 7.

2. Taking fully into account the opinion referred to in paragraph 1, the Commission, if it considers that an excessive deficit exists, shall address an opinion and a recommendation to the Council in accordance with Article 104(5) and (6).

3. The Council shall decide on the existence of an excessive deficit in accordance with Article 104(6), within three months of the reporting dates established in Article 4(2) and (3) of Regulation (EC) No. 3605/93. When it decides, in accordance with Article 104(6), that an excessive deficit exists, the Council shall at the same time make recommendations to the Member State concerned in accordance with Article 104(7).

4. The Council recommendation made in accordance with Article 104(7) shall establish a deadline of four months at the most for effective action to be taken by the Member State concerned. The Council recommendation shall also establish a deadline for the correction of the excessive deficit, which should be completed in the year following its identification unless there are special circumstances.

Article 4

1. Any Council decision to make public its recommendations, where it is established that no effective action has been taken in accordance with Article 104(8), shall be taken immediately after the expiry of the deadline set in accordance with Article 3(4) of this Regulation.

2. The Council, when considering whether effective action has been taken in response to its recommendations made in accordance with Article 104(7), shall base its decision on publicly announced decisions by the Government of the Member State concerned.

Article 5

Any Council decision to give notice to the participating Member State concerned to take measures for the deficit reduction in accordance with Article 104(9) shall be taken within one month of the Council decision establishing that no effective action has been taken in accordance with Article 104(8).

Article 6

Where the conditions to apply Article 104(11) are met, the Council shall impose sanctions in accordance with Article 104(11). Any such decision shall be taken no later than two months after the Council decision giving notice to the participating Member State concerned to take measures in accordance with Article 104(9).

Article 7

If a participating Member State fails to act in compliance with the successive decisions of the Council in accordance with Article 104(7) and (9), the decision of the Council to impose sanctions, in accordance with paragraph 11 of Article 104, shall be taken within ten months of the reporting dates pursuant to Regulation (EC) No. 3605/93 as referred to in Article 3(3) of this Regulation. An expedited procedure shall be used in the case of a deliberately planned deficit which the Council decides is excessive.

Article 8

Any Council decision to intensify sanctions, in accordance with Article 104(11), other than the conversion of deposits into fines under Article 14 of this Regulation, shall be taken no later than two months after the reporting dates pursuant to

Regulation (EC) No. 3605/93. Any Council decision to abrogate some or all of its decisions in accordance with Article *104*(12) shall be taken as soon as possible and in any case no later than two months after the reporting dates pursuant to Regulation (EC) No. 3605/93.

SECTION 3   ABEYANCE AND MONITORING

Article 9

1. The excessive deficit procedure shall be held in abeyance:
– if the Member State concerned acts in compliance with recommendations made in accordance with Article *104*(7),
– if the participating Member State concerned acts in compliance with notices given in accordance with Article *104*(9).

2. The period during which the procedure is held in abeyance shall be included neither in the ten month period referred to in Article 7 nor in the two month period referred to in Article 6 of this Regulation.

Article 10

1. The Commission and the Council shall monitor the implementation of action taken:
– by the Member State concerned in response to recommendations made under Article *104*(7),
– by the participating Member State concerned in response to notices given under Article *104*(9).

2. If action by a participating Member State is not being implemented or, in the Council's view, is proving to be inadequate, the Council shall immediately take a decision under Article *104*(9) or Article *104*(11) respectively.

3. If actual data pursuant to Regulation (EC) No. 3605/93 indicate that an excessive deficit has not been corrected by a participating Member State within the time limits specified either in recommendations issued under Article *104*(7) or notices issued under Article *104*(9), the Council shall immediately take a decision under Article *104*(9) or Article *104*(11) respectively.

SECTION 4   SANCTIONS

Article 11

Whenever the Council decides to apply sanctions to a participating Member State in accordance with Article *104*(11), a non-interest-bearing deposit shall, as a rule, be required. The Council may decide to supplement this deposit by the measures provided for in the first and second indents of Article *104*(11).

Article 12

1. When the excessive deficit results from non-compliance with the criterion relating to the government deficit ratio in Article *104*(2)(a), the amount of the first deposit shall comprise a fixed component equal to 0.2% of GDP, and a variable component equal to one tenth of the difference between the deficit as a percentage of GDP in the preceding year and the reference value of 3% of GDP.

2. Each following year, until the decision on the existence of an excessive deficit is abrogated, the Council shall assess whether the participating Member State concerned has taken effective action in response to the Council notice in

accordance with Article *104*(9). In this annual assessment the Council shall decide, in accordance with Article *104*(11), and without prejudice to Article 13 of this Regulation, to intensify the sanctions, unless the participating Member State concerned has complied with the Council notice. If an additional deposit is decided, it shall be equal to one tenth of the difference between the deficit as a percentage of GDP in the preceding year and the reference value of 3% of GDP.

3. Any single deposit referred to in paragraphs 1 and 2 shall not exceed the upper limit of 0.5% of GDP.

Article 13

A deposit shall, as a rule, be converted by the Council, in accordance with Article *104*(11), into a fine if two years after the decision to require the participating Member State concerned to make a deposit, the excessive deficit has in the view of the Council not been corrected.

Article 14

In accordance with Article *104*(12), the Council shall abrogate the sanctions referred to in the first and second indents of Article *104*(11) depending on the significance of the progress made by the participating Member State concerned in correcting the excessive deficit.

Article 15

In accordance with Article *104*(12), the Council shall abrogate all outstanding sanctions if the decision on the existence of an excessive deficit is abrogated. Fines imposed in accordance with Article 13 of this Regulation will not be reimbursed to the participating Member State concerned.

Article 16

Deposits referred to in Articles 11 and 12 of this Regulation shall be lodged with the Commission. Interest on the deposits, and the fines referred to in Article 13 of this Regulation constitute other revenue referred to in Article 269 of the Treaty and shall be distributed among participating Member States without a deficit that is excessive as determined in accordance with Article *104*(6) in proportion to their share in the total GNP of the eligible Member States.

SECTION 5   TRANSITIONAL AND FINAL PROVISIONS

Article 17

For the purpose of this Regulation and for as long as the United Kingdom has a budgetary year which is not a calendar year, the provisions of Sections 2, 3 and 4 of this Regulation shall be applied to the United Kingdom in accordance with the Annex.

Article 18

This Regulation shall enter into force on 1 January 1999.

This regulation shall be binding in its entirety and directly applicable in all Member States.

Done at Brussels, 7 July 1997.

ANNEX

TIME LIMITS APPLICABLE TO THE UNITED KINGDOM

1. In order to ensure equal treatment of all Member States, the Council, when taking decisions in Sections 2, 3 and 4 of this Regulation, shall have regard to the different budgetary year of the United Kingdom, with a view to taking decisions with regard to the United Kingdom at a point in its budgetary year similar to that at which decisions have been or will be taken in the case of other Member States.

2. For the provisions specified in Column I below there shall be substituted the provisions specified in Column II.

COLUMN I	COLUMN II
'three months of the reporting dates established in Article 4(2) and (3) of Council Regulation (EC) No. 3605/93' (Article 3(3))	'five months after the end of the budgetary year in which the deficit occurred'
'the year following its identification' (Article 3(4))	'the budgetary year following its identification'
'ten months of the reporting dates pursuant to Council Regulation (EC) No. 3605/93 as referred to in Article 3(3) of this Regulation' (Article 7)	'twelve months from the end of the budgetary year in which the deficit occurred'
'the preceding year' (Article 12(1))	'the preceding budgetary year'

Resolution of the European Council on Growth and Employment

Amsterdam, 17 June 1997

The European Council, meeting in Amsterdam on 16 June 1997,
RECALLING the conclusions of the Essen European Council, the Commission's initiative for 'Action on Employment: A Confidence Pact', the Dublin Declaration on Employment,
has adopted the following guidelines.

INTRODUCTION

1. It is imperative to give a new impulse for keeping employment firmly at the top of the political agenda of the Union. EMU and the Stability and Growth Pact will enhance the Internal Market and will foster a non-inflationary macro-economic environment with low interest rates, thereby strengthening conditions for economic growth and employment opportunities. In addition, we will need to strengthen the links between a successful and sustainable Economic and Monetary Union, a well-functioning Internal Market and employment. To that

end, it should be a priority aim to develop a skilled, trained and adaptable workforce and to make labour markets responsive to economic change. Structural reforms need to be comprehensive in scope, as opposed to limited or occasional measures, so as to address in a coherent manner the complex issue of incentives in creating and taking up a job.

Economic and social policies are mutually reinforcing. Social protection systems should be modernized so as to strengthen their functioning in order to contribute to competitiveness, employment and growth, establishing a durable basis for social cohesion.

This approach, coupled with stability based policies, provides the basis for an economy founded on principles of inclusion, solidarity, justice and a sustainable environment, and capable of benefiting all its citizens. Economic efficiency and social inclusion are complementary aspects of the more cohesive European society that we all seek.

Taking account of this statement of principles, the European Council calls upon all the social and economic agents, including the national, regional and local authorities and the social partners, to face fully their responsibilities within their respective sphere of activity.

DEVELOPING THE ECONOMIC PILLAR

2. The Treaty, in particular Articles 98 and 99, provides for close co-ordination of the Member States' economic policies, referred to in Article 4 of the Treaty. While primary responsibility in the fight against unemployment rests with the Member States, we should recognize the need both to enhance the effectiveness and to broaden the content of this co-ordination, focusing in particular on policies for employment. To this end, several steps are necessary.

3. The broad guidelines of the economic policies will be enhanced and developed into an effective instrument for ensuring sustained convergence of the economic performances of the Member States. Within the framework of sound and sustainable macro-economic policies and on the basis of an evaluation of the economic situation in the EU and in each Member State, more attention will be given to improving European competitiveness as a prerequisite for growth and employment, so as to, among other objectives, bring more jobs within the reach of the citizens of Europe. In this context, special attention should be given to labour and product market efficiency, technological innovation and the potential for small and medium-sized enterprises to create jobs. Full attention should also be given to training and education systems including life-long learning, work incentives in the tax and benefit systems and reducing non-wage labour costs, in order to increase employability.

4. Taxation and social protection systems should be made more employment friendly and by that improving the functioning of labour markets. The European Council stresses the importance for the Member States of creating a tax environment that stimulates enterprise and the creation of jobs. These and other policies for employment will become an essential part of the broad guidelines, taking into account national employment policies and good practices arising from these policies.

5. The Council is therefore called upon to take the multi-annual employment

programmes, as envisaged in the Essen procedure, into account when formulating the broad guidelines, in order to strengthen their employment focus. The Council may make the necessary recommendations to the Member States, in accordance with Article 99(4) of the Treaty.

6. This enhanced co-ordination of economic policies will complement the procedure as envisaged in the new Title on Employment in the Treaty, which provides for the creation of an Employment Committee, which is asked to work together closely with the Economic Policy Committee. The Council should seek to make those provisions immediately effective. In both procedures the European Council will play its integrating and guiding role, in accordance with the Treaty.

7. The European Union should complement national measures by systematically examining all relevant existing Community policies, including Trans-European Networks and Research and Development programmes, to ensure that they are geared towards job creation and economic growth, while respecting the Financial Perspectives and the Inter-Institutional Agreement.

8. The European Council has agreed concrete action on making maximum progress with the final completion of the Internal Market: making the rules more effective, dealing with the key remaining market distortions, avoiding harmful tax competition, removing the sectoral obstacles to market integration and delivering an Internal Market for the benefit of all citizens.

9. Whereas the task of the European Investment Bank, as stated in Article 267 of the Treaty, is to contribute, by having recourse to the capital market and utilizing its own resources, to the balanced and steady development of the common market in the interest of the Community, we recognize the important role of the European Investment Bank and the European Investment Fund in creating employment through investment opportunities in Europe. We urge the EIB to step up its activities in this respect, promoting investment projects consistent with sound banking principles and practices, and more in particular:
– to examine the establishment of a facility for the financing of high-technology projects of small and medium-sized enterprises in co-operation with the European Investment Fund, possibly making use of venture capital with involvement of the private banking sector;
– to examine its scope of intervention in the areas of education, health, urban environment and environmental protection;
– to step up its interventions in the area of large infrastructure networks by examining the possibility of granting very long-term loans, primarily for the large priority projects adopted in Essen.

10. The Commission is invited to make the appropriate proposals in order to ensure that, upon expiration of the ECSC Treaty in 2002, to use the revenues of outstanding reserves for a research fund for sectors related to the coal and steel industry.

11. This overall strategy will maximize our efforts to promote employment and social inclusion and to combat unemployment. In doing so, job promotion, worker protection and security will be combined with the need for improving the functioning of labour markets. This also contributes to the good functioning of EMU.

RENEWED COMMITMENT

12. The European Council invites all parties, namely the Member States, the Council and the Commission, to implement these provisions with vigour and commitment.

The possibilities offered to social partners by the Social Chapter, which has been integrated into the new Treaty, should serve to underpin the Council's work on employment. The European Council recommends social dialogue and the full use of present Community law concerning the consultation of social partners, including, where relevant, in processes of restructuring, and taking into account national practices.

13. Together, these policies allow the Member States to build on the strengths of the European construction to co-ordinate their economic policies effectively within the Council so as to create more jobs and pave the way for a successful and sustainable stage three of Economic and Monetary Union in accordance with the Treaty. The European Council asks social partners to fully face their responsibilities within their respective sphere of activity.

Charter of Fundamental Rights

As noted earlier, the Charter of Fundamental Rights is a recent document being 'proclaimed' at the Nice Summit of the European Council in December 2000. It emerged out of a series of debates concerning the role and position of fundamental rights within the EU. These had been taking place in and between the member states, among academics and within the EP. Moreover, fundamental rights had been gaining prominence in the case law of the ECJ. Indeed, as Macía notes, the ECJ has long claimed that respect for fundamental rights is an integral part of the general principles of Community law. In the European Treaties too matters concerning fundamental rights were being given increasing prominence, whether it be in the preambles to the SEA and the TEU, the role of the EU in promoting human rights and fundamental freedoms as part of the CFSP, the conferral of rights on EU citizens as part of the TEC's provisions concerning citizenship or the TEU's reference in ex Article F(2) (now Article 6) that the EU should 'respect fundamental rights, as guaranteed by the European Convention for the Protection of Human Rights and Fundamental Freedoms . . . and as they result from the constitutional traditions common to the Member States, as general principles of Community law'.

As the final reference makes clear, in determining what should be understood by fundamental rights the EU has long been guided by non-EU documents, notably the European Convention on Human Rights (ECHR) adopted by the Council of Europe in 1950. However, although the member states are signatories to this, neither the EU nor the EC is. And according to the ECJ in Opinion 2/94, the EC cannot accede to the ECHR without an amendment to the TEC, something which Finland was keen to see realized through Nice.

Although Opinion 2/94 disappointed those who wished to see greater prominence given to fundamental rights within the EU, the issue was on the agenda of the 1996 IGC, although here too supporters of an EU bill of rights were to be frustrated. Nevertheless the TA did, as we have seen earlier in the *Guide*, give the fundamental rights a boost through the insertion of Article 13 TEC, a 'watershed' in the eyes of McGoldrick in the evolution of human rights in the EU. Amsterdam also inserted Article 7, subsequently revised by Nice, allowing for a member state's voting rights to be suspended where a serious and persistent breach of human rights and fundamental freedoms is determined. A clear list of rights, however, was still lacking.

Then in June 1999 the Cologne European Council announced that the fundamental rights applicable at the level of the EU should be consolidated in a charter and made more evident. The charter would include the rights and freedoms guaranteed by the ECHR, those derived from the constitutional traditions of the member states. Account would also be taken of the economic and social rights set out in the Council of Europe's European Social Charter as well as the EC's own Charter of Fundamental Social Rights of Workers. The aim was to present the charter to the Nice European Council where consideration would be given to whether it should be incorporated into the EU's treaty base.

Work on the charter began formally in January 2000 when the so-called 'convention' charged with drawing it up met for the first time. Its composition, agreed at the Tampere European Council in October 1999, consisted of 15 representatives of the member-state governments, one representative of the Commission president, 16 MEPs and 30 members of national parliaments. In all this was 62 people. In addition there were four observers, two each from the ECJ and the Council of Europe. As many commentators have pointed out, such a convention was highly innovative, no European text having previously been drawn up by a body composed of such a collection of representatives. Its significance is discussed by de Búrca.

The work of the convention consisted of 17 meetings culminating in the adoption of the charter on 2 October 2000. It was then unanimously approved by the European Council at Biarritz, where it became clear that the charter, for the time being at least, would remain a non-binding document. This was mainly thanks to strong resistance from Denmark, the UK and Ireland to the charter being incorporated into or alluded to in the EU's treaty base. Consequently, following approval by the EP (14 November 2000) and the Commission (6 December 2000), the charter was simply 'solemnly proclaimed' at Nice by the presidents of the Commission, Council and EP. It was then published in the *Official Journal*.

The text comprises 54 articles divided into seven chapters and preceded by a preamble. The chapters cover dignity, freedoms, equality, solidarity, citizens' rights, justice and general provisions. Each article is titled to indicate its contents. As envisaged, many of the rights contained in these chapters derive from the ECHR. Others are, as the Commission points out in its guide to the charter, based on other charters and documents, provisions of the TEC and the case law of the ECJ.

The preamble, like those of the TEC and TEU, invokes the idea of 'ever closer union' among the peoples of Europe and declares the EU to be founded on 'the indivisible, universal values of human dignity, freedom, equality and solidarity'. Having then asserted the principles of democracy and the rule of law, the individual is declared to be 'at the heart of [the EU's] activities', as evidenced by citizenship and the creation of an area of freedom, security and justice. Further drawing on the content and language of the TEC and TEU, reference is then made to all this having respect for the diversity of cultures and traditions within the EU as well as the identities and organization of the member states. This is followed by allusions to balanced and sustainable development, the four freedoms of the Single Market, the need to make rights more visible, the powers and tasks of the EC and EU, the principle of subsidiarity and the various sources drawn on for the rights contained in the charter. The preamble concludes by noting that the rights listed entail responsibilities and duties with regard to other persons, to the human community, and to future generations.

Having provided the justification, purpose and context of the charter, Chapter I on dignity spells out the first set of rights which include those to life (reference being included to non-use of the death penalty), physical and mental integrity including a ban on the cloning of human beings, and the prohibition of torture and slavery. Chapter II then lists freedoms, including the rights to liberty and security; privacy; the protection of personal data; marry and start a family; freedom of thought, conscience and religion; freedom of expression and information; assembly and association; academic freedom; education, employment; conduct a business; own property; asylum; and protection in the event of removal.

Rights relating to equality follow in Chapter III. These go beyond issues of equality before the law, non-discrimination and gender equality to include rights of the child, of the elderly and of disabled people. Workers' and consumers' rights then make up the bulk of the rights contained in Chapter IV on solidarity. Others include the right of access to preventive health care. Yet not all areas addressed in Chapter IV contain explicit rights. Instead, with environmental and consumer protection, high levels are to be ensured by the EU. In the case of social security benefits and social services only entitlement to these is recognized and respected.

This brings us to Chapter V on citizens' rights, where the charter in effect simply summarizes rights enshrined in the TEC. Chapter VI on justice relies more heavily on the ECHR and the case law deriving from it, establishing as it does the right to an effective remedy and to a fair trial, the presumption of innocence and right of defence, the principles of legality and proportionality of criminal offences and penalties, and the right not to be tried or punished twice in criminal proceedings for the same criminal offence. The final chapter, that containing the general provisions, notes the scope of the charter being the institutions and bodies of the EU and the member states. As if to emphasize the fact that the charter draws on existing rights and practices, Article 51 notes that it does not establish any new power or task for the EC or EU, or modify any of the powers or tasks defined by 'the Treaties'. The final two provisions concern the level of protection afforded by the charter, noting that rights and freedoms cannot be restricted or adversely affected by the latter, and prohibiting the abuse of the rights contained in the charter.

In all, the charter appears as a seemingly innocuous presentation of existing rights and freedoms enjoyed by EU citizens. Nevertheless, as noted, there was considerable opposition to making it legally binding, something which would have significant implications as Engel and others argue. This has not stopped the ECJ from referring to it. As early as February 2001 reference was made to the charter in Advocate-General Tizzano's opinion in the *BECTU* case. And, given the Declaration on the Future of the Union (No. 23 TN), the question of its legal status will not be going away. It is slated for consideration in the 2004 IGC, and there should be no practical difficulties in making the charter legally binding, the convention having drafted the text 'as if' it would be adopted. The issue of incorporation is essentially a political decision. Whether or not such a decision will be taken remains to be seen. All the same, the charter exists and cannot be ignored.

PREAMBLE

The peoples of Europe, in creating an ever closer union among them, are resolved to share a peaceful future based on common values.

Conscious of its spiritual and moral heritage, the Union is founded on the indivisible, universal values of human dignity, freedom, equality and solidarity; it is based on the principles of democracy and the rule of law. It places the individual at the heart of its activities, by establishing the citizenship of the Union and by creating an area of freedom, security and justice.

The Union contributes to the preservation and to the development of these common values while respecting the diversity of the cultures and traditions of the peoples of Europe as well as the national identities of the Member States and the organisation of their public authorities at national, regional and local levels; it seeks to promote balanced and sustainable development and ensures free movement of persons, goods, services and capital, and the freedom of establishment.

To this end, it is necessary to strengthen the protection of fundamental rights in the light of changes in society, social progress and scientific and technological developments by making those rights more visible in a Charter.

This Charter reaffirms, with due regard for the powers and tasks of the Community and the Union and the principle of subsidiarity, the rights as they result, in particular, from the constitutional traditions and international obligations common to the Member States, the Treaty on European Union, the Community Treaties, the European Convention for the Protection of Human Rights and Fundamental Freedoms, the Social Charters adopted by the Community and by the Council of Europe and the case-law of the Court of Justice of the European Communities and of the European Court of Human Rights.

Enjoyment of these rights entails responsibilities and duties with regard to other persons, to the human community and to future generations.

The Union therefore recognises the rights, freedoms and principles set out hereafter.

CHAPTER I   DIGNITY

Article 1   Human dignity

Human dignity is inviolable. It must be respected and protected.

Article 2   Right to life

1. Everyone has the right to life.

2. No one shall be condemned to the death penalty, or executed.

Article 3   Right to the integrity of the person

1. Everyone has the right to respect for his or her physical and mental integrity.

2. In the fields of medicine and biology, the following must be respected in particular:

– the free and informed consent of the person concerned, according to the procedures laid down by law,

– the prohibition of eugenic practices, in particular those aiming at the selection of persons,

– the prohibition on making the human body and its parts as such a source of financial gain,

– the prohibition of the reproductive cloning of human beings.

Article 4   Prohibition of torture and inhuman or degrading treatment or punishment

No one shall be subjected to torture or to inhuman or degrading treatment or punishment.

Article 5   Prohibition of slavery and forced labour

1. No one shall be held in slavery or servitude.

2. No one shall be required to perform forced or compulsory labour.

3. Trafficking in human beings is prohibited.

CHAPTER II   FREEDOMS

Article 6   Right to liberty and security

Everyone has the right to liberty and security of person.

Article 7   Respect for private and family life

Everyone has the right to respect for his or her private and family life, home and communications.

Article 8   Protection of personal data

1. Everyone has the right to the protection of personal data concerning him or her.

2. Such data must be processed fairly for specified purposes and on the basis of the consent of the person concerned or some other legitimate basis laid down by law. Everyone has the right of access to data which has been collected concerning him or her, and the right to have it rectified.

3. Compliance with these rules shall be subject to control by an independent authority.

Article 9   Right to marry and right to found a family

The right to marry and the right to found a family shall be guaranteed in accordance with the national laws governing the exercise of these rights.

Article 10   Freedom of thought, conscience and religion

1. Everyone has the right to freedom of thought, conscience and religion. This right includes freedom to change religion or belief and freedom, either alone or in community with others and in public or in private, to manifest religion or belief, in worship, teaching, practice and observance.

2. The right to conscientious objection is recognised, in accordance with the national laws governing the exercise of this right.

Article 11   Freedom of expression and information

1. Everyone has the right to freedom of expression. This right shall include freedom to hold opinions and to receive and impart information and ideas without interference by public authority and regardless of frontiers.

2. The freedom and pluralism of the media shall be respected.

Article 12   Freedom of assembly and of association

1. Everyone has the right to freedom of peaceful assembly and to freedom of association at all levels, in particular in political, trade union and civic matters, which implies the right of everyone to form and to join trade unions for the protection of his or her interests.

2. Political parties at Union level contribute to expressing the political will of the citizens of the Union.

Article 13 Freedom of the arts and sciences

The arts and scientific research shall be free of constraint. Academic freedom shall be respected.

Article 14 Right to education

1. Everyone has the right to education and to have access to vocational and continuing training.

2. This right includes the possibility to receive free compulsory education.

3. The freedom to found educational establishments with due respect for democratic principles and the right of parents to ensure the education and teaching of their children in conformity with their religious, philosophical and pedagogical convictions shall be respected, in accordance with the national laws governing the exercise of such freedom and right.

Article 15 Freedom to choose an occupation and right to engage in work

1. Everyone has the right to engage in work and to pursue a freely chosen or accepted occupation.

2. Every citizen of the Union has the freedom to seek employment, to work, to exercise the right of establishment and to provide services in any Member State.

3. Nationals of third countries who are authorised to work in the territories of the Member States are entitled to working conditions equivalent to those of citizens of the Union.

Article 16 Freedom to conduct a business

The freedom to conduct a business in accordance with Community law and national laws and practices is recognised.

Article 17 Right to property

1. Everyone has the right to own, use, dispose of and bequeath his or her lawfully acquired possessions. No one may be deprived of his or her possessions, except in the public interest and in the cases and under the conditions provided for by law, subject to fair compensation being paid in good time for their loss. The use of property may be regulated by law in so far as is necessary for the general interest.

2. Intellectual property shall be protected.

Article 18 Right to asylum

The right to asylum shall be guaranteed with due respect for the rules of the Geneva Convention of 28 July 1951 and the Protocol of 31 January 1967 relating to the status of refugees and in accordance with the Treaty establishing the European Community.

Article 19 Protection in the event of removal, expulsion or extradition

1. Collective expulsions are prohibited.

2. No one may be removed, expelled or extradited to a State where there is a serious risk that he or she would be subjected to the death penalty, torture or other inhuman or degrading treatment or punishment.

CHAPTER III   EQUALITY

Article 20   Equality before the law

Everyone is equal before the law.

Article 21   Non-discrimination

1. Any discrimination based on any ground such as sex, race, colour, ethnic or social origin, genetic features, language, religion or belief, political or any other opinion, membership of a national minority, property, birth, disability, age or sexual orientation shall be prohibited.

2. Within the scope of application of the Treaty establishing the European Community and of the Treaty on European Union, and without prejudice to the special provisions of those Treaties, any discrimination on grounds of nationality shall be prohibited.

Article 22   Cultural, religious and linguistic diversity

The Union shall respect cultural, religious and linguistic diversity.

Article 23   Equality between men and women

Equality between men and women must be ensured in all areas, including employment, work and pay. The principle of equality shall not prevent the maintenance or adoption of measures providing for specific advantages in favour of the under-represented sex.

Article 24   The rights of the child

1. Children shall have the right to such protection and care as is necessary for their well-being. They may express their views freely. Such views shall be taken into consideration on matters which concern them in accordance with their age and maturity.

2. In all actions relating to children, whether taken by public authorities or private institutions, the child's best interests must be a primary consideration.

3. Every child shall have the right to maintain on a regular basis a personal relationship and direct contact with both his or her parents, unless that is contrary to his or her interests.

Article 25   The rights of the elderly

The Union recognises and respects the rights of the elderly to lead a life of dignity and independence and to participate in social and cultural life.

Article 26   Integration of persons with disabilities

The Union recognises and respects the right of persons with disabilities to benefit from measures designed to ensure their independence, social and occupational integration and participation in the life of the community.

CHAPTER IV   SOLIDARITY

Article 27   Workers' right to information and consultation within the under-taking

Workers or their representatives must, at the appropriate levels, be guaranteed information and consultation in good time in the cases and under the conditions provided for by Community law and national laws and practices.

Article 28   Right of collective bargaining and action

Workers and employers, or their respective organisations, have, in accordance with Community law and national laws and practices, the right to negotiate and conclude collective agreements at the appropriate levels and, in cases of conflicts of interest, to take collective action to defend their interests, including strike action.

Article 29   Right of access to placement services

Everyone has the right of access to a free placement service.

Article 30   Protection in the event of unjustified dismissal

Every worker has the right to protection against unjustified dismissal, in accordance with Community law and national laws and practices.

Article 31   Fair and just working conditions

1. Every worker has the right to working conditions which respect his or her health, safety and dignity.

2. Every worker has the right to limitation of maximum working hours, to daily and weekly rest periods and to an annual period of paid leave.

Article 32   Prohibition of child labour and protection of young people at work

The employment of children is prohibited. The minimum age of admission to employment may not be lower than the minimum school-leaving age, without prejudice to such rules as may be more favourable to young people and except for limited derogations.

Young people admitted to work must have working conditions appropriate to their age and be protected against economic exploitation and any work likely to harm their safety, health or physical, mental, moral or social development or to interfere with their education.

Article 33   Family and professional life

1. The family shall enjoy legal, economic and social protection.

2. To reconcile family and professional life, everyone shall have the right to protection from dismissal for a reason connected with maternity and the right to paid maternity leave and to parental leave following the birth or adoption of a child.

Article 34   Social security and social assistance

1. The Union recognises and respects the entitlement to social security benefits and social services providing protection in cases such as maternity, illness, industrial accidents, dependency or old age, and in the case of loss of employment, in accordance with the rules laid down by Community law and national laws and practices.

2. Everyone residing and moving legally within the European Union is entitled to social security benefits and social advantages in accordance with Community law and national laws and practices.

3. In order to combat social exclusion and poverty, the Union recognises and respects the right to social and housing assistance so as to ensure a decent existence for all those who lack sufficient resources, in accordance with the rules laid down by Community law and national laws and practices.

Article 35   Health care

Everyone has the right of access to preventive health care and the right to benefit from medical treatment under the conditions established by national laws and practices. A high level of human health protection shall be ensured in the definition and implementation of all Union policies and activities.

Article 36   Access to services of general economic interest

The Union recognises and respects access to services of general economic interest as provided for in national laws and practices, in accordance with the Treaty establishing the European Community, in order to promote the social and territorial cohesion of the Union.

Article 37   Environmental protection

A high level of environmental protection and the improvement of the quality of the environment must be integrated into the policies of the Union and ensured in accordance with the principle of sustainable development.

Article 38   Consumer protection

Union policies shall ensure a high level of consumer protection.

CHAPTER V   CITIZENS' RIGHTS

Article 39   Right to vote and to stand as a candidate at elections to the European Parliament

1. Every citizen of the Union has the right to vote and to stand as a candidate at elections to the European Parliament in the Member State in which he or she resides, under the same conditions as nationals of that State.

2. Members of the European Parliament shall be elected by direct universal suffrage in a free and secret ballot.

Article 40   Right to vote and to stand as a candidate at municipal elections

Every citizen of the Union has the right to vote and to stand as a candidate at municipal elections in the Member State in which he or she resides under the same conditions as nationals of that State.

Article 41   Right to good administration

1. Every person has the right to have his or her affairs handled impartially, fairly and within a reasonable time by the institutions and bodies of the Union.

2. This right includes:

– the right of every person to be heard, before any individual measure which would affect him or her adversely is taken;

– the right of every person to have access to his or her file, while respecting the legitimate interests of confidentiality and of professional and business secrecy;

– the obligation of the administration to give reasons for its decisions.

3. Every person has the right to have the Community make good any damage caused by its institutions or by its servants in the performance of their duties, in accordance with the general principles common to the laws of the Member States.

4. Every person may write to the institutions of the Union in one of the languages of the Treaties and must have an answer in the same language.

Article 42   Right of access to documents

Any citizen of the Union, and any natural or legal person residing or having its registered office in a Member State, has a right of access to European Parliament, Council and Commission documents.

Article 43   Ombudsman

Any citizen of the Union and any natural or legal person residing or having its registered office in a Member State has the right to refer to the Ombudsman of the Union cases of maladministration in the activities of the Community institutions or bodies, with the exception of the Court of Justice and the Court of First Instance acting in their judicial role.

Article 44   Right to petition

Any citizen of the Union and any natural or legal person residing or having its registered office in a Member State has the right to petition the European Parliament.

Article 45   Freedom of movement and of residence

1. Every citizen of the Union has the right to move and reside freely within the territory of the Member States.

2. Freedom of movement and residence may be granted, in accordance with the Treaty establishing the European Community, to nationals of third countries legally resident in the territory of a Member State.

Article 46   Diplomatic and consular protection

Every citizen of the Union shall, in the territory of a third country in which the Member State of which he or she is a national is not represented, be entitled to protection by the diplomatic or consular authorities of any Member State, on the same conditions as the nationals of that Member State.

CHAPTER VI   JUSTICE

Article 47   Right to an effective remedy and to a fair trial

Everyone whose rights and freedoms guaranteed by the law of the Union are violated has the right to an effective remedy before a tribunal in compliance with the conditions laid down in this Article.

Everyone is entitled to a fair and public hearing within a reasonable time by an independent and impartial tribunal previously established by law. Everyone shall have the possibility of being advised, defended and represented.

Legal aid shall be made available to those who lack sufficient resources in so far as such aid is necessary to ensure effective access to justice.

Article 48   Presumption of innocence and right of defence

1. Everyone who has been charged shall be presumed innocent until proved guilty according to law.

2. Respect for the rights of the defence of anyone who has been charged shall be guaranteed.

Article 49   Principles of legality and proportionality of criminal offences and penalties

1. No one shall be held guilty of any criminal offence on account of any act or omission which did not constitute a criminal offence under national law or international law at the time when it was committed. Nor shall a heavier penalty be imposed than that which was applicable at the time the criminal offence was committed. If, subsequent to the commission of a criminal offence, the law provides for a lighter penalty, that penalty shall be applicable.

2. This Article shall not prejudice the trial and punishment of any person for any act or omission which, at the time when it was committed, was criminal according to the general principles recognised by the community of nations.

3. The severity of penalties must not be disproportionate to the criminal offence.

Article 50   Right not to be tried or punished twice in criminal proceedings for the same criminal offence

No one shall be liable to be tried or punished again in criminal proceedings for an offence for which he or she has already been finally acquitted or convicted within the Union in accordance with the law.

CHAPTER VII   GENERAL PROVISIONS

Article 51   Scope

1. The provisions of this Charter are addressed to the institutions and bodies of the Union with due regard for the principle of subsidiarity and to the Member States only when they are implementing Union law.
They shall therefore respect the rights, observe the principles and promote the application thereof in accordance with their respective powers.

2. This Charter does not establish any new power or task for the Community or the Union, or modify powers and tasks defined by the Treaties.

Article 52   Scope of guaranteed rights

1. Any limitation on the exercise of the rights and freedoms recognised by this Charter must be provided for by law and respect the essence of those rights and freedoms. Subject to the principle of proportionality, limitations may be made only if they are necessary and genuinely meet objectives of general interest recognised by the Union or the need to protect the rights and freedoms of others.

2. Rights recognised by this Charter which are based on the Community Treaties or the Treaty on European Union shall be exercised under the conditions and within the limits defined by those Treaties.

3. In so far as this Charter contains rights which correspond to rights guaranteed by the Convention for the Protection of Human Rights and Fundamental Freedoms, the meaning and scope of those rights shall be the same as those laid down by the said Convention. This provision shall not prevent Union law providing more extensive protection.

Article 53   Level of protection

Nothing in this Charter shall be interpreted as restricting or adversely affecting human rights and fundamental freedoms as recognised, in their respective fields of application, by Union law and international law and by international agreements to which the Union, the Community or all the Member States are party, including the European Convention for the Protection of Human Rights and Fundamental Freedoms, and by the Member States' constitutions.

Article 54   Prohibition of abuse of rights

Nothing in this Charter shall be interpreted as implying any right to engage in any activity or to perform any act aimed at the destruction of any of the rights and freedoms recognised in this Charter or at their limitation to a greater extent than is provided for herein.

vi   Looking Back at the Existing Treaties

Discussion of accession treaties, not to mention the satellite Community treaties and statutes, reminds us that the TEC and the TEU are only part of the EU's treaty base. This remains a multiform affair, each element of which has its place and needs to be remembered in considering the European Treaties. And their very number makes it clear that, whatever their overall role in the Union, they remain very much treaties. Even if they are often of different types, are negotiated within frameworks and precedents laid down by the Union and its founding documents and deal with policy and institutional issues, they are still agreements among member states. They are a distinct subspecies of traditional international compacts with which they have much in common in terms of shape and status.

Treaty making, in other words, is still a process dominated not, as so much press comment implies, by Brussels Eurocrats but by the member states and their governments. Moreover, these are neither united nor consistent in their approach. Hence decisions on treaties are subject to outside circumstances and pressures, often originating in public opinion inside the member states. It is the complications caused by these conflicting pressures which account for the ambiguities and complexities we find in the treaties themselves. So the European Treaties are neither simply the whims of out-of-touch leaders nor just the results of earlier EU decisions. They are highly political bargains made within both pressing political backgrounds and the special contexts of the EU and the EC.

One of the most important of these contexts is the fact that, generally, as at Nice, what is being negotiated is not a new constitutive creation but an amendment of the existing key treaties. This is one reason why outsiders find it so hard to come to terms with what is being done. Much criticism of 'Maastricht' and 'Nice' is actually directed, as Weiler pointed out, at what is in earlier documents. And, at Nice, there was a further confusion between the IGC treaty agreements proper and the other, non-treaty-based, decisions the European Council summit made before it went into full IGC mode. It was clear that neither the Conservative front bench nor their political opposites at the head of the Irish 'no' movement really understood the difference. This makes it easier to attack the treaty but infinitely more difficult to sort out exactly what should be revised, and how.

All this offers three justifications for our strategy in the *Guide*. Printing the treaties in a non-official format which can be found on the shelves of ordinary bookshops has, firstly, acquired a new validity following the furore over Nice. In Ireland the 'no' campaign made much of the fact that, since the text was only available to computer nerds, not enough time was given for ordinary people to become familiar with it. Secondly, Nice also points up the value of looking at what is actually in the European Treaties as such and what their wording appears to mean rather than accepting at face value generalized assumptions about integration which misunderstand or ignore the treaties. Thirdly, Nice also highlighted the importance of the TEU and the TEC within both the treaty base and the development of European integration. They are the treaties which contain, or hint at, the issues which most concern people about Europe.

However, even after going through the two key European Treaties in detail, it is clear that they still leave unresolved some of the problems identified at the start of the *Guide*: the inter-relations of Union and Community, the readability of treaties and their limited comprehensiveness, not to mention the very different political attitudes they provoke. Equally, they are very much in evolution. Thus they changed markedly at Amsterdam and could change further, albeit less substantially, after Nice. This makes it hard to draw firm lessons about their dynamics and status. However, it is clear that their evolution is a highly political matter and that they are neither treated nor function as a full constitution for the Union.

The Key European Treaties

Although all the treaties are in some degree necessary to the existence of the overall 'European construction', there should be no doubt that the TEU and the TEC are its essential cornerstones. When official documents talk of the 'treaties on which the Union is founded' it is these that they normally have in mind. Together the TEC and the TEU give the construction its supra-national dimension – the essential frameworks, rules and understandings which create the transforming context of inter-governmental bargaining. Take them away and the construction would implode. Without them, there would be no shape and no sense of order.

Unfortunately, they do not provide these in an altogether logical or hierarchical way. While most of the institutional framework is in the TEC, this interacts with the pillar structure established by the TEU. Equally, the Union's key axioms are divided between the two treaties. And they are not always as neatly cross-referenced as is the case with subsidiarity. In the same way the preferences of the member states are confusingly enshrined in both treaties. Beyond this, the rank order of the two is unclear and it is not possible to say precisely which one takes precedence. Increasingly the TEU seems to have emerged as the overarching and dynamic document but the TEC cannot be dismissed. This is partly because, as we have just said, all European Treaties are necessary to the treaty base. It is also because power in the Union is intimately linked to the institutional provisions of the TEC, as both the negotiations for and the responses to Nice showed. So understanding the Union demands that we see the TEU and TEC as documentary Siamese twins.

Within this symbiotic relationship, what seems to emerge is that the contribution of the TEU is an increasingly significant one. Its status has increased over the last few years moving away from being simply a treaty constituting a new and separate body to being the treaty which now clearly sets the overall tone and direction of the integration enterprise. This is a reflection of the fact that it is shorter, more political and more concerned with principle and procedure than the TEC. It also gives the Union as a whole its shape. None the less, it is neither fully nor well articulated. The TEU has therefore been described as an overcoat for the Union, although a waistcoat might be a more appropriate description since, while it provides a front and a back, it now merely has empty openings where the Union's Community arms are concerned.

Equally, the TEU serves very much as a statement about the role of the member states in a way which the TEC does not. It is for this reason that there has been virtually no movement on ideas of merging the two treaties because to do this would be seen as enhancing supra-nationalism. Hence, its constitutive role remains extremely important given that 'Union' is now the term used by most people to describe the whole enterprise. This looseness of expression is, in fact, a reflection of both the way the Union and the TEU have evolved in recent years and of the convoluted relationship between the two bodies and their constitutive treaties.

Turning to the TEC, we have a treaty which today plays more of a supportive role than it used to do. Originally it provided the main inspiration for integration and the supra-national institutions which gave this effect. Today, it continues to provide the institutional basis for the Union, although it shares the task of controlling the institutions with the TEU. It also supplies almost all the policy prescriptions for the Union (CFSP being the obvious exception), the things which often matter most to ordinary people. At the same time the TEC gives the Union its legal capacities both at home and in its dealings with other forces. And, clearly, without these the Union as a whole could not function.

This accounts for the fact that the TEC is longer, more dense and certainly more complex than the TEU. So, despite the fact that it carries the Union's basic concepts and citizenship, it has a less constitutional feel than the TEU. None the less, it is far more closely related with ordinary life through the way it both creates and responds to the workings of Community law. Hence, its shared organs are of vital importance to the Union as a whole. Yet despite the significance of the TEC as the activating element of the Union, there can be little question but that the existence of two treaties is problematic.

Recurring Problems

The first problem they present is, not surprisingly, the fact that they do not actually resolve the question of what the Community, and especially the Union, are. Nor do they make clear the exact relations between them. Despite their apparent Siamese-twin relationship the two remain distinct in many ways, as the previous discussion shows. Consequently, the Union does not have the luxury of a unitary structure. However, so closely inter-related are the Union and the Community that it is often very difficult to decide which body is acting and where the ultimate authority is to be found. As the late Vincent Wright observed of the French Constitution of 1958, it dodges the crucial question of where power lies. This does not help transparency. The basic blueprints of the Union, to put it another way, are somewhat fuzzy.

Nor does the nature of the texts themselves help things. Yes they have been tidied up and now read more tightly than before but, even so, they are still not an easy read. They contain so many subtle little caveats and cross-references that their import is not always immediately apparent, especially to those who are unfamiliar with the grammar of such legal documents. And, as at Nice, the way they are set out as amendments to a gamut of treaties not printed alongside the changes can make them even more opaque. Indeed, Brok claimed that the Irish voted 'no' because of such complications although if they could not easily get hold of the text this could hardly have been the case.

In any case, as Commissioner Barnier has remarked, the European Treaties are not deliberately complicated so as to discourage readers but because of the inter-governmental compromises involved in what has been a very up-and-down process of treaty amend-ment. States drop bits into treaties so as to satisfy domestic constituencies – thus creating the so-called 'Christmas-tree effect'. Moreover, because of their own fears and rivalries, they can fail to use their influence over the process to sort out infelicities in case these reopen difficult questions. Equally, the treaties have to be formal documents both because of the subject material they cover, notably economic management, and because of the fact that their contents have to be legally enforceable.

What makes things worse is that, as has already become clear, the European Treaties are not self-contained or self-explanatory documents. They have many gaps which have to be filled by other decisions or legal rulings. These, like outside reactions, can change the way they are understood. In other words, we have to take account not just of the words themselves but of the way they are 'read' in real life. There are two problems here. On the one hand, few look at the treaties as documents. References to their contents can often be surprisingly sketchy. Debate focuses on the structures and processes to which they give rise along with other changes made to the Union's material constitution. Little thought is given to their legal packaging. And, in any case, legal provisions are not always an accurate indicator of actual behaviour.

On the other, the changes made by IGCs to the European Treaties are often assessed in very different not to say contradictory ways. As has become clear earlier in the *Guide*, Eurosceptic critics are more likely to pay attention to the details of the treaties than supporters. The former tend to be uniformly hostile to what they see as yet further infringements of national sovereignty whereas the latter usually start by criticizing what the states agree for not going far enough and then finish by seeing it as a masterpiece of integration, as Eijsbouts says. All this means that the Treaties remain problematic documents.

Evolving Uncertainties

A further difficulty is that the European Treaties are also, in a way, increasingly moving targets. There has been little chance for people to become accustomed to them because they have constantly been surrounded with scaffolding and screening. A clear view of the existing structures can often be obscured by preparations for the next phase of treaty reform. Whereas the SEA made few amendments, Maastricht made huge changes yet had less than three years to bed them in before it was overtaken by Amsterdam. This proved to be a long drawn-out process and one which made more alterations than was often realized, both substantively and technically. Yet, it aroused very little popular concern.

Nice, conversely, made far fewer changes and these were often matters of degree and not principle. They were also more focused on the TEC than on the TEU. Even less than Amsterdam was it a constitutive treaty. And Neunreither would say that not only was it not innovative but that it was the most path dependent of the recent treaties. That is to say that it mainly recorded what was already agreed or being done. None the less, it was Nice which fell foul of a now refreshed populist opposition responding to the way that successive treaty amendments add to the Union's complexity.

Yet that opposition can itself be seen as partly the cause of its own frustrations over the contents and character of the treaty draft. Treaties are not made by bureaucrats in ivory towers in Brussels but by elected leaders, their officials and advisers. As we have already suggested, fear of public disapproval is one of the things which makes governments play hard ball and end up making the tortuous compromises which so bemuse public opinion. Putting this right actually involves improving domestic political communications as well as those of the Union.

Equally, the assumption of some of the leaders of the Irish 'no' movement that it is only the hardness of heart of the negotiators which prevents agreement on a simple and acceptable treaty flies in the face of most of the evidence adduced in the *Guide*. Treaty making in the context of the EU is no easy matter. This is due not only to the many political forces involved, and to the way European Treaties are negotiated, but also to the treaties' status. They are treaties first and foremost even if they serve constitutional purposes. Developments since Nice have, in other words, made it clear that the European Treaties remain only a partial constitution for the Union. And this is true however we define a constitution.

Current arguments thus point firstly to the continuing dispute about the status of the European Treaties and whether they should give way to a 'proper' European Constitution. This very much raises the question of whether the member states are, or wish to remain, the 'masters of the treaties'. Secondly, the arguments show that even though the negotiators of Nice felt that they had managed to avoid bequeathing any 'leftovers' to the future, they actually helped – albeit involuntarily – to open up a far wider debate about the nature, future and dynamics of the Union. And in this debate the European treaties will remain an essential if ambiguous element, and one which will require constant explanation.

Whether we have adequately explained them as they presently are is up to readers to decide. However, we have tried. And we would be delighted to receive suggestions of better interpretations, whether directly or through academic channels. At least then we could have the kind of debate on what the treaties actually say and do which is so often lacking even among contributions to the 'debate on the future of Europe'.

vii Towards Further European Treaties?

The Community and Union have now spent the last third of their existence thinking about altering the European Treaties and their contents. And this process is certainly going to continue beyond Nice. Indeed, although the Treaty of Nice sought to open the way for a further, relatively focused, debate about further changes, things have moved on since then. To begin with, there is now some uncertainty about whether Nice itself will finally be ratified in its existing form. Moreover, the Irish 'no' in June 2001 raised all kinds of hares about the future of the Union and complicated both the post-Nice process and responses to it. Many of the latter suggest that the so-called 'debate on the future of Europe' will have to cope with far more issues than were originally envisaged in December 2000 and in more divisive circumstances. And there is no certainty about how any results of the debate should be negotiated or packaged.

With a whole range of actors and interests involved in all this it is very hard to estimate the prospects for further treaty reform. However, the likelihood is that those who are baying for a new 'constitution' for Europe will again be disappointed and probably rightly so. Hence the present messy condominium will continue. And this means that some form of the European Treaties will be with us for a while yet.

Ratifying Nice?

The ratification process started unproblematically with, paradoxically, the Danes moving rapidly and successfully to approve the treaty without a referendum. It also went through the French Parliament without much difficulty. Yet then, on the same day that the

Spaniards started consideration of the treaty and a second Labour electoral victory removed any real likelihood of a negative decision in the United Kingdom, the Irish rejected the treaty by 54% to 46%, admittedly on a low turnout and for contradictory motives. The rejection came as a surprise to many, though insiders, both supporters and opponents, had suspected that the polls may have been misleading.

Three kinds of reasons seem to have lain behind the vote. Firstly, it had much to do with internal Irish politics: referendum fatigue; criticism of a government which had signed up to the Partnership for Peace without seeking public endorsement and then failed to campaign effectively and energetically for Nice; and the emergence of a battle hardened 'anti' movement reinforced by a strengthening Sinn Fein. Indeed Sinott and Thomsen argue that what really needs to be explained is not the 'no' vote, which was actually slightly down on 1998, but why former 'yes' voters abstained. The inability of the 'yes' campaign to mobilize its supporters, leaving them open to contrary arguments and, possibly, a lack of understanding is seen as crucial. It is a classic example of both a popular lack of European engagement and of an inability of elites to generate such engagement.

None the less, secondly, there were a number of identity questions beginning with a fear about a loss of influence in an EU led by large states, whether using enhanced co-operation or the new mainstream provisions. Greens like Gormley argued strongly that the Union must continue on the basis of absolute equality between states, irrespective of size. And, contrary to UK Euroscepticism, Irish fears were that participation in the new Union would be helpful to NATO and to the detriment of neutrality. Equally, though some of the leaders denied it, there was no doubt that the 'no' campaign played on fears of monetary loss, whether through the ending of subsidies, net contributions or tax harmonization. The social geography of rejection with the largest majorities in the rural west underline this. At the same time, Irish identity was seen as morally at risk thanks to the way that the Charter of Fundamental Rights might be used to impose abortion and divorce on the country.

Thirdly, there were a number of economic policy issues. Criticism of Irish budgetary policies was much resented, especially when it seemed to point to interventionist social programmes as unhappily flagged by the French Socialist (PS) prime minister, Lionel Jospin, in the run-up to the vote. Some observers believe that prosperity and better relations with the UK have encouraged the spread of anti-European neo-liberalism from across the Irish Sea. Amongst the many working-class voters who turned it down fear of immigration also played a part, even though some of the migrants might be from good Catholic countries like Poland. Whatever the reasons, and whatever the turnout, the result was the same and presented the Union with a real problem, just as the Danes had in 1992.

In fact, all kinds of suggestions were made about how to proceed. Other hostile forces thus climbed on the bandwagon and, unsuccessfully, demanded referenda in Austria, France and the United Kingdom. For many the answer was to abandon Nice and return to the drawing board. This was because the treaty was both flawed in itself and no longer legally sustainable. However, opinions differed as to what should be sketched out on the drawing board. For enthusiasts like J.-L. Bourlanges MEP and the Union of European Federalists (UEF) it would be a much more radical integrationist matter. The latter argued that the Irish had rejected an inter-governmental Europe and this should be respected. This assumption would come as some surprise to Anthony Coughlan and his Irish supporters, who argue that the problem with Nice is that it will lead to a two-tier Europe, and they want a single-tier EU in which all states are equal and have a veto. In any case the UEF believes it was therefore up to the 15 governments to come up with a more appealing political project for the future of Europe at Laeken. They assume that this will involve a 'convention' and a constitution before 2003.

A slightly more realistic assessment comes from people like Riccardi, the editorialist of *Agence Presse Europe*, whose answer is to adopt a more radical agenda on the assumption that Ireland and other doubting states would stand aside, allowing other states to ratify a parallel new treaty which would be activated when a limited number of states approved it. Again this seems to ignore political realities not just in Ireland but in most other countries of the EU. Hence, for the even more extreme leader writer of *The Federalist* splits and crises, and even the denouncing of the treaties, are the price to be paid for creating a necessary European federation. This might be created on the basis of six to eight states. It would be impossible among 15 to 25. Contrary to the federationists' post-war belief in popular support, their successors look to governments to do all this.

The contrary view comes from SOS democracy and some of the leaders of the 'no' campaign, who argue that there should be a simpler treaty creating a less centralized and intrusive Union, reversing the tendencies of the 1990s. This is something they believe could be rapidly and easily negotiated. Such a belief ignores both the existence of the counter-project – which sees the treaty form as the problem – and the technical difficulties involved in such a negotiation. None the less, the Irish decision gave the idea new strength.

A number of ideas about how the road block on the way to enlargement might be by-passed were also canvassed. One idea was to drop Nice and rely on the accession treaties under negotiation to push the same solutions through, something which would have infinitely complicated the treaty base and further dented the Union's credibility. Another possibility was to revert to the Amsterdam protocol and use this to push through necessary institutional changes. In the event, member-state governments made it absolutely clear that there would be no renegotiating the painfully agreed Nice deal, especially 18 months before final ratification was necessary for enlargement. To do so would, on the one hand, reopen the Pandora's box of conflicts between large and small member states and, on the other, be bound to fail, given the fact that the Irish opposition was so variegated and often concerned with things which were not actually in the treaty. Moreover, it would send a terrible signal to the candidate countries.

In fact the Union has adopted something of a Micawber-like approach, waiting for something Irish to turn up and refraining from the kind of threatening moves embarked on so counter-productively by President Mitterrand in 1992. Indeed, the official response was very low key and laid back. And, to a large extent, this has been echoed in much of the press. The assumption seems to be that if the treaty is re-presented after the creation of a national forum, the holding of a general election and with declarations on military commitments, abortion and, less convincingly, the powers of the Union, the Irish will approve it if properly persuaded. And, by then, the other member states, who also have a democratic right to do so, should also have ratified the Treaty. However, the Irish government will have first to win a general election and see off a possible legal challenge to the constitutionality of calling a second referendum. Whether this strategy will work remains to be seen. If it does not, and Nice cannot be acted on directly, there will be real problems. However, it is unlikely that the Irish opposition will get what it wants from any new deal.

As it is, by late July 2001, although three states had ratified and others like the UK were well advanced, six states had not even commenced ratification proceedings. However, whether or not Nice as such is ratified many of its decisions will find their way into the treaties in some form or another. This reinforces, as we said at the outset, our decision to continue with the *Guide* on a post-Nice basis. Even if our original assumption that it would eventually come into effect proves incorrect, knowing what the treaties would have been like had it been ratified will still be useful.

Debating the Future of Europe

In any case, all this has cut across the emerging debate on the future of Europe. This has a number of roots and meanings. Of the former, a major stimulus to the underlying ambitions for further integration that had accompanied both the 1996 and 2000 IGCs was the long-term model of a future Union evoked in controversial major speeches in 2000 by Joschka Fischer, Jacques Chirac and Tony Blair. The Commission's own thoughts about 'governance' in the aftermath of the fall in 1999 of the Santer Commission and the pressures of enlargement have also played a part. Then, in the run-up to Nice, pressures from the German *Länder* for a limitation to Brussels' incursions on their autonomy gave the idea a further push.

So Nice gave a formal endorsement to the idea of further discussions on a selection of issues related to the next stage of Union development and enlargement (see Declaration No. 23 TN). This was done because of concerns that the changes made at Nice would not be sufficient either to make the enlarged Union work well or to satisfy the aspirations of its citizens. Consequently it wanted to encourage as many people as possible to start thinking about the future shape of the Union so that this could better reflect popular desires and thus be more accountable. The treaty recognized the failure of post-Amsterdam attempts to woo citizens over by more relevant policies and endorsed the need for a deeper and wider debate about the future of the Union. This was to be encouraged by the Swedish and Belgian presidencies through discussions with academic, business, political and social interests, together with representatives of national parliaments and the candidate states. Out of this came an interim report at Gothenburg and this was to be followed, at the Laeken European Council in December 2001, by a declaration on the best method of continuing the debate. The Belgian government has already set up a group of 'Wise Men' – Giuliano Amato, Jean-Luc Dehaene, Jacques Delors, Bronislaw Geremek and David Miliband – to help it prepare for Laeken although this will not produce a report and the decision will be that of the presidency alone.

Four issues were singled out at Nice for consideration, beginning with how to establish and monitor a more precise delimitation of powers between the European Union and the member states. This is the delimitation-of-competences question and, as such, relates to subsidiarity. The second is what to do about the status of the new Charter of Fundamental Rights, so as to make EU citizens more aware of their rights, and the third is how to involve national parliaments more in the governance of the Union so as to reinforce national democracy. The final question of the four was whether to simplify the treaties without changing their meaning and, if so, how. However, it was implicitly accepted that other issues could be addressed.

This had the virtue of giving some precision to the much evoked but rarely defined and usually unclear concept of a 'debate'. It also, for the first time, gave it some kind of organizational basis, although the provisions were still somewhat vague. Yet so far the debate – which was launched on 7 March 2001 – has neither got very far nor conformed to the template laid down at Nice. In its first or open debate phase the Commission sponsored a website where enthusiasts, people worried about Turkey, and rabid English Europhobes, have given vent to their prejudices. There have been a number of conferences, some public meetings and a few contributions from academics, institutions and politicians. The Dutch government has presented a paper to the States General. Other events are planned in some countries, though elections have held things back in Italy and the United Kingdom. Little of this has yet come together to make a real public impact. Even at Gothenburg the Swedish presidency's report was a barely remarked annex which did little more than inventory sporadic national initiatives and canvass the possibility of a forum – similar but not identical to the convention which produced the Charter of Fundamental Rights – to ensure that the second and more focused stage of the debate prepares the agenda for the IGC. The report foresaw a need for a group of 'Wise Men' to help with this.

In any case, the European Parliament and others have sought to take over the process. Originally disappointed by the Nice treaty, the EP has come round to accept it because it offers the possibility of a second bite at the cherry of deeper integration. Hence, MEPs have made progress on what they chose to call the 'Future of Europe Debate', rather than the post-Nice process, a condition for approving Nice. By progress they mean moves to constitutionalize the treaties in part by making the Charter of Fundamental Rights a binding part of it. They want, moreover, to do this through a convention rather than an IGC. This should in turn lead to the development of the European social model, including a European tax facility; to elevating the Commission to the role of a European government, perhaps with a directly elected president; and to a bicameral legislature with strengthened powers for the EP itself. Finally, they also want an enhanced EU role in the world. And they looked to the Belgian presidency to lead the way to this 'political Europe' with its new legitimacy, by its proposals to the Laeken European Council. They also appear to hope that this will not give any ground to ideas of specifying competences or involving national parliaments further since these are seen as regressive and anti-European.

All this was badly received in Ireland as a telling speech by the Irish Attorney-General in June 2001 showed. In fact the Irish vote had changed the dimensions of the whole debate in two ways. On the one hand, it ensured that there will be a much wider agenda than was originally envisaged. On the other, it called into question the assumption that the debate was likely to lead to further integration. In doing this it brought to light the way the debate originated in two contradictory aspirations. Nice reflected both the desire of those who want to go further and the wish of the German *Länder* and some UK opinion to prevent further loss of autonomy by enshrining a (restrictive) list of EU powers. Initial responses from the first camp to the Irish vote have, as we have already implied, suggested that they see no need to accommodate views which differ from their own. This impression is reinforced by the 2001 Benelux Memorandum on the Future of Europe, which restates the now rather tired integrationist conventional wisdom of the last 15 years.

This suggests that getting agreement, whether on method or on outcome, will not be easy either in the second stage of the public debate in 2002 or in the IGC proper. The two are, of course, closely related in the minds of both camps. So further fierce argument between federationists and those who are now being described as sovereignists is likely since behind the detailed questions lies the issue of what the European Union is or should be. And, on this, there is no real agreement as yet. It is too early for the Union to decide its final form and destination. As Schmitter has pointed out, if we asked the peoples of Europe to choose between federationist and confederationist constitutional options – or what has been called 'power Europe' and 'area Europe' – they are likely to embrace both, assuming they vote at all, leading to a deliciously Alice in Wonderland Union.

Towards Further Treaties?

Will the debate lead to anything? And what forms might the outcome take, substantively and technically? The answer to the first seems to be yes. Something will emerge from it, though whether the people will actually respond to the questions presently being asked of them is unclear. But it is unlikely that things will go on exactly as they are now. Circumstances and political pressures will ensure that this is not so.

However, the likelihood that there will be an agreed outcome with a clear-cut choice made between these two polar opposites is zero. This is because, on the one hand, the forces in opposition are so many and so various, and none has the ability to dictate to the Union as a whole. Only some kind of compromise is feasible. In any case, outside events and local difficulties are all too likely to complicate things. And we have to remember that new members and other candidate countries will also be playing a role.

On the other hand, the reality is, as the *Guide* should have made clear, that the debate is far too polarized. The Union is a complicated condominium embracing both supra-national and inter-governmental elements. And, while it is not a federation, it is already happily federal in the sense that it seeks, in a messy way, to share responsibilities among all levels of authority and participation in the Union. Shifting this to either a clear-cut authoritative federation or to a mere free-trade area in which all powers are repatriated (and there is no possibility of further concerted action) is neither feasible nor desired. There are more realistic and attractive models such as network Europe, the constitutional order of states or Wessels' ever closer fusion. What is likely to emerge will no doubt fit none of these exactly, but the lesson of the *Guide* must be that some kind of substantive halfway house is the only real possibility for the Union given its present political balance. Although this is unlikely to be any simpler and more comprehensible than the present situation, it is something with which most people could live.

To move on to the last part of the second question, the technical form of any new arrangements, this rather suggests that, as seasoned observers like Neunreither and Weiler argue, we will not finish up with a constitution as such. For although there are good arguments of principle in its favour these are outweighed by the absence of the necessary political conditions. There is, in other words, no evidence that the majority of citizens are willing to exchange their existing status for the clarity, empowerment and rights promised by a European Constitution. Indeed, it could be a very counter-productive turn-off, given the propensity to boredom with institutional questions. Equally, as Galloway says, the EU does have a constitution of sorts and it works, so why fix it? Despite the assumptions of some enthusiasts we have no guarantee that a constitution would actually be written in a more comprehensible way than the treaties. Given the variety of competing interests and the openness of the suggested drafting process, the opposite could well be true.

To say this, however, does not mean that there will be no change in the present treaties. If there is enough agreement, and this is a big if, then some of the questions raised by the Nice Declaration on the Future of the Union may get an answer. Moreover, enlargement is likely to demand far more changes than we realize today, especially if, as some think, Nice is basically a holding operation for the existing member states. In any case, assuming that Nice is ratified, it is a kind of MOT certificate for the enlarging Union. And such certificates do not last for ever. So, even if the Nice arrangements do not unravel, there could be further change whether before 2004 or after.

This could include some form of simplification, building on the many ideas already canvassed and catalogued in Annex 3. However, there are very narrow limits to what can be achieved in this direction without risking potentially destabilizing conflicts. So the likelihood is that we will still be left with a series of European Treaties. If the ratification of the TN gets held up and enlargement speeds up, then there could be new accession treaties ahead of the ratification of Nice, which would be confusing and complicated. This would especially be so if states not considered in the present list of 27, such as Norway and Switzerland, come up fast on the outside and overtake laggards with weightings different from theirs. And, of course, in 2002, the TECSC will expire. So there could be significant changes to the treaty base almost irrespective of the outcome of the 'debate on the future of Europe'.

However, the debate will certainly continue. And, no doubt, as for the last 20 years, both federationists and sovereignists will query the contents and complexities of the treaties. Because the Union is a recent and very deliberate construction, as opposed to an organic community, its character comes from changes made to its structures. This exacerbates political argument but the two views can cancel each other out, leaving the in-between ambiguities of the existing European Treaties to guide the Union. In any case, getting away from ongoing treaty change may not, as the *Guide* has already suggested, be easy. Continuing debate, leading to further revision at the margins, seems the more likely outcome.

viii Postscript

In the short term, between the submission of the manuscript and the completion of the *Guide*, the European Treaties did not disappear from public view. However, they did not enjoy the place that might have been expected. In fact, discussion was relatively low key especially where Nice was concerned and often obscured by other issues whether related to the 2004 agenda or to outside events. None the less, questions about the European Treaties were returned to the public agenda by the Laeken Declaration of 15 December 2001. Yet, despite talk of everything being changed by this, it seems unlikely that either the European Treaties or the Union itself will depart from their existing paths of complex betwixt and betweenness.

The second half of 2001 saw ratification of Nice proceed smoothly, even if there was little further by way of indication from the Irish as to how they would overcome the referendum's 'no'. Spain, Austria, Germany, Portugal and the UK all approved Nice. In the first two there were no contrary votes and elsewhere opposition was usually small. In the UK the Commons divided on party lines. By the end of the year, more than half the states had therefore ratified the Treaty. Belgium, Finland, Italy, the Netherlands and Sweden had also commenced their processes. Only Greece delayed matters until the New Year and there was no evidence of serious opposition.

In Ireland things were different. Opposition remained. Hence, the government proceeded cautiously, seeking to improve information and understanding by creating a 'National Forum on Europe' for parliamentarians and others to receive presentations from both the 'yes' and 'no' camps. There was also continued talk of the government seeking new Danish-style declarations from the EU on military neutrality, abortion and the limits to EU authority. The first would emphasize that participation in the European Rapid Reaction Force was voluntary and that non-participating states would not be expected to pay for it while the second would seek to counter charges that the Charter of Fundamental Rights could be used to bring abortion into Ireland. The third element would presumably be a further statement on EU respect for the rights of member states though there was no mention of this in the Laeken Declaration. The government also talked of other domestic measures including improved *Dáil* scrutiny of EU legislation. The question of what would happen if this strategy fails remained unanswered.

One effect of the Irish 'no' was to make critics of Nice re-evaluate the Treaty. They came to think – as had doubters after Maastricht and Amsterdam – that, despite its flaws, it did offer a solution to some problems. Things would be much more difficult without it especially for candidate countries. So Nice was 'a nice try' which had to be approved to allow enlargement to continue. Hence, while attacks on voting arrangements continued and the EP and others still sniped at the Treaty from time to time, pro-European opinion increasingly came to stress its merits, notably its legal reforms. Commentators like Shaw and Yataganas argued it was a further small step in the EU's piecemeal constitutional development. And, in the view of the UK Foreign Office and others, it did not involve anything like the creation of a 'superstate' but gave the UK more say. This kind of nuanced verdict was very evident in the Federal Trust's *The Treaty of Nice Explained*.

Beyond Nice, the second half of 2001 also saw some progress with the Future of Europe debate. Most attention was concentrated on the mechanisms for treaty amendment, the traditional wider agenda of institutional change and on ideas of constitutionalizing the treaties. A major debate on the future of Europe did not really materialize. The formal debate, launched in March 2001, proved a rather limited affair despite the hopes that it would bring in civil society and candidate countries. To begin with, it was limited to enthusiasts with neither the general public nor the media showing much interest. Contributions to the 'Futurum' website rarely related to either Nice or its four issues but often rehearsed old arguments on topics such as Cyprus. Second, the debate did not produce vital and agreed new ideas. At best it was worthy but banal, at worst it merely encouraged existing – and opposing – prejudices. And third, not every country took it very seriously, the UK being amongst the least active despite the new government's efforts to stress the value of the EU.

It is not surprising, therefore, that the debate did not greatly illuminate the four key issues entrusted to it at Nice. To begin with there was surprisingly little discussion of the Charter of Fundamental Rights though some MEPs like Berthu called for it to be subordinated to the ECHR. However, the EP remained committed to consolidating it into the treaties and the Danish Foreign Minister saw this as a way of stressing that the EU was more than merely an economic body and was subject to international norms.

There was more movement on the role of national parliaments even though some in the EP regarded this as a threat to itself and not, as did Ludlow and others, as a way of reconnecting the EU with national political elites. Ideas of involving national parliaments in the Council when this is acting in legislative mode, of making Commissioners report weekly to national parliaments, holding national elections on the same day as EP elections, involving MEPs in national parliamentary scrutiny and of creating joint national–EP specialist committees were all canvassed, along with the merits of COSAC. However, there was little support for Blair's second chamber although the idea of involving parliaments in deciding whether the EU should legislate or not did seem to attract some support.

Thus, where the question of defining the EU's competences was concerned, Blair called for proper guarantees against centralization and for subsidiarity through national parliamentary involvement. Ludlow also suggested that member-state responsibilities could be clarified in any treaty revision. And Prodi accepted that the question of what the EU should do had to be faced. But Lamassoure's reports to the EP showed that allocating competences was a very complicated problem since the European Treaties do not presently provide a very clear division of powers. Hence clarifying them could require a wholesale rewriting of the treaties.

Simplification was another rather ignored subject and one which was often conducted in ignorance of the attempts already made by the European University Institute and elsewhere to do this. None the less, even doubting MEPs like Beazley were willing to concede the need for codification. And the UK government, having sought to rewrite the treaties in a new 297-word version, promised to produce a fuller, simpler version of the main European Treaties for the people. Bonde also saw this as a way of ensuring national control of the EU. Conversely Ludlow argued for a basic treaty to enhance legitimacy and flexibility.

In fact, debate in the second half of 2001 preferred to concentrate on topics beyond those suggested at Nice. Hence, there was much interest in the way the next stage of the debate would be organized. There was, as anticipated, a good deal of pressure, led by the EP, for the creation of a new 'Convention' to take charge of this. Secondly, the debate often preferred to consider a much wider agenda. This was true of contributions from Delors' *Notre Europe* foundation, from the EP and its parties, from the Benelux and other governments and from a major Jean Monnet Conference in Brussels in October. Suggestions made included merging the Union and the Community or at least communitarizing the pillars or giving the former legal personality. Equally there was talk of reforming the European Council, the Presidency system and, especially, the existing General Affairs Council. Even the Tories saw the virtues of having a more stable and specialist co-ordinating ministerial body in Brussels. There were also many calls to slim the Commission down and have its President elected by the EP or even the populace at large so that it became a 'legitimate government for Europe'. Some also wanted to see Europol, a Public Prosecutor and a Law Council added to the institutional set-up, if not a European-wide police service and identity card. And, not surprisingly, there was pressure to universalize QMV and co-decision. However, there was little talk of policy change except for more economic co-ordination in the light of EMU. The EP also demanded a much greater voice in this. Equally, it sought more influence in external policy, something which went along with a general desire to strengthen the CFSP and its officials. Yet there was, at the same time, some realization that all this would be too much for some states. Hence, Delors and others talked of allowing an advance guard to go ahead and Barnier of writing a right of secession into the treaties.

This tied in with a third, more significant, concern. The second half of 2001 thus heard increasing talk of constitutionalization of the treaties as well as a renewed Franco-German commitment to a European Constitution. As before what was meant was not wholly clear and there were academic arguments about whether a constitution as such – assuming there is such a thing – is feasible or necessary. For some it was not credible without a European state or a European demos and for others it was unnecessary since the EU's existing legal bases, including national charters, already provide a constitution. None the less, majority opinion continued to argue that it was both possible and necessary to turn the European Treaties into something superior, more autonomous, more binding and more concerned with principle. The Centre for European Reform also put forward the idea of the EU having its own mission statement.

For those who believe in closer integration the argument was that doing this would enhance legitimacy and transparency because a constitution would clarify outcomes, powers and rights. It would make the EU both more comprehensible and more comforting to ordinary people, symbolizing popular cohesion. Equally, if it did not require unanimous ratification, it could provide a means of leaving doubters behind. However, some of those who thought this way were also aware that there were risks in this approach. Constitutionalizing would probably expose the policy *acquis* to attack. It could also make the EU too rigid. And if it were either too abstract or too detailed it could easily alienate the very people it was supposed to win over.

Moreover, constitutionalization was, as often in the past, also espoused by those whose political ambitions were somewhat different. Dashwood, Vibert and others saw it as a means of reassuring the people that the EU would not threaten them by specifying and circumscribing its powers to those required by its basic aims. Equally it could provide an easier framework for enlargement than current provisions. In any case, wiser heads were aware that it was unrealistic to believe that there was either sufficient need, time or will to produce any constitution by 2004, let alone one reducing member states' powers. At best a basic treaty, without claims to superior status, might be possible in the minds of Griller, Ludlow and others. Yet even this could be problematic.

Further reasons why the Future of Europe debate did not evolve in the ways assumed in December 2000 can be found in the way that the EU itself developed. To begin with, Nice was partly obscured by the Commission's White Paper on Governance of July 2001. This set out ways of increasing accountability, effectiveness and participation in the everyday working of the Union without treaty changes. Once this was put out to consultation it attracted a good deal of attention. And it was picked up by the Laeken Summit as a parallel track to be pursued in reforming the EU.

More importantly, the EU had other things on its mind. On the one hand, it had to give considerable attention to things like enlargement – which became increasingly likely to be a 'big bang' matter of up to ten states at once and not the drip-feed process assumed by Nice. Equally, the coming of the final stage of EMU increasingly obsessed the press and public opinion as well as elites. On the other hand, the events of 11 September 2001 forced the Union and its states to focus on external questions such as terrorism and underdevelopment.

Some of this awareness of the changing world order showed itself in the Laeken Declaration on the Future of the European Union which was approved without great difficulty by the European Council in December 2001. The Declaration (available at www.europa.en.int/futurum/document/offtextdoc151201), which was the first item in the summit conclusions, is an unusual document, more philosophical than legislative and raising as many questions as it answers. The questions raised are broader, with a different priority, from those listed at Nice and derive from an unusual willingness to accept criticism of the EU. And they are set in a clearer and more purposeful context than is common. However, their import is not clear since the Declaration can be read in many ways from, at one extreme as a rolling back of the EU commitment, through various compromises to a yet more integrationist plan. So its results are hard to predict despite claims that it was a real turning point in EU history.

The Declaration's starting point is that the EU has moved from being largely an economic concern to something more political. And it now finds itself at a crossroads having virtually succeeded in uniting and pacifying the continent but needing to protect its successes against two new challenges. The first is trying to bring its operations closer to citizens and their aspirations. These are seen as contradictory, both demanding more effective action and rejecting over-intrusive regulation. The second is to try and do more to shoulder responsibilities for stability and essential democratic values in a world which the terrorist attacks on the US had shown to be more divided, threatening and uncertain than had been appreciated. In other words the aim must be a simpler and stronger Union.

Meeting the first challenge was seen as requiring three reforms, beginning with a better division of responsibilities between states and the EU in line with the Nice provisions. However, this is now seen as raising wider questions about how to make the division more transparent, whether tasks should be re-allocated to different levels, and how to avoid both the perils of 'creeping competence' and of veto stagnation. Secondly, the EU's instruments may need to be simplified given the way laws and treaties have been piled one on top of another. This may require a clearer hierarchy of EU acts.

Even more significant is a third category of reforms needed to make the Union both more effective and more democratically acceptable. These could involve changes to the way the Commission President and MEPs are selected. It could also involve increasing QMV and reforming co-decision and the operation of the Council and other posts. The question of bringing national parliaments in to police subsidiarity is also raised along with questions about strengthening the CFSP. Otherwise enhancing the EU's position in the world is not given much attention reflecting the way the Declaration has largely grown out of the post-Nice agenda.

Another Nice issue, simplification or, as it is somewhat misleadingly called, constitutionalization, is tackled. The Declaration accepts that there are too many treaties and they are too complicated. So it raises the question of whether things can be made simpler by merging the EC and the EU or by dividing the texts into a basic and an implementing treaty. Only in this context is there mention of the remaining Nice issue, the position of the Charter of Fundamental Rights. There is also the thought that, in the long run, all this could lead to some kind of constitutional text, apparently one stressing values.

To help the 2004 IGC adjudicate on these issues the Laeken European Council also agreed to create an advisory 'Convention' to meet from 1 March 2002 under the chairmanship of Valéry Giscard d'Estaing, the former French President and MEP, assisted by a representative steering committee and a cross-institutional secretariat. Composed of one representative of each head of government or state, two MPs per member state, sixteen MEPs, two Commissioners, six representatives of the Committee of the Regions and of the Economic and Social Committee, together with up to 39 representatives from the candidate countries and other observers, the Convention is to decide its own procedure and to consult as it chooses. But it has to be public. It can also draw on what is loosely described as a Forum – an undefined network of academic, business and other non-governmental bodies representing civil society – something rarely picked up in UK commentaries. However, it must report to the European Council notably by presenting a final document, whether an agreed text or, more likely, a series of ideas. What the 2004 IGC will do with this is not made clear.

Although this has been hailed as marking the beginning of a new era, it would be unwise to expect too much change. To begin with, if Nice is not ratified, the post-Laeken process will be called into question even if ways and means are found of keeping both shows on the road. And overriding an Irish veto will sit oddly with Laeken's desire to respond to citizens' needs. Moreover, given the very different forces and opinions involved in the process it will be all too easy for the IGC to disregard the Convention's views, unpopular though this might be in EP circles. Conflicting ideas and member-state interests suggest that there will not be a clear-cut and final solution to the question of what the EU will be, merely another evolutionary compromise adjustment along a road with no clear or obvious end. The Convention thus got off to a slow and poorly publicized start in Spring 2002. It had some difficulties agreeing its form, agreeing an agenda, and coping with the concerns of candidate countries, eurosceptics, regions, small states and wider social interests. The Union is therefore likely to remain a complex and mixed body.

None the less, the European Treaties constituting it will change. Partly this is because they will, perhaps as a result of the governance debate, be read in different ways. They will also presumably be altered by Nice, accession treaties and the 2004 IGC. The question is whether such changes will be accepted and helpful. Even attempts at simplification could add yet more unpopular complexity. In other words, treaty-making is likely to remain a more difficult process than outsiders tend to think.

VI Annexes

Annex 1   Bibliographic and Other Sources

Understanding the European Treaties is not something which can be achieved simply by
reading one book. A whole range of sources is required to bring out their myriad facets
and interpretations. An indicative guide to such sources is provided here. We provide,
first, listings for the actual treaty texts, followed by indications of alternative versions of
the treaties referred to in Annex 3. The major element is the bibliography of books and
articles. There is also a listing of relevant ECJ cases and finally, since texts are increasingly
available on the internet, details of some useful websites.

1a: Sources for the Treaties

As well as being available on the Union's website, the treaties are available in a whole
range of hard copy versions. For example, the Council of Europe's *European Yearbook*
normally prints them. Some of these are published by the Union itself or by its member
states, others are commercially produced, sometimes with comments. They fall into two
main categories: prints of the founding treaties and editions of the agreements emerging
from IGCs. They are arranged in this way here.

Founding Treaties

Consolidated Treaties (Luxembourg: OOPEC, 1997)
Constantinescu, V. et al., *Traité Instituant la Communauté Economique Européenne; commentaire
article par article* (Paris: Economica, 1992)
Lenz, C. O., et al., *EG Vertrag zur Gründung der EG* (2. Aufl) (Köln: Bundesanzeizer, 1999)
Nelson, S. (ed.), *The Convoluted Treaties II: Treaty Establishing the European Economic Com-
munity* (Oxford: Nelson and Pollard, 1993)
*Official Journal of the European Communities Treaty on European Union, together with the
complete text of the Treaty establishing the European Community, OJ* C224, 31 August 1992
The Rome, Maastricht and Amsterdam Treaties (Brussels: Euroconfidentiel, 1999)
Selected Instruments Taken from the Treaties (Luxembourg: OOPEC, 2000)
Les Traités de Rome, Maastricht et Amsterdam (Paris: La Documentation Française, 1998)
Treaties establishing the European Communities (Luxembourg: OOPEC, 1973)
Treaties establishing the European Communities, abridged edition (Luxembourg: OOPEC, 1987)
Treaties and Alliances of the World, 7th edition (Letchworth: Harper, 2002)

Treaty on European Union – Maastricht

Agence Europe Treaty on European Union, *Europe Documents* No. 1759/60, 7 February 1992 (and No. 1759/60 bis, 26 February 1992)

Belmont European Policy Centre, *The New Treaty on European Union* (Brussels: Belmont European Policy Centre, 1992)

Church, C. H. and Phinnemore, D., *European Union and European Community* (Hemel Hempstead: Harvester Wheatsheaf, 1995)

Cloos, J., Weyland, J. et al., *Le Traité de Maastricht: Genèse, Analyse, Commentaires* (Brussels: Etablissements Emile Brulyant, 1994)

Constantinescu, V. et al., *Traité sur l'Union Européenne* (Paris: Economica, 1995)

Corbett, R., *The Maastricht Treaty* (London: Longman, 1993)

Council of the European Communities, Commission of the European Communities, *Treaty on European Union* (Luxembourg: OOPEC, 1992)

Duffy, P. and Yves de Cara, J. *European Union – The Lawyers' Guide* (London: Longman, 1992)

Europa Union, *Europäische Gemeinschaft – Europäische Union: Die Vertragstexte von Maastricht* (Bonn: Presse- und Informationsamt der Bundesregierung/Europa Union, 1992)

European Information Service, 'Treaty on European Union', *European Report*, No. 1746, 22 February 1992

Groeben, H. von der et al., *Beitrag über die Europäische Union von Maastricht mit Schlußfolgerungen des Europäischen Rates von Lissabon* (Baden-Baden: Nomos Verlagsgesellschaft, 1992)

Hunnings, N. M. and MacDonald Hill, J., 'The Treaty on European Union', *Common Market Law Review*, 63 (11), 1992, 573–792

Journaux officiels *Traité sur l'Union Européenne* (Paris: Imprimerie Nationale, 1992)

'Maastricht – The Treaty on European Union', *The Sunday Times*, 11 October 1992

Treaty on European Union (Luxembourg: OOPEC, 1992)

Treaty on European Union, *Official Journal of the European Communities*, C 191, 29 July 1992

Treaty on European Union, together with the complete text of the treaty establishing the European Community, *Official Journal of the European Communities*, C 224, 31 August 1992

Vertrag über die Europäische Union, Bulletin, No. 16 (Bonn: Presse- und Informationsamt der Bundesregierung, 1992)

Amsterdam

Berthu, G. and Sonchet, D., *Le Traité d'Amsterdam* (Paris: Guibert, 1998)

Cowgill, B., *The Treaty of Amsterdam in Perspective* (Stroud: British Management Data Foundation, 1999)

Duff, A., *The Treaty of Amsterdam: Text and Commentary* (London: Sweet and Maxwell/Federal Trust, 1997)

European Policy Centre, *Making Sense of Amsterdam* (Brussels: European Policy Centre, 1997)

Revue du Marche Commune et de l'Union Européenne (1998) *Treaty of Amsterdam* (Luxembourg: OOPEC, 1997)

Treaty of Amsterdam amending the Treaty on European Union, the Treaties establishing the European Communities and certain related acts, signed at Amsterdam, 2 October 1997, *Official Journal of the European Communities*, C 340, 10 November 1997

Nice

Aalt, W. and Verhey, L., 'The EU Charter: Text and Structure', *Maastricht Journal of European and Comparative Law*, 8 (1), 2001, 11–32

Berthu, G., *Traité de Nice* (Paris: de Guibert, 2001)

Cuadrado, M. M. (ed.), *Estructura Politica de la Union Europea* (Madrid: Universidad Complutense, 2001)

Feus, K. (ed.), *The EU Charter of Fundamental Rights* (London: Federal Trust, 2000)

Feus, K. (ed.), *The Treaty of Nice Explained* (London: Federal Trust, 2001)

Galloway, D., *The Treaty of Nice and Beyond: Realities and Illusions of Power in the EU* (Sheffield: UACES/Sheffield Academic Press, 2001)

The Treaty of Nice (Stroud: British Management Data Foundation, 2001)

Treaty of Nice (Luxembourg: OOPEC, 2001)

Treaty of Nice amending the Treaty on European Union, the Treaties establishing the European Communities and certain related acts, *Official Journal of the European Communities*, C 80, 10 March 2001

Supplementary Acts and Treaties

Act concerning the Conditions of Accession and the Adjustments to the Treaties – Accession to the European Communities of the Kingdom of Denmark, Ireland and the United Kingdom of Great Britain and Northern Ireland, *Official Journal of the European Communities*, L 73, 27 March 1972

Act concerning the Conditions of Accession and the Adjustments to the Treaties – Accession to the European Communities of the Kingdom of Spain and the Portuguese Republic, *Official Journal of the European Communities*, L 302, 15 November 1985

Act concerning the Conditions of Accession and the Adjustments to the Treaties – Accession to the European Communities of the Hellenic Republic, *Official Journal of the European Communities*, L 291, 19 July 1979

Act concerning the Conditions of Accession and the Adjustments to the Treaties – Accession to the European Union of the Republic of Austria, the Republic of Finland and the Kingdom of Sweden, *Official Journal of the European Communities*, C 241, 29 August 1994

Act concerning the election of the representatives of the European Parliament, *Official Journal of the European Communities*, L 278, 8 October 1976

Agreement on the European Economic Area, *Official Journal of the European Communities*, L 1, 1 January 1994

Convention of 13 November 1962 amending the Treaty establishing the European Economic Community, *Official Journal of the European Communities*, 150, 1 October 1964

Council Decision on the system of the European Communities Own Resources, *Official Journal of the European Communities*, L 293, 12 November 1994

Decision of the Council of the European Communities of 1 January 1973 adjusting the documents concerning the accession of new Member States to the European Communities, *Official Journal of the European Communities*, L 2, 1 January 1973

Decision of the Council of the European Union of 1 January 1995 adjusting the documents concerning the accession of new Member States to the European Union, *Official Journal of the European Communities*, L 1, 1 January 1995

Documents concerning the accession of the Republic of Austria, the Republic of Finland, and the Kingdom of Sweden to the European Union (Luxembourg: OOPEC, 1995)

Documents concerning the accessions to the European Communities of the Kingdom of Denmark, Ireland and the United Kingdom of Great Britain and Northern Ireland, the Hellenic Republic, the Kingdom of Spain and the Portuguese Republic (Luxembourg: OOPEC, 1987)

European Union: Selected instruments taken from the Treaties (Luxembourg: OOPEC, 1999)

Single European Act, *Bulletin of the European Communities*, Supplement 2/86, 1986

Single European Act, *Official Journal of the European Communities*, L 169, 29 June 1987

Treaty amending certain budgetary provisions of the Treaties establishing the European Communities and of the Treaty establishing a single Council and a single Commission of the European Communities, *Official Journal of the European Communities*, L 2, 2 January 1971

Treaty amending certain financial provisions of the Treaty establishing the European Communities and of the Treaty establishing a single Council and a single Commission of the European Communities, *Official Journal of the European Communities*, L 359, 31 December 1977

Treaty amending, with regard to Greenland, the Treaties establishing the European Communities, *Official Journal of the European Communities*, L 29, 1 February 1984

Treaty establishing a single Council and a single Commission of the European Communities, *Official Journal of the European Communities*, 152, 13 July 1967

1b: Alternative Versions of the Treaties

As Annex 3 will show, there have been a whole series of attempts to reform the European Treaties, dating back to the 1980s. The most important of these are listed below. None of them has been formally adopted. However, they do show the varied thinking that has gone on in the past about the treaties and may be of use in the run up to 2004.

Algieri, F. and the Bertelsmann Group in the Centre for Applied Policy, University of Munich, *A Basic Treaty for the European Union*, May 2000 (via www.cap.unimuenchen.de)

Basler Thesen fur die kunftige Verfassung Europas (Université de Basle, Institute of European Studies: Basler Schriften zur Europaïschen Integration 18, 1995)

Bogdandy, A. von et al., *A Unified and Simplified Model of the European Communities Treaties and the Treaty on European Union in Just One Treaty* (Luxembourg: European Parliament Directorate-General for Research, September 1996)

Caportorti, F. et al., *The European Union Treaty: Commentary on the Draft Adopted by the EP on 14 February 1984* (Oxford: Clarendon, 1986)

Church, C. and Yates, L., 'Getting the Packaging Right', *European Access*, 1995/96 (December), 7–9

Convention of Young European Citizens *Constitution of the European Union*, 20 July 2001 (published on the Future of Europe Website (http://europa.eu.int/futurum/documents/contrib/const fr.pdf) in September 2001)

Dashwood, A. and Ward, A. (eds.), 'CELS (Cambridge) E.C. Treaty Project', *European Law Review*, 22 (5), 1997, 395–516

European Constitutional Group, *A Proposal for a European Constitution* (London: European Policy Forum, 1993)

Feus, K., *A Simplified Treaty for the EU?* (London: Federal Trust, 2001)

Goulard, S. and Lequesne, C., *Une constitution européenne si et seulement . . .* (Paris: IEP/CERI, 2001)

Herman, F., *Draft report on the Constitution of the European Union* (Committee on Institutional Affairs, PE 203.601-EWPR2342434101) September 1993

'Our Constitution for Europe', *The Economist*, 28 October 2000, 17–22

Pinder, J., *The Constitution of the EU*, unpublished mss, available from the author

Raux, J., *Pour un Traité fondamentale de portée constitutionelle*, paper presented to the Jean Monnet Conference, Brussels, 1998

Robert Schumann Centre, *A Unified and Simplified Model of the European Communities* (Florence: EUI, 1996)

Robert Schumann Centre, *Re-organisation of the Treaties: Final Report plus Basic Treaty* (Florence: EUI, 2000)

Touscuz, J. et al., *Pacte Fondamental de l'Union Européenne* (Nice: CERCI, September 2001) (via www.cerci.org)

Treaties and the Treaty on European Union in Just One Treaty (Luxembourg: EP Directorate-General for Research, 1996)

Version Consolidée des Traités, 2 vols (Brussels: Secretariat General du Conseil, 2000)

Vibert, F., *Europe: A Constitution for the Millennium* (Aldershot: Dartmouth, 1995)

Villa Faber Group, *Thinking Enlarged* (Munich: Bertelsmann Foundation and Centre for Applied Policy Research, November 2001)

1c: Books and Articles

Abeysuriya, L., *An Assessment of the New European Union* (Kendal: The author, 1997)

Ackrill, R. W., ' CAP Reform 1999: A Crisis in the Making', *Journal of Common Market Studies*, 31 (2), 2000, 343–353

Alexander, L. (ed.), *Constitutionalism* (Cambridge: Cambridge University Press, 1998)

Allen, D., ' "Who speaks for Europe?" The Search for an Effective and Coherent External Policy', in Peterson, J. and Sjursen, H. (eds.), *A Common Foreign Policy for Europe?* (London: Routledge, 1998), 41–58

Allen, D., 'Cohesion and the Structural Funds: Transfers and Trade-Offs', in Wallace, H. and Wallace, W. (eds.), *Policy-Making in the European Union*, 4th edn (Oxford: Oxford University Press, 2000), 242–264

Allott, P., 'The Crisis of European Constitutionalism', *Common Market Law Review*, 34 (3), 1997, 439–490

Alter, K., 'Who are the "Masters of the Treaty": European Governments and the ECJ', *International Organization*, 52 (1), 1998, 121–147

Amtenbrink, F. et al., 'Stability and Growth Pact: Placebo or Panacea?', *European Business Law Review*, 8 (10), 1997, 202–210 and 233–238

Anderson, C. and Kaltenthaler, K., 'The Dynamics of Public Opinion', *European Journal of International Relations*, 2 (2), 1996, 175–199

Andrews, W. G., *Constitutions and Constitutionalism* (New York: Van Nostrand, 1965)

Areilza, J. M. de, 'Enhanced Co-operation in the Treaty of Amsterdam', Harvard University Jean Monnet Papers 13/1998

Armstrong, K. A., 'Governance and the Single European Market', in Craig, P. and Búrca, G. de (eds.), *The Evolution of EU Law* (Oxford: Oxford University Press, 1999), 745–789

Arnull, A., 'Taming the Beast? The Treaty of Amsterdam and the Court of Justice', in O'Keefe, D. and Twomey, P. (eds.), *Legal Issues of the Amsterdam Treaty* (Oxford: Hart, 1999), 109–122

Arnull, A., *The European Union and its Court of Justice* (Oxford: Oxford University Press, 1999)

Arnull, T. 'Renumbering the Treaties: another fine mess . . .', *European Law Review*, 24 (5), 1999, 443–444

Aust, A., *Modern Treaty Law and Practice* (Cambridge: Cambridge University Press, 2000)

Bainbridge, T., *The Penguin Companion to European Union*, new edition (London: Penguin, 1998)

Baldwin, R. et al., *Nice Try: Should the Treaty of Nice be Ratified?* (London: CEPR, 2001)

Barendt, E., 'Is there a United Kingdom Constitution?', *Oxford Journal of Legal Studies*, 17 (1), 1997, 137–146

Barents, R., 'Some Observations on the Treaty of Amsterdam', *Maastricht Journal of European and Comparative Law*, 4 (4), 1997, 332–345

Barents, R., 'Some Observations on the Treaty of Nice', *Maastricht Journal of European and Comparative Law*, 8 (2), (2001), 121–132

Barnard, C., 'Article 13: Through the Looking Glass of Union Citizenship', in O'Keefe, D. and Twomey, P. (eds.), *Legal Issues of the Amsterdam Treaty* (Oxford: Hart, 1999), 375–394

Barnard, C., 'EC "Social Policy" ', in Craig, P. and Búrca, G. de (eds.), *The Evolution of EU Law* (Oxford: Oxford University Press, 1999), 479–516

Barnard, C., *EC Employment Law*, 2nd edn (Oxford: Oxford University Press, 2000)

Barnier, M., 'Europe's Future: Two Steps and Three Paths – A Personal Note' Brussels, 8 June 2000. See also *Agence Presse Europe*, 1 June 2001 (7975), 5

Baun, M., *An Imperfect Union: The Maastricht Treaty and the New Politics of European Integration* (Boulder CO: Westview, 1996)

Beaumont, P. and Walker, N. (eds.), *Legal Framework of the Single European Currency* (Oxford: Hart 1999)

Beaumont, P and Weatherill, S., *EU Law*, 3rd edn (London: Penguin, 1999)

Beazley, C., 'A British View of European Constitution', in Feus, K. (ed.), *A Simplified Treaty for the European Union?* (London: Federal Trust, 2001), 85–90

Bell, M., 'The New Article 13 EC Treaty: A Sound Basis for European Anti-Discrimination Law?', *Maastricht Journal of European and Comparative Law*, 6 (1), 1999, 5–23

Bellamy, R., Bufacchi, V. and Castiglione, D. (eds.), *Democracy and Constitutional Culture in the Union of Europe* (London: Lothian, 1995)

Berglöf, E., 'The Nice Treaty Should be Ratified – Then Repaired', *European Affairs*, 2 (4), 2001, 74–79

Bertelsmann Group for Policy Research, *A Basic Treaty for the European Union: Draft Version for the Reorganisation of the Treaties* (Munich: Centre for Applied Policy Research, 2000)

Berthu, G. (with Souchet, D.), *Traité d'Amsterdam contre la démocratie* (Paris: de Guibert, 1998)

Best, E. et al. (eds.), *Rethinking the European Union IGC 2000 and Beyond* (Maastricht: EIPA, 2000)

Bieber, R., *Draft of a Consolidated Treaty of the European Union*, EP Directorate-General for Research, Political Series Working Papers, W-16, 1996

Bieber, R. and Amarelle, C., 'Simplification of European Law', *Columbia Journal of European Law*, 5 (1), 1998, 15–37

Blair, A., *Dealing with Europe: Britain and the Negotiation of the Maastricht Treaty* (Aldershot: Ashgate, 1999)

Blin, O., 'L'article 113 CE après Amsterdam', *Revue du Marché commun et de l'Union européenne*, 420, 1998, 447–456

Blondel, J., *Comparative Government. An Introduction*, 2nd edn (Hemel Hempstead: Prentice Hall, 1995)

Boeles, P., 'Parliamentary and Judicial Control in Matters of Asylum and Immigration under the Treaty of Amsterdam', in Heukels, T. et al. (eds.), *The European Union after Amsterdam: A Legal Analysis* (The Hague: Kluwer Law International, 1998), 215–226

Bogdandy, A. von, 'The Legal Case for Unity: The European Union as a Single Organization with a Single Legal System', *Common Market Law Review*, 36 (5), 1999, 887–910

Bogdandy, A. von and Ehlermann, C.-D., 'Consolidation of the European Treaties: Feasibility, Costs and Benefits', *Common Market Law Review*, 33 (6), 1996, 1107–1116

Bogdandy, A. von and Nettesheim, M., 'Ex Pluribus Unum: Fusion of the European Communities into the European Union', *European Law Journal*, 2 (3), 1996, 267–289

Bogdanor, V. (ed.), *Constitutions in Democratic Politics* (Aldershot: Gower, 1988)

Bonde, J.-P., *The Nice Treaty Explained*, www.EUObserver.com, 30 May 2001

Bonnor, P. G., 'The European Ombudsman: a Novel Source of Soft Law in the European Union', *European Law Review*, 25 (1), 2000, 39–56

Bonvicini, G., 'Making European foreign policy work', in Westlake, M. (ed.) *The European Union Beyond Amsterdam* (London: Routledge, 1998), 61–75

Bourgeois, J. H. J., 'Competition Policy and Commercial Policy', in Maresceau, M. (ed.), *The European Community's Commercial Policy after 1992 – The Legal Dimension* (Dordrecht: Martinus Nijhoff, 1993), 113–133

Bourlanges, J.-L. and Martin, D., *Report on the Functioning of the Treaty on European Union with a view to the 1996 Intergovernmental Conference – Implementation and Development of the Union*, European Parliament Session Documents A4-0102, Strasbourg, 4 May 1995

Bourrinet, J., 'Vers une citoyenneté: aspects économiques', *Revue du Marché commun et de l'Union économique*, 362, 1992, 772–776

Boyce, B., 'The Democratic Deficit of the EC', *Parliamentary Affairs*, 46 (4), 1993, 458–477

Bradley, K. St C., 'The European Parliament and Treaty Reform: Building Blocks and Stumbling Blocks', in O'Keefe, D. and Twomey, P. (eds.), *Legal Issues of the Amsterdam Treaty* (Oxford: Hart, 1999), 123–140

Brok, E., cited in *Agence Presse Europe* 10 January 2001 (7877) p. 4: 14 February 2001 (7902) p. 6 and 28 February 2001 (7912) p. 5

Buchan, D., *Europe: The Strange Superpower* (Aldershot: Dartmouth, 1993)

Bulmer, S., *Council of Ministers and European Council: Two Faced Institution in a Federal Order* (Manchester: EPRU Working Paper, 1991)

Bulmer, S. and Armstrong, K., *The Governance of the Single European Market* (Manchester: Manchester University Press, 1988)

Búrca, G. de, 'The Drafting of the European Union Charter of Fundamental Rights', *European Law Review*, 26 (2), 2001, 126–138

Búrca, G. de, 'The Institutional Development of the EU: A Constitutional Analysis', in Craig, P. and Búrca, G. de (eds.), *The Evolution of EU Law* (Oxford: Oxford University Press, 1999), 55–81

Burchell, J. and Lightfoot, S., *The Greening of the EU* (Sheffield: UACES/Sheffield Academic Press, 2001)

Canor, I., '*Primus Inter pares.* Who is the Ultimate Guardian of Human Rights in Europe?', *European Law Review*, 25 (1), 2000, 2–21

Capotorti, F. et al., *The European Union Treaty – Commentary on the Draft Adopted by the European Parliament on 14 February 1984* (Oxford: Clarendon Press, 1986)

Chalmers, D., 'Inhabitants in the Field of EC Environmental Law', in Craig, P. and Búrca, G. de (eds.), *The Evolution of EU Law* (Oxford: Oxford University Press, 1999), 653–692

Chalmers, D. and Szyszcak, E., *European Union Law* (Aldershot: Ashgate, 1999)

Charter of Fundamental Rights of the European Union, OJ C364, 18 December 2000

Chirac, J. *Notre Europe – Discours prononcé devant le Bundestag* (Berlin: 27 June 2000)

Christiansen, T. and Jørgensen, K. E., 'The Amsterdam Process: A Structurationist Perspective on EU Treaty Reform', *European Integration online Papers (EIoP)*, 3 (1), 1999 (http://eiop.or.at/eiop/texte/1999-001a.htm)

Church, C. H., *European Integration Theory in the 1990s* (London: UNL European Dossier, 1996)

Church, C. H. and Phinnemore, D., *European Union and European Community: A Handbook and Commentary on the Post-Maastricht Treaties* (Hemel Hempstead: Harvester Wheatsheaf, 1995)

Churchill, R. R., *EEC Fisheries Law* (Dordrecht: Martinus Nijhoff, 1987)

Cini, M. and McGowan, L., *Competition Policy in the European Union* (Basingstoke: Macmillan, 1998)

Cloos, J. et al., *Le Traité de Maastricht: Genèse, Analyse, Commentaires* (Brussels: Etablissements Emile Brulyant, 1994)

Close, G., 'The Legal Basis for the Consumer Protection Policy of the EEC and Priorities for Action', *European Law Review*, 8 (4), 1983, 221–240

Cohn-Bendit, D., 'A European Magna Carta', *Guardian*, 10 November 2000, 23

Collins, A. M., 'Freedom through Security? The Third Pillar', *Irish Journal of European Law* 7 (1), 1998, 43–63

Conference of the Representatives of the Governments of the Member States, *The European Union Today and Tomorrow – Adapting the European Union for the Benefit of its Peoples and Preparing it for the Future: A General Outline for a Draft Revision of the Treaties, Dublin II, Conf 2500/96* (Brussels: Council of the European Union)

Conference of the Representatives of the Governments of the Member States, *Treaty of Amsterdam amending the Treaty on European Union, the Treaties Establishing the European Communities and Certain Related Acts – Descriptive Summary* (Brussels: Council of the European Union, 1997)

Conference of the Representatives of the Governments of the Member States, *Treaty of Amsterdam amending the Treaty on European Union, the Treaties Establishing the European Communities and Certain Related Acts* (Brussels: Council of the European Union, 1997)

Conference of the Representatives of the Governments of the Member States, *Consolidated Draft Treaty Texts, SN600/97(C101)* (Brussels: Council of the European Union, 1997)

Conseil de l'Union Européenne, *Note pour le Groupe de Réflexion: Simplification des Traités, SN/513/95 (REFLEX 14)* (Brussels: Conseil de l'Union Européenne, 1995)

Corbett, R., *The Maastricht Treaty* (London: Longman, 1993)

Council of the European Union, *Draft Treaty of Amsterdam, CONF/4001/97* (Brussels: Council of the European Union, 1997)

Council of the European Union, *Efficient Institutions after Enlargement: Options for the Intergovernmental Conference – Presidency Report*, 13636/99, Brussels, 7 December 1999

Craig, P., 'Constitutions, Constitutionalism and the European Union', *European Law Review*, 7 (2), 2001, 125–150

Craig, P., 'The Nature of the Community: Integration, Democracy and Legitimacy', in Craig, P. and Búrca, G. de (eds.), *The Evolution of EU Law* (Oxford: Oxford University Press, 1999), 1–54

Cram, L., et al. (eds.), *Developments in the European Union* (Basingstoke: Macmillan, 1999)

Cremona, M., 'External Economic Relations and the Amsterdam Treaty', in O'Keefe, D. and Twomey, P. (eds.), *Legal Issues of the Amsterdam Treaty* (Oxford: Hart, 1999), 225–248

Cremona, M., 'External Relations and External Competence: The Emergence of an Integrated Policy', in Craig, P. and Búrca, G. de (eds.), *The Evolution of EU Law* (Oxford: Oxford University Press, 1999), 137–175

Curtin, D., 'The Constitutional Structure of the Union: a Europe of Bits and Pieces', *Common Market Law Review*, 30 (1), 1993, 17–69

Curtin, D. M. 'The Fundamental Principle of Open Decision-making and EU (Political) Citizenship', in O'Keefe, D. and Twomey, P. (eds.), *Legal Issues of the Amsterdam Treaty* (Oxford: Hart, 1999), 71–92

Curtin, D. and Dekker, I., 'The EU as a "Layered" International Organization: Institutional Unity in Disguise', in Craig, P. and Búrca, G. de (eds.), *The Evolution of EU Law* (Oxford: Oxford University Press, 1999), 83–136

Damro, C., 'Building an International Identity: the EU and Extraterritorial Competition Policy', *Journal of European Public Policy*, 8 (2), 2001, 208–226

Dashwood, A., 'The Limits of EC Power', *European Law Review*, 21 (1), 1996, 113–128

Dashwood, A., 'External Relations Provisions of the Amsterdam Treaty', *Common Market Law Review*, 35 (5), 1998, 1019–1045

Dashwood, A., 'States in the European Union', *European Law Review*, 23 (2), 1998, 200–216

Dashwood, A., 'External Relations Provisions of the Amsterdam Treaty', in O'Keefe, D. and Twomey, P. (eds.), *Legal Issues of the Amsterdam Treaty* (Oxford: Hart, 1999), 201–224

Dashwood, A., 'The constitution of the European Union after Nice: Law-making Procedures', *European Law Review*, 26 (3), 2001, 215–238

Dashwood, A. and Hillion, C. (eds.), *The General Law of E.C. External Relations* (London: Sweet and Maxwell, 2000)

Dashwood, A. and Ward, A. (eds.), 'CELS (Cambridge) E.C. Treaty Project', *European Law Review*, 22 (5), 1997, 395–516

Dastoli, P. V., 'European Constitution and Federalism after Nice: a New Chance or Requiem for a Myth?', unpublished paper, 2001

Davidson, I., 'Action Plan to Cut the Euro Nonsense', *Financial Times*, 5 January 1995

de Schoutheete, P., 'Restructuring the European Treaties', *Challenge Europe – On-Line Journal*, 25 May 2000, www.theepc.be

de Witte, B., 'The Pillar Structure and the Nature of the European Union: Greek Temple or French Gothic Cathedral?', in Heukels, T. et al. (eds.), *The European Union after Amsterdam: A Legal Analysis* (The Hague: Kluwer Law International, 1998), 51–68

de Witte, B., 'The Legal Status of the Charter: Vital Question or Non-issue?' *Maastricht Journal of European and Comparative Law*, 8 (1), 2001, 81–89

de Witte, B., 'Clarifying the Delimitation of Powers', unpublished paper submitted to *Europe 2004, Le Grand Débat*, Action Jean Monnet Brussels, 15 October 2001

Dehousse, F., *Les resultats de la Conference intergouvernmentale* (Brussels: CRISP, 1997)

Dehousse, F., 'European Institutional Architecture after Amsterdam: Parliamentary System or Regulatory Structure?', *Common Market Law Review*, 35 (3), 1998, 595–627

Dehousse, F., *Amsterdam: The Making of a Treaty* (London: Kogan Page, 1999)

Dehousse, F., 'The IGC Process and Results', in O'Keefe, D. and Twomey, P. (eds.), *Legal Issues of the Amsterdam Treaty* (Oxford: Hart, 1999), 93–108

Dehousse, F., 'Amsterdam: Success or Failure? A Personal View', in Monar, J. and Wessels, W. (eds.), *The European Union after the Treaty of Amsterdam* (London: Continuum, 2001), 45–55

Demaret, P., 'The Treaty Framework', in O'Keefe, D. and Twomey, P. (eds.) *Legal Issues of the Maastricht Treaty* (London: Chancery Lane Law, 1994), 3–12

den Boer, M., 'Area of Freedom, Security and Justice: Bogged Down by Compromise', in O'Keefe, D. and Twomey, P. (eds.), *Legal Issues of the Amsterdam Treaty* (Oxford: Hart, 1999), 303–322

den Boer, M., 'The Incorporation of Schengen into the TEU: A Bridge too Far?', in Monar, J. and

Wessels, W. (eds.), *The European Union after the Treaty of Amsterdam* (London: Continuum, 2001), 298–318

den Boer, M. and Wallace, W., 'Justice and Home Affairs: Integration through Incrementalism?', in Wallace, H. and Wallace, W. (eds.), *Policy-Making in the European Union*, 4th edn (Oxford: Oxford University Press, 2000), 493–519

Devuyst, Y., 'The EC's Common Commercial Policy and the Treaty on European Union – An Overview of the Negotiations', *World Competition*, 16 (2), 1992, 67–80

Devuyst, Y., 'Treaty Reform in the EU', *Journal of European Public Policy*, 5 (4), 1998, 615–631

Dimitrakopoulos, G. and Leinen, J., *Report on the European Parliament's Proposals for the Intergovernmental Conference*, A5-0086/2000, Strasbourg, 27 March 2000

Dinan, D., *Encyclopaedia of the European Union* (London: Macmillan, 1998)

Dinan, D., 'Treaty Change in the EU: The Amsterdam Experience', in Cram, L. et al. (eds.) *Developments in the European Union* (London: Macmillan, 1999), 290–310

Dobson, L., *What has Nice ever done for us the Citizens?*, paper presented to the UACES Research Conference, Bristol, 16–17 September 2001

Dodd, T. et al., 'The European Communities (Amendment) Bill: Implementing the Amsterdam Treaty', *House of Commons Library Research Paper* No. 97/112, 5 November 1997

Dooge, J. and Keatinge, P. (eds.), *What the Treaty of Nice Means* (Dublin: Institute of European Affairs, 2001)

Dorau, C., *Die Verfassungsfrage der Europäischen Union* (Baden-Baden: Nomos, 2001)

Dragone, S., 'La codification communautaire techniques et procédures', *Revue du Marche Unique Européen*, 1998/1, 77–94

Duff, A. (ed.), *The Treaty of Amsterdam: Text and Commentary* (London: Federal Trust/Sweet and Maxwell, 1997)

Duff, A., *The Treaty of Nice*, www.andrewduffmep.org/Press%20Releases/PR090101.html

Duhamel, O., *Report on the Constitutionalisation of the Treaties*, A5-0289/2000, Strasbourg, 12 October 2000

Duke, S., 'From Amsterdam to Kosovo: lessons for the future of CFSP', *EIPASCOPE*, 1999/2, 2–15

Duke, S., 'After the Applause Stops: Nice's Aftermath and the Prospects for CESDP', *EIPASCOPE*, 2001/1, 24–26

Duvigneau, J., 'From Advisory Opinion 2/94 to the Amsterdam Treaty: Human Rights Protection in the European Union', *Legal Issues of European Integration*, 2/1994, 61–91

Dyson, K., *Elusive Union* (London: Longman, 1994)

Dyson, K. and Featherstone, K., *The Road to Maastricht: Negotiating Economic and Monetary Union* (Oxford: Oxford University Press, 1999)

Eaton, M. R., 'Common Foreign and Security Policy', in O'Keefe, D. and Twomey, P. (eds.), *Legal Issues of the Amsterdam Treaty* (Oxford: Hart, 1999), 215–225

EC Commission, *A Basic Treaty for the European Union*, COM(2000)434 final, Brussels, 12 July 2000

EC Commission, *Adapting the Institutions to Make a Success of Enlargement*, Brussels, 10 November 2000

EC Commission, *How the Charter was drawn up – The sources of rights*, 2001 (Brussels: EC Commission, 2001) (europa.eu.int/comm/justicehome/unit/charte/en/charter02.html)

Edwards, G. and Pijpers, A. (eds.), *The Politics of European Treaty Reform* (London: Pinter, 1997)

Ehlermann, C.-D., 'Differentiation, Flexibility, Closer Cooperation: The New Provisions of the Amsterdam Treaty', Robert Schuman Centre Working Paper, Florence, 1997

Eijsbouts, T., 'Constitutional Sedimentation', *Legal Issues of European Integration*, 1996, 52–60

Eikenberg, K., 'Article 296 (ex 233) E.C. and external trade in strategic goods', *European Law Review*, 25 (2), 2000, 117–138

Elazar, D., 'Constitution Making. The Pre-eminently Political Act', in Banting, K. and Simeon, R. (eds.), *The Politics of Constitutional Change in Industrial Nations* (London: Macmillan, 1985), 232–250

Engel, C., 'The European Charter of Fundamental Rights: A Changed Political Opportunity Structure and its Normative Consequences', *European Law Review*, 7 (2), 2001, 151–170

EP Directorate-General for Research, 'The Simplification of the EU Treaties and the IGC of 1996', EP Directorate-General for Research, Political Series Working Papers, W-17/rev. 1995

EP Directorate-General for Research, 'A Unified and Simplified Model of the European Communities Treaties and the Treaty on European Union in Just One Treaty', EP Directorate-General for Research, Legal Series Working Papers, W-9, 1996

European Central Bank, *Annual Report 2000* (Frankfurt: ECB, 2001)

European Commission (ed.), *40 Years of the Treaties of Rome: or the Capacity of the Treaties to Advance the European Integration Process* (Brussels: Brulyant, 1999)

European Constitutional Group, *European Constitutional Settlement: Draft Report* (London: European Policy Forum, 1993)

European Policy Centre, *Brief Article by Article Summary of the Treaty of Nice* (Document 384) www.theepc.be

European Policy Centre, *Making Sense of the Amsterdam Treaty* (Brussels: European Policy Centre, 1997)

European Policy Centre, *The Process leading to the IGC: The Europe We Need* (Brussels: European Policy Centre, 28 September 2001)

European University Institute – Robert Schuman Centre for Advanced Studies, *Reorganisation of the Treaties: Basic Treaty of the European Union – Draft* (Florence: European University Institute, May 2000).

Evangelisti, F., 'The Role of National Parliaments in the Creation of the Area of Freedom, Security and Justice: An Italian Point of View', in O'Keefe, D. and Twomey, P. (eds.), *Legal Issues of the Amsterdam Treaty* (Oxford: Hart, 1999), 323–328

Evans, A., *A Textbook on European Union Law* (Oxford: Hart, 1998)

Falkner, G., 'The Council or the Social Partners? EC Social Policy between Diplomacy and Collective Bargaining', *Journal of European Public Policy*, 7 (5), 2000, 705–724

Falkner, G., 'How Pervasive are Euro-Politics? Effects of EU Membership on a New Member State', *Journal of Common Market Studies*, 31 (2), 2000, 225–250

Featherstone, K., 'The Political Dynamics of Economic and Monetary Union', in Cram, L. et al. (eds.), *Developments in the European Union* (Basingstoke: Macmillan, 1999), 311–329

Felsenthal, D. S. and Machover, M., *The Treaty of Nice and Qualified Majority Voting*, http://www.lse.ac.uk/Depts/cpnss/projects/niceqmv.pdf (June 2000)

Fennelly, N., 'Pressing the Legal Coherence within the New Treaty', *Maastricht Journal of European and Comparative Law*, 5 (2), 1998, 185–199

Fennelly, N., 'The Area of "Freedom, Security and Justice" and the European Court of Justice – A Personal View', *International and Comparative Law Quarterly*, 49 (1), 1999, 1–14

Feus, K. (ed.), *A Simplified Treaty for the European Union?* (London: Federal Trust, 2001)

Fenn, J. E., *Constitutions in Crisis* (Oxford: Oxford University Press, 1991)

Finer, S. et al., *Comparing Constitutions*, 2nd edn (Oxford: Oxford University Press, 1996)

Fischer, J., 'From Confederacy to Federation: Thoughts on the Finality of European Integration', Speech to the Humboldt University, Berlin, 12 May 2000

Fischer, K. H., *Der Vertrag von Nizza: Text und Kommentar* (Baden-Baden: Nomos, 2001)

Flynn, L., 'Competition Policy and Public Services in EC Law after the Maastricht and Amsterdam Treaties', in O'Keefe, D. and Twomey, P. (eds.), *Legal Issues of the Amsterdam Treaty* (Oxford: Hart, 1999), 185–199

Flynn, L., 'The Implications of Article 13 EC – After Amsterdam, Will Some Forms of Discrimination be More Equal Than Others?', *Common Market Law Review*, 36 (6), 1999, 1127–1152

Foreign and Commonwealth Office, *The European Union Treaties in under 300 words* (London: Foreign and Commonwealth Office, 2001)

Forster, A., *Britain and the Maastricht Negotiations* (Basingstoke: Macmillan, 1999)

Forster, A. and Wallace, H., 'Common Foreign and Security Policy: From Shadow to Substance?', in Wallace, H. and Wallace, W. (eds.), *Policy-Making in the European Union*, 4th edn (Oxford: Oxford University Press, 2000), 461–491

Forthergill, S., 'The Premature Death of EU Regional Policy?', *European Urban and Regional Studies*, 5 (2), 1997, 183–188

Frazer, T., 'The New Structural Funds, State Aids and Interventions in the Single Market', *European Law Review*, 20 (1), 1994, 3–19

Gammie, G., 'Note by Counsel to the Speaker: The Treaty on European Union' in *Fifteenth Report from the Select Committee on European Legislation* (London: HMSO, 1992), xl–lx

Gardener, B., *European Agriculture: Policies, Productions and Trade* (London: Routledge, 1996)

Gavechan, J., 'Amsterdam: L'échec de la hierarchie des normes', *Revue du Droit Française et Etrangère*, 35 (1), 1998, 1–20

General Secretariat of the Council, *Explanatory Report from the General Secretariat of the Council on the Simplification of the Community Treaties*, OJ C353, 20 November 1997

Gerkrath, J., *L'Emergence d'un droit constitutionnel pour l'Europe* (Brussels: Editions de l'Université de Bruxelles, 1998)

Gold, M. (ed.), *The Social Dimension: Employment Policy in the European Community* (Basingstoke: Macmillan, 1993)

Goldschmidt, P. I. B. and Lanz, C., 'Maybe Definitely – Definitely Maybe? EC Competition Law – Is the Time Ripe for Reform?', *EIPASCOPE*, 2, 2001, 16–22

Golub, J., 'In the Shadow of the Vote: Decision-Making in the European Community', *International Organisation*, 53 (4), 1999, 733–764

Gormley, L. W., 'Reflections on the Architecture of the European Union after the Treaty of Amsterdam', in O'Keefe, D. and Twomey, P. (eds.), *Legal Issues of the Amsterdam Treaty* (Oxford: Hart, 1999), 57–70

Gourlay, C. and Remacle, E., 'The 1996 IGC: the Actors and their Interaction', in Eliassen, K. A. (ed.), *Foreign and Security Policy in the European Union* (London: Sage, 1998), 59–93

Grabbe, H., *Preparing the EU for 2004* (London: Centre for European Reform, 2001)

Grant, W., *The Common Agricultural Policy* (London: Macmillan, 1997)

Granturco, T., 'La genèse de l'intégration de la culture au sein des compétences communautaires', *Journal of European Integration History*, 5 (2), 2000, 109–126

Gray, M., 'Negotiating EU Treaties: the Case for a New Approach', in Best, E. et al. (eds.), *Rethinking the European Union: IGC 2000 and Beyond* (Maastricht: EIPA, 2000), 263–280

Gray, M. and Stubb, A., 'Keynote Article: the Treaty of Nice – Negotiating a Poisoned Chalice?', in Edwards, G. and Wiessala, G. (eds.), *The European Union: Annual Review of the EU 2000/2001* (Oxford: Blackwell, 2001), 5–23

Gray, T. S., 'The Common Fisheries Policy of the European Union', *Environmental Politics*, 6 (4), 1997, 150–158

Greaves, R., ' EC Transport Law and Policy: a Status Report', in Dashwood, A. and Ward, A. (eds.), *The Cambridge Yearbook of European Legal Studies II – 1999* (Oxford: Hart, 2000), 261–284

Griffiths, R. T., *Europe's First Constitution – The European Political Community, 1952–54* (London: Federal Trust, 2000)

Griller, S., 'The Constitutional Architecture' in *Europe 2004, Le Grand Débat* (Brussels: Action Jean Monnet, 2002), 47–73

Grilli, E. R., *The European Community and the Developing Countries* (Cambridge: Cambridge University Press, 1993)

Guérot, U., 'Eine Verfassung für Europa', *Internationale Politik*, 56 (2), 2001, 28–36

Guggenbühl, A., 'A Contemplative View on the First Pillar of the New European Union', *EIPASCOPE*, 2, 1997, 1–6

Guiraudon, V., 'European Integration and Migration Policy: Vertical Policy-making as Venue Shopping', *Journal of Common Market Studies*, 31 (2), 2000, 251–271

Haan, F. de and Eijffinger, S. C. W., 'The Democratic Accountability of the European Central Bank: A Comment on Two Fairy-tales', *Journal of Common Market Studies*, 33 (3), 2000, 393–407

Haenel, H., 'Une Constitution pour l'Union Européenne', *Delegation du Senat Français pour l'Union Européenne – Rapport d'Integration 363 (2000–2001)* (2001)

Hahn, H. J., 'The Stability Pact for European Monetary Union: Compliance with Deficit Limit as a Constant Legal Duty', *Common Market Law Review*, 35 (1), 1998, 77–100

Hailbronner, K., *Immigration and Asylum Law and Policy in the European Union* (Dordrecht: Kluwer Law International, 2000)

Halbroch, G., 'Comitology after Amsterdam', *EIPASCOPE*, 3, 1997, 2–7

Hancher, L., 'Community, State and Market', in Craig, P. and Búrca, G. de (eds.), *The Evolution of EU Law* (Oxford: Oxford University Press, 1999), 721–743

Hantrais, L., *Social Policy in the European Union* (Basingstoke: Macmillan, 1995)

Harden, I., 'The Constitution and its Discontents', *British Journal of Political Science* 21 (4), 1991, 489–510

Harmsen, R. and Reinhardt, N., 'Negotiating the Intergovernmental Conferences', in Larres, K. and Meehan, E. (eds.), *Uneasy Allies: British–German relations and European Integration since 1945* (Oxford: Oxford University Press, 2000), 277–298

Hartley, T. C., *The Foundations of European Community Law*, 4th edn (Oxford: Oxford University Press, 1998)

Hayes-Renshaw, F. and Wallace, H., *The Council of Ministers* (Basingstoke: Macmillan, 1997)

Healey, N. M., 'European Monetary Union: One Money, One Europe', in Lynch, P. et al. (eds.), *Reforming the European Union: from Maastricht to Amsterdam* (Harlow: Longman, 2000), 87–107

Hedemann-Robinson, M., 'The Area of Freedom, Security and Justice with Regard to the UK, Ireland and Denmark: The "Opt-in Opt-outs" Under the Treaty of Amsterdam', in O'Keefe, D. and Twomey, P. (eds.), *Legal Issues of the Amsterdam Treaty* (Oxford: Hart, 1999), 289–302

Hervey, T. K., 'Legal Issues Concerning the *Barber* Protocol', in O'Keefe, D. and Twomey, P. (eds.), *Legal Issues of the Maastricht Treaty* (Oxford: Hart, 1999), 329–337

Hervey, T. K., 'Putting Europe's House in Order: Racism, Race Discrimination and Xenophobia after the Treaty of Amsterdam', in O'Keefe, D. and Twomey, P. (eds.), *Legal Issues of the Amsterdam Treaty* (Oxford: Hart, 1999), 329–350

Hession, M. and Macrory, R., 'Maastricht and the Environmental Policy of the Community: Legal Issues of a New Environment Policy', in O'Keefe, D. and Twomey, P. (eds.), *Legal Issues of the Maastricht Treaty* (Oxford: Hart, 1999), 151–167

Hillion, C., 'Institutional Aspects of the Partnership between the European Union and the Newly Independent States of the Former Soviet Union: Case Studies of Russia and Ukraine', *Common Market Law Review*, 37 (5), 2000, 1211–1235

Hix, S., 'The Study of the European Community: The Challenge to Comparative Politics', *West European Politics*, 17 (1), 1994, 1–30

Hix, S., *The Political System of the European Union* (Basingstoke: Macmillan, 1999)

Hix, S., 'Executive Selection in the European Union: Does the Commission President Investiture Procedure Reduce the Democratic Deficit?', in Neunreither, K. and Wiener, A. (eds.), *European Integration after Amsterdam: Institutional Dynamics and Prospects for Democracy* (Oxford: Oxford University Press, 2000), 95–111

Hoffman, S., 'Towards a Common European Foreign and Security Policy?', *Journal of Common Market Studies*, 31 (2), 2000, 189–198

Holmes, M. (ed.), *The Eurosceptical Reader* (Basingstoke: Macmillan, 1996)

Howe, M., *From Maastricht to Amsterdam* (London: Centre for Policy Studies, 1997)

Howe, M. and Shrimpton, M., *The EC, Denmark and the Masstricht Treaty* (London: Great College Street papers, December 1992)

Hrbek, R., 'Die deutschen Länder und das Vertragswerk von Nizza', *Integration*, 24 (2), 2001, 102–113

Hurwitz, A., 'The 1990 Dublin Convention: a Comprehensive Assessment', *International Journal of Refugee Law* 11 (4), 1999, 646–677

Ingersent, K. et al., *The Reform of the Common Agricultural Policy* (London: Macmillan, 1998)

Jacqué, J.-P., 'La Simplification et le Consolidation des Traités', *Revue Trimestrielle du Droit Européenne*, 1997, 905–921

Jessurun d'Oliveira, H. U., 'Nationality and the European Union after Amsterdam', in O'Keefe, D. and Twomey, P. (eds.), *Legal Issues of the Amsterdam Treaty* (Oxford: Hart, 1999), 395–412

Johnston, A., 'Judicial Reform and the Treaty of Nice', *Common Market Law Review*, 38 (3), 2001, 499–523

Junge, K., *Flexibility, Enhanced Co-operation and the Treaty of Amsterdam* (London: Kogan Page, 1999)

Keating, M. and Jones, B. (eds.), *Regions in the European Community* (Oxford: Clarendon, 1985)

Keatinge, P., 'Strengthening the Foreign Policy Process', in Tonra, B. (ed.), *Amsterdam: What the Treaty Means* (Dublin: Institute of European Studies, 1997), 97–106

Kenner, J., 'Employment and Macroeconomics in the EC Treaty: a Legal and Political Symbiosis', *Maastricht Journal of European and Comparative Law*, 7 (4), 2000, 375–397

Kenner, J., 'The Paradox of the Social Dimension', in Lynch, P. et al. (eds.), *Reforming the European Union: from Maastricht to Amsterdam* (Harlow: Longman, 2000), 108–129

King, A., *Does the UK still Have a Constitution?* (London: Sweet and Maxwell, 2001)

Koutrakos, P., 'Is Article 297 a "Reserve of Sovereignty"?', *Common Market Law Review*, 37 (6), 2000, 1339–1362

Kuijper, P. J., 'Some Legal Problems Associated with the Communitarization of Policy on Visas, Asylum and Immigration under the Amsterdam Treaty and Incorporation of the Schengen Acquis', *Common Market Law Review*, 37 (2), 2000, 345–366

Küsters, H. J., 'The Origins of the EEC Treaty', in Serra, E. (ed.), *The Relaunching of Europe and the Treaties of Rome* (Brussels: Brulyant, 1989), 211–238

Laffan, B., *The Finances of the European Union* (Basingstoke: Macmillan, 1997)

Laffan, B., 'Becoming a Living Institution: The Evolution of the European Court of Auditors', *Journal of Common Market Studies*, 37 (3), 1998, 251–260

Laffan, B. and Shackleton, M., 'The Budget: Who Gets What, When, and How', in Wallace, H. and Wallace, W. (eds.), *Policy-Making in the European Union*, 4th edn (Oxford: Oxford University Press, 2000), 211–241

Lamassoure, A., 'For a European Constitutional Process', in Feus, K. (ed.), *A Simplified Treaty for the European Union?* (London: Federal Trust, 2001), 71–76

Lamassoure, A., 'Working Document on the Division of Powers between the Union and the Member States', *European Parliament Committee on Constitutional Affairs* 15 March 2001 (PE 294.757)

Lambert, H., 'Building a European Asylum Policy under the "First Pillar" of the Consolidated Treaty Establishing the European Community', *International Journal of Refugee Law*, 11 (2), 1999, 329–337

Lane, J. E., *Constitutions and Political Theory* (Manchester: Manchester University Press, 1996)

Lane, R., *EC Competition Law* (Harlow: Longman, 2000)

Langrish, S., 'The Treaty of Amsterdam: Selected Highlights', *European Law Review*, 23 (1), 1998, 3–19

Lasok, D. and Bridge, J. W., *Law and Institutions of the European Community*, 6th edn (London: Butterworths, 1994)

Leibfried, S. and Pierson, P., 'Social Policy: Left to Courts or Markets', in Wallace, H. and Wallace, W. (eds.), *Policy-Making in the European Union*, 4th edn (Oxford: Oxford University Press, 2000), 267–292

Leinen, J. and Méndez de Vigo, I., *Report on the Laeken European Council and the future of the Union*, A5-0368/2001, Strasbourg, 23 October 2001

Lejeune, Y. (ed.), *Le Traité d'Amsterdam. Espoirs et déceptions* (Brussels: Brulyant, 1998)

Lenaerts, K., 'Fundamental Rights in the European Union', *European Law Review*, 25 (6), 2000, 575–600

Lenaerts, K. and van Nuffel, P., *Constitutional Law of the European Union* (London: Sweet and Maxwell, 1999)

Lequesne, C., 'Quota Hopping: The Common Fisheries Policy Between States and Markets', *Journal of Common Market Studies*, 38 (5), 2000, 779–793

Lequesne, C., 'The Common Fisheries Policy: Letting the Little Ones Go?', in Wallace, H. and Wallace, W. (eds.), *Policy-Making in the European Union*, 4th edn (Oxford: Oxford University Press, 2000), 345–372

Lequesne, C., 'The European Commission: A Balancing Act between Autonomy and Dependence', in Neunreither, K. and Wiener, A. (eds.), *European Integration after Amsterdam: Institutional Dynamics and Prospects for Democracy* (Oxford: Oxford University Press, 2000), 36–51

Leslie, P., 'Abuses of Asymmetry: Privilege and Exclusion', in Neunreither, K. and Wiener, A. (eds.), *European Integration after Amsterdam: Institutional Dynamics and Prospects for Democracy* (Oxford: Oxford University Press, 2000), 192–217

Liebfried, S. and Pierson, P. (eds.), *European Social Policy: Between Fragmentation and Integration* (Washington, DC: Brookings, 1995)

Lippert, B. and Stevens-Ströhmann, R., *German Unification and EC Integration: German and British Perspectives* (London: Pinter/Royal Institute of International Affairs, 1993)

Livingstone, S., *The European Convention on Human Rights* (Oxford: Oxford University Press, 1999)

Lodge, J., 'Contribution', *Challenge Europe – European Policy Centre On Line Journal*, 21 May 2000 (www.theepc.be)

Lodge, J. and Flynn, V., 'The CFSP After Amsterdam: The Policy Planning and Early Warning Unit', *International Relations*, 14 (1), 1998, 7–21

Loth, W., 'La mise en oeuvre des Traités de Rome', in European Commission (ed.), *40 Years of the Treaties of Rome: or the Capacity of the Treaties to Advance the European Integration Process* (Brussels: Brulyant, 1999), 41–46

Louis, J.-V., 'The European Union's Constitutional Muddle: Which Way Forward?', in Monar, J. and Wessels, W. (eds.), *The European Union after the Treaty of Amsterdam* (London: Continuum, 2001), 87–95

Loveland, I., 'Political Sovereignty and the EU', *Parliamentary Affairs*, 49 (4), 1996, 517–535

Ludlow, P., 'Recasting the European Political System, 1950–1996', *CEPS Review*, Summer 1996, 25–33

Ludlow, P., 'The European Council at Nice: Neither Triumph nor Disaster', *A View from Brussels: A Commentary on the EU*, No. 10 (Brussels: Centre for European Policy Studies, 2001)

Ludlow, P., *2004 and Beyond: A Commentary on the EU* (Brussels: Centre for European Policy Studies, 2001)

Ludlow, P. and Ersbøll, N., *Preparing for a Larger Union* (Brussels: CEPS, 1994)

Lynch, P., 'Flexibility and Closer Cooperation: Evolution or Entropy', in Lynch, P. et al. (eds.), *Reforming the European Union: from Maastricht to Amsterdam* (Harlow: Longman, 2000), 200–216

Machan, M., 'A Nice Trip', *EPC European Challenge On Line Journal*, 21 April 2001

Macía, L. C., 'A Charter of Fundamental Rights for the European Union?', in Best, E. et al. (eds.), *Rethinking the European Union: IGC2000 and Beyond* (Maastricht: European Institute of Public Administration, 2000), 185–205

Macrory, R., 'The Amsterdam Treaty: an Environmental Perspective', in O'Keefe, D. and Twomey, P. (eds.), *Legal Issues of the Amsterdam Treaty* (Oxford: Hart, 1999), 171–184

Madgwick, P. and Woodhouse, D., *The Law and Politics of the Constitution of the United Kingdom* (Hemel Hempstead: Harvester Wheatsheaf, 1995)

Maher, I., 'Competition Law and Intellectual Property Rights: Evolving Formalism', in Craig, P. and Búrca, G. de (eds.), *The Evolution of EU Law* (Oxford: Oxford: University Press, 1999), 597–624

Majone, G., *Regulating Europe* (London: Routledge, 1996)

Mancini, G., 'The Making of a Constitution for Europe', *Common Market Law Review*, 26 (4), 1989, 595–614

Mare, T. de la, 'Article 177 in Social and Political Context', in Craig, P. and Búrca, G. de (eds.), *The Evolution of EU Law* (Oxford: Oxford University Press, 1999), 215–260

Maresceau, M. (ed.), *The European Community's Commercial Policy after 1992 – The Legal Dimension* (Dordrecht: Martinus Nijhoff, 1993)

Marr, A., 'Why Europe Needs a Constitution', CER article June/July 1999

Maus, D. and Passelecq, O. (eds.), *Le Traité d'Amsterdam face aux constitutions nationales* (Paris: La Documentation Française, 1998)

McDonagh, B., *Original Sin in a Brave New World* (Dublin: IEA, 1998)

McGoldrick, D., 'The European Union after Amsterdam: An Organization with General Human Rights Competences?', in O'Keefe, D. and Twomey, P. (eds.), *Legal Issues of the Amsterdam Treaty* (Oxford: Hart, 1999), 249–270

McGowan, F., 'Competition Policy: The Limits of the European Regulatory State', in Wallace, H. and Wallace, W. (eds.), *Policy-Making in the European Union*, 4th edn (Oxford: Oxford University Press, 2000), 115–147

McKay, D., 'Policy Legitimacy and Institutional Design: Comparative Lessons for the European Union', *Journal of Common Market Studies*, 31 (1), 2000, 25–44

McKay, H. (ed.), *In Search of New Constitutions* (Edinburgh: Edinburgh University Press, 1995)

McLaren, L. M., 'Turkey's Eventual Membership of the EU: Turkish Elite Perspectives on the Issue', *Journal of Common Market Studies*, 31 (1), 2000, 117–130

McMahon, J. A., 'The EC Banana Regime, the WTO Rulings and the ACP; Fighting for Economic Survival?', *Journal of World Trade*, 23 (4), 1998, 101–114

Meehan, E., *Citizenship and the European Community* (London: Sage, 1993)

Meehan, E., 'Europeanization and Citizenship', *Yearbook of European Studies 14* (Amsterdam: Rodopi, 2000), 157–178

Metcalfe, L., 'Reforming the Commission', *EIPASCOPE*, 3, 1999, 3–9

Meunier, S. and Nicolaïdes, K., 'Who Speaks for Europe? The Delegation of Trade Authority in the EU', *Journal of Common Market Studies*, 37 (3), 1999, 477–501

Middlemas, K., *Orchestrating Europe* (London: Fontana, 1995)

Miller, V., *Intergovernmental Conference 2000: the Main Agenda*, House of Commons Research Paper 00/49, 19 April 2000

Miller, W. et al., *Political Culture in Contemporary Britain* (Oxford: Clarendon, 1996)

Missiroli, A., *CFSP, Defence and Flexibility* (Paris: WEU Institute Chaillot Paper 38, February 2000)

Monar, J., 'The EU's Foreign Affairs System', *European Foreign Affairs Review*, 2 (4), 1997, 13–36

Monar, J., 'An Emerging Regime of European Governance for Freedom, Security and Justice', ESRC One Europe or Several? Programme Briefing Note, 2/99, November 1999

Monar, J., 'An "Area of Freedom, Justice and Security"? Progress and Deficits in Justice and Home Affairs', in Lynch, P. et al. (eds.), *Reforming the European Union: from Maastricht to Amsterdam* (Harlow: Longman, 2000), 142–161

Monar, J., 'Continuing and Building on Amsterdam: The Reforms of the Treaty of Nice', in Monar, J. and Wessels, W. (eds.), *The European Union after the Treaty of Amsterdam* (London: Continuum, 2001), 321–334

Monar, J., 'Justice and Home Affairs after Amsterdam: The Treaty Reforms and the Challenge of their Implementation', in Monar, J. and Wessels, W. (eds.), *The European Union after the Treaty of Amsterdam* (London: Continuum, 2001), 267–295

Monar, J. and Wessels, W. (eds.), *The European Union after the Treaty of Amsterdam* (London: Continuum, 2001)

Monnet, J., *Memoirs* (London: Collins, 1978)

Moravcsik, A., *The Choice for Europe: Social Purpose and State Power from Messina to Maastricht* (London: UCL Press, 1998)

Moravcsik, A. and Nicolaïdes, K., 'Explaining the Treaty of Amsterdam: Interests, Influences, Institutions', *Journal of Common Market Studies*, 37 (1), 1999, 59–85

Moravcsik, A. and Nicolaïdes, K., 'Federal Ideals and Constitutional Realities', *Journal of Common Market Studies* Annual Review, 1998

More, G., 'The Principle of Equal Treatment: From Market Unifier to Fundamental Right', in Craig, P. and Búrca, G. de (eds.), *The Evolution of EU Law* (Oxford: Oxford University Press, 1999), 517–553

Morgan, R., 'The European Community: the Constitution of a Would be Polity', in Bogdanor, V. (ed.), *Constitutions in Democratic Politics* (Aldershot: Gower, 1988), 367–379

Moxon-Browne, E., 'Social Europe', in Lodge, J. (ed.), *The European Community and the Challenge of the Future*, 2nd edn (London: Pinter, 1993), 152–162

Nash, F., 'The United Kingdom and the European Union', in Stanyer, J. and Hampshire Monk, I. (eds.), *Contemporary Political Studies III* (London: Political Studies Association, 1996), 739–750

Nentwich, M. and Falkner, G., 'The Treaty of Amsterdam: Towards a New Institutional Balance', *European Integration online Papers (EIoP)*, 1 (15), 1997 (http://eiop.or.at/eiop/texte/1997-015a.htm)

Neunreither, K., 'Political Representation in the European Union: A Common Whole, Various Wholes, or Just a Hole?', in Neunreither, K. and Wiener, A. (eds.), *European Integration after Amsterdam: Institutional Dynamics and Prospects for Democracy* (Oxford: Oxford University Press, 2000), 129–149

Neunreither, K., 'The European Union at Nice: A Minimalist Approach to a Historic Challenge', *Government and Opposition*, 36 (2), 2001, 184–208

Neuwahl, N. A., 'The Place of the Citizen in the European Construction', in Lynch, P. et al. (eds.), *Reforming the European Union: from Maastricht to Amsterdam* (Harlow: Longman, 2000), 183–199

Newman, M., *Democracy, Sovereignty and the EU* (London: Hurst, 1996)

Neyer, J., 'Justifying Comitology: The Promise of Deliberation', in Neunreither, K. and Wiener, A. (eds.), *European Integration after Amsterdam: Institutional Dynamics and Prospects for Democracy* (Oxford: Oxford University Press, 2000), 112–128

Nicoll, W. and Salmon, T., *Understanding the European Union* (London: Longman, 2000)

Notre Europe, *A Wake-Up Call for Europe* (Paris: Notre Europe, 15 October 2001)

O'Keefe, D., 'Recasting the Third Pillar', *Common Market Law Review*, 32 (4), 1995, 893–920

O'Keefe, D., 'Can the Leopard Change its Spots?: Visas, Immigration and Asylum following Amsterdam', in O'Keefe, D. and Twomey, P. (eds.), *Legal Issues of the Amsterdam Treaty* (Oxford: Hart, 1999), 271–288

O'Keefe, D., 'Union Citizenship', in O'Keefe, D. and Twomey, P. (eds.), *Legal Issues of the Maastricht Treaty* (Oxford: Hart, 1999), 87–107

O'Leary, S., 'The Free Movement of Persons and Services', in Craig, P. and Búrca, G. de (eds.), *The Evolution of EU Law* (Oxford: Oxford University Press, 1999), 377–416

O'Reilly, D. O. and Stone Sweet, A., 'The Liberalization and Reregulation of Air Transport', *Journal of European Public Policy*, 5 (3), 1998, 447–466

O'Riordan, M., 'Employment', in Tonra, B. (ed.), *Amsterdam: What the Treaty Means* (Dublin: Institute of European Studies, 1997), 67–75

Padoa-Schioppa, A., 'The Institutional Reforms of the Amsterdam Treaty', *The Federalist*, 40 (1), 1998, 8–25

Padoan, P. C., ' EU Employment and Social Policy after Amsterdam: Too Little or Too Much?', in Monar, J. and Wessels, W. (eds.), *The European Union after the Treaty of Amsterdam* (London: Continuum, 2001), 207–226

Palmer, J., 'The EU after Nice: One Step Forward, Two Steps Back', Document (364), 201, www.theepc.be

Parsons, C., 'Domestic Interests, Ideas and Integration: The French Case', *Journal of Common Market Studies*, 31 (1), 2000, 45–70

Patterson, L. A., 'Biotechnology Policy: Regulating Risk and Risking Regulation', in Wallace, H. and Wallace, W. (eds.), *Policy-Making in the European Union*, 4th edn (Oxford: Oxford University Press, 2000), 317–343

Payne, D. C., 'Policy-Making in Nested Institutions: Explaining the Conservation Failure of the EU's Common Fisheries Policy', *Journal of Common Market Studies*, 31 (2), 2000, 303–324

Peel, Q., 'Europe's Guaranteed Gridlock', *Financial Times*, 9 July 2001, 23

Peers, S., 'Banana Split: WTO Law and Preferential Agreements in the EC Legal Order', *European Foreign Affairs Review*, 4 (2), 1999, 195–214

Peers, S., '*Caveat Emptor*? Integrating the Schengen *Acquis* into the European Union Legal Order', in Dashwood, A. and Ward, A. (eds.), *The Cambridge Yearbook of European Legal Studies II – 1999* (Oxford: Hart, 2000), 87–123

Peers, S., 'Justice and Home Affairs: Decision-making after Amsterdam', *European Law Review*, 25 (2), 2000, 183–191

Pernice, I., 'Multilevel Constitutionalism and the Treaty of Amsterdam: European Constitution-Making Revisited?', *Common Market Law Review*, 36 (4), 1999, 703–750

Pernice, I., 'Dividing and Defining Competences', unpublished presentation to the Heinrich Böll Stiftung, 10 November 2000

Pernice, I. and Mayer, F., 'De la constitution composée de l'Europe', *Revue trimestrielle de droit européen*, 36 (4), 2000, 623–647

Pescatore, P., 'La Constitution, son contenu, son utilité', *Zeitschrift für Schweizerisches Recht*, 111 (1), 1992, 54–55

Petersen, N., *The Danish Referendum on the Treaty of Amsterdam*, ZEI Discussion Paper C17 (Bonn: Zentrum für Europäische Integrationsforschung, 1998)

Peterson, J. and Sjursen, H., 'Conclusion: the Myth of the CFSP?', in Peterson, J. and Sjursen, H. (eds.), *A Common Foreign Policy for Europe?* (London: Routledge, 1998), 169–185

Petite, M., 'The Treaty of Amsterdam', *Jean Monnet Papers*, 98 (2), 1998 (http://www.jeanmonnet-program.org)

Philip Morris Institute, *Does Europe Need a Constitution?* (Brussels: PMI, 1996)

Phinnemore, D., *Association: Stepping-Stone or Alternative to EU Membership?* (Sheffield: UACES/Sheffield University Press, 1999)

Piris, J. C., 'Does the European Union Have a Constitution? Does it Need One?', *European Law Review*, 24 (4), 1999, 557–585

Polakiewicz, J., *Treaty Making in the Council of Europe* (Strasbourg: Council of Europe, 1999)

Pollack, M., 'Creeping Competence: The Expanding Agenda of the European Community', *Journal of Public Policy*, 14 (2), 1994, 95–145

Pollack, M., 'The End of Creeping Competence? EU Policy-Making Since Maastricht', *Journal of Common Market Studies*, 38 (3), 2000, 519–538

Pollack, M. A., 'A Blairite Treaty: Neo-Liberalism and Regulated Capitalism in the Treaty of Amsterdam', in Neunreither, K. and Wiener, A. (eds.), *European Integration after Amsterdam: Institutional Dynamics and Prospects for Democracy* (Oxford: Oxford University Press, 2000), 266–289

Pond, E., 'A New Constitution for the Old Continent?', *The Washington Quarterly*, 24 (4), 2001, 29–40

Randall, E., 'European Union Health Policy With and Without Design: Serendipity, Tragedy and the Future of EU Health Policy', *Policy Studies*, 21 (2), 2000, 133–164

Rau, J., 'Plea for a Constitution: Speech to the European Parliament', http://eng.bundespraesident.de/dokumente/Rede/ix_59100.htm

Raux, J., 'Pour Un Traité fondamentale de portée constitutionelle', paper presented to Jean Monnet Conference, Brussels 1998

Rees, G. W., 'Common Foreign and Security Policy and Defence: a Lost Opportunity', in Lynch, P. et al. (eds.), *Reforming the European Union: from Maastricht to Amsterdam* (Harlow: Longman, 2000), 162–179

Rees, W., Neuwahl, N. and Lynch, P. (eds.), *Reforming the European Union* (London: Longman, 2000)

Reflection Group, '*A Strategy for Europe': Final Report from the Chairman of the Reflection Group on the 1996 Intergovernmental Conference* (Brussels: Reflection Group, 1995)

Regelsberger, E. and Wessels, W., 'The CFSP Institutions and Procedures: a Third Way for the Second Pillar', *European Foreign Affairs Review*, 1 (1), 1996, 29–54

Reich, N., 'A European Constitution for Citizens', *European Law Journal*, 3 (2), 1997, 131–164

Richardson, T., 'The Trans-European Network: Environmental Policy Integration in the European Union', *European Urban and Regional Studies*, 4 (4), 1997, 333–346

Rieger, E., 'The Common Agricultural Policy: Politics against Markets', in Wallace, H. and Wallace, W. (eds.), *Policy-Making in the European Union*, 4th edn (Oxford: Oxford University Press, 2000), 179–211

Roberts-Thompson, P., ' EU Treaty Referendums and the European Union', *Journal of European Integration*, 23 (2), 2001, 105–137

Ross, M., 'Article 16 E.C. and Services of General Interest: from Derogation to Obligation?', *European Law Review*, 25 (1), 2000, 22–38

Sapir, A., 'Trade Regionalism in Europe: Towards an Integrated Approach', *Journal of Common Market Studies*, 31 (1), 2000, 151–162

Sbragia, A. M., *Europolitics* (Washington, DC: Brookings, 1994)

Sbragia, A. M., 'Environmental Policy: Economic Constraints and External Pressures', in Wallace, H. and Wallace, W. (eds.), *Policy-Making in the European Union*, 4th edn (Oxford: Oxford University Press, 2000), 293–316

Schepers, S., 'The Legal Force of the Preamble to the EEC Treaty', *European Law Review*, 6 (5), 1981, 356–361

Schilling, T., 'Treaty or Constitution', *Maastricht Journal of European and Comparative Law*, 3 (1), 1996, 47–68

Schmid, C. U., *Ways Out of the Maquis Communautaire: On Simplification and Consolidation and the Need for a Restatement of European Primary Law* (Florence: European University Institute Working Paper RSC No. 99/6, 1999), II

Schmitter, P. C., *How To Democratize the EU . . . and Why Bother?* (Lanham, MD: Rowman and Littlefield, 2000)

Sciarra, S., 'The Employment Title in the Amsterdam Treaty: A Multi-language Legal Discourse', in O'Keefe, D. and Twomey, P. (eds.), *Legal Issues of the Amsterdam Treaty* (Oxford: Hart, 1999), 157–170

Scott, J., *EC Environmental Law* (London: Longman, 1998)

Scott, J., 'Regional Policy: An Evolutionary Perspective', in Craig, P. and Búrca, G. de (eds.), *The Evolution of EU Law* (Oxford: Oxford University Press, 1999), 625–652

Secrétariat Général du Conseil, *Version Consolidée des Traités – Volumes I et II* (Brussels: Secrétariat Général du Conseil, 2000)

Secretariat Working Party: Task Force on the Intergovernmental Conference, *Simplification of the Union Treaties and the 1996 Intergovernmental Conference*, Political Series W-16 (Luxembourg: European Parliament Directorate-General for Research, October 1995)

Secretariat Working Party: Task Force on the Intergovernmental Conference, *Draft of a Consolidated Treaty of the European Union*, Political Series W-17/rev. (Luxembourg: European Parliament Directorate-General for Research, March 1996)

Sedelmeier, U., 'East of Amsterdam: The Implications of the Amsterdam Treaty for Eastern Enlargement', in Neunreither, K. and Wiener, A. (eds.), *European Integration after Amsterdam: Institutional Dynamics and Prospects for Democracy* (Oxford: Oxford University Press, 2000), 218–236

Seidel, M., 'Constitutional Aspects of the Economic and Monetary Union', in Snyder, F. (ed.), *Constitutional Dimensions of European Economic Integration* (The Hague: Kluwer Law International, 1996), 43–53

Serra, E. (ed.), *The Relaunching of Europe and the Treaties of Rome* (Brussels: Brulyant, 1989)

Shackleton, M., 'The Politics of Codecision', *Journal of Common Market Studies*, 31 (2), 2000, 325–342

Shapiro, M., 'The European Court of Justice', in Craig, P. and Búrca, G. de (eds.), *The Evolution of EU Law* (Oxford: Oxford University Press, 1999), 321–347

Shaw, J., 'Twin-track Social Europe – the Inside Track', in O'Keefe, D. and Twomey, P. (eds.), *Legal Issues of the Amsterdam Treaty* (Oxford: Hart, 1999), 295–311

Shaw, J., 'From the Margins to the Centre: Education and Training Law and Policy', in Craig, P. and Búrca, G. de (eds.), *The Evolution of EU Law* (Oxford: Oxford University Press, 1999), 555–595

Shaw, J., 'Constitutional Settlements and the Citizen after the Treaty of Amsterdam', in Neunreither, K. and Wiener, A. (eds.), *European Integration after Amsterdam: Institutional Dynamics and Prospects for Democracy* (Oxford: Oxford University Press, 2000), 290–317

Shaw, J., 'The Treaty of Nice: Legal and Constitutional Implications', *European Public Law*, 7 (2), 2001, 195–215

Sherlock, A., *The European Union and the European Convention on Human Rights* (Oxford: Oxford University Press, 2001)

Sinott, R., *A Knowledge of the EU in Irish Public Opinion* (Dublin: Institute of European Affairs, Occasional Paper 5, 1995)

Sinott, R. and Thomsen, S., 'Reasons for "No" to Nice not the right question' http://www.europe2020.org/fr/irish/

Smith, B. and Wallace, W., 'Constitutional Deficits of EU Justice and Home Affairs: Transparency, Accountability and Judicial Control', in Monar, J. and Wessels, W. (eds.), *The European Union after the Treaty of Amsterdam* (London: Continuum, 2001), 125–149

Smith, F., 'Renegotiating Lomé: the Impact of the World Trade Organisation on the European

Community's Development Policy after the *Bananas* Conflict', *European Law Review*, 25 (3), 2000, 247–263

Smith, M. P., 'Autonomy by the Rules: The European Commission and the Development of State Aid Policy', *Journal of Common Market Studies*, 36 (1), 1998, 55–78

Snyder, F., ' EMU Revisited: Are We Making a Constitution? What Constitution Are We Making?', in Craig, P. and Búrca, G. de (eds.), *The Evolution of EU Law* (Oxford: Oxford University Press, 1999), 417–477

Snyder, F., 'The Union's Unfinished Constitution', paper presented to the Jean Monnet Symposium on the IGC, April 2000

Snyder, F. G., *Law of the Common Agricultural Policy* (London: Sweet and Maxwell, 1985)

Solana, J., 'Foreword', in D. Galloway, *The Treaty of Nice and Beyond* (Sheffield, UACES/Sheffield Academic Press, 2001), 7–8

Spiro, H. J., *Government by Constitution* (New York, Random House, 1959)

Stavridis, S., *ESDP after Nice* (Catania: Jean Monnet Working papers 2001/3)

Stefanou, C. and Xanthaki, H., *A Legal and Political Interpretation of Articles 224 and 225 of the Treaty of Rome: The FYROM Cases* (Aldershot: Ashgate, 1997)

Stein, E., 'Lawyers, Judges and the Making of a Transnational Constitution', *American Journal of International Law*, 75 (1), 1981, 1–27

Steiner, J., *Textbook on EC Law*, 4th edn (London: Blackstone, 1994)

Stevens, A. and Stevens, H., *Brussels Bureaucrats: The Administration of the European Union* (Basingstoke: Palgrave, 2001)

Stevens, C., 'Trade with Developing Countries: Banana Skins and Turf Wars', in Wallace, H. and Wallace, W. (eds.), *Policy-Making in the European Union*, 4th edn (Oxford: Oxford University Press, 2000), 401–426

Stone Sweet, A. and Sandholtz, W., 'European Integration and Supranational Governance', *Journal of European Public Policy*, 4 (3), 1997, 1–24

Streit, M. E. and Müssler, W., 'The Economic Constitution of the European Community – "From Rome to Maastricht" ', in Snyder, F. (ed.), *Constitutional Dimensions of European Integration* (The Hague: Kluwer Law International, 1996), 109–147

Stubb, A. C.-G., 'Negotiating Flexible Integration in the Amsterdam Treaty', in Neunreither, K. and Wiener, A. (eds.), *European Integration after Amsterdam: Institutional Dynamics and Prospects for Democracy* (Oxford: Oxford University Press, 2000), 153–174

Stuyck, J., 'European Consumer Law after the Treaty of Amsterdam: Consumer Policy In or Beyond the Internal Market?', *Common Market Law Review*, 37 (2), 2000, 367–400

Svensson, A.-C., *In the Service of the European Union: the Role of the Presidency in Negotiating the Amsterdam Treaty 1995–97* (Uppsala: Acta Universitatis Upsaliensis, 2000)

Sverdrup, U., 'Precedents and Present Events in the European Union: An Institutional Perspective on Treaty Reform', in Neunreither, K. and Wiener, A. (eds.), *European Integration after Amsterdam: Institutional Dynamics and Prospects for Democracy* (Oxford: Oxford University Press, 2000), 241–265

Szyszcak, E., 'The New Parameters of European Labour Law', in O'Keefe, D. and Twomey, P. (eds.), *Legal Issues of the Amsterdam Treaty* (Oxford: Hart, 1999), 141–156

Telo, M. and Magnette, P. (eds.), *De Maastricht à Amsterdam* (Brussels: Editions Complexe, 1999)

Temple Lang, J., 'The Duties of Cooperation of National Authorities and Courts under Article 10 E.C.: Two More Reflections', *European Law Review*, 26 (1), 2001, 84–93

Thagesen, R. and Matthews, A., 'The EU's Common Banana Regime: An Initial Evaluation', *Journal of Common Market Studies*, 35 (4), 1997, 615–627

Toggenburg, G., 'A Rough Orientation Through the Delicate Relationship: The European Union's Endeavours for (its) Minorities', *European Integration Online Papers*, 4 (16), 2000 (via http://eiop.or.at/eiop.texte/2000-016a.htm)

Toth, A. G., 'The Legal Effect of the Protocols Relating to the United Kingdom, Ireland and Denmark', in Heukels, T. et al. (eds.), *The European Union after Amsterdam: A Legal Analysis* (The Hague: Kluwer Law International, 1998), 227–252

Tournier, J.-C., *Mieux Comprendre la traité d'Amsterdam* (Paris: Editions d'Organisation, 1999)

'The Treaty of Amsterdam: Neither a Bang nor a Whimper', *Common Market Law Review*, 34 (4), 1997, 767–772

Tsoukalis, L., 'Economic and Monetary Union: Political Conviction and Economic Uncertainty', in Wallace, H. and Wallace, W. (eds.), *Policy-Making in the European Union*, 4th edn (Oxford: Oxford University Press, 2000), 149–178

'Tulips or Nettles from Amsterdam?', *European Law Review*, 22, 1997, 289–290

Twomey, P., 'Constructing a Secure Space: The Area of Freedom, Security and Justice', in O'Keefe, D. and Twomey, P. (eds.), *Legal Issues of the Amsterdam Treaty* (Oxford: Hart, 1999), 351–374

'Union without constitution', *Common Market Law Review*, 34 (5), 1997, 1105–1111

Usher, J., *EC Institutions and Legislation* (London: Longman, 1998)

Usher, J., *General Principles of EC Law* (London: Longman, 1998)

Usher, J., 'Economic and Monetary Union – A Model for Flexibility?', in Dashwood, A. and Ward, A. (eds.), *The Cambridge Yearbook of European Legal Studies I – 1998* (Oxford: Hart, 1999), 39–75

Vibert, F., 'The Case for a Constitution', unpublished Paper presented to the UACES Conference *Legitimacy and Accountability in the European Union after Nice*, Birmingham University, 5–6 July 2001

Vincenzi, C., *Law of the European Community*, 2nd edn (London: Financial Times/Pitman, 1999)

von Kyaw, D., 'Weichenstellungen des EU-Gipfels von Nizza', *Internationale Politik*, 56 (2), 2001, 5–12

Wachsmann, P., 'Les Droits de l'homme', *Revue Trimestrielle du Droit Européenne*, 33 (4), 1997, 883–902

Waddington, L., 'Article 13 EC: Mere Rhetoric or Harbinger of Change', in Dashwood, A. and Ward, A. (eds.), *The Cambridge Yearbook of European Legal Studies I – 1998* (Oxford: Hart, 1999), 175–197

Waddington, L., 'Throwing Some Light on Article 13 EC Treaty', *Maastricht Journal of European and Comparative Law*, 6 (1), 1999, 1–4

Wallace, H., 'Flexibility: a Tool of Integration or a Restraint on Disintegration', in Neunreither, K. and Wiener, A. (eds.), *European Integration after Amsterdam: Institutional Dynamics and Prospects for Democracy* (Oxford: Oxford University Press, 2000), 175–191

Wallace, W., 'Collective Governance: the EU Political Process', in Wallace, H. and Wallace, W. (eds.), *Policy-Making in the European Union*, 4th edn (Oxford: Oxford University Press, 2000), 523–542

Ward, I., 'Amsterdam and the Continuing Search for Community', in O'Keefe, D. and Twomey, P. (eds.), *Legal Issues of the Amsterdam Treaty* (Oxford: Hart, 1999), 41–56

Ward, I., 'Beyond Constitutionalism: the Search for a European Political Imagination', *European Law Journal*, 7 (1), 2000, 24–40

Watson, P., 'Social Policy after Maastricht', *Common Market Law Review*, 30 (3), 1993, 481–513

Weale, A. et al., *Environmental Governance in Europe: An Ever Closer Ecological Union?* (Oxford: Oxford University Press, 2000)

Weatherill, S., *EC Consumer Law and Policy* (London: Longman, 1997)

Weatherill, S., 'Safeguarding the *Acquis Communautaire*', in Heukels, T. et al. (eds.), *The European Union after Amsterdam: A Legal Analysis* (The Hague: Kluwer Law International, 1998), 153–178

Weatherill, S., 'Consumer Policy', in Craig, P. and Búrca, G. de (eds.), *The Evolution of EU Law* (Oxford: Oxford University Press, 1999), 693–720

Weatherill, S., ' "If I'd Wanted you to Understand I Would Have Explained it Better": What is the Purpose of the Provisions on Closer Co-operation Introduced by the Treaty of Amsterdam?', in O'Keefe, D. and Twomey, P. (eds.), *Legal Issues of the Amsterdam Treaty* (Oxford: Hart, 1999), 21–40

Weatherill, S. and Beaumont, P., *EC Law: The Essential Guide to the Legal Workings of the European Community* (London: Penguin, 1996)

Weidenfeld, W. (ed.), *Maastricht in der Analyse* (Gütersloh: Verlag Bertelsmann Stiftung, 1994)

Weidenfeld, W. (ed.), *Nizza in der Analyse* (Gütersloh: Verlag Bertelsmann Stiftung, 2001)

Weiler, J., 'Prologue: Amsterdam and the Quest for Constitutional Democracy', in O'Keefe, D. and Twomey, P. (eds.), *Legal Issues of the Amsterdam Treaty* (Oxford: Hart, 1999), 1–20

Weiler, J. H. H., 'The Transformation of Europe', *Yale Law Journal*, 100, 1991, 2403–2483

Weiler, J. H. H., 'The Anatomy of the Community Legal Order: Through the Looking Glass', in Weiler, J. H. H., *The Constitution of Europe* (Cambridge: Cambridge University Press, 1999), 286–323

Weiler, J. H. H., 'The Constitution of the Common Market Place: Text and Context in the Evolution of the Free Movement of Goods', in Craig, P. and Búrca, G. de (eds.), *The Evolution of EU Law* (Oxford: Oxford University Press, 1999), 349–376

Weizsäcker, R. V., Dehaene, J.-L. and Simon, D., *The Institutional Implications of Enlargement* (Report to the European Commission, Brussels: 18 October 1999)

Welsh, J. M., 'A Peoples' Europe', *Politics*, 13 (2), 1993, 25–31

Wessels, W., 'Der Amsterdamer Vertrag – Durch Stückwerksreformen zu einer effizienteren, erweiterten und föderalen Union?', *Integration*, 20 (3), 1997, 117–135

Wessels, W., 'The Amsterdam Treaty in Theoretical Perspective: Which Dynamics at Work?', in Monar, J. and Wessels, W. (eds.), *The European Union after the Treaty of Amsterdam* (London: Continuum, 2001), 70–84

Wessels, W., 'Nice Results: the Millennium IGC in the EU's Evolution', *Journal of Common Market Studies*, 39 (2), 2001, 197–219

Westlake, M., *The EU beyond Amsterdam* (London: Routledge, 1999)

White, R. C. A., 'Defining a Constitution for the European Union', in Lynch, P. et al. (eds.), *Reforming the European Union: from Maastricht to Amsterdam* (Harlow: Longman, 2000), 217–231

Whiteford, E. A., 'Social Policy after Maastricht', *European Law Review*, 18 (3), 1993, 202–222

Whitman, R., 'The New Treaty of Amsterdam and the Future of the EU', *Comparative Political Studies* (Exeter: Political Studies Association, 1997)

Whittle, R., 'Disability Discrimination and the Amsterdam Treaty', *European Law Review*, 23 (1), 1998, 50–58

Wiener, A., 'Forging Flexibility – The British "No" to Schengen', *European Journal of Migration and Law*, 1, 1999, 441–463

Wincott, D., 'Is the Treaty of Maastricht an Adequate "Constitution" for the European Union?', *Public Administration*, 72 (4), 1994, 573–590

Wincott, D., *The Treaty of Maastricht: an Adequate 'Constitution' for the European Union?*, (University of Warwick: European Public Policy Institute Occasional Paper 93/6, 1993)

Winn, N., 'The Proof of the Pudding is in the Eating: the EU "Joint Action" as an Effective Foreign Policy Instrument?', *International Relations*, 13 (6), 1997, 19–32

Wishlade, F., 'Competition Policy or Cohesion Policy by the Back Door? The Commission guidelines on National Regional Aid', *European Competition Law Review*, 6, 1998, 343–357

Wolf, Philip L., *Comparative Constitutions* (London: Macmillan, 1972)

Woolcock, S., 'European Trade Policy: Global Pressures and Domestic Constraints', in Wallace, H. and Wallace, W. (eds.), *Policy-Making in the European Union*, 4th edn (Oxford: Oxford University Press, 2000), 373–399

Wouters, J., 'Amsterdam, Parts Two and Three', *Maastricht Journal of European and Comparative Law*, 4 (4), 1997, 328–331

Yataganas, X. A., 'The Treaty of Nice: the Sharing of Power and the Institutional Balance in the European Union – A Continental Perspective', *European Law Review*, 7 (3), 2001, 242–291

Young, A. R., 'The Adaptation of European Foreign Economic Policy: From Rome to Seattle', *Journal of Common Market Studies*, 31 (1), 2000, 93–116

Young, A. R. and Wallace, H., 'The Single Market: A New Approach to Policy', in Wallace, H. and Wallace, W. (eds.), *Policy-Making in the European Union*, 4th edn (Oxford: Oxford University Press, 2000), 85–114

Zilioli, C. and Selmayr, M., 'The External Relations of the Euro Area: Legal Aspects', *Common Market Law Review*, 36 (2), 1999, 273–349

Zwaan, J. de, 'Community Dimensions of the Second Pillar', in Heukels, T. et al. (eds.), *The European Union after Amsterdam: A Legal Analysis* (The Hague: Kluwer Law International, 1998), 179–193

Zwaan, J. de, 'Opting in and Opting out of Rules Concerning the Free Movement of Persons: Problems and Practical Arrangements', in Dashwood, A. and Ward, A. (eds.), *The Cambridge Yearbook of European Legal Studies I – 1998* (Oxford: Hart, 1999), 107–124

Zwaan, J. de and Vrouenraets, M., 'The Future of the Third Pillar: An Evaluation of the Treaty of Amsterdam', in Heukels, T. et al. (eds.), *The European Union after Amsterdam: A Legal Analysis* (The Hague: Kluwer Law International, 1998), 203–214

1d: ECJ Cases

Administration des Douanes et Droits Indirects v. *Léopold Legros and others* (Case C-163/90), *European Court Reports*, 1992, I-4625

Barber v. *Guardian Royal Exchange* (Case 262/88), *European Court Reports*, 1990, I-1889

Beus v. *Hauptzollamt München* (Case 5/67), *European Court Reports*, 1968, 83

Bickel and Franz (Case 274/96), *European Court Reports*, 1998, I-7637

Brasserie du Pêcheur and Factortame (Case C-46 and C-48/93), *European Court Reports*, 1996, I-1029

British American Tobacco Co. Ltd. v. *Commission* (Cases 142/84 and 156/84) *European Court Reports*, 1987, 4487

Broadcasting, Entertainment, Cinematographic and Theatre Union (BECTU) v. *Secretary of State for Trade and Industry* (Case C-173/99), *European Court Reports*, 2001, I-4881

Campus Oil v. *Ministry for Industry and Energy* (Case 72/83), *European Court Reports*, 1984, 2727

Carvel v. *Council* (Case T-194/94), *European Court Reports*, 1995, II-2767

Collins and Patricia Im- und Export v. *Imtrat and EMI Electrola* (Case C-92/92), *European Court Reports*, 1993, I-5145

Commission v. *Council (AETR)* (Case 22/70), *European Court Reports*, 1971, 263

Commission v. *Council (Airport Transit Visas)* (Case C-170/96), *European Court Reports*, 1998, I-2763

Commission v. *Council (ERASMUS)* (Case 242/87), *European Court Reports*, 1989, 1425

Commission v. *France (Re Italian Table Wines)* (Case 42/82), *European Court Reports*, 1983, 2729

Commission v. *Greece* (Case C-120/94), *European Court Reports*, 1996, I-1513

Commission v. *Netherlands* (Case C-68/89), *European Court Reports*, 1991, I-2637

Commission v. *United Kingdom (Re Tachographs)* (Case 128/78), *European Court Reports*, 1979, 419

Commission v. *Council* (Case C-170/96), *European Court Reports*, 1998, I-2763

Commission v. *France* (Case C-265/95), *European Court Reports*, 1997, I-6959

Compassion in World Farming (Case C-1/96 831), *European Court Reports*, 1998, I-1251

Costa v. *Ente Nazionale per l'Energia Elettrica (ENEL)* (Case 6/64), *European Court Reports*, 1964, 585

Council v. *European Parliament* (Case 34/86), *European Court Reports*, 1986, 2155

Council v. *European Parliament* (Case C-284/90), *European Court Reports*, 1992, I-2277

Defrenne v. *SABENA* (Case 43/75), *European Court Reports*, 1976, 455

Defrenne v. *SABENA* (No. 3) (Case 149/77), *European Court Reports*, 1978, 1365

Department of Health and Social Security v. *Barr and Montrose Holdings* (C-355/89), *European Court Reports*, 1991, I-3479

Deutsche Babcock Handel GmbH v. *Hauptzollamt Lübeck-Ost* (Case 328/85), *European Court Reports*, 1987, 5119

European Parliament v. *Council* (Case 13/83), *European Court Reports*, 1985, 1513

European Parliament v. *Council* (Case C-70/88), *European Court Reports*, 1990, I-2041

Europemballage Corp. and Continental Can Co. Inc. v. *Commission* (Case 6/72), *European Court Reports*, 1973, 215

Firm Foto Frost (Case 314/85), *European Court Reports*, 1987, 4199

France v. *European Parliament* (Case C-345/95), *European Court Reports*, 1995, I-5215

France v. *UK* (Case 141/78), *European Court Reports*, 1979, 2923

François de Coster v. *Collège des Bourgmestres et Echevins de Watermael-Boitsfort* (Case 17/00) – not yet published

Francovich v. *Italian State* (Case C-6/90 and C-9/90), *European Court Reports*, 1992, I-5337

Germany v. *European Parliament and Council* (Case 376/98), *European Court Reports*, 2000, I-2247

Gilly v. *Directeur des Services Fiscaux du Bas-Rhin* (Case 336/96), *European Court Reports*, 1998, I-2793

Government of Gibraltar v. *Council and Commission* (Case 298/89), *European Court Reports*, 1993, I-3605

Grau Gomis and Others (167/94R), *European Court Reports*, 1995, I-1023

Gravier v. *City of Liège* (Case 293/83), *European Court Reports*, 1985, I-593

Groupement des Industries Sidérurgiques Luxembourgeoises v. *High Authority* (Cases 7 and 9/54), *European Court Reports*, 1955–56, 53

Imm Zwartveld (Case 2/88), *European Court Reports*, 1990, I-3365

Kalanke v. *Freie Hansestadt Bremen* (Case 450/93), *European Court Reports*, 1995, I-3051

Keck (Bernard) and *Daniel Mithouard*, Criminal Proceedings Against (Joined Cases 267/91 and 268/91), *European Court Reports*, 1993, I-6097

Kleinwort Benson Ltd v. *City of Glasgow District Council* (Case C-346/93), *European Court Reports*, 1995, I-615

Kramer (Cornelius) and Others (Cases 3, 4 and 6/76), *European Court Reports*, 1976, 1279

Lancry v. *Direction Générale des Douanes* (Case 363/93), *European Court Reports*, 1994, I-3957

Les Verts – Parti Ecologiste v. *European Parliament* (Case 194/83), *European Court Reports*, 1986, 1339

Levin v. *Staatssecretaris van Justice* (Case 53/81), *European Court Reports*, 1982, 1035

Luisi v. *Ministereo del Tesoro* (Case 286/82), *European Court Reports*, 1984, 377

Marshall v. *Southampton and South West Area Health Authority* (No. 2) (Case C-271/91), *European Court Reports*, 1993, I-4367

Merckx and Neuhuys v. *Ford Motor Company Belgium* (Case C-171/94), *European Court Reports*, 1996, I-1253

Ministère Publique v. *Lucas Asjes and Others* (*Nouvelles Frontières*) (Joined Cases C-209–213/84), *European Court Reports*, 1986, 1425

Mr and Mrs F. v. *Belgian State* (Case 7/75), *European Court Reports*, 1975, 679

Nold v. *Commission* (Case 4/73), *European Court Reports*, 1974, 491

NV Algemene Transport – en Expeditie Onderneming Van Gend en Loos v. *Nederlandse Administratie der Belastingen* (Case 26/62), *European Court Reports*, 1963, 1

Opinion 1/91 on EEA Agreement between the Community, on the one hand, and the countries of the European Free Trade Association, on the other, relating to the creation of the European Economic Area, *European Court Reports*, 1991, I-6079

Opinion 1/94 on the Agreement Establishing the World Trade Organization, *European Court Reports*, 1994, I-5267

Opinion 2/94 on Accession of the European Communities to the European Human Rights Convention, *European Court Reports*, 1996, I-1759

Procureur de Roi v. *Dassonville* (Case 8/74), *European Court Reports*, 1975, 837

Procureur de Roi v. *Royer* (Case 48/75), *European Court Reports*, 1976, 497

Pubblico Ministereo v. *Manghera* (Case 59/75), *European Court Reports*, 1976, 91

Regina v. *Secretary of State for the Home Department, ex parte Gallagher* (Case C-175/94), *European Court Reports*, 1995, I-4253

Regina v. *Bouchereau* (Case 30/77), *European Court Reports*, 1977, 1999

Regina v. *Henn and Darby* (Case 34/79), *European Court Reports*, 1979, 3795

Regina v. *Secretary of State for Transport, ex parte Factortame* (Case 221/89), *European Court Reports*, 1991, I-3905

Rewe-Zentrale v. *Bundesmonopolverwaltung für Branntwein* (*Cassis de Dijon*) (Case 120/78), *European Court Reports*, 1979, 649

Reyners v. *Belgian State* (Case 2/74), *European Court Reports*, 1974, 631

Roquette Frères v. *Council* (*Isoglucose*) (Case 138/79), *European Court Reports*, 1980, 3333

Rui Alberta Pereira Roque v. *His Excellency the Lieutenant Governor of Jersey* (Case C-171 /96), *European Court Reports*, 1998, I-4607

Sacchi (Case 155/73), *European Court Reports*, 1974, 409

SGEEM and Etroy / EIB (Case C-370/89), *European Court Reports*, 1992, I-6211

Simmenthal SpA v. *Commission* (Case 92/78), *European Court Reports*, 1979, 777

Sotgiu v. *Deutsche Bundespost* (Case 152/73), *European Court Reports*, 1994, 153

Stanley George Adams v. *Commission* (Case 145/83), *European Court Reports*, 1985, 257

Thijssen v. *Contraladienst voor de Verzekeringen* (Case 42/92), *European Court Reports*, 1993, I-4047

Van Duyn v. *Home Office* (Case 41/74), *European Court Reports*, 1974, 1337

1e: Online Sources

As well as traditional books and articles, the Internet is another increasingly important source of information on the European Treaties and related subjects. However, normal critical caution is necessary since not everything on the net is correct or unbiased. Moreover, information can often be out of date. It can also be withdrawn or relocated without warning or indication of any new home. While we have tried to ensure that the URLs for external websites referred to in this book are both correct and appropriate at the time of going to press we can make no guarantee that they will remain so.

The EU is, like many foreign governments, now 'on line' to a very large extent. Indeed it claims that its website – Europa – is the world's largest. It can be accessed via http:// europa.eu.int and related sites. The Europa website, restructured in 2000 and accessible in all EU official languages, provides among other things the text of recent treaties, policy statements, descriptions of the EU's institutions, access to databases and a 'what's new' section.

On the treaties and related matters such subsites as EUR-Lex (http://europa.eu.int/ eur-lex/en/index.html), which contains EU legislation, the future of Europe debate (*http:// europa.eu.int/futurum/index_en.htm*) and the ECJ's database of cases (http://curia.eu.int/ en/jurisp/index.htm) are of great importance and value. Rapid posting of official documents is, in fact, one of the internet's main contributions to information about Europe. There are also databases on previous IGCs, details of forthcoming legislation and speeches on the treaties etc. The EU's public relations statements, of course, are subject to the same health warnings as all others.

The Europa site also has links to the various institutions' own sites. Most presidencies also have websites of their own. And of course there is a great deal of material on national governmental websites, now conveniently accessible from Europa as well as directly through the abc facility under 'governments'. Other European organizations, like the Council of Europe (http://www.coe.fr), also have often useful sites, most of which can be accessed without restriction.

There is also a whole range of useful academic and think-tank sites, such as EuroInternet which has access to a whole range of papers on European Integration (*http://eiop.or.at/ eiop/*). Most universities have their own links to European information while the

European University Institute in Florence (http://www.iue.it) is another key source. Similarly useful URLs include the following:

www.fedtrust.org.uk
www.uni-mannheim.de/users/ddz/edz/eedz.html
www.lib.berkeley.edu/GSSI/eu.html
www.theepc.be
www.uaces.org
www.euractiv.com
www.jeanmonnetprogram.org
http://eurotext.ulst.ac.uk:8017/
www.consuniv.org/cue.html
www.igcc.ucsd.edu/publications/policy_papers/
www.ejil.org/journal
www.europe2020.org
www.europanet.org
http://members.tripod/com/~WynGrant/WynGrantCAPpage.html

Beyond this there are a whole range of news services, both free and subscription-based, which carry useful information. Free services include Euractiv, European Observer and, up to a point, European Voice. However, these have their own political slants. Paid services include Agence Presse Europe, KnowEurope, EIS, EU Direct and EU Interactive.

The debate on the future of Europe can be followed via *europa.eu.int/futurum* and *european-convention.eu.int*, the latter being linked to the forum's URL.

Annex 2   Amendments to the TEC and the TEU

Throughout the *Guide* the evolutive nature of the European Treaties is very apparent. Keeping track of the actual changes made is not easy. So, we offer here a series of tables showing how the two key documents – the Treaty establishing the European Community and the Treaty on European Union – have altered over the years. Then, after a consideration of the way they have been renumbered as part of an ongoing move to restructure the European Treaties so as to make them more comprehensible and appealing, similar reference tables are provided for the two minor European Treaties: TECSC and TEAEC.

2a: Amendments to the TEC: Reference Table

The TEC has changed considerably since it was signed in 1957. Through various treaty amendments its shape and structure have been altered, its overall length has increased from 248 articles to the current 318 and most of its provisions have been renumbered. Table 2A charts the evolution of each article which has appeared in the Treaty.

In the first column are all the articles in the 1957 TEC as well as those added prior to the TEU, for example by the SEA in 1987. The second column lists all articles which appeared in the TEC following amendments introduced by the TEU and TA in the 1990s but keeps, for clarity, the original pre-consolidation numbering. The third column lists all articles according to their current numbering, incorporating additions brought about by Nice. In the fourth column, an indication of the current content of each part, title, chapter and section of the TEC is provided.

In the column 'Miscellaneous Amendments', the table identifies changes to the TEC introduced in the years prior to the SEA by, for example, the Merger Treaty. Such changes tend to be restricted to a few articles. The same is true of the amendments listed in the sixth column, which indicates where articles have been affected by the acts of accession and associated decisions of the Council which came into force in 1973, 1981, 1986 and 1995. Here and in the subsequent columns abbreviations are used to signal whether the article or element of the Treaty in question has been amended (A), inserted (I), repealed (R), deleted (D), moved (M) or renumbered (RN) or, indeed, if a wholly new article has been inserted (NI).

Following on from the acts of accession, the table then indicates in the next four columns the impact of the four key amending treaties on the TEC. These are the SEA, the TEU, the TA and the TN. The final column contains notes concerning either the new location of moved articles or the origin of certain inserted articles which in effect have simply been moved from elsewhere in the treaty.

While the table may appear to provide a complete overview of amendments, some changes are not indicated. First there are those changes which simply provided for the substitution of terms throughout the treaty. These are the amendments brought about by Article 3(1) SEA, which substituted 'European Parliament' for 'Assembly' throughout the treaty, and Article G(A)(1) TEU, which replaced the term 'European Economic Community' with 'European Community'. Second, since almost all articles were affected by Article 12 TA and the renumbering of the treaty's provisions, this amendment is not recorded in the TA column. A full list of abbreviations follows the table.

Table 2A   The evolution of the Treaty establishing the European Community

Pre-TEU	Post-TA	Current	Current Content	Misc. Amendments	AA	SEA	TEU	TA	TN	Notes
Preamble	*Preamble*	*Preamble*	*Preamble*					A		
Part One	**Part One**	**Part One**	**Principles**							
1	1	1					A	A	A	
2	2	2					A	A		
3	3	3					I	A	A	
	3a	4					I	I		
	3b	5					A	I	I	
	3c	6					I	I		
4	4	7		amended by CFP			A	A	A	
	4a	8					I	I		
	4b	9					I	I		
5	5	10				A	D	A		
	5a	11				I	RN	I		
		11a				I	RN	A		
6	6	12					RN	R		
6a	6a	13					RN	A		
7	7	14					RN	R	A	
8a	7a	15					RN	A		
8b	7b	16					RN	R		
8c	7c									
	7d									
Part Two	**Part Two**	**Part Two**	**Citizenship of the Union**				I	I		
8	17	17					I	A	A	
8a	18	18					I	A	A	
8b	19	19					I	A	A	
8c	20	20					I	A		
8d	21	21					I	A		
8e	22	22					I	A		

Part Two Title I	Part Three Title I	Part Three Title I	Community Policies / Free movement of goods	RN
			Community Policies / Free movement of goods	
9	9	23		A
10	10	24		A
11	11			R
Chapter 1	*Chapter 1*	*Chapter 1*	*The Customs Union*	A
Section 1	*Section 1*			D
12	12	25		A
13	13			R
14	14			R
15	15			R
16	16			R
17	17			R
Section 2	*Section 2*	*Section 2*		D
18	18			R
19	19			R
20	20			R
21	21			R
22	22			R
23	23			R
24	24			R
25	25			R
26	26			R
27	27			R
28	28	26		A
29	29	27		A
Chapter 2	*Chapter 2*	*Chapter 2*	*Prohibition of quantitative restrictions*	A
30	30	28		A
31	31			R
32	32			R
33	33			R
34	34	29		A
35	35			R
36	36	30		A

Pre-TEU	Post-TA	Current	Current Content	Misc. Amendments	AA	SEA	TEU	TA	TN	Notes
37	37	31							A	
Title II	Title II	Title II	*Agriculture*					A		
38	38	32						A		
39	39	33								
40	40	34						A		
41	41	35								
42	42	36								
43	43	37						A		
44	44							R		
45	45							R		
46	46	38								
47	47							R		
Title III	Title III	Title III	*Free movement of persons, services and capital*					R		
Chapter 1	*Chapter 1*	*Chapter 1*	*Workers*					A		
48	48	39					A	A		
49	49	40				A	A	A		
50	50	41								
51	51	42						A		
Chapter 2	*Chapter 2*	*Chapter 2*	*Right of establishment*					A		
52	52	43						A		
53	53							R		
54	54	44				A	A	A		
55	55	45						A		
56	56	46				A	A	A		
57	57	47				A	A	A		
58	58	48								
Chapter 3	*Chapter 3*	*Chapter 3*	*Services*					A		
59	59	49				A		A		
60	60	50								
61	61	51						A		
62	62							R		
63	63	52						A		

(1)	(2)	(3)	Status
64	64	53	A
65	65	54	
66	66	55	
Chapter 4	Chapter 4	Chapter 4 Capital and payments	A
67	67		R
68	68		R
69	69		R A
70	70		R A
71	71		R
72	72		R
73	73		R
	73a		
	73b	56	I
	73c	57	I
	73d	58	I
	73e	59	I R
	73f	60	I
	73g		I
	73h		I R
	Title IIIa	Title IV Visa, asylum, immigration and other policies related to free movement of persons	I
	73i	61	I
	73j	62	I
	73k	63	I
	73l	64	I
	73m	65	I
	73n	66	I
	73o	67	I
	73p	68	I A
	73q	69	I
Title IV	Title IV	Title V Transport	
74	74	70	A
75	75	71	A
76	76	72	A
77	77	73	A

Pre-TEU	Post-TA	Current	Current Content	Misc. Amendments	AA	SEA	TEU	TA	TN	Notes
78	78	74							A	
79	79	75							A	
80	80	76								
81	81	77								
82	82	78								
83	83	79							A	
84	84	80				A			A	
Part Three Title I	Title V	Title VI	Common rules on competition, taxation and approximation of laws				RN			
Chapter 1	Chapter 1	Chapter 1	*Rules on competition*							
Section 1	Section 1	Section 1	*Rules applying to undertakings*							
85	85	81						A		
86	86	82								
87	87	83						A		
88	88	84								
89	89	85						D		
90	90	86						R		
Section 2	Section 2							RN		
91	91							A		
Section 3	Section 3	Section 2	*Aids granted by States*				A			
92	92	87					A			
93	93	88								
94	94	89								
Chapter 2	Chapter 2	Chapter 2	*Tax provisions*					A		
95	95	90								
96	96	91								
97	97							R		
98	98	92				A	A			
99	99	93								
Chapter 3	Chapter 3	Chapter 3	*Approximation of laws*				A			
100	100	94						A		

		New	Title / Chapter				
100a	100a	95		I	A		A
100b	100b			I			R
	100c				I		R
	100d				A		A
101	101	96		I	A		
102	102	97		I	I		
Title II	**Title VII**	**Title VI**	**Economic and monetary policy**		RN	RN	
Chapter 1	*Chapter 1*	*Chapter 1*	*Economic policy*	I	NI	RN	
102a	102a	98		RN	D		
Chapter 2	*Chapter 2*				A		A
103	103	99		RN	I		
Chapter 3	103a	100			D		
104	104	101			NI		
	104a	102			I		
	104b	103			I		
	104c	104			I		
	Chapter 2		*Monetary policy*		A		
105	105	105			I		
106	105a	106			A		
107	106	107			A		
108	107	108			A,M		see 109h
	109h				A		
109	108	109			I		
	108a				A,M		see 109i
	109i				I	A	
Chapter 3	109		*Institutional provisions*		I		
	Chapter 3				I		
	109a	112			I		
	109b	113			I		
	109c	114			I		
	109d	115			I		
Chapter 4	*Chapter 4*		*Transitional provisions*		I		A
	109e	116			I		

Pre-TEU	Post-TA	Current	Current Content	Misc. Amendments	AA	SEA	TEU	TA	TN	Notes
	109f	117					I	A		
	109g	118					I	I		amended ex 108
	109h	119					I	I		amended ex 109
	109i	120					I	I		
	109j	121					I	I		
	109k	122					I	I		
	109l	123					I	I	A	
	109m	124					I	I		
	Title VIa	Title VIII	Employment				I	I		
	109n	125						I		
	109o	126						I		
	109p	127						I		
	109q	128						I		
	109r	129						I		
	109s	130						I		
Chapter 4	Title VII	Title IX	Common commercial policy			RN	RN			
110	110	131								
111							R			
112	112	132					A	A	A	
	113	133					A	A	A	
114							R			
115	115	134					A			
116	116						R			
Title III	Title VIIa	Title X	Customs co-operation				I	I		
	116	135								
Chapter 1	Title VIII	Title XI	Social policy, education, vocational training and youth				RN			
Chapter 1	Chapter 1	Chapter 1								
117	117	136						A		
118	118	137					A	A	A	
118a	118a	138				I	A	M		see amended 118
	118a							NI		
118b	118b	139				I		A	A	

		Subject		Amendment codes / notes
	118c		140	I
119	119		141	A
	119a		142	I — ex 120
120	120		143	M — see 119a
121	121		144	I — NI
122	122		145	
Chapter 2	Chapter 2	*The European Social Fund*	Chapter 2	
123	123		146	A, A
124	124		147	A, A
125	125		148	A, A
Chapter 3	Chapter 3	*Education, vocational training and youth*	Chapter 3	I
126	126		149	I, A
127	127		150	I, A
128	Title IX — 128	Culture	Title XII — 151	I, A
Title IV — 129	Title X — 129	Public health	Title XIII — 152	A,M — NI — see 198d
	Title XI — 129a	Consumer protection	Title XIV — 153	I, A
	Title XII — 129b	Trans-European networks	Title XV — 154	I, A
	129c		155	I
	129d		156	I
130	Title XIII — 130	Industry	Title XVI — 157	I, A
Title V	Title XIV — 198e	Cohesion	Title XVII — 198e	A,M — RN — see 198e
130a	130a		158	I — A
130b	130b		159	I — A
130c	130c		160	I — A
130d	130d		161	I — A
130e	130e		162	I — A

Pre-TEU	Post-TA	Current	Current Content	Misc. Amendments	AA	SEA	TEU	TA	TN	Notes
Title VI	Title XV	Title XVIII	Research and technological development			I	RN			
	130f	163				I	A			
	130g	164				I	A			
	130h	165				I	A			
	130i	166				I	A	A		
	130j	167				I	A,RN			
	130k	168				I	RN			
	130l	169				I	RN			
	130m	170				I	A,RN			
	130n	171				I	A,RN			
	130o					I	R			
	130p	172				I	A,RN	A		
	130q	173				I	I			
Title VII	Title XVI	Title XIX	Environment			I	RN			
	130r	174				I	A	A		
	130s	175				I	A	A	A	
	130t	176				I	A			
Title XVII	Title XVII	Title XX	Development co-operation				I	I		
	130u	177					I			
	130v	178					I			
	130w	179					I	A		
	130x	180					I			
	130y	181					I			
		Title XXI	Economic, financial and technical co-operation with third countries				I		I	
		181a					I		I	
Part Four	Part Four	Part Four	Association of the overseas countries and territories							
				amended by GT						
131	131	182			A			A		
132	132	183								
133	133	184						A		
134	134	185								

Old article	New article	Amendments	Notes
135	186		
136	187		
136a	188	A	inserted by GT
Part Five / Title I	Part Five / Title I		Institutions of the Community
Chapter 1 / Section 1	Chapter I / Section 1		Provisions governing the institutions / The institutions / The European Parliament
137	189	A A	
138¹	190	A L,A A,A* A	repealed by AEP
138a	191	I	
138b	192	I	
138c	193	I	
138d	194	I	
138e	195	I	
139	196		amended by MT
140	197		
141	198		
142	199		
143	200		
144	201	A	
Section 2	Section 2		The Council
145	202	A A	
146	203	A I A	repealed by MT
147	204	I I	repealed by MT
148	205	A A*	
149	—	M,R, A A*	see 189a, 189c
150	206	A	
151	207	A I A A	repealed by MT
152	208	I A	
153	209	A	
154	210	A I	repealed by MT
Section 3	Section 3		The Commission
155	211	A	
156	212	I I	repealed by MT
157	213	A A* I A*	repealed by MT

Pre-TEU	Post-TA	Current	Current Content	Misc. Amendments	AA	SEA	TEU	TA	TN	Notes
158	158	214		repealed by MT			I	A	A	
159	159	215		repealed by MT			I	A	A	
160	160	216		repealed by MT			I			
161	161	217		repealed by MT	A		I		NI	
162	162	218		repealed by MT			I			
163	163	219		repealed by MT			I	A	A	
Section 4	*Section 4*	*Section 4*	*The Court of Justice*							
164	164	220		A – OJ L2,1.1.73			A	A	A	
165	165	221		A – OJ L318, 28.11.74	A		A	A	A	
166	166	222			A			A	A	
167	167	223		A – OJ L2,1.1.73	A				A	
168	168	224			A				M,NI	see amended 223
168a	168a	225				I	A		M,NI	see new 224
		225a							I	
169	169	226								
170	170	227								
171	171	228					A			
172	172	229					A			
		229a								
173	173	230					A	A	I	
174	174	231					A	A	A	
175	175	232					A			
176	176	233					A			
177	177	234					A			
178	178	235								
179	179	236								
180	180	237					A			
181	181	238								
182	182	239								

Old	New	Provision					Notes
183	240						
184	241						
185	242						
186	243						
187	244						
188	245		A			A	
Section 5	*Section 5*	*The Court of Auditors*				A	
188a	246		I				
188b	247		I		A	A	ex 206(2–10)
188c	248		I		A	A	ex 206a
Chapter 2	*Chapter 2*	*Provisions common to several institutions*					
189	249		A			A	amended ex 149(1)(3)
189a	250		I				
189b	251		I		A		
189c	252		I				amended ex 149(2)
190	253		A				
191	254		A	I		A	
191a	255						
192	256						
Chapter 3	*Chapter 3*	*The Economic and Social Committee*					
193	257		A		A		
194	258				A		
195	259				A		
196	260		A				
197	261		A		A		
198	262		A		A		
Chapter 4	*Chapter 4*	*The Committee of the Regions*					
198a	263		I	A	A	A	
198b	264		I		A		
198c	265		I		A		
Chapter 5	*Chapter 5*	*The European Investment Bank*					
198d	266		I			A	amended ex 129

Pre-TEU	Post-TA	Current	Current Content	Misc. Amendments	AA	SEA	TEU	TA	TN	Notes
	198e	267								
Title II	Title II	Title II	Financial provisions				I			amended ex 130
199	199	268					A			
200	201	269					R			
201	201a	270					A			
202	202	271					I			
203	203	272		amended by CBP, CFP						
204	204	273		amended by CBP, CFP						
205	205	274					A	A		
205a	205a	275		inserted by CFP						
206	188b			amended by CBP, CFP	A		M			see 188b
	206	276					I	A		amended ex 206b
206a	188c			inserted by CFP			M,R			see 188c
206b	206			inserted by CFP			M,R			see 206
207	207	277								
208	208	278								
209	209	279		amended by CFP			A	A		
209a	209a	280					I	A	A	
Part Six	Part Six	Part Six	General and final provisions							
210	210	281								
211	211	282								
212	212	283		repealed by MT				I		
213	213	284								
	213a	285						I		
	213b	286						I		
214	214	287								
215	215	288					A			
216	216	289								
217	217	290							A	
218	218	291		repealed by MT				I		
219	219	292								

			Codes
220	220	293	
221	221	294	A
222	222	295	
223	223	296	A
224	224	297	
225	225	298	
226	226	299	R A A
227	227	300	A A
228	228	301	A I A
	228a		
229	229	302	A A
230	230	303	
231	231	304	A A
232	232	305	
233	233	306	
234	234	307	A
235	235	308	
236	236	309	R A I A A A
	237		
238	238	310	R
239	239	311	R
240	240	312	A
241	241		R
242	242		R
243	243		R
244	244		R
245	245		R
246	246		R
Final	**Final**	**Final Provisions**	
247	247	313	
248	248	314	A
Annexes	**Annexes**	**Annexes**	A
I	I	Tariff headings	D

Pre-TEU	Post-TA	Current	Current Content	Misc. Amendments	AA	SEA	TEU	TA	TN	Notes
II	II	I	Agricultural products	A – OJ 7, 30.1.1961					A	
III	III		Invisible transactions				A	D		
IV	IV	II	Overseas countries and territories	A – OJ 150, 1.10.1965; A – GT	A				A	

Notes: [1] Following repeal by the Merger Treaty the provisions of Article 190 (ex 138) were to be found in Article 14 of the Act concerning the election of the representatives of the European Parliament (1976). These were amended by successive accession treaties and the TEU before being inserted into the TEC by the TA.

Abbreviations:

A   amended
A*   amendment envisaged by Protocol on the enlargement of the European Union (2001)
D   deleted
I   inserted
M   provisions moved
NI   new insertion
R   repealed
RN   renumbered
AA   acts of accession (whether 1972, 1980, 1985 or 1994) and including the Council decisions adjusting those acts following the Norwegian 'no' votes in 1972 and 1994
AEP Act concerning the election of the representatives of the European Parliament (1976)
CBP Treaty amending certain budgetary provisions of the Treaties establishing the European Communities and of the Treaty establishing a single Council and a single Commission of the European Communities (1970)
CFP Treaty amending certain financial provisions of the Treaty establishing the European Communities and of the Treaty establishing a single Council and a single Commission of the European Communities (1977)
GT   Greenland Treaty (Treaty amending, with regard to Greenland, the Treaties establishing the European Communities) (1984)
MT   Merger Treaty (Treaty establishing a single Council and a single Commission of the European Communities) (1965)
SEA Single European Act (1986)
TA   Treaty of Amsterdam (1997)
TEU Treaty on European Union (1992)
TN   Treaty of Nice (2001)

2b: Amendments to the TEU: Reference Table

Although a much younger Treaty than the TEC, the TEU has in its first 10 years also undergone significant changes. These have been brought about by Amsterdam and Nice, resulting in a renumbered and slightly longer treaty. Table 2B charts the evolution of each article.

Column 1 lists all the articles as numbered when the TEU was signed in 1992. The second column lists all current articles using the post-TA numbering and the third column indicates the current content of each title. The fourth column identifies changes to the TEU introduced by the Treaty of Amsterdam TA, noting whether the article or title was amended (A), inserted (I), deleted (D), moved (M), renumbered (RN) or retitled. Since all articles were affected by Article 12 (TA) and the renumbering of the treaty's provisions, this amendment is not recorded. The same abbreviations are used in column 5 to indicate the impact of the Treaty of Nice (TN) and the envisaged consequences of the Protocol on the Enlargement of the European Union. The final column contains notes indicating, primarily, the results of the restructuring brought about by the TA to Titles V and VI. A full list of abbreviations follows the table.

Table 2B   The evolution of the Treaty establishing the European Union

TEU 1992	Post-TA numbering	Current Content	TA 1997	TN 2000	Notes
Preamble	*Preamble*		A		
Title I	Title I	Common provisions			
Article A	Article 1		A		
Article B	Article 2		A		
Article C	Article 3		A		
Article D	Article 4				
Article E	Article 5		A		
Article F	Article 6		A		
	Article 7		I	A	
Title II	Title II	Provisions amending the TEC, with a view to establishing the EC			
Article G	Article 8				
Title III	Title III	Provisions amending the TECSC			
Article H	Article 9				
Title IV	Title IV	Provisions amending the TEAEC			
Article I	Article 10				
Title V	Title V	Provisions on a common foreign and security policy	RS		
Article J.1			A		to Articles 11 and 12
Article J.2					to Articles 15, 16 and 19(1)
Article J.3			A		to Articles 13(1), 14(2–3) (5–7), 23(2)
Article J.4			A		to Article 17(1)(4–5)
Article J.5			A		to Articles 18(1–3) and 19(2)

TEU 1992	Post-TA numbering	Current Content	TA 1997	TN 2000	Notes
Article J.6					to Article 20
Article J.7					to Article 21
Article J.8			A		to Article 13(1–2), 22(1–2), 23(1), 25
Article J.9					to Article 27
Article J.10			D		
Article J.11			A		to Article 28(1–2)
	Article 11				
	Article 12				
	Article 13				
	Article 14				
	Article 15				
	Article 16				
	Article 17			A	
	Article 18				
	Article 19				
	Article 20				
	Article 21				
	Article 22		I		
	Article 23		I	A*	
	Article 24		I	A	
	Article 26		I	A	
	Article 27a			I	
	Article 27b			I	
	Article 27c			I	
	Article 27d			I	
	Article 27e			I	
	Article 28		I		
Title VI	Title VI	Provisions on police and judicial co-operation in criminal matters	RS, RN		
Article K.1					to Article 29
Article K.2			A		to Article 33 and Article 63 (1) TEC
Article K.3			A		to Article 34
Article K.4			A		to Articles 34 and 36
Article K.5			A		to Article 37
Article K.6			A		to Article 39
Article K.7			M		to Articles 43–45
Article K.8			A		to Article 41
Article K.9			A		to Article 42
	Article 29			A	
	Article 30		I		
	Article 31		I	A	
	Article 32		I		
	Article 33				
	Article 34			A*	
	Article 35		I		
	Article 36				
	Article 37				
	Article 38		I		

TEU 1992	Post-TA numbering	Current Content	TA 1997	TN 2000	Notes
	Article 39				
	Article 40		I		
	Article 40a			I	
	Article 40b			I	
	Article 41				
	Article 42				
	Title VII	Provisions on enhanced co-operation	I	RN	
	Article 43		I	A	
	Article 43a			I	
	Article 43b			I	
	Article 44		I	A	
	Article 44a			I	
	Article 45		I	A	
Title VII	Title VIII	Final provisions	RN		
Article L	Article 46		A	A	
Article M	Article 47		A	A	
Article N	Article 48		A		
Article O	Article 49		A		
Article P	Article 50				
Article Q	Article 51				
Article R	Article 52				
Article S	Article 53		A		

Abbreviations:

A	amended
A*	amendment envisaged by Protocol on the enlargement of the European Union (2001)
D	deleted
I	inserted
M	provisions moved
RN	renumbered, renamed
RS	restructured
TA	Treaty of Amsterdam (1997)
TEU	Treaty on European Union (1992)
TN	Treaty of Nice (2001)

Annex 3   Reforming and Revising the European Treaties

The majority of the *Guide* deals with the key treaties as they are but their actual nature means that many people would like to see them changed. The fact that the Union is ultimately regulated by a whole series of complicated, imperfectly related and frequently misunderstood treaties, negotiated by and among the member states, may be a fact of life but it is an uncomfortable one for many commentators. As Annex 2 has made clear, it has produced an incessant stream of changes to both the main European treaties, making them very hard to keep track of and necessitating too much cross-referencing. Moreover, at Amsterdam the established numbering was reorganized, making it hard to relate the treaties to the vast literature on the Union which had been cast using the earlier numbering. These changes are set out in Tables 3A and 3B in the appendix to this annex (pp. 715–26). Such incessant changes, whether substantive or in numbering, have also robbed the treaties of some of their initial clarity and elegance.

Alongside the actual negotiation of the new treaties there has been a consistent stream of often controversial attempts to revise them. For most people this has normally been very much a fringe issue, and even some specialists regard it as excessively 'tedious and technocratic', it being quite possible to understand the treaties without knowing about such attempts which, after all, have been largely unsuccessful. Yet they do say something about how the treaties are both negotiated and understood. And the post-Nice agenda has brought these questions to the fore, with its call for discussion of simplifying the treaties and the associated talk of constitutionalizing them. Such questions concerning the shape of the treaties are definitely on the official, if not the public, EU agenda and warrant our examination so as to make clear the background from which the present discussions have evolved.

Criticisms of the Treaties

There are two main reasons why the shape, as well as the contents, of the treaties have made observers uncomfortable. The first is the political conviction of some that the Community and Union are an imperfect answer to Europe's needs for democracy and efficacy. This is because they are built on inter-governmental treaties, of which the member states remain 'the masters' to the exclusion of the collective interest. Many believe that, as well as being changed to strengthen the power of the Union and its institutions, such vital treaties should be drafted in a more open and democratic way, closer to that which is found in most states. This links up with a desire to produce a kind of 'constitutional patriotism' – or '*Verfassungspatriotismus*', as the Germans call it – among the peoples of Europe. At present the fragmented, limited and obscure nature of the treaties makes it hard for ordinary citizens to understand, esteem or support them, thus depriving the EU and EC of autonomy and legitimacy. Nor do the European Treaties guarantee freedom within the Union. Seen from this perspective, what is needed is a clear, comprehensive political document to appeal to the citizens of Europe.

So, although this is anathema to many supporters of national rights, the argument is often made that the Union should be given a new legal basis, emerging from a new amending procedure, so as to send it further down the road of integration. In other words, the demand is that the Union should acquire a 'proper' constitution and become a self-sufficient federation. This is notwithstanding the contrary legal claim that the

Union already does have a constitution in the treaties. Such demands are, moreover, posited on the assumption that, were the Union to acquire a constitution, it could be of only one type, modelled on the classic representative state. But there are also those who want to constitutionalize the treaties in order to prevent any further accretions of power at the centre. This contrast underlies the decisions made at Nice about the future of the Union.

These basic political desires to alter the legal basis of Union integration link up with a second, more recent, realization that the treaties are technically flawed. There are 20 treaties, involving 1,000 articles and numerous protocols, not to mention sheaves of declarations. And, like EC law in general, they lack a clear hierarchy signifying which are the most significant. (Introducing such a hierarchy was on the agenda after Maastricht but was not acted on.) Equally, these treaties do not say who does what. So they remain, in the eyes of many, too complicated, too numerous, too prolix, often too outdated and too opaque. They cannot be easily understood, used or legally relied on.

All this causes difficulties for today's Union, irrespective of future aspirations. In the eyes of many they create constitutional chaos and Byzantine structures within the Union, making it hard both to understand and to operate. And, even for those who do not want to see the Union become a centralized federation, these are problems which ought to be remedied here and now. Tidying up the treaties and the way they are amended so as to impose clarity and collective responsibility might, in any case, be a way of depoliticizing the amendment process, thereby avoiding incessant and politically sensitive ratifications such as those which followed Maastricht.

This urge to tidy up the Union's primary law extends beyond the treaties. Since the Edinburgh summit in 1992 there has been an ongoing programme to improve the quality of legislative drafting in the EC. This involves reorganizing Community legislation by making it more compact and readable. The commitment to do this was underlined by a Council resolution of 8 June 1993 and a 1994 inter-institutional agreement (IIA). The process has been slowly pursued by the Commission, which has collapsed a variety of texts into single, more rational documents. The Commission has also produced a number of reports on the progress of the programme, assisted by a series of guidelines and action programmes such as SLIM and BEST. Reports on the progress achieved are regularly presented to European Councils, as was the case at Nice.

Roads to Reform and Revision

Since the 1980s there has been a complicated dialectic between the two pressures for treaty change noted, the ambitiously political reformist and the cautiously pragmatic revisionist. Sometimes they have worked together, at others they have pointed in different ways. And often the urge to radical reform has only resulted in limited revisions. In any case, they have helped to produce at least five different approaches to recasting and improving the treaties.

The first of these involves trying to subordinate the existing treaties to a new and superior constitutional type structure and document. This idea of relegating the treaties really began with the EP's draft European Union Treaty of 1984. However, before the idea got anywhere it was overtaken by two more technical drives, not to replace but to rationalize the treaties whether, secondly, by codifying them into a few more logically ordered texts or, thirdly, by just tidying up and simplifying the existing documents. Proposals to do the former were quite common prior to IGC 1996 and they were then, to some extent, facilitated by the IGC. More significantly, the TA sought to rationalize the treaties by purging and consolidating them without changing their legal value. The Nice Declaration on the Future of the Union seems to hint at further moves.

Since Amsterdam there have been further developments. Fourthly, came the call for the treaties to be split into two, one part dealing with principles and the other with policies. The latter would be open to easier amendment than at present. This was explored but not acted on. Hence it was overtaken by a fifth development, the talk of 'constitutionalizing' the treaties, not in the legal sense but in a political way, perhaps in concert with a further drive towards making major changes in the nature, status and operation of the Union as urged by Joschka Fischer, Jacques Chirac and the EP in the spring of 2000. For some of those involved in the argument, the 'post-Nice process' should lead not to the rather limited changes apparently envisaged at Nice but to a more radical development of this sort. This would probably also involve adding the Charter of Fundamental Rights to the revised constitutional document.

Before looking at these five pathways and what happened along them, we need to be clear about the terms used to describe them. Unfortunately, the terms used to describe such revisions to the treaties are often applied in careless and sometimes contradictory ways. For the Commission, 'simplification' is a matter of tidying up existing texts by repealing or amending obsolete and other otiose elements and amending misleading wordings, cross-references and headings, while 'consolidation' is a related process involving the physical insertion of new and amended provisions into existing treaty texts and repealing unnecessary acts. It can also involve rearranging simplified texts in a more comprehensible way and, where necessary, renumbering. All this is normally supposed to be done without changing either the content or the status of the legislation. In treaty terms this is a limited process since it involves no major structural changes. Sometimes this can be described as codification.

However, since the 1970s, 'codification' has usually been seen as a way of melding a number of texts together into one, more manageable, new document, which will contain a legislative 'code' for the domain in question. The 1993–4 decisions noted above laid down the way this should be done. Dragone suggests that there are three aspects to this: regrouping directives; modifications which do not otherwise change the substance; and formally repealing the acts thus absorbed. In other words, this too is supposed to be done without upsetting the status quo. Where the treaties are concerned, codification is fairly similar save that amendments to individual treaties have been dealt with in different ways and, since there have only been proposals so far, no treaties have actually been repealed as a result of codification, as opposed to consolidation.

This makes it clear that codification is a more radical process, even if usage does not always reflect this fact. 'Recasting' can also be used to describe adopting a new act in place of an existing, much-amended one. Unfortunately these distinctions are not always observed even in Union practice. Authorities can, indeed, start with one meaning of a term and then switch to another. Here we try and keep to the Commission's normal definitions.

'Relegating' the Treaties

The first significant attempt to restructure the treaties took the form of seeking to relegate the treaties by subordinating them to a new and overarching constitutional treaty which, in turn, would set up a body which would embrace the existing institutional structures.

This, of course, was a highly political move since it involved substantial alteration to the status and nature of the various Communities. Thus, in the 1950s the Parliamentary Assembly of the ECSC, using the opening provided by Article 38 of the Treaty establishing the European Defence Community, drew up a new draft accord embodying a 'statute' for a proposed 'supra-national' European Political Community. This, now conveniently examined by Griffiths, would, once it was adopted by state representatives meeting in an IGC, not merely have created an interesting institutional structure but provided for the absorption of the European Defence Community and the ECSC while building on the TECSC provisions for coal and steel sectors. An unofficial draft constitution for a 'United States of Europe' also circulated at about this time.

More significantly, several versions of an overarching treaty were proposed during the Fouchet negotiations of the early 1960s when de Gaulle's France sought to superimpose an inter-governmental umbrella over the various communities. This was to be designated 'a Union of States' but would have had similar organs to the Community save for having a Council consisting of heads of government, as well as at least two committees of ministers. The other five members also wrote a Court of Justice into their version. Financing would have been by national donation. The 'Union's' objectives were essentially diplomatic and defence orientated, although it was envisaged that the new Union would eventually subsume the existing communities.

This idea died a death. So did thoughts, in the preamble to the 1965 Merger Treaty, of going on to unify the treaties as well as the institutions. Equally, in the 1970s, although there was vague discussion of related reforms including a 1979 call by Willy Brandt for a European Constitution, no real attempt was made to recast the European treaties. Meanwhile the treaty base did, as we have already seen, grow with the addition of new accession, budgetary and parliamentary acts.

The resulting complexity explains why, in the 1980s, there were more emphatic efforts at change. Initially, and most significantly, there were continuing attempts within the Community mainstream to solve the problem by creating new overarching structures, both documentary and institutional. The stimulus for this came first from the Genscher–Colombo Plan of 1981, which proposed a draft 'European Act' that it was hoped would be endorsed by the European Council. This had many echoes of the Fouchet proposals since it both concentrated on diplomatic, cultural and related matters and made similar institutional proposals, talking vaguely of the step-by-step creation of a European Union, open to other states, but involving little more than a closer co-ordination of the EC and EPC under the leadership of the European Council. However, the latter would have been required to establish closer relations with the EP. The Council of Ministers would also have seen its role change in much the same way as in the Fouchet Plan. But essentially the treaties would not have been changed. All of this did, in fact, have some effect on the member states as it led to the 1983 Stuttgart Declaration. This proposed considering establishing a Union in some five years' time.

For many this was just a revival of inter-governmentalism. And, in the view of radical integrationists like former Commissioner Altiero Spinelli, this offered no future to Europe. Hence he helped to persuade the now directly elected EP to see itself as a constituent assembly. So it set up a Committee on Institutional Affairs which, in 1984, with the help of some leading legal figures produced a draft European Union Treaty which the EP then approved. The draft was a simple framework agreement of 87 articles divided into six parts: The Union; Objectives and Methods of Action; Institutional Arrangements; Policies; Finances; and Final Provisions.

It involved several changes to the status quo. To begin with it meant the addition of a new and superior constitutional document. The suggestion was that items in the existing treaties would remain in force until amended by the new body, according to new supra-national procedures. Secondly, it proposed the creation of a new body, the Union, to which consenting High Contracting Parties would accede and which would take over the patrimony of the Community. Its institutions were to include the European Council, thus recognizing what was already happening inside the Community. This was also true of the way in which the main lines of ECJ jurisprudence were included in the treaty.

The Union was to have two working methods: common action using the EC mechanisms and co-operation among the member states. However, though this preserved a kind of pillar element inside the Union, the latter could pre-empt national sovereignty and transfer policy areas to the common action mode. The Union would also have its own citizenship, external policy and funds even though it was described as a body established among states, somewhat anticipating the actual post-Maastricht EU. What would happen to non-participating member states while all this was going on was not made clear. In any event this was not acted on although, as we have seen, its existence encouraged other constitutional developments in the Union.

In the mid-1990s the EP returned to the charge. Moved by what it saw as the inter-governmental imperfections of Maastricht and the inaccessible and incomprehensible way its changes were expressed, it again toyed with the idea of relegating the treaties. The Committee on Institutional Affairs tabled a draft constitution in early 1993 which was then developed and ultimately debated in February 1994. The draft involved a preamble and 47 articles divided into six parts: Principles; Competences; Institutions; Functions and Means; External Relations; and Final Provisions. Although it was seen as ultra-federal and did include a section on human rights, it was actually quite a restrained framework document. Thus it stressed the role of the member states and their continuing legislative rights while also making the European Council a full institution. However, it only needed the approval of four-fifths of the states before it came into effect while revision would be by a special constitutional law. Given that there was provision for secession the implication was that those countries which did not accept it would be forced out.

Despite the fact that the treaty could have been a much more radical proposal the EP did not adopt it. In fact the assembly almost did not vote on it at all. In the end it merely took note of the project and nothing more was heard of the draft. The post-Maastricht popular unease did not encourage action on such ambitious and politically controversial ideas.

This did not stop outsiders suggesting new constitutional settlements. Indeed, between Maastricht and Nice there was a wide and continuing unending debate about constitutional matters, mainly on the other side of the Channel. As we have already seen, for lawyers the treaties either always were or have become a constitution, partly through the decisions of the ECJ and partly from the emergence of a new multi-level constitutional law in which the Union had subsumed the Community. Enthusiasts for integration have argued that the Union needs a constitution, understood as a single document with more authority, more democratic origins and more overall status than the existing treaties. Conversely, the aim for some was to restrain precisely such tendencies. The same divisions also appeared after Nice as discussions about the long-term future of the EU and the 2004 IGC got under way. And then, as before, most debate concentrated on the principles of such a constitution, especially where central decision-making is concerned.

However, at least five actual examples of what such a constitution might be were offered. Three of these, from John Pinder, the Basel Institute of European Studies and, most recently, Professor Jean Touscouz of the University of Nice provide versions of a more integrated arrangement. The first is a brief document which would leave the existing treaties and laws unchanged, while the other two embody some elements of the present European treaties. The Swiss draft, the product of a post-graduate seminar, consists of 80 new articles, divided into a long preamble and seven sections, beginning with basic rights and organs and excluding most policies. The whole is accompanied by a series of commentaries. The Touscouz 'avant projet' of a Founding Pact for a new 'European Organization' thus incorporates the bare bones of the existing treaties. These would be formally abrogated, although much of their contents would be enshrined as protocols. States which failed to ratify would be excluded from the new body but would be able to conclude association agreements with the Organization.

Two others, from the European Constitutional Group and, more recently, the *Economist*, rather enlist the ideas of 'constitutional economics' so as to limit competency creep. They thus seek to place severe limits on the power of the institutions and devise a series of checks and balances to ensure that power rests ultimately with the member states. This can involve the creation of new parliamentary bodies to help in this task. None the less, all of these suggestions symbolize a growing belief that, for whatever reason, the Union needs a set of superior rules to the treaties. Yet, despite their attractive brevity, none of them has been acted on. The failure of all these proposals to reform by relegating along with the more mainstream suggestions meant, of course, that the technical difficulties of the existing treaties remained to be tackled.

Codifying the Treaties

So the idea of relegating the treaties gave way to more modest and realistic ideas. Initially, these focused on codifying the existing treaties. This was taken to mean condensing several texts into fewer versions, thereby making them more manageable and appealing. The idea, which involves revision more than reform, was later acted on during and after the 1996 IGC.

As a result there were a number of academic examinations of ways in which the treaties might be reformulated, essentially without changing their contents and status. But, while member-state governments were to prove unwilling to risk such experiments upsetting the ratification of the changes actually agreed, they did allow the Council Secretariat to continue working on codified versions. These were to emerge in the spring of 2000. However, the resultant drafts attracted but little attention, either then or when the post-Nice process started. This was partly because, by the time they were published, one by-product of codification, the idea of simplification, had long since rationalized the texts of the existing treaties, purging, consolidating and renumbering them, thereby giving them more of a constitutional flavour. It was also partly because new constitutional debates were already occupying many minds in the run-up to Nice.

Much of the drive for codification must be put down to the EP. At roughly the same time as it decided not to take up its 1994 draft constitution it commissioned a report from Roland Bieber of the University of Lausanne as part of its preparations for the 1996 IGC. Having inventoried 15 texts, which yielded over 1,000 articles, Bieber sought to simplify the treaties by suppressing unnecessary and duplicate clauses, and then to regroup them in a more coherent and constitutional way, and all this without changing the existing legal situation. In the event he eliminated or replaced 742 articles, ending up with a 316-article codified treaty. This was divided into seven sections: Basic Principles; Rights; Relations with Member States; CFSP and External Relations; Institutions and Finance; Activities; and Final Provisions. Observers thought this was certainly more manageable structurally, although somewhat long and still preserving the original problematic style of writing. However, the main problem was that although aiming to respect the substance of the treaties, or working *au droit constant* as the French jargon has it, some of his changes actually went beyond this, as with his fusing of Community and Union (with the latter being given legal personality) and his demotion of key policies to a protocol.

This was one reason why the EP commissioned a further exercise from the European University Institute (EUI) in 1996. This was to be a more technical and limited attempt to see if the existing treaties could be codified and made more readable and transparent. The team, under Ehlermann and von Bogdandy, produced two drafts, one merging all four treaties and the other simply bringing the TEC and the TEU together. The latter was provided in case the first was felt to be politically unacceptable. It also pointed the way towards 2002 when the TECSC would lapse.

Both variants involved some elimination of obsolete provisions, consolidation of identical clauses and minor rephrasing in the light of the new structures. Both had a very similar structure, being divided into five parts: Principles; Civic Rights; Institutional Provisions; Procedures (including activities and instruments); and General and Final Provisions. Significantly this inverts the order of all the constitutive European Treaties, except the TECSC, and gives the institutional provisions more prominence. In the first variant – which ran to 512 articles – activities was subdivided into EC, CFSP, JHA, TEAEC and TECSC elements, whereas in the second the last two were omitted. This meant that the second was shorter, with only 190 articles, as well as having some minor amendments to cover the missing elements.

A third version came from the Centre for European Legal Studies in Cambridge a year later under the direction of Alan Dashwood and was published in the *European Law Review*. This restricted itself to the TEC alone and sought to modernize it by removing obsolete articles, clarifying obscurities and, more significantly, writing in key decisions of the Court of Justice which have fleshed out gaps in the treaty. At the same time the treaty was reordered into four parts: The Community Order; Citizenship; Community Activities; and General and Final Provisions. Each of these was given a new system of numbering which started afresh in each part, thus allowing for easier amendment. However, articles which are unchanged are not reprinted although there is a useful legal commentary. Yet, although it was conceived as a 'restatement' – a semi-official rephrasing such as those developed in the USA – which brought the treaties into line with case law, it also had political implications, notably in the new emphasis given both to the institutions and to external relations by the way the clauses were reformulated.

While this was never seriously intended for use, this was not true of the codification efforts associated with Amsterdam itself. Acting on a mandate from the Dublin summit, the Council Legal Service and others set to work, alongside the negotiations proper, to see what could be done to tidy up the treaties and then condense them into single texts. Both tasks were accomplished, but only the first was acted on at the time. None the less, the work carried out is significant, given the talk of further simplification ahead of IGC 2004.

In seeking to codify the treaties the Legal Service decided not to use either the Lausanne or the Florence drafts, partly because they actually introduced controversial changes to the status of the Union in the case of the former and partly because they were too long and therefore off-putting in the latter. At best the drafters were willing to fuse the three Communities and to give the treaties a slightly more constitutional feel. But the Union and the pillars had to stay.

Their work led to a series of reports in March and May 1997 which showed that the task of codifying without changing the actual treaty was feasible. However, although the text was largely ready it was rejected by the IGC negotiators quite late in the day. The reason for this was that the Secretariat rightly assumed that the new compilations would have to be ratified, following a short IGC and a *mise à jour* after the Amsterdam summit. The political view was that this was too risky because it could confuse things, and perhaps even jeopardize ratification by exposing more basic elements of the EU's operations to public debate.

None the less, Declaration No. 42 TA encouraged the Secretariat to carry on with its experimental technical work and allowed it to publish its results, although noting that they would have no legal value. Once the TA and the two consolidated treaties had been finalized the task was indeed taken up. It was largely completed by the end of 1998 – at least in a French version – but in the event was not published (and then without any fanfare) until March 2000. It was published then, partly at Commission suggestion, to get it into the public domain before substantive negotiations were fully engaged lest it complicate matters, particularly with the work being done on the Charter of Fundamental Rights.

What emerged was two variants. The first melded together the TEU and the TEC. This was done by dividing the Treaty into six 'books'. Book I was the Common Dispositions of the TEU and Book II covered the TEC, albeit in a different order from that which it enjoys at present, principles and institutions appearing much more prominently at the start. Books III, IV and V covered the CFSP, PJCCM and enhanced co-operation. The remaining elements of the TEU then appeared as the Final Dispositions or Book VI. All this was unchanged in the amalgam, the four treaties with specific elements of the TEAEC and the TECSC being added as protocols, thus avoiding duplication but allowing for the excision of the latter in due course.

In the event, of course, no action was taken on the drafts. This was because, although they were only revisions of the treaties in substance, symbolically and structurally they seemed to many too close to a reform. Hence the potential for complication by having so many variants available, which some of us feared, never actually developed. Indeed, as already suggested, hardly anybody noticed that they had been published.

The same lack of interest, perhaps surprisingly, was to beset the associated work of simplification successfully undertaken at Amsterdam. Yet the tidying up then undertaken was significant both in itself and in the consolidated versions of the TEU and TEC which it produced. The rationalizing side of Amsterdam, to which we have already drawn attention, deserves to be better appreciated. Yet, it seems often to be left out of account when further attempts at simplification are discussed.

Simplifying the Treaties

This third approach to treaty restructuring had its roots in the broader process of treaty reform which began in the run-up to the 1996 IGC. The Bieber Report to the EP started by looking for redundant or duplicate clauses, so as to allow codification. The report understood simplification to involve mainly reorganizing the Union's primary law structure so that there was a clear distinction between 'constitutional' and 'technical' elements. But it also involved, firstly, removing lapsed or repeat references and, secondly, better drafting and numbering. However, much of this was lost sight of in the drive to produce a single text out of the many treaties.

The real impetus for simplification came from the IGC process. This owed much to the concern for transparency and clarity which emerged, even amongst British MPs, from the post-Maastricht crisis. The idea of simplification was supported by most of the institutions. It was thus referred to the Westendorp Reflection Group. Believing that the actual texts should be improved as much as possible the group sought the advice of the Council Secretariat as to the feasibility of doing this *au droit constant*. The Secretariat's note of October 1995 followed Bieber in seeing simplification as part of a broader reorganization to remedy both the increasing complexity and the decreasing user-friendliness of the treaties. And, throughout the months leading up to the Amsterdam summit, the kind of simplification which actually resulted seems to have been very secondary to thoughts of a wider revision and recasting of the European Treaties.

The note canvassed three options: simplifying, codifying (or 'consolidating' as it was then unhelpfully termed) and restructuring. The first could involve three elements: eliminating redundant articles, redrafting so as to make the text more reader-friendly and removing some substantive complications such as those created by the proliferation of decision-making procedures. However, since the last two risked making political decisions, as did codifying or restructuring, it is not surprising that the Secretariat argued that only the first would avoid substantive change and political risks. Codifying and restructuring were even more problematic in this respect. The Reflection Group accepted this advice and recommended that 'Union law should be more accessible. The 1996 IGC should [therefore] result in a simpler treaty.' Although it did not give great attention to the issue its 'Annotated Agenda' made it clear that some members, like Elizabeth Gigou, wanted to go further than this and make more sweeping changes, including abstracting a shorter 'charter' from the existing treaties possibly through a special working group.

The Turin summit merely accepted that the question of whether it would be possible to 'simplify and consolidate the treaties' needed to be explored. Doing this was given further encouragement by the Florence European Council which called for all possible ways of simplifying the treaties to be explored so that the goals and operations of the Union could be made more comprehensible to the public. So simplification became an item on the agenda of IGC 1996 and attracted the support of at least eight states whose initial statements came out in favour of removing obsolete clauses, improving the clarity of the drafting and making the whole thing more concise and unified. The UK position was to welcome this in principle but to point out the danger of changing the substance of the treaties, and hence the political balance, in doing so.

The IGC again sought the advice of the Council Secretariat. Its assessments underlined the concerns raised by the UK government. Such fears were noted in the three reports on the subject it produced in early May, mid-July and late November 1996. The first report drew on work done in the Secretariat over the winter and set out the options for codifying, restructuring and simplifying, or making the texts more user-friendly. Restructuring was seen as necessary to cope with the likely length of any merged treaties. Where simplification as such was concerned, the report insisted that this should not involve rewriting, even if this might actually improve transparency. It was also suggested that, to avoid confusion, any changes arising from simplification should not only be separated in the treaty from the substantive changes agreed at Amsterdam but should also be supported by consolidated and renumbered versions of the treaties, making it clear what effects the simplification process actually had.

In its second report the Secretariat sought to flesh out its case and respond to questions raised by the delegations. It insisted on the need to limit the simplification exercise so as to ensure that no political change resulted. So, even though changes in decision-making, the pillar structure and the legal personality of the Union would have helped clarity they would not be considered unless, and until, the IGC consciously agreed to alter things. They could be then swept up by the ongoing simplification process. Following an IGC discussion on 3–4 September 1996 this in fact continued and lists of possible changes were circulated. None the less, codification experiments seem to have remained the main concern, with delegations deciding that they did not want to proliferate yet more protocols. A final report was tabled by the Secretariat on 21 November setting out a suggested approach along with outline versions of a reformed treaty. None of these sought to merge the Union and the Community, but even when unifying only some of the treaties at least 143 articles could be saved. Simplification of wording was ruled out and it was also suggested that whichever form of renumbered, simplified and restructured treaty was agreed should be placed in the second part of the final act. At this stage the Secretariat still saw the revised version as having legal force.

Things were not sufficiently advanced to be included in the draft Irish treaty and the presidency in its conclusions merely restated the problem of the unwieldy nature of the treaty base. It noted that there was both a general agreement on pursuing the simplification work, providing the *acquis* was not reopened, especially where the pillar structure was concerned, and also assuming this did not delay the negotiations. This led to a Friends of the Presidency Group working alongside the IGC proper on the details of simplification of the two treaties and the attached protocols. Declarations were left aside as historical records. However, there was even some willingness to consider codifying the treaties on the basis of work already submitted by the Council Secretariat, providing this was kept separate from the substantive negotiations on treaty changes. This was something the Dutch presidency was very keen on, although they recognized that it was replete with difficulties in a way which simplification as such was not. Textual changes were by then agreed.

So, by the time the Dutch presented their draft treaty on 30 May it was agreed that the amendments for simplifying the treaties would form the second part of the Treaty of Amsterdam. The presidency also stated that this 'must be complemented by a codification of all the relevant Treaties'. The intention was that this would be done speedily after the signature of the Amsterdam treaty. In the event it was not.

Shortly before the Amsterdam summit the delegations finally rejected the idea of codification because they feared that the other changes they hoped to agree would be put at risk by any attempt to achieve 'the treaty to end all treaties'. Having a separate and binding reorganized treaty submitted at the same time as the Amsterdam changes could cause confusion and might suggest that the whole European enterprise needed reapproval, thus inviting rejection. So all the draft treaty could say in its Section VI was that 'proposed amendments', already circulated to the conference, 'should form the second part of the Treaty of Amsterdam'. There was also a proposed declaration stating that the High Contracting Parties should work expeditiously on a non-binding codification of all the treaties.

When Amsterdam finally appeared it did, as we have already implied, three things. The first of these was to list over 100 textual changes to the original treaties. This involved removing obsolete references in the TEC, TECSC and the TEAEC to such things as target dates, transition periods and defunct bodies. This meant that 47 articles in the TEC were excised and 60 partially purged. At the same time four basic acts were repealed along with two annexes and nine protocols. Three other auxiliary documents were also modified. Finally, there was some minor redrafting to ensure that the cross-references to altered articles were correct and that the language reflected the changes. Thus in Article 3 TEC the term 'prohibition' replaced the original 'elimination'. A commentary in the *OJ* explained what the changes actually made to the TEC were and why they were done.

Similar alterations were made to the TECSC and the TEAEC whereas the TEU, being much newer, was not affected.

Secondly, while taking account of the substantive changes made at Amsterdam, the revisers prevented the Amsterdam treaty as such from getting in the way. They reduced it to the barest essentials so that it is very much a window treaty which shows changes made to the basic European Treaties. And they also incorporated some previous acts into the treaties proper, thus treating the treaty base much more as a unity. However, despite the Secretariat's hopes for giving the new versions full legal status, the original European Treaties retain their validity and any disputes arising from the simplification process will be resolved by the ECJ. In the view of Jacqué this meant that any charges of complications applied only to the political decisions taken at Amsterdam and not to the revisions.

Thirdly, rather than just leaving the old treaties with a more up-to-date text, the Friends of the Presidency both altered the structure of the treaties to take account of the changes and provided working versions incorporating all the amendments made at Amsterdam. Eliminating articles left gaps, requiring articles to be moved up and headings changed. This was done and the whole thing was renumbered. The Group also took the opportunity of renumbering and reorganizing the TEU in a more systematic way, following on the changes made to it at Amsterdam. The tables in the appendix to this annex show exactly what was done to the TEC and TEU as a result.

And rather than simply listing the changes made, as had often been the case in the past, consolidated versions of the two treaties were published. These were attached to the final act as 'illustrative' texts. The idea was that readers would get a better idea of what had been done. Codification, as already noted, disappeared from view.

All this may have been highly technical and it may have left odd imperfections in the text, but it was both a large-scale revision and a significant one. The 1996 IGC gave the idea of simplification both its first real airing and initial substance. It also reinforced the transparency of the treaty revision process and produced a technically improved set of treaties. It was also successful, up to a point, in the sense that the renumbering caused far less disruption and dismay than had been expected by some. However, it has caused complications for the Courts and the legal community, not to mention unwary students. Equally, the uncertain legal status of the 'working versions' does not seem to have given rise to any difficulties. The EUI in Florence did think that making these the only binding version might be a way ahead for treaty reform but this was not followed up. It also expressed some surprise that the simplification process had led to the elimination of items which, according to Article 10 of Amsterdam, remained legally effective.

Generally, in fact, the changes attracted very little support and not much more attention. In the run-up to the 2000 IGC both the Italian government and the Commission acknowledged that Amsterdam had made some progress and could be built on. However, even the consolidated versions were felt to be still too long. And, as we have already noted, there was no interest in the codification process.

Others of a more reformist mind were, implicitly, more critical as their demands for further simplification in the run-up to the 2000 IGC show. Thus the EP and the French presidency were still talking rather generally of simplification of the texts in the spring of 2000 and Nicole Fontaine, President of the EP, in July insisted on the need for a simplification process starting after Nice and building not on Amsterdam but on what was being done in other quarters. In other words, it soon became clear that the Amsterdam changes had not satisfied either those 'revisers' who wanted a clearer, simpler and more readable text or those 'reformers' who wanted to make more radical changes to the contents, organization and status of the treaties. For the EP, Amsterdam had only simplified the treaties 'to a certain degree' and, despite its efforts the structure of the treaties was still very much out of tune with the needs of democracy, closeness to the citizens and transparency. Hence, in the run-up to the 2000 IGC, there were calls, first for 'splitting' the treaties and then for wider changes. Thus, when Mme Fontaine talked of radical simplification of the treaties as a task for the future, she had in mind something wider than merely textual tidying.

Even so, any observations, even tangential, on the Amsterdam simplification process were unusual. As one commentator said, 'a final section on the simplification and consolidation of the treaties is tedious and technical and of interest only to specialists. Few lay people read treaties, however well written.' However, Amsterdam did provide the texts which everyone now uses, despite their less than complete legal status, and nobody has thought of undoing the changes then made. As the EUI observed, the consolidated versions were bound to impose themselves. None the less, whereas relegating and codifying had not really delivered, simplification was achieved.

Splitting the Treaties

The main thought was to go beyond technical simplification as such and tackle some of the other issues raised by the Council Secretariat's reports. However, the first of these, the idea of splitting the treaties, was to prove a rather short fourth road to treaty reform. The idea, which drew on both the technical and the political concerns about the treaties, briefly flourished between the autumn of 1999 and the summer of 2000 but ran into three obstacles. The first was that the proposed division proved almost impossible in practice, so that a different type of restructuring had to be adopted. Even so, secondly, in 2000 there was no real political will to do this, just as in the 1996 IGC there had been no desire to complicate the substantive negotiations by what was a complex (and politically loaded) exercise. And, finally, the idea was rather obscured by other ideas of treaty reform, including those arising from the Charter of Rights which was being negotiated at the time.

The idea of splitting the treaties into two documents, one dealing with general principles, together with institutional arrangements, and the other with less contentious, mainly policy-oriented questions, was initially raised by the Council Secretariat in its 1995 paper for the Westendorp Reflection Group. It mentioned it as part of a possible broader merging and restructuring of the treaties. Something similar was then canvassed by the Commission in its submissions to the 1996 IGC. Although the IGC chose not to follow up the idea, it did not go away. Firstly, it was evoked in the *European Law Review* by Arnull in 1999 as a way of remedying the disturbances caused by renumbering. He wondered whether further upheaval might be avoided by developing a core treaty with a series of individually modifiable protocols covering specific policy questions.

While he was pessimistic about the chances of this being done in 2000 the three Wise Men, under former Belgian Premier Jean-Luc Dehaene, were more positive. They had been appointed earlier that year to advise Prodi on the IGC agenda. Their report started from the current method of treaty reform which, they argued, meant incessant change. And this not merely caused political difficulties inside states during ratification but created legal uncertainty. For not only did the rules change very frequently but the changes were seen as increasing centralized EU responsibilities. They did not believe that this would be acceptable or effective in a much-enlarged Union.

The answer, therefore, might be to distinguish between the various elements of the treaties, separating them out into a basic treaty which could be changed only by unanimity as at present, and a separate text or texts containing policy material. The latter could be amended more easily. They believed, perhaps a tad generously, that the EUI had shown this could be done and recommended that the EUI along with the Commission and Council Legal Services might be invited to look at the idea. Their view was supported by others, notably the International Commission for the Reform of the Institutions (ICRI) report which talked of 'distilling from the existing Treaty base a more accessible basic document on key institutional roles, key principles and key procedures'. The Centre for European Reform believed that this would help to demystify the EU and avoid the blockages likely to be caused by essaying ratification in a vastly enlarged Union. Hence, it should be done either now or as an add-on to the next treaty amendment. The EP also took up the notion as part of a plea for the constitutionalization of the treaties. It believed that this implied first unifying the treaties and then dividing them into a 'constitutional' statement and a second document 'defining other areas' which could be revised more easily.

In its November 1999 statement the Commission argued that easier amendment would be needed in an enlarged Union and that this was linked to splitting the treaties into a basic text and an implementing one. It was also very aware of the difficulties of doing this without changing the existing division of powers with the Union. However, if it could be done it would make the treaties more democratic while also ensuring that the Union's essentially evolutionary nature could continue, which, if all treaty reforms had to be unanimous, it could not do. Hence it had asked the EUI to see what could be done in this direction, reserving the right to make further proposals if the EUI was successful. The merits of the idea also figured in the Commission's formal endorsement of the IGC in January 2000. And versions of how it might be done were provided by the already-mentioned Touscouz draft and by the Bertelsmann Foundation.

The latter argued that the elements for a new, readable, basic treaty were already present in the existing treaties, so there was no need for a 'big bang' revision. They came up with a 107-article treaty in eight parts: Principles; Rights; Union–Member State Relations; Institutions; Legislation; Closer Cooperation; Finance; and Final. Although the report dodged the question of whether to abandon the EU/EC distinction the treaty involved a double mixing of TEU and TEC provisions both generally and in specific articles. Wordings were not, however, changed. What would happen to the articles in the existing treaties which would be excluded from the basic document is not made wholly clear. This pointed to some of the difficulties involved in the idea of splitting.

None the less, the idea was taken up by the Italian and Benelux governments in their initial position papers on the IGC. The former talked enthusiastically of splitting the treaties into a constitutional and a policy part. The former would cover principles, institutions, the separation of powers, and decision-making. The latter said that the IGC ought to look at the idea, though the Dutch themselves saw a basic treaty as a longer-term objective. Other governments, including the UK and Finnish, were even less keen to see it on the agenda at this stage and most never mentioned the idea.

Hence, once the negotiations got under way, very little was heard of splitting the treaties, even though the EUI sent a preliminary report to the Commission on 6 March 2000. And the Portuguese presidency was not moved to try to get it onto the agenda. Equally, the EP's resolution of 13 April saw 'splitting' as simply a secondary effect of constitutionalization. The way that Fischer and Chirac went on to raise other questions about future changes to the treaties also helped to play down its importance.

None the less, the EUI went ahead with its work and finally produced a report and two treaties in mid-May 2000. It concentrated on the TEU and the TEC since the TECSC was about to expire. However, instead of splitting them on a functional basis it provided two new-style treaties. This, it believed, was the best way to deal with the rambling nature of the treaty base. In fact it did not actually mention the idea of splitting in its final report.

What it offered, firstly, was a basic treaty to replace the TEU. This reflected the approach advocated by legal experts prior to 1996. The basic treaty contained sections on Foundations, Fundamental Rights, Citizenship, Pillars II and III, Institutional and Financial Provisions, Flexibility, Final Provisions and Objectives (including activities and policies). In fact the EUI offered two versions, one sketching out the main lines and the other setting out policies in more detail. The revisers clearly had great difficulty in providing clear objectives for the various policies in a way which the basic treaty required and had to invent new formulas on occasion. They also decided to concentrate on the composition of the institutions and not their decision-making and functioning. The two resulting versions ran to 70 or 95 clauses (as they were called) with two special protocols on the CFSP and PJCCM. The treaties were printed both as texts and as a commented version explaining what had been done.

The second major offering was a revised version of the TEC which was much closer to the existing text, the symbolic importance of which was well recognized by the revisers. It had six parts: Principles; Citizenship; Policies; Association; Institutions; and General and Final Provisions. Thus it somewhat overlapped the basic treaty as well as containing material, often relating to internal organization, which was not felt worthy of inclusion in the former.

None of this attracted much attention. Thus, while the Commission accepted that the EUI had shown that a fundamental treaty could be produced without changing the existing legal situation, it withheld immediate judgment. This was used by the member-state governments to avoid taking a position on such a sensitive idea. The Portuguese presidency made no direct reference to the reports at Fiera, just sweeping aside the idea of 'splitting' as too technically complex to be considered by the IGC. There was no objection to this when the European Council met. However, in June the Belgian Senate voted 107–21 in favour of the principle.

When the Commission pronounced on 14 July it criticized the fact that even the consolidated treaties still mixed principle and policy detail so that a 'genuine re-organization' was needed to provide the Union with 'basic instruments which reflect as clearly as possible the balances on which European integration is based'. It did not therefore comment on the EUI's actual choices, confining itself to outlining and support-ing the latter's objective of producing a reorganized treaty. This would be based on the law as it stood but the reorganization could be extended to other elements of EC primary law, including other treaties. It believed that the EUI had shown that this was possible. So it was up to the IGC to decide whether to start work on it, although it recognized that this could not be done by December. It therefore recommended that Nice lay down a timetable and a procedure for doing so.

The Commission position, in other words, implicitly dropped the idea of splitting the treaties, accepting that there were better ways of reorganizing them. Indeed, it now talked of having asked the EUI to draw up a 'basic text'. This highlights the fact that, given the number of treaties, splitting can only really happen after some form of consolidation, a point not sufficiently appreciated by early enthusiasts for the idea. Moreover, the Commission did suggest that the basic treaty did not say enough about institutions or policies, a thought echoed by de Schoutheete, who was one of the revising team. This, in turn, points up the fact that, for some states, policies are as much basic principles as some of the more obviously 'constitutional' elements of the treaties, if not more so. Equally, decision-making is essential to the political balance of the Union.

The Commission also suggested that more minor adjustments to tie the two texts together seemed to be needed. In fact, there are some other problems about the EUI's drafts. To begin with, they do not eliminate the duplication of treaties and the overlap between the two is potentially confusing. And the status of the basic treaty with the two pillars being added on as protocols might be seen as changing the Union's inter-governmental elements, not to mention the status of the treaties themselves. None the less, although this is a minimalist exercise, it is, as de Schoutheete says, clearer, more logically organized and more transparent than the existing drafts. It also effectively writes *finis* to the idea of splitting as such. However, despite its virtues it was seen as too time consuming.

Given these problems and the lack of enthusiasm for the idea, the incoming French presidency did not take up the Commission's invitation to consider starting work on a restructured treaty there and then. It took no formal action at first, although Hubert Védrine, the French foreign-affairs minister, did express sympathy with such ideas. However the idea was formally ruled out in the early autumn. This was despite the fact that alternative treaty ideas were then circulating back in France.

This message seems to have got across even if there was little further academic or political comment on the EUI draft. In like manner, little attention was paid to the second major EUI report on modes of revision, a question also raised by the Dehaene panel but kept separately. The report, which was published on 28 July 2000, again does not refer to splitting but canvasses the possibility both of allowing more non-IGC revision of the treaties and an improvement of the amendment procedures contained in Article 48 TEU. This would make the process of change less rigid and less destabilizing than might otherwise be the case in an enlarged Union. The Maastricht experience was very much in the minds of the authors.

The Commission did not formally respond to this although Barnier talked of synergies between the EUI's ideas and other things on the EU agenda. And even in the new year Prodi was to canvass such a division as part of a wider change to the treaties. Hence, during the autumn and in the run-up to Nice, the idea of technical changes to the treaties within *droit constant*, more or less vanished. To an extent this was because the presidency in mid-September ruled the idea out, a stance confirmed at Biarritz. It was also because attention switched to the Charter of Fundamental Rights and questions of values. This opened up wider concerns such as those present in the EP 25 October resolution on constitutionalizing the treaties. This took note of the EUI's work both as background factor and as showing the feasibility of moving forward to a clearer and simpler consti-tutional treaty.

This caused no reaction in the United Kingdom but then, in late November 2000, the EUI's texts were rediscovered by the BBC, perhaps because of the Foreign Policy Centre's pamphlet on treaty reform, and gave rise to a brief but heated flurry of insults about constitutions for a superstate. This too soon died away just as the idea of splitting had done. However, aspirations to improve the treaties remained very much alive. And Nice was to give them a new shape and dynamic.

Constitutionalizing the Treaties

Although the idea of splitting the treaties proved no panacea, the underlying impulse to streamline and restructure the treaties did not go away. In fact, discussions about such reforms, and about the way in which treaty amendments were arrived at, continued throughout the run-up to Nice. There was often much talk of what was described as 'constitutionalizing' the treaties, something on which the EP was increasingly insistent. And, although it did not get exactly what it wanted, the Nice European Council in December 2000 did agree that some aspects of treaty reform should figure on the agenda both for the post-Nice debate and for the 2004 IGC. However, its reasons for agreeing this may well prove to be at variance with the assumptions of most of those who have been calling for the constitutionalization of the treaties.

The idea emerged somewhat before the idea of splitting but did not really take off until 2000. And what exactly is meant by 'constitutionalization' is not always clear. These are just two of the problems facing the idea. As a result it is far from certain that the 2004 process will actually lead to a major reform of the treaties as such.

The idea of going beyond anything that Amsterdam might do by way of tidying up the treaties goes back to the discussions of simplification in the EP, the EUI and the Council Secretariat in the mid-1990s. There had also been a proposal for a 'Founding Treaty' from Jean Raux of the University of Rennes. Then, in May 1998 the European Movement called for a constitution for Europe. This was echoed by the presidents of the Czech Republic, Germany and Italy in 1999. British political commentators like Andrew Marr and Nick Harvey, the Liberal Democrat MP, also took up the idea during that year.

Their argument was that the treaties were too complicated, did too little to restrain competition between the institutions and were too unsettled. Turning them, whether now or later, into a more settled constitution which would spell out the rules of the game so that people could understand it would be necessary if they were ever able to come to accept its powers and feel involved with it alongside their own national politics. The Dehaene report also worried about the instability and insecurity which came from too-frequent treaty amendments and looked to see the treaties placed on a different status from other parts of Community legislation.

More important was the encouragement which came from the EUI and the EP. The former's *Quelle Charte Constitutionnelle?*, originally prepared for the EP, canvassed three ways to make the treaties more constitutional: replacing them within a new overarching charter, enriching their constitutional substance or changing the way in which they were revised. This led in part to the November 1999 Dimitrakopoulos–Leinen report which argued strongly for a process of constitutional reform to be initiated through the Commission presenting a draft treaty to the IGC and going on to involve the EP on equal terms with the member states. It wanted to see the emergence of a simplified, rationalized and intelligible treaty based on extracting core elements from the mass of treaties, adding references to human rights and relegating policy details to separate protocols. Prior to this Andrew Duff MEP had proposed a complex process for drafting a constitution.

The EP built on this the following autumn when it accepted the Duhamel report on 'Constitutionalizing the Treaties'. This argued that the structure of the treaty base was out of line with the needs of democratic simplicity and should be replaced by a single framework treaty: clear, concise (since it would contain only key rules) and consolidating the Union with the three Communities. The resolution also laid down a somewhat complicated process for achieving this through an initial tidying up of the treaty followed by a convention in which the Commission and the EP would play a large part along with outside forces. Final approval would also involve the latter as well as referenda in all concerned states, thus hinting that some might be left outside.

Although the IGC did not directly act on such suggestions, the idea of such treaty development received a good deal of political and academic support in the summer and autumn of 2000. Not merely did Fischer and Chirac use the term 'constitution' in their groundbreaking speeches but Chris Patten in May 2000 came out in favour of a constitutional limitation on the powers and prospects of the Union so as to remove a major Eurosceptic claim that everything flowed towards Brussels. The Commission itself also talked in June 2000 of further changes to the treaties since, even after consolidation, they were still too long, too illogical and too distant from the actual balance of forces in the Union. They needed to be reduced to something more manageable, albeit with only limited retouching of the text. The dynamism generated by the convention then drafting the Union's Charter of Fundamental Rights and Freedoms gave a further boost to the idea as did pressure from the German *Länder* and Mark Leonard of the Foreign Policy Centre in London.

A number of, mainly French, academics also reinforced the trend with a series of papers, offering a defence of the idea of a constitution as such against talk of constitutional treaties, and, in the case of Touscouz, the outlines of a possible draft. This would abrogate the treaties while bringing in some non-treaty material. And it accepted that such rationalization could not be done *au droit constant*. Alongside this there was a growing theoretical discussion of 'constitutionalism' as the way to develop not only democracy and civil rights within the Union but also understandings of the Union as a polity. Constitutionalism was seen as the opposite of tyranny and arbitrary rule and, in the view of Dobson, as a way of involving European citizens in the Union's politics. Daniel Cohn-Bendit also stepped into the debate with his call for a European Magna Carta.

Not everyone agreed with this. Many politicians, including Delors, attacked the idea, notably in a seminar run by the Philip Morris Institute (PMI). Delors himself observed that 'a good treaty was better than a bad constitution'. Heavyweight academics like Weiler also weighed-in against the idea, arguing that in technical terms the EU already had the legal essentials of a constitution and what it lacked was not formalization but popular acceptance and involvement. Eurosceptics in the UK also came out strongly against ideas of a constitution, whether in the form of the Charter of Fundamental Rights or ideas of rationalizing the treaties.

Despite this, the promptings for a constitutional solution continued after the Nice Declaration on the Future of the Union made 'a simplification of the treaties with a view to making them clearer and better understood without changing their meaning'. Thus Chirac and Schröder went on talking of the need for a basic law or constitution, as did the German president. Prodi also spoke of dividing the treaties into a brief, transparent treaty and an implementing appendix while the Party of European Socialists, looking towards 2004, called for radical simplification of the treaties: reducing their number, adding the Charter of Fundamental Rights to them and changing their revision procedure. Quentin Peel in the *Financial Times* argued that the transfer of sovereignty had reached its limits and the Union faced a choice between further clumsy inter-governmentalism, as at Nice, or a clear-cut constitutional settlement, limiting the powers of Brussels. Even a conservative MEP like Christopher Beazley saw some virtue in the idea.

Yet, if the pressure for a constitutional-style revision of the treaties was to continue unabated into 2001, it was far from clear what this actually implied. Constitutionalization seems to mean a variety of things, which is hardly surprising given the variety of meanings the term can have. Intensive discussions are going on in academic and political circles about what it means in contexts beyond the state. It can involve making clear the locus of decision-making, attributing the level of competencies, making interest representation explicit and establishing full popular legitimacy. For Lamassoure in 2001 it involves a new base of legitimacy, a new stress on rights, a revised approach to the competencies of the Union and, most significantly, a new ratification process. A constitution would come into effect when a given number of states accepted it, allowing a 'vanguard' to by-pass more reluctant states. It is thus a very political conception.

From this perspective it seems also to have less to do with the Union's material structures and more to do with a constitution as a set of superior (and more hierarchically arranged) rules and especially with creating a codified document bringing together the current European Treaties. So, on the one hand, the pressure is for a more readable and straightforward document and on the other for the expression of a popularly endorsed core of principles for a European polity.

Hence, while ideas of merging the Union with the three Communities and of changing decision-making modes clearly figure in the aspirations of many of those wishing to constitutionalize the treaties, they are a minor theme. This is partly because many wish to see no change in the status quo and expect rationalization to be carried out *au droit constant*. This limits the possibility of material change. It is also partly because the real concern is with the status of the treaties.

Thus, on the one hand, what many seem to want to give the treaties is a more emphatic impact as the guarantor of rights and rules in the way that national constitutions are. They want to see a treaty which is directly binding on citizens and is the expression of their privileges as Europeans. From this flows both the desire to make the Charter the first part of a revised treaty and the stress on citizenship, superior rules and values. This can often be linked with the desire to create a formal 'hierarchy of norms' of which the revised treaty would be the apex. And, obviously, all this requires popular democratic endorsement. However, while many see the enhancing of the treaties as a way of linking with the citizens, others see it as a way of limiting the powers conferred on the institutions, and a way of entrenching the division of powers, the rights of member states and the principle of subsidiarity.

On the other hand, and this is the main gravamen of those who wish to see further integration, constitutionalization means replacing the treaties by a new document. And this is not merely for the sake of simplicity but because such a document can enshrine the popular will. What many want is to see the treaties unified, by eliminating many documents and adding case law. At the same time they want to see the resulting document purged of policy and secondary matters, so that a core of basic principles on the rules of the game are clearly visible. These would include institutions, objectives and rights. Of course the new rules could be used to constrain the institutions and not just to empower them further.

Finally, constitutionalization should also result in better presentation, possibly including a new preamble, a more approachable style and the elimination of unnecessary complications. Such changes would make the new treaty not merely more comprehensible in an abstract sense but, by making it more accessible to the citizens of Europe, attract more popular support. It would legitimize authority and both empower and educate the citizenry. In the minds of some, this could lead to the people being called on to ratify it and thus give a new mandate to their representatives. Revising the mode of treaty amendment is, of course, a major element of the desire to constitutionalize the treaties although it does not appear in the Benelux governments' memo of late June 2001. This stresses the community method, giving the Union legal personality, reforming the institutions on a traditional executive legislative model (with the population electing the president of the Commission), increasing QMV and enhancing the Union's external influence. This represents a considerable shift away from the existing situation.

Such a change would also involve a qualitative leap away from incremental change and the idea of conferred powers towards a Union which is a self-confident and sustaining civic polity. In other words, constitutionalization usually means enhancing the status of a revised founding treaty both in terms of its legal and regulatory standing and of its democratic legitimacy. The member states would thus cease to be 'the masters of the treaties'. However, for others, constitutionalization can also be a means of preventing precisely such an eventuality. Equally, there was little certainty that any such develop-ments were possible.

The fact that the very idea rests on such contradictory political aspirations is one of the two main problems facing the attempt to constitutionalize the treaties. While Duhamel argues that a constitution would be a way of heading off threats to limit the power of the Union since 'one cannot govern with treaties' and Dastoli says that one is needed to end the minimalism inherent in the claim that, thanks to the ECJ, the Union already has a constitution, some others of this persuasion have warned against going too far down the constitutional road. This is in case the exercise is used as an excuse for reversing integration. Alarm bells have thus been rung by suggestions that, in any revision, the treaties should no longer commit the signatories to 'ever closer union'. Equally, talk of involving national parliaments in the process can cause alarm. In fact the EP sees talk of competencies and the role of national parliaments as pointing in a very different direction from that in which they want to go. So, interestingly, the Constitutional Affairs Commit-tee decided not to offer a report on treaty revision, and made no real comment on the subject in its March 2001 working paper.

The difficulty of reconciling these conflicting views emerges in the draft constitution produced by the 'Convention of Young European Citizens' in mid-July 2001 and posted on the EP's website in the following autumn. This offers a 105-clause constitution for the Union – the Community being somewhat overlooked – divided into 10 titles. Many of these derive from the Charter of Fundamental Rights. They are written in simple if somewhat broad terms. However, although the draft keeps the existing institutional set-up it points in different directions. Thus it insists on the one hand that national constitutions must conform to that of the Union while on the other providing that all decisions in the Council be taken on the basis of one state, one vote.

Beyond this there are a number of technical problems. One is posed by the fact that Amsterdam has already pre-empted all the easy and uncontroversial changes. And respecting the status quo effectively rules out any substantive changes or rewriting in a simpler style. This might appear to make things simpler but could easily create new uncertainties and confusions since life is not always as simple as people would like, particularly in the Union. Spelling out the present subtle balances, as Geoffrey Howe told the PMI Seminar, may actually cause new conflicts and objections. Another uncertainty comes from the fact that repealing the many accession treaties could have unfortunate side-effects by playing down the way these both add new legitimacy and underline the fact that these are treaties between states and not a domestic constitution. A third is how (and when) any such changes are to be co-ordinated with the alterations likely to emerge from debate on the other three major issues on the agenda for 2004, let alone from any others likely to emerge from the wide consultations now under way after the Irish decision to reject the Nice treaty. The way that, as noted, the Laeken Declaration made the idea of a constitution a long-term possibility merely added to the argument.

Reforming the European Treaties

So the prospects of either constitutionalizing reformers or the revising authors of Nice achieving their aims are not all that good, as we have already suggested. If the contending forces do not cancel each other out, the technical difficulty of changing the treaties may still defeat both of them. Getting agreement on a set of constitutional values may not be possible at this stage of the Union's development. Equally, whether it is actually possible to reform the treaties without upsetting the status quo remains to be established.

In any case, even though 70% of the population are said by Eurobarometer to be in favour of a constitution for the Union, realists might argue that in this age of declining interest in politics, even the most striking changes to the treaties are unlikely to be noticed, let alone produce any major changes in outlook. Even the most readable treaty can be ignored. If, as some authorities say, institutional changes are an immense turn-off, then public opinion could ignore them, no matter how 'simple' they may become. And, as the Irish referendum shows, when public opinion does take up such European issues, its response cannot merely differ from what is assumed by the protagonists in the debate but be in direct and embarrassing contradiction to their desires. So, as we have already suggested, it may not be all bad news if the Union is compelled to persevere with messy constitutional documents of uncertain status.

None the less, the subject of treaty reform does matter and this for at least three reasons. To begin with, it is through the treaties that major changes to the Union take place, and are likely to continue to do so. And the treaties set the tone for the rest of Community legislation and action. Secondly, the whole question of what the Union is and where it is going is embedded in approaches to treaty restructuring. Finally, as this discussion has shown, there are well-organized, if contradictory, political forces who will ensure that the question remains on the European agenda.

So, getting away from ongoing treaty change may not, as the *Guide* has already suggested, be easy, always assuming we wish to do so. There are still unresolved questions about the shape of the European Treaties, both political and technical. However, the practical difficulties are considerable. And, as we have seen, the Irish decision has raised the political temperature where the treaties are concerned. So an end to discussions of treaty reform and revision is far from in sight.

Appendix – Consolidation and Simplification: TEU and TEC Concordance Tables

One of the most significant impacts of the Treaty of Amsterdam on the European Treaties was to renumber the articles contained in the TEU and TEC. To assist users of the treaties, Amsterdam had, as an annex, 'Tables of Equivalence' supposedly indicating the new numbering of the articles. The tables were, however, misleading since the 'previous numbering' which they listed referred to the article numbers after amendments had been introduced by Amsterdam. For example, it listed Articles J.12–J.18 TEU, thus implying they could be found in the pre-Amsterdam TEU. This was not the case. Similarly, it listed under 'previous numbering' Articles K.10–K.17 TEU even though these were inserted into the treaty by the TA.

Although the tables of equivalence did indicate where new articles had been inserted, thus seeking to clarify matters, the fact that Amsterdam, in amending provisions, particularly in the TEU, had moved various clauses and references to previous numbering could be wholly misleading. A good example is Article J.2 TEU which, in its post-Amsterdam form, contains elements of the original Articles J.5, J.6 and J.9(1) TEU. It does not contain any provisions from the original Article J.2 TEU.

The following concordance tables depart from the often confusing approach adopted in the tables of equivalence annexed to the TA by setting out more clearly the impact which Amsterdam has actually had. They start, in their first columns, with the numbering of the treaty articles prior to the TA's adoption. The second column then indicates the impact of Amsterdam before noting in the third column where the original provisions, amended or otherwise, appeared prior to the renumbering exercise. It is in the second and third columns where additions to the TEU and TEC introduced at Amsterdam are also recorded. In the final column we have the new numbering assigned to articles by the TA. So as to provide as complete a possible picture of the two treaties, additions (but not amendments) by the Treaty of Nice are also noted. These can be identified via the use of italics and '(TN)' in the second column. A fuller schematic account of how the two treaties have been affected by Amsterdam, Nice and other amendments has already been provided in Annex 2 above.

Table 3A   Concordance table, Treaty on European Union

Pre-TA	Impact of TA	Numbering Post-TA	Simplified Numbering
Preamble		*Preamble*	*Preamble*
Title I		Title I	Title I
Article A	amended	Article A	*Article 1*
Article B	amended	Article B	Article 2
Article C	amended	Article C	Article 3
Article D	–	Article D	Article 4
Article E	amended	Article E	Article 5
Article F	amended	Article F	Article 6
	new	Article F.1	Article 7
Title II		Title II	Title II
Article G	–	Article G	*Article 8*
Title III		Title III	Title III
Article H	–	Article H	*Article 9*
Title IV		Title IV	Title IV
Article I	–	Article I	*Article 10*
Title V	restructured	Title V	Title V
Article J.1 (1–2)(4)	amended	Article J.1 (1)	*Article 11*
Article J.1 (3)	amended	Article J.2	Article 12
Article J.2 (1)	–	Article J.6	Article 16
Article J.2 (2)	amended	Article J.5	Article 15
Article J.2 (3)	–	Article J.9 (1)	Article 19 (1)
Article J.3 (1)	amended	Article J.3 (1)	Article 13 (1)
Article J.3 (2)	amended	Article J.13 (2)	Article 23 (2)
Article J.3 (3–7)	amended	Article J.4 (2–3)(5–7)	Article 14 (2–3)(5–7)
Article J.4 (1–2)(4–6)	amended	Article J.7 (1)(4–5)	Article 17 (1)(4–5)
Article J.4 (3)	deleted		
Article J.5 (1–3)	amended	Article J.8 (1–3)	Article 18 (1–3)
Article J.5 (4)	–	Article J.9 (2)	Article 19 (2)
Article J.6	–	Article J.10	Article 20
Article J.7	–	Article J.11	Article 21
Article J.8 (1–2)	amended	Article J.3 (1–2)	Article 13 (1–2)
Article J.8 (2)	amended	Article J.13 (1)	Article 23 (1)
Article J.8 (3–4)	–	Article J.12 (1–2)	Article 22 (1–2)
Article J.8 (5)	–	Article J.15	Article 25
Article J.9	–	Article J.17	Article 27
Article J.10	deleted		
Article J.11	amended	Article J.18 (1–2)	Article 28 (1–2)
	new	Article J.12	Article 22
	new	Article J.13	Article 23
	new	Article J.14	Article 24

Pre-TA	Impact of TA	Numbering Post-TA	Simplified Numbering
	new	Article J.16	Article 26
	new (TN)		*Article 27a*
	new (TN)		*Article 27b*
	new (TN)		*Article 27c*
	new (TN)		*Article 27d*
	new (TN)		*Article 27e*
	new	Article J.18 (3–4)	Article 28 (3–4)
Title VI	restructured	Title VI	Title VI
Article K.1	amended	Article K.1	*Article 29*
	new	Article K.2	Article 30
	new	Article K.3	Article 31
	new	Article K.4	Article 32
Article K.2(1)	amended	Article 73k (1) TEC	*Article 63 (1) TEC*
Article K.2(2)	amended	Article K.5	Article 33
Article K.3	amended	Article K.6	Article 34
Article K.4(1–2)	–	Article K.8	Article 36
Article K.4(3)	amended	Article K.6	Article 34
	new	Article K.7	Article 35
Article K.5	amended	Article K.9	Article 37
	new	Article K.10	Article 38
Article K.6	amended	Article K.11	Article 39
	new	Article K.12	Article 40
Article K.7	to new Title VIa		
	new (TN)		*Article 40a*
	new (TN)		*Article 40b*
Article K.8	amended	Article K.13	*Article 41*
Article K.9	amended	Article K.14	Article 42
Title VIa	new	Title VIa	Title VII
	new	Article K.15	Article 43
	new (TN)		*Article 43a*
	new (TN)		*Article 43b*
	new	Article K.16	Article 44
	new (TN)		*Article 44a*
	new	Article K.17	Article 45
Title VII		Title VII	*Title VIII*
Article L	amended	Article L	Article 46
Article M	–	Article M	*Article 47*
Article N	–	Article N	Article 48
Article O	amended	Article O	*Article 49*
Article P	–	Article P	Article 50
Article Q	–	Article Q	Article 51
Article R	–	Article R	Article 52
Article S	amended	Article S	Article 53

Table 3B   Concordance table, Treaty establishing the European Community

Pre-TA	Impact of TA	Numbering Post-TA	Simplified Numbering
Preamble		*Preamble*	*Preamble*
Part One		**Part One**	**Part One**
Article 1		Article 1	Article 1
Article 2	amended	Article 2	Article 2
Article 3	amended	Article 3	Article 3
Article 3a		Article 3a	Article 4
Article 3b		Article 3b	Article 5
	new	Article 3c	Article 6
Article 4		Article 4	Article 7
Article 4a		Article 4a	Article 8
Article 4b		Article 4b	Article 9
Article 5		Article 5	Article 10
	new	Article 5a	Article 11
	new (TN)		*Article 11a*
Article 6		Article 6	Article 12
	new	Article 6a	Article 13
Article 7	repealed		
Article 7a		Article 7a	Article 14
Article 7b	repealed		
Article 7c		Article 7c	Article 15
	new	Article 7d	Article 16
Part Two		**Part Two**	**Part Two**
Article 8		Article 8	Article 17
Article 8a	amended	Article 8a	Article 18
Article 8b		Article 8b	Article 19
Article 8c		Article 8c	Article 20
Article 8d	amended	Article 8d	Article 21
Article 8e		Article 8e	Article 22
Part Three		**Part Three**	**Part Three**
Title I		**Title I**	**Title I**
Article 9		Article 9	Article 23
Article 10		Article 10	Article 24
Article 11	repealed		
Chapter 1		*Chapter 1*	*Chapter 1*
Section 1	deleted		
Article 12		Article 12	Article 25
Article 13	repealed		
Article 14	repealed		
Article 15	repealed		
Article 16	repealed		
Article 17	repealed		
Section 2	deleted		
Article 18	repealed		
Article 19	repealed		
Article 20	repealed		
Article 21	repealed		
Article 22	repealed		
Article 23	repealed		
Article 24	repealed		
Article 25	repealed		
Article 26	repealed		

Pre-TA	Impact of TA	Numbering Post-TA	Simplified Numbering
Article 27	repealed		
Article 28		Article 28	Article 26
Article 29		Article 29	Article 27
Chapter 2		*Chapter 2*	*Chapter 2*
Article 30		Article 30	Article 28
Article 31	repealed		
Article 32	repealed		
Article 33	repealed		
Article 34		Article 34	Article 29
Article 35	repealed		
Article 36		Article 36	Article 30
Article 37		Article 37	Article 31
Title II		Title II	Title II
Article 38		Article 38	Article 32
Article 39		Article 39	Article 33
Article 40		Article 40	Article 34
Article 41		Article 41	Article 35
Article 42		Article 42	Article 36
Article 43		Article 43	Article 37
Article 44	repealed		
Article 45	repealed		
Article 46		Article 46	Article 38
Article 47	repealed		
Title III		Title III	Title III
Chapter 1		*Chapter 1*	*Chapter 1*
Article 48		Article 48	Article 39
Article 49		Article 49	Article 40
Article 50		Article 50	Article 41
Article 51	amended	Article 51	Article 42
Chapter 2		*Chapter 2*	*Chapter 2*
Article 52		Article 52	Article 43
Article 53	repealed		
Article 54		Article 54	Article 44
Article 55		Article 55	Article 45
Article 56	amended	Article 56	Article 46
Article 57	amended	Article 57	Article 47
Article 58		Article 58	Article 48
Chapter 3		*Chapter 3*	*Chapter 3*
Article 59		Article 59	Article 49
Article 60		Article 60	Article 50
Article 61		Article 61	Article 51
Article 62	repealed		
Article 63		Article 63	Article 52
Article 64		Article 64	Article 53
Article 65		Article 65	Article 54
Article 66		Article 66	Article 55
Chapter 4		*Chapter 4*	*Chapter 4*
Article 67	repealed		
Article 68	repealed		
Article 69	repealed		
Article 70	repealed		
Article 71	repealed		
Article 72	repealed		

Pre-TA	Impact of TA	Numbering Post-TA	Simplified Numbering
Article 73	repealed		
Article 73a	repealed		
Article 73b		Article 73b	Article 56
Article 73c		Article 73c	Article 57
Article 73d		Article 73d	Article 58
Article 73e	repealed		
Article 73f		Article 73f	Article 59
Article 73g		Article 73g	Article 60
Article 73h	repealed		
	new	Title IIIa	Title IV
	new	Article 73i	Article 61
	new	Article 73j	Article 62
	new	Article 73k	Article 63
	new	Article 73l	Article 64
	new	Article 73m	Article 65
	new	Article 73n	Article 66
	new	Article 73o	Article 67
	new	Article 73p	Article 68
	new	Article 73q	Article 69
Title IV		Title IV	Title V
Article 74		Article 74	Article 70
Article 75	amended	Article 75	Article 71
Article 76		Article 76	Article 72
Article 77		Article 77	Article 73
Article 78		Article 78	Article 74
Article 79		Article 79	Article 75
Article 80		Article 80	Article 76
Article 81		Article 81	Article 77
Article 82		Article 82	Article 78
Article 83		Article 83	Article 79
Article 84		Article 84	Article 80
Title V		Title V	Title VI
Chapter 1		*Chapter 1*	*Chapter 1*
Section 1		*Section 1*	*Section 1*
Article 85		Article 85	Article 81
Article 86		Article 86	Article 82
Article 87		Article 87	Article 83
Article 88		Article 88	Article 84
Article 89		Article 89	Article 85
Article 90		Article 90	Article 86
Section 2	deleted		
Article 91	repealed		
Section 3	renumbered	*Section 3*	*Section 2*
Article 92		Article 92	Article 87
Article 93		Article 93	Article 88
Article 94		Article 94	Article 89
Chapter 2		*Chapter 2*	*Chapter 2*
Article 95		Article 95	Article 90
Article 96		Article 96	Article 91
Article 97	repealed		
Article 98		Article 98	Article 92
Article 99		Article 99	Article 93
Chapter 3		*Chapter 3*	*Chapter 3*

Pre-TA	Impact of TA	Numbering Post-TA	Simplified Numbering
Article 100		Article 100	Article 94
Article 100a	amended	Article 100a	Article 95
Article 100b	repealed		
Article 100c	repealed		
Article 100d	repealed		
Article 101		Article 101	Article 96
Article 102		Article 102	Article 97
Title VI		Title VI	Title VII
Chapter 1		*Chapter 1*	*Chapter 1*
Article 102a		Article 102a	Article 98
Article 103		Article 103	Article 99
Article 103a		Article 103a	Article 100
Article 104		Article 104	Article 101
Article 104a		Article 104a	Article 102
Article 104b		Article 104b	Article 103
Article 104c		Article 104c	Article 104
Chapter 2		*Chapter 2*	*Chapter 2*
Article 105		Article 105	Article 105
Article 105a		Article 105a	Article 106
Article 106		Article 106	Article 107
Article 107		Article 107	Article 108
Article 108		Article 108	Article 109
Article 108a		Article 108a	Article 110
Article 109		Article 109	Article 111
Chapter 3		*Chapter 3*	*Chapter 3*
Article 109a		Article 109a	Article 112
Article 109b		Article 109b	Article 113
Article 109c		Article 109c	Article 114
Article 109d		Article 109d	Article 115
Chapter 4		*Chapter 4*	*Chapter 4*
Article 109e		Article 109e	Article 116
Article 109f		Article 109f	Article 117
Article 109g		Article 109g	Article 118
Article 109h		Article 109h	Article 119
Article 109i		Article 109i	Article 120
Article 109j		Article 109j	Article 121
Article 109k		Article 109k	Article 122
Article 109l		Article 109l	Article 123
Article 109m		Article 109m	Article 124
	new	Title VIa	Title VIII
	new	Article 109n	Article 125
	new	Article 109o	Article 126
	new	Article 109p	Article 127
	new	Article 109q	Article 128
	new	Article 109r	Article 129
	new	Article 109s	Article 130
Title VII		Title VII	Title IX
Article 110		Article 110	Article 131
Article 112		Article 112	Article 132
Article 113	amended	Article 113	Article 133
Article 115		Article 115	Article 134
	new	Title VIIa	Title X
	new	Article 116	Article 135

Pre-TA	Impact of TA	Numbering Post-TA	Simplified Numbering
Title VIII		Title VIII	Title XI
Chapter 1		*Chapter 1*	*Chapter 1*
Article 117	amended	Article 117	Article 136
Article 118	amended	Article 118c	Article 140
Article 118a	amended	Article 118	Article 137
	new	Article 118a	Article 138
Article 118b	amended	Article 118b	Article 139
Article 119		Article 119	Article 141
Article 120		Article 119a	Article 142
	new	Article 120	Article 143
	new (TN)		Article 144
Article 122		Article 122	Article 145
Chapter 2		*Chapter 2*	*Chapter 2*
Article 123		Article 123	Article 146
Article 124		Article 124	Article 147
Article 125	amended	Article 125	Article 148
Chapter 3		*Chapter 3*	*Chapter 3*
Article 126		Article 126	Article 149
Article 127	amended	Article 127	Article 150
Title IX		Title IX	Title XII
Article 128	amended	Article 128	Article 151
Title X		Title X	Title XIII
Article 129	amended	Article 129	Article 152
Title XI		Title XI	Title XIV
Article 129a	amended	Article 129a	Article 153
Title XII		Title XII	Title XV
Article 129b		Article 129b	Article 154
Article 129c	amended	Article 129c	Article 155
Article 129d	amended	Article 129d	Article 156
Title XIII		Title XIII	Title XVI
Article 130		Article 130	Article 157
Title XIV		Title XIV	Title XVII
Article 130a	amended	Article 130a	Article 158
Article 130b		Article 130b	Article 159
Article 130c		Article 130c	Article 160
Article 130d		Article 130d	Article 161
Article 130e	amended	Article 130e	Article 162
Title XV		Title XV	Title XVIII
Article 130f		Article 130f	Article 163
Article 130g		Article 130g	Article 164
Article 130h		Article 130h	Article 165
Article 130i	amended	Article 130i	Article 166
Article 130j		Article 130j	Article 167
Article 130k		Article 130k	Article 168
Article 130l		Article 130l	Article 169
Article 130m		Article 130m	Article 170
Article 130n		Article 130n	Article 171
Article 130o	amended	Article 130o	Article 172
Article 130p		Article 130p	Article 173
Title XVI		Title XVI	Title XIX
Article 130r	amended	Article 130r	Article 174
Article 130s	amended	Article 130s	Article 175

Pre-TA	Impact of TA	Numbering Post-TA	Simplified Numbering
Article 130t		Article 130t	Article 176
Title XVII		Title XVII	Title XX
Article 130u		Article 130u	Article 177
Article 130v		Article 130v	Article 178
Article 130w	amended	Article 130w	Article 179
Article 130x		Article 130x	Article 180
Article 130y		Article 130y	Article 181
	new (TN)		*Title XXI*
	new (TN)		*Article 181a*
Part Four		**Part Four**	**Part Four**
Article 131		Article 131	Article 182
Article 132		Article 132	Article 183
Article 133		Article 133	Article 184
Article 134		Article 134	Article 185
Article 135		Article 135	Article 186
Article 136		Article 136	Article 187
Article 136a		Article 136a	Article 188
Part Five		**Part Five**	**Part Five**
Title I		Title I	Title I
Chapter 1		*Chapter 1*	*Chapter 1*
Section 1		*Section 1*	*Section 1*
Article 137	amended	Article 137	Article 189
Article 138	amended	Article 138	Article 190
Article 138a		Article 138a	Article 191
Article 138b		Article 138b	Article 192
Article 138c		Article 138c	Article 193
Article 138d		Article 138d	Article 194
Article 138e		Article 138e	Article 195
Article 139		Article 139	Article 196
Article 140		Article 140	Article 197
Article 141		Article 141	Article 198
Article 142		Article 142	Article 199
Article 143		Article 143	Article 200
Article 144		Article 144	Article 201
Section 2		*Section 2*	*Section 2*
Article 145		Article 145	Article 202
Article 146		Article 146	Article 203
Article 147		Article 147	Article 204
Article 148		Article 148	Article 205
Article 150		Article 150	Article 206
Article 151	amended	Article 151	Article 207
Article 152		Article 152	Article 208
Article 153		Article 153	Article 209
Article 154		Article 154	Article 210
Section 3		*Section 3*	*Section 3*
Article 155		Article 155	Article 211
Article 156		Article 156	Article 212
Article 157		Article 157	Article 213
Article 158	amended	Article 158	Article 214
Article 159		Article 159	Article 215
Article 160		Article 160	Article 216
Article 161		Article 161	Article 217

Pre-TA	Impact of TA	Numbering Post-TA	Simplified Numbering
Article 162		Article 162	Article 218
Article 163	amended	Article 163	Article 219
Section 4		*Section 4*	*Section 4*
Article 164		Article 164	Article 220
Article 165		Article 165	Article 221
Article 166		Article 166	Article 222
Article 167		Article 167	Article 223
Article 168		Article 168	Article 224
Article 168a		Article 168a	Article 225
	new (TN)		*Article 225a*
Article 169		Article 169	Article 226
Article 170		Article 170	Article 227
Article 171		Article 171	Article 228
Article 172		Article 172	Article 229
	new (TN)		*Article 229a*
Article 173	amended	Article 173	Article 230
Article 174		Article 174	Article 231
Article 175		Article 175	Article 232
Article 176		Article 176	Article 233
Article 177		Article 177	Article 234
Article 178		Article 178	Article 235
Article 179		Article 179	Article 236
Article 180		Article 180	Article 237
Article 181		Article 181	Article 238
Article 182		Article 182	Article 239
Article 183		Article 183	Article 240
Article 184		Article 184	Article 241
Article 185		Article 185	Article 242
Article 186		Article 186	Article 243
Article 187		Article 187	Article 244
Article 188		Article 188	Article 245
Section 5		*Section 5*	*Section 5*
Article 188a		Article 188a	Article 246
Article 188b		Article 188b	Article 247
Article 188c	amended	Article 188c	Article 248
Chapter 2		*Chapter 2*	*Chapter 2*
Article 189		Article 189	Article 249
Article 189a		Article 189a	Article 250
Article 189b	amended	Article 189b	Article 251
Article 189c		Article 189c	Article 252
Article 190		Article 190	Article 253
Article 191		Article 191	Article 254
	new	Article 191a	Article 255
Article 192		Article 192	Article 256
Chapter 3		*Chapter 3*	*Chapter 3*
Article 193		Article 193	Article 257
Article 194		Article 194	Article 258
Article 195		Article 195	Article 259
Article 196		Article 196	Article 260
Article 197		Article 197	Article 261
Article 198	amended	Article 198	Article 262
Chapter 4		*Chapter 4*	*Chapter 4*
Article 198a	amended	Article 198a	Article 263

Pre-TA	Impact of TA	Numbering Post-TA	Simplified Numbering
Article 198b	amended	Article 198b	Article 264
Article 198c	amended	Article 198c	Article 265
Chapter 5		*Chapter 5*	*Chapter 5*
Article 198d		Article 198d	Article 266
Article 198e		Article 198e	Article 267
Title II		Title II	Title II
Article 199		Article 199	Article 268
Article 201		Article 201	Article 269
Article 201a		Article 201a	Article 270
Article 202		Article 202	Article 271
Article 203		Article 203	Article 272
Article 204		Article 204	Article 273
Article 205	amended	Article 205	Article 274
Article 205a		Article 205a	Article 275
Article 206	amended	Article 206	Article 276
Article 207		Article 207	Article 277
Article 208		Article 208	Article 278
Article 209		Article 209	Article 279
Article 209a	amended	Article 209a	Article 280
Part Six		Part Six	Part Six
Article 210		Article 210	Article 281
Article 211		Article 211	Article 282
Article 212		Article 212	Article 283
Article 213		Article 213	Article 284
	new	Article 213a	Article 285
	new	Article 213b	Article 286
Article 214		Article 214	Article 287
Article 215		Article 215	Article 288
Article 216		Article 216	Article 289
Article 217		Article 217	Article 290
Article 218		Article 218	Article 291
Article 219		Article 219	Article 292
Article 220		Article 220	Article 293
Article 221		Article 221	Article 294
Article 222		Article 222	Article 295
Article 223		Article 223	Article 296
Article 224		Article 224	Article 297
Article 225		Article 225	Article 298
Article 226	repealed		
Article 227	amended	Article 227	Article 299
Article 228	amended	Article 228	Article 300
Article 228a		Article 228a	Article 301
Article 229		Article 229	Article 302
Article 230		Article 230	Article 303
Article 231		Article 231	Article 304
Article 232		Article 232	Article 305
Article 233		Article 233	Article 306
Article 234		Article 234	Article 307
Article 235		Article 235	Article 308
Article 236	amended	Article 236	Article 309
Article 238		Article 238	Article 310
Article 239		Article 239	Article 311
Article 240		Article 240	Article 312

Pre-TA	Impact of TA	Numbering Post-TA	Simplified Numbering
Article 241	repealed		
Article 242	repealed		
Article 243	repealed		
Article 244	repealed		
Article 245	repealed		
Article 246	repealed		
Final Provisions		**Final Provisions**	
Article 247		Article 247	Article 313
Article 248		Article 248	Article 314

Annex 4   Amendments to the TECSC and TEAEC

Tables 4A and 4B allow readers to chart the evolution of provisions contained in the TECSC and TEAEC. All articles which have undergone amendment or repeal or which have been inserted in the relevant Treaty are listed in column 1. Readers can then ascertain from the next six columns the impact of five amending treaties (CCI, MT, CBP, CFP and SEA) as well as acts of accession (AA). An indication is given as to whether the treaties amended (A), inserted (I) or repealed (R) the article concerned. The four remaining columns summarize the impact of the TEU, the TA and the TN before noting where further details of the provision can be found. Where, in this final column, reference is made to an article in the TEC or TEU which contains identical or almost identical provisions, the post-TA numbering of the TEC and TEU is used. A full list of abbreviations follows each table.

Table 4A   The evolution of the Treaty establishing the European Coal and Steel Community

Art. (1)	CCI (2)	MT (3)	CBP (4)	CFP (5)	SEA (6)	AA (7)	Impact of TEU (8)	Impact of TA (9)	Impact of TN (10)	Notes (11)
2								simplified		see Box 10, pp. 570–71
4								simplified		see Box 10, pp. 570–71
7	A						amended	amended		see Box 10, pp. 570–71
9		R				A	inserted amended Art. 10 MT			see Art. 213 TEC
10		R					inserted amended Art. 11 MT	amended para. 2	amended para. 2	see Art. 214(2) TEC
10		R					inserted amended Art. 11 MT	deleted para. 3		see Box 10, pp. 570–71
11		R				A	inserted amended Art. 14 MT		amended	see Art. 161 TEC
12		R					inserted amended Art. 12 MT		amended	see Art. 215 TEC
12a							new article			see Art. 217 TEC
13		R					inserted amended Art. 17 MT	new first para.	deleted first para.	see Art. 219 TEC
16		R					inserted amended Art. 15 MT	simplified		see Box 10, pp. 570–71
17		R					inserted Art. 18 MT			see Art. 212 TEC
18						A	new subparagraph			
20								new final para.	amended final para.	see Art. 189 TEC
20a							new article			see Art. 192 TEC
20b							new article			see Art. 193 TEC
20c							new article			see Art. 194 TEC
20d							new article			see Art. 195 TEC
21	A					A	amended para. 3	see footnote[1]	amended para. 5	see Art. 190(4) TEC
21								amended		see Box 10, pp. 570–71
22		A					amended third para.			
24		A								see Arts. 200–1 TEC
27		R				A	inserted amended Art. 2 MT			see Art. 203 TEC
27a							new article			see Art. 104 TEC
28						A				
29		R					inserted Art. 6 MT			see Art. 210 TEC
30								amended	amended para. 2	see Art. 207 TEC
30		R					inserted amended Art. 5 MT			
31									amended	see Art. 220 TEC

Article						Reference
32	A[2]	A	amended third para.		amended	see Art. 221 TEC
32a	I	A		simplified	amended	see Art. 222 TEC
32b	I	A			amended	see Art. 223 TEC
32c	I	A			amended	see Art. 224 TEC
32d	I		amended	amended	amended	see Art. 225 TEC
32e					new article	see Art. 225a TEC
33			amended	amended final para.	amended	see Art. 230 TEC
40		A	amended			
45		A	A		amended	see Art. 245 TEC
45a		A	inserted former Art. 78e			see Art. 246 TEC
45b		A	inserted former Art. 78e	simplified para. 3	amended	see Art. 247 TEC
45c			inserted former Art. 78f	amended	amended	see Art. 248 TEC
50				amended		see Box 10, pp. 570–71
52				repealed		see Box 10, pp. 570–71
56						see p. 569
76	R		inserted amended Art. 5 MT	amended		see Art. 291 TEC
78	A	A		amended		see Art. 272 TEC
78a	I	I				see Art. 271 TEC
78b	I	A				see Art. 273 TEC
78c	I		amended first para.	amended first para.		see Art. 276 TEC
78d	I	A				see Art. 275 TEC
78e	I		repealed, moved and amended			now Art. 45a–45b
78f	I		repealed, moved and amended			now Art. 45c
78g	I		new paras. 2 & 3	amended para. 1		see Art. 274 TEC
78h	I		new and reordered subparas.			see Art. 279 TEC
78i			new article			see Art. 280 TEC[3]
79	A[4]		amended para. (a)	amended		see Box 10, pp. 570–71
84				simplified		see Box 10, pp. 570–71
85				repealed		see Box 10, pp. 570–71
93	A			simplified		see Box 10, pp. 570–71
95	A			simplified		see Box 10, pp. 570–71

Art. (1)	CCI (2)	MT (3)	CBP (4)	CFP (5)	SEA (6)	AA (7)	Impact of TEU (8)	Impact of TA (9)	Impact of TN (10)	Notes (11)
96							repealed (see Art. 48 TEU)	new article	amended	see Art. 309 TEC
97								simplified		see Box 10, pp. 570–71
98							repealed			see Art. 49 TEU

Notes:

[1] The TA amendments to Article 21 are complex. First it amended the existing para. 3 and inserted a new para. 4. Articles 1, 2 and 3(1) of the Act concerning the election of the representatives of the European Parliament (*OJ* L278, 8 October 1976, as amended by successive acts of accession) were then inserted as paragraphs 1, 2 and 3, with the amended para. 3 and new para. 4 being renumbered paras. 4 and 5. The original paras. 1 and 2 were repealed by Article 14 of the 1976 Act noted.

[2] Article 32 also amended by Council Decision on 26 November 1974, *OJ* L318, 28 November 1974.

[3] Article 78i is identical to the pre-TA Article 209a TEC. Whereas the TA amended the latter, no amendment was made to Article 78i.

[4] Also amended by Article 1 of the Treaty amending, with regard to Greenland, the Treaties establishing the European Communities, *OJ* L29, 1 February 1985.

Abbreviations:

A   amended
R   repealed
I   inserted
AA   Acts of accession (whether 1972, 1980, 1985 or 1994)
CBP   Treaty amending certain budgetary provisions of the Treaties establishing the European Communities and of the Treaty establishing a single Council and a single Commission of the European Communities (1970)
CCI   Convention on Certain Institutions Common to the European Communities (1957)
CFP   Treaty amending certain financial provisions of the Treaty establishing the European Communities and of the Treaty establishing a single Council and a single Commission of the European Communities (1975)
MT   Merger Treaty (Treaty establishing a single Council and a single Commission of the European Communities) (1965)
SEA   Single European Act (1986)
TA   Treaty of Amsterdam (1997)
TEU   Treaty on European Union (1992)
TN   Treaty of Nice (2001)

Table 4B   The evolution of the Treaty establishing the European Atomic Energy Community

Art. (1)	MT (2)	CBP (3)	CFP (4)	SEA (5)	AA (6)	Impact of TEU (7)	Impact of TA (8)	Impact of TN (9)	Notes (10)
3			I			amended			see Art. 7 TEC
76							simplified		see Box 14, pp. 578–9
93							simplified		see Box 14, pp. 578–9
94							repealed		see Box 14, pp. 578–9
95							repealed		see Box 14, pp. 578–9
98							simplified		see Box 14, pp. 578–9
100							repealed		see Box 14, pp. 578–9
104							amended		see Box 14, pp. 578–9
105							amended		see Box 14, pp. 578–9
106							simplified		see Box 14, pp. 578–9
107							amended	amended final para.	see Art. 189 TEC
107a						new article			see Art. 192 TEC
107b						new article			see Art. 193 TEC
107c						new article			see Art. 194 TEC
107d						new article			see Art. 195 TEC
108	A				A	amended para. 3	see footnote[1]	amended para. 5	see Art. 190(4) TEC
109	A					added new subpara.			see Art. 196 TEC
114									see Art. 201 TEC
116	R				A	inserted amended Art. 2 MT			see Art. 203 TEC
117	R					inserted amended Art. 3 MT			see Art. 204 TEC
118					A				see Art. 205 TEC
121	R					inserted amended Arts 4–5 MT	amended	amended para. 2	see Art. 207 TEC
123	R					inserted amended Art. 6 MT			see Art. 210 TEC
125	R					inserted amended Art. 18 MT			see Art. 212 TEC
126	R				A	inserted amended Art. 10 MT			see Art. 213 TEC
127	R					inserted amended Art. 11 MT	amended para. 2	amended para. 2	see Art. 214(2) TEC
127	R					inserted amended Art. 11 MT	deleted para. 3		see Box 14, pp. 578–9
128	R					inserted amended Art. 12 MT		amended	see Art. 215 TEC
129	R					inserted amended Art. 13 MT			see Art. 216 TEC
130	R				A	inserted amended Art. 14 MT		amended	see Art. 217 TEC

Art. (1)	MT (2)	CBP (3)	CFP (4)	SEA (5)	AA (6)	Impact of TEU (7)	Impact of TA (8)	Impact of TN (9)	Notes (10)
131	R					inserted amended Arts. 15–16 MT	amended		see Art. 218 TEC
132	R					inserted amended Art. 17 MT		deleted first para.	see Art. 219 TEC
133	R					repealed (again)			
134					A				
136					A	amended		amended	see Art. 220 TEC
137²								amended	see Art. 221 TEC
138					A		simplified	amended	see Art. 222 TEC
139					A			amended	see Art. 223 TEC
140								amended	see Art. 224 TEC
140a				I	A	amended paras. 1–3			see Art. 225 TEC
140b								new article	see Art. 225a TEC
143						new para. 2			see Art. 228 TEC
146						amended	amended	amended	see Art. 230 TEC
160				A				amended	see Art. 245 TEC
160a						new article			see Art. 246 TEC
160b					A	inserted amended Art. 180	simplified para. 3	amended	see Art. 247 TEC
160c						inserted former Art. 180a	amended	amended	see Art. 248 TEC
163								amended	see Art. 254 TEC
165				A				amended	see Art. 257 TEC
166					A			amended	see Art. 258 TEC
167						amended		amended para. 1	see Art. 259 TEC
168						amended			see Art. 260 TEC
170							amended		see Art. 262 TEC
172						repealed paras. 1–3			see Art. 269 TEC
173						new article			see Art. 270 TEC
173a						new article			
177		A	A						see Art. 272 TEC
178		I	A						see Art. 273 TEC
179						amended	amended		see Art. 274 TEC

Art.							Reference
179a			A				see Art. 275 TEC
180		A	I	repealed, moved and amended			now Art. 160b
180a			I	repealed, moved and amended			now Art. 160c
180b			I	inserted new paras. 2–3			see Art. 276 TEC
181			A		amended para. 1	amended	see Art. 277 TEC
183				amended para. 3	simplified		see Art. 279 TEC
183a				new article			see Art. 280 TEC[3]
186	R[4]						see Art. 283 TEC
190	R						see Art. 290 TEC
191					inserted amended Art. 28 MT	amended	see Art. 291 TEC
198			A[5]	amended para. (a)	amended		see Box 14, pp. 578–9
199					simplified		see Box 14, pp. 578–9
201				amended			see Art. 304 TEC
204				repealed (see Art. 48 TEU)	new article	amended	see Art. 309 TEC
205				repealed			see Art. 49 TEU
206				amended	amended		see Art. 310 TEC
209				repealed			see Box 14, pp. 578–9
210				repealed			see Box 14, pp. 578–9
211				repealed			see Box 14, pp. 578–9
212				repealed			see Box 14, pp. 578–9
213				repealed			see Box 14, pp. 578–9
214				repealed			see Box 14, pp. 578–9
215				repealed			see Box 14, pp. 578–9
216				repealed			see Box 14, pp. 578–9
217				repealed			see Box 14, pp. 578–9
218				repealed			see Box 14, pp. 578–9
219				repealed			see Box 14, pp. 578–9
220				repealed			see Box 14, pp. 578–9

Art. (1)	MT (2)	CBP (3)	CFP (4)	SEA (5)	AA (6)	Impact of TEU (7)	Impact of TA (8)	Impact of TN (9)	Notes (10)
221							repealed		see Box 14, pp. 578–9
222							repealed		see Box 14, pp. 578–9
223							repealed		see Box 14, pp. 578–9
225							amended		see Art. 314 TEC

Notes:

[1] The TA amendments to this article are complex. First it amended the existing para. 3 and inserted a new para. 4. Articles 1, 2 and 3(1) of the Act concerning the election of the representatives of the European Parliament (OJ L278, 8 October 1976, as amended by successive Acts of Accession) were then inserted as paragraphs 1, 2 and 3, with the amended para. 3 and new para. 4 being renumbered paras. 4 and 5. The original paras. 1 and 2 were repealed by the Article 14 of the 1976 Act noted.

[2] Article 137 also amended by Council Decision on 26 November 1974, OJ L318, 28 November 1974.

[3] Article 280 is identical to the pre-TA Article 209a TEC. Whereas the TA amended the latter, no amendment was made to Article 280.

[4] Replaced by Article 24(1) of the Merger Treaty. Whereas other provisions of the Merger Treaty have been inserted into the TEAEC, this has not. The TA did insert amended provisions into Article 283 TEC.

[5] Also amended by Article 1 of the Treaty amending, with regard to Greenland, the Treaties establishing the European Communities, OJ L29, 1 February 1985.

Abbreviations:

A	amended
R	repealed
I	inserted

AA	Acts of accession (whether 1972, 1980, 1985 or 1994)
CBP	Treaty amending certain budgetary provisions of the Treaties establishing the European Communities and of the Treaty establishing a single Council and a single Commission of the European Communities (1970)
CCI	Convention on Certain Institutions Common to the European Communities (1957)
CFP	Treaty amending certain financial provisions of the Treaty establishing the European Communities and of the Treaty establishing a single Council and a single Commission of the European Communities
MT	Merger Treaty (Treaty establishing a single Council and a single Commission of the European Communities) (1965)
SEA	Single European Act (1986)
TA	Treaty of Amsterdam (1997)
TEU	Treaty on European Union (1992)
TN	Treaty of Nice (2001)

Index

Where pages numbers appear in italic, this indicates treaty text

READ MORE IN PENGUIN

In every corner of the world, on every subject under the sun, Penguin represents quality and variety – the very best in publishing today.

For complete information about books available from Penguin – including Puffins, Penguin Classics and Arkana – and how to order them, write to us at the appropriate address below. Please note that for copyright reasons the selection of books varies from country to country.

In the United Kingdom: Please write to *Dept. EP, Penguin Books Ltd, Bath Road, Harmondsworth, West Drayton, Middlesex UB7 0DA*

In the United States: Please write to *Consumer Services, Penguin Putnam Inc., 405 Murray Hill Parkway, East Rutherford, New Jersey 07073-2136*. VISA and MasterCard holders call 1-800-631-8571 to order Penguin titles

In Canada: Please write to *Penguin Books Canada Ltd, 10 Alcorn Avenue, Suite 300, Toronto, Ontario M4V 3B2*

In Australia: Please write to *Penguin Books Australia Ltd, 487 Maroondah Highway, Ringwood, Victoria 3134*

In New Zealand: Please write to *Penguin Books (NZ) Ltd, Private Bag 102902, North Shore Mail Centre, Auckland 10*

In India: Please write to *Penguin Books India Pvt Ltd, 11 Community Centre, Panchsheel Park, New Delhi 110017*

In the Netherlands: Please write to *Penguin Books Netherlands bv, Postbus 3507, NL-1001 AH Amsterdam*

In Germany: Please write to *Penguin Books Deutschland GmbH, Metzlerstrasse 26, 60594 Frankfurt am Main*

In Spain: Please write to *Penguin Books S. A., Bravo Murillo 19, 1°B, 28015 Madrid*

In Italy: Please write to *Penguin Italia s.r.l., Via Vittorio Emanuele 45/a, 20094 Corsico, Milano*

In France: Please write to *Penguin France, 12, Rue Prosper Ferradou, 31700 Blagnac*

In Japan: Please write to *Penguin Books Japan Ltd, Iidabashi KM-Bldg, 2-23-9 Koraku, Bunkyo-Ku, Tokyo 112-0004*

In South Africa: Please write to *Penguin Books South Africa (Pty) Ltd, P.O. Box 751093, Gardenview, 2047 Johannesburg*